CHINA

6th Edition

Where to Stay and Eat for All Budgets

Must-See Sights and Local Secrets

Ratings You Can Trust

Fodor's Travel Publications New York, Toronto, London, Sydney, Auckland

www.fodors.com

FODOR'S CHINA

Editor: Margaret Kelly

Editorial Contributors: Stephanie Butler, Liana Cafolla, Joanna Cantor, Chris Cottrell, Cherise Fong, Nels Frye, Chris Horton, Helena Iveson, Hannah Lee, Helen Luk, Zoe Li, Zoe Mak, Michael Manning, Eileen Wen Mooney, Paul Mooney, Lisa Movius, Dominique Rowe, Elyse Singleton, Michael Standaert, Dave Taylor, Albert Wong.

Production Editor: Astrid deRidder
Maps & Illustrations: Mark Stroud and David Lindroth, *cartographers*; Bob Blake, Rebecca Baer, *map editors;* William Wu, *information graphics*
Design: Fabrizio La Rocca, *creative director*; Guido Caroti, Siobhan O'Hare, *art directors*; Tina Malaney, Chie Ushio, Ann McBride, Jessica Walsh, *designers*; Melanie Marin, *senior picture editor;* Moon Sun Kim, *cover designer*
Cover Photo Farmer walking on terraced rice field, Longsheng Guangxi region: Daryl Benson/Masterfile
Production Manager: Angela L. McLean

6th Edition

ISBN 978-1-4000-0825-4

ISSN 1070-6895

SPECIAL SALES

This book is available at special discounts for bulk purchases for sales promotions or premiums. Special editions, including personalized covers, excerpts of existing books, and corporate imprints, can be created in large quantities for special needs. For more information, write to Special Markets/Premium Sales, 1745 Broadway, MD 6-2, New York, New York 10019, or e-mail specialmarkets@randomhouse.com.

AN IMPORTANT TIP & AN INVITATION

Although all prices, opening times, and other details in this book are based on information supplied to us at press time, changes occur all the time in the travel world, and Fodor's cannot accept responsibility for facts that become outdated or for inadvertent errors or omissions. So **always confirm information when it matters,** especially if you're making a detour to visit a specific place. Your experiences—positive and negative—matter to us. If we have missed or misstated something, **please write to us.** We follow up on all suggestions. Contact the China editor at editors@fodors.com or c/o Fodor's at 1745 Broadway, New York, NY 10019.

PRINTED IN THE UNITED STATES OF AMERICA

10 9 8 7 6 5 4 3 2 1

Be a Fodor's Correspondent

Your opinion matters. It matters to us. It matters to your fellow Fodor's travelers, too. And we'd like to hear it. In fact, we need to hear it.

When you share your experiences and opinions, you become an active member of the Fodor's community. That means we'll not only use your feedback to make our books better, but we'll publish your names and comments whenever possible. Throughout our guides, look for "Word of Mouth," excerpts of your unvarnished feedback.

Here's how you can help improve Fodor's for all of us.

Tell us when we're right. We rely on local writers to give you an insider's perspective. But our writers and staff editors—who are the best in the business—depend on you. Your positive feedback is a vote to renew our recommendations for the next edition.

Tell us when we're wrong. We're proud that we update most of our guides every year. But we're not perfect. Things change. Hotels cut services. Museums change hours. Charming cafés lose charm. If our writer didn't quite capture the essence of a place, tell us how you'd do it differently. If any of our descriptions are inaccurate or inadequate, we'll incorporate your changes in the next edition and will correct factual errors at fodors.com immediately.

Tell us what to include. You probably have had fantastic travel experiences that aren't yet in Fodor's. Why not share them with a community of like-minded travelers? Maybe you chanced upon a beach or bistro or B&B that you don't want to keep to yourself. Tell us why we should include it. And share your discoveries and experiences with everyone directly at fodors.com. Your input may lead us to add a new listing or highlight a place we cover with a "Highly Recommended" star or with our highest rating, "Fodor's Choice."

Give us your opinion instantly at our feedback center at www.fodors.com/feedback. You may also e-mail editors@fodors.com with the subject line "China Editor." Or send your nominations, comments, and complaints by mail to China Editor, Fodor's, 1745 Broadway, New York, NY 10019.

You and travelers like you are the heart of the Fodor's community. Make our community richer by sharing your experiences. Be a Fodor's correspondent.

Tim Jarrell, Publisher

CONTENTS

MAPS

Fodor's Features

CONTENTS

ABOUT THIS BOOK

Our Ratings
Sometimes you find terrific travel experiences and sometimes they just find you. But usually the burden is on you to select the right combination of experiences. That's where our ratings come in.

As travelers we've all discovered a place so wonderful that its worthiness is obvious. And sometimes that place is so experiential that superlatives don't do it justice: you just have to be there to know. These sights, properties, and experiences get our highest rating, **Fodor's Choice,** indicated by orange stars throughout this book.

Black stars highlight sights and properties we deem **Highly Recommended,** places that our writers, editors, and readers praise again and again for consistency and excellence.

By default, there's another category: any place we include in this book is by definition worth your time, unless we say otherwise. And we will.

Disagree with any of our choices? Care to nominate a place or suggest that we rate one more highly? Visit our feedback center at www.fodors.com/feedback.

Budget Well
Hotel and restaurant price categories from ¢ to $$$$ are defined in the opening pages of each chapter. For attractions, we always give standard adult admission fees; reductions are usually available for children, students, and senior citizens. Want to pay with plastic? **AE, D, DC, MC, V** following restaurant and hotel listings indicate whether American Express, Discover, Diners Club, MasterCard, and Visa are accepted.

Restaurants
Unless we state otherwise, restaurants are open for lunch and dinner daily. We mention dress only when there's a specific requirement and reservations only when they're essential or not accepted—it's always best to book ahead.

Hotels
Hotels have private bath, phone, TV, and air-conditioning and operate on the European Plan (aka EP, meaning without meals), unless we specify that they use the Continental Plan (CP, with a Continental breakfast), Breakfast Plan (BP, with a full breakfast), or Modified American Plan (MAP, with breakfast and dinner) or are all-inclusive (including all meals and most activities). We always list facilities but not whether you'll be charged an extra fee to use them, so when pricing accommodations, find out what's included.

Many Listings
- ★ Fodor's Choice
- ★ Highly recommended
- ✉ Physical address
- ✣ Directions
- 📫 Mailing address
- ☎ Telephone
- 📠 Fax
- 🌐 On the Web
- 📧 E-mail
- 🎫 Admission fee
- ⏲ Open/closed times
- Ⓜ Metro stations
- 💳 Credit cards

Hotels & Restaurants
- 🏨 Hotel
- 🛏 Number of rooms
- 👍 Facilities
- 🍽 Meal plans
- ✕ Restaurant
- ✍ Reservations
- 🚬 Smoking
- 🍷 BYOB
- ✕🏨 Hotel with restaurant that warrants a visit

Outdoors
- 🏌 Golf
- ⛺ Camping

Other
- 👶 Family-friendly
- ⇨ See also
- ✉ Branch address
- ☞ Take note

WHAT'S WHERE

1 Beijing. Beijing is in massive flux and the construction never stops. Feel the ancient pulse beneath the current clamor—rock up to Tiananmen Square or get an early start in the Forbidden City.

2 Beijing to Shanghai: Hebei, Shandong, Anhui, Jiangsu. Discover a cultural and natural treasure trove—Huangshan peaks are islands in a sea of clouds and canal-laced Suzhou is the Venice of the Orient.

3 Shanghai. In the 1920s Shanghai was known as the Whore of the Orient, but we like to think of her as a classy lady who knows how to have a good time. The party stopped for a few decades after the revolution, but now Shanghai is back in swing.

4 East Coast: Zhejiang, Fujian. Fujian's Xiaman is an undiscovered pearl with all the history, culture, and infrastructure of more popular tourist magnets. Zhejiang's Hangzhou is the famous southernmost city of the Grand Canal.

5 Hong Kong. A city of contrasts—east and west, old and new, work hard and play harder. Long nights of bar-hopping are offset by tai chi sessions at dawn.

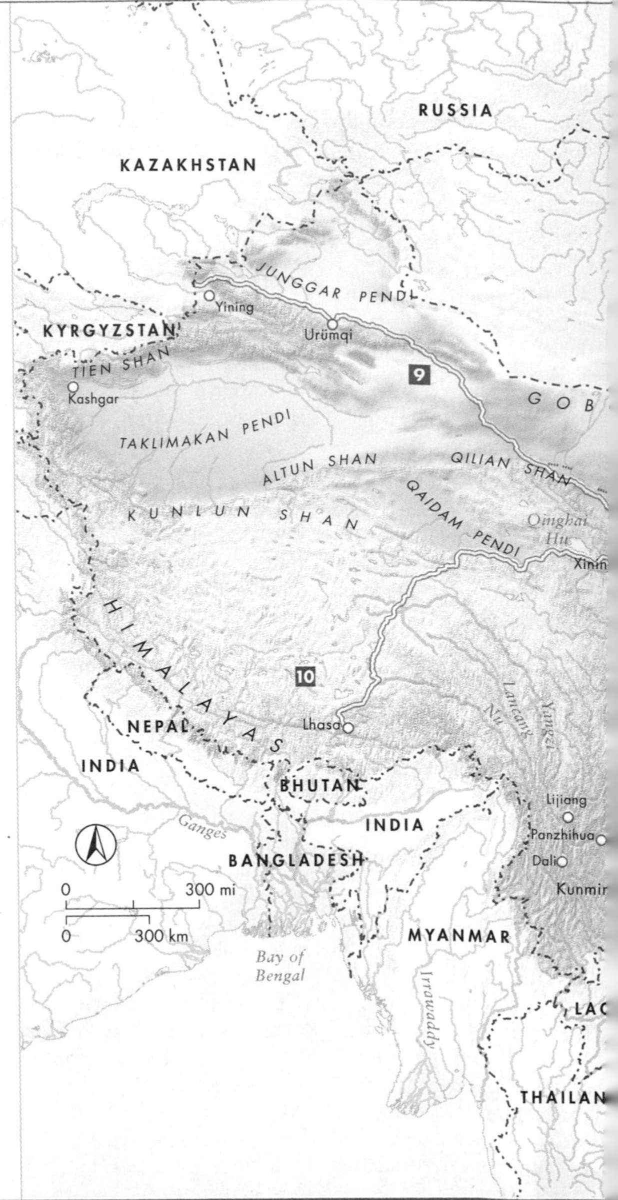

6 Pearl River Delta: Guangzhou and Shenzhen. The word engine is used metaphorically to describe the Pearl River Delta region, but the vibrations are still palpable here in China's industrial hub.

7 Southwest: Guangxi, Guizhou, Yunnan. The mountains are high and the emperor is far away. If you're looking to take a walk on the wild tribal side, then any and all of these three provinces should be high on your to-visit list.

8 Sichuan, Chongqing. China's latest industrial revolution is happening in faraway Sichuan and Chongqing, where the Three Gorges Dam, while hotly debated, remains a stunning sight.

9 The Silk Road. Shaanxi, Gansu, Qinghai: Distant and mysterious, this was ancient China's lifeline to the outside world. Visit the country's last remaining walled cities—Xian is fascinating for its cultural and its historical importance.

10 Tibet. The roof of the world is not the most accessible place, but that's changing thanks to the new train line connecting Lhasa to major cities throughout China.

QUINTESSENTIAL CHINA

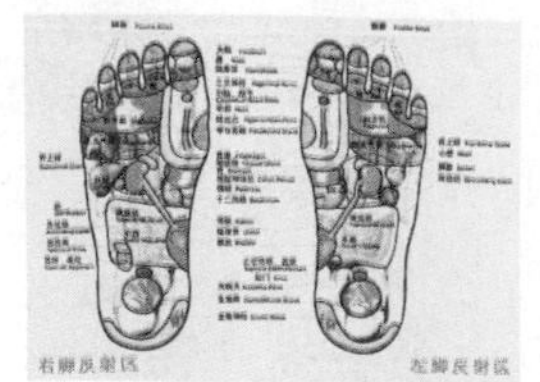

Chinese Chess

Xiangqi is similar in some ways to international chess, but the differences that are culturally interesting. Western Kings roam the board, but Chinese emperors can't leave the castle (a central box in the rear three rows of the board). Xiangqi has no bishops but instead the shi, who stay inside the palace to protect the king. Naturally, the culture that invented gunpowder has artillery on their chessboards; the cannons can jump across the board for devastating long-range strikes. Similar pieces include horses, which function similar to western horses (though they can't jump over blocking pieces). The chariots move like rooks. One of the most interesting differences is that the common soldiers (bing) become more efficient once they hit enemy soil, engaging in lateral guerrilla warfare tactics that western pawns can only dream of.

Reflexology

Foot massage spas are all becoming the rage in China, but if you thought this was a new trend brought on by an upwardly (and naturally more footsore) Chinese populace, think again. While Western medicine sees the foot as mere locomotion, practitioners of traditional Chinese reflexology think that bodily health is reflected in the sole. Each organ is connected to a specific reflex point on the foot. With precise and skillful manipulation of these points, vital functions can be stimulated, toxins eliminated, blood circulation improved, and nerves soothed. If your masseuse is skilled, they'll be able to give you a fairly accurate health diagnosis after just a few minutes of looking at the bottoms of your feet. Are you a smoker? Do you suffer from indigestion? Have you been sleeping poorly? Your feet tell all.

Chinese culture is rich, diverse, and will hit you like a ton of bricks. Keep an open mind while you're traveling because this will be an experience of a lifetime.

China Beyond the Han

If America is a melting pot, then China is a massive huo guo, a bubbling hot pot of diverse meats, spices, and vegetables, held together, if you will, by the unifying broth that are the Han Chinese. Officially there are 56 ethnic minorities that make up the great Chinese nation. Though small in number relative to the Han, these minorities have historically been a force to be reckoned with. Rulers of the last dynasty (the Qing) were Manchus. Though Chinese history is rife with examples of inter-tribal war and Han incursion into non-Han territory (Tibet being the latest and most famous example), the revolution, in theory, leveled the playing field. Traveling through areas less dominated by the Han Chinese offers views of the far different from the usual Beijing-Shanghai-Three Gorges tour.

All the Tea in China

For a vast majority of the Chinese people the day begins and ends with tea. Whether its being savored in a delicate ceremonial porcelain cup or slurped out of a glass mason jar, you can bet that the imbiber takes tea consumption seriously. Ask a Chinese person about the best tea and the answer will very likely depend on where they're from. The highly prized Pu'er tea has a dark color and heavy, almost earthy flavor. It gets its name from the region of southern Yunnan province where it's grown. Fujian produces the best Wulong teas, thanks to the high mountains and favorable climate. Wulong is usually served with much ceremony. Perhaps the most expensive tea in China is a variant of green tea from the Longjing ("Dragon Well") region of Hangzhuo. Longjing tea is served in clear glasses, so one can watch the delicate dance of the long, thin leaves as they float to the top.

IF YOU LIKE

Strolling Around Pedestrian Malls

In a China increasingly filled with cars, pedestrian malls are becoming all the rage, and for good reason—not only is the air and noise pollution less oppressive when there are no cars around, but also dodging taxis tends to detract from one's shopping enjoyment.

Wangfujing, Beijing. This is considered to be the gold standard of urban Chinese pedestrian malls. This shopping Mecca of restaurants, department stores, and some of the most upscale clothing shops in Asia is just a stone's throw away from the plaza in which Chairman Mao announced communist China's birth. Be aware, Wangfujing is crawling with "art touts," whose job is to lure visitors into local painting shops for an exhibition that usually turns into a sales pitch.

Nanjing Dong Lu, Shanghai. This is the "in" place to spend and be seen. However, avoid the stretch midday in summer, as the bright white street heats up like the inside of a solar panel.

Shangxiajiu, Guangzhou. For sensory stimulation, visit this massive warren of buildings and shops in the heart of old Guangzhou, where the overall decibel level hovers around deafening. Small storefronts sell delicious dried fruit samples and there are a few quiet back alleys to explore.

Causeway Bay, Hong Kong. If you want to understand why the Chinese use ren shan ren hai (people mountain people sea) to describe a crowd scene, visit Causeway Bay any night of the week. Fashion galore and restaurants of all description make this neighborhood a people magnet.

Contemporary Art

China has one of the most vibrant, eclectic, and often downright avant-garde art scenes this side of Paris. Beijing is arguably the center of China's contemporary art scene, and it's in China's capital that well-known artists like sculptor Wang Guangyi (who blends propaganda and icons from the cultural revolution for what some consider cynical effect) and painter Feng Mengbo (whose hallmarks include mixing oil painting and computer graphics) ply their trades.

Dashanzi 798 Art District, Beijing. This former military electronics complex in Beijing's Chaoyang district houses dozens of galleries and the workshops of many of the city's up-and-coming artists.

Shanghart Gallery, Shanghai. Opened in 1996, the Shanghart Gallery is among the most "in" places for contemporary art in the city. As always, competition between Shanghai and Beijing is fierce, and while nobody in China seriously considers Shanghai a contender for the art crown of China, that doesn't stop the Pearl of the Orient from trying.

Guangdong Museum of Art, Guangzhou. Denizens of the Pearl River Delta, though normally thought of as caring more about making money than art, have a number of museums and galleries worth visiting. This museum is well respected throughout China.

He Xiangning Museum, Shenzhen. This beautiful new museum in the Overseas Chinese Town district hosts an annual exhibit each autumn featuring the best works of art students from all over China.

Bicycling

In the not too distant past, China was known as "The Bicycle Kingdom," but as cars become more popular, the iconic sea of bicycles that once filled the avenues of Beijing and Shanghai has dried to a trickle.

But this doesn't mean that bicycling enthusiasts should lose heart. While the two-wheeled herd has thinned out considerably, you'll hardly be riding alone. Most hotels will be able to help you out with bicycle rentals, or a brand new flying pigeon (the bike of China) should only set you back a few hundred Yuan.

Beijing. Though notorious for its bad air and automobile gridlock, the capital is still our favorite urban bicycling ground. Its wide avenues and impossible-to-maneuver-by-car back alleyways make it an ideal city to tour by bicycle.

Xian. The city center is small enough to make it perfect for exploring by bike. For a unique experience, take a tour on top of the city wall, the only one left fully intact in all of China.

Shanghai. The Pearl of the Orient is also two-wheel friendly, though you'll be asked to dismount and walk along the Nanjing pedestrian area.

Chengdu. The greenest city in China is also as flat as a Ping-Pong table, which makes it one of our favorites for exploring by bike.

Sculptures and Tombs

The ancient Egyptians may be best at burying their dead kings in gaudy opulence, but the Chinese give them a run for their money when it comes to craftsmanship for the post-mortem care of royalty.

Terracotta Warriors, Xian. The Terracotta warriors are perhaps the best known example of sculptures-as-tomb-guardians in the world. These meticulously crafted soldiers were created as part of the elaborate funeral ritual of the first Qing emperor, buried in the ground outside of what would later become the Silk Road city of Xian, and only discovered millennia later by a modern-day farmer tilling soil.

Ming Tomb, Nanjing. The Ming emperors were particularly interested in making sure that their resting places were both remembered and protected. The Nanjing Ming Tomb was Built as a burial site for the emperor Hong Wu, the warrior monk who established the Ming Dynasty, and is guarded by a grand procession of stone animals—real and mythical—all kneeling in tribute to the emperor as they guard his remains for all eternity.

Tomb of the Southern Yue Kings, Guangzhou. Construction workers breaking ground to build Guangzhou's China hotel were in for quite a shock when they came across an intact underground tomb belonging to the ancient emperor Wen Di. The discovery was interesting in that it led histo[illegible] to reevaluate the area's place [illegible] dynastical history. Tho[illegible] ery barely hindered the hotel, the [illegible] faithfully [illegible] the [illegible] mu[illegible]

[illegible] cov- [illegible] ion of [illegible] ot merely [illegible] asures form the Nan Yue

IF YOU LIKE

Antique Villages Come to Life

China is filled with ancient towns and villages, and a fairly recent trend has been the gentrification (sometimes closer to Disneyfication) of historically or culturally significant towns in the name of preservation. Other places, however, look closer to the way they did hundreds of years ago.

Lijiang, Yunnan Province. Though a fun place to visit, with its tribal themed café, guesthouses, and CD stores, Lijiang is pretty much a for-tourists-only kind of place, but the architecture is still pretty cool.

Fuli, Guangxi Province. Just a quick skip up the river from Yangshuo (itself in the midst of a radical "Disneyfication"), Fuli doesn't seem to have changed much since Sun Yat-sen visited nearly a century ago. This Ming-era town gives visitors a good idea of how local people lived hundreds of years ago.

Gulangyu island, Xiamen. Though the area by the ferry pier has been renovated, most of this car-free island off the coast of Xiamen feels not so much "faux run-down" as genuinely feral, with colonial-era buildings in varied states of glorious disrepair. The beaches on the north side of the island are also quite good for swimming.

Dapeng Ancient City, Shenzhen. Located just a few miles outside of China's new-
-st and most modern metropolis, the
walled ancient city of Dapeng—which
-ed military personnel and their
sou- charged with defending China's
dyna- -st during the Ming and Qing
worth -n unpolished gem well

Taking It to the Extreme

An increasing number of Middle Kingdom visitors are coming not merely to see the Great Wall but to engage in more adrenalin-intensive activities (jumping over the Great Wall on a skateboard, for example). This new breed of China traveler will be happy to hear that adventure sports are alive and well in the People's Republic.

The Great Wall, Huang Hua. This crumbling section of the wall, just a few hours outside of Beijing, is far more rugged than the more tourist-popular Badaling section, and offers amazing views and seriously challenging climbs.

Rock Climbing, Yangshuo. Yangshuo has become a major "in" spot for aficionados of rock climbing, and the area has hundreds of routes for climbers of all levels. Possibly one of the most challenging routes is the inside track of Moon Hill, which draws some of the world's best climbers each year.

Long Distance Bicycling. Rural touring is exploding in China, and an increasing number of western visitors are choosing to see the country not by train or tour bus, but by bicycle. Bike Asia runs tours for all levels of experience and endurance, from the rolling hills of Guangxi and Guizhou, to the serious-riders-only mountains of Tibet.

Wind Surfing, Qingdao. It's no accident that this seaside city in Northeast China was chosen to host the Olympic sailing events of 2008. The shape of the beaches combined with average wind speeds makes Qingdao an ideal place for those who get their kicks sailing.

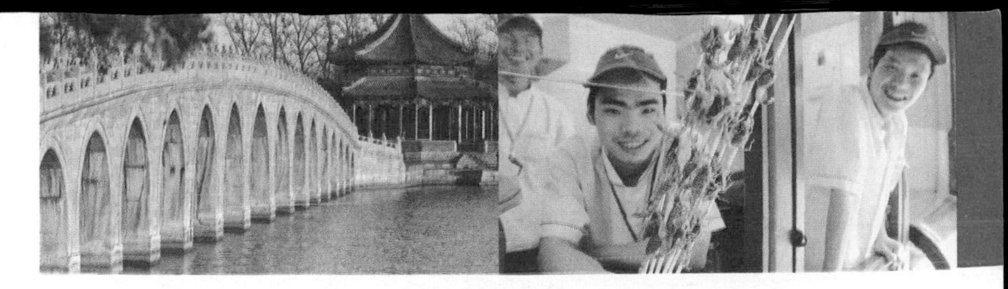

Visiting Specters

There are some places in China where you get the distinct feeling that you're not alone, places where the eyes of those long gone seem to be watching you, probing you with a certain ... curiosity. Its only natural that a country that measures its age in millennia would have many such places.

Summer Palace, Beijing. Visitors to the residence of Cixi, located in the Summer Palace outside Beijing, have noted that they feel a certain sense of disquiet, as if the "Old Buddha" (as the last empress of China was called) herself were still hanging around. Well known for her canny political sense, it is entirely likely that the Old Buddha still returns to keep an eye on the comings and goings of foreign barbarians in China—a big issue during her reign. Though today she's merely a specter of her former glorious self, we advise visitors to be reverent in her home nonetheless.

Hakka Enclosures, Shenzhen. Eerie presences have been reported roaming around inside the Longgang Hakka Enclosures on the outskirts of Shenzhen. Though the former stronghold and dwelling of the proud Hakka people has been converted into a museum, its been done so in a way so unobtrusive that visitors almost get the sense that the homes within are still occupied, and that their former residents might return at any moment. And they just might at that, so consider yourselves a guest of China's guest people (as the Hakka are known), and tread lightly through their domain.

Adventurous Dining

Much has been written about the cuisine of China, and for a very good reason—it's some of the best (and most laden with variety) to be found on the planet. Most visitors will be happy to stick with well-known dishes, such as Peking duck or kung pao chicken, but for those who want a culinary walk on the wild side, might we suggest a few less known regional favorites?

Stinky Tofu, Fujian. Though it's hotly contested whether this highly odiferous dish originated first in Fujian or later in Taiwan, the overpowering snack is readily available on both sides of the Taiwan straits. Cubes of tofu fermented and deep fried to a crispy brown, the dish smells like extremely ripe cheese. Best enjoyed by those who prefer their food on the pungent side.

Yak Butter Tea, Yunnan, Tibet. This beverage is ubiquitous throughout both Tibet and the higher mountain regions of Yunnan province. Thick and tangy, the main ingredients of yak butter tea are, as the name suggests, yak butter. Though its adherents drink it by the gallon, considering it delicious and healthy, unsuspecting imbibers have likened its flavor to melted blue cheese, or even wood polish.

Stewed Chicken Feet, Guangzhou. To a Cantonese chef, nothing should ever go to waste, and the claws of the humble chicken, stewed until the fat an[illegible]ies are nearly dripping from i[illegible]y dim is considered a cruc[illegible] sum feast.

GREAT ITINERARIES

BEIJING & THE SILK ROAD

Day 1: Welcome to Beijing

Beijing is the cultural heart of China and the nation's top travel destination. Try to catch the daily flag-raising ceremony in Tiananmen Square. Most first-time visitors to China are drawn here as soon as they recover from the jet lag. As you watch goose-stepping People's Liberation Army soldiers march from the Forbidden City into the world's largest public square under the watchful eye of Mao Zedong, you'll know you're not in Kansas anymore. After the flag-raising, take a stroll around the square and soak in the atmosphere. And of course, a tour of the Forbidden City is an essential Beijing experience.

Logistics: Avoid unlicensed taxi touts who approach you in Beijing's airport. Proceed to the taxi stand outside, where a ride to your hotel should cost in the range of Y100. Tiananmen Square is best approached on foot or by subway, as taxis aren't allowed to let you off anywhere nearby.

Day 2: The Great Wall

If you're really pressed for time, you could visit the Badaling section of the Great Wall in an afternoon, but we recommend a day-trip out to the more impressive sections at Mutianyu, Simatai, or Jinshanling.

Logistics: The most economical way to ...ch any section of the Great Wall is by rus... ...our bus. If you don't want to be privat... ...ever, you're better off hiring ...tation for the day.

Day 3: J... ...Empire

Beijing is d... ...rous imperial palaces and p... The lovely Summer Palace ... ...est

has come to symbolize the decadence that brought about the fall of the Qing dynasty. The Temple of Heaven is considered to be the most perfect example of Ming dynasty architecture and is a great place to take a break from the frenetic pace of the capital.

Logistics: These imperial sites will each take about three or four hours to tour properly, and are best reached by taxi. There's no need to ask the driver to wait, though, as plenty of taxis are constantly coming and going.

Day 4: Capital Entertainment

Beijing is teeming with cultural performances, fabulous restaurants, and sprawling outdoor markets. If you're looking to do some souvenir shopping, plan on spending a few hours at Beijing Curio City or the Silk Alley Market in the Chaoyang District. In the evening, music enthusiasts will want to take in a glass-shattering performance of Beijing Opera. If that's not your thing, experience the city's more modern nightlife around Qianhai Lake, where fashionable bars and shops stay open late.

Logistics: Unless you're willing to try your luck on one of Beijing's public buses, these destinations are best reached by taxi.

Days 5–8: Xian, China's Ancient Capital

For most of China's history, Xian was the nation's capital. As the starting point for the Silk Road, the area is packed with historically significant destinations, most of which can be covered in just a few days. One entire day should be devoted to visiting the Terracotta Warriors Museum and surrounding sites located east of the city. The famous warriors, built to protect China's first emperor in the afterlife, are

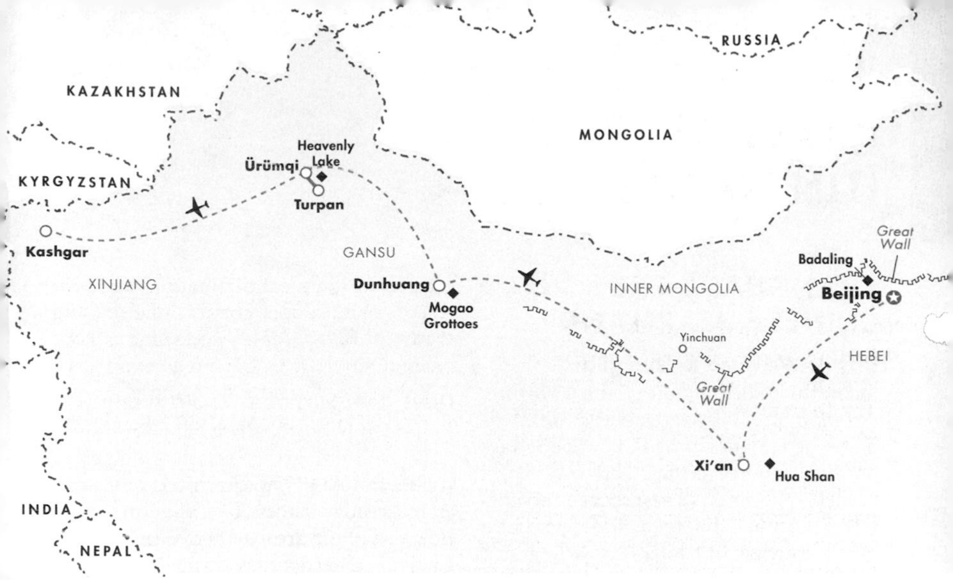

only part of a huge tomb complex that stretches for miles. If you've got the time, we also recommend a day-trip to the spectacular peaks of Hua Shan.

Logistics: Flights from Beijing to Xian take about two hours with very frequent departures. Trains depart from Beijing's West Rail Station and take 12 hours. Most sites within Xian can be reached by foot. The Terracotta Warriors and Hua Shan are located east of Xian, so you'll want to book a tour or catch one of the cheap public buses.

Travel Note:

If you're not interested in continuing farther west along the Silk Road, Xian is the perfect transportation hub from which to catch a flight or train to Lhasa, Chengdu, Shanghai or any other destination of your choice.

Days 9–10: Dunhuang

Once the border between China and the unknown barbarian lands to the west, Dunhuang was also a major stop for merchants and religious pilgrims traveling the Silk Road. Filled with more than 1,000 years of Buddhist carvings, the Mogao Grottoes are widely considered to be the best surviving example of early religious art in China.

Logistics: Flights from Xian to Dunhuang take three hours and depart regularly during the busy summer months, less often in the off-season.

Days 11–14: Urumqi & Turpan

Xinjiang is China's vast western frontier, where the pagodas and temples of the East melt into the bazaars and minarets of Central Asia. The capital of Urumqi is certainly interesting as far as large cities go in China, but for a real taste of the region you'll want to head out to the countryside. Heavenly Lake is perhaps the most beautiful body of water in the whole country. The small city of Turpan provides a fascinating look into the Silk Road history that once defined the area and the Uyghur minority way of life that dominates today. If you've got an extra couple of days, head even farther west to Kashgar, closer to Baghdad than Beijing in both distance and culture.

Logistics: During the busy summer season, flights regularly connect Dunhuang with Urumqi. Other times of the year you'll need to make the long journey by train or make a connecting flight in Lanzhou or Xian. There are multiple daily flights between Urumqi and Kasghar, as well as between Urumqi and Beijing.

GREAT ITINERARIES

SHANGHAI & THE CHINESE HEARTLAND

Day 1: Welcome to Shanghai

Shanghai is all about the country's future, not its past. Once you've settled in, your first stop should be the Bund, Shanghai's unofficial tourist center. This waterfront boulevard is the city's best spot for people-watching and culinary exploration. For a bird's-eye view of China's sprawling economic capital, head across the Huangpu River toward Pudong, where you can mount either the Oriental Pearl Tower or the Jinmao Tower. There's also the Yu Garden, where you can relax among carefully designed landscaping and traditional architecture evoking the China of yore.

Logistics: Unless you fear cutting-edge technology, you'll want to take the ultra-fast maglev train from the airport into the city center. Shanghai is suprisingly easy to navigate on foot, although taxis are ubiquitous if your feet get tired. To get between the Bund and Pudong, the Y2 ferry across the Huangpu River departs every 10 minutes.

Day 2: Paris of the East

Shanghai's colonial history adds immeasurably to the city's charm. Be sure to visit the French Concession. Whether you're a fan of colonial architecture or enjoy sipping cappuccino in quiet cafés, this is a pleasant area to spend time. Walk through Xintiandi, where restored traditional houses mix with bars, boutiques, and small museums. Spend some time searching for the perfect souvenir on the Nanjing Lu. Alternatively, you could brush up on your Chinese history at the Shanghai Museum, one of the finest in the country.

Logistics: All of these destinations are clustered together in a square mile located west of the Bund, easily accessible on foot or by taxi.

Days 3–4: Suzhou & Zhouzhuang

Regarded by the Chinese in ancient times as heaven on earth, Suzhou manages to retain many of its charms despite the encroaching forces of modernization. Enjoy strolling through perfectly designed gardens and temples along the gently flowing branches of the Grand Canal. Luckily, Suzhou is close enough to work well as a day-trip. Riding on a gondola past the Zhouzhuang's signature tile-roof wooden houses, you'll understand why it was called the "Venice of the East." If you've only got one day to get out of Shanghai, the area's water villages should be your destination.

Logistics: Transportation between Shanghai and Suzhou is most conveniently available by bus, of either the intercity or tourist variety; seats on a tourist coach to Zhouzhuang are also easily booked. If you're planning to visit both destinations, you'll probably want to spend the night at a hotel in Suzhou.

Days 5–8: Huang Shan

China's top natural scenic attraction, Huang Shan (Yellow Mountain) is an impossibly beautiful collection of 72 jagged peaks famous for grotesquely twisted pine trees and unusual rock formations. This area has provided the inspiration for generations of Chinese poets and artists, which is why its vistas and valleys may seem so familiar to you. There are numerous paths to the top, either by foot or by cable car. To take part in Huang Shan's essential experience, spend a night at one of the mountaintop guesthouses before

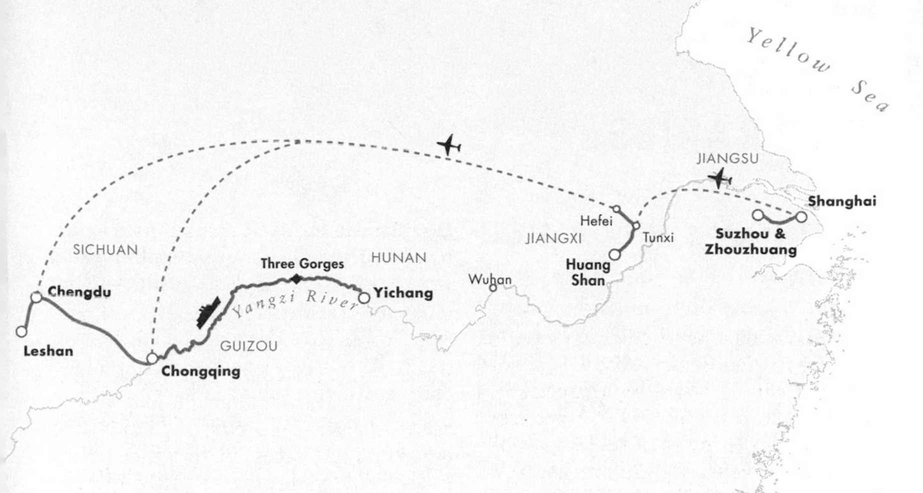

waking at dawn to watch the sun rise over an eerie sea of fog.

Logistics: Unless you're willing to spend 10 or more hours on a bus from Shanghai, your best bet is to fly into Huang Shan's airport located nearby in the town of Tunxi. There's no need to book a tour of the mountain, as paths and scenic viewpoints are all well marked in English.

Day 9-10: Chengdu

As the capital of Sichuan Province, Chengdu has long been one of China's great cultural centers. Famous for its fiery local cuisine, the city has also managed to partially maintain a pleasant atmosphere of yesteryear. Essential sites include the Buddhist Wenshu Monastery and for animal lovers, the Giant Panda Breeding Research Base. No matter how little time you have available to spend here, make the day-trip south to Leshan to see the world's largest stone-carved Buddha. With toes the size of a small bus, the seated Grand Buddha is impressive to say the least.

Logistics: Like most tourist hubs, the airport near Huang Shan offers fairly frequent flights to major cities such as Chengdu only during the busy warmer months. You may find it easier to connect through Hefei or Shanghai. All hotels and travel agencies in Chengdu can book tours to Leshan, or you can travel on your own by public bus.

Travel note: If you're pressed for time and are set on cruising the Yangzi River, skip Chengdu and fly directly to Chongqing.

Days 11–14: The Three Gorges

Despite rising water levels caused by construction of the Three Gorges Dam, a cruise along the Yangzi River through the Three Gorges is impressive. Along the way, you'll pass soon-to-be-submerged abandoned metropolises that were humming with life only a few years ago as well as their modern counterparts built on higher ground. Be sure to book yourself on a luxury boat catering to foreigners, or you'll end up spending three days on a damp, rat-infested ship. Don't miss a visit to the Little Three Gorges, where monkeys play near the water's edge.

Logistics: Boats depart from Chongqing, a three- or four-hour drive east of Chengdu. If you book your tour in Chengdu, transportation to Chongqing is almost always included. Most cruises disembark at Yichang in Hubei Province, where you can get a flight back to most travel hubs.

GREAT ITINERARIES

SOUTHERN CHINA & TIBET

Day 1: Welcome to Hong Kong

Despite the city's return to Chinese rule in 1999, Hong Kong is still a world away from the mainland. To get a feel for the city, take a ride on the Star Ferry, connecting Hong Kong Island with Kowloon. The ferry offers the best possible views of the business district's skyline. Don't miss the smoke-filled Man Mo Temple and Hong Kong's famous assortment of antiques shops and art galleries. Ride the very steep tram to the summit of Victoria Peak, with views of the entire harbor.

Logistics: The new airport is connected to Kowloon and Hong Kong island by express train, taking about 30 minutes. Taxis are available everywhere, although much of the city can be explored by foot. The tram to Victoria Peak is open until midnight.

Day 2: Getting Out of the City

While the business districts clustered around the harbor feature some of the world's densest urban jungle, Hong Kong also has a relaxed natural side. The express ferry to Lantau can whisk you away from the city in about 40 minutes. Arriving at the town of Mui Wo, you can catch a bus to the island's top two attractions: Po Lin Monastery, featuring the world's tallest outdoor bronze statue of Buddha, and Tai O, an old fishing village dotted with terrific seafood restaurants. For even greater solitude, take the ferry to one of the smaller Outer Islands.

Logistics: Ferries for Lantau leave from either the Star Ferry Terminal or the Outlying Districts Services Pier just to the west. On the island, private buses travel between all of the main attractions.

Day 3: Macau

Even with a recent push to become Asia's Las Vegas, Macau is still decidedly quieter and more traditional than Hong Kong. The slower pace of development has left much of the city's colonial charm intact. Start with a visit to Largo do Senado (Senate Square), paved with Portuguese-style tiles and surrounded by brightly colored colonial buildings. The city is home to two beautiful churches, São Domingos and São Paulo, the latter featuring exhibits on the early history of Asian Christianity.

Logistics: TurboJets from Hong Kong to Macau depart frequently and at all times of the day, making the trip in about an hour. If you're not comfortable traveling around the city by taxi, book a tour before you leave Hong Kong.

Days 4–8: Yangshuo & Longshen

The scenery in northern Guangxi Province is some of the most beautiful in all of China. Dotted with dramatic groupings of sheer limestone karst mountains, visitors often find themselves loath to leave. You'll see more of the countryside by taking the four-hour Li River Cruise down to Yangshuo as soon as possible. Yangshuo is a laid-back town popular with backpackers, and an excellent base from which to explore natural sites like Green Lotus Peak and Moon Hill. If you've got more time, head back through Guilin to the town of Longsheng, home to the famously photogenic Dragon's Backbone Rice Terraces.

Logistics: For a flight to Guilin you'll need to get to the airport in Shenzhen, just over the border. This can be done by taking a train followed by an airport bus, or by catching the direct TurboJet ferry from Kowloon.

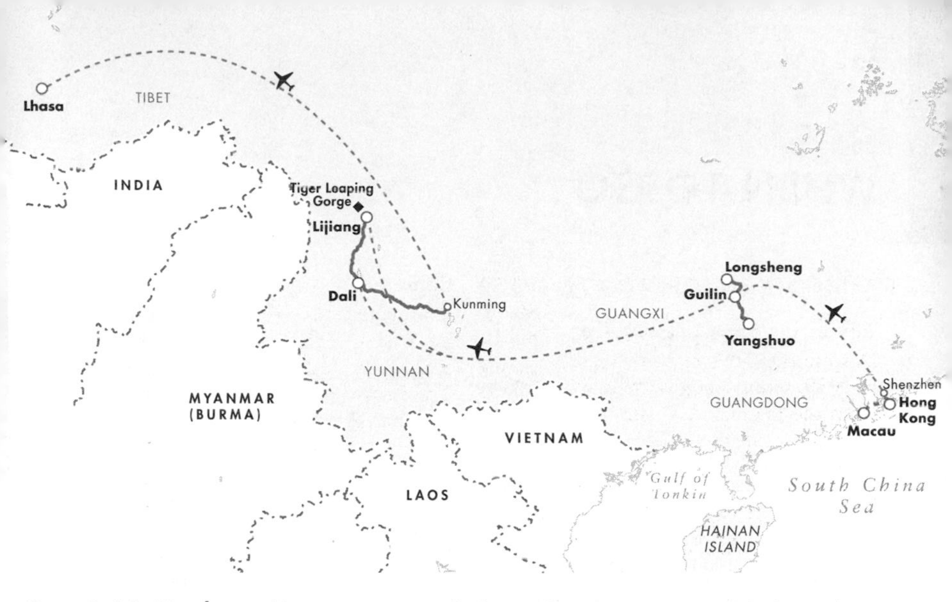

Days 9–14: Northwest Yunnan

Sandwiched between the Tibetan Plateau and Myanmar, foreigners have long been attracted to this area for its mix of minority cultures and stunning natural beauty. Dali, beside the waters of Erhai Lake, is home to the Bai people who settled here 4,000 years ago; the elegant Three Pagodas north of town are one of China's most iconic images. Farther north lies Lijiang, capital of the Naxi people and the only place in the country where traditional Chinese music is said to survive in its original form. The highlight of the region is Tiger Leaping Gorge, one of the deepest river gorges in the world and a popular two- or three-day hike.

Logistics: Most flights from Guilin to either Dali or Lijiang connect through the regional capital. Travel between these destinations is by public bus or tour coach.

Days 15–18: Lhasa

Lhasa is the capital of a nation within a nation, with only tenuous ties to the rest of China. These ties have increased considerably with the opening of the train line to Tibet, yet the city is still unique. Start your tour of the city with a walk around the Barkhor followed by a visit to Jokhang Temple, respectively Tibetan Buddhism's holiest pilgrimage circuit and holiest religious site. Don't miss the Sera Monastery, where monks hold animated theological debates every afternoon. Climb the long steps to the Potala Palace, followed by a visit to what was once the world's largest monastic complex, Drepung Monastery. If you only spend one day outside of Lhasa, make the two-hour trip to the mountaintop Ganden Monastery, with awe-inspiring views of the surrounding Lhasa River Valley. The five-day roundtrip between Lhasa and Everest Base Camp with a number of stops along the way is the essential Tibet experience.

Logistics: Multiple daily flights connect Kunming with Lhasa. Sites within Lhasa are accessible on foot or by taxi. Travel to sites outside Lhasa, like Everest Base Camp, must be arranged through an official tour operator.

Travel Note: Those wishing to visit Tibet can easily book flight or train tickets from most major transportation hubs.

WHEN TO GO

Although temperatures can be scorching, summer is the peak tourist season, and hotels and transportation can be very crowded. If you're traveling during peak season, try to book several months in advance.

The weather is better and the crowds not quite as dense in late spring and early fall, although you need to be prepared for rain. It's easy enough to buy a poncho or an umbrella when you're on the road.

Winter is bitterly cold and not conducive to travel in much of the country, especially North. However, the southern most reaches remain moderate throughout the winter. Try to avoid traveling around Chinese New Year and other national holidays if possible. Many businesses in China shut down and it will seem like the entire population is traveling with you—hotels will be booked solid and major sights will feel like Times Square on New Year's Eve.

Regardless of the weather, avoid traveling during the National Week holiday in October and International Labor Day in May. The entire country goes on vacation and most major destinations resemble mosh pits.

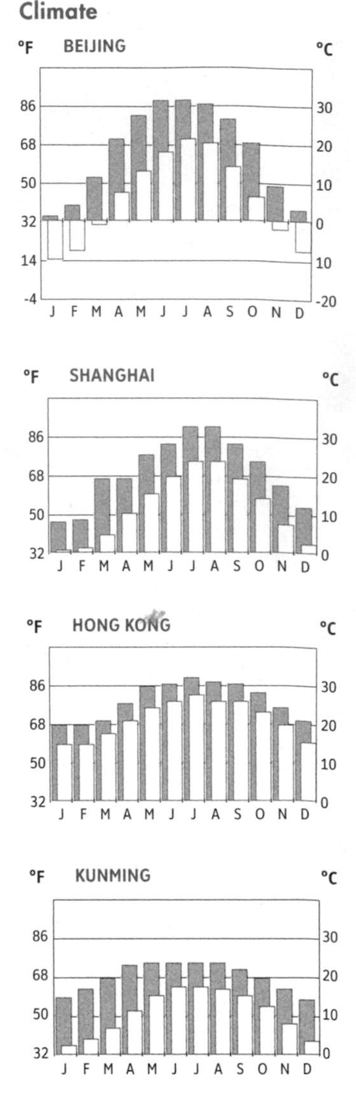

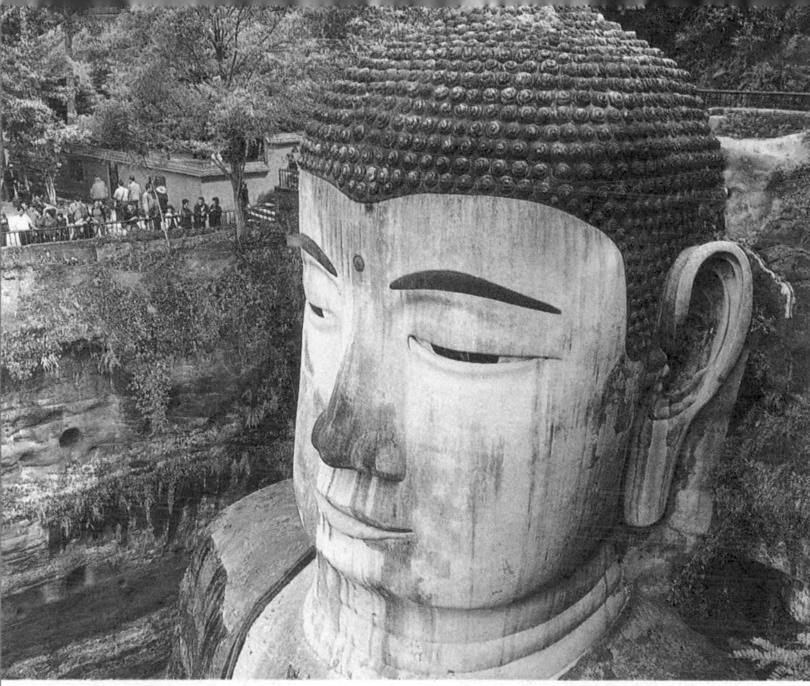
Giant Buddha Statue, Leshan

THE AGE OF EMPIRES

When asked his opinion on the historical impact of the French Revolution, Chairman Mao quipped, "It's too early to tell." Though a bit tongue in cheek, China does measure its history in millennia, and in its grand timeline, interactions with the West have been mere blips.

According to historical records, Chinese civilization stretches back to the 15th century BC—markings found on turtle shells carbon dated to around 1500 BC bear some similarity to modern Chinese script. China then resembled city-states rather than a unified nation. Iconic figures such as Lao Tzu (the father of Taoism), Sun Tzu (author of the *Art of War*), and Confucius lived during this period. Generally, 221 BC is accepted as the beginning of Imperial China, when the city-states united under various banners.

Over the next 2,200 years (give or take a few), China alternated between periods of harmony and political upheaval. Its armies conquered new territory and were in turn conquered by external invaders (most of whom wound up themselves being assimilated).

By the early 18th century, the long, slow decline of the Qing—the last of China's Imperial dynasties—was already in progress, making the ancient nation ripe for exploitation by rising European powers. The Imperial era ended with the forced abdication of child Emperor Puyi (whose life is chronicled in Bernardo Bertolucci's *The Last Emperor*), and it's here that the history of modern China, first with the founding of the republic under Sun Yat-sen and then with the establishment of the People's Republic under Mao Zedong, truly begins.

Writing Appears

1500BC 1200BC 900BC

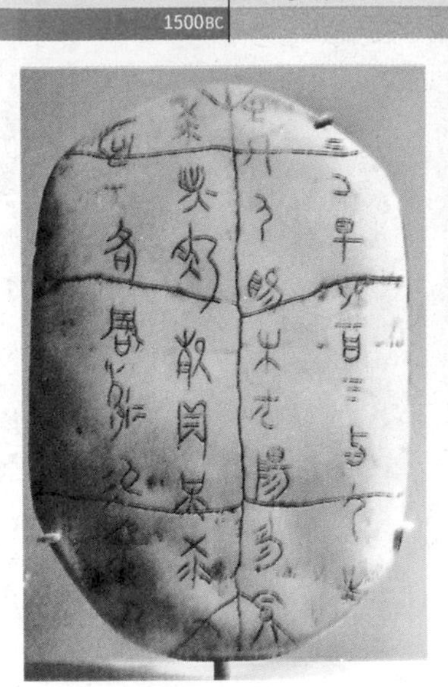

(left) Oracle shell with early Chinese characters. (top, right) The Great Wall stretches 4,163 miles from east to west. (bottom, right) Confucius was born in Qufu, Shandong.

circa 1500 BC

Writing Appears

The earliest accounts of Chinese history are still shrouded in myth and legend, and it wasn't until 1959 that stories were verified by archaeological findings. For millennia, people formed communities in the fertile lands of what is now central China. The first recorded Chinese characters are said to have been developed 3,500 years ago. Though sometimes referred to as the Shang Dynasty, this period was more of a precursor to modern Chinese dynasties than a truly unified kingdom.

722–475 BC

The Warring States Period

China was so far from unified that these centuries are collectively remembered as the Warring States Period. As befitting such a contentious time, military science progressed, iron replaced bronze, and weapons material improved. Some of China's greatest luminaries lived during this period, including the father of Taoism, Lao-tzu, Confucius, and Sun-Tzu, one of the greatest military tacticians and the author of the infamous *Art of War,* which is still studied in military academies around the world.

221–207 BC

The First Dynasty

The Qin Dynasty eventually defeated all of the other warring factions thanks to their cutting-edge military technology, namely the cavalry. The Qin were also called Ch'in, which may be where the word China first originated. The first Emperor, Qin Shi-huang, unified much of the lands and established a legal code and vast bureaucracy to hold it together. The Qin dynasty also standardized the written and spoken language and introduced a common currency.

(left) Terracotta warriors in Xian, on the Silk Road. (top right) Buddha statue, Maijishan Cave in Tianshui, Gansa. (bottom left) Sun Tzu, author of The *Art of War*.

In order to protect his newly unified country, Qin Shihuang ordered the creation of the massive Great Wall of China, which was built and rebuilt over the next 1,000 years. He was also a sculpture enthusiast and commissioned a massive army of stone soldiers to follow him into the afterlife. Buried with him, these terra-cotta warriors would remain hidden from the eyes of the world for two thousand years, until they were found by a farmer digging in a field just outside of Xian. These warriors are among the most important archaeological finds of the 20th century.

220–265 BC

Buddhism Arrives

Emperor Qin's dreams of a unified China fell apart, and eventually the kingdom split into three warring factions. But what was bad for stability turned out to be good for literature. The Three Kingdoms Period is still remembered in song and story. *The Romance of the Three Kingdoms* is as popular among Asian bookworms as the *Legend of King Arthur* is among Western readers. It's still widely read and has been translated into almost every language. Variations of the story have been adapted for manga, television series, and video games.

The Three Kingdoms period was filled with court intrigue, murder, and massive battles that, while exciting to read about centuries later, weren't much fun at the time. Armies ravaged the countryside, and most people lived and died in misery. Perhaps it was the carnage and disunity of the time that turned the country into a magnet for forces of harmony; it was during this period that Buddhism was first introduced into China, traveling over the Himalayas from India, via the Silk Road.

Religion Diversifies

600 800 1000

(left) Genghis Khan conquered much of China. (top, right) Islamic lecture at madrassa classroom inside Dongguan mosque, Xinning. (bottom, right) Kublai Khan was the first Mongol Emperor of China.

618–845 Religion Diversifies

Chinese spiritual life continued to diversify. Nestorian Monks from Asia Minor arrived bearing news of Christianity, and Saad ibn Abi Waqqas (a companion of the Prophet Muhammad) supposedly visited the Middle Kingdom to spread the word of Islam. During this era, Wu Zetian, onetime concubine, seized power from the Tang Dynasty and became the first (and only) woman to assume the title of emperor. She ruled for 25 years through puppet emperors and finally, for 15 years as Emperor Shengshen.

1271–1368 Ghengis Invades

In Xanadu did Kublai Khan a stately pleasure dome decree . . .

Or so goes the famed Coleridge poem. But Kublai's grandfather Temujin (better known as Ghengis Khan) had bigger things in mind. One of the greatest war tacticians in history, he united the restive nomads of Mongolia's grassy plains and eventually sacked, looted, and pillaged much of the known west and most of the Chinese landmass. By the time Ghengis died in 1227, his grandson was well-tutored and ready to take on the rest of China.

By 1271, Kublai had established a capital in a landlocked city that would only much later become known as Beijing. This marks the beginning of the first (but not last) non-Han dynasty. Kublai Khan kept fighting southward and by 1279, Guangzhou fell to the Mongols, and Khan became the ultimate monarch of China. Though barbarians at heart, the Mongols must be credited for encouraging the arts and a number of early public works projects, including extending the highways and grand canals.

The Mongols | Ming Dynasty | Qing Dynasty
1400 | 1600 | 1800

(left) Statue of admiral Zheng He. (top right) Forbidden City in Beijing (bottom right) Child emperor Puyi.

1368–1644

Ming Dynasty

Many scholars believe that the Mongols' inability to relate with the Han is what ultimately pushed the Han to rise up and overthrow them. The reign of the Ming Dynasty was the last ethnically Han Dynasty to rule over a unified China. At its apex, the Bright Empire encompassed a landmass easily recognized as China, even by today's mapmakers. The Ming Emperors built a huge army and navy, refurbished the agricultural system, and printed many books using movable type long before Gutenberg. In the 13th century, Emperor Yongle began construction of the famous Forbidden City in Beijing, a veritable icon of China.

Also during the Ming Dynasty, China's best known explorer, Zheng He, plied the seven seas in massive treasure fleets that dwarfed in size and range the ships of Christopher Columbus. A giant both in stature and persona, Admiral Zheng (who was also a eunuch) spent two decades expanding China's knowledge of the world outside of its already impressive borders. He traveled as far as India, Africa, and (some say) even the coast of the New World.

1644–1911

Qing Dynasty

The final dynasty represented a serious case of minority rule. They were Manchus from the northeast. The early Qing dynasty was a brutal period as forces loyal to the new emperor crushed those loyal to the old. The Qing Dynasty peaked in the mid-to-late 18th century but soon after, its military powers began to wane. In the 19th century, Qing control weakened and prosperity diminished. By 1910 China was fractured, a baby sat on the Imperial throne, and the Qing Dynasty was on its deathbed.

(left) Portrait of Marshal Chiang Kai-shek with his wife. (top, right) Mao Zedong on December 6, 1944. (bottom, right) Sun Yat-sen.

1834–1860 The Opium Wars

European powers were hungry to open new territories up for trade, but the Qing weren't buying. The British East India Company, strapped for cash, realized they could sell opium in China at huge profits. The Chinese government quickly banned the nefarious trade and in response, a technologically superior Britain declared war. After a humiliating defeat in the first Opium War, China was forced to cede Hong Kong. Other foreign powers followed with territorial demands of their own.

1912–1949 Republican Era

China's Republican period was chaotic and unstable. The revolutionary Dr. Sun Yat-sen—revered by most Chinese as the father of modern China—was unable to build a cohesive government without the aid of regional warlords and urban gangsters. When he died of cancer in 1925, power passed to Chiang Kai-shek, who set about unifying China under the Kuomintang. What began as a unified group of both left- and right-wingers quickly deteriorated, and by the mid-1920s, civil war between the Communists and Nationalists was brewing.

The '30s and '40s were bleak decades for the Chinese people, caught between a vicious war with Japan and periodic clashes between Kuomintang and Communist forces. After Japan's defeat in 1945, China's civil war kicked into high gear. Though the Kuomintang were armed with superior weapons and backed by American money, the majority of Chinese people rallied behind the Communists. Within four years, the Kuomintang were driven off the mainland to Taiwan, where the Republic of China exists to the present day.

(top left) Illiterate soldiers are taught about Mao's *Little Red Book* in Beijing December 1966. (top right) Central Shenzhen, Guangdong (bottom left) Poster of Mao's slogans.

1949–Present

The People's Republic

On October 1, 1949, Mao Zedong declared from atop Beijing's Gate of Heavenly Peace that "The Chinese People have stood up." And so the People's Republic of China was born. The Communist party set out to overhaul China's ancient feudal system, emphasizing class struggle, redistribution of wealth, and elimination of foreign dominance. The next three decades would see a massive, often painful transformation of Chinese society from feudalism into the modern age.

The Great Leap Forward was a disaster—Chinese peasants were encouraged to cram 100 years of industrial development into as many weeks. Untenable decisions led to industrial and agricultural ruin, widespread famine, and an estimated 30 million deaths. The trauma of this period, however, pales in comparison to The Great Proletarian Cultural Revolution. From 1966–1976, fear and zealotry gripped the nation as young revolutionaries heeded Chairman Mao's call to root out class enemies. During this decade, millions died, millions were imprisoned, and much of China's accumulated religious, historical, and cultural heritage literally went up in smoke.

Like a phoenix rising from its own ashes, China rose from its own self-inflicted destruction. In the early 1980s, Deng Xiao-ping took the first steps in reforming China's stagnant economy. With the maxim "To Get Rich is Glorious," Deng loosened central control on the economy and declared Special Economic Zones, where the seeds of capitalism could be incubated. Two decades later, the nation is one of the world's most vibrant economic engines. Though China's history is measured in millennia, her brightest years may well have only just begun.

Experience Beijing

THE HEART OF THE DRAGON

Watching traditional Beijing opera is a colorful and memorable way to spend an evening.

WORD OF MOUTH

"[Jinghsan Park] is a beautiful park teeming with people. . . .We walked around for hours watching people kick around the feathered weighted thing . . . people dancing, people doing a ribbon routine, people doing exercise programs, and people like us just walking around watching others."

—lynclarke

www.fodors.com/forums

WELCOME TO BEIJING

TOP REASONS TO GO

★ **The Forbidden City:** Built by more than 200,000 workers, it's the largest palace in the world and has the best-preserved and most complete collection of imperial architecture in China.

★ **Tiananmen Square:** The political heart of modern China, the square covers 100 acres, making it the largest public square in the world.

★ **Temple of Heaven:** One of the best examples of religious architecture in China, the sprawling, tree-filled complex is a pleasant place for wandering: watch locals practice martial arts, play traditional instruments, and enjoy ballroom dancing on the grass.

★ **Magnificent Markets:** So much to bargain for, so little time! Visit outdoor Panjiayuan (aka the Dirt Market), the Silk Alley Market, or the Yashow Market.

★ **Summer Palace:** This garden complex dates back eight centuries, to when the first emperor of the Jin Dynasty built the Gold Mountain Palace on Longevity Hill.

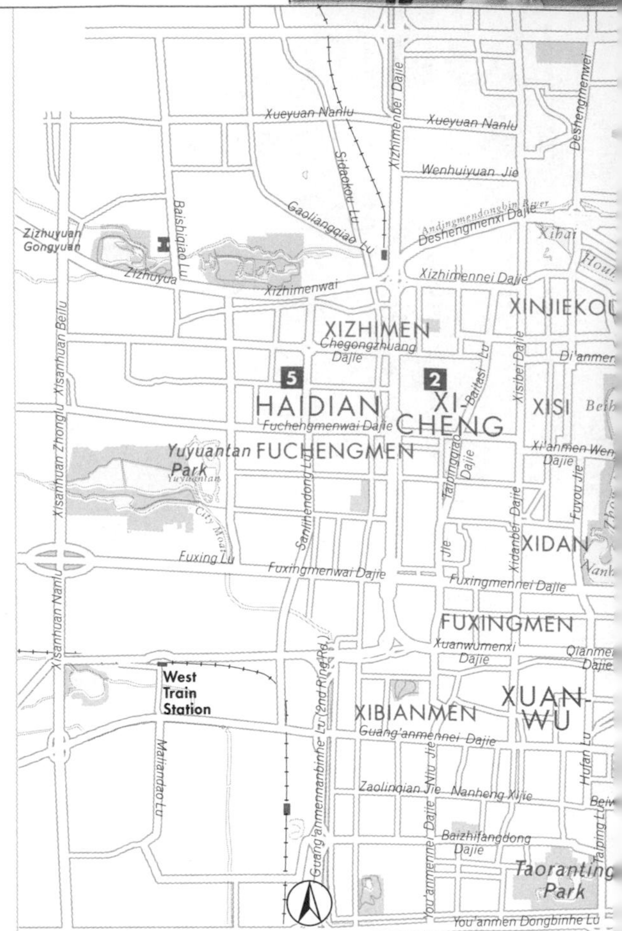

1 Dongcheng District. Dongcheng ("east district") encompasses the Forbidden City, Tiananmen Square, Wangfujing (a major shopping street), the Lama Temple, and many other historical sights dating back to imperial times.

2 Xicheng District. Xicheng ("west district"), west of Dongcheng, includes Beihai Park, former playground of the imperial family, and a series of connected lakes bordered by willow trees, courtyard-lined hutongs, and lively bars.

3 Southern Districts: Chongwen and Xuanwu. These areas have some of the city's oldest neighborhoods and a long history of folk arts, with opera theaters and acrobatic shows still staged here. The Chongwen District also has some of the city's most famous restaurants.

4 Chaoyang District. Chaoyang is the biggest and busiest district, occupying the areas north, east, and south of the eastern Second Ring Road. It's home to foreign embassies, multinational companies, the Central Business District, and the Olympic Park.

5 Haidian District. Haidian is the technology and university district. It's northwest of the Third Ring Road and packed with shops selling electronics and students cramming for the next exam.

GETTING ORIENTED

Laid out like a target with ring roads revolving around a bull's-eye, with **Chang'an Jie** ("Eternal Peace Street") cutting across the middle, Beijing sprawls outward from the central point of the **Forbidden City.** The ring roads are its main arteries and, along with Chang'an Jie, you will find yourself traveling them just about anytime you go from one place to another aboveground. As you explore Beijing, you'll find that taxis are often the best way to get around. However, if the recently expanded subway system goes where you're headed, it's often a faster option than dealing with traffic. The city is divided into 18 municipal and suburban districts (*qu*). Only six of these districts are the central stomping grounds for most visitors; this chapter focuses on those districts.

BEIJING PLANNER

Visitor Centers

China International Travel Service (CITS), an official government agency, maintains offices in many hotels and at some tourist venues. The Beijing Tourism Administration maintains a 24-hour hotline for tourist inquiries and complaints, with operators fluent in English.

Beijing Tourism Administration (☎ *010/6513–0828* 🌐 *english.visitbeijing.com.cn*)

China International Travel Service (✉ *28 Jianguomenwai Dajie, Chaoyang District* ✣ *Across from the Friendship Store* ☎ *010/6515–8565* 🌐 *www.cits.net*)

Beijing Temperatures

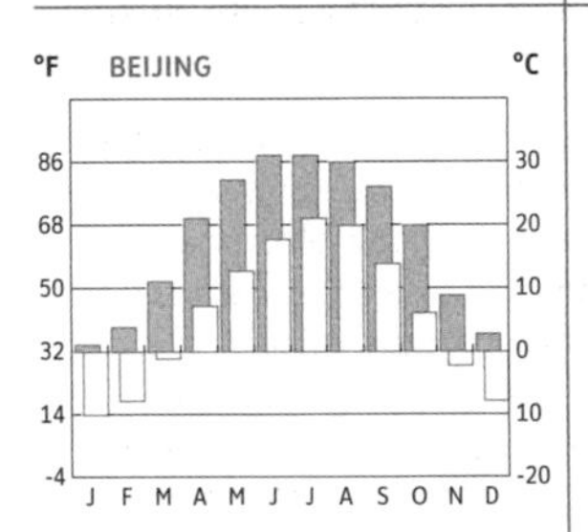

When to Go

The best time to visit Beijing is spring or early fall, when the weather is pleasant and crowds are a bit smaller. Book at least one month in advance for travel during these two times of year. In winter, Beijing's Forbidden City and Summer Palace can look fantastical and majestic when the traditional tiled roofs are covered with a light dusting of snow and the venues are devoid of tourists.

Avoid the two long national holidays: Chinese New Year, which ranges from mid-January to mid-February; and National Day holiday, the first week of October. Millions of Chinese travel during these weeks, making it difficult to book hotels, tours, and transportation.

How's the Weather?

The weather in Beijing is at its best in September and October, with a good chance of sunny days and mild temperatures. Winters are cold, but it seldom snows. Although hotels are usually well heated, some restaurants may be poorly heated, so be prepared with a warm sweater when dining out. Late April through June is lovely, but come July the days are hot and excruciatingly humid with is a greater chance of rain. Spring is also the time of year for Beijing's famous dust storms.

Getting Here

The Beijing Capital International Airport (PEK) is 27 km (17 mi) northeast of the city center. The easiest way to get from the airport to Beijing is by taxi. When you arrive, head for the clearly labeled taxi line just outside the terminal, beyond a small covered parking area. Ignore offers from touts trying to coax you away from the line—they're privateers looking to rip you off.

Most major hotels have personnel at the airport able to arrange a car or minivan. Another option is the newly built Airport Line subway which departs from T2 and T3 and goes to Dongzhimen station on the northeast corner of the Second Ring Road, on the edge of central Beijing, for only 20 minutes travel time at a price of Y25.

Getting Around

On Foot: Though traffic has put a cramp in Beijing's walking style, meandering remains one of the best ways to experience the capital—especially the old *hutongs*.

By Bike: Some 3,000 new automobiles take to the streets of the capital every week and have made biking more dangerous. Fortunately, most streets have wide, well-defined bike lanes often separated by an island of hedges. Bikes can be rented at many hotels and next to some subway stations.

By Subway: Beijing now has eight lines, including an extension to the main Olympic venues and an express line to the airport. Most tourist spots are close to Line 1, which runs east–west through Tiananmen Square, and Line 2, which runs in a loop tracing Beijing's ancient city walls (and the Second Ring Road). The subway runs from about 5 AM to midnight daily. Fares are Y2 per ride for any distance and transfers are free. Stations are marked in both Chinese and English, and stops are announced in both languages.

By Taxi: Beijing's taxi companies are shifting to newer cars. In the daytime, flag-fall for taxis is Y10 for the first 3 km (2 mi) and Y2 per km thereafter. The rate rises to Y3 per km on trips over 15 km and after 11 PM, when the flag-fall also increases to Y11. Few taxi drivers speak English, so ask your hotel concierge to write down your destination in Chinese.

Street Vocabulary

Below are some terms you'll see over and over again. These words will appear on maps and street signs, and they are part of the name of just about every place you go:

Dong is east, **xi** is west, **nan** is south, **bei** is north, and **zhong** means middle. **Jie** and **lu** mean street and road, respectively, and **da** means big.

Gongyuan means park. Jingshan Park is also called Jingshan Gongyuan.

Nei means inside and **wai** means outside. You will often come across these terms on streets that used to pass through a gate. Andingmen Nei Dajie, for example, is the section of the street located inside the Second Ring Road (where the gate used to be), whereas Andingmen Wai Dajie is the section outside the gate.

Qiao, or bridge, is part of the place name at just about every entrance and exit on the ring roads.

Men, meaning door or gate, indicates a street that once passed through an entrance in the old wall that surrounded the city until it was mostly torn down in the 1960s. The entrances to parks and some other places are also referred to as *men*.

EXPLORING BEIJING

Updated by Michael Manning

BEIJING IS A VIBRANT JUMBLE of neighborhoods and districts. The city was transformed almost overnight in preparation for the 2008 Olympics, often leveling lively old *hutongs* (alleyway neighborhoods) to make way for the glittering towers that dwarf their surroundings. Still, day-to-day life seems to pulse the same Beijing blood.

Laid out like a target with ring roads revolving around a bull's-eye, with **Chang'an Jie** ("Eternal Peace Street") cutting across the middle, Beijing sprawls outward from the central point of the **Forbidden City.** The ring roads are its main arteries and, along with Chang'an Jie, you will find yourself traveling them just about anytime you go from one place to another aboveground. As you explore Beijing, you'll find that taxis are often the best way to get around. However, if the recently expanded subway system goes where you're headed, it's often a faster option than dealing with traffic, which has become increasingly congested in recent years with the rise of private automobiles.

The city is divided into 18 municipal and suburban districts (*qu*). Only six of these districts are truly urban and are the central stomping grounds for most visitors: **Dongcheng, Xicheng, Chongwen, Xuanwu, Chaoyang,** and **Haidian.**

ESSENTIALS

Airport Information **Beijing Capital International Airport (PEK)** (☎ *010/6454–1100* 🌐 *www.bcia.com.cn*).

Bus Contact **Beijing Public Transportation Corporation** (🌐 *www.bjbus.com*).

Embassy **U.S. Embassy** (✉ *3 Xiushui Bei Jie, Chaoyang District* ☎ *010/6532–3431 Ext. 229 or 010/6532–3831 Ext. 264* 📠 *010/6532–2483* 🌐 *beijing.usembassy-china.org.cn*).

General Emergency Contacts **Fire** (☎ *119*). **Police** (☎ *110*). **Medical Emergency** (☎ *120*). **Traffic Accident** (☎ *122*).

Medical Assistance **Asia Emergency Assistance Center** (*private* ✉ *2-1-1 Tayuan Diplomatic Office Bldg., 14 Liangmahe Nan Lu, Chaoyang District* ☎ *010/6462–9112 during office hrs, 010/6462–9100 after hrs*). **Beijing United Family Health Center** (*private* ✉ *2 Jiangtai Lu, near Lido Hotel, Chaoyang District* ☎ *010/5927–7000, 010/5927–7120 for emergencies* 🌐 *www.unitedfamilyhospitals.com*). **China Academy of Medical Science (Peking Union Hospital)** (*public* ✉ *1 Shui Fu Yuan, Dongcheng District* ☎ *010/6529–5284*). **Hong Kong International Medical Clinic** (*private* ✉ *Office Tower, 9th fl., Hong Kong Macau Center-Swissotel, 2 Chaoyangmen Bei Da Jie, Chaoyang District* ☎ *010/6553–2288* 🌐 *www.hkclinic.com*). **SOS International** (*private* ✉ *Building C, BITIC Leasing Center, 1 North Road, Xing Fu San Cun, Chaoyang District* ☎ *010/6462–9199* 🌐 *www.internationalsos.com*).

Pharmacies **Beijing United Family Health Center** (*private* ✉ *2 Jiangtai Lu, near Lido Hotel, Chaoyang District* ☎ *010/5927–7000, 010/5927–7120 for emergencies* 🌐 *www.unitedfamilyhospitals.com*). **International Medical Center (IMC)** (*private* ✉ *Beijing Lufthansa Center, Room 106, 50 Liangmaqiao Lu, Chaoyang District* ☎ *010/6465–1907* 🌐 *www.imcclinics.com*). **Watsons** (✉ *Holiday Inn Lido Hotel,*

Jichang Lu, Chaoyang District ✉ *Full Link Plaza, 18 Chaoyangmenwai Dajie, Chaoyang District*) can also be found in most large shopping centers.

Postal Services **International Post and Telecommunications Office** (✉ *Jianguomen Bei Dajie, Chaoyang District* ☎ *010/8478–0200*). **DHL** (☎ *010/8458–0178* 🌐 *www.cn.dhl.com*). **FedEx** (☎ *010/6464–8855* 🌐 *www.fedex.com*). **UPS** (☎ *800/820–8388* 🌐 *www.ups.com*).

DONGCHENG DISTRICT

Dongcheng district, with its idyllic hutongs and plethora of historical sights, is one of Beijing's most pleasant areas. It's also one of the smaller districts in the city, which makes it easy to get around. A day exploring Dongcheng will leave you feeling like you've been introduced to the character of the capital. From the old men playing chess in the hutongs to the sleek, chauffeured Audis driving down Chang'an Jie, to the colorful shopping on Wangfujing, Dongcheng offers visitors a thousand little tastes of what makes Beijing a fascinating city.

HIGHLIGHTS

From **Wangfujing's** glitzy mall at **Oriental Plaza** to the incense-laden **Lama Temple** and immense **Ditan Park,** Dongcheng has plenty to offer visitors looking for closely packed Beijing thrills. The district is situated north and east of the **Forbidden City,** which is not to be missed by any first-time visitor. The great palace is fronted by **Tiananmen Square.** Aside from its historic sites and the massive hotels and office buildings that line major thoroughfares, Dongcheng is a mostly residential district increasingly made up of shiny high-rises.

GETTING HERE AND GETTING AROUND

Dongcheng is easily accessible by subway, with stops along most of its perimeter: Tiananmen East station to Jianguomen on Line 1 forms the south side of this district; Jianguomen to Gulou Dajie on Line 2 forms the district's north and east sides. Line 2 stops at the Lama Temple, the Ancient Observatory, Wangfujing, and Tiananmen Square. Taxi travel during peak hours (7 to 9 AM and 5 to 8 PM) is difficult. At other times, traveling by taxi is affordable, convenient, and the fastest option (especially at noon, when much of the city is at lunch, and after 10 PM). Renting a bike to see the sites is also a good option. ⚠ **If you rent a bike, be extremely cautious of traffic, and rent a helmet.** Bus travel within the city, especially during rush hours, is laborious and should be avoided unless you speak or read Chinese

SIGHTS

❸ Fodor's Choice ★ **Confucius Temple (with the Imperial Academy).** This tranquil temple to China's great sage has endured nearly eight centuries of additions and restorations. The complex is now combined with the Imperial Academy next door, once the highest educational institution in the country. Two carved stone drums, dating to the Qianlong period (1735–96) flank the Gate of Great Accomplishment. In the Hall of Great Perfection you'll find the central shrine to Confucius. Check out the huge collection of ancient

Confucius Temple (with the Imperial Academy) **3**
Ditan Park **2**
Donghuamen Night Market **8**
Drum & Bell Towers **1**
Jingshan Park **6**
Lama Temple (Yonghe Temple) **4**
Nanxincang **5**
Tiananmen Square **7**

BEIJING'S SUBWAY

The subway in Beijing is faster and cheaper than a taxi. Most first-time visitors to Beijing stick to the original two lines, which provide access to the most popular areas, and the airport extension. **Line 1** runs east and west along Chang'an Jie past the China World Trade Center, Jianguomen (an embassy district), the Wangfujing shopping area, Tiananmen Square and the Forbidden City, Xidan (another major shopping location), and the Military Museum before heading out to the far western suburbs. **Line 2** (the loop line) runs along a sort of circular route around the center of the city shadowing the Second Ring Road. Important destinations include the Drum and Bell Towers, Lama Temple, Dongzhimen (with a connection to the airport express), Dongsishitiao (near Sanlitun and the Worker's Stadium), Beijing Train Station, and Qianmen (Front Gate) south of Tiananmen Square. Free transfers between Line 1 and 2 can be made at either Fuxingmen or Jianguomen stations.

If you are near the Second Ring Road or on Chang'an Jie, the subway stops just about every half-mile, and you'll spot the entrances (with blue subway logos) dotting the streets. Each stop is announced in English and Chinese, and clearly marked signs are in English or pinyin at each station. Transferring between lines is easy and free, with the standard Y2 ticket including travel between any two destinations. When planning a trip on Line 13, make sure you transfer from the correct station. If your destination is on the west side of the line, leave from Xizhimen; if it's on the east side of the line, leave from Dongzhimen.

Subway tickets can be purchased from electronic kiosks and ticket windows in every station. Fid the button that says "English," insert your money, and press another button to print. Single-ride tickets cost Y2, and unless you want a pocketful of coins you'll need to pay with exact change; the machines don't accept Y1 bills, only Y1 coins.

In the middle of each subway platform is map of the Beijing subway system along with a local map showing the exits. Subway cars have a simplified diagram of the line you're riding above the doors.

Trains can be very crowded, especially during rush hour, and it's not uncommon for people to push onto the train before exiting passengers can get off. Be wary of pickpockets.

⚠**The subway system is not convenient for people with disabilities. In some stations, there are no escalators, and sometimes the only entrance or exit is via steep steps.**

musical instruments. Like in Buddhist and Taoist temples, worshippers can offer sacrifices (in this case, to a mortal, not a deity).

A cemetery of stone tablets, or stelae, stand like rows of creepy crypts in the front and main courtyards of the temple. On the front stelae you can barely make out the names of thousands of scholars who passed imperial exams. Another batch of stelae, carved in the mid-1700s to record the *Thirteen Classics*, philosophical works attributed to Confucius, line the west side of the grounds.

The Imperial Academy was established in 1306 as a rigorous training ground for high-level government officials, the academy was notorious, especially during the early Ming Dynasty era, for the harsh discipline imposed on scholars perfecting their knowledge of the Confucian classics. This tranquil temple to China's great sage has endured close to eight centuries of additions and restorations. It is now combined with the Imperial Academy (next door), once the highest educational institution in the country. ✉ *Guozijian Lu off Yunghegong Lu near Lama Temple, Dongcheng District* ☎ *010/8401–1977* 🎫 *Y10* ⏲ *Daily 8:30–5* Ⓜ *Yonghegong.*

❷ **Ditan Park** *(Temple of Earth Park)*. In the 16th-century park is the square altar where emperors once made sacrifices to the earth god and the Hall of Deities. This is a lovely place for a stroll, especially if you're already near the Drum Tower or Lama Temple. ✉ *Yonghegong Jie, just north of Second Ring Rd., Dongcheng District* ☎ *010/6421–4657* 🎫 *Y2* ⏲ *Daily* 6 AM–*9* PM.

❶ ★ **Drum Tower.** *(Gulou)* Until the late 1920s, the 24 drums once housed in this tower were Beijing's timepiece. Sadly, all but one of these huge drums have been destroyed, and the survivor is in serious need of renovation. Kublai Khan built the first drum tower on this site in 1272. You can climb to the top of the present tower, which dates from the Ming Dynasty. Old photos of hutong neighborhoods line the walls beyond the drum; there's also a scale model of a traditional courtyard house. The nearby **Bell Tower,** renovated after a fire in 1747, offers fabulous views of the hutongs from the top of a long, narrow staircase. The huge 63-ton bronze bell, supported by lacquered wood stanchions, is also worth seeing. ✉ *North end of Dianmen Dajie, Dongcheng District* ☎ *010/6404–1710* 🎫 *Y20 for Drum Tower, Y15 for Bell Tower* ⏲ *Daily 9–4:30* Ⓜ *Guloudajie.*

❻ **Jingshan Park** *(Coal Hill Park)*. This park was built around a small peak formed from earth excavated from the Forbidden City's moats. Ming rulers ordered the hill's construction to improve the feng shui of their new palace to the south. Climb a winding stone staircase past peach and apple trees to Wanchun Pavilion, the park's highest point. On a clear day, it has unparalleled views of the Forbidden City and the Bell and Drum Towers. Chongzhen, the last Ming emperor, is said to have hanged himself at the foot of Coal Hill as his dynasty collapsed in 1644. ✉ *Jingshanqian Dajie, opposite the north gate of the Forbidden City, Xicheng District* ☎ *010/6404–4071* 🎫 *Y2* ⏲ *Daily* 6 AM–*10* PM.

❹ Fodor's Choice ★ **Lama Temple (Yonghe Temple).** Beijing's most visited religious site and one of the most important functioning Buddhist temples in Beijing, this Tibetan Buddhist masterpiece has five main halls and numerous galleries hung with finely detailed *thangkhas* (painted cloth scrolls). The entire temple is decorated with Buddha images—all guarded by somber lamas (monks) dressed in brown robes. Originally a palace for Prince Yongzheng, it was transformed into a temple once he became the Qing's third emperor in 1723. The temple flourished under Emperor Qianlong, housing some 500 resident monks; only about two dozen monks live in the complex today. This was once the official "embassy" of Tibetan Buddhism in Beijing.

With statues of Maitreya, the future Buddha, and Weitou, China's guardian of Buddhism, The Hall of Heavenly Kings is worth a slow stroll. In the courtyard beyond, a pond with a bronze mandala represents paradise. The Buddhas of the Past, Present, and Future hold court in the Hall of Harmony. Look on the west wall where an exquisite silk *thangkha* of White Tara—the embodiment of compassion—hangs. Images of the Medicine and Longevity Buddhas line the Hall of Eternal Blessing. In the Pavilion of Ten Thousand Fortunes, gaze up at the breathtaking 26-meter (85-foot) Maitreya Buddha, which was carved from a single sandalwood block. ✉ *12 Yonghegong Dajie, Beixingqiao, Dongcheng District* ☎ *010/6404–4499* ✉ *Y25* ⊙ *Daily 9–4:30* Ⓜ *Yonghegong.*

❼ Fodor'sChoice ★ **Tiananmen Square.** The world's largest public square, and the very heart of modern China, Tiananmen Square owes little to grand imperial designs and everything to Mao Zedong. Young protesters who assembled here in 1919 as part of the May Fourth Movement established a tradition of patriotic dissent, which was repressed in 1989. Today the square is packed with sightseers, families, and undercover policemen. Although formidable, the square is a little bleak, with no shade, benches, or trees. Come here at night for an eerie experience—it's a little like being on a film set. You can try your hand at flying a kite. Itinerant vendors sell kites of all kinds.

At the height of the Cultural Revolution, hundreds of thousands of Red Guards crowded the square; in June 1989, the square was the scene of tragedy when student demonstrators were killed. At dawn, watch the military guard raise China's flag. Wide-eyed visitors converge on Tiananmen Square each day to watch soldiers goose stepping out of the Forbidden City.

The square is sandwiched between two grand gates: the Gate of Heavenly Peace (Tiananmen) to the north and the Front Gate (Qianmen) in the south. Along the western edge is the Great Hall of the People. The National Museum of China lies along the eastern side. The Monument to the People's Heroes, a 125-foot granite obelisk, commemorates those who died for the revolutionary cause of the Chinese people. ✉ *Bounded by Changan Jie to the north and Xuanwumen Jie to the south, Dongcheng District* ✉ *Free* ⊙ *24-hours year-round* Ⓜ *Tiananmen East.*

EXPERIENCES

GETTING TO KNOW MAO

Tiananmen Square is likely one of the first places you'll visit when you arrive in Beijing. For good reason, too: this square is the ultimate symbol of modern China. At the height of the Cultural Revolution, hundreds of thousands of Red Guards crowded the square, chanting Mao's name and waving his Little Red Book. In June 1989 the square was the scene of tragedy when hundreds of student demonstrators were killed by troops breaking up a pro-democracy protest. While exploring the

Continued on page 48

THE FORBIDDEN CITY

Palace of Heavenly Purity

Undeniably sumptuous, the Forbidden City, once home to a long line of emperors, is Beijing's most enduring emblem. Magnificent halls, winding lanes, and stately courtyards await you—welcome to the world's largest palace complex.

As you gaze up at roofs of glazed-yellow tiles—a symbol of royalty—try to imagine a time when only the emperor ("the son of God") was permitted to enter this palace, accompanied by select family members, concubines, and eunuch-servants. Now, with its doors flung open, the Forbidden City's mysteries beckon.

The sheer grandeur of the site—with 800 buildings and more than 8,000 rooms—conveys the pomp and circumstance of Imperial China. The shady palaces, musty with age, recall life at court, where corrupt eunuchs and palace officials schemed and bored concubines gossiped.

Building to Glory

Under the third Ming emperor, Yongle, 200,000 laborers built this complex over the course of 14 years, finishing in 1420. Yongle relocated the Ming capital to Beijing (from Nanjing in the south) to strengthen China's northern frontier. After Yongle, the palace was home to 23 Ming and Qing emperors, until the dynastic system crumbled in 1911.

In imperial times, no buildings were allowed to exceed the height of the palace. Moats and massive timber doors

protected the emperor. Gleaming yellow roof tiles marked the vast complex as the royal court's exclusive dominion. Ornate interiors displayed China's most exquisite artisanship, including ceilings covered with turquoise-and-blue dragons, walls draped with priceless scrolls, intricate cloisonné screens, sandalwood thrones padded in delicate silks, and floors of golden-hued bricks. Miraculously, the palace survived fire, war, and imperial China's collapse.

More Than Feng Shui

The Forbidden City embodies Feng Shui, architectural principles used for thousands of years throughout China. Each main hall faces south, opening to a courtyard flanked by lesser buildings. This symmetry repeats itself along a north–south axis that bisects the imperial palace, with a broad walkway paved in marble. This path was reserved exclusively for the emperor's sedan chair. Even court ministers, the empress, and favored concubines were required to trod on pathways and pass through doors set to either side of the Imperial Way.

Take a close look at gates, doors, and woodwork here: most structures have nails in a 9 x 9 formation. Nine is the largest odd number less than the number 10, so it's considered both lucky and important.

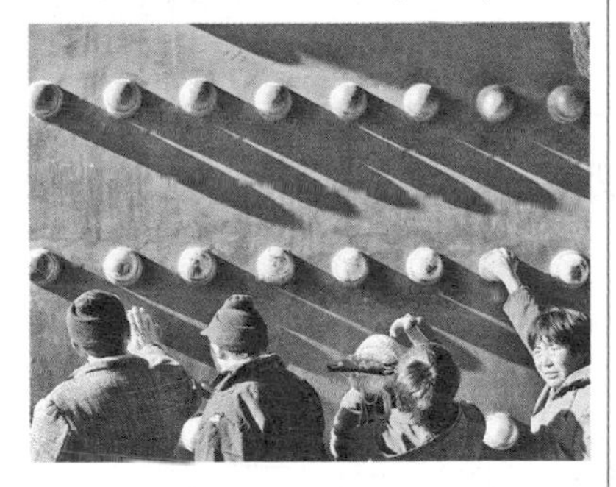

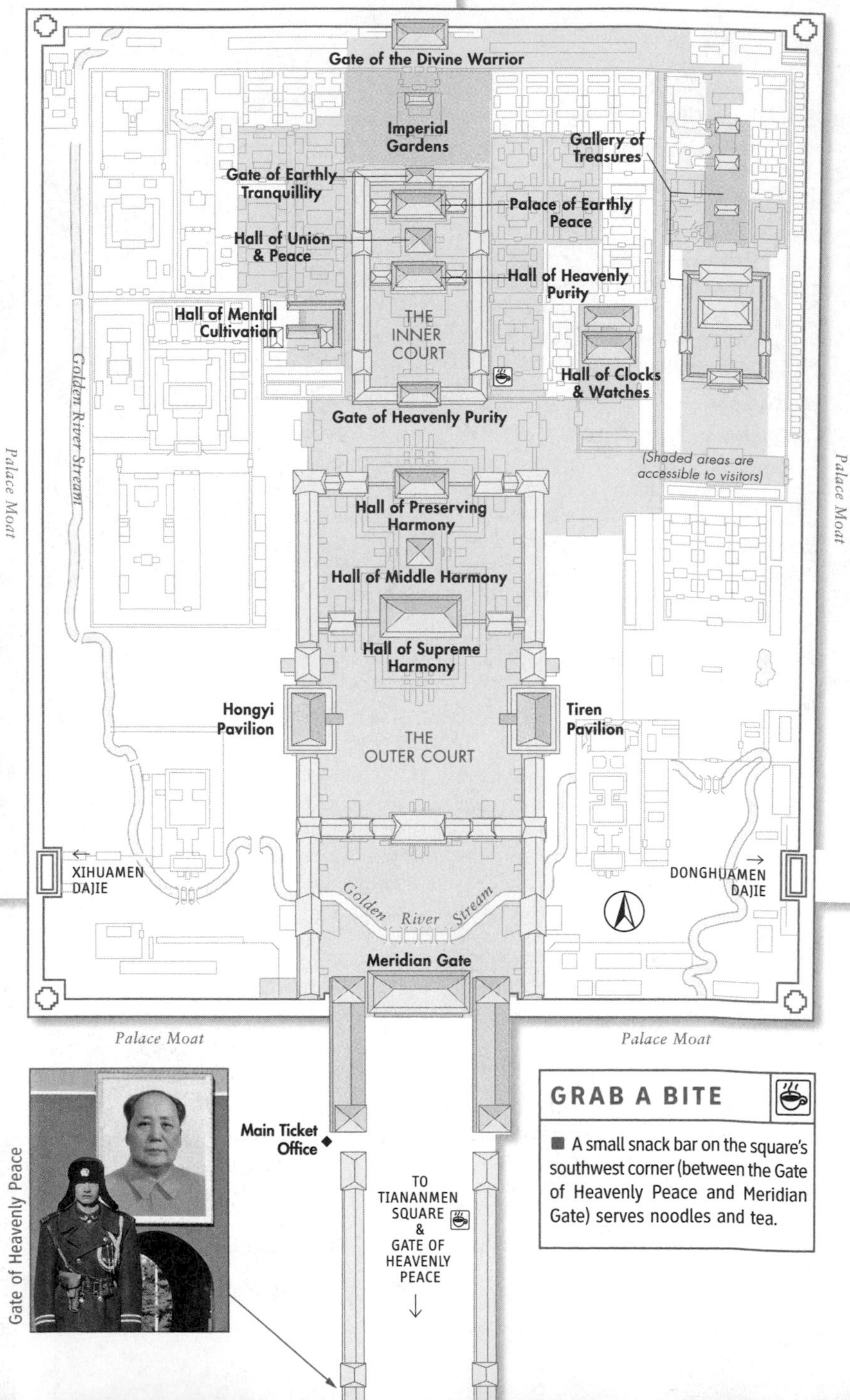

GRAB A BITE

■ A small snack bar on the square's southwest corner (between the Gate of Heavenly Peace and Meridian Gate) serves noodles and tea.

WHAT TO SEE

The most impressive way to reach the Forbidden City is through the **Gate of Heavenly Peace** (Tiananmen), connected to Tiananmen Square. The Great Helmsman himself stood here to establish the People's Republic of China on October 1, 1949.

The **Meridian Gate** (Wumen), sometimes called Five Phoenix Tower, is the main southern entrance to the palace. Here, the emperor announced yearly planting schedules according to the lunar calendar; it's also where errant officials were flogged. The main ticket office and audio-guide rentals are just west of this gate.

The central entrance of the Meridian was reserved for the emperor. The one day the empress was allowed to walk through it was her wedding day.

THE OUTER COURT

The **Hall of Supreme Harmony** (Taihedian) was used for coronations, royal birthdays, and weddings. Bronze vats, once kept brimming with water to fight fires, ring this vast expanse. The hall sits atop three stone tiers with an elaborate drainage system with 1,000 carved dragons. On the top tier, bronze cranes symbolize longevity. Inside, cloisonné cranes flank the imperial throne, above which hangs a heavy bronze ball—placed there to crush any pretender to the throne.

Take a close look at the bronze vats and you'll see the telltale scratch marks of greedy foreign soldiers who scraped the gold with their bayonets.

Emperors greeted audiences in the **Hall of Middle Harmony** (Zhonghedian). It also housed the royal plow, with which the emperor would turn a furrow to commence spring planting.

The highest civil service examinations, which were personally conducted by the emperor, were once administered in the **Hall of Preserving Harmony** (Baohedian). Behind the hall, a 200-ton marble relief of dragons, the palace's most treasured stone carving, adorns the staircase.

The Hall of Supreme Harmony was the site of many imperial weddings.

A short jaunt to the right is **Hall of Clocks and Watches** (Zhongbiaoguan), where you'll find a collection of early timepieces. It's pure opulence: there's a plethora of jeweled, enameled, and lacquered timepieces (some astride elephants, others implanted in ceramic trees). Our favorites? Those crafted from red sandalwood. *(Admission: Y10)*

You'll see that lions in the palace live in pairs. A female lion playing with a cub symbolizes imperial fertility. A male lion, sitting majestically with a sphere beneath his paw, represents power.

Marble dragons will greet you behind the Hall of Preserving Harmony.

DID YOU KNOW?

- 24 emperors and two dynasties ruled from within these labyrinthine halls.
- The emperor was the only non-castrated male allowed in the eastern and western palaces. This served as proof that any pregnant concubine was carrying the royal one's baby.
- If you prepared for your trip by watching Bertolucci's *The Last Emperor*, you may recognize the passage outside the Hall of Mental Cultivation: this is where young Puyi rode his bike in the film.
- Women can enter the Forbidden City for half price on March 8, International Women's Day.
- When it was first built in the 15th century, the palace was called the Purple Forbidden City; today, its official name is the Ancient Palace Museum (Gugong Bowuguan); often it's shortened simply to Gugong.

The Hall of Heavenly Purity

THE INNER COURT

Now you're approaching the very core of the palace. Several emperors chose to live in the Inner Palace with their families. The **Hall of Heavenly Purity** (Qianqinggong) holds another imperial throne; the **Hall of Union and Peace** (Jiaotaidian) was the venue for the empress's annual birthday party; and the **Palace of Earthly Peace** (Kunninggong) was where royal couples consummated their marriages. The banner above the throne bizarrely reads DOING NOTHING.

On either side of the Inner Palace are six western and six eastern palaces—the former living quarters of concubines, eunuchs, and servants. The last building on the western side, the **Hall of Mental Cultivation** (Yangxin-dian), is the most important of these; starting with Emperor Yongzheng, all Qing Dynasty emperors attended to daily state business in this hall.

AN EMPEROR CHEAT SHEET

JIAJING (1507–1567)

Ming Emperor Jiajing was obsessed with Taoism, which he hoped would give him longevity, but which also led him to ignore state affairs for 25 years. His other fixation was the pursuit of girls: his 18 concubines conspired to strangle him in his sleep, but their plot was uncovered. Nearly all of the girls, and their families, were killed.

YONGZHENG (1678–1735)

The third emperor of the Qing Dynasty, Yongzheng was tyrannical but efficient. He became emperor amid rumors that he had forged his father's will. He appeased his brothers by promoting them, but then proceeded to murder and imprison anyone who posed a challenge, including his own brothers, two of whom died in prison.

Animal ornaments decorate the corners of many roofs—the more animals, the more important the building.

The Gallery of Treasures (Zhenbaoguan), actually a series of halls, has breathtaking examples of imperial ornamentation. The first room displays candleholders, wine vessels, tea sets, and a golden pagoda commissioned by Qing emperor Qian Long in honor of his mother. A cabinet on one wall contains the 25 imperial seals. Jade bracelets, golden hair pins, and coral fill the second hall; carved jade landscapes a third. *(Admission: Y10)*

HEAD FOR THE GREEN

North of the Forbidden City's private palaces, beyond the **Gate of Earthly Tranquillity**, lie the most pleasant parts of the Forbidden City: the **Imperial Gardens** (Yuhuayuan), composed of ancient cypress trees and stone mosaic pathways. During festivals, palace inhabitants climbed the Hill of Accumulated Elegance. You can exit the palace at the back of the gardens through the park's **Gate of the Divine Warrior** (Shenwumen).

FAST FACTS

Address: The main entrance is just north of the Gate of Heavenly Peace, which faces Tiananmen Square on Chang'an Jie.

Phone: 010/8513-2255

Web site: www.dpm.org.cn

Admission: Y60

Hours: Oct. 16—Apr. 15, daily 8:30—4:30; Apr. 16—Oct. 15, daily 8:30—5

UNESCO Status: Declared a World Heritage Site in 1987.

- You must check your bags prior to entry and also pass through a metal detector.
- The palace is always packed with visitors, but it's impossibly crowded on national holidays.
- Allow 2—4 hours to explore the palace. There are souvenir shops and restaurants inside.
- You can hire automated audio guides at the Meridian Gate for Y40 and a Y100 returnable deposit.

CIXI (1835–1908)

The Empress Dowager served as de facto ruler of China from 1861 until 1908. She entered the court as a concubine at 16 and soon became Emperor Xianfeng's favorite. She gave birth to his only son to survive: the heir apparent. Ruthless and ambitious, she learned the workings of the imperial court and used every means to gain power.

PUYI (1906–1967)

Puyi, whose life was depicted in Bertolucci's classic *The Last Emperor*, took the throne at age two. The Qing dynasty's last emperor, he was forced to abdicate after the dynasty fell. During an attempted restoration in 1917, he held the throne for 12 days. Puyi was forced out of the Imperial City in 1924 by a warlord.

CLOSE UP

Best Beijing Tours

Beijing Hikers. This outfitter offers guided group and private hiking trips aimed at expat hikers and tourists. *139/1002–5516 or 138/1016–5056 www.beijinghikers.com.*

Beijing Hutong Tourist Agency. This agency was one of the first to offer guided pedicab tours of Beijing's back-alleys, with glimpses of old courtyard houses and daily Beijing life. *26 Di'anmen Xidajie, Dongcheng District 010/6615–9097.*

China Culture Club. With well-informed English-speaking guides, CCC is popular with those looking for more than just the standard tour highlights. *Kent Center, 29 Anjialou, Liangmaqiao Road, Chaoyang District 010/6432–9341, 010/6432–1041 weekends www.chinaculture center.org.*

China International Travel Service. CITS is China's official travel agency, dating to 1954. *28 Jianguomenwai Dajie, Chaoyang District Across from the Friendship Store 010/6515–8565 www.cits.net.*

CycleChina. If a guided three-hour afternoon bicycle tour of a hutong or a trip through Beijing sitting in a motorbike sidecar sounds like fun, call CycleChina. *12 Jingshan East Street, Dongcheng District Across from the east gate of Jingshan Park 010/6402–5653, 139/1188–6524 www.cyclechina.com.*

Kingdom Bicycle. Offering bicycle rentals and suggested itineraries covering some of Beijing's lesser known historical sites, Kingdom is a great resource. *North Garden office, B402, Oriental Plaza, Wangfujing, Dongcheng District 133/8140–0738 (English), 010/6522–9478 www. bicyclekingdom.com.*

WildChina. This foreign-managed travel company is probably the best in China. *Room 801, Oriental Place, 9 East Dongfang Lu, North Dongsanhuan Lu, Chaoyang District 010/6465–6602 www.wild china.com.*

square, you'll have a chance to gaze up at a portrait of Chairman Mao, a man who inspired both intense love and hate during his lifetime.

Some three decades after his passing, Mao Zedong continues to evoke radically different feelings among the Chinese. Was he the romantic poet-hero who helped the Chinese stand up? Or was he a monster whose wrenching policies caused the deaths of millions of people? Born into a relatively affluent farming family in Hunan in 1893, Mao became active in politics at a young age; he was one of the founding members of the Chinese Communist Party in 1921. When the People's Republic of China was established in 1949, Mao served as chairman of the party and of the state. After initially improving the economy, he launched radical economic, political, and agricultural programs in the mid-1950s—often against the advice of his closest comrades—causing serious damage to the nation. The party's official assessment is that Mao was 70% correct and 30% incorrect. His critics, however, reverse this ratio.

AN ANCIENT GRANARY

5 If you have a few hours, visit **Nanxincang,** China's oldest existing granary dating back to the Yongle period (1403–24). Located on Dongsi Shitiao, it is just one block west of the Second Ring Road. This valuable historical site is now Beijing's latest entertainment venue, the new home to three art galleries, a teahouse, and several bars and restaurants.

The structures at Nanxincang—just 10 years younger than those of the Forbidden City—were among the more than 300 granaries that existed in this area during imperial days to meet the increasing demands of the capital. Have a glass of wine on the second floor of Yuefu, an audio and book shop, where you can admire the old interior, then have dinner at one of the excellent restaurants in the compound. **Sifang Jie** (☎ *010/6409–6403*) specializes in dishes from southwest China. **Fanqian Fanhou** (☎ *010/6409–6510*) has wonderful cheap Taiwanese cuisine. **Rain Club** (☎ *010/6409–6922* M *Dongsi Shitiao*) offers fancier East-meets-West fusion cuisine.

> **WANGFUJING SHOPPING**
>
> Beijing's premier shopping street simply glistens with new malls and department stores (namely those at the Oriental Plaza). This pedestrian-only lane overflows with spending opportunities for locals and visitors alike, spanning the shopping spectrum from Adidas to Tiffany's to snack shops and souvenir stalls.

EVENING MUNCHIES

Crunchy deep-fried scorpions and other tasty critters are sold at the **Donghuamen Night Market,** at the northern end of Wangfujing's wide walking boulevard. We'll admit: this is more of a place to look at and perhaps photograph food rather than devour it. Hawkers also serve up deep-fried starfish, plus a variety of insects and other hard-to-identify food items. Most street-market food is usually safe to eat as long as it's hot. The row of interesting outdoor evening stalls makes for an intriguing walk with great photo ops.

XICHENG DISTRICT

Xicheng district is home to an eclectic mix of a few of Beijing's favorite things: delicious food, venerable hutongs and old courtyard houses, charming lakes, and engaging nightlife. The lakes at Shichahai are fun for all ages, both day and night. Take a boat ride on the lake in the warmer months, or ice-skate here in the cold winter months.

Our top experience? Taking a walk or bicycle tour of the surrounding hutongs: there is no better way to scratch the surface of this sprawling city (before it disappears!) than by exploring the hutongs lined by courtyard houses. Wander in and out of historical sites in the area, such as Prince Gong's palace, the courtyard house of famed opera legend Mei Lanfang (⇨ *see "Beijing Opera" in this chapter)*, and the Drum and Bell Towers (which fall right between Dongcheng and Xicheng). In the evening, find a restaurant or bar with a view of the lake.

HIGHLIGHTS

Shichahai, a collection of lakes, comprises Xicheng's foremost attractions. Shichahai's southernmost lakes, **Nanhai** ("south lake") and **Zhonghai** ("middle lake"), are due west of the Forbidden City. Together they form Zhongnanhai, a government compound for China's top leaders that is off-limits to the public. **Beihai** ("north lake") is in Beihai Park, once an imperial playground, north of Zhongnanhai: it features classic imperial gardens and murky lotus-flower-filled waters traversed by walkways of intricate woodwork.

To the north of Beihai is **Qianhai** ("front lake"). **Houhai** ("rear lake") is a commercialized yet wonderful lake surrounded by chic bars, good restaurants, and tempting shops. **Soong Ching-ling's former residence**, a lovely spot once inhabited by the wife of the father of modern China, Sun Yat-sen, is on the northeastern side of **Houhai.**

Xicheng's other main attraction is **Xidan,** an area full of shopping malls and boutiques selling clothing and accessories.

GETTING HERE AND GETTING AROUND

The district to the north and west of the Forbidden City, Xicheng is a natural hop, skip, and a jump from Dongcheng.The Line 1 subway stops include Tiananmen West, Xidan, and Fuxingmen while Line 2 makes stops from Fuxingmen to the Drum Tower (Gulou), following Xicheng's perimeter. Xizhimen is a major terminus with access to the northwest via subway. **■TIP→ Houhai and Beihai Park are more conveniently reached by taxi.**

SIGHTS

❹ ★ **Beihai Park** *(North Sea Park)*. A white Tibetan dagoba is perched on a small island just north of the south gate. Also at the south entrance is the **Round City,** which contains a white-jade Buddha, and an enormous jade bowl given to Kublai Khan. Nearby, the well-restored **Temple of Eternal Peace** houses a variety of Buddhas. Climb to the dagoba from Yongan Temple. Once there, you can pay an extra Y1 to ascend the Buddha-bedecked **Shanyin Hall.**

The lake is Beijing's largest and most beautiful public waterway. On summer weekends the lake teems with paddle boats. The **Five Dragon Pavilion,** on Beihai's northwest shore, was built in 1602 by a Ming dynasty emperor who liked to fish under the moon. ✉ *Beihai Nan Men, Weijin Lu, Xicheng District* ☎ *010/6404–0610* 💴 *Y10; extra fees for some sights* ⏲ *Daily 6 AM–10 PM.*

Qianhai and Houhai. Most people come to these lakes, along with Xihai to the northwest, to stroll and enjoy the shoreside bars and restaurants. In summer you can boat, fish, and even, on occasion, windsurf. In winter sections of the frozen lakes are fenced off for skating. Easily combined with a trip to Beihai Park or the Bell and Drum Towers. ✉ *North of Beihai Lake, Xicheng District.*

❶ **Museum of Antique Currency.** This museum in a tiny courtyard house showcases a small but impressive selection of rare Chinese coins. Explanations are in Chinese only. Also in the courtyard are coin and

Beihai Park 4

Museum of Antique Currency 1

Prince Gong's Mansion 3

Soon Ching-ling's Former Residence 2

curio dealers. ✉*Deshengmen Jianlou, Bei'erhuan Zhonglu, Xicheng District* ☎*010/6201–8073* 🎟*Y20* ⏲*Tues.–Sun. 9–4.*

SILVER INGOT BRIDGE

Known as **Yind Ding Qiao** in Chinese, this Ming Dynasty Bridge is named for its shape, which resembles a silver ingot turned upside down. It divides Qianhai and Houhai at the lakes' most narrow point. ✉*Xicheng District.*

❸ **Prince Gong's Palace** *(Gong Wang Fu)*. This grand compound sits in a neighborhood once reserved for imperial relatives. Built in 1777 during the Qing Dynasty, it fell to Prince Gong—brother of Qing emperor Xianfeng and later an adviser to Empress Dowager Cixi—after the original inhabitant was executed for corruption. With nine courtyards joined by covered walkways, it was once one of Beijing's most lavish residences. The largest hall offers summertime Beijing opera and afternoon tea to guests on guided hutong tours. Some literary scholars believe this was the setting for *Dream of the Red Chamber,* China's best-known classic novel. ✉*17 Qianhai Xijie, Xicheng District* ☎*010/6618–0573* 🎟*Y20* ⏲*Daily 9–4.*

❷ **Soong Ching-ling's Former Residence** *(Song Qingling Guju)*. Soong Ching-ling (1893–1981) was the youngest daughter of the wealthy, American-educated bible publisher, Charles Soong. At the age of 18, disregarding her family's strong opposition, she eloped to marry the much older Sun Yat-sen. When her husband founded the Republic of China in 1911, Soong Ching-ling became a significant political figure. In 1924 she headed the Women's Department of the Nationalist Party. Then in 1949 she became the vice president of the People's Republic of China. Throughout her career she campaigned tirelessly for the emancipation of women. Indeed, the rights of modern-day Chinese women owe a great deal to her. This former palace was her residence and work place and now houses a small museum, which documents her life and work. ✉*46 Houhai Beiyan, Xicheng District* ☎*010/6404–4205* 🎟*Y20* ⏲*Daily 9–4.*

EXPERIENCES

SHOPPING ON THE CHEAP

Less than 2 km (1 mi) west of the Forbidden City, the massive shopping area of Xidan swarms with local shoppers and bargain-hunters. Socks, trousers, hats, dresses, and t-shirts galore!

A TASTE OF OLD BEIJING

Time seems to be standing still in Xicheng's ancient neighborhoods. A street stand sells steamed meat buns beside a parked cart piled high with watermelons. Peddlers shout out while, at the corner, boys crowd around a hawker with dozens of small woven baskets, the size of plums. Inside are crickets. A gaggle of grandmothers sits on short stools nearby, some holding grandchildren, others snoozing in the sun. Pedicabs glide by, on constant prowl for passengers. Along the lake, elderly men are absorbed in the same pastimes that their ancestors enjoyed a century ago. One group is playing Chinese chess, another mah-jongg—the sound of clicking tiles can be heard long before you reach the spot. Elsewhere, a group of men admire birds perched in cages hanging from trees.

WELCOME TO THE HUTONG

For long-time residents of Beijing, there is nothing more emblematic of the city than these idyllic—but quickly disappearing—courtyard houses and hutongs. Never bypass an intriguing alleyway: strolls into the hutong frequently reveal ancient neighborhoods; brick and timber homes; courtyards full of children, *laobaixing* (ordinary folk), and, in winter, mountains of cabbage and coal.

Hutongs have been around for more than 700 years. Traditional courtyard houses are also an important part of the allure of hutongs. The designs of the houses were a symbol of the owner's rank and social status. Homes with elaborate Chinese-style gates with spreading eaves are the former residences of imperial officials or businessmen. The homes of commoners have simple square-topped gates.

One of the best places to explore Beijing's hutongs is the Houhai area, which was home to nobles during the Qing Dynasty. Walk around the lake and plunge into any small lane and just keep wandering around this maze of alleyways. **■TIP→ The Silver Ingot Bridge, which separates the front and rear lakes, is a good place to start.** An easy way to visit the hutongs is with the **Beijing Hutong Tourist Agency** (*⊠26 Di'anmen Xidajie ☎010/6615–9097*). To experience the inside of one of the beautiful *siheyuan,* or courtyard houses of the Qing dynasty, have dinner at the Red Capital Club, The Source, Baijia Dazhaimen, or Gui Gongfu.

SOUTHERN DISTRICTS: CHONGWEN AND XUANWU

The sights in this part of town are ancient reminders of the Beijing that once was—a more religious and artistically inspired Beijing, a Beijing as rich in culture and history as it was in resources and political power. This area is crowded with small shops, European architecture, opera and acrobatic theaters, and street performers and magicians. A lazy stroll through Source of Law Temple or Antiques Street (Liulichang) on a quiet afternoon is sure to remind you of the city's past.

HIGHLIGHTS

Qianmen Dajie (a walking street) runs north–south from Qianmen ("Front Gate") at Tiananmen Square, separating the two districts. The ancient, breathtaking **Temple of Heaven,** which has wonderful examples of Ming dynasty architecture, is a must-visit for first timers. The **Source of Law Temple** is a peaceful old Zen temple that's still operational. **Ox Street** and the **Niujie Mosque** are about all that remains of Beijing's old Muslim neighborhoods.

Liulichang (Antiques Street) is Beijing's historical art street, where the Ming and Qing dynasty literati used to swap stories and books. Now a bustling antiques market, Liulichang has great shopping if you're looking for Chinese art or art supplies.

GETTING HERE AND GETTING AROUND

South of the Forbidden City, the Chongwen and Xuanwu districts occupy the area enclosed by the Second Ring Road and Chang'an Jie. The southern portion of the Line 2 subway runs across the northern

Front Gate (Qianmen) 4

Ming Dynasty City Wall Ruins Park 5

Niujie (Ox Street) Mosque 1

Ruifuxiang Silk Shop 3

Source of Law Temple 2

Temple of Heaven 6

CLOSE UP

Fringe Art: The Dashanzi 798 Art District

If you are keen to see what the city's art scene has to offer beyond calligraphy, the Dashanzi 798 Art District boasts a thriving contemporary art community. Exploration of social taboos, use of digital media, and clever installations are juxtaposed among more orthodox forms of canvas paintings and photography. Some efforts may seem like knockoffs of American pop art, and Mao references run rampant, but this level of expression is still evolving for the public arena. Complete freedom of expression is not tolerated and governmental closings are not unheard of. Chinese artists have also learned the benefits of subversive subtlety.

Built in the 1950s, the factory was a major industrial project designed by East German architects backed by Soviet aid. The factory's decline started in the 1980s, just as Beijing's contemporary art scene began to emerge. The massive relocation of pollutant factories outside the city in preparation for the 2008 Summer Olympic Games accelerated the decline of the area's manufacturing roots. Meanwhile, students and artists take over deserted factories to establish their own galleries and studios. The recent government declaration of Dashanzi as a protected arts district has paved the way for a resurgence of new, inventive local galleries, as well as design studios, restaurants, cafés, and bars. The annual Dashanzi International Arts Festival—held each May—continues to draw international attention to the 798 area.

The Dashanzi compound is immensely walkable; keep in mind this is solely a pedestrian affair unless you arrive by private car. Cabs are not allowed to enter the compound. Though it's open on weekdays (except Monday), most people visit on weekends, when throngs of locals and foreigners congregate to see what's on display.

Directions to Dashanzi: Traveling from the city by car, take the Dashanzi (#2) exit off the Airport Expressway. Just as you come to the end of the exit ramp, ask the driver to stop at the intersection. Cross the road and walk against oncoming traffic until you see 797 Microphone. Enter through the main gate, onto Jiuxianqiao Road. **■TIP→ It may be helpful to ask your hotel staff to instruct the taxi driver before you set off.** ✉ *4 Jiuxianqiao Rd., Dashanzi,Chaoyang District* ☎ *010/6438–4862 or 010/6437–6248* 🌐 *www.798space.com.*

To get a feel for what sells abroad, drop by internationally owned galleries such as White Space Beijing or Art Seasons. These established galleries house perennially hot artists such as Liu Fei, Zhao Bo, and Chen Ke. Time-Zone 8 Book Shop is an avant-garde bookshop in the heart of Dashanzi.

—by Katharine Mitchell

fringe of these districts, making stops at Beijing Train Station, Chongwenmen, Qianmen, Hepingmen, Xuanwumen, and Changchun Jie. Line 5 stops at the Temple of Heaven and runs north–south with transfers to Line 1 at Dongdan, and transfers to Line 2 at Chongwenmen and the Lama Temple.

For destinations in the south of Chongwen and Xuanwu, it's smart to take a taxi as things are more spread out and it may be hard to find your way on foot.

SIGHTS

5 **Ming Dynasty City Wall Ruins Park.** This enlightening walk follows Chongwenmen Dong Dajie behind the train station. This rebuilt section of Beijing's grand old inner city wall was reconstructed with the original bricks returned by Beijing residents who had taken them to build their own structures when the city wall was torn down in the 1960s. It's a well-lit area, flanked by a wide strip of grass with paths full of city residents walking dogs, flying kites, and practicing tai chi. The eastern terminus is the imposing **Dongbianmen Watch Tower,** which houses several art galleries. ✉ *Chongwenmen Dong Dajie, just east of the Chongwenmen subway stop, Chongwen District* Ⓜ *Chongwenmen.*

1 **Niujie (Ox Street) Mosque.** Originally built during the Liao Dynasty in 996, Beijing's oldest and largest mosque sits at the center of the Muslim quarter and mimics a Chinese temple from the outside, with its hexagonal wooden structure. Inside, arches and posts are inscribed with Koranic verse, and a special moon tower helps with determining the lunar calendar. At the rear of the complex is a minaret from which a muezzin calls the faithful to prayer. Because Muslims must pray in the direction of Mecca, which from Beijing is toward the west, the main prayer hall opens onto the east. The main prayer hall is open only to Muslims and can fit up to 1,000 worshippers. All visitors must wear long trousers or skirts and keep their shoulders covered. Women are not permitted to enter some areas.

Fodor's Choice ★

Standing opposite the main entrance, and serving to prevent ghosts from entering the mosque, The Spirit Wall is covered with carved murals on the premise that ghosts can't turn sharp corners. Two dark tombs with Chinese and Arabic inscriptions are kept in one of the small courtyards. They belonged to two Persian imams who came to preach at the mosque in the 13th and 14th centuries. From the Tower for Viewing the Moon, imams (the prayer leaders of a mosque) measure the beginning and end of Ramadan, Islam's month of fasting and prayer. Ramadan beings when the imam sights the new moon, which appears as a slight crescent. ✉ *88 Niu Jie, Xuanwu District* 🎫 *Y10* ⏲ *Daily 8–sunset.*

4 **Front Gate** *(Qianmen).* From its top looking south, you can see that the Front Gate is actually two gates: Sun-Facing Gate (Zhengyangmen) and Arrow Tower (Jian Lou), which was, until 1915, connected to Zhengyangmen by a defensive half-moon wall. The central gates of both structures opened only for the emperor's biannual ceremonial trips to the Temple of Heaven. The gate now defines the southern edge of Tiananmen Square. ✉ *Xuanwumen Jie, Xuanwu District* Ⓜ *Qianmen.*

2 **Source of Law Temple** *(Fayuan Si).* Also a school for monks—the Chinese Buddhist Theoretical Institute houses and trains them here—the temple functions within the boundaries of current regime policy. You can observe both elderly practitioners chanting mantras in the main prayer halls, as well as robed students kicking soccer balls in a side

courtyard. Before lunch the smells of vegetarian stir-fry tease the nose. The dining hall has simple wooden tables set with cloth-wrapped bowls and chopsticks. Dating from the 7th century but last rebuilt in 1442, the temple holds a fine collection of Ming and Qing statues, including a sleeping Buddha and an unusual grouping of copper-cast Buddhas seated on a 1,000-petal lotus. ✉ *7 Fayuan Si Qianjie, Xuanwu District* ☎ *010/6353–4171* 🎫 *Y5* ⏲ *Daily 8:30–3:30.*

❻ Fodor'sChoice ★ **Temple of Heaven.** The Temple of Heaven, where emperors once performed important rites, began in the early 15th century under Yongle, whom many call the "architect of Beijing." Set in a huge, serene, mushroom-shaped park southeast of the Forbidden City, the Temple of Heaven is surrounded by splendid examples of Ming Dynasty architecture. The temple's hallmark structure is a magnificent blue-roofed wooden tower, built in 1420. It burned to the ground in 1889 and was immediately rebuilt using Ming architectural methods (and timber imported from Oregon). The building's design is based on the calendar: 4 center pillars represent the seasons, the next 12 pillars represent months, and 12 outer pillars signify the parts of a day. Together these 28 poles, which correspond to the 28 constellations of heaven, support the structure without nails. A carved dragon swirling down from the ceiling represents the emperor.

Shaped like a semicircle on the northern rim to represent heaven and square on the south for the earth, the grounds were once believed to be the meeting point of the two. The area is double the size of the Forbidden City and is still laid out to divine rule: buildings and paths are positioned to represent the right directions for heaven and earth. This means, for example, that the northern part is higher than the south.

The Temple of Heaven was a site for imperial sacrifices, meant to please the gods so they would generate bumper harvests. A long, twisting platform, the Long Corridor once enclosed the animal-killing pavilion, the Long Corridor was traditionally hung with lanterns on the eve of sacrifices. Today it plays host to scores of Beijingers singing opera, playing cards and chess, and fan dancing. On the western edge of the grounds, the Hall of Abstinence is where the emperor would retreat three days before the ritual sacrifice.

Just inside the south gate, the Round Altar, a three-tiered, white-marble structure, was where the emperor worshipped the winter solstice; it's based around the divine number nine. If there aren't many other visitors, stand in the center and shout to hear a strange audio effect.

Cross the divine pathway on the Danbi Bridge to the Hall of Prayer for Good Harvests. The middle section was once reserved for the Emperor of Heaven, who was the only one allowed to step foot on the eastern side, while aristocrats and high-ranking officials walked on the western strip. ✉ *Yongdingmen Dajie (South Gate), Xuanwu District* ☎ *010/6702–8866* 🎫 *All-inclusive ticket Y35; entrance to park only Y15* ⏲ *Daily 8–6; ticket booth closes 4:30* PM.

EXPERIENCES

THE MUSLIM QUARTER

Urban renewal has wiped out much of Beijing's old Muslim Quarter, which dates back to the 900s. The main survivor is the **Niujie (Ox Street) Mosque,** which was built in 996; it is often crowded with members of Beijing's Muslim community. Like other mosques in China, the Niujie Mosque looks like a traditional Buddhist temple with the addition of inscriptions in Arabic. A few Muslim shops—mainly halal restaurants and butchers—remain in the neighborhood, which is now dominated by high-rise apartment buildings.

MYSTERIES OF THE TEMPLE

An almost-magical wall encircling the Imperial Vault of Heaven, the Echo Wall allows you to eavesdrop. Extreme quiet is needed to hear the effect. Also, on the courtyard's step are three echo stones, which play with handclaps.

The number nine was regarded as a symbol of the power of the emperor. Nine or multiples of nine are used in the designs of palaces and temples. If you count studs on palace gates, for example, there are usually nine rows of nine.

DAZHALAN'S DELIGHTS

Dazhalan, a street and neighborhood in Xuanwu, immediately southwest of the Forbidden City, is packed with people, cars, and bicycles—each competing for the limited space on its narrow streets, already crowded with hawkers' stands and overflowing restaurants. Dive into the hutong and you are immediately rubbing elbows with the masses. Many *laozihao,* or old brand-name shops, continue to do a booming business here.

❸ The **Ruifuxiang Silk Shop** (✉ *5 Dazhalan Dajie* ☎ *010/6303–5313*), established in 1893, has thick bolts of silk, cotton, cashmere, and wool piled high, in more colors than you'll find in a box of crayons: chartreuse, candy-pink, chocolate brown, fresh-cut-grass green—you name it. Clerks deftly cut yards of cloth while tailors take measurements for colorful *qipaos* (traditional gowns). In this corner of Beijing, life seems to continue much as it did a century ago.

CHAOYANG DISTRICT

Chaoyang is where you'll find a lot of the action in Beijing: the nightlife in this district is positively sizzling. The bars and clubs are vibrant and full of Chinese office workers and university students as well as foreigners including expats, English teachers, and embassy staff. During the day, all these people work in this area, as it's home to the CBD (Central Business District), as well as the embassies and the residences of the people who run Beijing's portion of the global economy.

HIGHLIGHTS

From shopping at **Yashow Market** to partying in **Sanlitun,** Chaoyang has a little of everything. **Jianguomen** is Beijing's first embassy area, with some good foreign restaurants, but mostly quiet blocks of gated embassy compounds; in the center there is lovely **Ritan Park,** with its winding

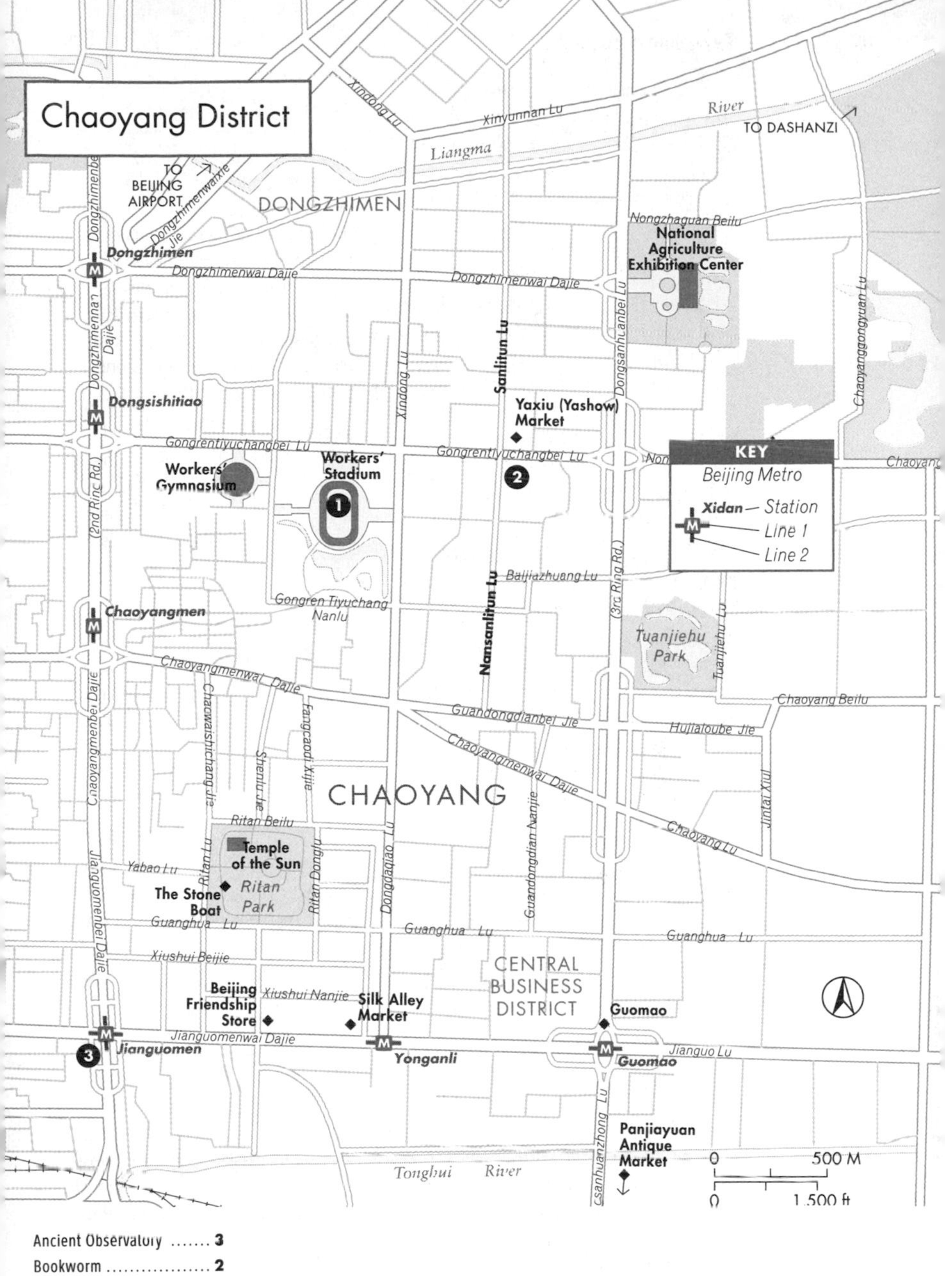

Ancient Observatory 3

Bookworm 2

Workers' Stadium 1

paths, lotus-flower ponds, climbing wall, and even a few restaurants and bars. The **Olympic Park** is also technically in Chaoyang, but it feels like a district unto itself.

The fast-rising **Central Business District** (CBD) encompasses the China World Trade Center and a slew of new and impressive skyscrapers, such as the CCTV Tower, the multimillion-dollar complex that's a continuous loop of horizontal and vertical sections, and locals have taken to calling it the "boxer shorts" or "bird's legs" building. Opposite the China World Trade Center is Jianwai Soho, a collection of gleaming white high-rises in a nicely laid-out complex with dozens of restaurants and shops.

RITAN PARK EATS

If you're near Ritan Park and need a nighttime pick-me-up, check out **The Stone Boat,** on the west side of the park alongside the lake. In a beautiful location overlooking the lake, it offers coffee, tea, juices, and mixed drinks along with simple snacks. On the weekends during the warmer months, it also features local music talent. If that's not your cup of tea, try **Vics** (☎ *010/6593–6215*) or **Mix** (☎ *010/6530–02889*), both just inside the north gate of the Workers' Stadium.

North of Ritan Park is the **Workers' Stadium** complex, where many of the biggest visiting acts perform. The famous Sanlitun Bar Street is several blocks east of Workers' Stadium and runs north–south; this is the area that's known for great bars catering to foreigners, expats, and young Chinese.

For shopping, check out **Yashow Market** (also called Yaxiu Shichang), a former department store that's been turned into five floors of small shops mainly selling pirated products. Or head to the so-called **Silk Alley Market,** which is no longer an alley; a mall has been erected near the Yonganli subway station. There's a street of restaurants and bars growing up next to the flower market at **Nurenjie** (aka Ladies' Street). At nearby Lucky Street, there's a string of Asian, Western, and Chinese restaurants and coffee shops. Also, be sure to check out the **Panjiayuan Antique Market,** which is known for more than just antiques—it's a great place to shop for knickknacks, old books, art, posters, baskets, and gifts. For the artsy visitors, check out the **798 Art District,** which is in an old factory complex full of galleries and nightlife spots.

GETTING HERE AND GETTING AROUND

The heart of Chaoyang district is accessible via lines 1 and 2 on the subway, but the district is huge and the sites are broadly distributed. Taking taxis between sites is usually the easiest way to get around. The 798 Art District is especially far away from central Beijing, and so a taxi is also the best bet (about Y30 from the center of town). Buses go everywhere, but they are slow and very crowded.

SIGHTS

❸ **Ancient Observatory.** This squat tower of primitive stargazing equipment peeks out next to the elevated highways of the Second Ring Road. It dates to the time of Genghis Khan, who believed that his fortunes could be read in the stars. Many of the bronze devices on display were gifts from Jesuit missionaries who arrived in Beijing and shortly thereafter ensconced themselves as the Ming court's resident stargazers. The main astronomical devices are arranged on the roof; inside, the dusty exhibition rooms shelter ancient star maps with information dating back to the Tang Dynasty. Writhing bronze dragon sculptures adorn some of the astronomy pieces on the black-brick roof of Jianguo Tower, the main building that houses the observatory. Among the sculptures are an armillary sphere to pinpoint the position of heavenly bodies and a sextant to measure angular distances between stars, along with a celestial globe.

To China's imperial rulers, interpreting the heavens was key to holding onto power; a ruler knew when an eclipse would occur, or he could predict the best time to plant crops. Celestial phenomena like eclipses and comets were believed to portend change; if left unheeded they might cost an emperor his legitimacy—or mandate of heaven. *2 Dongbiaobei Hutong, Jianguomenwai Dajie, Chaoyang District 010/6524 2202 Y10 Daily 9–4 Jianguomen.*

EXPERIENCES

NIGHTLIFE

A steady stream of Beijing's beautiful people passes through the north gate of the **Workers' Stadium**, drawn toward the hip-hop music that throbs from several of the bars that have displaced spaces once devoted to basketball and Ping-Pong. The crowd runs the gamut from Chinese college kids to well-heeled Beijing tycoons to Mongolian prostitutes, plus expats and foreign diplomats. Downstairs in Vics it's wall-to-wall people: drinking, dancing, or lost in conversation. A young woman, French beret pulled down over her eyes, leans against her boyfriend; an older woman straight from the society pages of Hong Kong's newspapers sips wine. There's even a Chinese Elvis, his hair defying physics to remain aloft inches into the air. Welcome to the new China.

SANLITUN BAR STREET

This is one of the hottest streets in the city. Plenty of bars, pubs, and dance spots amp the energy up here, with more refined venues filling out the southern section of the street. Enjoy a drink or meal, along with some great books, at **The Bookworm**, in the first alley on Sanlitun South Street. Readings and musical events take place throughout the week here, usually in the evenings.

HAIDIAN DISTRICT

In the last decade or so, with the Chinese Internet and tech booms, the rise of the middle class, and, with it, university education, Haidian has become an educational- and techno-mecca. The major IT players are all located here (including offices of Microsoft, Siemens, NEC, and Sun). If you want to escape modern life, never fear: Haidian is a huge district, and the outer areas house many interesting cultural sites—in fact, it's the juxtaposition of the Summer Palace, and, say, nearby Zhongguan-

CLOSE UP

The 2008 Olympic Games

The 2008 Summer Olympics changed the face of Beijing: just about everywhere you look, you'll find signs of the feverish development boom that began when the games were awarded to the city in 2001. Whole city blocks were razed to make way for state-of-the-art Olympic venues, new hotels, and modern buildings. The city is now the scene of brash, breathtaking structures.

BEIJING CAPITAL AIRPORT, TERMINAL 3

Address: Beijing Capital Airport

Architects: Norman Foster, the preeminent British architect responsible for Hong Kong's widely respected airport

BEIJING LINKED HYBRID

Address: Adjacent to the northeast corner of the Second Ring Road

Architects: New York–based Steven Holl, who won awards for his Museum of Contemporary Art in Helsinki, Finland, and Li Hu, who helped design China's first contemporary museum in Nanjing

CCTV (CENTRAL CHINESE TELEVISION) TOWER AND CULTURAL CENTER

Address: 32 Dong San Huan Zhong Lu (32 East Third Ring Middle Road)

Architects: Rem Koolhaas (a Dutch mastermind known for his outlandish ideas and successful Seattle Public Library) and Ole Scheeren (Koolhaas's 30-something German protégé)

NATIONAL STADIUM ("BIRD'S NEST")

Address: Beijing Olympic Park at Bei Si Huan Lu (North Fourth Ring Road).

Architects: Herzog and de Meuron of Switzerland, who won the prestigious Pritzker Prize for work at London's Tate Modern and the Ricola Marketing Building in Laufen, Switzerland

NATIONAL SWIMMING CENTER (THE "WATERCUBE")

Address: Beijing Olympic Park

Architects: PTW, the Australian firm that cut its teeth on venues for the 2000 Games in Sydney

GRAND NATIONAL THEATER

Address: Xi Chang'an Jie (just west of Tiananmen Square)

Architect: French-born Paul Andreu, who designed the groundbreaking Terminal 1 of Paris's Charles de Gaulle airport in 1974

cun (the technology hub) that really makes the Haidian district the exemplification of new China.

HIGHLIGHTS

Zhongguancun is the technology neighborhood, with dozens of big-name corporate headquarters next to malls (such as **Hailong Shopping Mall**) offering cheap shopping and high-quality computer components and electronics. The many universities in Haidian have lent a huge, energetic student presence and an international atmosphere to the entire district, and to the **Wudaokou** area in particular, which has a vibrant nightlife and dining scene dominated by students.

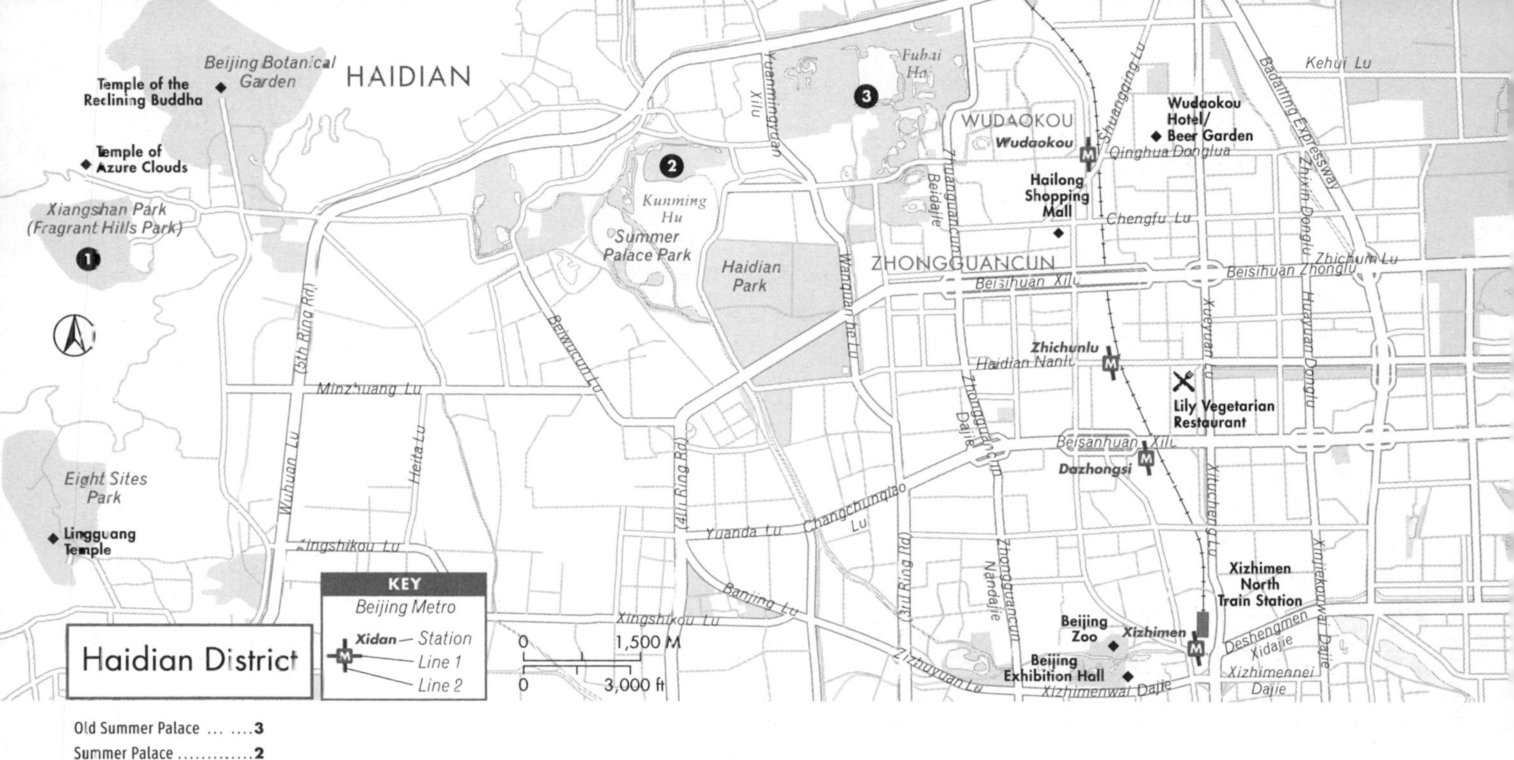

Old Summer Palace 3
Summer Palace 2
Xiangshan Park (Fragrant Hills Park) 1

TIANJIN

Tianjin (96 km [60 mi] east of Beijing) is a huge port city of 10 million people known to Beijingers for its *baozi* (steamed buns), wonderful antiques market, and international architecture, including British, French, American, German, Japanese, Russian, Italian, Austrian-Hungarian, and Belgian examples. For the best antiques shopping in China, head to Tianjin on a Wednesday evening train, check into your hotel, have dinner, and go to bed so you can wake up early for the **Shenyangdao Antiques Market,** which opens at 4 AM every Thursday and is well picked over by mid-morning. When buying at Shenyangdao, be wary of items dubbed genuine antiques. They do exist, but are very rare; even the prettiest, oldest looking pieces can be fake. Some are made with antique wood that has been recently recycled into "antiques" by skilled artisans. The casual collector should remember: buy things because you like them, not because you think they are inherently valuable. Feel free to haggle relentlessly. Trains (Y30) to Tianjin leave Beijing Station every hour from 6 AM until 5:30 PM, and buses (Y25) leave around the clock.

There are lots of fascinating sites in Haidian. The **Summer Palace,** the **Old Summer Palace,** the **Fragrant Hills Park,** and the **Beijing Botanical Garden** all call this district home; these are just a few of the more popular ones. The **Beijing Zoo** is here, too, but it's a bit behind the times.

GETTING HERE AND GETTING AROUND

Occupying the northwest corner of the city, the sprawling district of Haidian is Beijing's science, technology, and university district; it also houses numerous cultural sites. As you plan your visit to this district, keep in mind that Haidian is geographically large, and traveling between sites will require a taxi ride. Subway Line 13 stops at Wudaokou, the heart of Haidian; if Line 4 is open by the time you visit Beijing, it promises stops at both the Beijing Zoo and the Old Summer Palace. Otherwise, the Summer Palace, Old Summer Palace, Fragrant Hills Park, and the Beijing Botanical Garden are all rather far away in the northwest of the city and are best reached by taxi. To save money, take the train to the Xizhimen (or Wudaokou) subway station and take a taxi from there.

SIGHTS

❶ **Xiangshan Park** *(Fragrant Hills Park).* This hillside park northwest of Beijing was once an imperial retreat. From the eastern gate you can hike to the summit on a trail dotted with small temples. If you're short on time, ride a cable car to the top. ✉ *Haidian District* ☎ *010/6259–1155* *Y10; one-way cable car, Y60* ⏲ *Daily 6–6.*

❸ ★ **Old Summer Palace.** Once a grand collection of palaces, this complex was the emperor's summer retreat from the 15th century to 1860, when it was looted and blown up by British and French soldiers. The Western-style buildings—patterned after Versailles in France—were added during the Qing Dynasty and designed by Jesuits. Beijing has chosen to preserve the vast ruin as a "monument to China's national humiliation," though the patriotic slogans that were once scrawled on the rubble have now been cleaned off. The palace is made up of three idyllic parks: Yuanmingyuan (Garden of Perfection and Light) in the west, Wanchunyuan (Garden of 10,000 Springs) in the south, and Changchunyuan (Garden of Everlasting Spring), where the European ruins of marble palaces can be found, in the east. You can take a boat out on Fuhai Lake. Paddle your way around this charming lake, thick with pink lilies, the occasional sunken fountain, island pavilions, and stone-arched bridges.

SEE HOW CIXI LIVED

Her home, in the Hall of Joyful Longevity, is near the beginning of the Long Corridor. The residence is furnished and decorated as Cixi left it. Her private theater, called the Grand Theater Building, just east of the hall, was constructed for her 60th birthday and cost 700,000 taels of silver. At the west end of the beautiful lake you'll find the Marble Boat, which Cixi built with money meant for the Chinese navy.

The Labyrinth, an engraved concrete wall maze, known as Huanghuazhen (Yellow Flower), twists and turns around a European-style pavilion. Recently restored and just to the left of the west gate of Changchunyuan, it was once the site of lantern parties during mid-autumn festivals. Palace maids would race each other to the pavilion carrying lotus lanterns. Scramble over the stones of Changchunyuan, which are like a surreal graveyard to European architecture. The ruins of ornately carved columns, squat lion statues, and crumbling stone blocks lie like fallen dominoes. The park costs an extra Y15 to enter, but it's well worth it. ✉ *Qinghuan Xi Lu, (just northeast of the Summer Palace), Haidian District* ☎ *010/6265–8207* 🎫 *Park Y10; extra Y15 fee for sites* ⏲ *Daily 7–7.*

❷ Fodor's Choice ★ **Summer Palace.** Emperor Qianlong commissioned this giant royal retreat for his mother's 60th birthday in 1750. Anglo–French forces plundered, then burned, many of the palaces in 1860 and funds were diverted from China's naval budget for the renovations. Empress Dowager Cixi retired here in 1889. Nine years later, she imprisoned her nephew, Emperor Guangxu, after his reform movement failed. In 1903, she moved the seat of government from the Forbidden City to the Summer Palace from which she controlled China until her death in 1908.

Nowadays, the place is undoubtedly romantic. Pagodas and temples perch on hillsides; rowboats dip under arched stone bridges; and willow branches brush the water. The greenery provides a welcome relief from the loud, bustling city. It's also a fabulous history lesson. You can see firsthand the results of corruption: the opulence here was bought with siphoned money as China crumbled while suffering repeated humiliations at the hands of colonialist powers. The entire gardens were for the Empress Dowager's exclusive use. UNESCO placed the Summer Palace on its World Heritage list in 1998.

Inside the Hall of Benevolent Longevity is where Cixi held court and received foreign dignitaries. It is said that the first electric lights in China shone here. Just behind the hall and next to the lake is Hall of Jade Ripples, where Cixi kept the hapless Guangxu under guard while she ran China in his name. The ceiling and wooden rafters of the Long Corridor are richly painted with thousands of scenes from legends and nature—be on the lookout for Sun Wukong (the Monkey King). The wooden walkway skirts the northern shoreline of Kunming Lake for about half a mile until it reaches the marble boat. Cixi's home, in the Hall of Joyful Longevity, is near the beginning of the Long Corridor. The residence is furnished and decorated as Cixi left it. Her private theater, called the Grand Theater Building, just east of the hall, was constructed for her 60th birthday and cost 700,000 taels of silver.

WORD OF MOUTH

"There's no need to join a tour of the Summer Palace. Just ask the hotel to write down your destination in Chinese, flag a cab, and show the cabbie where you want to go. When you pay your entrance fee at the gate, you can buy a booklet with a map. From there, just stroll as whim takes you—a nice contrast to being led around by a tour guide. You'll need a good half day."

—Neil_Oz

Longevity Hill is strung with pagodas and temples, including the impressive Tower of the Fragrance of Buddha, Glazed Tile Pagoda, and the Hall that Dispels Clouds, this is the place where you can escape the hordes of visitors—take your time exploring the lovely northern side of the hill.

You can hire a boat on Kunming Lake. This giant body of water extends southward for 3 km (2 mi); it's ringed by tree-lined dikes, arched stone bridges, and numerous gazebos. In winter, you can skate on the ice. The less-traveled southern shore near Humpbacked Bridge is an ideal picnic spot. At the west end of the lake you'll find the Marble Boat, which doesn't actually float and was built by the Dowager Empress Cixi with money meant for the navy. ✉ *Yiheyuan Lu and Kunminghu Lu, Haidian District* ✣ *12 km (7½ mi) northwest of downtown Beijing* ☎ *010/6288–1144* 🌐 *www.summerpalace-china.com (Chinese only)* 🎫 *Y60 summer all-inclusive, Y50 winter* ⏲ *Daily 6:30–8 (ticket office closes at 6 PM).*

EXPERIENCES

SHOPPING FOR THE GOODS

When you're done with lunch and sightseeing, hop a cab to **Hailong Shopping Mall:** go in and explore—the five-story shopping mall has every kind of computer or electronic device you could possibly want, often at deep discounts. ■ **TIP→ Be careful when buying software, though, as most of it is pirated and is illegal to bring it back to the United States.**

QUICK EATS IN WUDAOKOU

There are plenty of restaurants on campus and around Zhongguancun, but the coolest places to eat in Haidian are in Wudaokou. Try excellent and innovative Korean barbecue at **Hanguokeli** (✉ *35 Chengfu Lu* ☎ *010/6256–3749* Ⓜ *Wudaokou*). Another hopping eatery is **Youle** (✉ *On Shuangqing Lu, just off Chengfu Lu* ☎ *010/5872–2028*), a Japanese noodle house on the first floor of Weixin Guoji Dasha, or the Weixin International Mansion. Not to be missed is the beer garden at the **Wudaokou Hotel** on Chengfu Lu, one block east of the subway station. The **Bridge Café** (☎ *010/8286–7206*), also on Chenfu Lu one block west of the subway station, serves up great sandwiches, salads, and desserts popular with the student crowd.

WHERE TO EAT

By Eileen Wen Mooney
Updated by Zoe Li

China's economic boom revolutionized dining culture in Beijing. Today you can eat a wide variety of regional cuisines, including unusual, specialties from Yunnan, earthy Hakka cooking from southern China, Tibetan yak and *tsampa* (barley flour), numbingly spicy Sichuan cuisine, and chewy noodles from Shaanxi. The capital also offers plenty of international cuisine, including French, German, Thai, Japanese, Brazilian, Malaysian, and Italian, among others.

Peking duck is the capital's most well-known dish, but there's much more to the city's cuisine than just the famous fowl. Despite rising competition, traditional Beijing dining is making a comeback. Waiters whisk dishes through crowded, lively rooms furnished with wooden menu boards and lacquered square tables, while doormen, dressed in traditional cotton jackets, loudly announce each arrival and departure. Beijing-style eateries offer many little-known but excellent specialties, such as *dalian huoshao* (meat and vegetable-filled dumplings) and *zhajiangmian* (thick noodles with meat sauce). If you're adventurous, sample a bowl of intestines brewed in an aromatic broth mixed with bean curd, baked bread, and chopped cilantro.

Beijingers complement their meals with locally brewed beer, such as Yanjing or Beijing beer, or the fiery *erguoto,* an alcoholic beverage distilled from wheat and fermented sorghum. Or try *Suanmeitang,* a delightful nonalcoholic drink made from dried plums—it's perfect in summer. Imperial-style banquets, serving Manchu and Han dishes, offer an alternatively lavish dining experience.

LOGISTICS

People tend to eat around 6 PM, and, although the last order is usually taken around 9 PM, some places remain open until the wee morning hours. For reservations, book as far ahead as you can, and reconfirm as soon as you arrive. Tipping is not required, although some larger hotels add a 15% service charge to the bill. Small and medium-size venues only take cash payment, but more established restaurants usually accept credit cards.

CHINESE CUISINE

To help you navigate China's cuisines, we have used the following terms in our restaurant reviews.

Cantonese: A diverse cuisine that roasts and fries, braises and steams. Spices are used in moderation. Dishes include fried rice, sweet-and-sour pork, and roasted goose.

Chinese: Catch-all term used for restaurants that serve cuisine from multiple regions of China.

Chinese fusion: Any Chinese cuisine with international influences.

Chiu chow: Known for its vegetarian and seafood cusine, which are mostly poached, steamed, or braised. Dishes include *popiah* (non-fried spring rolls), baby oyster congee, and fish-ball noodle soup.

Hunan: Cooking methods feature stewing, frying, braising, and smoking. Flavors are spicy, with chili peppers, shallots, garlic, and dried and preserved condiments. Signature dishes are Mao's braised pork, steamed fish head with shredded chilies, and spicy eggplant in garlic sauce.

Macanese: An eclectic blend of southern Chinese and Portuguese cooking, featuring the use of salted dried fish, coconut milk, turmeric, and other spices. Common dishes are "African" barbecued chicken with spicy piri piri sauce, pork buns, and curried baked chicken.

Mandarin (Beijing): Dishes from Beijing typically are snack sized, featuring ingredients like dark soy paste, sesame paste, and sesame oil. Regional specialties include Peking duck, moo shu pork, and quick-fried tripe.

Northern Chinese (inner Mongolia and environs): Staples are lamb and mutton, preserved vegetables, and noodles, steamed breads, pancakes, stuffed buns, and dumplings. Common dishes are cumin-scented lamb, congee porridge with pickles, and Mongolian hotpot.

Sichuan (central province): Famed for bold flavors and spiciness from chilies and Sichuan peppercorns. Dishes include "dan dan" spicy rice noodles, twice-cooked pork, and tea-smoked duck.

Shanghainese: Cuisine characterized by rich flavors produced by braising and stewing, and the use of alcohol in cooking. Dumplings, noodles, and bread are served more than rice. Signature dishes are baby hairy crabs stir-fried with rice-cake slices, steamed buns and dumplings, and "drunken chicken."

Taiwanese: Diverse cuisine centers on seafood, pork, rice, soy, and fruit. Specialties include "three cups chicken" with a sauce made of soya, rice wine, and sugar; oyster omelets; cuttlefish soup; and dried tofu.

Tibetan: Cuisine reliant on foodstuffs grown at high altitudes, including barley flour; yak meat, milk, butter, and cheese; and mustard seed. Salted black tea with yak butter is a staple beverage.

Yunnan (southernmost province): This region's cuisine is noted for its use of vegetables, fruit, bamboo shoots, and flowers in its spicy preparations. Dishes include rice noodle soup with chicken, pork, and fish; steamed chicken with ginseng and herbs; and the cured Yunnan ham.

PRICES

Dining out is one of the great bargains in Beijing, where it's still possible to have a three-course meal with drinks for less than $10. As in other cities, drinks can push up the price of a meal, so study the drink options and costs carefully. Although one tea may cost Y40 a pot, another may just be Y10. A soda could be Y25 a glass, and a bottle of beer is just Y10.

	WHAT IT COSTS IN YUAN				
	¢	$	$$	$$$	$$$$
Restaurants	under Y40	Y40–Y80	Y81–Y120	Y121–Y180	over Y180

Prices are for a main course. Note: the term "main course" may not be appropriate for some restaurants, as Chinese dishes are normally shared.

DONGCHENG DISTRICT

$$ FRENCH **Café de la Poste.** In almost every French village, town, or city there is a Café de la Poste, where people go for a cup of coffee, a beer, or a simple family meal. This haunt lives up to its name: It's a steak-lover's paradise, with such favorites as finely sliced marinated beefsteak served with lemon-herb vinaigrette and steak tartare. If the next table orders banana flambé, we promise the warm scent of its rum will soon have you smitten enough to order it yourself. *58 Yonghegong Dajie, Dongcheng District* *010/6402–7047* *No credit cards* *Yonghegong.*

$$ CHINESE **Gui Gongfu.** Known as the "Lair of Queens" because two Qing empresses once lived here, this space was also home to the infamous Empress Dowager Cixi and her niece Logyu. A large courtyard house with wisteria and crab-apple trees in the garden make this ideal for dining alfresco in the summer. Some of the dishes are flavored with tea leaves and are accordingly named. *Lu Yu zhucha* is the restaurant's signature dish: Lu Yu is the author of the ancient *Book of Tea* and the dish is stir-fried beef with chilies and tea leaves. Green-tea flavored noodles and oolong spareribs are also excellent choices. This quiet restaurant attracts people keen to experience a bit of Old Beijing. *11 Fang Jia Yuan Hutong, Dongcheng District* *010/6512–7667* *AE, V.*

$$$$ CANTONESE Fodor's Choice ★ **Huang Ting.** Beijing's traditional courtyard houses, facing extinction as entire neighborhoods are demolished to make way for high-rises, provide the theme here. The walls are constructed from original *hutong* bricks taken from centuries-old courtyard houses that have been destroyed. This is arguably Beijing's best Cantonese restaurant, serving southern favorites such as braised shark fin with crab meat, seared abalone with seafood, and steamed scallop and bean curd in black-bean sauce. The dim sum is delicate and refined, and the deep-fried taro spring rolls and steamed pork buns are not to be missed. *The Peninsula, 8 Jinyu Hutong, Wangfujing, Dongcheng District,* *010/6512–8899 Ext. 6707* *AE, DC, MC, V* *Dongdan.*

$$$$ INTERNATIONAL ★ **Jing.** Consistently rated among the city's best, Jing serves up East–West fusion cuisine in an ultramodern setting replete with polished red wooden floors, cream-color chairs, and gauzy curtain dividers.

Where to Eat in Beijing
KEY
Beijing Metro
Station
Line 1
Line 2
XINJIEKOU
DONGCHENG
DI'ANMEN
DONGSI
XICHENG
XISI
XIDAN
DONGDAN
FUXINGMEN
QIANMEN
XUANWU
CHONGWEN
Lama Temple
Drum & Bell Tower
Gongwangfu
Beihai Park
Jingshan Park
Forbidden City
Tiananmen Square
Great Hall of the People
China National Museum
Mao Zedong Memorial Hall
Ancient Observatory
Beijing Train Station
Liulichang
Ox Street Mosque
Temple of Heaven
Tiantan Park
Taoranting Park
Guanyuan Park
Qingnianhu Park
Ditan Park
Xihai
Houhai
Qianhai
Beihai
Zonghai
Nanhai
Deshengmenxi Dajie
Deshengmendong Dajie
Andingmenxibin River
(2nd Ring Rd.)
Andingmendongbin
Xizhimennei Dajie
Ping'anlixi Dajie
Fuchengmenwai Dajie
Fuxingmennei Dajie
Xichangan Jie
Jianguomennei
Xuanwumendong Dajie
Qianmenxi Dajie
Qianmendong Dajie
Chongwenmenxi Dajie
Zhushikouxi Dajie
Zushikoudong Dajie
Guang'anmennei Dajie
Luomashi Dajie
Tiantan Lu
Nanheng Xijie
Beiwei Lu
Taoranting Lu
Tiyuguan Lu
Di'anmenxi Dajie
Di'anmendong Dajie
Zhangzizhong Lu
Jingshanhou Jie
Jingshanqian Jie
Xi'anmen Dajie
Wenjin Jie
Chaoyangmennei
Gulou Dongdajie
Jiaodaokou Dongdajie
Gulouxi Dajie
Dingfu
Anding Lu
Hepingli Beijie
Hepingli Zhongjie
Andeli Beijie
Ande Lu
Guowang Hutong
Doufuchi Hutong
Jiuguloulwai Dajie
Guloudwai Dajie
Jiugulou Dajie
Baochao Hutong
Beiluogu Xiang
Nan Luogu Xiang
Andingmennei Dajie
Jiaodaokounan Dajie
Yonghegong Dajie
Dongsibei Dajie
Dongsinan Dajie
Dongdanbei Dajie
Meishuguanhou Jie
Beichizi Dajie
Nanchizi Dajie
Nanheyan Dajie
Huatong Jie
Wangfujing Dajie
Jinyu
Xinjiekounan Dajie
Xinjiekoubei Dajie
Huguosi Jie
Deshengmennei Dajie
Xisibei Dajie
Xisinan Dajie
Xishiku Dajie
Xidanbei Dajie
Taipingqiao Dajie
Naoshikou Jie
Fuyou Jie
Fuyou Jie
Beixinhua Jie
Nanxinhua Jie
Qianmen Dajie
Tianqiaonan Dajie
Hufang Lu
Taiping Lu
Tiantandong Lu
Niu Jie
Chongwenmen
Chaoyangmen
Dongzhimennei
Dongzhimenbeixiao
Dongzhimennanxiao
Beijingzhan
Xizhimennanxiao

Alameda **29**
Aria **37**
Baijia Dayuan **1**
Bellagio **33**
The Bookworm **32**
Café Constance **27**
Café de la Poste **18**
Comptoirs de France Bakery **42**
Din Tai Fung **23**
Ding Ding Xiang **2, 22**
Fangshan **7**
Gaon **39**
Gui Gongfu **21**
Hai Wan Ju **44**
Han Cang **6**
Huang Ting **14**
Jing **13**
Jun Wangfu **30**
Kong Yi Ji **3**
La Dolce Vita **25**
La Galerie **35**
Lai Jin Yu Xuan **10**
Li Qun Roast Duck **11**
Makye Ame **36**
Mei Fu **4**
Nam Nam **28**
Noodle Bar **31**
Old Beijing Noodle King **12**
Paomo Guan **20**
Paulaner Brauhaus **26**
Red Capital Club **19**
Shaguo Ju **8**
Shin Yeh **34**
The Source **17**
South Silk Road **42**
Still Thoughts **16**
Taj Pavilion **38**
Three Guizhou Men **40**
Whampoa Club **9**
Yotsuba **24**
Yue Bin **15**
Yuxiang Renjia **41**
Zhang Qun Jia **5**

Signature appetizers include outstanding duck rolls, tiger prawns, and fragrant coconut soup. The fillet of barramundi and risotto with seared langoustines are standout main courses. For dessert, don't miss the warm chocolate cake with almond ice cream. There's also an excellent selection of international wines. ✉ *The Peninsula Beijing, 8 Jinyu Hutong, Wangfujing, Dongcheng District* ☎ *010/6523–0175 Ext. 6714* ▭ *AE, DC, MC, V* Ⓜ *Dongdan.*

$$ CHINESE

✕ **Lai Jin Yu Xuan.** A gem tucked inside Zhongshan Park on the west side of the Forbidden City, Lai Jin is known for its Red Mansion banquet, based on dishes from Cao Xueqin's classic 18th-century novel, *The Dream of the Red Chamber.* The two-level restaurant sits beside a small pond amid willow and peach trees. The two daily dishes are *qie xiang* (eggplant with nuts) and *jisi haozigan* (shredded chicken with crown-daisy chrysanthemum). After your meal, take a lazy stroll across the park to the nearby teahouse with the same name, where you can enjoy a cup of tea in the courtyard surrounded by ancient cypress and scholar trees. ✉ *Inside Zhongshan Park, on the west side of the Forbidden City, Dongcheng District* ☎ *010/6605–6676* ▭ *No credit cards.*

¢ NORTHERN CHINESE

✕ **Paomo Guan.** The bright red-and-blue bamboo shading the front porch of this adorable spot will immediately catch your eye. Paomo Guan focuses on *paomo*—a Shaanxi trademark dish. Guests break a large piece of unleavened flat bread into little pieces and then put them in their bowl. After adding condiments, the waiter takes your bowl to the kitchen where broth—simmered with spices, including star anise, cloves, cardamom, cinnamon sticks, and bay leaves—is poured over the bread bits. ✉ *59 Chaoyangmennei Nanxiaojie, Dongcheng District* ☎ *010/6525–4639* ▭ *No credit cards.*

$$$$ MANDARIN Fodor's Choice ★

✕ **Red Capital Club.** Occupying a meticulously restored courtyard home in one of Beijing's few remaining traditional neighborhoods, the Red Capital Club oozes nostalgia. Cultural Revolution memorabilia and books dating from the Great Leap Forward era adorn every nook of the small bar, while the theme of the dining room is imperial. The fancifully written menu reads like a fairy tale, with dreamily named dishes. "South of Clouds" is a Yunnan dish of fish baked over bamboo—it's said to be a favorite of a former Communist marshal. "Dream of the Red Chamber" is a fantastic eggplant dish cooked according to a recipe in the classic novel by the same name. ✉ *66 Dongsi Jiutiao, Dongcheng District* ☎ *010/6402–7150* ✍ *Reservations essential* ▭ *AE, DC, MC, V* ⊙ *No lunch.*

$ CHINESE ★

✕ **Still Thoughts.** Soft Buddhist chants hum in this clean, cheerful restaurant, which serves no meat. Carnivores may still be happy here, though, as much of the food is prepared to look and taste like meat. Try the crispy Peking "duck," or a "fish" (made of tofu skin) that even has scales carved into it. *Zaisu jinshen,* another favorite, has a filling that looks and tastes like pork. It is wrapped in tofu skin, deep-fried, and coated with a light sauce. ✉ *18A Dafosi Dongjie, Dongcheng District* ☎ *010/6400–8941* ▭ *No credit cards.*

$$$$ SICHUAN Fodor's Choice ★

✕ **The Source.** The Source serves a set menu of Sichuan specialties, completely changing it every two weeks. The menu includes several appetizers, both hot and mild dishes, and a few surprise concoctions from the chef. On request, the kitchen will tone down the spiciness. The Source's location was once the backyard of a Qing Dynasty general regarded by the Qing court as "The Great Wall of China" for his military exploits. The grounds have been painstakingly restored; an upper level overlooks a small garden filled with pomegranate and date trees. The central yard's dining is serene and acoustically protected from the hustle and bustle outside. ✉*14 Banchang Hutong, Kuanjie, Dongcheng District* ☎*010/6400–3736* ✍*Reservations essential* ▭*AE, DC, MC, V.*

¢ MANDARIN **✕Yue Bin.** On a narrow alley opposite the National Museum of Art, Yue Bin's home-style cooking attracts neighborhood residents as well as hungry museum-goers. In business since 1949, it has managed to maintain its popularity throughout decades. The no-frills dining room is just big enough for half a dozen spotless tables. Don't leave without trying *suanni zhouzi*, pork elbow in a marinade of raw garlic and vinegar; the *guota doufuhe*, bite-size tofu stuffed with minced pork; or the *wusitong*, a roll of duck and vegetables. ✉*43 Cuihua Hutong, Dongcheng District* ☎*010/6524–5322* ▭*No credit cards.*

XICHENG DISTRICT

$$$$ MANDARIN ★ **✕Fangshan.** In a traditional courtyard villa on the shore of Beihai, you can get a taste of China's imperial cuisine. Established in 1925 by three royal chefs, Fangshan serves dishes once prepared for the imperial family, based on recipes gathered across China. The chef is best known for its filled pastries and steamed breads—traditional snack foods developed to satisfy Empress Dowager Cixi's sweet tooth. To experience Fangshan's exquisite imperial fare, order one of the banquet-style set meals at Y500 per person. Be sure to make reservations two or three days in advance. ✉*Beihai Park, northwest of the Forbidden City, Xicheng District* ☎*010/6401–1879* ✍*Reservations essential* ▭*AE, DC, MC, V* Ⓜ*Tiananmen West.*

$ CHINESE Fodor'sChoice ★ **✕Han Cang.** In the mood for something other than the ubiquitous home-style Beijing or Sichuan fare? Try Hakka cuisine. Specialties like *sanbei ya* (three-cup duck), *yanju* (salt-baked) shrimp, and *zhi bao luyu* (fish baked in aluminum foil) are served at this casual restaurant, flanked by the many watering holes around Houhai. If you're in a group, be sure to book one of the tables on the second floor so you enjoy views of the lake. ✉*Shichahai Dongan, Houhai, across the street from the north gate of Beihai Park, Xicheng District* ☎*010/6404–2259* ✍*Reservations essential* ▭*No credit cards.*

$ CHINESE **✕Kong Yi Ji.** Named for the down-and-out protagonist of a short story by Lu Xun (China's most famous writer), this restaurant is set behind a small bamboo forest. Upon entering, the first thing you'll see is a bust of Lu Xun. The old-fashioned menu, which is traditionally bound with thread, features some of the dishes made famous in the story, such as *huixiang dou*, or aniseed-flavored broad beans. A wide selection of *huangjiu*, sweet rice wine, is served in heated silver pots; it's sipped from a special ceramic cup. ✉*South shore of Shichahai, Deshengmennei Dajie, Xicheng District* ☎*010/6618–4915* ✍*Reservations not accepted* ▭*AE, MC, V.*

$$$$ CHINESE Fodor's Choice ★

✕ **Mei Fu.** In a plush, restored courtyard on Houhai's south bank, Mei Fu oozes intimate elegance. The interior is filled with antique furniture and velvet curtains punctuated by pebbled hallways and waterfalls. Black-and-white photos of Mei Lanfang, China's most famous opera star, who performed female roles, hang on the walls. Diners choose from set menus, starting from Y300 per person, which feature typical Jiangsu and Zhejiang cuisine, such as fried shrimp, pineapple salad, and tender leafy vegetables. A Y200 (per person) lunch is also available. ⊠*24 Daxiangfeng Hutong, south bank of Houhai Lake, Xicheng District* ☎*010/6612–6845* ✍*Reservations essential* ▭*MC, V.*

$ MANDARIN

✕ **Shaguo Ju.** Established in 1741, Shaguo Ju serves a simple Manchu favorite—*bairou,* or white-meat pork, which first became popular 300 years ago. The first menu pages list all the dishes cooked in the *shaguo* (the Chinese term for a casserole pot). The classic *shaguo bairou* consists of strips of pork neatly lined up, concealing bok choy and glass noodles below. Shaguo Ju emerged as a result of ceremonies held by imperial officials and wealthy Manchus in the Qing Dynasty, which included sacrificial offerings of whole pigs. The meat offerings were later given away to the nightwatch guards, who shared the "gifts" with friends and relatives. Such gatherings gradually turned into a small business, and white meat became very popular. ⊠*60 Xisi Nan Dajie, Xicheng District* ☎*010/6602–1126* ▭*No credit cards* Ⓜ*Xidan.*

$$$$ CHINESE

✕ **Whampoa Club.** Following the success of his restaurant in Shanghai, culinary mastermind Jereme Leung brings his New Chinese cuisine to Beijing. Housed in a sumptuously restored traditional courtyard house, the restaurant is one of the most beautiful in the city. The food of northern China is fine-tuned with modern twists. For example, the Beijing salad of cabbage doused in pungent mustard is paired with sweet lime jelly and buttery scallop sashimi. After dinner, head to the sleek black bar for a Beijing-inspired cocktail made with local baijiu liquor. ⊠*23A Jinrong Jie, Xicheng* ☎*10/8808–8828* ▭*AE, DC, MC, V.*

$$$$ CHINESE

✕ **Zhang Qun Jia.** You may never guess that behind the old fading wooden door with the number 5 written on it, set on "Bending Pipe Street," lies a gourmet restaurant. "Zhang Qun's Home" began as a place where the artist and friends could relax. Soon it turned into a small restaurant, serving the home-style specialties of her native Suzhou. Light shining through a small skylight, scattered books and fresh-cut flowers create the welcoming feeling of a friend's home. The aroma and taste of the spring onion in the noodles is captivating. The set meal costs Y200 to Y600 a person, and includes a large number of appetizers, hot dishes, and a dessert, all selected by Ms. Zhang. ⊠*5 Yandai Xiejie, Houhai, Xicheng District* ☎*010/8404–6662* ✍*Reservations not accepted* ▭*No credit cards.*

SOUTHERN DISTRICTS: CHONGWEN AND XUANWU

$$ MANDARIN Fodor's Choice ★

✕ **Li Qun Roast Duck Restaurant.** Juicy, whole ducks roasting in a traditional oven greet you upon entering this simple courtyard house. It's a family-run affair, far from the crowds and commercialism of Quanjude, Beijing's most famous Peking duck eatery. Li Qun is a choice option for those who enjoy a good treasure hunt: the restaurant is hidden deep in a hutong neighborhood. It should take about 10 minutes to walk there from Chongwenmen Xi Dajie, though you may have to stop several times and ask for directions. It's so well known by locals, however, that when they see foreigners coming down the street, they automatically point in the restaurant's direction. Sure, the restrooms and dining room are a bit shabby, but the place is charming. Ask for an English menu and feast to your heart's content! ✉*11 Beixiangfeng, Zhengyi Lu, Chongwen District* ☎*010/6705–5578* *Reservations essential* *No credit cards* Ⓜ*Chongwen.*

WORD OF MOUTH

"We liked the Liqun Roast Duck Restaurant. . . . Beijing Duck is roasted, but the crispy skin is served separately, along with pancakes, sliced green onions, and a dipping sauce. By the way, I found that rice wasn't always provided as a matter of course, so you may have to ask for it—the word is mifan, pronounced mee-FAHN."
–Neil_Oz

¢ MANDARIN

Old Beijing Noodle King. Close to the Temple of Heaven, this noodle house serves hand-pulled noodles and traditional local dishes in a lively old-time atmosphere. Waiters shout across the room to announce customers arriving. Try the tasty *zhajiang* noodle accompanied by meat sauce and celery, bean sprout, green beans, soy beans, sliver of cucumber, and red radish. ✉*29 Chongwenmen Dajie, Hongqiao Market, Chongwen District* ☎*010/6705–6705* *Reservations not accepted* *No credit cards.*

CHAOYANG DISTRICT

$$$ BRAZILIAN Fodor'sChoice ★

Alameda. Specializing in Brazilian fare, Alameda serves simple but delicious food. The weekday Y60 lunch specials are one of the best deals in town. Their menu is light yet satisfying, with plenty of Latin influences. Crowds seek out the *feijoada*—Brazil's national dish—a hearty black-bean stew with pork and rice, served only on Saturdays. The glass walls and ceiling make it a bright, pleasant place to dine, but magnifies the din of the crowded room. ✉*Sanlitun Beijie, by the Nali shopping complex, Chaoyang District* ☎*010/6417–8084* *AE, MC, V.*

$$$$ INTERNATIONAL ★

Aria. Aria's outdoor dining is secluded within neatly manicured bushes and roses, providing a perfectly quiet lunch spot amid Beijing's frenetic downtown. Sample the fish fillet topped with crispy pork skin. The best deal at this elegant restaurant is the weekday business lunch: for just Y198 you can enjoy a soup or salad, main course, dessert, and coffee or tea. Renaissance-style paintings decorate the walls. There is a posh dining area and bar on the first floor, and more intimate dining at the top of the spiral staircase. Live jazz enlivens the evenings. ✉*2/F China World Hotel, 1 Jianguomenwai Dajie, Chaoyang District* ☎*010/6505–2266 Ext. 38* *AE, MC, V* Ⓜ*Guomao.*

$ TAIWANESE ★

Bellagio. Chic Bellagio is a bright, trendy-but-comfortable restaurant serving up typical Sichuan dishes with a Taiwanese twist. A delicious choice is their *migao* (glutinous rice with dried mushrooms and dried shrimp, stir-fried rice noodles, and meatball soup). You can finish your meal with a Taiwan-style crushed ice and toppings of red bean, green bean, mango, strawberry, or peanut. Bellagio is open until 4 AM, making it a favorite with Beijing's chic clubbing set. The smartly dressed all-female staff—clad in black and white—have identical short haircuts. ✉*6 Gongti Xilu, Chaoyang District* ☎*010/6551–3533* ✍*Reservations essential* ▭*AE, MC, V.*

$ CAFÉ ★ ✕**The Bookworm.** We love this Beijing hot spot when we're craving a double-dose of intellectual stimulation and good food. Thousands of English-language books fill the shelves and may be borrowed for a fee or read inside. New books and magazines are also for sale. This is a popular venue for guest speakers, poetry readings, and live-music performances. The French chef offers a three-course set lunch and dinner. For a nibble, rather than a full meal, sandwiches, salads, and a cheese platter are also available. ✉*Building 4, Nan Sanlitun Lu, Chaoyang District* ☎*010/6586–9507* ▭*No credit cards.*

$$ GERMAN ✕**Café Constance.** The opening of Café Constance, a German bakery, brought excellent rye, pumpernickel, and whole-wheat breads to Beijing. The hearty "small" breakfast begins with coffee, fresh fruit, muesli, unsweetened yogurt, eggs and bacon; the big breakfast adds several cold cuts and breads and rolls. This is a true winner if you're looking for a good breakfast, simple meal, or a good cup of java and dessert. ✉*Lucky St. B5andC5, 29 Zaoying Lu, Chaoyang District* ☎*010/5867–0201* ▭*AE, MC, V.*

$ FRENCH ✕**Comptoirs de France Bakery.** This contemporary French-managed café serves a variety of sandwiches, excellent desserts, coffees, and hot chocolates. Besides the standard Americano, cappuccino, and latte, Comptoirs has a choice of unusual hot-chocolate flavors, including banana, Rhum Vieux, and Cointreau. In the Sichuan peppercorn–infused hot chocolate, the peppercorns float in the brew, giving it a pleasant peppery aroma. ✉*China Central Place, Building 15, N 102, 89 Jianguo Rd. (just northeast of Xiandai Soho), Chaoyang District* ☎*010/6530–5480* ▭*No credit cards.*

$$$ SHANGHAINESE Fodor's Choice ★ ✕**Din Tai Fung.** The arrival of Din Tai Fung—one of Taipei's most famous restaurants—was warmly welcomed by Beijing's food fanatics. The restaurant's specialty is *xiaolong bao* (juicy buns wrapped in a light unleavened-dough skin and cooked in a bamboo steamer), which are served with slivers of tender ginger in a light black vinegar. Xiaolong bao have three different fillings: ground pork, seafood, or crabmeat. If you can, leave some room for the scrumptious tiny dumplings packed with red-bean paste. This restaurant is frequented by both Beijing's up-and-coming middle class and old Taiwan hands, who are fervently loyal to its delicate morsels. ✉*24 Xinyuan Xili Zhongjie, Chaoyang District* ☎*010/6462–4502* ▭*AE, MC, V.*

$$$ KOREAN ✕**Gaon.** A quirky mixture of classic and contemporary decor backdrop traditional Korean food with a modern twist. Korean savory "pancakes" are normally too heavy to have with a big meal, but at Gaon they are small and served as appetizers. The *bulgogi* (beef mixed with mushrooms and scallion and served on a hot plate) is subtle yet tasty. We promise you won't leave the restaurant hungry. ✉*5/F, East*

Tower, Twin Towers, B-12 Jianguomenwai Dajie, Chaoyang District ☎*010/5120–8899* ▭*MC, V* Ⓜ*Yonganli.*

¢ CHINESE ✕**Hai Wan Ju.** Haiwan means "a bowl as deep as the sea," fitting for this eatery that specializes in crockery filled with hand-pulled noodles. The interior is simple, with traditional wooden tables and benches. A *xiao er* (a "young brother" in a white mandarin-collar shirt and black pants) greets you with a shout, which is then echoed in a thundering chorus by the rest of the staff. The clanking dishes and constant greetings re-create the busy atmosphere of an old teahouse. There are two types of noodles here: *guoshui,* noodles that have been rinsed and cooled; and *guotiao,* meaning "straight out of the pot," which is ideal for winter days. Vegetables, including diced celery, radish, green beans, bean sprouts, cucumber, and scallion, are placed on individual small dishes. Nothing tastes as good as a hand-pulled noodle: it's doughy and chewy, a texture that can only be achieved by strong hands repeatedly stretching the dough. ✉*36 Songyu Nanlu, Chaoyang District* ☎*010/8731–3518* ▭*AE, MC, V.*

$ CANTONESE ✕**Jun Wangfu.** Tucked inside Chaoyang Park, Jun Wangfu excels in classical Cantonese fare; it's frequented by Hong Kong expats. The comprehensive menu includes steamed tofu with scallops, spinach with taro and egg, crispy goose, roast chicken, and steamed fish with ginger and scallion. The fresh baked pastry filled with *durian* (a spiny tropical fruit with a smell so notoriously strong it is often banned from being brought aboard airplanes) is actually a mouthwatering rarity—don't be scared off by its overpowering odor. ✉*19 Chaoyang Gongyuan Nanlu, east of Chaoyang Park south gate, Chaoyang District* ☎*010/6507–7888.*

$$ ITALIAN ★ ✕**La Dolce Vita.** The food lives up to the name here: a basket of warm bread is served immediately, a nice treat in a city where good bread is hard to come by. The tough decision is between ravioli, tortellini, and oven-fired pizza. The rice-ball appetizer, with cheese and bits of ham inside, is fantastic. ✉*8 Xindong Lu North, Chaoyang District* ☎*010/6468–2894* ▭*AE, MC, V.*

$$ CHINESE ✕**La Galerie.** Choose between two outdoor dining areas: one a wooden platform facing the bustling Guanghua Road; the other well hidden in the back, overlooking the greenery of Ritan Park. Inspired Cantonese food and dim sum fill the menu: *Changfen* (steamed rice noodles) are rolled and cut into small pieces then stir-fried with crunchy shrimp, strips of lotus root, and baby bok choy, accompanied by sweet soybean, peanut, and sesame pastes. The *xiajiao* (steamed shrimp dumplings) envelop juicy shrimp and water chestnuts. ✉*South gate of Ritan Park, Guanghua Rd., Chaoyang District* ☎*010/8563–8698* ▭*AE, MC, V* Ⓜ*Jianguomen.*

$ TIBETAN ✕**Makye Ame.** Prayer flags lead you to the second floor entrance of this Tibetan restaurant, where a pile of mani stones and a large prayer wheel greet you. Long Tibetan Buddhist trumpets, lanterns, and handicrafts decorate the walls, and the kitchen serves a range of hearty dishes that run well beyond the staples of yak-butter tea and *tsampa* (roasted barley flour). Try the vegetable *pakoda* (a deep-fried dough pocket filled with vegetables), curry potatoes, or roasted lamb spareribs. Heavy wooden tables with brass corners, soft lighting, and Tibetan textiles make this an especially soothing choice. ✉ *11 Xiushui Nan Jie, 2nd floor, Chaoyang District* ☎ *010/6506–9616* ▭ *MC, V* Ⓜ *Jianguomen.*

$ VIETNAMESE ✕ **Nam Nam.** A sweeping staircase to the second floor, a tiny indoor fish pond, wooden floors, and posters from old Vietnam set the scene in this atmospheric restaurant. The light, delicious cuisine is paired with speedy service. Try the chicken salad, beef noodle soup, or the raw or deep-fried vegetable or meat spring rolls. The portions are on the small side, though, so order plenty. Finish off your meal with a real Vietnamese coffee prepared with a slow-dripping filter and accompanied by condensed milk. ✉ *7 Sanlitun Jie, Sanlitun, Chaoyang District* ☎ *010/6468–6053* ▭ *AE, MC, V.*

$ CHINESE ✕ **Noodle Bar.** With a dozen seats surrounding the open kitchen, this petite dining room is a giant when it comes to flavor. The stark menu lists little more than beef brisket, tendon, and tripe, which are stewed to chewy perfection and complemented with noodles hand-pulled right before your eyes. For those seeking a moment of respite in Beijing's busy Sanlitun district, this is the place for a light lunch and a quick noodle-making show. The service is efficient and friendly. ✉ *Courtyard 4, Gongti Beilu, Chaoyang District* ☎ *010/6501–8882* ▭ *AE, MC, V.*

$$ GERMAN ✕ **Paulaner Brauhaus.** Traditional German food is dished up in heaping portions at this spacious, bright restaurant in the Kempinski Hotel. Wash it all down with delicious Bavarian beer made right in the restaurant: try the Maibock served in genuine German steins. In summer, you can enjoy your meal outdoors in the beer garden. ✉ *Kempinski Hotel, 50 Liangmaqiao Lu, Chaoyang District* ☎ *010/6465–3388* ▭ *AE, MC, V.*

$$$ TAIWANESE Fodor's Choice ★ ✕ **Shin Yeh.** The long line proves that Shin Yeh diners are hooked. The focus here is on Taiwanese flavors and freshness. *Caipudan* is a scrumptious turnip omelet. *Fotiaoqiang* ("Buddha jumping over the wall") is a delicate soup with medicinal herbs and seafood. Last but definitely not least, try the *mashu,* a glutinous rice cake rolled in ground peanut. Service is friendly and very attentive. ✉ *6 Gongti Xilu, Chaoyang District* ☎ *010/6552–5066* ▭ *AE, MC, V.*

$ YUNNAN ✕ **South Silk Road.** Serving the specialties of southwest China's Yunnan province in a minimalist setting, South Silk Road is a joy. Servers in the colorful outfits of the Bai minority guide you to a sprawling dining room resembling a factory loft. The paintings of Fang Lijun, its artist-owner, are displayed on the walls. Treebark salad, sliced sausages with Sichuan peppercorn, and *qiguoji* (a clay-pot soup with tonic herbs) are all tasty. One of the house specialties is *guoqiao mixian* ("crossing the bridge" noodles): a scorching bowl of broth, kept boiling by a thin layer of hot oil on top. The fun lies in adding small slivers of raw fish, chicken, ham, and rice noodles, which cook instantly in the pot. Female diners take note: the floor of the restaurant's upper level is made of glass, so don't wear a skirt when you dine here! ✉ *Building D, Soho New Town, 88 Jianguo Lu, Chaoyang District* ☎ *010/8580–4286* ▭ *AE, MC, V* Ⓜ *Dawang Lu.*

$ INDIAN ✕ **Taj Pavilion.** Beijing's best Indian restaurant, Taj Pavilion serves up all the classics, including chicken tikka masala, *palak panir* (creamy spinach with cheese), and *rogan josht* (tender lamb in curry sauce).

Consistently good service and an informal atmosphere make this a well-loved neighborhood haunt. ✉ *China World Trade Center, L-1 28 West Wing, 1 Jianguomenwai Dajie, Chaoyang District* ☎ *010/6505–5866* ▭ *AE, MC, V* Ⓜ *Guomao.*

$ CHINESE ✕ **Three Guizhou Men.** The popularity of this ethnic cuisine prompted three Guizhou friends to set up shop in Beijing. There are many dishes here to recommend, but among the best are "beef on fire" (pieces of beef placed on a bed of chives over burning charcoal) accompanied by ground chilies, spicy lamb with mint leaves, and *mi doufu,* a rice-flour cake in spicy sauce. ✉ *Jianwai SOHO, Bldg. 7, 39 Dong Sanhuan Zhonglu, Chaoyang District* ☎ *010/5869–0598* ▭ *AE, MC, V* Ⓜ *Guomao.*

$$$$ JAPANESE Fodor's Choice ★ ✕ **Yotsuba.** This tiny, unassuming restaurant is arguably the best Japanese restaurant in town. It consists of a sushi counter—manned by a Japanese master working continuously and silently—and two small tatami-style dining areas, evoking an old-time Tokyo restaurant. The seafood is flown in from Tokyo's Tsukiji fish market. Reservations are a must for this dinner-only Chaoyang gem. ✉ *2 Xinyuan Xili Zhongjie, Chaoyang District* ☎ *010/6467–1837* ✍ *Reservations essential* ▭ *AE, MC, V* ⊗ *No lunch.*

$ SICHUAN Fodor's Choice ★ ✕ **Yuxiang Renjia.** There are many Sichuan restaurants in Beijing, but if you ask native Sichuanese residents, Yuxiang Renjia is their top choice. Huge earthen vats filled with pickled vegetables, hanging bunches of dried peppers and garlic, and simply dressed servers evoke the Sichuan countryside. The restaurant does an excellent job of preparing provincial classics such as *gongbao jiding* (diced chicken stir-fried with peanuts and dried peppers) and *ganbian sijidou* (green beans stir-fried with olive leaves and minced pork). Thirty different Sichuanese snacks are served for lunch on weekends, all at very reasonable prices. ✉ *5/F, Lianhe Daxia, 101 Chaowai Dajie, Chaoyang District* ☎ *010/6588–3841* ▭ *AE, MC, V* Ⓜ *Chaoyangmen.*

HAIDIAN DISTRICT

$$$$ MANDARIN ✕ **Baijia Dayuan.** Staff dressed in rich-hued, traditional outfits welcome you at this grand courtyard house. Bowing slightly, they'll say *"Nin jixiang"* ("May you have good fortune"). The mansion's spectacular setting was once the garden of Prince Li, son of the first Qing emperor. Cao Xueqin, the author of the Chinese classic *Dream of the Red Chamber,* is said to have lived here as a boy. Featured delicacies include bird's nest soup, braised sea cucumber, abalone, and authentic imperial snacks. On weekends, diners are treated to short, live performances of Beijing opera. ✉ *15 Suzhou St., Haidian District* ☎ *010/6265–4186* ✍ *Reservations essential* ▭ *MC, V.*

$$ ASIAN ✕ **Ding Ding Xiang.** Hot pot restaurants are plentiful in northern China, but few do it better than Ding Ding Xiang. A variety of meats, seafood, and vegetables can be cooked in a wide selection of broths (the wild mushroom broth is a must for mycophiles). Should you be visiting Beijing in the bitter winter months, look forward to paper-thin lamb slices dipped in a bubbling pot of broth. Despite the surly service

and gaudy decor, this place is perennially crowded. ✉*Bldg 7, Guoxing Jiayuan, Shouti Nanlu, Haidian District* ☎*010/8835–7775* ▭*No credit cards* ✉*14 Dongzhong Jie, DongzhimenwaiDongcheng District* ☎*10/6417–2546* ▭*AE, MC, V.*

WHERE TO STAY

By Eileen Wen Mooney

Communism closed the doors on the opulent accommodations once available to visiting foreigners in Beijing. Functional concrete boxes served the needs of the few "fellow travelers" admitted into the People's Republic of China in the 1950s and '60s. By the late 1970s, China's lack of high-quality hotels had become a distinct embarrassment; the only answer seemed to be opening the market to foreign investment. Many new hotels were built to handle the 2008 Olympic crowds and they are bound to change the landscape even more in the coming years.

A multitude of polished palaces await you, with attentive service, improved amenities—such as conference centers, health clubs, and nightclubs—and, of course, rising prices. "Western-style" comfort, rather than history and character, is the main selling point for Beijing's hotels. Some traditional courtyard houses have been converted into small hotels—they offer a quiet alternative to the fancier establishments.

RATES

For the 2008 Olympics, there was an explosion of new hotels, and many existing hotels spruced themselves up. This is great news for travelers. Today you have an amazing choice of places to stay, including comfortable budget hotels, quaint courtyard inns, hip boutique hostelries, and the gleaming towers of international chains. Rates are generally quoted for the room alone; breakfast, whether Continental or full, is usually extra. We've noted at the end of each review if breakfast is included in the rate ("CP" for Continental breakfast daily and "BP" for full breakfast daily). All hotel prices listed are based on high-season rates. There may be significant discounts on weekends and in the off-season. It's usually not difficult finding a hotel in Beijing, so booking two weeks in advance should suffice.

Discounts on room rates can reach 40% during quieter times of the year, which come in winter and summer. In general, five-star hotels will be as expensive as those in other major Western cities, but small three- and four-star hotels can be a bargain in Beijing. You can sometimes get good deals by booking online through agents such as Ctrip 🌐*www.ctrip.com*, which has both English and Chinese Web sites.

China is one of the few remaining places in the world where tipping is not the norm. The exception: bellboys will expect a tip for carrying your bags to your room—give about Y10 per bag.

	WHAT IT COSTS IN YUAN				
	¢	$	$$	$$$	$$$$
Hotels	under Y700	Y700–Y1,100	Y1,101–Y1,400	Y1,401–Y1,800	over Y1,800

Prices are for two people in a standard double room in high season, excluding 10% to 15% service charge.

DONGCHENG DISTRICT

¢–$ Fodor'sChoice ★ **Banqiao No. 4.** It may seem impossible, but Banqiao No. 4 is a well-preserved courtyard house with an unbeatable central location. You might expect this stylish lodging to be expensive, but the rates are quite reasonable. Set in an old neighborhood with many intertwined alleyways, this hotel is only a few minutes walk to the metro station, and a 20-minute bike ride to the Lama Temple, Confucian Temple, and Beihai Park. In addition to tastefully furnished rooms, Banqiao 4 offers thoughtful extras like Wi-Fi access. The hotel has two suites that are perfect for families, with a large bed and a sofa bed. There is no restaurant, but the hotel is a 10-minute walk to Gui Jie and its dozens of eateries. **Pros:** reasonable prices, large rooftop terrace. **Cons:** some bathrooms are small. ✉ *4 Banqiao Hutong, Beixinqiao, Dongcheng District,* ☎ *10/8403–0968* *16 rooms, 2 suites* *In-room: Wi-Fi* *AE, DC, MC, V* Ⓜ *Beixinqiao* *BP.*

$$ Fodor'sChoice ★ **Côté Cour S.L.** This 14-room boutique hotel is in a grand old courtyard house in an atmospheric hutong. The style is a perfect blending of East and West, blending a traditional feel with modern comforts. The accommodations have antique stone tile floors, comforters made with special silk from southern China, and sinks fashioned from traditional Chinese ceramics. There are also high-tech touches like flat-screen TVs and wireless Internet connections. One of the nicest parts of the hotel is the lounge, where Continental breakfast is served in the morning and drinks are offered in the evening. The room has floor-to-ceiling windows and the walls are decorated with wonderful contemporary art. A staircase leads to the roof terrace with wonderful glimpses of neighboring courtyard houses shaded under green foliage. **Pros:** traditional courtyard lodging, intimate feel, lovely terrace. **Cons:** no restaurant, no pool. ✉ *70 Yan Yue Hutong, Dongcheng District,* ☎ *10/6512–8020* 🌐 *www.hotelcotecoursl.com* *14 rooms* *In-room: safe, Wi-Fi. In-hotel: bar, laundry service, no-smoking rooms* *AE, D, DC, MC, V* Ⓜ *Dengshikou (Exit A)* *CP.*

$$$–$$$$ Fodor'sChoice ★ **The Emperor.** On a tree-lined avenue, the Emperor is a short walk from the Forbidden City, Tiananmen Square, and the famous shopping area Wangfujing. It's amongst traditional temples and houses, making it a tranquil oasis in the midst of a fast-evolving metropolis. Though fronted by a classical brick facade, the hotel features a cutting-edge interior by a team of internationally renowned designers. Its rooms boast a modern aesthetic, and have wall-mounted flat-screen TVs, wireless Internet connections, and butler service. Shi, the chic restaurant, serves fusion cuisine creatively prepared by Chinese chef John Hao, who puts a

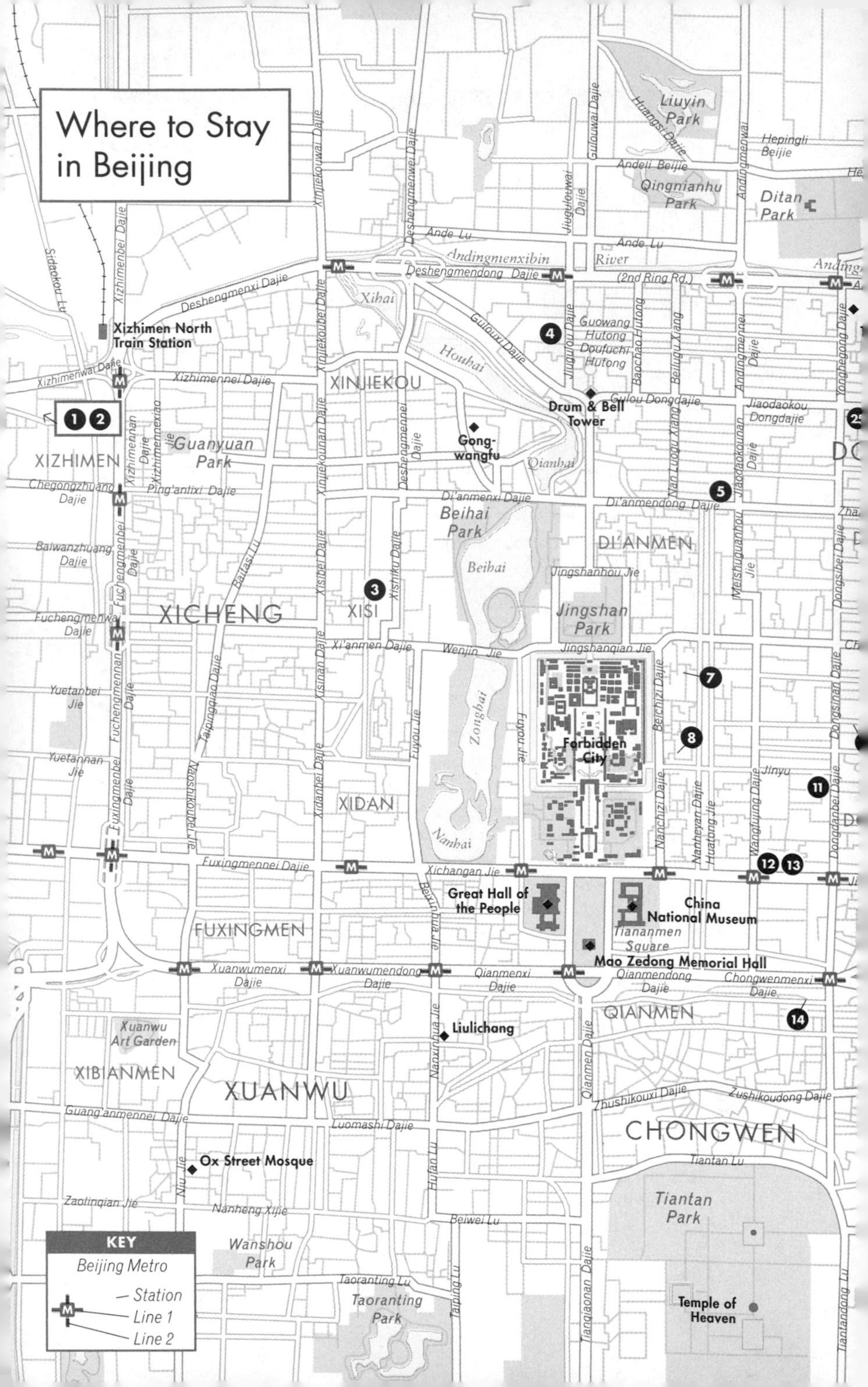
Where to Stay in Beijing
Xizhimen North Train Station
XIZHIMEN
XINJIEKOU
XICHENG
XISI
XIDAN
FUXINGMEN
XUANWU
XIBIANMEN
DI'ANMEN
QIANMEN
CHONGWEN
Liuyin Park
Qingnianhu Park
Ditan Park
Guanyuan Park
Beihai Park
Beihai
Jingshan Park
Zongbai
Nanhai
Xihai
Houhai
Qianhai
Forbidden City
Drum & Bell Tower
Gongwangfu
Great Hall of the People
China National Museum
Tiananmen Square
Mao Zedong Memorial Hall
Liulichang
Ox Street Mosque
Xuanwu Art Garden
Wanshou Park
Taoranting Park
Tiantan Park
Temple of Heaven
Ande Lu
Andingmenxibin River
Deshengmendong Dajie
(2nd Ring Rd.)
Deshengmenxi Dajie
Xizhimenwai Dajie
Xizhimennei Dajie
Gulouxi Dajie
Gulou Dongdajie
Guowang Hutong
Doufuchi Hutong
Jiaodaokou Dongdajie
Di'anmenxi Dajie
Di'anmendong Dajie
Ping'anlixi Dajie
Chegongzhuang Dajie
Baiwanzhuang Dajie
Fuchengmenwai Dajie
Yuetanbei Jie
Yuetannan Jie
Xi'anmen Dajie
Wenjin Jie
Jingshanhou Jie
Jingshanqian Jie
Fuxingmennei Dajie
Xichangan Jie
Xuanwumenxi Dajie
Xuanwumendong Dajie
Qianmenxi Dajie
Qianmendong Dajie
Chongwenmenxi Dajie
Zhushikouxi Dajie
Zhushikoudong Dajie
Guang'anmennei Dajie
Luomashi Dajie
Tiantan Lu
Zaolinqian Jie
Nanheng Xijie
Beiwei Lu
Taoranting Lu
Hepingli Beijie
Andeli Beijie
Huangsi Dajie
Gulouwai Dajie
Jiugulouwai Dajie
Jiugulou Dajie
Baochao Hutong
Beiluogu Xiang
Nan Luogu Xiang
Andingmennei Dajie
Jiaodaokounan Dajie
Meishuguanhou Jie
Yonghegong Dajie
Dongsibei Dajie
Dongsinan Dajie
Dongdanbei Dajie
Beichizi Dajie
Nanchizi Dajie
Nanheyan Dajie
Huatong Jie
Wangfujing Dajie
Jinyu
Xinjiekouwai Dajie
Deshengmennei Dajie
Xinjiekoubei Dajie
Xinjiekounan Dajie
Deshengmennei Dajie
Xishiku Dajie
Xisibei Dajie
Xisinan Dajie
Xidanbei Dajie
Fuyou Jie
Beixinhua Jie
Nanxinhua Jie
Hufan Lu
Taiping Lu
Qianmen Dajie
Tianqiaonan Dajie
Tiantandong Lu
Niu Jie
Xizhimenbei Dajie
Sidaokou Lu
Xizhimennan Dajie
Xizhimennanxiao Jie
Fuchengmenbei Dajie
Fuchengmennan Dajie
Fuxingmenbei Dajie
Baitasi Lu
Taipingqiao Dajie
Naoshikoubei Jie
KEY
Beijing Metro
Station
Line 1
Line 2

Beijing Airport
28 29
Zoujiazhuang Xilu
Zuojiazhuang Dongjie
Beisanhuan Donglu (3rd Ring Rd.)
Hepingli Dongjie
Bahe River
Xibahe Nanlu
Zuojiazhuang
Xianheyuan Lu
Dongzhimenwaixie Jie
Xindong Lu
Shunyuan Jie
Liangma River
Liangmahe Nanlu
26
27
Nanguan Park
Dongzhimenbeixiao Jie
Dongzhimenbei Dajie
DONGZHIMEN
Dongzhimennei Dajie
Dongzhimenwai Dajie
Dongzhimennan Dajie
Xindong Lu
Sanlitun Lu
Dongsanhuanbei Lu
Dongsi Tiao
Gongrentiyuchangbei Lu
24
22
Workers' Stadium
23
(3rd Ring Rd.)
Yaojiayuan Lu
Nansanlitun Lu
Tuanjiehu Park
Dongzhimennanxiao Jie
Dajie
Chaoyangmenwai Dajie
Guandongdianbei Jie
Chaoyangmenbei Dajie
Chaoyangmennanxiao Jie
Ritan Beilu
Ritan Park
Dongdaqiao Lu
CHAOYANG
21
Guanghua Lu
20
Xiushui Beijie
Jianguomenbei Dajie
16
Xiushui Nanjie
17
18
Jianguomenwai Dajie
Beijingzhan
Ancient Observatory
15
19
Beijingzhangdong Jie
Tonghui River
Chongwenmendong Dajie
Dongsanhuanzhong Lu
City Moat
0
1,000 M
0
3,000 ft
Guangqumenwai Lu
Guangqumennanbinhe Lu
Guangming Lu
Jinsong Lu
(2nd Ring Rd.)
Dongsanhuannan Lu
Longtan Park

modern spin on traditional local dishes. On the roof, the Yin bar offers breathtaking views over the Forbidden City. Also on the roof is the hotel's spa, an all-glass structure offering amazing city views. **Pros:** best rooftop terrace in the city, views of the Forbidden City, unique design of rooms. **Cons:** restaurant is on the expensive side. ✉ *33 Qihelou Jie, Dongcheng District,* ☎ *10/6526–5566* 🌐 *www.theemperor.com.cn* *46 rooms, 9 suites* *In-room: safe, Wi-Fi. In-hotel: restaurant, bar, spa, Wi-Fi* *AE, D, DC, MC, V* Ⓜ *Tiananmen Dong* *EP.*

$$$$ ★ **Grand Hyatt Beijing.** This mammoth complex includes an upscale shopping mall, a cinema screening films in English, and a wide range of inexpensive eateries. Rooms and suites, many with floor-to-ceiling windows, are decorated with comfortable cherry-wood furnishings. The hotel's Olympic-size swimming pool is surrounded by lush vegetation, waterfalls, statues, and comfortable teak chairs and tables. Over the pool, a "virtual sky" ceiling imitates different weather patterns. The gym is equipped with state-of-the-art exercise equipment. The Red Moon on the lobby level is one of the city's chicest bars, and has live music every night. The hotel is within walking distance to Tiananmen Square and the Forbidden City. **Pros:** efficient service, plenty of shopping, impressive pool. **Cons:** small rooms, hard mattresses, pricey Internet. ✉ *1 Dongchang'an Jie, corner of Wangfujing, Dongcheng District,* ☎ *010/8518–1234* 🌐 *www.beijing.grand.hyatt.com* *825 rooms, 155 suites* *In-room: safe, refrigerator, Wi-Fi. In-hotel: 3 restaurants, bar, pool, gym, Wi-Fi, no-smoking rooms* *AE, DC, MC, V* Ⓜ *Wangfujing* *EP.*

$–$$ Fodor's Choice ★ **Hotel Kapok.** Just a few blocks from the east gate of the Forbidden City, this hotel is quite a find. One of a growing number of boutique hotels in Beijing, it is the work of local architect Pei Zhu, who came up with the minimalist design. Rooms are large and nicely designed, and have all the modern amenities of more expensive hotels. The entrance to some rooms face small bamboo and pebble gardens. **Pros:** cozy and comfortable rooms, near top tourists sites, close to shopping. **Cons:** no pool. ✉ *16 Donghuamen, Dongcheng District,* ☎ *10/6525–9988* 🌐 *www.hotelkapok.com* *89 rooms* *In-room: Wi-Fi. In-hotel: restaurant, Wi-Fi* *AE, D, DC, MC, V* Ⓜ *Tiananmen East* *EP.*

$$$$ Fodor's Choice ★ **Legendale.** Those fond of a classic ambience will be drawn to the Legendale, surrounded by some of the city's best-preserved hutongs. The hotel's palatial architecture is done up in rich blues, golds, and burgundies, exuding an Old-World elegance. The breathtaking gilded staircase winds upward, creating a theatre-like ambience with balconies at each level and a dome-like atrium drawing in an abundance of natural light. Sparkling and ornate crystal chandeliers dangle from the high ceilings; an antique Parisian fireplace is the centerpiece in the opulent lobby. Camoes, with its hand-painted white and blue mural depicting a seafaring scene from old Portugal, offers Mecanese and Portuegese cuisine. Petrus, a French restaurant, has a large wine collection, and Macao focuses on Chinese fare. **Pros:** plenty of pampering, in a great neighborhood. **Cons:** stratopheric prices. ✉ *90–92 Jinbao Street, Dongcheng District,* ☎ *10/8511–3388* 🌐 *www.legendalehotel.com* *390 rooms, 81 suites* *In-room: safe, refrigerator, Internet.*

In-hotel: 3 restaurants, pool, laundry service, Wi-Fi ▭*AE, DC, MC, V* Ⓜ*Dengshikou* 🍴*EP.*

¢–$ **LüSongyuan.** In 1980, the China Youth Travel Service set up this delightful courtyard hotel on the site of an old Mandarin's residence. The traditional wooden entrance is guarded by two *menshi* (stone lions). Inside are five courtyards decorated with pavilions, rockeries, and greenery. Rooms are basic, with large windows. There are no self-service cooking facilities, but it has a reasonable Chinese restaurant. It's all about location here: you're in the middle of an ancient neighborhood, within walking distance to Houhai, and just a block away from many restaurants on Nan Luogu Xiang. **Pros:** convenient location, near restaurants. **Cons:** cluttered courtyard, unenthusiastic service. ✉*22 Banchang Hutong, Kuanjie, Dongcheng District,* ☎*010/6401–1116* *55 rooms* *In-hotel: restaurant, bar, Internet terminal, Wi-Fi* ▭*AE, DC, MC, V* 🍴*EP.*

WORD OF MOUTH

"The five nights spent at the Peninsula didn't disappoint. We were upgraded to an "executive" floor, which entitled us to perks such as happy hour, computers, and breakfast. There is an excellent detailed map of the surrounding area in the Peninsula stationery folder in the room desk. We ate at the Peninsula's Hutong restaurant Huang Ting, which was good." —Marija

$$$–$$$$ ★ **Peninsula Beijing.** Guests at the Peninsula Beijing enjoy an impressive combination of modern facilities and traditional luxury. A waterfall cascades through the spacious lobby, which is decorated with well-chosen antiques. Rooms have teak-and-rosewood flooring, colorful rugs, and gorgeous wood furnishings. There are high-tech touches like custom bedside control panels that let you adjust lighting, temperature, and the flat-screen TVs. Food fanatics, take note: one on-site restaurant, Jing, serves delicious East-meets-West fusion food. Huang Ting, a second restaurant, provides a rustic setting for some of Beijing's tastiest dim sum. Work off the meals in the fully equipped gym or swimming pool—or take the 10-minute walk to the Forbidden City. If you're less ambitious, relax in the hotel's spa. The Peninsula's arcade has designer stores, including Chanel, Jean Paul Gaultier, and Tiffany & Co. **Pros:** near the Forbidden City, close to sightseeing, restaurants and shopping, rooms are impeccable. **Cons:** lobby is too dark, hectic atmosphere. ✉*8 Jinyu Hutong (Goldfish La.), Wangfujing, Dongcheng District,* ☎*010/8516–2888* 🌐*www.peninsula.com* *525 rooms, 59 suites* *In-room: safe, refrigerator, Wi-Fi. In-hotel: 2 restaurants, room service, bar, tennis court, pool, gym, spa, laundry service, Wi-Fi* ▭*AE, DC, MC, V* Ⓜ*Dongdan* 🍴*EP*

$$$$ **Raffles Beijing Hotel.** Singaporean designer Grace Soh and her team transformed this hotel into a vivid, modern space while retaining its history. Crystal chandeliers illuminate the lobby, and the grand white staircase is enveloped in a royal-blue carpet. The atrium is adorned with 13 large cloth lanterns in olive green, plum, purple, and yellow—a welcome change to the ubiquitous red. The presidential suite is one of the largest, most luxurious accommodations in Beijing. For dining, choose between French and Italian restaurants. The Writer's Bar is

replete with large leather armchairs and dark, polished floors. This is a great location for visitors who plan to do some sightseeing: Tiananmen Square, the Forbidden City, and Wangfujing are all nearby. **Pros:** near the Forbidden city, close to night market, wonderful French cuisine. **Cons:** restaurants very pricey, poor service. ☒*33 Dongchang'an Jie, off Wangfujing Dajie, Dongcheng District,* ☎*010/6526–3388* ⊕*www.beijing.raffles.com* *171 rooms, 24 suites* *In-room: refrigerator, Wi-Fi. In-hotel: 2 restaurants, room service, bar, pool, Wi-Fi* ▭*AE, DC, MC, V* Ⓜ*Wangfujing.*

$$ Fodor'sChoice ★ **Red Capital Residence.** Beijing's first boutique courtyard hotel is located in a carefully restored home in Dongsi Hutong. Each of the five rooms is decorated with antiques and according to different themes, including the Chairman's Suite, the two Concubine's Private Courtyards, and the two Author's Suites (one inspired by Edgar Snow, an American journalist who lived in Beijing in the 1930s and 1940s, and the other by Han Suyin, a famous Japanese novelist). There is a cigar lounge where you can sit on original furnishings used by China's early revolutionary leaders, as well as a wine bar in a Cultural Revolution–era bomb shelter. Special arrangements can also be made for guests to tour Beijing at night in Madame Mao's Red Flag limousine. **Pros:** intimate feel, friendly service, plenty of atmosphere. **Cons:** small rooms, limited facilties. ☒*9 Dongsi Liutiao, Dongcheng District,* ☎*010/6402–7150* ⊕*www.redcapitalclub.com.cn* *5 rooms* *In-hotel: bar, laundry service* ▭*AE, DC, MC, V* *CP.*

$–$$ **Zhuyuan Hotel** *(Bamboo Garden Hotel).* This charming hotel was once the residence of Kang Sheng, a sinister character responsible for "public security" during the Cultural Revolution, Kang nevertheless had fine taste in art and antiques, some of which are on display. The Bamboo Garden cannot compete with the high-rise crowd when it comes to amenties, but its bamboo-filled gardens make it a treasure for those looking for a true Chinese experience. It's within walking distance to the colorful Houhai, or Rear Lakes, area. The neighborhood is perfect if you want to experience the lifestyles of ordinary Beijingers. **Pros:** traditional feel, interesting neighborhood. **Cons:** courtyard is underused, pricey for what you get. ☒*24 Xiaoshiqiao Hutong, Jiugulou Dajie, Dongcheng District,* ☎*010/5852–0088* *40 rooms, 4 suites* *In-hotel: restaurant, bar, bicycles, laundry service* ▭*AE, DC, MC, V* Ⓜ*Gulou.*

XICHENG DISTRICT

$$$$ ★ **Ritz-Carlton Beijing, Financial Street.** With an inspired East-meets-West decor, the Ritz-Carlton is ideal for travelers looking for a little extra. With ample amounts of glass and chrome, the Ritz-Carlton could be mistaken for many of the city's sleek financial buildings. The interior is stylish and contemporary, with crystal mythological animals to provide good luck. Greenfish Café offers a great contemporary buffet that includes low-calorie fare, and the chef at Cepe produces homemade pasta with phenomenal sauces and other Italian fare. The enormous health club has an indoor pool and a spa with six treatment rooms. The

hotel is located in the western part of the city on the up-and-coming Financial Street, which is being touted as the city's Wall Street. **Pros:** impeccable service, luxurious atmosphere, spacious rooms. **Cons:** far from the city's attractions. ✉ *18 Beijing Financial St., Xicheng District,* ☎ *010/6601–6666* 🌐 *www.ritzcarlton.com* *253 rooms, 33 suites* *In-room: safe, Wi-Fi. In-hotel: 3 restaurants, room service, bar, pool, gym, spa, Wi-Fi* *AE, DC, MC, V* Ⓜ *Fuchengmen* *EP.*

SOUTHERN DISTRICT: CHONGWEN

$–$$ ★ **Courtyard Beijing.** Merging Eastern and Western culture and style, the Courtyard is situated at the heart of the nation's capital. Guests have easy access to many of Beijing's historical sites, and it's connected to the huge New World Shopping Center, one of the busiest in the city, selling a wide variety of international and domestic name-brand products. One problem is that this is a super-congested part of the city. However, there's a subway station just one block away, making quick escapes to quieter areas quite easy. ✉ *3C Chongwenmenwai Dajie, Chongwen District,* ☎ *010/6708–1188* *010/6708–1808* 🌐 *www.courtyard.com/bjscy* *283 rooms, 16 suites* *Restaurant, babysitting, satellite TV, children's pool, sauna, fitness room, laundry service, Internet* *AE, DC, MC, V* Ⓜ *Chongwenmen.*

CHAOYANG DISTRICT

$$–$$$ ★ **Courtyard by Northeast Beijing.** Located between the Lido Commercial District and Wangjing High Tech Park, this hotel has a good location for business travelers. The spacious and stylish rooms are equipped with high-tech touches like LCD TVs and high-speed Internet access. The 24-hour fitness center features an indoor swimming pool and whirlpool bathed in natural light. Upgrade to the executive level and you can get free Continental breakfast and evening cocktails. The open-kitchen MoMo Café serves a variety of international dishes, while MoMo 2 Go offers sandwiches and salads. **Pros:** good value, ideal location for people doing business in the city's northeast. **Cons:** far from the tourist sites. ✉ *101 Jingshun Road, Chaoyang District,* ☎ *010/5907–6666* 🌐 *courtyardbeijingnortheast.com* *258 rooms, 43 suites* *In-room: refrigerator, Wi-Fi. In-hotel: restaurant, bar, pool, gym* *AE, DC, MC, V* *EP* Ⓜ *None.*

$ **Gloria Plaza Hotel.** This hotel is situated in the Jianguomenwai commercial center, not far from the embassy district. From the hotel, it's just a 10-minute walk to the Ancient Observatory, the Silk Market, the Friendship Store, and to the Red Gate Gallery, which exhibits contemporary Chinese art in one of the few remaining towers of the old city wall. A restored section of the city wall begins at the Red Gate Gallery, making for a pleasant stroll. The simple rooms have good city views. The Sports City Café broadcasts sports events from around the world and serves up decent American food. Sampan offers decent dim sum. **Pros:** centrally located, close to subway. **Cons:** a bit run-down. ✉ *2 Jiangguomen Nan Dajie, Chaoyang District,* ☎ *010/6515–8855* *www.gphbeijing.com* *432 rooms, 50 suites* *In-room: safe, Internet. In-hotel: 2 restaurants, room service, bar, pool, gym, laundry service* *AE, DC, MC, V* *EP* *Jianguomen.*

$$$$ Fodor's Choice ★ **Hotel G.** This vibrant and stylish design is just minutes from the major commercial district. The mid-century modern design uses subtle Chinese accents to add an understated glamour. Its 110 rooms have designations that are easy to remember when booking: Good (studio), Great (deluxe studio), Greater (suite), and Greatest (deluxe suite). Rooms have a colorful and almost funky atmoshphere. There's a split-level rooftop Mediterranean restaurant with a Tibetan-style tent and open fireplace, a sleek Japanese restaurant, and a glamorous lobby bar for cocktails. Hotel G claims to make the best hamburger in town, using Argentinian premium beef with a choice of more than dozen cheeses and sauce toppings. **Pros:** adjacent to one of the hottest nightlife areas, chic design. **Cons:** too colorful for some, can be noisy. *7 Gongti Xilu, Chaoyang District,* *10/6552–3600* *www.hotel-g.com* *110 rooms* *In-room: safe, refrigerator, Wi-Fi. In-hotel: 3 restaurants, gym* *AE, D, MC, V* *None* *EP.*

$ **Jianguo Hotel.** The Jianguo Hotel has maintained its friendly feel for years and continues to attract many diplomats, journalists, and business executives. Nearly half the rooms have balconies overlooking busy Jianguomenwai Dajie. The sunny atrium lobby is furnished with comfortable cushioned rattan sofas and chairs. Charlie's Bar, a longtime favorite, has a good lunch buffet, and Flo Justine's is one of the city's best French restaurants. The gym and pool facilities, however, are very basic. The hotel is a reasonably priced alternative for those attending conferences at the more expensive China World Hotel, just one block away. **Pros:** central location, reasonable rates. **Cons:** limited amenities, rooms are small. *5 Jianguomenwai Dajie, Chaoyang District,* *010/6500–2233* *www.hoteljianguo.com* *462 rooms, 54 suites* *In-room: safe, refrigerator. In-hotel: 4 restaurants, bar, pool, laundry service, Wi-Fi, no-smoking rooms* *AE, DC, MC, V* *EP* *Yonganli.*

$–$$ **Jinglun Hotel.** The rooms of the elegantly refurbished Jinglun Hotel are decorated in a minimalist style. Just a 10-minute drive to Tiananmen Square, and a few minutes from the China World Trade Center, the Jinglun is a well-appointed business and leisure hotel with competitive prices. The tiny, crowded lobby gives way to simple rooms with white-linen beds accented by dark purple, olive-green, and yellow cushions. **Pros:** sleek design, unimpeded city views, great location. **Cons:** small rooms. *3 Jianguomenwai Dajie, Chaoyang District,* *010/6500–2266* *www.jinglunhotel.com* *642 rooms, 126 suites* *In-room: safe, refrigerator, Wi-Fi. In-hotel: restaurant, bar, pool, gym, bicycles, Wi-Fi* *AE, DC, MC, V* *BP* *Yonganli.*

$–$$ **Kempinski Hotel.** This fashionable hotel is part of the Lufthansa Center, so you're close to shopping. It's also within walking distance of the Sanlitun neighborhoos, with its dozens of bars and restaurants. There is an excellent German restaurant here, the Paulaner Brauhaus, which has its own microbrewery. A deli, with an outstanding bakery frequented by expats, is also on-site. We love Kranzler's Coffee Shop, which has an excellent Sunday brunch. A gym and swimming pool are on the 18th floor. **Pros:** excellent service, easy access to the airport. **Cons:** far from attractions, no subway. ✉ *50 Liangmaqiao Lu, Chaoyang District,* ☎ *010/6465–3388* 🌐 *www.kempinski-beijing.com* *526 rooms, 114 suites* *In-room: safe, Internet. In-hotel: 6 restaurants, room service, bars, pool, gym, bicycles, laundry service* *AE, DC, MC, V* *EP* Ⓜ *None.*

$$$–$$$$ ★ **Kerry Centre Hotel.** This hotel is close to the city's embassy and business district, making it an excellent choice for business travelers, It's also well-situated for anyone who wants to be near shopping. What really distinguishes the Kerry from the rest of the pack is the amazing health club. With a full-service fitness center, a jogging track, squash and tennis courts, a spa, and, of course, a pool, it's *the* health club of choice for expats living in Beijing. Centro, the lobby bar, is arguably the most popular hotel bar in the city. The free wireless Internet throughout the lobby, including in the bar and restaurants, is an added plus. **Pros:** reasonably priced luxury, great location, first-class swimming pool and sports facilities. **Cons:** small rooms, poor food, congested area. ✉ *1 Guang Hua Lu, Chaoyang District,* ☎ *010/6561–8833* 🌐 *www.shangri-la.com* *487 rooms, 23 suites* *In-room: safe, refrigerator, Internet. In-hotel: 2 restaurants, bar, tennis courts, pool, gym, Wi-Fi* *AE, DC, MC, V* *EP* Ⓜ *Guomao.*

$$$–$$$$ **Kunlun Hotel.** Topped by a revolving restaurant, this 28-story tower is a bit over the top. The hotel was named for the Kunlun Mountains, a range between northwestern China and northern Tibet that features prominently in Chinese mythology. The lovely rooms are spacious, with nice touches like slippers and robes. The superior suites, with hardwood floors, marble baths, and chic furnishings, are the most attractive. The hotel restaurant serves great Shanghai-style food as well as reliable Thai and Japanese fare in very nicely designed venues. The Kunlun, close to Beijing's rising new diplomatic area, is popular with Chinese business travelers. This shouldn't be your top choice if sightseeing is your priority. **Pros:** imposing lobby, restful rooms. **Cons:** far from the sites. ✉ *2 Xinyuan Nan Lu, Sanlitun, Chaoyang District,* ☎ *010/6590–3388* 🌐 *www.hotelkunlun.com* *701 rooms, 50 suites* *In-room: Internet. In-hotel: 6 restaurants, bar, pool, gym, Wi-Fi* *AE, DC, MC, V* *EP.*

$$$$ Fodor's Choice ★ **Park Hyatt Beijing.** The 63-story tower has plenty of pampering. Imagine your own spa-inspired bathroom with an oversize rain showerhead, deep-soaking tub, and heated floors. The rooms themselves are large and functional, with expansive desks fitted with international power outlets and wireless access. The rooftop bar, designed to resemble a Chinese lantern, has dramatic views of the city. The restaurant features international cuisine and 360-degree views of Beijing. **Pros:** spectacular views of the city, centrally located. **Cons:** pricey. ✉ *2 Jianguomenwai Dajie, Chaoyang District,* ☎ *10/8567–1234* *237 rooms, 18 suites* 🌐 *beijing.park.hyatt.com* *In-room: safe, refrigerator, Wi-Fi. In-hotel: restaurant, bar, pool, laundry service, Wi-Fi* *AE, D, DC, MC, V* Ⓜ *Guomao* *EP.*

$$$$ Fodor's Choice ★ **St. Regis.** Considered by many to be the best hotel in Beijing, the St. Regis is a favorite of business travelers and visiting dignitaries. This is where Uma Thurman and Quentin Tarantino relaxed while filming of *Kill Bill.* You won't be disappointed: the luxurious interiors combine classical Chinese elegance and modern furnishings. The Press Club Bar, with its wood paneling, overflowing bookcases, and grand piano, feels like a private club. The Japanese restaurant has tasty, moderately priced lunch specials. The Astor Grill is known for its steak and seafood dishes, and Danielli's serves authentic Italian food. We went back for seconds of waffles with fresh blueberries at the incredible breakfast buffet. The St. Regis health club is arguably the most unique in Beijing: the equipment is state-of-the-art; the Jacuzzi is supplied with natural hot spring water pumped up from deep beneath the hotel; and the glass-atrium swimming pool, with plenty of natural light, is a lovely place for a relaxing swim. An added plus is that it's just a 10-minute taxi ride from the Forbidden City. If you can afford it, this is the place to stay. **Pros:** ideal location, near public transportation, lots of restaurants nearby. **Cons:** the little extras really add up here. ☒ *21 Jianguomenwai Dajie, Chaoyang District,* ☎ *010/6460–6688* 🌐 *www.stregis.com/beijing* *258 rooms, 102 suites* *In-room: refrigerator, Wi-Fi. In-hotel: 5 restaurants, bar, tennis court, pools, gym, spa, bicycles, laundry service, Wi-Fi, parking (paid), no-smoking rooms* 💳 *AE, DC, MC, V* Ⓜ *Jianguomen.*

$$$–$$$$ **Swissôtel.** In the large, impressive marble lobby you can enjoy jazz every Friday and Saturday evening. Rooms have high-quality, European-style furnishings in cream and light grey, plus temperature controls and coffeemakers. The hotel health club has an atrium-style swimming pool and an outdoor tennis court. The Western coffee shop has one of the best hotel buffets in Beijing. It's a short walk to the bustling Sanlitun bar area and the Nanxincang complex of restaurants, which are housed in a former Ming dynasty granary. A subway entrance is just outside the hotel's front door. **Pros:** lovely lobby, great amenties. **Cons:** far from most sites, mediocre food. ☒ *2 Chaoyangmennei Dajie, Dongsishiqiao Flyover Junction (Second Ring Rd.), Chaoyang District,* ☎ *010/6553–2288* 📠 *010/6501–2501* 🌐 *www.swissotel-beijing.com* *430 rooms, 50 suites* *In-room: safe, refrigerator, Internet. In-hotel: 2 restaurants, room service, bar, pool, tennis court, gym, laundry service, no-smoking rooms* 💳 *AE, DC, MC, V* Ⓜ *Dongsi Shitiao.*

$–$$ **Traders Hotel.** Inside the China World Trade Center complex, this hotel is connected to a shopping mall. The hotel is a favorite of international business travelers who appreciate its central location, good service, and top-notch amenities. On top of all that, it's an excellent value. Rooms are done up in muted colors and have queen- or king-size beds. Guests have access to an excellent health club. **Pros:** moderately priced for a business hotel, near plenty of shopping. **Cons:** small lobby. ☒ *1 Jianguomenwai Dajie, Chaoyang District,* ☎ *010/6505–2277* 🌐 *www.shangri-la.com* *570 rooms, 27 suites* *In-room: safe, refrigerator, Internet. In-hotel: 2 restaurants, bar, no-smoking rooms* 💳 *AE, DC, MC, V* *EP* Ⓜ *Guomao.*

¢ **Zhaolong International Youth Hostel.** If partaking in Beijing's lively nightlife scene is on your itinerary, consider this comfortable youth hostel in Sanlitun for your stay. The hostel offers spic-and-span rooms with two to six beds each, a reading room, a kitchen, and bicycle rentals. **Pros:** as cheap as it gets, clean and comfortable. **Cons:** just the basics. ✉ *2 Gongti Bei Lu, Sanlitun, Chaoyang District,* ☎ *010/6597–2299 Ext. 6111* 🌐 *www.zhaolonghotel.com.cn* *30 rooms* *In-room: no phone, no TV. In-hotel: bar, laundry facilities* *AE, MC, V* *CP* Ⓜ *Tuanjiehu/Nongzhanguan.*

HAIDIAN DISTRICT

$ **Friendship Hotel.** The name is telling, as the hotel was built in 1954 to house foreigners, mostly Soviets, who had come to help rebuild the nation. This is one of the largest garden-style hotels in Asia. The architecture is traditional Chinese, and the public spaces are classic and elegant. Rooms are large, but they are filled with somewhat outdated furnishings. With 14 restaurants, an Olympic-size pool, and a driving range, the hotel aims to be a one-stop destination. Its location far from the main tourist trail means that it's better situated for people who need to be close to the university area. **Pros:** a bit of history, good location in northwest Beijing. **Cons:** away from the city center. ✉ *3 Baishiqiao Lu, Haidian District,* ☎ *010/6849–8888* 🌐 *www.bjfriendshiphotel.com/english/index.asp* *1,700 rooms, 200 suites* *In-room: refrigerator, Ethernet. In-hotel: 14 restaurants, bar, tennis courts, pools, gym* *AE, DC, MC, V* *EP.*

$$$ **Shangri-La Hotel.** Set in delightful landscaped gardens, the Shangri-La is a wonderful retreat for business travelers and those who don't mind being far from the city center. A new tower, called the Valley Wing, was completed in 2007. Each room is designed to have a garden or city view. The hotel's Blue Lobster is headed by Chef de Cuisine Brian McKenna, and offers an exciting molecular gastronomy and innovative cuisine. **Pros:** lovely gardens, excellent amenties. **Cons:** far from the city center. ✉ *29 Zizhuyuan Lu, Haidian District,* ☎ *010/6841–2211* 🌐 *www.shangri-la.com* *670 rooms, 32 suites* *In-room: safe, refrigerator, Wi-Fi. In-hotel: 7 restaurants, room service, pool, gym, laundry service, Wi-Fi, parking (free)* *AE, DC, MC, V* *EP.*

BEIJING AIRPORT AREA

$$ **Sino-Swiss Hotel.** This contemporary hotel overlooks a gorgeous outdoor pool surrounded by trees, shrubs, and colorful umbrellas. All the rooms and public areas are completely up-to-date. The restaurant Mongolian Gher offers barbecue and live entertainment inside a traditional yurt (a tentlike structure), whereas the Swiss Chalet serves familiar Continental food on the outdoor terrace. Just five minutes from the airport, the Sino-Swiss Hotel is convenient if you have an early-morning flight or get stuck at the airport. **Pros:** good dining options, near the airport. **Cons:** far from the downtown attractions. ✉ *9 Xiao Tianzhu Nan Lu, Beijing Capital Airport, Shunyi County,* ☎ *010/6456–5588* 🌐 *www.sino-swisshotel.com* *408 rooms, 35 suites* *In-room: safe, refrigerator, Internet. In-hotel: 4 restaurants, bars, tennis courts, pools, gym, laundry service* *AE, DC, MC, V* *BP.*

ARTS AND NIGHTLIFE

Updated by Helena Iveson

No longer Shanghai's staid sister, Beijing is reinventing herself as a party town with just a smattering of the pretensions of her southern sibling. There's now a venue for every breed of boozer, from beer-stained pub to designer cocktail lounge and everything in between. There are also more dance clubs than you can count. An emerging middle class means that you'll find most bars have a mixed crowd and aren't just swamps of expatriates, but there will be spots where one or the other set will dominate.

Beijing has an active, if not international-standard, stage scene. There's not much to see in English, although the opening of The Egg, properly known as the National Center for the Performing Arts, may change that. Music and dance transcend language boundaries, and Beijing attracts some fine international composers and ballet companies for the crowds. For a fun night on the town that you can enjoy no other place in the world, Beijing Opera, acrobatics, and kung-fu performances remain the best bets.

THE ARTS

The arts in China took a long time to recover from the Cultural Revolution (1966–76), and political works are still generally avoided. Film and theater reflect an interesting mix of modern and avant-garde Chinese and Western influences. On any given night in Beijing, you can see a drama by the famous playwright Lao She, a satire by a contemporary Taiwanese playwright, or a stage version of *Animal Farm.*

All of the free-listings magazines will have reviews of plays as well as concerts and dance performances; *Time Out Beijing* and *The Beijinger* carry the most critical and comprehensive coverage. The cheapest seats start at around Y50 and can go up to over Y1,000 for world-class international ballets and musicals.

As most of the stage is inaccessible to non-Chinese speakers, visitors to Beijing are more likely to hunt out the big visual spectacles, such as Beijing Opera or kung-fu displays. These long-running shows are tailored for travelers: your hotel will be able to recommend performances and venues, and will likely be able to help you book tickets.

ACROBATICS AND KUNG FU

Chaoyang Theater. This newly renovated space is the queen bee of acrobatics venues, especially designed to unleash oohs and ahhs. Spectacular individual and team acrobatic displays involving bicycles, seesaws, catapults, swings, and barrels are performed here nightly. ✉ *36 Dongsanhuan Bei Lu, Chaoyang District* ☎ *010/6507–2421* 🌐 *www.acrobatics.com.cn* Ⓜ *Hujialou.*

Fodor's Choice ★ **The Red Theatre.** If it's Vegas-style stage antics you're after, the Legend of Kung Fu show is what you want. Extravagant martial arts are complemented by neon, fog, and heavy-handed sound effects. Shows are garish but also sometimes glorious. ✉ *44 Xingfu Da Jie, Chongwen*

District ☎*101/6710–3671* 🌐*www.chunyi-kungfu.com* Ⓜ*Tiantan Dong Men.*

Tianqiao Acrobatic Theater. The Beijing Acrobatics Troupe of China famous for weird, wonderful shows. Content includes a flashy show of offbeat contortions and tricks, with a lot of high-wire action. ✉*30 Beiwei Lu, Xuanwu District* ☎*010/8315–6300* Ⓜ*None.*

ART GALLERIES

Artist Village Gallery. If you'd like a real change of pace from the city art scene, hire a driver or join a tour to visit the Artists' Village in the eastern suburbs of Beijing. More than 500 artists live and work in studio spaces, peasant homes, and old buildings in and around the central village of Songzhuang. Though a trip out to the Artist Village can take a chunk out of your day, the trip is worth it. The countryside is a stark contrast to the city, and the art is of excellent quality. The gallery itself displays local works in a modern, well-appointed building. Visits are by appointment only, so talk with your hotel concierge before booking a car. ✉*1 Chunbei, Ren Zhuang, Tongxian Songzhuang* ☎*139/0124–4283 or 010/6959–8343* 🌐*www.artistvillagegallery.com* Ⓜ*None.*

The Courtyard Gallery. Although the space here is minuscule—it's in the basement of the Courtyard Restaurant—this gallery still manages to attract some of the most sought-after names in contemporary Chinese art, such as Wang Qingsong, Zhang Dali, and the Gao Brothers. ✉*95 Donghuamen Dajie, Dongcheng District* ☎*010/6526–8882* 🌐*www.courtyard-gallery.com* Ⓜ*Tiananmen East.*

Red Gate Gallery. This gallery, one of the first to open in Beijing, displays and sells modern Chinese paintings and sculpture in the extraordinary space of the old Dongbianmen Watchtower, a centuries-old landmark. ✉*Dongbianmen Watchtower, Second Ring Rd. at Jianguomen, Chongwen District* ☎*010/6525–1005* 🌐*www.redgategallery.com* Ⓜ*Jianguomen.*

MUSIC

Beijing Concert Hall. Beijing's main venue for Chinese and Western classical-music concerts also hosts folk dancing and singing, and many celebratory events throughout the year. The venue is the home of the China National Symphony Orchestra. ✉*1 Bei Xinhua Jie, Xicheng District* ☎*010/6605–5812.*

Fodor's Choice ★ **Forbidden City Concert Hall.** With a seating capacity of 1,400, this is one of Beijing's largest concert halls. It is also one of the most well-appointed, with plush seating and top-notch acoustics. Despite the modern building, you'll walk through ancient courtyards to get to the hall—highly romantic. ✉*In Zhongshan Park, Xichangan Jie, Xicheng District* ✥*on the west side of Tiananmen Square* ☎*010/6559–8285* Ⓜ*Tiananmen West.*

MAO Live House. This is the place to come for a glimpse into Beijing's cutting-edge music scene. The small space is managed by a Japanese music label that pride themselves on seeking out interesting new bands.

Continued on page 100

BEIJING OPERA

"OPULENT" MAY BE AN UNDERSTATEMENT

For hundreds of years, Beijing opera troupes have delighted audiences—from members of the royal court to marketplace crowds at makeshift stages—with rich costumes, elaborate makeup, jaw-dropping acrobatics, and tales of betrayal and intrigue.

Nowadays, the weird and wonderful operas staged in Beijing's customized theaters are more than likely of the Jing Ju style, which emerged during the Qing Dynasty. There are more than 350 other kinds of Chinese opera, each distinguished by different dialects, music, costumes, and stories.

Why go? For the same amount of time as a movie (and about $20 per person), a night at the opera guarantees you a glimpse at China's past—not to mention a fascinating mix of drama, color, movement, and sound.

INTRODUCING BEIJING OPERA

A RICH & CURIOUS HISTORY

To master the art of Beijing opera's leaping acrobatics, stylized movements, sword dances, and dramatic makeup techniques, actors begin their grueling training as young children. The work pays off: nowhere else in the world can you see a performer in heavy, opulent costume, so artfully singing, miming, turning flips, and brandishing swords.

Opera instrumentation consists of the percussive Wuchang, that is, the gongs, drums, cymbals, and wooden clappers that accompany exaggerated body movements and acrobatics, and the melodic Wenchang, including the Chinese fiddle (*erhu*), the lutelike *pipa*, horns, and flutes.

Neophytes may find two hours of the staccato clanging and nasal singing of Beijing opera hard to take (and most young Chinese fed on a diet of western-style pop agree). But this dramatic, colorful experience might be one of the most memorable of your trip.

FALSETTOS & BACK FLIPS & GONGS, OH MY!

Beijing opera was born out of a wedding between two provincial opera styles from Anhui and Hubei in the 19th century—during China's last dynasty, the Qing Dynasty. It also borrowed from other regional operas and Kunqu, a 500-year-old Chinese musical-theater style. Even though Beijing opera is relatively young, many of its stories are extracted from epics written as far back as the 12th century.

After Mao Zedong took the helm in 1949, opera was molded to reflect the ideals of Chinese communism. The biggest changes occurred under Mao's wife, Jiang Qing, during the Cultural Revolution (1966–1976). Traditional operas were banned; only the so-called eight model plays could be staged. These starred people in plain work clothes singing about the glories of Communism. Traditional opera was reinstated gradually following Mao's death in 1976.

TIP→ If you're especially keen to follow the opera closely, choose a theater that displays English subtitles above the stage. Don't mind if things get lost in translation? Sit back and enjoy—the stage antics will be entertainment enough.

MEI LANFANG: GAY ICON & OPERA HERO(INE)

Born in Beijing into a family of performers, Mei Lanfang (1894–1961) perfected the art of female impersonation during his five decades on stage. He is credited with popularizing Beijing opera overseas and was so hip in his day that there was a brand of cigarettes named after him. *The Worlds of Mei Lanfang* (2000) is an American-made documentary about the star, with footage of his performances. You can visit his house at 9 Huguosijie, Xicheng District. Y10 Tues.–Sun. 9–4 010/6618–3598 www.meilanfang.com.cn.

Mei Lanfang's gender-bending chops earned him a special place in the hearts of gay activists.

ALL GUSSIED UP

All smiles: elaborate swirls and designs make for quite a done-up countenance.

Towering headdresses and flowing, cotton-candy-soft beards are all part of Beijing opera culture.

The richly embroidered silks in Beijing opera—called *xing tou*—are largely based on Ming Dynasty fashions. These nearly fetishistic costumes are key to identifying each character. The emperor is draped in a yellow robe with a colorful dragon on the back; scholars usually dress in blue and wear a cap with wings; generals don padded armor with bold embroidery; and bandits are often adorned in black capes and trousers.

Painstakingly detailed costumes and towering, bejeweled headdresses enhance the movements of the actors. For example, soldiers wear helmets with pheasant plumes that are waggled and brushed through the air. Cascading sleeves—called water sleeves—are waved and swept to express sorrow or respect.

PAINTED FACES

There are more than 1,000 different kinds of makeup patterns used in Beijing opera. Colors symbolize character traits. For example, red conveys bravery or loyalty, white signifies treachery, yellow suggests brutality, black stands for integrity or fierceness, and purple expresses wisdom. Bandits often have blue faces; gods and spirits are marked with gold and silver.

FACE CHANGING (BIAN LIAN)

A specialty of Sichuan opera (Chuan Ju) is the art of face changing, where actors swap masks with lightning speed. One method is to blow into a tiny box of colored powder to camouflage the switch. More spectacular is the mask-pulling routine, in which several masks are painted on thin fabric and attached to the face. Flicking a cloak or sleeve allows the performer to pull the masks off as needed. Masters whisk through as many as 10 masks in 20 seconds.

NOW YOU KNOW

The two most famous Beijing operas are *Peony Pavilion* and *Farewell My Concubine.*

In contrast to the ostentatious costumes, Beijing opera sets are quite sparse: the traditional stage is a simple platform with a silk backdrop.

THE FOUR MAJOR PLAYERS

There are four archetypal characters in Beijing opera: Sheng, Dan, Jing, and Chou. Each one can have variations. The Dan roles, for example, include Qingyi, a shy maiden, and the more promiscuous Huadan. A performer typically devotes a lifetime to perfecting one role.

During the Qing Dynasty, women were banned from performing, so men played the Dan role. These female impersonators were often the most popular actors. Women began performing again in the 1930s; nowadays most female roles are played by women.

SHENG Male characters: Scholars, statesmen

CHOU Clowns: Not always good-natured, wears white patches around eyes/nose

JING Warriors: The roles with the most elaborately painted faces

DAN Female characters: Coquettes, old ladies, warriors, maidens

WHERE TO WATCH

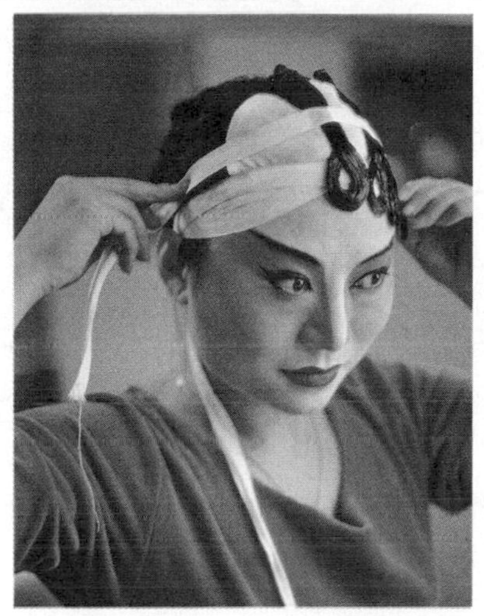

Embellished eyebrows, perfect tendrils of hair, and striking lips—a performer prepares for the show.

Shorter shows put on at venues such as Liyuan Theater are full of acrobatics and fantastic costumes. You can catch an opera performance any night of the week in Beijing, but there will be more options on weekends. Shows usually start around 7 PM and cost between 50 and 200 Yuan. All the free-listing magazines have information, and staff at your hotel can recommend performances and help book tickets. You can also buy tickets online through ⊕ www.piao.com.cn; register online and pay by credit card or cash on delivery, or phone ☎ 010/6417-7845. Piao.com.cn will send the tickets to your hotel. ■ TIP→ **You can also get a taste of Chinese opera for free before you spring for tickets if you have access to a television: nonstop opera is broadcast on CCTV channel 11.**

★ CHANG'AN GRAND THEATER At this contemporary theater, like at a cabaret, you sit at tables and can eat and drink while watching lively, colorful performances of Beijing opera. ■ TIP→ **A great perk? English subtitles appear above the stage.** ✉ 7 Jianguomennei Dajie, Dongcheng District ☎ 010/6510-1310

HUGUANG GUILDHALL The city's oldest Beijing opera theater, the Guildhall has staged performances since 1807. The hall has been restored to display its original architecture. Although it's the most atmospheric place to take in an opera, it's not the liveliest. The last we heard, the Huguang monkey king was looking washed out. ✉ 3 Hufangqiao, Xuanwu District ☎ 010/6351-8284 ⊕ www.beijinghuguang.com

LAO SHE TEAHOUSE Performances vary, but usually include Beijing opera and such arts as acrobatics, magic, or comedy. The teahouse is named after Lao She, a playwright and novelist who died in 1966. ✉ 3 Qianmenxi Dajie, 3rd floor, Xuanwu District ☎ 010/6303-6830 ⊕ www.laosheteahouse.com

★ Fodor's Choice LIYUAN THEATER Though it's unashamedly touristy, it's our top pick. You can watch performers put on makeup before the show (come early) and then graze on snacks and sip tea while watching English-subtitled shows. Glossy brochures complement the crooning. ✉ Qianmen Hotel, 175 Yongan Lu, Xuanwu District ☎ 010/6301-6688 Ext. 8860 or 010/6303-2301

TIANQIAO HAPPY TEAHOUSE In an old, traditional theater, the teahouse hosts Beijing operas as well as acrobatics, jugglers, and contortionists. ✉ 113 Tianqiao Shichang, Xuanwu District ☎ 010/6303-9013

RENT IT: *FAREWELL MY CONCUBINE*

Before your trip, rent Chen Kaige's *Farewell My Concubine*, a 1993 film that follows the life, loves, and careers of two male opera performers against a background of political turmoil. It also depicts the brutality of opera schools, where children were forced to practice grueling routines (think splits, balancing water jugs, and head stands).

The sound system is excellent and so are the drinks prices. ✉ *111 Gulou Dongdajie, Dongcheng District* ☎ *010/6402–5080* 🌐 *www.maolive.com* Ⓜ *Beixin Qiao.*

THEATER

Beijing Exhibition Theater. Chinese plays, Western and Chinese operas, and ballet performances are staged in this Soviet-style building that's part of the Exhibition Center complex. ✉ *135 Xizhimenwai Dajie, Xicheng District* ☎ *010/6835–4455* Ⓜ *Xizhimen.*

China National Puppet Theater. Shadow and hand-puppet shows convey traditional stories—it's lively entertainment for children and adults alike. This venue also attracts overseas performers, including the Moscow Puppet Theater. ✉ *1 Anhuaxili, Chaoyang District* ☎ *010/6425–4849* Ⓜ *None.*

Fodor's Choice ★ **National Centre for Performing Arts.** Architecturally, the giant silver dome is stunning, and interior holds a state-of-the-art opera house, a music hall, and a theater. The Egg offers a world-class stage for national and international performers, but you can only explore inside if you have a ticket. ✉ *2 Xi Chang'an Jie, Xicheng District* ☎ *010/6655–0988* 🌐 *www.chncpa.org* Ⓜ *Tiananmen West.*

NIGHTLIFE

Beijing has spent the last decade shaking off its grim Communist image and putting the neon into its nightlife. Sanlitun—the heart of Beijing's nightlife—has spread its party presence around Gongti and Houhai. Sanlitun Jiuba Jie, or "Bar Street," offers mainly crass live-music pubs; it's quite popular with locals. On Gongti West Gate, a stream of pumping dance clubs have attracted some big-name DJs—Tiesto, Felix Da Housecat, and Paul Oakenfold, among others. The city's main gay club, Destination, is also here.

Houhai, once a quiet lakeside neighborhood home to Beijing's *laobaixing* (ordinary folk), has exploded into a bumping bar scene. This is a great place to come for a drink at dusk: park yourself on an outdoor seat and enjoy. There are a few hidden gems here, but most of the bars are bland and expensive, with disappointingly weak drinks. Stick to the bottled beer to get your money's worth. The *hutong*, or mazelike neighborhoods, around the lake also hide some cute bars.

BARS AND DANCE CLUBS

DONGCHENG AND XICHENG DISTRICTS (INCLUDING HOUHAI)

★ **Drum and Bell.** This bar has a perfect location—right between the Drum and Bell towers. The terrace is a comfy perch for a summer afternoon drink, where you scan the surrounding hutong rooftops. Don't get too plastered, though, because the staircase down is very steep. On the ground floor there are jumbles of sofas tossed with Cultural Revolution memorabilia. ✉ *41 Zhonglouwan Hutong, Dongcheng District* ☎ *010/8403–3600* Ⓜ *Gulou.*

★ **East Shore Live Jazz Café.** The closest thing Beijing has to New Orleans is this bar. Expect cigar smoke, velvet drapes, sepia photographs of jazz greats, and plenty of vintage instruments on display. Owner, local jazz legend Liu Yuan, says he wants to use the bar to promote homegrown jazz talents. On top of the live swing and jazz, the bar boasts the best views of Houhai, either through the floor-to-ceiling windows (complete with telescope) in the bar or from the small, sparsely furnished rooftop. ⚠ **There are no guardrails on the roof, so drink and step with extreme care.** ✉ *Qianhai Nanyan Lu, 2nd fl., next to the Post Office, Xicheng District* ☎ *010/8403–2131* Ⓜ *None.*

Fodor's Choice ★ **No Name Bar.** The first bar to open in Houhai is still around, even though its neighbors have already been torn down. It's very relaxed: many expats still list No Name as their favorite bar in the city. The service is refreshingly low-key—a nice change from the sycophantic staff at neighboring venues—and it's all tumbledown elegance with rattan and potted plants. Locals refer to it by the owner's name: Bai Feng. Anyone from tourists to old China hands can be found here. ✉ *3 Qianhai East Bank, Xicheng District* ☎ *010/6401–8541* Ⓜ *None.*

★ **Yugong Yishan.** This Beijing institution, in its second location, is a chilled-out bar run by two local music fans. It plays host to a range of live bands playing everything from blues to jazz to Afro-Caribbean beats, and attracts an equally diverse crowd. It occasionally charges an entrance fee, depending on the entertainment. Don't bother with the cocktails—instead, nod your head along to the music while sipping a good old Tsingdao beer. ✉ *3-2 Zhangzizhong Lu, Dongcheng District* ☎ *010/6404–2711* Ⓜ *Zhang Zizhong Lu.*

CHAOYANG DISTRICT

Centro. We don't always warm up to hotel bars, but this one is decidedly different. It's huge and luxurious, with cavernous wine cellars—and it also has some of the city's favorite cocktail mixologists. Come for the early evening happy hour, when excellent cocktails are two-for-one and feast your eyes on the nouveau riche showing off their labels. ✉ *1/F Kerry Center Hotel, 1 Guanghua Lu, Chaoyang District* ☎ *010/6561–8833 Ext. 42* Ⓜ *Jintaixizhao.*

The Den. This bar's attraction is sports on the wide-screen TVs. The owner runs the city's amateur rugby club, so you'll find players and their supporters drinking rowdily. Open 24 hours a day, it's guaranteed to be buzzing every night. ✉ *4 Gongti Donglu, next to the City Hotel, Chaoyang District* ☎ *010/6592–6290* Ⓜ *Tuanjie Hu.*

Face. Stylish without being pretentious, Face is justifiably popular. The complex has a multitude of restaurants, but the real gem is the bar. Grab a lounge bed surrounded by silky drapes, take advantage of the happy hour drink specials, and enjoy some premier people-watching. ✉ *26 Dongcaoyuan, Gongti Nan Lu, Chaoyang District* ☎ *010/6551–6788* Ⓜ *None.*

Fodor's Choice ★ **Q Bar.** George and Echo's cocktails—strong, authentic, and not super expensive—are a small legend here in Beijing. This tucked-away lounge adds an unpretentious note to an evening out. Don't be put off by the fact it's in a bland motel stuck in the 1980s. The drinks are worth it (especially the whiskey sours). ✉ *Top floor of Eastern Inn Hotel, Sanlitun Nan Lu, Chaoyang District* ☎ *010/6595–9239* Ⓜ *Tuanjie Hu.*

Saddle Cantina. For a touch of Mexico, head to this terra-cotta-colored venue in downtown Beijing. It's packed on summer evenings thanks to its large terrace, perfect for downing one of the brilliant margaritas. The service is friendly, and the house band will have you tapping your feet. ✉ *81 Sanlitun Bei Lu, Chaoyang District* ☎ *010/6400–4330* Ⓜ *Tuanjie Hu.*

Fodor'sChoice ★ **Song.** Beijing's best bar and club for grown-ups, Song has über-cool music and a fantastic wooden interior designed to resemble a rice terrace. The funky clientele isn't too full of itself, and the great cocktails add to the fun. ✉ *9 Guanghua Lu, Chaoyang District* ☎ *010/6587–1311* Ⓜ *None.*

★ **Stone Boat.** This watering hole is a pavilion-style hut on the edge of a pretty lake in Ritan Park. There are dainty ducks, feisty fishermen, and park joggers to observe while you sip chilled white wine. This is one of Beijing's nicest outdoor bars, as long as you don't mind having to use the public toilets opposite the building. The bar is livelier on weekends, when it often hosts live musicians from Xinjiang. ✉ *Lakeside, southwest corner of Ritan Park, Chaoyang District* ☎ *010/6501–9986* Ⓜ *Jianguomen.*

The Tree. For years now, expats have crowded this bar for its Belgian beer, wood-fired pizza, and quiet murmurs of conversation. If you want pasta instead of pizza, its sister restaurant, Nearby the Tree, is, well, nearby, 100 meters southeast. ✉ *43 Sanlitun Beijie, Chaoyang District* ☎ *010/6415–1954* Ⓜ *Tuanjie Hu.*

CHAOYANG WEST GATE

i-Ultra Lounge. The Block 8 complex, which includes this happening lounge, two restaurants, and a rooftop "beach," single-handedly made the area hip, attracting crowds of dressed-to-the-nines partygoers wanting to see and be seen. The lounge's purple and gray interior can seem pretentious, especially the catwalk-style entrance which turns everyone into a potential supermodel, but it's always fun. Weekends are given over to pumping house music. ✉ *8 Chaoyang Gongyuan Xi Lu, Chaoyang District* ☎ *010/6508–8585* Ⓜ *None.*

The World of Suzie Wong. It's no coincidence this bar is named after a 1957 novel about a Hong Kong prostitute. Come here late at night and you'll find a healthy supply of modern Suzie Wongs and a crowd of expat clients. The sleaze factor is enhanced by its 1930s opium-den design, with China-chic beds overrun with cushions. Suzie Wong's, however, has a reputation for mixing a more-than-decent cocktail. ✉ *1A South Nongzhanguan Lu, Chaoyang West Gate, Chaoyang District* ☎ *010/6593–6049.*

SHOPPING

Updated by Nels Frye

Large markets and malls in Beijing are generally open from 9 AM to 9 PM. Weekdays are always less crowded, and smaller shops tend to be quieter just after lunch, when many Chinese people (including some merchants) take a rest. If a shop looks closed (the lights are out or the owner is resting), don't give up. Many merchants conserve electricity or take catnaps if the store is free of customers. Just knock or offer the greeting "*ni hao.*"

Major credit cards are accepted in pricier venues catering to Westerners. Cash is the driving force here, and ATMs abound. Before accepting those Mao-faced Y100 notes, most vendors hold them up to the light, tug at the corners, and rub their fingers along the surface. In some department stores, you must pay at a central payment counter.

Shops frequented by foreigners sometimes have an employee with some fluency in English. But money remains the international language. In many cases, the shop assistant will still whip out a calculator, look at you thoughtfully, then type in a starting price. You're expected to counter with your offer. Punch in your dream price. The clerk will come down Y10 or Y20 and so on. Remember that the terms "yuan," "kuai," and "RMB" are often used interchangeably.

MALLS AND DEPARTMENT STORES

Beijing Friendship Store. The Beijing Friendship Store is like a date you invite to family gatherings: it's reliable, well-groomed, and respectable, yet utterly boring. Years ago, this was the only place sanctioned to sell foreign goods, but with so many cheaper and more glamorous options now, this old mainstay has lost its allure. (There are even rumors it will be demolished in the near future.) However, if the thought of bargaining in a loud, crowded market makes your head hurt, or if you're on a single-sweep shopping spree for goods of guaranteed quality, then the Friendship Store will be your haven. Don't miss the bookstore, which stocks the *International Herald Tribune* and books on politics and contemporary literature. ✉*17 Jianguomenwai Dajie, Chaoyang District* ☎*010/6500–3311* Ⓜ*Jianguomen.*

★ **China World Shopping Mall.** Rising up alongside the China World Trade Center, the two towers of Guomao rule the roost with tiers of top-flight designers, such as **Prada, Marc Jacobs, Hermès,** and **Dior.** For quality souvenirs, check out **Tian Fu,** a branch of the famous Chinese tea sellers, or **Emperor,** which sells silk bedding and table linens. ✉*1 Jianguomenwai Dajie, Chaoyang District* ☎*010/6505–2288* Ⓜ*Guomao.*

The Kerry Centre Mall. Part of a hotel complex, the Kerry Centre Mall comprises a group of small but top-notch clothing shops, in addition to two golf stores, a post office, and an international food court. Lush piles of silk and wool carpets from Xinjiang and Henan provinces line the walls of **Aladdin Jia Ju Carpets.** On the mall's entrance level, **Dave's Custom Tailoring** turns out quality men's suits in about 10 days. A few doors down, **Mystery Garments** embellishes linens and silks with

Chinese embroidery from Guizhou. ✉1 *Guanghua Rd., Chaoyang District* ☎*010/8529–9450* Ⓜ*Guomao.*

Lufthansa Youyi Shopping Center. A high-end shopping mall attached to the ritzy Kempinski Hotel, this center is popular with expat parents, who rave about the selection of children's clothing and baby goods on the sixth floor. International dealers in crystal and glass applaud the jewels and vases sold at **Liuligongfang** on the first floor. ✉*52 Liangmaoqiao Lu, Chaoyang District* ☎*010/6465–1188* Ⓜ*Liangmaqiao.*

★ **Malls at Oriental Plaza.** This enormous shopping complex originates at the southern end of Wangfujing, where it meets Chang'an Jie, and stretches a city block east to Dongdan Dajie. A true city within a city, it's conveniently organized by "street" names, such as Gourmet Street (aka the Food Court) and Sky Avenue. Upscale shops include **Kenzo** and **Allea,** which have some of the best men's accessories between Tokyo and Naples. ✉*1 Dongchang'an Jie, Dongcheng District* ☎*010/8518–6363* Ⓜ*Wangfujing.*

Wangfujing Department Store. Wangfujing's grand dame continues to attract large crowds with stores selling everything from jewelry to clothing to sports equipment. ✉*255 Wangfujing Dajie, Dongcheng District* ☎*010/6522–3388* Ⓜ*Wangfujing.*

MARKETS

Beijing Curio City. This complex has four stories of kitsch and curio shops and a few furniture vendors, some selling authentic antiques. Prices are high (driven up by free-spending tour groups), so don't be afraid to lowball your offer. If you are looking for antiques, try **Dong Fang Yuan** (# 111). ✉*Dongsanhuan Nan Lu, Exit Third Ring Rd. at Panjiayuan Bridge, Chaoyang District* ☎*010/6774–7711* Ⓜ*Jinsong.*

★ **Hongqiao Market** *(Pearl Market).* Hongqiao is full of tourist goods, knockoff handbags, and cheap watches, but it's best known for its three stories of pearls, hence its nickname. Freshwater, seawater, black, pink, white: the quantity is overwhelming and quality varies by stall. Prices range wildly, though the cheapest items are often fakes. Fanghua Pearls (No. 4318), on the fourth floor, displays quality necklaces and earrings, with photos of Barbara Bush and Margaret Thatcher shopping there to prove it. Fanghua has a second store devoted to fine jade and precious stones. As a bonus, hold your nose and dive into the fish and meat market in the basement: a veritable aquarium of sea cucumbers, crab, dragon shrimp, squid, and eel. ✉*Tiantan Lu, between Chongemenwai Lu and Tiyuguan Dajie, east of the northern entrance to Temple of Heaven, Chongwen District* ☎*010/6711–7630* Ⓜ*Tiantang Dongmen.*

Fodor's Choice ★ **Panjiayuan Antiques Market.** Every weekend, the sun rises over thousands of pilgrims rummaging in search of antiques and the most curious of curios. With more than 3,000 vendors crowding an area of 48,500 square meters, not every jade bracelet, oracle bone, porcelain vase, and ancient screen is authentic, but most people are here for the reproductions anyway. Behold the bounty: watercolors, scrolls, calligraphy, Buddhist statues, opera costumes, old Russian SLR cameras, curio cabinets, Tibetan jewelry, tiny satin lotus-flower shoes, rotary telephones, jade dragons, antique mirrors, infinite displays of "Maomorabilia." If you're buying jade, first observe the Chinese customers, how they hold a flashlight to the milky-green stone to test its authenticity. As with all Chinese markets, bargain with a vengence, as many vendors inflate their prices astronomically for *waiguoren* ("outside country people"). A strip of enclosed stores forms a perimeter around the surprisingly orderly rows of open air stalls. The friendly owner of the eponymous **Li Shu Lan** decorates her shop (# 24-D) with antiques from her *laojia,* or countryside hometown. Stop by the **Bei Zhong Bao Pearl Shop** (# 7-A) for medium-quality freshwater pearls cultivated by the Hu family. Also here are a sculpture zoo, book bazaar, reproduction-furniture shops, and a two-story market stashing propaganda posters and Communist literature. Show the taxi driver the Chinese characters for Panjiayuan Shichang. ✉ *Third Ring Rd. at Panjiayuan Bridge, Chaoyang District* Ⓜ *Jinsong.*

Ritan Office Building Market. Don't let the gray-brick and red-trim exterior fool you: the offices inside the Ritan Building are strung with racks of brand-name dresses and funky-fab accessories. Unlike the tacky variations made on knockoff labels sold in less-expensive markets, the collections here, for the most part, retain their integrity—perhaps because many of these dresses are actually designer labels. They're also more expensive, and bargaining is discouraged. Of note, the owner Liu Xingxing tailors and sells Hunan silk qipaos (# 1019). The **Ruby Cashmere Shop** (# 1009) sells genuine cashmere sweaters and scarves at reduced prices. Upstairs, the burning incense and bright red walls of **You Gi** (# 2006) provide a welcome atmosphere for perusing an overpriced but eccentric collection of Nepalese and Indian clothing and jewelry. ✉ *15A Guanghua Lu, just east of the south entrance to Ritan Park, opposite the Vietnam Embassy, Chaoyang District* ☎ *010/8561–9556* Ⓜ *Yonganli.*

Fodor's Choice ★ **Silk Alley Market.** Once a delightfully chaotic sprawl of hundreds of outdoor stalls, the Silk Alley Market is now corralled inside a huge shopping center. The government has been cracking down on an increasing number of certain copycat items, so if you don't see that knockoff Louis Vuitton purse or Chanel jacket, just ask; it might magically appear from a stack of plastic storage bins. You will face no dearth, however, of knockoff Pumas and Nikes or Paul Smith polos. Chinese handicrafts and children's clothes are on the top floors. Bargain relentlessly, check carefully the quality of each intended purchase, and guard your wallet against pickpockets. ✉ *8 Xiushui Dong Jie, Chaoyang District* ☎ *139/0113–6086 or 010/5169–9003* 🌐 *www.xiushui.com.cn* Ⓜ *Yonganli.*

★ **Yaxiu Market** *(Yashow Market).* Especially popular among younger Western shoppers, Yaxiu is yet another indoor arena stuffed to the gills with low-quality knockoff clothing and shoes. Prices are slightly cheaper than Silk Alley, but the haggling no less cruel. Don't be alarmed if you see someone sniffing sneakers or suede jackets: they're simply testing whether the leather is real. The giant sign outside this bustling clothes market near Sanlitun reads Yashow, but it's written YAXIU in pinyin. ✉ *58 Gongti Bei Lu, Chaoyang District* ☎ *010/6416–8699* Ⓜ *Tuanjiehu.*

Zhaojia Chaowai Market. Beijing's best-known venue for affordable antiques and reproduction furniture houses scores of independent vendors who sell everything from authentic Qing Dynasty–era chests to traditional baskets, ceramics, carpets, and curios. Be sure to bargain; vendors routinely sell items for less than half their starting price. ✉ *43 Huawei Bei Li, Chaoyang District* ☎ *010/6770–6402* Ⓜ *Jinsong.*

SPECIALTY SHOPS

BOOKS

★ **The Bookworm.** Book lovers, hipsters, and aspiring poets take note: this lending library and bookstore offers a spacious second-story reading room with a full café and bar. All are welcome to browse: the magazine and new-books section are a stupendous sight for English-starved travelers. The store frequently hosts poetry readings and lectures. ✉ *4 Sanlitun Nan Lu, set back slightly in a parking lot, Chaoyang District* ☎ *010/6586–9507* 🌐 *www.beijingbookworm.com* Ⓜ *Tuanjiehu.*

Foreign Languages Bookstore. Head directly to the third floor, which is reserved for imported publications. Classics perpetually roost on the shelves of this state-owned shop, but best sellers, biographies, and decent books about China also make the cut (though don't expect to read anything on the Tiananmen Square incidents). Find maps, Chinese-language learning materials, and children's books here, too. ✉ *235 Wangfujing Dajie, Dongcheng District* ☎ *010/6512–6903* Ⓜ *Wangfujing.*

CHINESE MEDICINE

★ **Tongrentang.** A first-time consultation with a Chinese doctor can feel a bit like a reading with a fortune-teller. With one test of the pulse, many traditional Chinese doctors can describe the patient's medical history and diagnose current maladies. China's most famous traditional Chinese medicine shop, Tongrentang, is one of the oldest establishments on Dashilan. Palatial, hushed, and dimly illuminated, this 300-year-old old shop even smells healthy. Browse the glassed displays of deer antlers and pickled snakes, dried seahorses and frogs, and delicate tangles of roots with precious price tags of Y48,000. ■ **TIP→ If you don't speak Chinese and wish to have a consultation with a doctor, bring along a translator.** ✉ *24 Dashilan, Qianmen, Exit C, Chongwen District* Ⓜ *Qianmen.*

COMPUTERS AND ELECTRONICS

Bainaohui Computer Shopping Mall. Next door to the Wonderful Electronic Shopping Mall is Bainao, which means "one hundred computers." (The Chinese word for computer translates literally as "electric brain.") Home to hundreds of laptops and PCs, this retail mall is crammed with vendors. ✉ *10 Chaoyangmenwai Da Jie, Chaoyang District* ☎ *010/6599–5912* Ⓜ *Chaoyangmen.*

Wonderful Electronic Shopping Mall. Cameras, tripods, flash disks, and MP3s (called MP-San in Chinese) abound. If you forgot the USB cable for your digital recorder or need extra camera batteries, this is the place. ✉*12 Chaoyangmenwai Da Jie, Chaoyang District* ☎*010/8561–4335* Ⓜ*Chaoyangmen.*

EARLY-BIRD CATCHES

A common superstition in Chinese markets is that if you don't make a sale with your very first customer of the day, the rest of the day will go badly. So set out early, and if you know you're the first customer of the day, bargain relentlessly.

FASHION DESIGNERS AND BOUTIQUES

Heyan'er. He Yan's design philosophy is stated in her label: BU YAN BU YU, or NO TALKING. Her linen and cotton tunics and collarless jackets speak for themselves. From earth tones to aubergine hues and peacock patterns, He Yan's designs echo traditional Tibetan styles. ✉*15–2 Gongti Bei Lu* ☎*010/6415–9442* Ⓜ*Dongsishitiao* ✉*Holiday Inn Lido, 6 Fangyuan Xi Lu* ☎*010/6437–6854* Ⓜ*Sanyuanqiao.*

The Red Phoenix. In this cramped-but-charming Sanlitun showroom, fashion diva Gu Lin designs embroidered satin qipaos, cropped jackets, and men's clothing for stylish foreigners and China's *xin xin ren lei* (literally the "new, new human being," referring to the country's latest flock of successful young professionals). ✉*30 Sanlitun Bei Jie* ☎*010/6416–4423* Ⓜ*Tuanjiehu.*

Tianshang Studio. Fashion designer Huang Yue produces hand-tailored men's and women's suits, wedding gowns, and coats out of luscious fabrics (Y2,000 and up). Huang is one of the few designers to successfully blend traditional styles and haute couture. Prices are higher that what many visiting Beijing are used to, but are justified, given the quality of the materials and workmanship. ✉*Opposite to Tongli, Sanlitun Beijie* ☎*010/6417–1093* Ⓜ*Tuanjiehu.*

JEWELRY

Shard Box Store. The signature collection here includes small to mid-size jewelry boxes fashioned from the broken shards of antique porcelain. Supposedly the shards were collected during the Cultural Revolution, when scores of antique porcelain pieces were smashed in accordance with the law. Birds, trees, pining lovers, and dragons decorate these affordable ceramic-and-metal containers, which range from Y20 to Y200. ✉*1 Ritan Bei Lu, near the Holiday Inn Lido, Chaoyang District* ☎*010/8561–3712* Ⓜ*Yong'anli* ✉*2 Jiangtai Lu* ☎*010/5135–7638* Ⓜ*Sanyuanqiao.*

Treasure House. In the Embassy District, Treasure House has a modest but slick collection, including silver cuff links and charms inscribed with the Chinese symbols for happiness and longevity. ✉*1 Sanlitun Beixiaojie* ☎*010/8451–6096* Ⓜ*Yong'anli.*

EXPLORING TEA STREET

Tea Street. Maliandao hosts the ultimate tea party every day of the week. Literally hundreds of tea shops perfume the air of this prime tea-shopping district, west of the city center. Midway down this near-mile-long strip looms the **Teajoy Market,** the Silk Alley of teas. Unless you're an absolute fanatic, it's best to visit a handful of individual shops, crashing tea parties wherever you go. Vendors will invite you to sit down in heavy wooden chairs to nibble on pumpkin seeds and sample their large selections of black, white, oolong, jasmine, and chrysanthemum teas. Prices range from a few kuai for a decorative container of loose green tea to thousands of yuan for an elaborate gift set. Tea Street is also the place to stock up on clay and porcelain teapots and service sets. Green and flower teas are sold loose; black teas are sold pressed into disks and wrapped in natural-colored paper. Despite the huge selection of drinking vessels available, you'll find that most locals prefer to drink their tea from a recycled glass jar. ✉ *Located near Guanganmen Wai Dajie, Xuanwu District* Ⓜ *Xuanwumen.*

SILK AND FABRICS

Beijing Silk Shop. Since 1830, the Beijing Silk Shop has been supplying the city with quality silks and fabrics. To reach the shop, walk all the way down Dashilan, then head directly onto Dashilan West Street. ■ **TIP→ Two larger stores on Dashilan specialize in silk. Ruifuxiang, at No. 5, is housed in a beautiful two-story building, as is Century Silk Store at No. 33.** ✉ *50 Dashilan Xi Jie, Xuanwu District* ☎ *010/6301–6658* Ⓜ *Qianmen.*

Beijing Yuanlong Silk Corporation. Jars of silkworm pupa and baskets of cocoons greet you on the second floor of Yuanlong. A tour guide will walk you through the silk quilt-making process while women in white lab coats demonstrate how to clean, soak, and stretch the silk of cocoons. It's touristy but fun, especially if you've never seen the process. Silk quilts and duvets are for sale, and there's an on-site tailor for specialty items. ■ **TIP→ You should avoid this spot entirely if tour buses are lined-up in the parking lot.** ✉ *55 Tiantan Lu, between the north gate of Temple of Heaven Park and Hongqiao, Chongwen District* ☎ *010/6705–2451* Ⓜ *Qianmen.*

China Star Silk Store. In the Wangfujing area, this is a great place to consider buying a *qipao*, the traditional Chinese silk dress. ✉ *133 Wangfujing Dajie, Dongcheng District* ☎ *010/6525–7945* Ⓜ *Wangfujing.*

Daxin Textiles Co. For a wide selection of all types of fabrics, from worsted wools to sensuous silks, head to this shop. Tailors turn the fabric into wearable, if low-quality, garments. ✉ *Northeast corner of Dongsi, Dongcheng District* ☎ *010/6403–2378* Ⓜ *Dongsi.*

SIDE TRIPS FROM BEIJING

Updated by Paul Mooney

Not only is Beijing a fascinating city to visit, but its outskirts are packed with history- and culture-laden sites for the admirer of early empires and their antiquities. First and foremost, a trip to the Great Wall is a must—you simply can't miss it! After the Great Wall, there are a variety of wonderful things to do and see: you can go horseback riding at Yesanpo, take a dip at the beach and gorge yourself with fresh seafood in Beidaihe, or travel to Laolongtou (the Old Dragon's Head), and see another section of the Great Wall in all its majesty as it collides with the ocean.

WORD OF MOUTH

"In several visits to Beijing I have used Jane Yeo as a private guide. She has a masterful knowledge of Beijing, its history, and sights. Her English is excellent. She can accommodate single travelers as well as groups and will customize a tour to exactly what you would like to see. She also knows wonderful restaurants and places to shop. Her fees are reasonable. My expectations are always exceeded, and my traveling companions have also been pleased with her services. Her website is www.janeyeotours.com." –eastwest

Buddhist temples and ancient tombs, as well as historical bridges and anthropological digs, are all located within a few hours of Beijing. For all these sites, getting there is half the fun—traveling through rural China, even for a day trip, is always something of an adventure.

THIRTEEN MING TOMBS

48 km (30 mi) north of Beijing.

A narrow valley just north of Changping is the final resting place for 13 of the Ming Dynasty's 16 emperors (the first Ming emperor was buried in Nanjing; the burial site of the second one is unknown; and the seventh Ming emperor was dethroned and buried in an ordinary tomb in western Beijing). Ming monarchs once journeyed here each year to kowtow before their clan forefathers and make offerings to their memory. The area's vast scale and imperial grandeur convey the importance attached to ancestral worship in ancient China.

The road to the Thirteen Ming Tombs begins beneath an imposing stone portico that stands at the valley entrance. Beyond the entrance, the **Shenlu** (*Y16 Daily 9–5:30*), or Spirit Way, once reserved for imperial travel, passes through an outer pavilion and between rows of stone sculptures—imperial advisers and huge, serene elephants, lions, horses, and other creatures—on its 7-km (4½-mi) journey to the burial sites. The spirit way leads to **Changling** (*010/6076–1886 Y30*), the head tomb built for Emperor Yongle in 1427. The designs of Yongle's great masterpiece, the Forbidden City, are echoed in this structure. The tomb is open daily from 8:30 to 4:30. Changling and a second tomb, **Dingling** (*010/6076–1424 Y60 Mar.–June and Sept.–Nov.; Y40 July and Aug. and Dec.–Feb.*), were rebuilt in the 1980s and opened to the public. Both complexes suffer from over-restoration and overcrowding, but

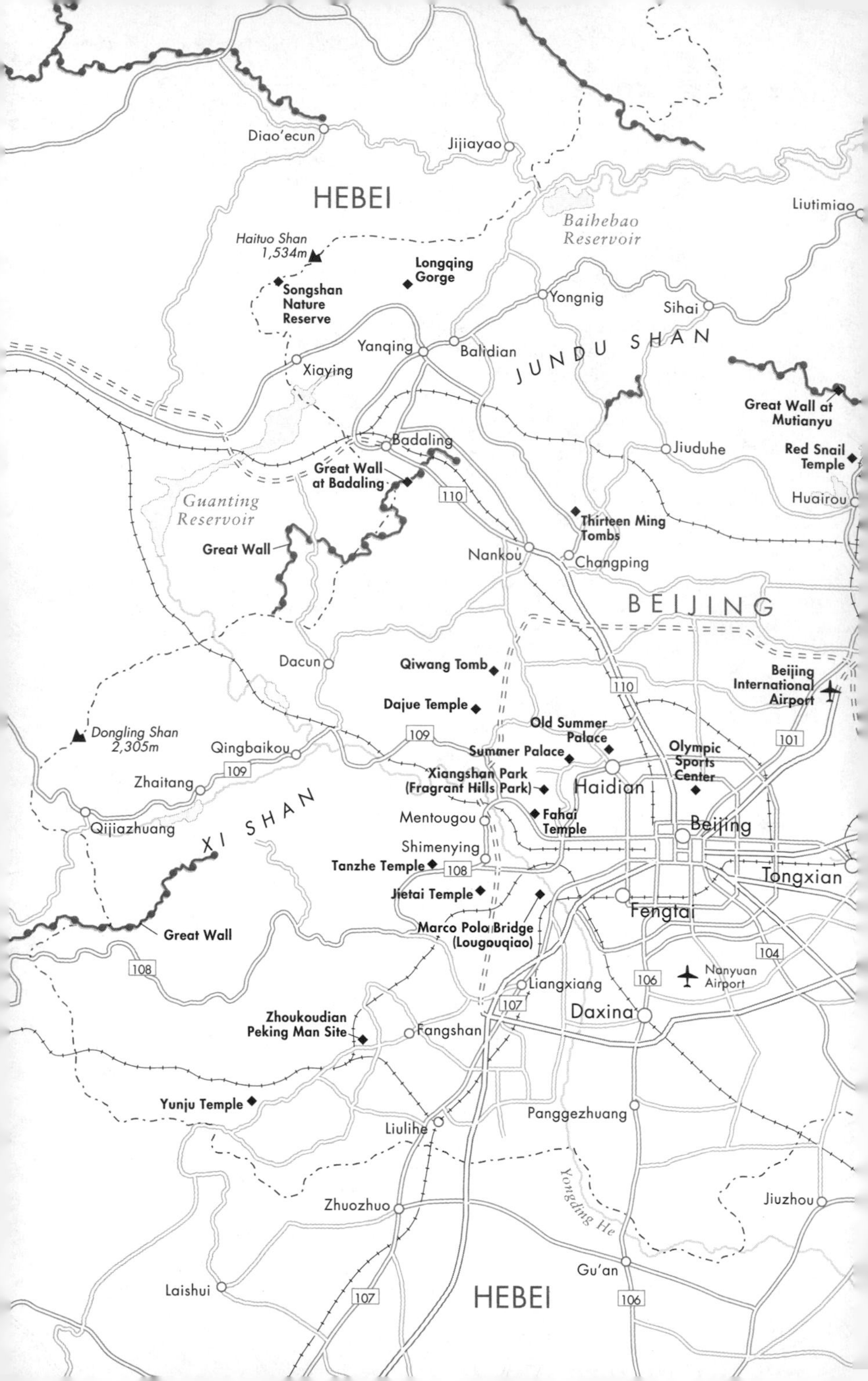

Diao'ecun
Jijiayao
HEBEI
Liutimiao
Baihebao
Reservoir
Haituo Shan
1,534m
Longqing
Gorge
Songshan
Nature
Reserve
Yongnig
Sihai
Yanqing
Balidian
JUNDU SHAN
Xiaying
Great Wall at
Mutianyu
Badaling
Jiuduhe
Red Snail
Temple
Great Wall
at Badaling
110
Huairou
Guanting
Reservoir
Thirteen Ming
Tombs
Great Wall
Nankou
Changping
BEIJING
Dacun
Qiwang Tomb
110
Beijing
International
Airport
Dajue Temple
Old Summer
Palace
Dongling Shan
2,305m
109
Olympic
Sports
Center
101
Qingbaikou
Summer Palace
109
Xiangshan Park
(Fragrant Hills Park)
Zhaitang
Haidian
Fahai
Temple
Qijiazhuang
Mentougou
Beijing
XI SHAN
Shimenying
Tanzhe Temple
108
Tongxian
Jietai Temple
Fengtai
Marco Polo Bridge
(Lougouqiao)
Great Wall
104
108
106
Nanyuan
Airport
Liangxiang
107
Daxina
Zhoukoudian
Peking Man Site
Fangshan
Yunju Temple
Panggezhuang
Liulihe
Yongding He
Zhuozhuo
Jiuzhou
Gu'an
Laishui
107
106
HEBEI

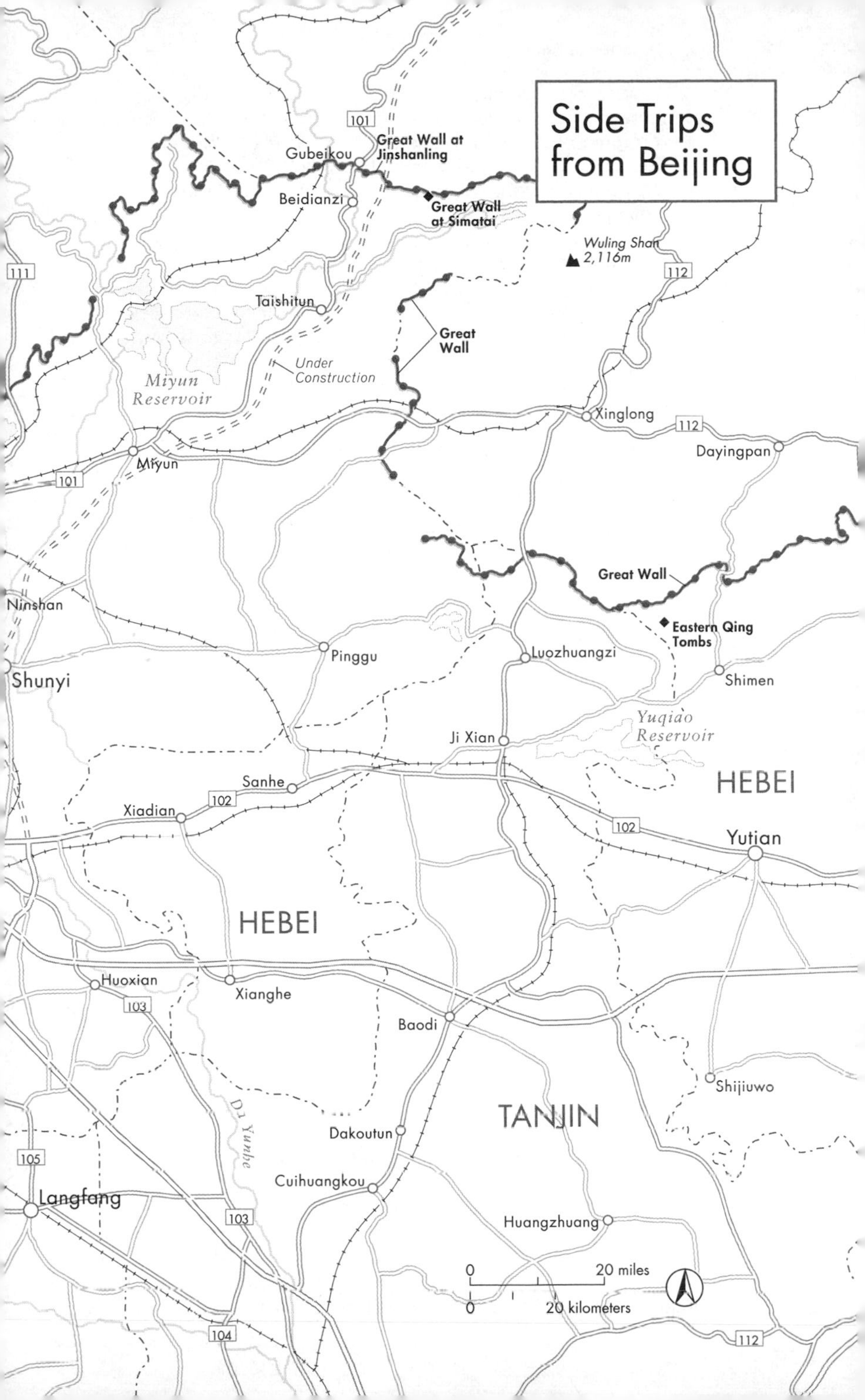

Side Trips from Beijing
101
Great Wall at Jinshanling
Gubeikou
Beidianzi
Great Wall at Simatai
Wuling Shan 2,116m
111
112
Taishitun
Great Wall
Under Construction
Miyun Reservoir
Xinglong
112
Dayingpan
Miyun
101
Great Wall
Ninshan
Eastern Qing Tombs
Pinggu
Luozhuangzi
Shunyi
Shimen
Yuqiao Reservoir
Ji Xian
HEBEI
Sanhe
102
Xiadian
102
Yutian
HEBEI
Huoxian
Xianghe
103
Baodi
Shijiuwo
Da Yunhe
TANJIN
Dakoutun
105
Cuihuangkou
Langfang
103
Huangzhuang
0
20 miles
0
20 kilometers
104
112

they're worth visiting if only for the tomb relics on display in the small museums at each site. Dingling is particularly worth seeing because this tomb of Emperor Wanli is the only Ming Dynasty tomb that has been excavated. Unfortunately, this was done in 1956 when China's archaeological skills were sadly lacking, resulting in irrecoverable losses. Nonetheless, it is interesting to compare this underground vault with the tomb of Emperor Qianlong at Qingdongling. Dingling is open daily from 8:30 to 5:30. Allow ample time for a hike or drive northwest from Changling to the six fenced-off **unrestored tombs,** a short distance farther up the valley. Here, crumbling walls conceal vast courtyards shaded by pine trees. At each tomb, a stone altar rests beneath a stela tower and burial mound. In some cases the wall that circles the burial chamber is accessible on steep stone stairways that ascend from either side of the altar. At the valley's terminus (about 5 km [3 mi] northwest of Changling), the **Zhaoling tomb** (*Y30*) rests beside a traditional walled village. This thriving hamlet is well worth exploring.

Picnics amid the Ming ruins have been a favorite weekend activity among Beijing-based diplomats for nearly a century. The signs prohibiting this activity are largely ignored; if you do choose to picnic here, though, be sure to carry out all trash. ⊠*Near Changping, Changping County.*

FAHAI TEMPLE

20 km (12 mi) west of Beijing.

The stunning works of Buddhist mural art at Fahai Temple, which underwent extensive renovation and reopened in 2008, are among the most underappreciated sights in Beijing. Li Tong, a favored eunuch in the court of Emperor Zhengtong (1436–49), donated funds to construct Fahai Temple in 1443. The project was highly ambitious: Li Tong invited only celebrated imperial and court painters to decorate the temple. As a result, the murals in the only surviving chamber of that period, Daxiongbaodian (the Mahavira Hall), are considered the finest examples of Buddhist mural art from the Ming Dynasty. Sadly, statues of various Buddhas and one of Li Tong himself were destroyed during China's Cultural Revolution.

The most famous of the nine murals in Mahavira Hall is a large-scale triptych featuring Guanyin (the Bodhisattva of Compassion) and Wenshu (the Bodhisattva of Marvelous Virtue and Gentle Majesty) in the center, and Poxian (the Buddha of Universal Virtue) on either side. The depiction of Guanyin follows the theme of "moon in water," which compares the Buddhist belief in the illusoriness of the material world to the reflection of the moon in the water. Typically painted with Guanyin are her legendary mount Jin Sun and her assistant Shancai Tongzi. Wenshu is often presented with a lion, symbolic of the bodhisattva's wisdom and strength of will, while Poxian is shown near a six-tusked elephant, each tusk representing one of the qualities that leads to enlightenment. On the opposite wall is the *Sovereign Sakra and Brahma* mural, with a panoply of characters from the Buddhist canon.

Continued on page 122

THE GREAT WALL

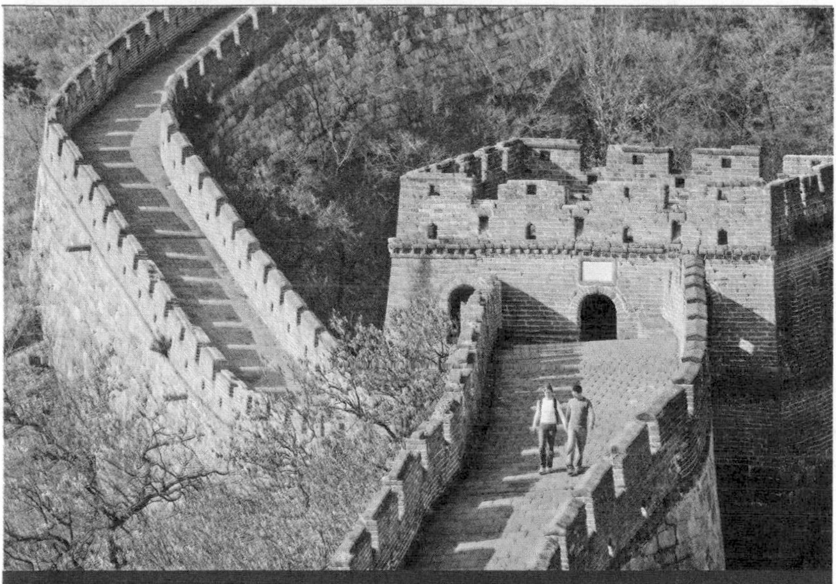

■ One misconception is that the Great Wall is the only man-made structure visible from space. We say there's no better way to see it than up close.

■ Sections of this magnificent, ancient wall were built from the 5th century BC until the 17th century AD.

■ The Great Wall is the longest man-made structure on earth. It was designated a UNESCO World Heritage Site in 1987.

For some people, the Great Wall is the main reason for a trip to China; for any visitor to Beijing, it's a must-see. Originally intended to keep foreigners out, the world's most famous wall has become the icon of an increasingly open nation. One of the country's most accessible attractions, the Great Wall promises both breathtaking scenery and cultural illumination. As you explore this snaking structure, often compared to a dragon, try to imagine the monumental task of building such a behemoth, and how imposing it must have appeared from horseback, to a nomadic invader trying to penetrate its near-perfect strategic location. Even for those who have conquered it, the Great Wall still has a way of defying imagination.

HISTORY & MYSTERY

Built by successive dynasties over two millennia, the Great Wall isn't one structure built at one time, but a series of defensive installations that shrank and grew. Especially vulnerable spots were more heavily fortified, while some mountainous regions were left un-walled altogether. The actual length of the wall remains a topic of considerable debate: at its longest, some estimates say the protective cordon spans 6,437 km (4,000 mi)—a distance wider than the United States. Although attacks, age, and pillaging (not to mention today's tourist invasion) have caused the crumbling of up to two-thirds of its length, new sections are being uncovered even today.

As kingdoms scrambled to protect themselves from marauding nomads, portions of wall cropped up, leading to a motley collection of northern borders. It was the first emperor of a unified China, Qin Shi-huang (circa 259–210 BC), founder of the Qin Dynasty, who linked these fortifications into a single network. By some accounts, Qin mustered nearly a million people, or one-fifth of China's workforce, to build this massive barricade, a mobilization that claimed countless lives and gave rise to many tragic folktales.

The Ming Dynasty fortified the wall like never before: for an estimated 5,000 km (3,107 mi), it stood 26 feet tall and 30 feet wide at its base. However, the wall failed to prevent the Manchu invasion that toppled the Ming in 1644. That historical failure hasn't tarnished the Great Wall's image, however. Although China once viewed it as a model of feudal oppression, the Great Wall is now touted as the national symbol. "Love China, Restore the Great Wall," declared Deng Xiaoping in 1984. Since then large sections have been repaired and opened to visitors, turning it also into a symbol of the tension between preservation and restoration in China.

AN ETERNAL WAIT

One legend concerns Lady Meng, whose husband was kidnapped on their wedding night and forced to work on the Great Wall. She traveled to the work site to await his return, believing her determination would bring him back. She waited so long that, in the end, she turned into a rock, which to this day stands at the head of the Great Wall in the beautiful seaside town of Qinhuangdao.

MATERIALS & TECHNIQUES

During the 2nd century BC, the wall was largely composed of packed earth and piled stone.

Some sections, like those in the Taklimakan Desert, were fortified with twigs, sand, and even rice (the jury's still out on whether workers' remains were used, as well).

The more substantial brick-and-mortar ruins that wind across the mountains north of Beijing date from the Ming Dynasty (14th–17th centuries). Some Ming mortar kilns still exist in valleys around Beijing.

YOUR GUIDE TO THE GREAT WALL

As a visitor to Beijing, you simply must set aside a day to visit one of the glorious Great Wall sites just outside the capital. The closest, Badaling, is just an hour from the city's center—in general, the farther you go, the more rugged the terrain. So choose your adventure wisely!

BADALING, the most accessible section of the Great Wall, is where most tours go. This location is rife with Disneylike commercialism, though: from the cable car you'll see both the heavily reconstructed portions of wall and crowds of souvenir stalls.

If you seek the wall less traveled, book a trip to fantastic **MUTIANYU**, which is about the same distance as Badaling from Beijing. You can enjoy much more solitude here, as well as amazing views from the towers and walls.

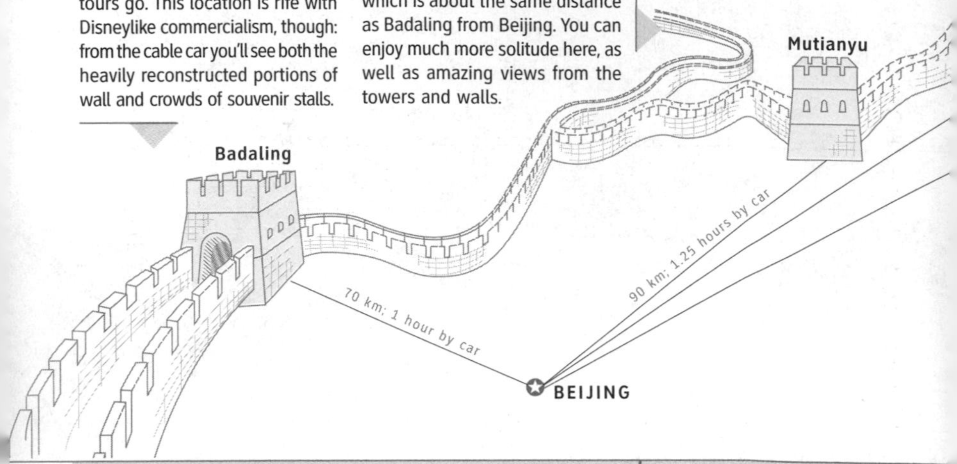

Badaling

Mutianyu

70 km; 1 hour by car

90 km; 1.25 hours by car

BEIJING

TRANSPORTATION

CARS: The easiest and most comfortable way to visit the wall is by private car. Though taxis are occasionally willing to make the trip to more accessible sections like Badaling and Mutianyu, most hotels can arrange a four-passenger car and an English-speaking driver for Y400–Y600 (about 8 hours). Settle details in advance, and remember that it's polite to invite your driver to eat meals with you. To ensure your driver doesn't return to Beijing without you, pay after the trip is over.

TOURS: In addition to the tour buses that gather around Tiananmen Square, most hotels and tour companies offer trips (in comfortable, air-conditioned buses or vans) to Badaling, Mutianyu, Simatai, and Jinshanling. ■ **TIP→-Smaller, private tours are generally more rewarding than large bus trips.** Trips will run between Y100 and Y500 per person, but costs vary depending on the group size, and can sometimes be negotiated. Wherever you're headed, book in advance.

TOUR OPERATORS

OUR TOP PICKS

■ **CITS (China International Tour Service)** runs bus tours to Badaling and private tours to Badaling, Mutianyu, and Simatai. (Y400, Y500, Y600 per person) ✉1 Dongdan Bei DAJIE, Dongcheng District ☎010/6522–2991 🌐www.cits.net

■ **Beijing Service** leads private guided tours by car to Badaling, Mutianyu, and Simatai (Y420–Y560 per person for small groups of 3-4 people). ☎010/5166–7026 ✉travel@beijingservice.com 🌐www.beijingservice.com

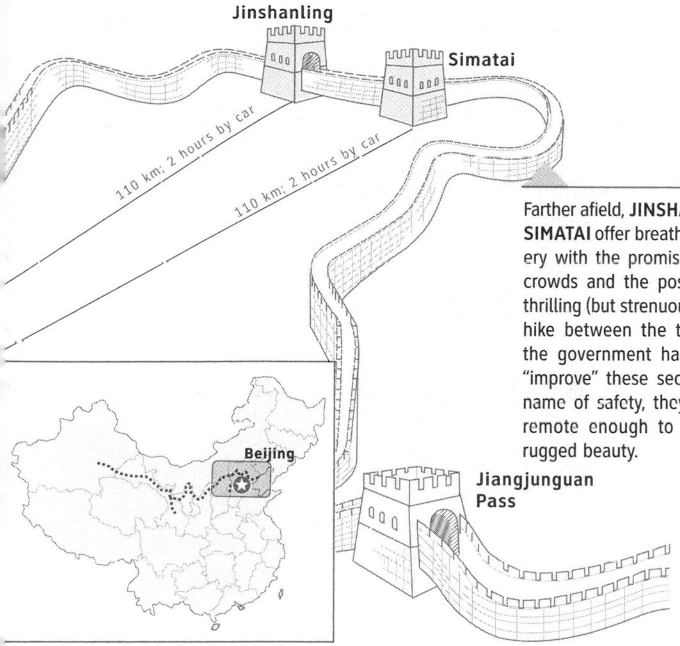

Farther afield, **JINSHANLING** and **SIMATAI** offer breathtaking scenery with the promise of smaller crowds and the possibility of a thrilling (but strenuous) four-hour hike between the two. Though the government has started to "improve" these sections in the name of safety, they're still just remote enough to retain their rugged beauty.

■ **Great Wall Adventure Club** organizes private bus and car trips to Jinshanling–Simatai (Y380–Y650) and Mutianyu (Y160–Y350). ☎138/1154-5162 ✉greatwall@greatwalladventure.com 🌐www.greatwalladventure.com

ADDITIONAL TOURS

■ **Abercrombie & Kent** also offers pricey personalized group tours to the wall. Call for prices. ☎010/6507-7125 🌐www.abercrombiekent.com

■ **Cycle China** runs good guided hiking tours of the unrestored Wall at Jiankou, as well as personalized tours to Simatai and Mutianyu. (Y-50–Y750 for minimum of 5 people). ☎010/6402-5653, 🌐www.cyclechina.com

■ **David Spindler**, a Great Wall expert, runs private tours to various sites. Contact him for prices, schedules, and details through Wild China ☎010/6465-6602 Ext. 314 ✉info@wildchina.com 🌐www.wildchina.com

■ **Dragon Bus Tours**, which picks up at major hotels, has tours to Badaling (with Ming Tombs), Mutianyu, and a bus to Simatai—with an occasional stop at a souvenir factory. (Y280–350; Y350-Y500 for Simatai) ☎010/6515-8565 ✉service@beijinghighlights.com

■ **Gray Line/Panda Tours**, with branches in a dozen high-end hotels in Beijing, runs bus tours to Badaling (and Ming Tombs), Mutianyu, and Simatai—but beware of stops at souvenir factories. (Y280 per person) ✉4 fl., Shuang'an Dashi, 421 Beisanhuan, haidian ☎010/6525-8372 🌐www.pandatourchina.cn

GREAT WALL AT BADALING

GETTING THERE

Distance: 70 km (43 mi) northwest of Beijing, in Yanqing County

Tours: Beijing Service, CITS, Dragon Bus Tours, Gray Line/ Panda Tours

By Car: A car for four people to Badaling should run no more than Y600 for five hours, sometimes including a stop at the Thirteen Ming Tombs.

By Bus: It's hard to wander south of Tiananmen Square without encountering the many buses going to Badaling. Choose wisely: look for the 1 or 5 bus at Qianmen, across from the southeastern corner of Tiananmen Square (departs 6:30 AM–11:30 AM for Y12–Y18 per person).

FAST FACTS

Phone: 010/6912–1383

Hours: Daily 6:30 AM–7 PM

Admission: Y40 Apr.–Nov.; cable car is an additional Y35 one-way, Y50 round-trip

Web Site: www.badaling.gov.cn

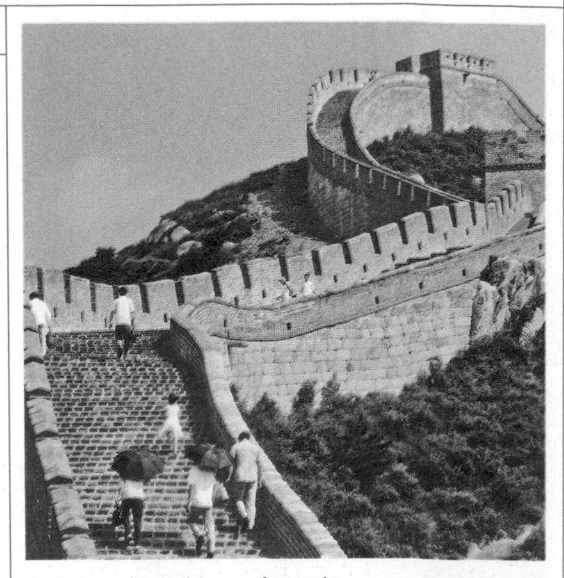

Only one hour by car from downtown Beijing, the Great Wall at Badaling is where visiting dignitaries go for a quick photo-op. Postcard views abound here, with large sections of the restored Ming Dynasty brick wall rising majestically to either side of the fort. In the distance, portions of the early-16th-century Great Wall disintegrate into more romantic but inaccessible ruins.

Badaling is convenient to the Thirteen Ming Tombs and outfitted with tourist-friendly facilities, so it's popular with tour groups and is thus often crowded, especially on weekends. ■ **TIP→ People with disabilities find access to the wall at Badaling better than elsewhere in the Beijing area.** You can either take the cable car to the top, or you can walk up the gently sloping steps, relying on handrails if necessary. On a clear day you can see for miles across leafy, undulating terrain from atop the battlements. The admission price also includes access to the China Great Wall Museum and the Great Wall Circle Vision Theater.

■ **TIP→ Most tours to Badaling will take you to the Thirteen Ming Tombs, as well. If you don't want a stop at the tombs—or at a tourist-trapping jade factory or herbal medicine center along the way—be sure to confirm the itinerary before booking.**

GREAT WALL AT MUTIANYU

GETTING THERE

Distance: 90 km (56 mi) northeast of Beijing, in Huairou County

Tours: CITS, Gray Line/Panda Tours, Great Wall Adventure Tour

By Car: A car to Mutianyu should cost no more than Y600 for the day—it takes about an hour to get there.

By Bus: Take Bus 916/936 from Dongzhimen to Huairou (Y5). From there take a minibus to Mutianyu (Y25–Y30) or hire a taxi to take you there and back to the bus station (about Y50 each way, Y100–Y150 round-trip after bargaining). On weekends and national holidays, the tourist Bus 6 from outside the South Cathedral at Xuanwumen goes directly to Mutianyu (Y50, leaves 6:30–8:30 AM).

FAST FACTS

Phone: 010/6162–6873 or 010/6162–6022

Hours: Daily 7 AM–6:30 PM

Admission: Y40 (students half-price); chairlift, Y35; cable car, Y50 one-way, Y55 with toboggan descent

Fodor's Choice Slightly farther from downtown Beijing than Badaling, the Great Wall at Mutianyu is more spectacular and, despite the occasional annoyances of souvenir stands, significantly less crowded. This long section of wall, first built during the Northern Qi Dynasty (6th century) and restored and rebuilt throughout history, can offer a solitary Great Wall experience, with unforgettable views of towers winding across mountains and woodlands. On a clear day, you'll swear you can see the deserts of Mongolia in the distance.

The lowest point on the wall is a strenuous one-hour climb above the parking lot. As an alternative, you can take a cable car on a breathtaking ride to the highest restored section (this is how President Bill Clinton ascended in 1998), from which several hiking trails descend. Take a gorgeous 1½-hour walk east to reach another cable car that returns to the same parking lot. Mutianyu is also known for its toboggan run.

■TIP→ For those taking a car, the road from Huairou, a suburb of Beijing, to Mutianyu folows a river upstream and is lined with restaurants selling fresh trout. In addition, Hongluo Temple is a short drive from the bottom of the mountain.

GREAT WALL AT SIMATAI

GETTING THERE

Distance: At around 110 km (68 mi) northeast of Beijing, Simatai is farther than Badaling and Mutianyu, but is well worth the trip—the road runs through lovely farmland, and few visitors make the trek.

Tours: Most hotels offer tours here, as do CITS, Gray Line/Panda Tours, and Great Wall Adventure Tour.

By Car: A car to Simatai should be no more than Y800 for the day. If you plan to hike from Jinshanling to Simatai, or vice versa, have your car drop you off at one and pick you up at the other.

By Bus: Take the early-morning Bus 916 from the bus station at Dongzhimen (Y20), starting at 6 AM. On weekends and holidays, a luxury bus leaves Qianmen at 8:30 AM (Y85 round-trip) and leaves Simatai at 3 PM.

FAST FACTS

Phone: 010/6903–5025 or 010/6903–1051

Hours: Daily 8 AM–5 PM

Admission: Y40; cable car, Y30 one-way, Y50 round-trip. If you hike to Jinshanling, you will have to buy another Y5 ticket at the border.

★ Remote and largely unrestored, the Great Wall at Simatai is ideal if you're seeking adventure. Near the frontier garrison at Gubeikou, the wall traverses towering peaks and hangs precariously above cliffs. Be prepared for no-handrails hiking, tough climbs, and unparalleled vistas. Several trails lead to the wall from the parking lot.

In summer, a cable car takes you two-thirds of the way up; from there it's a steep 40-minute climb to the summit. Heading east from the Miyun reservoir at a moderate pace will take you to Wangjing Ta, the 12th watchtower, after about 3 hours. For a longer hike, head west over the bridge toward the restored Jinshanling section.

The hike to Jinshanling is a strenuous 9 km (5.6 mi), usually taking around 4 hours up and down sublime sections of the wall. Be aware that crossing to Jinshanling costs Y5. People who wish to hike from one to the other often ask their driver to wait for them at their destination. (Note that hikers usually go from Jinshanling to Simatai, where buses back to Beijing are easier to find.)

GREAT WALL AT JINSHANLING

GETTING THERE

Distance: 110 km (68 mi) northeast from Beijing

Tours: CITS, Cycle China, Gray Line/Panda Tours, Great Wall Adventure Tour

By Car: A car should be no more than Y800; the ride is about two hours. If you plan to hike from Jinshanling to Simatai, as many do, it makes sense to be dropped off at Jinshanling and have your car pick you up at Simatai.

By Train: Take train L671, which departs at 7:25 AM from Beijing North Railway Station, to Gubeikou; there switch to a local minibus or taxi to Jinshanling.

By Bus: Take a minibus from Dongzhimen long-distance bus station to Miyun (Y8) and then change to a local bus or taxi. Or take a Chengde-bound bus from Dongzhimen and get off at Jinshanling; a cab can bring you to the entrance for Y10.

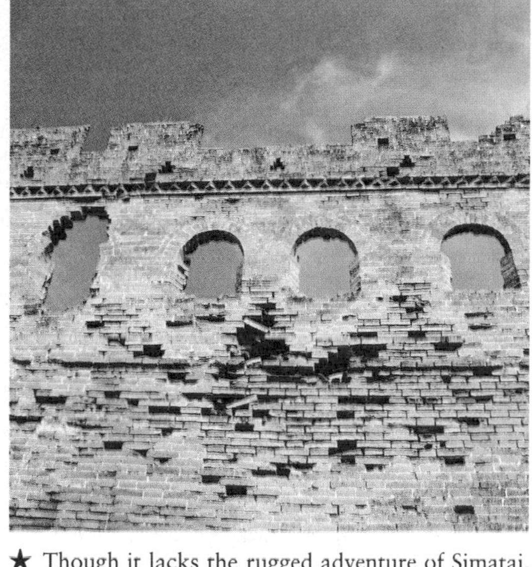

★ Though it lacks the rugged adventure of Simatai, Jinshanling is perhaps the least restored of the major Great Wall sections near Beijing, as well as the least visited. Besides being the starting point for a fantastic four-hour hike to Simatai, Jinshanling also serves as one of the few sections of the Great Wall on which you can camp overnight.

A starry night here is gorgeous and unforgettable—go with a tour group such as Cycle China. Don't forget to pack a piece of charcoal and paper to make rubbings of bricks that still bear the stamp of the date they were made.

FAST FACTS

Phone: 031/1883–0222 or 0138/3144–8986

Hours: Daily 8 AM–5 PM

Admission: Y50; Y50 for overnight stays. If you hike to Simatai, you will have to buy another Y5 ticket at the border.

GREAT WALL MARATHON

Not for the faint of heart, the Great Wall Marathon (and half marathon) takes place each May. The marathon covers approximately 6.5 km (4 mi) of the Great Wall, with the rest of the course running through lovely valleys in rural Tianjin. 🌐 www.great-wall-marathon.com

YESANPO & BEIDAIHE

Yesanpo (150 km [90 mi] northeast of Beijing) is a sleepy village between Beijing and neighboring Hebei province. Go here if you're craving a slower-paced scene and some outdoor fun. The accommodations aren't first class, but there are plenty of great things to do. Leave Beijing from Beijing West Station for the two-hour ride. Traditionally, locals have houses with extra rooms for guests, and owners will strive to make your stay as comfortable as possible. A clean room with two beds and an air-conditioner should run you no more than Y150. There are also a few hotels on the main street by the train station with rooms running approximately Y200. This scenic town is nestled in a valley. The area is best toured on horseback, and horses are available for rent for Y300 per day (with a guide), or Y100 for an hour or so. Yesanpo is also known for its whole barbecued lamb. Train 6095 leaves Beijing West station at 6:20 AM and takes three hours. They return three times daily.

Chairman Mao's and the party's favorite spot for sand, sun, and seafood, **Beidaihe** (250 km [170 mi] northeast of Beijing), is one of China's premier beach resorts (though it's definitely no Bali). This crowded spot is just a 2½-hour train ride from Beijing Station. Nearly every building in town has been converted to a hotel, and every restaurant has tanks of pick-your-own seafood lining the street.

The murals were painted during the time of the European Renaissance, and though the subject matter is traditional, there are comparable experiments in perspective taking place in the depiction of the figures, as compared with examples from earlier dynasties. Also of note is a highly unusual decorative technique; many contours in the hall's murals, particularly on jewelry, armor, and weapons, have been set in bold relief by the application of fine gold threads.

The temple grounds are also beautiful, but of overriding interest are the murals themselves. Visitors stumble through the dark temple with rented flashlights (free with your ticket). Viewing the murals in this way, it's easy to imagine oneself as a sort of modern-day Indiana Jones unraveling a story of the Buddha as depicted in ancient murals of unrivaled beauty. Fahai Temple is only a short taxi ride from Beijing's Pingguoyuan subway station. ✉*Moshikou Lu, take an approximate Y12-taxi ride from Pinguoyuan subway station directly to the temple, Shijingshan District, Beijing* ☎*010/8871–5776* 🎫*Y20* ⏲*Daily 9–4.*

Eunuchs have played an important role throughout Chinese history, often holding great influence over affairs of state, yet surprisingly little is known about them. The **Beijing Eunuch Culture Exhibition Hall** near the magnificent **Tian Yi Mu,** begins to redress this lack of information. Tian Yi (1534–1605) was only nine when he was castrated and sent into the service of the Ming emperor Jiajing. He spent the next 63 years of his life serving three emperors and rose to one of the highest ranks in the land, the Director of Ceremonies. His tomb, though not as magnificent as the Thirteen Ming Tombs, nonetheless befits a man of such high social status. Particularly noteworthy in the tomb complex are the stone carvings around the base of the central mound depicting ancient anecdotes. The four smaller tombs on either side belong to other eunuchs who wished to pay tribute to Tian Yi by being buried in the same compound with him.

The small exhibition hall at the front of the tomb complex contains limited background information, most of it in Chinese, about famous eunuchs. Keep an eye out for the ancient Chinese character meaning "to castrate," which resembles two knives, one inverted, side by side. Also here is a list of all the temples in Beijing that were founded by eunuchs. The hall and tomb are a five-minute walk from Fahai Temple; just ask people the way to Tian Yi Mu. ✉ *80 Moshikou Lu, Shijingshan District, Beijing* ☎ *010/8872–4148* 🎫 *Y8* ⏲ *Daily 9–5.*

JIETAI TEMPLE

★ *35 km (22 mi) west of Beijing.*

On a wooded hill west of Beijing, Jietai Temple is one of China's most famous ancient Buddhist sites. Its four main halls occupy terraces on a gentle slope up to Ma'an Shan (Saddle Hill). Originally built in AD 622, it's been used for the ordination of Buddhist novices since the Liao dynasty. The temple complex expanded over the centuries and grew to its current scale in a major renovation conducted by devotees during the Qing Dynasty (1644–1912). The temple buildings, plus three magnificent bronze Buddhas in the Mahavira Hall, date from this period. There is also a huge, potbellied Maitreya Buddha carved from the roots of what must have been a truly enormous tree. To the right of this hall, just above twin pagodas, is the Ordination Terrace, a platform built of white marble and topped with a massive bronze Sakyamuni (Buddha) seated on a lotus flower. Tranquil courtyards, where ornate stelae and well-kept gardens bask beneath the Scholar Tree and other ancient pines, add to the temple's beauty. Many modern devotees from Beijing visit the temple on weekends. ✉ *Mentougou County* ☎ *010/6980–6611* 🎫 *Y35* ⏲ *Daily 8–4:30.*

EN ROUTE

Farther along the road past Jietai Temple, **Tanzhe Temple** is a Buddhist complex nestled in a grove of *zhe* (cudrania) trees. Established around AD 400 and once home to more than 500 monks, Tanzhe was heavily damaged during the Cultural Revolution; it has since been restored, but if you look closely at some of the huge stone tablets, or *bei*, littered around the site you'll see that many of the inscriptions have been destroyed. The complex makes an ideal side trip from Jietai Temple or Marco Polo Bridge. ✉ *10 km (6 mi) northeast of Jietai Temple, 45 km (28 mi) west of Beijing, Mentougou County* ☎ *010/6086–2500* 🎫 *Y35* ⏲ *Daily 8–4:30.*

MARCO POLO BRIDGE

16 km (10 mi) southwest of Beijing's Guanganmen Gate.

Built in 1192 and reconstructed after severe flooding during the Qing Dynasty, this impressive span—known as Marco Polo Bridge because it was praised by the Italian wayfarer—is Beijing's oldest bridge. Its 11 segmented stone arches cross the Yongding River on what was once the imperial highway that linked Beijing with central China. The bridge's marble balustrades support nearly 485 carved stone lions that decorate elaborate handrails. Note the giant stone slabs that comprise the bridge's original roadbed. Carved imperial stelae at either end of the span commemorate the bridge and surrounding scenery.

The Marco Polo Bridge is best remembered in modern times as the spot where invading Japanese armies clashed with Chinese soldiers on June 7, 1937. The assault began Japan's brutal eight-year occupation of eastern China, which ended with Tokyo's surrender at the end of World War II. The bridge has become a popular field-trip destination for Beijing students. On the Beijing side of the span is the **Memorial Hall of the War of Resistance Against Japan.** Below the bridge on the opposite shore, local entrepreneurs rent horses (the asking price is Y120 per hour, but you should bargain) and lead tours of the often-dry grassy riverbed. ✉*Near Xidaokou, Fengtai District, Beijing* ☎*010/8389–3919* 🎫*Free* ⏲*Daily 8:30–6.*

ZHOUKOUDIAN PEKING MAN SITE

48 km (30 mi) southwest of Beijing.

This area of lime mines and craggy foothills ranks among the world's great paleontological sites (and served as the setting for Amy Tan's *The Bonesetter's Daughter*). In 1929 anthropologists, drawn to Zhoukoudian by apparently human "dragon bones" found in a Beijing apothecary, unearthed a complete cranium and other fossils dubbed homo erectus pekinensis, or Peking Man. These early remains, believed to be nearly 700,000 years old, suggest (as do similar *Homo erectus* discoveries in Indonesia) that humankind's most recent ancestor originated in Asia, not Europe (though today some scientists posit that humans evolved in Africa first and migrated to Asia). A large-scale excavation in the early 1930s further unearthed six skullcaps and other hominid remains, stone tools, evidence of fire, plus a multitude of animal bones, many at the bottom of a large sinkhole believed to be a trap for woolly rhinos and other large game. Sadly, the Peking Man fossils disappeared under mysterious circumstances during World War II, leaving researchers only plaster casts to contemplate. Subsequent digs at Zhoukoudian have yielded nothing equivalent to Peking Man, although archaeologists haven't yet abandoned the search. Trails lead to several hillside excavation sites. A small museum showcases a few (dusty) Peking Man statues, a collection of Paleolithic artifacts, two mummies, and some fine animal fossils, including a bear skeleton and a saber-toothed tiger skull. Because of the importance of Peking Man and the potential for other finds in the area, Zhoukoudian is a UNESCO World Heritage Site, but it may not be of much interest to those without a particular inclination for the subject. If you should find yourself here with little to do after your museum visit and the few dig locations, consider a little hike into the surrounding hills, which are named the Dragon Bone Mountains. ✉ *Zhoukoudian* ☎ *010/6930–1272* 🎫 *Y30* ⏲ *Daily 8:30–4:30.*

YUNJU TEMPLE

75 km (47 mi) southwest of Beijing.

Yunju Temple is best known for its mind-boggling collection of 14,278 minutely carved Buddhist tablets. To protect the Buddhist canon from destruction by Taoist emperors, the devout Tang-era monk Jing Wan carved Buddhist scriptures into stone slabs that he hid in sealed caves in the cliffs of a mountain. Jing Wan spent 30 years creating these tablets until his death in AD 637; his disciples continued his work for the next millennium into the 17th century, thereby compiling one of the most extensive Buddhist libraries in the world. A small pagoda at the center of the temple complex commemorates the remarkable monk. Although the tablets were originally stored inside Shijing Mountain behind the temple, they are now housed in rooms built along the temple's southern perimeter.

Four central prayer halls, arranged along the hillside above the main gate, contain impressive Ming-era bronze Buddhas. The last in this row, the Dabei Hall, displays the spectacular *Thousand-Arm Avalokiteshvara*. This 13-foot-tall bronze sculpture—which actually has 24 arms and five heads and stands in a giant lotus flower—is believed to embody boundless compassion. A group of pagodas, led by the 98-foot-tall Northern Pagoda, is all that remains of the original Tang complex. These pagodas are remarkable for their Buddhist reliefs and ornamental patterns. Heavily damaged during the Japanese occupation and again by Maoist radicals in the 1960s, the temple complex remains under renovation. ✉ *Off Fangshan Lu, Nanshangle Xiang, Fangshan County* ☎ *010/6138–9612* 🎫 *Y40* ⏲ *Daily 8:30–5 summer, 8:30–4:30 winter.*

EASTERN QING TOMBS

Fodor's Choice ★

125 km (78 mi) east of Beijing.

Modeled on the Thirteen Ming Tombs, the Eastern Qing Tombs replicate the Ming spirit ways, walled tomb complexes, and subterranean burial chambers. But they're even more extravagant in their scale and grandeur, and far less touristy. The ruins contain the remains of five emperors, 14 empresses, and 136 imperial concubines, all laid to rest in a broad valley chosen by Emperor Shunzhi (1638–61) while on a hunting expedition. By the Qing's collapse in 1911, the tomb complex covered some 46 square km (18 square mi) of farmland and forested hillside, making it the most expansive burial ground in all China.

The Eastern Qing Tombs are in much better repair than their older Ming counterparts. Although several of the tomb complexes have undergone extensive renovation, none is overdone. Peeling paint, grassy courtyards, and numerous stone bridges and pathways convey a sense of the area's original grandeur. Often, visitors are so few that you may feel as if you've stumbled upon an ancient ruin unknown beyond the valley's farming villages.

Of the nine tombs open to the public, two are not to be missed. The first is **Yuling,** the resting place of the Qing Dynasty's most powerful sovereign, Emperor Qianlong (1711–99), who ruled China for 59 years. Beyond the outer courtyards, Qianlong's burial chamber is accessible from inside Stela Hall, where an entry tunnel descends some 20 meters (65 feet) into the ground and ends at the first of three elaborately carved marble gates. Beyond, exquisite carvings of Buddhist images and sutras rendered in Tibetan adorn the tomb's walls and ceiling. Qianlong was laid to rest, along with his empress and two concubines, in the third and final marble vault, amid priceless offerings looted by warlords early in the 20th century.

Dingdongling was built for the infamous Empress Dowager Cixi (1835–1908). Known for her failure to halt Western-imperialist encroachment, Cixi once spent funds allotted to strengthen China's navy on a traditional stone boat for the lake at the Summer Palace. Her burial compound, reputed to have cost 72 tons of silver, is the most elaborate (if not the largest) at the Eastern Qing Tombs. Many of its stone carvings are considered significant because the phoenix, which symbolized the female, is level with, or even above, the imperial (male) dragon—a feature, ordered, no doubt, by the empress herself. A peripheral hall paneled in gold leaf displays some of the luxuries amassed by Cixi and her entourage, including embroidered gowns, jewelry, imported cigarettes, and even a coat for one of her dogs. In a bow to tourist kitsch, the compound's main hall contains a wax statue of Cixi sitting Buddha-like on a lotus petal flanked by a chambermaid and a eunuch.

The Eastern Qing Tombs are a two- to three-hour drive from the capital. The rural scenery is dramatic, and the trip is one of the best full-day excursions outside Beijing. Consider bringing a bed sheet, a bottle of wine, and boxed lunches, as the grounds are ideal for a picnic. ✉ *Near Malanguan, Hebei province, Zunhua County* ☎ *0315/694–5348* 🎫 *Y120* 🕒 *Daily 8–5 summer, 8:30–4:30 winter.*

ENGLISH	PINYIN	CHINESE
EXPLORING		
Ancient Observatory		
Beihai Park	Běihǎi gōngyuán	北海公园
Bell Tower	Zhōng lóu	钟楼
Chaoyang District	Cháoyáng qū	朝阳区
Chongweng District	Chóngwén qū	崇文区
Confucius Temple	Kǒngmiào	孔庙
Ditan Park (Altar of the Earth)	Dìtán gōngyuán	地坛公园
Dongcheng District	Dōngchéng qū	东城区
Donghuamen Night Market	Dōnghuāmén yèshì	东华门夜市
Drum Tower	Gǔlóu	鼓楼
Forbidden City	Gùgōng	故宫
Great Hall of the People	Rénmín dàhuìtáng	人民大会堂
Haidian District	Hǎidiàn qū	海淀区
Houhai (Back Lake)	Hòuhǎi	后海
Jingshan Park (Coal Hill)	Jǐngshān gōngyuán	景山公园
Lama Temple	Yōnghégōng	雍和宫
Liulichang	Liúlíchǎng	琉璃厂
Mao Zedong Memorial Hall	Máozhǔxí jìniàntáng	毛主席纪念堂
Ming City Wall Ruins Park	Míng chéngqiáng yízhǐ gōngyuán	明城墙遗址公园
Monument to the People's Heroes	Rénmínīngxíong ǐnìanbēi	人民英雄纪念碑
Museum of Antique Currency	Gǔdàiqiánbì bówùguǎn	古代钱币博物馆
Nanhai (south lake)	Nánhǎi	南海
Old Summer Palace	uánmíngyuán	圆明园
Ox Street Mosque	Niújiē qīngzhēnsì	牛街清真寺
Prince Gong's Palace	Gōngwángfǔ	恭王府
Qianhai (Front Lake)	Qiánhǎi	前海
Silver Ingot Bridge	Yíndìng qiáo	银锭桥
Soong Ching-ling's Former Residence	Sòng Qìnglíng qùjū	宋庆龄故居
Source of Law Temple	Fǎyuánsì	法源寺
Summer Palace	Yíhéyuán	颐和园
Taxi	chū zū chē	出租车
Temple of Heaven	Tiāntán	天坛
Tian'anmen Square	Tiānānmén guǎngchǎng	天安门广场

ENGLISH	PINYIN	CHINESE
Wangfujing	Wángfǔjǐng	王府井
Worker's Stadium	Gōngrén tǐyùcháng	工人体育场
Xiangshan Park (Fragrant Hills)	Xiāngshān gōngyuán	香山公园
Xicheng District	Xīchéng qū	西城区
Xidan (Shopping Area)	Xīdān	西单
Xuanwu District	Xuānwǔ qū	宣武区
WHERE TO EAT		
Aria	Ālìyǎ	阿郦雅
Assaggi	Chángshì	尝试
Baijia Dayuan	Báijiā dà zháimén	白家大宅门
Bellagio	Lùgǎng xiǎo zhèn	鹿港小镇
The Bookworm	Shūchóng	书虫
Café de la Poste	Yúnyóu yì	云游驿
Comptoirs de France Bakery	Fǎpài	法派
Ding Ding Xiang	Dǐngdǐngxiāng	鼎鼎香
Din Tai Fung	Dǐngtàifēng	鼎泰丰
La Dolce Vita	Tiánmìshēnghuó	甜蜜生活
Fangshan	Fǎngshàn	仿膳
La Galerie	Zhōngguó yìyuàn	中国艺苑
Gaon	Gāoēn	高恩
Gui Gongfu	Guìgōngfǔ	桂公府
Hai Wan Ju	Hǎiwǎnjū	海碗居
Han Cang	Háncāng	汉仓
Huang Ting	Huángting	凰庭
Jing	Jīng	京
Jun Wangfu	Jūnwángfǔ	君王府
Kong Yi Ji	Kǒngyǐjǐ	孔乙己
Lai Jin Yu Xuan	Láijīn yǔxuān	来今雨轩
Li Qun Roast Duck Restaurant	Lìqún kǎoyādiàn	利群烤鸭店
Makye Ame	Mǎjíāmǐ	玛吉阿米
Mei Fu	Méi fǔ	梅府
Noodle Bar	Miàn bā	面吧
Old Beijing Noodle King	lǎo Běijīng zhájiàngmiàn dàwáng	老北京炸酱面大王
Paomo Guan	pào mó guǎn	泡馍馆
Paulaner Brauhaus	Pǔlānà píjiǔ fāng cāntīng	普 拉那啤酒坊餐厅
Qin Tangfu	Tíntáng fǔ	秦唐府

ENGLISH	PINYIN	CHINESE
The Red Capital Club	Xīnhóngzī jùlèbù	新红资俱乐部
Shaguo Ju	Shāguō jū	沙锅居
Shin Yeh	Xīnyè	欣叶
South Silk Road	Chámăgŭdào	茶马古道
The Source	Dōujiāngyuán	都江源
Still Thoughts Vegetarian Restaurant	Jìngsī sùshí fāng	静思素食坊
Taj Pavilion	Tàijī lóu	泰姬楼
Three Guizhou Men	Sāngeguìzhōurén	三个贵州人
Whampoa Club	Huángpŭ huì	黄埔会
Yotsuba	Sìyè	四叶
Yue Bin Restuarant	Yuèbīn fànguăn	悦宾饭馆
Yuxiang Renjia	Yúxiāngrénjiā	渝乡人家
Zhang Qun Jia	Zhāngqúnjiā	张群家
WHERE TO STAY		
Banqiao No. 4	Bănqiáo sì hào	板桥4号
Côté Cour S.L	Péngyuàn sìhé bīnguăn	朋院四合宾馆
Courtyard Beijing	Běijīng Wànyí jiŭdiàn	北京万怡酒店
Crowne Plaza Beijing	Běijīng guójì yìyuàn	北京国际艺苑
The Emperor	Huángjīa yìzhàn	皇家驿栈
Friendship Hotel	Yŏuyì bīnguăn	友谊宾馆
Gloria Plaza Hotel	Běijīng Kăilái dà jiŭdiàn	北京凯莱大酒店
Grand Hyatt	Běijīng Dōngfāngjūnyuè jiŭdiàn	北京东方君悦酒店
Hotel G	Běijīng jí zhàn	北京极栈
Hotel Kapok	Mùmiánhuā jiŭdiàn	木棉花酒店
Jianguo Hotel	Jiànguó fàndiàn	建国饭店
Jinglun Hotel	Jīnglún fàndiàn	京伦饭店
Kempinski	Kăibīnsījī fàndiàn	凯宾斯基饭店
Kerry Centre Hotel	Běijīng Jiālĭ zhōngxīn fàndiàn	北京嘉里中心饭店
Kunlun Hotel	Běijīng Kūnlún fàndiàn	北京昆仑饭店
Legendale	Lìjùn jiŭdiàn	励骏酒店
LüSongyuan	Lŭsōngyuán bīnguăn	侣松园宾馆
Park Hyatt Beijing	Běijīng Bòyuè jiŭdiàn	北京柏悦酒店
Peninsula Beijing	Wángfŭ Bàndăo jiŭdiàn	王府半岛酒店
Raffles Beijing Hotel	Běijīng fàndiàn Láifóshì	北京饭店莱佛士
Red Capital Residence	Xīnhóngzī kèzhàn	新红资客栈

ENGLISH	PINYIN	CHINESE
Ritz-Carlton Financial Street	Běijīng Jīnróng jiē Lìsīkǎ'ěrdùn jiǔdiàn	北京金融街丽思卡尔顿酒店
Shangri-La Hotel	Běijīng Xiānggélǐlā fàndiàn	北京香格里拉饭店
Sino-Swiss Hotel	Běijīng Guódū dàfàndiàn	北京国都大饭店
St. Regis	Běijīng guójì jùlèbù fàndiàn	北京国际俱乐部饭店
Swissôtel	gǎngao zhōngxīn Ruìshì jiǔdiàn	港澳中心瑞士酒店
Traders Hotel	Guómào fàndiàn	国贸饭店
Zhaolong International	Zhàolóng qīngnián lǚshè	兆龙青年旅
Zhuyuan Hotel	Zhúyuán bīnguǎn	竹园宾馆
ARTS & NIGHTLIFE		
Bainaohui Computer Shopping Mall	Baìnaǒhuìdiànnaǒ guǎngchǎng	百脑会电脑广场
Beijing Concert Hall	Běijīng yīnyuètīng	北京音乐厅
Beijing Exhibition Theater	Běijīng zhǎnlǎnguǎn jùchǎng	北京展览馆剧场
Centro	Xuànkù	炫酷
Chaoyang Theater	Cháoyáng jùchǎng	朝阳剧场
China National Puppet Theater	Zhōngguó guójiā mùǒujùyuà	中国国家木偶剧院
The Courtyard Gallery	Sìheyuàn huàláng	四合院画廊
The Den	Dūnhuáng	敦煌
Drum and Bell	Gǔzhōng kāfēiguǎn	鼓钟咖啡馆
East Shore Live Jazz Café	Dōng'àn kāfēi	东岸咖啡
Face	Fēi sè	飞色
Forbidden City Concert Hall	Zhōngshān gōngyuán yīnyuètáng	中山公园音乐堂
i-Ultra Lounge (Block 8)	8 Hào gōngguǎn	8号公馆
MAO Live House	Guāngmáng	光芒
National Centre for Performing Arts	Guójiā dàjùyuàn	国家大剧院
No Name Bar (Bai Feng's)	Wúmíng jiǔbā	无名酒吧
Red Gate Gallery at the Watch Tower	Hóngmén huàláng	红门画廊
The Red Theatre	Hóng jùchǎng	红剧场
Saddle Cantina	Mòxīgē cāntīng	墨西哥餐厅
Song	Sòng	颂
Stone Boat	Shífǎng	石舫
The Tree	Yǐnbìdeshù	隐蔽的树
The World of Suzie Wong	Sūxīhuáng jùlèbù	苏西黄俱乐部
Yugong Yishan	Yúgōngyíshān	愚公移山

ENGLISH	PINYIN	CHINESE
SHOPPING		
Beijing Curio City	Beǐjīng gǔwán chéng	北京古玩城
Beijing Friendship Store	Yoǔyì shāngdiàn	北京友谊商店
Beijing Yuanlong Silk Corporation	(Yuánlóng) cìxiù	刺绣
The Bookworm	Shūchóng	书虫
China Star Silk Store	Míngxīng zhōngshì fúzhuāngdiàn	明星中式服装店
China World Shopping Mall	Zhōngguó guójì maòyì zhōngxīn	中国国际贸易中心
Daxin Textiles Co.	Dàxīn fǎngzhī	大新纺织
Foreign Langauges Bookstore	Waìwén shūdiàn	外文书店
Heyan'er	Héyán fúzhuāng diàn	何燕服装店
Hongqiao Market	Hóngqiaó shìchǎng	红桥市场
Lufthansa Youyi Shopping Center	Yānshā Yoǔyì shāngchéng	燕莎友谊商城
Malls at Oriental Plaza	Dōngfāng guǎngchǎng	东方广场购物中心
Panjiayuan Antique Market	Pānjiāyuán shìchǎng	潘家园市场
The Red Phoenix	Hóngfènghuáng fúzhuāng	红凤凰服装工作室
Ritan Office Building Market	Rìtán shāngwù loú	日坛商务楼
Shard Box Store	Shèndégé	慎 德阁
Silk Alley Market	Xiùshuǐ shìchǎng	秀水市场
Tianshang Studio	Tiānshang gōngzuòshì	添裳工作室
Tongrentang	Tóngréntáng	同仁堂
Treasure House	Baǒyuèzāi	宝月斋
Wonderful Electronic Shopping Mall	Lándaǒ dàshà	蓝岛大厦
Yaxiu Market	Yǎxiù shìchǎng	雅秀市场
Zhaojia Chaowai Antique Market	Zhaòjiā Cháowài gǔdiǎnjiājù shìchǎng	赵家朝外古典家具市场
SIDE TRIPS		
Beidaihe	Běidàihé	北戴河
Eastern Qing Tombs	Qīngdōnglíng	清东陵
Fahai Temple	Fǎhǎi sì	法海寺
The Great Wall	Chángchéng	长城
Jietai Temple	Jiètái sì	戒台寺
Marco Polo Bridge	Lúgōu qiáo	卢沟桥
Tanzhe Temple	Tánzhè sì	潭哲寺
Thirteen Ming Tombs	Míng Shísānlíng	明十三陵
Tianjin	Tiānjīn	天津

ENGLISH	PINYIN	CHINESE
Yesanpo	Yěsān pō	野三坡
Yunju Temple	Yúnjū sì	云居寺
Zhaoling tomb	Zhāo líng	昭陵
Zhoukoudian Peking Man Site	Zhōukǒudiàn Běijīngrén xiànchǎng	周口店北京人现场

Beijing to Shanghai

HEBEI, SHANDONG, JIANGSU & ANHUI

Working the land in the Jiangxi province.

WORD OF MOUTH

"One of the highlights of my China trip was a visit to the Yellow Mountain (Huangshan). I went there in October. . . . Huangshan is the most beautiful mountain I've seen."

—kim_Lee

WELCOME TO BEIJING TO SHANGHAI

Delicately carved ornaments on the roof of the Bailin Zen Buddhist Temple in Shijiazhuang, Hebei.

TOP REASONS TO GO

★ **Qingdao:** Life's a beach in China's premier seaside city. Enjoy some of the country's best seafood and wash it down with Tsingtao beer, the local brew. Stroll around the well-preserved architecture from the days when the Germans were in charge.

★ **Huangshan:** Yellow Mountain's towering granite peaks overlooking rice paddies and green fields have been a place of pilgrimage for centuries.

★ **Chengde:** Originally a summer retreat for an emperor, this town's magnificent temples, parks, and palaces now attract weekenders hunting for culture.

★ **Suzhou:** Classical gardens and a network of crisscrossing canals run throughout the moated city.

★ **Tongli:** A fine example of a town built on water, Tongli is a wonderful place to wander around. Quaint side streets and alleyways open onto canals and bridges.

1 Anhui. It may be one of China's poorest provinces, but it's rich in sublime mountain scenery at Huangshan. The peaks are a sacred site in China; ascend the photogenic summit to understand why.

2 Hebei. Wrapped around the nation's capital, Hebei's attractions are definitely worth a side trip. Chengde is home to an impressive display of imperial architecture, and in warm weather, the seaside resorts of Beidaihe and Shanhaiguan become playgrounds for middle-class Chinese.

3 Jiangsu. Brimming with history, Jiangsu's attractions include stately monuments, memorials to horrific massacres, ancient peaks, and elegant gardens. Nanjing was the country's capital for six dynastic periods. Nearby Suzhou is renowned for its splendid gardens.

Altar inside imperial mausoleum, Nanjing Jiangsu.

The winding paths up Huangshan are sometime treacherous but always spectacular.

4 Shandong. Take a pilgrimage to Taishan, the most revered of all China's sacred mountains, or Qufu, the birthplace of Confucius. For the more earthly pleasures of sun, beer, and Bavarian architecture, don't miss the oceanside city of Qingdao, China's windsurfing (and drinking) capital.

GETTING ORIENTED

Stretching from Hebei, which is culturally and geographically Northern China, to the more refined province of Jiangsu, Eastern China is accessible thanks to a well-developed tourist infrastructure. All four provinces have air and rail links to the major transport hubs of Beijing and Shanghai. As you travel from north to south, you'll have a chance to judge for yourself if Chinese stereotypes are accurate: Northerners are viewed as typically taller with light skin, and are thought to be very fond of wheat-based foods like noodles and bread. Southerners, on the other hand, are thought of as shorter and darker, and rice is their staple. This vague cultural border lies somewhere between Beijing and Shanghai.

BEIJING TO SHANGHAI PLANNER

When to Go

No matter the month, there's great weather in some part of this region. In spring and summer, head to the coast at Qingdao and farther north, Beidaihe and Shanåhaiguan. Save the arduous ascents up Huangshan and Taishan for autumn, when the crowds and temperatures have died down.

Traveling a country of 1.3 billion is difficult is when the 1.3 billion are also on vacation. The eastern region of China is heavily populated, and during the two weeklong public holiday periods, it seems like everyone takes to the road (or train, or plane).

Avoid traveling during the Chinese New Year, which is based on the lunar calendar and usually falls at the end of January. The weeklong National Day holiday at the start of October can easily be avoided with a bit of planning.

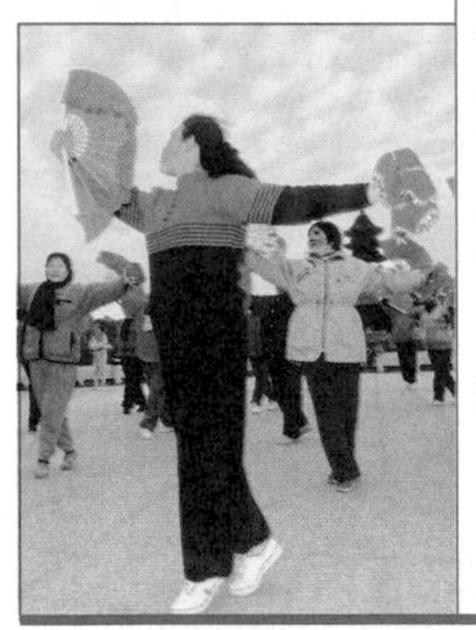

World Heritage Sites

It's not surprising that a country that counts its history in millennia would also have 33 UNESCO World Heritage sites—and seven of them in this region alone.

The newest additions are the two traditional villages of Xidi and Hongcun in Anhui. UNESCO states that they "preserve to a remarkable extent the appearance of nonurban settlements of a type that largely disappeared or was transformed during the last century."

In Jiangsu, UNESCO has acknowledged Suzhou for its nine classical gardens. Farther north, another site that blends harmoniously into nature is Chengde's Mountain Resort's vast complex of palaces, temples, and imperial gardens.

In addition to Taishan, Shandong Province has the temple, cemetery, and family mansion of Confucius in Qufu on the UNESCO list. The Qufu complex of monuments has managed to retain its outstanding artistic and historic character.

What to Buy

For centuries, buyers from around the world lusted after the luxury fabrics produced in Suzhou. Silk-spinning worms were in such high demand that to take one abroad was punishable by death. The Suzhou Arts and Crafts Museum exhibits some of the most accomplished silk embroideries you'll find in China. Another place to stop by is the Suzhou Silk Museum Shop.

The mountain vistas at Huangshan and Taishan have inspired artists for centuries. Painters flock here, and the most serious of them camp out for weeks at a time. A lot of the best artwork goes to Shanghai or Beijing, but good works are available in Tunxi near Huangshan or Tai'an, the gateway to Taishan.

Nanjing is a convenient place to pick up traditional crafts from Jiangsu, including teapots, carvings, flowing silks, folk paper cuttings, and copies of the lavish embroidered robes once worn by emperors.

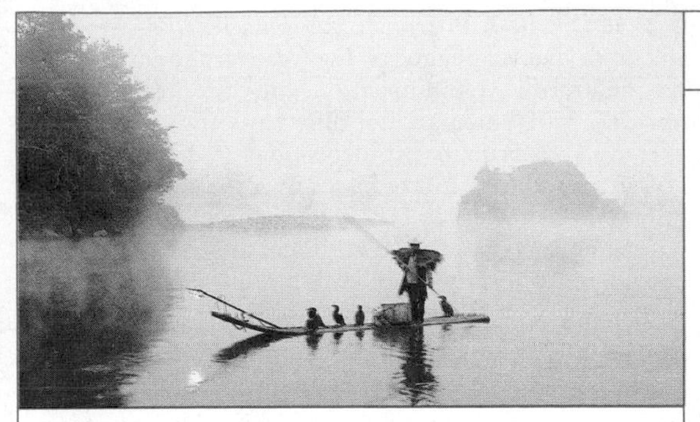

Getting Here and Around

Air Travel. Besides the major international airports in Beijing and Shanghai, other domestic air hubs include Nanjing, Qingdao, and Shijiazhuang. Distances between sights are not long in this region.

Bus Travel. With even more destinations and departures than the rail system, buses can be essential for trips of less than 4 or 5 hours. Buses vary wildly in terms of quality and comfort, but sometimes there's just no other option.

Train Travel. China's excellent rail system is probably your best bet for getting around this region. The distances aren't quite long enough for air travel, and trains offer a greater variety of departure times and destinations. Tickets can be purchased either through your hotel or at the stations, although the lines are long and vendors can be curt with non-Chinese speakers.

DINING AND LODGING PRICE CATEGORIES IN YUAN				
¢				
Restaurants				
under Y25	Y25–Y49	Y50–Y99	Y100–Y165	over Y165
Hotels				
under Y700	Y700–Y1,099	Y1,100–Y1,399	Y1,400–Y1,800	over Y1,800

Restaurant prices are for a main course, excluding tax and tips. Hotel prices are for a standard double room, including taxes.

Food Facts

Every locality has ita own specialties—wild game such as deer and hare in Chengdu, or Qufu's Confucius-family-style cuisine, a drawn-out banquet featuring dishes that have been refined over 2,000 years.

Dishes in and around Shanghai emphasize fresh ingredients, aroma, and tenderness. Shallots and garlic are frequently used so don't expect subtlety. In the coastal haven of Qingdao, seafood is the catch of the day.

Jiangsu cuisine, also called Huaiyang cuisine, is popular along the lower reaches of the Yangtze River. Fish and crustaceans are the main ingredients, and the food is light, fresh, and slightly sweet.

Inland in Anhui, food is famously salty, relying heavily on preserved ham and soy sauce to enhance flavors. Try *Bagongshan doufu jiao,* a dish of minced pork wrapped in tofu or *qingceng bing,* which means thousand-layer pancakes. They're made of ham, eggs, and spring onions.

If you're not a meat eater, don't miss the vegetarian options in or near any Buddhist temple. Chefs manipulate tofu, wheat gluten, and vegetables to create interpretations of meat that even a voracious carnivore will appreciate.

Updated by Michael Manning

WITH DIZZYING SPEED, CHINA IS transforming itself. A visit today is completely unlike one five years ago, or five years from now. With modern transportation, reliable communication, and comfortable lodgings, the eastern provinces of China are not difficult to travel through. However, modernization has brought problems. In cities like Nanjing, the air quality is often so bad that a haze hangs over the city. With car traffic increasing, crossing streets has become a game of chance. But this entire region is the epicenter of the New China, the epitome of the Old China, and is as exciting as anywhere in the country.

At the same time, the area's history persists in solemn tombs, monuments, and elegant gardens. This is where Confucius was born, and where the Great Wall meets the sea. Described by Marco Polo as the noblest city in the world, Hangzhou is famous for West Lake, which has long inspired poets, painters, and other artists. The largest artificial waterway in the world, the Grand Canal, extends from Beijing to Hangzhou. Nearby Suzhou is famous for its many well-preserved gardens. Classic scenery is also at Huangshan, one of China's traditional Five Famous Mountains, in Anhui province. The mountain's peaks rise from the mist and have inspired whole schools of Chinese painting.

HEBEI

Many visitors travel through Hebei without a backward glance on the way to and from the capital, but the province has several sites worth a detour. Chengde is a must for history buffs and fans of the outdoors. The town's glory days were during the 18th century when the Emperor Kangxi made the town his summer retreat and hunting ground, filling the place with a palace and temples. The emperors may be long gone, but the town still serves as a holiday destination, now for busloads of Beijing residents. Farther south, the seaside resorts of Beidaihe and Shanhaiguan, where the Great Wall meets the sea, give foreign visitors the rare opportunity to mingle with Chinese vacationers.

CHENGDE

4 hrs (230 km [140 mi]) by train northeast of Beijing; 7 hrs (470 km [291 mi]) by train southwest of Shenyang.

An increasingly common stop on the China tour circuit, some visitors regard Chengde as one of the highlights of their trip. With the Wulie River running through the town and the Yanshan Mountains serving as an impressive backdrop, Chengde is filled with magnificent examples of imperial architecture that make it well worth the journey.

Chengde was just another village until the Qing Dynasty emperor Kangxi stumbled upon it during a hunting trip. Now it is a UNESCO World Heritage site, home to one of the largest intact imperial gardens in China, the magnificent Mountain Resort, and the Eight Outer Monasteries. Although children enjoy romping through the imperial gardens,

Beijing to Shanghai
INNER MONGOLIA
INNER MONGOLIA
Chengde
see detail map
Great Wall
Jining
LIAONING
Liaodong Bay
Start of the Great Wall
BEIJING
Changping
BEIJING
Shanhaiguan
Beidaihe
Tangshan
Tianjin
TIANJIN
Dalian
Baoding
Bohai Bay
Korea Bay
HEBEI
Hejian
Cangzhou
Shijiazhuang
Hengshui
SHANXI
Yantai
Weihai
Laizhou Bay
Dezhou
River
Laiyang
Xingtai
Ru Shan
Ji'nan
Zibo
Weifang
Handan
Liaocheng
Mt. Tai
Ti'an
Qingdao
see detail map
SHANDONG
Yellow
Qufu
Rizhaoshi
Jining
Xinxiang
Heze
Linyi
Haizhou Bay
Yellow Sea
Zhengzhou
Kaifeng
Lianyungang
Shangqiu
Xuzhou
HENAN
Qingjiang
JIANGSU
Bengbu
Yangzhou
Nanjing
see detail map
Nantong
Hefei
Changzhou
Wuxi
Shanghai
Lake Tai
Dabie Mountain
ANHUI
SHANGHAI
HUBEI
River
Suzhou
see detail map
Wangpan Bay
Wuhan
Yangtzi
Hangzhou
0
100 mi
0
100 km
Huangshan
ZHEJIANG
Tunxi
JIANGXI

there's little else to entertain younger visitors. It's best to visit in summer or early autumn, as some tourist facilities close in the off-season.

GETTING HERE AND AROUND

Most tourists arrive on the N211 direct train, which departs Beijing West Rail Station at 6:30 AM. About an hour outside of Beijing, look out the window for a glimpse of the Great Wall.

There are also buses every 20 minutes from Beijing's Dongzhimen bus station.

BY AIR Chengde's tiny airport is set for an upgrade that will connect the city with other popular tourist destinations around China. Until then, your best bet is to fly into Beijing; Qinhuangdao's airport is slightly closer, but it's difficult to find flights to or from most other destinations.

BY BUS Long-distance buses are uncomfortable and slow, but they're the only transport linking Chengde with Beidaihe and Shanhaiguan via Qinhuangdao. Several daily buses make this trip, all departing from Chengde's long-distance bus station near the Shenghua Hotel. Buses to Beijing also depart from this station.

BY TAXI Chengde is a small city, so you shouldn't have to pay more than Y10 to get anywhere in town.

BY TRAIN Chengde is on a northern rail line between Beijing and Shenyang. The journey takes 4½ hours from the capital. No trains run between Chengde and Beidaihe or Shanhaiguan.

TOURS

All hotels in Chengde run tours covering the main sites, at least during the high season. An English-speaking guide costs around Y100. Chengde's branch of the China International Travel Service (CITS) charges about Y300 to hire a car with an English-speaking guide/driver for the day.

ESSENTIALS

Air Contacts **Qinhuangdao Airport Ticket Office** (✉ *169 Yingbin Lu, Qinhuangdao* ☎ *0335/306–2579*).

Bus Contacts **Chengde Long-Distance Station** (✉ *Wulie Lu at Xinhua Lu* ☎ *0314/212–3588*).

Medical Assistance **Chengde Chinese-Western Hospital** (✉ *12 Xi Da Jie* ☎ *0314/202–2222*).

Train Contacts **Chengde Train Station** (✉ *Chezhan Lu*).

Visitor and Tour Info **Chengde CITS** (✉ *11 Zhonghua Lu* ☎ *0314/202–7483*).

EXPLORING CHENGDE

It isn't worth spending much time wandering around the city, but the massive size of the Mountain Resort, twice as large as Beijing's Summer Palace, means you will be doing plenty of walking. The other monasteries are close to the city.

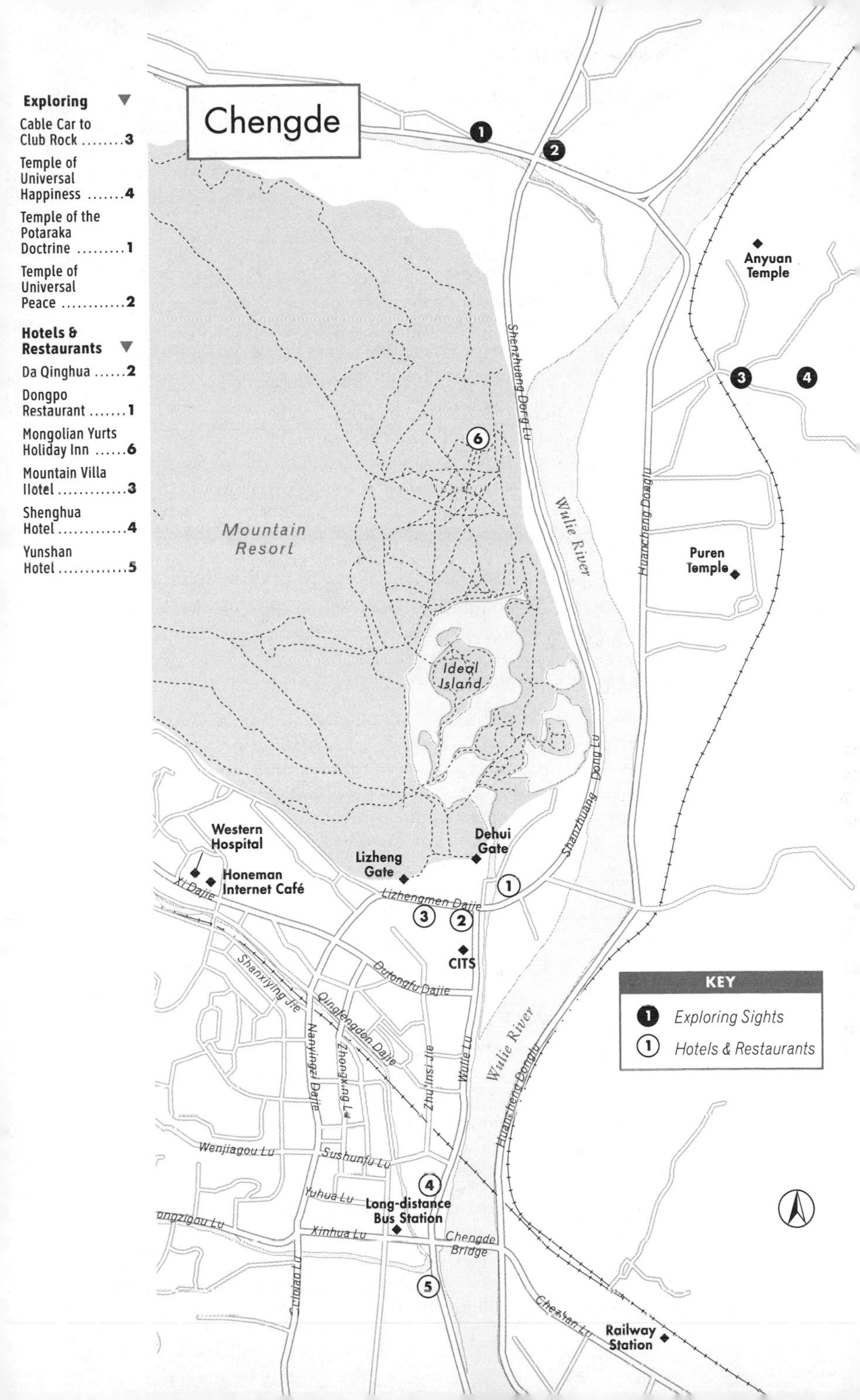

Chengde
Exploring
Cable Car to Club Rock 3
Temple of Universal Happiness 4
Temple of the Potaraka Doctrine 1
Temple of Universal Peace 2
Hotels & Restaurants
Da Qinghua 2
Dongpo Restaurant 1
Mongolian Yurts Holiday Inn 6
Mountain Villa Hotel 3
Shenghua Hotel 4
Yunshan Hotel 5
Mountain Resort
Ideal Island
Shenzhueng Dong Lu
Wulie River
Huancheng Donglu
Anyuan Temple
Puren Temple
Shanzhuang Dong Lu
Western Hospital
Honeman Internet Café
Xi Dajie
Lizheng Gate
Dehui Gate
Lizhengmen Dajie
CITS
Dutongfu Dajie
Shanxiying Jie
Qingfengdon Dajie
Nanyingzi Dajie
Zhongxing Lu
Zhu'insi Jie
Wulie Lu
Wulie River
Huancheng Donglu
Wenjiagou Lu
Sushunfu Lu
Yuhua Lu
Long-distance Bus Station
Xinhua Lu
Chengde Bridge
Chezhan Lu
Railway Station
KEY
Exploring Sights
Hotels & Restaurants

MAIN ATTRACTIONS

Fodor'sChoice ★ At the **Mountain Resort** *(Bishu Shanzhuang)*, Emperor Kangxi ordered construction of the first palaces in 1703. Within a decade, dozens of ornate temples, pagodas, and spectacular gardens were spread over 1,500 acres. By the end of the 18th century, nearly 100 imperial structures filled the town.

Besides luxurious quarters for the emperor and his court, great palaces and temples were completed to house visiting dignitaries and to impress them with the grandeur of the Chinese empire. Its interconnected palaces, in different architectural styles, reflect China's diversity. Replicas of famous temples representing China's religions stand on hillsides surrounding the palace as though paying homage to the court.

Numerous buildings remain; some have been restored but many have grass coming up through the cracks. Only eight of the temples are open for visitors (two of the originals were demolished, and another two are dilapidated). Some rooms have been lovingly restored and display period furniture, ornaments, and costumed mannequins frozen in time. The surrounding landscape of lakes, grassy meadows, and cool forests is lovely for a stroll. Mountains in the northern half of the park and a giant pagoda in the center afford panoramas of the city of Chengde to the south and the temples to the north and east. The Mountain Resort and the temples are so big that even with a massive influx of summer tourists they don't feel crowded. ✉ *Center of town* ☎ *0314/202–5918* 🎫 *Summer, Y90; winter, Y60* ⏲ *Daily 7* AM*–6* PM.

Viewing Chengde's **Eight Outer Monasteries** from above, it looks as though Emperor Kangxi built a Disneyland for China's religions. Originally there were a dozen temples, and each was built to reflect the architectural styles of a different minority group. The Eight Outer Monasteries are grouped on the eastern and northern slopes of the Mountain Resort in two different sections near the Wulie River. The eastern temples of Anyuan, Pule, and Puren can be reached by bus number 10 from the Mountain Resort, and the northern temples of Putuozongcheng, Xumifushou, Puning Si, Puyou, and Shuxiang can be reached by taking bus number 6 from the same place. Only Puning Si is still in use by monks. ✉ *North of the Imperial Summer Villa* 🎫 *Y20–Y50* ⏲ *Daily 8–6.*

❷ On the western bank of the Wulie River, the **Temple of Universal Peace** (*Puning Si* ✉ *Puning Si Lu* 🎫 *Summer, Y50; winter, Y40* ⏲ *Daily 8–6*) is an interesting blend of traditional Chinese temple and Buddhist monastery. The fascinating compound is well worth a visit, particularly to see the awe-inspiring 72-foot tall statue of Guanyin, a Buddhist deity of compassion, the tallest wooden statue in the world. The temple was built in 1755 during the reign of Emperor Qianlong and modeled on the Samye Temple, the earliest Buddhist monastery in Tibet.

❶ The **Temple of the Potaraka Doctrine** (*Putuozongcheng Miao* ✉ *Shizhigou Lu* 🎫 *Summer, Y40; winter, Y30* ⏲ *Daily 8–6*) is modeled on the Potala Monastery in Lhasa, which is why it is known as the Little Potala. The temple, started in 1767, is the largest of the eight surviving temples in Chengde. Inside the imposing gate is a pavilion housing three stelae, the largest one inscribed in Han, Manchu, Mongolian, and Tibetan languages.

> **WORD OF MOUTH**
>
> "The outer temples, especially Xumifushou and the Potala (which are within walking distance of each other), are really excellent. There are several casual eating places under an awning in front of the Potala that are good for lunch."
>
> —someotherguy

4 The **Temple of Universal Happiness** (*Pule Si* ⊠ *East of Mountain Resort* *Summer, Y30; winter, Y20* *Daily 8–6*) was built in 1766 when the imagery of Tibetan and Mongol Buddhism played an important role in the political and cultural arenas, especially in court circles. The architecture of the main building, the Pavilion of the Brilliance of the Rising Sun (Xuguangge) is similar to Beijing's Temple of Heaven. Look for the high, square, boxlike ceilings with a wooden Tibetan-style mandala motif. On top of the building's outer walls were eight brilliantly painted pagodas supported by lotus flower stands, only one of which remains. The lotus traditionally represents purity and is a common motif in Buddhist temples.

IF YOU HAVE TIME

A cable car and a hiking trail lead up to **Club Rock** *(Bangchui Feng)*, a phallic protrusion that spawned a local legend: if the rock should fall, so will the virility of local men. *Y25* *Daily 8–6.*

WHERE TO EAT

Given Chengde's role as a royal hunting ground, it's no surprise that the local specialty is wild game. Venison, rabbit, and pheasant are prepared at many restaurants. The town is also known for its medicinal beverages. Try almond juice if you suffer from asthma, or date juice for stomach problems.

¢–$ CHINESE — ✕ **Da Qinghua.** Overlooking Lizheng Gate, this cheerful place with a rustic wooden exterior is a good choice if you want to sample local dishes. Try the specialty: homemade dumplings filled with pheasant and local mushrooms. The picture menu helps—the staff does not speak English. To find it, look for the dragons on the building's exterior. ⊠ *19 Lizhengmen Da Jie* ☎ *0314/202–3611* *No credit cards.*

$–$$ SICHUAN — ✕ **Dongpo Restaurant.** With one branch near Dehui Gate (east of Lizheng Gate) and two others around town, Dongpo serves hearty Sichuan fare. There's no English menu, but classics like *gongbao jiding* (chicken with peanuts) and *niurou chao tudou* (beef and potatoes) are available. ⊠ *Shanzhuang Dong Lu* ☎ *0314/210–6315* *No credit cards.*

WHERE TO STAY

¢ — **Mongolian Yurts Holiday Inn.** This hotel (no relation to the chain) is made up of 30 yurts. They may not be the type used by Genghis Khan—they are made of concrete—but they can sleep two or three people and have modern touches like television sets. Located inside the Mountain Resort, this makes for a peaceful and unusual stay. The restaurant continues the Mongolian theme so expect plenty of mutton on the menu. **Pros:** great location, quiet, it's a yurt. **Cons:** it's a yurt. ⊠ *Inside the*

Mountain Resort ☎*0314/216–3094* *30 yurts* *In-room: no a/c. In-hotel: restaurant* *No credit cards* *Closed Nov.–Mar.*

¢–$ **Mountain Villa Hotel.** This hotel has perhaps the best location in town: opposite the main gate of the Mountain Resort. The reception area is impressive, if a little gaudy, with a massive chandelier hanging overhead. Some of the guest rooms are beginning to look a little tired, so ask to see a few before you decide. The cheerful staff and a full array of services make this an excellent choice if you're making a quick visit. **Pros:** excellent location. **Cons:** could use a renovation. ✉*11 Lizhengmen,* ☎*0314/209–1188* *390 rooms, 10 suites* *In-room: safe. In-hotel: 6 restaurants, bar, gym, bicycles* *AE, DC, MC, V.*

¢–$$ **Shenghua Hotel.** A tower of glass and steel, the city's newest luxury hotel soars 14 stories. Although the reception areas are dark, the rooms have plenty of windows. An excellent restaurant serves local specialties such as lightly battered stir-fried venison. The bilingual tour operator on staff can help you plan tours of the region. **Pros:** reliable services, near bus and train stations. **Cons:** a bit far from Mountain Resort and monasteries. ✉*22 Wulie Lu* ☎*0314/227–1000* *www.shenghuahotel.com* *111 rooms* *In-room: safe, refrigerator, dial-up. In-hotel: 3 restaurants, bar, gym, concierge, laundry service* *AE, DC, MC, V.*

¢ **Yunshan Hotel.** Despite a facade that resembles a waffle, the Yunshan Hotel has a pleasing interior design. An octagonal lobby capped with a massive skylight leads to nicely furnished guest rooms. Two restaurants—one serving Chinese food, the other Western food—make this a reliable choice. A few English speakers at the tour desk can help arrange tours. **Pros:** decent restaurants, spacious rooms for price. **Cons:** located away from attractions. ✉*2 Banbishan Lu* ☎*0314/205–5588* *230 rooms* *In-room: safe. In-hotel: 2 restaurants, bar, gym, spa* *AE, DC, MC, V.*

NIGHTLIFE AND THE ARTS

Puning Song and Dance (✉*Temple of Universal Peace, Puning Si Lu* ☎*0314/216–2007*) has an hour-long show that is a little touristy, but it's a great way to see the Temple of Universal Peace lighted up at night. The Y150 admission includes transport to and from your hotel.

BEIDAIHE

4 hrs (260 km [160 mi]) by express train east of Beijing; 5 hrs (395 km [245 mi]) by train southwest of Shenyang; 1 hr (35 km [22 mi]) by minibus southwest of Shanhaiguan.

English railway engineers came across this small fishing village in the 1890s. Not long after, wealthy Chinese and foreign diplomats were visiting in droves. After Mao Zedong came to power, the new rulers developed a taste for sea air. Today the seaside retreat has an interesting mix of beach kitsch and political posturing (watch out for the rousing propaganda posters along the beachfront). Beidaihe is terrifyingly crowded during the summer and practically empty the rest of the year.

GETTING HERE AND AROUND

Most visitors come directly from Beijing, and the train is the most convenient option. There are nine double-decker tourist trains each day, and the journey takes about three hours. The train station in Beidaihe is not in the center of town. If you arrive late at night, taxi drivers may try to charge exorbitant rates.

BY AIR The nearest airport is 5 km (3 mi) away at Qinhuangdao, with infrequent flights to Dalian, Nanjing, Shanghai, Taiyuan, and Yantai.

BY BOAT AND FERRY Qinhuangdao is one of the biggest harbors in China. Destinations include Dalian (14 hours), Shanghai (28 hours), Qingdao (12 hours), and Tianjin (18 hours). Contact CITS in Qinhuangdao for prices and schedules.

BY BUS An excellent minibus service runs between Beidaihe, Qinhuangdao, and Shanhaiguan. Buses leave every 30 minutes, cost Y6, and make frequent stops. The bus station in Beidaihe is at the intersection of Heishi Lu and Haining Lu. Buy tickets on the bus.

BY TRAIN Trains traveling up the coast from Beijing all pass through Beidaihe, Shanhaiguan, and Qinhuangdao.

ESSENTIALS

Air Contacts **Qinhuangdao Airport** (✉ *169 Yingbin Lu, Qinhuangdao* ☎ *0335/306–2579*).

Boat and Ferry Contacts **Qinhuangdao CITS** (✉ *100 Heping Dajie, Qinhuangdao* ☎ *0335/323–1117*). **Qinhuangdao Tourism Bureau** (✉ *11 Gangcheng Dajie, Qinhuangdao* ☎ *0335/366–1001*).

Bus Contacts **Beidaihe Station** (✉ *Beining Lu and Haining Lu* ☎ *0335/418–3077*).

Medical Assistance If you are ill in Beidaihe, go to Qinhuangdao—it has superior medical facilities. **Qinhuangdao Hospital** (✉ *281 Hebei Lu, Qinhuangdao* ☎ *0335/404–1695*).

Train Contacts **Beidaihe Train Station** (✉ *Chezhan Lu*).

Visitor and Tour Info The closest tourism center is in Qinhuangdao. **Qinhuangdao CITS** (✉ *100 Heping Dajie, Qinhuangdao* ☎ *0335/323–1117*). **Qinhuangdao Tourism Bureau** (✉ *11 Gangcheng Dajie, Qinhuangdao* ☎ *0335/366–1001*).

EXPLORING BEIDAIHE

The best way to get around on a sunny day is to rent a bicycle and cruise up and down the seafront.

Emperor Qin Shi Huang's Palace *(Qinhuang Gong)* is a 20th-century replica built in homage to the first Qin Dynasty emperor's visit to Beidaihe. Rooms here contain mannequins in period costumes, impressive weapons, and embroideries. ✉ *Near Shan Zhuang* 💴 *Y30* ⏲ *Daily 8–5.*

North of the middle beach is **Lianfeng Hill Park** *(Lianfengshan Gongyuan)*, where quiet paths through a pine forest lead to the **Guanyin Temple** (Guanyin Si). Look for the aviary, known as the Birds Singing Forest. There are also good views of the sea from the top of Lianfeng Hill. ✉ *West* *side of town* ☎*0335/404–1591* *Y25* ⏲*Daily 8–5.*

WHERE TO STAY AND EAT

In summer, seafood restaurants line the beach, and you only need to point at the most appetizing thing squirming in red buckets for the waiter to serve up a delicious fresh meal. A plateful of fresh mussels should cost about Y15, fresh crabs a little more. More good seafood restaurants are clustered on Haining Lu near the beach.

> **BIKING**
>
> Bikes are available from the **Beidaihe Guesthouse for Diplomatic Missions** (✉*1 Baosan Lu* ☎*0335/428–0000*). It costs about Y30 for half a day and you will need to leave either a deposit of around Y200.

¢–$$ ECLECTIC **Kiesslings.** Opened by Austrians six decades ago, this is the town's only foreign-owned restaurant. It serves both Chinese and Western dishes, but is best known for its tasty baked goods at breakfast. Its decor is a little old-fashioned, but that is part of its charm. The restaurant is usually open from May through September, but call ahead to make sure. ✉*Dongjing Lu, behind Beidaihe Guesthouse for Diplomatic Missions* ☎*0335/404–1043* *No credit cards.*

$ **Beidaihe Guesthouse for Diplomatic Missions** *(Beidaihe Waijiao Renyuan Binguan)*. Catering to foreign visitors, the guesthouse has several staff members who speak English remarkably well. Reflecting its past as a lodging for Russian diplomats, it has a building reserved for "distinguished guests." The attractive complex, made up of low-slung buildings from the 1960s, is set among cypresses and pines in a peaceful spot overlooking its own private beach. Rates for more expensive rooms include breakfast. **Pros:** the classic Beidaihe experience. **Cons:** some older buildings could use renovation. ✉*1 Baosan Lu* ☎*0335/428–0000* *153 rooms, 12 suites* *In-hotel: restaurant, bar, tennis court, gym, beachfront, laundry service* *AE, DC, MC, V* ⏲*Closed Nov.–Mar.*

¢ **Jinshan Hotel.** On a quiet stretch of sand, this hotel is made up of five two-story buildings linked by tree-lined paths. The rooms are clean and comfortable, although they are beginning to show their age. One of the town's branches of the China International Travel Service (CITS) is on the premises. Stay here in summer, as few of the facilities are open low season. **Pros:** on the beach. **Cons:** some rooms are worn. ✉*4 Dongsan Lu,* ☎*0335/404–1338* *267 rooms* *In-hotel: 2 restaurants, bar, gym* *AE, DC, MC, V.*

SHANHAIGUAN

1 hr (35 km [22 mi]) by minibus northeast of Beidaihe; 5 hrs (280 km [174 mi]) by minibus east of Beijing; 5 hrs (360 km [223 mi]) southwest of Shenyang.

On the northern tip of the Bohai Coast, Shanhaiguan is the end of the road for the Great Wall. This is where the eastern end of the massive structure plunges into the sea. During the Ming Dynasty, Shanhaiguan was fortified to prevent hordes of mounted Manchurian warriors from pushing to the south. Now local tourists swarm the town during the summer. An impressive wall still surrounds the old town, though the warriors on the battlements are now mannequins.

GETTING HERE AND AROUND

Some trains from Beijing to Beidaihe continue on to Shanhaiguan, but they are the slower trains and take around 5 hours. To save time, catch a train to the nearby town of Qinhuangdao, about 3 hours from Beijing. From Qinhuangdao, take a bus or a taxi to Shanghaiguan.

BY AIR The nearest airport is in the industrial city of Qinhuangdao.

BY BUS An excellent minibus service runs from Shanhaiguan to Beidaihe and Qinhuangdao. Buses leave every 30 minutes, cost Y6, and make frequent stops. The bus station in Beidaihe is at the intersection of Heishi Lu and Haining Lu. Buy tickets on the bus.

BY TAXI The half-hour taxi ride between Beidaihe and Shanhaiguan costs about Y80.

BY TRAIN Shanhaiguan has the fewest of trains, so it's worth booking a ticket to Qinhuangdao and then catching a bus to Shanhaiguan.

ESSENTIALS

Air Contacts **Qinhuangdao Airport** (✉ *169 Yingbin Lu, Qinhuangdao* ☎ *0335/306–2579*).

Boat and Ferry Contacts **Qinhuangdao CITS** (✉ *100 Heping Dajie, Qinhuangdao* ☎ *0335/323–1117*). **Qinhuangdao Tourism Bureau** (✉ *11 Gangcheng Dajie, Qinhuangdao* ☎ *0335/366–1001*).

Bus Contacts **Shanhaiguan Station** (✉ *Xinkai Xi Lu* ☎ *0335/502–3879*).

Medical Assistance **Qinhuangdao Hospital** (✉ *281 Hebei Lu, Qinhuangdao* ☎ *0335/404–1695*).

Train Contacts **Shanhaiguan Train Station** (✉ *Off Nanguan Da Jie*).

EXPLORING SHANHAIGUAN

MAIN ATTEACTIONS

The **First Gate Under Heaven** *(Tianxiadiyiguan)* is the city's eastern portal. Walking along the top (you have to pay an extra Y2, but it's worth it), you can gaze down at the fortifications and imagine how intimidating they must have been to potential invaders. Not that it worked forever: the Manchus overran the city in 1644. Through binoculars, you can see remaining sections of the Great Wall snaking up nearby mountains. ✉ *East side of the city* 🎫 *Y40, includes admission to Great Wall Museum* ⏲ *Daily 8:30–8.*

The **Great Wall Museum** *(Changcheng Bowuguan)*, housed in a Qing Dynasty–style building past the First Gate Under Heaven, has a diverting collection of historic photographs and cases full of military artifacts, including the fierce-looking weaponry used by attackers and defenders. There are some English captions, but they are not everywhere. ✉ *South of First Gate Under Heaven* 🎫 *Y40, includes admission to First Gate Under Heaven* ⏲ *Daily 7–4.*

One way to leave behind the crowds at Old Dragon Head is to climb the wall as it climbs **Jiao Mountain** *(Jiao Shan)*, about 4 km (2½ mi) from the city. The beginning of the section has been retrofitted with handrails and ladders up the sides of watchtowers, but you can keep climbing until you reach the "real" wall. On a clear day, the view makes it worth the effort. There is no public transportation, but Jiao Shan is only a 10-minute taxi ride from Shanhaiguan. *Y15, Y20 for cable car Daily 8–5.*

Legend has it that the Great Wall once extended into the Bohai Sea, ending with a giant carved dragon head. The structure that today is called **Old Dragon Head** *(Lao Long Tou)* has been totally rebuilt. It's still a dramatic sight, with the Great Wall jutting out into the sea with waves smashing at its base. On the beach there are motorboats that will take you out to snap a few photos. Some Ming Dynasty naval barracks have also been re-created, and you can dress up in imperial costumes and pretend you're a naval officer. *Y50 Daily 8–5.*

IF YOU HAVE TIME

About 8 km (5 mi) down the coast from Old Dragon Head is **Mengjiangnu Miao,** a shrine commemorating a local legend. As the story goes, a woman's husband died while building the Great Wall. She wept as she searched for his body, and in sympathy the Wall split open before her, revealing the bones of her husband and others buried within. Overcome with grief, she threw herself into the sea. The temple has statues of the woman, a symbol of wifely dedication. The shrine is a 10-minute taxi ride northeast of town. *Y30 Daily 7–4.*

WHERE TO STAY AND EAT

¢–$ CHINESE **Wang Yan Lou.** Probably the most upmarket option in town, Wang Yan Lou serves excellent local seafood. Don't be put off by the bland exterior or the plastic tablecloths—the food is better than appearances would suggest. The menu is only in Chinese. *Guancheng Xi Lu No phone No credit cards.*

¢ **First Pass Hotel.** Built to resemble a mansion from the time of the Qing Dynasty, this hotel is one of the best in Shanhaiguan. The owners have put a great deal of effort into the common areas, with ornate woodwork on the balconies and colorful lanterns lighting the corridors at night, but the guest rooms are basic. The restaurant, in one of the many courtyards, serves standard northern Chinese cuisine, so expect dumplings for breakfast and noodles for lunch. **Pros:** the best option in a town without many options. **Cons:** rooms not as nice as lobby. *1 Dong Da Jie 0335/513–2188 120 rooms In-room: no TV. In-hotel: restaurant, laundry service No credit cards.*

¢ **North Street Hotel.** Inside the city wall, this family-run lodging is a great deal as long as you don't expect too many comforts. Clean but shabby rooms are clustered around a pretty courtyard. The place may be a little noisy if the hotel is full. Still, the hotel has a lot more atmosphere than many nearby establishments. **Pros:** inexpensive. **Cons:** worn rooms and fixtures. *2 Mujia Hutong 0335/505–1680 64 rooms In-room: no phone, no TV No credit cards.*

CLOSE UP

Extreme Climbs on the Great Wall

If you want to walk around the Great Wall, but avoid the hordes of tourists, persistent postcard sellers, and Kentucky Fried Chicken outlets, then Huanghua is your best bet.

Huanghua is a rugged, unrestored part of the wall about 37 mi (60 km) from Beijing. Here the wall lies in two sections, almost 7 mi (11 km) long. A reservoir divides the two parts and local fishermen are always at work among the parapets and beacon towers.

In summer, the whole area is buried in swathes of yellow flowers (*huang hua*). In winter, the sections can be icy and too dangerous to climb.

A SENSE OF HISTORY

According to legend, the Ming Dynasty general who oversaw construction spared no expense. He ended up being beheaded for going over budget. But thanks to his thoroughness, you feel as if you're walking through the past as you huff up those steep inclines. There is almost no rebuilt brickwork here (aside from an initial walkway that allows you to safely ascend onto the wall). Be aware that the natural weathering of the bricks makes the climb a little precarious. This reason alone keeps the tour buses away, so it's a worthwhile trade-off.

THE COST

Not long ago, the main danger at Huanghua wasn't the crumbling bricks or sheer drops, but the locals keen to extort an entrance fee from visitors. They sometimes carried pitchforks and other sharp implements for added incentive. The government stamped that practice out, and now everyone must pay a flat rate of Y25.

GETTING THERE

Despite being only 37 mi (60 km) from Beijing, there are no direct public transportation options. However, it does not take much effort to reach Huanghua. From Beijing's Dongzhimen long-distance bus station, catch Bus 916 to Huairou, which leaves every 20 minutes from 5:30 AM to 6:30 PM. If the traffic is awful, this can take up to 3 hours; at the minimum it takes about 70 minutes. When you arrive at the transit station, taxi drivers will find you before you even get off the bus, all keen to take you on the remaining 30-minute journey to the wall. If you are an avid bargainer, you can hire a taxi for Y40 per car.

Another option is to hire a car for the day to take you to Huanghua from Beijing: expect to pay at least Y400. You can approach any taxi driver or ask your hotel to help arrange this.

SHANDONG

More than 93 million people call Shandong home, and an annual influx of domestic tourists considerably adds to that number. Most flock to this region for Qingdao, China's most attractive coastal city and best known for its beer (known in the West as Tsingtao) and Bavarian architecture, the well-preserved town of Qufu, home of the philosopher Confucius, and Mount Tai, the most revered of all China's sacred mountains.

REGIONAL TOURS

Qingdao CITS can organize tours around Shandong as well as within the Qingdao area. Shandong Rainbow International Tours can help you choose a tour in Shandong or other parts of China. They can also take care of arrangements for independent travel.

Tour Contacts **Qingdao China International Travel Service** (*6F, A Yuyuan Building, 73 Hong Kong Xi Lu, Qingdao* *0532/8386–3960* *www.citsqd.net/en*). **Shandong Rainbow International Tours** (*22 Yanerdao Lu, Rm 2404, Qingdao* *0532/8607–6607* *www.tourinchina.cn/english*).

JI'NAN

3 to 4½ hrs (500 km [220 mi]) by train south of Beijing; 3–4 hrs (395 km [245 mi]) by train west of Qingdao.

It may be Shandong's provincial capital, but Ji'nan is overshadowed in almost every way by its coastal rival, Qingdao. However, this modern and easygoing place is an enjoyable transit point to other destinations. A good place to stay if you are going to visit the nearby Qufu, Taishan, or Qingdao, Ji'nan can be enjoyed in its own right, particularly for its many springs, which have earned the city the nickname Spring City.

In 1901, Ji'nan was hauled into the 20th century by the construction of a railway line linking it to Qingdao. German, English, and Japanese companies found Ji'nan to be a convenient place to do business. A few buildings they had built are still in the downtown area (although they are increasingly overshadowed by new shopping centers and hotels).

Ji'nan's three main sites are Thousand Buddha Mountain, Big Bright Lake, and Gushing from the Ground Spring. These and a handful of other attractions easily occupy visitors for a day or so.

GETTING HERE AND AROUND

Your best option to travel from Beijing is to catch one of the four daily D-coded express trains, the first of which leaves the Beijing South Train Station at 8:20 AM and the last of which departs at 7:25 PM. The trip take just a little more than three hours. A first-class ticket costs Y183, and second class is Y153. There are buses, but the journey can take more than 7 hours.

BY AIR Regular flights link Ji'nan Yaoqiang Airport with Beijing, Shanghai, Hong Kong, and other major Chinese cities. The airport is 40 km (25 mi) northeast of downtown Ji'nan. The journey takes 45 minutes in a taxi and costs around Y100.

BY BUS Regular buses link Ji'nan with Mount Tai's nearest city, Tai'an (1 hour), and Qufu (3 hours). Buses ply the route between Ji'nan and Qingdao every 20 minutes, taking 4 to 5 hours.

BY TRAIN Ji'nan is on the Beijing–Shanghai line and the Beijing–Qingdao line, so there is no shortage of trains. On an express train, the journey from the capital takes between 3 and 4½ hours. Tai'an, the city nearest Mount Tai, is also on the Beijing–Shanghai rail line.

ESSENTIALS

Air Contacts **Ji'nan Yaoqiang Airport** (*Near Yaoqiang Village 0531/96888*).

Bus Contacts **Ji'nan Long-Distance Bus Station** (*23 Jiluo Lu 0531/96369*). **Tai'an Bus Station** (*139 Dongyue Dajie, opposite the train station 0538/833–2938*). **Qufu Bus Station** (*Shen Dao Lu and Jingxuan Lu 0537/441–1241*).

Medical Assistance **Shengli Hospital** (*324 Jingwu Lu 0531/793–8911*).

Train Contacts **Ji'nan Station** (*Jingyi Jie 0531/8601–2520*). **Tai'an Station** (*Yingzhe Dajie 0538/210–8600*).

Visitor and Tour Info **Ji'nan CITS** (*6th fl., Building 30, 1 Jiefang Lu 0531/8292–7071*). **Ji'nan Tourist Service** (*86 Jingshi Lu 800/420–8858 www.travelshandong.us*).

EXPLORING JI'NAN

Ji'nan's downtown area is relatively compact, with the Hucheng River looping through its center. Thousand Buddha Mountain overlooks the city from the southeast. The grid of streets south of the main railway station, which bear the most European influence, are worth walking by foot. The rest of the sites are best reached via taxi.

Legends about **Big Bright Lake** *(Daming Hu)* have been around for nearly 1,500 years. Water from springs fill the lake, which in turn empties into the Gulf of Bohai. Small temples surround the large lake, making it a great place for a stroll. *Daming Hu Lu www.daminglake.com/english Y30 Daily 6:30–6.*

Gushing from the Ground Spring *(Baotu Quan)*. Ji'nan's nickname is the City of Springs because of the more than 100 natural springs that once dotted the landscape. Many have since dried up, but Baotu Quan is still flowing, making the adjacent park attractive and lush. The water is said to be ideal for making tea; try it out at the Wangheting Teahouse, just east of the spring. *Quancheng Lu Y40 Daily 7–9.*

One interesting architectural legacy of the foreign occupation is an imposing redbrick **Protestant Church,** with its landmark twin towers. Built in 1927, it is still in use. *425 Jing Si Lu.*

NEED A BREAK?

Shandong Elite Teahouse (*9 Qianfoshan Lu*) makes for a lovely break any time of day. The teahouse serves many varieties of tea at polished wooden tables. The exquisite traditional Chinese teahouse setting is decorated with lattice wooden paneling, vases, and musical instruments.

On the southern outskirts of the city is **Thousand Buddha Mountain** *(Qianfoshan)*, one of the country's most sacred religious sites. It was called Mt. Li in ancient times. In the early days of Sui Dynasty many statues were chiseled into the rock, and it became known as Thousand Buddha Mountain. It is still the focus of religious festivals, although most of the statues have been lost to the ravages of time and the Cultural Revolution. If visiting in March or September, look out for the park's temple fairs. Getting to the top of the mountain requires a 30-minute climb or a ride on the cable car (Y25 round-trip). Either way you'll be rewarded with a good view of Ji'nan—air quality permitting. For your child, there's an excellent slide to whiz you back to the bottom. ✉ *18 Jing Shiyi Lu, off Qianfoshan Lu* *Y30* *Daily 6 AM–6 PM.*

WHERE TO EAT

¢–$ CHINESE **Foshan Yuan.** Near Thousand Buddha Mountain is this excellent restaurant specializing in vegetarian recreations of traditional dishes. Try the crispy duck or the three-cup chicken and you'll be amazed at how perfectly the kitchen captures the flavors of the original dishes. Whatever you order, make sure to sample the very tasty spicy carrot dumplings. There is—unusual for these parts—an English menu. The restaurant closes at 9 PM, when the staff prepares food for homeless people. ✉ *Foshan Yuan Jie* ☎ *0531/8602–7566* *No credit cards.*

¢–$ SHANGHAINESE **Jiu Wan Ban.** On a street filled with 24-hour joints, this cheerful place is the one locals rate as the best. You choose from pre-plated platters of fresh local fish, which are then cooked as you watch. Try the seafood version *xiaolongbao,* the little dumplings that are a specialty of Shanghai. ✉ *18 Chaoshan Jie* ☎ *0531/8612–7228* *No credit cards.*

¢–$ CHINESE **Yuan Jiudian.** On the bustling street in the center of the city, this homey kitchen serves up good local favorites like *di san xian,* a mix of potatoes, peppers, and eggplant fried in a soy-flavored sauce. The roast duck is also tasty. The staff does not speak English, but is patient with foreigners. ✉ *Eastern end of Foshan Jie* ☎ *0531/8252–8577* *No credit cards.*

WHERE TO STAY

$$–$$$ ★ **Crowne Plaza Ji'nan.** The city's newest hotel is already ranked among the best in China. The armload of awards it has collected is understandable, as this hotel in the heart of the shopping district is a great choice for business or leisure travelers. The English-speaking staff provides remarkably good service. The guest rooms are spacious and decorated in relaxing shades of oatmeal and cream; the bathrooms are excellent, with deep tubs and separate showers. With three bars, the hotel serves as a lively hub for the city's expat community. **Pros:** top-quality amenities, excellent location, great for business and leisure travelers. **Cons:** pricey public Internet access. ✉ *3 Tianditan Jie* ☎ *0531/8602–9999* *www.ichotelsgroup.com* *227 rooms, 79 suites* *In-room: refrigerator, ethernet. In-hotel: 6 restaurants, room service, bars, pool, gym, laundry service, no-smoking rooms* *AE, DC, MC, V.*

¢–$ **Silver Plaza Quancheng Hotel.** Located in the center of the city, this business hotel is a great place to stay even if you're not in town to close a deal. The common areas are bright and welcoming, and the rooms are spacious and relaxing. Try to avoid those overlooking the street, as these can be noisy. The restaurant serves up good renditions of local specialties and has an English menu. The service can be a bit brusque, mainly because of the huge number of people coming through the door. **Pros:** good restaurants, good value. **Cons:** some rooms can be noisy. ✉ *2 Nanmen Jie St.* ☎ *0531/8692–4815* *350 rooms* *In-hotel: restaurant, room service, bar, gym* *AE, DC, MC, V.*

$$–$$$$ **Sofitel Silver Plaza Ji'nan.** This 49-story cylinder in the center of town looks like a tube of lipstick. Inside a lobby incorporates classical design elements like massive marble columns and chandeliers, and a violinist serenades guests as they arrive. The elegant guest rooms are spacious, but the marble bathrooms, which come with separate tub and shower, are on the small side. Among its six restaurants, try the rooftop Silver Sky Revolving Restaurant. There's a panoramic view of the city, to a hearty buffet dinner, and live music. There is regular shuttle service to the airport. **Pros:** excellent views, good Western food. **Cons:** smoke smell in some no-smoking rooms. ✉*66 Luoyuan Dajie* ☎*0531/8606–8888* 🌐*www.sofitel.com/asia* *220 rooms, 106 suites* *In-room: refrigerator, ethernet. In-hotel: 6 restaurants, room service, bar, pool, gym, concierge, laundry service, airport shuttle* 💳*AE, DC, MC, V.*

NIGHTLIFE

Banjo (✉*54 Foshan Jie*) is a pleasant bar that has become a fixture for local expats. It's set among a row of Chinese, Japanese, and Korean restaurants that are very lively at night. For a touch of the Irish, head to the **Downtown Café** (✉*11 Foshan Jie*), which has a menu of pub grub and a wide selection of beers.

SHOPPING

Shandong Curio's City (✉*283 Quancheng Lu*) is a cluster of small antiques shops huddled around an attractive courtyard. Jade, jewelry, and local antiques are beautifully displayed.

Shen's Embroidery Arts (✉*66 Luoyuan Dajie* ☎*0531/8981–6158*) is in the lobby of the Sofitel Silver Plaza, but don't write it off as another lackluster hotel gift shop. The embroidered paintings are extremely labor intensive, making them unusual, though expensive, souvenirs.

SIDE TRIP TO MOUNT TAI

Reaching 5,067 feet above sea level, **Mount Tai** *(Taishan)* is the most venerated of the five sacred mountains of China. A destination for pilgrims for 3,000 years, the mountain was named a UNESCO World Heritage Site in 1987. Confucius is said to have climbed the mountain and said as he scanned the horizon: "The world is very small." Much later, the Marxist Mao Zedong reached the top and even more famously said: "The East is red." If you are keen to reach a ripe old age, legend has it that climbing Mount Tai means you'll live to 100. It is possible to climb the cut-stone steps to the summit in a day, but many people prefer to stay overnight on the mountain. The classic photo—sunrise over the cloud-hugged mountainside—is actually a rare sight because of the mist. Human sacrifices were made on the summit, but today you will only encounter large crowds throughout the year.

GETTING HERE AND AROUND

Mount Tai is near the town of Tai'an, a major stop on the Shanghai-Beijing railway. Dozens of trains travel through Tai'an daily. Buses from Ji'nan to Tai'an leave the bus terminal opposite the main train station every 25 minutes between 5 AM and 6 PM. From any spot in Tai'an, a taxi to Taishan takes less than 15 minutes and costs about

Y10. ⊠*About 50 km (30 mi) south of Ji'nan* *Dec. 1–Jan. 31, Y100; Feb. 1–Nov. 30, Y125.*

WHERE TO STAY

¢–$ **Shenqi Hotel.** It's the only real hotel on the summit but it's overpriced considering the barely adequate rooms. Still, there are unusual extras such as a bell that rings when it's time to get up for sunrise. **Pros:** perfect place to watch the sunrise on Mount Tai. **Cons:** overpriced, very basic rooms. ⊠*Summit of Mount Tai* ☎*0538/822–3866* *66 rooms* *In-hotel: restaurant, bar, laundry facilities* *AE, DC, MC, V.*

CONFUSING CONFUCIUS

Many locals claim to be direct descendants of Confucius, and they take great pride in their heritage. Although the philosopher would have raised an eyebrow, the townspeople sell Confucius-brand cookies, wine, and many other items.

SIDE TRIP TO QUFU

Qufu is the birthplace of the country's most famous philosopher, Confucius, and so it's of massive significance to the Chinese people. Confucius's impact was immense in China, and his code of conduct was to dominate daily life until it fell out of favor during the Cultural Revolution. His teachings—that son must respect father, wife must respect husband, ordinary citizens must respect officials—were swept away by Mao Zedong because of their associations with the past. Qufu suffered greatly during the Cultural Revolution, with the Red Guards smashing statues and burning buildings. But the pendulum has swung back, and Confucius's teachings are back in favor. It's a lovely place, with timbered houses surrounded by the town walls.

GETTING THERE AND AROUND

Regular buses run trips from Ji'nan to Qufu. The Qufu Bus Station is south of the town center at the intersection of Shen Dao and Jingxuan Lu.

EXPLORING QUFU

Within the city walls, the **Confucius Temple** is a cluster of temples that occupy about a fifth of the city center. The 466 buildings cover more than 50 acres, making this one of the largest architectural complexes left from ancient China, comparable to Beijing's Forbidden City or Chengde's Summer Resort. The Hall of Great Achievements is one of the most ornate of the temples; don't miss its 28 stone pillars carved with dragons. The courtyards are full of gnarled trees and the many memorial halls have fine calligraphy, stone columns, and old furnishings on display. ⊠*Banbi Jie* *Feb. 16–Nov. 14, Y90; Nov. 15–Feb. 15, Y80* *Daily 8–5.*

Adjacent to the Confucius Temple is the **Confucius Family Mansion.** Although not as big as the Confucius Temple, the private home consists of around 450 rooms. It dates from the 16th century and illustrates the power and glory enjoyed by Confucius's descendants. ⊠*Banbi Jie* *Feb. 16–Nov. 14, Y60; Nov. 15–Feb. 15, Y50* *Daily 8–5.*

Confucius and his descendants have been buried in this tree-shaded cemetery for the past 2,000 years. Surrounded by a 10-km (6-mi) wall, **Confucian Forest** has more than 100,000 pine and cypress trees. It's one of the only places in the city where you can escape the crowds. ✉ *Lindao Lu* *Feb. 16–Nov. 14, Y40; Nov. 15–Feb. 15, Y30* *Daily 8–5.*

WISEMAN PASS

If you want to soak up as much Confucianism as possible during your visit to Qufu, get a ticket that grants access to all three sites. During high season, that's Y150 for a ticket that covers the Confucius Temple, Confucius Family Mansion, and the Confucian Forest, saving you Y40. The low season price is Y130 as opposed to Y160 for individual tickets.

WHERE TO STAY

¢ **Queli Hotel.** A short walk to the Confucius Temple and Confucius Family Mansio, this hotel is a good choice for an overnight in Qufu. The traditional Chinese architecture is attractive, though the rooms are plain and have small bathrooms. The restaurant puts out a good spread: the local specialty is a somewhat shortened version of a 196-course banquet traditionally served only to emperors. **Pros:** very convenient for sightseeing. **Cons:** very simple accommodations, basic amenities. ✉ *1 Queli Lu,* ☎ *0537/486–6818* *150 rooms* *In-hotel: restaurant, bar, gym, laundry service, no elevator* *AE, DC, MC, V.*

QINGDAO

6–8 hrs (540 km [335 mi]) by train or 2 hrs by plane southeast of Beijing; 3–6 hrs by train (310 km [192 mi]) east of Ji'nan.

Qingdao has had a turbulent century, but it's emerged as one of China's most charming cities. It was a sleepy fishing village until the end of the 19th century, when Germany, using the killing of two German missionaries as a pretext, set up another European concession to take advantage of Qingdao's coastal position. The German presence lasted only until 1914, but locals continued to build German-style houses, and large parts of the old town make visitors feel as if they have stumbled into a town in the Black Forest. Unlike many cities that had foreign concessions, Qingdao has recognized the historical value of these buildings and is now enthusiastic about preserving them. With its seafront promenades, winding colonial streets, and pretty parks, Qingdao is probably China's best city for strolling.

Home to the country's best-known beer, Tsingtao, Qingdao is very accommodating when it comes to alcohol consumption. (Look for beer being sold on the streets in plastic bags.) But wine drinkers should take heart, as the region is also developing a much-talked-about wine industry.

The city is a destination for golfers, having many of the country's best courses. But Qingdao added a new sport of note when hosted the sailing events of the 2008 Olympics in the new Qingdao Sailing Center. Bei-

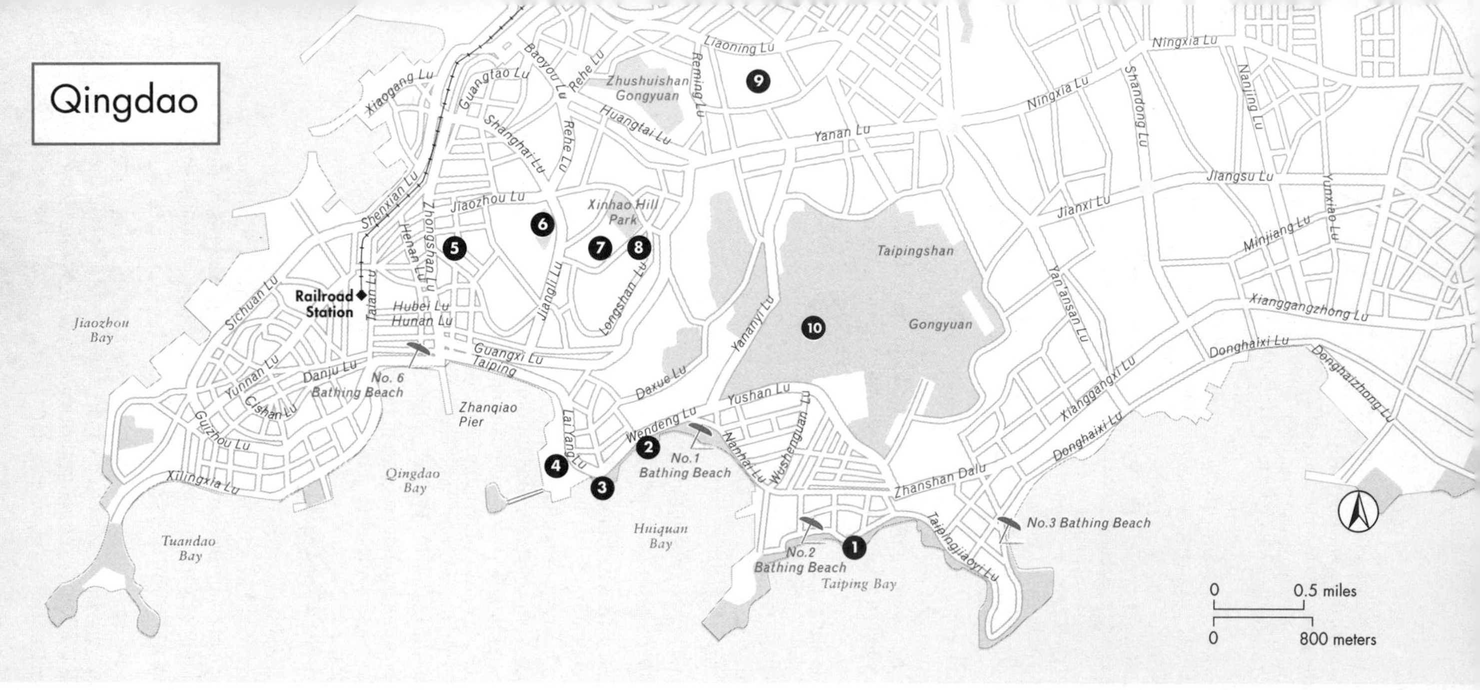

Catholic Church (Tianzhu Jiaotang) 5
German governor's residence (Qingdao Ying Binguan) 8
Guanhaishan Park 6
Huashi Lou 1
Lu Xun Park (Lu Xun Gongyuan) 3
Navy Museum (Haijun Bowuguan) 4
Protestant Church (Jida Jiaotang) 7
Sun Yat-sen Park (Zhongshan Gongyuan) .. 10
Tsingdao Beer Factory 9
Underwater World 2

jing invested a whopping $370 million for its world-class International Sailing Center.

WORD OF MOUTH

"I'd take the train (from Beijing to Jinan) because it is fast (5 hours), clean, comfortable, and more reliable. In China, it's extremely unusual if a train is more than 30 minutes late. I have been on so many Chinese trains and my impression is that 99% of them are right on time." —comrade

GETTING HERE AND AROUND

A comfortable way to get to Qingdao is aboard one of the several daily D-coded express trains that link Qingdao to Beijing (6 hours). It's best to buy tickets from travel agents or through your hotel, as lines are long and there are few English speakers at the station.

The long-distance bus terminal is opposite the train station. Taxis are a cheap way to get around. Getting anywhere in town will generally cost less than Y30.

BY AIR Qingdao Liuting Airport is 30 km (19 mi) north of the city. In a taxi, the journey takes 40 minutes and costs around Y80. Some hotels have airport shuttles. Direct flights link Qingdao with Osaka and Seoul, as well as Hong Kong and other major Chinese cities.

BY BOAT AND FERRY If time is not a consideration, going to Incheon in South Korea (four boats a week) or Shimonoseki in Japan (once every two weeks) is possible. For up-to-date information, consult a travel agent or the schedule at the passenger ferry terminal.

BY BUS Buses travel between Ji'nan and Qingdao every 20 minutes; the trip is four to five hours.

BY TRAIN Direct trains link Qingdao with Ji'nan (3 hours), Beijing (6 hours), and Shanghai (10 hours).

ESSENTIALS

Air Contacts **Qingdao Liuting Airport** (✉ *Near Liuting Village* ☎ *0532/8471–5777* 🌐 *www.qdairport.com*).

Boat and Ferry Contacts **Qingdao Ferry Terminal** (✉ *6 Xinjiang Lu, 1 mi (2 km) north of the train station* ☎ *0532/8282–5001*).

Bus Contacts **Qingdao Long-Distance Bus Station** (✉ *2 Wenzhou Lu* ☎ *0532/8371–8060*).

Medical Assistance **Qingdao Municipal Hospital** (✉ *5 DongHai Zhong Lu* ☎ *0532/8593–7600*).

Train Contacts **Qingdao Station** (✉ *2 Tai'an Lu* ☎ *0532/8297–5423*).

Visitor and Tour Info **Qingdao CITS** (✉ *6F, A Yuyuan Dasha Office Building, 73 Xianggang Zhong Lu* ☎ *0532/8386–3960*). **Qingdao Tourism Administration** (✉ *7 Minjiang Lu* ☎ *0532/8591–2029*).

EXPLORING QINGDAO

MAIN ATTRACTIONS

5 A landmark in Qingdao is the **Catholic Church** *(Tianzhu Jiaotang)*, with its towering 200-foot twin steeples and red-tile roof. It was built by the

Germans in 1934 and was badly damaged during the Cultural Revolution. Now though, it's a relaxing and peaceful place. ✉ *15 Zhejiang Lu* 🎫 *Y6* ⏲ *Mon.–Sat. 8–5, Sun. 10–5.*

❽ The striking former **German Governor's Residence** *(Qingdao Ying Binguan)* was transformed into a museum in 1996. Built in 1903 as the official residence of the governor-general of the then-German concession, it is set on a hill overlooking the old city. The interior is warm and welcoming, with wood paneling and a wide staircase leading from the foyer up to the bedrooms. Among the famous leaders who stayed here is a Who's Who of names from recent Chinese history: Mao Zedong, Zhou Enlai, and Deng Xiaoping ✉ *26 Longshan Lu, below Xinhao Hill Park* 🎫 *Y15* ⏲ *Daily 8:30–4:30.*

❶ After the German Governor's Residence, the castle-like **Huashi Lou** is Qingdao's second most famous example of traditional German architecture. It was built as a villa for a Russian aristocrat but soon became a retreat for the governor. Look out for wedding parties using the grounds as a backdrop for their photos. ✉ *18 Huanghai Lu* 🎫 *Y6.5* ⏲ *Daily 8–5:30.*

❼ Qingdao's **Protestant Church** *(Jidu Jiaotang)* is easy to spot: look out for the large green spire resembling those topping medieval castles. It was built in 1910 at the southwest entrance of Xinhao Hill Park. If you climb up to the bell tower, you are rewarded with an excellent view. ✉ *15 Jiangsu Lu* 🎫 *Mon.–Sat. Y5; free on Sun* ⏲ *Daily 8:30–4:30.*

NEED A BREAK?

It may bear more than a passing resemblance to a certain Seattle-based chain, but SPR (✉ *29 Taiping Lu* ☎ *0532/8299–6699* 💳 *No credit cards*) is a homegrown chain. Relax with a cappuccino or fill up on a slice of pizza.

❿ The largest of the city's parks, **Sun Yat-sen Park** *(Zhongshan Gongyuan)*, named for Dr. Sun Yat-sen, has plenty of exotic plants. It's pretty throughout the year, but is at its best in spring. ✉ *28 Wendeng Lu* 🎫 *Y12* ⏲ *Daily 5 AM–9 PM.*

❾ Beer fans should make a pilgrimage to the **Tsingdao Beer Factory** *(Tsingdao Pijiu Chang)*. A guide walks you through the facility, then gives you a multitude of freshly made beer samples. There is also an excellent museum on the history of the brewery, built in 1903 by—who else?—the Germans. ✉ *56 Dengzhou Lu* ☎ *0532/383–3437* 🎫 *Y50* ⏲ *Daily 8:30–4:30.*

IF YOU HAVE TIME

❻ **Guanhaishan Park** *(Guanhaishan gongyuan)* is tiny but charming. This was where the German high officials practiced their golf swing while looking down over the rest of the city. ✉ *15 Guanhai Er Lu* 🎫 *Free* ⏲ *Daily 7–5.*

❸ Built in 1929, **Lu Xun Park** *(Lu Xun Gongyuan)* faces the rocky coastline of Huiquan Bay. It was named in 1950 for the distinguished Chinese writer and commentator Lu Xun. ✉ *West end of No. 1 Bathing Beach* 🎫 *Y5* ⏲ *Daily 8–5.*

4 In the upper yard of the **Navy Museum** *(Haijun Bowuguan)* you'll find an indoor exhibition documenting the history of the Chinese navy. Outside are the big guns, including Russian-made fighter planes, fixed-turret and antiaircraft naval guns, rockets, tanks, ground artillery, naval vessels (including three moored in the adjacent harbor), and even an old biplane. The displays are dusty, so this museum is for hard-core naval fans only. ✉ *8 Lai Yang Lu* ☎ *0532/286–6784* *Y30* *Daily 8:30–5.*

RAISE A GLASS

The **International Beer Festival,** held every summer, is Qingdao's biggest event of the year, with gallons of beer from all over the world available for tasting. You may not see any lederhosen, but it's still great fun. The **Cherry Festival** takes place in April and May. In early September the **Mt. Daze Grape Festival** celebrates the fruit of the vine.

2 Children will be enthralled by one of the city's newest attractions, **Underwater World** *(Qingdao Haidi Shijie)*. The facility claims to have the world's largest aquarium, and it is kept filled with exotic creatures from the deep. Especially popular is an underwater tunnel where you can see sharks swim over your head. ✉ *1 Laiyang Lu* ☎ *0532/8289–2187* *Y120* *Daily 8:30–5.*

WHERE TO EAT

It's no surprise that Qingdao's specialty is seafood. Locals flock to Minjiang Lu, where the time between choosing a fish from tanks and having it arrive steaming on your plate is about three minutes.

When choosing a restaurant, look for displays of Qingdao's new sanitation rating "smiley face" logos. A green smiling logo means the restaurant has high sanitation standards; a yellow neutral face means there are a few problems; a red frown face indicates very poor sanitation. Establishments that have received yellow and red face icons are given a period of time in which to improve, but you may want to avoid those as long as you see anything less than a smile!

$–$$ SEAFOOD **Cui Zhu Yuan.** Don't be offended when you're brought a bib and plastic gloves when you walk into this brightly lighted restaurant. You'll need them for the signature dish: tiny lobsters served in a rich, spicy sauce. There might be some work getting to the fleshy bits, but that's half the fun. Other Qingdao specialties, like spicy clams, are excellent. ✉ *129 Minjiang Lu* ☎ *0532/8576–5286* *No credit cards.*

$–$$ CHINESE **Guo Fu Cheng.** On a street lined with lively eateries, this inexpensive hot-pot restaurant stands head and shoulders above the rest. You and your dining companions will all have a private hot pot, so you can choose what meat and seafood to add to the steaming liquid. If you don't want to do all the work yourself, the kitchen is happy to take care of things. Be warned: the spicy hot pot is *seriously* spicy. ✉ *72 Yunxiao Lu, off Minjiang Lu* ☎ *0532/8578–7018* *No credit cards.*

$$–$$$ FRENCH **La Villa** *(La Wei La Faguo Canting)*. It may have an Italian name, but this French restaurant serves up reliable renditions of classic dishes such as coq au vin. The French-trained chef also cooks steaks and other hearty fare. The

cozy wooden interior makes this popular with local expats. ✉5 *Xianggang Zhong Lu* ☎*0532/8388–6833* ▭*DC, MC, V.*

$$–$$$ SEAFOOD ✕**Qingdao Restaurant** *(Qingdao Caiguan)*. At this popular restaurant you wander around displays of uncooked dishes laid out on ice and tanks filled with mussels and crabs, all ready to be whisked away to the kitchen and cooked to order. The decor isn't exciting, but the food is excellent and the service is doting. ✉*17 Aomen Lu* ☎*0532/8388–0098* ▭*DC, MC, V.*

IN THE NEWS

Qingdao also has a lively foreign-restaurant scene, but places tend to open and close very quickly. Get a copy of the local expat magazine *Redstar* from your hotel for the latest information, or check out their Web site (🌐*www.myredstar.com*) for reviews, recommendations, and happenings around town.

¢–$ SEAFOOD ✕**Zhong Shan Restaurant.** In the same neighborhood as the Catholic Church, this spartan but spotless place is where locals come for seafood. The restaurant is in an attractive building from the 1930s, and its price list seems to be from the same era. A bowl of seafood wontons is Y5, and a large plate of fresh oysters with a garlic-and-vinegar dip is yours for an astounding Y18. ✉*46 Hunan Road, at Zhongshan Lu* ☎*0532/8287–9073* ▭*No credit cards.*

WHERE TO STAY

¢ **Badaguan Hotel.** If your priority is peace and quiet, this hotel in the scenic Badaguan neighborhood is a good choice. Set in established gardens, it feels miles away from the hustle and bustle of the city. The guest rooms look a little dusty, but are otherwise more than adequate. The location near Number 2 Beach makes up for any deficiencies. **Pros:** a bargain for beautiful ocean views in an out-of-the-way location. **Cons:** outside of city center. ✉*19 Zhengyangguan Lu* ☎*0532/8203–8666* *300 rooms* *In-room: Ethernet. In-hotel: restaurant, tennis court, gym* ▭*AE, DC, MC, V.*

$$–$$$ **Crowne Plaza.** The tallest building in the eastern end of the city, the Crowne Plaza towers over the competition. The service is attentive, especially considering the massive number of guests that constantly stream through the doors. The rooms in the cylindrical tower are spacious, and some have views of the ocean and the new Olympic Sailing Center. The hotel is adjacent to a ritzy shopping center filled with outposts of Prada and Louis Vuitton. **Pros:** beautiful ocean views in some rooms, excellent restaurants. **Cons:** some rooms are poorly ventilated. ✉*76 Xianggang Zhong Rd.* ☎*0532/8571–8888* 🌐*www.crowneplaza.com* *388 rooms* *In-room: refrigerator, Ethernet. In-hotel: 5 restaurants, room service, bar, tennis court, pool, gym, airport shuttle* ▭*AE, DC, MC, V.*

$–$$ **Huiquan Dynasty Hotel.** Opposite the city's most popular beach, this well-established hotel revels in its enviable location. Diners at the 25th-floor revolving restaurant enjoy great views of the ocean. It's worth paying for a room overlooking the ocean, as the rooms in the rear overlook a busy road. There is a branch of the CITS travel agency on the premises. **Pros:** great ocean views from some rooms, very convenient

(top) The Juyongguan section of the Great Wall of China is considered one of the three greatest passes. The others are Jiayuguan Pass and Shanhai Pass. (bottom) The Bailin Buddhist Temple in Shijiazhuang, Hebei.

(top) Take a sunrise camel trip on the Silk Road in Dunhuang, Gansu. (bottom) Pudong, literally "the east side of the river," is Shanghai's financial, economic, and commercial center.

(top) Located in the remote town of Xiahe, the Labrang Monastery is a little piece of Tibet along the Gansu-Qinghai border. (bottom) A colorful Chinese New Year celebration.

(top) In the Longsheng Longji Rice Terraces in Guangxi, patterns have been cut into the hills up to a height of 2,625 feet. (bottom left) Native son Chow Yun-Fat in *Crouching Tiger, Hidden Dragon.* (bottom right) Cormorant fishermen on the Li River near Guilin train their birds to do all the work.

(top left) The Chinese introduced tea to the world; learn all about it at the Flagstaff House Museum of Tea Ware, Hong Kong. (top right) *Manpower* sculpture by Rosanna Li, Grotto Fine Art gallery, Hong Kong. (bottom) The new China is crackling with energy, and crossing the street can sometimes be a dangerous sport.

(top) In the heyday of colonial encroachment, the Bund was Shanghai's main drag, with 52 architectural styles including Gothic, Baroque, and Romanesque. (bottom) In Cantonese opera, makeup and hair give clues to the characters' personality.

(top) The Great Buddha in Leshan, Sichuan, is a UNESCO World Heritage Site and the largest buddha in the world. Each of its big toes are 28 feet long. (bottom left) Architects and designers strive for auspicious feng shui in Hong Kong. (bottom right) In the countryside, the traditional blue Mao uniforms are still fairly common.

Nine-Dragon Wall at Beihai Park in Beijing is one of three walls of its kind in China. Built in 1756 during the Qing Dynasty, the famous wall has nine dragons playing in the clouds.

beach access. **Cons:** some rooms have a musty odor. ✉6 *Nanhai Lu* ☎*0532/8287–1122* *405 rooms* *In-room: Ethernet. In-hotel: 2 restaurants, room service, bar, pool, tennis courts, gym, laundry service* *AE, DC, MC, V.*

$$–$$$ **Shangri-La.** Only a block from the scenic coastline, the Shangri-La is also close to some of the best shopping and eating in town. Legions of bellboys wait to take you and your luggage up to your well-appointed room. Q Bar, popular with local expats, is a stylish place for a pre-dinner drink. Upgrade to the new Valley Wing for well-appointed rooms and excellent personalized service. **Pros:** convenient to beach. **Cons:** restaurants and shops a little far from the hotel on foot. ✉9 *Xiang Gang Zhong Lu* ☎*0532/388–3838* *www.shangri-la.com* *402 rooms* *In-room: refrigerator, Ethernet. In-hotel: 3 restaurants, room service, bar, tennis court, pool, gym* *AE, DC, MC, V.*

NIGHTLIFE AND THE ARTS

In a German-style building dating from the 1930s, **Café Roland** (✉9 *Taiping Jiao Er Lu* ☎*0532/8387–5734*) has a lovely wooden interior and a view of Number 3 Beach. The **Sailing Club and Bar** (✉6 *Nanhai Lu* ☎*0532/8286–4645*) lets you enjoy a quiet drink or some well-prepared seafood as you gaze at the sailboats floating past. It's easy to imagine yourself transported to somewhere in Europe. But for the best beer in town, head to the source: **Tsingdao Brewery Bar** (✉56 *Dengzhou Lu* ☎*0532/8383–3437*). Things can get rowdy because the prices are intentionally kept low, but if cost is more of a consideration than ambieânce, this can be an excellent night out.

SPORTS AND THE OUTDOORS

Chinese visitors come to Qingdao in the tens of thousands for the beaches. Each of the seven sandy beaches that run along the coast for more than 6 mi (10 km) have a variety of facilities ranging from changing rooms to kiosks renting inflatable toys. Sometimes the water quality isn't the greatest, so it's worth inquiring at your hotel.

BEACHES

Number 1 Beach is the busiest, and in summer it can be difficult to find a place for your towel. If your goal is peace and quiet, head to **Number 2 Beach,** as fewer Chinese tourists venture out that way. In the summer, watch out for the armies of brides and bridegrooms using the beaches as backdrops for their wedding photos.

GOLF

The 18-hole **Qingdao International Golf Club** (✉*Songling Lu* ☎*0532/8896–0001*) is 20 minutes from downtown. It has driving ranges, a pro, and a fine-dining restaurant. Booking ahead, especially on weekends, is recommended.

WATER SPORTS

With the sailing center for the 2008 Olympics, the Qingdao waterfront is completely transformed. Besides the athletic facilities, there are a conference center, a luxury hotel, a cruise-ship terminal, a yacht club, and a marina. There are also several other places that will help you get on or in the water.

Near Number 1 Beach, **Qingdao Qinhai Scuba Diving Club** (✉ *5 Huiquan Lu* ☎ *0532/8387–7977*) is the only government-certified diving club in northern China. All equipment is provided, and you can get your diving certificate in 12 classes.

The Sailing Club and Bar (✉ *6 Nanhai Lu* ☎ *0532/8286–4645*) has sailing and windsurfing equipment for rent in the summer. The prices are very reasonable, ranging from Y80 to Y200 an hour for a boat. Instructors are available for an extra fee. If the water is too cold for you, there are wet suits available.

One of the country's largest yacht clubs, **Yinhai International Yacht Club** (✉ *30 Donghai Zhong Lu* ☎ *0532/8588–6666* 🌐 *www.yinhai.com.cn*) has more than 30 yachts for rent, and offers lessons to beginners and more experienced sailors. The club is in the east of town, near the Olympic Sailing Center.

SHOPPING

The north end of Zhongshan Lu has a cluster of antiques and cultural artifacts shops. The largest antiques shop is the **Qingdao Arts and Crafts Store** (✉ *212 Zhongshan Lu* ☎ *0532/8281–7948*), with four floors of porcelain, scroll paintings, silk, gold, jade, and other stones. The **Cultural Relics Store** (✉ *40 Zhongshan Lu* ☎ *0532/8285–4435*) is also worth a look.

Very near the Catholic Church is **Michael's** (✉ *15 Zhejiang Lu* ☎ *0532/8286–6790*), a gallery specializing in calligraphy.

SIDE TRIPS FROM QINGDAO

Rising to a height of more than 3,280 feet, **Mount Lao** *(Laoshan)* is nearly as famous as the province's other famous mountain, Mount Tai. A place of pilgrimage for centuries, Laoshan once had 9 palaces, 8 temples, and 72 convents. Many of these places have been lost over the years, but a number of the temples remaining are worth a look for their elegant architecture and their excellent views out to sea. With sheer cliffs and cascading waterfalls, the beautiful mountain is widely recognized in China as a source of the country's best-known mineral water (a vital ingredient in the local brew, Tsingtao). It's possible to see the mountain's sights in less than a day. Tourist buses to Laoshan leave from the main pier in Qingdao. ✉ *40 km (25 mi) east of Qingdao* 🎫 *Apr. 1–Oct. 31, Y70; Nov. 1–Mar. 31, Y50* ⏲ *Daily 7–5.*

Near Laoshan is **Huadong Winery,** Shandong's best winery. Although not as famous as the province's brewery, it has nevertheless already won a string of prizes. Some judge the chardonnay, grown from vines imported from France in the 1980s, to be on par with those from California. You can taste not only the different wines, but also the grapes the wines are made from. The beautiful scenery alone makes this a worthwhile side trip from Qingdao. Visit the winery's **Qingdao Office** (✉ *15 Donghai Xi Lu* ☎ *0532/8387–4778*) to book a tour. ✉ *Nanlong Kou* ☎ *0532/8881–7878.*

JIANGSU

Coastal Jiangsu is defined by water. This eastern province is crossed by one of the world's great rivers, the mystical Yangtze, and has a coastline stretching hundreds of miles along the Yellow Sea. Jiangsu is also home to the Grand Canal, an ancient feat of engineering. This massive waterway, the longest ancient canal in the world with some parts dating from the 5th century BC, allowed merchants to ship the province's plentiful rice, vegetables, and tea to the north. Within the cities, daily life was historically tied to the water, and many old neighborhoods are still crisscrossed by countless small canals.

As a result of its trading position, Jiangsu has long been an economic and political center of China. The founder of the Ming Dynasty established the capital in Nanjing, and it remained there until his son moved it back north to Beijing. Even after the move, Nanjing and Jiangsu retained their nationwide importance. After the 1911 revolution, the province once again hosted the nation's capital, in Nanjing.

Planning a trip in the province is remarkably easy. The cities are close together, and connected by many buses and trains. Autumn tends to be warm and dry, with ideal walking temperatures. Spring can be rainy and windy, but the hills burst with blooms. Summers are infamously oppressive, hot, and humid. The winter is mild, but January and February are often rainy.

REGIONAL TOURS

Jiangsu Huate International Travel Service has a number of guides who speak English. Jinling Business International Travel Service offers a range of options for travelers. The company has its own fleet of comfortable cars with knowledgeable drivers. It can arrange trips throughout the region.

Tour Contacts **Jiangsu Huate International Travel Service** (✉ *33 Jinxiang He Lu, Nanjing* ☎ *025/8337–8695* 🌐 *english.hitravels.com*). **Jinling Business International Travel Service** (✉ *Jinling Hotel, 2 Hanzhong Lu, Nanjing* ☎ *025/8473–0501*).

NANJING

2–2½ hrs (309 km [192 mi]) by fast train west of Shanghai; 4½ hrs by normal train.

The name *Nanjing* means "Southern Capital," and for six dynastic periods, as well as during the country's tenure as the Republic of China, the city was China's administrative capital. Never as successful a capital as Beijing, the locals chalk up the failures of several dynasties here to bad timing, but it could be that the laid-back atmosphere of the Yangtze Delta just isn't as suited to political intrigue as the north.

Nanjing offers travelers significantly more sites of historical importance than Shanghai. One of the most impressive is the massive Ming Dynasty sections of the city wall, built to surround and protect the city in the

14th century. There are also a number of traditional monuments, tombs, and gates that reflect the glory of Nanjing's capital days.

The city lies on the Yangtze, and the colossal Second Bridge or the more subdued park at Swallow Rock are great places for viewing the river. The sheer amount of activity on the river is testimony to its continued importance as a corridor for shipping and trade. Downtown, the streets are choked with traffic, but the chaotic scene is easily avoided with a visit to any of the large parks. You can also take a short taxi ride to Ziin (Purple) Mountain where quiet trails lead between Ming Tombs and the grand mausoleum of Sun Yat-sen.

GETTING HERE AND AROUND

Regular daily flights connect Nanjing with all other major Chinese cities. The airport is located just 36 km (22 mi) from the city center.

Bus travel in this area of China is considerably more comfortable than elsewhere, thanks to a network of highways linking the cities and a fleet of luxury buses with comfortable seats and air-conditioning. Train travel is another good option, and there are frequent departures to many destinations in Jiangsu. Getting around Nanjing by taxi is both fast and inexpensive, though taxi drivers generally cannot speak any English, so be prepared with the address of your destination written in Chinese. For the more adventurous, bicycles can be rented from some small hotels and tourist agencies; the city is very bicycle-friendly with mostly flat roads and many dedicated bicycle lanes. The Nanjing subway is quick, comfortable, and extremely inexpensive, with distance-based fares starting at Y2.

■ TIP→ The best way to explore some of Nanjing's tourist destinations, once you're on Purple Mountain, is aboard the tourist bus that runs from the train station to Ming Tomb, Sun Yat-sen Botanical Gardens, Sun Yat-sen Mausoleum, and Spirit Valley Pagoda. Fare is Y3.

BY AIR Most flights from Europe or North America go through Shanghai or Beijing before continuing on to Nanjing's Lukou Airport, but there are direct flights from Asian hubs like Seoul, Singapore, Nagoya, and Bangkok. From Nanjing, several flights leave daily for Shanghai, Beijing, Guangzhou, Xiamen, Wuhan, and Hong Kong; flights leave daily for Xi'an, Chengdu, and Zhengzhou.

Taxis from Nanjing Lukou Airport, 36 km (22 mi) southwest of the city, should take between 20 and 30 minutes. The fare should be between Y90 and Y120.

BY BUS Buses departing from or going to other Jiangsu destinations, such as Shanghai, Suzhou, and Yangzhou, are both frequent and comfortable. Nanjing's main long-distance bus station lies west of the railway station at Zhongyang Men.

The trip to Shanghai take between 3 and 4 hours, and the trip to Suzhou can take as little as 2 hours; buses to both cities depart from the Zhongshan Nan Road Bus Station. Buses bound for Yangzhou leave frequently from the main long-distance bus station and take an hour.

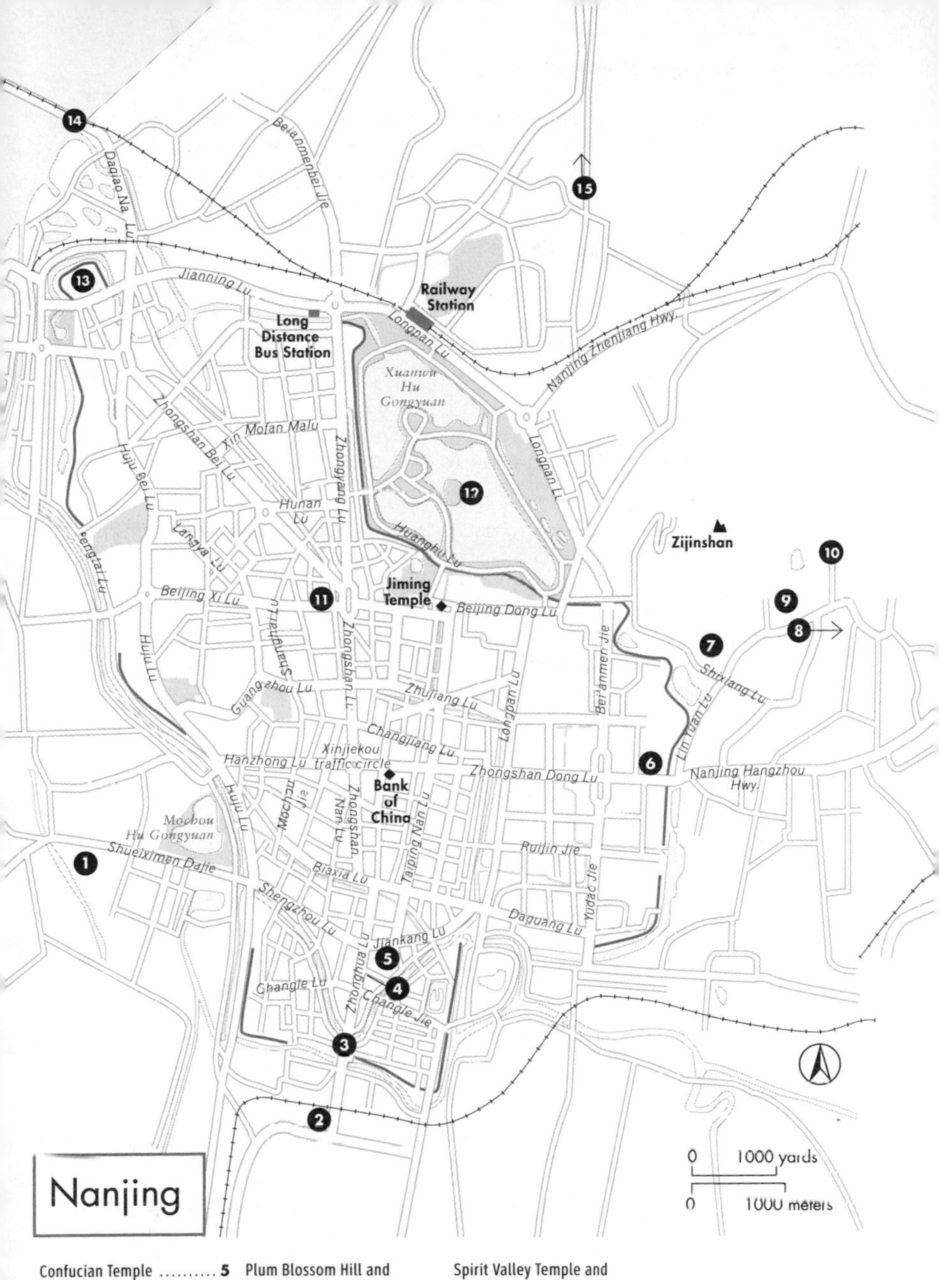

Confucian Temple 5
Drum Tower 11
Ming Tomb 9
Nanjing Massacre Memorial 1
Nanjing Museum 6
Plum Blossom Hill and Sun Yat-sen Botanical Gardens 7
Rain Flower Terrace and Martyrs Memorial 2
South Gate of City Wall 3
Swallow Rock 15
Spirit Valley Temple and Pagoda 8
Sun Yat-sen Memorial 10
Taiping Heavenly Kingdom Museum 4
Xuanwu Lake Park 12
Yangtze River Bridge 14
Yuejiang Lou Tower 13

BY TRAIN Trains can be a convenient way to get to Nanjing, but be mindful of what kind of ticket you buy—all trains are not created equal. The K- or T-coded tickets are for faster trains; local trains can take two or three times longer to reach a destination. High-speed D-coded trains are the fastest, usually serving two major destinations with few stops in between. Trains depart for Shanghai about every half hour and take between 2 and 4 hours.

TOURS

Major hotels will often arrange a tour guide for a group. Nanjing China Travel Service can arrange almost any type of tour of the city.

ESSENTIALS

Air Contacts Air China (☎ *025/8449–9378* 🌐 *www.airchina.com.cn/en/index.jsp*). **Dragonair** (☎ *025/8331–1999 Ext. 810* 🌐 *www.dragonair.com*). **Nanjing Lukou Airport** (✉ *Jiangning Qu* ☎ *025/248–0063*).

Bus Contacts Nanjing Bus Station (✉ *Jianing Lu and Zhongyang Lu* ☎ *025/8550–4973*).

Medical Assistance First Aid Station (✉ *231 Zhongshan Lu* ☎ *025/8663–3858*).

Train Contacts Nanjing Train Station (✉ *Long Pan Lu* ☎ *025/8582–2222*).

Visitor and Tour Info CITS (✉ *202/1 Zhongshan Bei Lu* ☎ *025/8342–8999* 🌐 *www.citsnjview.com*). **Nanjing China Travel Service** (✉ *12 Baixin Building, Baizi Ting, south of the Drum Tower* ☎ *025/8336–6582*).

EXPLORING NANJING

MAIN ATTRACTIONS

5 **Confucian Temple** *(Fuzimiao)*. The traditional-style temple overlooks the Qinhuai, a tributary of the Yangtze. The surrounding area is the city's busiest shopping and entertainment district and lit with neon at night. The back alleys behind the temple, once home to China's most famous district of courtesans, now house a toy market and excellent curio shops. This area has the best bazaars for souvenirs and crafts. Evening tours of the Qinhuai River leave from in front of the temple. The cost is Y40 per person. ✉ *Zhongshan Lu and Jiankang Lu, on the Qinhuai River* 🎫 *Y15* 🌐 *www.njfzm.com* ⏲ *Daily 8:30–5:30.*

9 **Ming Tomb** *(Ming Xiaoling)*. The ancient tomb of the founder of the Ming Dynasty, called Tomb of Filial Piety, is one of the largest burial mounds in China. The emperor Hong Wu, who chose Nanjing for the Ming Dynasty capital, was born a peasant and orphaned early on. He became a monk and eventually led the army that overthrew the Yuan Dynasty. Visitors approach the tomb through a grand entrance of stone animals. The lions, elephants, camels, and mythical creatures kneel in tribute to the emperor and stand as guardians to the tomb. Winding paths behind them make the Ming Tomb area a rewarding place to explore, but as in all Chinese tombs the entrance is hidden to foil looters. For a detailed history, buy a book at the entrance shop; English signage is sparse. ✉ *Mingling Lu, on Purple Mountain* 🎫 *Y70* ⏲ *Daily 8:30–5.*

Fodor's Choice ★

❶ **Nanjing Massacre Memorial** *(Datusha Jinianguan)*. In the winter of 1937, Japanese forces occupied Nanjing. In the space of a few days, thousands of Chinese were killed in the chaos, which became commonly known as the "Rape of Nanjing." This monument commemorates the victims, many of whom were buried in mass graves. Be advised, however: this is not for the squeamish. Skeletons have been exhumed from the "Grave of Ten Thousand" and are displayed with gruesomely detailed explanations as to how each lost his or her life. The memorial also displays artifacts from the Sino-Japanese reconciliation after World War II, which ended the conflict between the two countries on a less strident, more hopeful note. To get here, take Bus 7 or 37 from Xinjiekou. ✉*418 Shui Ximen Da Jie, west of Mouchou Lake Park* ☎*025/8650–1033* 🌐*www.nj1937.org* 🎫*Free* ⏲*Tues.–Sun. 8:30–4:30.*

 **Nanjing Museum** *(Nanjing Bowuguan)*. With one of the largest and most impressive collections in China, the Nanjing Museum has excellent displays that set objects in historical context. For instance, beside the shelves of ancient pottery there is a re-created kiln to illustrate how traditional objects were formed. The permanent collection includes excellent works in jade, silk, and bronzes. There's also a treasure room with some eye-popping displays. In a modern hall the museum's curators have pushed the envelope—and pushed some buttons—with some controversial temporary exhibitions. ✉*Zhongshan Dong Lu, inside Zhongshan Gate, east of the city center* ☎*025/8480–2119* 🎫*Y20* ⏲*Daily 9–4:30.*

 **South Gate of City Wall** *(Zhonghua Men)*. Built as the linchpin of the city's defenses, this is less of a gate than a complete fortress, with multiple courtyards and tunnels where several thousand soldiers could withstand a siege. It was even attacked; armies wisely avoided it in favor of the less heavily fortified areas to the north. Today bonsai enthusiasts have displays in several of the courtyards. ✉*Southern end of Zhonghua Lu, south side of city wall* 🎫*Y20* ⏲*Daily 8–6.*

 **Spirit Valley Temple and Pagoda** *(Linggu Si and Linggu Ta)*. The temple commemorates Xuan Zang, the monk who brought Buddhist scriptures back from India. Farther up the hill is a nine-story granite pagoda with a staircase that spirals up the central pillar. The top is dizzyingly high. This pagoda was built as a solemn memorial to those killed by the Nationalists in 1929; today, vendors sell plastic balloons to throw off the top balcony. Also on the grounds is the brick Beamless Hall, which was constructed without any wood or beams to support it. The magnificent 14th-century architecture is now given over to propagandistic "historical" reenactments. Although the temple and pagoda aren't worth a special trip, they are close to Ming Tomb and other attractions around Purple Mountain. ✉*Ta Lu, southeast of Sun Yat-sen Memorial* ☎*025/8444–6111* 🎫*Pagoda Y15, temple Y2* ⏲*Sept.–May, daily 8:30–5, June–Aug., daily 6:30 AM–6:30 PM.*

❹ **Taiping Heavenly Kingdom Museum** *(Taiping Tianguo Lishi Bowuguan)*. Commemorating a particularly fascinating period of Chinese history, this museum follows the life of Hong Xiuquan, a Christian who led a peasant revolt in 1859. He ultimately captured Nanjing and ruled for 11 years. Hong, who set himself up as emperor, claimed to be the younger brother of Jesus. On display are artifacts from the period. After browsing the museum, you can walk around the grounds of the Ming Dynasty garden compound that houses the museum. During the day, it is the calmest spot in Nanjing. In the evening from 6 to 11 there are performances of opera and storytelling. Reasonably priced English-speaking guides make up for the lack of English signage. ✉*128 Zhanyuan Lu, beside the Confucian Temple* ☎*025/5223–8687* 🎫*Museum only Y10, including performance Y50* ⏲*Daily 8:30–5.*

CAUTION

Be careful when crossing the street—look both ways, look again, and keep looking as you cross. Nanjing has seen an explosion of private auto ownership in the past decade, and no comparable program of driver education. Pedestrians may have the green walk light, but they are generally not given the right of way when cars make right turns, and running red lights is not uncommon. Motorbikes and bicycles ignore all lights and signage as a rule, and even take over the sidewalks.

⓬ **Xuanwu Lake Park** *(Xuanwu Hu Gongyuan).* More lake than park, this pleasant garden is bounded by one of the longer sections of the monumental city wall, which you can climb for a good view of the water. Purple Mountain rises in the east, and the glittering skyscrapers of modern Nanjing are reflected on the calm water. Causeways lined with trees and benches connect several large islands in the lake. Small pedal boats can be rented for Y15/hour. ✉*Off Hunan Lu, in the northeast corner of the city, outside the city wall* 🎫*Y20* ⏲*Daily 8–8.*

IF YOU HAVE TIME

⓫ **Drum Tower** *(Gulou).* The traditional center of ancient Chinese cities, the 1382 Drum Tower housed the drums used to signal important events, from the changing of the guard to an enemy attack or a fire. Today it holds only one drum. If you're in the area, you can duck inside to see the first-floor art exhibition. ✉*1 Dafang Xiang, beside Gulou People's Square* ☎*025/8663–1059* 🎫*Y5* ⏲*Daily 8:30 AM–5:30 PM.*

❼ **Plum Blossom Hill and Sun Yat-sen Botanical Gardens** *(Meihuashan and Zhongshan Zhiwuyuan).* This hillside explodes with plum blossoms in early spring. The garden is a nice place for a picnic, but is only worth a special trip when the flowers are in bloom. The exhibits at the botanical gardens, on the other hand, are a rewarding experience for anyone interested in the flora of China. ✉*1 Shixiang Lu, northeast of Nanjing Museum* 🎫*Y50* ⏲*Daily 6:30 AM–6:30 PM.*

❷ **Rain Flower Terrace and Martyrs Memorial** *(Yuhua Tai Lieshi Lingyuan).* The terrace gets its name from the legend of Yunzhang, a 15th-century Buddhist monk who supposedly pleased the gods so much with his recitation of a sutra that they showered flowers on this spot. The site was used for a more grim purpose in the 1930s, when the Nationalists used it to execute their left-wing political enemies. The site was transformed into a memorial park with massive statues of heroic martyrs, soaring obelisks, flower arrangements of the hammer and sickle, and a moving museum that uses personal objects to convey the lives of some of those executed here. ✉*215 Yuhua Lu, outside Zhonghua Gate* 🌐*www.cnbg.net/default_en.asp* 🎫*Y35* 🕑*Park daily 7* AM*–10* PM, *memorial daily 8–5:30.*

PEDESTRIAN STREETS

In the **Confucius Temple Area** *(Fuzimiao)* are souvenir and shopping streets around the Qinhuai River. ✉*By the intersection of Zhongshan Lu and Jiankang Lu.*

Hunan Road is a section of streets filled with snacks, shops, and restaurants. ✉*Hunan Lu, west of Zhongshan North Rd. and east of Zhongyang Lu.*

In the **Xinjiekou City Center**, around the big malls and shopping centers are several bustling walking streets. ✉*Xinjiekou between Huaihai Lu and Zhongshan Lu.*

⓯ **Swallow Rock** *(Yanzi Ji)*. North of the city, this small park overlooking the Yangtze is worth the trip. Paths wind up the hill to several lookout points for what may be Nanjing's best view of this great river. The park's name comes from the massive boulder over the water. The rock is well-known because the famous Chinese poet Li Bai was once inspired to write a poem here; the poem is now etched into the rock. To get here, take Bus 8 to the last stop. ✉*Northeast of Mount Mufu, on the Yangtze* 🎫*Y15* 🕑*Daily 7:30–6.*

❿ **Sun Yat-sen Memorial** *(Zhongshan Ling)*. Acknowledged by the Nationalist and Communist governments alike, the father of modern China lies buried in a delicately carved marble sarcophagus. His resting place is the center of a solemn and imposing monument to the ideas that overthrew the imperial system. On the mountain are steep trails up the pine-covered slopes that feel worlds away from the bustle of Nanjing. A popular destination for Chinese tourists, the mausoleum gets crowded on weekends. ✉*Lingyuan Lu, east of the Ming Tomb* 🎫*Y40* 🕑*Sept.–May, daily 8:30–5, June–Aug., daily 6* AM*–6:30* PM.

⓮ **Yangtze River Bridge** *(Changjiang Daqiao)*. Completed in 1968 at the height of the Cultural Revolution, the bridge is decorated in stirring Socialist-realist style. Huge stylized flags made of red glass rise from the bridge's piers, and groups of giant-size peasants, workers, and soldiers stride forward heroically. The Great Bridge Park lies on the south side. From here you can take an elevator from the park up to a small museum. ✉*End of Daqiao Nan, northwest section of the city* 🎫*Free* 🕑*Daily 9–5.*

⓭ **Yuejiang Lou Tower.** This massive tower complex, built in the new millennium in Ming Dynasty style, looks out over a broad sweep of the Yangtze River. The founding emperor of the Ming Dynasty wrote a poem describing his plans to have a tower built here where he could view the river. Other imperial business got in the way, and for several centuries the building remained on paper. The grand tower and its surrounding buildings were built in 2001 in a historically accurate style, but it somehow seems too sterile. ✉202 *Jianning Lu, northwest corner of the city* ☎*025/5880–3977* *Y30* ⏲*Daily 8–6.*

WHERE TO EAT

For more information on bars and restaurants in Nanjing, pick up a copy of the local bilingual *Map Magazine* at your hotel. Printed monthly, it has the latest listings and reviews of many popular spots in the city, as well as upcoming cultural events.

> **THAT'S THE TICKET**
>
> If you'll be seeing a number of sights in Nanjing, a yearly ticket is a bargain. There are two different cards. The Garden Card (Y120) provides admission to Swallow Rock, South Gate of the City Wall, the Taiping Heavenly Kingdom Museum, and the Sun Yat-sen Botanical Gardens. The Purple Mountain Card (Y100) covers admission to Ming Tomb, Sun Yat-sen Mausoleum, and the Spirit Valley Temple and Pagoda. The cards can be bought at any of these spots. All you need is a passport and an ID-size photo.

$$–$$$ SICHUAN Fodor's Choice ★ ✕**Baguo Buyi.** Nanjing cuisine is generally mild, but if you are craving something spicy, Baguo Buyi is one of the best places to try authentic Sichuan cuisine. The food is searingly hot, in sharp contrast to the sweeter flavors of eastern Chinese cuisine. The stew of beef and yellow tofu is delicious, as is the steamed river fish served in a caldron of peppercorns. The spicy crab is another favorite with locals. The dining room is decorated with traditional wood carvings and antique furniture, and the restaurant occasionally hosts Sichuan opera "face-changing" performances. ✉*211 Longpan Zhong Lu, at Yixian Qiao* ☎*025/8460–8801* ▭*No credit cards.*

$$–$$$ CONTINENTAL ✕**Blue Marlin.** Palladian windows and a broad arched ceiling distinguish this dining room. The owner attended culinary school in Germany, which is why the place serves European-influenced cuisine. Specials include fish, steak, pasta—even foie gras. While the dishes are not spectacular, the food is consistent and the portions large. Contact the restaurant for information on live music performances, which are held in the bar. ✉*8 Changjiang Hou Jie, across from the Nanjing Library* ☎*025/8453–7376* ▭*No credit cards.*

$$–$$$ CHINESE ★ ✕**Dingshan Meishi Cheng.** One of Nanjing's finest restaurants and a popular choice among locals, Dingshan Meishi Cheng serves local cuisine in a traditional setting. The food here is not as hot as that from Sichuan, nor as sweet as that from Shanghai. There's a set-price menu that includes 4 cold dishes, 4 hot dishes, and a whopping 18 small dessert dishes, all for Y60. ✉*5 Zhanyuan Lu, near Confucian Temple* ☎*025/5220–9217* ▭*AE, MC, V.*

$$–$$$ CHINESE ✕**Hong Ni Restaurant.** It's hard to miss the Hong Ni—its facade lights up the neighborhood with a three-story neon extravaganza. Although the exterior is pure Las Vegas, the cuisine is excellent Yangzi Delta food from neighboring Zhejiang province. Prices are reasonable and everything is served in a sleek dining room. The seafood dish is highly recommended. It's downtown, near the Xinjiekou traffic circle, and many members of the staff speak English. ✉*23 Hongwu Lu* ☎*025/8689–9777* ▭*No credit cards.*

$–$$ VEGETARIAN **Jimingsi Vegetarian Restaurant.** Inside the Jiming Temple, this establishment cooks up Chinese fare with absolutely no meat. Although the menu lists pork, fish, chicken, and goose dishes, the food is all vegetarian. The chefs use tofu, wheat gluten, and vegetables to create tasty interpretations of meat. An English menu features a limited selection of the best dishes. Tofu threads and the Sichuan "fish" are recommended. This restaurant is noteworthy more for its view of the temple grounds than its food, but overall it's well worth a visit. ✉*Jiming Temple, off Beijing Dong Lu, south of Xuanwu Lake Park* ☎*025/8771–3690* ▭*No credit cards* ⊙*No dinner.*

$$–$$$ VEGETARIAN **Pure Lotus Vegetarian Restaurant.** Set a few kilometers outside the city center, this vegetarian restaurant is as much a feast for the eyes as the stomach. Completely vegetarian, the creativity of the chefs in preparing the "meat" dishes is matched by their stunning presentation. There is an English menu, but the poetic names for dishes can be confusing, so ask your server for his or her recommendations. The restaurant has a pleasant, peaceful atmosphere in which to rest and recover from the urban clamor outside. ✉*99 Shitou Cheng Road, Shuimu Qinghuai Block, Building 1C, opposite back gate of the Nanjing Arts College* ☎*025/8375–2306* ▭*No credit cards.*

$$ CHINESE ★ **Shizi Lou.** Anchoring the strip of restaurants of Shizi Qiao, near the Shanzi Road Market, Shizi Lou is a great introduction to Huaiyang fare. Resembling an indoor market, you can walk between stands and point to the dishes you want to sample. The "stinky tofu" is very good and not as malodorous as it's billed. The place is famous for local meatballs, with a dozen types from which to choose. ✉*29 Hunan Lu, near Shizi Bridge* ☎*025/8360–7888* ▭*No credit cards.*

WHERE TO STAY

$–$$ Fodor'sChoice ★ **Celebrity City Hotel.** You won't forget you're in China when you step through the door at this modern hotel. The hotel combines the best of the East (elegant bamboo and silk brocade) and the West (sleek glass and steel). Three good restaurants are here, one serving spicy Hunan food, one re-creating the feasts of the imperial past (for imperial prices), and the third with good Korean and Japanese food. Half of one floor is dedicated to mah-jongg rooms. Rooms aren't palatial, but they are well designed, with sleek furnishings, privacy, and high ceilings. **Pros:** attentive service, unique decor. **Cons:** guest services not as extensive as at other luxury establishments. ✉*30 Zhongshan Bei Lu* ☎*025/8312–3333* *368 rooms, 77 suites* *In-hotel: 3 restaurants, 2 bars, pool, gym, no-smoking rooms* ▭*AE, MC, V.*

$–$$$ **Central Hotel.** This lodging caters to travelers by arranging day tours in and around Nanjing. The 24-hour travel desk also sets up tours to more distant destinations. Rooms are modern, stylish, and reasonably priced. After a long day of sightseeing, the sleek sauna and beautiful star-shaped courtyard pool are inviting. **Pros:** good value, convenient location. **Cons:** standard rooms noticeably lower quality than executive rooms. ✉*75 Zhongshan Lu* ☎*025/8473–3888* *354 rooms, 22 suites* *In-hotel: 2 restaurants, bar, pool, gym* ▭*AE, MC, V.*

$–$$ **Grand Hotel.** This elliptical building in the center of town is a good base for seeing the sights. It overlooks the busy shopping centers and office buildings in the commercial center of the city. Along with standard amenities, it has a good Western restaurant. **Pros:** family friendly (babysitting services available), helpful staff. **Cons:** some rooms and facilities need renovations. ✉*208 Guangzhou Lu* ☎*025/8331–1999* 🌐*www.njgrandhotel.com* *305 rooms, 11 suites* *In-hotel: 5 restaurants, bar, tennis court, pool, gym* *AE, DC, MC, V.*

$$$–$$$$ **Jinling Hotel.** Nanjing's best-known hotel has a great location in the center of the city. It's a huge modern building connected to a shopping center. The travel agency on the first floor provides friendly and efficient service. On the second floor is the most authentic Japanese food in town. The guest rooms have every comfort, including high-speed Internet, an in-room safe, and 24-hour room service. **Pros:** luxurious accommodations, attentive service, wide array of shopping and other facilities. **Cons:** expensive. ✉*2 Xinjiekou* ☎*025/8471–1888 or 025/8472–2888* 🌐*www.jinlinghotel.com/en* *592 rooms, 33 suites* *In-hotel: 9 restaurants, bar, gym, pool, sauna, beauty salon* *AE, MC, V.*

¢–$ **Lakeview Xuanwu Hotel.** This modern hotel's guest rooms have excellent views of Xuanwu Lake. If you don't feel like venturing far for dinner, the 20th-floor revolving restaurant serves an all-you-can-eat buffet with Western and Chinese cuisine. The hotel can also help you arrange day trips around the city. **Pros:** great views, good value. **Cons:** service can be slow, some outdated facilities. ✉*193 Zhongyang Lu* ☎*025/8335–8888* 🌐*www.xuanwu.com.cn* *258 rooms, 47 suites* *In-hotel: 6 restaurants, bar, gym* *AE, DC, MC, V.*

$–$$ **Mandarin Garden Hotel.** Although many hotels of its caliber seem impersonal, this well-appointed establishment is warm and friendly. Its setting on the north side of the Confucian Temple keeps you far from the noise of the city. The excellent rooftop bar affords a good view of the skyline. The Galaxy Restaurant on the second floor serves Cantonese food. Guests are treated to an excellent breakfast buffet. **Pros:** excellent location, friendly staff. **Cons:** furnishings getting old, some amenities not quite deluxe. ✉*9 Zhuang Yuan Jing* ☎*0255/220–2555 or 0255/220–2988* *477 rooms, 24 suites* *In-hotel: 12 restaurants, bar, pool, gym, no-smoking rooms* *AE, MC, V.*

¢ **Nanjing Hotel.** Built in 1936, the old-fashioned hotel surrounded by lawns and trees seems pleasantly out of place in such a busy area of town. The staff is well trained and friendly. A separate section has simpler, less attractive rooms but for half the standard rate. Rooms have different amenities, so ask to see a few before you decide. **Pros:** inexpensive, all basic amenities. **Cons:** some advertised amenities not available in certain rooms. ✉*259 Zhongshan Bei Lu,* ☎*025/8682–6666* *310 rooms, 14 suites* *In-hotel: 3 restaurants, gym* *AE, MC, V.*

$$$ **Sheraton Nanjing Kingsley Hotel and Towers.** Top-rate facilities make this attractive hotel a favorite among business travelers; if you're not on an expense account, the prices may seem steep. The rooms are as comfortable as in any Sheraton. It's also home to one of just two Irish pubs in Nanjing, Danny's, with Guinness on tap and a group of expat regulars. **Pros:** many amenities for business travelers, very comfortable rooms. **Cons:** more for business than leisure travel,

expensive. ✉169 Hanzhong Lu, ☎025/8666–8888 🌐www.sheraton.com 350 rooms In-hotel: 2 restaurants, bars, tennis court, pool, gym, no-smoking rooms ▭AE, DC, MC, V.

IN THE NEWS

A stunning new home for the Nanjing Public Library was completed and officially opened in December 2007. It is one of the largest libraries in Asia, with more than 7 million volumes and an impressive collection of ancient texts.

NIGHTLIFE

Nanjing's nightlife centers around the 1912 neighborhood, named for the year the Republic of China was founded. A few dozen restaurants, bars, and clubs are packed into several blocks at the intersection of Taiping Lu and Changjiang Lu, a 15-minute walk northeast of the city center. Locals start with dinner, relax over drinks, charge up with coffee, hit the dance floor at a trendy club, stagger out to a late-night tea shop, and catch a cab back home—all without ever having to cross a lane of traffic. All the bars get going by about 10 PM, and close at 2 AM.

A highlight of the club scene, **Red Club** (✉*Off Taiping Lu* ☎*025/8452–2568*) has a bar and dance floor downstairs. **Scarlet Bar** (✉*Changjiang Hou Lu, off Taiping Lu* ☎*025/8335–1916*) is a longstanding favorite popular with expats for its excellent music. At **Swank** (✉*Off Taiping Lu* ☎*No phone*), the dance floor is packed with a trendy crowd.

★ **Base 77** (✉*129 Hanzhong Lu* ☎*025/8470–2006*) has the best live music in town. The house band is remarkably versatile, even incorporating instruments like the mandolin and fiddle. **Behind the Wall** (✉*150 Shanghai Lu* ☎*025/8391–5630*) is a great escape from the smoke and noise of most Chinese bars and a popular expat hangout. It doubles as a Mexican restaurant during the day, which is why the staff can mix a mean margarita. For an expertly poured pint in a foreign-run Irish pub, check out the hot new **Finnegan's Wake** (✉*South Zhongshan Lu, 6 Cinnalane* ☎*130/5762–3789* 🌐*www.finneganswake.com.cn/*), not far from the Confucius Temple.

SHOPPING

The best place to buy traditional crafts, art, and souvenirs is the warren of small shops in the center of the city. The lavish embroidered robes once worn by the emperors were traditionally produced in Nanjing, and the **Brocade Research Institute** (✉*240 Chating Dong Jie, behind Nanjing Massacre Memorial* ☎*025/8651–8580*) has a fascinating museum and workshop where the brocades are still produced using massive traditional looms. Their gift shop sells beautiful examples of traditional brocade.

Nanjing is a convenient place to pick up many of the traditional crafts of Jiangsu—purple sand teapots, flowing silks, interesting carvings, and folk paper cuttings. The **Nanjing Arts & Crafts Company** (✉*31 Beijing Dong Lu* ☎*025/5771–1189*) has a range of items, from jade and lacquerware to tapestries. Prices are high but so is quality.

In the courtyard of the Confucian Temple, the **Chaotian Gong Antique Market** (✉*Zhongshan Lu and Jiankang Lu* ☎*No phone*) has an array of curios, from genuine antiques to fakes of varying quality. Vendors' opening prices can border on the ludicrous, especially with foreign customers, but some good-natured bargaining can yield good buys. The market is open every day, but is liveliest on weekend mornings.

The **Shanxi Lu Night Market** (✉*Hunan Lu and Matai Jie* ☎*No phone*) has all sorts of odd items and some good finds waiting to be unearthed by savvy shoppers.

Northwest of the Drum Tower, the **Fabric Market** (✉*215 Zhongshan Bei Lu* ☎*No phone*) sells silks, linen, and traditional cotton fabrics. Bargaining is necessary, but the prices are reasonable. A good basic ballpark to pay is Y40 to Y60 per meter of silk. The vendors can also arrange tailoring.

YANGZHOU

1 hr (106 km [66 mi]) northeast of Nanjing, 3½ hrs (300 km [185 mi]) from Shanghai.

Yangzhou has quietly transformed itself into one of the most pleasant cities in Eastern China. With a population of half a million—minuscule by Chinese standards—the town has a laid-back feel. Yangzhou is small enough to be seen in one day, but is charming enough to make you want to linger for a few days.

Because of its location on the Grand Canal, Yangzhou flourished in the Tang Dynasty. Drawing on thousands of years as a trade center for salt and silk, Yangzhou maintains a cosmopolitan feel. Indeed, some of the most interesting sites in Yangzhou demonstrate a blending of cultures: Japanese relations are evidenced in the monument to Jianzhen, a monk who helped spread Buddhist teachings to Japan. European influence is seen in the Sino-Victorian gardens of He Yuan, and Persian contact is preserved in the tomb of Puddahidin, a 13th-century trader and descendant of Mohammed.

GETTING HERE AND AROUND

The best way to get to or from Yangzhou is by bus. It lies on the Beijing–Shanghai and Nanjing–Nantong highways. Huaihai Road Bus Station has departures from 6:30 in the morning until 6:30 in the evening. Suzhou is 230 km (143 mi) south, about 2 hours away. Shanghai, about 300 km (186 mi) away, takes 3½ hours. Trains to Yangzhou are not as convenient as the bus.

BY AIR Currently, there is no airport in Yangzhou but there are rumors of plans to build one. Check with a travel agent before you go.

BY BUS Frequent bus service runs between Yangzhou and Nanjing and Suzhou, and on to Shanghai. Most routes have air-conditioned buses. The Yangzhou bus station is about 6 km (4 mi) west of the city.

BY TRAIN There is a train station in Yangzhou, but only the slower trains stop here. If you are coming from nearby Nanjing or Zhenjiang, a train is a good option.

TOURS

Hotels are the chief source of tourist information in Yangzhou. Not only for the young, China Youth Travel in Yangzhou can put together any kind of trip, from morning boat rides around Slender West Lake to evening cruises down the Great Canal. The staff speaks English, and has the most experience working with foreign travelers.

ESSENTIALS

Bus Contacts **Yangzhou Bus Station** (✉ *Jiangyang Zhong Lu* ☎ *0514/8786–1812*).

Medical Assistance **Yangzhou No. 1 People's Hospital** (✉ *45 Taizhou Lu* ☎ *0514/8790–7353*).

Train Contacts **Yangzhou Train Station** (✉ *Wenhe Xi Lu* ☎ *0514/8268–6282*).

Visitor and Tour Info **Yangzhou China Youth Travel Agency** (✉ *6 Siwangting Lu* ☎ *0514/8793–3876*).

EXPLORING YANGZHOU

MAIN ATTRACTIONS

The **Da Ming Temple** *(Daming Si)* is one of the more interesting Buddhist shrines in Eastern China. Maybe the most arresting detail is the mural behind the main laughing Buddha image, where an image of the gender-bending god Guanyin stands on a turtle's head. Another highlight on the temple grounds is the Fifth Spring Under Heaven. Most of the ancient Tang Dynasty springs are no longer usable, but this one still flows. The high mineral content of the water makes it especially suited for tea, which you can sip in a small teahouse overlooking the temple gardens. Also on the grounds is a Tang-style monument to a Chinese missionary who traveled to Japan, Jian Zhen. ✉ *8 Pingshan Tang Lu, next to Slender West Lake* ☎ *0514/8734–0720* 🎫 *Mar.–June and Sept.–Nov., Y45; Dec.–Feb., and July–Aug., Y30* ⏲ *Daily 7:45–5.*

Rather than flowers, **Ge Garden** *(Ge Yuan)* is planted with over 60 varieties of bamboo and is a virtual rainbow of greens. There are yellow stalks, striped stalks, huge treelike stands, and dwarf bamboo with delicate leaves. The emerald stalks stand out against whitewashed walls and black undulating rooflines. Note the loose bricks in the path, arranged to clack as you walk. Catch your breath with a cup of tea in the tea hall. ✉ *10 Yangfu Dong Lu, east of Yangzhou Hotel* ☎ *0514/8736–5553* 🌐 *www.ge-garden.net/english/* 🎫 *Mar.–May and Sept.–Nov., Y40; June–Aug. and Dec.–Feb., Y30* ⏲ *Daily 7:15–6.*

Originally part of a river, **Slender West Lake** *(Shou xi hu)* was created during the Qing Dynasty by rich salt merchants hoping to impress the emperor on his visit to Yangzhou. The park is planted in willows, bamboo, and flowers, and can be enjoyed briskly in 45 minutes or savored for a full afternoon. Pavilions, tearooms, and bowed bridges are all about the grounds. The **fishing terrace** is where the emperor decided he'd try his hand at angling. The merchants reportedly had their servants wade into the lake and hook a fish on each line he cast. Another mark left by the emperor is in the form of the **White Pagoda,** actually a *dagoba,* a Buddhist monument shaped like a bottle. The emperor casually remarked that Slender West Lake only lacked a dagoba like the one in Beijing. By the time the sun shone through the morning mist, there was the emperor's dagoba—more or less. The permanent structure was completed much later. Apparently all the flattery had the desired effect, because Yangzhou prospered up until the 20th century as a center of trade in China. ✉ *28 Da Hongqiao Lu, in the northern part of the city* ☎ *0514/8733–0189* 🌐 *www.shouxihu.com/sxhen/index.php* 🎟 *Mar.–May and Sept.–Nov., Y80; June–Aug. and Dec.–Feb., Y60* ⏲ *Daily 7–6.*

Fodor's Choice ★ Unremarkable when it was built, **Wang's Residence** *(Wangshi Xiaoyuan)* is now one of Yangzhou's highlights. This courtyard house was one of many large private homes owned by Yangzhou's prosperous merchant class. It alone was spared the wrath of the Cultural Revolution because it had been converted into a factory. The highlight is the detailed carvings, chief among them the crisscrossing bamboo design carved in layers out of *nanmu,* a glimmering wood now extinct in this area of China. There's even a bomb shelter in the small inner garden that serves as a reminder of the Japanese invasion. English translations are few, but there are a few guides who can lead in English—however, the house speaks for itself. ✉ *14 Di Gong Di, between Taizhou Lu and Guoqing Lu* ☎ *0514/8732–8869* 🎟 *Y15* ⏲ *Daily 8–5:30.*

IF YOU HAVE TIME

The **Garden Tomb of Puhaddin** *(Puhading Mu)* faces the Grand Canal, from where you climb a stairway to a graveyard of marble slab headstones. In the back is a garden with a charming pavilion that blends Chinese and Muslim design, with Arabic inscriptions. Largely ignored by local tourists, a visit to the garden tomb is an eye-opening look at Chinese history. ✉ *Laopai Lu at Quanfu Lu, near Jiefang Bridge* 🎟 *Y10* ⏲ *Daily 7:30–4:30.*

Dating from the 1880s, the Victorian-influenced **He Garden** *(He Yuan)* is notable for its melding of European and Chinese architecture. While Ge Garden flows in traditional style, He Garden has a more rigid design. However, the attention to detail and perspective subtly brings together design values of East and West, making the garden more than a mere imitation of European design. ✉ *66 Xuning Men Dalu, southeast corner of the city* ☎ *0514/8723–2360* 🎟 *Y40* ⏲ *Daily 7:30–5:30.*

WHERE TO EAT

¢–$ CHINESE ✕ **De Yue Restaurant.** Started 20 years ago with just six tables, this sprawling restaurant is a testament to the quality of the food. Specialties include salted goose, flaky white fish, and shrimp in rice wine. ✉ *139 Wen Chang Lu* ☎ *0514/8734–3833* ▭ *No credit cards.*

$–$$ CHINESE ✕ **Fu Chun Teahouse.** With history going back more than a century, Fu Chun serves traditional local food. It's best known for its desserts; try the sweet rice buns, layer cakes, or any of their other bite-size snacks.

CLOSE UP

Adopting in China

For some, the gardens, the architecture, the history, and the scenery are all secondary reasons to visit Yangzhou. Theirs is a more personal and momentous trip. On the outskirts of town there is a white-tiled compound called the Yangzhou Social Welfare Institute. This is where American parents and Chinese children come together to form families. Since Chinese law began promoting foreign adoption in 1991, there has been a huge surge in the number of families adopting from China. More than 50,000 children have been brought to the United States from China over the past 15 years.

Over 95% of children in orphanages are female. There persists a strong preference for boys, especially in rural areas. This is largely due to a combination of bias and traditional social structures whereby girls marry out and males help provide for the family. An unintended consequence of the One Child Policy exacerbates prejudices against women. Some Chinese parents, desperate to have a male child, take drastic measures like gender-selective abortion and even abandon their girls on the steps of orphanages.

The first wave of American-adopted Chinese girls are already teens. As they come of age, their trans-racial families face unique challenges as they grapple with questions of racial and cultural identity. Support groups, social organizations, and even specialized heritage tour groups address these questions and assist children in learning more about their places of birth.

For more information on adoption in China:

Families with Children from China (*www.fwcc.org*) runs listservs and provides a wealth of resources on adoption. Tour information is available from the nonprofit group **Our Chinese Daughters Foundation** (*www.ocdf.org*). **The China Centre of Adoption Affairs** (*CCAA www.china-ccaa.org*) is the Chinese government's official source for procedural and legal information. *Adoptive Families* (*www.adoptivefamilies.com*) is a magazine on general adoption issues.

Wash it all down with flavorful green tea. *35 Desheng Qiao Lu* *0514/8723–3326* *No credit cards.*

WHERE TO STAY

$–$$ **Metropark Hotel.** This modern hotel is conveniently located in the city center. Past the grand lobby are guest rooms with Asian-inspired decor. The helpful staff can arrange a car and driver if you want to explore the area. **Pros:** friendly staff, great location, clean and comfortable rooms. **Cons:** more geared toward business travelers. *559 Wenchang Quanfu Lu* *0514/8732–2888* *www.metroparkhotels.com* *242 rooms, 25 suites* *In-room: safe, Ethernet. In-hotel: 4 restaurants, bar, gym* *AE, MC, V.*

¢–$ **XiYuan Hotel.** Rooms at this hotel border on drab and are quite small, but the location, near Slender West Lake and many restaurants and stores, is convenient. Staff are friendly and helpful but speak limited English. **Pros:** a bargain compared to other upscale hotels in Yangzhou, convenient central location. **Cons:** language barrier with staff, quality of rooms. ✉ *1 Feng Le Shang Jie* ☎ *0514/8780–7888* 🌐 *www.xiyuan-hotel.com* *270 rooms, 12 suites* *In-hotel: 4 restaurants, gym, tennis courts, no-smoking rooms* 💳 *AE, MC, V.*

¢–$ **Yangzhou Hotel.** Although this hotel looks a little worn around the edges, it does have a prime location overlooking the canals. Frequent discounts make it a real bargain. If you like going to bed early though, ask for a room facing away from the street. One of the city's biggest nightclubs is next door, and the noise can continue past midnight. **Pros:** nice views, inexpensive. **Cons:** noisy, staff can be indifferent. ✉ *5 Feng Le Shang Jie* ☎ *0514/8780–5888* *150 rooms, 6 suites* *In-hotel: restaurant, bar, pool* 💳 *AE, MC, V.*

REPLANTING GARDENS

The sad story is that many of the country's historic gardens have been recently pieced back together. Most were ravaged during the Cultural Revolution, when for years Red Guard troops were encouraged to smash China's heritage to pieces. To this day, China is still replanting gardens, repairing temples, and restoring historic architecture.

NIGHTLIFE

The two best nightlife options are near the Yangzhou Hotel. At **Banana Night Club** (✉ *15 Fengle Shangjie* ☎ *0514/735–3650*) a DJ spins tunes for a mostly local crowd. The laid-back **Cellar Bar** (✉ *8 Fengle Shangjie* ☎ *0514/8736–7713*) has a good mix of locals and expats and features a pool table. The beer is cheap, and the service is friendly.

SUZHOU

Approximately 3½ hrs (225 km [140 mi]) by train on Nanjing–Shanghai rail line southeast of Nanjing, or 1 hr (84 km [52 mi]) by train west of Shanghai.

Suzhou has long been known as a place of culture, beauty, and sophistication. It produced scores of artists, writers, and politicians over the centuries, and it developed a local culture based on refinement and taste. Famous around the world for its carefully designed classical gardens, Suzhou's elegance extends even to its local dialect—Chinese often say that two people arguing in the Suzhou dialect sounds more pleasant than lovers talking in standard Chinese.

Unlike in other cities in Eastern China, glass-and-steel office parks have been barred from the old city center here, and this preservation makes Suzhou a pleasant place to explore. There is excellent English signage on the roads, and the local tourism board has even set up a convenient information center to get you on the right track.

Only an hour outside of Shanghai, the tourist trail here is well-worn and during the high season you will find yourself sharing these gardens with packs of foreign and domestic tour groups. It's worth getting up early to hit the most popular places before the crowds descend.

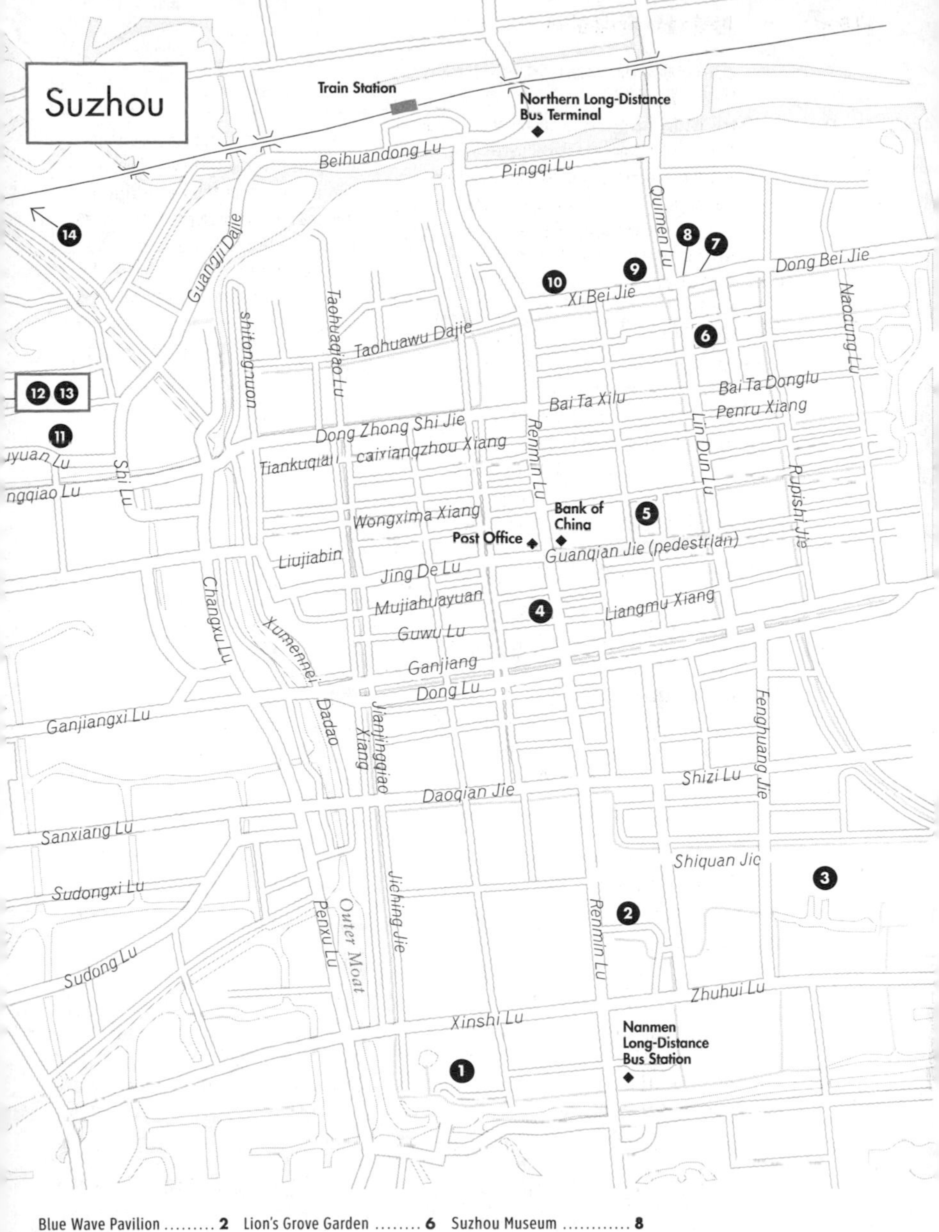

Blue Wave Pavilion **2**
Hanshan Temple **13**
Humble Administrator's Garden **7**
Joyous Garden **4**
Lingering Garden **11**
Lion's Grove Garden **6**
Master of the Nets Garden **3**
North Temple Pagoda **10**
Pan Gate **1**
Suzhou Arts and Crafts Museum **9**
Suzhou Museum **8**
Temple of Mystery **5**
Tiger Hill **14**
West Garden Temple **12**

GETTING HERE AND AROUND

Buses bound for Nanjing (2 hours) and Yangzhou (3 hours) depart from the North Bus Station. Frequent trains to Nanjing take two to three hours. It's a popular route, so be sure to buy tickets in advance. Trains to Yangzhou take 3½ hours.

> **WATER WHEELS**
>
> The old city is circled by a moat, and you can take an "aquatic bus" that leaves from the bus station. The cost is Y15 per person.

Buses to Shanghai take about an hour. Trains, which depart about every 20 minutes, take anywhere from 40 minutes to 1½ hours.

BY AIR Suzhou is served by Shanghai's airports, Hongqiao and Pudong International Airports. Hongqiao Airport is about 86 km (53 mi) from Suzhou, and shuttle buses run throughout the day. The trip takes less than 2 hours. If you are coming into Pudong, buses that make the 120-km (65-mi) trip from the airport about once an hour.

BY BUS Bus service between Suzhou and Nanjing is frequent. The Suzhou bus station is just outside the Pingmen Gate.

BY TRAIN Nanjing and Suzhou are on the same rail line, which continues on to Shanghai. Tickets can be purchased through your hotel. At the stations, the lines are long and vendors curt with non-Chinese speakers.

ESSENTIALS

Air Contacts **China Eastern Airlines** (✉*192 Renmin Lu* ☎*0512/6522–2788* 🌐*www.ce-air.com*). **China Southern Airlines** (✉*943 Renmin Lu* ☎*0512/6524–3437* 🌐*www.cs-air.com/en*).

Bus Contacts **Suzhou Bus Station** (✉*29 Xihui Lu* ☎*0512/6753–0686*).

Medical Assistance **People's Hospital No. 2** (✉*26 Daoqian Jie* ☎*0512/6522–3691*).

Train Contacts **Suzhou Train Station** (✉*Beihuan Xi Lu* ☎*0512/6753–2831*).

Visitor and Tour Info **CITS** (✉*18 Da Jing Xiang* ☎*0512/6511–7505* 🌐*english.citssz.com*).

EXPLORING SUZHOU

Suzhou is threaded by a network of narrow waterways. The canals that now seem quaint were once choked with countless small boats ferrying goods between the city's merchants. All of these small channels lead eventually to imperial China's main conduit of trade and travel, the **Grand Canal** *(Da Yunhe)*, which passes through the outskirts of town. The **Precious Belt Bridge** (Baodai Qiao) is an ancient bridge of 53 arches that bound over Tantai Lake where it meets the Grand Canal. ✉*Beyond Pingmen Gate, north on Renmin Lu.*

MAIN ATTRACTIONS

❷ **Blue Wave Pavilion** *(Canglang Ting)*. The Blue Wave Pavilion is the oldest existing garden in Suzhou, dating back more than 900 years to the Song Dynasty. With a simple design, the garden grounds feel a little wilder than the relative newcomers. The central pond is an expansive stretch

> **WORD OF MOUTH**
>
> "The main sights of Suzhou are its classic garden. It also has pretty intact city walls with no high-rise inside the old city. It's also famous for its silk knit centers. There are several water towns near Suzhou, and between Suzhou and Shanghai that are quite interesting." —rkkwan

of water that reflects the upturned eaves of the surrounding buildings. Over 100 different lattice designs shading the windows provide visual variety as you saunter the long corridor over the water. A rocky hill rises in the center of the pond, atop which stands the square Blue Wave Pavilion. The **Pure Fragrance Pavilion** showcases Qing Dynasty furniture at its most extreme; the entire suite is created from gnarled banyan root. ✉ *East of Renmin Lu, between Shiquan Jie and Xinshi Lu* 🎫 *Apr. 16–Oct. 30, Y20; Oct. 31–Apr. 15, Y15* ⏲ *Daily 8–5.*

7 **Humble Administrator's Garden** *(Zhuo Zheng Yuan)*. More than half of Suzhou's largest garden is taken up by ponds and lakes. The garden was built in 1509 by Wang Xianjun, an official dismissed from the imperial court. He chose the garden's name from a Tang Dynasty line of poetry reading "humble people govern," perhaps a bit of sarcasm considering the grand scale of his private residence. ✉ *178 Dongbei Jie, 1 block east of Lindun Lu* ☎ *0512/6751–0286* 🌐 *www.szzzy.cn* 🎫 *Apr. 16–Oct. 30, Y70; Oct. 31–Apr. 15, Y50* ⏲ *Daily 7:30–5:30.*

Fodor's Choice ★

11 **Lingering Garden** *(Liu Yuan)*. Windows frame other windows, undulating rooflines recall waves, and a closed corridor transforms into a room open to the pond at this interesting garden. The compound provides an endless array of architectural surprises: in a corner an unexpected skylight illuminates a planted nook; windows are placed to frame bamboo as perfectly as if they were painted. The **Mandarin Duck Hall** is particularly impressive, with a lovely moon gate engraved with vines and flowers. In the back of the garden stands a 70-foot-tall rock moved here from Lake Taihu. Ongoing solo musical performances on erhu and zither enliven the halls. ✉ *79 Liuyuan Lu, west of the moat* ☎ *0512/6557–9466* 🌐 *www.gardenly.com* 🎫 *Apr. 16–Oct. 30, Y40; Oct. 31–Apr. 15, Y30* ⏲ *Daily 7:30–5:30 (last ticket sold at 5).*

6 ★ **Lion's Grove Garden** *(Shizi Lin)*. This garden uses countless gnarled formations from nearby Lake Taihu to create a surreal moonscape. A labyrinth of man-made caves surrounds a small lake. There's a popular local saying that if you talk to rocks, you won't need a psychologist, making this garden a good place to spend a 50-minute hour. A tearoom on the second floor of the main pavilion overlooks the lake. ✉ *23 Yuanlin Lu, 3 blocks south of the Humble Administrator's Garden* ☎ *0512/6727–8316* 🌐 *www.szszl.com* 🎫 *Y30* ⏲ *Daily 8:15–5:30.*

3 ★ **Master of the Nets Garden** *(Wangshi Yuan)*. All elements of Suzhou style are here in precise balance: rock hills, layered planting, and charming pavilions overlooking a central pond. The garden is a favorite spot on tour group itineraries. To avoid the crowds, visit in the evening, when you can saunter from room to room enjoying traditional opera, flute,

and dulcimer performances—as the master himself might have enjoyed. Performances are held from mid-March to mid-November. ✉*11 Kuo Jia Tou Gang, west of Shiquan Lu* ☎*0512/6529–3190* 🌐*www.szwsy.com* 🎫*Apr. 16–Oct. 30, Y30; Oct. 31–Apr. 15, Y20* ⏲*Daily 7:30–5 (last ticket sold at 4:30).*

WORD OF MOUTH

"Go to Souzhou and spend a few days there, explore the gardens and perhaps make day trips to the water towns, e.g. Tongli."

—Nywoman

5 **Temple of Mystery** *(Xuanmiao Guan).* One of the best-preserved Taoist compounds, the Temple of Mystery backs a large square that is now a lively market. Founded in the 3rd century, the temple is a rare example of a wooden structure that has lasted centuries, with parts from the 12th century. Fortunately, it suffered little damage in the Cultural Revolution and retains a splendid ceiling of carefully arranged beams and braces painted in their original colors. Taoist music is performed throughout the day. ✉*Guanqian Jie* ☎*0512/6777–5479* 🎫*Y10; with Taoist music and flying cymbals performance Y35* ⏲*Daily 8:30–5.*

14 **Tiger Hill** *(Huqiu).* This hill is the burial place of the King of the State of Wu, who founded the city in 514 BC. At the top of the approach is a huge sheet of stone called **Thousand Man Rock,** where legend has it that the workers who built the tomb were thanked for their work with an elaborate banquet. The wine, alas, was drugged, so they died to keep the secret of the tomb's entrance. Modern archaeologists think they have discovered it hidden under the artificial lake. The secret may be out, but the king's wish to rest in peace is ensured by the fact that excavating the tomb would bring down the fragile Song Dynasty pagoda that stands above. The **Leaning Pagoda** is one of the most impressive monuments in Suzhou, with Persian influence evident in the arches and other architectural elements. A helpful audio guide explains many of the park's legends. ✉*Huqiu Lu, northwest of the city* ☎*0512/6532–3488* 🎫*Apr. 16–Oct. 30, Y60; Oct. 31–Apr. 15, Y40* ⏲*Daily 7:30–5.*

IF YOU HAVE TIME

13 **Hanshan Temple** *(Hanshan Si).* Best known as a subject of one of the Tang Dynasty's most famous poems, which described the sound of its massive bell at midnight, this large, pristinely painted temple may leave those unfamiliar with the ancient poetry feeling a little underwhelmed. The place has the frenetic feel of a tourist attraction, rather than the serenity of a temple. Literary pilgrims can line up to ring the temple bell themselves for an extra charge. ✉*24 Hanshan Si Nong* ☎*0512/6533–6634* 🎫*Apr. 16–Oct. 30, Y20; Oct. 31–Apr. 15, Y15* ⏲*Daily 8–5.*

4 **Joyous Garden** *(Yi Yuan).* The youngest garden in Suzhou, Joyous Garden was built in 1874. It borrows elements from Suzhou's other famous garden: rooms from the Humble Administrator's, a pond from the Master of the Nets. The most unusual feature in the garden is an oversize mirror, inspired by the founder of Zen Buddhism, who stared at a wall for years to find enlightenment. The garden's designer hung the mirror opposite a pavilion, to let the building contemplate its own reflection.

From April to October, the garden doubles as a popular teahouse in the evening. ✉*343 Renmin Lu, 1 block south of the Temple of Mystery* ☎*0512/6524–9317* 🎟*Y15* ⏲*Daily 7:30* AM*–midnight.*

❿ **North Temple Pagoda** *(Beisi Ta)*. One of the symbols of ancient Suzhou, this temple towers over the old city. This complex has a 1,700-year history, dating to the Three Kingdoms Period. The wooden pagoda has nine levels; you can climb as high as the eighth level for what might be the best view of Suzhou. Within the grounds are the Copper Buddha Hall and Plum Garden, which, built in 1985, lacks the history and the complexity of Suzhou's other gardens. ✉*Xibei Jie and Renmin Lu, 2 blocks west of Humble Administrator's Garden* ☎*0512/6753–1197* 🎟*Y15; Y10 more to climb pagoda* ⏲*Mar.–Oct., daily 7:45–6.*

❶ **Pan Gate** *(Pan Men)*. Traffic into old Suzhou came both by road and canals, so the city's gates were designed to control access by both land and water. This gate—more of a small fortress—is the only one that remains. In addition to the imposing wooden gates on land, a double sluice gate can be used to seal off the canal and prevent boats from entering. A park is filled with colorful flowers, in contrast to the subdued traditional gardens elsewhere in the city. A small platform extends over a pond where voracious carp turn the water into a thrashing sheet of orange and yellow as they compete for food that tourists throw down. You can climb the **Ruiguang Pagoda,** a tall, slender spire originally built more than 1,000 years ago. ✉*1 Dong Dajie, southwest corner of the old city* ☎*0512/6526–0004* 🎟*Panmen Gate Y25; Ruigang Pagoda Y6* ⏲*Daily 8–4:45.*

❾ **Suzhou Arts and Crafts Museum.** The highlight here is watching artists in action. They carve jade, cut latticework fans from thin sheets of sandalwood, and fashion traditional calligraphy brushes. Perhaps most amazing is the careful attention to detail of the women embroidering silk. The attached shop is a good place to pick up quality crafts. ✉*58 Xibei Jie, between Humble Administrator's Garden and the North Pagoda* ☎*0512/6753–4874* 🎟*Y15* ⏲*Daily 9–5.*

❽ **Suzhou Museum.** This is the most modern building to emerge amid a neighborhood of traditional architecture. The museum is the valedictory work for 90-year-old modernist master I.M. Pei. A controversy erupted over whether to allow Pei to construct the glass-and-steel structure in historical Suzhou. Like his crystal pyramid in the courtyard of the Louvre, this building thrives on juxtapositions of old and new. The museum houses historical objects from Suzhou's ancient past and an impressive collection of Ming and Qing Dynasty paintings and calligraphy. ✉*204 Dongbei Jie, next to Humble Administrator's Garden* ☎*0512/6757–5666* 🌐*www.szmuseum.com* 🎟*Free; English language docent tours Y100* ⏲*Daily 9–5.*

⓬ **West Garden Temple** *(Xi Yuan Si)*. This temple is most notable for the **Hall of 500 Arhats** (Wubai Luohan Tang), which houses 500 gold-painted statues of these Buddhist guides. They are humorous carvings: one struggling with dragons, another cradling a cat. ✉*8 Xiwan Lu, across from Lingering Garden* 🎟*Y25* ⏲*Daily 7–5.*

CLOSE UP

Exploring the Water Villages

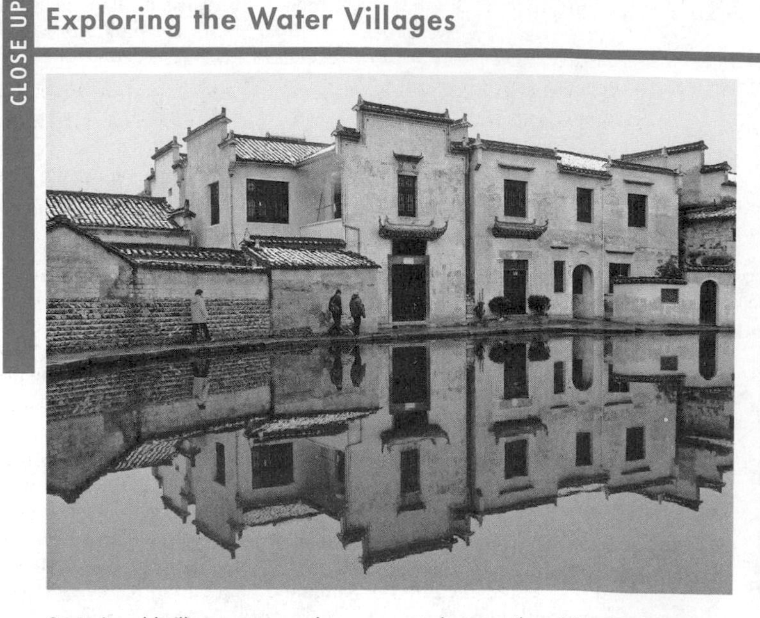

Centuries-old villages, preserved almost in their original state, are scattered around Suzhou. Bowed bridges span narrow canals, as traditional oared boats paddle by, creating an almost perfect picture of a way of life long past. A trip to one of these villages will probably be a highlight of your trip to Eastern China.

Be careful which village you choose, though. The tourist dollars that flow in may have saved these villages from the wrecking ball, but they have also changed their character to differing degrees. Those closest to the larger cities can be the most swamped by tour groups. Trekking to an out-of-the-way destination can pay off by letting you find a village that you will have all to yourself.

The most famous of the water villages is undoubtedly **Zhouzhuang.** Its fame is partly due to its proximity, just 45 minutes from Suzhou and an hour away from Shanghai. As a result, more than 2.5 million visitors head to the water village of Zhouzhuang each year to catch a glimpse of old China. Its charm is reduced by the sheer number of tourists who elbow their way through the streets. Next to the "ancient memorial archway," which isn't ancient at all, is a ticket window. The steep entrance fee of Y100 gets you into the water village-turned-gift shop.

Crowds aside, Zhouzhuang is fun for families. Several residences, some 500 years old, let you see what life was like in the Ming and Qing dynasties. There are several storefronts where you can see brick making, bamboo carving, and basket weaving—traditional crafts that up until recently were in widespread use throughout the countryside. The food is typical country fare, making it a nice break from the fancier cuisine of Suzhou and Shanghai. The most famous dish, a fatty cut of pork leg, is a bit oily for most Western palates. But there are also pickled vegetables and wild greens to sample. For crafts, skip the snuff bottles and teapots, which are of low quality. Opt for something you probably won't find elsewhere: homemade rice wine, rough-hewn ox-horn combs, and bamboo rice baskets.

Buses to Zhouzhuang leave from Suzhou's North Bus station every half hour between 7 AM and 5 PM. The 1½-hour trip costs Y18 to Y25.

The pick of the water villages is **Tongli,** 30 minutes from Zhouzhuang and 1½ hours from Suzhou. There's a slightly more reasonable entrance fee of Y80. A number of locals still live and work here, making this village seem more authentic than Zhouzhuang. The streets are cobbled, and the complete absence of cars makes Tongli feel like it's from a different era. You can still find yourself wandering on quaint side streets or creeping down impossibly narrow alleyways that open onto canals and bridges. Tongli is the largest of the water villages, imminently photographable, and a pleasure to explore. Near the entrance gate are several private homes offering beds, and throughout the village are tea shops and small tables set out in front of the canals. Hiring a boat (Y60 for up to 6 people) to float down the canals gives you a different perspective on the town.

A favorite spot in Tongli is Tuisi Garden, a slightly smaller version of the private courtyard parks found in Suzhou. Tongli is also home to the **Ancient Chinese Sexual Culture Museum,** housed in a former girl's school. The controversial exhibition of ancient erotic toys and art is the project of a retired university professor. ✉ *Entrance to town* ☎ *0512/6332–2973* 🎫 *Y20.*

Buses to Tongli leave from the square in front of Suzhou Train Station every 20 to 30 minutes between 7 AM and 5 PM. The journey is Y6 to Y10.

Even farther off the beaten path is **Luzhi,** about a half hour from Suzhou and Zhouzhuang. It is a popular tourist destination, but it is still relatively untouched by large tour groups and is a more peaceful water town experience. It has been described as a "museum of bridges." There are more than 40 here, in all different shapes and sizes. Many of the older women in the village preserve traditional customs, wearing traditional headdresses and skirts. Luzhi is also notable for the spectacular **Baosheng Temple** (✉ *Luzhi* ☎ *0512/6501–0011*), a yellow-walled compound built in 503 that is famous for its breathtaking collection of Buddhist arhats. Arranged on a wall of stone, these clay sculptures are the work of Yang Huizhi, a famous Tang Dynasty sculptor. They depict Buddhist disciples who have gained enlightenment; these works, made over 1,000 years ago, impart the character and artistry of their creator. The temple also features a well-preserved bell from the end of the Ming Dynasty. Luzhi-bound buses leave from the square in front of Suzhou Train Station every 30 minutes between 6:30 AM and 6:30 PM. The 40-minute drive is Y10.

WHERE TO EAT

Shiquan Jie is quickly becoming one of the city's restaurant hubs, with both Suzhou-style restaurants and Chinese regional cuisine from Xinjiang to Yunnan. Many offer English menus.

> **WORD OF MOUTH**
>
> "Once you get inside the old town, there are no motorized vehicles, just bikes and pedestrian traffic. Nothing really seems to be rebuilt here, so you can get a feel for the old ways of living, people still doing their laundry & washing vegetables in the canal. Stopped and had tea at a cute tea shop. Good local art here in Tongli, as well as inexpensive embroidered wall art." —quimbymoy

$$–$$$ CHINESE ★ **Deyuelou.** This restaurant has served Suzhou-style food for more than 400 years. The menu boasts a wide array of fish dishes and a particularly tasty *deyue tongji* (braised chicken). It also specializes in the ancient art of "garden foods"—an assortment of small dishes arranged to resemble various sorts of gardens, with foods portraying flowers, trees, and rocks. You can also try the local-style dim sum. ✉ *27 Taijian Nong and 8 Taijian Nong, south of the Temple of Mystery* ☎ *0512/6523–8940* ▭ *AE, MC, V.*

¢ CHINESE **Huangtianyuan.** Here the specialty is the local favorite of *gaotuan* (rice gluten), made by pounding rice to a fine paste. In business since 1821, the eatery's menu changes with the seasons. A year-round house specialty is *babao fan* (or "eight treasure rice," a syrupy rice with various sweets, nuts, and fruit bits). The sweets come in all sizes and colors, including green rice balls and red bean-filled dumplings. The desserts are subtly sweet, not the sugary concoctions that Westerners are used to. ✉ *86 Guanqian Jie* ☎ *0512/6770–4427* ▭ *No credit cards.*

$$–$$$ CHINESE ★ **Pine and Crane** *(Songhelou).* The food is the type once served on riverboats during banquet cruises—hence the popular designation "boat food." A particularly good dish is the *songshu guiyu,* or "squirrel-shaped Mandarin fish." (Don't let the English translation turn you off: it's a sweet-and-sour boneless fried river fish.) The other fish dishes are just as delicious. ✉ *72 Taijian Nong, south of the Temple of Mystery* ☎ *0512/6770–0688* ▭ *AE, MC, V.*

WHERE TO STAY

$–$$ **Bamboo Grove Hotel.** A modern hotel that caters to international travelers, the Bamboo Grove offers more amenities than you might expect. The three-story open lobby, the stylish garden courtyard, and vast restaurant are attractive places to relax. The guest rooms are comfortable but beginning to show their age, and are in need of refurbishment. The hotel's bamboo logo pops up everywhere, from the backs of chairs to the cute cotton robes hanging in the closets. **Pros:** convenient central location, good Chinese restaurant. **Cons:** dingy furnishings and carpet. ✉ *168 Zhuhui Lu* ☎ *0512/6520–5601* 🌐 *www.bg-hotel.com* *319 rooms, 37 suites* *In-room: safe, Ethernet. In-hotel: 2 restaurants, room service, bar, tennis courts, pool, gym, concierge, laundry service, public Internet, no-smoking rooms, refrigerator* ▭ *AE, DC, MC, V.*

$–$$ ★ **Gloria Plaza Hotel Suzhou.** From the watercolor paintings lining the halls to the cascading waterfall windows of its Sampan Restaurant, the

Gloria Plaza Hotel stands out as an inviting property. The large standard rooms dwarf the furniture inside; rooms on the executive floor fill the space better by adding a pullout couch. The hotel is alongside one of Suzhou's charming canals, which leads to the Humble Administrator's Garden, and just a five-minute walk from Guanqian Jie's restaurants and nightclubs. The business facilities are useful for anyone who wants to stay connected. **Pros:** great breakfast, convenient location for tourists. **Cons:** carpets and furnishings need replacing. ✉*535 Ganjiang Dong Lu* ☎*0512/6521–8855* 🌐*www.gphsuzhou.com* *281 rooms, 13 suites* *In-room: safe, dial-up. In-hotel: 2 restaurants, room service, bar, gym, concierge, laundry service, public Internet, no-smoking rooms* *AE, DC, MC, V.*

¢–$ **Lexiang Hotel.** Catering mainly to Chinese guests, this hotel is filled with furnishings in a classical Chinese style. It's down the street from the Joyous Garden and a block from the beautiful Temple of Mystery. **Pros:** good location, inexpensive. **Cons:** basic facilities. ✉*18 Dajingxi ang* ☎*0512/6522–8888* *0512/6801–3408* *197 rooms, 15 suites* *In-room: Ethernet, refrigerator. In-hotel: 3 restaurants, bar, gym* *AE, MC, V.*

$ **Nanyuan Guest House.** After a day of exploring Suzhou's gardens, return to a garden of your own. The 10 acres surrounding the Nanyuan Guest House are pleasantly planted with bamboo, and rocks and ponds are sprinkled throughout its courtyards. The selling point, however, is the location two blocks from the Master of the Nets Garden. The apricot-and-mauve rooms are spread among six buildings. **Pros:** beautiful grounds. **Cons:** inadequate facilities for business travelers. ✉*249 Shiquan Jie,* ☎*0512/6778–6778* *0512/6778–6888* *97 rooms, 7 suites* *In-hotel: 2 restaurants, room service, bar, laundry service, public Internet, refrigerator* *AE, DC, MC, V.*

$$–$$$$ Fodor's Choice ★ **Sheraton Suzhou Hotel & Towers.** Suzhou's most luxurious hotel has a two-story stone entrance topped by a pagoda lobby that is modeled after the Pan Gate. (If you want to compare, it sits behind the hotel.) The garden views from the courtyard-facing rooms are stunning. Guests have access to a fitness center and a striking Roman-style pool. But for a nightly rate that is twice the average Chinese monthly salary, the accommodations are not huge, Internet access is only available in the most expensive rooms, and the location is less than central. The Garden Brasserie presents an Asian-style buffet, and high tea is served on weekends. **Pros:** beautiful architecture and gardens, spacious rooms. **Cons:** pricey, fewer amenities than most hotels in its class. ✉*259 Xinshi Lu,* ☎*0512/6510–3388* 🌐*www.sheraton-suzhou.com* *328 rooms, 30 suites* *3 restaurants, room service, bar, pool, gym, concierge, laundry service, executive floor, public Internet, no-smoking rooms* *AE, DC, MC, V.*

¢–$ Fodor's Choice ★ **Suzhou Hotel.** On Perfect 10 Street, this hotel has a location to match. It is a short walk from the Master of the Nets Garden and a stretch of restaurants, bars, and clubs. In the Chinese-style suites, lovely moon gates separate the bedrooms from the sitting areas. The guest rooms are tastefully appointed. The inner-facing rooms overlook a garden. Even with the window open, the only noise is the croaking of frogs in a pond.

The hotel is popular with tour groups. **Pros:** excellent location, pleasant gardens. **Cons:** some rooms in need of refurbishment, can be crowded with large tour groups. ✉*115 Shiquan Jie,* ☎*0512/6520–4646* 📠*0512/6520–5191* *283 rooms, 23 suites* *In-hotel: 2 restaurants, room service, bar, gym, laundry service, no-smoking rooms, refrigerator* 💳*AE, MC, V.*

NIGHTLIFE AND THE ARTS

NIGHTLIFE

At night, Perfect Ten Street, the stretch of Shiquan Jie between Renmin Lu and Hengfeng Lu is home to a thriving cluster of bars and clubs.

Despite the suggestive name, **Action Bar** (✉*699 Shiquan Jie* ☎*0512/6219–8066*) is a nothing-fancy place with a drop-in feel. **Pulp Fiction** (✉*Shiquan Jie, east of Hengfeng Lu* ☎*0512/6520–8067*) is Suzhou's main expat bar, so you can be sure there are dartboards and pool tables. It also hosts live music and organizes quirky events. At the top of a flight of stairs is **Whiskey Jack's** (✉*150 Shiquan Jie* ☎*0512/6526–7626*) where bands play regularly.

THE ARTS

Mid-March to mid-November, there are traditional opera and music performances at the **Master of the Nets Garden** (✉*Shiquan Jie* ☎*0512/6529–3190*). The nightly concerts begin at 7:30 and cost is Y80. The show presents a taste of various scenes from opera, as well as an opportunity to hear classical Chinese instruments.

SHOPPING

Districts around the gardens and temples teem with silk shops and outdoor markets. The city's long history of wealth and culture have encouraged a tradition of elegant and finely worked craft objects. One of the best-known crafts is double-sided embroidery, where two separate designs are carefully stitched on both sides of a sheet of silk. The city is also famous for its finely latticed sandalwood fans. Both are available at the Suzhou Arts and Crafts Museum. The area outside the gate of the Master of the Nets Garden has dozens of small stalls selling curios and inexpensive but interesting souvenirs.

The **Friendship Store** (✉*504 Renmin Lu* ☎*0512/6523–6165*) has a selection of local products in silk, wood, and jade. Quality is good but better deals can be had elsewhere. Since 1956 the **Suzhou Cultural Relics Store** (✉*1208 Renmin Lu* ☎*0512/6523–3851*) has been selling antiques, calligraphy, jades, and other items. You can get jewelry and carvings at the **Suzhou Jade Carving Factory** (✉*33 Baita Xi Lu* ☎*0512/6727–1224*).

Near the North Pagoda, the **Suzhou Silk Museum Shop** (✉*661 Renmin Lu* ☎*0512/6753–4941*) is really the reason to come to the Silk Museum. For local artworks and calligraphy, visit the **Wumen Artstore** (✉*105 Liuyuan Lu* ☎*0512/6533–4808*).

ANHUI

Eastern China's most rural province, Anhui has a rugged terrain that forces families to fight their hardscrabble farmland for every acre of harvest. Today it remains significantly poorer than its neighbors, with an average income half of that in neighboring Zhejiang. But what Anhui lacks in material wealth, it makes up for in splendid natural landscape. Travelers here enjoy countryside largely untouched by the last century. Near Huangshan (Yellow Mountain), towering granite peaks loom over green fields, and round-shouldered water buffalo plow the flooded rice paddies.

The foothills of Huangshan have a remarkable wealth of historical architecture. Tiny communities dot the landscape in Shexian and Yixian counties. Many of these villages were far enough out of the way that even the zealous Red Guards of the Cultural Revolution left them alone. Today there are whole villages that remain exactly as they have been for 200 years.

Anhui boasts significant contributions to Chinese civilization. Of the treasures of classical Chinese education, Anhui produces the most famous paper and ink. Hui opera, an ancient musical form developed in the province, was a major influence in Beijing Opera. Hui cuisine is considered one of the country's finest culinary traditions, making use of mountain vegetables and simple, bold flavors.

Most of the province's attractions for tourists lie in the south, accessible from Shanghai, Hangzhou, and Nanjing.

REGIONAL TOURS

Nearby Nanjing is a good place in which to make arrangements for your travels in Anhui, particularly around Huangshan. For organized tours and other arrangements, contact **Jiangsu Huate International Travel Service** (✉*33 Jinxiang He Lu, Nanjing* ☎*025/8337–8695* 🌐*english.hitravels.com*).

HUANGSHAN (YELLOW MOUNTAIN)

5½ hrs (250 km [155 mi]) by train west of Nanjing; 3½ hrs by long-distance bus.

Fodor'sChoice ★ Eastern China's most impressive natural landscape, Huangshan has peaks that rise like islands through roiling seas of clouds. A favorite retreat of emperors and poets of old, its peaks have inspired some of China's most outstanding artworks and literary endeavors. They were so beguiling that years of labor went into their paths, which are actual stone steps rising up—sometimes gradually into the forest, sometimes sharply through a stone tunnel and into the mist above. Since 1990, the area has been a UNESCO World Heritage Site.

The common English translation—Yellow Mountain—is misleading. Huangshan is not a single mountain, but rather a series of peaks that stretches across four counties. To complicate matters, the name is not a reference to color. The region was originally called the "Black

Mountains," but a Tang Dynasty emperor renamed it to honor Huangdi, the Yellow Emperor. And according to legend, it was from these slopes that he rode off to heaven on the back of a dragon.

The mountain is renowned for its gnarled stone formations, crooked pines, and seas of mists. Most of these trees and rocks have names; some are obvious, whereas others require dedicated squinting and a leap of the imagination. Generations of Chinese poets and travelers have humanized these peaks and forests through this practice, and left their indelible mark on the area.

Be forewarned, though: Huangshan has its own weather. More than 200 days a year, precipitation obscures the famous views. It can be sunny below, but up in the mountains it's raining. But even on the foggiest of days the wind is likely to part the mist long enough to make out mysterious peaks. *Mar. 1–Nov. 30, Y200; Dec. 1–Feb. 28, Y120.*

GETTING HERE AND AROUND

Most long-distance transportation, including trains and airplanes, arrives in Tunxi, the largest city near Yellow Mountain. Be aware, however, that Tunxi is still 1 to 1½ hours away from Yellow Mountain. Minibuses to Tangkou and other destinations around the base of the mountain leave from the plaza in front of Tunxi's train station. The cost should be Y15 to Y30. There are also plenty of taxi drivers who are happy to offer their services, usually for around Y70 per carload.

Some buses from Nanjing, Hangzhou, and Shanghai go directly to Tangkou, the entrance at the base of the mountain. The airport is close to Tunxi, about a Y15 to Y20 cab ride from the mountain.

BY AIR If you plan to fly to Yellow Mountain, you'll land at the Huangshan City Airport near Tunxi, about 1 to 1½ hours away. There are direct flights to Beijing, Guangzhou, Shanghai, and Ji'nan.

BY TAXI AND MINIBUS In Tunxi, minibuses and taxis that congregate around the train station will take you to Yellow Mountain. For about Y20 they will drop you at the main gate at the bottom of the mountain or at the beginning of the climbing section.

BY TRAIN Trains travel to Tunxi, where you can catch a minivan or taxi to Yellow Mountain. The ride takes about an hour.

TOURS

Tours up the mountain are unnecessary. A better bet is to buy a good map from one of the local vendors and chart the path you want to take. Some Tunxi companies offer trips that include accommodations for little more than the cost of the admission price to the park. And there's no need to spend the day with strangers—you can hike on your own, joining the rest of the group in time to catch the bus back.

The Tunxi branches of China Travel Service (CTS) can arrange transportation and book a place to stay on the mountain. It also has info on getting out and exploring the surrounding countryside. You can also get info from China International Travel Service, or CITS.

ESSENTIALS

Nearly all services are 1½ hours away in Tunxi.

Medical Assistance **Beihai Medical Center** (✉ *Across from Beihai Hotel, Huangshan* ☎ *0559/558-2555*). **Jade Screen Tower First-Aid Station** (✉ *Jade Screen Tower Hotel* ☎ *0559/558-2288*).

Visitor and Tour Info **CTS** (✉ *12 Qianyuan Bei Lu, Tunxi* ☎ *130/1312-1152* ✉ *1Binjiang Xi Lu, Tunxi* ☎ *0559/231-8319* 🌐 *www.chinatravelservice.com*). **Huangshan Travel Net** (✉ *27 Xin'an North Rd., Tunxi District, Huangshan* ☎ *0559/251-2155 or 0559/251-2133* 🌐 *www.uhuangshan.com*).

HUANGSHAN TRAVEL NET

The best place for current information about the region is the English-language Huangshan Travel Net, run in conjunction with the local CTS. The site is the brainchild of CTS's Victor Zhang, one of the area's most knowledgeable guides. He has arranged tea tours, bike tours, and architecture tours. The site allows users to plan their own trip to the mountain. Resources and bookings for Tunxi are also available.

EXPLORING HUANGSHAN

There are two primary hiking routes up the mountain. The Eastern Steps, a straightforward path through forests, is both the shortest and the easiest. The Southern Steps (some guidebooks call these the Western Steps, which causes confusion with another set of steps used primarily by porters) require more effort, but they pay off with remarkable scenery. The steep, winding path reveals sheer peaks and precipitous lookouts over mist-enshrouded valleys.

Climbing up is physically taxing, but climbing down is mentally exhausting, requiring far more concentration. If you have the time and the leg muscles, it's nice to ascend the South Steps, where the scenery stretches before you. The views are a good excuse to stop and catch your breath.

EASTERN STEPS

The Eastern Steps begin at the **Cloud Valley Temple Cable Car Station.** The cable car takes eight minutes to traverse what takes hikers three or more hours. Large windows provide an aerial view of the mountain and bamboo forests below. This area was once home to several monasteries, nunneries, and temples. By the beginning of the 20th century they had been abandoned, but the name Cloud Valley Temple Area remains. *High season, Y80; low season, Y65* ⏲ *Weekdays 6:30* AM*–4:30* PM*, weekends 6:30* AM*–5* PM.

The Eastern Steps are quicker than the Southern Steps, but the scenery isn't as rewarding and there are fewer scenic side routes. Along the way is a **Fascinating Pavilion,** most notable as a rest stop along the way. There's a short half-hour side hike to **Pipeng,** with a good view out over a number of the smaller eastern peaks. By the time you reach **Cloud Valley,** the landscape that makes Huangshan famous begins to come into view. **Beginning to Believe Peak** is the start of the awe-inspiring landscape, and the first true majestic vista on this path.

SOUTHERN STEPS

The steep Southern Steps are by far the tougher path. However, the climb pays off with great views. There are also some beautiful side trails. Although the Eastern Steps feel like a walk through the woods, the Southern Steps truly feel like an ascent into the clouds. The steps begin around the Hot Springs, at the **Mercy Light Temple** area. **Midway Mountain Temple** has facilities to rest, eat, and even stay overnight, but no temple. It's here that the splendor of Huangshan comes into full view. At the **Three Islands at Penglai,** a trio of peaks poke out from a sea of mist. If you're feeling energetic, a side tour of **Heavenly Capital Peak** affords spectacular views out over the rest of the range. The effort is worth a try even if it looks cloudy, because the mist can sometimes clear by the time you get to the top. This may not be the highest peak in the range, but it is one of the steepest.

The **Jade Screen Cable Car** runs parallel to the Southern Steps, leaving riders close to the Welcoming Guests Pine. It can close unexpectedly in inclement weather. *High season, Y66; low season, Y56* *Weekdays 6:30 AM–4:30 PM, weekends 6:30 AM–5 PM.*

THE SUMMIT

The entrance to the summit area is announced by the **Welcoming Guest Pine,** a lone pine clinging to the edge of a cliff, one branch outstretched. Behind it, a sheer stone slope rises out of the clouds. Continuing up, you can climb **Lotus Peak,** the tallest in the province. A walk through **Turtle Cave,** an arched pathway straight through the hillside, brings the weary traveler to **Bright Top Peak,** slightly lower than Lotus, and an easier climb.

The newly opened **Xihai Grand Canyon** loop starts at the Cloud Dispelling Pavilion and ends at the Haixin Ting Pavilion. Rock formations called "Upside Down Boot" and "Lady Playing Piano" may be clumsily named, but they are stunning. The farther along you walk, the fewer travelers you'll come across. At the southern end of the loop, near Haixin, the trail reaches the **Immortal's Walk Bridge,** a dizzying arch over the misty abyss that leads to a terrace on one of the mountain's spires. A huge landscape spreads out beneath, without a single tour group in sight.

A highlight of any trip is sunrise, visible from several places on the mountain. Most hikers arrive well after dawn, but you'll be rewarded with the spectacle of Huangshan materializing from the shadows if you arrive just before first light. A popular spot near the Beihai Hotel is the **Dawn Pavilion.** There are several less crowded peaks with equally good views a little farther from the hotels. **Refreshing Terrace, Lion Peak,** and **Red Cloud Peak** all provide unobstructed views of the rising sun.

Compared to the ascent, the summit area is relatively level, but there is still a good amount of stair-climbing. It takes about three to four hours to walk the full summit circle, and considerably more if you take side trails.

WHERE TO EAT

Five areas of Huangshan offer lodging. Tangkou, a village that has sprung up to serve mountain climbers, has the most for travelers, including hotels, restaurants, grocery stores, and shops to gear up for the long climb ahead. Tangkou sits near the front gate of the park, and buses run regularly to the trailheads for both the Southern and Eastern steps. If you want to take the shorter route up the Eastern Steps, the Cloud Valley Temple Area is a convenient option. The Hot Springs area has been reopened after renovation, and is a much more pleasant option than Tangkou.

> **BE PREPARED**
>
> Most paths are well-maintained with good steps and sturdy handrails, but Huangshan still has sheer drop-offs and steep, uneven, rain-slicked steps. A walking stick (sturdy wooden dragon-head staffs are on sale around the mountain) will help steady your ascent. It can get very cold on the peaks and rain can come unexpectedly. Dress in layers, and consider bringing a hooded sweatshirt to stay warm.

Several small, basic huts are along the Southern Steps, but it would be better to push to the end of the path to the hotels in the Summit Area. Although these lodgings are more expensive than those below, they are your only option if you want to catch the sunrise. As a bonus, you'll have the dew-drenched forests to yourself for a few hours before the latecomers arrive. Reservations are strongly recommended, especially for weekends; this is a popular destination for Chinese travelers, as well as those from Japan and Korea.

$$–$$$ CHINESE **✕Celebrity's Banquet.** The best restaurant on the summit, Celebrity's Banquet celebrates local culture with a range of traditional Hui dishes. Soups of dried vegetables, jellied tofu, braised pork, and a delicately flavored pumpkin soup shouldn't be missed. ✉*Xihai Hotel, Grand Canyon Loop, Summit Area* ☎*0559/558–8888* ▭*AE, MC, V.*

$$–$$$ CHINESE **✕Tangzhen Hotel Restaurant.** This budget hotel is nothing to write home about, but the food is especially good. Locals come from all around the area to dine here. Specialties include cured mandarin fish, pork with bamboo, and mountain stone frogs. ✉*At the main entrance to Huangshan, Tangkou* ☎*0559/556–2665* ▭*No credit cards.*

WHERE TO STAY

$$–$$$ **Baiyun Hotel.** This hotel offers comfortable rooms and a good location on the summit—a short walk away from Bright Top Peak. An excellent restaurant downstairs serves great river fish, as well as mountain vegetables and mushroom dishes. **Pros:** good location, great restaurant. **Cons:** few amenities. ✉*Tianhai Area, Summit Area* ☎*0559/558–2708* *80 rooms, 1 suite* *In-hotel: restaurant, bar* ▭*AE, MC, V.*

$$ **Beihai Hotel.** This is one of the nicest places to stay on the mountain. A few extras like the sauna are a welcome end to a day of hiking. The rooms are set among rhododendrons and azaleas on the hillside. Ask for the front-facing rooms, which have better views—and rent for the same price as the rooms in the back. **Pros:** location. **Cons:** some rooms have unpleasant views. ✉*Huangshan Scenic Area, Summit Area*

☎0559/556–2555 📠0559/556–2996 137 rooms, 2 suites In-room: Dial-up, refrigerator. In-hotel: restaurant, bar ▭AE, MC, V.

¢–$$ **Huangshan Xingang Hotel.** Because practically every guest is coming up or down the mountain, the staff here is a great repository of knowledge of what to see, how to climb, and the best routes to take. Like most hotels in the area, this place has rooms that are somewhat small, but are clean and get lots of sun. They are good places to rest up for the climb ahead. **Pros:** great for a comfortable stop before your climb. **Cons:** basic amenities. ✉*At the main entrance to Huangshan, Tangkou ☎0559/556–1048 115 rooms, 2 suites In-hotel: restaurant, bar ▭AE, MC, V.*

$$–$$$$ **Jade Screen Tower.** The views from this hotel are unmatched, though like most of the hotels on the summit, the rooms are small. Nonetheless the location is good, at the top of the Southern Steps near the cable car station; it's the first proper hotel you'll reach after a long climb. **Pros:** great place to catch the sunrise. **Cons:** limited facilities. ✉*Past Welcoming Guest Pine, Summit Area ☎0559/558–2288 29 rooms, 1 suite In-hotel: 2 restaurants, no elevator ▭AE, MC, V.*

¢ **Peach Blossom Hotel.** A winding road takes you over a bridge and past a double waterfall to this resort between the main gate of the mountain park and the beginning of the Southern Steps. The no-frills rooms are clean and comfortable. The Peach Blossom also has great Chinese and Western food, with specialties like bamboo chicken. **Pros:** convenient to hot springs. **Cons:** not good for watching the sunrise. ✉*Huangshan Scenic Area, Hot Springs ☎0559/558–5666 141 rooms, 4 suites In-hotel: restaurant, bar ▭AE, MC, V.*

$$ **Yungu Hotel.** Tucked in among the trees, these traditional-style buildings blend well in the forest landscape. Cheaper than staying on the summit, the guest rooms here are also larger and better outfitted. **Pros:** charming surroundings. **Cons:** language barrier with some staff, hotel restaurant is not the best. ✉*Next to the cable-car station, Cloud Valley Temple Area, ☎0559/558–6444 100 rooms In-hotel: 2 restaurants, bar, gym. ▭AE, DC, MC, V.*

TUNXI

5½ hrs (250 km [155 mi]) by train west of Nanjing; 3½ hrs by long-distance bus.

Tunxi, also called Huangshan City, is the gateway to the Yellow Mountain area. Apart from being a transportation hub, Tunxi also has a charming strip of shops and restaurants and is a convenient place from which to take trips to Shexian and Yixian counties, famous for their historical architecture.

GETTING HERE AND AROUND

Unless you arrive on a long-distance bus bound for Tangkou, or have joined a chartered excursion to Yellow Mountain, your bus or train is probably bound for Tunxi, around 40 mi (65 km) from the mountain.

BY AIR From Huangshan City Airport near Tunxi flights travel daily to Beijing and Guangzhou, twice daily to Shanghai, and twice a week to Hong Kong. Taxies to the airport from Tunxi cost about Y15 to Y20.

BY BUS Buses are a convenient way of getting to Tunxi from Zhejiang, Jiangsu, and even Shanghai. Buses that run hourly from Hangzhou take 3½ hours and cost Y65. The route takes you through some gorgeous scenery. Buses from Nanjing take around 5 hours and cost Y80. From Shanghai, buses take eight to nine hours and cost Y120.

BY TRAIN Several trains depart daily for Nanjing, and there are two trains each day for Shanghai (12–13 hours, Y160).

TOURS

Guides are a good idea if you are exploring the countryside around Huangshan. CTS has private village tours in Yixian county and architecture tours in Shexian counties.

ESSENTIALS

Air Contacts Air China (✉ *23 Huashan Lu* ☎ *0559/953–4111* ✉ *49 Huangshan Donglu* ☎ *0559/254–1222* 🌐 *www.airchina.com.cn/en/index.jsp*). **Huangshan City Airport** (✉ *West of Tunxi on Yingbin Dadao* ☎ *0559/293–4111*).

Bus Contacts Tunxi Bus Station (✉ *95 Huangshan Dong Lu* ☎ *0559/235-3952*).

Medical Assistance People's Hospital of Huangshan City (✉ *4 Liyuan Lu, Huangshan* ☎ *0559/251–7036*).

Train Contacts Huangshan Train Station (✉ *Northern end of Qianyuan Beilu* ☎ *0559/211–6222*).

Visitor and Tour Info CITS (✉ *2 Binjiang Xi Lu* ☎ *0559/254–2110* 🌐 *www.huangshantour.com/english*). **CTS** (✉ *12 Qianyuan Bei Lu* ☎ *130/1312–1152 (English-speaking hotline)* ✉ *1Binjiang Xi Lu* ☎ *0559/231–8319* 🌐 *www.chinatravelservice.com*).

EXPLORING TUNXI

In Tunxi, the best place to pick up souvenirs is along **Old Street** *(Lao Jie)*. The street is quiet in the daytime, but comes alive in the early evening. Shops stay open until about 10 or 11. There's a lot of junk, but you may find some treasures.

WHERE TO STAY AND EAT

$–$$ Fodor'sChoice ★ ✕ **Diyilou.** All sorts of small dishes are sold at this lively shop. Diners order by pointing to sample dishes, so the lack of an English menu is no problem. With hundreds of dishes on rotation, there's something for everyone. Local specialties include tender bamboo shoots, four-mushroom soup, red-braised tofu, and a white mushroom-wrapped meatball that is not to be missed. ✉ *247 Tunxi Lao Jie, at Lao Jie* ☎ *0559/253–9797* 💳 *AE, MC, V.*

¢–$$ **Huashan Hotel.** This large hotel sits at a perfect location in Tunxi, just a block away from the shopping district of Old Street. The lobby is enormous, as are the guest rooms. Some are a bit musty; ask to see a few before you decide. The hotel restaurant is inexpensive and acceptable, but for a nicer meal venture out into the charming surroundings of Old Street. The service is thorough, if a little confused at times. **Pros:** great access to Old Street. **Cons:** staff's limited English, musty rooms. ✉*3 Yanan Lu, 1 block north of Old St.* ☎*0559/232–2888* *186 rooms, 14 suites* *In-room: Ethernet, refrigerator. In-hotel: 2 restaurants, tennis court, pool, gym* *AE, MC, V.*

SHOPPING

When shopping along Lao Jie, the best offerings are traditional calligraphy ink and paper. The best inkstones are sold at **Sanbai Yanzhai** (✉*173 Lao Jie* ☎*0559/253–5538*).

Another traditional craft is bamboo carving. The **Stone and Bamboo Shop** (✉*122 Lao Jie* ☎*0559/751–5042*) sells exquisite examples.

SIDE TRIP TO SHEXIAN COUNTY

Shexian County has been called a living architectural art museum because of its natural beauty and array of historical buildings. Over the centuries, it has inspired philosophers, poets, and painters. Today, there is no lack of tourists but it's a pleasant day trip from Tunxi.

GETTING HERE AND AROUND

Buses run throughout the day from the Tunxi long-distance bus station. The trip should take about 45 minutes and cost Y5. Once you get to Shexian Bus Station in Huizhou Old City, you can board a minibuses or take a taxi to outlying scenic spots. However, if you are traveling with several people, it will be well worth hiring a car and driver for the day. Many of these places are remote, and you may find the bulk of your day wasted waiting for minibuses or trying to find a taxi.

EXPLORING SHEXIAN COUNTY

Huizhou Old Town (✉*Shexian County Center* ☎*0559/653–1586* *Y15* *Daily 7:30–6:30*) boasts a centuries-old city wall and a magnificent four-sided memorial gate guarded by sculptures of frolicking lions.

The **Huashan Mysterious Grottoes** (✉*Between Xiongcun and Tunxi* ☎*0559/235–9888* *Y70* *Daily 7:30–6:30*) are a combination of natural caves and rooms carved into the rock. No one is quite certain when or why they were built, but they are impressive, and newly illuminated with colored lights.

The most famous series of **Memorial Arches** (✉*3 mi [5 km] west of Huizhou Old Town* ☎*No phone* *Y50* *Daily 8–5:30*) are in Tangyue village. Dating from the Ming and Qing dynasties, these archways represent traditional values like morality, piety, and *female* chastity.

Near Huizhou Old Town, **Yuliang Village** overlooks a Tang Dynasty dam with water gurgling over its sloped sides. Fishermen in wooden skiffs still make their living here. A narrow street parallel to the river is nice for a stroll. Most families leave their doors open, allowing a peak into homes where pages from magazines are used as wallpaper and aluminum foil is a common decoration. Inexpensive pedicabs travel from the Shexian bus station to Yuliang Village, or you can catch bus number 1 from the train station. ☎*No phone* *Y30* *Daily 7:30–6:30.*

SIDE TRIP TO YIXIAN COUNTY

A pleasant day trip from Tunxi, Yixian County is the site of some beautiful ancient architecture set in peaceful surroundings. But don't expect a quiet day with the village to yourself; Yixian County receives nearly 2.5 million visits per year. But don't let that deter you; the UNESCO World Heritage sites in the area offer a rare glimpse of what ancient Anhui may have been like and are stunningly photogenic.

GETTING HERE AND AROUND

To get to Yixian County destinations, take the buses that leave from in front of Tunxi's train station. They cost about Y10 and depart every 20 minutes. Because of a nearby military base, a police-issued travel permit costing Y50 is required for travel in Yixian County. The ticket offices at the gates of Xidi Village and Hongcun Village can take care of this for you. A passport is necessary to register for the permits.

EXPLORING YIXIAN COUNTY

An arched bridge leads to **Hongcun Village** (✉*Eastern Yixian County* ☎*0559/251–7464* 🎫*Y90* ⏲*Daily 6:30–6:30*). From above, the village is said to resemble a buffalo. Two 600-year-old trees mark its horns, a lake its belly, and even irrigation streams are its intestines. In recent years, a number of films have been partially shot here, including Ang Lee's *Crouching Tiger, Hidden Dragon*. Several large halls and old houses are open to tour. The Salt Merchants House is especially well preserved, with intricate decorations and carvings that were unharmed during the Cultural Revolution.

A UNESCO World Heritage site, **Xidi Village** (✉*Yixian Xidi Village* ☎*0559/515–4030* 🎫*Y80* ⏲*Daily 6:30–6:30*) is known for its exquisite memorial gate. There were once a dozen gates, but they were destroyed during the Cultural Revolution. The existing gate was left standing as a "bad example" to be criticized. There are several houses with excellent examples of brick carving and an impressive Clan Temple with massive ginkgo columns and beams.

ENGLISH	PINYIN	CHINESE CHARACTERS
HEBEI	HÉBĚI	河北
CHENGDE	Chéngdé	承德
Chengde Chinese-Western Hospital	Chéngdé zhōngxī jiéhé yīyuàn	承德中西结合医院
China International Tourist Service (CITS)	Zhōngguó guójì lǚxíngshè	中国国际旅行社
Club Rock	Bàngchuí fēng	棒槌峰
Da Qinghua Dumbling	Dàqīnghuà jiaózī	大清花饺子
Eight Outer Monasteries	Wàibā miào	外八庙
Hong Men Internet Bar	Hóngmén wāngbā	鸿门网吧
Mongolian Yurts Holiday Inn	Ménggùbāo dùjiàcūn	蒙古包度假村
Mountain Resort	bìshǔ shānzhuāng	避暑山庄
Mountain Villa Hotel	Shānzhuāng bīnguǎn	山庄宾馆
Shenghua Hotel	Shènghuá dà jiùdiàn	盛华大酒店
Temple of the Potaraka Doctrine	Pùtuózōngchéng sì	普陀宗乘寺
Temple of Universal Happiness	Pùlè sì	普乐寺
Temple of Universal Peace	Pùníng sì	普宁寺
BEIDAIHE	Béidàihé	北戴河
Beidaihe Waijiao Renyuan Binguan	Béidàihé wàijiāo rényuán bīnguǎn	北戴河外交人员宾馆
Emperor Qin Shi Huang's Palace	Qínhuáng gōng	秦皇宫
Guanyin Temple	Guānyīn sì	观音寺
Jinshan Hotel	Jīnshān Dà JiùDiàn	金山大酒店
Kiesslings	Qǐshìlín cāntīng	起士林餐厅
Lianfeng Hill Park	Líanfēngshān gōngyuán	联峰山公园
SHANHAIGUAN	Shānhǎiguān	山海关
cable car	lǎn chē	缆车
First Gate Under Heaven	Tīanxià dìyīguān	天下第一关
Great Wall Museum	Chángchéng bówùguǎn	长城博物馆
Jiao Mountain	Ji shān	角山
Jingshan Hotel	Jīngshān bīnguǎn	京山宾馆
Long Distance Bus Station	chángtǔ qìchēzhàn	长途汽车站
Longevity Mountain	Chángshoù shān	长寿山
Mengjiangnu Miao	Mèngjiāngnǔ miào	孟姜女庙
North Street Hotel	Běijīe zhāodàisùo	北街招待所
Old Dragon Head	Lǎolóngtóu	老龙头
Qinhuangdao Airport	Qínhuángdǎo jīcháng	秦皇岛机场

ENGLISH	PINYIN	CHINESE CHARACTERS
Wang Yan Lou	Wāngyān lóu	王严楼
Yangsai Hu	Yángsāihú	羊腮胡
SHANDONG	SHĀNDŌNG	山东
JI'NAN	Jǐnán	济南
Big Bright Lake	Dàmínghú	大明湖
Confucian Forest	Kǒnglín	孔林
Confucius Family Mansion	Kǒngfǔ	孔府
Confucius Temple	Kǒngmiào	孔庙
Foshan Jie	Fóshānjī	佛山街
Gushing from the Ground Spring	Bàotūquán	趵突泉
Long Distance Bus Station	chángtú qìchē zǒngzhàn	长途汽车总站
Long Distance Bus Station	chángtú qìchēzhàn	长途汽车站
Mount Tai	Tàishān	泰山
Protestant Church	Jīdū jiàotáng	基督教堂
Qufu	Qūfù	曲阜
Tai'an	Tài'ān	泰安
Tai'an Bus Station	Tài'ān qìchēzhàn	泰安汽车站
Thousand Buddha Mountain	Qiānfóshān	千佛山
Train Station	huǒchēzhàn	火车站
Train Station	huǒchēzhàn	火车站
Train Station	huǒchēzhàn	火车站
Yaoqiang Airport	Yáoqiáng jīchǎng	遥墙机场
QINGDAO	Qīngdǎo	青岛
Catholic Church	tiānzhǔ jiàotáng	天主教堂
Ferry Terminal	Qīngdǎo gǎngkèyùnzhàn	青岛港客运站
German Governor's Residence	Qīngdǎo yíngbīnguǎn	青岛迎宾馆
Guanhaishan Park	Guānhǎishān gōngyuán	观海山公园
Huadong Winery	Huádōng Bǎilì jiǔzhuāng	华东百利酒庄
Huashi Lou	Huāshílóu	花石楼
Liuting Airport	Liútíng jīchǎng	流亭机场
Long Distance Bus Station	chángtú qìchēzhàn	长途汽车站
Lu Xun Park	Lǔxùn gōngyuán	鲁迅公园
Minjiang Lu	Mǐnjiāng lù	闽江路
Mount Lao	Láoshān	崂山
Navy Museum	hǎijūn bówùguǎn	海军博物馆
Number 1 Beach	dìyī hǎishuǐyùchǎng	第一海水浴场

ENGLISH	PINYIN	CHINESE CHARACTERS
Number 2 Beach	dì'èr hǎishuǐyùchǎng	第二 海水浴场
Protestant Church	Jīdū jiàotáng	基督教堂
Sun Yat-sen Park	Zhōngshān gōngyuán	中山公园
Train Station	huǒchēzhàn	火车站
Tsingtao Beer Factory	Qīngdǎo píjiǔchǎng	青岛啤酒厂
Underwater World	Qīngdǎo hǎidǐ shìjiè	青岛海底世界
Zhongshan Lu	Zhōngshān lù	中山路
JAINGSU	JĪANGSU	江苏
NANJING	Nánjīng	南京
China Travel Service	Zhōngguó lǚxíngshè	中国旅行社
Confucian Temple	Fūzǐmiào	夫子庙
Drum Tower	Gǔlóu	鼓楼
Hunan Road	Húnán lù	湖南路
Lukou Airport	Lùkǒu jīchǎng	禄口机场
Ming Tomb	Míngxiàolíng	明孝陵
Nanjing Massacre Memorial	dàtúshā jìniànguǎn	大屠杀纪念馆
Nanjing Museum	Nánjīng bówùguǎn	南京博物馆
Plum Blossom Hill	Méihuā shān	梅花山
Rain Flower Terrace and	Yǔhuātái lièshìlíngyuán	雨花台烈士陵园
South Gate of City Wall	Zhōnghuá mén	中华门
Spirit Valley Temple and Pagoda	Línggǔsì, Línggǔtǎ	灵谷寺，灵谷塔
Sun Yat-sen Botanical Gardens	Zhōngshān zhíwùyuán	中山植物园
Sun Yat-sen Memorial	Zhōngshānlíng	中山陵
Swallow Rock	Yànzijī	燕子矶
Taiping Heavenly Kingdom Museum	Tàipíngtiānguó lìshǐ bówùguǎn	太平天国历史博物馆
Train Station	huǒchēzhàn	火车站
Xinjiekou	Xīnjiēkǒu	新街口
Xuanwu Lake Park	Xuánwǔhú gōngyuán	玄武湖公园
Yangtze River Bridge	Chángjiāng dàqiáo	长江大桥
Yuejiang Lou Tower	Yuèjiāng lóu	阅江楼
Zhongshan Nan Road Bus Station	Zhōngshān nán lù qìchēzhàn	中山南路汽车站
Zhongyangmen Bus Station	Zhōngyāng mén qìchēzhàn	中央门汽车站
YANGZHOU	Yángzhōu	扬州
China Youth Travel Agency	zhōngqīnglǚ	中青旅

ENGLISH	PINYIN	CHINESE CHARACTERS
Daming Temple	Dàmíngsì	大明寺
Garden Tomb of Puhaddin	Pŭhādīngmù	普哈丁墓
Ge Garden	Gèyuán	个园
He Garden	Héyuán	何园
Long Distance Bus Station	chángtú qìchēzhàn	长途汽车站
Slender West Lake	Shòu Xīhú	瘦西湖
Train Station	huŏchēzhàn	火车站
Wang's Residence	Wāngshì xiăoyuàn	汪氏小苑
SUZHOU	Sūzhōu	苏州
Ancient Chinese Sexual Culture Museum	gŭdài xìngwénhuà zhănshì	古代性文化展示
Baosheng Temple	Băoshèngsì	保圣寺
Blue Wave Pavilion	Cānglàngtíng	沧浪亭
Grand Canal	dàyùnhé	大运河
Hanshan Temple	Hánshānsì	寒山寺
Humble Administrator's Garden	Zhuōzhèngyuán	拙政园
Joyous Garden	Yíyuán	怡园
Lingering Garden	Líuyuán	留园
Lion's Grove Garden	Shīzilín	狮子林
Long Distance Bus Station	chángtú qìchēzhàn	长途汽车站
Luzhi	Lùzhí	甪直
Master of the Nets Garden	Wăngshīyuán	网师园
North Temple Pagoda	Bĕisìtá	北寺塔
Pan Gate	Pánmén	盘门
Shiquanjie Street	Shíquánjīe	十全街
Suzhou Arts & Crafts Museum	Sūzhōu gōngyìmĕishù bówùguăn	苏州工艺美术博物馆
Suzhou Museum	Sūzhōu bówùguăn	苏州博物馆
Temple of Mystery	Xuánmiàoguān	玄妙观
Tiger Hill	Hŭqiū	虎丘
Tongli	Tónglĭ	同里
Train Station	huŏchēzhàn	火车站
Water Villages	shuĭxiāng	水乡
West Garden Temple	Xīyuánsì	西园寺
Zhouzhuang	Zhōuzhuāng	周庄

ENGLISH	PINYIN	CHINESE CHARACTERS
ANHUI	ĀNHUĪ	安徽
HUANGSHAN	Huángshān	黄山
Cloud Valley scenic area	Yúngŭ jĭngqū	云谷景区
Cloud Valley Temple Cable Car	Yúngŭsì suŏdào	云谷寺索道
Hot Springs scenic area	wēnquán jĭngqū	温泉景区
Jade Screen Cable Car	Yùpíng suŏdào	玉屏索道
North Sea scenic area	Bĕihăi jĭngqū	北海景区
Tangkou	Tāngkŏu	汤口
Tianhai scenic area	Tiānhăi jĭngqū	天海景区
TUNXI	Túnxī	屯溪
Tunxi (Huangshan City)	Túnxī (Huángshān shì)	屯溪 （黄山市）
Bus Station	chángtú qìchēzhàn	长途汽车站
Huangshan City Airport	Huángshān shì jīchăng	黄山市机场
Train Station	huŏchēzhàn	火车站
Tunxi Old Street	Túnxī lăojiē	屯溪老街
SHEXIAN	Shè xiàn	歙县
Hongcun Village	Hóng cūn	宏村
Huashan Mysterious Grottoes	Huàshān míkū	华山谜窟
Huizhou Old Town	Huīzhōu lăochéng	徽州老城
Long Distance Bus Station	chángtú qìchēzhàn	长途汽车站
Tang Yue Memorial Arches	Tángyuè páilouqún	堂樾牌楼群
Train Station	huŏchēzhàn	火车站
Xidi Village	Xī dī	西堤
Yixian County	Yī xiàn	黟县
Yuliang Village	Yúliáng gŭzhèn	渔梁古镇

Shanghai

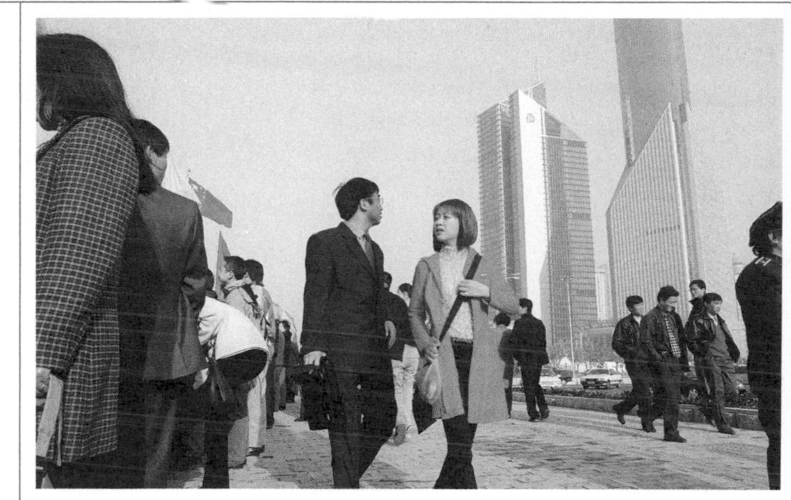

The hyper-modern skyline of the Pudong district.

WORD OF MOUTH

"On Taikang Street and in the Art Alley . . . there were all sorts of little shops and galleries selling clothing and jewelry, and various art materials, frames, paintings, sculpture, and antiques along with charming little cafes."

—wiselindag

www.fodors.com/forums

WELCOME TO SHANGHAI

TOP REASONS TO GO

★ **Skyline Views:** Head to the top of the 1960s *Jetsons* kitsch of the Pearl Tower or the pagoda-inspired Jin Mao, and count the cranes restructuring the city's skyline.

★ **Shanghai Museum:** The Bund and the glamorous Plaza 66 are the up and coming designer areas. If you want something more "Chinese," the boutiques in and around Xintiandi offer very stylish fusion pieces.

★ **Shopping Overload:** The Hong Kong Heritage Museum chronicles the city's history. On a Lantau Island hill, see the 242-ton Tian Tan Buddha statue sits in the lotus position beside the Po Lin Buddhist Monastery.

★ **Yu Garden:** When not too crowded, the Garden offers peace and beauty amid the clamor of the city, with rocks, trees, and walls curved to resemble dragons, bridges, and pavilions.

1 The Bund. Shanghai's famous waterfront boulevard is lined with art-deco buildings and souvenir stands. It's great for people-watching, being watched yourself, shopping for increasingly chic clothes, and sampling some of Shanghai's most famous restaurants. It's also where you'll get that postcard view of the futuristic skyline in Pudong.

2 Xintiandi. Shopping, bars, restaurants, and museums mix together in restored traditional *shikumen* (stone gate) houses. Xintiandi is a popular location for hanging out and people-watching, and there are a few great boutiques. The small museums have interesting exhibits related to Shanghai's and the Communist Party's history.

3 Former French Concession. Whether you're an architecture fanatic, a photographer, a romantic, or just plain curious, a wander through these streets is always a wonderful way to pass an afternoon. Fuxing Lu is a good long walk and the streets around Sinan Lu and Fuxing Park have some real architectural treats. Take your time and allow for breaks at cafés or in small boutiques.

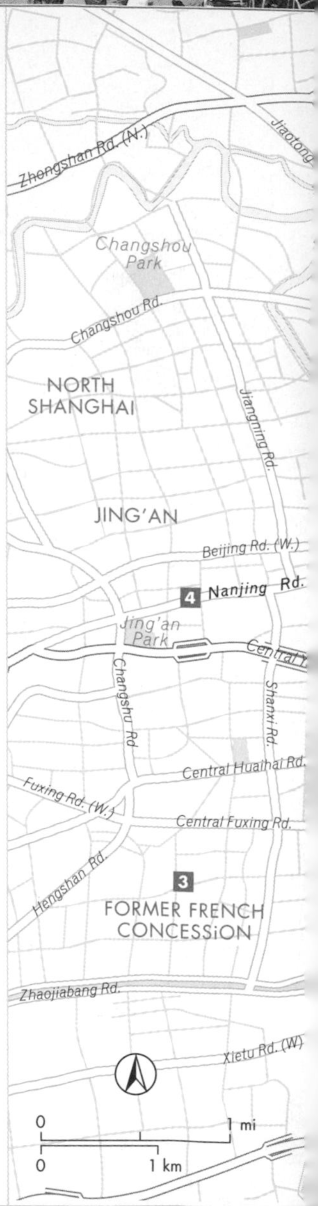

Lujiazui Financial Distirct, Pudong

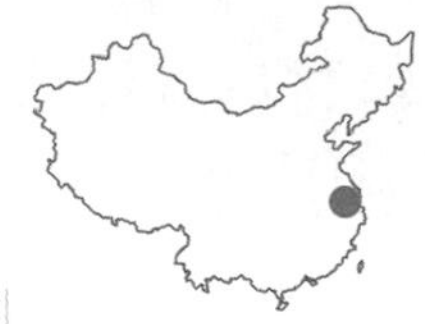

4 Nanjing Lu. People come from all over China to shop on what was once China's premier shopping street—and it sometimes feels as though they're all here at the same time. Although it's still a little tawdry, like a phoenix rising from the ashes, pedestrian-only Nanjing Dong Lu is undergoing a massive face-lift, and trendy designer boutiques are beginning to emerge alongside pre-1960s department stores and old-fashioned silk shops.

GETTING ORIENTED

Shanghai is fast and tough, so bring good shoes and a lot of patience. Don't expect the grandeur of ancient sights, but rather relish the small details like exquisitely designed art-deco buildings or laid-back cafés. Shanghai hides her gems well, so it's important to be observant and look up and around. The crowds of people and the constant change can make travelers weary, so take advantage of the wide range of eateries and convenient benches.

SHANGHAI PLANNER

City of the Future

As the most Westernized city in China after Hong Kong, Shanghai is at the forefront of China's modernization. Almost a quarter of the world's construction cranes stand in this city. Still, architectural remnants of a colonial past survive along the winding, bustling streets.

When to Go

The best time to visit Shanghai is early fall, when the weather is good and crowds diminish. Although temperatures are scorching and the humidity can be unbearable, summer is the peak tourist season, and hotels and transportation can get very crowded.

Avoid the two main national holidays, Chinese New Year (which ranges from mid-January to mid-February) and the National Day holiday (during the first week of October), when 1.3 billion people on the move.

Navigating

Shanghai is divided into east and west sides by the Huangpu River. The metro area is huge, but the city center is a relatively small district in Puxi (west of the river). On the east side lies the district that many think is Shanghai's future—Pudong (east of the river). The city is loosely laid out on a grid and most neighborhoods are easily explored on foot. Massive construction makes pavements uneven and the air dusty, but if you can put up with this, walking is the best way to really get a feel for the city and its people. Taxis are readily available and good for traveling longer distances, and the subway network is expanding every day.

Major east–west roads are named for Chinese cities and divide the city into *bei* (north), *zhong* (middle), and *nan* (south) sections. North–south roads divide the city into *dong* (east), *zhong* (middle), and *xi* (west) segments. The heart of the city is found on its chief east–west streets—Nanjing Lu, Huaihai Lu, and Yanan Lu.

■ TIP→ **Transport cards costing Y10 are available from the metro stations and can be charged with however much money you like. These can be used in taxis, on metros, and on some buses. They aren't discounted, but they'll save you time you would have spent joining queues and fumbling for cash.**

Navigating Vocabulary

Below are some terms you'll see on maps and street signs and in the name of most places you'll go:

Dong is east, **xi** is west, **nan** is south, **bei** is north, and **zhong** means middle. **Jie** and **lu** mean street and road, respectively, and **da** means big.

Qiao, or bridge, is part of the place name at just about every entrance and exit on the ring roads.

Men, meaning door or gate, indicates a street that passed through an entrance in the fortification wall that surrounded the city hundreds of years ago. The entrances to parks and some other places are also referred to as *men*. For example, Xizhimen literally means Western Straight Gate.

Getting Around

By Taxi: Taxis are plentiful, cheap, and easy to spot. Your hotel concierge can call for one by phone or you can hail one on the street. The available ones have a small lit-up sign on the passenger side. If you're choosing a cab from a line, peek at the driver's license on the dashboard. The lower the license number, the more experienced the driver. Drivers with a number below 200,000 can usually get you where you're going. Most cab drivers don't speak English, so it's best to give them a piece of paper with your destination written in Chinese. (Keep a card with the name of your hotel on it handy for the return trip.)

By Subway: The Shanghai's quick and efficient subway system—called the Shanghai Metro—is an excellent way to get around town, and the network is growing exponentially. More English maps and exit signs are also being included. The electronic ticket machines have an English option, too. In-car announcements for each station are given in both Chinese and English. Keep your ticket handy; you'll need to insert it into a second turnstile as you exit at your destination. Transport cards are swiped at entry and exit.

By Ferry: Ferries run around the clock every 10 minutes between the Bund and Pudong's terminal just south of the Riverside Promenade. The per-person fare is Y2 each way.

By Bus: Taking buses is not recommended as they are often crowded, slow, and nearly impossible to negotiate without speaking Chinese.

By Bike: Few hotels rent bikes, but you can inquire at bike shops or even corner stores, where the rate is around Y30 a day, plus a refundable deposit. Note that for about Y200 you can buy your own basic bike. Shanghai's frenzied traffic is not for the faint of heart, though fortunately most secondary streets have wide, well-defined bike lanes.

Opening Hours

Almost all businesses close for Chinese New Year and other major holidays.

Shops: Stores are generally open daily 10 to 7; some stores stay open as late as 10 PM, especially in summer.

Temples and Museums: Most temples and parks are open daily 8 to 5. Museums and most other sights are generally open 9 to 4, six days a week, with Monday being the most common closed day.

Banks and Offices: Most banks and government offices are open weekdays 9 to 5, but some close for lunch (between noon and 2). Bank branches and CITS tour desks in hotels often keep longer hours and are usually open Saturday morning. Many hotel currency-exchange desks stay open 24 hours.

Dragon Boat Day

2,000 years ago, a poet named Qu Yuan threw himself into the river in protest against the Emperor. To commemorate him, people now race dragon boats and eat *zongzi* (sticky rice dumplings). The date of the Dragon Boat Festival varies but is often in May or June.

EXPLORING SHANGHAI

SHANGHAI, OR "CITY ABOVE THE SEA," lies on the Yangzi River delta, and until 1842 it was a small fishing village. After the first Opium War the village was carved up into autonomous concessions administered concurrently by the British, French, and Americans.

In its heyday, Shanghai had the best art, the greatest architecture, and the strongest business in Asia. With dance halls, brothels, glitzy restaurants, international clubs, and a racetrack, it catered to the rich. The Paris of the East was known as a place of vice and indulgence. Amid this glamour and degradation the Communist Party held its first meeting in 1921.

In the 1930s and '40s, the city suffered raids, invasions, and occupation by the Japanese. After the war's end, Nationalists and Communists fought a three-year civil war for control of China. The Communists declared victory in 1949 and established the People's Republic of China. Between 1950 and 1980 Shanghai's industries soldiered on through periods of extreme famine and drought, reform, and suppression. Politically, the city was central to the Cultural Revolution and the Gang of Four's base. The January Storm of 1967 purged many of Shanghai's leaders, and Red Guards set out to destroy the "Four Olds": old ways of idea, living, traditions, and thought.

In 1972, with the Cultural Revolution still going, Shanghai hosted the historic meeting between Premier Zhou Enlai and U.S. president Richard Nixon. In 1990 China's leader, Deng Xiaoping, chose Shanghai as the center of the country's commercial renaissance, and it has again become one of China's most open cities ideologically, socially, culturally, and economically.

Today, beauty and charm coexist with kitsch and commercialism. From the colonial architecture of the Former French Concession to the forest of cranes and the neon-lit high-rises of Pudong, Shanghai is a city of paradox and change.

■ TIP→ Shanghai is a sprawling city with large districts. We have created a series of smaller neighborhoods, centered on the main attractions. You still need to know the official districts when dealing with hotels, taxis, and tourist resources, so official districts are listed at the end of each entry.

GETTING HERE

Shanghai has two major airports: most international flights go through the newer Pudong International Airport (PVG), which is 45 km (30 mi) east of the city, whereas many domestic routes operate out of the older Hongqiao International Airport (SHA), 15 km (9 mi) west of the city center.

Taking a taxi is the most comfortable way into town from Pudong International Airport. Expect to pay around Y120 to Y160 for the hour-long or so trip to Puxi; getting to the closer Pudong area takes 40 minutes and should cost no more than Y100. At rush hour, journey times can easily double.

From Hongqiao, a taxi to Puxi starts at Y30 and takes 30 to 40 minutes; expect an hour for the costlier trip to Pudong hotels. A taxi from one airport to the other takes about an hour and costs Y200 to Y240.

Many hotels offer free airport transfers to their guests. Otherwise, shuttle buses link Pudong Airport with a number of hotels (routes starting with a letter) and transport hubs (routes starting with a number) in the city center. Most services run every 10 to 20 minutes between roughly 7 AM and the last flight arrival (usually around midnight). Trips to Puxi take about 1½ hours and cost between Y19 and Y30. From Hongqiao, Bus 925 runs to People's Square, but there's little room for luggage. It costs Y4.

HEALTH AND SAFETY

Tap water in Shanghai is safe for brushing teeth. However, it contains a high concentration of metals, so you should buy bottled water to drink. Make sure food has been thoroughly cooked and is served to you fresh and hot; avoid vegetables and fruits that you haven't washed (in bottled or purified water) or peeled yourself. Shanghai's severely polluted air can bring on, or aggravate, respiratory problems. If you're a sufferer, take the cue from locals, who wear surgical masks, or a scarf or bandana as protection.

The most reliable places to buy prescription medication is at the 24-hour pharmacy at the World Link Medical Center and the Shanghai United Family Health Center *(⇨Medical Services, below)*. During the day, the Watson's chain is good for over-the-counter medication but has limited selection and poor service; it has dozens of branches around over town. Chinese pharmacies offer a fuller range of imported over-the-counter drugs and are usually open 24-hours; look for the green cross on a white sign.

There is little violent crime against tourists in China, partly because the penalties are severe for those who are caught—China's yearly death-sentence tolls run into the thousands. Single women can move about Shanghai without too much hassle. Handbag-snatching and pickpocketing do happen in markets and on crowded buses or trains.

Shanghai is full of people looking to make a quick buck. The most common scam involves people persuading you to go with them for a tea ceremony, which is often so pleasant that you don't smell a rat until several hundred dollars appear on your credit-card bill. "Art students" who pressure you into buying work is another common scam. Avoiding such scams is as easy as refusing *all* unsolicited services—be it from taxi or pedicab drivers, tour guides, or potential "friends."

Shanghai traffic is as manic as it looks, and survival of the fittest (or the biggest) is the main rule.

ESSENTIALS

Airport Information **Hongqiao International Airport** (☎ *021/6268–8918* 🌐 *www.shanghaiairport.com*). **Pudong International Airport** (☎ *021/9608–1388* 🌐 *www.shanghaiairport.com*).

Bike Rentals **Bohdi Bikes** (☎ *021/5266-9013 or 139/1875-3119* 🌐 *www.bohdi.com.cn*).

Bus Contacts **Shanghai Long Distance Bus Station** (✉ *North Square, Shanghai Railway Station, 1662 Zhongxing Lu, Zhabei* ☎ *021/6605-0000*).

Consulates **United States Consulate** (✉ *1469 Huaihai Zhong Lu, Xuhui* ☎ *021/6433-6880, 021/6433-3936 after-hours emergencies* ✉ *Citizen Services Section, Westgate Mall, 8th fl., 1038 Nanjing Xi Lu, Jing'an* ☎ *021/3217-4650* 🌐 *shanghai.usconsulate.gov*).

Emergency Contacts **Fire** (☎ *119*). **International SOS Medical Services 24-hour Alarm Center** (☎ *021/6295-0099*). **Police** (☎ *110, 021/6357-6666 [English]*). **Shanghai Ambulance Service** (☎ *120*).

Ferry Contacts **China-Japan International Ferry Company** (✉ *908 Dongdaming Lu, Hongkou* ☎ *021/6595-7988*). **China International Travel Service** (*CITS* ☎ *021/6289-8899* 🌐 *www.cits.com.cn*). **Pudong–Puxi ferry** (✉ *Puxi dock, the Bund at Jinling Lu, Huangpu* ✉ *Pudong dock, 1 Dongchang Lu, south of Binjiang Da Dao, Pudong*). **Shanghai Ferry Company** (☎ *021/6537-5111 or 021/5393-1185* 🌐 *www.shanghai-ferry.co.jp*).

Medical Services **Huadong Hospital** (✉ *Foreigners' Clinic, 2F, 221 Yanan Xi Lu, Jing'an* ☎ *021/6248-3180 Ext. 30106*). **Huashan Hospital** (✉ *Foreigners' Clinic, 15F, 12 Wulumuqi Zhong Lu, Jing'an* ☎ *021/6248-9999 Ext. 2531 for 24-hour hotline*). **Shanghai East International Medical Center** (✉ *551 Pudong Nan Lu., Pudong* ☎ *021/5879-9999* 🌐 *www.seimc.com.cn*).

Shanghai United Family Health Center (*private;* ✉ *1139 Xian Zia Lu, Changning* ☎ *021/5133-1900, 021/5133-1999 emergencies* 🌐 *www.unitedfamilyhospitals.com*). **SOS International Shanghai Office** (✉ *Sun Tong Infoport Plaza, 22nd fl., Unit D-G, 55 Huaihai Xi Lu, Xuhui* ☎ *021/6295-0099 emergencies* 🌐 *www.internationalsos.com*).

World Link Medical Center (✉ *Room 203, West Tower, Shanghai Center, 1376 Nanjing Xi Lu, Jing'an Hongqiao Clinic* ✉ *Mandarin City, 1F, Unit 30, 788 Hongxu Lu, Minhang Jian Qiao Clinic* ✉ *51 Hongfeng Lu, Jian Qao, Pudong* ☎ *021/6445-5999*).

Postal Services **Post Office** (✉ *276 Suzhou Bei Lu, Hongkou* ✉ *Shanghai Center, 1376 Nanjing Xi Lu, Jing'an* ✉ *133 Huaihai Lu, Xuhui* ☎ *021/6393-6666 Ext. 00*). ✉ *105 Tianping Lu*).

Subway Contacts **MagLev Train** (☎ *021/2890-7777* 🌐 *www.smtdc.com*). **Shanghai Metro Passenger Information** (☎ *021/6318-9000* 🌐 *www.shmetro.com*).

Train Contacts **Shanghai Railway Station** (✉ *303 Moling Lu, Zhabei* ☎ *021/6317-9090*). **Shanghai South Railway Station** (✉ *Between Liuzhou Lu and Humin Lu, Xuhui* ☎ *021/5435-3535*).

Visitor Info **China International Travel Service (CITS)** (✉ *1277 Beijing Xi Lu, Jing'an* ☎ *021/6289-4510* 🌐 *www.cits.net*). **Shanghai Tourist Information Services** (✉ *Yu Garden, 149 Jiujiaochang Lu, Huangpu* ☎ *021/6355-5032* ✉ *Hongqiao International Airport* ☎ *021/6268-8899*).

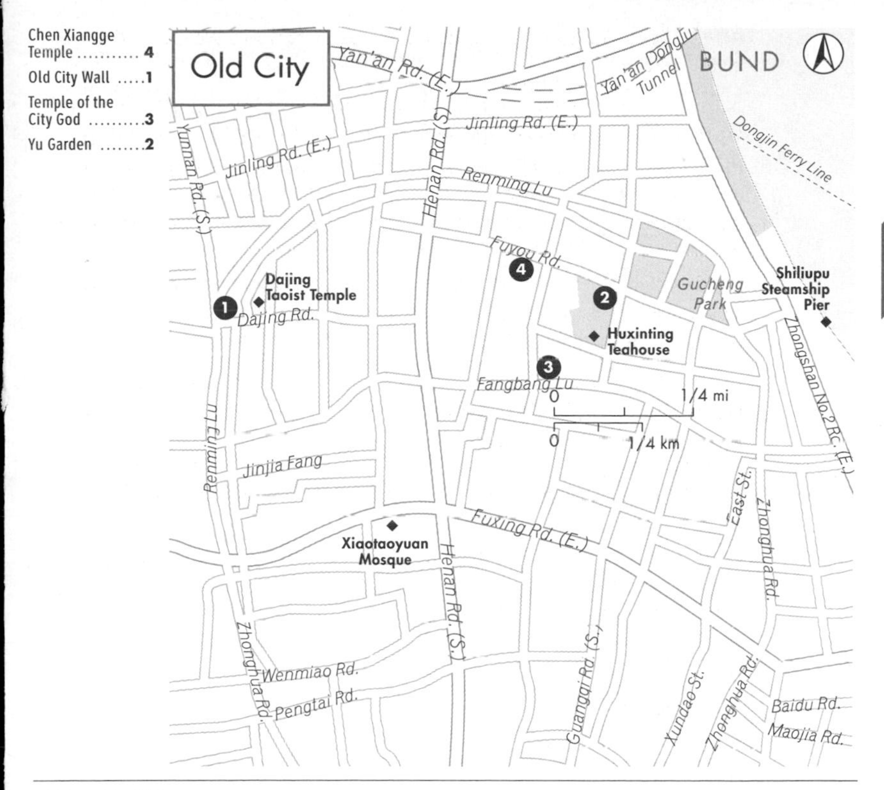

OLD CITY

Tucked away in the east of Puxi are the remnants of Shanghai's Old City. Once encircled by a thick wall, a fragment of which still remains, the Old City has a sense of history among its fast disappearing old *shikumen* (stone gatehouses), temples, and markets. Delve into narrow alleyways where residents still hang their washing out on bamboo poles and chamber pots are still in use. Burn incense with the locals in small temples, sip tea in a teahouse, or get a taste of Chinese snacks and street food. This is the place to get a feeling for Shanghai's past, but you'd better get there soon, as the wrecker's ball knows no mercy.

GETTING AROUND

This area could take a very long afternoon or morning as it's a good one to do on foot. Browsing the shops in and around the Yu Garden might add a couple of hours. At press time, Shanghai's ever expanding metro system had not yet reached Old City. However, it's a short walk east from Nanjing Dong Lu station on Line 2, and a slightly longer walk south from Huangpi Nan Lu on Line 1. **■TIP→ Taxis are nearly impossible to find in this area when you want to leave.**

SIGHTS

❹ **Chen Xiangge Temple.** If you find yourself passing by this tiny temple on your exploration of the Old City, you can make an offering to Buddha with the free incense sticks that accompany your admission. Built in 1600 by the same man who built Yu Garden, it was destroyed during the Cultural Revolution and rebuilt in the 1990s. The temple is now a nunnery, and you can often hear the women's chants rising from the halls beyond the main courtyard. ✉*29 Chenxiangge Lu, Huangpu* ☎*021/6320–0400* *Y5* *Daily 7–4.*

❶ **Old City Wall.** The Old City used to be completely surrounded by a wall, built in 1553 as a defense against Japanese pirates. Most of it was torn down in 1912, except for one 50-yard-long (40-meter-long) piece that still stands at Dajing Lu and Renmin Lu. You can walk through the remnants and check out the rather simple museum nearby, which is dedicated to the history of the Old City (the captions are in Chinese). Stroll through the tiny neighboring alley of Dajing Lu for a lively panorama of crowded market life in the Old City. ✉*269 Dajing Lu, at Renmin Lu, Huangpu* ☎*021/6326–6171* *Y5* *Daily 9–4:30.*

❸ **Temple of the City God** *(Chenghuang Miao)* lies at the southeast end of the bazaar. This Taoist Temple of the City God was built during the early part of the Ming Dynasty and was later destroyed by fire in 1924. The main hall was rebuilt in 1926 and has been renovated many times over the years. Inside are gleaming gold figures, and atop the roof you'll see statues of crusading warriors—flags raised, arrows drawn. ✉*Xi Dajie Lu, Huangpu* ☎*021/6386–8649* *Y10* *Daily 8:30–4:30.*

EXPERIENCES

❷ **Yu Garden.** Since the 18th century, this complex, with its traditional red walls and upturned tile roofs, has been a marketplace and social center where local residents gather, shop, and practice *qi gong* in the evenings. Although a bit overrun by tourists and not as impressive as the ancient palace gardens of Beijing, Yu Garden is a piece of Shanghai's past, and one of the few old sights left in the city.

Fodor's Choice ★

To get to the garden itself, you must wind your way through the bazaar. The garden was commissioned by the Ming Dynasty official Pan Yunduan in 1559 and built by the renowned architect, Zhang Nanyang, over 19 years. When it was finally finished it won international praise as "the best garden in southeastern China." In the mid-1800s the Society of Small Swords used the garden as a gathering place for meetings. It was here that they planned their uprising with the Taiping rebels against the French colonists. The French destroyed the garden during the first Opium War, but the area was later rebuilt and renovated.

Winding walkways and corridors bring you over stone bridges and carp-filled ponds and through bamboo stands and rock gardens. Within the park are an **old opera stage,** a **museum** dedicated to the Society of Small Swords rebellion, and an **exhibition hall,** opened in 2003, of Chinese calligraphy and paintings. One caveat: the park is almost always thronged with Chinese tour groups, especially on weekends. As with most sights in Shanghai, don't expect a tranquil time alone. ✉*218*

Anren Lu, bordered by Fuyou Lu, Jiujiaochang Lu, Fangbang Lu, and Anren Lu, Huangpu ☎*021/6326–0830 or 021/6328–3251* 🌐*www.yugarden.com.cn* 🎟*Y40* ⏲*Gardens, daily 8:30–5.*

XINTIANDI AND CITY CENTER

Xintiandi is Shanghai's showpiece restoration project. Reproduction shikumen houses contain expensive bars, restaurants, and chic boutiques. It's at its most magical on a warm night when locals, expats, and visitors alike pull up a chair at one of the outside seating areas and watch the world go by. Nearby, the area around People's Square has some magnificent examples of modern and historical architecture and a smattering of some of Shanghai's best museums. The adjoining People's Park is a pleasant green space where it's possible to escape the clamor of the city for a while.

GETTING AROUND

People's Square metro station is at present the main point of convergence for Shanghai's metro lines. The underground passageways can be confusing, so it's best to take the first exit and then find your way aboveground. Xintiandi is a block or two south of Line 1's Huangpi Nan Lu metro station.

The sights in this area are divided into two neat clusters—those around People's Square and those around Xintiandi. You can easily walk between the two in 20 minutes. Visiting all the museums in the People's Square area could take a good half day. Xintiandi's sights don't take very long at all, so you could go before dinner, check out the museums, and then settle down for a pre-dinner drink.

SIGHTS

Fodor's Choice ★ **Dongtai Lu Antiques Market.** A few blocks east of Xintiandi, antiques dealers' stalls line the street. You'll find porcelain, Victrolas, jade, and anything else worth hawking or buying. The same bowls and vases pop up in multiple stalls, so if your first bargaining attempt isn't successful, you'll likely have another opportunity a few stores down. Prices have shot up over the years, and fakes abound, so be careful what you buy. ✉*Off Xizang Lu, Huangpu* ⏲*Daily 10–6.*

⓬ **Site of the First National Congress of the Communist Party.** The secret meeting on July 31, 1921, that marked the first National Congress was held at the Bo Wen Girls' School, where 13 delegates from Marxist, Communist, and Socialist groups gathered from around the country. Today, ironically, the site is surrounded by Xintiandi, Shanghai's center of conspicuous consumption. The upstairs of this restored shikumen is a well-curated museum explaining the rise of communism in China. Downstairs lies the very room where the first delegates worked. It remains frozen in time, the table set with matches and tea cups. ✉*374 Huangpi Nan Lu, Luwan* ☎*021/5383–2171* 🎟*Free, audio tour Y10* ⏲*Daily 9–4.*

 **Grand Theater.** The spectacular front wall of glass shines as brightly as the star power in this magnificent theater. Its three stages host the

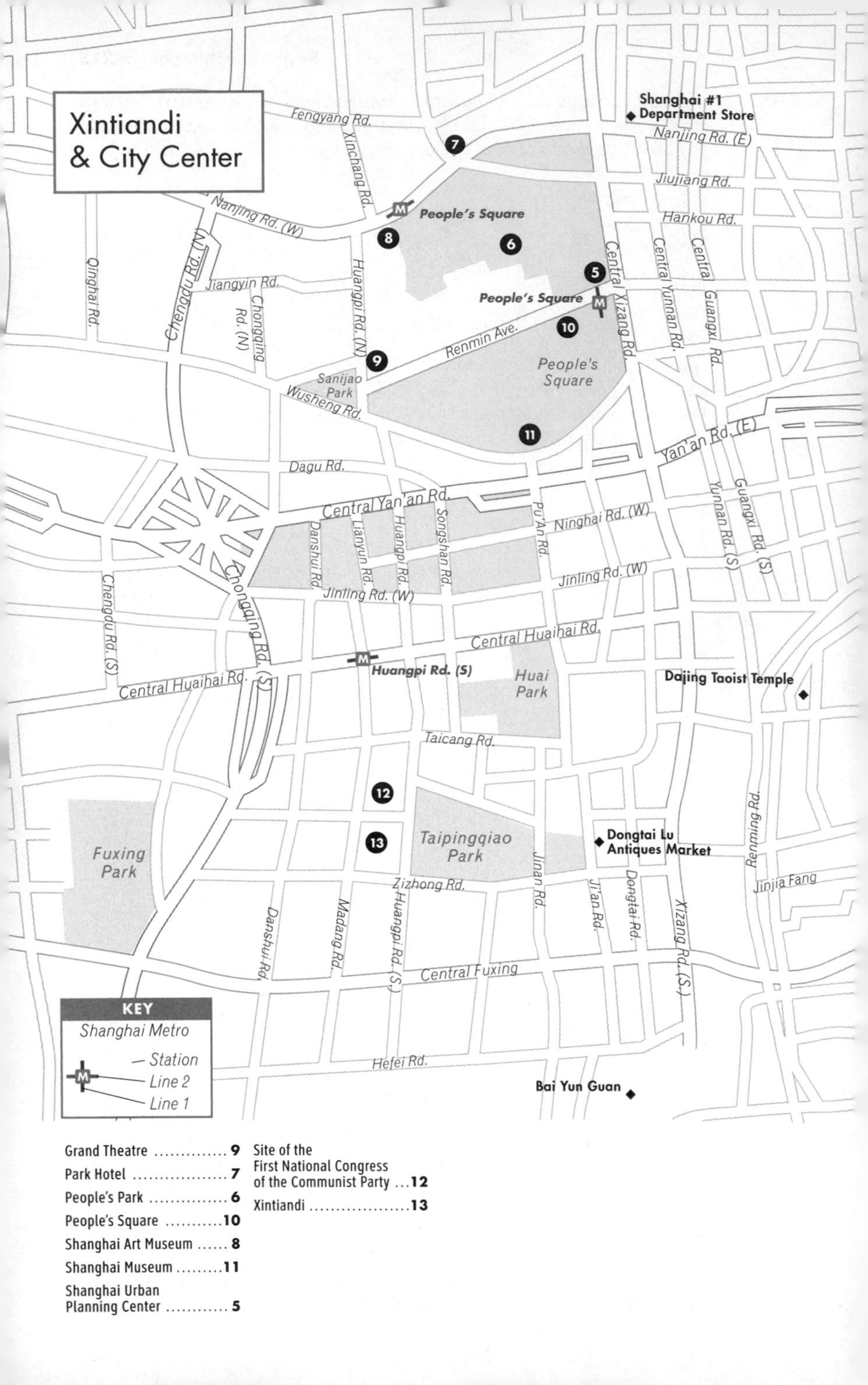
Xintiandi & City Center
Fengyang Rd.
Xinchang Rd.
Shanghai #1 Department Store
Nanjing Rd. (E)
Jiujiang Rd.
Hankou Rd.
Nanjing Rd. (W)
People's Square
Central Xizang Rd.
Central Yunnan Rd.
Central Guangxi Rd.
Qinghai Rd.
Chengdu Rd. (N)
Jiangyin Rd.
Chongqing Rd. (N)
Huangpi Rd. (N)
Renmin Ave.
People's Square
Sanijao Park
Wusheng Rd.
Yan'an Rd. (E)
Dagu Rd.
Central Yan'an Rd.
Danshui Rd.
Lianyun Rd.
Huangpi Rd.
Songshan Rd.
Pu'An Rd.
Ninghai Rd. (W)
Yunnan Rd. (S)
Guangxi Rd. (S)
Chengdu Rd. (S)
Chongqing Rd. (S)
Jinling Rd. (W)
Central Huaihai Rd.
Huangpi Rd. (S)
Huai Park
Dajing Taoist Temple
Taicang Rd.
Renming Rd.
Fuxing Park
Taipingqiao Park
Dongtai Lu Antiques Market
Jinjia Fang
Zizhong Rd.
Jinan Rd.
Ji'an Rd.
Dongtai Rd.
Xizang Rd. (S.)
Danshui Rd.
Madang Rd.
Huangpi Rd. (S.)
Central Fuxing
KEY
Shanghai Metro
Station
Line 2
Line 1
Hefei Rd.
Bai Yun Guan
Grand Theatre 9
Park Hotel 7
People's Park 6
People's Square 10
Shanghai Art Museum 8
Shanghai Museum 11
Shanghai Urban Planning Center 5
Site of the First National Congress of the Communist Party ...12
Xintiandi 13

best domestic and international performances. The dramatic curved roof atop a square base is meant to invoke the Chinese traditional saying, "the earth is square and the sky is round." ■**TIP→ See it at night.** ✉*300 Renmin Dadao, Huangpu* ☎*021/6386–8686* 🌐*www.shgtheatre.com.*

3

7 **Park Hotel.** This art-deco structure overlooking People's Park was originally the tallest hotel in Shanghai. Completed in 1934, it had luxury rooms, a nightclub, and chic restaurants. Today it's more subdued, and the lobby is the most vivid reminder of its glorious past. It was also apparently an early inspiration for famous architect I.M. Pei (of the glass pyramids at the Louvre). ✉*170 Nanjing Xi Lu, Huangpu* ☎*021/6327–5225* 🌐*www.parkhotel.com.cn.*

6 **People's Park.** In colonial days, this park was the northern half of the city's racetrack. Today the 30 acres of flower beds, lotus ponds, and trees are crisscrossed by a large number of paved paths. There's also an art gallery, the **Museum of Contemporary Art,** and a bar and restaurant, **Barbarossa,** inside. ✉*231 Nanjing Xi Lu, Huangpu* ☎*021/6327–1333* *Free* ⏲*Daily 6–6 in winter and 5–7 in summer.*

10 **People's Square.** Once the southern half of the city's racetrack, Shanghai's main square has become a social and cultural center. The **Shanghai Museum** is inside it, and the Municipal Offices, Grand Theater, and Shanghai Urban Planning Center surround it. During the day, visitors and residents stroll, fly kites, and take their children to feed the pigeons. In the evening, kids roller-skate, ballroom dancers hold group lessons, and families relax together. Weekends here are especially busy. ✉*Best place to enter is at Xizang Lu/Renmin Dadao Huangpu.*

Fodor'sChoice ★

5 **Shanghai Urban Planning Center.** To understand the true scale of Shanghai and its ongoing building boom, visit the Master Plan Hall of this museum. Sprawled out on the third floor is a 6,400-square-foot planning model of Shanghai—the largest model of its kind in the world—showing the metropolis as city planners expect it to look in 2020. You'll find familiar existing landmarks like the Pearl Tower and Shanghai Center as well as future sites like the so-called Flower Bridge, an esplanade over the Huangpu River being built for Expo 2010. ✉*100 Renmin Dadao, Huangpu* ☎*021/6372–2077* 🌐*www.supec.org* *Y30 unless there is a special exhibition* ⏲*Mon.–Thurs. 9–5, Fri.–Sun. 9–6, last ticket sold 1 hr before closing.*

EXPERIENCES

FALL IN LOVE WITH XINTIANDI

13 **Xintiandi.** By WWII, around 70 percent of Shanghai's residents lived in shikumen or "stone gatehouses." Over the last two decades, most have been razed in the name of progress, but this 8-acre collection of stone gatehouses was renovated into an upscale shopping and dining complex and renamed Xintiandi, or "New Heaven on Earth." The restaurants are busy from lunchtime until past midnight, especially those with patios for watching the passing parade of shoppers. Just off the main thoroughfare is the visitor center and the **Shikumen Museum** (✉*House 25, North Block, 123 Xingye Lu, Luwan* ☎*021/3307–0337*), a shikumen

Fodor'sChoice ★

restored to 1920s style and filled with furniture and artifacts collected from nearby houses. Exhibits explain the European influence on shikumen design, the history of the Xintiandi renovation, as well as future plans for the entire 128-acre project. ✉*181 Taicang Lu, Luwan* ✣*Bordered by Taicang Lu, Madang Lu, Zizhong Lu, and Huangpi Nan Lu* ☎*021/6311–2288* 🌐*www.xintiandi.com* 🎫*Museum Y20* ⏲*Museum, daily 10:30–10:30.*

WORD OF MOUTH

"I must suggest the Shanghai Museum! That was one of the highlights of the trip. We could have stayed there for hours."

—Wanda1

DISCOVER THE ART SCENE

8 **Shanghai Art Museum.** At the northwest corner of People's Park, the former site of the Shanghai Library was once a clubhouse for old Shanghai's sports groups, including the Shanghai Race Club. The building is now the home of the state-run Shanghai Art Museum. Its permanent collection includes paintings, calligraphy, and sculpture, but its rotating exhibitions have favored modern artwork. There's a museum store, café, and a rooftop restaurant. ✉*325 Nanjing Xi Lu, at Huangpi Bei Lu, Huangpu* ☎*021/6327–2829* 🌐*www.sh-artmuseum.org.cn* 🎫*Varies, depending on exhibition. Generally Y20* ⏲*Daily 9–4.*

11 **Shanghai Museum.** Truly one of Shanghai's treasures, this museum has the country's premier collection of relics and artifacts. Eleven galleries exhibit Chinese artistry in all its forms: paintings, bronzes, sculpture, ceramics, calligraphy, jade, Ming and Qing Dynasty furniture, coins, seals, and art by indigenous populations. Its bronze collection is one of the best in the world, and its dress and costume gallery showcases intricate handiwork from several of China's 52 minority groups. If you opt not to rent the excellent acoustic guide, information is well presented in English. You can relax in the museum's pleasant tearoom or buy postcards, crafts, and reproductions of the artwork in the bookshop. ✉*201 Renmin Da Dao, Huangpu* ☎*021/6372–3500* 🌐*www.shanghaimuseum.net* 🎫*Free, Y20 for Chinese acoustic guide, Y40 for foreign language acoustic guide* ⏲*Daily 9–4.*

Fodor's Choice ★

THE BUND AND NANJING DONG LU

The city's most recognizable sightseeing spot, the Bund, on the bank of Shanghai's Huangpu River, is lined with massive foreign buildings that predate 1949. Some of these buildings have been developed into hip "lifestyle" complexes with spas, restaurants, bars, galleries, and designer boutiques. The Bund is also an ideal spot for that photo of Pudong's famous skyline. Leading away from the Bund, Nanjing Dong Lu is slowly returning to being the stylish street it once was, and it's a popular shopping spot for the locals. Some of the adjacent streets still have a faded glamour. The best time to visit is at night to stroll the neon-lit pedestrian road.

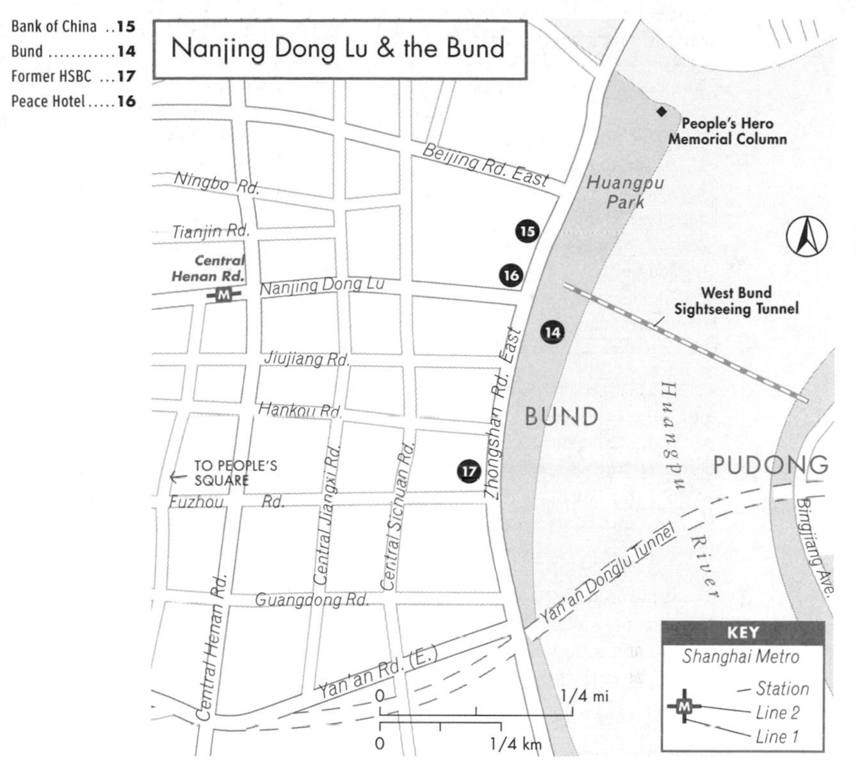

3

GETTING AROUND

The simplest way to get here is to take metro Line 2 to Nanjing Dong Lu station, and then head east for the Bund or west for the main shopping area of Nanjing Dong Lu. Alternatively, you can get off at People's Square station and walk east.

SAFETY

As in any tourist area, there are pickpockets. Not so much a safety issue as an annoyance are the "art students" who invite you to see paintings; avoid this as not only will you be subject to the hard sell, but the paintings are also overpriced and usually of poor quality.

SIGHTS

14 Fodor's Choice ★ **The Bund.** Shanghai's waterfront boulevard best shows both the city's pre-1949 past and its focus on the future. Today the municipal government has renovated the old buildings of this most foreign face of the city, highlighting them as tourist attractions, and even tried for a while to sell them back to the very owners it forced out after 1949. Currently, the area is undergoing a massive transformation including the closure of half the lanes of traffic along the waterfront and a revamp of the northern area near Suzhou Creek.

On the riverfront side of the Bund, Shanghai's street life is in full force. The city rebuilt the promenade, making it an ideal gathering place

A BRIEF HISTORY

The district's name is derived from the Anglo-Indian and literally means "muddy embankment." In the early 1920s the Bund became the city's foreign street: Americans, British, Japanese, French, Russians, Germans, and other Europeans built banks, trading houses, clubs, consulates, and hotels in styles from neoclassical to art deco.

As Shanghai grew to be a bustling trading center in the Yangzi Delta, the Bund's warehouses and ports became the heart of the action. With the Communist victory, the foreigners left Shanghai, and the Chinese government moved its own banks and offices here.

On the riverfront side of the Bund, Shanghai's street life is in full force. The city rebuilt the promenade, making it an ideal gathering place for both tourists and residents. In the morning, just after dawn, the Bund is full of people ballroom dancing, doing aerobics, and practicing kung fu, qi gong, and tai chi. The rest of the day people walk the embankment, snapping photos of the Oriental Pearl Tower, the Huangpu River, and each other. Be prepared for the aggressive souvenir hawkers; while you can't completely avoid them, try ignoring them or telling them *"bu yao,"* which means "Don't want." In the evenings lovers come out for romantic walks amid the floodlit buildings and tower. ✉*5 blocks of Zhongshan Dong Yi Lu between Jinling Lu and Suzhou Creek, Huangpu.*

EXPERIENCES

FIND ART DECO ON THE BUND

⓯ **Bank of China.** Here, old Shanghai's Western architecture (British art deco in this case) mixes with Chinese elements. In 1937 it was designed to be the highest building in the city and surpassed the neighboring Cathay Hotel (now the Peace Hotel) by a hair, except for the green tower on the Cathay's roof. ✉*23 The Bund, Zhongshan Dong Yi Lu, Huangpu* ☎*021/6329–1979.*

⓱ **Former Hong Kong and Shanghai Bank Building (HSBC).** One of the Bund's most impressive buildings—some say it's the area's pièce de résistance—the domed structure was built by the British in 1921–23, when it was the second-largest bank building in the world. After 1949 the building was turned into Communist Party offices and City Hall; now it is used by the Pudong Development Bank. In 1997 the bank made the news when it uncovered a beautiful 1920s Italian-tile mosaic in the building's dome. In the 1950s the mosaic was deemed too extravagant for a Communist government office, so it was covered by white paint, which protected it from being found by the Red Guards during the Cultural Revolution. It was then forgotten until the Pudong Development Bank renovated the building. If you walk in and look up, you'll see the circular mosaic in the dome—an outer circle painted with scenes of the cities where the HSBC had branches at the time: London, Paris, New York, Bangkok, Tokyo, Calcutta, Hong Kong, and Shanghai; a middle circle made up of the 12 signs of the zodiac; and the center painted with a large sun and Ceres, the Roman goddess of abundance. ✉ *12 The Bund, Zhongshan Dong Yi Lu, Huangpu* ☎ *021/6161–6188* 🎫 *Free* ⏲ *Weekdays 9–5:30, weekends 9–5.*

16 ★ **Peace Hotel** *(Heping Fandian)*. This hotel at the corner of the Bund and Nanjing Lu is among Shanghai's most treasured old buildings. If any establishment will give you a sense of Shanghai's past, it's this one. Its high ceilings, ornate woodwork, and art-deco fixtures are still intact, and hopefully will remain so once the current renovations have finished, and the ballroom evokes old Shanghai cabarets and gala parties.

The south building was formerly the Palace Hotel. Built in 1906, it is one of the oldest buildings on the Bund. The north building, formerly the Cathay Hotel, built in 1929, is more famous historically. It was known as the private playroom of its owner, Victor Sassoon, a wealthy landowner who invested in the opium trade. The Cathay was actually part of a complete office and hotel structure collectively called Sassoon House. Victor Sassoon himself lived and entertained his guests in the green penthouse. The hotel was rated on a par with the likes of Raffles in Singapore and the Peninsula in Hong Kong. It was *the* place to stay in old Shanghai; Noel Coward wrote *Private Lives* here. Though the hotel is closed for renovation, as of this printing, you can still see the hotel's art deco exterior. ✉ *20 Nanjing Dong Lu, Huangpu.*

FORMER FRENCH CONCESSION

With its tree-lined streets and crumbling old villas, the Former French Concession is possibly Shanghai's most atmospheric area. It's a wonderful place to go wandering and make serendipitous discoveries of stately architecture, groovy boutiques and galleries, or cozy cafés. Here, much of Shanghai's past beauty remains, although many of the old buildings are in desperate states of disrepair. One of the major roads through this area, Huaihai Lu, is a popular shopping location with shops selling international and local brands. It's also where many of Shanghai's restaurants, bars, and clubs are located, so if you are looking for an evening out, head to this area.

GETTING AROUND

This is a lovely area to walk around, so it might be best to leave cabs behind and go on foot. The only site that is at a distance is Soong Qingling's Former Residence, which is a bit farther down Huaihai Lu. Any of the four Line 1 metro stops (Huangpi Nan Lu, Shaanxi Nan Lu, Changshu Lu, or Hengshan Lu) will land you somewhere in the French Concession area.

SIGHTS

18 **Fuxing Park.** The grounds of this European-style park—known as French Park before 1949—provide a bit of greenery in crowded Shanghai. Here you'll find people practicing tai chi and lovers strolling hand in hand. ✉ *105 Fuxing Zhong Lu, Luwan* ☎ *021/5386–1069* 🎫 *Free* ⏲ *Daily 6 AM–6 PM.*

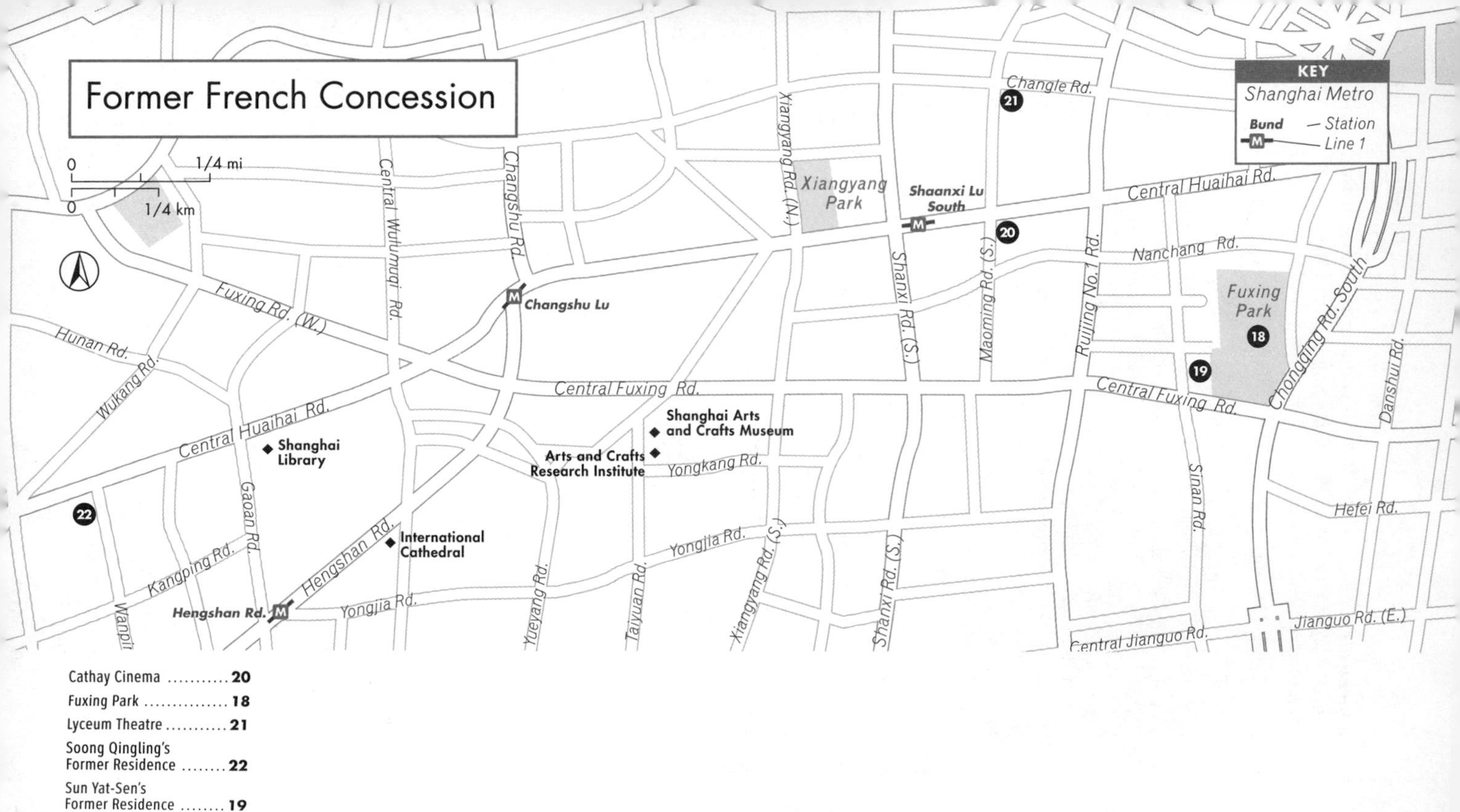

Former French Concession
0
1/4 mi
0
1/4 km
KEY
Shanghai Metro
Bund
— Station
Line 1
Changle Rd.
Central Huaihai Rd.
Xiangyang Park
Xiangyang Rd. (N.)
Shaanxi Lu South
Nanchang Rd.
Fuxing Park
Chongqing Rd. South
Danshui Rd.
Changshu Rd.
Central Wulumuqi Rd.
Changshu Lu
Fuxing Rd. (W.)
Hunan Rd.
Wukang Rd.
Shanxi Rd. (S.)
Maoming Rd. (S.)
Ruijing No.1 Rd.
Central Fuxing Rd.
Shanghai Arts and Crafts Museum
Arts and Crafts Research Institute
Yongkang Rd.
Shanghai Library
Sinan Rd.
Hefei Rd.
Gaoan Rd.
International Cathedral
Hengshan Rd.
Kangping Rd.
Yongjia Rd.
Xiangyang Rd. (S.)
Yueyang Rd.
Taiyuan Rd.
Hengshan Rd.
Wanpi
Central Jianguo Rd.
Jianguo Rd. (E.)
Cathay Cinema 20
Fuxing Park 18
Lyceum Theatre 21
Soong Qingling's Former Residence 22
Sun Yat-Sen's Former Residence 19

EXPERIENCES

SEE HOW THEY LIVED

22 **Soong Qingling's Former Residence.** While she first came to national attention as the wife of Dr. Sun Yat-sen, Soong Qingling became revered in her own right for her dedication to the Communist Party. Indeed, many mainland Chinese regard her as the "Mother of China." (On the other hand, Soong's sister, Meiling, married Chiang Kai-shek, who was the head of the Nationalist government from 1927 to 1949, at which point the couple fled to Taiwan.) This three-story house, built in 1920 by a German ship owner, was Soong's primary residence from 1948 to 1963. It has been preserved as it was during her lifetime and includes her 4,000 books in the study and furniture in the bedroom that her parents gave as her dowry. The small museum next door has some nice displays from Soong Qingling and Sun Yat-sen's life, including wedding pictures from their 1915 wedding in Tokyo. ✉*1843 Huaihai Zhonglu, Xuhui* ☎*021/6437–6268* 🌐*www.shsoong-chingling.com* 🎫*Y20* 🕓*Daily 9–4:30.*

19 **Sun Yat-sen's Former Residence.** Dr. Sun Yat-sen, the father of the Chinese republic, lived in this two-story house for six years, from 1919 to 1924. His wife, Soong Qingling, continued to live here after his death until 1937. Today it's been turned into a museum, and tours are conducted in Chinese and English. ✉*7 Xiangshan Lu, Luwan* ☎*021/6437–2954* 🎫*Y20* 🕓*Daily 9–4:30.*

FIND ART DECO

20 **Cathay Cinema.** Once part of millionaire Victor Sassoon's holdings, the art-deco Cathay Cinema was one of the first movie theaters in Shanghai. The building still serves as a theater, showing a mix of Chinese and Western films. ✉*870 Huaihai Zhonglu, at Maoming Nan Lu, Luwan* ☎*021/5404–0415* 🌐*www.guotaifilm.com.*

21 **Lyceum Theatre.** In the days of old Shanghai, the Lyceum was the home of the British Amateur Drama Club. The old stage got a face-lift in 2003 and is still in use as a concert hall. ✉*57 Maoming Nan Lu, Luwan* ☎*021/6217–8530.*

NANJING XI LU AND JING'AN

Shanghai's glitziest malls and some five-star hotels are along the main street in this area, Nanjing Xi Lu. So, if you're into designer threads, luxury spas, or expensive brunches, you can satisfy your spending urges and max out your credit here. For those of a more spiritual bent, Jingan Temple, whose reconstruction is finally pretty much finished, is one of Shanghai's largest temples. The small Jingan Park across the street is popular with couples. Behind the temple is an interesting network of back streets.

GETTING AROUND

Sights are thin in this area, but if you like international designer labels, this is where you can work the plastic. Metro Line 2 takes you to **Jingan Si** station. If you want to take a taxi afterward, joining the line at the **Shanghai Centre/Portman Ritz-Carlton** is a good idea, especially when it's raining.

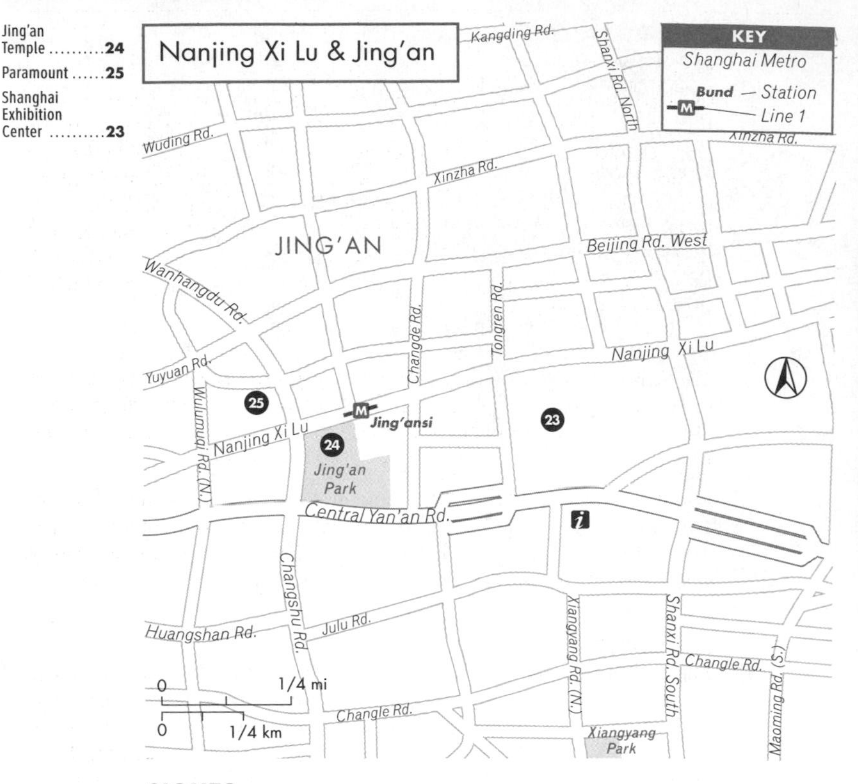

SIGHTS

❷❹ **Jingan Temple.** Originally built about AD 300, the Jingan Temple has been rebuilt and renovated numerous times. The temple's Southern-style halls, which face a central courtyard, gleam with new wood carvings of elephants and lotus flowers, but the hall interiors have stark, new concrete walls, and feel generally antiseptic. The temple's main draw is its copper Hongwu bell, cast in 1183 and weighing in at 3.5 tons. *✉1686 Nanjing Xi Lu, next to the Jingan Si subway entrance, Jing'an ☎021/6256–6366 Y10 Daily 7:30–5.*

❷❺ **Paramount.** Built in 1933, socialites referred to the Paramount as the finest dance hall in Asia. Now, at night, the domed roof of this art-deco dance hall glow blue and inside people dance the afternoon and the night away. *✉218 Yuyuan Lu, Jing'an ☎021/6249–8866 Varies depending on the dance session time Daily.*

❷❸ **Shanghai Exhibition Center.** This mammoth piece of Russian architecture was built as a sign of Sino-Soviet friendship after 1949. Today, it hosts conventions and special touring exhibitions. The complex has a restaurant that caters largely to tour groups. *✉1000 Yanan Zhonglu, Jing'an ☎021/6279–0279 Daily 9–4.*

PUDONG

Shanghai residents used to say that it was better to have a bed in Puxi than an apartment in Pudong, but the neighborhood has come a long way in recent years from a rural area to one that represents a futuristic city of wide boulevards and towering skyscrapers topped by the almost complete Mori Tower, fondly referred to as "the bottle-opener." Apartments here are some of the most expensive in Shanghai. Although a little on the bland side, it is home to expat compounds designed in a medley of bizarre architectural styles, international schools, and malls. However, there are quite a few sites here worth visiting, particularly if you have children.

GETTING AROUND

The Bund Tourist Tunnel is a strange and rather garish way of making the journey under the Huangpu River to Pudong. You might get a few laughs from the light displays. Otherwise, you can take the metro on Line 2 to Lujiazui, or catch the ferry from the Bund.

Pudong is not a walking-friendly area as there are large, rather featureless distances between the sights. You can either take the metro to get around or jump in a cab. If you visit all the sights, you could easily spend a day out here.

EXPERIENCES

CHECK OUT CHINA'S FUTURE

30 ★ **Jinmao Tower** *(Jinmao Dasha)*. This gorgeous 88th-floor (8 being the Chinese number implying wealth and prosperity) industrial art-deco pagoda houses what is currently the highest hotel in the world—the Grand Hyatt Shanghai takes up the 53rd to 87th floors. The 88th-floor observation deck, reached in 45 seconds by two high-speed elevators, offers a 360-degree view of the city. The Jinmao combines the classic 13-tier Buddhist pagoda design with postmodern steel and glass. Check out the Hyatt's dramatic 33-story atrium or the Cloud Nine bar on the 87th floor. ✉ *88 Shiji Dadao, Pudong* ☎ *021/5047–0088* 🎫 *Observation deck Y70* ⏲ *Daily 8 AM–10 PM.*

27 ★ **Oriental Pearl Tower.** The tallest tower in Asia (1,535 feet or 468 meters) has become the pride and joy of the city, a symbol of the brashness and glitz of today's Shanghai. This UFO-like structure is especially kitschy at night, when it flashes with colored lights against the classic beauty of the Bund. Its three spheres are supposed to represent pearls (as in "Shanghai, Pearl of the Orient"). An elevator takes you to observation decks in the tower's three spheres. Go to the top sphere for a 360-degree bird's-eye view of the city, or grab a bite in the Tower's revolving restaurant. On the bottom floor is the Shanghai History Museum. ✉ *1 Shiji Da Dao, Pudong* ☎ *021/5879–1888* 🎫 *Y150 including the museum* ⏲ *Daily 8 AM–9:30 PM.*

USE YOUR LEGS

Century Park. This giant swathe of green in Pudong is a great place to take children as it has a variety of vehicles for hire, good flat paths for rollerblading, and pleasure boats. On a fine day, pack a picnic as

BEST CITY TOURS

Here are some day tour options that might help you get your bearings on that stressful first afternoon.

BOAT TOURS

Huangpu River boat tours afford a great view of Pudong and the Bund, but after that it's mostly ports and cranes.

Huangpu River Cruises launches several small boats for one-hour daytime or night time cruises. The company also runs a 3½-hour trip up and down the Huangpu River between the Bund and Wusong, where the Huangpu meets the Yangzi River. You'll see barges, bridges, and factories, but not much scenery. All tours depart from the Bund at 239 Zhongshan Dong Lu. Purchase all tickets at the dock or through CITS; prices range Y50 to Y150. ✉ *153 Zhongshan Dong Er Lu (the Bund), Huangpu* ☎ *021/6374–4461.*

Shanghai Oriental Leisure Company runs 40-minute boat tours along the Bund from the Pearl Tower's cruise dock in Pudong. Prices range from Y50 to Y70, and tickets can be purchased at the gate to the Pearl Tower. Follow the brown signs from the Pearl Tower to the dock. ✉ *Oriental Pearl Cruise Dock, 1 Shiji Dadao, Pudong* ☎ *021/5879–1888.*

Shanghai Scenery Co., Ltd. This company owns three boats that run one-hour tours along the Huangpu River starting from Yangzijiang Dock. Day tours cost Y50 and night tours, Y88–Y98. ✉ *108 Huangpu Rd., Huangpu* ☎ *021/6356–1932* 🌐 *www.shanghaiscenery.com.*

BUS TOURS

Grayline Tours has escorted half- and full-day coach tours of Shanghai as well as one-day trips to Suzhou, Hangzhou, and other nearby water-side towns. Prices range from around Y250 to Y1,000. ✉ *A19, 2F Youth Centre Plaza, 1888 Hanzhong Lu, Putuo 200070* ☎ *021/6150–8061* 🌐 *www.graylineshanghai.com.*

Jinjiang Tours runs a full-day bus tour of Shanghai that includes the French Concession, People's Square, Jade Buddha Temple, Yu Garden, the Bund, and Xintiandi. Tickets cost Y2,400 lunch included. ✉ *161 Chang Le Lu, Luwan* ☎ *021/6415–1188* 🌐 *www.jjtravel.com.*

HERITAGE TOURS

Shanghai Jews. This half-day tour is available daily in Hebrew or English and takes visitors to the sites of Shanghai's Jewish history. The cost is Y400 per person. ☎ *1300/214–6702* 🌐 *www.shanghai-jews.com.*

there are designated picnic areas as well as woods and grass to play on. ✉ *1001 Jinxiu Lu, Pudong* ☎ *021/3876–0588* 🌐 *www.centurypark.com.cn* 🎫 *Y10* 🕓 *Daily 7 AM–6 PM.*

26 **Riverside Promenade.** Although the park that runs 2,750 yards (2,514 meters) along the Huangpu River is sugary-sterile in its experimental suburbia, it still offers the most beautiful views of the Bund. You can stroll on the grass and concrete and view a perspective of Puxi unavailable from the west side. If you're here in the summer, you can ENJOY WADING, as a sign indicates, in the chocolate-brown Huangpu River from the park's wave platform. ✉ *Bingjiang Dadao, Pudong* 🎫 *Free.*

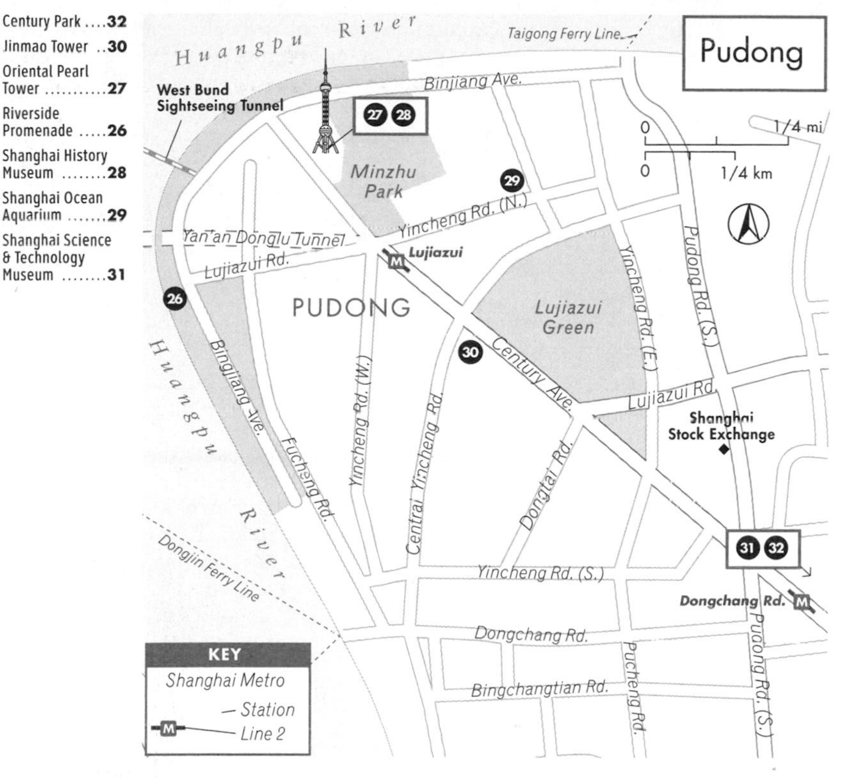

FOR THE KIDS

(28) ★ **Shanghai History Museum.** This impressive museum in the base of the Pearl Tower recalls Shanghai's pre-1949 history. Inside you can stroll down a re-created Shanghai street circa 1900 or check out a streetcar that used to operate in the concessions. Dioramas depict battle scenes from the Opium Wars, shops found in a typical turn-of-the-20th-century Shanghai neighborhood, and grand Former French Concession buildings of yesteryear. ✉ *1 Shiji Dadao, Pudong* ☎ *021/5879–1888* 🎟 *Y35* ⏲ *Daily 8–9:30.*

(29) **Shanghai Ocean Aquarium.** As you stroll through the aquarium's 12,000-foot-long (3,658-meter-long) clear, sightseeing tunnel, you may feel like you're walking your way through the seven seas—or at least five of them. The aquarium's 10,000 fish represent 300 species, 5 oceans, and 4 continents. You'll also find penguins and species representing all 12 of the Chinese zodiacal animals, such as the tiger barb, sea dragon, and seahorse. ✉ *1388 Lujiazui Ring Road, Pudong* ☎ *021/5877–9988* 🌐 *www.sh-aquarium.com* 🎟 *Y120 adults, Y80 children* ⏲ *9 AM–6 PM;* ⏲ *9 AM–6 PM; July and August, Chinese New Year and May and October holidays.*

(31) **Shanghai Science and Technology Museum.** This museum, a favorite attraction for kids in Shanghai, has more than 100 hands-on exhibits in its six

main galleries. Earth Exploration takes you through fossil layers to the earth's core for a lesson in plate tectonics. Spectrum of Life introduces you to the animal and plant kingdoms within its simulated rain forest. Light of Wisdom explains basic principles of light and sound through interactive exhibits, and simulators in AV Paradise put you in a plane cockpit and on television. Children's Technoland has a voice-activated fountain and miniature construction site. In Cradle of Designers, you can record a CD or assemble a souvenir. Two IMAX theaters and an IWERKS 4D theater show larger-than-life movies, but mostly in Chinese. All signs are in English; the best times to visit are weekday afternoons. ✉ *2000 Shiji Dadao, Pudong* ☎ *021/6854–2000* 🌐 *www.sstm.org.cn* 🎟 *Y60; there are separate prices for the IMAX and IWERKS* ⏲ *Tues.–Sun. 9–5:15.*

NORTH SHANGHAI

Although often neglected in favor of their more glamorous neighboring areas, the northern Shanghai districts of Putuo, Hongkou, and Zhabei still offer some interesting sights. Hongkou District, particularly, is still relatively undeveloped and unchanged, and buildings from the past are still visible behind cheap clothing stores. An area with an interesting history, it has the most sights worth seeing as well as the lush green sweep of Lu Xun Park. The old buildings and warehouses around Suzhou Creek, which feeds into the Huangpu, are slowly being turned into a hip and happening arty area, particularly the M50 development. Also in Putuo District is another one of Shanghai's main temples, the Jade Buddha Temple.

GETTING AROUND

North Shanghai's sights are in three distinct areas. The galleries at M50 open later in the morning, so it may be best to head to some other sites first. Many of them are closed on Mondays. Qipu Lu also gets very busy as the day goes on and is unbearable on weekends.

For the Jade Buddha Temple and M50, you can hop off the metro Line 3 or 4 at Zhongtan Lu, and then it's a short walk to M50 and a longer one to Jade Buddha. You can take the Pearl Line to East Baoxing Lu and Hongkou Stadium for Lu Xun Park and Duolun Lu. The best way to get around is by taxi.

SIGHTS

(36) **Duolun Lu.** Designated Shanghai's "Cultural Street," Duolun Road takes you back in time to the 1930s, when the 1-km-long (½-mi-long) lane was a favorite haunt of writer Lu Xun and fellow social activists. Bronze statues of those literary luminaries dot the lawns between the well-preserved villas and row houses, whose first floors are now home to antiques shops, cafés, and art galleries. As the street takes a 90-degree turn, its architecture shifts 180 degrees with the seven-story stark gray **Shanghai Doland Museum of Modern Art.** ✉ *Off Sichuan Bei Lu, Hongkou.*

33 ★ **Jade Buddha Temple.** Completed in 1918, this temple is fairly new by Chinese standards. During the Cultural Revolution, in order to save the temple when the Red Guards came to destroy it, the monks pasted portraits of Mao Zedong on the outside walls so the Guards couldn't tear them down without destroying Mao's face as well. The temple is built in the style of the Song Dynasty, with symmetrical halls and courtyards, upturned eaves, and bright yellow walls. The temple's great treasure is its 6½-foot-tall (2-meter-tall) seated Buddha made of white jade with a robe of precious gems, originally brought to Shanghai from Burma. Other Buddhas, statues, and frightening guardian gods of the temple populate the halls, as well as a collection of Buddhist scriptures and paintings. The monks who live and work here can sometimes be seen worshipping. It's madness at festival times. ✉ *170 Anyuan Lu, Putuo* ☎ *021/6266–3668* 🌐 *www.yufotemple.com* 🎫 *Y30* 🕑 *Daily 8–4:30.*

37 **Ohel Moishe Synagogue and Huoshan Park.** Currently called the Jewish Refugee Memorial Hall of Shanghai, the Ohel Moishe Synagogue served as the spiritual heart of Shanghai's Jewish ghetto in the 1930s and '40s. In this sanctuary-turned-museum, whose restoration was completed in 2008, visitors can see a reconstruction of the main room of the synagogue and see artworks inspired by the story of Jews in Shanghai. An outside building has photos, newspaper clippings and a film (narrated in Chinese).

Around the corner, down a lane just as well preserved, Huoshan Park bears a memorial tablet in the immigrants' honor. ✉ *62 Changyang Lu, Hongkou* ☎ *021/6541–5008* 🎫 *Y50* ⏲ *Mon.–Sat. 9 AM–4 PM.*

EXPERIENCES

MODERN ART FIX

34 **M50** is a cluster of art galleries and artists studios by Suzhou Creek. This is home to some of Shanghai's hottest galleries and where you will see works from China's best artists as well as new and not so well-known ones. There are also a couple of shops selling music and art supplies and a branch of Shirtflag. Don't be shy about nosing around—there are galleries in many floors of these old factories and warehouses and sometimes artists will be around for a chat. ✉ *50 Moganshan Lu, Putuo* 🎫 *Free* ⏲ *Daily although most galleries are closed on Mon. Opening times vary depending on the gallery.*

35 **Shanghai Doland Museum of Modern Art.** Opened in December 2003, this is Shanghai's first official venue for modern art. The six-story museum's 14,400 square feet of exhibition space include a tiny shop selling art books and a metal spiral staircase that's a work of art in itself. The exhibitions, which change frequently, are cutting edge for Shanghai. They've showcased electronic art from American artists, examined gender issues among Chinese, and featured musical performances ranging from Chinese electronica to the *dombra,* a traditional Kazak stringed instrument. ✉ *27 Duolun Lu, Hongkou* ☎ *021/6587–2530* 🎫 *Varies according to the exhibition* ⏲ *Daily 10–5:30.*

XUJIAHUI AND SOUTH, HONGQIAO AND GUBEI

Buyers throng into the large malls in the shopping precinct at Xujiahui, which shines with neon and giant billboard advertisements. Down the road are the districts of Hongqiao and Gubei where wealthy expats live in high-walled compounds and drive huge SUVs. You're likely to find a larger concentration of Western-style restaurants and supermarkets here if you are feeling homesick.

GETTING AROUND

Metro Line 1 takes you right into the depths of the Grand Gateway Mall at Xujiahui. The other sights are fairly far-flung, so it might be a good idea to jump into a taxi. If you are going to places like the Shanghai Botanical Gardens from the center of town, be prepared for a large taxi bill. Otherwise, you can get off at Shanghai South Railway Station.

SIGHTS

40 **Longhua Martyrs Cemetery** may seem a tranquil place now, but it has had a bloody history. It has been the execution site of many Communists, particularly during the Guomingdang crackdown in 1927. Nowadays, it's full of large Soviet-style sculpture and immaculate lawns. The most chilling is the small, unkempt, grassy execution area accessed by a tunnel where the remains of murdered Communists were found with leg irons still on in the 1950s. ✉ *180 Longhua Lu, Xuhui* ☎ *021/6468–5995* 🌐 *www.slmmm.cn* 🎫 *Y1* ⏲ *Daily 6–5, Museum 9–4.*

TEE OFF

Some 20 clubs dot the countryside within two hours of downtown Shanghai. All clubs run on a membership basis, but most allow nonmembers to play when accompanied by a member.

Grand Shanghai International Golf and Country Club. This club has a Ronald Fream–designed 18-hole championship course and driving range. ✉ *18 Yangcheng Zhonglu, Yangcheng Lake Holiday Zone, Kunshan City, 215347, Jiangsu Province* ☎ *0512/5789–1999* 🌐 *www.grandshanghaigolf.com.cn.*

Shanghai Binhai Golf Club. Peter Thomson designed the Scottish links-style, 27-hole course at this club in Pudong. Another 27 holes are on the books. ✉ *Binhai Resort, Baiyulan Dadao, Nanhui County* ☎ *021/3800–1888 (reservation hotline)* 🌐 *www.binhaigolf.com.*

Shanghai International Golf and Country Club. This 18-hole course designed by Robert Trent Jones Jr. is Shanghai's most difficult. There are water hazards at almost every hole. ✉ *961 Yin Zhu Lu, Zhu Jia Jiao, Qingpu District* ☎ *021/5972–8111.*

Shanghai Links Golf and Country Club. This Jack Nicklaus–designed 18-hole course is about a 45-minute ride east of downtown. It's open to the public on Tuesday for Ladies' Day. ✉ *1600 Linghai Lu, Tianxu Township, Pudong* ☎ *021/5897–3068* 🌐 *www.shanghailinks.com.cn.*

Shanghai Riviera Golf Resort. The late Bobby J. Martin designed this 18-hole course and driving range. ✉ *277 Yangtze Lu, Nanxiang Town, Jiading District* ☎ *021/5912–6888* 🌐 *www.srgr.cn.*

Shanghai Silport Golf Club. This club hosts the Volvo China Open. Its 27-hole course on Dianshan Lake was designed by Bobby J. Martin; 9 holes designed by Roger Packard opened in 2004. ✉ *1 Xubao Lu, Dianshan Lake Town, Kunshan City, Jiangsu Province* ☎ *0512/5748–1111* 🌐 *www.silport.com.cn.*

Shanghai Sun Island International Club. You'll find a 27-hole course designed by Nelson & Haworth plus an excellent driving range at this club. ✉ *2588 Shantai Lu, Zhu Jia Jiao, Qingpu District* ☎ *021/6983–3001* 🌐 *www.sunislandclub.com.*

Tianma Country Club. Tianma is the most accessible course to the public. Its 18 holes have views of Sheshan Mountain. ✉ *3958 Zhaokun Lu, Tianma Town, Songjiang District* ☎ *021/5766–1666* 🌐 *www.tianmacc.com.*

Tomson Shanghai Pudong Golf Club. The closest course to the city center, Tomson has 18 holes and a driving range designed by Shunsuke Kato. ✉ *1 Longdong Dadao, Pudong* ☎ *021/5833–8888* 🌐 *www.tomsongolf.com.*

39 ★ **Longhua Temple** *(Longhua Si)*. Shanghai's largest and most active temple has as its centerpiece a seven-story, eight-sided pagoda. While the temple is thought to have been built in the 3rd century, the pagoda dates from the 10th century; it's not open to visitors. Near the front entrance of the temple stands a three-story bell tower, where a 3.3-ton bronze bell is rung at midnight every New Year's Eve. Along the side corridors of

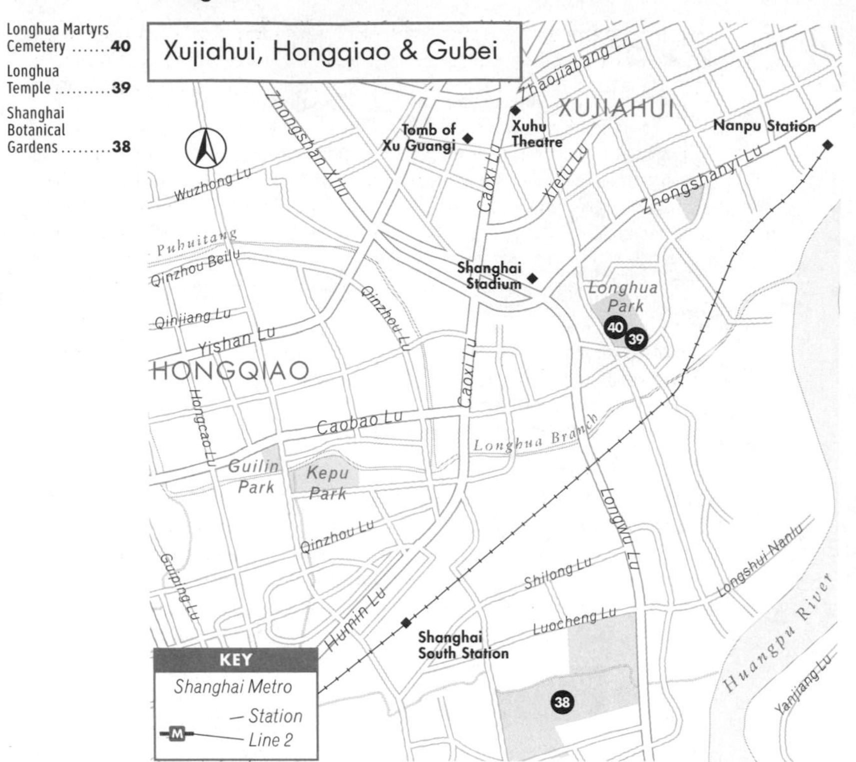

the temple you'll find the Longhua Hotel, a vegetarian restaurant, and a room filled seven rows deep with small golden statues. The third hall is the most impressive. Its three giant Buddhas sit beneath a swirled red and gold dome. ✉*2853 Longhua Lu, Xuhui* ☎*021/6456–6085 or 021/6457–6327* 🎫*Y10 with free incense* ⏲*Daily 7–4:30.*

38 **Shanghai Botanical Gardens.** Spread over 200 acres, the garden has areas for peonies and roses, azaleas, osmanthus, bamboo and orchids, and medicinal plants. Its Penjing Garden is among the world's best. *Penjing* translates as "pot scenery," and describes the Chinese art of creating a miniature landscape in a container. More than 2,000 bonsai trees line the Penjing Garden's courtyards and corridors. The Chinese Cymbidium Garden has more than 300 varieties. Within the Grand Conservatory are towering palms and more than 3,500 varieties of tropical plants. ✉*1111 Longwu Lu, Xuhui* ☎*021/5436–3369* 🌐*www.shbg.org* 🎫*Y15 for entrance through main gate only* ⏲*Daily 7–5.*

WHERE TO EAT

Updated by David Taylor

You'll notice most Chinese restaurants in Shanghai have large, round tables. The reason becomes clear the first time you eat a late dinner at a local restaurant and are surrounded by jovial, laughing groups of people toasting and topping off from communal bottles of beer, sharing cigarettes, and spinning the lazy Susan loaded with food. Whether feting guests or demonstrating their growing wealth, hosts will order massive, showy spreads.

Shanghai's standing as China's most international city is reflected in its dining scene. You can enjoy *jiaozi* (dumplings) for breakfast, foie gras for lunch, and Kobe beef teppanyaki for dinner. It's traditional to order several dishes, plus rice, to share among your party. Tipping is not expected, but sophistication comes at a price. Although you can at Chinese restaurants for less than Y40, even simple Western meals cost a more Western price.

Most restaurants in Shanghai offer set lunches—multicourse feasts—at a fraction of the usual price. Also, check out the "Restaurant Events" section of *That's Shanghai,* or *Smartshanghai.com,* which list dining discounts and promotions around town.

ON THE MENU

Shanghainese food is fairly typical Chinese, with dark, sweet, and oily dishes served in great abundance. The dish sizes can be quite small—it's not unusual for two diners to polish off six dishes plus rice. The drink of choice is *huangjiu,* or yellow wine. It's a mild-tasting sweetish rice wine, which pairs well with the local cuisine.

Shanghai is full of fine restaurants from around the world, but sometimes the finest dining experience in the city can be had with a steamer tray of *xiaolongbao* (Shanghai's signature dumplings—small steamed buns filled with pork and crab meat in broth) matched with a cold beer. River fish is often the highlight (and most expensive part) of the meal, and hairy crab is a seasonal delicacy.

MEAL TIMES

Dinner hours in restaurants begin at around 5 PM, but often carry on late into the night. Many of the classic, local restaurants popular with the Shanghainese only close after the last diners have left, which sometimes keeps them open until the wee hours of the morning. Generally, though, dinner is eaten between 6 and 11 PM.

PRICES

Even in the fanciest restaurants, main courses are unlikely to cost more than US$35. However, famous restaurants charge as much as the international market will bear—prices that often don't reflect the quality of the dining experience. If you're looking for an excellent meal and you don't care about the restaurateur's name, then exceptional dining experiences can be had for half the price.

Great local food can be found for laughably cheap prices ($1 to $5 per dish), even in fairly nice restaurants. The experience of eating at a small, unknown restaurant is pure China.

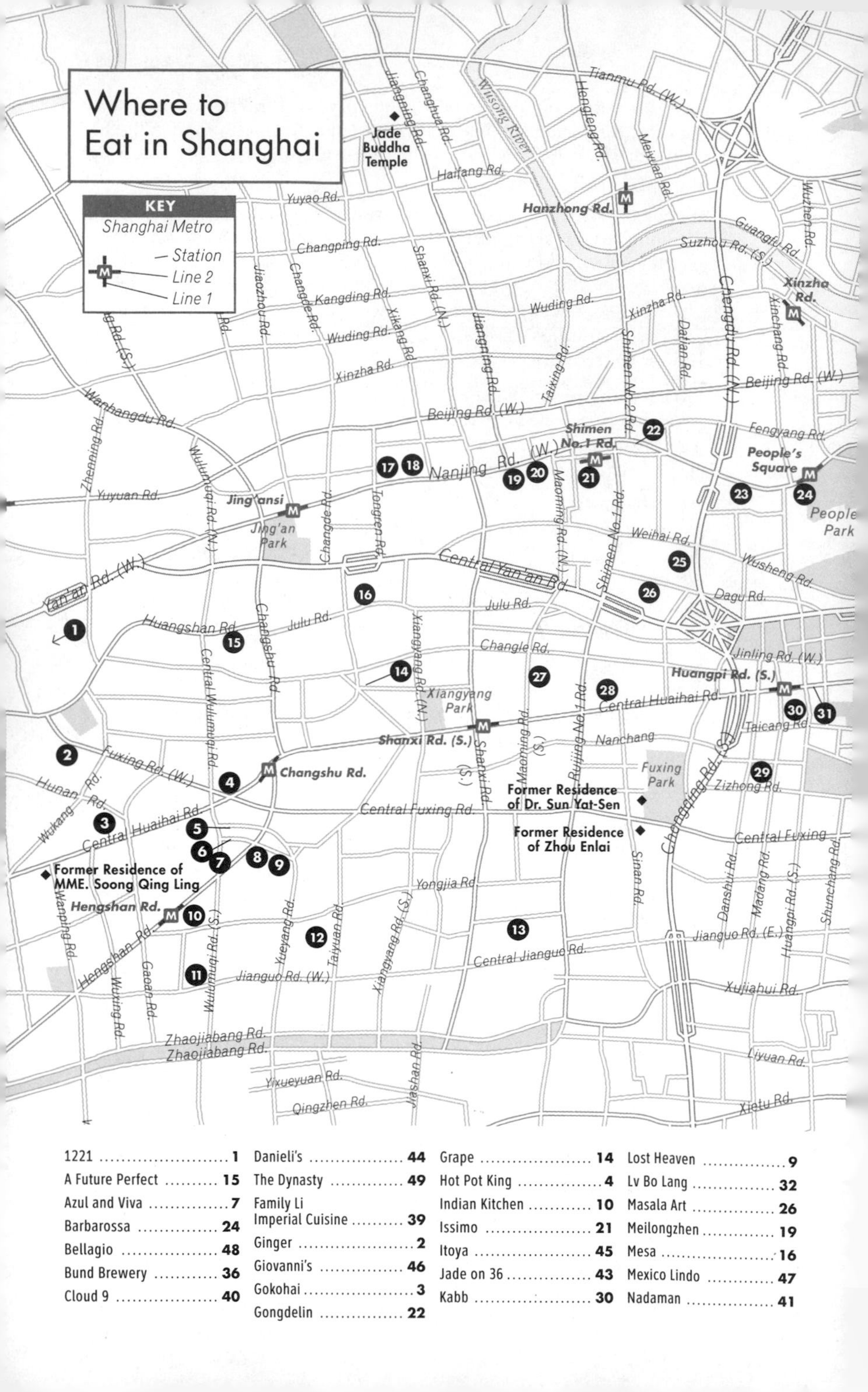

1221 1
A Future Perfect 15
Azul and Viva 7
Barbarossa 24
Bellagio 48
Bund Brewery 36
Cloud 9 40
Danieli's 44
The Dynasty 49
Family Li Imperial Cuisine 39
Ginger 2
Giovanni's 46
Gokohai 3
Gongdelin 22
Grape 14
Hot Pot King 4
Indian Kitchen 10
Issimo 21
Itoya 45
Jade on 36 43
Kabb 30
Lost Heaven 9
Lv Bo Lang 32
Masala Art 26
Meilongzhen 19
Mesa 16
Mexico Lindo 47
Nadaman 41

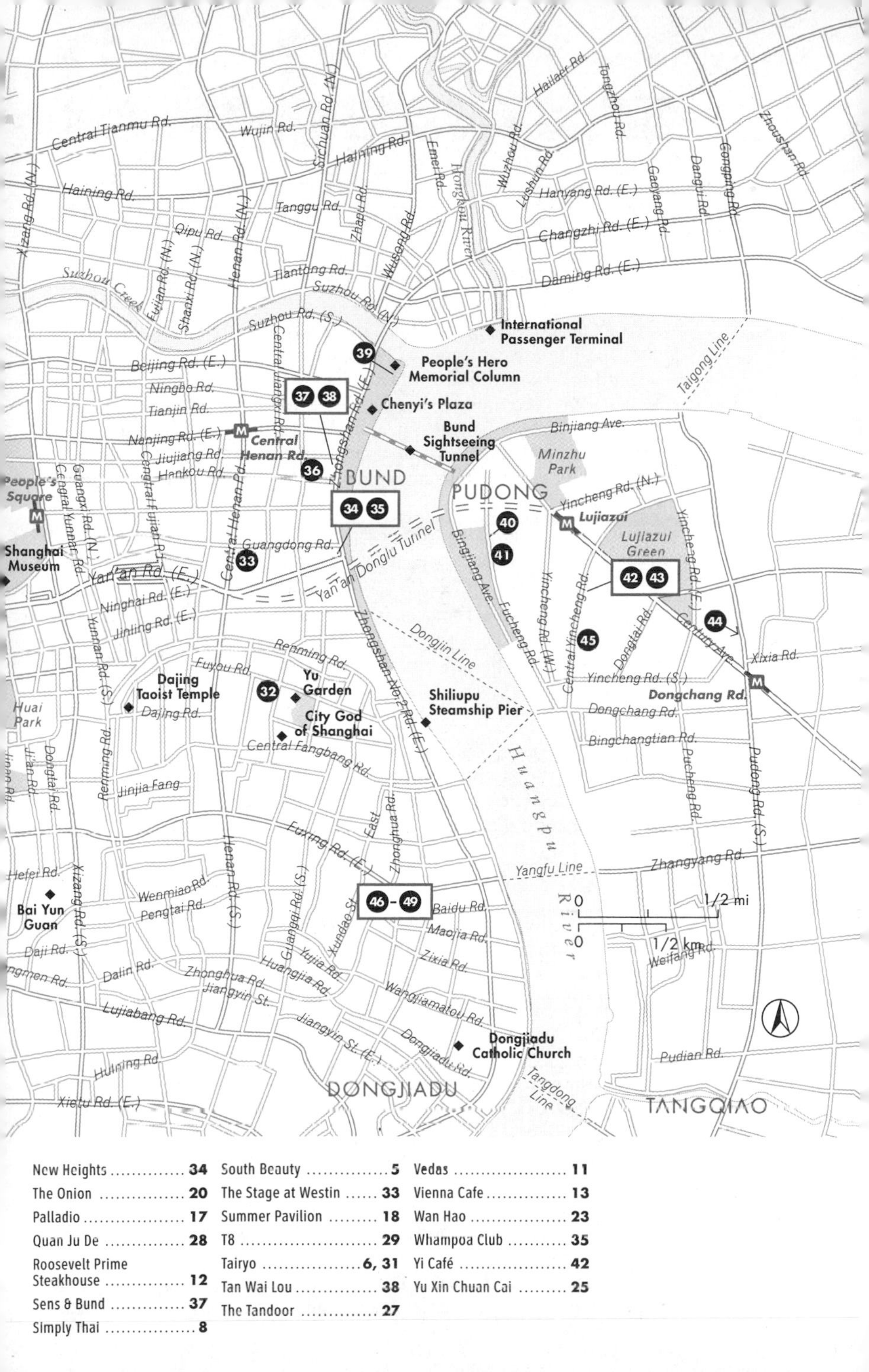

New Heights 34
The Onion 20
Palladio 17
Quan Ju De 28
Roosevelt Prime Steakhouse 12
Sens & Bund 37
Simply Thai 8
South Beauty 5
The Stage at Westin 33
Summer Pavilion 18
T8 29
Tairyo 6, 31
Tan Wai Lou 38
The Tandoor 27
Vedas 11
Vienna Cafe 13
Wan Hao 23
Whampoa Club 35
Yi Café 42
Yu Xin Chuan Cai 25

WHAT IT COSTS IN YUAN					
	¢	$	$$	$$$	$$$$
Restaurants	under Y40	Y40–Y80	Y81–Y150	Y151–Y300	over Y300

Prices are for a main course at dinner.

OLD CITY

Narrow and crowded, the Old City is all that's left of old China in Shanghai. The area is home to the spectacular Yuyuan Gardens, and is a good location to find traditional-style food in an authentic environment. We recommend that the adventurous go out into the side streets around Fangbang Lu in search of authentic Chinese snacks. **■ TIP→ When dining in these small local restaurants always ask the price first—with no English menu, many sellers in this area aren't above raising the price after your first bite.**

$$ CHINESE **✕ Lv Bo Lang.** A popular stop for visiting dignitaries, Lv Bo Lang (pronounced "Lü Bo Lang") is a perfect photo op of a restaurant. The traditional three-story Chinese pavilion with upturned eaves sits next to the Bridge of Nine Turnings in the Yu Garden complex. The food is good but not great, with many expensive fish choices on the menu. Among the best dishes are the crab meat with bean curd, the braised eggplant with chili sauce, and the sweet *osmanthus* cake, made with the sweetly fragrant flower of the same name. ✉ *115 Yuyuan Lu, Huangpu* ☎ *021/6328–0602* ✍ *Reservations essential* ▭ *AE, DC, MC, V.*

The center of the gastronomic city, the City Center and Xintiandi contain some of the finest restaurants in the city, like T8, the JW Marriott's restaurants, and the trendy Barbarossa.

XINTIANDI AND CITY CENTER

The center of the gastronomic city, the City Center and Xintiandi contain some of the finest restaurants in the city, like T8 and the trendy Barbarossa.

$$ MIDDLE EASTERN **✕ Barbarossa.** Modern Middle Eastern food in a setting taken from the *Arabian Nights,* Barbarossa is a popular evening destination. The decoration is amazing, albeit possibly flammable, with billowing draperies swathing the space, and the food and service are reasonable. At around 10 PM, Barbarossa becomes a club, so don't aim for a late dinner unless you like mingling with the party people. ✉ *People's Square, 231 Nanjing Xi Rd., next to the Shanghai Art Museum, Luwan* ☎ *021/6318–0220* ▭ *AE, DC, MC, V.*

$–$$ AMERICAN **✕ Kabb.** Serving burgers, salads, and other standards of American food, this café in Xintiandi is distinguished for its superb location. The food is good, but without distinction, though the portions are massive. Service is slightly indifferent, and the pricing is rather high for such pedestrian fare. However, it does fill the bill for a quick lunch on the sidewalk tables. ✉*Xintiandi, 181 Taicang Lu, 5 Xintiandi Bei Li, Luwan* ☎*021/3307–0798* ▭*AE, DC, MC, V.*

$$$ INTERNATIONAL Fodor'sChoice ★ ✕**T8.** A veteran of the Shanghai fine dining scene, T8 has garnered its share of headlines for its stunning interior and inspired contemporary cuisine. The restaurant occupies a traditional shikumen house within Xintiandi and has modernized the space with raw stone floors, carved-wood screens, and imaginative lighting that transforms shelves full of glasses into a modern-art sculpture. The show kitchen turns out exciting fusion dishes from fresh seasonal ingredients. Like the clientele, the wine list is exclusive, with many labels unavailable elsewhere in Shanghai. ✉*Number 8, North Block, Xintiandi, Lane 181 Taicang Lu, Luwan* ☎*021/6355–8999* *Reservations essential* ▭*AE, DC, MC, V* *No lunch Monday.*

$$ JAPANESE ✕**Tairyo.** Teppanyaki has invaded Shanghai. More down to earth than a sophisticated sushi bar, teppanyaki (Japanese barbecue) includes sushi, sashimi, barbecued meats, and a wide variety of Western and Eastern dishes. It does serve à la carte, but at Y150 for all you can eat and drink, Tairyo's main attraction is obvious. Just walk in, take a seat at the grill, and indulge while the chef prepares your dinner as you watch. We recommend the Mongolian King Steak, but the menu has English and pictures, so pick and choose. This is a perfect no-effort dinner destination. Private rooms are available for groups larger than seven (reservations essential). ✉*Hong Kong New World Plaza, South Building, 283 Huaihai Rd., 3rd fl., Luwan* ☎*021/6390–7244* ▭*AE, DC, MC, V.*

$$$–$$$$ CANTONESE ✕**Wan Hao.** On the 38th floor of the JW Marriott overlooking People's Square, Wan Hao is an elegant and relatively inexpensive Chinese restaurant. It specializes in Cantonese dishes, though the menu contains other popular options like Peking Duck and spicy chicken. The food is good without being exceptional, and the ambience is pleasant. Look to the seasonal dishes for the freshest options; the kitchen team is always updating the menu. Servings tend to be on the small side—Chinese-style—despite the Western place settings, so expect to order several dishes per person. If you're unsure about your order, the staff is happy to help. ✉*JW Marriott at Tomorrow Square, 38th fl., 399 Nanjing Xi Lu, Luwan* ☎*021/5359–4969* ▭*AE, DC, MC, V.*

NANJING DONG LU AND THE BUND

The Bund is the heart of modern Shanghai, with the colonial history of Puxi facing the towering steel and glass of Pudong. The stellar view of the river and Pudong has attracted some of the finest restaurant development in town. However, many visitors complain that the Bund restaurants are more style than substance. We find that it's well worth your effort to experience what this area has to offer.

$$ AMERICAN ★ ✕**Bund Brewery.** Ostensibly a brew pub, the Bund Brewery is more popular as an off-Bund dinner alternative. The food is modern, well-portioned pub fare, and the service reasonably attentive. It's a good choice for an unpretentious meal after a day's Bund sightseeing, or before heading out the clubs for the evening. ✉ *11 Hankou Lu, Huangpu* ☎*021/6321–8447* ▭*AE, DC, MC, V.*

$$$$ MANDARIN
Family Li Imperial Cuisine. This spectacular restaurant, a newer branch of the famous Beijing Imperial restaurant, deserves a visit despite high prices (set menus begin at Y600). Using family recipes smuggled from the Forbidden City a century ago, Family Li gives the closest thing to a taste of imperial food. There are only nine rooms, and only set menus are served. Reservations more than 24 hours in advance are a must. ✉ *Huangpu Park, 500 East Zhongshan Yi Rd., Huangpu* ☎ *021/5308–1919* *Reservations essential* *AE, DC, MC, V.*

$$$ AMERICAN ★
New Heights. Perched atop prestigious Three on the Bund, New Heights is a surprisingly unpretentious restaurant. With a gorgeous terrace overlooking the river and a solid menu of generally North American standard fare, this is an excellent destination for the weary Bund tourist. We recommend it for a late lunch basking in the afternoon sun on the terrace. Try the hamburger with a cold beer. ✉ *Three on the Bund, 7th fl., 3 Zhong Shan Dong Yi Rd., Huangpu* ☎ *021/6321–0909* *AE, DC, MC, V.*

$$–$$$ ECLECTIC ★
The Stage at Westin. Although The Stage is usually a fairly standard 5-star buffet, it is also home to Shanghai's most popular Sunday Champagne Brunch. Costing almost Y500 and booked 2 to 3 weeks in advance, the brunch at the Westin has become an institution. Check it out if you feel the need for some decadent indulgence. ✉ *Level 1, The Westin Shanghai Bund Center, 88 Henan Zhong Rd., Huangpu* ☎ *021/6335–0577 Reservations essential* *AE, DC, MC, V.*

$$$$ FRENCH
Sens & Bund. The Shanghai branch of the France-based Jardin du Sens Group, Sens & Bund serves contemporary Mediterranean cuisine overlooking the Huangpu. The food is good, the service well-trained, and the ambience relaxing. The prices are quite high, but the overall quality and consistency makes this a better choice than many of its neighbors. Ask for a river view table. ✉ *Bund 18, 1 Zhongshan Dong Yi Rd., 6th fl., Huangpu* ☎ *021/6323–9898* *AE, DC, MC, V.*

$$ CHINESE FUSION
Tan Wai Lou. Bund18's Chinese restaurant, Tan Wai Lou, serves up nouveau-Cantonese cuisine in a refined setting. The food is good and well presented, though the non-Chinese service can be a little jarring for a diner expecting a classic Chinese meal. Still, the seafood is very fresh and the view of the Huangpu spectacular. ✉ *Bund18, 5th fl., 18 Zhongshan Dong Yi Rd., Huangpu* ☎ *021/6339–1188* *Reservations essential* *AE, DC, MC, V.*

$$$ CHINESE FUSION
Whampoa Club. A popular member of the Bund scene, Whampoa Club is nouveau Chinese at its best. With a focus on fresh seafood and interesting interpretations of Shanghai classics, this is a destination worth checking out. As befits a celebrity venue, prices are steep, but generally worth the expense. ✉ *Three on the Bund, 4th fl., 17 Guangdong Lu, 4th fl., Huangpu* ☎ *021/6321–3737* *Reservations essential* *AE, DC, MC, V.*

$$ SICHUAN
Yu Xin Chuan Cai. Yu Xin offers fantastic Sichuan food and is extremely popular with the locals. Each of the two locations seats hundreds and is always full. Book ahead, or be prepared to wait around 30 to 60 minutes for a table. Try the tea-smoked duck. ✉ *3F, 333 South Cheng Du Lu and 5F, No. 399, Jiu Jiang Lu, Huangpu*

☎021/5298–0438, 021/5298–0439 (Cheng Du Lu), 021/6361–1777 (Jiu Jiang Lu) Reservations essential ▭Local only.

FORMER FRENCH CONCESSION

$$ INTERNATIONAL Fodor'sChoice ★ **A Future Perfect.** Hidden away down a little lane off Huashan Road, AFP has the kind of terrace space that most Shanghai-restaurant owners can only dream of: spacious, tranquil, yet intimate. It is a must for those hot afternoons and evenings in Shanghai when you need a break from shopping and sightseeing and deserve some good food and good drinks. We recommend being adventurous; the menu is fresh and there is plenty to satisfy any tastes. AFP has an on-site bakery and serves breakfast every morning. *⊠16, La. 351, Huashan Lu, Xuhui ☎021/6248–8020 ▭AE, DC, MC, V.*

WORD OF MOUTH

"One small shop had two vats of boiling broth whereby each person takes a basket and fills it with whatever food they want to eat . . . I picked some pork meat, two types of mushrooms, cabbage and thin noodles. The cook finished off the soup with some hot sauce and other spices."
—monicapileggi

$$ INTERNATIONAL Fodor'sChoice ★ **Azul and Viva.** In creating his continent-hopping New World cuisine, owner Eduardo Vargas drew upon his globe-trotting childhood and seven years as a restaurant consultant in Asia. As a result, the menus in Azul, the tapas bar downstairs, and Viva, the restaurant upstairs, feature a delicious, delicate balance of flavors that should please any palate. Classics like beef carpaccio contrast cutting-edge dishes like coffee-glazed pork. Lunch and weekend brunch specials are lower priced. The relaxed, romantic interior—dim lighting, plush pillows, and splashes of color against muted backdrops—invites you to take your time on your culinary world tour. *⊠18 Dongping Lu, Xuhui ☎021/6433–1172 ▭AE, DC, MC, V.*

$–$$ CAFÉ **Ginger.** Tucked away in the avenues of the French Concession, Ginger is a European-flavored café. Small and intimate, Ginger is a place for conversations over lunch, or a relaxing afternoon coffee. We recommend having your drinks in the tiny enclosed terrace, for a rare tranquil Shanghai moment. *⊠299 Fuxing Xi Lu, near Huashan Lu, Xuhui ☎021/6433–9437 ▭AE, DC, MC, V.*

$–$$ JAPANESE **Gokohai.** Possibly the best shabu-shabu restaurant in Shanghai, Gokohai is a hidden gem. Shabu-shabu is Japanese hotpot—each diner gets a pot and chooses a selection of meats (served in enormous, sombrero-shaped piles) and vegetables to cook in the broth. You'll need to ask for the all-you-can-eat deal for Y88 (drinks not included), because it is not mentioned on the menu. *⊠1720 Huaihai Lu, near Wuxing Lu, Xuihui ☎021/6471–7657 Reservations recommended ▭Local only.*

¢–$ CHINESE ★ **Grape.** Entry-level Chinese food at inexpensive prices has been Grape's calling card since the mid-1980s. This cheerful two-story restaurant remains a favorite among expatriates and travelers wandering the Former French Concession. The English menu, with photos, includes such recognizable fare as sweet-and-sour pork and lemon chicken as well as delicious dishes like garlic shrimp and *jiachang doufu* (home-style bean curd), all of which are served with a smile. ✉*55 Xinle Lu, Luwan* ☎*021/5404–0486* ▭*No credit cards.*

¢–$ CHINESE ✕**Hot Pot King.** *Huo guo,* or hotpot, is a popular Chinese ritual of at-the-table cooking, in which you simmer fresh ingredients in a broth. Hot Pot King reigns over the hotpot scene in Shanghai because of its extensive menu as well as its refined setting. The most popular of the 17 broths is the yin-yang, half spicy red, half basic white pork-bone broth. Add in a mixture of veggies, seafood, meat, and dumplings for a well-rounded pot, then dip each morsel in the sauces mixed tableside by your waiter. The minimalist white and gray interior has glass-enclosed booths and well-spaced tables, a nice change from the usual crowded, noisy, hotpot joints. ✉*1416 Huaihai Rd., 2nd fl., Xuhui* ☎*021/6473–6380* ▭*AE, DC, MC, V.*

¢–$ INDIAN ✕**Indian Kitchen.** The Indian chefs working their magic in the show kitchen provide the entertainment while you wait for a table at this tremendously popular restaurant. Delicious butter chicken marsala and tandoor-cooked chicken tikka taste as good as they look in the picture menu, which is packed with classic Indian dishes. The many bread selections include taste bud tingling spring onion *parotas* (fried flat bread). Two blocks from the Hengshan Lu metro station and bar neighborhood, Indian Kitchen is a convenient dining spot. ✉*572 Yongjia Lu, Xuhui* ☎*021/6473–1517* ✍*Reservations essential* ▭*AE, DC, MC, V.*

$–$$ YUNNAN ★ ✕ **Lost Heaven.** Lost Heaven serves Yunnan cuisine—Southern Chinese from the borders of Myanmar and Cambodia. The food is reminiscent of Thai cuisine, and well-prepared, while the dining room evokes Yunnan architecture despite its location in the middle of the French Concession. Service is acceptable without being polished. Certainly worth a look. ✉ *38 Gao You Lu, near Fuxing Xi Lu, Luwan* ☎*021/6433–5126* ▭ *AE, DC, MC, V.*

$$–$$$ INTERNATIONAL ✕ **Mesa.** Nestled on the quiet residential street Julu Lu, Mesa is a little hard to find. The unassuming facade is backed with a stark minimalist decor, which belies the sophistication of the seasonal menu. The cuisine is contemporary, meaning the chef has been allowed to experiment, and the results are impeccable. The wine list is comprehensive, with an excellent by-the-glass selection, and not overpriced. ✉*748 Julu Lu, Luwan* ☎*021/6289–9108* ⏲*No lunch Monday. Brunch Saturday and Sunday, 9:30–4. Babysitting available for brunch* ▭*AE, DC, MC, V.*

$–$$ MANDARIN ✕**Quan Ju De.** The original Beijing branch of this restaurant has been *the* place to get Peking duck since 1864. This Shanghai branch opened in 1998, but the Peking duck is just as popular here. Few dishes are more definitively Chinese than Peking duck, the succulent, slow-roasted bird that is never quite properly prepared overseas. The ambience here is "old Chinese" to the point of absurdity, complete with hostesses dressed in traditional imperial outfits including platform tasseled shoes and flashy headpieces, and with lattice screens scattered throughout the dining room. The menu has both pictures and English text to explain the different types of duck available. One minor drawback is the size of the portions. There are no half-ducks on the menu, and a full duck is rather a lot for two people. ✉786 *Huaihai Zhonglu, 4th fl., Luwan* ☎*021/5404–5799* ✍*Reservations essential* ▭*AE, DC, MC, V.*

$$$–$$$$ AMERICAN Fodor'sChoice ★ ✕ **Roosevelt Prime Steakhouse.** Located in thc historic Marshall Mansions of the French Concession, Roosevelt offers the best steak in the city (and quite possibly the country) in a relaxed steakhouse ambience. The meat is USDA Prime, cooked to your specification in an imported stone oven. These steaks are not cheap, ranging in price from Y300 to Y1,200 for the Porterhouse, though regular mains are considerably more reasonable. Try the mac and cheese with black truffle, and the excellent Caesar salad. ✉*160 Taiyuan Lu, Xuhui* ☎*021/6433–8240* ▭*AE, DC, MC, V.*

$–$$ THAI Fodor'sChoice ★ ✕ **Simply Thai.** Unpretentious Thai fare at moderate prices has earned this restaurant a loyal expat clientele. Customers flock to the tree-shaded patio to savor such favorites as green and red curries (on the spicy side) and stir-fried rice noodles with chicken (on the tame side). The appetizers are all first-rate, especially the crispy spring rolls and samosas. The wine list includes a half-dozen bottles under Y200, a rarity in Shanghai. The branch in Xintiandi is a bit noisier but features the same great food and prices. ✉*5C Dongping Rd., Xuhui* ☎*021/6445–9551* ✍*Reservations essential* ▭*AE, DC, MC, V.*

$–$$ SICHUAN ★ ✕ **South Beauty.** The elegant interior and spicy fare are both worth beholding at South Beauty. As the sliding-glass front door opens—revealing a walkway between two cascading walls of water—it splits the restaurant's trademark red Chinese-opera mask in two. Likewise, the menu is split down the middle between cooler Cantonese cuisine and sizzling hot Sichuan fare. Don't be fooled: even dishes with a one-pepper rating, like sautéed baby lobster, will singe your sinuses. ✉*28 Taojiang Lu, Xuhui* ☎*021/6445–2581* ✍*Reservations essential* ▭*AE, DC, MC, V.*

$$–$$$ INDIAN ✕ **The Tandoor.** Don't miss the unbelievable *murgh malei kebab* (tandoori chicken marinated in cheese and yogurt mixture), or try some vegetable curries—*palak aloo* (spinach with peas) or *dal makhani* (lentil). Decorated with mirrors, Indian artwork, and Chinese characters dangling from the ceiling, the restaurant is ingeniously designed to show the route of Buddhism from India to China. The management and staff, all from India, remain close at hand throughout the meal to answer questions and attend to your needs. ✉*Jinjiang Hotel, South Building, 59 Maoming Nan Lu, Luwan* ☎*021/6472–5494* ✍*Reservations essential* ▭*AE, DC, MC, V.*

$ INDIAN ★ ✕ **Vedas.** In the heart of the Old French Concession, Vedas is a popular destination for quality Indian food at affordable prices. Decor is dark and comfortable. The menu focuses on northern Indian cuisine, and the hand-pulled naan bread, thick and succulent curries, fiery vindaloos, and house-made chutneys are excellent. Vedas is extremely popular, and always bustling. Don't expect an intimate, tranquil dining experience, but do expect spectacular food and great service in a pleasant if busy environment. ✉*550 Jianguo Xi Lu, Xuhui* ☎*021/6445–8100* ✍*Reservations essential* ▭*AE, DC, MC, V.*

$–$$ CAFÉ Fodor'sChoice ★ **Vienna Café.** Coffee, cakes, and excellent breakfasts, Vienna is a Shanghai institution, for those in the know. This is not a trendy café, nor is it trying to be anything other than an Austrian coffee house. With wood-paneled main room and a tiny solarium, this is perfect place for a Sunday breakfast. Try an Einspanner with the Sachertorte, and never mind the effects to your waistline. ✉*25 Shaoxing Lu, near Ruijin Er Lu, Xuhui* ☎*021/6445–2131* ▭*No credit cards.*

NANJING XI LU AND JING'AN

$–$$ SHANGHAINESE ★ ✕ **1221.** This stylish but casual eatery is a favorite of hip Chinese and expatriate regulars. The dining room is streamlined chic, its crisp white tablecloths contrasting the warm golden walls. Shanghainese food is the mainstay, with a few Sichuan dishes. From the extensive 26-page menu (in English, pinyin, and Chinese), you can order dishes like sliced *you tiao* (fried bread sticks) with shredded beef, a whole chicken in a green-onion soy sauce, and *shaguo shizi tou* (pork meatballs). ✉*1221 Yanan Xi Lu, Changning* ☎*021/6213–6585 or 021/6213–2441* ✍*Reservations essential* ▭*AE, DC, MC, V.*

¢–$ VEGETARIAN Fodor'sChoice ★ ✕ **Gongdelin.** A two-story gold engraving of Buddha pays tribute to the origins of the inventive vegetarian dishes this restaurant has served for 80 years. Chefs transform tofu into such surprising and tasty creations as mock duck, eel, and pork. The interior is just as inspired, with Ming-style, wood-and-marble tables; metal latticework; and a soothing fountain. Tables fill up quickly after 6 PM, so either arrive early or buy some goodies to go at the take-out counter. ✉*445 Nanjing Xi Lu, Huangpu* ☎*021/6327–0218* ▭*AE, DC, MC, V.*

$$$–$$$$ ITALIAN ★ ✕ **Issimo.** Located in JIA hotel and run by Salvatore Cuomo, Issimo is a great (albeit upmarket) Italian restaurant. The food is well-prepared and plentiful (all pastas are for two), and the ambience is as exquisite as a designer boutique venue should be. The menu is small and focused on seasonal offerings and the wine list excellent. Reservations are recommended. ✉*JIA Hotel, 2nd fl., 931 West Nanjing Lu, entrance on Taixing Lu, Jingan* ☎*021/6287–9009* ▭*AE, DC, MC, V.*

$ INDIAN ✕ **Masala Art.** A rising star of the Indian dining scene, Masala Art is a little hard to find but worth the effort. Serving excellent breads and sublime curries in an understated dining area, Masala Art wins praise for fine food at very reasonable prices. ✉*397 Dagu Lu, Jing'an* ☎*021/6327–3571* ✍*Reservations essential* ▭*AE, DC, MC, V.*

$$$ SHANGHAINESE Fodor'sChoice ★ ✕ **Meilongzhen.** Probably Shanghai's most famous restaurant, Meilongzhen is one of the oldest dining establishments in town, dating from 1938. The building served as the Communist Party headquarters in the 1930s, and the traditional Chinese dining rooms still have their intricate woodwork, and mahogany and marble furniture. The exhaustive menu has more than 80 seafood options, including such traditional Shanghainese fare as Mandarin fish, and dishes with a more Sichuan flair, like shredded spicy eel and prawns in chili sauce. Since this is a stop for most tour buses, expect a wait if you haven't booked ahead. ✉*No. 22, 1081 Nanjing Xi Lu, Jing'an* ☎*021/6253–5353* ✍*Reservations essential* ▭*AE, DC, MC, V.*

$-$$ CANTONESE **The Onion.** On the high-traffic sector of Nanjing Xi Lu, Onion is a simple concept Cantonese restaurant, serving quality Cantonese dishes at reasonable prices. The decor is light and airy, with well-spaced tables and efficient service. The menu is extensive and bilingual, with lunch specials and dim sum. This is a very low-stress restaurant, and a great destination for a simple and satisfying meal. *881 Nanjing Xi Lu, 3rd fl., Jing'an 021/6267–5477 No credit cards.*

$$-$$$ ITALIAN **Palladio.** As befits the showcase Italian Restaurant at the Ritz, the award-winning Palladio is simply excellent. With a seasonal menu and positively obsequious service, this restaurant will always satisfy your senses—though it might also deplete your wallet. Set lunches begin at Y198, and dinners soar into the heady heights. *Portman Ritz-Carlton, 1376 Nanjing Xi Lu, Jing'an 021/6279–7188 Reservations essential AE, DC, MC, V.*

$$$-$$$$ CANTONESE **Summer Pavilion.** Helmed by Ho Wing, the former chef of Hong Kong's famed Jockey Club, Summer Pavilion serves delicious Cantonese specialties ranging from simple dim sum to delicacies such as shark fin, bird's-nest soup, and abalone. As befits the Portman Ritz-Carlton, the restaurant's dining room is elegant, with black and gold accents and a raised platform that makes you feel as though you're center stage—a sense heightened by the attentive servers, who stand close at hand, but not too close, anticipating your needs. *Portman Ritz-Carlton, 2nd fl., 1376 Nanjing Xi Lu, Jing'an 021/6279–8888 Reservations essential AE, DC, MC, V.*

PUDONG

$$-$$$ CONTEMPORARY **Cloud 9.** Pudong can be an intimidating concrete jungle, with little respite in sight. If you're looking for refreshment on your Pudong safari, try Cloud 9 on the 87th floor of the Hyatt. Be aware, this is not a cheap lounge—there is a dress code, but the view is spectacular. Kick back and drink in the city laid out beneath you, while nibbling at their tasty Asian-inspired tapas and snacks. *Grand Hyatt, 87th fl., 88 Shiji Dadao, Pudong 021/5049–1234 Reservations essential AE, DC, MC, V.*

$$-$$$ ITALIAN ★ **Danieli's.** One of the finest Italian restaurants in the city, Danieli's is worth the commute to Pudong. The intimate dining area is spacious without being overwhelming, and the staff is very well trained. Their business lunch is famed for its speed and quality, but it is at dinner that Danieli's really shines. The menu is well balanced with seasonal dishes, and boasts an excellent five-course set menu. Prices can be expensive, especially for wine, but it is worth the money. *St. Regis, 889 Dongfang Lu, Pudong 021/5050–4567 Reservations essential No lunch Sat. AE, DC, MC, V.*

$-$$ JAPANESE **Itoya.** The waitstaff's precision teamwork makes dining at Itoya a pleasure. Servers pause to greet all guests in unison. You're handed a hot towel upon sitting down and instantly after finishing your meal. The menu sticks to traditional Japanese fare: tempura, sushi, sashimi. In line with its location directly across from the Grand Hyatt's entrance, the restaurant also has several budget-busting items such as

Kobe beef and lobster sashimi. ✉ *178 Huayuan Shiqiao Lu, Pudong* ☎ *021/5882–9679* ▭ *AE, DC, MC, V.*

$$$$ INTERNATIONAL Fodor'sChoice ★ ✕ **Jade on 36.** This is a restaurant that must be experienced to be believed. Perched on the 36th floor of the Shangri-La tower, the Jade lounge/restaurant is simply beautiful. There is no à la carte menu; instead, diners choose from a selection of set menus named simply by colors and sizes. The cuisine is innovative and extremely fresh, the service impeccable, and the view pleasant. Menus vary from five to eight courses, with an emphasis on fresh seafood and tender meats. The jumbo shrimp in a jar is especially enjoyable, as is the signature lemon tart. It's an expensive indulgence, but worth every penny. ✉ *Pudong Shangri-La, 36th fl., 33 Fu Cheng Lu, Pudong* ☎ *021/6882–8888* ▭ *AE, DC, MC, V.*

$$$–$$$$ JAPANESE ✕ **Nadaman.** Sleekly elegant and stylized, Nadaman is modern Japanese dining taken to its extreme. The accents of raw granite merged into a formalized designer interior reflect the restaurant's origins in the modern Tokyo, looking almost overdesigned. With a focus on freshness and presentation, Nadaman gives diners superb cuisine at a price tag to match. The sushi is some of the finest in the city. ✉ *Pudong Shangri-La, 2nd fl., 33 Fu Cheng Lu, Pudong* ☎ *021/6882–8888* ✍ *Reservations essential* ▭ *AE, DC, MC, V.*

$$$ ECLECTIC ✕ **Yi Café.** Popular and busy, the Yi Café at the Shangri-La is open-kitchen dining at its finest, serving a world of cuisines. The Yi Café is very popular with the Lujiazui business set, as well as local diners for the quality and variety of the food. It's a great place to people-watch over a selection of the finest dishes Asia has to offer. This experience doesn't come cheap, at Y268 per person, but it's worth it. The restaurant slightly under-represents Western cuisine, focusing more on Asian dishes. ✉ *Pudong Shangri-La, 2nd fl., 33 Fu Cheng Lu, Pudong* ☎ *021/6882–8888* ▭ *AE, DC, MC, V.*

HONGQIAO AND GUBEI

¢–$ TAIWANESE ✕ **Bellagio.** Taiwanese expatriates pack the bright, sunlit dining room of Bellagio for an authentic taste of home. Red fabric–covered chairs and black streamlined tables contrast the white walls and decorative moldings. Waiters, chic in black sweaters, move efficiently between the closely spaced tables. The menu includes such traditional entrées as three-cup chicken as well as 25 noodle dishes spanning all of Southeast Asia. Save room for dessert: shaved-ice snacks are obligatory Taiwanese treats and come in 14 varieties. ✉ *778 Huangjin Cheng Dao, by Gubei Lu, Changning* ☎ *021/6278–0722* ✍ *Reservations not accepted* ▭ *AE, DC, MC, V.*

$–$$ CANTONESE ✕ **The Dynasty.** Although its cuisine is mostly Cantonese, Dynasty does serve some other regional fare, such as first-rate Peking duck and Sichuan-influenced hot-and-sour soup. The Cantonese seafood dishes, especially the prawns and lobster, are particularly good, and the shrimp *jiaozi* (dumplings) are delicious. Keyhole cutouts in the subdued pewter walls showcase Chinese vases and artifacts. Thick carpets mute any hotel noise, but the prices quickly remind you this is indeed a hotel restaurant. ✉ *Renaissance Yangtze, 2099 Yanan Xi Lu, Changning* ☎ *021/6275–0000* ✍ *Reservations essential* ▭ *AE, DC, MC, V.*

$$–$$$ ITALIAN ★ ✕ **Giovanni's.** Its Italian courtyard with a penthouse view provides a wonderful backdrop for Giovanni's traditional Italian fare. The antipasta and calamari are delicious, and the pastas are served perfectly al dente. Seasonal promotions keep the menu fresh. ✉ *Sheraton Grand Tai Ping Yang, 27th fl., 5 Zunyi Nan Lu, Changning* ☎ *021/6275–8888* ✍ *Reservations essential* ▭ *AE, DC, MC, V.*

$–$$ MEXICAN ✕ **Mexico Lindo.** Fiery fare in a south-of-the-border setting has made Mexico Lindo Cantina & Grill the best entry on Shanghai's limited Mexican-dining scene. This Spanish-style casa is hidden off Hongmei Lu, down a tiny alley that's evolved into a well-respected restaurant row. In addition to tacos, fajitas, and quesadillas, the menu includes spicy prawns—rated three peppers—and a tasty one-pepper carnita pork burrito. A stairway mural depicts farm workers as well as fiesta revelers, whose ranks you can join with the eight margaritas and eight tequilas on the drink menu. ✉ *Villa 1, 3911 Hongmei Lu, Changning* ☎ *021/6262–2797* ✍ *Reservations essential* ▭ *AE, DC, MC, V.*

WHERE TO STAY

Updated by David Taylor

Shanghai's stature as China's business capital means that its hotels cater primarily to business clientele and can be divided into two categories: modern Western-style hotels that are elegant and nicely appointed; or hotels built during the city's glory days, which became state-run after 1949. The latter may lack great service, modern fixtures, and convenient facilities, but they often make up for it in charm, tradition, history, and value.

Judging by the number of five-star and Western chain hotels now in Shanghai, the city has proven just how grandly it has opened to the outside world. The Grand Hyatt, JW Marriott, Westin, Portman Ritz-Carlton, and St. Regis aren't merely hotels; they're landmarks on the Shanghai skyline. Even the historic properties that make up the other half of Shanghai's hotel market feel the pressure to update their rooms and facilities. And as Shanghai speeds up its preparations for the World Expo in 2010, newcomers, like the Conrad, Jumeirah, and Park Hyatt, are setting the bar even higher with their ultramodern settings and top-notch service.

RESERVATIONS AND RATES

Increasing competition means there are bargains to be had, especially during the low season from November through March. Avoid traveling during the three national holidays—Chinese New Year (mid-January to mid-February), Labor Day (May 1), and National Day (October 1)—when rooms and prices will be at a premium.

Rates are generally quoted for the room alone; breakfast, whether Continental or full, usually is extra. All hotel prices listed here are based on high-season rates.

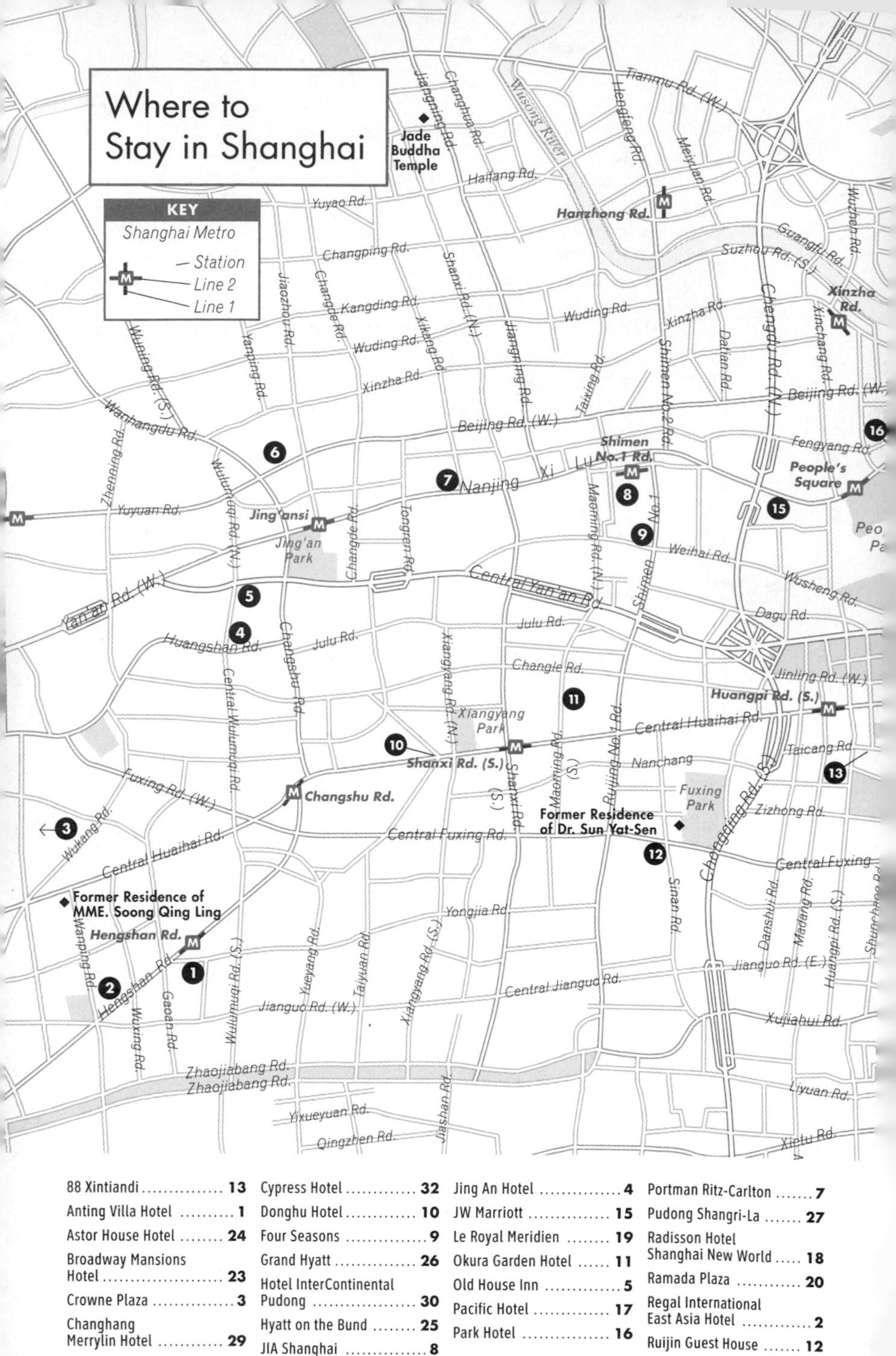
Where to Stay in Shanghai
KEY
Shanghai Metro
Station
Line 2
Line 1
Jade Buddha Temple
Hanzhong Rd.
Xinzha Rd.
Shimen No.1 Rd.
People's Square
Jing'ansi
Jing'an Park
Xiangyang Park
Shanxi Rd. (S.)
Changshu Rd.
Huangpi Rd. (S.)
Fuxing Park
Former Residence of Dr. Sun Yat-Sen
Former Residence of MME. Soong Qing Ling
Hengshan Rd.
Wusong River
Tianmu Rd. (W.)
Jiangning Rd.
Changhua Rd.
Hengfeng Rd.
Meiyuan Rd.
Haifang Rd.
Yuyao Rd.
Changping Rd.
Kangding Rd.
Wuding Rd.
Xinzha Rd.
Beijing Rd. (W.)
Nanjing Xi Lu
Yan'an Rd. (W.)
Central Yan'an Rd.
Julu Rd.
Changle Rd.
Central Huaihai Rd.
Fuxing Rd. (W.)
Central Fuxing Rd.
Jianguo Rd. (W.)
Central Jianguo Rd.
Zhaojiabang Rd.
Yixueyuan Rd.
Qingzhen Rd.
Chengdu Rd. (N.)
Chongqing Rd. (S.)
Shimen No.2 Rd.
Ruijin No.1 Rd.
Sinan Rd.
88 Xintiandi 13
Anting Villa Hotel 1
Astor House Hotel 24
Broadway Mansions Hotel 23
Crowne Plaza 3
Changhang Merrylin Hotel 29
Cypress Hotel 32
Donghu Hotel 10
Four Seasons 9
Grand Hyatt 26
Hotel InterContinental Pudong 30
Hyatt on the Bund 25
JIA Shanghai 8
Jing An Hotel 4
JW Marriott 15
Le Royal Meridien 19
Okura Garden Hotel 11
Old House Inn 5
Pacific Hotel 17
Park Hotel 16
Portman Ritz-Carlton 7
Pudong Shangri-La 27
Radisson Hotel Shanghai New World 18
Ramada Plaza 20
Regal International East Asia Hotel 2
Ruijin Guest House 12

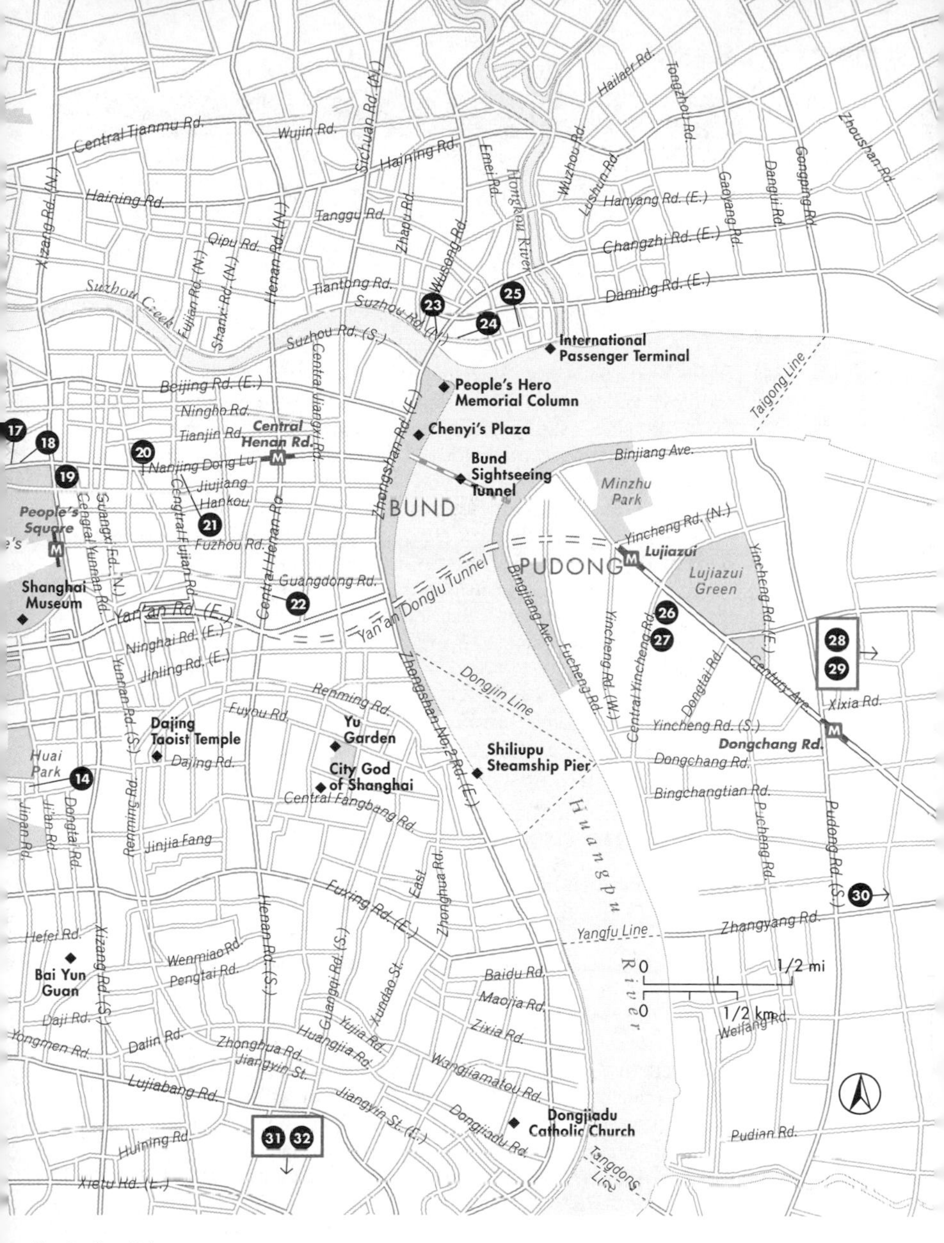

Sheraton Grand Tai Ping Yang **31**

Sofitel Hyland **21**

Somerset Grand **14**

St. Regis **28**

URDN **6**

The Westin Shanghai **22**

WHAT IT COSTS IN YUAN					
	¢	$	$$	$$$	$$$$
Hotels	under Y700	Y700–Y1,100	Y1,101–Y1,400	Y1,401–Y1,800	over Y1,800

Prices are for two people in a standard double room in high season, excluding 10%–15% service charge.

OLD CITY

$$$$ **The Westin Shanghai.** With its distinctive room layouts, glittering glass staircase, and 90-plus works of art on display, the Westin Shanghai is a masterpiece near the majestic Bund. Crowne Deluxe rooms are miniature suites; sliding doors divide the sitting area, bathroom, and bedroom (the only problem is that all these divisions make the rooms feel on the small side). Luxurious amenities include rain-forest showers, extra deep tubs, and Westin's trademark Heavenly Bed. Pampering continues at the Banyan Tree spa—China's first—and the Sunday champagne brunch at the Stage restaurant is considered the best in town by Shanghai's glitterati. **Pros:** very attentive service. **Cons:** expensive for what you get; far from most shopping. ✉ *Bund Center, 88 Henan Zhonglu, Huangpu* ☎ *021/6335–1888 or 888/625–5144* 📠 *021/6335–2888* 🌐 *www.westin.com/shanghai* *570 rooms, 24 suites* *In-room: safe, Wi-Fi, refrigerator. In-hotel: 3 restaurants, room service, bar, pool, gym, spa, concierge, laundry service, executive floor, parking (no fee), no-smoking rooms* 💳 *AE, DC, MC, V.*

XINTIANDI AND CITY CENTER

$$$$ **88 Xintiandi.** Although it targets business travelers, 88 Xintiandi is a shopper's and gourmand's delight. The boutique hotel is in the heart of Xintiandi, its balconies overlooking the top-dollar shops and restaurants below. The rooms, all mini- or full-size suites with kitchens, are likewise upscale. Beds are elevated on a central, gauze-curtained platform; sitting areas have large flat-screen TVs and DVD players. Stylish wood screens accent the rooms and common areas. Deluxe rooms and the executive lounge overlook man-made Lake Taipingqiao. Guests can further indulge at the 88 Spa and Gym, with full fitness facilities and two treatment rooms. **Pros:** prime location in Xintiandi; interesting traditional Chinese decor. **Cons:** occasionally slack service; street noise gets in. ✉ *380 Huangpi Nan Lu, Luwan* ☎ *021/5383–8833* 📠 *021/5353–8877* 🌐 *www.88xintiandi.com* *12 suites, 41 rooms* *In-room: safe, kitchen, refrigerator, DVD, Wi-Fi. In-hotel: restaurant, room service, bar, pool, gym, concierge, laundry service, parking (fee), no-smoking rooms* 💳 *AE, DC, MC, V.*

$$$$ **JW Marriott.** For the best views in Puxi, look no further. The JW Marriott's futuristic 60-story tower on the edge of People's Square turns heads with its 90-degree twist, which divides the executive apartments below from the 22-story hotel above. The interior follows classic lines with subtle Chinese accents. Celadon vases, wedding boxes, and

WHICH NEIGHBORHOOD?

Shanghai may have an excellent subway system and cheap, plentiful taxis, but if you want to take full advantage of Shanghai's popular tourist sights, restaurants, and nightlife opt to stay in downtown **Puxi,** incorporating the quiet, leafy green Former French Concession, the historical promenade of the Bund, and the bustling shopping street of Nanjing Dong Lu. From these neighborhoods you'll have easy access to all of Shanghai's dynamic neighborhoods.

FORMER FRENCH CONCESSION

Sneak away from the city's frenetic energy in one of the historical hotels tucked down the Former French Concession's tree-lined streets. Excellent restaurants and shopping abound, the neighborhood's relaxing atmosphere can be a nice break after a hectic day of sightseeing. A short cab or metro ride takes you straight to any of the city's sights on The Bund and Nanjing Dong Lu.

HONGQIAO DEVELOPMENT ZONE

Hongqiao is not a destination for leisure travelers. A combination of residential complexes and business offices, Hongqiao lacks many sights or restaurants. Unless business brings you here or you have an early flight from the Hongqiao airport, there aren't many reasons to stay so far from the action.

THE BUND AND NANJING DONG LU

Breathtaking views of the Pudong skyline, skyscrapers juxtaposed with Victorian architecture, and easy access to great shopping and some of the city's best restaurants are just a few reasons to stay here. Best of all, most major sites, from the Bund to the Shanghai Museum, are all within comfortable walking distance. If you want to see modern Shanghai, this is the place to be.

PUDONG

Although Pudong—with its shiny new skyscrapers and wide boulevards—can feel impersonal, and it's too far from downtown Puxi for some, it has some of the city's best hotels, all close to Pudong International Airport. Phenomenal views of the Bund are a major bonus. But if you stay here, be prepared to spend at least 30 minutes shuttling back and forth to Puxi (and it could take even longer during rush hour as millions of locals compete to flag down taxis or squeeze into subway cars almost overflowing with commuters).

ornamental jades complement the soft green-and-yellow palette and warm fiddleback wood in the spacious rooms, but the real eye-catcher is the amazing cityscape vista from every room. The largely business clientele appreciates the one-touch "At Your Service" call button, and the Mandara Spa, indoor and outdoor pools, excellent restaurants, JW Lounge (with 60-plus martinis), and proximity to many of the major tourist attractions are big draws for leisure travelers. **Pros:** fantastic location; great views. **Cons:** expensive given the quality of service. ⊠*399 Nanjing Xi Lu, Huangpu* ☏*021/5359–4969 or 888/236–2427* *021/6375–5988* *www.jwmarriottshanghai.com* *305 rooms, 37 suites* *In-room: safe, Wi-Fi, refrigerator. In-hotel: 3 restaurants, room* *service, bar, pools, gym, spa, concierge, laundry service, executive floor, parking (fee), no-smoking rooms* ▭*AE, DC, MC, V.*

$ **Pacific Hotel.** This 1926 property has done an admirable job of preserving its charm. The marble lobby and the downstairs bar, decorated with art-deco leather chairs and archived photos of 1920s Shanghai, sweep you back to the city's glory days. In the original Italian-style front building, 6th- and 7th-floor rooms have wood floors, ornate molded ceilings, and great views of People's Park. Bathrooms, though, are rather institutional. The smaller rooms in the rear building lack the fine detail and views but are still comfortable and are a bit quieter. Amenities fall short, and soundproofing could be better, but the hotel's proud history, prime location, and prices make it an appealing choice. **Pros:** near People's Park. **Cons:** erratic service; aging property. ✉*108 Nanjing Xi Lu, Huangpu* ☎*021/6327–6226* 📠*021/6372–3634* *177 rooms, 5 suites* *In-room: safe (some), refrigerator, Ethernet. In-hotel: restaurant, room service, bars, spa, laundry service, parking (fee).* ▭*AE, DC, MC, V.*

$$ **Park Hotel** *(Guoji Fandian).* Once Shanghai's tallest building, the 20-story Park Hotel is now dwarfed on the Puxi skyline and eclipsed by other hotels whose glory days are present instead of past. Recently named a China Cultural Heritage Site, this 1934 art-deco structure overlooking People's Park still has great views and a musty charm, particularly in its restored marble lobby. Rooms are clean and bright, with prints of historic buildings from around the world. But bathrooms are tiny, and the hotel's limited English service and facilities have definitely slipped to second-rate. **Pros:** central location; heritage property. **Cons:** aging rooms; inadequate service. ✉*170 Nanjing Xi Lu, Huangpu* ☎*021/6327–5225* 📠*021/6327–6958* *225 rooms, 25 suites* *In-room: safe, refrigerator, Wi-Fi. In-hotel: 3 restaurants, bars, gym, concierge, laundry service, parking (no fee), no-smoking rooms* ▭*AE, DC, MC, V.*

$$$$ **Radisson Hotel Shanghai New World.** A prominent figure not only on People's Square, but also on the Shanghai skyline, the flying-saucer dome-topped Radisson New World is best known for its revolving restaurant, Epicure on 45. Rooms are divided between the lower Park Tower and the higher City Tower. Park Tower rooms are more expensive but have the best views, facing People's Square. Though the hotel caters primarily to business travelers, suites—each with a huge living room, kitchen/dining room, and spacious bath—are convenient for families. In addition, most rooms have flat-screen TVs. Many travelers still prefer the tranquil garden setting of the Radisson's Xingguo hotel in the French Concession, but it cannot compete with the New World's central location and city views. ■ **TIP→ Ask about special weekend packages.** **Pros:** prime location. **Cons:** dark decor, taxis not readily available. ✉*88 Nanjing Xi Lu, Xuangpu* ☎*021/6359–9999* 📠*021/6358–9705* 🌐*www.radisson.com/shanghaicn_newworld* *429 rooms, 91 suites* *In-room: safe, Internet, refrigerator. In-hotel: 3 restaurants, room service, bar, pool, gym, spa, concierge, laundry service, parking (fee), no-smoking rooms* ▭*AE, DC, MC, V.*

$$$ **Somerset Grand.** Designed as serviced apartments for expats, the Somerset Grand's suites are great for families wanting extra space plus the usual hotel amenities. The twin 34-story towers have 334 one- to three-bedroom suites, ranging from 890 to 2,500 square feet (82 to 232 square meters). (One-bedroom suites have only one king-size bed.) The units feel homey, with blue-and-pink floral comforters and rugs, and a small kitchen. Kids can burn off steam at the pool and in the playroom. There's a great French restaurant and coffee shop on the grounds; the hotel is two blocks from the restaurants, shops, and movie theater at Xintiandi and 10 minutes to the subway. **Pros:** suites; good for kids. **Cons:** institutional decor. *8 Jinan Lu, Luwan 021/6385–6888 021/6384–8988 www.the-ascott.com 334 suites In-room: safe, kitchen, refrigerator, Internet. In-hotel: tennis courts, pool, gym, concierge, laundry facilities, laundry service, parking (fee), no-smoking rooms AE, DC, MC, V.*

THE BUND AND NANJING DONG LU

$$$$ ★ **Hyatt on the Bund.** Located at the North End of the Bund near the banks of the Suzhou River, the Hyatt on the Bund offers beautifully appointed rooms in an airy and modern building. This is a location which will only improve in value as the government continues its modernization of the Bund, but for now, it is a little awkward on its own. However, the main Bund is just a short walk across the bridge, and the Hyatt on the Bund is reasonably accessible to most of the city. A major point of interest is the spectacular Vue bar, with its expansive vistas and rooftop hottub. **Pros:** beautiful facilities; excellent restaurant. **Cons:** uninteresting neighborhood. *199 Huangpu Lu, near Wuchang Lu and the Bund, Bund 021/6393–1234 021/6393–1313 www.shanghai.bund.hyatt.com 600 rooms, 31 suites In-room: safe, Ethernet, refrigerator. In-hotel: 4 restaurants, room service, bars, pool, gym, spa, laundry service, executive floor, airport shuttle, no-smoking rooms AE, DC, MC, V.*

DRINK AND A VIEW

The hopping Noah's Bar on the 6th floor [of Captain Hostel] has views of the Pudong skyline that rival those from much pricier lodgings.

$$$$ Fodor's Choice ★ **Le Royal Meridien.** Dominating the foot of the Nanjing Pedestrian Street, the Meridien has changed the face of Puxi hospitality. High ceilings, massive rooms, excellent amenities, and attentive staff make this a premium destination. Ask for a park view—the "Bund" view overlooks four blocks of run-down Shanghai, but the view over People's Park is simply wonderful. However, the large banks of small elevators can make navigating the hotel's many levels a little frustrating. **Pros:** location; excellent facilities. **Cons:** service hiccups; annoying elevator system. *505 Nanjing Dong Lu, Huangpu 021/3318–9999 www.lemeridien.com.cn 646 rooms, 115 suites In-room: safe, Internet, refrigerator, available Internet. In-hotel: 4 restaurants, room service, bars, pool, gym, spa, laundry service, executive floor, airport shuttle, parking (fee), no-smoking rooms AE, DC, MC, V.*

$$$–$$$$ Fodor's Choice ★ **Ramada Plaza.** With its ornate lobby resembling a European opera house, the Ramada Plaza Shanghai brings a touch of grandeur to the Nanjing Road pedestrian walkway. Statues of Greek gods reign from atop intricate inlaid tables. Soaring marble columns direct the eye skyward to a stained-glass skylight. Although the fair-sized rooms lack any great views, they do face in toward a dramatic atrium, topped by yet another and the executive lounge. An indoor swimming pool, one of the largest in Shanghai, is housed inside an addition reminiscent of an ancient Chinese palace. Given the lush setting and ace location, the Ramada Plaza is a good value for the money. **Pros:** location; you can usually get a room for less than the rack rate if you inquire while reserving. **Cons:** no views. ✉ *719 Nanjing Dong Lu, Huangpu* ☎ *021/6350–0000 or 800/854–7854* ℻ *021/6350–6666* 🌐 *www.ramadainternational.com* *376 rooms, 36 suites* *In-room: safe, Wi-Fi. In-hotel: 4 restaurants, room service, bar, pool, gym, spa, concierge, laundry service, executive floor, parking (no fee), no-smoking rooms, Internet* *AE, DC, MC, V.*

$$$ **Sofitel Hyland.** Directly on the Nanjing Road pedestrian mall, the Sofitel Hyland is a convenient base for shopping and exploring the city center and the Bund. The rooms in this 30-story French-managed hotel are somewhat small but have been spruced up with prints of Chinese emperors and small replicas of terra-cotta warrior statues. The top-floor Sky Lounge serves Sunday brunch amid views of the Bund and downtown, and Le Pub 505 brews up its own beer. **Pros:** location. **Cons:** small rooms and poor frontage. ✉ *505 Nanjing Dong Lu, Huangpu* ☎ *021/6351–5888* ℻ *021/6351–4088* 🌐 *www.accorhotels-asia.com* *299 rooms, 73 suites* *In-room: safe, refrigerator, Internet. In-hotel: 3 restaurants, room service, bars, pool, gym, spa, laundry service, executive floor, airport shuttle, parking (fee), no-smoking rooms* *AE, DC, MC, V.*

FORMER FRENCH CONCESSION

$$ **Anting Villa Hotel.** Two blocks from the metro and the Hengshan Road–nightlife district, the Anting Villa Hotel is a convenient and surprisingly quiet retreat tucked away down a small side street. Superior rooms in the 10-story hotel tower have been refurbished in a "Spanish style" with garishly bright red pillowcases and leather-covered furniture; some rooms now come with flat-screen TVs. It's worth it to pay a little extra for a garden-view room with vistas of the cedar-shaded grounds and namesake 1932 Spanish-style villa. Although English service is limited, the hotel's staff is eager and friendly. **Pros:** central location; eager-to-please service. **Cons:** a little faded; can be hard to communicate. ✉ *46 Anting Lu, Xuhui* ☎ *021/6433–1188* ℻ *021/6433–9726* 🌐 *antingvilla.sinohotel.com* *135 rooms, 11 suites* *In-room: safe, refrigerator, Wi-Fi. In-hotel: restaurant, room service, gym, laundry service, parking (no fee), no-smoking rooms* *AE, DC, MC, V.*

$$$$ **Crowne Plaza.** This hotel on the far western side of the Former French Concession makes up for its out-of-the-way location with service. The staff here is among the friendliest in town and makes guests, mostly

business travelers, feel at home. Though the hotel's rooms are not as elegant as those of its competitors, it does have the biggest club lounge in Shanghai, with a mezzanine floor and a sleek black marble-topped bar. **Pros:** good service; amenity-packed. **Cons:** you'll need taxis to get to and from the hotel. ✉*400 Panyu Lu, Xuhui* ☎*021/6280–8888 or 800/227–6963* 🌐*www.shanghai.crowneplaza.com* *488 rooms, 12 suites* *In-room: safe, kitchen (some), refrigerator, Internet. In-hotel: 4 restaurants, room service, bars, pool, gym, executive floor, parking (no fee), no-smoking rooms* *AE, DC, MC, V.*

3

$$$ **Donghu Hotel.** Just off the frenzied shopping street of Huaihai Road, the Donghu Hotel remains one of Shanghai's best preserved hotels from the city's 1920s heyday. The hotel's seven buildings have a surprising array of restaurants—Korean barbecue and Japanese, in addition to the standard Chinese and Western fare—an indoor pool, and a wide variety of room options. "Superior" rooms in Building 7 don't quite live up to their title and are simply furnished with twin beds and rather mismatched yellow wallpaper and red carpet. We suggest the Donghu deluxe rooms across the street at Building 1; with their traditional Chinese furniture and dark-wood paneling, these spacious rooms make you feel as if you've stepped back in time. **Pros:** traditional and elegant; numerous dining options. **Cons:** poor service and upkeep. ✉*70 Donghu Lu, Xuhui* ☎*021/6415–8158* 🌐*www.donghuhotel.com* *240 rooms, 30 suites* *In-room: safe (some), Wi-Fi. In-hotel: 6 restaurants, room service, pool, gym, concierge, laundry service, parking (fee), Internet* *AE, DC, MC, V.*

$$$–$$$$ **Jing An Hotel.** The weekly chamber-music concert in its lobby is just one example of how the Jing An Hotel has retained its elegance and charm after 70 years. In a 1½-acre garden, the Spanish-style main building's lobby has beautiful stained-glass windows. The ornate upstairs dining rooms often host prominent city officials. Although facilities are lacking compared to the newer hotels in town and the rooms in the Jing An New Building should be avoided at all costs (bathrooms are barely the size of a closet), the hotel's proximity to the subway line and its lush Former French Concession setting make this oft-overlooked property a winner. **Pros:** near public transportation; beautiful surroundings. **Cons:** poorly maintained facilities; inconsistent service. ✉*370 Huashan Lu, Xuhui* ☎*021/6248–0088* *021/6249–6100* 🌐*www.jinganhotel.net* *210 rooms, 17 suites* *In-room: safe, refrigerator, Internet. In-hotel: 2 restaurants, room service, bars, gym, concierge, laundry service, airport shuttle, parking (fee), no-smoking rooms* *AE, DC, MC, V.*

SIZE MATTERS

Elaborately carved wooden door frames and lintels [at Jing An Hotel] direct the eye upward toward the 10-foot (3-meter) ceilings that make for some of the most spacious hotel rooms in Shanghai.

$ Fodor's Choice ★ **Old House Inn.** Hidden down a small lane, Old House Inn is one of Shanghai's few boutique hotels and a must if you're looking for a personalized experience that the larger hotels just can't offer. What this tiny gem lacks in amenities (there's no elevator, gym, concierge, or business facilities), it makes up for with its authentic Chinese style and charm. All rooms are decorated with antique dark-wood furniture and traditional porcelains, and the friendly staff is so eager to please that they'll even run down to the end of the lane and find you a taxi. Adjacent to the hotel is the swanky A Future Perfect restaurant, popular with both expats and trendy locals for its outdoor café. ■**TIP→ Book well in advance to snag one of the moderately priced king-size rooms.** **Pros:** quaint and quiet; extremely helpful staff. **Cons:** small; limited services. ✉*No. 16, Lane 351, Huashan Lu, Xuhui* ☎*021/6248–6118* 🌐*www.oldhouse.cn* *12 rooms* *In-room: safe, refrigerator, Internet. In-hotel: no elevator, restaurant, bar, laundry service, parking (no fee)* *AE, DC, MC, V.*

UNIQUE SPOT

Old House Inn is one of Shanghai's few boutique hotels and a must if you're looking for a personalized experience that the larger hotels just can't offer.

$$$$ **Okura Garden Hotel.** Its parklike setting in the heart of the French Concession makes this 33-story Garden Hotel a favorite Shanghai retreat, especially for Japanese travelers familiar with the Okura Group name. The first three floors, which were once old Shanghai's French Club, have been restored, with cascading chandeliers, frescoes, and art-deco details at every turn. Average-size standard rooms are simply furnished with silk wallpaper and European-style furniture and, unlike deluxe rooms and suites, lack flat-screen TVs. The romantic third-floor terrace bar overlooks the two-acre garden, and the Japanese and French restaurants serve excellent but high-priced food. For those who want to stay connected, cell phones are available for rent at the concierge desk. **Pros:** gorgeous surroundings; near French Concession and Nanjing Xi Lu. **Cons:** you'll pay a hefty fee for all the beauty. ✉*58 Maoming Nan Lu, Luwan* ☎*021/6415–1111* 🌐*www.gardenhotelshanghai.com* *478 rooms, 22 suites* *In-room: safe, refrigerator, Internet. In-hotel: 5 restaurants, room service, bars, tennis courts, pool, gym, concierge, laundry service, executive floor, airport shuttle, parking (no fee), no-smoking rooms* *AE, DC, MC, V.*

$$$$ **Regal International East Asia Hotel.** Its exclusive Shanghai International Tennis Center is the Regal's trump card among five-star hotels. The center has 10 tournament courts as well as one of the city's best health clubs (it's not only huge, but all cardio machines come with personal TVs). The spacious rooms were renovated in 2005 and have flat-screen TVs. Club rooms each have a curvilinear desk and ergonomic chair and a funky chaise longue; deluxe rooms have compact bathrooms with marble sinks and huge mirrors. The Hengshan Road metro station and the bar and restaurant district are just a block away, but there's plenty of entertainment downstairs at the hotel's 12-lane bowling alley and gorgeous Fragrance Chinese restaurant. **Pros:** easy access to public transportation and entertainment; lots of activities for nights you want to stay in. **Cons:** on a high-traffic bar street. ✉*516 Hengshan Lu, Xuhui* ☎*021/6415–5588* 🌐*www.regal-eastasia.com* *278 rooms, 22 suites* *In-room: safe, DVD (some), Internet. In-hotel: 3 restaurants, room service, bar, tennis courts, pool, gym, concierge, executive floor, parking (no fee), no-smoking rooms, Wi-Fi* *AE, DC, MC, V.*

$$$–$$$$ ★ **Ruijin Guest House.** Formerly the Morriss Estate, the Ruijin Hotel showcases how opulently *taipans* (expatriate millionaire businessmen) lived in Shanghai's heyday of the 1930s. Rooms within the two preserved villas—No. 1 and Old No. 3—are rich with detail: high ceilings, ornate plaster molding, bamboo-etched glass. The two other buildings are significantly shorter on charm but still overlook the verdant grounds, which are shared with several top-notch restaurants (as well as the once-hip Face bar) and provide direct access to the bars on Maoming Road. New No. 3 may lack the historic cache of the other buildings, but its standard rooms, which come with a king-size bed and hot tub, are definitely a steal. **Pros:** location. **Cons:** inconsistent facilities and service. ✉ *118 Ruijin Er Lu, Luwan* ☎ *021/6472–5222* 🖷 *021/6473–2277* 🌐 *www.shedi.net.cn/outedi/ruijin* *62 rooms, 20 suites* *In-room: safe, refrigerator, Internet. In-hotel: restaurant, room service, bars, laundry service, parking (no fee), no-smoking rooms* 💳 *AE, DC, MC, V.*

3

NANJING XI LU AND JING'AN

$$$$ **The Four Seasons.** With palm trees, fountains, and golden-hued marble as warm as sunshine, the lobby of the Four Seasons establishes the hotel's theme as an elegant oasis in bustling downtown Puxi. Opened in 2002, this 37-story luxury hotel caters to its largely business clientele. It has impeccable service, a 24-hour business center, a gym, and butler service. The spacious rooms—just 12 to 15 per floor—include DVD/CD players, flat-screen TVs, safes big enough for a laptop, and marble showers and tubs (one of each). Nanjing Road and the Shanghai Museum are within a 10-minute walk, but there are convincing reasons to stay in: the Jazz 37 club; the exceptional Si Ji Xuan Cantonese restaurant; and **■ TIP→ you don't want to miss one of the spa's indulgent Balinese treatments. Pros:** beautiful building; amenity and entertainment heavy. **Cons:** amenities may discourage you from getting out of the hotel; slack service. ✉ *500 Weihai Lu, Jing'an* ☎ *021/6256–8888 or 800/819–5053* 🖷 *021/6256–5678* 🌐 *www.fourseasons.com* *360 rooms, 79 suites* *In-room: safe, refrigerator, DVD, Internet, Wi-Fi. In-hotel: 4 restaurants, room service, bar, pool, gym, spa, concierge, laundry service, executive floor, parking (fee), no-smoking rooms, Wi-Fi* 💳 *AE, DC, MC, V.*

$$$$ Fodor's Choice ★ **JIA Shanghai.** JIA is something else—a new paradigm in Shanghai hospitality. Discreetly housed in a vintage art deco building on Nanjing Xi Lu, JIA's unprepossessing exterior masks it's elegant and styled interior. The 55 rooms and suites are thoughtfully designed and just a touch over the top, making a stay in JIA an experience in itself. Every room is equipped with a kitchenette or kitchen for a pleasant, homey experience. Service is very good for China, though not quite world class yet. Generally, the experience is smooth and unobtrusive, welcoming guests without destroying the sense of comfortable privacy. Issimo, the in-house restaurant, is genuinely extraordinary, with impeccable interiors and superb food. The service is well trained and the menu small but very well thought out. **Pros:** exquisite design and unique setting; kitchenettes; privacy. **Cons:** no pool; no business center. ✉ *931 West*

Nan Jing Lu, near Tai Xing Lu (entrance on Tai Xing Lu), Jing'an ☎021/6217–9000 55 rooms In-room: kitchenette, refrigerator, DVD, Internet, Wi-Fi. In-hotel: 1 restaurant, room service, 1 bar, gym, laundry facilities, laundry service, public Wi-Fi, airport limo, no parking AE, D, DC, MC, V.

$$$$ **The Portman Ritz-Carlton.** Outstanding facilities and a high-profile location in the Shanghai Center have made the Portman Ritz-Carlton one of the city's top attractions since its opening in 1998. The 50-story hotel devotes three floors solely to its fitness center and another four to its executive club rooms. The two-story lobby—a popular networking spot and the location of the best afternoon tea in town—exudes cool refinement with its ebony, marble, and chrome touches. In addition to the Shanghai Center's surrounding shops, banks, airline offices, and restaurants, the hotel has its own deli and four top-notch restaurants. **Pros:** renovated in 2008 with plasma TVs, DVD players, and improved decor; superb location. **Cons:** very expensive; uneven service. *✉1376 Nanjing Xi Lu, Jing'an ☎021/6279–8888 or 800/241–3333 021/6279–8887 www.ritzcarlton.com 510 rooms, 68 suites In-room: safe, refrigerator, Internet. In-hotel: 4 restaurants, room service, bars, tennis court, pool, gym, concierge, laundry service, executive floor, parking (fee), no-smoking rooms AE, DC, MC, V.*

$$$$ Fodor's Choice ★ **URBN.** Innovatively designed and environmentally friendly, URBN is Shanghai's first carbon-neutral hotel. Made with environmentally sensitive technology and recycled materials, URBN is a truly unique place to stay. The service is attentive and well trained, making guests feel at home from the moment they step into the hotel's tree-shaded courtyard. The design is superb, with a leather-encased reception desk, slate decor, and a quiet, private bar on the top floor. URBN provides a wide variety of alternative entertainments, including Chinese cookery, calligraphy and tai chi classes, bike tours, and yoga lessons. **Pros:** eco-friendly; luxe setting, some of the best cocktails in town; elegant design. **Cons:** not terribly suitable for mobility impaired guests. *✉183 Jiaozhou Lu, near Beijing Xi Lu, Jing'an ☎021/5153–4600 021/5153–4610 www.urbnhotels.com 24 rooms, 2 suites In-room: safe, refrigerator, DVD, Internet. In-hotel: 1 restaurant, room service, bar, laundry service, executive floor, no-smoking rooms, Wi-Fi AE, DC, MC, V.*

PUDONG

¢–$ **Changhang Merrylin Hotel.** The Merrylin Corporation is better known throughout China for its restaurants than its hotels, and Changhang Merrylin Hotel's exceptional Chinese restaurant overshadows its fair-size inexpensive rooms. Decor aspires to European grandeur but comes off as amusingly tacky. Reliefs and golden statues of frolicking nymphs dominate the lobby, and rooms are decked out in gold-flecked wallpaper and crackled white-painted fixtures. Service can be brusque, but the location is within 3 blocks of the 10-story Next Age Department Store and metro Line 2 to Puxi. **Pros:** inexpensive; convenient to shopping and public transportation; delicious food in the restaurant. **Cons:** poor service. *✉818 Zhangyang Lu, Pudong ☎021/5835–5555*

021/5835–7799 192 rooms, 32 suites In-room: refrigerator, Internet (some). In-hotel: 3 restaurants, room service, bar, concierge, laundry service, airport shuttle, parking (fee) AE, DC, MC, V.

$$$$ ★ **Grand Hyatt.** Views, views, views are what this hotel is all about—occupying floors 53 through 87 of the spectacular Jin Mao Tower, the Grand Hyatt's interior is defined by art-deco lines juxtaposed with space-age grillwork and sleek furnishings and textures. The 33-story central atrium is a marvel in itself—a seemingly endless cylinder with an outer-space aura. Room amenities are space age as well: CAT 5 optical lines for laptop use; Internet connections on the flat-screen TV through a cordless keyboard; and three high-pressure shower heads in the bathroom. Views from the rooms are spectacular; corner rooms have two walls of pure glass for endless panoramas of the Oriental Pearl Tower, majesty of the Bund, and expanse of the city below. **TIP→ But watch out—being that high up puts you literally in the clouds and at the mercy of Shanghai's foggy weather. Pros:** beautiful rooms; hi-tech amenities make you feel like you're already in the future; fantastic city views. **Cons:** extremely pricy; no guarantee of clear views. *Jin Mao Dasha, 88 Shiji Dadao, Pudong 021/5049–1234 or 800/233–1234 www.shanghai.grand.hyatt.com 510 rooms, 45 suites In-room: safe, refrigerator, Internet, Wi-Fi. In-hotel: 5 restaurants, room service, bars, pool, gym, spa, concierge, laundry service, executive floor, parking (fee), parking (no fee) AE, DC, MC, V.*

$$$$ **Hotel InterContinental Pudong.** The pièce de résistance of the 24-story InterContinental is a nearly 200-foot-high Italian Renaissance–inspired atrium decorated with red Chinese lanterns that shines natural light onto the 19 guest floors, six of which are executive floors. A vivid coat of red livens up the hallways and spacious guest rooms, which all have separate tub and shower. The restaurants cater to a wide range of tastes: Japanese, Cantonese, Shanghainese, Chaozhou, and Continental. The open kitchen of Level One restaurant turns out a great lunch buffet with samples of all those cuisines. **Pros:** well-priced for its amenities. **Cons:** difficult location for exploration on foot. *777 Zhangyang Lu, Pudong 021/5831–8888 or 800/327–0200 021/5831–7777 www.shanghai.intercontinental.com 317 rooms, 78 suites In-room: safe, refrigerator, Internet. In-hotel: 4 restaurants, room service, bar, pool, gym, concierge, laundry service, executive floor, parking (fee), no-smoking rooms AE, DC, MC, V.*

$$$$ Fodor's Choice ★ **Pudong Shangri-La.** The Shangri-La occupies one of the most prized locations in Shanghai: overlooking the Huangpu River, opposite the Bund, near the Pearl Tower in Lujiazui. The hotel's breathtaking water's-edge views, white-glove service, and spacious rooms attract a mix of business and leisure travelers. The Shangri-La's two towers comprise the largest luxury hotel in Shanghai, with almost 1,000 guest rooms and 10 dining choices. Although rooms in Tower 2, behind the original hotel, come with 32-inch plasma TVs, DVD players, and fax machines, many return guests still prefer the rooms in Tower 1 for their gloriously unobstructed views of the Bund. **Pros:** fantastic property; good restaurants. **Cons:** expensive; not ideal for non-business travelers. *33 Fucheng Lu, Pudong 021/6882–8888 or 800/942–5050 021/6882–6688*

CLOSE UP

Spa Treatments

Around Shanghai are hundreds of blind massage parlors, inexpensive no-frills salons whose blind masseurs are closely attuned to the body's soft and sore spots. Be careful you haven't wandered into a brothel, though! At the other end of the spectrum lie the hotel spas, luxurious retreats where pampering is at a premium. Here are just a few of the massage outlets in Shanghai that can attend to your needs.

The **Banyan Tree Spa** (✉ *Westin Shanghai, 88 Henan Zhong Lu, 3rd fl., Huangpu* ☎ *021/6335–1888* 🌐 *www.banyantreespa.com*), the first China outpost of this ultraluxurious spa chain, occupies the third floor of the Westin Shanghai. The spa's 13 chambers as well as its treatments are designed to reflect *wu sing*, the five elemental energies of Chinese philosophy: earth, gold, water, wood, and fire. Relax and enjoy one of five different massages (Y820 plus service charge), facials, body scrubs, or indulgent packages that combine all three.

With instructions clearly spelled out in English, **Double Rainbow Massage House** (✉ *47 Yongjia Lu, Luwan* ☎ *021/6473–4000*) provides a cheap (Y45–Y80), nonthreatening introduction to traditional Chinese massage. Choose a masseur, state your preference for soft, medium, or hard massage, then keep your clothes on for a 45- to 90-minute massage. There's no ambience, just a clean room with nine massage tables.

Dragonfly (✉ *20 Donghu Lu, Xuhui* ☎ *021/5405–0008* 🌐 *www.dragonfly.com.cn*) is one in a chain of therapeutic retreat centers that has claimed the middle ground between expensive hotel spas and workmanlike blind-man massage parlors. Don the suede-soft treatment robes for traditional Chinese massage (Y135), or take them off for an aromatic oil massage (Y225).

The Three on the Bund complex includes the first **Evian Spa** (✉ *Three on the Bund, Zhongshan Dong Yi Lu, Huangpu* ☎ *021/6321–6622* 🌐 *www.threeonthebund.com*) outside of France. Its 14 theme rooms offer treatments from head to toe, and 9 different massages and a detox package (Y1,300) will ease the effects of pollution and late-night Shanghai partying.

With its exposed wood beams, unpolished bricks, and soothing fountains, the **Mandara Spa** (✉ *399 Nanjing Xi Lu, Huangpu 200003* ☎ *021/5359–4969* 🌐 *www.mandaraspa.com*) in the JW Marriott resembles a traditional Chinese water town. Face, beauty, and body treatments include the spa's signature Mandara massage (Y990), a 75-minute treatment in which two therapists administer a blend of five massage styles: Shiatsu, Thai, Lomi Lomi, Swedish, and Balinese.

Ming Massage (✉ *298 Wulumuqi Nan Lu, Xuhui* ☎ *021/5465–2501*) is a Japanese-style salon that caters to women, who receive a 20% discount daily from 11 to 4. Cross over the footbridge to one of five small treatment rooms for a foot, body, or combination "Ming" massage (Y178).

www.shangri-la.com 916 rooms, 65 suites In-room: safe, refrigerator, Internet. In-hotel: 8 restaurants, room service, bars, tennis court, pools, gym, spa, concierge, laundry service, executive floor, parking (fee), no-smoking rooms AE, DC, MC, V.

$$$$ Fodor's Choice ★ **St. Regis.** Every guest is a VIP at the St. Regis. The amphitheaterlike lobby sets the stage for the most indulgent hotel experience in Shanghai. The 318 rooms in this 40-story red-granite tower—its design lauded by *Architectural Digest*—spare no expense, with Bose wave radios, Herman Miller Aeron chairs, and rain-forest showers that give you the feeling of being under a waterfall. At 500 square feet (46 square meters), standard rooms compare to other hotels' suites. The two women-only floors are unique in Shanghai. Butlers address all your needs 24/7 (you can even contact them by e-mail) from in-room check-in to room service, and as part of a new program, they can arrange to escort guests personally to visit local artist studios. The hotel's location—15 minutes from the riverfront—is a drawback, but the fitness center and 24-hour gym, along with the remarkable Danieli's Italian restaurant, add to this pampering property's appeal. **Pros:** beautiful; service will make you feel like visiting royalty. **Cons:** far away from downtown. *889 Dong Fang Lu, Pudong 021/5050–4567 or 800/325–3589 021/6875–6789 www.stregis.com/shanghai 274 rooms, 44 suites In-room: safe, refrigerator, Internet, Wi-Fi. In-hotel: 3 restaurants, room service, bars, tennis court, pool, gym, spa, concierge, laundry service, parking (fee), no-smoking rooms AE, DC, MC, V.*

NORTH SHANGHAI

$$ **Astor House Hotel.** The oldest hotel in China, the Astor House Hotel does an admirable job of capturing the feeling of Victorian Shanghai. The lobby's dark-wood columns and vaulted ceilings are accented by potted orchids and photos of famous visitors from the hotel's illustrious past (including Charlie Chaplin, Ulysses Grant, and Albert Einstein). The hotel has maintained its popularity with both budget and business travelers with its spacious, high-ceilinged rooms, often decorated with historical memorabilia, that more than compensate for the hotel's lack of views. We especially like Executive Room A, with its hardwood floors, oriental carpet, and rain forest shower. **TIP→ Skip the renovated modern penthouse rooms—they lack the historical charm of the lower floors. Pros:** gorgeous building; good price. **Cons:** confused service; spartan furnishings. *15 Huangpu Lu, Hongkou 021/6324–6388 www.pujianghotel.com/index.htm 127 rooms, 3 suites In-room: safe (some), DVD (some), Internet. In-hotel: 2 restaurants, room service, bar, gym, concierge, laundry service, parking (no fee), no-smoking rooms AE, DC, MC, V.*

$ **Broadway Mansions Hotel.** One of Shanghai's revered old buildings, the Broadway Mansions Hotel has anchored the north end of the Bund since 1934. The worn wood furniture, industrial bathrooms, and steam radiators betray their age. In contrast, business rooms are strikingly modern, with cool gray-and-tan interiors, glass-topped desks and nightstands, and separate marble showers and tubs. River-view rooms cost

Y100 extra; request a higher floor to reduce the street noise. **Pros:** location; a sense of Shanghai history. **Cons:** service irregular; rooms worn. ✉*20 Suzhou Bei Lu, Hongkou* ☎*021/6324–6260 Ext. 2326* 🌐*www.broadwaymansions.com* *161 rooms, 72 suites* *In-room: safe (some), Internet. In-hotel: 2 restaurants, room service, bars, gym, laundry service, executive floor, airport shuttle, parking (no fee)* *AE, DC, MC, V.*

HONGQIAO AND GUBEI

$$–$$$ **Cypress Hotel.** Once part of tycoon Victor Sassoon's estate, the Cypress Hotel's shaded, stream-laced grounds remain a tranquil retreat in noisy Shanghai. From all of the hotel's rooms, you can look out over the garden and actually hear birdsong rather than car horns. The extensive health club boasts a swimming pool and outdoor tennis courts, which help to compensate for the hotel's limited English-speaking staff and location far from downtown Puxi. **Pros:** luxuriously quiet; beautiful environment. **Cons:** very far from downtown. ✉*2419 Hongqiao Lu, Hongqiao* ☎*021/6268–8868* *021/6268–1878* *141 rooms, 8 suites* *In-room: safe, refrigerator, Wi-Fi. In-hotel: 2 restaurants, room service, bar, tennis courts, pool, gym, laundry service, airport shuttle, parking (fee), no-smoking rooms* *AE, DC, MC, V.*

$$$$ Fodor's Choice ★ **Sheraton Grand Tai Ping Yang.** Even after 16 years, the Sheraton Grand is still the go-to hotel for savvy business travelers staying in Hongqiao. Formerly the Westin, this Japanese-managed property has four club floors, one-touch service by phone, and golf privileges at Shanghai International Golf Club. Oriental rugs, antique pottery, folding Chinese screens, and wooden masks and statues, all chosen by the hotel's general manager on his travels, add personal touches that cannot be found at any other hotel in town. Spacious standard rooms include large desks and ergonomic chairs, and the plush grand rooms have oriental carpets and overstuffed chairs in the separate bed and sitting rooms. A grand staircase sweeps you from the formal lobby up to the second floor and the exceptional Bauernstube deli. Giovanni's serves Italian food as impressive as its views from atop the 27th floor. **Pros:** beautifully decorated. **Cons:** far from downtown. ✉*5 Zunyi Nan Lu, Hongqiao* ☎*021/6275–8888 or 888/625–5144* *021/6275–5420* 🌐*www.sheratongrand-shanghai.com* *474 rooms, 22 suites* *In-room: safe, DVD, refrigerator, Internet. In-hotel: 5 restaurants, room service, bars, tennis court, pool, gym, concierge, laundry service, executive floor, parking (fee), no-smoking rooms, Wi-Fi* *AE, DC, MC, V.*

ARTS AND NIGHTLIFE

Updated by Lisa Movius

Fueled equally by expatriates and an increasingly adventurous population of locals, Shanghai boasts an active and diverse nightlife. Shanghai lacks the sort of performing-arts scene one would expect from a city its size, but it's getting there. Things like acrobatics are solely of interest to tourists; however, traditional forms of Chinese opera remain popular with older citizens and are even enjoying a resurgence among young people.

THE ARTS

For modern culture more in tune with Shanghai's vibe, head to the Shanghai Dramatic Arts Center. Despite being a state-owned institution, it manages to offset sumptuous historical epics with small, provocative plays that examine burning social issues like infidelity, divorce, finances, and AIDS. The center also does projects in conjunction with the city's handful of struggling but plucky modern-dance pioneers, who also perform at private venues like Zhijiang Dream Factory and Downstream Warehouse and, occasionally, on larger stages.

ACROBATICS

Shanghai Acrobatics Troupe. The Shanghai Acrobatics Troupe performs remarkable gravity-defying stunts at both the Shanghai Center Theater and Shanghai Circus World, a glittering gold and green dome located in the center of Jing'an that seats more than 1,600 people. ✉*Shanghai Center Theater, 1376 Nanjing Xi Lu, Jing'an* ☎*021/6279–8945* ✉*Shanghai Circus World, 2266 Gong He Xin Lu, Zhabei* ☎*021/6652–7750* ⏲*Shows daily at 7:30* PM *Y50–Y150.*

CHINESE OPERA

Kunju Opera Troupe. Kun opera, or Kunju, originated in Jiangsu Province more than 400 years ago. Because of the profound influence it exerted on other Chinese opera styles, it's often called the mother of Chinese opera. Its troupe and theater are located in the lower part of the Former French Concession. ✉*9 Shaoxing Lu, Luwan* ☎*021/6437–1012* *Y20–Y50* ⏲*Performances Sat. at 1:30.*

Yifu Theatre. Not only Beijing Opera, but also China's other regional operas, such as Huju, Kunju, and Yueju, are performed regularly at this theater in the heart of the city center. Considered the marquee theater for opera in Shanghai, it's just a block off People's Square. Call the box office for schedule and ticket information. ✉*701 Fuzhou Lu, Huangpu* ☎*021/6351–4668.*

DANCE AND CLASSICAL MUSIC

★ **Downstream Warehouse.** Experimental-dance troupe Niao and other avant-garde dance and theater performers use this small, underground space for rehearsals and occasional performances. ✉*Longcao Lu, La. 200, No. 100, 3rd fl., Xujiahui* ☎*021/5448–3368.*

Jing An Hotel. Every Sunday, the Shanghai Symphony Orchestra performs chamber music in the lobby of the Jing An Hotel. Past concerts have included pieces by Bach, Ravel, and Chinese composer Huang Yongxi. ✉*San Diego Hall, Jing An Hotel, 370 Huashan Lu, Jing'an* ☎*021/6248–1888 Ext. 687* *Y20.*

Shanghai Center Theater. This stage serves as a home to tourist favorites the **Shanghai Acrobatic Troupe** and has hosted performers such as the Israel Contemporary Dance Group and Wynton Marsalis. The building's distinct bowed front was designed to resemble the Marriott Marquis Theater in New York's Times Square. ✉*Shanghai Center, 1376 Nanjing Xi Lu, Jing'an* ☎*021/6279–8663.*

Shanghai Concert Hall. City officials spent $6 million in 2003 to move this 73-year-old hall two blocks to avoid the rumble from the nearby highway. Only then did they discover that they had moved it to sit over an even more rumbling subway line. Oops. It's the home of the Shanghai Symphony Orchestra and also hosts top-level classical musicians from around China and the world. ✉ *523 Yanan Dong Lu, Jing'an* ☎ *021/6386–9153.*

THEATER

Lyceum Theatre. Although the renovation of Shanghai's oldest theater sadly replaced the dark wood with glaring marble and glass, the design of the space makes for an intimate theater experience. The Lyceum regularly hosts drama and music from around China as well as smaller local plays and Chinese opera performances. ✉ *57 Maoming Nan Lu, Luwan* ☎ *021/6217–8539.*

★ **Majestic Theatre.** Once Asia's largest movie theater, this elegantly restored, beautiful 1930s art-deco gem regularly presents top-ticket theater from China's major troupes, as well as novelty acts and some Western performances. The venue does not have an affiliated drama troupe, so the space is open to all sundry comers. ✉ *66 Jiangning Lu, Jing'an* ☎ *021/6217–4409.*

Fodor's Choice ★ **Shanghai Dramatic Arts Center.** Shanghai's premier theater venue and troupe, with several busy stages, the Dramatic Arts Center presents an award-winning lineup of its own original pieces, plus those of other cutting-edge groups around China. It also stages Chinese-language adaptations, sometimes very inventive, of Western works, such as a festival of Samuel Beckett works reinterpreted through Chinese opera. It also invites a steady lineup of renowned international performers, such as the Royal Shakespeare Company. Despite being a state-owned institution, the Shanghai Dramatic Arts Center manages to offset sumptuous historical epics with small, provocative plays that examine burning social issues like infidelity, divorce, finances, and AIDS. ✉ *288 Anfu Lu, Xuhui* ☎ *021/6473–4567* 🌐 *www.china-drama.com.*

Zhijiang Dream Factory. A small private commercial theater in the trendy Tonglefang New Factories, Zhijiang stages a mixture of its own, visiting international, and collaborative theater and dance productions, as well as frequent rock concerts. It primarily targets young, white collar Shanghainese. ✉ *28B Yuyao Lu, New Factories Building 10, 4F, Jing'an* ☎ *021/6255–4062.*

NIGHTLIFE

BARS

XINTIANDI AND CITY CENTER

Barbarossa. Above the lily pond in People's Park and next to the MoCA, this beautiful Moroccan restaurant switches into a bar at night. Usually quiet and classy, it switches to hot, hip, and hopping on weekend nights, especially in summertime. ✉ *231 Nanjing Xi Lu, Huangpu* ☎ *021/6318–0220.*

LOCAL BREWS

Northern Chinese swear by their Baijiu, a strong, usually sweet clear liquor, but Shanghainese opt for milder poison. Most beloved is Huangjiu, a brown brew from Shaoxing with a mild taste that resembles whiskey, which may explain why the latter is the most popular foreign liquor among locals. Huangjiu's quality is determined by whether it was brewed 2, 5, or 10 years ago. It is usually served warm, sometimes with ginger or dried plum added for kick.

Beer is also widely consumed; although there is a Shanghai Beer brand, it is cheap, very bitter, and mostly found in the suburbs. More common are Suntory, or Sandeli, a local brewery opened by the Japanese brand, and Reeb (yes, it's meant to be "beer" spelled backward), or Li Bo. Most bars, however, serve Qingdao and imports like Tiger, Heineken, and Budweiser, which are more expensive. More premium imported beers can also be had, but the markup is steep.

TMSK. Short for Tou Ming Si Kao, this exquisitely designed little bar is an aesthete's dream. Glisteningly modern, TMSK is stunning—as are the prices of its drinks. ✉ *Xintiandi North Block, Unit 2, House 11, 181 Taicang Lu, Luwan* ☎ *021/6326–2227.*

THE BUND AND NANJING DONG LU

Bar Rouge. In the trendy, upscale Bund 18 complex, Bar Rouge is the destination du jour of Shanghai's beautiful people. It has retained that distinction for a surprisingly long time. Pouting models and visiting celebrities are among the regular clientele. ✉ *Bund 18 7F, 18 Zhongshan Dong Lu, Huangpu* ☎ *021/6339–1199.*

Number Five. One of the few unpretentious bars on the Bund, Five wears its position in the basement of the Glamour Bar with pride. Affordable drinks, generously proportioned pub food, Wednesday Swing-dancing nights, and sports broadcasts attract a crowd of dedicated regulars. ✉ *20 Guangdong Lu, BF, the Bund, Huangpu* ☎ *021/6289–9108.*

★ **Three on the Bund.** The sophisticated Three complex, suitably enough, encloses three different bars: the swanky, dark-wood paneled **Bar JG** on the 4th floor; the sleek white **Laris** on the 6th floor; and the more casual **New Heights/Third Degree** on the 7th floor. ✉ *3 Zhongshan Dong Lu, Huangpu* ☎ *021/6321–0909.*

FORMER FRENCH CONCESSION

★ **Arch Bar and Café.** For an artsy expatriate circle, head to Arch. Its location in Shanghai's copy of the Flatiron building and in a popular residential district attracts architects and design professionals. ✉ *439 Wukang Lu, Xuhui* ☎ *021/6466–0807.*

Fodor's Choice ★ **Cotton's.** This friendly, laid-back favorite moved many times before settling into the current old garden house. Busy without being loud, Cotton's is a rare place where you can have a conversation with friends—or make some new ones. ✉ *132 Anting Lu, Xuhui* ☎ *021/6433–7995.*

Face. Once the see-and-be-seen place in Shanghai, Face's hipster clientele has mostly moved to Manifesto with former owner Charlie, leaving it mostly a tourist destination. But it's still beautiful: candlelit tables outside and a four-poster bed inside are the most vied-for spots in this colonial villa with Indonesian furnishings. ✉*Bldg. 4, Ruijin Hotel, 118 Ruijin Er Lu, Luwan* ☎*021/6466–4328.*

O'Malley's. The most beloved of Shanghai's Irish pubs—not that there's much competition—O'Malley's has the requisite Guinness on tap and live Irish music. Its outdoor beer garden packs in crowds in the summer and during broadcasts of European soccer and rugby matches. ✉*42 Taojiang Lu, Xuhui* ☎*021/6474*

★ **Time Passage.** Shanghai has always been a place more inclined toward slick nightclubs and posh wine bars than mellow, conversation dives, but Time Passage has always been the exception. Cheap beers, friendly service, and a cool, if grungy, atmosphere makes it the best way to start—or end—a night on the town. ✉*Huashan Lu, La. 1038, No. 183, Xuhui, by Fuxing Lu* ☎*021/6240–2588.*

NANJING XI LU AND JING'AN

★ **Manifesto.** The mastermind behind Face opened this coolly minimalist yet warmly welcoming space and took most of his clientele with him. Popular with foreigners and local white-collars alike, it serves up standard cocktails plus excellent tapas from its sister restaurant Mesa. ✉*748 Julu Lu, Jing'an* ☎*021/6289–9108.*

PUDONG

B.A.T.S. *(Bar at the Shangri-La).* Tucked away in the basement of the Shangri-La, B.A.T.S.'s crowd ebbs and flows depending on the quality of the band. The cavelike brick-walled space has diner-style booths arranged around a large central bar. ✉*Pudong Shangri-La, 33 Fucheng Lu, Pudong* ☎*021/6882–8888.*

★ **Cloud 9.** Perched on the 87th floor of the Grand Hyatt, Cloud 9 is the highest bar in the world. It has unparalleled views of Shanghai from among—and often above—the clouds. The sky-high views come with sky-high prices: ■**TIP→ There's a two-drink minimum in the evening, so go in the late afternoon to avoid this.** The class is offset with kitsch, as Chinese fortune-tellers and various artisans ply their skills to customers. ✉*Grand Hyatt, 88 Shiji Dadao, Pudong* ☎*021/5049–1234.*

★ **Jade on 36.** This gorgeous, swanky spot in the new tower of the Pudong Shangri-La has swish drinks in a swish setting. Exquisite design and corresponding views (when Shanghai's pollution levels cooperate) have made Jade popular with the *in* set. ✉*Pudong Shangri-La, Tower 2, 36F 33 Fucheng, Pudong* ☎*021/6882–3636.*

HONGQIAO AND GUBEI

Fodor's Choice ★ **The Door.** The stunningly extravagant interior of the Door distracts from the bar's overpriced drinks. Take in the soaring wood-beam ceilings, sliding doors, and the museum's worth of antiques as you listen to the eclectic house band, which plays modern, funky riffs on Chinese music on the *erhu, pipa,* and other traditional instruments. ✉*4F, 1468 Hongqiao Lu, Changning* ☎*021/6295–3737.*

DANCE CLUBS

XIANTIANDI AND CITY CENTER

Rojam. A three-level techno behemoth, Rojam is like a never-ending rave that bulges with boogiers and underground lounge lizards from the under-30 set. ✉*4/F, Hong Kong Plaza, 283 Huaihai Zhong Lu, Luwan* ☎*021/6390–7181.*

FORMER FRENCH CONCESSION

California Club. Celebrity guest DJs play everything from tribal to disco for the bold and beautiful crowd at this hip establishment. The club is part of the Lan Kwai Fong complex at Park 97, which also includes Baci and Tokio Joe's restaurants. ✉*Park 97, 2A Gaolan Lu, Luwan* ☎*021/5383–2328.*

The Shelter. Opened by a collective of Shanghai's leading DJs, the former bomb shelter basement is not for the claustrophobic, but is a favorite of Shanghai scenesters, with cheap drinks and low or no cover. ✉*5 Yongfu Lu, by Fuxing Lu, Luwan* ☎*021/6437–0400.*

NANJING XI LU AND JING'AN

Judy's Too. A veteran on the club scene, Judy's Too is infamous for its hard-partying, meat-market crowd. The den of iniquity was memorialized in Wei Hui's racy novel *Shanghai Baby.* ✉*78–80 Tongren Lu, Jing'an* ☎*021/6289–3715.*

The Lab. A conceptual space for Shanghai's DJs to practice their craft, the Lab also has special events and occasional barbecues on their rooftop terrace. ■ **TIP→ Patrons should bring their own booze, as no alcohol is served here.** The tradeoff is that most events are free. Enjoy the music while lolling on the terrace, or take a turn at showing off your spinning prowess. ✉*343 Jiaozhou Lu, Jing'an* ☎*021/5213–0877.*

Fodor's Choice ★ **Muse.** Picturesque warehouse grunge in the artsy Tonglefang New Factories makes Muse a hip-hop favorite. ✉*68 Yuyao Lu, New Factories, Jing'an* ☎*021/6218–8166.*

GAY–LESBIAN BARS AND CLUBS

Eddy's. Flamboyant, occasional drag queen Eddy has had to move his male-friendly bar all over the city over the years, but has found an apparently permanent home on this quiet stretch of Huaihai. ✉*1877 Huaihai Zhong Lu, Luwan* ☎*021/6282–0521.*

Pink Home. Pretty boys are always welcome at this happening home of the men's pick-up scene. ✉*18 Gaolan Lu, Xuhui* ☎*021/5383–2208.*

Vogue in Kevin's. At the heart of Shanghai's "alternative"—that is, gay—scene, Vogue in Kevin's is a popular party and pick-up spot. The circular bar is a good perch for people-watching. ✉*House 4, 916 Changle Lu, Xuhui* ☎*021/6248–8985.*

NIGHTLIFE LOW DOWN

Offerings range from world-class swank to dark and dingy dens or from young Shanghainese kids screaming experimental punk to Filipino cover bands singing "Hotel California" in a hotel basement. Prices, scenes, crowds, and ambience can range just as wildly.

Maoming Nan Lu has long been Shanghai's nightlife hub, with the slightly seedy offerings of the main drag contrasting with the classy, upscale venues—most notably, **Face**—in the adjacent Ruijin Guest House, a hotel complex that takes up an entire city block. It has mostly closed down, with the action migrating to the newer **Tongren Lu** bar street.

Tongren Lu does have some good clubs for those who like their nightlife on the wild side. The infamous **Julu Lu** bar street is still going strong. All three of these are crowded with "fishing girls," who ask gents to give them money to buy drinks in exchange for their company (or something more)—and then they either pocket the money or take a cut from the bar.

Those looking for less-blatant sexual commerce should head to the bar, restaurant, and shopping complex of **Xintiandi,** an old Shanghai pastiche and tourist favorite with an array of clean and pleasant but pricey bars. **The Bund** is gradually emerging as a center for upscale dining and drinking, and every year sees new, swank destinations debuting in its historic halls. **Hengshan Lu** and **Fuxing Park** also offer concentrations of bars and clubs.

KARAOKE

Karaoke is ubiquitous in Shanghai; most nights, the private rooms at KTV (Karaoke TV) establishments are packed with Shanghainese crooning away with their friends. Many KTV bars employ "KTV girls" who sing along with (male) guests and serve cognac and expensive snacks. (At most establishments, KTV girls are also prostitutes.)

Haoledi. Crowded at all hours with locals of all ages crooning pop favorites, the popular Haoledi chain has branches virtually everywhere. These listed are just a few of the outlets downtown. ✉ *1111 Zhaojiabang Lu, Xuhui* ☎ *021/6311–5858* ✉ *180 Xizang Zhong Lu, Luwan* ☎ *021/6311–5858* ✉ *438 Huaihai Zhong Lu, Luwan* ☎ *021/6311–5858.*

Party World. This giant establishment is one of Shanghai's most popular KTV bars, and among the few that's dedicated to the KTV instead of the KTV girls. ✉ *459 Wulumuqi Bei Lu, Jing'an* ☎ *021/6374–1111* ✉ *109 Yandan Lu, inside Fuxing Park, Luwan* ☎ *021/5306–3888* ✉ *68 Zhejiang, Huangpu* ☎ *021/6374–1111.*

LIVE MUSIC

XINTIANDI AND CITY CENTER

CJW. The acronym says it all: cigars, jazz, and wine are what this swank lounge is all about. Its second location atop the Bund Center has a breathtaking view of the river. ✉ *Xintiandi, House 2, 123 Xingye Lu, Luwan* ☎ *021/6385–6677* ✉ *Bund Center 50F, 222 Yanan Dong Lu, Huangpu* ☎ *021/6329–9932.*

FORMER FRENCH CONCESSION

★ **Club JZ.** JZ continues its role as the king of Shanghai's jazz offerings. Various house bands and stellar guest performers mix it up nightly. ✉ *46 Fuxing Xi Lu, Xuhui* ☎ *021/6431–0269.*

Cotton Club. A dark and smoky jazz and blues club, the Cotton Club is an institution in Shanghai and still one of the best places to catch live jazz. ✉ *8 Fuxing Xi Lu, Xuhui* ☎ *021/6437–7110.*

★ **House of Blues and Jazz.** Decked out in memorabilia from Shanghai's jazz era of the 1930s, Blues and Jazz would be a great bar even without the music. But the several nightly sets make it a must visit. ✉ *60 Fuzhou Lu, Huangpu* ☎ *021/6437–5280*

NANJING XI LU AND JING'AN

★ **Jazz 37.** The Four Seasons' jazz bar matches its penthouse view with a stylish interior. Grab a canary-yellow leather chair by the white grand piano for some top-quality live jazz. ✉ *The Four Seasons, 37F, 500 Weihai Lu, Jing'an* ☎ *021/6256–8888.*

NORTH SHANGHAI

Bandu Music. An unpretentious café and bar in the M50 art compound, Bandu sells hard-to-find CDs and holds concerts of traditional Chinese folk music every Saturday night. ✉ *50 Moganshan Lu, Unit 11, 1F, Zhabei* ☎ *021/6431–0269.*

Live Bar. Another grungy rock dive catering to students and serving up cheap beer and loud music, Live Bar features heavy punk, metal, and hardcore sounds as well as pop and folk rock. ✉ *721 Kunming Lu, Yangpu* ☎ *021/2833–6764.*

XUJIAHUI AND SOUTH SHANGHAI

★ **288/The Melting Pot.** With live music of varying styles nightly, and up and coming rockers on weekend, this laid-back bar is a favorite with a range of rockers and office fodder, Chinese and foreigners alike. ✉ *288 Taikang Lu, Xuhui* ☎ *021/ 6467–9900.*

Fodor'sChoice ★ **Yuyintang.** No one or thing has done as much to bring Shanghai rock out from the underground and into the open as has the Yuyintang collective. Headed by sound engineer and former musician Zhang Haisheng, the group started organizing regular concerts around town and eventually opened their own space. Regular concerts, usually on Friday and Saturday nights or Sunday afternoons, spotlight the best and latest in Chinese music. ✉ *1731 Yanan Xi Lu, but entered on Kaixuan Lu, Little White Building in Tianshan Park, Xuhui* ☎ *021/5237–8662* 🌐 *www.yuyintang.org.*

SHOPPING

Updated by Elyse Singleton

Shanghai gets up late and opening hours really vary. Local supermarkets open early, but malls don't usually open until 10 and boutiques at 11 AM. The upside is stores tend to stay open later, with many closing at 10 PM. Markets generally start earlier, at around 8:30 or 9:30 AM, and close at around 6 PM. Most stores are open seven days a week. ■ **TIP→ Shopping here is a voyage of discovery that is best done on foot so as to discover the little surprises, especially in areas like the former French Concession.**

XINTIANDI AND CITY CENTER

ANTIQUES

★ **Dong Tai Antique Shop.** Friendly owner Mr. Liu sells a range of lamps, gramophones, fans, and other electrical equipment salvaged from Shanghai's glorious past. Some of his stock has been bought by chic restaurants like M on the Bund, and most are in some kind of working order. A small glass lamp base will set you back about Y100 if you stand your ground. ✉ *11 Dongtai Lu, Luwan* ☎ *021/6385–8793.*

BOOKS AND ART SUPPLIES

Chaterhouse Books. An oasis for the starved reader, this bookstore stocks a good range of magazines in English and other languages and English books, including children's books and a comprehensive selection of travel guides. ✉ *Shop B1-K Shanghai Times Square, 99 Huaihai Zhong Lu, Luwan* ☎ *021/6391–8237* 🌐 *www.chaterhouse.com.cn Shop 68, 6F Super Brand Mall, 168 Lujiazui Xi Lu, Pudong* ☎ *021/5049–0668 Shop 202B, 2F Shanghai Centre, 1376 Nanjing Xi Lu, Huangpu* ☎ *021/6279–7633.*

GIFTS

Fodor's Choice ★ **Shanghai Museum Shop.** The selection of books on China and Chinese culture at the main store is impressive, and there are some children's books. Expensive reproduction ceramics are available as well as smaller gift items such as magnets, scarves, and notebooks. Cool purchases like a Chinese architecture–ink stamp (Y90) make great gifts. A delicate bracelet with Chinese charms costs Y150. ✉ *Shanghai Museum, 201 Renmin Dadao, Huangpu* ☎ *021/6372–3500* ✉ *123 Taicang Lu, Luwan* ☎ *021/6384–7900.*

NANJING DONG LU AND THE BUND

ANTIQUES

Shanghai Antique and Curio Store. A pleasant departure from the touristy shops in the area, this government-owned store is an excellent place to gauge whether you are being taken for a ride elsewhere. Goods start with small pieces of embroidery, and range from ceramics to wedding baskets (traditionally used to hold part of the bride's dowry). Some of the pieces may not be taken out of the country, as a sign in the ceramics store warns. ✉ *240 Guangdong Lu, Huangpu* ☎ *021/6321–5868.*

TOP SHOPPING STOPS

Duolun Lu is a pedestrian street in Shanghai's historic Hongkou. Not only is it lined with examples of old architecture and home to a modern-art gallery, but its stalls and curio stores are ripe for browsing.

Moganshan Lu, a complex near Aomen Lu, once housed poor artists. It is now being developed and repackaged as M50, a hot new art destination with galleries, cafés, and stores moving in to make this a happening place to shop and hang out.

Taikang Lu is a former factory district that's now home to artists and designers. It has a hip and laid-back vibe, particularly on weekdays, and is fast becoming Shanghai's SoHo. You won't find Andy Warhols at the International Artists Factory, but there is definitely some worthwhile shopping.

In **Xintiandi,** exclusive and expensive stores are housed in reproduction traditional Shikumen buildings. Get ready to work that plastic.

Xujiahui, where six major shopping malls and giant electronics complexes in Puxi converge, looks like it's straight out of Tokyo. Shop 'til you drop, or play with the gadgets and compare prices at the electronics shops.

Yu Garden, a major tourist haunt in the Old Town area of Shanghai, can be overwhelming, but hard bargaining brings rewards. The amount and variety of goods for sale here are phenomenal. It is continually expanding as vendors move out of old buildings in the surrounding areas.

Also check out these streets that specialize in specific traditional products: **Fenyang Lu** and **Jinling Lu** for musical instruments; **Changle Lu** and **Maoming Lu** for *qipao* (Chinese-style dresses); and **Fuzhou Lu** for books and art supplies, including calligraphy supplies.

3

ART

★ **Studio Rouge.** A small but well-chosen collection of mainly photography and paintings by emerging and established artists crowd this simple space. Look for Studio Rouge M50 in Moganshan Lu; it houses the works of more international artists. ✉*17 Fuzhou Lu, Huangpu* ☎*021/6323–0833ß* ✉*Building 7, 50 Moganshan Lu, Putuo* ☎*1380/174–1782 (mobile).*

BOOKS AND ART SUPPLIES

Yangzhenhua Bizhuang. Calligraphy supplies at excellent prices—fine brushes start at just Y2—can be purchased at this long-established shop. It still has the original glass counters and dark-wood shelves and a staff that relaxes at the back with tea and pumpkin seeds. ✉*290 Fuzhou Lu, Huangpu* ☎*021/6322–3117.*

CERAMICS

Blue Shanghai White. The eponymous colored ceramics here are designed and hand-painted by the owner, and are made in Jingdezhen, once home to China's imperial kilns. Some larger pieces are made with wood salvaged from demolition sites around Shanghai. Prices start at Y60 for a cup to Y30,000 for a screen with ceramic panels. ✉*17*

Fuzhou Lu, Room 103, Huangpu ☎*021/6323–0856* ⊕*www.blue-shanghaiwhite.com.*

CLOTHING AND SHOES

Bund 18. The glamorous collection of shops here sells high-end designer clothing and accessories such as Marni, Ermenegildo Zegna, Cartier, and Giorgio Armani. The boutique **Younik** stands out by specializing in Shanghai-based designers, including Lu Kun. ✉*18 Zhongshan Dong Yi Lu, Huangpu* ☎*021/6323–7066* ⊕*www.bund18.com.*

★ **Suzhou Cobblers.** Beautifully embroidered handmade shoes and slippers with quirky designs such as cabbages are sold alongside funky bags made from rice sacks. Children's shoes are also available. Also sold here are sweet knitted toys and children's sweaters. ✉*17 Fuzhou Lu, Room 101, Huangpu* ☎*021/6321–7087* ⊕*www.suzhou-cobblers.com.*

PEARLS AND JEWELRY

Ling Ling Pearls and Jewelry. Traditional pearl necklaces and inexpensive fashion jewelry that is hipper than the competition stand out here. Pearl and stone combinations are priced high, but large discounts are often given sans haggling. The shop is in **Pearl City,** among the other pearl and jewelry sellers. ✉*2F, Pearl City, 558 Nanjing Dong Lu, 2nd fl., Huangpu* ☎*021/6322–9299*

★ **Amy Lin's Pearls and Jewelry.** Friendly owner Amy Lin has sold pearls to European first ladies and American presidents but treats all her customers like royalty. Her shop amongst the fake bags at Fenshine Plaza has inexpensive trinket bracelets, strings of seed pearls, and stunning Australian seawater pearl necklaces. ✉ *Shop 30, 3F, Fenshine Fashion and Accessories Plaza, 580 Nanjing Xi Lu, Huangpu* ☎*021/5228–2372 or* ⊕*www.amy-pearl.com.*

FORMER FRENCH CONCESSION

ANTIQUES

Brocade Country. The English-speaking owner, Liu Xiao Lan, has a Miao mother and a broad knowledge of her pieces. The Miao sew their history into the cloth and she knows the meaning behind each one. Many pieces are antique-collector's items and Ms. Liu has also started designing more wearable items. Antique embroidery can cost an arm and a leg, but smaller embroidery pieces are affordable and flat and easy to slip into a suitcase. ✉*616 Julu Lu, Jing'an* ☎*021/6279–2677.*

★ **Madame Mao's Dowry.** This covetable collection of mostly revolutionary-propaganda items from the '50s, '60s, and '70s is sourced from the countryside and areas in Sichuan province and around Beijing and Tianjin. Mixed in are hip designs from local and international designers. Although this could be your one-stop shopping experience, remember this is communism at capitalist prices: expect to pay Y800 for a small Revolution-era teapot and around Y1,800 for a Revolution-era mirror. ✉*207 Fumin Lu, Luwan* ☎*021/65403–3551* ⊕ *www.madame-maos-dowry.com* ✉*Gallery: 50 Moganshan Lu, Building 6, 5th fl., Putuo* ☎*021/6276–9932.*

CARPETS

Torana House. Two stories here are filled with carpets handmade by Tibetan artisans in rural areas using top-quality wool and featuring auspicious symbols. This is also a good place to pick up an antique piece from Tibet or Xinjiang. ✉*164 Anfu Lu, Xuhui* ☎*021/5404–4886* 🌐*www.toranahouse.com.*

CLOTHING AND SHOES

Boutique Cashmere Lover. The small collection of wickedly soft cashmere and blends is contemporary in design; some have Chinese details. ✉*248 Taikang Lu, No. 31, Luwan* ☎*021/6473–7829.*

WHO ARE THE MIAO?

Famous for their intricate embroidery work, the Miao are one of the oldest ethnic-minority groups in China and one of the largest groups still in southwest China. The Miao may have existed as early as 200 BC, in the Han Dynasty. It's not only the Miao, however, who are accomplished embroidery artists. Many ethnic-minority groups in southwestern China make pieces of similar quality.

Feel. The qipao may be a traditional Chinese dress, but Feel makes it a style for modern times as well with daring cut-outs and thigh skimming designs. ✉*La. 210, No. 3, Room 110, Taikang Lu, Luwan* ☎*021/5465–4519 or 021/6466–8065* ✉*Shop 305, The Loft, 508 Jiashan Lu, Luwan* ☎*021/5465–9319.*

insh and Helen Li *(In Shanghai).* A local designer sells cheeky clothes that are not for the fainthearted at these two locations. Skirts barely cover bottoms, but there are cute takes on traditional qipao, as well as a more lifestyle oriented range in the streetside store. It's a good place for T-shirts featuring stylish Chinese-inspired designs. ✉*200 Taikang Lu, Luwan* ☎*021/6466–5249* 🌐*www.insh.com.cn* ✉*11A, Lane 210, Taikang Lu* ☎*021/6415–7877.*

L'Atelier Mandarine. Clothing and accessories focus on children and lounging. The French designer uses natural fabrics such as silk, cotton, and cashmere for her own designs as well as stocking other local labels. The simple and chic designs let the quality of the fabric speak for itself. ✉*Studio No. 318, No. 3, La. 210, Taikang Lu, Luwan* ☎*021/6473–5381.*

★ **Shanghai Tang.** This is one of China's leading fashion brands with distinctive acid-bright silks, soft-as-a-baby's-bottom cashmere, and funky housewares. Sigh at the beautiful fabrics and designs and gasp at the inflated prices. ✉*Xintiandi 15, North Block 181, Taicang Lu, Luwan* ☎*021/6384–1601* ✉*JinJiang Hotel, Shop E, 59 Maoming Nan Lu, Luwan* ☎*021/5466–3006* ✉*Shangri-La Hotel, Lobby Level, 33 Fucheng Lu, Pudong* ☎*021/5877–6632* 🌐*www.shanghaitang.com.*

★ **Shanghai Trio.** Chinese fabrics mixed with French flair, irresistible children's clothes in bright colors and sweet little kimonos, great utilitarian satchels that scream urban chic, and crafty necklaces are the stars of this range. The shop has expanded recently to accommodate a housewares collection, with items such as blankets at Y800. ✉*Xintiandi, 181 Taicang Lu, Luwan* ☎*021/6355–2974* 🌐*www.shanghaitrio.com.cn.*

GIFTS AND HOUSEWARES

Harvest Studio. Drop in to watch the Miao women with their distinctive hair knots embroidering, and sometimes singing. This studio sells Miao-embroidered pillows, purses, and clothing as well as the silver jewelry that traditionally adorns the Miao ceremonial costume. They also have a funky range of contemporary cotton and jersey pieces. ✉ *3 La. 210, Room 118, Taikang Lu, Luwan* ☎ *021/6473–4566.*

Jooi. This Danish-owned design studio focuses on bags and accessories in fabrics ranging from industrial felt to shiny patent. Now, it also incorporates Nest, devoted to eco-friendly products. ✉ *Studio 201, International Artist Factory, La. 210, Taikang Lu, Luwan* ☎ *021/6473–6193* 🌐 *www.jooi.com.*

TEA

Shanghai Huangshan Tea Company. The nine Shanghai locations of this teashop sell traditional Yixing teapots as well as a huge selection of China's best teas by weight. The higher the price, the better the tea. ✉ *605 Huaihai Zhonglu, Luwan* ☎ *021/5306–2974.*

PUDONG

MALLS

Super Brand Mall. At 10 stories, this is one of Asia's largest malls. It has a massive Lotus supermarket along with a mind-boggling array of international shops and food stops and a movie complex. It can be overwhelming if you don't love to shop. ✉ *168 Lujiazui Lu, Pudong* ☎ *021/6887–7888* 🌐 *www.superbrandmall.com.*

Xinmei Union Square. Smaller, newer, and funkier than Pudong's other malls, Xinmei focuses on hip foreign brands such as Miss Sixty, G-Star Raw, Fornarina, and Swatch. ✉ *999 Pudong Nan Lu, Pudong* ☎ *021/5134–1888.*

NORTH SHANGHAI

ANTIQUES

Henry Antique Warehouse. This company is the antique Chinese–furniture research, teaching, and training institute for Tongji University. Part of the showroom sometimes serves as an exhibition hall for the modern designs created jointly by students and the warehouse's 50 craftsmen. Wandering through the pieces on display is a trek through Chinese history; from intricately carved traditional altar tables to 1920s art deco furniture. ✉ *796 Suining Lu, Changning* ☎ *021/5219–4871* 🌐 *www.antique-designer.com.*

ART

1918 Artspace. Excellent up-and-coming artists such as Jin Shan are showcased at this independent gallery's warehouse space. ✉ *78 Changping Lu, Putuo* ☎ *021/5228–6776* 🌐 *www.1918artspace.com.*

★ **M50.** This complex on Moganshan Lu is one of the hippest places in Shanghai. Get down to these old warehouses and hang out with

Continued on page 278

MARKETS

A GUIDE TO BUYING SILK, PEARLS & POTTERY

Chinese markets are hectic and crowded, but great fun for the savvy shopper. The intensity of the bargaining and the sheer number of goods available are pretty much unsurpassed anywhere else in the world.

Nowadays wealthier Chinese may prefer to flash their cash in department stores and designer boutiques, but generally, markets are still the best places to shop. Teens spend their pocket money at cheap clothing markets. Grandparents, often toting their grandchildren, go to their local neighborhood food market almost daily to pick up fresh items such as tofu, fish, meat, fruit, and vegetables. Markets are also great places to mix with the lo-cals, see the drama of bargaining take place, and watch as the Chinese banter, play with their children, challenge each other to cards, debate, or just lounge.

Some markets have a mish-mash of items, whereas others are more specialized, dealing in one particular ware. Markets play an essential part in the everyday life of the Chinese and prices paid are always a great topic of conversation. A compliment on a choice article will often elicit the price paid in reply and a discussion may ensue on where to get the same thing at an even lower cost.

GREAT FINDS

The prices we list below are meant to give you an idea of what you can pay for certain items. Actual post-bargaining prices will of course depend on how well you haggle, while pre-bargaining prices are often based on how much the vendor thinks he or she can get out of you.

PEARLS

Many freshwater pearls are grown in Taihu; seawater pearls come from Japan or the South Seas. Some have been dyed and others mixed with semiprecious stones. Designs can be pretty wild and the clasps are not of very high quality, but necklaces and bracelets are cheap. Post-bargaining, a plain, short strand of pearls should cost around Y40.

ETHNIC-MINORITY HANDICRAFTS

Brightly colored skirts from the Miao minority and embroidered jackets from the Yunnan area are great boho souvenirs. The heavy, elaborate jewelry could decorate a side table or hang on a wall. Colorful children's shoes are embellished with animal faces and bells. After bargaining, a skirt in the markets should go for between Y220 to Y300, and a pair of children's shoes for Y40 to Y60.

RETRO

Odd items from the hedonistic '20s to the revolutionary '60s and '70s include treasures like old light fixtures and tin advertising signs. A rare sign such as one banning foreigners from entry may cost as much as Y10,000, but small items such as teapots can be bought for around Y250. Retro items are harder to bargain down for than mass-produced items.

"MAOMORABILIA"

The Chairman's image is readily available on badges, bags, lighters, watches, ad infinitum. Pop-art–like figurines of Mao and his Red Guards clutching red books are kitschy but iconic. For soundbites and quotes from the Great Helmsman, buy the Little Red Book itself. Pre-bargaining, a badge costs Y25, a bag Y50, and a ceramic figurine Y380. Just keep in mind that many posters are fakes.

CERAMICS

Most ceramics you'll find in markets are factory-made, so you probably won't stumble upon a bargain Ming Dynasty vase, but ceramics in a variety of colors can be picked up at reasonable prices. Opt for pretty pieces decorated with butterflies, or for the more risqué, copulating couples. A bowl-and-plate set goes for around Y25, a larger serving plate Y50.

BIRDCAGES

Wooden birdcages with domed roofs make charming decorations, with or without occupants. They are often seen being carried by old men as they promenade their feathered friends. A pre-bargaining price for a medium-sized wooden cage is around Y180.

PROPAGANDA AND COMIC BOOKS

Follow the actions of Chinese revolutionary hero, Lei Feng, or look for scenes from Chinese history and lots of *gongfu* (Chinese martial arts) stories. Most titles are in Chinese and often in black and white, but look out for titles like *Tintin and the Blue Lotus*, set in Shanghai and translated into Chinese. You can bargain down to around Y15 for less popular titles.

SILK

Bolts and bolts of silk brocade with blossoms, butterflies, bamboo, and other patterns dazzle the eye. An enormous range of items made from silk, from purses to slippers to traditional dresses, are available at most markets. Silk brocade costs around Y35 per meter, a price that is generally only negotiable if you buy large quantities.

JADE

A symbol of purity and beauty for the Chinese, jade comes in a range of colors. Subtle and simple bangles vie for attention with large sculptures on market stalls. A lavender jade Guanyin (Goddess of Mercy) pendant runs at Y260 and a green jade bangle about Y280 before bargaining.

MAH-JONGG SETS

The clack-clack of mah-jongg tiles can be heard late into the night on the streets of most cities in summer. Cheap plastic sets go for about Y50. Far more aesthetically pleasing are ceramic sets in slender drawers of painted cases. These run about Y250 after bargaining, from a starting price of Y450. Some sets come with instructions, but if not, instructions for the "game of four winds" can be downloaded in English at www.mahjongg.com.

SHOPPING KNOW-HOW

When to Go

Avoid weekends if you can and try to go early in the morning, from 8 AM to 10 AM, or at the end of the day just before 6 PM. Rainy days are also good bets for avoiding the crowds and getting better prices.

Bringin' Home the Goods

Although that faux-Gucci handbag is tempting, remember that some countries have heavy penalties for the import of counterfeit goods. Likewise, that animal fur may be cheap, but you may get fined a lot more at your home airport than what you paid for it. Counterfeit goods are generally prohibited in the United States, but there's some gray area regarding goods with a "confusingly similar" trademark. Each person is allowed to bring in one such item, as long as it's for personal use and not for resale. For more details, go to the travel section of www.cbp.gov. The HM and Revenue Customs Web site, www.hmrc.gov.uk, has a list of banned and prohibited goods for the United Kingdom.

⚠ The Chinese government has regular and very public crackdowns on fake goods, so that store you went to today may have different items tomorrow. In Shanghai, for example, pressure from the Chinese government and other countries to protect intellectual property rights led to the demise of one of the city's largest and most popular markets, Xiangyang.

BEFORE YOU GO

- Be prepared to be grabbed, pushed, followed, stared at, and even to have people whispering offers of items to buy in your ear. In China, personal space and privacy are not valued in the same way as in the West, so the invasion of it is common. Move away but remain calm and polite. No one will understand if you get upset anyway.
- Many Chinese love to touch foreign children, so if you have kids, make sure they're aware of and prepared for this.
- Keep money and valuables in a safe place. Pickpockets and bag-slashers are becoming common.
- Pick up a cheap infrared laser pointer to detect counterfeit bills. The light illuminates the hidden anti-counterfeit ultraviolet mark in the real notes.
- Check for fake items, e.g. silk and pearls.
- Learn some basic greetings and numbers in Chinese. The local people will really appreciate it.

HOW TO BARGAIN

Successful bargaining requires the dramatic skills of a Hollywood actor. Here's a step-by-step guide to getting the price you want and having fun at the same time.

DO'S

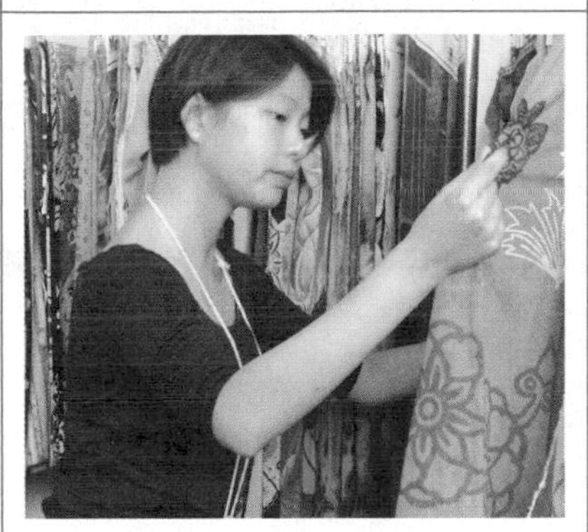

Browsing in a silk shop

- Start by deciding what you're willing to pay for an item.
- Look at the vendor and point to the item to indicate your interest.
- The vendor will quote you a price, usually by punching numbers into a calculator and showing it to you.
- Here, expressions of shock are required from you, which will never be as great as those of the vendor, who will put in an Oscar-worthy performance at your prices.
- Next it's up to you to punch in a number that's around 25% of the original price—or lower if you feel daring.
- Pass the calculator back and forth until you meet somewhere in the middle, probably at up to (and sometimes less than) 50% of the original quote.

DONT'S

Chinese slippers at a ladies' market

- Don't enter into negotiations if you aren't seriously considering the purchase.
- Don't haggle over small sums of money.
- If the vendor isn't budging, walk away; he'll likely call you back.
- It's better to bargain if the vendor is alone. He's unlikely to come down on the price if there's an audience.
- Saving face is everything in China. Don't belittle or make the vendor angry, and don't get angry yourself.
- Remain pleasant and smile often.
- Buying more than one of something gets you a better deal.
- Dress down and leave your jewelry and watches in the hotel safe on the day you go marketing. You'll get a lower starting price if you don't flash your wealth.

SHANGHAI MARKETS

Antiques Market of Shanghai Old Town God Temple. (Huabao Building). Prices are high due to the prime location of this basement market in the main Yu Garden shopping complex. Shop No. 22 has revolution-era materials, including an original Little Red Book. No. 200 has textiles and embroidery. ✉ *Yu Garden, 265 Fangbang Zhonglu, Huangpu* ✣ *On the corner of Fangbang Lu* ☎ *021/6355–9999* ⏲ *Daily 10 AM–6 PM.*

Cang Bao Antiques Building (Cang Bao Lou). During the week, you can browse four floors of booths that sell everything from Mao paraphernalia to real and fake antique porcelain. There are pearls in a wide range of colors and styles, starting from Y10 for a simple bracelet. Curios and other jewelry are on the ground floor, and check out the third floor for old photos, clothing, books, and obscure household kitsch. On Sunday the action starts long before sunrise when, according to a local saying, only ghosts should be awake, hence the market's nickname: *guishi* or "ghost market." Hawkers from the provinces arrive early to lay out their goods on the sidewalk or inside on the fourth floor. Ivory, jade, and wood carvings are among the many goods sold here, all at negotiable prices. ✉ *457 Fangbang Zhonglu, Huangpu* ✣ *End of Fangbang Lu near the gate to Henan Zhong Lu* ⏲ *Weekdays 9–5:30, weekends 5 AM–5:30 PM.*

★ Fodor's Choice **Dongtai Lu Market.** Mao statues, tiny shoes for women with bound feet (though foot-binding is rarely practiced in China anymore), ethnic minority-crafted clothing and embroidery, ceramic bracelets, gramophones —it's all here. This is one of the best places in town to buy gifts and souvenirs, and it's within walking distance of the shops at Xintiandi. Most of the stalls sell similar items, so your bargaining power is high as you can just walk to another store if you don't like the price. Real antiques are rare. Squeeze behind the stalls to check out the shops in the back. ✉ *Dongtai Lu (near Xizang Lu)* ☎ *021/5306–8888* ✣ *Just west of Xizang Lu* ⏲ *Daily 10–6.*

Fuyou Gate Market. This department-store-meets-market with a wild variety of items spreads over three floors. On the ground floor, No. 128 sells brightly colored Chinese folk textiles, including children's shoes, and on the second floor, shop No. 1 sells Korean stationery. ✉ *427 Fuyou Lu, Huangpu* ✣ *Take bus No. 66 from Xizang Nan Lu* ⏲ *Daily 7 AM–5:30 PM.*

Fuyuan Market. The first floor of this market, also in theYu Garden area, specializes in Chinese medicine. You can get jujube seeds for insomnia and kudzu vine flower for hangovers, or just wander around and marvel at the weird-looking ginseng. ✉ *338 Fuyou Lu, Huangpu* ✣ *Across the street and just east of Fuyou Gate Market* ⏲ *Daily 7 AM–5:30 PM.*

Pu'an Lu Children's Market. A mecca for parents, children, and doting relatives, this underground market sells toys, accessories, shoes, and clothing for kids. Hunt out French and Swedish clothing brands, and big-name toy manufacturers such as Lego and Barbie, as well as some beautiful Japanese wooden toys. You might find a pretty dress for Y29 or a small wooden Noah's ark for Y35. ✉ *10 Pu'an Lu Lu, Luwan* ✣ *Take metro line 1 to Huangpi Nan Lu and walk east down Huaihai Lu a few blocks, then turn left* ⌚ *Daily 9:30 AM–6:30 PM.*

Qi Pu Clothing Wholesale Market. Three large buildings (and counting) are stuffed to the rafters with cheap clothing here. It's good for children's clothes, but women's clothing tends to be very petite, and shoe lovers with big feet will be heartbroken. You're most likely to come away with fake designer sneakers and a T-shirt printed with misspelled or vaguely obscene English. ✉ *168 and 183 Qipu Lu, by Henan Bei Lu, Zhabei* ✣ *Take bus No. 66 from Xizang Nan Lu to Qipu Lu, or take the long walk north from the Henan Zhong Lu metro stop* ⌚ *Daily 6 AM–6 PM.*

★ Fodor's Choice **South Bund Soft-Spinning Material Market.** The unusual name alludes to the veritable treasure chest of fabrics, from lurid synthetics to silk brocades, spread over three floors. Shop No. 313 can produce embroidery based on a digital image for Y40, while Nos. 231, 399, 353, 161 are Aladdin's caves of buttons and braids. No. 189 has masses of silk brocade from a negotiable Y35 per meter. Most stores have a tailoring service with prices starting at Y40 for a shirt and Y50 for a pair of pants. Be warned: the tailoring is very hit or miss. Opt for a tailor whose display clothes are similar to those you want to have made. ✉ *399 Lujiabang Lu, Huangpu* ✣ *Near the Zhongshan Er Lu end of Lujiabang Lu* ⌚ *Daily 8:30 AM–6 PM.*

Shanghai Tan Shangsha. If craft and sewing is your bag, then heaven truly awaits at this first floor haberdashery market. With feathers, zippers, and every imaginable decoration imaginable, you will find at Aladdin's Cave of sewing and craft supplies. In general, it's a wholesale market, so the sellers are downright unfriendly when it comes to small purchases but they will sell to you eventually. If you've had enough of their attitude tip out into the surrounding side streets for more creative treats. ✉ *388 Renmin Lu, ground floor* ⌚ *7:30 AM–5:30 PM.* ☎ *021/6323–0833*

Wenmiao Book Market. The Sunday book market at Shanghai's only Confucian temple is worth a look for old propaganda material, comic books, and other cheap paperbacks mainly in Chinese. Look about under the tables for the cheapest items or flip through someone else's photo album. You can pick up a propaganda magazine for Y15 and then head out to the street to eat or have sticker photos made. ✉ *Wenmiao Lu, off Huaihai Lu, Huangpu* ⌚ *Sun. 10 AM–4 PM* 🎫 *Y1.*

WHERE TO EAT

Street vendors selling snacks and meals surround most markets. Wenmiao market has a particularly good selection of street food, including cold noodles served from carts, fried meat on sticks, and in summer, fresh coconut milk. At the South Bund Soft-Spinning Market, on Nancang Jie, you'll find similar offerings. Rumor has it that you can even eat snake there; look for the baskets outside the small food vendors' stores. Dongtai Lu is close to Xintiandi, where you can choose from a wide selection of cafés, bars, and restaurants.

■ TIP→ Avoid tap water, ice, and uncooked food. Cooked food from street vendors is generally safe unless it looks like it has been sitting around for a while.

the crowds. It's a great place to spend time wandering around the smaller galleries, chatting to the artists and dealers, and seeing China's more established artists' work as well. ✉*50 Moganshan Lu, Putuo* ☎*021/6266–0963* 🌐*www.m50.com.cn.*

ShanghART. The city's first modern-art gallery, ShanghART is *the* place to check out the work of art-world movers and shakers such as Ding Yi, Xue Song, and Shen Fan. Here you can familiarize yourself with Shanghai's young contemporary avant-garde artists. The gallery represents around 30 local artists as well as putting on great shows and openings in its adjacent H Space. They sell some catalogs of artists they represent and of past shows. ✉*50 Moganshan Lu, Putuo* ☎*021/6359–3923* 🌐*www.shanghartgallery.com* ✉*F-Space 315–317, 800 Guoshu Dong Lu, Yangpu* ☎*021/5506–5989.*

TEA

Tianshan Tea City. This place stocks all the tea in China and then some. More than 300 vendors occupy the three floors. You can buy such famous teas as West Lake dragon well tea and Wuyi red-robe tea, and the tea set to serve it in. ✉*520 Zhongshan Xi Lu, Changning* ☎*021/6259–9999* 🌐*www.dabutong.com.*

XUJIAHUI AND SOUTH SHANGHAI

ANTIQUES

★ **Hu & Hu Antiques.** Co-owner Marybelle Hu worked at Taipei's National Palace Museum as well as Sotheby's in Los Angeles before opening this shop with sister-in-law Lin in 1998. Their bright, airy showroom contains Tibetan chests and other rich furniture as well as a large selection of accessories, from lanterns to mooncake molds. Their prices are a bit higher than their competitors, but so is their standard of service. ✉*Alley 1885, 8 Caobao Lu, Minhang* ☎*021/3431–1212* 🌐*www.hu-hu.com.*

ENGLISH	PINYIN	CHINESE
EXPLORING		
Bank of China	Zhōngguó yínháng	中国银行
Bund	Wàitān	外滩
Cathay Cinema	guótài diànyǐngyuàn	國泰電影院
Century Park	shìjì gōngyuán	世紀公園
Chen Xiangge Temple	chén xiāng gé	陳Xiangge寺
Dongtai Road Antiques Street	Dōngtái lù	东台路
Duolun Road	Duōlún lù	多伦路
Former Hong Kong and Shanghai Bank Building	Pǔdōng fāzhǎn yínháng	浦东发展银行
Fuxing Park	Fùxīng gōngyuán	复兴公园
Grand Theater	Shànghǎi dàjùyuàn	上海大剧院
Grayline Tours	huīxiàn lǚyóu	灰线旅游
Huangpu River Cruises	Pǔjiang yóulan	浦江游览
Jade Buddha Temple	Yùfósì	玉佛寺
Jinjiang Tours	Jǐnjiāng lǚyóu	锦江旅游
Jinmao Tower	jinmào dàshà	金茂大廈
Longhua Temple	lónghuá sì	龍華寺
Longhua Martyrs Cemetery	lónghuá lièshì língyuán	龍華烈士陵園
Lyceum Theatre	Lánxīn dàxìyuàn	兰馨大戏院
M50	Chūnmíng yìshù chanyËyuan	春明艺术产业园
Nanjing Road	Nánjīng lù	南京路
Nanjing Dong (East) Road	Nánjīng dōng lù	南京东路
Nanjing Xi Lu (Nanjing West Road)	Nánjīng xī lù	南京西路
Old City Wall	dàjìng gé	老城牆
Oriental Pearl Tower	dōngfāng míngzhū diànshìtǎ	東方明珠電視塔
Paramount	bǎilèmén	派拉蒙
Park Hotel	Guójì fàndiàn	国际饭店
Peace Hotel	Hepíng fàndiàn	和平饭店
People's Park	rénmín guǎngchǎng	人民公園
People's Square	rénmín góngyuán	人民广场
Shanghai Art Museum	Shŕnghǎi bówůguǎn	上海美術館
Shanghai Botanical Gardens	Shŕnghǎi zhíwuyuán	上海植物園
Shanghai Jews	Shànghǎi yoÛtàirÈn	上海犹太人
Shanghai Museum	Shŕnghǎi bówùguǎn	上海博物館

ENGLISH	PINYIN	CHINESE
Shanghai Ocean Aquarium	Shŕnghăi hăiyáng shuĭzúguăn	上海海洋水族館
Shanghai Oriental Leisure Company	Shànghăi mĭngzhū shuĭshàng yúlè fāzhān yǒuxiàn gōngsī	上海明珠水上娱乐发展有限公司
Shanghai Scenery Co.	Shànghăi fēngcăi	上海风采
Shanghai Science and Technology Museum	Shànghăi kējìguăn	上海科技館
Shanghai Sightseeing Bus Centre	Shànghăi lǚyóu jísàn zhōngxīn	上海旅游集散中心
Shanghai Urban Planning Center	Shŕnghăi chéngshí gūihuà zhănlănguăn	上海城市規劃中心
Xintiandi	Xīntiāndì	新天地
Yu Gardens	Yùyuān	豫园
WHERE TO EAT		
1221	Yīèrèryī cāntīng	1221餐厅
Barbarossa	Bābālùshā	芭芭露莎
Bellagio	Băilègōng	百乐宫
Cloud 9	Jiŭchòngtiān	九重天
The Dynasty	Mănfúlóu	满福楼
Family Li Imperial Cuisine	Lìjiā cài	历家菜
Ginger Café	Jīngé kā fēi	金格咖啡
Giovanni's	Jífànnísī	吉范尼斯
Gokohai	Yùxiānghaĭ	钰香海
Gongdelin	Gōngdélín	功德林
Grape	Pútáoyuán	葡萄园
Hot Pot King	Láifúlóu	来福楼
Indian Kitchen	Yìndù xiăochú	印度小厨
Itoya	Yīténgjiā	伊藤家
Jade on 36	Fĕicuìsānshíliù	翡翠36
Kabb	Kăibóxī	凯博西
Lost Heaven	Huāmătiāntáng	花马天堂
Masala Art	Xiāngliàoyìshù	香料艺术
Meilongzhen	Méilóngzhèn	梅龙镇
Mesa	Méisà cāntīng	梅萨餐厅
Mexico Lindo Restaurant	Língdé Mòxīgē cāntīng	灵得墨西哥餐厅
New Heights	Xīnshìjiăo Cāntīng jiŭláng	新视角餐厅酒廊
The Onion	Yángcōng cāntīng	洋葱餐厅
Palladio	Pàlánduǒ	帕兰朵

ENGLISH	PINYIN	CHINESE
Quan Ju De	Quánjùdé	全聚德
Roosevelt Prime Steakhouse	Luósīfú dǐngjí níupaíguǎn	罗斯福顶级牛排馆
Sens & Bund	Yǎdé	雅德
Simply Thai	Tiāntài cāntīng	天泰餐厅
South Beauty	Qiàojiāngnán	俏江南
The Stage At Westin Restaurant	Wǔtaí cān tīng	舞台餐厅
Summer Pavilion	Xiàyuàn	夏苑
T8	T bā	T 8
Tairyo	Tailáng	太郎
The Tandoor	Tiāndōulǐ Yìndù cāntīng	天都里印度餐厅
Vienna Café	Weíyěnà kā fēi	维也纳咖啡
Wan Hao	Wànháo	万豪
Whampoa Club	Huángpǔhuì	黄埔会
Yi Café	Yí kāfēi	怡咖啡
Yu Xin Chuan Restaurant	Yúxìn chuāncaì	渝信川菜
WHERE TO STAY		
88 Xintiandi	88 xīntiāndì jiǔdiàn	88 新天地酒店
Anting Villa Hotel	Antíng biéshù huāyuán jiǔdiàn	安亭别墅花园酒店
Astor House Hotel	Pǔjiāng fàndiàn	浦江饭店
Broadway Mansions	Shànghǎi dàshà	上海大厦
Crowne Plaza	Yínxīng Huángguān Jiàrì Jiǔdiàn	银星皇冠假日酒店
Cypress Hotel	Longbài fàndiàn	龙柏饭店
Donghu Hotel	Dōnghú Bīnguǎn	東湖賓館
Four Seasons Hotel	Sìjì jiǔdiàn	四季酒店
Grand Hyatt	Shànghǎi jīnmào jūnyuè dàjiǔdiàn	上海金茂君悦大酒店
Hotel InterContinental	Jǐnjiāngtāngchén zhōujì dàjiǔdiàn	锦江汤臣洲际大酒店
JIA	Shànghǎijiā jiǔdiàn	上海家酒店
Jinjiang Hotel	Jǐnjiāng fàndiàn	锦江饭店
JW Marriott	J.W.wànháo jiǔdiàn	JW 万豪酒店
Le Royal Meridien	Shànghǎi Shìmàohuángjiāàiměi jiǔdiàn	上海世茂皇家艾美酒店
Okura Garden Hotel	Huāyuán fàndiàn	花园饭店
Old House Inn	Lǎoshíguāng jiǔdiàn	老时光酒店
Pacific Hotel	Jīnmén dàjiǔdiàn	金门大酒店
Park Hotel	Guójì fàndiàn	国际饭店

ENGLISH	PINYIN	CHINESE
The Portman Ritz-Carlton	Bōtèmàn Lìjiā jiǔdiàn	波特曼丽嘉酒店
Pudong Shangri-La	Pǔdōng Xiānggélǐlā jiǔdiàn	浦东香格里拉酒店
Radisson Hotel Shanghai New World	Xīnshìjiè Lìshēng dàjiǔdiàn	新世界丽笙大酒店
Ramada Plaza	Nánxīn Yǎhuáměidá dàjiǔdiàn	南新雅华美达大酒店
Regal International East Asia	Fùháo Huánqiúdōngyà jiǔdiàn	富豪环球东亚酒店
Ruijin Guest House	Ruìjīn bīnguǎn	瑞金宾馆
Sheraton Grand Tai Ping Yang	Shànghǎi tàipÌngyang Dàfàndiàn	上海太平洋大饭店
Somerset Grand	Shèngjiè gāojí fúwù gōngyù	盛捷高级服务公寓
The St. Regis	Shànghǎi Ruìjí Hóngtà dàjiǔdiàn	上海瑞吉红塔大酒店
URBN	YàyuË jiǔdiàn	雅悦酒店
The Westin Shanghai	Wēisītīng dàfàndiàn	威斯汀大饭店
ARTS & NIGHTLIFE		
Arch Bar and Cafe	Jiǔjiān jiǔbā	玖间酒吧
Bandu Music	Bàndù yīnyuè	半度音乐
Barbarossa	Bābālùshā jiǔbā	巴巴路莎酒吧
B.A.T.S. (in Pudon Shangri-La)	Biānfú jiǔbā (Pǔdōng Xiānggélǐlā Diàn)	蝙蝠酒吧（浦东香格里拉店）
California Club	Jiālìfúníyà jiǔbā	加利福尼亚酒吧
Club JZ	Chúncuì juéshìyuè jiǔbā	纯粹爵士乐酒吧
Cotton Club	Miánhuā jùlèbù	棉花俱乐部
Cotton's	Miánhuā jiǔbā	棉花酒吧
The Door	Qiánmén jiǔbā	乾门酒吧
Downstream Warehouse	Xiàhémǐcāng	下河米仓
Haoledi	Hǎolèdī KTV	好乐迪KTV
House of Blues and Jazz	Bùlǔsī yǔ juéshì zhīwū	布鲁斯与爵士之屋
Jade on 36 (in Pudon Shangri-La)	Fěicuì 36 jiǔbā (Pǔdōng Xiānggélǐlā diàn)	翡翠36酒吧（浦东香格里拉店）
Jazz 37 (in Four Seasons)	Juéshì 37 jiǔbā (sìjì jiǔdiàn nèi)	爵士37酒吧四季酒店内）
Jing An Hotel	Jìng'ān bīnguǎn	静安宾馆
Kunju Opera Troupe	Shànghǎi kūnjùtuán	上海昆剧团
The Lab	Shíyànshì	实验室
Live Bar	Xiànchǎng jiǔbā	现场酒吧
Lyceum Theatre	Lánxīn dàxìyuàn	兰馨大戏院
Majestic Theatre	Měiqí dàxìyuàn	美琪大戏院
Number Five	Waitān wǔhào jiǔbā	外滩五号酒吧
O'Malley's	Oumǎlì jiǔbā	欧玛莉酒吧

ENGLISH	PINYIN	CHINESE
Party World	Qiánguì KTV	钱柜KTV
Rojam	Luójié jiǔbā	罗杰酒吧
Shanghai Acrobatics Troupe	Shànghǎi aájìtuán	上海杂技团
Shanghai Center Theater	Shànghǎi shāngchéng jùyuàn	上海商城剧院
Shanghai Concert Hall	Shànghǎi yīnyuètīng	上海音乐厅
Shanghai Dramatic Arts Center	Shànghǎi huàjù yìshù zhōngxīn	上海话剧艺术中心
Three on the Bund	Wàitān sānhào	外滩三号
Time Passage	Zuotianjintianmingtian jiǔbā	昨天今天明天酒吧
TMSK (short for Tou Ming Si Kao)	Tòumíngsīkǎo jiǔbā	透明思考酒吧
Yifu Theatre	Yìfū wǔtái	逸夫舞台
Yuyintang	Yùyīntáng	育音堂
SHOPPING		
1918 Artspace	Yījiǔyībā yìshù kōngjiān	一九一八 艺术空间
Amy Lin's Pearls and Jewelry	ìmǐnlínshì zhūbǎo	艾敏林氏珠宝
Blue Shanghai White	Hǎishàngqīnghuā	海上青花
Brocade Country	Jǐnxiufǎng	锦绣纺
Bund 18	Wàitān shíbā hào	外滩十八号
Chaterhouse Books	Sānlián shūdiàn	三联书店
Dongtai Antique Shop	Dōngtái gǔwāndiàn	东台古玩店
Double Rainbow Massage House	Shuāngchǎihong ànmúo	双彩虹按摩
Dragonfly	Yōuting bǎojiàn huìsuǒ	悠亭保健会所
Evian Spa	Yīyún shuǐliáo	依云水疗
Feel	Jīnfěnshìjiā	金粉世家
Henry Antique Warehouse	Hànruì gǔdiǎn jiājù	汉瑞古典家俱
Hu & Hu Antiques	ǔyuè jiājù	古悦家俱
Insh	Yīngshàng gōngmào	莺裳工贸
Jooi	Ruìyì	瑞逸
Ling Ling Pearls & Jewelry	ínglíng zhūbǎo	玲玲珠宝
M50	Chūnmíng yìshù chanyĚyuan	春明艺术产业园
Madame Mao's Dowry	LMáotaì shèjì	毛太设计
Mandara Spa	Màndámèng shuǐliáo	蔓达梦水疗
Ming Massage	Míngyī ànmó	明一按摩
Shanghai Antique and Curio Store	Shànghǎi wénwù shāngdiàn	上海文物商店
ShanghArt	Xiánggénà huàláng	香格纳画廊

3

ENGLISH	PINYIN	CHINESE
Shanghai Huangshan Tea Company	Shànghǎi huángshān cháyè yǒuxiàn gōngsī	上海黄山茶叶有限公司
Shanghai Museum Shop	Shànghǎi bÛowˇugǔan shāngdiàn	上海博物馆商店
Shanghai Tang	Shànghǎitān	上海滩
Shanghai Trio	Shànghǎi zǔhé	上海组合
Studio Rouge	Hóngzhài dāngdài yìshù huàláng	红寨当代艺术画廊
Super Brand Mall	Zhèngdà guǎngchǎng	正大广场
Tianshan Tea City	Dàbùtóng Tiānshān chāchéng	大不同天山茶城
Torana House	Túlánnà	图兰纳
Xinmei Union Square	xīnméi liánhé guǎngchǎng	新梅聯合廣場

Eastern China

ZHEJIANG AND FUJIAN

4

The main canal ir the Zhejiang province.

WORD OF MOUTH

"After our lunch we walked along West Lake [in Hangzhou] and took a ride on a boat and visited two of the islands in the lake. . . . Both islands were lush with gardens, bridges, and pagodas. The sun was setting as we continued on to the northeast."

—monicapileggi

WELCOME TO EASTERN CHINA

Chinese tour boat in West Lake.

TOP REASONS TO GO

★ **Hangzhou Teatime:** Sip sublime Longjing tea and buy silk in the footsteps of Marco Polo at Hangzhou's romantic West Lake.

★ **Qiantian Tidal Bore:** Marvel at one of nature's most enthralling spectacles: the mighty tidal-bore at the mouth of Zhejiang's Qiantian River.

★ **Shaoxing Wine:** Dramatized by one of China's most famous writers Lu Xun, Shaoxing wine is celebrated throughout the region. Potent for sure, Shaoxing wine is de rigeur for local dining.

★ **Hakka Roundhouses:** The founder of modern China, Dr. Sun Yat-sen, came from China's proud Hakka minority people, whose ancient tradition of rounded-home architecture is now treasured for its graceful lines and organic construction material. As these people succumb to China's fast-paced economic changes, this legacy of living is quickly disappearing.

1 Hangzhou. Described by Marco Polo as the finest and noblest city in the world, Hangzhou is famous for the beautiful West Lake. In recent years, Hangzhou has also emerged as one of China's most vibrant cities. Outside the city, visit the plantations that produce the area's famous Longjing tea, or stroll in forested hills to take in the views of the surrounding area.

2 Shaoxing. Shaoxing is famed for its historic homes and many traditional bridges. This small, well-preserved town is perhaps the best place to experience the historic atmosphere of a traditional Yangzi Delta town. Visit the stunning Figure 8 Bridge, which is indeed shaped like a figure eight and was erected more than 800 years ago.

Local women picking some of China's most famous tea—Longjing was a favorite of Mao's and one of the most expensive brews in Hangzhou.

Elderly Hakka woman.

3 Xiamen. With a bird's-eye view of the Taiwan Straight, Xiamen is poised to profit from the windfall of increased economic activity between Taiwan and the mainland. Famous for its party atmosphere and popular with young ex-pats, Xiamen's trendy clubs and upscale restaurants are becoming as commonplace as the city's famous beaches and botanical gardens.

GETTING ORIENTED

With thousands of miles of coastline, the provinces of Zhejiang and Fujian are the rounded belly section of China's east coast. Indeed, their shores front the East China Sea and the South China Sea. Zhejiang Province's primary ports of call are the cities of Ningbo and Hangzhou, both of which are within two hours of Shanghai by bus. Hangzhou is also famous as the southernmost city of the Grand Canal. Directly south of Zhejiang is the lush and mountainous province of Fujian. With its proximity with the Taiwan Straight, the wealthy coastal cities of Fujian are convenient to each other, but the province's mountainous interior make them a long train trip away from the rest of the region.

EASTERN CHINA PLANNER

Follow the Coast

Few tour routes these days have exclusive planners just for China's central coast, which is a pity. After all, the provinces of Zhejiang and Fujian have much on offer for bicyclists, hikers, ocean swimmers, and windsurfers. And as one of China's first Special Economic Zones, Xiamen is currently awash with cash but still hasn't lost its old-world charm. Fall and spring are the ideal times to visit the region. Spring, especially April and May, has very comfortable temperatures and the trees and flowers are in full bloom. Hot and muggy summer is not the best time to visit. The region has a long and very pleasant fall season—moderate weather and clear skies lasting into early December. Chinese tourists flood in during the two "Golden Week" holidays at the start of May and October, so try to avoid those two weeks.

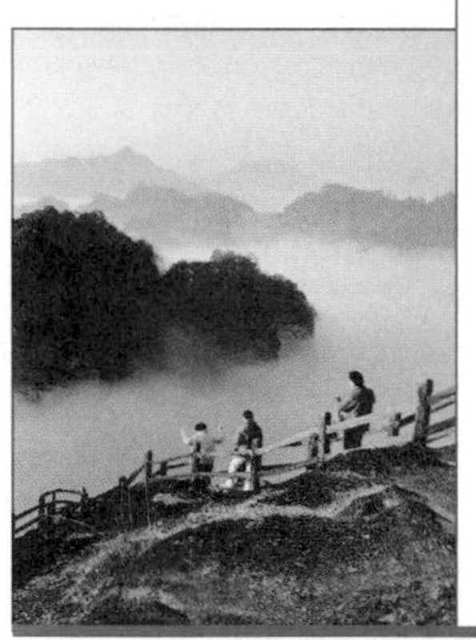

With the Kids

Travel by the most comfortable option possible. If there is a tourist train or bus available, take it. Traveling on local transport is hot, crowded, and often unpleasant, especially for kids.

China maintains very lax standards about personal safety, so always keep an eye on your children. Things to look out for are missing railings on stairs, pools, towers, and cliffs, poor footing, unprotected cooking implements, and hazardous traffic.

The Chinese, especially the older generations, love children. Don't lose your cool if older people approach your children and want to touch their hair, faces, and hands. They are just curious, and can be gently redirected away from your children.

West Lake is the Best

A famous poem that says, "Of all the lakes, north, south, east and west, the one at West Lake is the best." Start exploring where Pinghai Road meets Harbin Road in the northeastern part of the lake. There's a fabulous boardwalk with weeping willows, restaurants, and a lakeside teahouse.

Wending north, you can cross the street to ascend a small hill capped with the Baochu Pagoda. Here, the views of West Lake are some of the best in the city. Once you climb down, you can venture to the Baidi and Sudi Causeways, through the middle of the lake. Don't miss the classical Lingyin Temple, nestled in the nearby hills.

Take a guided boat from the southern shore by night, when the Three Pools Mirroring the Moon pagoda is alight. This stone pagoda has six incised circles. When candles are set inside them, the light appears as romantic moons.

Getting Here and Around

Shanghai is generally the best place to begin exploring Eastern China. It has good amenities, and with two airports and train stations, it offers myriad connectors across the country. Do not travel by bus unless it's absolutely necessary: even the smaller cities can be reached by rail. Most major travel agents in Shanghai speak English. If you want to make Hangzhou your base, many cheap flights are available, although choice of destinations is more limited. Talk to your travel agent for the best deals.

Money Matters

Prices are negotiable everywhere except supermarkets. Do not accept prices quoted in foreign currency, and never pay more than you think the article is really worth. Tourist markups can hit 1,000 percent in major attractions. Don't be afraid to shout "*Tai gui le!*" ("too expensive"), laugh at the seller, and walk away. He or she will probably call you back with a better price.

China is not a tipping country; however, tips constitute the majority of a tour guide's income.

WHAT IT COSTS IN YUAN				
¢	$	$$	$$$	$$$$
Restaurants				
under Y25	Y25–Y49	Y50–Y99	Y100–Y165	over Y165
Hotels				
under Y700	Y700–Y1,099	Y1,100–Y1,399	Y1,400–Y1,800	over Y1,800

Restaurant prices are for a main course, excluding tax and tips. Hotel prices are for a standard double room, including taxes.

When to Go

Eastern China has mildly cool winters (the temperature rarely dips below zero) and long, hot summers. The monsoon period extends from April through June, and typhoons can strike at any time through the late summer and autumn. If at all possible avoid traveling around the big Chinese national festivals (National Day, Oct. 1; May Day, May 1; and the Lunar New Year, late January or early February).

On the Menu

Zhejiang cuisine is often steamed or roasted and has a more subtle, salty flavor; specialties include yellow croaker with Chinese cabbage, sea eel, drunken chicken, and stewed chicken. In Shaoxing locals traditionally start the day by downing a bowl or two of *huang jiu* (rice wine), the true breakfast of champions. Shaoxing's most famous dish is its deep-fried *chou dofu,* or stinky tofu. Try it with a touch of the local chili sauce.

The cuisine of Fujian has its own characteristics. Spareribs are a specialty, as are soups and stews using a soy and rice-wine stock. The coastal cities of Fujian offer a wonderful range of seafood, including river eel with leeks, fried jumbo prawns, and steamed crab.

4

Updated by David Taylor

A MICROCOSM OF THE FORCES at play in contemporary China is presented in the provinces on the eastern coast of the country. The past's rich legacy and the challenges and aspirations for China's future combine in a present that is dizzying in its variety and speed of transformation.

Zhejiang has always been a hub of culture, learning, and commerce. The cities, with their elegant gardens, elaborate temples, and fine crafts, evoke the sophisticated and refined world of classical China's literati. Since the Southern Song Dynasty (1127–79), large numbers of Fujianese have emigrated around Southeast Asia. As a result, Fujian province has strong ties with overseas Chinese. In 1979 Fujian was allowed to form the first Special Economic Zone (SEZ)—a testing ground for capitalist market economy—at Xiamen. Today Xiamen is a pleasant city with a vibrant economy.

ZHEJIANG

The province of Zhejiang showcases the region's agricultural prowess and dedication to nature, even as it is one of the most populous urban regions of China. The capital city of Hangzhou is famous for its West Lake, which is visited by millions of tourists annually. A center of culture and trade, Zhejiang is also one of China's wealthiest provinces. Hangzhou served as one of the eight ancient capital cities of the country, after the Song Dynasty rulers fled Jurchen invaders. Throughout history, the city also benefited from its position as the last stop on the Grand Canal, the conduit for supplying goods to the imperial north.

Shaoxing showcases another aspect of Zhejiang life. The small-town flavor of this city-on-canals remains, despite a growing population. Several high-profile figures helped put Shaoxing on the map, including former Premier Zhou Enlai, and novelist Lu Xun.

Geographically, the river basin's plains in the north near Shanghai give way to mountains in the south of the province. Besides grain, the province also is recognized in China for its tea, crafts, silk production, and long tradition of sculpture and carving.

HANGZHOU

180 km (112 mi) southwest of Shanghai.

Residents of Hangzhou are immensely proud of their city, and will often point to a classical saying that identifies it as an "earthly paradise." Indeed, Hangzhou is one of the country's most enjoyable cities. The green spaces and hilly landscape that surround the city make Hangzhou unique in Eastern China. Add to the experience a thriving arts scene, sophisticated restaurants, and vibrant nightlife, and Hangzhou vies with nearby Shanghai as the hippest city in the East.

GETTING HERE AND AROUND

Hangzhou is best accessed by train, with the tourist express taking around an hour from Shanghai. Buses will get you to Shanghai in 2 hours or to Suzhou in 2½ hours. Hangzhou has several bus stations

spread around the city serving different destinations—buses to Shanghai use the East Bus Station, whereas those to Suzhou use the North Bus Station.

BY AIR Hangzhou Xiaoshan International Airport, about 27 km (17 mi) southeast of the city, has frequent flights to Hong Kong, Guangzhou, and Beijing, which are all about 2 hours away. There are also flights to other major cities around the region.

Major hotels offer limousine service to the airport. Taxis to the airport cost around Y120. A bus (Y15 per person) leaves from the CAAC office on Tiyuchang Lu every 30 minutes between 5:30 AM and 8:30 PM.

BY BOAT AND FERRY You can travel overnight by ferry between Hangzhou and Suzhou on the Grand Canal. Tickets are available through CITS or at the dock. It's a slow trip, and it's at night.

Many boats ply the waters of West Lake. Ferries charge Y35 for trips to the main islands. They depart when there are enough passengers, usually every 20 minutes. Small private boats charge Y80 for up to four people, but you can choose your own route. You can head out on your own boat for Y20, but you can't dock at the islands. Prices are fixed, but boat operators often try to overcharge you.

BY BUS Hangzhou is the bus hub for the province and has four stations. The West Bus Station (Xi Zhan) has several buses daily to the Yellow Mountain, as well as to Nanjing. The East Bus Station (Dong Zhan) is the town's biggest, with several hundred departures per day to destinations like Shaoxing (1 hr), Suzhou (2½ hrs), and Shanghai (2 hrs). About 9 km (5 mi) north of the city is the North Bus Station (Bei Zhan), where there are buses to Nanjing (4 to 4½ hours).

Within Hangzhou, in addition to regular city buses, a series of modern, air-conditioned buses connects most major tourist sights. Bus Y1 connects Baidi Causeway, Solitary Hill Island, Yue Fei Mausoleum, the Temple of the Soul's Retreat, and Orioles Singing in the Willow Waves. Bus Y3 runs to Precious Stone Hill, the China National Silk Museum, and the China Tea Museum.

BY TAXI Hangzhou's clean, reliable taxi fleet makes it easy to get from West Lake to farflung sights like the Temple of the Soul's Retreat and the China Tea Museum (Y30–Y45).

BY TRAIN Travel between Shanghai and Hangzhou is very efficient. Fast trains take about an hour, while local trains take two or more. The train station can be chaotic, but hotel travel desks can often book advance tickets for a small fee. Trains also run to Suzhou (3 hours), Nanjing (5½ hours), and most cities in Fujian.

TOURS

Hotels can set up tours of the city's sights. You can also hire a car, driver, and translator through CITS, which has an office east of West Lake in the building of the Zhejiang Tourism Board. It's relatively inexpensive, and you'll be privy to discounts you wouldn't be able to negotiate for yourself. Smaller travel services tend to be less reliable and less experienced with the needs of foreign travelers.

Taxi drivers at the train station or in front of hotels will often offer tours. Although these can be as good as official ones, your driver's knowledge of English is often minimal.

ESSENTIALS

Air Contacts CAAC (✉ *390 Tiyuchang Lu* ☎ *0571/8515–4259*). **Dragonair** (✉ *Radisson Plaza Hotel Hangzhou, 5th floor, 333 Ti Yu Chang Lu* ☎ *0571/8506–8388*). **Hangzhou Xiaoshan International Airport** (✉ *Hangzhou Xiaoshan District* ☎ *0571/8666–1234*).

Bank Bank of China (✉ *140 Yan An Lu* ☎ *0571/8501–8888*).

Boat and Ferry Contacts CITS (✉ *Huancheng Bei Lu* ☎ *0571/8515–3360*).

Bus Contacts East Bus Station (✉ *71 Genshan Xi Lu* ☎ *0571/8694–8252, 0571/8696–4011 for tickets*). **North Bus Station** (✉ *766 Moganshan Lu* ☎ *0571/8604–6666, 0751/8809–7761 for tickets*). **West Bus Station** (✉ *357 Tianmushan Lu* ☎ *0571/8522–2237*).

Medical Assistance Hangzhou Red Cross Hospital (✉ *208 Huancheng Dong Lu* ☎ *0571/5610–9588*). **Zhejiang Medical University Affiliated Hospital No. 1** (✉ *261 Qingchun Lu* ☎ *0571/8707–2524*).

Train Information Hangzhou Train Station (✉1 *Huan Cheng Dong Lu, near intersection of Jiang Cheng Lu and Xihu Da Dao* ☎*0571/8782–9418*).

Visitor and Tour Info Hangzhou Travel and Tourism Bureau (✉*484 Yanan Lu* ☎*0571/8515–2645*). **Zhejiang CITS** (✉*1 Shihan Lu* ✥*next to the Hangzhou Tourism Bureau* ☎*0571/8516–0877*). **Zhejiang Comfort Travel** (✉*Shangri-La Hotel Hangzhou, 78 Beishan Lu* ☎*0571/8796–5005*). **Zhejiang Women's International Travel Service** (✉*1 508 Wensan Lu* ☎*0571/8822–5166*).

RENT A BIKE

Shaded by willow trees, West Lake is one of the country's most pleasant places for bicycling. This path, away from car traffic, is also a quick way to move between the area's major sights. Numerous bike-rental shops are around Orioles Singing in the Willow Waves Park. The rental rate is about Y10 per hour. A deposit and some form of identification are required.

4

EXPLORING HANGZHOU

WEST LAKE ATTRACTIONS

West Lake *(Xihu)*. With arched bridges stretching over the water, West Lake is the heart of leisure in Hangzhou. Originally a bay, the whole area was built up gradually throughout the years, a combination of natural changes and human shaping of the land. The shores are idyllic and imminently photographable, enhanced by meandering paths, artificial islands, and countless pavilions with upturned roofs.

Two pedestrian causeways cross the lake: **Baidi** in the north and **Sudi** in the west. They are both named for two poet–governors from different eras who invested in landscaping and developing the lake. Ideal for strolling or biking, both walkways are lined with willow and peach trees, crossed by bridges, and dotted with benches where you can pause to admire the views. ✉*East of the city, along Nanshan Lu*.

The Bai Causeway ends at the largest island on West Lake, **Solitary Hill Island** *(Gushan)*. A palace for the exclusive use of the emperor during his visits to Hangzhou once stood here. On its southern side is a small, carefully composed park around several pavilions and a pond. A path leads up the hill to the **Seal Engraver's Society** (*Xiling Yinshe* ☎*0571/8781–5910* 🎫*Y5* ⏲*Daily 9–5*). Professional carvers will design and execute seals. The society's garden has one of the best views of the lake. Solitary Hill Island is home to the **Zhejiang Provincial Museum** (*Zhejiang Bowuguan* ☎*0571/8797–1177* 🌐*www.zhejiangmuseum.com* 🎫*Free* ⏲*Weekdays 8:30–4:30*). The museum has a good collection of archaeological finds, as well as bronzes and paintings. ✉*West Lake* 🎫*Free* ⏲*Daily 8–dusk*.

NEED A BREAK?

On the crest of the hill inside the Seal Engraver's Society is a small teahouse where you can drink local teas. Order a cup and have a seat on the hilltop veranda. The view will make clear why locals have loved this place for centuries.

Fodor's Choice ★

On the southeastern shore of West Lake is the **Evening Sunlight at Thunder Peak Pagoda** *(Leifeng Xizhao)*. Local legend says that the original Thunder Peak Pagoda was constructed to imprison a snake-turned-human who lost her mortal love on West Lake. The pagoda collapsed in 1924, perhaps finally freeing the White Snake. A new tower, completed in 2002, sits beside the remains of its predecessor. There's a sculpture on each level, including a carving that depicts the tragic story of the White Snake. The foundation dates to AD 976 and is an active archaeological site, where scientists uncovered a miniature silver pagoda containing what is said to be a lock of the Buddha's hair; on display in a separate hall. The view of the lake is breathtaking, particularly at sunset. ✉ *15 Nanshan Lu* ☎ *0571/8796–4515* 🌐 *www.leifengta.com.cn* 🎫 *Y40* 🕒 *March 16–Nov. 15, daily 8 AM–9 PM; Nov. 16–Mar. 15, daily 7:30 AM–5:30 PM; last admission 30 mins before closing.*

WORD OF MOUTH

"About touring Hangzhou—this last time I finally succumbed to paying for a ride in those open, golf-cart-like vehicles. It was wonderful. I wish I had done this on my very first trip to Hangzhou. The motorized carts—with a fringe on the top—circle completely around West Lake. One entire circle costs 40 Yuan (slightly less than $5) per person." —easytraveler

On the southern side of the lake is the man-made island of **Three Pools Reflecting the Moon** *(Santan YinGyue)*. Here you'll find walkways surrounding several large ponds, all connected by zigzagging bridges. Off the island's southern shore are three stone Ming Dynasty pagodas. During the Mid-Autumn Moon Festival, held in the middle of September, lanterns are lit in the pagodas, creating the three golden disks that give the island its name. Boats costing between Y35 and Y45 run between here and Solitary Hill Island. ✉ *West Lake* 🎫 *Y20* 🕒 *Daily 7–5:30.*

The slender spire of Protecting Chu Pagoda rises atop **Precious Stone Hill** *(Baoshi Shan)*. The brick and stone pagoda is visible from about anywhere on the lake. From the hilltop, you can see around West Lake and across to Hangzhou City. Numerous paths from the lakeside lead up the hill, which is dotted with Buddhist and Taoist shrines. Several caves provide shade from the hot summer sun. ✉ *North of West Lake.*

Along the eastern bank of the lake is **Orioles Singing in the Willow Waves** *(Liulang Wenying)*, a nice place to watch boats on the lake. This park comes alive during the Lantern Festival, held in the winter. Paper lanterns are set to float on the river, under the willow bows. ✉ *Near the intersection of Hefang Jie and Nanshan Lu.*

OTHER MAIN ATTRACTIONS

From worm to weave, the **China National Silk Museum** *(Zhongguo Sichou Bowuguan)* explores traditional silk production, illustrating every step of the way. By the end, you'll comprehend the cost of this fine fiber made from cocoons of mulberry-munching larvae. On display are looms, brocades, and a rotating exhibit of historical robes from different Chinese dynasties. The first-floor shop has the city's largest selection of silk, and sells it by the meter. The museum is south of West Lake, on the road to Jade Emperor Hill. ✉ *73-1 Yuhuangshan Lu* ☎ *0571/8706–2129* 🌐 *www.chinasilkmuseum.com* 🎫 *Free* 🕒 *Daily 8:30–4:30.*

★ The fascinating **China Tea Museum** *(Zhongguo Chaye Bowuguan)* explores all the facets of China's tea culture, such as the utensils used in the traditional ceremony. Galleries contain fascinating information about the varieties and quality of leaves, brewing techniques, and gathering methods, all with good English explanations. A shop also offers a range of tea for sale, without the bargaining you'll encounter at Dragon Well Tea Park. ✉*Off Longjing Lu, north of Dragon Well Tea Park* 🌐*www.teamuseum.cn* *Free* ⏲*Daily 8:30 AM–4:30 PM.*

Equally celebrated as West Lake, and a short ride southwest of the lake is **Dragon Well Tea Park** *(Longjing Wencha)*, set amid rolling tea plantations. This park is named for an ancient well whose water is considered ideal for brewing the famous local Longjing tea. Distinguishing between varieties and grades of tea can be confusing for novices, especially under the high pressure of the eager hawkers. It is worth a preliminary trip to the nearby tea museum to bone up first. The highest quality varieties are very expensive, but once you take a sip you will taste the difference. Opening prices are intentionally high, so be sure to bargain. ✉*Longjing Lu, next to Dragon Well Temple.*

4

Fodor'sChoice ★ One of the major Zen Buddhist shrines in China, the **Temple of the Soul's Retreat** *(Lingyin Si)* was founded in AD 326 by Hui Li, a Buddhist monk from India. He looked at the surrounding mountains and exclaimed, "This is the place where the souls of immortals retreat," hence the name. This site is especially notable for religious carvings on the nearby **Peak That Flew from Afar** (Feilai Feng). From the 10th to the 14th century, monks and artists sculpted more than 300 iconographical images on the mountain's face and inside caves. Unfortunately, the destruction wrought by the Red Guards during the Cultural Revolution is nowhere more evident than here. The temple and carvings are among the most popular spots in Hangzhou. To avoid the crowds, try to visit during the week. The temple is about 3 km (2 mi) southwest of West Lake. ✉*End of Lingyin Lu* ☎*0571/8796–9691* *Park Y35, temple Y30* ⏲*Park daily 5:30 AM–6 PM, temple daily 7–5.*

IF YOU HAVE TIME

Atop **Moon Mountain** (Yuelin Shan) stands the impressive **Pagoda of Six Harmonies** *(Liuhe Ta)*. Those who climb to the top of the seven-story pagoda are rewarded with great views across the Qiantang River. Originally lanterns were lighted in its windows, and the pagoda served as a lighthouse for ships navigating the river. On the 18th day of the 8th lunar month, the pagoda is packed with people wanting the best seat for Qiantang Reversal. On this day the flow of the river reverses itself, creating large waves that for centuries have delighted observers. Behind the pagoda in an extensive park is an exhibit of 100 or so miniature pagodas, representing every Chinese style. The pagoda is 2½ km (1½ mi) south of West Lake. ✉*Fuxing Jie, on the Qiantang River* *Y15* ⏲*Daily 6 AM–6:30 PM.*

In the hills southwest of the lake is **Running Tiger Spring** *(Hupao Quan)*. According to legend, a traveling monk decided this setting would be a perfect location for a temple, but was disappointed to discover that there was no source of water. That night he dreamed of two tigers that ripped up the earth around him. When he awoke he was lying next to a spring. On the grounds is an intriguing "dripping wall," cut out of the mountain. Locals line up with jugs to collect the water that pours from its surface, believing the water has special qualities—and it does. Ask someone in the temple's souvenir shop to float a coin on the surface of the water to prove it. ✉*Hupao Lu, near the Pagoda of Six Harmonies* 🎫*Y15* ⏲*Daily 6* AM*–6* PM.

FOR THE KIDS

One of our favorite child-friendly places is the garden behind the Pagoda of Six Harmonies in Hangzhou. Climbing the stairs of the seven-story Pagoda. Visit the garden and play among the miniature re-creations of China's most famous pagodas and temples. This park is an ideal place to picnic. The pagoda is 2½ km (1½ mi) south of West Lake. (✉*Fuxing Jie, on the Qiantang River* 🎫*Y30* ⏲*Daily 6–6:30.*

At the foot of Qixia Hill is **Yellow Dragon Cave** *(Huanglong Dong)*, famous for a never-ending stream of water spurting from the head of a yellow dragon. Nearby is a garden and a stage for traditional Yue opera performances that are given daily. In a nearby grove you'll see examples of rare "square bamboo." ✉*Shuguang Lu* ☎*0571/8798–5860* 🎫*Y15* ⏲*Daily 7:30–6.*

Near Solitary Hill Island stands the **Yue Fei Mausoleum** *(Yue Fei Mu)*, a shrine to honor General Yue Fei (1103–42), who led Song armies against foreign invaders. As a young man, his mother tattooed his back with the commandment to "Repay the nation with loyalty." This made Yue Fei a hero of both patriotic loyalty and filial piety. At the height of his success, a jealous rival convinced the emperor to have Yue Fei executed. A subsequent leader pardoned the warrior and enshrined him as a national hero. Statues of Yue Fei's accusers kneel in shame nearby. Traditionally, visitors would spit on statues of the traitors, but a recent sign near the statue asks them to glare instead. ✉*Beishan Lu, west of Solitary Hill Island* 🎫*Y25* ⏲*Daily 7:30–6.*

WHERE TO EAT

$$ INDIAN ✕**Haveli.** A sign of the city's cosmopolitan atmosphere, Nanshan Lu is home to several good international restaurants. The best of these is this authentic Indian restaurant, with a solid menu of dishes ranging from lamb vindaloo to chicken tandoor cooked in a traditional oven. End your meal with a fantastic mango-flavored yogurt drink. Choose between the dining room with a high peaked ceiling and exposed wood beams or the large patio. A belly dancer performs nightly. ✉*77 Nanshan Lu, south of Orioles Singing in the Willow Waves* ☎*0571/8702–9177* ✍*Reservations essential* 💳*AE, DC, MC, V.*

"If just relaxing is the aim, then Hangzhou is a better choice than Shanghai, I'd say, but three nights would almost certainly be enough." —PeterN_H

CLOSE UP

The Qiantang Tidal Bore

During the autumnal equinox, when the moon's gravitational pull is at its peak, huge waves crash up the Qiantang River. Every year at this time, crowds gather at a safe distance to watch what begins as a distant line of white waves approaching. As it nears, it becomes a towering, thundering wall of water.

The phenomenon, known as a tidal bore occurs when strong tides surge against the current of the river. The Qiantang Tidal Bore is the largest in the world, with speeds recorded up to 25 mi an hour, and heights of 30 feet. The Qiantang has the best conditions in the world to produce these tidal waves. Incoming tides are funneled into the shallow riverbed from the Gulf of Hangzhou. The bell shape narrows and concentrates the wave. People have been swept away in the past, so police now enforce a strict viewing distance.

$$–$$$ CHINESE FUSION Fodor's Choice ★ ✕**Louwailou Restaurant.** Back in 1848, this place opened as a fish shack on West Lake. Business boomed and it became the most famous restaurant in the province. Specializing in Zhejiang cuisine, Louwailou makes special use of lake perch, which is steamed and served with vinegar sauce. Another highlight is the classic *su dongpo* pork, slow cooked in yellow-rice wine and tender enough to cut with chopsticks. Hangzhou's most famous dish, Beggar's Chicken, is wrapped in lotus leaves and baked in a clay shell. It's as good as it sounds. ✉*30 Gushan Lu, southern tip of Solitary Hill Island* ☎*0571/8796–9682* ▭*AE, MC, V.*

$–$$ VEGETARIAN ✕**Lingyin Si Vegetarian Restaurant.** Inside the Temple of the Soul's Retreat, this restaurant has turned the Buddhist restriction against eating meat into an opportunity to invent a range of delicious vegetarian dishes. Soy replaces chicken and beef, meaning your meal is as benevolent to your health as to the animal world. ✉*End of Lingyin Si Lu western shore of West Lake* ☎*0571/8796–9691* ▭*No credit cards* ⏲*No dinner.*

¢–$$$ CHINESE FUSION ✕**Zhiweiguan Restaurant.** In business for nearly a century, this restaurant's bustling first floor is a pay-as-you-go dim-sum counter. You point to order a bamboo steamer filled with their famous dumplings or a bowl of wonton soup. The second floor is for proper dinner, where the menu is full of well-prepared fish dishes. ✉*83 Renhe Lu, east side of West Lake* ☎*0571/8701–8638* ▭*No credit cards.*

WHERE TO STAY

¢ **Dong Po Hotel.** This budget business hotel is clean and comfortable. The smaller rooms are rather utilitarian, but the location in the center of town—two blocks from the lake and two blocks from the night market—makes this a good choice. **Pros:** convenient location, low price. **Cons:** small and boring rooms, poor service. ✉*52 Renhe Lu* ☎*0571/8706–9769* *99 rooms, 3 suites* *In-hotel: restaurant* ▭*MC, V.*

$$ **Dragon Hotel.** Within walking distance of Precious Stone Hill and the Yellow Dragon Cave, this hotel stands in relatively peaceful and attractive surroundings. It's a massive place, but feels much smaller because its buildings are spread around peaceful courtyards with ponds, a waterfall,

and a gazebo. Two towers house the medium-size guest rooms, which are decorated in pale greens and blues. Although it has plenty of facilities, the hotel lacks the polish of its Western competitors. **Pros:** good location, newly renovated. **Cons:** indifferent service, little English is spoken. ✉ *120 Shuguang Lu, at Hangda Lu* ☎ *0571/8799–8833* 🌐 *www.dragon-hotel.com* *499 rooms, 29 suites* *In-room: safe, dial-up. In-hotel: 4 restaurants, room service, bar, tennis court, pool, gym, bicycles, concierge, laundry service, no-smoking rooms, Ethernet, refrigerator* *AE, DC, MC, V.*

¢ **Hangzhou Overseas Chinese Hotel.** A budget hotel with a five-star location, the Overseas Chinese Hotel is steps from West Lake. The chipped woodwork and beige color scheme make it less flashy than its competitors, but the low price makes this hotel a good pick. Rooms on the fifth floor have the best views over the water. You can hire a car and driver through the hotel to tour the outlying area. **Pros:** phenomenal location, good price. **Cons:** dingy decor, inadequate dining. ✉ *39 Hubin Lu* ☎ *0571/8768–5555* *218 rooms, 4 suites* *In-room: safe. In-hotel: 5 restaurants, bars, laundry service, refrigerator* *AE, DC, MC, V.*

$$$–$$$$ Fodor'sChoice ★ **Hyatt Regency Hangzhou.** Hangzhou's newest luxury hotel, the Hyatt Regency combines careful service, comfortable rooms, and a great location. A large pool overlooks West Lake. Inside there's a day spa, as well as excellent Chinese and Western restaurants. About two blocks north is Hubing Yi Park Boat Dock, where you can catch boats that ply the lake. The rooms are sleekly furnished, and the beds are truly soft. Ask for a room on an upper floor for an unobstructed view. **Pros:** gorgeous view, good service, excellent pool. **Cons:** location could be quieter, long check-in time. ✉ *28 Hu Bin Lu* ☎ *0571/8779–1234* 🌐 *www.hyatt.com* *390 rooms, 23 suites* *In-room: safe, Ethernet. In-hotel: 3 restaurants, room service, bars, tennis court, pool, gym, spa, concierge, children's programs (ages 1–12), laundry service, no-smoking rooms, refrigerator* *AE, DC, MC, V.*

$$$–$$$$ **Lakeview Wanghu Hotel.** True to its name, this hotel has good views of the water from its position near the northeastern shore of West Lake. It's oriented toward business travelers, which is why it emphasizes its meeting facilities and 24-hour business center. An on-site travel agency employs several guides who specialize in working with English-speaking travelers. **Pros:** good location, convenient travel services. **Cons:** poor customer service, small rooms. ✉ *2 Huancheng Xi Lu* ☎ *0571/8707–8888* 🌐 *www.wanghuhotel.com* *348 rooms, 9 suites* *In-hotel: 2 restaurants, bar, pool, gym* *AE, MC, V.*

$$$–$$$$ Fodor'sChoice ★ **Shangri-La Hotel Hangzhou.** Set on the site of an ancient temple, the Shangri-La is a scenic and historic landmark. The hotel's 40 hillside acres of camphor and bamboo trees merge seamlessly into the nearby gardens and walkways surrounding West Lake. Spread through two wings, the large rooms have a formal feel, with high ceilings and heavy damask fabrics. Request a room overlooking the lake. The gym and restaurants are all top caliber. A first floor garden bar is an elegant spot to relax with a drink. **Pros:** excellent location, staff speaks fluent English. **Cons:** poor customer service, long check-in times. ✉ *78 Beishan Lu* ☎ *0571/8797–7951* 🌐 *www.shangri-la.com* *355 rooms, 37 suites*

CLOSE UP

Art for Art's Sake

The contemporary arts scene in Hangzhou grows by the year, with a mix of national and international artists calling Hangzhou home. For current art exhibits, grab a copy of *In Touch* (☎ *0571/8763–0035* 🌐 *www.intouchzj.com*), an English-language magazine available in many hotels and coffee shops.

Some of the country's hottest artists show their work at **Contrasts** (✉ *No. 20-2b Hubin Lu* ☎ *0571/8717–2519* 🌐 *www.contrastsgallery.com*).

At **Loft 49** (✉ *49 Hangyin Lu* ☎ *0571/8823–8782* 🌐 *www.loft49.cn*), industrial spaces have been transformed into studios for the cutting-edge artists, sculptors, and architects. This former printing factory has free galleries and a café.

Frequent exhibits of painting and sculpture are on display at **Red Star** (✉ *280 Jianguo Nan Lu* ☎ *0571/8770–3888* 🌐 *www.redstarhotel.com*).

In-room: safe, dial-up. In-hotel: 3 restaurants, room service, bar, tennis court, pool, gym, bicycles, concierge, laundry service, executive floor, airport shuttle, no-smoking rooms, Ethernet, refrigerator ▭ *AE, DC, MC, V.*

$$$$ ★ **Sofitel Westlake Hangzhou.** A stone's throw from West Lake, this high-end hotel is in a lively neighborhood of restaurants, bars, and shops. Gauzy curtains and etched-glass and -wood columns divide the distinctive lobby, distinguished by a gold-and-black mural of the city's landmarks. The rooms—most of which have lake views—are thoughtfully designed, with sleek oval desks, fabric-covered headboards, and a glass privacy screen in the bathroom. A Roman-style pool overcomes its drab basement location. The hotel is a block north of Orioles Singing in the Willow Waves. **Pros:** good location, helpful staff. **Cons:** small rooms, many rooms with poor views. ✉ *333 Xihu Dadao,* ☎ *0571/8707–5858* 🌐 *www.accor.com* *186 rooms, 15 suites* *In-room: safe, dial-up, Wi-Fi. In-hotel: 4 restaurants, room service, bar, pool, gym, spa, concierge, laundry service, executive floor, airport shuttle, no-smoking rooms, refrigerator* ▭ *AE, DC, MC, V.*

NIGHTLIFE AND THE ARTS

The city's most exciting bar is the **Travelers Pub** (✉ *176 Shuguang Lu* ☎ *0571/8796–8846*), the only venue for live jazz and folk music. A bohemian crowd gathers here during the week, and on weekends hipsters fill the place to capacity. There's even a bulletin board for those looking to meet fellow travelers and artists looking for collaborators.

The laid-back **Kana Pub** (✉ *152 Nanshan Lu* ☎ *0571/8706–3228*) is an expat favorite for its well-mixed cocktails, live music, and friendly proprietor. The personable staff at the **Shamrock** (✉ *70 Zhongshan Zhong Lu* ☎ *0571/8702–8760*), the city's first Irish pub, serves Guinness and Kilkenny pints, bottled-beer specials, along with great food.

Yue opera performances take place daily from 8:45 AM to 11:30 AM and 1:45 PM to 4:30 PM at the **Yuanyuan Minsu Theater** (✉ *69 Shuguang Lu*

☎*0571/8797–2468*), at the Yellow Dragon Cave. The performances are free with the Y15 park admission.

SHOPPING

The best souvenirs to buy in Hangzhou are green tea and silk, but all sorts of wooden crafts, silk fans and umbrellas, and antiques are sold in small shops sprinkled around town. For the best Longjing tea, head to Dragon Well Tea Park or the China Tea Museum. Around town, especially along Yan'an Lu, you can spot the small tea shops by the wok-like tea roasters at the entrances.

China Silk City (*Zhongguo Sichou Cheng* ✉*217 Xinhua Lu, between Fengqi Lu and Tiyuchang Lu* ☎*0571/8510–0192*) sells silk ties, pajamas, and shirts, plus silk straight off the bolt. A combination health-food store and apothecary, **Fulintang** (✉*147 Nanshan Lu* ☎*0571/8702–6639*) sells herbs and other health-enhancing products. About three blocks north of the China Tea Museum, the **Xihu Longjing Tea Company** (✉*108 Longjing Lu* ☎*0571/8796–2219*) has a nice selection of Longjing tea.

The **Night Market** (✉*Renhe Lu, east of Huansha Lu*) has Hangzhou's best late-night snacks, and you'll find accessories of every kind—ties, scarves, pillow covers—as well as knockoff designer goods and fake antiques. It's open nightly 6 PM–10:30 PM.

SHAOXING

68 km (42 mi) east of Hangzhou.

★ Shaoxing is alive in the Chinese imagination thanks to the famous writer Lu Xun, who set many of his classic works in this sleepy southern town. A literary revolutionary, Lu Xun broke tradition by writing in the vernacular of everyday Chinese, instead of the stiff, scholarly prose previously held as the only appropriate language for literature.

Today, much of the city's charm is in exploring its narrow cobbled streets. The older sections of the city are made of low stone houses, connected by canals and crisscrossed by arched bridges. East Lake is no match for the grandeur of Hangzhou's West Lake, but its bizarre rock formations and caves make for interesting tours. Shaoxing is also famous for its celebrated yellow-rice wine, used by cooks everywhere.

GETTING HERE AND AROUND

The most reliable and comfortable way to travel to Shaoxing is by train. Regular train and luxury bus services run to Shaoxing from Hangzhou and Shanghai a few times a day.

BY BUS Hangzhou's East Bus Station has dozens of buses each day to Shaoxing. In Shaoxing, buses to Hangzhou leave from the main bus station in the north of town, at the intersection of Jiefang Bei Lu and Huan Cheng Bei Lu. Luxury buses take about an hour.

BY TAXI Although Shaoxing is small enough that walking is the best way to get between many sights, the city's small red taxis are relatively inexpensive. Most trips are Y15.

BY TRAIN Trains between Hangzhou and Shaoxing take about an hour, but do not leave as frequently as buses. The Shaoxing Train Station is 2½ km (1½ mi) north of the city, near the main bus station.

WORD OF MOUTH

"I asked a Shaoxing taxi driver about 'stinky tofu' and got a dissertation in response. Stinky tofu is either a religion or an all-consuming passion in Shaoxing, I haven't quite figured it out yet! "
—easytraveler

ESSENTIALS

Bus Contacts Shaoxing North Bus Station (✉ *2 Jiefang Bei lu* ☎ *0575/8513-0794*).

Medical Assistance Shaoxing People's Hospital (✉ *61 Shaoxing Dongjie* ☎ *0575/8822-8888*).

Bank Bank of China (✉ *568 Zhongxing Bei Lu* ☎ *0575/8514-3571*).

Train Contacts Shaoxing Train Station (✉ *Shaoxing Chezhan Lu* ☎ *0575/8802-2584*).

Visitor and Tour Info *www.shaoxing.gov.cn/en/index.htm.*

EXPLORING SHAOXING

MAIN ATTRACTIONS

The city's quiet northern neighborhoods are amenable to wandering, with several historic homes and temples that are now preserved as museums. The largest is the **Cai Yuanpei's House** (✉ *13 Bifei alley, Xiaoshan Lu* ☎ *0575/8511-0652* *Y5* *Daily 8–5*). The owner was a famous educator during the republic, and his family's large compound is decorated with period furniture.

In a city of bridges, **Figure 8 Bridge** *(Bazi Qiao Bridge)* is the city's finest and best known. Its long, sloping sides rise to a flat crest that looks like the character for eight, an auspicious number. The bridge is over 800 years old and is draped with a thick beard of ivy and vines. It sits in a quiet area of old stone houses with canal-side terraces where people wash clothes and chat with neighbors. ✉ *Bazi Qiao Zhi Jie, off Renmin Zhong Lu.*

The **Lu Xun Family Home** *(Lu Xun Gu Ju)* was once the stomping grounds of literary giant and social critic Lu Xun. The extended Lu family lived around a series of courtyards. Nearby is the local school where Lu honed his writing skills. Explore a traditional Shaoxing home and see some beautiful antique furniture. This is a popular destination, so it's wise to book a tour in high season. Consult your concierge for details. ✉ *398 Lu Xun Zhong Lu, 1 block east of Xianhen Hotel* ☎ *0575/8513-2080* *Free with ID or passport* *Daily 8:30–5.*

IF YOUR HAVE TIME

Near the Figure 8 Bridge is the bright pink **Catholic Church of St. Joseph,** dating from the turn of the 20th century. A hybrid of styles, the Italian-inspired interior is decorated with passages from the Bible in Chinese calligraphy. ☒*Bazi Qiao Zhi Jie, off Renmin Zhong Lu.*

The narrow **East Lake** *(Dong Hu)* runs along the base of a rocky bluff rising up from the rice paddies of Zhejiang. The crazily shaped cliffs were used as a rock quarry over the centuries, and today their sheer gray faces jut out in sheets of rock. You can hire a local boatman to take you along the base of the cliffs in a traditional black awning boat for Y40. ☒*Yundong Lu, 3 km (2 mi) east of the city center* *Y25* *Daily 7:30–5:30.*

The **Zhou Enlai Family Home** (☒*369 Laodong Lu* ☎*0575/8513–3368* *Y18* *Daily 8–5*) belonged to the first premier of Communist China, who came from a family of prosperous Shaoxing merchants. Zhou is credited with saving some of China's most important historical monuments from destruction at the hands of the Red Guards during the Cultural Revolution. The compound, a showcase of traditional architecture, has been preserved and houses exhibits on Zhou's life, ranging from his high-school essays to vacation snapshots with his wife.

WHERE TO EAT

¢–$ CHINESE FUSION

✕ **Sanwei Jiulou.** This restaurant serves up local specialties, including warm rice wine served in Shaoxing's distinctive tin kettles. Relaxed and distinctive, it's in a restored old building and appointed with traditional wood furniture. The second story looks out over the street below. ☒*2 Lu Xun Lu* ☎*0575/8893–5578* *No credit cards.*

¢ CHINESE

✕ **Xianheng Winehouse** *(Xianheng Jiudian).* Shaoxing's most famous fictional character, the small-town scholar Kong Yiji, would sit on a bench here, dining on wine and boiled beans. Forgo the beans, but the fermented bean curd is good, especially with a bowl of local wine. ☒*179 Lu Xun Zhong Lu, 1 block east of the Sanwei Jiulou* ☎*0575/8511–6666* *No credit cards.*

WHERE TO STAY

$–$$

Shaoxing International Hotel *(Shaoxing Guoji Dajiudian).* Surrounded by pleasant gardens, this hotel offers bright, well-appointed rooms and a range of facilities. It's near the West Bus Station. **Pros:** reasonable price. **Cons:** no Internet, dated decor. ☒*100 Fushan Xi Lu* ☎*0575/516–6788* *302 rooms* *In-hotel: 2 restaurants, tennis court, pool, gym, refrigerator* *AE, DC, MC, V.*

$–$$

Shaoxing Xianheng Hotel. Conveniently located near many of the city's restaurants, the Shaoxing Xianheng offers modern, comfortable rooms and good service. **Pros:** centrally located, good value. **Cons:** inconsistent English, some rooms need updating. ☒*680 Jiefang Nan Lu* ☎*0575/8806–8688* *221 rooms, 8 suites* *In-hotel: 2 restaurants, bar, tennis court, pool, gym* *AE, MC, V.*

CLOSE UP

What's Cooking

Shaoxing secured its place in the Chinese culinary pantheon with Shaoxing wine, the best yellow-rice wine in the country. Although cooks around the world know the nutty-flavored wine as a marinade and seasoning, in Shaoxing the fermented brew of glutinous rice is put to a variety of uses, from drinking straight up (as early as breakfast) to sipping as a medicine (infused with traditional herbs and remedies). Like grape wines, Shaoxing mellows and improves with age, as its color deepens to a reddish brown. It is local custom to bury a cask when a daughter is born and serve it when she marries.

The wine is excellent accompaniment to Shaoxing snacks such as pickled greens, and the city's most popular street food *chou doufu,* which means "stinking tofu." The golden-fried squares of tender tofu taste great, if you can get past the pungent odor. Also, look for dishes made with another Shaoxing product, fermented bean curd. With a flavor not unlike an aged cheese, it's rarely eaten by itself, but complements fish and sharpens the flavor of meat dishes.

4

SHOPPING

On the shopping street called **Lu Xun Zhong Lu,** in addition to calligraphy brushes, and fans, scrolls, and other items decorated with calligraphy, look for shops selling the local tin wine pots. The traditional way of serving yellow-rice wine, the pots are placed on the stove to heat up wine for a cold winter night. Also popular are traditional boatmen's hats, made of thick waterproof black felt.

FUJIAN

One of China's most beautiful provinces, Fujian has escaped the notice of most visitors. This is because the region, though not too far off the beaten path, is usually passed over in favor of more glamorous destinations like Hong Kong or Shanghai. The city of Xiamen is clean and beautiful, and the surrounding area has some of the best beaches north of Hainan. And Gulangyu is a rarity in modern China: a tree-filled island with undisturbed colonial architecture and absolutely no cars.

XIAMEN

200 km (124 mi) southwest of Fuzhou; 500 km (310 mi) northeast of Hong Kong.

By Chinese standards, Xiamen is a new city: its history only dates to the late 12th century. Xiamen was a stronghold for Ming loyalist Zheng Chenggong (better known as Koxinga), who later fled to Taiwan after China was overrun by the Qing. Xiamen's place as a dynasty-straddling city continues to this day due to its proximity to Taiwan. Some see Xiamen as a natural meeting point between the two sides in the decades-long separation. Only a few miles out to sea are islands that

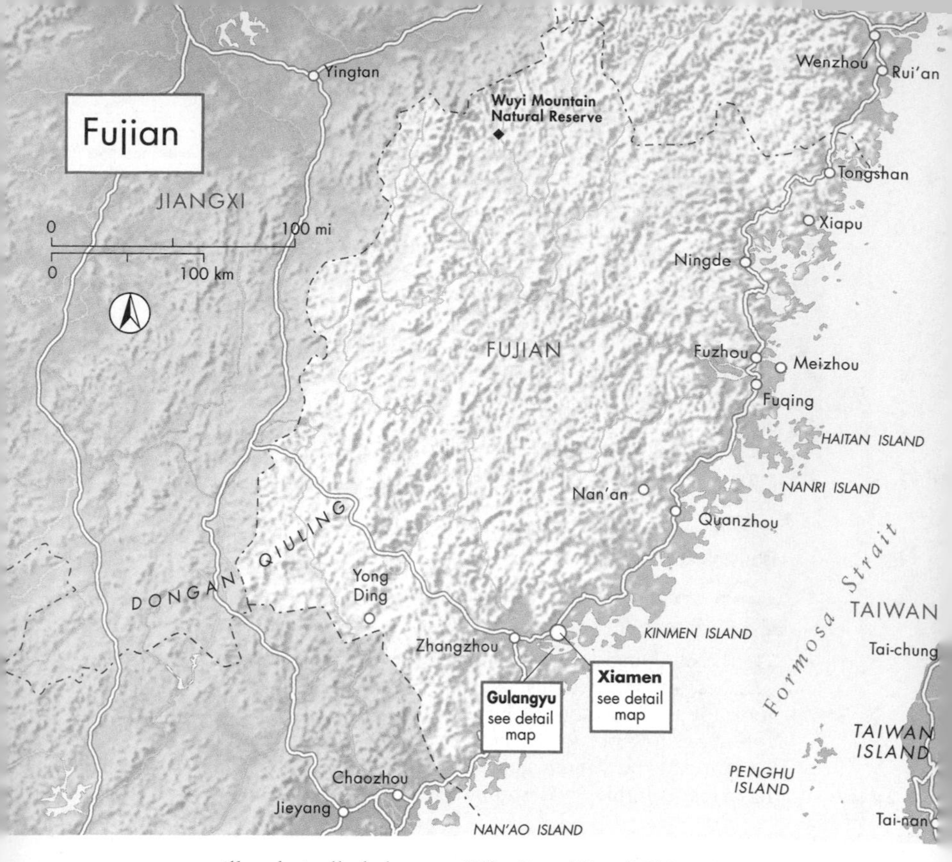

still technically belong to "The Republic of China," as Taiwan is still officially known.

Xiamen is today one of the most prosperous cities in China, with beautiful parks, amazing temples, and waterfront promenades that neatly complement the port city's historic architecture. Xiamen has a number of wonderful parks and temples well worth visiting.

GETTING HERE AND AROUND

The best way to reach Xiamen is by plane. The city is also accessible by long-distance train or sleeper bus, but these types of transportation entail much longer travel times.

BY AIR Xiamen Airport, one of the largest and busiest in China, lies about 12 km (7 mi) northeast of the city. A taxi from downtown should cost no more than Y60. Most carriers service Xiamen, which has connections to many cities in China, as well as international destinations like Jakarta, Manila, Penang, and Singapore.

BY BUS Xiamen has luxury bus service to all the main cities along the coast as far as Guangzhou and Shanghai. The long-distance bus station is on Hubin Nan Lu, just south of Yuandang Lake.

BY TAXI In Xiamen, taxis can be found around hotels or on the streets; they're a convenient way to visit the sights on the edge of town. Most taxi drivers do not speak English, so make sure that all your addresses are written in Chinese. Any hotel representative will do this for you.

BY TRAIN Rail travel to and from Xiamen isn't as convenient as in many other cities. Many journeys involve changing trains at least once. The railway station is about 3 km (2 mi) northeast of the port; bus service between the station and port is frequent.

4

ESSENTIALS

Air Contacts Dragonair (✉ *Seaside Bldg., Jiang Dao Lu, Xiamen* ☎ *0592/202–5433*). **Philippine Airlines** (✉ *Xiamen Airport* ☎ *0592/239–4729* 🌐 *www.philippineairlines.com*). **Xiamen Airlines** (✉ *22 Dailiao Lu, Xiamen* ☎ *0592/602–2961* 🌐 *www.xiamenair.com.cn*). **Xiamen Airport** (☎ *0592/602–0017*).

Banks Bank of China (✉ *10 Zhongshan Lu* ☎ *0592/506–6466*). **HSBC** (✉ *189 Xiahe Lu* ☎ *0592/239–7799*).

Bus Contacts Long-Distance Bus Station (✉ *56 Hubin Nan Lu* ☎ *0592/203–1246*).

Internet Javaromas (✉ *31-13 Jianye Lu* ☎ *0592/514–5677*).

Medical Assistance Lifeline Medical System (✉ *Hubin Bei Lu Xiamen* ☎ *0592/203–2834*).

Train Contacts Xiamen Train Station (✉ *Xiahe Lu* ☎ *0592/203–8888*).

Visitor and Tour Info CTS (✉ *2 Zhongshan Lu* ☎ *0592/212–6917* ✉ *Hubin Bei Lu* ☎ *0592/505–1022*).

EXPLORING XIAMEN

MAIN ATTRACTIONS

❺ The rather hilly **Hong Shan Park** *(Hong Shan Gong Yuan)* has a small Buddhist temple, a lovely waterfall, and beautiful views of the city and the harbor. There's also a lovely tea shop serving Iron Buddha tea, a Fujian specialty. ✉ *Siming Nan Lu, near Nanputuo Temple* 🎫 *Free.*

❷ **Nanputuo Temple** *(Nanputuo Si)* dates from the Tang Dynasty. It has been restored many times, most recently in the 1980s, following the Cultural Revolution. Built in the exuberant style that visitors to Taiwan will find familiar, it has roofs that are decorated with brightly painted flourishes of clustered flowers, sinewy serpents, and mythical beasts. Pavilions on either side of the main hall contain tablets commemorating the suppression of secret societies by the Qing emperors. As the most important of Xiamen's temples, it is nearly always the center of a great deal of activity as monks and worshippers mix with tour groups. Attached to the temple complex is an excellent vegetarian restaurant. To get here, take Bus 1 or 2 from the port. ✉ *Siming Nan Lu, next to Xiamen University* 🎫 *Y3* ⏲ *Daily 7:30 AM–6:30 PM.*

❶ Housed in a fascinating mix of traditional and colonial buildings close to Nanputuo Temple is **Xiamen University** *(Xiamen Daxue)*. It was founded in the 1920s with the help of Chinese people living abroad. The **Museum of Anthropology** *(Renlei Bowuguan)*, dedicated to the study of

Continued on page 312

SPIRITUALITY IN CHINA

Even though it's officially an atheist nation, China has a vibrant religious life. But what are the differences between China's big three faiths of Buddhism, Taoism, and Confucianism? Like much else in the Middle Kingdom, the lines are often blurred.

Walking around the streets of any city in China in the early 21st century, it's hard to believe that only three decades ago the bulk of the Middle Kingdom's centuries-old religious culture was destroyed by revolutionary zealots, and that the few temples, mosques, monasteries, and churches that escaped outright destruction were desecrated and turned into warehouses and factories, or put to other ignoble uses. Those days are long over, and religion in China has sprung back to life. Even though the official line of the Chinese Communist Party is that the nation is atheist, China is rife with religious diversity.

Perhaps the faith most commonly associated with China is Confucianism, an ethical and philosophical system developed from the teachings of the sage Confucius. Confucianism stresses the importance of relationships in society and of maintaining proper etiquette. These aspects of Confucian thought are associated not merely with China (where its modern-day influence is dubious at best, especially in a crowded subway car), but also with East Asian culture as a whole. Confucianism also places great emphasis on filial piety, the respect that a child should show an elder (or subjects to their ruler). This may account for

(left) Offering up joss sticks.
(below) The Yong he Gong Lama temple in Beijing.

Confucianism's status as the most officially tolerated of modern China's faiths.

Taoism is based on the teachings of the *Tao Te Ching*, a treatise written in the 6th century BC, and blends an emphasis on spiritual harmony with that of the individual's duty to society. Taoism and Confucianism are complementary, though to the outsider, the former might seem more steeped in ritual and mysticism. Think of it this way: Taoism is to Confucianism as Catholicism is to Protestantism. Taoism's mystic quality may be why so many westerners come to China to study "the way," as Taoism is sometimes called.

Buddhism came to China from India in the first century AD and quickly became a major force in the Middle Kingdom. The faith is so ingrained here that many Chinese openly scoff at the idea that the Buddha wasn't Chinese. In a nutshell, Buddhism teaches that attachment leads to suffering, and that the best way to alleviate the world's suffering is to purify one's mind, to abstain from evil, and to cultivate good. In China, there are three major schools: the Chinese school, embraced mainly by Han Chinese; the Tibetan school (or Lamaism) as practiced by Tibetans and Mongolians; and Theravada, practiced by the Dai and other ethnic minority groups in the southwest of the country.

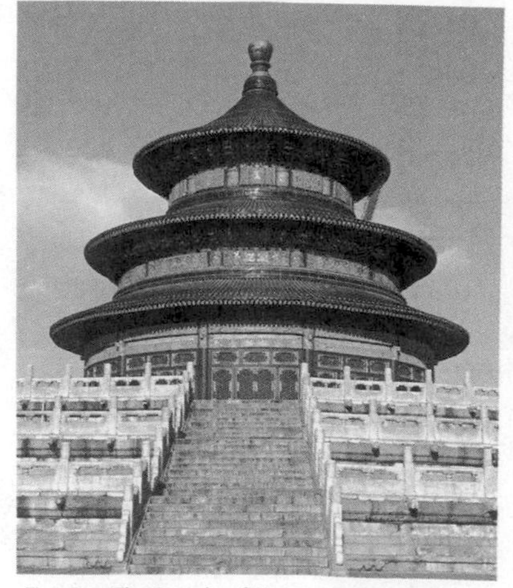
Tian Tan, The Temple of Heaven in Beijing.

TEMPLE FAUX PAS

Chinese worshippers are easygoing. Even at the smallest temple or shrine, they understand that some people will be visitors and not devotees. Temples in China have relaxed dress codes, but you should follow certain rules of decorum.

- You're welcome to burn incense, but it's not required. If you do decide to burn a few joss sticks, take them from the communal pile and be sure to make a small donation. This usually goes to temple upkeep or local charities.

The Buddha

- When burning incense, two sticks signify marriage, and four signify death.
- Respect signs reading NO PHOTO in front of altars and statues. Taoist temples seem particularly sensitive about photo taking. When in doubt, ask.
- Avoid stepping in front of a worshipper at an altar or censer (where incense is burned).
- Speak quietly and silence mobile phones inside of temple grounds.
- Don't touch Buddhist monks of the opposite sex.
- Avoid entering a temple during a ceremony.

TEMPLE OBJECTS

For many, temple visits are among the most culturally edifying parts of a China trip. Large or small, Chinese temples incorporate a variety of objects significant to religious practice.

INCENSE

Incense is the most common item in any Chinese temple. In antiquity, Chinese people burned sacrifices both as an offering and as a way of communicating with spirits through the smoke. This later evolved into a way of showing respect for one's ancestors by burning fragrances that the dearly departed might find particularly pleasing.

BAGUA

Taoist temples will have a bagua: an octagonal diagram pointing toward the eight cardinal directions, each representing different points on the compass, elements in nature, family members, and more esoteric meanings. The bagua is often used in conjunction with a compass to make placement decisions in architectural design and in fortune-telling.

"GHOST MONEY"

Sometimes the spirits need more than sweet- smelling smoke, and this is why many Taoists burn "ghost money" (also known as "hell money"), a scented paper resembling cash. Though once more popular in Taiwan and Hong Kong (and looked upon as a particularly capitalist superstition on the mainland), the burning of ghost money is now gaining ground throughout the country.

CENSER

Every Chinese temple will have a censer in which to place joss sticks, either inside the hall or out front. Larger temples often have a number of them. These large stone or bronze bowls are filled with incense ash from hundreds of joss sticks placed by worshippers. Some incense censers are ornate, with sculpted bronze rising above the bowls.

STATUES

Chinese temples are known for being flexible, and statues of various deities and mythical figures. Confucius is usually rendered as a wizened man with a long beard, and Taoist temples have an array of demons deities.

PRAYER WHEEL

Used primarily by Tibetan Buddhists, the prayer wheel is a beautifully embossed hollow metal cylinder mounted on a wooden handle. Inside the cylinder is a tightly wound scroll printed with a mantra. Devotees believe that the spinning of a prayer wheel is a form of prayer that's just as effective as reciting the sacred texts aloud.

CHINESE ASTROLOGY

According to legend, the King of Jade invited 12 animals to visit him in heaven. As the animals rushed to be the first to arrive, the rat snuck a ride on the ox's back. Just as the ox was about to cross the threshold, the rat jumped past him and arrived first. This is why the rat was given first place in the astrological chart. Find the year you were born to determine what your astrological animal is.

RAT

1924 · 1936 · 1948 · 1960 · 1972 · 1984 · 1996 · 2008

Charming and hardworking, Rats are goal setters and perfectionists. Rats are quick to anger, ambitious, and lovers of gossip.

OX

1925 · 1937 · 1949 · 1961 · 1973 · 1985 · 1997 · 2009

Patient and soft-spoken, Oxen inspire confidence in others. Generally easygoing, they can be remarkably stubborn, and they hate to fail or be opposed.

TIGER

1926 · 1938 · 1950 · 1962 · 1974 · 1986 · 1998 · 2010

Sensitive, and thoughtful, Tigers are capable of great sympathy. Tigers can be short-tempered, and are prone to conflict and indecisiveness.

RABBIT

1927 · 1939 · 1951 · 1963 · 1975 · 1987 · 1999 · 2011

Talented and articulate, Rabbits are virtuous, reserved, and have excellent taste. Though fond of gossip, Rabbits tend to be generally kind and even-tempered.

DRAGON

1928 · 1940 · 1952 · 1964 · 1976 · 1988 · 2000 · 2012

Energetic and excitable, short-tempered and stubborn, Dragons are known for their honesty, bravery, and ability to inspire confidence and trust.

SNAKE

1929 · 1941 · 1953 · 1965 · 1977 · 1989 · 2001 · 2013

Snakes are deep, possessing great wisdom and saying little. Snakes can often be vain and selfish while retaining sympathy for those less fortunate.

HORSE

1930 · 1942 · 1954 · 1966 · 1978 · 1990 · 2002 · 2014

Horses are thought to be cheerful and perceptive, impatient and hot-blooded. Horses are independent and rarely listen to advice.

GOAT

1931 · 1943 · 1955 · 1967 · 1979 · 1991 · 2003 · 2015

Wise, gentle, and compassionate, Goats are elegant and highly accomplished in the arts. Goats can also be shy and pessimistic, and often tend toward timidity.

MONKEY

1932 · 1944 · 1956 · 1968 · 1980 · 1992 · 2004 · 2016

Clever, skillful, and flexible, Monkeys are thought to be erratic geniuses, able to solve problems with ease. Monkeys are also thought of as impatient and easily discouraged.

ROOSTER

1933 · 1945 · 1957 · 1969 · 1981 · 1993 · 2005 · 2017

Roosters are capable and talented, and tend to like to keep busy. Roosters are known as overachievers, and are frequently loners.

DOG

1934 · 1946 · 1958 · 1970 · 1982 · 1994 · 2006 · 2018

Dogs are loyal and honest and know how to keep secrets. They can also be selfish and stubborn.

PIG

1935 · 1947 · 1959 · 1971 · 1983 · 1995 · 2007 · 2019

Gallant and energetic, Pigs have a tendency to be single-minded and determined. Pigs have great fortitude and honesty, and tend to make friends for life.

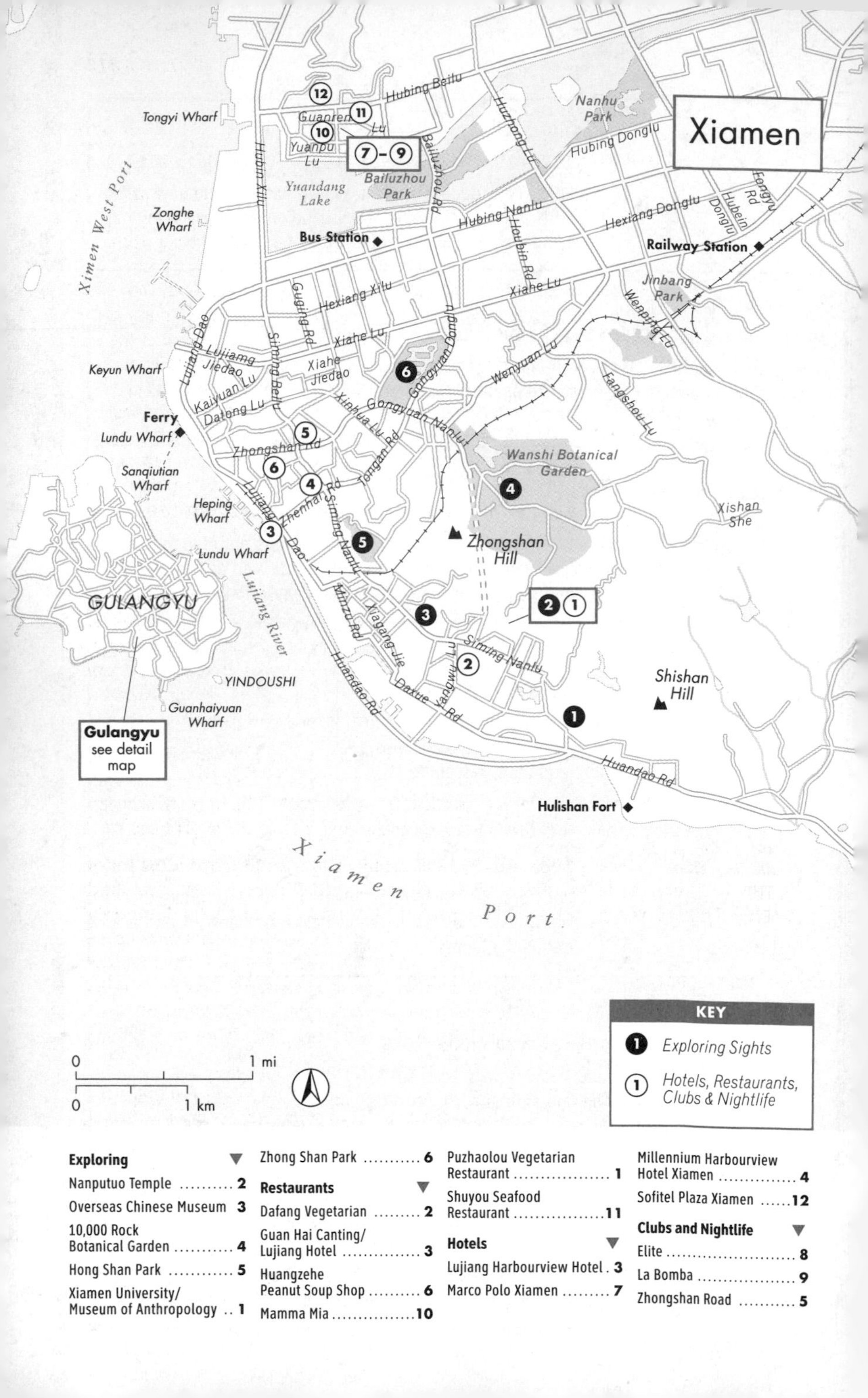
Xiamen
Hubing Beilu
Guanren Lu
Yuanpu Lu
Tongyi Wharf
Hubin Xilu
Bailuzhou Rd
Huzhong Lu
Nanhu Park
Hubing Donglu
Yuandang Lake
Bailuzhou Park
Ximen West Port
Zonghe Wharf
Bus Station
Hubing Nanlu
Houbin Rd
Hexiang Donglu
Hubein Donglu
Fongyu Rd
Railway Station
Jinbang Park
Hexiang Xilu
Guging Rd
Xiahe Lu
Wenping Lu
Wenyuan Lu
Gongyuan Donglu
Siming Beilu
Lujiang Jiedao
Lujiang Dao
Xiahe Jiedao
Keyun Wharf
Kaiyuan Lu
Datong Lu
Xinhua Lu
Gongyuan Nanlu
Fangshou Lu
Ferry
Lundu Wharf
Zhongshan Rd
Tongan Rd
Wanshi Botanical Garden
Sanqiutian Wharf
Zhenhai Rd
Siming Nanlu
Heping Wharf
Xishan She
Zhongshan Hill
Lundu Wharf
Lujiang River
GULANGYU
Minzu Rd
Xiagang Jie
Yangwu Lu
Siming Nanlu
YINDOUSHI
Shishan Hill
Huandao Rd
Daxue Rd
Guanhaiyuan Wharf
Gulangyu see detail map
Huandao Rd
Hulishan Fort
Xiamen Port
KEY
Exploring Sights
Hotels, Restaurants, Clubs & Nightlife
0 1 mi
0 1 km
Exploring
Nanputuo Temple 2
Overseas Chinese Museum 3
10,000 Rock Botanical Garden 4
Hong Shan Park 5
Xiamen University/ Museum of Anthropology 1
Zhong Shan Park 6
Restaurants
Dafang Vegetarian 2
Guan Hai Canting/ Lujiang Hotel 3
Huangzehe Peanut Soup Shop 6
Mamma Mia 10
Puzhaolou Vegetarian Restaurant 1
Shuyou Seafood Restaurant 11
Hotels
Lujiang Harbourview Hotel 3
Marco Polo Xiamen 7
Millennium Harbourview Hotel Xiamen 4
Sofitel Plaza Xiamen 12
Clubs and Nightlife
Elite 8
La Bomba 9
Zhongshan Road 5

the Neolithic era, is one of the most popular destinations. It has a very good collection of fossils, ceramics, paintings, and ornaments. It's open daily 8:30 to 11 and 3 to 5. ✉ *End of Siming Nan Lu.*

❹ Surrounding a pretty lake, the **10,000 Rock Botanical Garden** *(Wanshi Zhiwuyuan)* has a fine collection of more than 4,000 species of tropical and subtropical flora, ranging from eucalyptus and bamboo trees to orchids and ferns. There are several pavilions, of which the most interesting are those forming the **Temple of the Kingdom of Heaven** *(Tianjie Si).* ✉ *Huyuan Lu, off Wenyuan Lu* 🎫 *Y10* ⏲ *Daily 8–6.*

> **WIRED ON THE BEACH**
>
> Xiamen has at least a dozen laid-back cafés with wireless networks. Recently, China's largest wine importer, ASC Wines, began pouring a steady stream of fine vino into the island of old Amoy. Yet Xiamen's main attraction is still its subdued beach scene. One of the best places for an endless Xiamen summer is Siming, just east of downtown. Framed by mountains and defined by clean beaches, its sunsets are timeless. The beaches of Gulangyu island are another favorite, since cars have been banned from the isle.

IF YOU HAVE TIME

❸ In the southern part of the city, the **Overseas Chinese Museum** *(Huaqiao Bowuguan)* was founded by the wealthy industrialist Tan Kah-kee. Three halls illustrate, with the help of pictures and documents, personal items, and relics associated with the great waves of emigration from southeastern China during the 19th century. ✉ *493 Siming Nan Lu* ☎ *0592/208–5345* 🎫 *Free* ⏲ *Tues.–Sun. 9:30* AM*–4* PM.

❻ Commemorating Dr. Sun Yat-sen, **Zhong Shan Park** *(Zhong Shan Gong Yuan)* is centered around a statue to the great man. There is a small zoo, lakes, and canals you can explore by paddleboat. The annual Lantern Festival is held here. ✉ *Zhong Shan Lu and Zhenhai Lu* 🎫 *Free.*

OFF THE BEATEN PATH

Jinmen. History buffs will be fascinated by a trip around this remnant of China's bitter civil war. Though barely a stone's throw from mainland China, this island is still controlled by Taiwan. As of this writing only Xiamen residents are allowed to visit Jinmen, so tour boats only come close enough to let you see Taiwanese guards patrolling the shores or call out to the Taiwanese fishermen netting the waters. However, talks are continually underway between the two sides, and it's entirely possible that rules might be relaxed, allowing casual tourists to visit this cold-war outpost. Tours cost about Y80 per person.

Hakka Roundhouses *(Yong Ding Tu Lou).* Legend has it that when these four-story-tall structures were first spotted by the American military, fear spread that they were silos for some unknown gigantic missile. They were created centuries before by the Hakka, or "Guest People," an offshoot of the Han Chinese who settled all over southeastern China. These earthen homes are made of raw earth, glutinous rice, and brown sugar, reinforced with bamboo and wood. They are the most beautiful example of Hakka architecture. The roundhouses are in Yong Ding, 210 km (130 mi) northwest of Xiamen. To get here, take a bus from

Xiamen to Longyan, then transfer to a minibus headed to Yong Ding. ✉ *Yong Ding* 🎫 *Y20.*

WHERE TO EAT

Although Xiamen is known for its excellent seafood, the city's Buddhist population means it has excellent vegetarian cuisine. Xiamen is probably the best place outside of Taiwan to experience Taiwanese cuisine, and many restaurants advertise their *Taiwan Wei Kou* and *Taiwan Xiao Chi,* meaning "Taiwanese flavor" and "Taiwanese snacks."

> **WORD OF MOUTH**
>
> "Xiamen's main attractions are the warren of streets of the old port area, in which it is easy (and pleasant) to get lost, and the islet of Gulang (Gulang Yu), which has the best-preserved collection of treaty port-era mansions in China, and which still permits no cars."
>
> –PeterN_H

¢–$ VEGETARIAN ✕ **Dafang Vegetarian Restaurant.** Across from Nanputuo Temple, this reasonably priced restaurant is popular with students. But don't just come for the low prices—it also has excellent food. Try the sweet and sour soup or the mock duck. English menus are available. ✉ *3 Nanhua Lu* ☎ *0592/209–3236* ▭ *No credit cards.*

$–$$ SEAFOOD ✕ **Guan Hai Canting.** On the rooftop of the waterfront Lujiang Hotel, this terrace restaurant has beautiful views over the bay. The Cantonese chef prepares delicious seafood dishes and dim-sum specialties like sweet pork buns and shrimp dumplings. ✉ *54 Lujiang Lu, across from ferry terminal* ☎ *0592/266–2398* ▭ *AE, MC, V.*

¢ CHINESE FUSION ✕ **Huangzehe Peanut Soup Shop.** Peanuts get the star treatment at this restaurant near the waterfront. Peanut soups, peanut sweets, and even peanut dumplings show off the culinary potential of the humble goober. ✉ *24 Zhongshan Lu* ☎ *0592/212–5825* ▭ *No credit cards.*

$–$$ ITALIAN ✕ **Mamma Mia.** Across from the Marco Polo Xiamen hotel, Mamma Mia serves authentic Italian specialties like risotto, gnocchi, and several different types of pasta. There's also a beautiful bar on the third floor where you can sink into plush chairs. ✉ *1 Jianye Lu* ☎ *0592/536–2662* ▭ *AE, MC, V.*

$–$$ VEGETARIAN ✕ **Puzhaolou Vegetarian Restaurant.** The comings and goings of monks add to the atmosphere at this restaurant next to the Nanputuo Temple. Popular dishes include black-fungus soup with tofu and stewed yams with seaweed. You won't find any English menus, so ask for one of the picture menus. ✉ *Nanputuo Temple, 515 Siming Nan Lu* ☎ *0592/208–5908* ▭ *No credit cards.*

$$–$$$ SEAFOOD ★ ✕ **Shuyou Seafood Restaurant.** Shuyou means "close friend," and that's how you're treated at this upscale establishment. Considered one of the best seafood restaurants in China (and certainly in Xiamen), Shuyou serves fresh seafood in an opulent setting. Downstairs, the tanks are filled with lobster, prawns, and crabs, and upstairs diners feast on seafood dishes cooked in Cantonese and Fujian styles. If you're in the mood for other fare, the restaurant is also known for its excellent Peking duck and goose liver. ✉ *Hubin Bei Lu, between Marco Polo and Sofitel hotels* ☎ *0592/509–8888* ▭ *AE, MC, V.*

WHERE TO STAY

$–$$ **Lujiang Harbourview Hotel.** In a refurbished colonial building, this hotel has an ideal location opposite the ferry pier and the waterfront boulevard. A rooftop-terrace restaurant looks over the straits. Many of the rooms have ocean views. **Pros:** phenomenal location, good prices. **Cons:** limited English is spoken, rooms are small. ✉*54 Lujiang Lu* ☎*0592/202–2922* 🖷*0592/202–4644* *153 rooms, 18 suites* *In-room: safe, Ethernet. In-hotel: 4 restaurants, bar* ▭*AE, MC, V.*

$$$ **Marco Polo Xiamen.** Standing between the historic sights and the commercial district, the Marco Polo has an excellent location. The hotel's glass-roof atrium makes the lobby bar a nice place to relax after a day's sightseeing. Nightly entertainment includes a dance band from the Philippines. The guest rooms are comfortable and well appointed. **Pros:** good location, helpful staff. **Cons:** noise, poor reservation service. ✉*8 Jianye Lu* ☎*0592/509–1888* 🌐*www.marcopolohotels.com* *246 rooms, 38 suites* *In-room: safe, Ethernet. In-hotel: 3 restaurants, bar, pool, gym, no-smoking rooms* ▭*AE, MC, V.*

$$–$$$$ ★ **Millenium Harbourview Hotel Xiamen.** With an excellent location overlooking the harbor, this hotel is among the best in the city. Rooms are spacious and comfortable, and the staff is friendly and attentive. The hotel's restaurants are particularly good, and the first-floor coffee shop is the only place in Xiamen to get a good New York–style deli sandwich. Golfers will want to have a drink at the first-floor bar, which has a small putting green. **Pros:** excellent service, travel agents. **Cons:** noise, some rooms very dark. ✉*12-8 Zhenhai Lu* ☎*0592/202–3333* 🌐*www.millenniumhotels.com/cn/millenniumxiamen/index.html* *334 rooms, 7 suites* *In-room: safe, Ethernet. In-hotel: 4 restaurants, bar, pool, gym, no-smoking rooms* ▭*AE, MC, V.*

$$$–$$$$ **Sofitel Plaza Xiamen.** The newest (and costliest) luxury hotel in Xiamen, the Sofitel Plaza has a beautiful art-deco lobby. Though not on the beach, many of the hotel's nicely appointed guest rooms have a beautiful view of nearby Lake Yuandang. The Oasis Bar is popular with Xiamen's trendy set. The guest rooms, with dark-wood furnishings, are beautiful and modern. **Pros:** convenient location, good service, very clean. **Cons:** far from the beach. ✉*19 Hubin Bei Lu* ☎*0592/507–8888* 🌐*www.sofitel.com* *383 rooms, 48 suites* *In-room: safe, Ethernet. In-hotel: restaurant, bar, pool, gym, airport shuttle, no-smoking rooms* ▭*AE, MC, V.*

NIGHTLIFE AND THE ARTS

The stretch of Zhongshan Lu near the ferry pier is charming in the evening when the colonial-style buildings are lighted with gentle neon. This waterfront promenade is a popular spot for young couples walking arm in arm. There are a few small pubs where people stop for drinks.

The dimly lit **La Bomba** (✉*Jianye Lu, 1 block north of Marco Polo Xiamen hotel* ☎*0592/531–0707*) has live rock bands on the weekends.

The upscale **Elite** (✉*Jianye Lu, 1 block north of Marco Polo Xiamen hotel* ☎*0592/533–0707*) has a dance floor and a lounge where you can check out the crowd.

4

SPORTS AND THE OUTDOORS

Xiamen offers some excellent hiking opportunities. Most notable of these are the hills behind the Nanputuo Temple, where winding paths and stone steps carved into the sheer rock face make for a fairly strenuous climb. For a real challenge, hike from Nanputuo Temple to 10,000 Rock Garden. If you're still in the mood for a climb after spending a few hours enjoying the garden's beautiful landscape, another more serpentine trail (a relic of the Japanese occupation) leads to Xiamen University. The hike takes the better part of an afternoon.

The area around Xiamen has fine public beaches. Sunbathers abound nearly anywhere along Huandao Lu, the road that circles the island.

GULANGYU

5 minutes by boat from Xiamen.

The best way to experience Gulangyu's charm is to explore its meandering streets, stumbling across a particularly distinctive old mansion or the weathered graves of missionaries and merchants. These quiet back alleys are fascinating to wander, with the atmosphere of a quiet Mediterranean city, punctuated by touches of calligraphy or the click of mah-jongg tiles to remind you where you really are. And unlike most Chinese communities, you won't take your life in your hands when crossing the street because cars are banned on Gulangyu. This island is easy to reach by ferry from Xiamen.

GETTING HERE AND AROUND

Boats to the island run from early in the morning until midnight and depart from the ferry terminal across from the Lujiang. Electric buses are available on the island.

BY BOAT AND FERRY Ferry service from the Xiamen Ferry dock starts at 5:45 AM, with departures every 10–15 minutes, and costs Y8. The ferry does not run after midnight, so check the last departure time before you leave Xiamen to avoid getting stranded.

TOURS

The best—and really, the only—way to see Gulangyu is on foot. Take a morning or afternoon to climb up the narrow, winding streets to see the hundreds of colonial-era mansions (ranging from restored to ramshackle) that are the heart of this fabulous treasure trove of late-19th- and early-20th-century architecture. A good guide is Vivian Wang (☎*0592/13959–228225*), a native of the area.

ESSENTIALS

Many sights on Gulangyu charge admission fees, but a tour about the island's electric bus includes admission to all sites included on the tour. Island ATMs are available near major tourist sites, but it is best to do your banking before heading out.

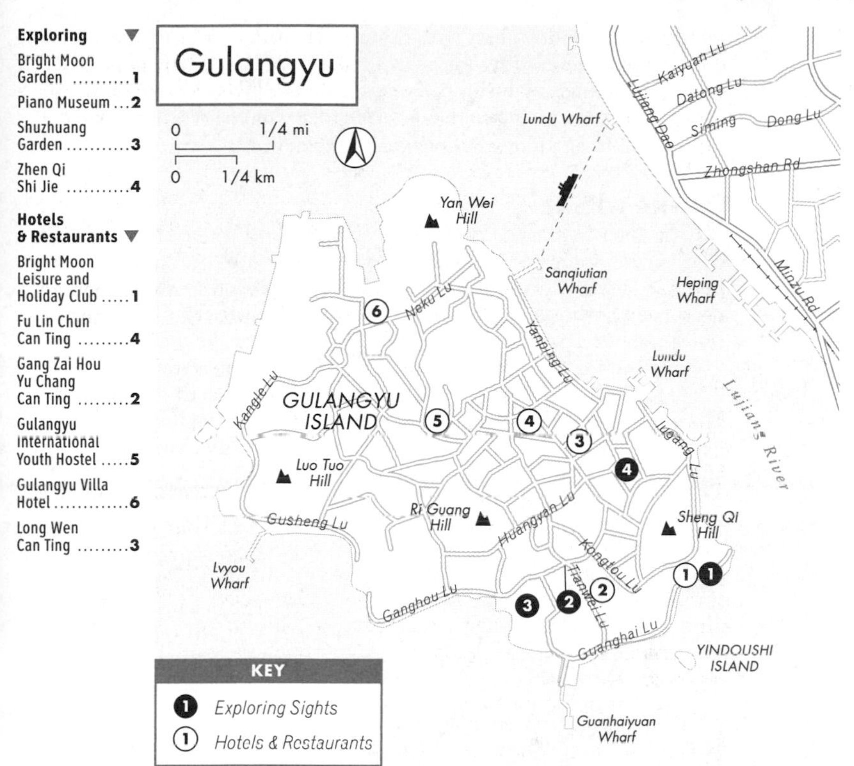

EXPLORING GULANGYU

2 Gulangyu holds a special place in the country's musical history, thanks to the large number of Christian missionaries who called the island home in the late 19th and early 20th centuries. Gulangyu has more pianos per capita than anyplace else in China, with one home in five having one. "Chopsticks" to Chopin—and everything in between—can be heard being played by the next generation's prodigies. The **Piano Museum** *(Island of Drumming Waves)* is a must for any music lover. *⊠45 Huangyan Lu ☎0592/206–0238 🎫Y30 ⏲Daily 8:15–5:15.*

1 From the ferry terminal, turn left and follow oceanfront Tianwei Lu until you come to **Bright Moon Garden** *(Haoyue Yuan)*. The garden is a fitting seaside memorial to Koxinga, and a massive stone statue of the Ming general stares eastward from a perch hanging over the sea. *⊠Tianwei Lu ☎No phone 🎫Y15 ⏲Daily 8–7.*

3 Continuing along Tianwei Lu, you'll come to **Shuzhuang Garden** *(Shuzhuang Huayuan)*. The garden is immaculately kept and dotted with pavilions and bridges, some extending out to rocks just offshore. *⊠Tianwei Lu ☎No phone 🎫Y40 ⏲Daily 8–7.*

4 Skillfully mixing history and oddities, **Zhen Qi Shi Jie** is one of the country's odder museums. Part of the museum displays the usual historical

information about Fujian and Taiwan. The other part is a veritable museum of oddities, offering pickled genetic mutations like two-headed snakes, conjoined twin sheep, and a few live exhibits like gigantic tortoises. The room of ancient Chinese sex toys will please some and mystify others. ⊠*38 Huangyan Lu and 4 Donghua Lu* ☎*0592/206–9933* *Y50* *Daily 8–6.*

WHERE TO EAT

¢–$ SEAFOOD **Fu Lin Chun Can Ting.** Serving home-style seafood cooked to order, this closet-size restaurant is almost always packed with locals during peak hours. If it comes from the sea, you'll find it here, with steamed crab, deep-fried shrimp, and whole fish served in a variety of tantalizing styles. ⊠*109 Long Tou Lu* ☎*0592/206–2847* *No credit cards.*

$ SEAFOOD **Gang Zai Hou Yu Chang Can Ting.** The name of this restaurant means "Behind Gang Zai Beach," which gives you a clue as to the short distance seafood travels from the ocean to the plate. Gang Zai Hou serves excellent oyster soup, steamed crabs, and just about anything else that swims. ⊠*14 Gang Hou Lu* ☎*0592/206–3719* *No credit cards.*

$ SEAFOOD **Long Wen Can Ting.** Serving fresh seafood dishes, this large restaurant near the ferry terminal is popular with tourists from Taiwan. The chef unabashedly admits to being an enthusiastic consumer of his own cuisine—never a bad sign. Specialties include whole steamed fish, oyster soup, and a wide variety of seafood dishes. The decor is traditional Chinese. ⊠*21 Long Tou Lu* ☎*0592/206–6369* *No credit cards.*

WHERE TO STAY

$ **Bright Moon Leisure and Holiday Club.** Located in Bright Moon Garden, this lovely little hotel consists of nine wooden houses perched on seaside cliffs. What the place lacks for in amenities it more than makes up with amazing views. **Pros:** quiet, fantastic views. **Cons:** simple amenities, limited English. ⊠*3 Zhangzhou Lu,* ☎*0592/206–9730* *0592/206–3401* *15 rooms* *In-hotel: beachfront, laundry service, no elevator* *AE, MC, V.*

¢ **Gulangyu International Youth Hostel.** If you're strapped for cash, you'd be hard-pressed to find cheaper accommodations. In the former German Embassy, this place retains a bit of its Bavarian feel. High-ceiling rooms have beds, desks, and antique-lighting fixtures. **Pros:** extremely inexpensive. **Cons:** simple accommodations, no air-conditioning. ⊠*18 Lu Jiao Lu,* ☎*0592/206–6066* *0592/206–6022* *6 rooms* *In-room: no a/c (some). In-hotel: laundry facilities, public Internet, no elevator* *No credit cards.*

¢ **Gulangyu Villa Hotel.** On the west side of the island, this peaceful hotel has clean but simple rooms. There is a decent Chinese restaurant on the premises. **Pros:** quiet and clean. **Cons:** limited English. ⊠*14 Gusheng Lu,* ☎*0592/206–0160 or 0592/206–3280* *0592/206–0165* *75 rooms* *In-hotel: restaurant, laundry service* *No credit cards.*

ENGLISH	PIN YIN	CHINESE CHARACTERS
ZHEJIANG	**ZHÈJIĀNG**	**浙江**
HANGZHOU	Hángzhōu	杭州
Baidi	Báidī	白堤
China National Silk Museum	Zhōngguósīchóubówùguǎn	中国丝绸博物馆
China Silk City	Zhōngguósīchóuchéng	中国丝绸城
China Tea Museum	Zhōngguócháyèbówùguǎn	中国茶叶博物馆
Dong Po Hotel	Dōngpōbīnguǎn	东坡宾馆
Dragon Hotel	Huánglóngfàndiàn	黄龙饭店
Dragon Well Tea Park	Lóngjǐngwénchá	龙井闻茶
Evening Sunlight at Thunder Peak Pagoda	Léifēngxīzhào	雷锋夕照
Fulintang	Fúlíntáng	福林堂
Gushan Island	Gūshāndǎo	孤山岛
Hangzhou Aquarium	Hángzhōuhǎidǐshìjiè	杭州海底世界
Hangzhou Overseas Chinese Hotel	Hángzhōuhuáqiáofàndiàn	杭州华侨饭店
Huanglong Dong Yuanyuan Mingsu Yuan Theater	Huánglóngdòngyuányuánbínsúyuán	黄龙洞圆缘民俗园
Hyatt Regency Hangzhou	Hángzhōukǎiyuèjiǔdiàn	杭州凯悦酒店
Kana Pub	Kánàjiǔbā	卡那酒吧
Lingyin Si Vegetarian Restaurant	Língyǐnsìsùzhāi	灵隐寺素斋
Liulang Wenying Park	Liǔlàngwényínggōngyuán	柳浪闻莺公园
Louwailou Restaurant	Lóuwàilóu	楼外楼
Moon Mountain	Yùelúnshān	月轮山
night market	Yèshì	夜市
Orioles Singing in the Willow Waves	Liǔlàngwényíng	柳浪闻莺
Pagoda of Six Harmonies	Liùhétǎ	六和塔
Peak That Flew from Afar	Fēiláifēng	飞来峰
Precious Stone Hill	Bǎoshíshān	宝石山
Protecting Chu Pagoda	Bǎoshūtǎ	宝俶塔
Redstar Hotel	Hángzhōuhóngxīngwénhuàdàshà	杭州红星文化大厦
Running Tiger Dream Spring	Hǔpǎomèngquán	虎跑梦泉
Seal Engraver's Society	Xīlìngyìnshè	西泠印社
Shamrock	Ai4er3lan2pi2jiu3ba1	爱尔兰啤酒吧
Shangri-La Hotel Hangzhou	Hángzhōuxiānggélǐlāfàndiàn	杭州香格里拉饭店
Sofitel Westlake Hangzhou	Hángzhōusuǒfēitèxīhúdàjiǔdiàn	杭州索菲特西湖大酒店
Sudi	Sūdī	苏堤

ENGLISH	PIN YIN	CHINESE CHARACTERS
Temple of the Soul's Retreat	Língyǐnsì	灵隐寺
Three Pools Reflecting the Moon	Sāntányìnyuè	三潭印月
Wanghu Hotel	Wànghúbīnguǎn	望湖宾馆
Xihu	Xīhú	西湖
Xihu Longjing Tea Company	Xīhúlóngjǐngcháyègōngsī	西湖龙井茶叶公司
Yellow Dragon Cave	Huánglóngdòng	黄龙洞
Yue Fei Mausoleum	Yuèfēimù	岳飞墓
Zhejiang Provincial Museum	Zhéjiāngshěngbówùguǎn	浙江省博物馆
Zhiweiguan Restaurant	Zhīwèiguān	知味观
Zhongshan Gongyuan	Zhōngshāngōngyuán	中山公园
SHAOXING	Shāoxìng	绍兴
Bazi Qiao Bridge	Bāzìqiáo	八字桥
CAAC	Zhōngguómínháng	中国民航
Cai Yuanpei's House	Càiyuánpéigùjūn	蔡元培故居
Catholic Church of St. Joseph	Tiānzhǔjiàotáng	天主教堂
Dragonair	Gǎnglónghángkōnggōngsī	港龙航空公司
East Bus Station	Hángzhōuqìchēdōngzhàn	杭州汽车东站
East Lake	Dōnghú	东湖
Hangzhou International Airport	Hángzhōuxiāoshānguójìjīchǎng	杭州萧山国际机场
Hangzhou Red Cross Hospital	Hángzhōuhóngshízìhuìyīyuàn	杭州红十字会医院
Hangzhou Travel and Tourism Bureau	Hángzhōushìlǚyóujún	杭州市旅游局
Lu Xun Family Home	Lǔxùngùjūn	鲁迅故居
Minhang Ticket Office	Mínhángshòupiàochù	民航售票处
North Bus Station	Hángzhōuqìchēběizhàn	杭州汽车北站
Sanwei Jiulou	Sānwèijiǔlóu	三味酒楼
Shaoxing People's Hospital	Shàoxīngrénmínyīyuàn	绍兴人民医院
Shaoxing International Hotel	Shàoxìngguójìdàjiǔdiàn	绍兴国际大酒店
Shaoxing Xianheng Hotel	Shàoxìngxúnhēngdàjiǔdiàn	绍兴咸亨大酒店
West Bus Station	Hángzhōuqìchēxīzhàn	杭州汽车西站
Xianheng Winehouse	Xánhēngjiǔdiàn	咸亨酒店
Zhejiang CITS	Zhèjiāngzhōngguóguójìlǚxíngshè	浙江中国国际旅行社
Zhejiang Medical University Affiliated Hospital No. 1	Zhèjiāngyīkēdàxuédìyīfùshǔyī yuàn	浙江医科大学第一附属医院
Zhejiang Women's International Travel Service	Zhèjiāngfùnǚguójìlǚxíngshè	浙江妇女国际旅行社
Zhou Enlai Family Home	Zhōuēnláigùjūn	周恩来故居

ENGLISH	PIN YIN	CHINESE CHARACTERS
FUJIAN	FÚ JIÀN	福建
XIAMEN CITY	xià mén shì	厦门市
10,000 Rock Botanical Garden	wàn shí zhí wù yuán	万石植物园
Dafang Vegetarian	dà fāng sù shí guǎn	大方素食馆
Elite	míng shì xiàn chǎng yīn yuè jiǔ bā	名仕现场音乐酒吧
Guan Hai Canting	guān hǎi cān tīng	观海餐厅
Hakka Roundhouses	kè jiā tǔ lóu	客家土楼
Hong Shan Park	huáng shān gōng yuán	黄山公园
Huangzehe Peanut Soup Shop	huáng zé hé huā shēng tāng diàn	黄则和花生汤店
Jinmen	jīn mén	金门
La Bomba	là bèng bā	辣蹦吧
Lujiang Hotel	lù jiāng bīn guǎn	鹭江宾馆
Nanputuo Temple	nán pǔ tuó sì	南普陀寺
Overseas Chinese Museum	huá qiáo bó wù guǎn	华侨博物馆
Puzhaolou Vegetarian Restaurant	pǔ zhào lóu sù cài guǎn	普照楼素菜馆
Shuyou Seafood Restaurant	shū yǒu hǎi xiān dà jiǔ lóu	舒友海鲜大酒楼
Sofitel Plaza Xiamen	suǒ fēi tè dà jiǔ diàn	索菲特大酒店
Xiamen University	xià mén dà xué	厦门大学
Zhong Shan Park	zhōng shān gōng yuán	中山公园
GULANGYU	gǔ làng yǔ	鼓浪屿
American Express	měi guó yùn tōng	美国运通
Bank of China	zhōng guó yín háng	中国银行
Bright Moon Garden	hǎo yuè yuán	皓月园
Bright Moon leisure and Holiday Club***	hǎo yuè xiū xián dù jià jū lè bù	皓月休闲度假俱乐部
China Travel Service	zhōng guó lv3 xíng shè	中国旅行社
CITS	zhōng guó guó jì lǚ xíng shè	中国国际旅行社
Dragonair	gǎng lóng háng kōng	港龙航空
Fu Lin Chun Can Ting	fú lín chūn cān tīng	福林春餐厅
Gang Zai Hou Yu Chang Can Ting	gǎng zái hòu yù chǎng cān tīng	港仔后浴场餐厅
Gulangyu International Youth Hostel	gǔ làng yǔ guó jì qīng nián lv3 shè	鼓浪屿国际青年旅舍
Gulangyu Villa Hotel	gǔ làng bié shù fàn diàn	鼓浪别墅饭店
Holiday Inn Crowne Plaza Har-bourview	hǎi jǐng huáng guān jià rì jiǔ diàn	海景皇冠假日酒店

ENGLISH	PIN YIN	CHINESE CHARACTERS
Long Hai White Beach Ancient Crater	lóng hăi bái tán huŏ shān kŏu	龙海白滩火山口
Long Wen Can Ting	lóng wén cān tīng	龙文餐厅
Long-distance bus station	cháng tú qì chē zhàn	长途汽车站
Marco Polo Xiamen	mă kĕ bō luó dà jiŭ diàn	马可波罗大酒店
Museum of Anthropology	rén lèi bó wù guăn	人类博物馆
Piano Museum	gāng qín bó wù guăn	钢琴博物馆
Public Security Bureau	gōng ān jú	公安局
Quanzhou	quán zhōu	泉州
Shuzhuang Garden	shū zhuāng huā yuán	菽庄花园
Temple of the Kingdom of Heaven	tiān jiè sì	天届寺
Tourist Complaint Hotline	lǚ yóu tóu sù rè xiàn	旅游投诉热线
Wanshi Botanical Garden	wàn shí zhí wù yuán	万石植物园
Zhen Qi Shi Jie	zhēn qí shì jiè	珍奇世界
Zhongshan Lu	zhōng shān lù	中山路

Hong Kong

CULTURE, COMMERCE, HIGH STYLE

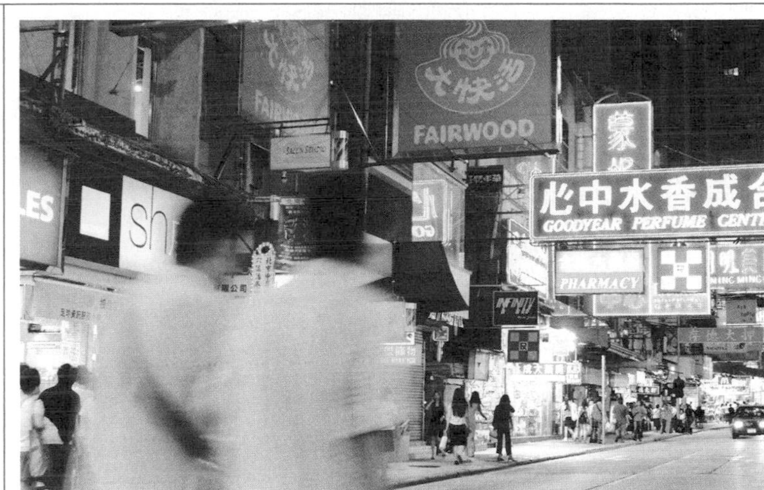

Retail temples in Kowloon; truly spiritual sights aren't far away, though.

WORD OF MOUTH

"We walked back along Shanghai Street, then checked out the markets for flowers, vegetables, seafood and bakeries on Reclamation Street. Ended up on Nathan Road, taking in the scene, the crowds, and the shops, enjoying our first day in Hong Kong."

—wiselindag

WELCOME TO HONG KONG

TOP REASONS TO GO

★ **Harbor Views:** The skyline that launched a thousand postcards. . . . See it on a stroll along the Tsim Sha Tsui waterfront, from a Star Ferry crossing the harbor, or from the top of Victoria Peak.

★ **Dim Sum:** As you bite into a moist *siu mai* it dawns on you why everyone says you haven't done dim sum until you've done it in Hong Kong.

★ **Cultural Immersion:** The Hong Kong Heritage Museum chronicles the city's history. On a Lantau Island hill, see the 242-ton Tian Tan Buddha statue sits in the lotus position beside the Po Lin Buddhist Monastery.

★ **Shopping as Religion:** At Kowloon's street markets, clothes, electronics, and souvenirs compete for space with food carts. Antiques fill windows along Hollywood Road.

★ **Horsing Around:** Every year, Hong Kongers gamble over US$10 billion, and the Happy Valley Racetrack is one of their favorite places to do it. As the horses pound along, thousands of punters scream themselves into a frenzy.

1 Hong Kong Island. It's only 78 square km (30 square mi), but it's where the action is, from high finance to nightlife to luxury shopping. The commercial districts—Western, Central, and Wan Chai—are on the north coast. Southside is home to small towns, quiet coves, and reserve areas. A 20-minute taxi ride from Central can have you breathing fresh air and seeing only greenery.

2 Kowloon. This peninsula on the Chinese mainland is just across from Central and bounded in the north by the string of mountains that give it its poetic name: *gau lung,* "nine dragons" (there are eight mountains, the ninth dragon was the emperor who named them). Kowloon—particularly the busy Tsim Sha Tsui district on the southern tip—has many of the territory's best hotels and a mind-boggling range of shopping options.

3 New Territories. The expanse between Kowloon and the Chinese border feels far removed from urban congestion and rigor. Nature reserves (many with great trails), temples, and traditional Hakka villages fill its 200 square mi. Conversely public housing projects have led to the creation of new town.

Ping Shan
Ha Tsuen
Lung Kwu Tan
Tuen Mun
TO GUANGZHOU
Airport Express
TO MACAU
CHEK LAP KOK
Hong Kong International Airport
Discovery Bay
LANTAU ISLAND
Mui Wo
4
Po Lin Monastery
Tian Tan Buddha
Sunset Peak 869m
Cheung Sha
Shek Pik
Tai Long Wan
TO MACAU
SHEK KWU CHAU

4 Outer Islands. Off the west coast of Hong Kong Island lie Lamma, Cheung Chau, and Lantau islands. Lantau, which is home to the Tian Tau Buddha, is connected by ferries to Hong Kong Island and by a suspension bridge to west Kowloon. More than 200 other islands also belong to Hong Kong.

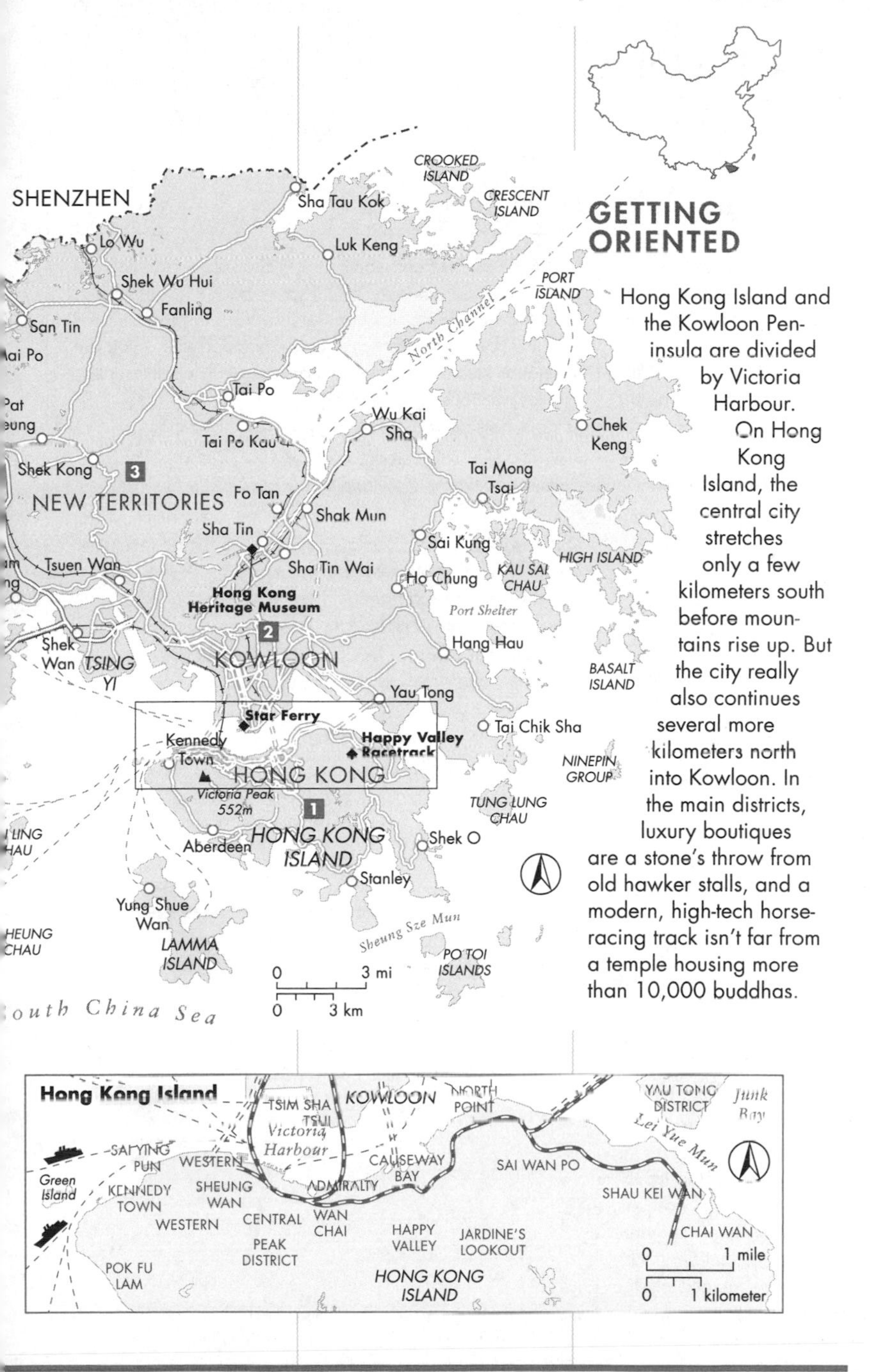

GETTING ORIENTED

Hong Kong Island and the Kowloon Peninsula are divided by Victoria Harbour.

On Hong Kong Island, the central city stretches only a few kilometers south before mountains rise up. But the city really also continues several more kilometers north into Kowloon. In the main districts, luxury boutiques are a stone's throw from old hawker stalls, and a modern, high-tech horse-racing track isn't far from a temple housing more than 10,000 buddhas.

HONG KONG PLANNER

Looks Deceive

On the surface it seems that every building is a sculpture of glass and steel and every pedestrian is hurrying to a meeting. But look past the shiny new surfaces to the ancient culture that gives the city its exotic flavor and its citizens their unique outlook.

Wording It Right

Learn a few basic Cantonese expressions like *"lei-ho?"* ("hi, how are you?") and *"mm-goi sai"* ("thanks very much"). The official languages are Chinese and English; most residents speak Cantonese. Mandarin—the "common language" of mainland China—is gaining in popularity here and in Macau, where the official languages are Chinese and Portuguese.

In hotels, major restaurants, and large stores, most people speak English. Many taxi and bus drivers and staffers in small shops, cafés, and market stalls do not.

Ask for directions from MTR employees or English-speaking policemen, identifiable by the red strips on their epaulets. Get your concierge to write down your destination in Chinese if you're headed off the main trail.

Navigating

- Hong Kong's streets seem utterly chaotic, but getting lost in Central is an achievement. If you manage it, get your bearings by looking up: orient yourself using the waterfront Two IFC skyscraper. In Kowloon, remember where you are in relation to Nathan Road, where the MTR (underground railway) stations are.
- The MTR, which links most of the areas you'll want to visit, is quick, safe, clean, and very user-friendly. The KCR transit system links Kowloon with areas in the New Territories.
- Pay with a rechargeable Octopus card. You can use it on the MTR, KCR, buses, trams, the Star Ferry, the Peak Tram—even at vending machines, convenience stores, fast-food restaurants, and the racetrack.
- It's often not worth taking the MTR for one stop, as stations are close. Walk or take a bus or tram.
- Most MTR stations have multiple exits, so consult the detailed station maps to determine which exit lets you out closest to your destination.
- If you're crossing Central, use the covered walkways that link its main buildings, thus avoiding stoplights, exhaust fumes, and weather conditions.
- On Hong Kong Island, Queen's Road changes its suffix every so often, so you get Queen's Road East, Queen's Road Central, and Queen's Road West. These suffixes, however, don't exactly correspond with the districts, so part of Queen's Road Central is actually in Western. As street numbers start again with each new section, be sure you know which part you're headed for, or better still, the intersecting street. The same goes for Des Voeux Road.

Good for Kids

Put the Zoological and Botanical Gardens, the Symphony of Lights, the Peak Tram, and a skyscraper climb atop your list. The Hong Kong Heritage Museum has a gallery where 4- to 10-year-olds can dress up in Hakka clothes and reconstruct pottery.

Ocean Park has a balance of toned-down thrills and high-octane rides, so you could take 3- or 4-year-olds right through to teenagers. Older kids might enjoy seeing candy-pink dolphins in their natural habitat on a Dolphin-watch half-day trip, and tropical birds fill the walk-through Edward Youde Aviary in Hong Kong Park.

Mall rats can make plenty of like-minded local friends at Times Square, Pacific Place, and Kowloon Tong's Festival Walk, all of which are safe places to wander.

Online Travel Tools

For a guide to what's happening in Hong Kong, check out the Hong Kong Tourist Board's (HKTB's) excellent site. For weather info, check out the Hong Kong Observatory. For political information plus news and interesting business links try the Hong Kong government site.

All About Hong Kong **Business in Hong Kong** (*www.gov.hk/en/business*): government-run site packed with advice. **Centamap** (*www.centamap.com*): online Hong Kong street maps so detailed they give street numbers and building names. **Hong Kong Government** (*www.gov.hk*). **Hong Kong Tourist Board** (*HKTB www.discoverhongkong.com*). **Hong Kong Weather** (*www.weather.gov.hk*).

Cultural Activities **HK Magazine** (*www.asia-city.com*): online version of a quirky weekly rag with the lowdown on just about everything happening in town. **Hong Kong Film** (*www.lovehkfilm.com*): all you need to know about Hongkollywood. **Hong Kong Leisure and Cultural Services Department** (*www.lcsd.gov.hk*): access Web sites for all of Hong Kong's museums and parks through this government portal.

Local Insight **Eat Drink Hong Kong** (*www.eatdrinkhongkong.com*): excellent online guide to Hong Kong's bars and restaurants. **Gay Hong Kong** (*www.gayhk.com*): comprehensive guide to the local scene. **Geoexpat** (*www.geoexpat.com*): local know-how from Hong Kong's large expat community. **Hong Kong Outdoors** (*www.hkoutdoors.com*): *the* authority on hiking, camping, and all things wild in Hong Kong.

When to Go

Hong Kong's high season, October through late December, sees sunny, dry days and cool, comfortable nights. January, February, and sometimes early March are cool and dank, with long periods of overcast skies. March and April can be either chilly and miserable or sunny and beautiful. By May the temperature is consistently warm and comfortable.

June through September are the cheapest months for one reason: they coincide with the hot, sticky, and very rainy typhoon (hurricane) season. Hong Kong is prepared for blustery assaults; if a big storm approaches, the airwaves crackle with information, and your hotel will post the appropriate signals (a No. 10 signal indicates the worst of winds, and a black warning is the equivalent for rain). This is serious business—bamboo scaffolding can come hurtling through the streets like spears, ships can sink in the harbor, and large areas of the territory can flood. Museums, shops, and transport shut down at signal No. 8.

HONG KONG TEMPERATURES

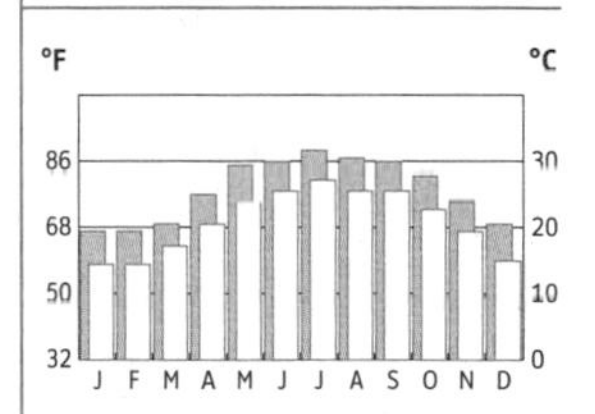

HONG KONG PLANNER

The Octopus

Public transportation options are many and varied—all are good, too. An "Octopus" stored-value card is by far the most convenient way to get around Hong Kong. It's used on all forms of public transport: you just swipe it over the ticket-gate sensor to deduct your fare, which will be cheaper than a regular one. You can buy an Octopus card (☎ *2266–2222* 🌐 *www.octopuscards.com*) in any MTR, KCR, or Airport Express Station. They cost HK$150, of which HK$50 is a refundable deposit, and the other HK$100 is for you to use. (If you return them in less than a month, you forfeit HK$7 of your deposit as a processing fee.) You can refill the cards at any ticket counter, at speedy machines in stations, or at a 7-11 or Wellcome supermarket, where you can also use them to pay for purchases.

Getting There

By Air. The sleek **Hong Kong International Airport (HKG)** (☎ *852/2181–8888* 🌐 *www.hkairport.com*) is universally referred to as Chek Lap Kok, which is where it's located. **Cathay Pacific** (☎ *800/233–2742 in U.S., 2747–1888 in Hong Kong* 🌐 *www.cathay-usa.com*) is Hong Kong's flagship carrier. Cathay has nonstop flights from Los Angeles and San Francisco on the west coast and from New York–JFK on the east. **Singapore Airlines** (☎ *800/742–3333 in U.S., 852/2520–2233 in Hong Kong* 🌐 *www.singaporeair.com*) offers direct flights to San Francisco and Newark. **Continental** (☎ *800/231–0856 in U.S., 852/3198–5777 in Hong Kong* 🌐 *www.continental.com*) also has a nonstop flight to Hong Kong from Newark.

Ground Transportation. The **Airport Express** train service (☎ *2881–8888 for MTR hotline* 🌐 *www.mtr.com.hk*) is the quickest way to and from the airport. High-speed trains whisk you to Kowloon in 19 minutes and Central in 24 minutes. **Citybus** (☎ *2873–0818* 🌐 *www.nwstbus.com.hk*) runs five buses ("A" precedes the bus number) from Chek Lap Kok to popular destinations. Taxis from the airport cost around HK$340 for Hong Kong Island destinations and HK$270 for Kowloon destinations, plus HK$5 per piece of luggage stored in the trunk. Two limo services in the arrivals hall, **Parklane** (☎ *2261–0303* 🌐 *www.hongkonglimo.com*) and **Intercontinental** (☎ *2261–2155* 🌐 *www.trans-island.com.hk*), range from HK$500 to HK$600.

The Ferry Experience

The **Star Ferry** (☎ *2367–7065* 🌐 *www.starferry.com.hk*) is a Hong Kong icon that's sailed across the harbor since 1888. Double-bowed, green-and-white vessels connect Central and Wan Chai with Kowloon in seven minutes, daily from 6:30 AM to 11:30 PM; the ride costs HK$2.20.

New World First Ferry (NWFF) (☎ *2131–8181* 🌐 *www.nwff.com.hk*) runs nine routes from Central to the islands of Lantau and Cheung Chau.

Getting Around

By Bus. A network of double-decker buses covers most of Hong Kong. When determining bus direction, buses ending with the letter "L" eventually connect to the Kowloon–Canton Railway; buses ending with the letter "M" connect to an MTR station; "A" enders go to the airport; and buses ending with the letter "X" are express.

Bus Information Citybus (☎ *2873–0818* 🌐 *www.citybus.com.hk*); Hong Kong Island, cross-harbor and airport routes. **Kowloon Motor Bus** (*KMB* ☎ *2745–4466* 🌐 *www.kmb.com.hk*) mainly serves Kowloon and New Territories. **Long Win Bus Company** (☎ *2261–2791* 🌐 *www.kmb.com.hk*) serves north Lantau, including Tung Chung. **New World First Bus** (☎ *2136–8888* 🌐 *www.nwfb.com.hk*) runs services on Hong Kong Island and in New Kowloon.

By Car. Frankly, you'd be mad to rent a car on Hong Kong Island or Kowloon. Maniac drivers, driving on the left, and traffic jams make driving here severely stress-inducing.

Heavy daytime traffic in Central and Tsim Sha Tsui means taxis aren't the best option. Outside these areas, or after dark, they're much more useful. Many drivers don't speak English so have your destination written in Chinese.

Information Hawk Rent-a-Car (☎ *2516–9822* 🌐 *www.hawkrentacar.com.hk*). **Parklane Limousine** (☎ *2730–0662* 🌐 *www.hongkonglimo.com*) rents Mercedes with drivers.

By Subway and Train. By far the best way to get around Hong Kong is on the Mass Transit Railway or MTR, which now provides all subway and train services in Hong Kong. Subways run every two to five minutes between 6 AM and 1 AM daily. Station entrances are marked with a dark red circle symbol containing the outline of a person with arms and legs outstretched in white.

You buy tickets from ticket machines or from English-speaking workers at the counters. Fares range from HK$3.60 to HK$23.50. A special Tourist MTR One-Day Pass (HK$50) allows you unlimited rides in a day.

The train network connects Kowloon to the eastern and western New Territories. Trains run every 5 to 8 minutes. Fares range from HK$3.70 to HK$47.50; you can pay by Octopus card or buy tickets from sales counters or ticket machines.

Information MTR (☎ *2881–8888* 🌐 *www.mtr.com.hk*).

Tramming it

Peak Tram. The **Peak Tram** (☎ *2849–6754* 🌐 *www.thepeak.com.hk*) is actually a funicular railway. Since 1888 it's been rattling up the 1,207 feet the hill from Central to Victoria Peak tram terminus. A steep ascent, on a clear day it offers fabulous panoramas. Both residents and tourists use it; most passengers board at the lower terminus between Garden Road and Cotton Tree Drive. (The tram has five stations.) The fare is HK$22 one way, HK$33 round-trip, and it runs every 15 minutes from 7 AM to midnight daily. A shuttle bus runs between the lower terminus and the Star Ferry.

Street Trams. Hong Kong Tramways (☎ *2548–7102* 🌐 *www.hktramways.com*) runs old-fashioned double-decker trams along the north shore of Hong Kong Island. Routes start in Kennedy Town (in the west), and go all the way through Central, Wan Chai, Causeway Bay, North Point, and Quarry Bay to Shau Kei Wan. A branch line turns off in Wan Chai toward Happy Valley, where horse races are held in season.

Destinations are marked on the front of each tram; board at the back and get off at the front, paying HK$2 regardless of distance (by Octopus or with exact change) as you leave. Although trams move slowly, for short hops between Central and Western or Admiralty they can be quicker than the MTR.

EXPLORING HONG KONG

By Victoria Patience and Eva Chui Loiterton
Updated by Cherise Fong

TO STAND ON THE TIP of Kowloon Peninsula and look across the harbor to the full expanse of the Hong Kong Island skyline is to see the triumph of ambition over fate. Whereas it took Paris and London 10 to 20 generations and New York six to build the spectacular cities seen today, in Hong Kong almost everything you see was built in the time since today's young investment bankers were born.

Hong Kong Island and Kowloon are divided physically and psychologically by Victoria Harbour. On Hong Kong Island, the central city goes only a few kilometers south into the island before mountains rise up, but on the Kowloon side, the city stretches several more kilometers north. In the main districts and neighborhoods, luxury boutiques are a stone's throw from old hawker stalls, and a modern, high-tech horse-racing track isn't far from a temple housing more than 10,000 buddhas.

If you're on Hong Kong Island and feeling disoriented, remember that the water is always north; in Kowloon it's always south. Central, Admiralty, and Wan Chai, the island's main business districts, are opposite Tsim Sha Tsui on the Kowloon Peninsula. West of Central are Sheung Wan and the other (mainly residential) neighborhoods that make up Western. Central backs onto the slopes of Victoria Peak, so the districts south of it—the Midlevels and the Peak—look down on it. Causeway Bay, North Point, Quarry Bay, Shau Kei Wan, and Chai Wan East run east along the shore after Wan Chai. Developments on the south side of Hong Kong Island are scattered: the beach towns of Shek O and Stanley sit on two peninsulas on the southeast; high-tech Cyberport, industrial Aberdeen, and Ap Lei Chau are to the west.

Kowloon's southern tip is the Tsim Sha Tsui district, which gives way to Jordan, Yau Ma Tei, Mong Kok, and Prince Edward. Northeast are the New Kowloon districts of Kowloon Tong, Kowloon City, and Wong Tai Sin, beyond which lie the eastern New Territories—mostly made up of mountainous country parks and fishing villages. The Sai Kung Peninsula juts out on the east, and Sha Tin New Town is north of New Kowloon, over Lion Rock Mountain. The Kowloon–Canton Railway and a highway run north of this to the Chinese border at Lo Wu.

PASSPORTS AND VISAS

Citizens of the United States need only a valid passport to enter Hong Kong for stays up to three months. You need at least six months' validity on your passport before traveling to Asia. Upon arrival, officials at passport control will give you a Hong Kong entry slip. Keep this slip safe; you must present it with your passport for your return trip home. If you're planning to pop over the border into mainland China, you must first get a visa.

SAFETY

Hong Kong is an incredibly safe place—day and night. The police maintain law and order, but a few pickpockets are still about, especially in Tsim Sha Tsui. So avoid carrying large amounts of cash or valuables with you, and you should have no problems.

Nearly all consumer dissatisfaction in Hong Kong stems from the electronics retailers in Tsim Sha Tsui. Get some reference prices online before buying, and always check the contents of boxed items before you leave the shop.

ESSENTIALS

Consulate U.S. Consulate General (✉ *26 Garden Rd., Central* ☎ *2523–9011* 🌐 *www.usconsulate.org.hk*).

Emergency Contacts Police, fire and ambulance (☎ *999*). **Hong Kong Police and Taxi Complaint Hotline** (☎ *2527–7177*).

Hospitals and Clinics Caritas Medical Centre (public) (✉ *111 Wing Hong St., Sham Shui Po, Kowloon* ☎ *3408–7911* 🌐 *www.ha.org.hk*). **Hong Kong Adventist Hospital** (private) (✉ *40 Stubbs Rd., Midlevels, Western* ☎ *2574–6211* 🌐 *www.hkah.org.hk*). **Hong Kong Central Hospital** (private) (✉ *1 Lower Albert Rd., Central* ☎ *2522–3141* 🌐 *www.hkch.org*). **Prince of Wales Hospital** (public) (✉ *30–32 Ngan Shing St., Sha Tin, New Territories* ☎ *2632–2211* 🌐 *www.ha.org.hk/pwh*). **Queen Elizabeth Hospital** (public) (✉ *30 Gascoigne Rd., Yau Ma Tei, Kowloon* ☎ *2958–8888*). **Queen Mary Hospital** (public) (✉ *102 Pok Fu Lam Rd., Pok Fu Lam, Western* ☎ *2855–3838* 🌐 *www.ha.org.hk/qmh*).

Pharmacies Watsons (☎ *2868–4388*).

Postal Services General Post Office (✉ *2 Connaught Rd., Central* ☎ *2921–2222* 🌐 *www.hongkongpost.com*). **Kowloon Central Post Office** (✉ *405 Nathan Rd., Tsim Tsa Shui*). **DHL** (☎ *2400–3388* 🌐 *www.dhl.com.hk*). **Federal Express** (☎ *2730–3333* 🌐 *www.fedex.com/hk_english*). **UPS** (☎ *2735–3535* 🌐 *www.ups.com*).

WESTERN

Western has been called Hong Kong's Chinatown, and though it's a strange-sounding epithet, there's a reason for it. The area is light-years from the dazzle of Central, despite being just down the road. And although developers are making short work of the traditional architecture, Western's colonial buildings, rattling trams, old-world medicine shops, and lively markets still recall bygone times.

THE TERRITORY

The Midlevels Escalator forms a handy boundary between Western and Central. Several main thoroughfares run parallel to the shore, each farther up the slope: Des Voeux Road (where the trams run), Queen's Road, Hollywood Road (where SoHo starts), and Caine Road (where the Midlevels begin). As to how far west Western goes, it technically reaches all the way to Kennedy Town, where the tram lines end, but there isn't much worth noting beyond Sheung Wan.

GETTING AROUND

The most atmospheric way to Sheung Wan is on a tram along Des Voeux Road. From Central or Admiralty, this is probably the quickest mode, too: no traffic, no subway lines, or endless underground walks. There are stops every two or three blocks. In addition, the Sheung Wan MTR station brings you within spitting distance of Western Market.

The Midlevels Escalator is fun up as far as SoHo. If you're going farther, take a bus or a cab it can take a good 20 minutes to reach the top. Buses 3, 40, and 40M run between the university and the IFC in Central, as does green Minibus 8. Both pass the top of Ladder Street. Expect a taxi from Central to the Midlevels to cost HK$20.

SIGHTS

❶ ★ **Hong Kong University Museum and Art Gallery.** Chinese harp music and a faint smell of incense float through its rooms. The small but excellent collection of Chinese antiquities includes ceramics and bronzes, some dating from 3,000 BC; fine paintings; lacquerware; and carvings in jade, stone, and wood. There are some superb ancient pieces: ritual vessels, decorative mirrors, and painted pottery. The museum has the world's largest collection of Nestorian crosses, dating from the Mongol Period (1280–1368). These belonged to a heretical Christian sect who came to China from the Middle East during the Tang Dynasty (618–907).

Usually two or three temporary exhibitions are on display: contemporary artists who work with traditional media are often featured. ■ **TIP→ Don't miss part of the museum: the collection is spread between the T. T. Tsui Building and the Fung Ping Shan Building, which you access via a first-floor footbridge.** The museum is out-of-the-way—20 minutes from Central via Buses 3A or 40M, or a 15-minute uphill walk from Sheung Wan MTR—but it's a must for the true Chinese-art lover. ✉ *94 Bonham Rd., Pokfulam, Western* ☎ *2241–5500* 🌐 *www.hku.hk/hkumag* 🎫 *Free* 🕒 *Mon.–Sat. 9:30–6, Sun. 1–6.*

❸ **Man Mo Temple.** It's believed to be Hong Kong Island's oldest temple, though no one knows exactly when it was built—the consensus is sometime around the arrival of the British in 1841. It's dedicated to the Taoist gods of literature and of war: Man, who wears green, and Mo, dressed in red. A haze of incense fills the small building—you first catch the fragrance a block away. Huge spirals of the stuff coil down from the ceiling as food for the ancestors. The temple bell, cast in Canton in 1847, and the drum next to it are sounded to attract the gods' attention when a prayer is being offered—give it a ring to make sure yours are heard. ■ **TIP→ To check your fortune, stand in front of the altar, ask a question, select a small bamboo cylinder, and shake it until a stick falls out. The number on the stick corresponds to a written fortune. Then go next door, where an English-speaking fortune-teller can tell you what it means for HK$20.** ✉ *Hollywood Rd. at Ladder St., Western* 🕒 *Daily 8–6* Ⓜ *Sheung Wan, Exit A2.*

EXPERIENCES

UPWARD MOBILITY

❺ The unimaginatively named Midlevels is midway up the hill between Victoria Peak and the Western and Central districts. A practical human mover, the **Midlevels Escalator** is a 1-km-long (½-mi-long) combination of escalators and walkways that provide free, glass-covered transport up or down the steep incline between Central and Midlevels. The trip provides a view of small Chinese shops, a wet market, the Jamia Mosque at Shelley Street, and gleaming residential high-rises. You're often so close to the apartments that it's impossible to avoid peering in. Starting at Staunton Street, the escalator cuts through the fashionable SoHo area, filled with cafés, bars, and boutiques.

Plan to ride the escalators up between 10:20 AM and midnight. From 6 to 10 AM they move downhill only, so commuters from Midlevels can get to work. After midnight the escalators shut down, and that equates to a long walk on steep steps. You can get off at any point and explore side streets where vendors sell porcelain, clothes, and antiques (not necessarily authentic). Most buildings have tiny makeshift altars to ancestors, usually made of colorful red paper with gold Chinese characters, with offerings of fruit and incense. ✉ *Enter across from Central Market, at Queen's Rd. Central and Jubilee St., Central* ⏲ *Daily 6 AM–11:30 PM.*

HEALTHY WAYS

❹ If you don't know your qi from your chin, and you're not sure if you need a dried seahorse or a live snake, head to the **Eu Yan Sang Medical Hall.** Glass cases at this reputable store display reindeer antlers, dried fungi, ginseng, and other medicinal mainstays. Grave but helpful clerks behind hefty wooden counters will happily sell you purported cures for anything from the common cold to impotence (the cure for the latter is usually slices of reindeer antler boiled into tea). ■ **TIP→ The Hong Kong Tourism Board runs free introductory classes on Chinese medicine here Wednesday at 2:30 PM.** From Sheung Wan MTR, walk left along Wing Lok Street, right into Wing Wo Street, then left onto Queen's Road Central. There are other smaller branches all over Hong Kong; try the one on 18 Russell Street in Causeway Bay for over-the-counter consultations in English. ✉ *152 Queen's Rd. Central, Western* ☎ *2544–3870, hotline 2544–3308* 🌐 *www.euyansang.com* ⏲ *Daily 9–7:30* Ⓜ *Sheung Wan MTR, Exit E2.*

⚠ **Chinese medicines aren't regulated by the Hong Kong government. Anything that sounds dubious or dangerous might be just that.**

❷ Brush up on traditional treatments at the **Hong Kong Museum of Medical Sciences.** The least morbid and most enlightening exhibits compare Chinese and western medical practices, and show Chinese medicines of both animal and plant origin. Elsewhere, dusty displays of old medical equipment send macabre thrills up your spine. Reaching this museum is a healthy experience in itself: you pant up several blocks' worth of stairs to the Edwardian building it's in. ■ **TIP→ The cheat's way of getting here is on the Midlevels Escalator: alight at Caine Road and walk west four or five blocks to Ladder Street. The museum is just down the first flight of stairs, on the left.** ✉ *2 Caine Lane, Western* ☎ *2549–5123* 🌐 *www.hkmms.org.hk* 🎫 *HK$10* ⏲ *Tues.–Sat. 10–5, Sun. 1–5.*

★ In colonial times **Bonham Strand,** a curving thoroughfare in the Sheung Wan district, was a major commercial hub. Sadly, its wooden shop fronts are falling victim to real estate development. The remaining few are medicinal mother lodes: wood-clad walls are lined with shelves of jars filled with pungent ingredients such as fungi, barks, and insects. These are consumed dried and ground up—infused in hot water or tea or taken as powder or pills. West of the intersection with Wing Lok Street, the original facades give way to those with big plate-glass windows displaying bundles of hairy-looking forked yellow roots—this is the heart of the ginseng wholesale trade. Ginseng is a broad-spectrum remedy that's a mainstay of Chinese medicine. Don't be surprised, though, to see Wisconsin-grown ginseng, a cheaper alternative to Chinese and Korean varieties, which are said to have more kick (or more kudos).

NO GIN, JUST TONIC

Downing a glass of herbal health tonic is a part of many a Hong Kongers' day. The pen-fronted stores that sell them are everywhere: look for small throngs of people surrounding counters full of ornate metal drums with taps on them. There are blends for flu, headaches, colds, and coughs as well as more serious complaints. Many stores have English labels; otherwise, tell the server your troubles, and he or she will run you off a glass of whatever works best. Most cost HK$6–HK$20 a dose. Chinese medicines aren't regulated by the Hong Kong government. Anything that sounds dubious might be just that.

★ A sharp but musty smell fills the air when you turn down **Wing Lok Street** or **Des Voeux Road West,** Sheung Wan streets renowned for their dried-seafood stores. Out of shop fronts spill sacks filled to bursting with dried and salted fish, seahorses, shrimp, and abalone—a shellfish that is to China what oysters are to the West. Foot-wide fungi, gleaming beans, wrinkly red prunes, nuts, and even rosebuds make up the rest of the stock. A grimmer offering lurks behind a few shopwindows: highly prized shark's fins, purported to be an aphrodisiac.

At Possession Street, where Queen's Road Central becomes **Queen's Road West,** shopwindows display what looks like clumps of fine vermicelli noodles, ranging in color from pale gold to rich chestnut. It's not pasta, though; these are birds' nests, another of Sheung Wan's intriguing specialties. They're used to make a highly prized (and correspondingly expensive) soup that tastes rather disappointingly like egg white.

In herb shops on Queen's Road West beyond the intersection with Hollywood Road, it's a tough call as to who's more wizened: the clerks or the dried goods they sell. Either way, these stores convey the longevity benefits of Chinese medicine. Forget the gleaming teak counters of Central's tony TCM boutiques, here the herbs, dried mushrooms, and other more mysterious ingredients are displayed in plastic jars and burlap sacks.

CENTRAL

Shopping, eating, drinking—Central lives up to its name when it comes to all of these. But it's also Hong Kong's historical heart, packed with architectural reminders of the early colonial days. They're in stark contrast to the soaring masterpieces of modern architecture that the city is famous for. Somehow the mishmash works. With the harbor on one side and Victoria Peak on the other, Central's views—once you get high enough to see them—are unrivaled. It's the liveliest district, packed with people, sights, and life.

■ **TIP→ In Hong Kong, the word "nightlife" is synonymous with Lan Kwai Fong, a few narrow lanes in Central filled with bars and clubs just up the hill from the intersection of Queen's Road Central and Pedder Street.**

THE TERRITORY

Central MTR station is a mammoth underground warren with a host of far-flung exits. A series of travelators join it with Hong Kong Station, under the IFC Mall, where Tung Chung line and Airport Express trains arrive and depart. Rattling old trams along Des Voeux Road have you at Sheung Wan, Admiralty, and Wan Chai in minutes. They continue to Causeway Bay, Happy Valley, and beyond.

GETTING AROUND

Central MTR station is a mammoth underground warren with a host of far-flung exits. A series of travelators join it with Hong Kong Station, under the IFC Mall, where Tung Chung line and Airport Express trains arrive and depart. Rattling old trams along Des Voeux Road have you at Sheung Wan, Admiralty, and Wan Chai in minutes. They continue to Causeway Bay, Happy Valley, and beyond. Bus routes to and from all over pass through Central's Exchange Square and under the Admiralty Centre in Admiralty.

5

Star Ferry vessels leave Pier 7 every 6 to 10 minutes 6:30 AM to 11:30 PM; the 7-minute trip costs HK$2.20 (upper deck). Regular and high-speed ferries run from the Outlying Islands Ferry Pier, in front of the IFC, every half hour 6 AM to midnight.

SIGHTS

8 ★ **Flagstaff House Museum of Tea Ware.** All that's good about British colonial architecture is in the simple white facade, wooden monsoon shutters, and colonnaded verandas of Flagstaff House. Over 600 pieces of delicate antique teaware from the Tang (618–907) through the Qing (1644–1911) dynasties fill rooms that once housed the commander of the British forces. ■ **TIP→ Skip the lengthy, confusing tea-ceremony descriptions; concentrate on the porcelain itself.** Look for the unadorned brownish purple clay of the Yixing pots: unglazed, their beauty hinges on perfect form. There's a carved wooden booth on the first floor where you can listen to traditional Chinese tea songs. The best place to put your Chinese tea theory into practice is the **Lock Cha Tea Shop** (☎ *2801–7177* 🌐 *www.lockcha.com*), in the K.S. Lo Gallery annex of Flagstaff House. It's half shop, half teahouse, so you can sample brews before you buy. Friendly, knowledgeable staffers prepare the tea gong-fu style at carved rosewood tables. Try the Tie Guan Yin, a highly aromatic green tea. ■ **TIP→ The Hong Kong Tourist Board runs tea appreciation classes at Lock Cha Tea Shop—phone the shop to book a spot.** ✉ *Hong Kong Park, 10 Cotton Tree Dr., Admiralty* ☎ *2869–0690* 🌐 *www.lcsd.gov.hk* 🎫 *Free* ⏲ *Wed.–Mon. 10–5* Ⓜ *Admiralty MTR, Exit C1.*

6 **Hong Kong Zoological and Botanical Gardens.** The city has grown around  the gardens, which opened in 1864, and though they're watched over

CLOSE UP

Leaves of the City

Get up early Hong Kong, and you'll see old men shuffling along Hong Kong's streets with their pet birds in tow. The destination? A teahouse for some warm brew and chat with pals birds chirping away from cages hung nearby.

But tea isn't just for old timers. Hot black tea comes free—usually in glass beakers that are constantly refilled—with all meals in Chinese restaurants. Pu-erh tea, which is known here as Bo Lei, is the beverage of choice at dim sum places. In fact, another way to say dim sum is *yum cha,* meaning "drink tea."

Afternoon tea is another local fixation. Forget cucumber sandwiches and petit fours. Here we're talking neighborhood joints with Formica tables, grumpy waiters, and menus only in Chinese. Most people go for nai cha made with evaporated milk. A really good cup is smooth, sweet, and hung with drops of fat. An even richer version, cha chow, is made with condensed milk. If *yuen yueng* (yin yang; half milk tea and half instant coffee) sounds a bit much, *ling-mun cha* (lemon tea) is also on hand. Don't forget to order butter toast or *daan-ta* (custard tarts).

The bubble (or boba) tea craze is strong. These cold brews contain pearly balls of tapioca or coconut jelly. There's also been a return to traditional teas. Chains such as Chinese Urban Healing Tea serve healthy blends in MTR stations all over town—giving Starbucks a run for its money.

by skyscrapers, a visit to them is still a delightful escape. Paths lined with semitropical trees, shrubs, and flowers wind through cramped zoo enclosures. Burmese python, Chinese alligator, Bornean orangutan, Bali mynah, ring-tailed lemur, and lion-tailed macaque are among its 500 birds, 70 mammals, and 70 reptiles from some 30 animal species. The Garden houses more than 1,000 species of plants indigenous to tropical and subtropical regions. Albany Road slices the park in half: birds and the greenhouse are on the eastern side, the other animals are to the west. A pedestrian underpass connects the two sides. ✉ *Upper Albert Rd. opposite Government House; enter on Garden Rd., Central* ☎ *2530–0107* 🌐 *www.lcsd.gov.hk/parks/hkzbg* 🎫 *Free* ⏲ *Zoo: daily 6* AM*–7* PM. *Gardens: daily 6* AM*–10* PM. *Greenhouse: daily 9–4:30.*

EXPERIENCES

HARBOR RIDE

❼ Fodor'sChoice ★ **Star Ferry.** Since 1898 the ferry pier has been the gateway to the island from Kowloon. If it's your first time in the city, you're all but required to cross the harbor and back on the Star Ferry. It's a beautiful trip on antiquated, character-full vessels. An evening ride is even better, when the city's neon and skyscrapers light up the skyline. The distinctive green-and-white vessels are beloved harbor fixtures. The new Central Star Ferry Terminal is at Piers 7 and 8 of the Outlying Islands Ferry Piers.

On ferries between Central and Tsim Sha Tsui, there are two classes: a first-class ticket (HK$2.20) gives you a seat on the roomier upper deck, with an air-conditioned compartment in front. Second-class seats (HK$1.70) are on the lower deck and tend to be noisy because they're near the engine room. ■ **TIP→ For trips from Central to Tsim Sha Tsui, seats on the eastern side have the best views.**

Across the way, the pier is a convenient starting point for any tour of Kowloon. As you face the bus station, Ocean Terminal, where luxury cruise ships berth, is on your left; inside this terminal, and in adjacent Harbour City, are miles of air-conditioned shopping arcades. ✉ *Central* ☎ *2767–7065* 🌐 *www.starferry.com.hk* ⏲ *Central to/from Tsim Sha Tsui, daily 6:30 AM–11:30 PM.*

THE PEAK

9 Fodor's Choice ★ **Peak Tram.** Hong Kong is very proud that its funicular railway is the world's steepest. Before it opened in 1880 the only way to get up to Victoria Peak, the highest hill overlooking Hong Kong Harbour, was to walk or take a bumpy ride in a sedan chair on steep steps. On the way up, grab a seat on the right-hand side for the best views of the harbor and mountains. The trams, which look like old-fashioned trolley cars, are hauled the whole way in seven minutes by cables attached to electric motors. En route to the upper terminal, 1,805 feet above sea level, the cars pass five intermediate stations. At times they seem to travel at an impossibly vertical angle.

At the top you enter the Peak Tower, a mall full of restaurants and shops. A viewing platform is on the mall's roof. Outside the Peak Tower, another mall faces you. Well-signed nature walks around the Peak are wonderful respites from the commercialism. Bus 15C, an antique double-decker with an open top, shuttles you to the Peak Tram Terminal from Central Pier 7 or on Connaught Road Central outside City Hall, every 30 minutes. ✉ *Between Garden Rd. and Cotton Tree Dr., Central* ☎ *2522–0922* 🌐 *www.thepeak.com.hk* 🎫 *HK$22 one way, HK$33 round-trip* ⏲ *Daily every 10–15 mins, 7:30 AM–midnight.*

As you step off the tram, the feeling that you left your stomach somewhere down in Central disappears. The cure? A sharp intake of breath and bout of sighing over the view. Whatever the time, whatever the weather, be it your first visit or your 50th, this is Hong Kong's one unmissable sight. ■ **TIP→ Before buying a return ticket down on the tram, consider taking one of the beautiful low-impact trails back to Central. There are also buses down.**

10 Fodor's Choice ★ **Victoria Peak's** Chinese name, Tai Ping Shan, means Mountain of Great Peace, and it certainly seems to inspire momentary hushed awe in visitors at the viewing point, a few yards left along the road from the tram terminal. Spread below you is a glittering forest of skyscrapers; beyond them the harbor and—on a clear day—Kowloon's eight mountains. On a rainy day wisps of cloud catch on the buildings' pointy tops; at night both sides of the harbor burst into color. Consider having dinner at one of the restaurants near the upper terminus. ■ **TIP→ Forsake all else up here and start your visit with the lookout point: there are a hundred other shopping ops in the world, but few views like this.**

5

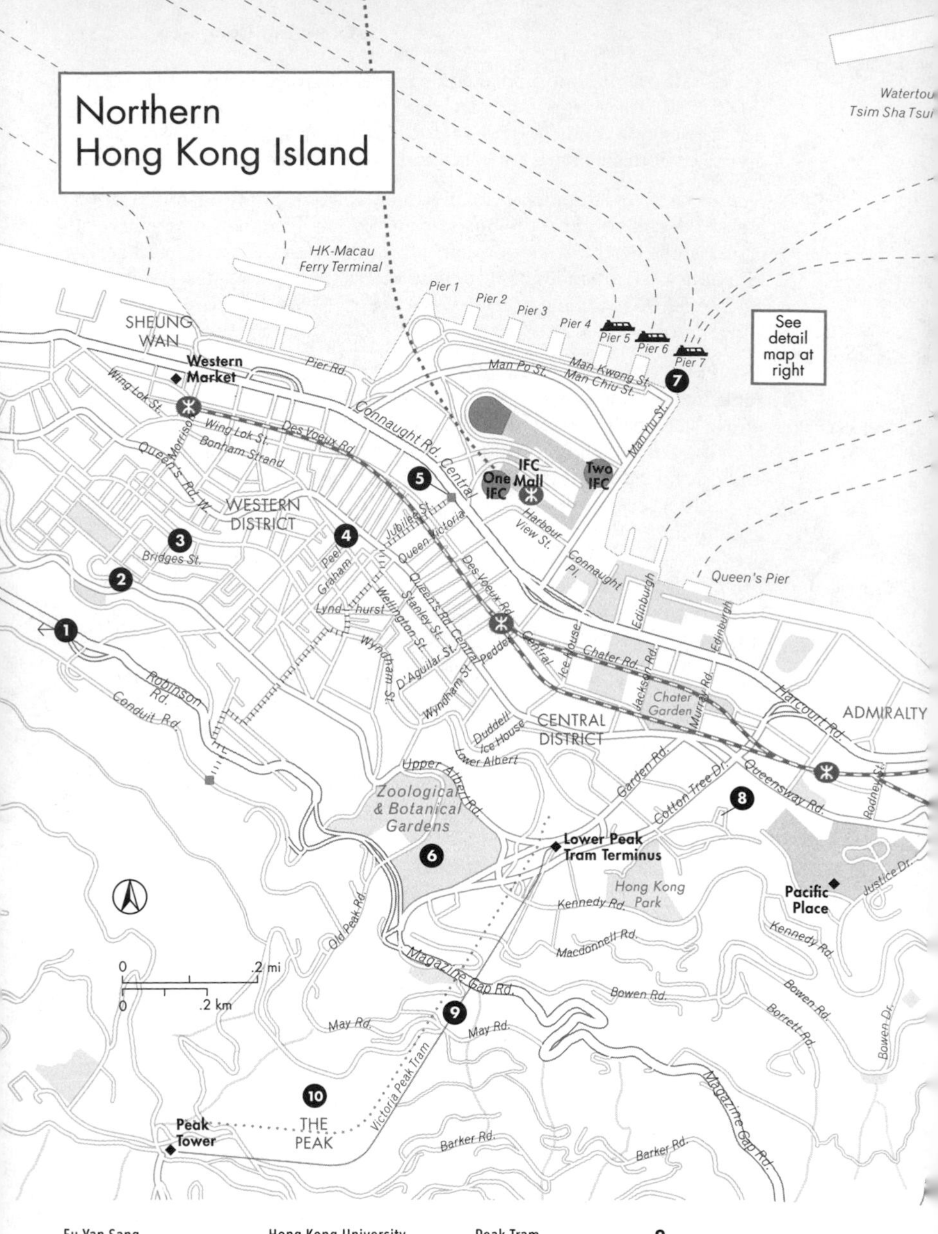

Eu Yan Sang Medical Hall **4**

Flagstaff House Museum of Tea Ware **8**

Happy Valley Racetrack **11**

Hong Kong Museum of Medical Sciences **2**

Hong Kong University Museum & Art Gallery **1**

Hong Kong Zoological & Botanical Gardens **6**

Law Uk Folk Museum **12**

Man Mo Temple **3**

Midlevels Escalator **5**

Peak Tram **9**

Star Ferry Pier **7**

Victoria Peak **10**

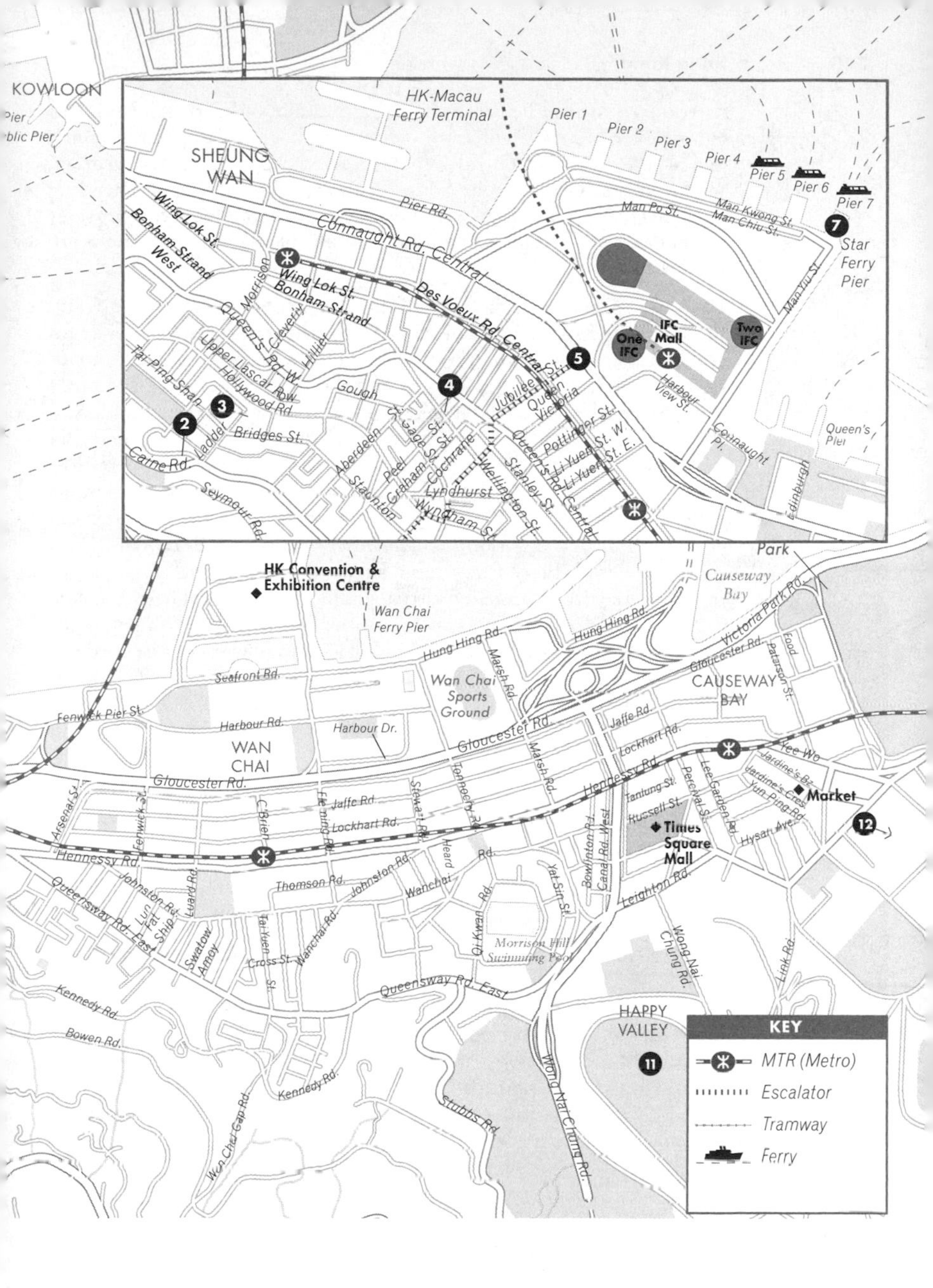
KOWLOON
HK-Macau Ferry Terminal
Pier 1
Pier 2
Pier 3
Pier 4
Pier 5
Pier 6
Pier 7
Star Ferry Pier
SHEUNG WAN
Pier Rd.
Connaught Rd. Central
Wing Lok St.
Bonham Strand West
Wing Lok St.
Bonham Strand
Des Voeux Rd. Central
Man Po St.
Man Kwong St.
Man Chiu St.
Man Yiu St.
IFC Mall
One IFC
Two IFC
Harbour View St.
Morrison
Queen's Rd. W.
Cleverly
Hillier
Upper Lascar Row
Hollywood Rd.
Tai Ping Shan
Gough
Ladder
Bridges St.
Caine Rd.
Seymour Rd.
Aberdeen
Gage St.
Peel
Graham St.
Cochrane
Staunton
Lyndhurst
Wyndham St.
Wellington St.
Stanley St.
Queen's Rd. Central
Jubilee St.
Queen Victoria
Pottinger St.
Li Yuen St. W.
Li Yuen St. E.
Connaught Pl.
Queen's Pier
Edinburgh
Park
Causeway Bay
HK Convention & Exhibition Centre
Wan Chai Ferry Pier
Hung Hing Rd.
Victoria Park Rd.
Gloucester Rd.
Paterson St.
Food
CAUSEWAY BAY
Seafront Rd.
Wan Chai Sports Ground
Marsh Rd.
Fenwick Pier St.
Harbour Rd.
Harbour Dr.
WAN CHAI
Jaffe Rd.
Lockhart Rd.
Yee Wo
Jardine's Bz.
Jardine's Cres.
Yun Ping Rd.
Hysan Ave.
Market
Hennessy Rd.
Lee Garden Rd.
Percival St.
Tanlung St.
Russell St.
Times Square Mall
Arsenal St.
Fenwick St.
O'Brien
Fleming Rd.
Stewart Rd.
Tonnochy Rd.
Heard
Bowrington Rd.
Canal Rd. West
Yat Sin St.
Johnston Rd.
Thomson Rd.
Wanchai
Luard Rd.
Lun Fat
Ship
Queensway Rd. East
Swatow
Amoy
Tai Yuen St.
Cross St.
Wanchai Rd.
Oi Kwan Rd.
Morrison Hill Swimming Pool
Leighton Rd.
Wong Nai Chung Rd.
Link Rd.
Kennedy Rd.
Bowen Rd.
HAPPY VALLEY
Stubbs Rd.
Wan Chai Gap Rd.
KEY
MTR (Metro)
Escalator
Tramway
Ferry

As you step off the Peak Tram, a sharp intake of breath and bout of sighing over the view will cure the feeling that you left your stomach somewhere down in Central. Whatever the time, whatever the weather, be it your first visit or your 50th, this is Hong Kong's one unmissable sight. ■ **TIP→ Before buying a return ticket down on the tram, consider taking one of the beautiful low-impact trails back to Central. There are also buses down.**

There are spectacular views in all directions on the **Peak Circle Walk,** an easy-going 3.5-km (2.2-mi) paved trail that starts at the Upper Tram Terminus. Start by heading north along fern-encroached Lugard Road. There's another stunning view of Central from the lookout, 20 minutes along, after which the road snakes west to an intersection with Hatton and Harlech roads. From here Lantau, Lamma, and—on incredibly clear days—Macau come into view. The longer option from here is to wind your way down Hatton to the University of Hong Kong campus in the Western district. The tacky **Peak Tower** (✉ *128 Peak Rd., Victoria Peak, Central* ☎ *2522–0668* 🌐 *www.thepeak.com.hk* ⏲ *10 AM–11 PM*) is packed with largely forgettable shops and restaurants. Kids might enjoy the free EA Experience virtual gaming room. Local heroes Jackie Chan and Michelle Yeoh are some of the famous faces resisting meltdown at Asia's first branch of London's famous wax works, **Madame Tussaud's** (☎ *2849–6966* 🌐 *www.madame-tussauds.com* 🎫 *HK$140* ⏲ *10 AM–10 PM*). The usual celebrity suspects—from Beckham to Marilyn—are here. The **Peak Galleria** mall scores high on nothing else but the cheese scale.

■ **TIP→ Bypass the overpriced tourist traps inside and head straight up the escalators to the rooftop Sky Terrace and Gallery, which looks down over the Pok Fu Lam country park and reservoir, and, on a clear day, Aberdeen.**

LANTAU ISLAND

A decade of manic development has made Lantau more than just "the place where the Buddha is." A mini-theme park at Ngong Ping keeps the Buddha company. Not to be outdone, Disney has opened a park and resort on the northeast coast. And there's the airport, built on a massive north coast reclamation. At 55 square mi, Lantau is almost twice the size of Hong Kong Island, so there's room for all this development and the laid-back attractions—beaches, fishing villages, and hiking trails—that make the island a great getaway.

THE TERRITORY

Most Lantau roads lead to Tung Chung, the north shore new town, close to Hong Kong International Airport. It's connected to Kowloon by the lengthy Tsing Ma Bridge, which starts near Hong Kong Disneyland, on Lantau's northeast tip.

The Tung Chung Road winds through mountains and connects north Lantau with the southern coast. Here, the South Lantau Road stretches from the town of Mui Wo in the east to Tai O in the west, passing Cheung Sha Beach, and Ngong Ping.

GETTING AROUND

The speediest way to Lantau from Central is the MTR's Tung Chung line (HK$18), which takes about half an hour. A trip by ferry is a 35-minute crossing from Central with great views.

New World First Ferry (☎*2131–8181* 🌐*www.nwff.com.hk*) vessels to Mui Wo leave every 30 to 40 minutes from Central's Pier 6 (HK$13–HK$25.50).

Bus routes are winding, and rides can be heart-stopping. There's service every half hour from Tung Chung and Mui Wo to Ngong Ping, more frequently to Tai O.

The most direct (and daring) way to Ngong Ping is the 25-minute trip on the **Ngong Ping 360 Skyrail** (☎*2109–9898* 🌐*www.np360.com.hk* *HK$58–68 one way; HK$88–98 round-trip* ⏲*Weekdays 10–6; Sat. 10–6:30; Sun. 9–6:30*).

You can reach Tung Chung by a red taxi from Kowloon or Central, but the long, toll-ridden trip will cost around HK$340 from Central. Blue taxis travel Lantau (but can't leave it)—and hairpin bends make costs add up.

5

SIGHTS

⓭ **Hong Kong Disneyland.** If you're expecting an Asian take on the Magic Kingdom, think again—this park on Lantau Island is aimed at mainland Chinese hungry for apple-pie Americana. It's as polished as all the other Disneys, and it has one big advantage: fewer visitors, which means shorter lines. You can go on every ride at least once and see all the attractions in a day. If your kids are theme park–savvy, the tame rides here won't win their respect. That said, there are loads for little kids. Space Mountain is the only attraction with a height restriction. ■ **TIP→ Hong Kong Disneyland operates a Fastpass system, which lets you jump the lines at the most popular attractions.**

You enter right into **Main St., USA,** an area paying tribute to early-20th-century small-town America. Shops—cute though they are—outnumber attractions here, so save lingering for the 3:30 PM parade, which winds up in the Town Square. Sleeping Beauty's castle, with its trademark turrets, is the gateway to faux-medieval **Fantasyland.** Choose from two spin-cycles—the Mad-Hatter's Teacups or Cinderella's Carousel—while you wait for your Winnie-the-Pooh Fastpass time.

Throbbing drums let you know you've hit **Adventureland,** on the park's south side. Landscapers have really run amok at attractions like Tarzan's Treehouse, on an island only accessible by rafts and the Jungle River Cruise. Inspired by the Bogart–Hepburn film *The African Queen,* this canopied boat ride takes you past "ancient" ruins, headhunters, and a volcano. Animated beasties—crocs, snakes, hippos, elephants, partying gorillas—will try to scare or squirt you, egged on by the boat's quipping skipper.

In **Tomorrowland** attractions look more like the *Jetsons* than the future. It's home to roller-coaster-in-the-dark Space Mountain, a humbled version of the original. ■ **TIP→ Shade is limited so take the lead from locals**

and make an umbrella your No. 1 accessory—use it as a parasol if the sun blazes down or the traditional way if it pours.

If you do one show, make it the *Festival of the Lion King*. Give your feet a rest but get your toes tapping with this energetic live performance of the animated film. The one place where Disney meets the East is at ye olde Corner Café. It may seem surreal, but run with it: the congee, curry, sushi, dim sum, stir fries, and kebabs are excellent, as theme-park food goes. If your kids are suspicious of far-flung fare, the Starliner Diner in Tomorrowland does burgers and fries.

The MTR is the quickest way here: take the Tung Chung line to Sunny Bay Station, then change to the Disneyland Resort Line, whose special trains have plush royal-blue seating and Mickey-shaped windows. Check opening hours online or by phone first, as they change monthly. ✉ *Lantau Island* ☎ *3550–3888* 🌐 *www.hongkongdisneyland.com* 🎫 *HK$350 weekends, holidays, and July and Aug.; HK$295 other days* 🕒 *Weekdays 10–8, weekends 10* AM*–11* PM Ⓜ *Disneyland Resort Station.*

⓮ Fodor's Choice ★ **Tian Tan Buddha.** Hong Kongers love superlatives, even if making them true requires strings of qualifiers. So the Tian Tan Buddha is the world's largest Buddha—that's seated, located outdoors, and made of bronze. It doesn't need the epithets: its vast silhouette against the sky is impressive. Steep stairs lead to the lower podium, essentially forcing you to stare up at all 242½ tons of Buddha as you ascend. (Note: the only way to the upper level, right under the Buddha, is through an underwhelming museum inside the podium. You only get a couple of feet higher up, so it's not worth the effort). At the top, cool breezes and fantastic views over Lantau Island await.

It's hard to believe today, but from its foundation in 1927 through the early '90s, the **Po Lin Monastery** was a true retreat, virtually inaccessible by road. These days, it's at the heart of Lantau's biggest attraction. The monastery proper has a gaudy and exuberantly commercial orange temple complex with a vegetarian restaurant—a clattering canteen with greasy, uninspiring fare (pick up sandwiches at the Citygate Mall, Tung Chung). It's the Buddha people come for. The peaceful **Wisdom Path** runs beside 38 halved, towering tree trunks arranged in an infinity shape on a gentle hillside. Each is carved with Chinese characters that make up the Heart Sutra, a 5th-century Buddhist prayer that expresses the doctrine of emptiness. The idea is to walk around the path—which takes 5 minutes—and reflect. To reach it, follow the signposted trail to the left of the Buddha. People were kicking up a fuss over this attraction before its first stone was laid. **Ngong Ping Village** is a money-making add-on to the Tian Tian Buddha. Indeed, if a trip here is a journey of enlightenment, then Nirvana is much easier to reach than previously thought. If you're hungry there's a Cantonese restaurant, an Asian-fusion place, and a branch of the local *gelatteria* Da Dolce. At the Ngong Ping Teahouse you can watch a tea ceremony and pastry making before partaking of both. ✉ *Ngong Ping, Lantau Island* ☎ *2109–9898 to Ngong Ping Village* 🎫 *Buddha: lower podium free, upper podium and museum HK$23 or free with meal ticket. Monastery and path*

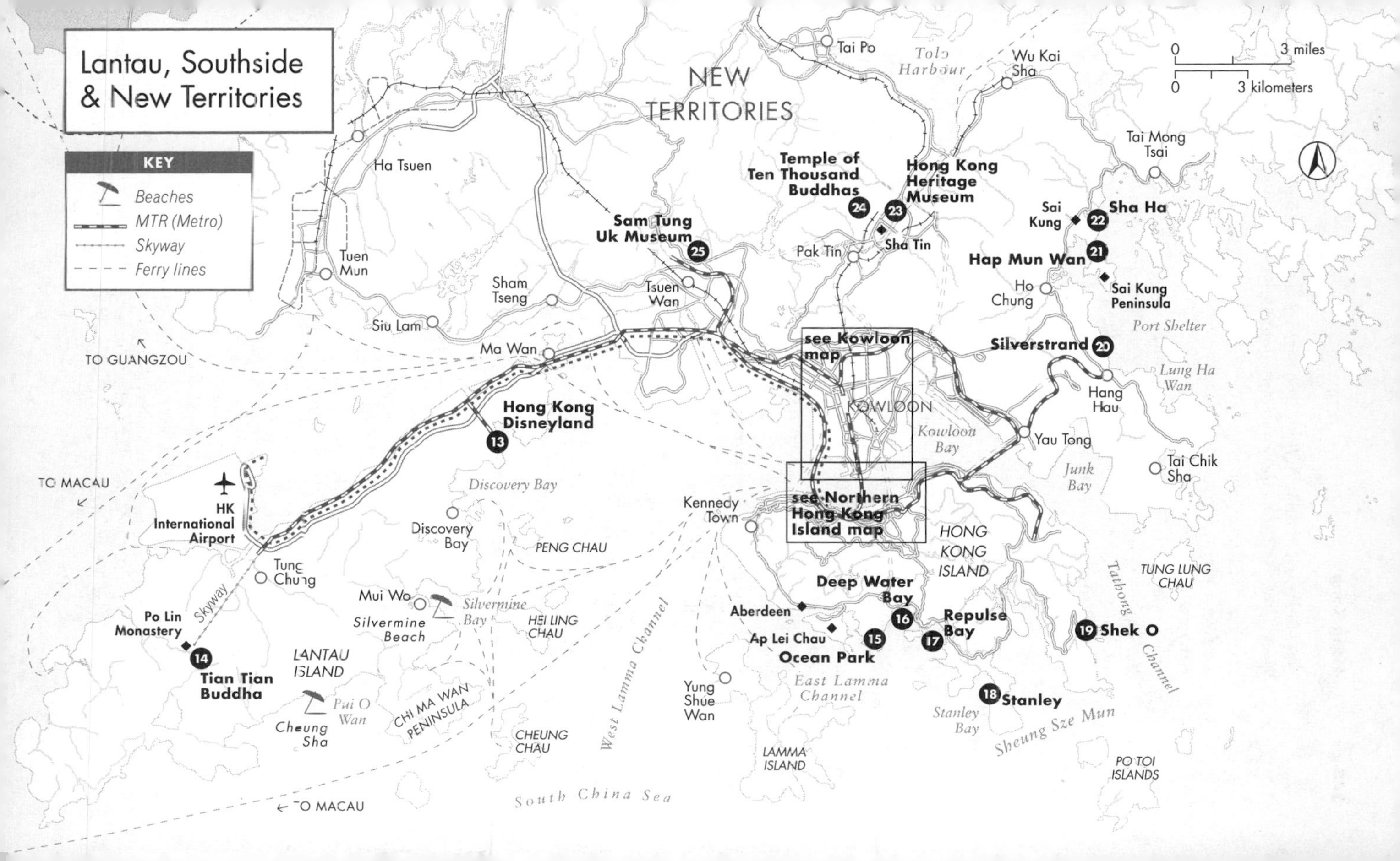
Lantau, Southside & New Territories
KEY
Beaches
MTR (Metro)
Skyway
Ferry lines
0
3 miles
0
3 kilometers
NEW TERRITORIES
Tai Po
Tolo Harbour
Wu Kai Sha
Tai Mong Tsai
Ha Tsuen
Temple of Ten Thousand Buddhas
24
Hong Kong Heritage Museum
23
Sha Tin
Pak Tin
Sai Kung
22
Sha Ha
21
Hap Mun Wan
Sai Kung Peninsula
Ho Chung
Sam Tung Uk Museum
25
Tuen Mun
Sham Tseng
Tsuen Wan
Siu Lam
Port Shelter
TO GUANGZOU
Ma Wan
see Kowloon map
Silverstrand
20
Lung Ha Wan
Hang Hau
KOWLOON
Kowloon Bay
Yau Tong
Hong Kong Disneyland
13
Tai Chik Sha
Junk Bay
TO MACAU
Discovery Bay
HK International Airport
Discovery Bay
Kennedy Town
see Northern Hong Kong Island map
HONG KONG ISLAND
PENG CHAU
Tung Chung
TUNG LUNG CHAU
Mui Wo
Silvermine Bay
Deep Water Bay
Skyway
Po Lin Monastery
Silvermine Beach
HEI LING CHAU
Aberdeen
16
Repulse Bay
Tathong Channel
19
Shek O
14
LANTAU ISLAND
Ap Lei Chau
15
Ocean Park
17
Tian Tian Buddha
West Lamma Channel
Yung Shue Wan
East Lamma Channel
18
Stanley
Pui O Wan
CHI MA WAN PENINSULA
Cheung Sha
Stanley Bay
Sheung Sze Mun
CHEUNG CHAU
LAMMA ISLAND
PO TOI ISLANDS
South China Sea
TO MACAU

free. Village HK$65. Village and return Skyrail HK$145 ⌚Buddha daily 10–5:30. Monastery and path daily dawn–dusk. Village weekdays 10–6, weekends 10–6:30.

EXPERIENCE

DOLPHIN-SPOTTING

Candy-pink dolphins might sound like something Disney cooked up, but Lantau's cutest residents are the endangered species *Sousa chinensis,* native to the Pearl River estuary. Only a few hundred are left, but ecotourism company **Hong Kong Dolphinwatch** (☎*2984–1414* 🌐*www.hkdolphinwatch.com*) guarantees you a sighting on their 2½-hour cruises (HK$320)—or a free second trip.

WAN CHAI, CAUSEWAY BAY AND BEYOND

The Happy Valley races are a vital part of Hong Kong life, so it's only fitting that they're in one of the city's most vital areas. A few blocks back from Wan Chai's new office blocks are crowded alleys where you might stumble across a wet market, a tiny furniture-maker's shop, or an age-old temple. Farther east, Causeway Bay pulses with Hong Kong's best shopping streets and hundreds of restaurants. At night, the whole area comes alive with bars, restaurants, and discos, as well as establishments offering some of Wan Chai's more traditional services (think red lights and photos of seminaked women outside).

THE TERRITORY

Wan Chai's trams run mostly along Hennessy Road, with a detour along Johnston Road at the neighborhood's western end. Queen's Road East runs parallel to these two streets to the south, and a maze of lanes connect it with Hennessy.

The thoroughfares north of Hennessy—Lockhart, Jaffe, and Gloucester, which is a freeway—are laid out in a grid. Causeway Bay's diagonal roads make it hard to navigate, but it's small; wander around, and before long you'll hit something familiar.

GETTING AROUND

Both Wan Chai and Causeway Bay have their own MTR stops, but a pleasant way to arrive from Central is on the tram along Hennessy Road. All the lines go through Wan Chai, but check the sign at the front if you're going beyond. Some continue to North Point and Shau Kei Wan, via Causeway Bay, while others go south to Happy Valley.

The underground stations are small labyrinths, so read the signs carefully to find the best exit. Traffic begins to take its toll on journey times farther east—the MTR is a better option for Shau Kei Wan and Chai Wan.

Star Ferries sail between Tsim Sha Tsui and Wan Chai every 8 to 20 minutes. They leave from the ferry pier just east of the convention center.

Like all of Hong Kong, Wan Chai isn't really dangerous at night, but single women strolling the streets in the wee hours might get unwanted attention from groups of drunk expats. Taxis are a good idea.

SIGHT

12 **Law Uk Folk Museum.** This restored Hakka house was once the home of the Law family, who arrived here from Guangdong in the mid-18th century. It's the perfect example of a triple-*jian,* double-*lang* residence. Jian are enclosed rooms—here, the bedroom, living room, and workroom at the back. The front storeroom and kitchen are the *lang,* where the walls don't reach up to the roof, and thus allow air in. Although the museum is small, informative texts outside and displays of rural furniture and farm implements inside give a powerful idea of what rural Hong Kong was like. It's worth a trip to bustling industrial Chai Wan, at the eastern end of the MTR, to see it. Photos show what the area looked like in the 1930s—these days a leafy square is the only reminder of the woodlands and fields that once surrounded this dwelling. ✉ *14 Kut Shing St., Chai Wan, Eastern* ☎ *2896–7006* 🌐 *www.lcsd.gov.hk/CE/Museum/History/en/luf.php* 🎫 *Free* ⏲ *Mon.–Wed., Fri. and Sat. 10–6, Sun., holidays 1–6* Ⓜ *Chai Wan, Exit B.*

5

EXPERIENCE

OFF TO THE RACES

Even if you're not a gambler, it's worth going to one of Hong Kong's two tracks just to experience the phenomenon. The "sport of kings" is run under a monopoly by the Hong Kong Jockey Club, one of the territory's most powerful entities. It's a multimillion-dollar-a-year business, employing thousands of people and drawing crowds that approach insanity in their eagerness to rid themselves of their hard-earned money. Profits go to charity and community organizations.

The season runs from September through June. Some 65 races are held at one of the two courses—on Saturday or Sunday afternoon 1 to 6 at Sha Tin and Wednesday night 7:15 to 11 at Happy Valley—which rank among the world's great horse-racing experiences.

In the public stands the vibe is electric and loud, thanks to feverish gamblers shouting and waving their newspapers madly. Both courses have huge video screens at the finish line, so you can see what's happening every foot of the way. ■ **TIP→ The HKTB's Come Horseracing tours begin at HK$690 and include transfers, lunch, and tips on picking a winner.**

11 Fodor's Choice ★ **Happy Valley Racecourse.** Hong Kong punters are the world's most avid horse-racing fans, and the beloved track in Happy Valley—opened soon after the British first arrived in the territory—is one of their headquarters. The roar of the crowd as the jockeys in bright silk colors race by is a must-see. The joy of the Happy Valley track, even for those who aren't into horses, is that it's smack in the middle of the city and surrounded by towering apartment blocks—indeed, people whose balconies hang over the backstretch often have parties on racing days. The track is a 10-minute walk from Causeway Bay MTR Exit A (Times Square). ✉ *Hong Kong Jockey Club, 1 Sports Rd., Happy Valley* ☎ *2966–8111* 🌐 *racecourses.hkjc.com* 🎫 *HK$10.*

Sha Tin Racecourse. Whether you enter Sha Tin by road or rail, you'll be amazed to find this metropolis in the middle of the New Territories. One of the so-called "new towns," Sha Tin underwent a population explosion starting in the mid-1980s that transformed it from a town of 30,000 to a city of more than a half million. The biggest attraction is the racecourse, which is newer and larger than the one in Happy Valley. In fact, it's one of the world's most modern courses and, as such, is the venue for all championship events, including some equestrian events for the 2008 Olympics. The easiest way to get here is by taxi, or you can catch the MTR to Kowloon Tong and transfer to the KCR train, which stops at the Racecourse Station on race days. A walkway from it takes you directly to the track. ✉ *Tai Po Rd., next to Racecourse KCR station, Sha Tin* ☎ *2966–6520* 🌐 *racecourses.hkjc.com* 🎫 *HK$10.*

SOUTHSIDE

For all the unrelenting urbanity of Hong Kong Island's north coast, its south side consists largely of green hills and a few residential areas around picturesque bays. With beautiful sea views, real estate is at a premium; some of Hong Kong's wealthiest residents live in beautiful houses and luxurious apartments here. Southside is a breath of fresh air—literally and figuratively. The people are more relaxed, the pace is slower, and there are lots of sea breezes.

TRANSPORTATION FROM CENTRAL TO . . .

Aberdeen: 30 minutes via Bus 70 or 91. (Apleichau is 15 minutes from Aberdeen on Bus 90B or 91; 10 minutes by sampan.)

Deep Water Bay: 20 minutes via Bus 6, 64, 260, or 6A.

Ocean Park: 30 minutes via Star Ferry Pier and Bus 629.

Repulse Bay: 30 minutes via Bus 6, 6A, 6X, 66, 64, or 260.

Shek O: 50 minutes via MTR to Shau Ki Wan and then Bus 9 to the last stop.

Stanley: 40 minutes via Bus 6, 6A, 6X, 66, 64, or 260.

Note that express buses skip Aberdeen and Deep Water Bay, heading directly to Repulse Bay and Stanley. Buses run less frequently in the evening, so it's more convenient to grab a taxi (they're everywhere).

SIGHT

⓯ ★ **Ocean Park.** When it comes to amusement parks, there's no question where Hong Kongers' loyalties lie. This marine-theme park embraces both high- and low-octane buzzes and spectacular zoological attractions; they even breed endangered species here. The park stretches out over 170 hilly acres, and you can gaze down at much of it from spookily silent cabins of the mile-long cable car that connects the tamer Lowlands area to the action-packed Headland. **■ TIP→ If all you fancy is roller-coasting, enter the park at the Tai Shue Wan Middle Kingdom entrance, and head straight up the escalator to Adventure Land. If you're planning to do everything, start at the main entrance.**

The highlights of the **Lowland Gardens** are the giant pandas, particularly the young siblings from China, Le Le and Ying Ying. Paths wind to other enclosures, including a cantilevered butterfly house where rare species are bred, and the traditional Chinese architecture of the Goldfish

Pagoda. Cross a rickety bridge to the lush undergrowth of the Amazing Amazon: its inhabitants are richly colored birds like toucans and flamingos.

Hong Kong's biggest roller coaster, the Dragon, is at the **Headland,** where the cable car stops. It might not quite be up to international standards, but it still loops the loops. There's also a Ferris wheel and swinging pirate ship here. If your kids are too small to get past Headland height restrictions, make for the old-school attractions at **Kids World.** There's a carousel as well as kid-size fairground stalls. You can also sneak in some learning at Dolphin University. (The first-ever dolphins born from artificial insemination were born in Ocean Park.)

More than 2,000 fish find their way around the Atoll Reef in **Marine Land,** where the newest exhibits are the Chinese Sturgeon Aquarium and Pacific Pier, which has more than 20 resident seals and sea lions. For sheer visual delight, the Sea Jelly Spectacular offers a colorful display in a dark environment. At the Ocean Theatre, dolphins and sea lions clown around with surprising grace. In **Adventure Land,** the Wild West–theme Mine Train was designed to feel rickety and screw-loose, which is probably why it rates highest on the scream-o-meter. Expect a light spraying or a heavy drenching at the Raging River: it all depends on your seat (and your luck). Rounding up the adrenaline boosts is the Abyss Turbo Drop, consisting, simply, of a 185-foot vertical plunge. It will definitely give you that sinking feeling.

Ocean Park is 30 minutes from Admiralty MTR or Central Star Ferry Pier by Citybus 629. Buses 70, 75, 90, 97, 260, 6A, and 6X also run from Central. ✉ *Tai Shue Wan Rd., Aberdeen, Southside* ☎ *2552–0291* 🌐 *www.oceanpark.com.hk* 🎫 *HK$208* ⏲ *Daily 10–6.*

EXPERIENCES

SUNBATHING

⑯ **Deep Water Bay.** On Island Road, just to the east of Ocean Park and all its amusements, this bay was the setting for the William Holden film *Love Is a Many Splendored Thing* (1955), and its deep coves are still lovely. Near Deep Water Bay are the manicured greens of the Deep Water Bay Golf Course, which is owned by the Hong Kong Golf Club. Not surprisingly, the area has become a multimillionaires' enclave and is home to Hong Kong's richest man, Li Ka-shing, a very private real estate tycoon. *From Exchange Square Bus Terminus in Central, take Bus 6, 64, 260, or 6A.*

■ TIP→ For a scenic route to Deep Water Bay, take Bus 70 from Central's Exchange Square to Aberdeen and change to Bus 73, which passes the beach en route to Stanley.

⑰ **Repulse Bay.** It's named after the British warship HMS *Repulse* not, as some local wags say, after its slightly murky waters. It was home of the now demolished Repulse Bay Hotel, which gained notoriety in December 1941 when Japanese clambered over the hills behind it, entered its gardens, and overtook the British, who were using the hotel as headquarters. Repulse Bay Verandah Restaurant & Bamboo Bar—a great place for British high tea—is a replica of the eating and drinking establishment that once graced the hotel. High tea costs HK$128 and is served weekdays from 3 to 5:30 and weekends from 3:30 to 5:30. You can also grab a bite at one of several Chinese restaurants and snack kiosks that dot the beach. The Lifesaving Club at the beach's east end resembles a Chinese temple, with large statues of Tin Hau, goddess of the sea, and Kwun Yum, goddess of mercy. ⚠ **If you opt for a meal in a seafood restaurant here or at any beach, note that physicians caution against eating raw shellfish because of hepatitis outbreaks.**

⓳ **Shek O.** This wide beach is almost Mediterranean in appearance with its low-rise houses and shops set prettily on a headland. In Shek O village you can find old mansions, small shops selling inflatable toys and other beach gear, and a few popular Chinese and Thai restaurants. Follow the curving path from the town square across a footbridge to the "island" of Tai Tau Chau, really a large rock with a lookout over the South China Sea. Little more than a century ago, this open water was ruled by pirates. Also near town is the Shek O Golf and Country Club and the superb Shek O Country Park, with great trails and bird-watching: look for Kentish plovers, reef egrets, and black-headed gulls, as well as the colorful rufus-backed shrike and the ubiquitous chatty bulbul. *From Central, take MTR to Shau Kei Wan, then take Bus 9 to last stop (about 30 min).*

⓲ **Stanley.** Notorious during World War II as the home of Japan's largest POW camps in Hong Kong, Stanley is now known primarily for its market, a great place for deals on knickknacks, ceramics, paintings, casual clothing, and sporting goods. The old police station, built in 1859, now houses a restaurant. Past the market, on Stanley Main Street, a strip of restaurants and pubs faces the bay. On the other side of the bay, a temple honoring Tin Hau, goddess of the sea, is wedged between giant modern housing estates.

Stanley's wide main beach is the site of Hong Kong's most popular dragon boat races, usually held in June, in which teams paddle out into the sea, turn around, and, at the sound of the gun, race ferociously back to shore. The beach is popular with the windsurfing, water-skiing, and wakeboarding crowd. *From Exchange Square Bus Terminus in Central, take Bus 6, 6A, 6X, 66, 64, or 260.*

SAIL AWAY: SAMPANS AND JUNKS

Named after an English lord, not the Scottish city, the Southside town of Aberdeen (30 minutes from Central via Bus 70 or 91) was once a pirate refuge. After World War II it became commercial as the *tanka* (boat people) attracted visitors to their floating restaurants. In the harbor are some 3,000 junks and sampans, still interspersed with floating restaurants, among them the famous Jumbo Kingdom, its faux-Chinese decorations covered in lights. The tanka still live on houseboats, and though the vessels look picturesque, conditions are depressing.

Elderly women with sea- and sun-weathered skin and croaking voices may invite you aboard a sampan for a harbor ride. It's better to go with one of the licensed operators that depart on 20-minute tours daily from

8 to 6 from the seawall opposite Aberdeen Centre. Tickets are HK$40. A tour lets you see how the fishing community lives and works and how sampans are also homes, sometimes with three generations on one small vessel. Ironically, about 110 yards away are the yachts of the Marina Club and the slightly less exclusive Aberdeen Boat Club.

You can also hire a junk to take you to outer islands: Cheung Chau, Lamma, Lantau, Po Toi, or the islands in Port Shelter, Sai Kung. Sailing on a large (up to 80 feet long), well-varnished, plushly appointed, air-conditioned junk—which can serve as a platform for swimmers and water-skiers—is a unique Hong Kong experience. Many local "weekend admirals" command these floating rumpus rooms, which are also known as "gin junks" because so much alcohol is often consumed aboard them.

Ap Lei Chau Island (Duck's Tongue Island), accessible via sampan or Bus 90B or 91 along the bridge that connects it with Aberdeen, has a yard where junks, yachts, and sampans are built, almost all without formal plans. With 86,800 people living on 1.3 square km (½ square mi), Ap Lei Chau is the world's most densely populated island.

■ TIP→ Look to your right when crossing the bridge for a superb view of the harbor and its countless junks.

The ritzy bar **aqua luna** (☎ *2116–8821* 🌐 *www.aqua.com.hk*) is on the *Cheung Po Tsai,* an impressive 28-meter junk named for a pirate and created by an 80-year-old local craftsman. It's slow but impressive, with magnificent red sails. A 45-minute cruise through Victoria Harbour costs HK$150 by day and HK$180 at night, which includes one drink. Departures are every afternoon at 1:30 and 2:30, then every hour on the half hour from 5:30 PM to 10:30 PM from Tsim Sha Tsui Pier, near the Cultural Centre, and 15 minutes later from Pier 9 in Central.

The ***Duk Ling*** (☎ *2573–5282* 🌐 *www.dukling.com.hk*) is a fully restored 50-year-old fishing junk whose large sails are a sight to behold. For HK$50, the HKTB offers visitors aged 3 to 75 one-hour sails from Kowloon Pier (Thursday at 2 PM and 4 PM, Saturday at 10 AM and noon) and from Central's Pier 9 (Thursday at 3 PM and 5 PM, Saturday at 11 AM and 1 PM). Register first at the HKTB Visitor Centres in Causeway Bay or Tsim Sha Tsui; when you do, bring your passport to prove you're from out of town.

HIKING

Fodor's Choice ★ **Dragon's Back.** One of the most popular trails crosses the "rooftop" of Hong Kong Island. Take the Peak Tram from Central up to Victoria Peak, and tackle as much or as little of the range as you feel like—there are numerous exits "downhill" to public-transport networks. Surprisingly wild country feels a world away from the urban bustle below, and the panoramas—of Victoria Harbour on one side, and South Island and outlying islands on the other—are spectacular. You can follow the trail all the way to the delightful seaside village of Shek O, where you can relax over an evening dinner before returning to the city by minibus or taxi. The most popular route, and shorter, is from Shek O Country

Park. Take the MTR from Central to Shau Kei Wan, then Bus 9, alight after the first roundabout, near the crematorium.

Wilson Trail. The 78-km-long (48-mi-long) trail runs from Stanley Gap on the south end of Hong Kong Island, through rugged peaks that have a panoramic view of Repulse Bay and the nearby Round and Middle islands, and to Nam Chung in the northeastern New Territories. You have to cross the harbor by MTR at Quarry Bay to complete the entire walk. The trail is smoothed by steps paved with stone, and footbridges aid with steep sections and streams. Clearly marked with signs and information boards, this popular walk is divided into 10 sections, and you can easily take just one or two (figure on three to four hours a section); traversing the whole trail takes about 31 hours.

Section 1, which starts at Stanley Gap Road, is only for the fit. Much of it requires walking up steep mountain grades. For an easier walk, try Section 7, which begins at Sing Mun Reservoir and goes along a greenery-filled, fairly level path that winds past the eastern shore of the Sing Mun Reservoir in the New Territories and then descends to Tai Po, where there's a sweeping view of Tolo Harbour. Other sections take you through the monkey forest at the Kowloon Hill Fitness Trail, over mountains, and past charming Chinese villages.

KOWLOON

There's much more to the Kowloon Peninsula than rock-bottom prices and goods of dubious provenance. Just across the harbor from Central, this piece of Chinese mainland takes its name from the string of mountains that bound it in the north: *gau lung*, "nine dragons" (there are actually eight mountains, the ninth represented the emperor who named them). Although less sophisticated and more wild than its island-side counterpart, Kowloon's dense, gritty urban fabric is the backdrop for Hong Kong's best museums and most interesting spiritual sights. And there's street upon street of hard-core consumerism in every imaginable guise.

THE TERRITORY

Kowloon's southernmost district is Tsim Sha Tsui (TST), home to the Star Ferry Pier. The waterfront extends a few miles to TST East. Shops and hotels line Nathan Road, which runs north from the waterfront through the market districts of Jordan, Yau Ma Tei, and Mong Kok.

New Kowloon is the unofficial name for the sprawl beyond Boundary Street. The district just north is Kowloon Tong. Two spiritual sights—Wong Tai Sin and Lok Fu—are a little farther east. The tongue sticking out into the sea to the south was the runway of the old Kai Tak Airport. Kowloon City is a stone's throw west.

GETTING AROUND

The most romantic way from Hong Kong Island to southern Tsim Sha Tsui (TST) is by Star Ferry. There are crossings from Central every 6 to 12 minutes and a little less often from Wan Chai.

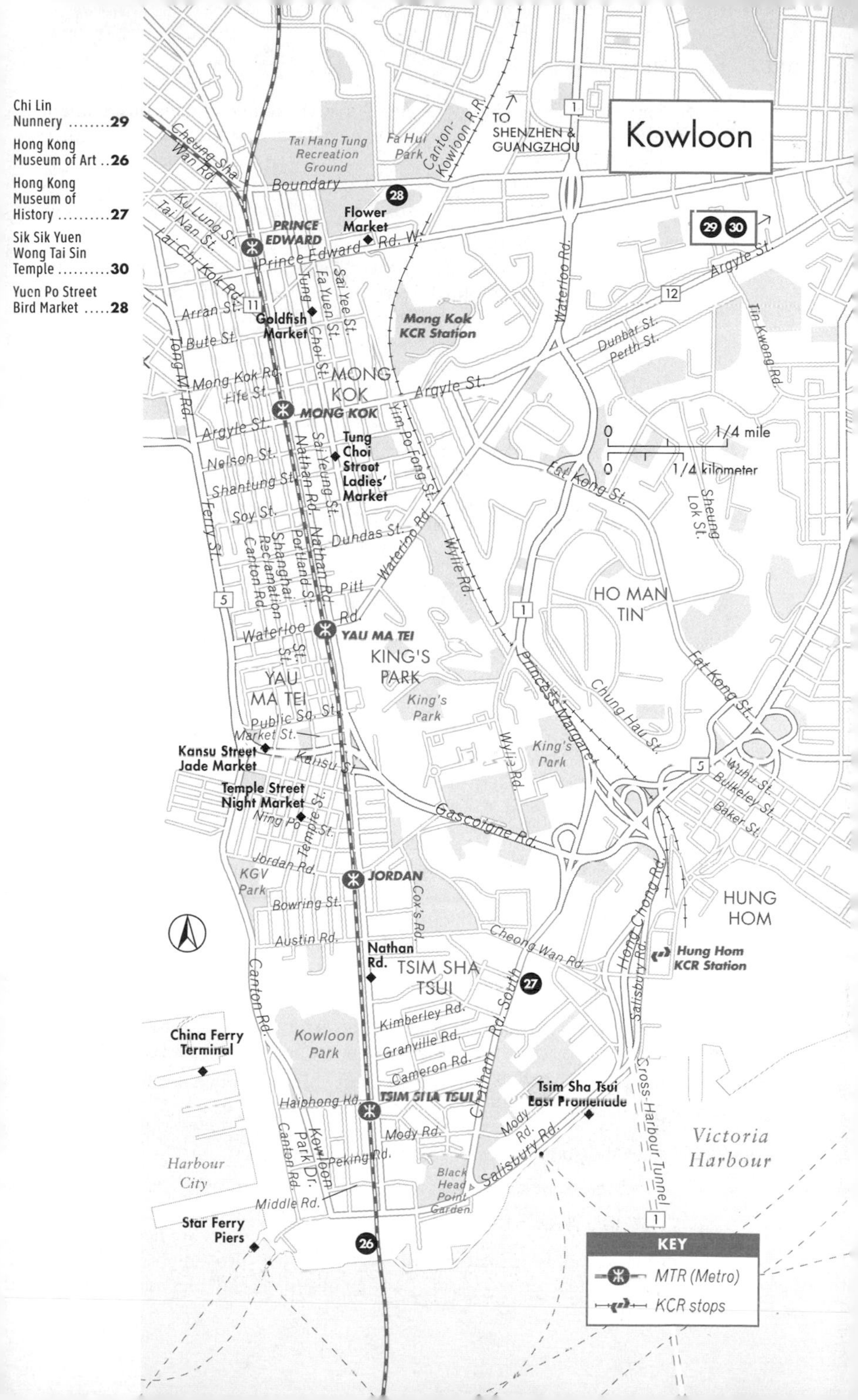
Kowloon
Chi Lin Nunnery 29
Hong Kong Museum of Art ..26
Hong Kong Museum of History 27
Sik Sik Yuen Wong Tai Sin Temple 30
Yucn Po Street Bird Market 28
TO SHENZHEN & GUANGZHOU
Tai Hang Tung Recreation Ground
Fa Hui Park
Canton-Kowloon R.R.
Boundary
Flower Market
PRINCE EDWARD
Prince Edward Rd. W.
Cheung Sha Wan Rd.
Ku Lung St.
Tai Nan St.
Lai Chi Kok Rd.
Arran St.
Goldfish Market
Bute St.
Tong Mi Rd.
Mong Kok Rd.
Fife St.
Tung Choi St.
Fa Yuen St.
Sai Yee St.
Mong Kok KCR Station
MONG KOK
Argyle St.
Waterloo Rd.
Dunbar St.
Perth St.
Tin Kwong Rd.
Nelson St.
Shantung St.
Soy St.
Sai Yeung St.
Nathan Rd.
Yim Po Fong St.
Tung Choi Street Ladies' Market
Ferry St.
Shanghai St.
Reclamation St.
Canton Rd.
Portland St.
Dundas St.
Pitt St.
Wylie Rd.
Tsui Kong St.
Sheung Lok St.
HO MAN TIN
YAU MA TEI
KING'S PARK
King's Park
Public Sq. St.
Market St.
Kansu St.
Kansu Street Jade Market
Temple Street Night Market
Ning Po St.
Temple St.
Princess Margaret
Chung Hau St.
Fat Kong St.
Gascoigne Rd.
Wuhu St.
Bulkeley St.
Baker St.
Jordan Rd.
JORDAN
KGV Park
Bowring St.
Austin Rd.
Cox's Rd.
Nathan Rd.
TSIM SHA TSUI
Cheong Wan Rd.
Hong Chong Rd.
Salisbury Rd.
HUNG HOM
Hung Hom KCR Station
Chatham Rd. South
China Ferry Terminal
Kowloon Park
Kimberley Rd.
Granville Rd.
Cameron Rd.
Haiphong Rd.
TSIM SHA TSUI
Tsim Sha Tsui East Promenade
Mody Rd.
Kowloon Park Dr.
Peking Rd.
Harbour City
Middle Rd.
Black Head Point Garden
Cross-Harbour Tunnel
Victoria Harbour
Star Ferry Piers
0 1/4 mile
0 1/4 kilometer
KEY
MTR (Metro)
KCR stops

TST is also accessible by MTR. Underground walkways connect the station with Kowloon-Canton Railway's Tsim Sha Tsui East terminus, where KCR East Rail trains depart every 10 to 15 minutes for the eastern New Territories. The Kowloon Airport Express station is amid a construction wasteland west of TST. One day it will connect with KCR West Rail; for now hotel shuttles link it to the rest of Kowloon.

The MTR is your best bet for Jordan, Yau Ma Tei, Mong Kok, Kowloon Tong, Lok Fu, and Wong Tai Sin. But you'll need a bus or cab to reach Kowloon Tong from Wong Tai Sin or TST East.

SIGHTS

28 ★ **Yuen Po Street Bird Garden.** The air fills with warbling and tweeting about a block from this narrow public garden. Around 70 stalls stretch down one side of it, selling all the birds, cages, and accessories a bird owner could need. More gruesome are the heaving bags of creepy-crawlies—old men tending the stalls lift larvae with chopsticks and pop them into the open mouths of baby birds. Birds are a favorite pet in Hong Kong, especially among the elderly, who often take them out for a "walk" in bamboo cages.

Plenty of free birds swoop in to gorge on spilled food and commiserate with imprisoned brethren. The garden was built to replace the old, mazelike Bird Market, which was closed down during the worst bird flu outbreaks. (Government sanitation programs mean the flu is no longer a threat, though all the vendors here ignore signs warning against contact with birds.) From the MTR station walk east along Prince Edward Road for three short blocks, then turn left onto Sai Yee Street, then right onto Flower Market Road, for an aromatic approach. The Bird Garden is at the end of this flower-market street. ✉ *Yuen Po St., Prince Edward, Kowloon* ☎ *2302–1762* 🌐 *www.lcsd.gov.hk/parks/ypsbg* 🎫 *Free* 🕐 *Daily 7 AM–8 PM* Ⓜ *Prince Edward, Exit B1.*

29 Fodor's Choice ★ **Chi Lin Nunnery.** Not a single nail was used to build this nunnery, which dates from 1934. Instead, traditional Tang Dynasty architectural techniques involving wooden dowels and bracket work hold its 228,000 pieces of timber together. Most of the 15 cedar halls house altars to bodhisattvas (those who have reached enlightenment)—bronze plaques explain each one.

Feng shui principles governed construction. The buildings face south toward the sea, to bring abundance; their backs are to the mountain, provider of strength and good energy. The temple's clean lines are a vast departure from most of Hong Kong's colorful religious buildings—here, polished wood and gleaming Buddha statues are the only adornments.

The Main Hall is the most imposing—and inspiring—part of the monastery. Overlooking the smaller second courtyard, it honors the first Buddha, known as Sakyamuni. The soaring ceilings are held up by 28 cedar columns, measuring 18 feet each. They also support the roof—no mean feat, given that its traditionally made clay tiles make it weigh 176 tons.

Courtyards and gardens, where frangipani flowers scent the air, run beside the nunnery. The gardens are filled with bonsai trees and artful rockeries. Nature is also present inside: the various halls and galleries all look onto two courtyards filled with geometric lotus ponds and manicured bushes. **■ TIP→ Consider combining Chi Lin Nunnery with a visit to Sik Sik Yuen Wong Tai Sin Temple, only one MTR stop or a short taxi ride away.** ✉ *5 Chi Lin Dr., Diamond Hill, Kowloon* ☎ *2354–1789* *Free* ⏲ *Nunnery daily 9–4:30, lotus-pond garden daily 7–7* Ⓜ *Diamond Hill, Exit C2.*

26 Fodor's Choice ★ **Hong Kong Museum of Art.** An extensive collection of Chinese art is packed inside this boxy tiled building on the Tsim Sha Tsui waterfront in Kowloon. It's a heady mix of things that make Hong Kong what it is: Ming ceramics, 2,000-year-old calligraphic scrolls, 1,100 works chronicling colonization, kooky contemporary canvases. Thankfully it's organized into thematic galleries with clear, if uninspiring, explanations. Hong Kong's biggest visiting exhibitions are usually held here.

5

Head to the Chinese Antiquities Gallery if Ming's your thing. A series of low-lit rooms on the third floor houses ceramics from Neolithic times through the Qing dynasty. Unusually, they're displayed by motif rather than by period: dragons, phoenixes, lotus flowers, and bats are some of the auspicious designs. Bronzes, jade, lacquerware, textiles, enamel, and glass ware complete this collection of decorative art.

In the Chinese Fine Art Gallery you get a great introduction to Chinese brush painting, often difficult for the Western eye to appreciate. Landscape paintings from the 20th-century Guangdong and Lingnan schools form the bulk of the collection, and modern calligraphy also gets a nod. **■ TIP→ Traditional Chinese landscape paintings are visual records of real or imagined journeys—a kind of travelogue. Pick a starting point and try to travel through the picture, imagining the journey the artist is trying to convey.**

The Contemporary Hong Kong Art Gallery showcases a mix of traditional Chinese and Western techniques—often in the same work. Paintings account for most of the pieces from the first half of the 20th century, when local artists used the traditional mediums of brush and ink in innovative ways. Western techniques dominate later work, the result of Hong Kong artists spending more time abroad.

There are educational rooms tucked away on the eastern side of every floor. Kids can emboss traditional motifs on paper or do brass rubbings; there are also free gallery worksheets in English. A good selection of reference books makes them useful learning centers for adults, too. Guided tours can help you to understand art forms you're not familiar with. There are general museum tours in English Monday through Saturday at 11 AM and 4 PM. Check the Web site for the schedule of more detailed visits to specific galleries—they change every month. If you prefer to tour alone, consider an English-language audio-guide: it's informative, if a little dry, and it costs only HK$10.

The museum is a few minutes' walk from either the Star Ferry or Tsim Sha Tsui MTR stop. ✉ *10 Salisbury Rd., Tsim Sha Tsui, Kowloon* ☎ *2721–0116* 🌐 *hk.art.museum* 🎟 *HK$10* ⏲ *Fri. and Sun.–Wed. 10–6, Sat. 10–8* Ⓜ *Tsim Sha Tsui MTR, Exit E.*

27 ★ **Hong Kong Museum of History.** A whopping HK$156 million went into making this museum engaging and educational. The permanent Hong Kong Story re-creates life as it was rather than simply displaying relics of it: indeed, actual artifacts are few. The museum's forte is clear explanations of spectacular life-size dioramas, which include village houses and a Central shopping street in colonial times. The ground-floor Folk Culture section is a Technicolor introduction to the history and customs of Hong Kong's main ethnic groups: the Punti, Hakka, and Hoklo. Upstairs, gracious stone-walled galleries whirl you through the Opium Wars and the beginnings of colonial Hong Kong. **■ TIP→ Unless you're with kids who dig models of cavemen and bears, skip the prehistory and dynastic galleries. Reserve energy for the last two galleries: a chilling account of life under Japanese occupation and a colorful look at Hong Kong life in the '60s.**

Budget at least two hours to stroll through—more if you linger in each and every gallery. Pick your way through the gift shop's clutter to find local designer Alan Chan's T-shirts, shot glasses, and notebooks. His retro-kitsch aesthetic is based on 1940s cigarette-girl images. To get here from the Tsim Sha Tsui MTR walk along Cameron Road, then left for a block along Chatham Road South. A signposted overpass takes you to the museum. ✉ *100 Chatham Rd. South, Tsim Sha Tsui, Kowloon* ☎ *2724–9042* 🌐 *hk.history.museum* 🎟 *HK$10; free Wed.* ⏲ *Mon. and Wed.–Sat. 10–6, Sun. and holidays 10–7* Ⓜ *Tsim Sha Tsui MTR, Exit B2.*

30 ★ **Sik Sik Yuen Wong Tai Sin Temple.** There's a very practical approach to prayer at one of Hong Kong's most exuberant places of worship. Here the territory's three major religions—Taoism, Confucianism, and Buddhism—are all celebrated under the same roof. You'd think that highly ornamental religious buildings would look strange with highly visible vending machines and LCD displays in front of them, but Wong Tai Sin pulls it off in cacophonic style. The temple was established in the early 20th century, on a different site, when two Taoist masters arrived from Guangzhou with the portrait of Wong Tai Sin—a famous monk who was born around AD 328—that still graces the main altar. In the '30s the temple was moved here; continuous renovations make it impossible to distinguish old from new.

Start at the incense-wreathed main courtyard, where the noise of many people shaking out *chim* (sticks with fortunes written on them) forms a constant rhythmic background. After wandering the halls, take time out in the Good Wish Garden—a peaceful riot of rockery—at the back of the complex. At the base of the complex is a small arcade where soothsayers and palm readers are happy to interpret Wong Tai Sin's predictions for a small fee. At the base of the ramp to the Confucian Hall, look up behind the temple for a view of Lion Rock, a mountain in the shape of a sleeping lion. ■ **TIP→ If you feel like acquiring a household altar of your own, head for Shanghai Street in Yau Ma Tei, the Kowloon district north of Tsim Sha Tsui, where religious shops abound.** ✉ *Wong Tai Sin Rd., Wong Tai Sin, Kowloon* ☎ *2327–8141* *Donations expected. Good Wish Garden: HK$2* ⏲ *Daily 7–5:30* Ⓜ *Wong Tai Sin, Exit B2 or B3.*

NEW TERRITORIES

Rustic villages, incense-filled temples, green hiking trails, pristine beaches—the New Territories have a lot to offer. Until a generation ago, the region was mostly farmland with the occasional walled village. Today, thanks to a government housing program that created "new towns" like Sha Tin and Tuen Mun with up to 500,000 residents, parts of the region are more like the rest of Hong Kong. Within its expansive 518 square km (200 square mi), however, you'll still feel far removed from urban congestion and rigor. Here you can visit the area's most lush parks and sneak glimpses into traditional rural life in the restored walled villages and ancestral clan halls.

5

THE TERRITORY

The New Territories border mainland China to the north and Sai Kung Peninsula to the east. Places worth visiting are a fair distance from each other, so day trips here take some planning—and some patience. You're definitely on "the other side," where few people speak English.

It's best to choose two or three sights to visit in a day, allowing 15 to 30 minutes of travel time between each, depending on whether you're going by bus or taxi.

GETTING AROUND

Between the bus, MTR, and the Kowloon–Canton Railway (KCR), you can get close to many sights. Set off on the MTR from Central to Tsuen Wan; from there, taxis, buses, and minibuses will take you to places such as the Yuen Yuen Institute and Tai Mo Shan. For Sha Tin and other spots in the east, take the MTR to Kowloon Tong; transfer to the KCR to Sha Tin station. To reach the Sai Kung Peninsula, take the MTR from Central to Choi Hung, then the green Minibus 1A to Sai Kung Town.

To tour at your own pace consider hiring a car and driver. **Ace Hire Car** (☎ *2893–0541*) charges HK$220 per hour (three-hour minimum).

For a HK$5 call charge, you can hire a cab from the **Hong Kong Kowloon Taxi Knowledge Association** (☎ *2574–7311*) to pick you up and take you anywhere in Hong Kong.

SIGHTS

㉓ Fodor's Choice ★ **Hong Kong Heritage Museum.** This fabulous museum is Hong Kong's largest, yet it still seems a well-kept secret: chances are you'll have most of its 10 massive galleries to yourself. They ring an inner courtyard, which pours light into the lofty entrance hall. There's lots of ground to cover: prioritize the New Territories Heritage, the T. T. Tsui Gallery, and the Cantonese Opera Halls, all permanent displays, and do the temporary history and art exhibitions if energy levels permit. ■ **TIP→ Try to time your arrival to coincide with one of the hourly (on the hour) English-language presentations in the ground-floor Orientation Theater.**

The New Territories Heritage Hall is packed with local history—6,000 years of it. See life as it was in beautiful dioramas of traditional villages—one on land, the other on water (with houses-on-stilts). There's also lots of info and artifacts related to religion and festivals. The last gallery documents the rise of massive urban New Towns. There's even a computer game where you can design your own.

In the T. T. Tsui Gallery of Chinese Art exquisite antique Chinese glass, ceramics, and bronzes fill nine hushed second-floor rooms. The curators have gone for quality over quantity. Look for the 4-foot-tall terra-cotta Horse and Rider, a beautiful example of the figures enclosed in tombs in the Han Dynasty (206 BC–AD 220). The Tibetan religious statues and *thankga* paintings are unique in Hong Kong.

The Cantonese Opera Hall is all singing, all dancing, and utterly hands-on. The symbolic costumes, tradition-bound stories, and stylized acting of Cantonese opera can be impenetrable: the museum provides simple explanations and stacks of artifacts, including century-old sequined costumes that put anything Vegas dreams up to shame. ■ **TIP→ Don't miss the opera hall's virtual makeup display, where you get your on-screen face painted like an opera character.**

Kids love the Children's Discovery Gallery, where hands-on activities for 4- to 10-year-olds include dressing up in traditional Hakka gear and putting a broken "archaeological find" back together. The Hong Kong Toy Story, charting more than a century of local toys, brings a whole new dimension to that Made in Hong Kong tag in the toy box.

The museum is a five-minute signposted walk from Che Kung Temple KCR Station. If the weather's good, walk back along the leafy riverside path that links the museum with the Sha Tin KCR Station, in New Town Plaza mall, 15 minutes away. ✉ *1 Man Lam Rd., New Territories, Sha Tin* ☎ *2180–8188* 🌐 *hk.heritage.museum* 🎫 *HK$20; HK$10 Wed.* ⏲ *Mon. and Wed.–Sat. 10–6, Sun. 10–7* Ⓜ *Che Kung or Sha Tin KCR.*

㉕ **Sam Tung Uk Museum.** A walled Hakka village from 1786 was saved from demolition to create this museum. It's in the middle of industrial Tsuen Wan, in the western New Territories, so its quiet whitewashed courtyards and small interlocking chambers contrast greatly with the nearby residential towers. Hakka villages were built with security in mind, and this one looks more like a single large house than a village. Indeed, most Hakka village names end in *uk,* which literally means "house"—Sam Tung Uk translates as "Three Beam House." Rigid symmetry dictated the village's construction: the ancestral hall and two common chambers form the central axis, which is flanked by the more private areas. The front door is angled to face west–southwest, in keeping with feng shui principles of alignment between mountain and water. Traditional furniture and farm tools are displayed in each room.

■ **TIP→ Head through the courtyards and start your visit in the exhibition hall at the back, where a display gives helpful background on Hakka culture and pre-industrial Tsuen Wan—explanations are sparse elsewhere. You can also try on a Hakka hat.** ✉ *2 Kwu Uk Lane, Tsuen Wan, New Territories* ☎ *2411–2001* 🌐 *www.heritagemuseum.gov.hk/english/branch_sel_stu.htm* 🎫 *Free* 🕙 *Wed.–Mon. 9–5* Ⓜ *Tsuen Wan, Exit B3.*

THE HAKKA

The Hakka or "guest" people from northeast China first arrived in Hong Kong during the late 17th century. They fiercely held on to their language and traditions, were dealt the worst lands, and were scorned by the local Punti community. Their farming lifestyle was notoriously tough; women worked the fields as hard as men (leading to a happy side effect of unbound feet). Even today the Hakka have a reputation for being hardworking and conscientious. In the New Territories you still might see traditionally dressed women in open-crown, broad-brimmed hats, circled by a curtain of black cloth.

24 ★ **Temple of Ten Thousand Buddhas.** You climb some 400 steps to reach this temple: but look on the bright side, for each step you get about 32 Buddhas. The uphill path through dense vegetation is lined with life-size golden Buddhas in all kinds of positions. If you're dragging bored kids along, get them to play "Spot the Celebrity Lookalike" on the way. ■ **TIP→ In summer bring water and insect repellent.** Prepare to be dazzled inside the main temple: its walls are stacked with gilded ceramic statuettes. There are actually nearly 13,000 Buddhas here, a few more than the name suggests. They were made by Shanghai craftsmen and have been donated by worshippers since the temple was built in the 1950s. Kwun Yum, goddess of mercy, is one of several deities honored in the crimson-walled courtyard.

Look southwest on a clear day and you can see nearby **Amah Rock,** which resembles a woman with a child on her back. Legend has it that this formation was once a faithful fisherman's wife who climbed the mountain every day to wait for her husband's return, not knowing he'd been drowned. Tin Hau, goddess of the sea, took pity on her and turned her to stone.

The temple is in the foothills of Sha Tin, in the central New Territories. Take Exit B out of the Sha Tin KCR station, walk down the pedestrian ramp, and take the first left onto Pai Tau Street. Keep to the right-hand side of the road and follow it around to the gate where the signposted path starts. ■ **TIP→ Don't be confused by the big white buildings on the left of Pai Tau Road. They are ancestral halls, not the temple.** ✉ *Off Pai Tau St., Sha Tin, New Territories* 🎫 *Free* 🕙 *Daily 9–5:30* Ⓜ *KCR East Rail: Sha Tin.*

EXPERIENCES

SUNBATHING

 **Hap Mun Wan.** Half Moon Bay is a brilliant, golden-sand beach on a grassy island near Sai Kung Town. It's one of the many small beaches among dozens of small islands near Sai Kung that are popular and easy to reach.

Bunn's Divers Institute (✉*188 Johnston Rd., Wan Chai* ☎*2574–7951*) runs outings for qualified divers to areas like Sai Kung. The cost of a day trip runs HK$580 for two sessions, one in the morning and another in the afternoon, and includes lunch, two tanks, and weights. Sampans to Half Moon depart from the Sai Kung waterfront, beside the bus station. If you're sharing a sampan with other passengers, remember the color of the flag on the roof: that's the color you need for your return ferry. Shared sampans cost HK$40. **■TIP➜ To cruise around the harbor, rent a *kaido* (pronounced "guy-doe," one of the small boats run by private operators for about HK$130 round-trip), and stop at tiny Yim Tin Tsai Island, which has a rustic Catholic mission church built in 1890.** *From Central, take MTR to Choi Hung, then green Minibus 1A to Sai Kung Town.*

㉒ **Sha Ha.** The sand isn't fine and golden, but the main reason people visit this beach is for the windsurfing. Sha Ha's waters are shallow, even far from shore, and ideal for beginning windsurfers. Feeling exhausted after a day out on the water tackling the wind? Grab something to eat at the restaurants and bars that dot the beach. You can take lessons or rent a board or even a kayak at the **Kent Windsurfing Centre** (✉*Sha Ha, Sai Kung* ☎*9733–1228*). Ask for Eddy. *From Central take MTR to Choi Hung, then green Minibus 1A to Sai Kung Town. It's a 10-min walk along the shore to Sha Ha.*

⑳ **Silverstrand.** Though rocky in spots, it has soft sand and is crowded on summer weekends. Walk down a steep set of steps to reach the small stretch of beach where families enjoy all manner of floating beds and tubes in the sea. Despite the heat, barbecuing is a popular beach activity here. The local style is to hold long forks laden with sausages, chicken wings, fish balls, or other finger food over the coals. *From Central, take MTR to Diamond Hill, then Bus 91. Alight at big roundabout.*

HIKING

Fodor's Choice ★ **MacLehose Trail.** Named after a former Hong Kong governor, the 97-km (60-mi) MacLehose is the grueling course for the annual charity event, the MacLehose Trailwalker. Top teams finish the hike in an astonishing 15 hours. Mere mortals should allow three to four days or simply tackle one section or another on a day hike or two.

This isolated trail through the New Territories starts at Tsak Yue Wu, beyond Sai Kung, and circles High Island Reservoir before breaking north. A portion takes you through the Sai Kung Country Park, Hong Kong's most beloved preserve, and up a mountain called Ma On Shan. Turn south for a high-ridge view, and walk through Ma On Shan Country Park. From here walk west along the ridges of the mountains known as the Eight Dragons, which gave Kowloon its name.

After crossing Tai Po Road, the path follows a ridge to the summit of Tai Mo Shan (Big Hat Mountain), which, at 3,140 feet, is Hong Kong's tallest mountain. On a clear day you can even see the spire of the Bank of China building in Central from here. Continuing west, the trail drops to Tai Lam Reservoir and Tuen Mun, where you can catch public transport back to the city. To reach Tsak Yue Wu, take the MTR to Choi Hung and then Bus 92 or 96R, or Minibus 1 to Sai Kung Town. From Sai Kung Town, take Bus 94 to the country park. **■TIP→ An easier way to access Tai Mo Shan is via an old military road. En route you'll see the old British barracks, now occupied by the People's Liberation Army. Take the MTR to Tsuen Wan and exit the station at Shiu Wo Street, then catch Minibus 82.**

To the east of Sha Tin, **Sai Kung Peninsula** has a few small towns and Hong Kong's most beloved nature preserve. The hikes through the hills surrounding High Island Reservoir are spectacular, and the beaches are among the territory's cleanest. Seafood restaurants dot the waterfront at Sai Kung town as well as the tiny fishing village of Po Toi O in Clear Water Bay. Take the MTR to Choi Hung and then Bus 92 or 96R, or Minibus 1 to Sai Kung Town. Instead of taking the bus, you can also catch a taxi along Clearwater Bay Road, which will take you into forested areas and land that's only partially developed with Spanish-style villas overlooking the sea. At Sai Kung Town, you can rent a sampan that will take you to one of the many islands in the area for a day at the beach. Sai Kung Country Park has several hiking trails that wind through majestic hills overlooking the water. This excursion will take a full day, and you should only go if it's sunny.

WHERE TO EAT

By Robin Goldstein

Stand your ground when faced with a barrage of 16-stroke Chinese characters. Don't wince at the steaming cauldron of innards or the rows of webbed duck feet that announce the corner restaurant's offerings. Be bold at the sight of a vicious cleaver beheading a roast suckling pig.

If you do, you'll find that the resulting crackles of pork fat and tender slices of meat—served with rice and some glistening greens—taste better than anything at the western-theme restaurant or pan-Chinese chain down the street. You know the one. It has the English-language menu and the empty tables.

At small, local restaurants specializing in Cantonese food, don't expect an English menu or knives and forks. (Tip: if you struggle with chopsticks, keep a plastic fork or spoon in your bag). The best advice is to follow the crowds. Choose a restaurant that's full, and don't be shy about pointing to an interesting dish at your neighbor's table. This is often the best way to order, since even when there is an English menu, local specialties may not be on it.

The pointing method of ordering comes in handy when you visit the small, brightly lit dives, many open into the wee hours, that specialize either in noodle soups or roast meats. At noodle-centric restaurants, fish-ball soup with ramen noodles is an excellent choice, and the goose, suckling pig, honeyed pork, and soy-sauce chicken are good bets at the roast-meat shops. A combination plate, with a sampling of meats and some greens on a bed of white rice, is a foolproof way to go.

Other than being adventurous, what's the best way to enjoy a memorable meal in Hong Kong? Remember that many fine-dining restaurants are in five-star hotels and shopping malls. Several of these restaurants, such as Dynasty and Caprice, offer seasonal menus or special chef's selections along with their standard à la carte options.

Finally, Hong Kong is the world's epicenter of dim sum. While you're here you must have at least one dim sum breakfast or lunch in a teahouse. Those steaming bamboo baskets you see conceal delicious dumplings, buns, and pastries—all as comforting as they are exotic.

SPICY SZECHUAN

Though it is more commonly know as *Sichuan* these days, the cooking style still features an eye-watering array of chilis and the ingredients are cooked slowly for an integrated flavor—the opposite of Cantonese food. Szechuan rice, bamboo, wheat, river fish, shellfish, chicken, and pork dishes are all prepared with plenty of salt, anise, fennel seed, chili, and coriander.

MEAL TIMES

Locals eat lunch between noon and 1:30 PM; dinner is around 8. Dim sum begins as early as 10 AM. Reservations aren't usually necessary except during Chinese holidays or at of-the-moment or high-end hotel restaurants like Alain Ducasse's SPOON or the Caprice. There are certain classic Hong Kong preparations (e.g., beggar's chicken, whose preparation in a clay pot takes hours) that require reserving not just a table, but the dish itself. Do so at least 24 hours ahead.

You'll also need reservations for a meal at one of the so-called private kitchens—unlicensed culinary speakeasies, which are often the city's hottest tickets. Book several days ahead, and if possible, join forces with other people. Some private kitchens only take reservations for parties of four, six, or eight.

PRICES

The ranges in our chart reflect prices of main courses on dinner menus (unless dinner isn't served). That said, the custom of sharing dishes affects the ultimate cost of your dinner. Further, we exclude outrageously expensive dishes—abalone, bird's nest soup, shark's fin soup—and seafood at market prices when we assign ranges to properties.

Don't be shocked when you get your bill and see that you've been charged for everything, including tea, rice, and those side dishes placed automatically on your table. Tips are expected (10% average gratuity) at most restaurants, even if the bill includes a service charge, which *won't* go to the waitstaff.

	WHAT IT COSTS IN HK$				
	¢				
AT DINNER	under HK$50	HK$50–HK$100	HK$101–HK$200	HK$201–HK$300	over HK$300

Prices are per person for a main course at dinner and do not include the customary 10% service charge.

WESTERN, CENTRAL AND THE ADMIRALTY

$$$$ FRENCH ✕**Amber.** When the Landmark Mandarin Oriental hotel opened in 2005, its aim was to be seen as the preeminent hotel on Hong Kong Island. It made sense that it would contain a flagship power-lunch restaurant that aspires to a similar level of impeccable, modern style. Chef Richard Ekkebus's tasting menu includes creative dishes such as Dungeness crab served in five different forms—jelly, salad, foam, bisque, and ice cream—and New Zealand langoustine with seared pork belly and purple artichokes. ✉*Landmark Mandarin Oriental Hotel, 15 Queen's Rd., Central* ☎*2132–0066* ▭*AE, DC, MC, V* Ⓜ*Central.*

$$$$ CONTEMPORARY ✕**Bo Innovation.** The mastermind behind this deservedly renowned and upscale "private kitchen" is Alvin Leung, who dubbed himself the "demon chef" and had that moniker tattooed on his arm. Leung set up Bo Innovation in Central in 2005 to serve what he calls "extreme Chinese" cuisine, applying molecular gastronomy, French, and Japanese cooking techniques to traditional Cantonese dishes. Three years later, the restaurant has moved to a bigger spot in Wan Chai with outdoor seating, but Leung's cooking remains quirky and hard to define. Some of his recent creations include an egg-tart martini, which turns the classic Hong Kong pastry into an eggnoglike drink with a crust around the rim in place of salt. The toro (tuna belly) sashimi topped with foie gras powder blends two rich flavors into one. The Australian Wagyu striploin with black-truffle *cheung fan,* or rice roll, is a winner. At dinner, choose between the eight-course tasting menu (HK$680) or the 12-course chef's menu (HK$1,080); it's not possible to dine à la carte. Tables are often full on Friday and Saturday, so book in advance. ✉*Shop No. 13, 2nd fl., J Residence, 60 Johnston Rd., Wan Chai* ☎*2850–8371* 🌐*www.boinnovation.com* ✍*Reservations essential* ▭*AE, DC, MC, V* ⏲*Closed Sun. No lunch Sat.* Ⓜ*Wan Chai.*

$$ ECLECTIC ✕**Café Deco Bar & Grill.** As is often the case where there's a captive audience, dining up at the Peak Galleria mall is a crapshoot. This huge eatery is no exception: you come for the views, not the food. The best strategy might be to come here in time for sunset, hit Café Deco just for drinks and appetizers, and enjoy the vistas; then head down to the city for dinner. Dishes on the overly ambitious menu traverse five or six continents, and are dramatically prepared by chefs in open kitchens (which will, at least, amuse the kids). Oysters are good and the pizza is okay, but you should avoid the insipid Southeast Asian fare and overpriced steaks. When you book (and you must), be sure to request a table with a view, as many tables in the place have none, which defeats the purpose of coming. ✉*1st fl., Peak Galleria, 118 Peak Rd., The Peak, Central* ☎*2849–5111* 🌐*www.cafedecogroup.com* ✍*Reservations essential* ▭*AE, DC, MC, V.*

$$$$ ECLECTIC ✕**café TOO.** The innovative café TOO introduces all-day dining and

WORD OF MOUTH

"Cafe TOO is certainly the best buffet in Hong Kong . . . if the mango souffle is available among the dessert offerings, by all means have it!" —Ben Vickery

"Café Deco is definitely tourist oriented and very noisy. But the view from a window table is divine." —Paul

drama with seven separate cooking "theaters" and a brigade of 30 chefs. The liveliness and bustle make it a good place to stop for breakfast or lunch. Take your pick from seafood, sushi, and sashimi; Peking duck and dim sum; a carving station for roasts, poultry, and game; noodles and pastas; and pizzas, curries, tandoori, antipasto, cured meats, salads, or sandwiches. You can even have a late-night snack here from 10:30 PM to midnight. ✉*7th fl., Island Shangri-La hotel, Pacific Place, Supreme Court Rd., Admiralty* ☎*2820–8571* 🌐*www.shangri-la.com* 💳*AE, DC, MC, V* Ⓜ*Admiralty.*

$$$ AMERICAN ✕ **Dan Ryan's.** If, after a few days of goose web and thousand-year egg, you have a sudden burger craving, this is the place. You'll find good approximations of the kind expats dream about when they think of the States. The popular bar and grill is often standing room only, so call ahead for a table. Apart from burgers, steaks, and ribs, the menu offers a smattering of international dishes—pasta and the like—but we recommend that you stay away from anything complicated (and certainly anything with fish) and stick to the simple, rib-sticking fare, served up without fuss or formality. ✉*114 Pacific Place, 88 Queensway, Admiralty* ☎*2845–4600* 🌐*www.danryans.com* *Reservations essential* 💳*AE, DC, MC, V* Ⓜ*Admiralty.*

$$$ ITALIAN ✕ **DiVino.** This ultracool wine bar feels like something straight out of Milan, bringing with it small plates for casual snacking and mixed platters ideal for sharing. Not surprisingly, it's popular with the drinks-after-work crowd—and you get complimentary savory treats with your wine from 6 to 8 PM. But don't underestimate the cuisine: the tailor-made cold-cut platters, for starters, are superb. The cheese board is served with crusty, oven-warm bread. Pasta main courses include Gorgonzola and black-truffle penne and pumpkin gnocchi with sage and ricotta cheese. The place also stays open for revelry late into the evening. ✉*Shop 1, 73 Wyndham St., Central* ☎*2167–8883* 🌐*www.divino.com.hk* 💳*AE, DC, MC, V* ⊗*No lunch Sun.* Ⓜ*Central.*

WORD OF MOUTH

"Quite popular with the after-work crowd, DiVino makes for an energizing start to a big night out in Hong Kong" —Nicole

$$–$$$ PAN-ASIAN ✕ **dragon-i.** If you can stomach the scene at this scenester hangout, an evening at dragon-i can be a memorable experience. The hip interior is a window into the world of Hong Kong's beautiful people. A velvet rope shows up at some point each evening, and the models all put in an appearance on Wednesday nights (and along follows everyone else). Happily, the Japanese and traditional Cantonese cuisines generally keep up—just don't come with lofty expectations, and be prepared to spend a lot for small portions. Dim sum lunch on the terrace is a lower-impact way to go. ✉*Basement fl., The Centrium, 60 Wyndham St., Central* ☎*3110–1222* 🌐*www.dragon-i.com.hk* *Reservations essential* 💳*AE, DC, MC, V* ⊗*Closed Sun.* Ⓜ*Central.*

$$$ ECLECTIC ✕ **Jimmy's Kitchen.** One of the oldest restaurants in Hong Kong, Jimmy's opened in 1928 and serves comfort food from around the world to a loyal clientele in a private-club atmosphere. Neither the food nor the decor has changed much in the last 30 years. Its handy location just

off Queen's Road in Central and a menu that offers a wide selection of both western and Asian dishes including borscht, goulash, bangers and mash, curry, and burgers have made Jimmy's a favorite with both Chinese and western locals as well as tourists looking for a taste of home. It's not cheap, but it's a good choice for a night out with friends, especially if your group's cravings are pulling you in different directions. ✉*Basement, South China Bldg., 1–3 Wyndham St., Central* ☎*2526–5293* ▭*AE, DC, MC, V* Ⓜ *Central.*

ANCIENT CHINESE SECRET

If you keep an open mind about food, you can lose yourself in the magic of a cuisine whose traditions have been braising for millennia. It, like many of Hong Kong's residents, has its roots in Guangdong (Canton) Province. Cantonese cooks believe that the secret to bringing out the natural flavors of food is to cook it quickly at very high temperatures. The resulting dishes are then served and eaten immediately.

$$$ ECLECTIC

Lumiere. Modern, sexy Lumiere, in the IFC Mall, bills itself as a "Szechuan Bistro and Bar," and its menu blends Sichuan and South American cuisines. Although main courses are Sichuan in inspiration, like spicy jumbo crab claws, the starters include ceviche. Another signature dish is seared Chilean sea bass in Sichuan style. Also getting high marks is the unique cocktail list at the long bar, which overlooks the harbor. Drinks are classified into "fruity," "creamy," "dry," and "sweet-and-sour," and also categorized by strength. Here, too, there's South America to thank, as in a "Caipiritini" (a mix of caipirinha and martini)—or, if you prefer, there's always the 1970 Pétrus. ✉*3101–3107, podium level 3, International Finance Center Mall, Central* ☎*2393–3933* 🌐*www.cuisinecuisine.hk* ▭*AE, DC, MC, V* Ⓜ*Central.*

$$$ CANTONESE Fodor'sChoice ★

Lung King Heen. It's made a serious case for being the best Cantonese restaurant in Hong Kong—and consequently, the world. Where other contenders tend to get too caught up in prestige dishes, and hotel restaurants in name-brand chefs, here there's a complete focus on taste. When you try a little lobster-and-scallop dumpling, or a dish of housemade XO sauce that is this divine, you will be forced to reevaluate your entire conception of Chinese cuisine. ✉*Podium 4, Four Seasons Hotel, 8 Finance St., Central* ☎*3196–8880* 🌐*www.fourseasons.com* *Reservations essential* ▭*AE, DC, MC, V* Ⓜ*Central.*

¢ CANTONESE

Mak's Noodles Limited. Mak's looks like any other Hong Kong noodle shop, but it's one of the best known in town, with a reputation that belies its humble decor. The staff is attentive, and the menu includes some particularly inventive dishes, such as tasty pork-chutney noodles. The real test of a good noodle shop, however, is its wontons, and here they're fresh, delicate, and filled with whole shrimp. And don't miss the *sui kau,* filled with minced chicken and shrimp. ✉*77 Wellington St., Central* ☎*2854–3810* ▭*No credit cards* Ⓜ*Central.*

$$$$ FRENCH

Restaurant Pétrus. Commanding breathtaking views atop the Island Shangri-La, Restaurant Pétrus scales the upper Hong Kong heights of prestige, formality, and price. This is one of the city's few flagship hotel restaurants that have not attempted to reinvent themselves as fusion;

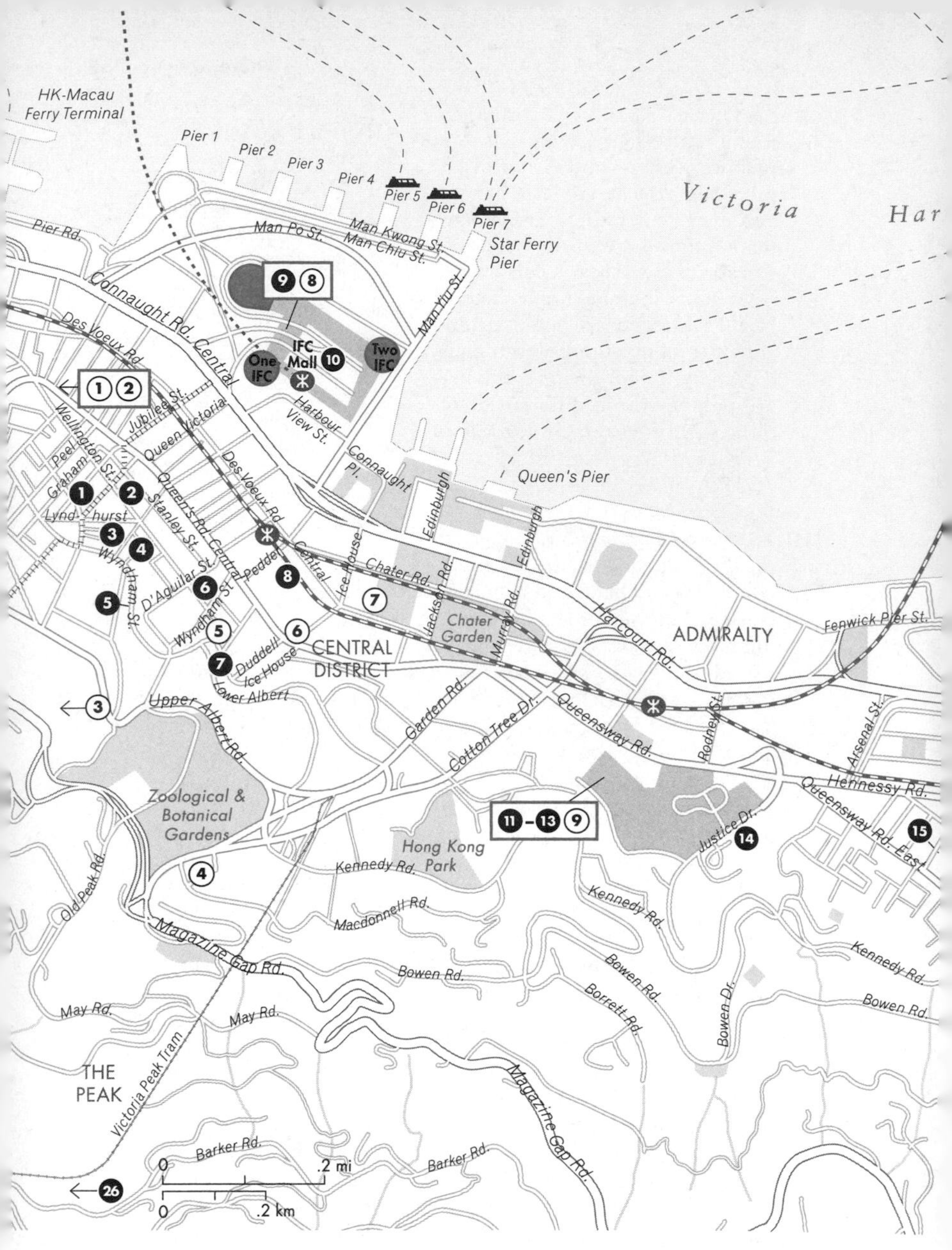

Restaurants ▼

Amber	8
Bebek Bengil 3	18
Bo Innovation	7
Café Deco Bar & Grill	26
café TOO	13
Che's Cantonese Restaurant	16
Cinecittà	14
Dan Ryan's	11
Dim Sum	25
DiVino	3
dragon-i	5
Gitone Fine Arts	15
Hay Hay	17
Jimmy's Kitchen	6
Lucy's	24
Lumiere	10
Lung King Heen	9
Mak's Noodles Limited	2
OVOlogue	20
Restaurant Pétrus	12
Shek O Thai Seafood Restaurant	23
ToTT's Asian Grill & Bar	21
Victoria City Seafood	19
Xiao Nan Guo	22
Yellow Door Kitchen	1
Yung Kee	4

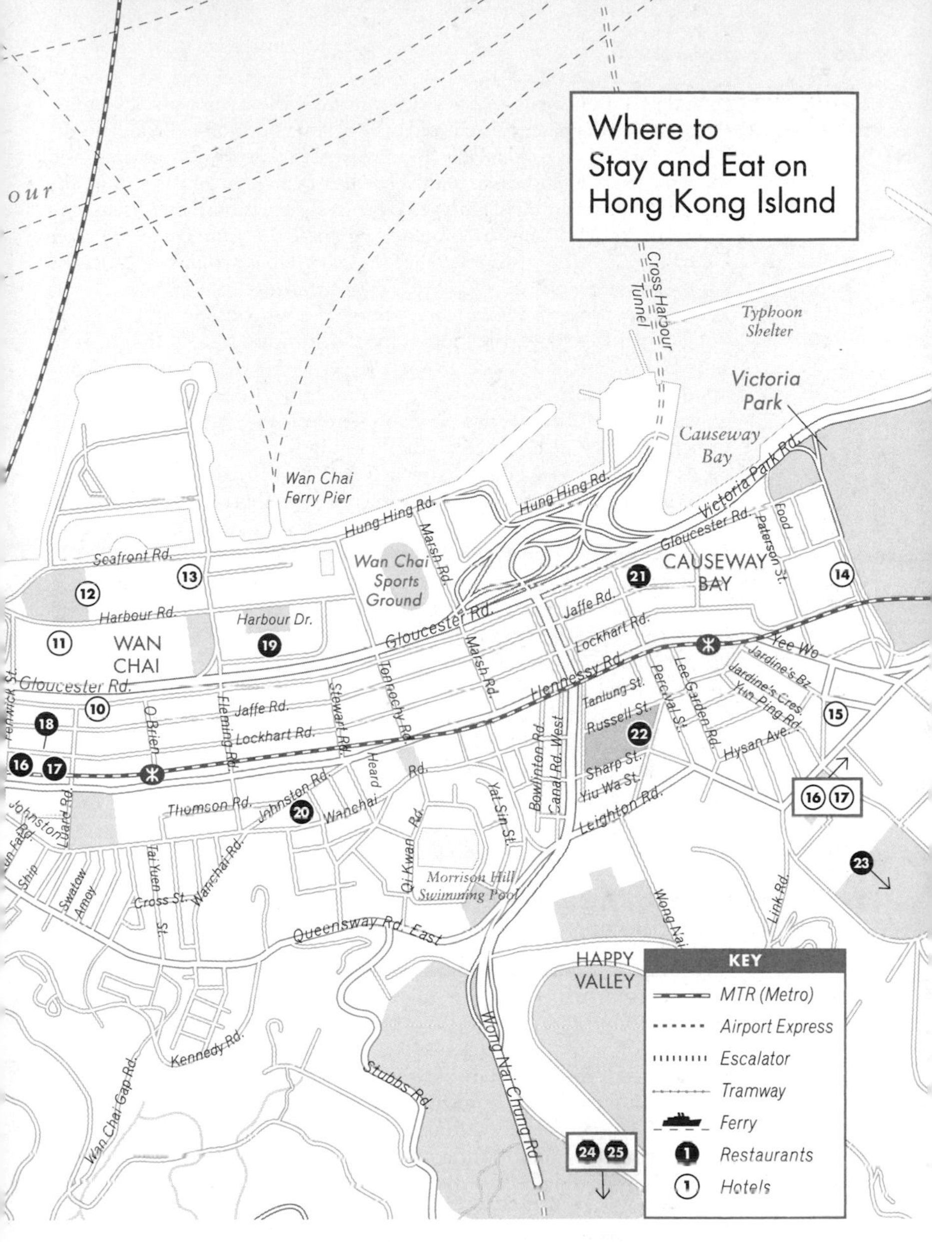

Hotels ▼

Bishop Lei International House **3**

Four Seasons **8**

Garden View YWCA **4**

Grand Hyatt **12**

The Harbourview **11**

Hotel Jen **1**

Ice House **5**

Island Shangri-La **9**

Jia Hotel **15**

Lan Kwai Fong Hotel **2**

Landmark Mandarin Oriental **6**

Luk Kwok **10**

Mandarin Oriental Hong Kong **7**

Metropark Hotel **16**

Park Lane **14**

Renaissance Harbour View **13**

Rosedale on the Park **17**

sometimes, traditional French haute cuisine is what you want. Likewise, the design of the place is in the old-school restaurant-as-ballroom mode. The kitchen has a particularly good way with (surprise!) foie gras, and the wine list is memorable, with verticals of Chateau Pétrus among the roughly 1,000 celebrated vintages. The dress here is business casual—no jeans or sneakers. ✉ *56th fl., Island Shangri-La, Pacific Place, Supreme Court Rd., Admiralty* ☎ *2820–8590* 🌐 *www.shangri-la.com* ✍ *Reservations essential* 💳 *AE, DC, MC, V* Ⓜ *Admiralty.*

$$–$$$ CANTONESE ✕ **Yung Kee.** Close to Hong Kong's famous dining district of Lan Kwai Fong, Yung Kee has turned into a local institution since it first opened shop as a street-food stall in 1942. It serves authentic Cantonese cuisine amid riotous decor and writhing gold dragons. Locals come for roast goose with beautifully crisp skin and tender meat, as well as dim sum. Other specialty dishes include the "cloudy tea" smoked pork, which needs to be reserved a day in advance, and deep-fried prawn with mini crab roe. More adventurous palates may wish to check out the thousand-year-old preserved eggs. ✉ *32–40 Wellington St., Central* ☎ *2522–1624* 🌐 *www.yungkee.com.hk* 💳 *AE, DC, MC, V* Ⓜ *Central.*

$$$ SICHUAN ✕ **Yellow Door Kitchen.** A sunny, casual Sichuan private kitchen (unlicensed restaurant), the Yellow Door is still one of the most talked-about places to eat in SoHo, even though it's been open since 2002. The space is down-home and personal, with good food and good feelings. Many of the spices and ingredients are shipped in from Sichuan province to create such wonders as bean curd and meat cooked in spicy Sichuan sauce and a memorable stuffed Hangzhou-style "8-treasure duck," which is stuffed with sticky rice and braised. The HK$288 set dinner is great value. ✉ *6th fl., 37 Cochrane St., SoHo, Central* ☎ *2858–6555* 🌐 *www.yellowdoorkitchen.com.hk* ✍ *Reservations essential* 💳 *AE, DC, MC, V* ⊗ *Closed Sun. No lunch Sat.* Ⓜ *Central.*

WAN CHAI AND CAUSEWAY BAY

$$ INDONESIAN ✕ **Bebek Bengil 3** *(Dirty Duck Diner)*. Inspired by a tiny but legendary institution in Bali, this re-creation in the heart of Wan Chai similarly specializes in crispy duck, marinated for 36 hours in an age-old recipe of spices. The seating is *sala*-style (at a low table, sitting on pillows on the floor), on an outside terrace overlooking bustling Lockhart Road. Familiar Indonesian dishes like *nasi goreng* (spicy noodles) and beef *rendang* (a spicy concoction with ginger, lemongrass, and coconut milk) are on the menu. Finish with drinks at BB's lively sister establishment on the ground floor, the Klong Bar & Grill. ✉ *5th fl., The Broadway, 54–62 Lockhart Rd., Wan Chai* ☎ *2217–8000* 🌐 *www.elite-concepts.com* 💳 *AE, DC, MC, V* Ⓜ *Wan Chai.*

$–$$ CANTONESE ✕ **Che's Cantonese Restaurant.** Smartly dressed locals in the know head for this casually elegant dim sum specialist, which is in the middle of the downtown bustle yet well concealed on the fourth floor of an office building. From the elevator, you'll step into a classy Cantonese world. It's hard to find a single better dim sum dish than Che's crispy pork buns, whose sugary baked pastry conceals the brilliant saltiness of stewed pork within. Other dim sum to try include panfried turnip cake; rich, tender braised duck web (foot) in abalone sauce; and a refreshing dessert of cold pomelo and sago with mango juice for a calming end to an exciting meal. ✉ *4th fl., The Broadway, 54–62 Lockhart Rd., Wan Chai* ☎ *2528–1123* 💳 *AE, DC, MC, V* Ⓜ *Wan Chai.*

$$$ ITALIAN Fodor'sChoice ★ ✕**Cinecittà.** Come here for fine Roman cuisine in this up-and-coming foodie enclave just around the corner from Pacific Place. As the name suggests, the theme is Italia cinema, centered on Fellini and his works. The interior is mostly white and glass, the atmosphere trendy and elegant, and the food always top-notch. Order from the menu or ask the chef to compose a tasting selection for you. Pastas are homemade and are excellent. Come to admire the fashionistas, show off your glad rags, or just to focus on the fabulous food. ✉ *9 Star St., Wan Chai* ☎ *2529–0199* 🌐 *www.elite-concepts.com* 💳 *AE, DC, MC, V* Ⓜ *Wan Chai.*

$–$$ CANTONESE ✕**Dim Sum.** This elegant jewel breaks with tradition and serves dim sum all day and night. The original menu goes beyond common Cantonese morsels like *har gau* (steamed shrimp dumplings), embracing dishes more popular in the north, including chili prawn dumplings, Beijing onion cakes, and steamed buns. Lobster bisque and abalone dumplings are also popular. Lunch reservations are not taken on weekends, so there's always a long line. Arrive early, or admire the antique telephones and old Chinese posters while you wait. Even if it feels somewhat contrived, it's worth it. ✉ *63 Sing Woo Rd., Happy Valley* ☎ *2834–8893* 💳 *AE, MC, V* Ⓜ *Happy Valley.*

$$$ SHANGHAINESE ✕**Gitone Fine Arts.** Highly recommended by locals, this pottery-studio-cum-restaurant-speakeasy has acquired quite a following since its 1995 opening. An artistic couple runs the studio and gallery, and turn it into a cozy, unlicensed "private dining" restaurant at night. The menu varies completely from day to day, but there are generally both Shanghainese and Cantonese options. Go for the Shanghai-style meal, as this is the specialty—it will include up to 16 small courses making up a long night of adventurous tasting. The pork leg braised in sweet soy, when available, is outstanding; it's a Shanghainese classic. Booking is essential, and unless you get lucky on a particular night, you must have at least a group of four. ✉ *Ground fl., shop GB, 27–28, Site B, Lei King Wan, 45–47 Tai Hong St., Sai Wan Hoi* ☎ *2527–3448 or 2525–6077* ✍ *Reservations essential* 💳 *AE, DC, MC, V* Ⓜ *Sai Wan Ho.*

¢ CANTONESE ✕**Hay Hay.** The best food in Hong Kong can hide out in the dingiest storefronts, and nowhere is this more true than at Hay Hay, a restaurant whose business card contains not a word of English. Surprisingly, though, an English menu lurks somewhere in the back office, but you shouldn't bother with it. Instead, just point to what looks good on other tables—it's likely to be a delicious plate of rice, sweet, tender roast goose or pork, and greens; or an exemplary noodle soup with slices of roast meat resting on top. Apply the hot sauce liberally, and don't expect the staff to speak English. ✉ *72–86 Lockhart Rd., corner of Ward St., Wan Chai* ☎ *2143–6183* 💳 *No credit cards* Ⓜ *Wan Chai.*

$$ CANTONESE ✕**OVOlogue.** Located in one of Hong Kong's last remaining colonial buildings, this stylish and innovative Cantonese restaurant offers an elegant respite from the hectic shopping streets of Wan Chai. The menu includes dim sum with a few novel additions, as well as a selection

of popular Cantonese dishes. The decor—1920s Shanghai style—is exquisitely executed and evokes a bygone Chinese era. This is a good choice for diners who want to try Cantonese cuisine and dim sum in beautiful surroundings. ✉ *3rd fl., Renaissance Harbour View, 1 Harbour Rd., Wan Chai* ☎ *2802–8888 Ext. 6971* ▭ *AE, DC, MC, V* Ⓜ *Wan Chai.*

WORD OF MOUTH

"Located on the 34th floor of the Excelsior with window views of Causeaway Bay and Admiralty, ToTT's is an experience for all the senses." —cjbryant

$$$$ INTERNATIONAL ✕ **ToTT's Asian Grill & Bar.** The funky interior—zebra-stripe chairs, a central oval bar, and designer tableware—is matched by the East-meets-West cuisine at this restaurant on top of the Excelsior hotel, which looks down on Causeway Bay and the marina. It's one of the very best dinner views in town, with a fun, lively vibe to boot. Best on the menu are steaks, with excellent imported meat cooked properly to order; there's also an extensive wine list. Live music kicks in late during the evening, offering a chance to burn a few calories on the dance floor. ✉ *Excelsior Hotel, 281 Gloucester Rd., Causeway Bay* ☎ *2837–6786* ▭ *AE, DC, MC, V* Ⓜ *Causeway Bay.*

$$$ SEAFOOD ✕ **Victoria City Seafood.** This perennially popular restaurant excels at Cantonese dim sum, Shanghainese, and seafood. It's a big, bright, banquet-style space, generally packed with large groups. Not to be missed are the spectacular soup dumplings with hairy-crab roe; steamed blood with leek and egg tarts; and stir-fried rice rolls with XO sauce. Seafood, which you select live from the tank, might include whitebait in chili sauce, steamed prawns in vinegar sauce, whole local garoupa with ginger, or crab cooked with fried garlic. There's an Admiralty branch, too. ✉ *Sun Hung Kai Center, 30 Harbour Rd., Wan Chai* ☎ *2827–9938* ✉ *5th fl. Citic Tower, 1 Tim Mei Ave., Admiralty* ☎ *2877–2211* ▭ *AE, DC, MC, V* Ⓜ *Wan Chai.*

$$ SHANGHAINESE ✕ **Xiao Nan Guo.** First, a disclosure: this is a chain restaurant. But in this case it's not a bad thing, since it's part of a Shanghai chain, and you want your Shanghainese food to be authentic. In the years since it came to Hong Kong, Xiao Nan Guo has developed a serious following, particularly for dim sum. The feeling is casual and unpretentious, with a bright, expansive, bustling dining room lined with round tables. The focus is really on the food: soup dumplings are excellent, as you'd expect, but don't forget about the fatty "Lion's Head" meatballs, or the pork belly. ✉ *Shop 1301, 13th fl., Times Sq., 1 Matheson Rd., Causeway Bay* ☎ *2506–0009* ✉ *Shop 1201, 12th fl., Times Sq., 1 Matheson Rd., Causeway Bay* ▭ *AE, DC, MC, V* Ⓜ *Causeway Bay.*

SOUTHSIDE

$$$ MEDITERRANEAN Fodor's Choice ★ ✕ **Lucy's.** Turn left after Delifrance to find this warm, intimate eatery, hidden inside the famous Stanley Market and rarely uncovered by tourists. You may feel like you've walked into someone's house when you enter the small, shabby-chic dining room, but Lucy's is a professionally run restaurant offering excellent, home-cooked food. Try the delicious

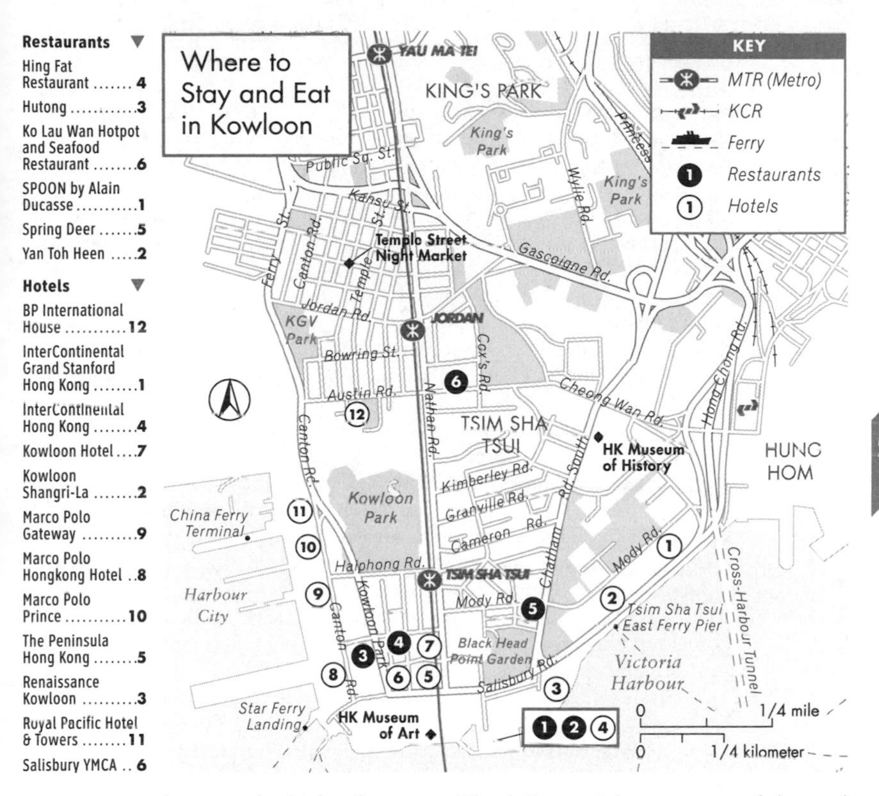

homemade chicken liver pate. The daily specials are a very safe bet and often include risottos and grilled or roasted meat; there are also plenty of fresh fruits and veggies on the menu. Desserts, especially the pecan pudding with toffee cream sauce, are not to be missed. More upscale than most of the beachside restaurants here and with oodles more character, Lucy's is a perfect end to a relaxed day browsing in the market, and easily your best bet in Stanley. ✉*Ground fl., 64 Stanley Main St., Southside, Stanley* ☎*2813–9055* ▭*MC, V.*

$ ASIAN Fodor'sChoice ★

✕ **Shek O Chinese Thai Seafood Restaurant.** The seaside village of Shek O lies past Stanley, and is worth a trip for the large sandy beach and fresh local seafood. For the quality and variety of food, this casual eatery is an all-time favorite. Come here for simple seaside dining at its best—the menu is extensive and everything's good and fresh—but prepare for plastic tables and toilets that are best approached with caution. This is a great spot for relaxing and dining with friends or family for a very reasonable price. ✉*303 Shek O Village, main intersection, next to bus stop, Southside, Shek O* ☎*2809–4426* ▭*AE, DC, MC, V.*

5

KOWLOON

WHAT IS BEIJINGESE?

This hearty fare is designed for the chilly climate of northern China—noodles, dumplings, and breads are more evident than rice. Peking duck is a perennial favorite. Firm flavors—such as garlic, ginger, and leek—are popular.

¢–$ CANTONESE **Hing Fat Restaurant.** So many simple roast meat and noodle soup shops are around lower Nathan Road that it can be hard to choose one. The popular Hing Fat is a reliable choice both for soup dumplings and for Cantonese-style roast meats—and the place is open all night, which is a definite plus. If you've made a long night of it, plop down here among the locals for late-night refueling within easy reach of the big Tsim Sha Tsui hotels. ✉ *Ground fl., 8–10 Ashley Rd., Tsim Sha Tsui, Kowloon* ☎ *2736–7788* ▭ *No credit cards* Ⓜ *Tsim Sha Tsui.*

$$$–$$$$ NORTHERN CHINESE Fodor'sChoice **Hutong.** It's not hard to see why Hutong is one of the hottest tables in Hong Kong: it has some of the most imaginative food in town, yet it's completely Chinese. Meanwhile, its spot at the top of the dramatic One Peking Road tower overlooks the entire festival of lights that is the Island skyline. Best among a sensational selection of northern Chinese creations are crispy, deboned lamb ribs, whose crackling skin conceals a deep, tender gaminess within. More subtle is Chinese spinach in a well-developed herbal ginseng broth, and delicate scallops with fresh pomelo. If you have just one meal in Hong Kong, make certain it's here. And remember to reserve well in advance. ✉ *28th fl., 1 Peking Rd., Tsim Sha Tsui, Kowloon* ☎ *3428–8342* 🌐 *www.aqua.com.hk* ✍ *Reservations essential* ▭ *AE, DC, MC, V* Ⓜ *Tsim Sha Tsui.*

$$ CANTONESE Fodor'sChoice ★ **Ko Lau Wan Hotpot and Seafood Restaurant.** Those seeking authentic Cantonese hotpot need not look further. Locals flock here for the tender beef and a wide selection of seafood, served in small slices that you cook at your table in a piping-hot soup (the satay broth and the coconut broth with pork are particularly tasty.) The owner runs his own fish farm in the seaside district of Sai Kung—no wonder the cuttlefish or shrimp balls and the yellow tail, amberjack, and abalone sashimi are all so tantalizingly fresh. The adventurous should try the geoduck, a giant clam, popular among Hong Kongers, which can be eaten raw with soy sauce and wasabi or slightly cooked in a soup. ✉ *1st fl., Vincent Commercial Building, 21–23 Hillwood Rd., Tsim Sha Tsui, Kowloon* ☎ *3520–3800* 🌐 *www.hotpotexpress.com* ▭ *MC, V* ⏲ *No lunch; 6 PM–3 AM daily Jordan.*

WORD OF MOUTH

"SPOON is a great concept, beautifully done food, amazing view and wonderful staff. Could not ask for a better restaurant." —Jenniene

$$$$ FRENCH **SPOON by Alain Ducasse.** Even if culinary legend Alain Ducasse is not exactly presiding over this kitchen, his inspiration is felt at this sleek restaurant, especially in preparations such as steamed foie gras, which balances the richness of seared foie gras with the resilience of a cold terrine de foie gras. Despite the occasional Asian flavor (seaweed pesto and shiitake mushrooms), the menu is contemporary French, liberally employing lobster, truffle, and other luxury ingredients with a

keen sense of balance. The best, if priciest, way to go is the multicourse tasting menu. The tables overlooking the harbor provide a romantic setting—or reserve the kitchen-side chef's table for a completely different experience. ✉ *Lobby level, Hotel InterContinental Hong Kong, 18 Salisbury Rd., Tsim Sha Tsui, Kowloon* ☎ *2313–2256* 🌐 *hongkong-ic.intercontinental.com* ✍ *Reservations essential* 💳 *AE, DC, MC, V* Ⓜ *Tsim Sha Tsui.*

$$
MANDARIN
✕ **Spring Deer.** With shades of pastel blue and green in a somber interior, and waiters in bland uniforms, this Peking duck specialist looks like something out of 1950s communist Beijing. The crowd, too, is hilariously old-school, which only adds to your duck experience. You'll see locals with noodle dishes, stir-fried wok meat dishes, and so forth, and they're good, but the Peking duck is the showstopper—it might be the best in town. Even the peanuts for snacking, which are boiled to a delectable softness, go above and beyond the call of duty. ✉ *1st fl., 42 Mody Rd., Tsim Sha Tsui, Kowloon* ☎ *2366–401 or 2366 5839* 💳 *AE, DC, MC, V* Ⓜ *Tsim Tsa Shui.*

$$$$
CANTONESE
Fodor's Choice ★
✕ **Yan Toh Heen.** This Cantonese restaurant in the Hotel InterContinental sets formal elegance against expansive harbor views, and its food is at the top of its class in town. Exquisite is hardly the word for the place settings, all handcrafted with green jade. Equally successful are dim sum, sautéed Wagyu beef with mushrooms and shishito pepper (a mild green chili pepper), and exemplary braised whole abalone in oyster sauce. The vast selection of seafood—the largest range in Hong Kong—transcends the usual tank to offer such exotic fishes as maori and green wrasse and shellfish like red coral crab, cherrystone clam, and sea whelk. Shorts are not allowed. ✉ *Lower level, Hotel InterContinental Hong Kong, 18 Salisbury Rd., Tsim Sha Tsui, Kowloon* ☎ *2313–2243* 🌐 *hongkong-ic.intercontinental.com* ✍ *Reservations essential* 💳 *AE, DC, MC, V* Ⓜ *Tsim Sha Tsui.*

WHERE TO STAY

By Robin Goldstein

Whether you are a business traveler or a casual tourist, you will inevitably be caught up with the manic pace of life here. Luckily, Hong Kong's hotels are constantly increasing their efforts to make you feel at home, so you can enjoy wonderful views of either city life or the world-famous harbor free from stress.

It's rare to find a hotel without the latest technologies, be they iPod docks, Wi-Fi, or the latest ayurvedic spa treatments. Yet space is at a premium, so rooms are smaller than what you may be used to at home, but the better hotels use innovative design to ward off claustrophobia. Reserve well in advance, and plan to pay dearly. Room shortages mean that the age of the under-$100 hotel room is vanishing; top spots run $500 to $600.

RESERVATIONS AND RATES

Book well in advance, especially for March or September to early December, high seasons for conventions. Most hotels have reliable Internet booking systems; phone reservations are also accepted, and receptionists speak English. Most hotels operate on the European plan, with no meals included. All rooms have private baths unless indicated otherwise. We always list the facilities available, but we don't specify whether they cost extra; so when pricing accommodations, always ask what's included and what's not.

WHAT IT COSTS IN HK$

	¢				
FOR TWO PEOPLE	under HK$700	HK$700–HK$1,100	HK$1,101–HK$2,100	HK$2,101–HK$3,000	over HK$3,000

Prices are for two people in a standard double room in high season, excluding 10% service charge and a 3% government tax.

WESTERN, CENTRAL AND THE ADMIRALTY

WORD OF MOUTH

"Bishop Lei is fantastic value for Hong Kong. The location is great (about a 2 minute walk from the moving sidewalk), the bus is outside the door, the front desk staff are helpful, and it's about a 40 minute walk to the top of the Peak." —Anna

$ Fodor'sChoice ★ **Bishop Lei International House.** Owned and operated by the Catholic diocese of Hong Kong, this guesthouse is up the Midlevels Escalator at the top of SoHo. Rooms are quite small but functional, and half have harbor views. Although it's economically priced, there is a fully equipped business center, a workout room, a pool, and a restaurant serving Chinese and western meals. **Pros:** walking distance to SoHo and Lan Kwai Fong, good value. **Cons:** starting to show age. ✉ *4 Robinson Rd., Midlevels, Western* ☎ *2868–0828* ⊕ *www.bishopleihtl.com.hk* *104 rooms, 101 suites* *In-room: safe, refrigerator, Internet. In-hotel: restaurant, pool, gym, laundry service, no-smoking rooms* *AE, DC, MC, V* Ⓜ *Central.*

$$$$ **Four Seasons.** When the Four Seasons opened, in the shadow of the world's sixth-tallest building, there was a collective intake of breath: with the elegantly colorful Chinese-theme rooms and their more muted western counterparts, the place displays equal levels of effortless modern style, yet they're not about trendy minimalism; the *smallest* of them is a roomy 500 square feet. World-class linens, feng shui elevator banks, heated infinity pools, 42-inch plasma TVs, skyline-view hot-rock massages in the city's most cutting-edge spa, clairvoyant service, fantastic restaurants—and this list doesn't even include the holistic effect of staying in a place that's redefining the world's very notion of an urban luxury hotel. **Pros:** spacious rooms, great views, no luxury overlooked. **Cons:** having everything comes at a price. ✉ *International Finance Center, 8 Finance Rd., Central* ☎ *3196–8888* ⊕ *www.fourseasons.com* *399 rooms, 54 suites* *In-room: refrigerator, safe, DVD, Wi-Fi. In-hotel: 5 restaurants, room service, bars, pools, gym, spa, laundry service, Wi-Fi, no-smoking rooms* *AE, DC, MC, V* Ⓜ *Sheung Wan.*

$$ **Garden View YWCA.** Don't be put off by the name: this attractive cylindrical guesthouse on a hill overlooks the botanical gardens and harbor, and its well-designed rooms make excellent use of small irregular

shapes and emphasize each room's picture windows. If you want to do your own cooking, ask for a room with a kitchenette (which will include a microwave oven); if not, the coffee shop serves European and Asian food. You can also use the swimming pool and gymnasium in the adjacent YWCA. Garden View is a five-minute drive (Bus 12A or Minibus 1A) from Central and a few minutes from the Peak tram station. **Pros:** excellent price for convenient location, walking distance to city center. **Cons:** traffic can get pretty bad in the morning and early evenings due to a nearby school. ✉ *1 MacDonnell Rd., Midlevels, Western* ☎ *2877–3737* 🌐 *www.ywca.org.hk* *136 rooms* *In-room: kitchen (some), refrigerator, Internet. In-hotel: restaurant, pool, gym, laundry service, no-smoking rooms* 💳 *AE, DC, MC, V* Ⓜ *Central.*

$–$$ Fodor's Choice ★ **Hotel Jen.** This new hotel, which opened in early 2008 on the site of an old Novotel, has a sleek, Zen-like atmosphere, with lots of white and other calming neutral colors, beige wood, and plenty of natural light. Guest rooms have daybeds in front of their large windows, which are perfect for reading during the day as well as accommodating an extra person at night. Long desks accommodate those with work to get done, though Korean and Japanese tourists comprise a significant portion of the clientele here. The bright and uncluttered Sky Lounge, a lounge and bar area on the 28th floor for hotel guests, is generally not crowded and makes a nice place to relax with a magazine. If visiting Western's antiques stores is high on your itinerary, this is a great alternative to pricier boutique hotels. **Pros:** unbeatable value, relaxing atmosphere. **Cons:** no easy access to an MTR station, so not convenient for visiting other parts of Hong Kong; not for those seeking raucous nightlife. ✉ *508 Queen's Rd. W, Western* ☎ *2974–1234* 🌐 *www.hoteljen.com* *280 rooms, 5 suites* *In-room: safe, kitchen (some), refrigerator, DVD (some), Internet, Wi-Fi. In-hotel: restaurant, room service, bar, pool, gym, laundry service, Wi-Fi, parking (paid), no-smoking rooms* 💳 *AE, D, DC, MC, V.*

$ **Ice House.** Consider yourself lucky to be alive at the right time: the apart-hotel accommodation concept has finally hit Hong Kong, and at the Ice House, it's done right. These chic, modern studio apartments are available to rent by the day or week, not just by the month (which, by the way, is quite reasonable at around HK$14,000). Sunlight is plentiful, and the glass-cube showers are an amusing touch. The location is excellent, next to the Foreign Correspondents' Club and Lan Kwai Fong, and studios come with free unlimited broadband, direct phone line, and other business amenities. There's housekeeping service every day but Sunday. If you want to feel like you have a place of your own in town, the Ice House is a unique option. **Pros:** free broadband, great value if your needs are basic. **Cons:** no hotel-style pampering here. ✉ *38 Ice House St., Central* ☎ *2836–7333* 🌐 *www.icehouse.com.hk* *30 rooms* *In-room: kitchen, Internet. In-hotel: laundry service, no-smoking rooms* 💳 *AE, DC, MC, V.*

$$$$ **Island Shangri-La.** This trademark elliptical building has become an icon of Hong Kong, as has *The Great Motherland of China,* the world's largest Chinese landscape painting, which is housed in its glass atrium. The painting, which spans 16 stories, can be viewed from elevators soaring up and down through the atrium, carrying guests to their rooms,

The lobby of the deluxe hotel, affectionately known to locals as the "Island Shang," sparkles with more than 780 dazzling Austrian crystal chandeliers hanging from high ceilings and huge, sunlit windows. Take the elevator up from the 39th floor and see the mainland's misty mountains drift by. Rooms are some of the largest on Hong Kong Island and have magnificent views; all have large desks and all-in-one bedside control panels. For very upscale dining there's the scenic, formal French eatery Pétrus on the top floor, or for Chinese food, the classy Summer Palace. **Pros:** *The Great Motherland*, spectacular reputation for quality service, large rooms. **Cons:** it costs to be fabulous. ✉ *Two Pacific Place, Supreme Court Rd., Admiralty* ☎ *2877–3838, 800/942–5050 in U.S.* 🌐 *www.shangri-la.com* *531 rooms, 34 suites* *In-room: safe, refrigerator, DVD, Wi-Fi. In-hotel: 4 restaurants, room service, pool, gym, laundry service, Wi-Fi, parking (paid), no-smoking rooms* 💳 *AE, DC, MC, V* Ⓜ *Admiralty.*

$$$ Fodor's Choice ★ **Lan Kwai Fong Hotel.** This boutique hotel, which opened in 2006, is popular with journalists and designers who appreciate its contemporary Chinese decor and SoHo location. Rooms are decorated with Asian accents but avoid an overdone, theme-park look, and bathrooms are outfitted with rain showerheads. The hotel's location in the middle of the Western SoHo area, which is full of art galleries, antiques shops, and boutiques, is another major selling point; an open-air breakfast lounge capitalizes on these colorful surroundings. Pricier rooms have unobstructed harbor views, although avid people-watchers may prefer "city-view" rooms, which look onto the vibrant street life below. **Pros:** hotel and neighborhood have lots of character. **Cons:** narrow roads surrounding hotel are often congested. ✉ *3 Kau U Fong, Western* ☎ *3650–0000* 🌐 *www.lankwaifonghotel.com.hk* *162 rooms, 5 suites* *In-room: safe, kitchen (some), refrigerator, Internet, Wi-Fi. In-hotel: 2 restaurants, room service, bar, gym, laundry service, no-smoking rooms* 💳 *AE, D, DC, MC, V.*

$$$$ **Landmark Mandarin Oriental.** Hong Kong hotels are like computers: every year the new technology outdoes the old by such a staggering margin that you're left wondering why anyone would stick by their old models. The design of this boutique-size hotel is dazzling, and a complete departure from the Mandarin's standard MO. The three room types are named for their square footage; the midrange L600 is the most interesting, with a round bathroom fascinatingly placed at the center of the space. Everything from iPod docks to surround-sound speakers are controlled through your TV remote, and the 21,000-square-foot spa has Turkish baths and "rain forest" steam room. And all of this is implausibly concealed within the financial mitochondrion of the city. **Pros:** you can't get more central in Central. **Cons:** even more expensive than other high-end hotels in Central. ✉ *15 Queen's Rd. Central, Central* ☎ *2132–0188* 🌐 *www.mandarinoriental.com/landmark* *113 rooms* *In-room: refrigerator, DVD, Wi-Fi. In-hotel: 3 restaurants, room service, bar, pool, gym, spa, laundry service, Wi-Fi, no-smoking rooms.* 💳 *AE, DC, MC, V* Ⓜ *Central.*

$$$$ **Mandarin Oriental Hong Kong.** In September 2006, the legendary Mandarin, which has served the international elite since 1963, completed a

top-to-bottom renovation that included the installation of one of the city's most elaborate spas. The hotel is such a symbol of Hong Kong's colonial and financial history that rumors of the renovations sparked fierce debate amongst the business elite. However, the Mandarin has not lost its characteristic charm in the face of modernization; sumptuous materials and furnishings, like silky cognac drapes and leather armchairs in guest rooms, are the norm here, but now so are flat-panel LCDs and iPod docks. Everything you see, you want to touch. Five new categories of rooms, from "study" to "harbour," span a wider price range than ever before. On the 25th floor, rising high above the Central skyline, are renowned chef Pierre Gagnaire's French restaurant Pierre and the panoramic M Bar. Walking around the new spa area is a delight in itself, as every corridor, alleyway and room feels like a classic Oriental boudoir, concealing hidden delights. **Pros:** staying here is a classic Hong Kong experience, rooms have wonderful study areas. **Cons:** standard rooms are relatively small for a luxury hotel. ✉ *5 Connaught Rd., Central* ☎ *2522–0111* 🌐 *www.mandarin-oriental.com/hongkong* *434 rooms, 68 suites* *In-room: safe, Internet, Wi-Fi. In-hotel: 6 restaurants, room service, bars, pool, gym, spa, laundry service, Wi-Fi, no-smoking rooms* *AE, DC, MC, V* Ⓜ *Central.*

5

LANTAU ISLAND

$$ **Disney's Hollywood Hotel.** Like its pricier sister, the Disneyland Hotel, Disney's Hollywood Hotel could theoretically be viewed simply as one of Asia's best airport hotels. But that would hardly do justice to the creativity and attention to detail that so brightly color every aspect of your stay here. The theme is the golden age of Hollywood, and if you're from the United States you'll smile at the loving display of Americana here, from the New York–theme restaurant to the art-deco frontage of the cocktail lounge. Of course, this is Disneyland, and there are the Chef Mickey restaurants, too. There's a playroom, Malibu Toy Shop, as well as a number of activities for kids. Rooms are on the smaller side, and a bit more "Goofy" than they are at the Disneyland Hotel, with perhaps even greater appeal for the children. **Pros:** great value. **Cons:** cut off from Hong Kong attractions, which is not great if you get sick of Disneyland. ✉ *Hong Kong Disneyland Resort, Lantau Island* ☎ *1–830–830* 🌐 *www.hongkongdisneyland.com* *600 rooms* *In-room: safe, refrigerator, Internet. In-hotel: 3 restaurants, room service, bars, tennis court, pool, gym, spa, children's programs (ages 2–12), laundry service, no-smoking rooms* *AE, DC, MC, V.*

$$$ **Hong Kong Disneyland Hotel.** Modeled in Victorian style after the Grand Floridian in Florida's Walt Disney World Resort, this top-flight hotel is beautifully executed on every level, from the spacious rooms with balconies overlooking the sea to the topiary of Mickey's Maze, and grand, imposing ballrooms that wouldn't be out of place in a fairy-tale secret castle. There's a full daily schedule of activities, many aimed at children although adults may enjoy the horticulture tours; and downstairs, Disney characters meet and greet guests during the enormous buffet breakfast—a good way to get your kids to forgive you for the

three days you spent sampling geese hanging from their necks in Mong Kok. Don't overlook Disneyland as a place to stay before or after your early-morning or late-night flight—it's minutes from the airport. **Pros:** great for kids. **Cons:** overpriced compared to Disney's Hollywood. ✉*Hong Kong Disneyland Resort, Lantau Island* ☎*1–830–830* 🌐*www.hongkongdisneyland.com* *400 rooms* *In-room: safe, refrigerator, Internet. In-hotel: 3 restaurants, room service, bars, tennis court, pool, gym, spa, children's programs (ages 2–12), laundry service, parking (free), no-smoking rooms* ▭*AE, DC, MC, V.*

WORD OF MOUTH

"I found the Regal to be a very stylish, opulent, and relaxing haven after a very long day of flying." —Brian

$$$ **Regal Airport Hotel.** Ideal for passengers in transit, this is one of the largest airport hotels in the world. It's some distance from the city, but the efficient high-speed rail system can have you on Hong Kong Island in around 25 minutes, and a free shuttle bus can take you to Tsimshatsui, for a little longer depending on traffic. It's also connected directly to the passenger terminal by an air-conditioned, moving walkway. Consistently voted one of the best airport hotels in the world, it has a spa, opened in 2006, with an impressive range of treatments and private spa suites that allow guests to receive treatments in their own rooms. Some rooms have terrific views of planes landing from afar; those with balconies overlook the hotel's two swimming pools and make you feel like you're staying in a resort. **Pros:** can't get any closer to the airport than this, great amenities for an airport hotel. **Cons:** not convenient to Hong Kong sights. ✉*9 Cheong Ted Rd., Lantau Island* ☎*2286–8888* 🌐*www.regalhotel.com* *1,171 rooms, 32 suites* *In-room: safe, refrigerator, kitchen (some), Wi-Fi. In-hotel: 7 restaurants, room service, bar, pool, gym, laundry service, parking (paid), no-smoking rooms* ▭*AE, DC, MC, V.*

WAN CHAI AND CAUSEWAY BAY

$$$$ **Grand Hyatt.** A ceiling painted by Italian artist Paola Dindo tops the Hyatt's art-deco-style lobby, and black-and-white photographs of classic Chinese scenes hang on the walls. The elegant guest rooms have sweeping harbor views, many with interesting zigzag window frames; amenities include large interactive TVs with cordless keyboards. The One Harbour Road Cantonese restaurant is notable—as is JJ's nightclub and Thai restaurant—and the ground-floor breakfast buffet is a decadent feast. The Plateau spa has a Zen-like calm and there are extensive outdoor facilities. The hotel is especially convenient if you're spending time at the Hong Kong Convention and Exhibition Centre, which is connected to the building. **Pros:** excellent sports facilities, including tennis and squash courts and a driving range. **Cons:** no space in the minibar for your own items. ✉*1 Harbour Rd., Wan Chai* ☎*2588–1234* 🌐*www.hongkong.grand.hyatt.com* *512 rooms, 37 suites* *In-room: safe, Wi-Fi. In-hotel: 8 restaurants, room service, bars, tennis courts, pool, gym, spa, laundry service, Wi-Fi, parking (paid), no-smoking rooms* ▭*AE, DC, MC, V* Ⓜ *Wan Chai.*

$$ **The Harbourview.** This waterfront YMCA property has small but relatively inexpensive rooms near the Wan Chai Star Ferry Pier. Rooms are not luxurious but have recently been renovated and now have new TVs, curtains, and carpets; some have harbor views. However, the final stage of renovations, set to begin in 2009, will temporarily reduce the number of available rooms. The hotel is well placed if you want to attend cultural events in the evening: both the Arts Centre and the Academy for Performing Arts are next door. It's also just opposite the Hong Kong Convention and Exhibition Centre. The 16-story building provides free shuttle service to Causeway Bay and the Central Star Ferry. You can use the superb YMCA Kowloon facilities, just a short ferry ride away, for a small fee. **Pros:** use of YMCA facilities across the harbor, affordable rates for reliable service and decent rooms. **Cons:** not close to a metro station. ✉ *4 Harbour Rd., Wan Chai* ☎ *2802–0111* 🌐 *www.theharbourview.com.hk* *320 rooms* *In-room: refrigerator, Internet, Wi-Fi. In-hotel: restaurant, room service, laundry service, Wi-Fi, no-smoking rooms* *AE, DC, MC, V* Ⓜ *Wan Chai.*

5

$$$ **Jia.** The first boutique hotel designed by Philippe Starck in Asia is a wonder to behold, beginning with the (see-and-be) scene in the lobby, bar, and restaurant—one of the hippest places to drink or dine in town. Although the sculptural furniture and accompanying trendiness won't be everyone's cup of tea, this is still a groundbreaking concept that is helping to redefine the modern Hong Kong hotel landscape. It doesn't have rooms; rather, it has "apartments," with mini-kitchens, dining tables, and cookware. You can choose between smaller studios or the larger one-bedroom suites, which have separate bedrooms. At this writing, a new restaurant and bar are due to open by the end of 2009. **Pros:** trendy yet reasonably priced for the area. **Cons:** no on-site gym, only one dining option. ✉ *1–5 Irving St., Causeway Bay* ☎ *3196–9000* 🌐 *www.jiahongkong.com* *34 studios, 24 suites* *In-room: kitchen, DVD, Internet. In-hotel: restaurant, room service, bar, laundry service, Wi-Fi, no-smoking rooms* *AE, DC, MC, V* Ⓜ *Causeway Bay.*

Fodor's Choice ★

$$ **Luk Kwok.** This contemporary hotel and office tower designed by Hong Kong's leading architect, Remo Riva, replaced the Wan Chai landmark of the same name immortalized in Richard Mason's novel *The World of Suzie Wong*. The Luk Kwok's appeal, aside from its slightly kitschy classic Asian feel, is its proximity to the Hong Kong Convention and Exhibition Centre, the Academy for Performing Arts, and the Arts Centre. Guest rooms, in the building's 19th to 29th floors, are simply furnished; higher floors have mountain or city views. **Pros:** landmark sight, has a popular Chinese restaurant. **Cons:** Wan Chai's rowdy nightlife district not great for children. ✉ *72 Gloucester Rd., Wan Chai* ☎ *2866–2166* 🌐 *www.lukkwokhotel.com* *196 rooms, 4 suites* *In-room: safe, refrigerator, Internet, Wi-Fi. In-hotel: 2 restaurant, room service, bar, gym, laundry service, Wi-Fi, no-smoking rooms* *AE, DC, MC, V* Ⓜ *Wan Chai.*

$$ **Metropark Hotel.** At this contemporary hotel you'll get a prime location and unobstructed views for a lower cost than at many others. Most rooms, though not strikingly designed, have extensive views of either Victoria Park or the harbor through the floor-to-ceiling windows. The

tiny lobby leads into Vic's bar; the Café du Parc serves French-Japanese fusion cuisine. The rooftop pool may be too small for those seeking their daily exercise, but has a spectacular view of Victoria Park and the harbor. Free shuttle buses to and from the Hong Kong Convention and Exhibition Centre and the hub of Causeway Bay run throughout the day. **Pros:** spectacular views at an affordable price, next door to Victoria Park. **Cons:** boring interior design. ✉*148 Tung Lo Wan Rd., Causeway Bay* ☎*2600–1000* 🌐*www.metroparkhotel.com* *266 rooms, 56 suites* *In-room: safe, refrigerator, Internet, Wi-Fi (some). In-hotel: restaurant, room service, bar, pool, gym, spa, laundry service, Wi-Fi, no-smoking rooms* ▭*AE, DC, MC, V* Ⓜ*Causeway Bay.*

$$ **Park Lane.** With an imposing facade that wouldn't look out of place in London, this elegant hotel overlooks Victoria Park and backs onto one of Hong Kong Island's busiest shopping, entertainment, and business areas, Causeway Bay. There's a spacious and grand lobby and rooms have luxurious marble bathrooms, elegant handcrafted furniture, and marvelous views of the harbor, Victoria Park, or the city. The rooftop restaurant has a panoramic view and serves international cuisine with a touch of Asian flavor. **Pros:** in the central shopping district. **Cons:** always crowded. ✉*310 Gloucester Rd., Causeway Bay* ☎*2293–8888* 🌐*www.parklane.com.hk* *810 rooms, 33 suites* *In-room: safe, refrigerator, Internet. In-hotel: 4 restaurants, room service, bar, gym, laundry service, Wi-Fi, parking (paid), no-smoking rooms* ▭*AE, DC, MC, V* Ⓜ*Causeway Bay.*

$$$$ **Renaissance Harbour View.** Sharing the Hong Kong Convention and Exhibition Centre complex with the Grand Hyatt is this more-modest but attractive hotel. Guest rooms are medium size with plenty of beveled-glass mirrors that reflect the modern decor. Many rooms have good harbor views and all have high-speed Internet access. Grounds are extensive and include a large outdoor pool, gardens, a playground, and jogging trails, which makes this a good place to stay if you are with children. The wonderfully scenic, soaring lobby lounge has a live jazz band in the evening and is a popular rendezvous spot for locals and visiting businesspeople. **Pros:** you can't get any closer to the Convention Centre, excellent facilities. **Cons:** flanked by office buildings, so it can feel rather dead at night; no Wi-Fi in guest rooms. ✉*1 Harbour Rd., Wan Chai* ☎*2802–8888* 🌐*www.renaissancehotels.com/hkghv* *862 rooms, 53 suites* *In-room: safe, refrigerator, Internet. In-hotel: 3 restaurants, room service, bars, tennis courts, pool, gym, laundry service, Wi-Fi, parking (paid), no-smoking rooms* ▭*AE, DC, MC, V* Ⓜ*Wan Chai.*

$$ **Rosedale on the Park.** This "cyber boutique hotel," the first of its kind in Hong Kong, has lots of high-tech extras. All public areas have computers, and you can rent a printer, computer, or fax for use in your room, where you also have broadband Internet access and a cordless telephone that can be used anywhere on the property. Mobile phones are also available for rent during your stay. You're in Hong Kong, after all, so why not take advantage of all that technology? Although only the top few floors have park or stadium views, all rooms are bright and comfortable. Next to Victoria Park and only a five-minute walk to the MTR subway, it's a great location for shopping—and the price is one

of the best values for a hotel in the middle of Causeway Bay. Cheena, the Rosedale's contemporary Chinese restaurant, is a popular lunch spot which promises not to use MSG. **Pros:** free broadband access in guest rooms. **Cons:** not all rooms have Wi-Fi access. ✉*8 Shelter St., Causeway Bay* ☎*2127–8888* 🌐*www.rosedale.com.hk* *274 rooms, 45 suites* *In-room: safe, refrigerator, Internet, Wi-Fi (some). In-hotel: 2 restaurants, room service, bar, laundry service, no-smoking rooms* *AE, DC, MC, V* Ⓜ *Causeway Bay.*

KOWLOON

$$ **BP International House.** Built by the Boy Scouts Association, this hotel next to Kowloon Park offers an excellent value for the money. A portrait of association founder Baron Robert Baden-Powell, hangs in the spacious modern lobby. The hostel-like rooms are small and spartan but have regular hotel amenities and panoramic views of Victoria Harbour and clear views of the busiest part of Kowloon. Ask to see your room before settling in, as some rooms are better than others. A multipurpose hall hosts exhibitions, conventions, and concerts, and the health club is one of the biggest in town. Another attraction for budget travelers is the self-service coin laundry. There are Internet terminals available for use. **Pros:** efficient reception service, very good value. **Cons:** can get crowded with tour groups, rooms vary significantly. ✉*8 Austin Rd., Jordan, Kowloon* ☎*2376–1111* 🌐*www.bpih.com.hk* *529 rooms, 4 suites* *In-room: safe, refrigerator, Internet, Wi-Fi. In-hotel: 2 restaurants, gym, laundry facilities, laundry service, Wi-Fi, parking (paid), no-smoking rooms* *AE, DC, MC, V* Ⓜ *Jordan.*

$$$$ **InterContinental Grand Stanford Hong Kong.** More than half the rooms in this luxury hotel, the sibling of the larger InterContinental Hong Kong in downtown Tsim Sha Tsui, have an unobstructed harbor view. The elegant lobby is spacious, the staff is helpful and friendly, and the comfortable, modern rooms are decorated in warm earth tones with wood trim and large desks. Executive rooms have a direct-line fax machine and amenities include trouser presses. There isn't quite an executive floor, but the club lounge serves the same purpose. The restaurants, which are well known locally, include Mistral (Italian), Belvedere (regional French), and Tiffany's New York Bar, which celebrates the Roaring 1920s with antique furniture, Tiffany-style glass ceilings, and a live band. **Pros:** same quality service as the downtown InterContinental for a little less. **Cons:** not in the center of Tsim Sha Tsui, lacks the prestige of the downtown branch. ✉*70 Mody Rd., Tsim Sha Tsui East, Kowloon* ☎*2721–5161* 🌐*www.hongkong.intercontinental.com* *554 rooms, 25 suites* *In-room: safe, Wi-Fi. In-hotel: 4 restaurants, room service, bar, pool, gym, spa, laundry service, parking (paid), no-smoking rooms* *AE, DC, MC, V* Ⓜ *Tsim Sha Tsui.*

$$$$ **InterContinental Hong Kong.** Don't be fooled by its aging exterior; perhaps one of the most attractive hotels in Asia, the InterContinental Hong Kong is opulent inside and offers a panoramic view of the whole coast of Hong Kong Island. Coming here for a spectacularly conceived cocktail at 8 PM to take in the skyline light show, perhaps equivalent to tea at

5

the Peninsula, should be on your must-do list. The lobby has a delicious airy quality, and the impeccably modern rooms are just as exciting, with luxuriously large beds, desks with ergonomically designed chairs, and superlative showers in the bathrooms. Corner suites have 180-degree harbor views as well as spacious outdoor terraces. The restaurant lineup includes Nobu and SPOON by Alain Ducasse. **Pros:** sets the standard for luxury, executive lounge open to nonexecutive guests for an extra fee, exceptional spa. **Cons:** all this luxury has a high price tag. ✉*18 Salisbury Rd., Tsim Sha Tsui, Kowloon* ☎*2721–1211, 800/327–0200 in U.S.* 🌐*www.hongkong-ic.intercontinental.com* *495 rooms, 92 suites* *In-room: safe, refrigerator, Wi-Fi. In-hotel: 5 restaurants, room service, pool, gym, spa, laundry service, parking (paid), no-smoking rooms* *AE, DC, MC, V* Ⓜ*Tsim Sha Tsui.*

$$ **Kowloon Hotel.** The mirrored exterior and the chrome, glass, and marble lobby reflect the hotel's high-tech orientation. Kowloon means "nine dragons" in Cantonese, and is the theme here. Triangular windows and a pointed lobby ceiling, made from hundreds of handblown Venetian-glass pyramids, represent dragons' teeth. The Kowloon is the lesser sibling to the adjacent Peninsula hotel, so you can sign up for services at the Pen and charge them to your room account here; similarly, all the facilities at the Peninsula are open to you. Rooms are small, but each has a computer with free Internet service and fax. Airline information is displayed in the lobby *and* in each room. **Pros:** in-room fax and Wi-Fi, access to Peninsula facilities. **Cons:** internet access only free for the first 15 minutes even in executive club, small rooms. ✉*19–21 Nathan Rd., Tsim Sha Tsui, Kowloon* ☎*2929–2888* 🌐*www.harbour-plaza.com/klnh* *733 rooms, 7 suites* *In-room: safe, refrigerator, Wi-Fi. In-hotel: 3 restaurants, room service, laundry service, no-smoking rooms* *AE, DC, MC, V* Ⓜ*Tsim Sha Tsui.*

$$$ **Kowloon Shangri-La.** Catering mainly to business travelers, this upscale hotel has a 24-hour business center with teleconferencing facilities as well as some strange features, such as the elevator carpets that are changed at midnight to indicate the day of the week. You'll feel like a tycoon in the posh lobby; the guest rooms all have magnificent harbor or city views, and although it doesn't have quite the glamour or services (or the accompanying sky-high prices) of the Island Shangri-La, it's still a wonderful place to stay. Complimentary newspapers are delivered daily to your room; club rooms have combination fax/printer/copier/scanners, as well as in-room DVD players and even TVs in the bathroom. A wireless telephone system allows guests to receive calls throughout the hotel. Attention to detail and outstanding service, in a city where service is already tops, set this hotel apart. **Pros:** outstanding service, many amenities. **Cons:** no easy access to public transit. ✉*64 Mody Rd., Tsim Sha Tsui East, Kowloon* ☎*2721–2111, 866-565–5050-in U.S.* 🌐*www.shangri-la.com/kowloon* *700 rooms, 30 suites* *In-room: safe, refrigerator, DVD (some), Wi-Fi. In-hotel: 5 restaurants, room service, bar, pool, gym, laundry service, Wi-Fi, no-smoking rooms* *AE, DC, MC, V* Ⓜ*Tsim Sha Tsui East.*

$$$ **Marco Polo Gateway.** This 16-story hotel, popular with Japanese tour groups and corporate clients, is in the shopping and commercial area

along Canton Road and close to the Tsim Sha Tsui MTR station. Rooms here are showing their age and feel positively antiquated compared to other Hong Kong hotels in this price range. However, some rooms have a unique view of Kowloon Mosque dome rising above the trees on Nathan Road. The Gateway's greatest asset is its restaurant, La Brasserie, which serves French provincial cuisine in typical brasserie style (dark wood, long bar, leather seats, red-checkered tablecloths). The business center is well supplied, and the staff is helpful. You can use the pool, gym, and spa at the nearby Marco Polo Hongkong Hotel. **Pros:** French restaurant. **Cons:** rooms here are showing their age. ✉ *Harbour City, Canton Rd., Tsim Sha Tsui, Kowloon* ☎ *2113–0888* 🌐 *www.marcopolohotels.com* *433 rooms, 55 suites* *In-room: safe, refrigerator, Internet. In-hotel: 3 restaurants, room service, bar, laundry service, public Wi-Fi, parking (paid), no-smoking rooms* *AE, DC, MC, V* Ⓜ *Tsim Sha Tsui.*

WORD OF MOUTH

"We went back to Marco Polo a second time because of its great location and the comfortable room size. It's a bit on the expensive side, but you get what you pay for." —Daniel & Cynthia

$$$ **Marco Polo Hongkong Hotel.** Next to the Cultural Centre and part of the wharf-side Harbour City complex, this is the largest and best of three Marco Polo hotels along the same street (the other two share the pool, gym, and spa at this location). Spacious rooms have special touches such as a choice of 11 types of pillows and, for children, miniature bathrobes, mild shampoos, and rubber ducks. The hotel's location on the edge of Tsim Sha Tsui means that most rooms have sweeping views of Hong Kong Island, the sea, and Kowloon West, including the new ICC tower. The Marco Polo Hongkong enjoys a long-standing reputation among European and American travelers and is the official hotel for the Hong Kong Sevens' rugby players. The largest Oktoberfest in town takes place here, with more than 1,000 thigh-slapping, beer-swilling, fun-loving participants. **Pros:** the most affordable of the grand, harbor-view hotels. **Cons:** difficult or impossible to get a room here in late March during the Hong Kong Sevens tournament, boisterous crowds during Oktoberfest. ✉ *Harbour City, Canton Rd., Tsim Sha Tsui, Kowloon* ☎ *2113–0088* 🌐 *www.marcopolohotels.com* *664 rooms, 49 suites* *In-room: safe, refrigerator, Internet. In-hotel: 7 restaurants, room service, bar, pool, gym, spa, laundry service, parking (paid), no-smoking rooms* *AE, DC, MC, V* Ⓜ *Tsim Sha Tsui.*

$$$ **Marco Polo Prince.** Like its neighboring Marco Polo namesakes in the Harbour City complex (the Hongkong and Gateway), the Prince is convenient to upscale shops, cinemas, and the restaurants and shops of Tsim Sha Tsui. It's also near the China Hong Kong Terminal, where ferries, boats, and buses depart for mainland China. Most of the small but comfortable rooms overlook expansive Kowloon Park, and some suites have views of Victoria Harbour. By the end of 2009, all guest rooms should be refurbished with updated technology such as flat-screen TVs and cordless phones, making this the second choice of the three Marco Polos. The Spice Market restaurant has a Southeast Asian buffet and an

international menu. You can use the pool, gym, and spa at the Marco Polo Hongkong, a five-minute walk away. **Pros:** easy access to other Marco Polo hotels, Harbour City shopping complex, and China Ferry Terminal. **Cons:** no harbor views, not convenient to leave the building for gym and spa access. ✉ *Harbour City, Canton Rd., Tsim Sha Tsui, Kowloon* ☎ *2113–1888* 🌐 *www.marcopolohotels.com* *393 rooms, 49 suites* *In-room: safe, refrigerator, Internet. In-hotel: 4 restaurants, room service, bar, laundry service, Wi-Fi, parking (paid), no-smoking rooms* 💳 *AE, DC, MC, V* Ⓜ *Tsim Sha Tsui.*

$$$$ **The Peninsula Hong Kong.** Established in 1928, the Peninsula has long been synonymous with impeccable taste and colonial glamour. And many people adore this hotel. Rooms have been updated recently with the flat-screen TVs and DVD players, and the hotel's renowned Rolls-Royces were replaced with newer models in 2006, but don't expect a high-tech feel here—this hotel is for those with old-world tastes. The spa is decked out with faux-Roman statues that are all show without a sense of style. But at about US$600 for the cheapest harbor-view room, it seems the Peninsula's most modern feature is its price. However, views at the popular Philippe Starck–designed Felix restaurant on the rooftop are unrivaled and there is still the famous high tea in the lobby bar. **Pros:** old-world glamour. **Cons:** may just seem old to those with a more modern aesthetic. ✉ *Salisbury Rd., Tsim Sha Tsui, Kowloon* ☎ *2366–6251* 🌐 *www.peninsula.com* *300 rooms, 54 suites* *In-room: safe, kitchen (some), refrigerator, DVD, Internet, Wi-Fi. In-hotel: 8 restaurants, room service, bar, pool, gym, spa, laundry service, parking (free), no-smoking rooms* 💳 *AE, DC, MC, V* Ⓜ *Tsim Sha Tsui.*

$$$ **Renaissance Kowloon.** Part of a large shopping complex, and now a member of the Marriott chain, this popular hotel on the Tsim Sha Tsui waterfront has perfect views of Hong Kong Island from its upper club floors, rivaled only by the adjacent hotel InterContinental Hong Kong, part of the same complex. Long escalators lead from the shopping area to the hotel's large second-floor lobby. The comfortable, modern guest rooms are homey and have plenty of space for working and relaxing. Greenery surrounds the outdoor pool, which stays open throughout the year. The Panorama restaurant, one of three in the hotel, has one of the best harbor views in town. **Pros:** reasonably priced considering views and facilities. **Cons:** you'll have to walk through a maze of shopping malls to get to the metro station which can be frustrating during peak shopping hours. ✉ *22 Salisbury Rd., Tsim Sha Tsui, Kowloon* ☎ *2369–4111* 🌐 *www.marriott.com* *492 rooms, 53 suites* *In-room: safe, refrigerator, Wi-Fi (some). In-hotel: 3 restaurants, room service, bar, pool, gym, spa, laundry service, Wi-Fi, parking (paid), no-smoking rooms* 💳 *AE, DC, MC, V* Ⓜ *Tsim Sha Tsui.*

$$ **Royal Pacific Hotel and Towers.** On the Tsim Sha Tsui waterfront, the Royal Pacific is part of the Hong Kong China City complex, which includes the terminal for ferries to mainland China. Guest rooms are arranged in two blocks, the hotel and tower wings. Tower-wing rooms have harbor views and are luxuriously furnished, while more inexpensive hotel-wing rooms have Kowloon street and park views and are smaller but just as attractive. The hotel connects to Kowloon Park by a

footbridge and is close to shops and cinemas. It doesn't have an executive floor, but a club lounge providing a similar service. **Pros:** good location. **Cons:** not distinctive. ✉ *33 Canton Rd., Tsim Sha Tsui, Kowloon* ☎ *2736–1188* 🌐 *www.royalpacific.com.hk* *673 rooms, 34 suites* *In-room: safe, Internet. In-hotel: 4 restaurants, room service, bar, gym, laundry service, Wi-Fi, parking (paid), no-smoking rooms* 💳 *AE, DC, MC, V* Ⓜ *Tsim Sha Tsui.*

$$ **Salisbury YMCA.** This upscale YMCA is Hong Kong's most popular and is great value for your money. Next to the Peninsula and opposite the Cultural Centre, Space Museum, and Art Museum, it's in an excellent location for theater, art, and concert crawls. The pastel-color rooms have harbor views and broadband Internet access. The Y also has a chapel, a garden, dance halls, a children's library, and excellent health and fitness facilities including squash courts and two climbing walls. Neighborhood restaurants are cheap and good, and the shopping is great. **Pros:** same view as Peninsula guests for a quarter the price, enough indoor activities to occupy you for days should a tropical storm hit. **Cons:** lobby sometimes feels more like a student center. ✉ *41 Salisbury Rd., Tsim Sha Tsui, Kowloon* ☎ *2369–2211* 🌐 *www.ymcahk.org.hk* *301 rooms, 62 suites* *In-room: safe, Internet. In-hotel: 2 restaurants, room service, bar, pool, gym, laundry facilities, Wi-Fi, no-smoking rooms* 💳 *AE, DC, MC, V* Ⓜ *Tsim Sha Tsui.*

NIGHTLIFE SAVVY

Hong Kong is a surprisingly safe place, but as in every tourist destination the art of the tourist rip-off has been perfected. If you're unsure, visit places signposted as members of the Hong Kong Tourist Board (HKTB). For listings and quirky reviews of all that's on, pick up *Hong Kong Magazine*, distributed free in Central's bars and cafés each Thursday. The nightlife coverage in *BC Magazine* is almost as extensive. Another good source of nightlife and cultural information is the daily newspaper, the *South China Morning Post*. The free monthly newspaper *City News* lists City Hall performances and events.

5

AFTER DARK

By Eva Chui Loiterton
Updated by Dominique Rowe

A riot of neon, heralding frenetic after-hours action, announces Hong Kong's nightlife districts. Hectic workdays make way for an even busier nighttime scene. Clubs and bars fill to capacity, evening markets pack in shoppers looking for bargains, restaurants welcome diners, cinemas pop corn as fast as they can, and theaters and concert halls prepare for full houses.

The neighborhoods of Wan Chai, Lan Kwai Fong, and SoHo are packed with bars, pubs, and nightclubs that cater to everyone from the hippest trendsetters, to bankers ready to spend their bonuses, and more laid-back crowds out for a pint. Partying in Hong Kong is a way of life; it starts at the beginning of the week with a drink or two after work, progressing to serious barhopping, and clubbing if it's the weekend. Work hard, play harder is the motto here and people follow it seriously.

CENTRAL

On weekends, the streets of Lan Kwai Fong are liberated from traffic, and the swilling hordes from both sides of the street merge into one heaving organism. A five-minute walk uphill is SoHo. Back in the '90s, it took local businesses some effort to convince district councillors that the sometimes vice-associated moniker (which in this case stands for South of Hollywood Road) was a good idea, but Hong Kong is now proud of this *très* chic area, a warren of streets stuffed with commensurately priced restaurants, bars, and late-night boutiques. Midway between Lan Kwai Fong's madness and SoHo's glamour is the newly regenerated Wyndham Street, home to a sophisticated array of bars, nightclubs, and restaurants.

BARS

Barco. Had enough of the crowds and looking for a quiet drink and conversation that you can actually hear? Barco is the place. It's cozy, with a small lounge area and an even smaller courtyard in the back, and an assortment of board games if you're feeling playful. ✉*42 Staunton St., SoHo, Central* ☎*2857–4478* ⏲*Closes 1* AM.

★ **California.** Set in a semi-basement, but with large open windows at the top so the crowds in Lan Kwai Fong can easily peer inside, California is a slice of the West Coast for homesick expats or western visitors looking for a more familiar environment. It's almost an institution, having survived the notoriously high turnover rate in the area, and remains one of the busiest bars in the neighborhood. ✉*32–34 D'Aguilar St., Lan Kwai Fong, Central* ☎*2521–1345* ⏲*Closes 3* AM.

Club 71. This bohemian diamond-in-the-rough was named in tribute to July 1, 2003, when half a million Hong Kongers successfully rallied against looming threats to their freedom of speech. Tucked away on a terrace down a market side street, the quirky, unpretentious bar is a mainstay of artists, journalists, and left-wing politicians. ✉*B/F, 67 Hollywood Rd., Sheung Wan* ☎*2858–7071* ⏲*Closes 2* AM.

F.I.N.D.S. The name of this supercool restaurant and bar is an acronym of Finland, Iceland, Norway, Denmark, and Sweden. The striking decor is pale blue and white, with sparkling granite walls. There's a large outdoor terrace, with comfortable seating. About 30 premium vodkas are served. You can also try one of the many tasty themed cocktails with corny names such as the Edvard Munch, made with lime aquavit and ginger wine. ✉*2nd fl., LKF Tower, 33 Wyndham St., entrance of D'Aguilar St., Central* ☎*2522–9318* ⏲*Closes 3* AM.

Globe. Between Lan Kwai Fong and SoHo, the Globe is one of the few laid-back places in the area to knock back a beer or two with down-to-earth folks. It's the local pub for homesick expats who live in the area, and does a great Sunday roast. ✉*39 Hollywood Rd., Central* ☎*2543–1941* ⏲*Closes 2* AM.

Insomnia. It's *almost* open 24/7 (closing for only three hours from 6 to 9 AM), hence the name. Live music is what really draws people here; there's a small stage and a dance floor at the back, but you'll have to fight your way there on weekends through the perfumed women and suited men. You might have more breathing room if you stay near the front bar, by the arched windows. ✉ *38–44 D'Aguilar St., Lan Kwai Fong, Central* ☎ *2525–0957.*

Le Jardin. For an otherworldly, cosmopolitan vibe, check out this casual bar with a lovely outdoor terrace overlooking the gregarious alfresco dining lane known locally as "Rat Alley." Walk through the dining area, and up a flight of steps. It's a little tricky to find, but the leafy, fairy-lit setting is worth it. ✉ *1st fl., 10 Wing Wah La., Central* ☎ *2526–2717* ⏲ *Closes 3* AM.

Lei Dou. Meaning simply "here" in Cantonese, this otherworldly spot, hidden away in the heart of the action, is where those in the know (and those seeking discretion) come to wind down in style. Lei Dou's fans love it for its decadent, candlelit decor, down-tempo jazz, and comfortable seating. ✉ *Ground fl., 20–22 D'Aguilar St., Central* ☎ *2526–6628* ⏲ *Closes 3* AM.

5

Lux. The well-heeled drink martinis and designer beers at this swanky corner spot. It has a prime location in Lan Kwai Fong and is another great bar to people-watch; it also serves excellent food in booths at the back. ✉ *California Tower, 30–32 D'Aguilar St., Lan Kwai Fong, Central* ☎ *2868–9538* ⏲ *Closes 4* AM.

MO Bar. This plush bar in the Landmark Mandarin Oriental is where the banking set goes to relax. You'll pay top dollar for the martinis (up to HK$150), but the striking interior makes it worthwhile. A huge, red-light circle dominates an entire wall, the "O" being a Chinese symbol of shared experience. ✉ *The Landmark Mandarin Oriental, 15 Queen's Road Central, The Landmark, Central* ☎ *2132–0077* ⏲ *Closes 2* AM.

RED Bar. Although its shopping mall location, outdoor terrace self-service policy, and incongruous affiliation with the next-door gym may not seem appealing, once you arrive, you'll throw all your preconceived notions into the harbor. On the roof of IFC Mall, RED has breathtaking views of the city, making it a great place to grab an early dinner, and relax with a cocktail while watching the sunset. ✉ *Level 4, Two IFC, 8 Finance St., Central* ☎ *8129–8882* ⏲ *Closes 2* AM.

Staunton's Wine Bar & Cafe. Adjacent to Hong Kong's famous outdoor escalator is this popular bistro-style café and bar. Partly alfresco, it's the perfect place to people-watch. You can come for a drink at night, or for coffee or a meal during the day. It's also a Sunday-morning favorite for nursing hangovers over brunch. ✉ *10–12 Staunton St., SoHo, Central* ☎ *2973–6611* ⏲ *Closes 3* AM.

DISCOS AND NIGHTCLUBS

Azure. If Lan Kwai Fong's masses are wigging you out, head skywards to this fabulous and spacious club at the top of the 30-story Hotel LKF. With its 270-degree panorama of the harbor, pool table, DJ booth, dance space, and smokers' terrace, the venue manages to balance coolness with good, old fashioned fun. ✉ *29th fl., Hotel LKF, 33 Wyndham St., Central* ☎ *3518–9330* ⏲ *Closes 3* AM.

Club 97. As the first glitzy Lan Kwai Fong nightspot, Club 97 draws mobs of beautiful people. It started off life as a members-only club, but that rule has since been disregarded. The space is dominated by a circular bar in the center of the room, and has a small dance floor surrounded by cozy nooks. ✉ *9–11 Lan Kwai Fong, Central* ☎ *2186–1897* ⏲ *Closes 4* AM.

AFTER THE PARTY

The ever-reliable MTR shuts down at 1 AM, and taxis are your only way home after that. They can easily be flagged down on the street; when the light on the car roof is on, it's available for hire. If the cab has an "out of service" sign over its round "for hire" neon sign on the dashboard, it means it's a cross-harbor taxi.

★ **dragon-i.** A place to prance, pose, and preen, dragon-i is owned by local party-boy socialite Gilbert Yeung. The entrance is marked by an enormous birdcage (filled with real budgies and canaries) made entirely of bamboo poles. Have a drink on the wonderful alfresco deck by the doorway or step inside the rich, red playroom, which doubles as a restaurant in the early evening. Take a trip to the bathroom to see arguably the biggest cubicles in Hong Kong, with floor-to-ceiling silver tiles and double-height mirrored ceilings. ✉ *The Centrium, 60 Wyndham St., Central* ☎ *3110–1222* ⏲ *Closes 5* AM.

★ **Drop.** This pint-size gem is where celebrities party—usually until sunrise when they're in town. Hidden down an alley beside a hot dog stand, its location only adds an air of exclusivity to the speakeasy-like feel. Excellent fresh-fruit martinis are its forte. Drop has two incarnations: after-dinner cocktail lounge before midnight, and impenetrable fortress later on, so arrive early to avoid disappointment. ✉ *Basement, On Lok Mansion, 39–43 Hollywood Rd., entrance off Cochrine St., Central* ☎ *2543–8856* ⏲ *Closes 6* AM.

Yumla. This diminutive music bar features consistently good DJs playing to a tiny, explosive dance-floor crowd of locals and expats, and an adjacent "beer garden," which is actually a conveniently located public park. ✉ *Lower basement, 79 Wyndham St., Central* ☎ *2147–2382* ⏲ *Closes 4* AM.

GAY AND LESBIAN SPOTS

Propaganda. Off a quaint but steep cobblestone street, this is *the* most popular gay club in Hong Kong; its near-monopoly on the late-night scene is reflected in its steep cover charge (HK$180 Friday, HK$220 Saturday, including one drink). The art deco bar area is a pleasant schmooze-fest, with elegant booths and soft lighting, while the dance floor has lap poles on either side for go-go boys to flaunt their wares. It's pretty empty during the week; the crowds arrive well after midnight on weekends. The entrance is in an alleyway, Ezra Lane, which runs parallel to Hollywood Road. ✉ *1 Hollywood Rd., Central* ☎ *2868–1316* ⏲ *Closes 5:30* AM.

Volume. Nestled down a leafy residential staircase off Hollywood Road, Volume hosts a friendly, mixed crowd of gays, lesbians, and their friends, thanks to free entry and an open-door policy. New Arrivals Wednesdays are a staple of the scene, welcoming tourists and newbies, and attracting locals with free vodka between 7 and 9 PM. The entrance is just below street level, around the corner from the main road. ✉ *83–85 Hollywood R., Sheung Wan* ☎ *2857–7683* ⏲ *Closes late.*

MUSIC CLUBS

The Cavern. This large bar at the top of Lan Kwai Fong is a laid-back space where locals and tourists come to drink beer, eat peanuts, tap their feet to the cover bands, and watch the swelling streets from the pavement tables. ✉ *Shop 1, ground fl., LKF Tower, 33 Wyndham St., entrance on D'Aguliar St., Central* ☎ *2121–8969* ⏲ *Closes 4 AM.*

★ **Fringe Club.** The arts-minded mingle in this historic redbrick building that also houses the members-only Foreign Correspondents' Club, next door. The Fringe is the headquarters for Hong Kong's alternative arts scene and normally stages live music twice a week. ✉ *2 Lower Albert Rd., Central* ☎ *2521–7251* ⏲ *Closes 3 AM.*

WAN CHAI

Wan Chai is the pungent night flower of the nocturnal scene, where the way of life served as inspiration for the novel *The World of Suzie Wong*. It now shares the streets with hip wine bars, salsa nights, old men's pubs, and after-parties that continue past sunrise. The seedy "hostess bars" in this neighborhood are easy to spot and avoid, with curtained entrances guarded by old ladies on stools and suggestive names in neon. But some things never change: the busiest nights are still when there's a navy ship in the harbor, on an R&R stopover. Wednesday's ladies' night, with half-price drinks, is also a big draw.

BARS

Carnegie's. Named after the Scotsman and steel baron Andrew Carnegie, whose family sailed to America in the late 1800s, this rock-and-roll bar lives up to its name. Although Carnegie himself probably didn't imagine bar-top dancing to classic rock tunes at an establishment bearing his name, the Scottish owners feel that the spirit of his love of music lives on regardless. ✉ *53–55 Lockhart Rd., Wan Chai* ☎ *2866–6289* ⏲ *Closes 4 AM.*

Old China Hand. Once full of gritty booths and stark lighting, this pub now has a facade that opens onto the street, absorbing all the hustle and bustle of Lockhart Road. It's open 24/7, and has been here from time immemorial (as have some of its patrons, by the looks of it). The kitchen serves typical pub fare and is something of an institution for those wishing to sober up with greasy grub after a long night out. ✉ *104 Lockhart Rd., Wan Chai* ☎ *2865–4378.*

★ **Mes Amis.** In the heart of Wan Chai, on the corner of Lockhart and Luard roads, Mes Amis is a friendly bar that also serves good food. Its corner setting and open bi-fold doors mean that none of the action outside is missed, and vice versa—the perpetual crowd of patrons inside are on display to those on the street. ✉ *83 Lockhart Rd., Wan Chai* ☎ *2527–6680* ⏲ *Closes 6 AM.*

★ **1/5 nuevo.** Once one of Hong Kong's slickest nightspots, 1/5 moved down to street level in 2007 and morphed into a tapas lounge and cocktail bar, hence the addition of "nuevo" to its name. High-flyers, financiers, and expats populate this dark, sophisticated Star Street hangout. ✉ *9 Star St., Wan Chai* ☎ *2529–2300* ⏲ *Closes midnight.*

The Pawn. In a district plagued by controversial redevelopment, this attractive historic building, a former pawnshop, has been preserved with minimal fuss. The stylish interior is decorated with retro furniture, while a cranky old foosball table lends a fun, youth-club feel. The long balcony overlooking the iconic Hong Kong tramway is a great place for curious tourists to spy on bustling everyday life below. ✉ *62 Johnston Rd., Wan Chai* ☎ *2866–3444* ⏲ *Closes* 2 AM.

DISCOS AND NIGHTCLUBS

Joe Bananas. This disco and bar's reputation for all-night partying and general good times remains unchallenged. People dressed too casually are strictly excluded: no shorts, sneakers, or T-shirts (the only exception is the Rugby Sevens weekend when even Joe can't turn away the thirsty swarm). Arrive before 11 PM to avoid the line. ✉ *23 Luard Rd., Wan Chai* ☎ *2529–1811* ⏲ *Closes* 5 AM.

Tribeca. A self-proclaimed "New York–style nightclub," Tribeca occupies the space that formerly housed Manhattan and more recently Club Ing. Unlike many other nightclubs in Hong Kong, it has a huge space—one of the largest in the city—full of dance floors, bars, lounges, and the requisite VIP areas. The plush interior attempts to emulate a swanky nightclub in the Big Apple, and judging by the crowds who flock here, it's doing a good job. ✉ *4th fl., Convention Plaza, 1 Harbour Rd., Wan Chai* ☎ *2836–3690* ⏲ *Closes* 4 AM.

KOWLOON

Central and Wan Chai are undoubtedly the king and queen of nightlife in Hong Kong. If you're staying in a hotel, however, or having dinner across the water in Kowloon, Ashley Road and an out-of-the-way strip called Knutsford Terrace still make for a fun night out.

BARS

Aqua. Felix at the Peninsula Hotel has had a stronghold on the sophisticated bar-with-a-view competition for years, but now its crown has been handed over to Aqua. Inside One Peking, an impressive curvaceous skyscraper dominating the Kowloon skyline, this very cool bar is on the mezzanine level of the top floor. The high ceilings and raking glass walls offer up unrivaled views of Hong Kong Island and of the harbor filled with ferries and ships. ✉ *29th fl. and 30th fl., One Peking, 1 Peking Rd., Tsim Sha Tsui, Kowloon* ☎ *3427–2288* ⏲ *Closes* 2 AM.

Bahama Mama's. You'll find tropical rhythms at the Caribbean-inspired bar, where world music plays and the kitsch props include a surfboard over the bar and the silhouette of a curvaceous woman showering behind a screen over the restroom entrance. ✉ *4–5 Knutsford Terr., Tsim Sha Tsui, Kowloon* ☎ *2368–2121* ⏲ *Closes* 4 AM.

CLOSE UP

Hostess Clubs

The many hostess clubs found in Hong Kong are clubs in name only. Some of these are multimillion-dollar operations with plush interiors with hundreds of hostess-companions. Computerized clocks on each table tabulate companionship charges in timed units; the costs are clearly detailed on table cards, as are standard drink tabs. The clubs also have dozens of luxuriously furnished private rooms, with partitioned lounges and the ubiquitous karaoke setup. Local and visiting businessmen adore these rooms—and the multilingual hostesses. Business is so good that the clubs are willing to allow visitors *not* asking for companionship.

The better clubs are on a par with music lounges in deluxe hotels, though they cost a little more. Their happy hours start in the afternoon, when many have a sort of tea-dance ambience, and continue through to mid-evening. Peak hours are 10 PM to 4 AM. Think twice before succumbing to the city's raunchier hideaways. If you stumble into one, check out cover and hostess charges *before* you get too comfortable. Many so-called hostess clubs are in fact fronts for prostitution. In Wan Chai, for instance, hostess clubs are dotted among regular bars, too many to mention by name. But most, if not all of them are sad little places full of leering men watching girls with vacant expressions performing half-hearted pole dances dressed in leotards.

The reputable **Club BBoss** (✉ *Mandarin Plaza, Tsim Sha Tsui East, Kowloon* ☎ *2369–2883* ⏲ *Closes 4* AM) is Hong Kong's grandest and most boisterous hostess club, tended by a staff of more than 1,000, and frequented by local company executives. If your VIP room is too far from the entrance, you can hire an electrified vintage Rolls-Royce and purr around an indoor roadway. Be warned that this is tycoon territory—a bottle of brandy can cost HK$18,000.

5

★ **Delaney's.** Both branches of Hong Kong's pioneer Irish pub have Irish interiors that were shipped here, and the mood is as authentic as the furnishings. Guinness and Delaney's ale (a specialty microbrew) are on tap, and there are corner snugs (small private rooms) and an Irish menu. The crowd includes some genuine Irish regulars; get ready for spontaneous outbursts of fiddling and other Emerald Isle traditions. Happy hour runs from 5 to 9 PM daily. ✉ *Basement fl., 71–77 Peking Rd., Tsim Sha Tsui, Kowloon* ☎ *2301–3980* ✉ *Ground fl., One Capital Place, 18 Luard Rd., Wan Chai* ☎ *2804–2880* ⏲ *Closes 3* AM.

Fodor's Choice ★ **Felix.** High up in the Peninsula Hotel, this bar is immensely popular with visitors; it not only has a brilliant view of the island, but the interior was designed by the visionary Philippe Starck. Don't forget to check out the padded mini-disco room. Another memorable feature is the male urinals, situated right by glass windows overlooking the city. ✉ *28th fl., Peninsula Hong Kong, Salisbury Rd., Tsim Sha Tsui, Kowloon* ☎ *2920–2888* ⏲ *Closes 2* AM.

SHOPPING

By Victoria Patience and Sofia Suárez
Updated by Zoe Mak and Dominique Rowe

They say the only way to get to know a place is to do what the locals do. When in Rome, scoot around on a Vespa and drink espresso. When in Hong Kong, shop. Shopping is so sacred that sales periods are calendar events, and most stores close on just three days a year—Christmas Day and the first two days of Chinese New Year. Imagine that: 362 days of unbridled purchasing. Opening hours are equally conducive to whiling your life away browsing the racks: all shops are open until 7 or 8 PM; many don't close their doors until midnight.

It's true that the days when everything in Hong Kong was cheap are over. It *is* still a tax-free port, so you can get some good deals. But it isn't just about the savings. You might find a bargain or two elbowing your way through a chaotic open-air market filled with haggling vendors selling designer knockoffs, the air reeking of the *chou tofu* ("stinky" tofu) bubbling at a nearby food stand. But then you could find a designer number going for half the usual price in a hushed marble-floor mall, the air scented by designer fragrances worn by fellow shoppers. What's more, in Hong Kong, the two extremes are often within spitting distance of each other.

MALLS

If you are short on time, visiting one of Hong Kong's many malls might be the answer. On Hong Kong Island, the main ones are Cityplaza (Eastern); IFC (Central); Island Beverley (Causeway Bay); The Landmark (Central); Pacific Place, which contains the three lesser arcades of Admiralty Centre, United Centre, and Queensway Plaza (Admiralty); and Times Square (Causeway Bay). In Kowloon, just next to the Star Ferry, is Harbour City, encompassing the Ocean Terminal, Marco Polo Hong Kong Hotel Arcade, Ocean Centre, and Gateway Arcade. Farther flung malls include Festival Walk in Kowloon Tong and Langham Place in Mong Kok.

CHINESE DEPARTMENT STORES

★ **Chinese Arts and Crafts.** Head to this long-established mainland company to blitz through that tiresome list of presents in one fell swoop. It stocks a huge variety of well-priced brocades, silk clothing, carpets, and cheap porcelain. Incongruously scattered throughout the shops are specialty items like large globes with lapis oceans and landmasses inlaid with semiprecious stones for a mere HK$70,000. Other more accessible—and more packable—gifts include appliqué tablecloths and cushion covers or silk dressing gowns. ✉ *Pacific Place, Admiralty* ☎ *2827–6667* 🌐 *www.chineseartsandcrafts.com.hk* Ⓜ *Admiralty, Exit F* ✉ *Asia Standard Tower, 59 Queen's Rd., Central* Ⓜ *Central, Exit D2* ✉ *China Resources Bldg., 26 Harbour Rd., Wan Chai* Ⓜ *Wan Chai, Exit A5* ✉ *Star House, 3 Salisbury Rd., Tsim Sha Tsui, Kowloon* Ⓜ *Tsim Sha Tsui, Exit F* ✉ *JD Mall, 233 Nathan Rd., Jordan, Kowloon* Ⓜ *Jordan, Exit A.*

Sincere. Hong Kong's most eclectic department store stocks everything from frying pans to jelly beans. Run by the same family for more than a century, Sincere has several local claims to fame: it was the first store in Hong Kong to give paid days off to employees, the first to hire women in sales positions—beginning with the founder's wife and sister-in-law—and the first to establish a fixed-price policy backed up by the regionally novel idea of issuing receipts. Although you probably won't have heard of its clothes or cosmetic brands, you might come across a bargain. ✉ *173 Des Voeux Rd., Central* ☎ *2544–2688* 🌐 *www.sincere.com.hk* Ⓜ *Sheung Wan, Exit E3.*

TRICKS OF THE TRADE

Be wary of absurd discounts, which are designed purely to get you in the door. Product switches are also common—after you've paid, they pack a cheaper model. The consensus is to avoid electronics shops in Tsim Sha Tsui, whose fearsome reputation is well-earned. Check purchases carefully, ensuring clothes are the size you wanted, jewelry is what you picked, and electronics come with the plug and accessories you paid for. Shops displaying the Hong Kong Tourism Board's (HKTB) QUALITY TOURISM SERVICE sticker (an easily recognizable junk boat) are good bets.

Wing On. Great values on household appliances, kitchenware, and crockery have made Wing On a favorite with locals on a budget since it opened in 1907. It also stocks clothes, cosmetics, and sportswear, but don't expect to find big brands (or even brands you know). You *can* count on rock-bottom prices and an-off-the-tourist-trail experience, though. ✉ *211 Des Voeux Rd. Central, Sheung Wan, Western* ☎ *2852–1888* 🌐 *www.wingonet.com* Ⓜ *Sheung Wan, Exit E3* ✉ *Cityplaza, 18 Tai Koo Shing Rd., Tai Koo, Eastern* Ⓜ *Tai Koo, Exit D2* ✉ *Wing On Kowloon Centre, 345 Nathan Rd., Jordan, Kowloon* Ⓜ *Jordan, Exit A.*

Fodor's Choice ★ **Yue Hwa Chinese Products Emporium.** Its five floors contain Chinese goods, from clothing and housewares to tea and traditional medicine. The logic behind the store's layout is hard to fathom, so go with time to rifle around. As well as the predictable tablecloths, silk pajamas, and chopstick sets, there are cheap and colorful porcelain sets and offbeat local favorites like mini-massage chairs. The top floor is entirely given over to tea—you can pick up a HK$50 packet of leaves or an antique Yixing teapot stretching into the thousands. ✉ *301–309 Nathan Rd., Jordan, Kowloon* ☎ *3511–2222* 🌐 *www.yuehwa.com* Ⓜ *Jordan, Exit A* ✉ *55 Des Voeux Rd., Central* Ⓜ *Central, Exit B* ✉ *1 Kowloon Park Dr., Tsim Sha Tsui, Kowloon* Ⓜ *Tsim Sha Tsui, Exit E.*

MARKETS

Flower Market. Huge bucketfuls of roses and gerbera spill out onto the sidewalk along Flower Market Road, a collection of street stalls selling cut flowers and potted plants. Delicate orchids and vivid birds of paradise are some of the more exotic blooms. During Chinese New Year there's a roaring trade in narcissi, poinsettias, and bright yellow chrysanthemums, all auspicious flowers. ✉ *Flower Market Rd., off Prince Edward Rd. W, Mong Kok, Kowloon* ⏲ *Daily 7 AM–7:30 PM* Ⓜ *Prince Edward, Exit B1.*

Goldfish Market. Goldfish are considered auspicious in Hong Kong (though aquariums have to be positioned in the right place to bring good luck to the family), and this small collection of shops is a favorite local source. Shop fronts are decorated with bag upon bag of glistening, pop-eyed creatures, waiting for someone to take them home. Some of the fishes inside shops are serious rarities and fetch unbelievable prices. ✉ *Tung Choi St., Mong Kok, Kowloon* ⏲ *Daily 10–6* Ⓜ *Mong Kok, Exit B2.*

Jardine's Bazaar and Jardine's Crescent. These two small parallel streets are so crammed with clothing stalls it's difficult to make your way through. Most offer bargains on the usual clothes, children's gear, bags, and cheap souvenirs like chopstick sets. The surrounding boutiques are also worth a look for local and Japanese fashions, though the sizes are small. ✉ *Jardine's Bazaar, Causeway Bay* ⏲ *Daily noon–10 PM* Ⓜ *Causeway Bay, Exit F.*

Kansu Street Jade Market. Jade in every imaginable shade of green, from the milkiest apple tone to the richest emerald, fills the stalls of this Kowloon market. If you know your stuff and haggle insistently, you can get fabulous bargains. Otherwise, stick to cheap trinkets. Some of the so-called "jade" sold here is actually aventurine, bowenite, soapstone, serpentine, and Australian jade—all inferior to the real thing. ✉ *Kansu St. off Nathan Rd., Yau Ma Tei, Kowloon* ⏲ *Daily 10–4* Ⓜ *Yau Ma Tei, Exit C.*

★ **Ladies' Market.** Block upon block of tightly packed stalls overflow with clothes, bags, and knickknacks along Tung Choi Street in Mong Kok. Despite the name there are clothes for women, men, and children here. Most offerings are imitations or no-name brands; rifle around enough and you can often pick up some cheap and cheerful basics. Haggling is the rule here: a poker face and a little insistence can get you dramatic discounts. At the corner of each block and behind the market are stands and shops selling the street snacks Hong Kongers can't live without. Pick a place where locals are munching and point at whatever takes your fancy. Parallel **Fa Yuen Street** is Mong Kok's unofficial sportswear market. It's lined with small shops selling cut-price sneakers—some real, others not so real. To reach the market, walk two blocks east along Nelson Street from the Mong Kok MTR station. ✉ *Tung Choi St., Mong Kok, Kowloon* ⏲ *Daily noon–11 PM* Ⓜ *Mong Kok, Exit E.*

★ **Stanley Village Market.** This was once Hong Kong's most famed bargain trove, but its ever-growing popularity means that Stanley Village Market no longer has the best prices around. Still, you can pick up some good buys in sportswear and casual clothing if you comb through the stalls. Good value linens—especially appliqué tablecloths—also abound. Dozens and dozens of shops line a main street so narrow that awnings from each side meet in the middle, and on busy days your elbows will come in handy. Weekdays are a little more relaxed. One of the best things about Stanley Market is getting here: the winding bus ride from Central (route 6, 6X, 6A, or 260) or Tsim Sha Tsui (route 973) takes you over the top of Hong Kong Island, with fabulous views on the way. ✉*Stanley Village, Southside* ⏲*Daily 11–6.*

★ **Temple Street Night Market.** Each night, as it gets dark, the lamps strung between the stalls of this Yau Ma Tei street market slowly light up, and the air fills with the smells wafting from myriad food carts. Hawkers try to catch your eye by flinging clothes up from their stalls. Cantonese opera competes with pop music, and vendors' cries and shoppers' haggling fills the air. Adding to the color here are the fortune-tellers and the odd magician or acrobat who has set up shop in the street. Granted, neither the clothes nor cheap gadgets on sale here are much to get excited about, but it's the atmosphere people come for—any purchases are a bonus. The market stretches for almost a mile and is one of Hong Kong's liveliest nighttime shopping experiences. ✉*Temple St., Mong Kok, Kowloon* ⏲*Daily 5* PM*–midnight; best after 8* PM Ⓜ*Jordan, Exit A.*

FAKING IT

The Hong Kong government has seriously cracked down on designer fakes. Depending on how strict the police are being when you visit, you may not find the choice of knockoffs you were hoping for. Bear in mind that designer fakes are illegal, and as such you could get into trouble if you get caught with them going through customs.

5

SPECIALTY SHOPS

ART AND ANTIQUES

Alisan Fine Arts. In a quiet corner of the sleek Prince's Building shopping arcade is this established authority on contemporary Chinese artists. Styles range from traditional to modern abstract, and media include oil, acrylic, and Chinese ink. Founded in 1981 by Alice King, this was one of the first galleries in Hong Kong to promote the genre. ✉*3rd fl., Prince's Bldg., 10 Chater Rd., Central* ☎*2526–1091* 🌐*www.alisan.com.hk* Ⓜ*Central.*

Altfield Gallery. If only your entire home could be outfitted by Altfield. Established in 1980, the elegant gallery carries exquisite antique Chinese furniture, Asia-related maps and topographical prints, Southeast Asian sculpture, and decorative arts from around Asia, including silver artifacts and rugs. ✉*2nd fl., Prince's Bldg., 10 Chater Rd., Central* ☎*2537–6370* 🌐*www.altfield.com.hk* Ⓜ*Central.*

Chine Gallery. Dealing in antique furniture and rugs from China, and furniture from Japan, this dark, stylish gallery accommodates international clients by coordinating its major exhibitions with the spring and fall auction schedules of Christie's and Sotheby's. ✉*42A Hollywood Rd., Central* ☎*2543–0023* 🌐*www.chinegallery.com* Ⓜ*Central.*

Grotto Fine Art. Director and chief curator Henry Au-yeung writes, curates, and gives lectures on 20th-century Chinese art. His hidden gallery (hence the "grotto" in the name) focuses exclusively on local Chinese artists, with an interest in the newest and most avant-garde works. Look for paintings, sculptures, prints, photography, mixed-media pieces, and conceptual installations. ✉ *2nd fl., 31C–D Wyndham St., Central* ☎ *2121–2270* 🌐 *www.grottofineart.com* Ⓜ *Central.*

> **LAW ON YOUR SIDE**
>
> Although mainland law forbids that any item more than 120 years old leave China, the SAR isn't held to this rule. It's perfectly legal to ship your antique treasures home.

Hanart TZ Gallery. This is a rare opportunity to compare and contrast cutting-edge and experimental art from mainland China, Taiwan, and Hong Kong selected by one of the field's most respected authorities. Unassuming curatorial director Johnson Chang Tsong-zung also cofounded the Asia Art Archive and has curated exhibitions at the São Paolo and Venice biennials. ✉ *2nd fl., Henley Bldg., 5 Queen's Rd., Central* ☎ *2526–9019* 🌐 *www.hanart.com* Ⓜ *Central.*

Schoeni Art Gallery. Known for vigorously promoting Chinese art on a global scale, this gallery, founded by Manfred Schoeni in 1992, has represented and supported various artists from mainland China with styles ranging from neorealism to postmodernism. Manfred's daughter Nicole now pinpoints exciting new artists for her prominent clientele. Informative past exhibition catalogs are placed atop Chinese antiques, which are also presented in this huge space. You're likely to pass the Hollywood Road branch first, but Old Baily Street gallery is the better of the two. ✉ *Upper ground fl., 21–31 Old Bailey St., Central* ☎ *2525–5225* 🌐 *www.schoeni.com.hk* Ⓜ *Central.*

Teresa Coleman Fine Arts Ltd. You can't miss the spectacular textiles hanging in the window of this busy corner shop. Specialist Teresa Coleman sells embroidered costumes from the Imperial Court, antique textiles, painted and carved fans, jewelry, lacquered boxes, and engravings and prints. ✉ *79 Wyndham St., Central* ☎ *2526–2450* 🌐 *www.teresacoleman.com* Ⓜ *Central.*

Yue Po Chai Antique Co. One of Hollywood Road's oldest shops is at the Cat Street end, next to Man Mo Temple. Its vast and varied stock includes porcelain, stone carvings, and ceramics. ✉ *Ground fl., 132–136 Hollywood Rd., Central* ☎ *2540–4374* Ⓜ *Central.*

CLOTHING: HK COUTURE

Barney Cheng. One of Hong Kong's best-known, locally based designers, Barney Cheng creates haute couture designs and prêt-à-porter collections, infusing his glam, often sequined, pieces with wit. When the Kennedy Center in Washington, D.C., hosted an exhibition titled "The New China Chic," Cheng was invited to display his works alongside those by the likes of Vera Wang and Anna Sui. ✉ *12th fl., World Wide Commercial Bldg., 34 Wyndham St., Central* ☎ *2530–2829* 🌐 *www.barneycheng.com* Ⓜ *Central.*

Lu Lu Cheung. A fixture on the Hong Kong fashion scene for more than a decade, Lu Lu Cheung's designs ooze comfort and warmth. In both daytime and evening wear, natural fabrics and forms are represented in practical yet imaginative ways. ✉ *The Landmark, Central* ☎ *2537–7515* 🌐 *www.lulucheung.com.hk* Ⓜ *Central* ✉ *New Town Plaza, Shatin Centre St., New Territories, Shatin* Ⓜ *Shatin.*

Olivia Couture. The surroundings are functional, but the gowns, wedding dresses, and *cheongsams* by local designer Olivia Yip are lavish. With a growing clientele, including socialites looking to stand out, Yip is quietly making a name for herself and her Parisian-influenced pieces. ✉ *Ground fl., Bartlock Centre, 3 Yiu Wah St., Causeway Bay* ☎ *2838–6636* 🌐 *www.oliviacouture.com* Ⓜ *Causeway Bay.*

Ranee K. Designer Ranee Kok Chui-Wah's showrooms are scarlet dens cluttered with her one-off dresses and eclectic women's wear that bring new meanings to "when East meets West." Known for her quirky cheongsams and dresses, she has also collaborated with brands such as Furla and Shanghai Tang. Special clients and local celebrities enjoy her custom tailoring, too. ✉ *Ground fl., 16 Gough St., Central* ☎ *2108–4068* 🌐 *www.raneek.com* Ⓜ *Central.*

5

Fodor's Choice ★ **Shanghai Tang.** In addition to the brilliantly hued—and expensive—displays of silk and cashmere clothing, you'll find custom-made suits starting at around HK$5,000, including fabric from a large selection of Chinese silks. You can also have a cheongsam (a sexy slit-skirt silk dress with a Mandarin collar) made for HK$2,500 to HK$3,500, including fabric *(⇨ also Tailoring, below)*. Ready-to-wear Mandarin suits and unisex kimonos are all in the HK$1,500 to HK$2,000 range. Among the Chinese souvenirs are novelty watches with mah-jongg tiles or dim sum instead of numbers. There's a second location inside the Peninsula Hong Kong. ✉ *12 Pedder St., Central* ☎ *2525–7333* 🌐 *www.shanghaitang.com* Ⓜ *Central* ✉ *Peninsula Hong Kong, Salisbury Rd., Tsim Sha Tsui, Kowloon* Ⓜ *Tsim Sha Tsui.*

★ **Sin Sin Atelier.** Sin Sin represents the best of Hong Kong design. Her conceptual, minimalist clothes, jewelry, and accessories retain a Hong Kong character, while drawing from other influences—especially Japanese. Yet the pieces are ultimately a unique expression of her ebullient spirit. A regular performer in Hong Kong community theater, Sin Sin prefers to introduce her collections via unusual presentations such as modern dance performances rather than catwalk shows. She also has an art space directly across the road and a fine art gallery up the hill in SoHo. ✉ *Ground fl., 52 Sai St., off Hollywood Rd. at Cat St. end, Western* ☎ *2521–0308* 🌐 *www.sinsin.com.hk.*

Spy Henry Lau. Local bad boy Henry Lau brings an edgy attitude to his fashion for men and women. Bold and often dark, his clothing and accessories lines are not for the fainthearted. ✉ *1st fl., Cleveland Mansion, 5 Cleveland St., Causeway Bay* ☎ *2317–6928* 🌐 *www.spyhenrylau.com* Ⓜ *Causeway Bay* ✉ *Shop C, ground fl., 11 Sharp St., Causeway Bay* Ⓜ *Causeway Bay.*

CLOSE UP

The Choice Is Joyce

Local socialites and couture addicts still thank Joyce Ma, the fairy godmother of luxury retail in Hong Kong, for bringing must-have labels to the city. Others may be catching up, but her Joyce boutiques are still ultrachic havens outfitted with a *Vogue*-worthy wish list of designers and beauty brands.

Joyce Beauty. Love finding unique beauty products from around the world? Then this is the place for you, with cult perfumes, luxurious skin solutions, and new discoveries to be made. Bring your credit card—"bargain" isn't in the vocabulary here. ✉ *Times Square, 1 Matheson St., Causeway Bay* ☎ *2970–2319* Ⓜ *Causeway Bay* ✉ *G/F, New World Tower, 16–18 Queen's Rd. Central, Central* Ⓜ *Central* ✉ *Lane Crawford, IFC Mall, 8 Finance St., Central* Ⓜ *Central* ✉ *The Gateway, 3–27 Canton Rd., Tsim Sha Tsui, Kowloon* Ⓜ *Tsim Sha Tsui.*

Joyce Boutique. Not so much a shop as a fashion institution, Joyce Boutique's hushed interior houses the worship-worthy creations of fashion's greatest gods and goddesses. McCartney, Galliano, Dolce&Gabbana, Prada, Miyake: the stock list is practically a mantra. Joyce sells unique household items, too, so your home can live up to your wardrobe. ✉ *New World Tower, 16 Queen's Rd., Central* ☎ *2810–1120* 🌐 *www.joyce.com* Ⓜ *Central, Exit G* ✉ *Pacific Place, 88 Queensway, Admiralty* Ⓜ *Admiralty, Exit F* ✉ *Harbour City, Tsim Sha Tsui, Kowloon* Ⓜ *Tsim Sha Tsui, Exit F.*

Joyce Warehouse. Fashionistas who've fallen on hard times can breathe a sigh of relief. Joyce's outlet on Ap Lei Chau, the island offshore from Aberdeen in Southside, stocks last season's duds from the likes of Jil Sander, Armani, Ann Demeulemeester, Costume National, and Missoni. Prices for each garment are reduced by about 10% each month, so the longer the piece stays on the rack, the less it costs. Bus 90B gets you from Exchange Square to Ap Lei Chau in 25 minutes; then hop a taxi for the four-minute taxi ride to Horizon Plaza. ✉ *21/F, Horizon Plaza, 2 Lee Wing St., Southside* ☎ *2814–8313* ⏲ *Tues.–Sat. 10–6, Sun. noon–6.*

Vivienne Tam. You know it when you walk into a Vivienne Tam boutique—the strong Chinese-motif prints and modern updates of traditional women's clothing are truly distinct. Don't let the bold, ready-to-wear collections distract you from the very pretty accessories, which include footwear with Asian embellishments such as jade. Tam is one of the best-known Hong Kong designers and, even though she's now based outside the SAR, the city still claims her as its own. ✉ *Pacific Place, 88 Queensway, Admiralty* ☎ *2918–0238* 🌐 *www.viviennetam.com* Ⓜ *Admiralty* ✉ *Harbour City, Canton Rd., Tsim Sha Tsui, Kowloon* Ⓜ *Tsim Sha Tsui* ✉ *Festival Walk, 80 Tat Chee Ave., Kowloon Tong, Kowloon* Ⓜ *Central.*

CLOTHING: HK CASUAL

F.C.K. (Fashion Community Kitterick). One of the trendiest local chains sells several brands including Kitterick, Z by Kitterick, indu homme, K-2, a.y.k, and the Lab. These are clothes that Hong Kong's brand-conscious youth are happy to wear. ✉ *1st fl., Hong Kong Pacific Centre, 28 Hankow Rd., Tsim Sha Tsui, Kowloon* ☎ *2721–0836* 🌐 *www.kitterick.com.hk* Ⓜ *Tsim Sha Tsui.*

Giordano. Hong Kong's version of the Gap is the most established and ubiquitous local source of basic T-shirts, jeans, and casual wear. Like its U.S. counterpart, the brand now has a bit more fashion sense and slick ad campaigns, but still offers reasonable prices. A few of its hundreds of stores are listed here, but you'll have no problem finding one on almost every major street. A new line, **Giordano Concepts,** offers more stylish (and pricier) urban wear in neutral colors like black, gray, and white. Customer service is generally good, even if the young, energetic staff screeches "hello" then "bye-bye" at every customer in a particularly jarring way. ✉ *Ground fl., Capitol Centre, 5–19 Jardine's Crescent, Causeway Bay* ☎ *2923–7110* 🌐 *www.giordano.com.hk* Ⓜ *Causeway Bay* ✉ *Ground fl., Yu To Sang Bldg., 37 Queen's Rd., Central* Ⓜ *Central* ✉ *Ground fl., 74–76 Nathan Rd., Tsim Sha Tsui, Kowloon* Ⓜ *Tsim Sha Tsui.*

5

Giordano Ladies. If Giordano is the Gap, Giordano Ladies is the Banana Republic, albeit with a more Zen approach. It's clean-line modern classics in neutral black, gray, white, and beige; each collection is brightened by a single highlight color, red one season, blue the next, and so on. Everything is elegant enough for the office and comfortable enough for the plane. ✉ *1st fl., Capitol Centre, 5–19 Jardine's Crescent, Causeway Bay* ☎ *2923–7118* 🌐 *www.giordanoladies.com* Ⓜ *Causeway Bay* ✉ *Man Yee Bldg., 60–68 Des Voeux Rd., Central* Ⓜ *Central* ✉ *1st fl., Manson House, 74–78 Nathan Rd., Tsim Sha Tsui, Kowloon* Ⓜ *Tsim Sha Tsui.*

CLOTHING: TAILOR MADE

A-Man Hing Cheong Co., Ltd. People often gasp at the very mention of A-Man Hing Cheong in the Mandarin Oriental Hotel. For some it symbolizes the ultimate in fine tailoring with a reputation that extends back to its founding in 1898. For others it's the lofty prices that elicit a reaction. Regardless, this is a trustworthy source of European-cut suits, custom shirts, and excellent service. ✉ *Mezzanine, Mandarin Oriental, 5 Connaught Rd., Central* ☎ *2522–3336* Ⓜ *Central.*

Ascot Chang. This self-titled "gentleman's shirtmaker" makes it easy to find the perfect shirt, even if you could get a better deal in a less prominent shop. Ascot Chang has upheld exacting Shanghainese tailoring traditions in Hong Kong since 1955, and now has stores in New York, Beverly Hills, Manila, and Shanghai, in addition to offering online ordering and regular American tours. The focus here is on the fit and details, from 22 stitches per inch to collar linings crafted to maintain their shape. Among the countless fabrics, Swiss 200s two-ply Egyptian cotton by Alumo is one of the most coveted and expensive. Like many shirtmakers, Ascot Chang does pajamas, robes, boxer shorts, and women's blouses, too. It also has developed ready-made lines of shirts, T-shirts, neckties, and other accessories. ✉ *Prince's Bldg., 10 Chater Rd., Central* ☎ *2523–3663* 🌐 *www.ascotchang.com* Ⓜ *Central* ✉ *IFC*

Mall, 8 Finance St., Central Ⓜ *Central* ✉ *Peninsula Hong Kong, Salisbury Rd., Tsim Sha Tsui, Kowloon* Ⓜ *Tsim Sha Tsui* ✉ *New World Centre, InterContinental Hong Kong, 18–24 Salisbury Rd., Tsim Sha Tsui, Kowloon* Ⓜ *Tsim Sha Tsui.*

Blanc de Chine. Blanc de Chine has catered to high society and celebrities, such as actor Jackie Chan, for years. That's easy when you're housed on the second floor of an old colonial building (just upstairs from Shanghai Tang) and you rely on word of mouth. The small, refined tailoring shop neatly displays exquisite fabrics. Next door is the Blanc de Chine boutique filled with lovely ready-made women's wear, menswear, and home accessories. With newer stores in New York and Beijing, it appears the word is getting out. Items here are extravagances, but they're worth every penny. ✉ *Pedder Bldg., 12 Pedder St., Central* ☎ *2104–7934* 🌐 *www.blancdechine.com* Ⓜ *Central.*

David's Shirts Ltd. Like so many of its competitors, the popular David's Shirts has global reach and even a branch in New York City. But customers still enjoy the personalized service of a smaller business supervised by David Chu himself since 1961. All the work is done in-house by Shanghainese tailors with at least 20 years' experience each. There are more than 6,000 imported European fabrics to choose from, each prewashed. Examples of shirts, suits, and accessories—including 30 collar styles, 12 cuff styles, and 10 pocket styles—help you choose. Single-needle tailoring, French seams, 22 stitches per inch, handpicked, double-stitched shell buttons, German interlining—it's all here. Your details, down to on which side you wear your wristwatch, are kept on file should you wish to use its mail-order service in the future. ✉ *Ground fl., Wing Lee Bldg., 33 Kimberley Rd., Tsim Sha Tsui, Kowloon* ☎ *2367–9556* 🌐 *www.davidsshirts.com* ✉ *Mezzanine, Mandarin Oriental, 5 Connaught Rd., Central* Ⓜ *Central.*

Jantzen Tailor. You'll have to push past a lively crowd and eclectic shops in a mall preferred by Filipina domestic helpers to get to Jantzen. Catering to expatriate bankers since 1972, this reputable yet reasonable tailor specializes in classic shirts; it also makes suits and women's garments. The comprehensive Web site displays its commitment to quality, such as hand-sewn button shanks, Gygil interlining, and Coats brand thread. ✉ *2nd fl., United Chinese Bank Bldg, 31–37 Des Voeux Rd., Central* ☎ *2570–5901 or 2810–8080* 🌐 *www.jantzentailor.com* Ⓜ *Central.*

Linva Tailors. It's one of the best of the old-fashioned cheongsam tailors, in operation since the 1960s. Master tailor Mr. Leung takes clients through the entire process and reveals a surprising number of variations in style. Prices are affordable, but vary according to fabric, which ranges from basics to special brocades and beautifully embroidered silks. ✉ *38 Cochrane St., Central* ☎ *2544–2456* Ⓜ *Central.*

Maxwell's Clothiers Ltd. After you've found a handful of reputable, high-quality tailors, one way to choose between them is price. Maxwell's is known for its competitive rates. It's also a wonderful place to have favorite shirts and suits copied and for straightforward, structured women's shirts and suits. It was founded by third-generation tailor

Continued on page 404

IT SUITS YOU

No trip to Hong Kong would be complete without a visit to one of its world-famous tailors, as many celebrities and dignitaries can attest. In often humble, fabric-cluttered settings, customer records contain the measurements of notables such as George Clooney, Kate Moss, David Bowie, David Beckham, and Queen Elizabeth II.

Prince Charles, who has his pick of Savile Row craftsmen, placed a few orders while in the territory for the 1997 handover. When Bill Clinton passed through, word has it that tailors were up until 4 AM to accommodate him.

Like some of their international clientele, who often make up a third of their total business, a handful of tailors are famous themselves. They even go on world tours for their fans. Picking the right tailor can be daunting in a city where the phone book lists about 500 of them. A good suit will last for 20 years if cared for correctly. A bad one will probably leave your closet only for its trip to the thrift store. All the more reason to make thoughtful, educated choices.

TIP

The special economic zone of Shenzhen on the mainland, just a train ride away, is known for competitively priced and speedy tailoring. Quality doesn't always measure up, though, so buyer beware.

11 12 13 14 15 16 17 18 19 20 21 22

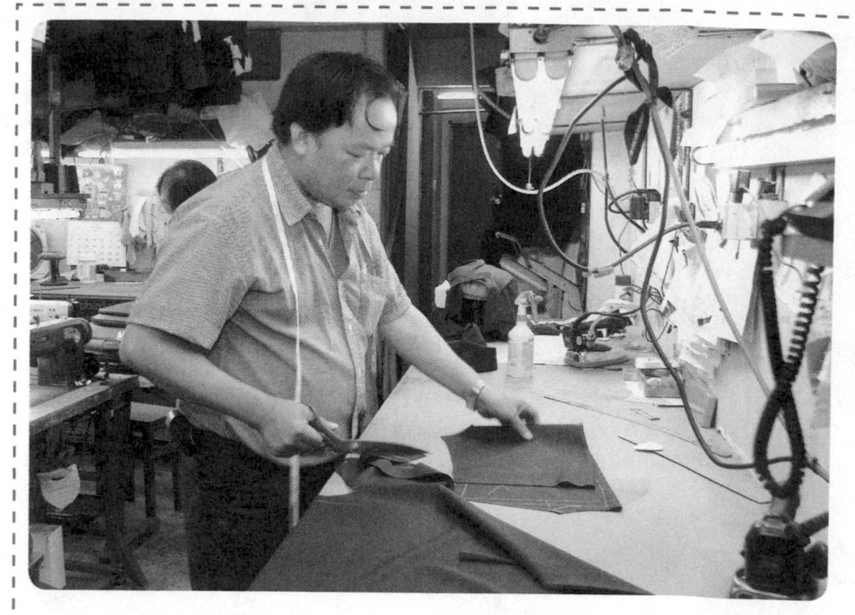

5 STEPS TO SIZING THINGS UP

If you've ever owned a custom-made garment, you understand the joy of clothes crafted to fit your every measurement. In Hong Kong, prices rival exclusive ready-to-wear brands.

Hong Kong is best known for men's tailoring, but whether you're looking for a classic men's business suit or an evening gown, these steps will help you size things up.

1. SET YOUR STYLE

Be clear about what you want. Bring samples—a favorite piece of clothing or magazine photos. Also, Hong Kong tailors are trained in classic, structured garments. Straying from these could lead to disappointment. There are three basic suit styles. Experienced tailors can advise on the best one for your shape.

The **American cut** is considered traditional by some, shapeless by others. Its jacket has notched lapels, a center vent, and two or three buttons. The trousers are lean, with flat fronts. The **British cut** also has notched lapels and two- or three-button jackets, but it features side vents and pleated trousers. The double-breasted **Italian cut** has wide lapels and pleated trousers—a look in remission these days.

2. CHOOSE YOUR FABRIC

You're getting a deal on workmanship, so consider splurging on, say, a luxurious blend of cashmere, mink, and wool. When having something copied, though, choose a fabric similar to the original. And buy for the

11 12 13 14 15 16 17 18 19 20 21 22

climate you live in, not the climate of your tailor. (How often will you wear seersucker in Alaska?) Take your time selecting: fabric is the main factor affecting cost.

Examine fabric on a large scale. Small swatches are deceiving. Those strong pinstripes might be elegant on a tiny card, but a full suit of them could make you look like an extra from *The Godfather*.

3. MEASURE UP

Meticulous measuring is the mark of a superior craftsman, so be patient. And for accuracy, stand as you normally would (you can't suck in that gut forever). Tailors often record your information, so you can have more garments sent to you without returning to Hong Kong. Still, double check measurements at home before each order.

4. PLACE YOUR ORDER

Consider ordering two pairs of trousers per suit. They wear faster than jackets, and alternating between two will help them last longer.

Most tailors require a deposit of 30%–50% of the total cost. Request a receipt detailing price, fabric, style, measurements, fittings, and production schedule. Also ask for a swatch to compare with the final product.

5. GET FIT

There should be at least two fittings. The first is usually for major alterations. Subsequent fittings are supposed to be for minor adjustments, but don't settle for less than perfect: keep sending it back until they get it right.

Bring the right clothes, such as a dress shirt and appropriate shoes, to try on a suit. Having someone you trust at the final fitting helps ensure you haven't overlooked anything.

Try jackets buttoned and unbuttoned. Examine every detail. Are shoulder seams puckered or smooth? Do patterns meet? Is the collar too loose or tight? (About two fingers' space is right.)

FINDING A TAILOR

- As soon as you arrive, visit established tailors to compare workmanship and cost.
- Ask if the work is bespoke (made from scratch) or made-to-measure (based on existing patterns but handmade according to your measurements).
- You get what you pay for. Assume the workmanship and fabric will match the price.
- A fine suit requires six or more days to create. That said, be wary but not dismissive of "24-hour tailors." Hong Kong's most famous craftsmen have turned out suits in a day.

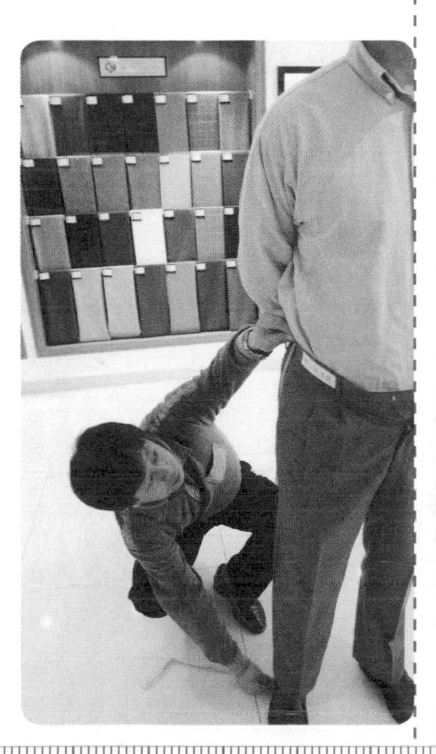

MEN'S TAILORING

Although most tailors can accommodate women—and a few even focus on womenswear (see listings)—Hong Kong tailors are best known for men's suits and shirts. Many shirtmakers also do pajamas, boxer shorts, and women's shirts. To help you with all the options, here are some basics.

JACKETS

Buttons: Plastic buttons can make exquisite tailoring look cheap. Select natural materials like horn. (No two natural buttons will be exactly alike.) Ask for extras, too.

Cuffs: The rule is the number of buttons on each cuff should match the total number on the front of the jacket.

Double- or Single-Breasted: Single-breasted jackets are more versatile: you can dress them up or down and wear them open or buttoned. Two buttons are most popular, but single-breasted jackets can have from one to four.

Lining: The interior (sleeves and pockets, too) should be lined with a beautifully stitched, high-quality fabric like silk. The lining affects both how the jacket falls and how readily it glides on and off.

Pockets: Standard jackets have straight pockets; modern designs have slanted ones. Both can be a slot style or have flaps, which may add girth. A small ticket pocket above a standard pocket is a nice touch.

Stitching: Handstitched lapels subtly show off fine tailoring; the discerning request handstitched buttonholes as well. At the first fitting, stitches should be snug and free of any fraying.

Vent: The vent was created to allow cavalry officers to sit in their saddles comfortably. Although you probably won't go riding in your suit, don't skip the vent. Unvented jackets simply aren't flattering.

SHIRTS

Back: The back can be plain or have a box, side, or inverted pleat.

Collars: Some are straight (pointed), others are rounded. Ask for removable stays; cleaning with them inside a collar causes points to fray. The English collar has a semi-cutaway style; a tab collar has a strip of fabric holding it in place. Button-down collars are more casual.

Cuffs: Cuffs should just show from beneath jacket sleeves. Styles include rounded, square, or angled with one or two buttons. The elegant French (or double) cuff is worn with cufflinks.

Fit: Tailors can make shirts snug or baggy, depending on your taste, and still avoid the ballooned look of mass-produced garments.

Front: You can choose a plain front or one with a placket. Pockets (optional) can go on the left or right and be monogrammed.

TROUSERS

Hems: Some argue cuffless or flat hems are formal; others consider them casual—even costume-like. It's your call. To accommodate shoes, hems are slightly shorter at the front.

Length: Prescribed lengths differ by style, but socks should remain hidden, and trousers should cover half to two-thirds of the shoe.

Pleats: Younger generations prefer flat-front trousers. Traditionalists like single or double pleats, which are roomier in the hips and thighs.

Pockets: Pockets cut on the diagonal are standard, but you can opt for horizontal or vertical designs. One or two (more casual) back pockets, with or without flaps, are also options.

Waist Details: You can request waist adjusters (internal buttons and straps that let you adjust the waist by about 2 inches) or waistband buttons for suspenders.

	Save	Splurge	Break the Bank
SUITS	HK$2,800 (Yuen's Tailor and Jantzen Tailor); HK$3,000 (Sam's Tailor)	HK$4,500 (Mode Elegante); HK$7,000 (Ascot Chang)	HK$8,000–HK$17,000 (A-Man Hing Cheong)
SHIRTS	HK$300 (Yuen's Tailor); HK$350 (Sam's Tailor).	HK$500 (Mode Elegante)	HK$700–HK$6,000 (Ascot Chang, HK$1,000 is average); HK$–00–HK$1,800 (A-Man Hing Cheong).

11 12 13 14 15 16 17 18 19 20 21 22 23 24 25 26 27 28 29 30

Ken Maxwell in 1961 and follows Shanghai tailoring traditions while also providing the fabled 24-hour suit upon request. The showroom and workshop are in Kowloon, but son Andy and his team take appointments in the United States, Canada, and Europe twice annually. The motto of this family business is, "Simply let the garment do the talking." ✉ *7th fl., Han Hing Mansion, 38–40 Hankow Rd., Tsim Sha Tsui, Kowloon* ☎ *2366–6705* 🌐 *www.maxwellsclothiers.com* Ⓜ *Tsim Sha Tsui.*

Mode Elegante. Don't be deterred by the somewhat dated mannequins in the windows. Mode Elegante is a favorite source for custom-made suits among women and men in the know. Tailors here specialize in European cuts. You'll have your choice of fabrics from the United Kingdom, Italy, and elsewhere. Your records are put on file so you can place orders from abroad. It'll even ship the completed garment to you almost anywhere on the planet. Alternatively, you can make an appointment with director Gary Zee, one of Hong Kong's traveling tailors who make regular visits to North America, Europe, and Japan. ✉ *11th fl., Star House, 3 Salisbury Rd., Tsim Sha Tsui, Kowloon* ☎ *2366–8153* 🌐 *www.modeelegante.com* Ⓜ *Tsim Sha Tsui.*

Fodor's Choice ★ **Sam's Tailor.** Unlike many famous Hong Kong tailors, you won't find the legendary Sam's in a chic hotel or sleek mall. But don't be fooled. These digs in humble Burlington House, a tailoring hub, have hosted everyone from U.S. presidents (back as far as Richard Nixon) to performers such as the Black Eyed Peas, Kylie Minogue, and Blondie. This former uniform tailor to the British troops once even made a suit for Prince Charles in a record hour and 52 minutes. The men's and women's tailor does accept 24-hour suit or shirt orders, but will take about two days if you're not in a hurry. Founded by Naraindas Melwani in the 1950s, "Sam" is now his son, Manu Melwani, who runs the show with the help of his own son, Roshan, and about 55 tailors behind the scenes. In 2004 Sam's introduced a computerized bodysuit that takes measurements without a tape measure. (It uses both methods, however.) These tailors also make annual trips to Europe and North America. (Schedule updates are listed on the Web site.) ✉ *Burlington House, 90–94 Nathan Rd., Tsim Sha Tsui, Kowloon* ☎ *2367–9423* 🌐 *www.samstailor.com* Ⓜ *Tsim Sha Tsui.*

★ **Shanghai Tang—Imperial Tailors.** Upscale Chinese lifestyle brand Shanghai Tang has the Imperial Tailors service in select stores, including the Central flagship. A fabulous interior evokes the charm of 1930s Shanghai, and gives an indication of what to expect in terms of craftsmanship and price. From silk to velvet, brocade to voile, fabrics are displayed on the side walls, along with examples of fine tailoring. The expert tailors here can make conservative or contemporary versions of the cheongsam. Men can also have a Chinese *tang* suit made to order. ✉ *Ground fl., 12 Pedder St., Central* ☎ *2525–7333* 🌐 *www.shanghaitang.com* Ⓜ *Central.*

W. W. Chan & Sons Tailors Ltd. Chan is known for excellent-quality suits and shirts, classic cuts, and has an array of fine European fabrics. It's comforting to know that you'll be measured and fitted by the same master tailor from start to finish. The Kowloon headquarters features a mirrored, hexagonal changing room so you can check every angle. Tailors from here travel to the United States several times a year to fill orders for its customers; if you have a suit made here and leave your address, they'll let you know when they plan to visit. ✉ *2nd fl., Burlington House, 92–94 Nathan Rd., Tsim Sha Tsui, Kowloon* ☎ *2366–9738* 🌐 *www.wwchan.com* Ⓜ *Tsim Sha Tsui.*

Yuen's Tailor. Need a kilt? This is where the Hong Kong Highlanders Reel Club comes for custom-made kilts. The Yuen repertoire, however, extends to well-made suits and shirts. The tiny shop is on an unimpressive gray walkway and is filled from floor to ceiling with sumptuous European fabrics. It's a good place to have clothes copied; prices are competitive. ✉ *2nd fl., Escalator Link Alley, 80 Des Voeux Rd., Central* ☎ *2815–5388* Ⓜ *Central.*

ELECTRONICS

Variety and novelty—not prices—are the reasons to buy electronic goods and accessories in Hong Kong these days. Products are often launched in this keen, active electronics market before they are in the United States and Europe. The street sweepers may wear old-fashioned rattan Hakka hats, but even they carry cutting-edge, almost impossibly tiny phones.

Broadway. Like its more famous competitor, Fortress, Broadway is a large electronic-goods chain. It caters primarily to the local market, so some staff members speak better English than others. Look for familiar-name-brand cameras, computers, sound systems, home appliances, and mobile phones. Just a few of the shops are listed here. ✉ *7th fl., Times Square, 1 Matheson St., Causeway Bay* ☎ *2506–0228* 🌐 *www.ibroadway.com.hk* Ⓜ *Causeway Bay* ✉ *3rd fl., Ocean Centre, Harbour City, Canton Rd., Tsim Sha Tsui, Kowloon* Ⓜ *Tsim Sha Tsui* ✉ *Ground fl., 78 Sai Yeung Choi St. S, Mong Kok, Kowloon* Ⓜ *Mong Kok.*

DG Lifestyle Store. An appointed Apple Center, DG carries Macintosh and iPod products. High-design gadgets, accessories, and software by other brands are add-ons that meld with the Apple design philosophy. ✉ *Times Square, 1 Matheson St., Causeway Bay* ☎ *2506–1338* 🌐 *www.dg-lifestyle.com* Ⓜ *Causeway Bay* ✉ *IFC Mall, 8 Finance St., Central* Ⓜ *Central* ✉ *Mega Box, Kowloon Bay, Kowloon* Ⓜ *Kowloon Bay.*

★ **Fortress.** Part of billionaire Li Ka-shing's empire, this extensive chain of shops sells electronics with warranties—a safety precaution that draws the crowds. It also has good deals on printers and accessories, although selection varies by shop. You can spot a Fortress by looking for the big orange sign. For the full list of shops, visit the Web site. ✉ *Times Square, 7th fl., 1 Matheson St., Causeway Bay* ☎ *2506–0031* 🌐 *www.fortress.com.hk* Ⓜ *Causeway Bay* ✉ *3rd fl., Ocean Centre, Harbour City, Canton Rd., Tsim Sha Tsui, Kowloon* Ⓜ *Tsim Sha Tsui* ✉ *Chung Kiu Commercial Bldg., 47–51 Shan Tung St., Mong Kok, Kowloon* Ⓜ *Mong Kok* ✉ *Lower ground fl., Melbourne Plaza, 33 Queen's Rd. Central, Central* Ⓜ *Central.*

★ **Wanchai Computer Centre.** You'll find honest-to-goodness bargains on computer goods and accessories in the labyrinth of shops here. And you can negotiate prices. Your computer can be put together by a computer technician in less than a day if you're rushed; otherwise, two days is normal. The starting price is HK$5,000 depending on the hardware, processor, and peripherals you choose. This is a great resource, whether you're a techno-buff who's interested in assembling your own computer (a popular pastime with locals), or a technophobe looking for discounted earphones. ✉ *130 Hennessy Rd., Wan Chai* ☎ *No phone* Ⓜ *Wan Chai.*

JEWELRY

Artland Watch Co Ltd. Elegant but uncomplicated, the interior of this established watch retailer is like its service. The informed staff will guide you through the countless luxury brands on show and in the catalogs from which you can also order. Prices here aren't the best in Hong Kong, but they're still lower than at home. ✉ *Ground fl., Mirador Mansion, 54–64B Nathan Rd., Tsim Sha Tsui, Kowloon* ☎ *2366–1074* Ⓜ *Tsim Sha Tsui* ✉ *Ground fl., New Henry House, 10 Ice House St., Central* Ⓜ *Central.*

Chocolate Rain. The collections—dreamed up by a Hong Kong fine arts graduate—consist of pieces handcrafted of recycled materials, jade, crystals, precious stones, and mother-of-pearl. The showroom also displays works by the designer's friends, and it doubles as a classroom for jewelry-making courses. ✉ *Ground fl., 34 Staunton St., SoHo, Central* ☎ *2975–8318* 🌐 *www.chocolaterain.com* Ⓜ *Central.*

Edward Chiu. Everything about Edward Chiu is *fabulous,* from the flamboyant way he dresses to his high-end jade jewelry. The minimalist, geometric pieces use the entire jade spectrum, from deep greens to surprising lavenders. He's also famous for contrasting black-and-white jade, setting it in precious metals and adding diamond or pearl touches. ✉ *IFC Mall, 8 Finance St., Central* ☎ *2525–2618* 🌐 *www.edwardchiu.com* Ⓜ *Central.*

Eldorado Watch Co Ltd. At this deep emporium of watch brands, seek the advice of one of the older staffers who look like they've been there since the British landed. Brands include: Rolex, Patek Philippe, Girard-Perregaux, etc. ✉ *Ground fl., Peter Bldg., 60 Queen's Rd., Central* ☎ *2522–7155* Ⓜ *Central.*

Qeelin. With ancient Chinese culture for inspiration and *In The Mood for Love* actress Maggie Cheung as the muse, something extraordinary was bound to come from Qeelin. Its name was cleverly derived from the Chinese characters for male ("qi") and female ("lin"), and symbolizes harmony, balance, and peace. The restrained beauty and meaningful creations of designer Dennis Chan are exemplified in two main collections: Wulu, a minimalist form representing the mythical gourd as well as the lucky number eight; and Tien Di, literally "Heaven and Earth," symbolizing everlasting love. Classic gold, platinum, and diamonds mix with colored jades, black diamonds, and unusual materials for a truly unique effect. A sweeter addendum to the collection was added recently in the form of Bo Bo, the panda bear. ✉ *IFC Mall, 8 Finance St., Central* ☎ *2389–8863* 🌐 *www.qeelin.com* Ⓜ *Central* ✉ *Peninsula Shopping Arcade, Salisbury Rd., Tsim Sha Tsui, Kowloon* Ⓜ *Tsim Sha Tsui.*

Ronald Abram Jewellers. Looking at the rocks in these windows can feel like a visit to a natural history museum. Large white- and rare-color diamonds sourced from all over the world are a specialty here, but the shop also deals in emeralds, sapphires, and rubies. With years of expertise, Abrams dispenses advice on both the aesthetic merits and the investment potential of each stone or piece of jewelry. ✉ *Mezzanine, Mandarin Oriental, 5 Connaught Rd., Central* ☎ *2810–7677* 🌐 *www.ronaldabram.com* Ⓜ *Central.*

Sandra Pearls. You might be wary of the lustrous pearls hanging at this little Jade Market stall. The charming owner, Sandra, does, in fact, sell genuine and reasonably priced cultured and freshwater pearl necklaces and earrings. Some pieces are made from shell, which Sandra is always quick to point out, and could pass muster among the snobbiest collectors. ✉ *Stalls 381 and 447, Jade Market, Kansu St., Yau Ma Tei, Kowloon* ☎ *9485–2895* Ⓜ *Yau Ma Tei.*

5

Super Star Jewellery. Discreetly tucked in a corner of Central, Super Star looks like any other small Hong Kong jewelry shop—with walls lined by display cases filled with the usual classic designs (old-fashioned to some) in predominantly gold and precious stones. What makes them stand out are the good prices and personalized service. The cultured pearls and mixed strands of colored freshwater pearls are not all shown, so ask Lily or one of her colleagues to bring them out. ✉ *The Galleria, 9 Queen's Rd. Central, Central* ☎ *2521–0507* Ⓜ *Central.*

TSL Jewellery. One of the big Hong Kong chains, TSL (Tse Sui Luen), specializes in diamond jewelry and manufactures, retails, and exports its designs. Its range of 100-facet stones includes the Estrella cut, which reflects nine symmetrical hearts and comes with international certification. Although its contemporary designs use platinum settings, TSL also sells pure, bright, yellow-gold items targeted at Chinese customers. ✉ *G9–10, Park Lane Shopper's Blvd., Nathan Rd., Tsim Sha Tsui, Kowloon* ☎ *2332–4618* 🌐 *www.tsljewellery.com* Ⓜ *Tsim Sha Tsui* ✉ *Ground fl., 35 Queen's Rd. Central, Central* Ⓜ *Central* ✉ *Ground fl., 1 Yee Woo St., Causeway Bay* Ⓜ *Causeway Bay.*

Tayma Fine Jewellery. Unusual colored "connoisseur" gemstones are set by hand in custom designs by Hong Kong–based jeweler Tayma Page Allies. The collection is designed to bring out the personality of the individual wearer, and includes oversize cocktail rings, distinctive bracelets, pretty earrings, and more. ✉ *Prince's Bldg., 10 Chater Rd., Central* ☎ *2525–5280* 🌐 *www.taymajewellery.com* Ⓜ *Central.*

SIDE TRIP TO MACAU

By Hiram Chu
Updated by Chris Cottrell and Cherise Fong

Enter the desperate, smoky atmosphere of a Chinese casino, where frumpy players bet an average of five times more than the typical Vegas gambler. Sit down next to grandmothers who smoke like chimneys while playing baccarat—the local game of choice—with visiting high rollers. Then step out of the climate-controlled chill and into tropical air that embraces you like a warm, balmy hug. Welcome to Macau.

The many contrasts in this tiny enclave of 552,000 people serve as reminders of how very different cultures have embraced one another's traditions for hundreds of years. Though Macau's population is 95% ethnic Chinese, there are still vibrant pockets of Portuguese and Filipino expats. And some of the thousands of Eurasians—who consider themselves neither Portuguese nor Chinese, but something in between—can trace the intermarriage of their ancestors back a century or two.

Macau's old town, while dominated by the buildings, squares, and cobblestone alleyways of colonial Portugal, is tinged with eastern influences as well, as in the Buddhist temple at the intersection of the Travessa de Dom Quixote and Travessa de Sancho Panca. In Macau you can spend an afternoon strolling the black sands of Hác-Sá Beach before feasting on a dinner of *bacalhau com natas* (dried codfish with a cream sauce), grilled African chicken (spicy chicken in a coconut-peanut broth—a classic Macanese dish), Chinese lobster with scallions, or fiery prawns infused with Indian and Malaysian flavors. Wash everything down with *Vinho Verde,* the crisp young wine from northern Portugal, and top it all off with a traditional Portuguese *pastel de nata* (egg-custard tart) and dark, thick espresso.

EXPLORING MACAU

Macau, a Special Administrative Region (SAR) of the People's Republic of China, is on the western bank of the Pearl River Delta, about an hour from Hong Kong by hydrofoil. It consists of the Macau Peninsula and Taipa and Coloane islands. The Cotai area, a glitzy, Vegas-like strip of hotels and casinos that began development in 2006, lies between Taipa and Coloane and virtually merges the two.

Most of Macau's population lives on the peninsula attached to mainland China. The region's most famous sights are here—Senado Square, the Ruins of St. Paul's, A-Ma Temple—as are most of the luxury hotels and casinos. As in the older sections of Hong Kong, cramped older buildings stand comfortably next to gleaming new structures. Most people visit Macau to gamble, eat cheap seafood, and shop without crowds. But don't overlook its timeless charms and unique culture, born from centuries of both Portuguese and Chinese influence.

TOURS

Depending on your mindset, tours of Macau can either be spontaneously joined or meticulously made-to-order. If you're just debarking for the day at the main ferry terminal, find the **Kamlon Travel** (✉ *Macau Ferry Terminal, Av. da Amizade* ☎ *853/2833–6611 or 853/2872–5813*) counter, where you can join a four- to five-hour tour of the peninsula's top attractions, departing daily at 11 AM and 12:45 PM.

For a tour of the islands, the **Venetian Travel Shop** (✉ *Shop 1028, Venetian Macao-Resort-Hotel* ☎ *853/8118–2930 or 853/8118–2833*) hosts daily tours from 9:15 to 1 that include the Taipa Houses Museum and the A-Ma Cultural Village on Coloane for MOP$250 per person.

Book at least one day in advance from one of many travel agents in Hong Kong. Browse your options at the travel counters of the main ferry terminals in either Macau or Hong Kong, or check 🌐 *www.macautourism.gov.mo* for a list of authorized travel agencies in Macau; some offer tours in multiple languages.

THE BASICS

Passports and Visas: To enter Macau, Americans, Canadians, and EU citizens need only a valid passport for stays of up to 90 days.

Currency: The Macanese pataca (MOP) has a fixed exchange rate of MOP$1.032 to HK$1—roughly MOP$7 to US$1. Patacas come in 10, 20, 50, 100, 500, and 1,000 MOP banknotes plus 1, 5, and 10 MOP coins. A pataca is divided into 100 avos. Hong Kong dollars are accepted in Macau on a 1:1 basis.

Language: Chinese and Portuguese are Macau's official languages. Cantonese and Mandarin are widely spoken.

5

Estoril Tours (✉ *Shop 3711, 3rd fl., Shun Tak Centre, 200 Connaught Rd., Central, Hong Kong* ☎ *2559–1028* 🌐 *www.estoril.com.mo*) will customize a private group tour, from bungee-jumping off the Macau Tower to wandering through Coloane Village or a day visiting museums.

GETTING HERE AND AROUND

Chances are you'll arrive at the Macau Ferry Terminal after sailing from Hong Kong. Hop into one of the many waiting casino or hotel shuttles and head straight downtown, less than 10 minutes away. From there it's a short walk to the city's historic center, along the short stretch of road named Avenida Almeida Ribeiro, more commonly known as San Ma Lo, which is Macau's commercial and cultural heart.

On a good day, you could drive from one end of Macau to the other in 30 minutes. This makes walking and bicycling ideal ways to explore winding city streets, nature trails, and long stretches of beach.

BY AIR International flights (from Asia) come into Macau, but there are no planes from Hong Kong. Sixteen-minute helicopter flights fly between Hong Kong's Shun Tak Centre and the Macau Ferry Terminal on East Asia Airlines; they leave every 30 minutes from 9:30 AM to 10:30 PM daily. Prices are HK$1,925 Monday to Thursday with a HK$200 surcharge on Friday, Saturday, Sunday, and holidays. Reservations are essential.

BY BUS Public buses are clean and affordable; trips to anywhere in the Macau peninsula cost MOP$2.50. Service to Taipa Island is MOP$3.30, and service to Coloane is MOP$5. Buses run 6:30 to midnight and require exact change upon boarding. But you can get downtown for free, via casino shuttles, from the official Border Gate crossing just outside mainland China, from the airport, and from the Macau Ferry Terminal.

BY CAR Like in Hong Kong, Macau motorists drive on the left-hand side of the road. Road signs are in Chinese and Portuguese only. Rental cars with Avis are available at the Mandarin Oriental Hotel. Regular cars go for MOP$900 on weekdays and MOP$1,200 on weekends.

BY FERRY Ferries run every 15 minutes with a reduced schedule from midnight to 7 AM. Prices for economy/ordinary and super/deluxe run HK$133 to HK$275. Weekday traffic is usually light, so you can buy tickets right before departure. Weekend tickets often sell out, so make reservations. You can book tickets up to 90 days in advance with China Travel Service (*www.ctshk.com*) or directly with CotaiJet or TurboJET by phone or online. Booking by phone requires a Visa card. You must pick tickets up at the terminal at least a half hour before departure.

Most ferries leave from Hong Kong's Shun Tak Centre Sheung Wan MTR Station in Central, though limited service is available from First Ferry at Kowloon's Tsim Sha Tsui Terminal. In Macau most ferries disembark from the main Macau Ferry Terminal, but CotaiJet services the terminal on Taipa Island. The trip takes one hour one way. Buses, taxis, and free shuttles to most casinos and hotels await on the Macau side

BY TAXI The best places to catch a cab are the major casinos—the Wynn, Sands, and Venetian. Carry a bilingual map or ask the concierge at your hotel to write the name of your destination in Chinese. All taxis are metered, and air-conditioned. The base charge is MOP$13 for the first 1½ km (1 mi) and MOP$1 per additional 600 feet. Trips between Coloane and either the Macau Peninsula or Taipa incur respective surcharges of MOP$5 or MOP$2. Drivers don't expect a tip.

ESSENTIALS

Air Contacts East Asia Airlines (*853/2872-7288 Macau Terminal, 2108-9898 Shun Tak Centre www.helihongkong.com*). **Macau International Airport** (*853/2886-1111 www.macau-airport.gov.mo*).

Car Rental Avis (*853/2833-6789 in Macau, 2926-1126 in Hong Kong www.avis.com*).

Ferry Contacts CotaiJet (*853/2885-0595 in Macau, 2359-9990 in Hong Kong cotaijet.com.mo*). **First Ferry** (*2131-8181 www.nwff.com.hk*). **TurboJET** (*2859-3333 information, 2921-6688 reservations www.turbojet.com.hk*).

Visitor and Tour Info Macau Government Tourist Office (*MGTO; Macau Ferry Terminal, Macau 853/2833-3000 www.macautourism.gov.mo Shun Tak Centre, 200 Connaught Rd., Central, Hong Kong 2857-2287*).

DOWNTOWN MACAU

Fodor's Choice ★ **Fortaleza da Guia.** The Guia Fortress, built between 1622 and 1638 on Macau's highest hill, was key to protecting the Portuguese from invaders. You can walk the steep, winding road up to the fortress or take a five-minute cable car ride from the entrance of Flora Garden on Avenida Sidonio Pais. Once inside the fort, notice the gleaming white Guia Lighthouse (you can't go inside, but you can get a good look at the exterior) that's lighted every night. Next to it is the Guia Chapel, built by Clarist nuns to provide soldiers with religious services. The chapel is no longer used for services but restoration work in 1998 uncovered elaborate frescoes that mix Western and Chinese themes. They're best seen when the morning or afternoon sun floods the chapel.

The elegant yellow and white building with Mughal architectural influences built onto a slope of Guia Hill is the **Quartel dos Mouros** (Moorish Barracks). It now houses the Macau Maritime Administration but originally was constructed in 1874 for Indian police regimens brought into the region, a reminder of Macau's historic relationship with the Indian city of Goa. ✉ *Guia Hill, Downtown* 🎫 *Free* ⏲ *Daily 9–5:30.*

Fodor'sChoice ★ **Largo do Senado.** The charming Senado Square, Macau's hub for centuries, is lined with neoclassical-style colonial buildings painted bright pastels. Only pedestrians are allowed on its shiny black-and-white tiles, and the alleys off it are packed with restaurants and shops. Take your time wandering. There are plenty of benches on which to rest after shopping and sightseeing. Come back at night, when locals of all ages gather to chat and the square is beautifully lit.

The magnificent yellow **Igreja de São Domingos** (St. Dominic's Church; ✉ *Largo de São Domingos, Downtown* ☎ *No phone* ⏲ *Daily 8–6*) beckons you to take a closer look. After a restoration in 1997, it's again among Macau's most beautiful churches, with a cream-and-white interior that takes on a heavenly golden glow when illuminated for services. The church was originally a convent founded by Spanish Dominican friars in 1587. In 1822, China's first Portuguese newspaper, *The China Bee,* was published here. The church became a repository for sacred art in 1834 when convents were banned in Portugal.

It's hard to ignore the imposing white facade of **Santa Casa da Misericordia** (✉ *2 Travessa da Misericordia 853/2857–3938 or 853/8399–6699* 🎫 *MOP$5* ⏲ *Mon.–Sat. 10–1 and 2–5:30*). Founded in 1569 by Dom Belchior, Macau's first bishop, the Holy House of Mercy is the China coast's oldest Christian charity, and it continues to take care of the poor with soup kitchens and health clinics, as well as providing housing for the elderly. The exterior is neoclassical, but the interior is done in a contrasting opulent, modern style. A reception room on the second floor contains paintings of benefactress Marta Merop.

The neoclassical **Edifício do Leal Senado** (*Senate Building;* ✉ *163 Av. de Almeida Ribeiro, Downtown* ☎ *853/2833–7676* 🎫 *Free* ⏲ *Tues.–Sun. 9–9*) was built in 1784 as a municipal chamber and continues to be used by the government today. An elegant meeting room on the first floor opens onto a magnificent library based on one in the Mafra Convent in Portugal, with books neatly stacked on two levels of shelves reaching to the ceiling. Art and historical exhibitions are frequently hosted in the beautiful foyer and garden.

★ **Macau Canidrome.** Asia's only greyhound track looks rundown and quaint compared to the bigger jockey club and glitzy casinos, but it offers a true taste of Macau in a more popular neighborhood near the

China border crossing. The Canidrome opened in 1932 and tends to attract a steady crowd of older gamblers several times a week for the slower-pace, lower-stakes gambling rush of betting on fast dogs chasing an electronic rabbit. Check out the parade of race dogs before each race. You can sit on benches in the open-air stadium, at tables in the air-conditioned restaurant, or in an upstairs box seat. ✉ *Av. do Artur Tamagnini Barbosa, at Av. General Castelo Branco, Downtown* ☎ *853/2833–3399, 853/2826–1188 to place bets* 🌐 *www.macauyydog.com* 🎫 *Public stands MOP$10, private boxes MOP$120* ⏲ *Mon., Thurs., and weekends 6 PM–11 PM; first race at 7:30.*

Macau Fisherman's Wharf. More of a distraction than an amusement park, this developing complex of minor attractions nonetheless has an old-world decadence. Its centerpiece is the Roman Amphitheatre, which hosts outdoor performances, but its main draws are the lively themed restaurants on the west side, such as AfriKana B.B.Q and Camões. Across from the toylike Babylon Casino, the Rocks Hotel heralds a series of themed accommodations to come. Children's rides and games, on the east end, include a role-playing war game and an underground video-game arcade. Come for the food, and stay after dark, as the Fisherman's Wharf is even more active at night. ✉ *Av. da Amizade, at Av. Dr. Sun Yat-Sen, Downtown* ☎ *853/8299–3300* 🌐 *www.fishermanswharf.com.mo* 🎫 *Admission free; rides and games MOP$20–MOP$200* ⏲ *Open 24 hours.*

Fodor's Choice ★ **Macau Tower Convention & Entertainment Centre.** Rising 1,000 feet above the peaceful San Van Lake, the world's 10th-largest freestanding tower recalls a similar structure in Auckland. And it should, as both were designed by New Zealand architect Gordon Moller. The Macau Tower offers a variety of thrills, including the Mast Climb, which challenges the daring and strong of heart and body with a two-hour climb on steel rungs 344 feet up the tower's mast for incomparable views of Macau and China. Other thrills include the Skywalk, an open-air stroll around the tower's exterior—without handrails; the SkyJump, an assisted, decelerated 765-foot descent; and the classic bungee jump. Prices range from MOP$388 for the Skywalk to MOP$1,688 for the Mast Climb, with extra charges for photos. More subdued attractions inside the tower are a mainstream movie theater and a revolving lunch and dinner buffet at the 360 Café. ✉ *Largo da Torre de Macau, Downtown* ☎ *853/8988–8656* 🌐 *www.macautower.com.mo.*

Fodor's Choice ★ **Ruínas de São Paulo** *(Ruins of St. Paul's Church)*. Only the magnificent, towering facade, with its intricate carvings and bronze statues, remains from the original Church of Mater Dei, built between 1602 and 1640 and destroyed by fire in 1835. The church, an adjacent college, and Mount Fortress, all Jesuit constructions, once formed East Asia's first western-style university. Now the widely adopted symbol of Macau, the ruins are a primary tourist attraction, with snack bars and antiques and other shops at the foot of the site.

Behind the facade of São Paulo is the **Museum of Sacred Art and Crypt** (☎ *No phone* 🎫 *Free* ⏲ *Daily 9–6*), which holds statues, crucifixes,

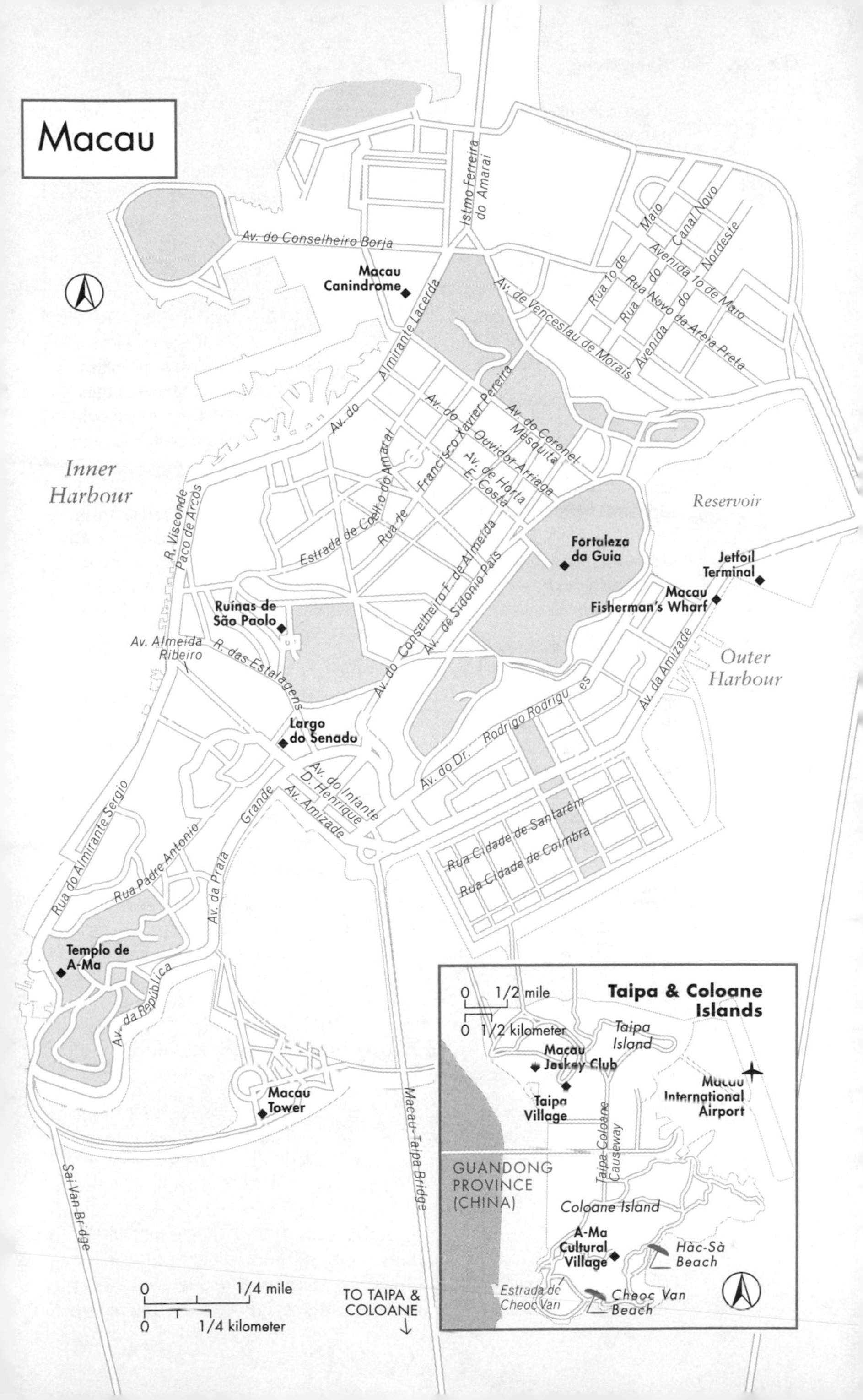
Macau
Av. do Conselheiro Borja
Istmo Ferreira do Amaral
Macau Canindrome
Av. do Almirante Lacerda
Av. de Venceslau de Morais
Rua 10 de Maio
Avenida 1o de Maio
Rua do Canal Novo
Rua Novo da Areia Preta
Avenida do Nordeste
Inner Harbour
R. Visconde Paco de Arcos
Estrada de Coelho do Amaral
Rua de Francisco Xavier Pereira
Av. do Ouvidor Arriaga
Av. de Horta E. Costa
Av. do Coronel Mesquita
Reservoir
Fortaleza da Guia
Jetfoil Terminal
Macau Fisherman's Wharf
Av. do Conselheiro F. de Almeida
Av. de Sidonio Pais
Ruínas de São Paolo
Av. Almeida Ribeiro
R. das Estalagens
Outer Harbour
Av. da Amizade
Av. do Dr. Rodrigo Rodrigues
Largo do Senado
Av. do Infante D. Henrique
Av. Amizade
Praia Grande
Rua do Almirante Sergio
Rua Padre Antonio
Av. da Praia
Rua Cidade de Santarém
Rua Cidade de Coimbra
Templo de A-Ma
Av. da República
Macau Tower
Sai Van Bridge
Macau-Taipa Bridge
0 1/4 mile
0 1/4 kilometer
TO TAIPA & COLOANE
Taipa & Coloane Islands
0 1/2 mile
0 1/2 kilometer
Taipa Island
Macau Jockey Club
Taipa Village
Macau International Airport
GUANDONG PROVINCE (CHINA)
Taipa Coloane Causeway
Coloane Island
A-Ma Cultural Village
Hàc-Sà Beach
Estrada de Cheoc Van
Cheoc Van Beach

and the bones of Japanese and Vietnamese martyrs. There are also some intriguing Asian interpretations of Christian images, including samurai angels and a Chinese Virgin and child.

The **Templo de Na Tcha** is a small Chinese temple built in 1888, during the Macauan plague. The hope was that Na Tcha Temple would appeal to a mythical Chinese character who granted wishes and could save lives. The **Troco das Antigas Muralhas de Defesa** (Section of the Old City Walls) is all that remains of Macau's original defensive barrier, and borders the left side of the Na Tcha Temple. These crumbling yellow walls were built in 1569 and illustrate the durability of *chunambo,* a local material made from compacted layers of clay, soil, sand, straw, crushed rocks, and oyster shells. ✉ *Top end of Rua de São Paulo, Downtown* ☎ *853/8399–6699* ⏲ *Daily 8–5.*

WORLD HERITAGE

The "Historic Centre of Macao" was listed as China's 31st UNESCO World Heritage Site in 2005. The term "center" is misleading as the site is really a collection of churches, buildings, and neighborhoods that colorfully illustrate Macau's 400-year history. Included in it are China's oldest examples of western architecture and the region's most extensive concentration of missionary churches.

Fodor's Choice ★ **Templo de A-Ma** *(A-Ma Temple).* Thought to be Macau's oldest building, this temple, properly Ma Kok Temple but known as A-Ma, is also one of Macau's most picturesque. The structure has its origins in the Ming Dynasty (1368–1644) and was influenced by Confucianism, Taoism, and Buddhism, as well as local religions. Vivid-red calligraphy on large boulders tells the story of the goddess A-Ma (also known as Tin Hau), the patron of fishermen. A small gate opens onto prayer halls, pavilions, and caves carved directly into the hillside. ✉ *Rua de São Tiago da Barra, Largo da Barra, Downtown* ⏲ *Daily 7–6.*

TAIPA

Taipa village's narrow, winding streets are packed with restaurants, bakeries, shop houses, temples, and other buildings with traditional South Chinese and Portuguese design elements. The aptly named Rua do Cunha (Food Street) has many great Chinese, Macanese, Portuguese, and Thai restaurants. Several shops sell homemade Macanese snacks, including steamed milk pudding, almond cakes, beef jerky, and coconut candy. A small public square hosts frequent music and dance performances by students and other local performers.

Macau Jockey Club. The MJC operates year-round, hosting an average of 100 races. A five-story, open-air grandstand accommodates as many as 15,000 spectators, and, of course, hundreds of private suites and VIP boxes for high rollers and celebrity visitors. All the facilities are top quality, and you can even get a great meal here. Horses have a comfortable lifestyle, too, with more than 1,250 air-conditioned stalls, an equine hospital, and an equine swimming pool. There's also a riding school for aspiring jockeys. Sand-track races are held weeknights at 7, and grass track races take place weekends at 2, except in summer when the heat and humidity forces all races to be held in the evenings. You can place bets at more than 80 stations throughout Macau and Hong Kong as well as through the Internet. If you opt to bet here, though, be sure to stop by the northeast exit to visit the large Four Face Buddha statue where you can say a short prayer for luck. ✉ *Estrada Governador Albano de Oliveira, Taipa* ☎ *853/821–188* 🌐 *www.macauhorse.com* *General admission is free, grandstand seating is MOP$20.*

COLOANE

Centuries ago, Coloane was a wild place, where pirates hid in rocky caves and coves, awaiting their chance to strike at cargo ships on the Pearl River. Early in the 20th century, the local government sponsored a huge planting program to transform Coloane from a barren place to a green one. The results were spectacular—and enduring. Today this island has green hills and clean sandy beaches.

Once connected to Taipa Island by a thin isthmus, Coloane is now almost completely fused with Taipa via the huge Cotai reclaimed land project, where the "Strip" is being constructed and scheduled for completion by 2010. Regardless of the recent development boom, Coloane remains the destination of choice for anyone seeking natural beauty and tranquility.

Fodor's Choice ★ **A-Ma Cultural Village.** A path just south of Seac Pai Van Park leads to A-Ma Cultural Village, a huge complex built in a traditional Qing Dynasty style. It pays homage to Macau's namesake, the goddess of the sea. The vibrancy and color of the details in the bell and drum towers, the tiled roofs, and the carved marble altars are truly awe-inspiring. It's as if you've been transported back to the height of the Qing Empire and can now see temples in their true state of greatness. Other remarkable details include the striking rows of stairs leading to Tian Hou Palace at the entrance. Each row features painstakingly detailed marble and stone carvings of auspicious Chinese symbols: a roaring tiger, double lions, five cranes, the double phoenix, and a splendid imperial dragon. The grounds here also have a recreational fishing zone and an arboretum with more than 100 species of local and exotic flora.

Behind A-Ma Cultural Village is the 560-foot-tall **Coloane Hill,** crowned by a gleaming white-marble statue of A-Ma (commemorating the year of Macau's handover), soaring 65 feet and visible from miles away. You can make the short hike up to the top or take one of the shuttle buses that leave from the foot of the hill every 30 minutes. ✉ *Off Estrada de Seac Pai Van Coloane Island South* ⏲ *Daily 8–6*

Cheoc Van Beach. Perfect for romantic walks, this beach is in a sheltered cove with a nice seafood restaurant to one side, the Marine Club with kayak rentals on the other side, and a charming pousada (historic inn) overlooking the ocean. Be warned that there are lots of stray, though generally friendly, dogs on this beach. ✉ *Off Estrada de Cheoc Van, Coloane Island South* ⏲ *Open 24 hours.*

Hác-Sá. Translated from the Chinese, hác-sá means "black sand," although the sands of the area's biggest beach are actually a deep gray.

Playgrounds, picnic areas, and restaurants are all within walking distance. Even if you don't stay at the resident five-star Westin Resort, you can use the public sports complex, which is equipped with an Olympic-size swimming pool, tennis courts, and other sports facilities, for a fee. Also nearby is the Hác-Sá Reservoir BBQ park with picnic and barbecue facilities, boat rentals, and water-sports outfitters. ✉ *Off Estrada de Hác Sá, Coloane Island South* ⏲ *Open 24 hours.*

WHERE TO EAT

	WHAT IT COSTS IN PATACAS				
	¢				
AT DINNER	under MOP$80	MOP$80–MOP$150	MOP$151–MOP$200	MOP$201–MOP$300	over MOP$300

Prices are for two main courses, a small side dish, and two beverages at dinner and do not include the customary 10% service charge.

$$$ PORTUGUESE Fodor's Choice ★ **A Lorcha.** Vastly popular A Lorcha (the name means "wooden ship") celebrates Macau's port heritage with a maritime theme for the menu. Don't miss the signature dish, Clams Lorcha Style, with tomato, beer, and garlic. Other classics include *feijoada* (Brazilian pork-and-bean stew), steamed crab, and perfectly smoky and juicy fire-roasted chicken. Remember to save room for the excellent Portuguese desserts, such as thick mango pudding and sinfully dense serradura. Watch for racers during the Grand Prix, as the Macanese owner Adriano is a fervent Formula fan. ✉ *289 Rua do Almirante Sérgio, Inner Harbour* ✉ *Rua do Almirate Sérgio, No. 289, AA, R/C, Macau* ☎ *853/2831–3193* ✍ *Reservations essential* ▭ *AE, MC, V* ⏲ *Closed Tues.*

$$ PORTUGUESE Fodor's Choice ★ **Dom Galo.** "Quirky" springs to mind when describing the colorful decor of Dom Galo, from plastic monkey puppets to funky chicken toys hanging from the ceilings. Near the MGM Grand, it draws a wide clientele, from graphic designers to gambling-compliance lawyers to 10-year-old Cantonese kids celebrating birthdays. The waitstaff is from the Philippines and the owner is Portuguese—which means service is usually spot-on. And the food is good: *insalada de polvo* (octopus salad), king prawns, and steak fries served with a tangy mushroom sauce. Pitchers of sangria are essential with any meal. So, too, are reservations. ✉ *Av. Sir Andars Ljung Stedt, Downtown* ☎ *853/2875–1383* ▭ *MC, V.*

$$ CANTONESE Fodor's Choice ★ **Fat Siu Lau.** Well known to both locals and Hong Kong visitors, Fat Siu Lau has kept its customers coming back since 1903 with delicious Macanese favorites and modern creations. For best results, try ordering whatever you see the chatty Cantonese stuffing themselves with on the surrounding tables, and you won't be disappointed. It will probably be whole curry crab, grilled prawns in a butter garlic sauce, and the famous roasted pigeon marinated in a secret marinade. The newer Fat Siu Lau 2 is on Macau Lan Kwai Fong Street and offers the same great food. ✉ *64 Rua da Felicidade, Downtown* ☎ *853/2857–3580* ✍ *Reservations essential* ▭ *MC, V.*

$$$$ SPANISH **La Paloma.** Specialties at this Spanish restaurant (formerly the Portuguese restaurant Os Gatos) firmly ensconced in the 17th-century Pousada de São Tiago include seafood paella, pigeon roasted or braised in three different sauces, Iberian Parma ham, pork sirloin, garoupa (grouper), and fresh sole. Don't miss the afternoon high tea, available from 3 to 6 daily, outside on the brick terrace shaded by hundred-year-old trees, in the air-conditioned interior with a view of the South China Sea, or even at the mirror-walled Paloma Bar built inside the ancient fortress. ✉*Pousada de São Tiago, Av. da República, Inner Harbour,* ☎*853/2896–8686* ▭*AE, DC, MC, V.*

$$$ MACANESE **Litoral.** One of the most popular local restaurants, Litoral serves authentic Macanese dishes that are simple, straightforward, and deliciously satisfying. Tastefully decorated with whitewashed walls and dark-wood beams, must-try dishes include the tamarind pork with shrimp paste, as well as codfish baked with potato and garlic, and a Portuguese vegetable cream soup. For dessert, try the *bebinca de leite,* a coconut-milk custard, or the traditional egg pudding, *pudim abade de priscos*. Various-priced set menus are also available, and reservations are recommended on weekends. ✉*261 Rua do Almirante Sergio, Inner Harbour* ☎*853/2896–7878* ▭*AE, MC, V.*

$$–$$$ SHANGHAINESE **Portas do Sol.** Originally a Portuguese restaurant, Portas do Sol has been transformed into a destination for exquisite dim sum and Chinese cuisine. Tiny, sweet Shanghainese pork buns, turnip cakes, steamed rice-flour crepes, and soup dumplings are some of the traditional fare, and there are some innovative new creations that look like miniature jewels on the plate. For dessert, you can choose from a wide variety of Chinese sweets, including coconut-milk sago pudding, double-boiled papaya with snow fungus (a tasteless mushroom that becomes gelatinous when cooked), and sweet red-bean porridge with ice cream. Evening diners may or may not appreciate the cabaret show and ballroom dancing. Reservations are a good idea on weekends as this place fills up with Hong Kong and mainland visitors. ✉*Hotel Lisboa, Av. da Amizade, Downtown* ☎*853/2888–3888* ▭*AE, MC, V.*

WHERE TO STAY

	WHAT IT COSTS IN PATACAS				
	¢				
FOR 2 PEOPLE	under MOP$300	MOP$300–800	MOP$800–1,000	MOP$1,000–1,500	over MOP$1,500

Prices are for two people in a standard double room on a typical Saturday night, not including 10% service charge and 5% tax.

MACAU

$$ **Hotel Lisboa.** Macau's infamous landmark, with its distinctive, labyrinthine interior architecture, rumored connections to organized crime, open prostitution, and no-limit VIP rooms, now stands in the shadow of its Grand Lisboa sister. The two are connected by a bridge and share facilities, such as the Grand's modern pool, gym, and spa. The advantages

to staying in the older structure are nostalgic value and lower price. And though the Grand Lisboa opened in early 2007, the Hotel Lisboa was renovated one year later, so the rooms are just as luxurious, with hardwood floors and Jacuzzi baths. Take your time to wander through the hotel's corridors displaying jade and artworks from Dr. Stanley Ho's private collection, before running into an ostentatiously gilded staircase. Many people come to the Lisboa expressly for its restaurants: Robuchon a Galera, Portas do Sol, and Chiu Chow (⇨ *Where to Eat*). **Pros:** historical interior, central location, superior restaurants, linked to the Grand Lisboa. **Cons:** old building, low ceilings, smoky casino. ✉*2–4 Av. de Lisboa, Downtown* ☎*853/2888–3888, 800/969–130 in Hong Kong* 🌐*www.hotelisboa.com* *1,000 rooms, 28 suites* *In-room: safe, DVD, Internet. In-hotel: 3 restaurants, room service, pool, gym, spa, laundry service, no-smoking rooms* *AE, DC, MC, V.*

$ **Hotel Sintra.** Just minutes away from Senado Square and right down the street from the New Yaohan department store, the Sintra is a good three-star antechamber to the Lisboan kingdom, with its own built-in Mocha minicasino accessible through the lobby. Its carpeted rooms are decorated in soothing brown-and-cream color schemes, while the staff is smartly dressed and helpful. Breakfast is an extra MOP$88 for an American buffet. **Pros:** in the heart of downtown, simple but tasteful decor. **Cons:** small rooms, small casino. ✉*Av. De Dom João IV, Downtown* ☎*853/710–111, 800/969–145 in Hong Kong* 🌐*www.hotelsintra.com* *240 rooms, 11 suites* *In-room: safe, refrigerator, Internet. In-hotel: restaurant, room service, Wi-Fi, no-smoking rooms* *AE, DC, MC, V.*

$$$ **Mandarin Oriental.** The Mandarin Oriental is synonymous with elegance and understated opulence, and its Macau location doesn't disappoint. This hotel is also widely known for deluxe treatments in the enormous spa complex next to the gorgeous, tropical swimming pool on the landscaped grounds. You'll feel like you're in a lush rain forest as you look out from the traditional Mediterranean architecture of the hotel. It even has tennis and squash courts. The hotel's renowned restaurants include the Café Bela Vista for its endless buffet, and Naam, the exquisite Thai restaurant popular with locals and visitors alike. **Pros:** classic luxury facilities, on-site rock climbing, kid's club. **Cons:** old casino, high-traffic location. ✉*956–1110 Av. da Amizade, Outer Harbour* ☎*853/8793–3261, 2881–1288 in Hong Kong, 800/526–6567 in U.S.* 🌐*www.mandarinoriental.com/macau* *388 rooms, 28 suites* *In-room: safe, refrigerator, Internet, Wi-Fi. In-hotel: 4 restaurants, room service, bar, tennis courts, pools, gym, spa, water sports, children's programs (ages 3–12), laundry service, Internet, Wi-Fi, no-smoking rooms* *AE, DC, MC, V.*

$$$ Fodor's Choice ★ **MGM Grand.** In Macau, the golden lion statue stands guard on the peninsula's southern coast, as guests penetrate into the MGM's spectacular Grande Praça (Grand Square), an 82-foot-tall floor-to-glass-ceiling space modeled after a Portuguese town square that serves as an inner courtyard and has fine dining under the stars. A few million Hong Kong dollars were invested in the permanent chandelier sculpture and original drawings by Dale Chihuly decorating the hotel lobby and

reception. Chihuly's glassworks line the hall linking the art gallery to the patisserie, giving it a warm pink glow, while the M Bar plays soft jazz and lounge music. The rooms are everything you'd expect in the way of comfort and elegance from a luxury accommodation, but it's the classy world around them, outside the casino, that distinguishes this hotel from the rest. **Pros:** tasteful architecture, Chihuly artwork, refined dining and lounge options. **Cons:** inseparable from the casino, which can get smoky and loud; high-traffic location. ✉ *Av. Dr. Sun Yat Sen, Downtown* ☎ *853/8802–8888* 🌐 *www.mgmgrandmacau.com* *494 rooms, 99 suites* *In-room: safe, refrigerator (some), DVD (some), Wi-Fi. In-hotel: 8 restaurants, room service, bars, pool, spa, laundry service, Wi-Fi, parking (paid), no-smoking rooms* 💳 *AE, MC, V.*

$$$$ Fodor's Choice ★ **Pousada de São Tiago.** The spirit of the structure's past life as a 17th-century fortress permeates every part of this romantic and intimate lodging, making it ideal for a honeymoon or wedding. Even the front entrance impressive: an ascending stone tunnel carved into the mountainside with water seeping through in quiet trickles. The pousada reopened in mid-2007 after a major renovation that consolidated accommodations into 12 modern luxury suites, each with Jacuzzi bathrooms and large balconies for room-service breakfast. Stop for high tea in the mirrored lounge, or sip a cocktail on the terrace under 100-year-old trees. **Pros:** all the modern comfort of a luxury hotel inside a 17th-century fortress, intimate, sunset views of the Inner Harbour. **Cons:** small pool, limited facilities, you'll need to call a taxi to go out. ✉ *Fortaleza de São Tiago da Barra, Av. da República, Inner Harbour* ☎ *853/2837–8111, 800/969–153 in Hong Kong* 🌐 *www.saotiago.com.mo* *12 suites* *In-room: Internet, Wi-Fi. In-hotel: restaurant, room service, bar, pool, laundry service, Internet, Wi-Fi, parking (free), no smoking rooms* 💳 *AE, MC, V.*

$$ **Rocks Hotel.** Opened on Christmas Eve, 2006, as the first in a series of theme hotels to come to the east end of Fisherman's Wharf, the posh-yet-quaint five-story Rocks Hotel is modeled after the charm of 18th-century Victorian England. Each room and suite is individually decorated, with a novelty old-fashioned bathtub in addition to a modern shower stall. Balconies offer low sea views on all sides. The extensive Asian and American breakfast buffet is worth looking forward to in the morning. The foyer itself is impressive, with its grand staircase under sparkling chandeliers, although it could use some real birds in the giant gilded cage to liven up the lobby. **Pros:** distinctive decor, low-key fine dining. **Cons:** no pool or spa, located inside an amusement park. ✉ *Macau Fisherman's Wharf, Outer Harbour* ☎ *853/2878–2782, 800/962–863 in Hong Kong* 🌐 *www.rockshotel.com.mo* *66 rooms, 6 suites* *In-room: safe, Internet. In-hotel: restaurant, room service, bar, gym, laundry service, Internet, parking (free), no-smoking rooms* 💳 *AE, DC, MC, V.*

$$$ **Sands Macao.** Las Vegas casino tycoon Sheldon Anderson's first venture in Macau, the Sands is nothing if not luxurious. Spacious rooms have deep, soft carpets, large beds, and huge marble bathrooms with Jacuzzis. If you opt to become a high-rolling member, you can stay in one of the 51 deluxe or executive suites, ranging in size from 650

to 1,300 square feet, with all-in-one remote-control plasma TV, karaoke, curtains, and lighting, plus personal butler service on request. VIP members also have privileges such as private helicopter and high-limit gaming rooms at both the Sands and Venetian casinos. But all guests can enjoy the outdoor heated pool on the sixth floor, as well as the exclusive sauna, spa, and salon. **Pros:** heated outdoor pool, across the street from Fisherman's Wharf. **Cons:** not as new as the Venetian, near lots of vehicle traffic. ✉ *203 Largo de Monte Carlo, Outer Harbour* ☎ *853/8983–3100* 🌐 *www.sands.com.mo* *258 rooms, 51 VIP suites* *In-room: safe, DVD, Wi-Fi. In-hotel: 7 restaurants, room service, bar, pools, gym, spa, laundry service, parking (paid)* *AE, MC, V.*

$$ Fodor'sChoice ★ **Sofitel Macau at Ponte 16.** Ever since its February 2008 opening, Ponte 16 has pioneered the revamp of Macau's retro western port into an emerging casino and commercial pole. The neighborhood may not be there yet, but Sofitel is Ponte 16's jewel in the crown, with lush, sleek suites and a giant, curvaceous pool, complete with cocktail and juice bar, just outside the indoor buffet lounge. Adventurous and up-and-coming, it has all the edgy perks—grab it while it's hot. **Pros:** giant outdoor pool with bar serving everything from fresh fruit to fine wine, some rooms have unique views of the Inner Harbour. **Cons:** in a still-developing neighborhood, heavy traffic outside. ✉ *Rua do Visconde Paço de Arcos, Inner Harbour* ☎ *853/8861–0016* 🌐 *www.sofitel.com* *389 rooms, 19 suites* *In-room: safe, DVD, Internet. In-hotel: restaurants, room service, bar, pool, gym, spa, laundry service, Internet, parking (free), no-smoking rooms* *AE, DC, MC, V.*

COLOANE

$ **Pousada de Coloane.** At Cheoc-Van Beach at the southernmost tip of Coloane Island, Pousada de Coloane offers a quiet, natural setting, nestled within the lush hills and mountains of Macau's south. There are ample opportunities for kayaking, hiking, and swimming. A long winding path paved with Portuguese azulejo tiles leads you to the spacious terrace overlooking the beach and is ideal for outdoor wedding receptions and other celebrations. Facilities include a pool, a fireplace, and a small bar in the restaurant. The open terrace garden and restaurant offers traditional Portuguese, Macanese, and Chinese favorites cooked in a heavy, home-style tradition, but there are also other seafood restaurants down on the beach. All 30 rooms have private hot tubs, cable TV, and balconies overlooking the beach, with the mountains of mainland China in the distance. **Pros:** intimate coastal location, sea-view balconies. **Cons:** limited facilities, no in-room Internet. ✉ *Cheoc Van Beach, Coloane Island South* ☎ *853/2888–2143* 🌐 *www.hotelpcoloane.com.mo* *30 rooms* *In-room: safe (some). In-hotel: restaurant, room service, bar, pool, laundry service, Internet, Wi-Fi, parking (free)* *MC, V.*

$$ Fodor'sChoice **Westin Resort.** Built into the side of a cliff, the Westin is surrounded by the black sands of Hác-Sá Beach and lapping waves of the South China Sea. This is where you truly get away from it all. Every room faces the ocean; the place glows as much because of the sunny tropical color scheme as from the sunshine. The vast private terraces are ideal for alfresco dining and afternoon naps. Guests also receive access

to Macau's renowned golf club, the PGA-standard, 18-hole Macau Golf and Country Club, which was built on the rocky cliffs and plateaus above the hotel. **Pros:** green surrounds, golf-club access, fun for kids. **Cons:** isolated location, limited access. ✉*1918 Estrada de Hác Sá, Coloane Island South* ☎*853/2887–1111, 800/228–3000 in Hong Kong* 🌐*www.westin-macau.com* *208 rooms, 20 suites* *In-room: safe, Internet. In-hotel: 3 restaurants, room service, bars, golf course, tennis courts, pools, gym, spa, beachfront, bicycles, laundry service, Internet, parking (free), children's programs (ages 3–12), no-smoking rooms* 💳*AE, DC, MC, V.*

AFTER DARK

Old movies, countless novels, and gossip through the years have portrayed Macau's nightlife as a combustible mix of drugs, wild gambling, violent crime, and ladies of the night. Up until the 1999 handover back to mainland China, this image of Macau was mostly accurate and worked to drive away tourists.

Outside of the casinos and a few restaurants, today's Macau shuts down after 11 PM. You can slip into any dark, elegant lounge bar inside the larger hotels, and enjoy live music and expensive cocktails, but don't expect much energy or big crowds. And most late-night saunas are glorified brothels, with "workers" from China, Vietnam, Thailand, and Russia.

CASINOS

Gone are the days of Macau's dark and dingy underground gaming parlors. One is no longer bound by Stanley Ho's iron grip on the gambling scene and there's now an emerging dreamland of opportunity for the bigwigs of Las Vegas to move in and spice up the competition. Over the past few years, American-style casinos have been mushrooming like mad, primarily in Macau's NAPE (zona *N*ova de *A*terros do *P*orto *E*xterior), or New Reclamation Area, in the Outer Harbour district between the main ferry terminal and the historic center.

But you don't have to be a hard-core gambler to enjoy browsing the glittering premises. While Dr. Ho has fought back sportingly, renovating older properties, partnering, and launching entirely new ones (e.g., the Grand Lisboa), it's the foreign exports that are most likely to please both casual tourists and serious players for their variety of gaming and other entertainment, relatively clean, well-lit atmosphere, free 24/7 accessibility, and overall glamour-resort experience. Homegrown newbie Ponte 16, however, is the one to watch.

THE SCENE

Gambling is lightly regulated, so there are only a few things to remember. No one under age 18 is allowed into casinos. Most casinos use Hong Kong dollars in their gaming and not Macau patacas, but you can easily exchange currencies at cashiers. High- and no-limit VIP rooms are available on request, where minimum bets range from HK$50,000 to HK$100,000 per hand. You can get cash from credit cards and ATMs

24 hours a day, and every casino has a program to extend additional credit to frequent visitors. Most casinos don't have strict dress codes outside of their VIP rooms, but men are better off not wearing shorts or sleeveless shirts. Minimum bets for most tables are higher than those in Las Vegas, but there are lower limits for slots and video gambling.

The players here may not look sophisticated, but don't be fooled. Chinese men and women have long embraced gambling, so many of Macau's gamblers are truly hard-core. Average bets are in the hundreds per hand, and many people gamble until they're completely exhausted or completely broke, usually the latter.

Macau is also famous for gambling's sister industries of pawnshops, loan sharks, seedy saunas, and prostitution. This underbelly is hidden, though. You won't encounter such things unless you seek them out.

THE CREAM OF THE CROP **Sands Macao** (✉ *203 Largo de Monte Carlo, Downtown* ☎ *853/2888-3333* 🌐 *www.sands.com.mo*). **MGM Grand** ✉ *Av. Dr. Sun Yat Sen, Downtown* ☎ *853/8802-8888* 🌐 *www.mgmgrandmacau.com*). **Wynn Macau** (✉ *Rua Cidade de Sintra, Downtown* ☎ *853/2888-9966* 🌐 *www.wynnmacau.com*). **Venetian Macao Resort Hotel** (✉ *Estrada da Baía de N. Senhora da Esperança, Cotai* ☎ *853/2882-8888* 🌐 *www.venetianmacao.com*).

THE LANDMARKS **Casino Lisboa** (✉ *Av. de Lisboa, Downtown* ☎ *853/2837-5111* 🌐 *www.hotelisboa.com*). **Crown Macau** (✉ *Av. de Kwong Tung, Taipa* ☎ *853/2886-8888* 🌐 *www.crown-macau.com*). **Galaxy StarWorld** ✉ *Av. da Amizade, Downtown* ☎ *853/2838-3838* 🌐 *www.galaxyentertainment.com*). **Grand Lisboa** (✉ *2-4 Av. de Lisboa, Downtown* ☎ *853/2838-5111* 🌐 *www.grandlisboa.com*).

Pearl River Delta

GUANGZHOU AND SHENZHEN

Pizhou Exhibition Hall in Guangzhou, Guangdong province.

WORD OF MOUTH

Shenzhen is a crazy place. It didn't exist other than small villages 30 years ago. Therefore the whole population consists of younger people looking for fortune and work, and sometimes their young kids. . . . Most of its population speaks only Putonghua.

—rkkwan

WELCOME TO PEARL RIVER DELTA

Sun Yat-sen Memorial Hall, Guangzhou.

TOP REASONS TO GO

★ **Feel the Buzz!:** This region is the undisputed engine driving China's economic boom, and whether you're in Guangzhou or Shenzhen, you're sure to feel the buzz of a Communist nation on a capitalist joyride.

★ **Explore the Ancient:** Though thoroughly modern, the Pearl River Delta has not lost touch with its ancient roots. From the temples of Guangzhou to the Ming Dynasty–walled city of Dapeng in Shenzhen, a journey through the PRD is a journey through the centuries.

★ **Soak Up Some Colonial Splendor:** Guangzhou's well-preserved examples of architecture date back to the 19th century, when European merchants amassed fortunes in the opium trade, and the buildings from which they once plied their trade still stand.

★ **Shopping! Shopping! Shopping!:** Need we say more?

Citic Plaza.

1 Guangzhou. After you've recovered from the initial confusion produced by the crowds, heavy traffic, and pollution, turn to the city's unique cuisine, sights, culture, and history, such as Colonial Shamian and the nearby White Cloud Mountain.

2 Shenzhen. Come to Shenzhen for excellent shopping and dining at affordable prices. Or head to Overseas Chinese Town to take in some art and culture. For those who enjoy a round or two of golf, the city's Mission Hills Golf Club promises to blow your mind.

GETTING ORIENTED

The Pearl River Delta is a massive triangle. Guangzhou is at the top, Shenzhen on the east corner, and Zhuhai on the west. The area as a whole is just a bit too spread out for any one corner to make a good base of operations from which to explore the others. We recommend beginning at one corner and making your way around. Guangzhou is fairly dense, so leave yourself three days in which to soak it all in before heading down to Shenzhen. From Shenzhen's Shekou Harbor it's a one-hour ferry ride to Zhuhai, which takes less than a day to explore before returning either back to Guangzhou or into nearby Macau or Hong Kong.

PEARL RIVER DELTA PLANNER

When To Go

When to go is a major question every traveler needs to ask themselves, and certainly in a place like the Pearl River Delta, where summer temperatures and humidity can make the area feel like the inside of a clothes dryer halfway through the dry cycle and winter brings an all-pervading chill and dampness.

The answer is spring and autumn, but this is complicated by a few factors. Unless you have friends in the hotel industry, don't even think about visiting Guangzhou during the annual spring trade fair, when hotel prices skyrocket.

Don't travel anywhere in China during the Golden Week holiday, which takes place annually from October 1 through 7. So what do we recommend? September, October (excluding Golden Week), and early to mid-November.

Cuisine

Most Cantonese dishes are stirfried or steamed, although roasted meats such as barbecued chicken and pork are also popular. Dim sum—literally meaning "touch your heart"—includes a huge selection of dumplings and pastries. Filled with meat and vegetables, they are a perfect way to start or end the day. When you go out to eat, go with as many people as you can find so that you can try as many different dishes as possible.

One Cantonese saying goes "anything with its back towards the sky is edible," and the idea is so inclusive that any animal or insects, including snakes, civet cats, and locusts, makes the list. The cuisine also makes use of every part of an animals body, including feet, tongues, and entrails. Be adventurious but make sure you know what you're eating! And stick to fully cooked dishes to avoid bacterial or parasitic infections, particularly during warm weather.

A few things to remember when eating chopsticks: do not stick your them vertically into your bowl of rice, this is thought to be unlucky because it resembles burning joss sticks connected with the death. Don't be surprised to hear people slurping and burping—these are totally acceptable behaviors not only in China, but in most of Asia as well. When eating rice, bring the edge of the bowl to your mouth and use your chopsticks to push the rice in.

Tours and Travel Arrangements

China Travel Services (☎ *852/2851–1700 or 852/2522–0450* 🌐 *www.ctshk.com/english/index.htm*) has 40 offices in Hong Kong, Kowloon, and the New Territories and can arrange just about any type of travel experience that might interest you in the Pearl River Delta. CTS can assist with visas and booking discount hotel rooms. They are open weekdays 9 AM to 7 PM, Saturday 9 AM to 5 PM, and Sunday and holidays 9:30 to 12:30 and 2 PM to 5 PM.

China International Travel Service Limited (*CITS* ☎ *8610/6522–2991* 📠 *8610/6522–1733* 🌐 *www.cits.cn/en/index.htm*). **Bestourchina** (🌐 *www.bestourchina.com*) is a sub-brand of CITS online business.

Avoid the Luohu Border-Crossing Crush

At Luohu (the main border crossing between Hong Kong and mainland China) the masses are funneled through a large three-story building. From the outside this building looks huge, but from the inside—especially when you're surrounded by a quarter million people waiting to be processed—the crossing is reminiscent of a scene from *Soylent Green*.

If you're going through Shenzhen enroute to or from Guangzhou, take the through train from Kowloon to Guangzhou. The immigration line at the Guangzhou East station is a comparative piece of cake, even on the worst days. It's possible to buy tickets on the fly on this commuter train, but we advise booking anywhere from a few hours to a day or two in advance.

If you're heading into Shenzhen, why not trade the mad crush of Luohu for an hour long ferry ride followed by a quick trip through the much less popular border crossing at Shekou Harbor? Although this won't bring you into downtown Shenzhen, you'll be no farther from attractions like the amusement parks and Mission Hills Golf Club.

DINING AND LODGING PRICE CATEGORIES IN YUAN

¢	$	$$	$$$	$$$$
Restaurants				
under Y25	Y25–Y49	Y50–Y99	Y100–Y165	over Y165
Hotels				
under Y700	Y700–Y1,099	Y1,100–Y1,399	Y1,400–Y1,800	over Y1,800

Restaurant prices are for a main course, excluding tax and tips. Hotel prices are for a standard double room, including taxes.

Ancient Days

Though Shenzhen City is barely three decades old, the areas outside the city are resplendent with examples of ancient Chinese culture. You'll want to take at least a day to explore the Longgang District, home to two examples modern and antique architecture existing side by side.

Like the rapidly disappearing hutong neighborhoods of Beijing, **Dapeng Fortress**—an ancient city—is a living museum. The old town contains homes, temples, shops, and courtyards that look pretty much the way they did when they were built over the course of the Ming (1368–1644) and Qing (1644–1911) dynasties. For the most part, the residences are occupied, the shops are doing business, and the temples are active houses of worship. Dapeng's ancient city is surrounded by an old stone wall, and entered through a series of gates.

Likewise, **Hakka Folk Customs Museum and Enclosures** are a very well-preserved example of an ancient walled community. The Hakkas built their homes inside of an exterior wall, complete with vertical-arrow slits for discouraging unwanted visitors. Many of the homes inside the fort are furnished, and visitors may get the feeling that the original inhabitants have just popped out for a bit of hunting and might come back any minute, crossbows cocked.

By Joshua Samuel Brown
Updated by Hannah Lee

THE PEARL RIVER DELTA IS China's workshop, its fastest-growing, ever-changing, and most affluent region. It's the industrial engine powering China's meteoric economic rise. You will find some of the greatest shopping, a flourishing nightlife, and a culinary scene, which most regions can only dream of.

The Pear River Delta is also among China's most polluted regions, and this is saying a lot. From the southern suburbs of Guangzhou city to the northern edge of Shenzhen, industry stretches in all directions. Tens of thousands of factories churn out the lion's share of the world's consumer products. This hyper-industry has polluted the entire area's soil, water, and air so badly that in Hong Kong (on the region's southern tip) pollution is an overriding public concern. On a bad day, the air quality in Guangzhou can actually be described as *abusive*. On top of all of this, much of the region is noisy and chaotic.

So why would the pleasure traveler even visit Pearl River Delta? The answers are myriad. History enthusiasts head to Guangzhou, Guangdong province's ancient capital, and the historic center of Cantonese culture and the revolution that overthrew the last dynasty. Gourmands flock to both Guangzhou and Shenzhen to indulge in some of the best examples of Chinese cuisine. Culture vultures visit the many temples, shrines, and museums scattered throughout the region. And shop-a-holics? A visit to the Pearl River Delta will quickly dismiss any lingering notions that China is still a nation bound by the tenets of Marx and Mao, secret police notwithstanding.

SAFETY

Avoid giving money to beggars. Take the usual precautions against appearing conspicuously wealthy, and carry with you only the amount of cash you need. Crowded places, such as stations and clubs, often harbor pickpockets, so keep your eyes on your bags and your wallet in your front pocket. If you see a local wearing a backpack on the front of his or her body, it's probably a good idea to do the same.

GUANGZHOU

120 km (74½ mi; 1½ hrs) north of Hong Kong.

Guangzhou (also known as Canton), the capital of Guangdong province, is both a modern boomtown and an ancient port city. This metropolis of over 7 million people has all the expected accoutrements of a competitive, modern Chinese city: skyscrapers, heavy traffic, efficient metro, and serious crowds. Guangzhou is an old city with a long history. Exploring its riverfront, parks, temples, and markets, one is constantly reminded the impact its irrepressible culture, language, and cuisine has made on the world.

In the early 20th century, Guangzhou was a hotbed of revolutionary zeal, first as the birthplace of the movement to overthrow the last dynasty (culminating in the 1911 Revolution), and then as a battleground between Nationalists and Communists in the years leading to

CLOSE UP

Underground in Guangzhou

Guangzhou's subway system is cheap, clean, and (unlike Beijing's) reasonably efficient. Divided into four lines that span both sides of the Pearl River, most of the areas of interest to casual visitors are found on lines 1 or 2 (the red and yellow lines on the maps).

The terminus of Line 1 is Guangzhou-dongzhan, or Guangzhou East Train Station, which is where trains leave for Hong Kong. This area is also the heart of the Tienhe, Guangzhou's newest financial district. Gongyuanqian is the interchange for lines 1 and 2. The most interesting temples and shrines are within walking distance of stations along Line 1, with signs in English pointing the way.

Ask your hotel concierge to give you an English subway map. ⇨*See subway map later in the chapter.* For walking-tour-friendly neighborhoods, we recommend Dongshankou station. This is a lovely little area with plenty of shopping opportunities. Tree-lined streets just off the avenue are filled with enclosed gardens and old houses with traditional architecture. The area surrounding the Linhex station is the most modern part of the city. This is a good neighborhood to walk around with your head tilted skyward.

Of course, if you really want to continue on an anti-car trip, get off at Gongyuanqian station (where Lines 1 and 2 intersect) and walk to the Beijing Road Pedestrian Mall: the hip, trendy, and carfree heart of young consumerism in Guangzhou.

the 1949 Communist revolution. Following the open-door policy of Deng Xiaoping in 1979, the port city was able to resume its role as a commercial gateway to China.

Rapid modernization during the 1980s and '90s has taken its toll not just on the environment but also on the pace of city life. On bad days the clouds of building-site dust, aggressive driving, shop touts, and persistent beggars can be overwhelming. But in Guangzhou's parks, temples, winding old-quarter backstreets, restaurants, river islets, and museums, the old city and a more refined way of life is never far away.

GETTING HERE AND AROUND

Most travelers enter Guangzhou either by train or plane. Long-distance trains pull in at the Guangzhou East Station. This station is also on the metro line. One-way tickets to or from Hong Kong cost between Y210 and Y250, and between Y130 and Y170 to Shenzhen.

Guangzhou is connected to Shenzhen (approximately 100 km [62 mi] to the south) by the aptly named Guangzhou–Shenzhen expressway. Buses from Guangzhou to Hong Kong leave from both the Guangzhou East Station and from major hotels such as the China and the Garden hotels, and cost about Y180.

Although taxis in Guangzhou are cheap and plentiful, traffic in the city is reaching nightmare proportions.

BY AIR Guangzhou's Baiyun Airport in Huada city currently offers 10 flights per day to both Hong Kong (Y670) and Beijing (Y1,240) between 9 AM

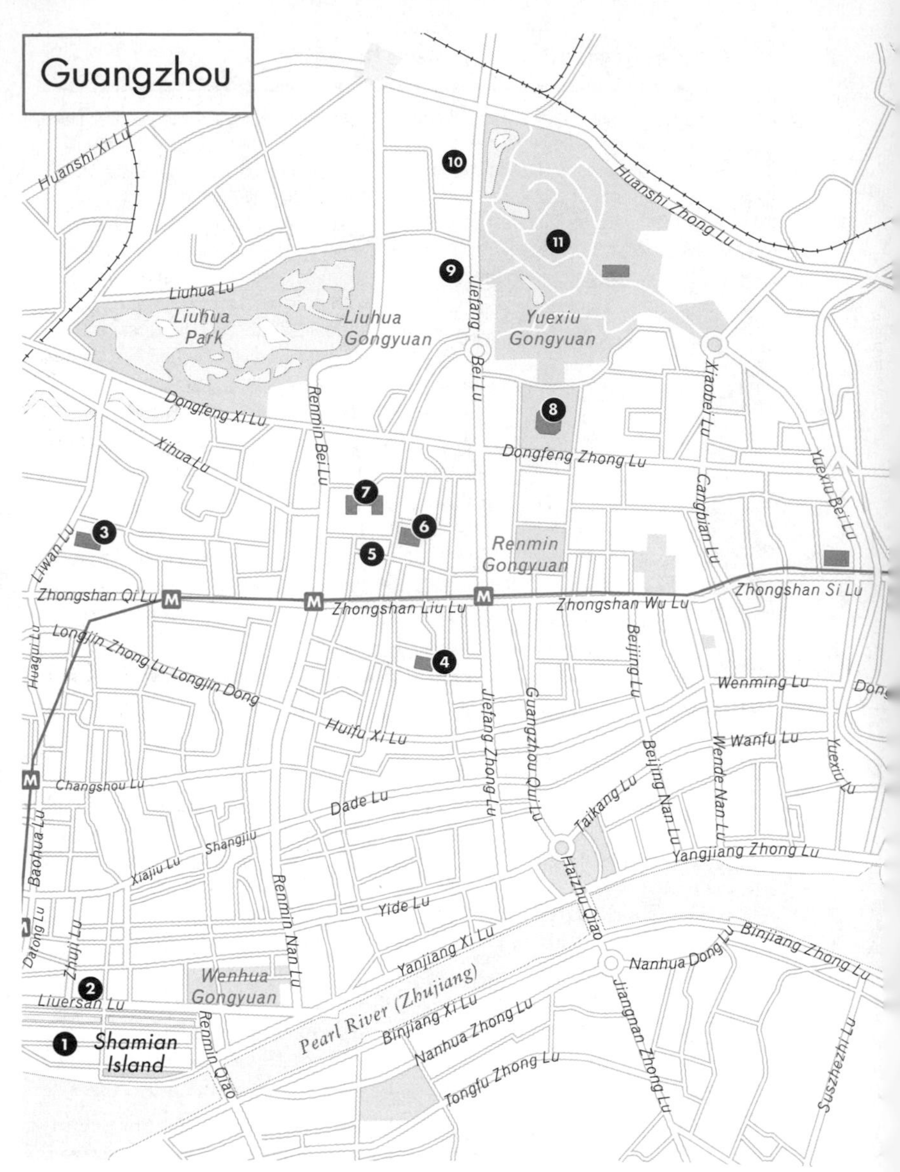

Bright Filial Piety Temple **7**	Mausoleum of the 72 Martyrs **13**	Sun Yat-sen Memorial Hall **8**
Chen Family Temple **3**	Memorial Garden for the Martyrs **12**	The Qingping Market **2**
Guangdong Museum of Art **15**	Orchid Garden **10**	Tianhe Stadium Complex **14**
Guangxiao Temple **5**	Shamian Island **1**	Tomb of the Southern Yue Kings **9**
Huaisheng Mosque **4**	Six Banyan Temple **6**	Yuexiu Park **11**

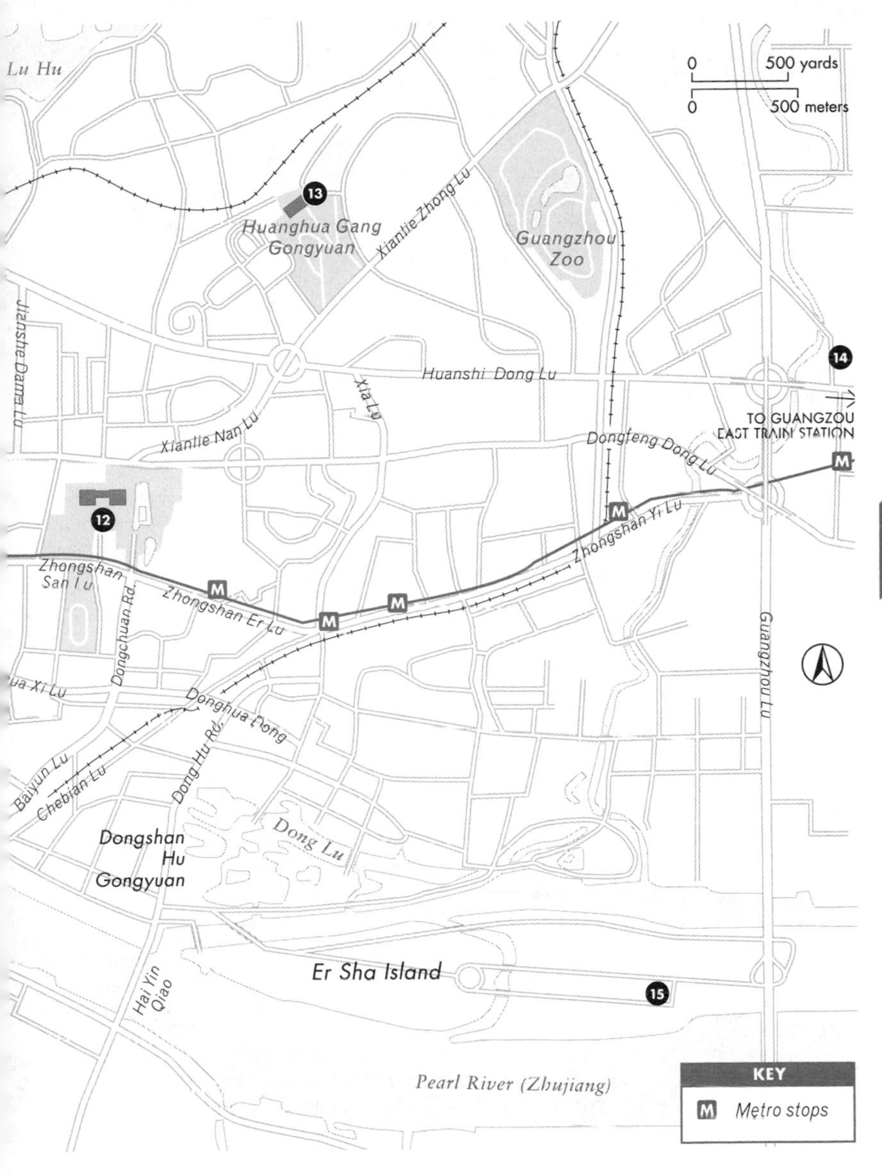
Lu Hu
0 500 yards
0 500 meters
Huanghua Gang Gongyuan
Xianlie Zhong Lu
Guangzhou Zoo
Jianshe Dama Lu
Huanshi Dong Lu
Xia Lu
Xianlie Nan Lu
TO GUANGZOU EAST TRAIN STATION
Dongfeng Dong Lu
Zhongshan Yi Lu
Zhongshan San Lu
Zhongshan Er Lu
Dongchuan Rd.
Guangzhou Lu
Donghua Dong
Dong Hu Rd.
Baiyun Lu
Chebian Lu
Dongshan Hu Gongyuan
Dong Lu
Er Sha Island
Hai Yin Qiao
Pearl River (Zhujiang)
KEY
Metro stops

6

and 9 PM. It has direct flights to Paris, Los Angeles, Singapore, Bangkok, Sydney, Jakarta, and Phnom Penh and a number of cities in North America.

WORD OF MOUTH

"There is a teahouse on a small island in the lake and they had the most extensive assortment of high-end Xixing teapots I've seen anywhere. They also had quite an assortment of teas." —Kathie

BY BUS Guangzhou Provincial Passenger Bus Station is the largest bus station in Guangdong province. Buses depart here daily to the neighboring Guangxi, Hunan, Fujian and Jiangxi provinces. There are also deluxe buses to Shenzhen, Hong Kong, and Macau. The easiest way from Guangzhou to Hong Kong is by the deluxe bus.

BY SUBWAY Guangzhou's clean and efficient underground metro currently has two lines connecting 36 stations, including the new East and old Central railway stations. Tickets range from Y2 to Y7.

BY TRAIN Five express trains (Y234 first-class, Y190 second-class) depart daily for Guangzhou East Railway Station from Hong Kong's Kowloon Station. The trip takes about 1¾ hours. The last train back to Hong Kong leaves at 5:25 PM. Trains between Shenzhen's Luohu Railway Station and Guangzhou East Railway Station run every hour and cost between Y80 and Y100.

REGIONAL TOURS

A popular tour company in Guangzhou is **GZL International Travel Service** (☎ *86020/8633* 🌐 *www.gzl.com.cn* ✉ *office@gzl.com.cn*).

ESSENTIALS

Air Contacts China Southern Airlines (✉ *181 Huanshi Lu, on left as you exit Guangzhou railway station (Guangzhou main station metro)* ☎ *020/95539 24-hr hotline* 🌐 *www.csair.com/en/index.asp*). **Baiyun Airport** (✉ *Airport International Office Building, South Area of Guangzhou Baiyun International Airport, 510470* ☎ *020/3606–6999 flight information* 🌐 *www.gbiac.net/en/index.html*). **Zhuhai International Airport** (☎ *0756/889–5494*).

Banks HSBC (✉ *G2, G/F, Garden Hotel, No.368 Huan Shi Dong Lu, Guangzhou 510064* ☎ *020/8313–1888* 🌐 *www.hsbc.com.cn*). **Bank of China** (✉ *197 Dongfeng Xilu 510180* ☎ *020/8333–8080* 🌐 *www.boc.cn*).

Bus Contacts Citybus (☎ *852/2873–0818*). **Guangdong Provincial Bus Station** (✉ *145 Huanshi Xi Lu* ☎ *020/8666–1297*). **Guangzhou Bus Station** (✉ *158 Huanshi Xi Lu* ☎ *020/8668–4259*). **Tianhe Bus Station** (✉ *Yuangang, Tianhe District* ☎ *020/8774–1083*).

Medical Assistance Shenzhen People's Hospital (✉ *Dongmen Rd. N, Shenzhen* ☎ *0755/2553–3018 Ext. 2553, 1387 (Outpatient Dept.)*.

Subway Contact Guangzhou Metro (☎ *020/8328–9033* 🌐 *www.gzmtr.com/en*).

Train Contacts Guangzhou East Railway Station (✉ *Lin Hezhong Rd., Tianhe District* ☎ *020/6134–6222*). **Guangzhou Railway Station** (✉ *Huanshi Lu* ☎ *020/6135–7222*).

EXPLORING GUANGZHOU

Guangzhou is a massive, sprawling metropolis divided into several districts and many more neighborhoods. Roughly speaking, the city is divided in half by the Pearl River, which runs from east to west and separates the Haizhu District (a large island) from the districts in the north. Most of the explorations we're recommending will keep you north of the Pearl River, since this is where the majority of the more culturally edifying parts of Guangzhou lie.

CULTURAL ATTRACTIONS

MAIN ATTRACTIONS

❷ **The Qingping Market** has undergone a few changes over the past few years; the sprawling cluster of stalls was once infamous for its wet market, a hotbed of animal slaughter. Though it always had a good selection of general knickknacks, as well as a large section of goods of various apothecarial value (ginseng, fungi, and herbs, as well as more cruelly obtained items like bear bile and essence of tiger prostate), the wet market scared all but the heartiest visitors away. Following SARS, the government decided to do away with the bloodier, less hygienic stalls. A large section of the old market was been cleared away to make room for a shiny new mall-like structure with stalls dedicated to sales of traditional medicines. The funkier and older outdoor section of the market still exists off to one side, but for the most part items on sale are of the flora and not the fauna variety. Merchants of tiger claws and bear bile are still engaged in their cruel trade on the base of the bridge leading to Shamian Island. Even though most of these merchants are dressed Tibetan style (perhaps to engender the sympathy of foreigners?) the majority of them are Han Chinese engaged in a despicable trade.

❶ **Shamian Island.** More than a century ago the Mandarins of Guangzhou designated a 44-acre sandbank outside the city walls in the Pearl River as an enclave for foreign merchants. The foreigners had previously lived and done business in a row of houses known as the Thirteen Factories, near the present Shamian, but local resentment after the Opium Wars—sometimes leading to murderous attacks—made it prudent to confine them to a protected area, which was linked to the city by two bridges that were closed at 10 every night.

The island soon became a bustling township, as trading companies from Britain, the United States, France, Holland, Italy, Germany, Portugal, and Japan built stone mansions along the waterfront. With spacious gardens and private wharves, these served as homes, offices, and warehouses. There were churches for Catholics and Protestants, banks, a yacht club, football grounds, a cricket field, and the Victory hotel.

Shamian was attacked in the 1920s but survived until the 1949 Revolution when its mansions became government offices or apartment houses and the churches were turned into factories. In recent years, however, the island has resumed much of its old character. Many colonial buildings have been restored, and both churches have been beautifully renovated and reopened to worshippers. Worth visiting is **Our Lady of Lourdes Catholic Church** (✉ *Shamian Dajie at Yijie*), with its cream-and-white

6

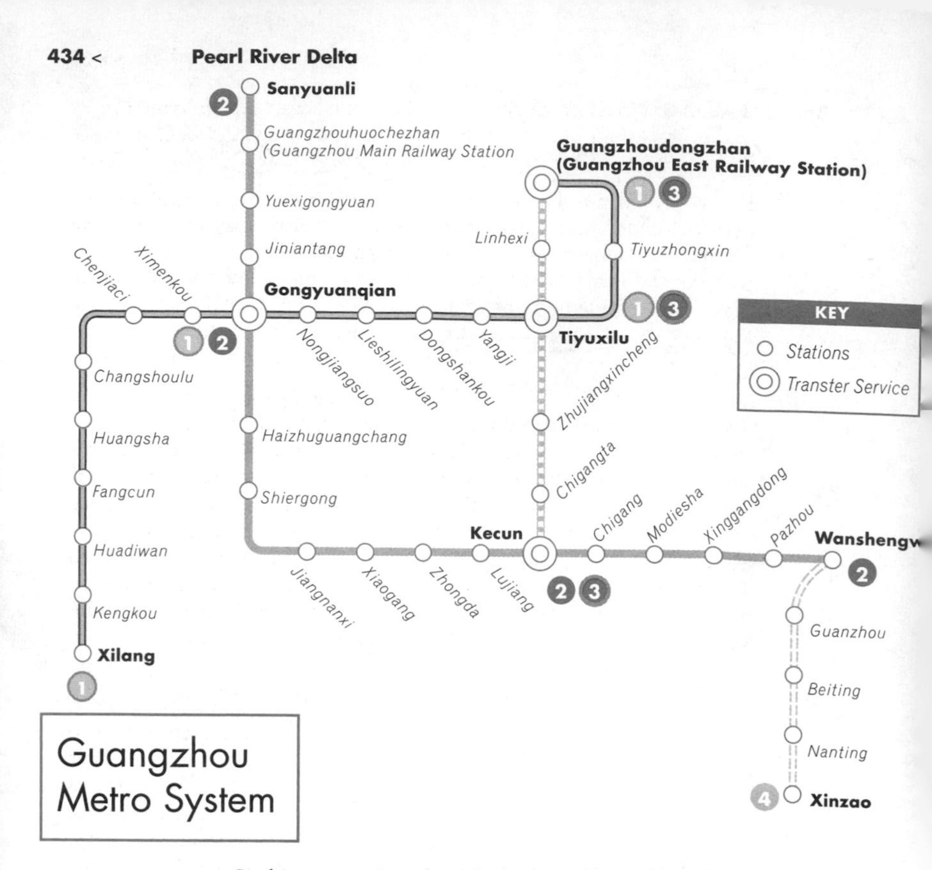

neo-Gothic tower. A park with shady walks and benches has been created in the center of the island, where local residents come to chat with friends, walk around with their caged birds, or practice tai chi.

NEED A BREAK?

Have an espresso in Chinese colonial splendor at the Shamian Island Blenz (✉ *46 Shamian Ave.*), across from Customs Hotel in a building dating back to the late Qing Dynasty. Comfy couches, strong coffee, and free Internet access are available in this old building that once housed Guangzhou's U.S. Bank in the pre-revolutionary days. Right on the park, Blenz is a great place to watch people practice tai chi and traditional Chinese fan dancing.

❼ **"Bright Filial Piety Temple"** *(Guangxiao Si)*. This is the oldest Buddhist temple in Guangzhou and by far the most charming. The gilded wooden laughing Buddha at the entrance heralds the temple's welcoming atmosphere. A huge bronze incense burner, wreathed in joss-stick smoke, stands in the main courtyard. Beyond the main hall, noted for its ceiling of red-lacquer timbers, is another courtyard with several treasures, among them a small brick pagoda said to contain the tonsure hair of Hui-neng (the sixth patriarch of Chan Buddhism), and a couple of iron pagodas, which are the oldest of their kind in China. Above them spread the leafy branches of a myrobalan plum tree and a banyan, called

Buddha's Tree because it is said Hui-neng became enlightened in its shade. ✉ *Corner of Renmin Bei and Guangxiao Lu, 2 blocks north of metro station Ximenkou, Liwan* Ⓜ *Ximenkou* 🎫 *Y5* ⏲ *Daily 6:30–5.*

❻ **Six Banyan Temple** *(Liu Rong Si Hua Ta)*. Look at any ancient scroll painting or lithograph by early Western travelers, and you'll see two landmarks rising above old Guangzhou. One is the minaret of the mosque; the other is the 56-meter (184-foot) pagoda of the Six Banyan Temple. Still providing an excellent lookout, the pagoda appears to have nine stories, each with doorways and encircling balconies. Inside, however, there are 17 levels. Thanks to its arrangement of colored, carved roofs, it is popularly known as the Flowery Pagoda.

The temple was founded in the 5th century, but because of a series of fires, most of the existing buildings date from the 11th century. It was built by the Zen master Tanyu and is still a very active place of worship, with a community of monks and regular attendance by Zen Buddhists. It was originally called Purificatory Wisdom Temple but changed its name after a visit by the Song Dynasty poet Su Dongpo, who was so delighted by six banyan trees growing in the courtyard that he left an inscription with the characters for six banyans. ✉ *Haizhu Bei Lu, south of Yuexiu Park, Liwan* 🎫 *Y10* ⏲ *Daily 8–5.*

6

IF YOU HAVE TIME

❸ **Chen Family Temple** *(Chen Jia Ci)*. The Chen family is one of the Pearl River Delta's oldest clans. In the late 19th century local members, who had become rich merchants, decided to build a memorial temple. They invited contributions from the Chens—and kindred Chans—who had emigrated overseas. Money flowed in from 72 countries, and no expense was spared. One of the temple's highlights is a huge ridgepole frieze. It stretches 90 feet along the main roof and depicts scenes from the epic *Romance of Three Kingdoms,* with thousands of figures against a backdrop of ornate houses, monumental gates, and lush scenery. Elsewhere in the huge compound of pavilions and courtyards are friezes of delicately carved stone and wood, as well as fine iron castings and a dazzling altar covered with gold leaf. The temple also houses a folk-arts museum and shop. ✉ *7 Zhongshan Qi Lu, Liwan* 🎫 *Y10* ⏲ *Daily 8:30–5* Ⓜ *Chengjia Ci metro station.*

❹ **Huaisheng Mosque** *(Huaisheng Si Guang)*. In the cosmopolitan era of the Tang Dynasty (618–907) a Muslim missionary named Abu Wangus, said to be an uncle of the prophet Mohammed, came to southern China. He converted many Chinese to Islam and built this mosque in Guangzhou. His tomb in the northern part of the city has been a place of pilgrimage for visiting Muslims, but the mosque is his best-known memorial. A high wall encloses the mosque, which is dominated by the smooth, white minaret. Rising to 33 meters (108 feet), it can be climbed using an interior spiral staircase, and the views from the top—where a muezzin calls the faithful to prayer—are spectacular. ✉ *Guangta Lu, 3 blocks southwest of the Gongyuanqian metro station, Liwan* 🎫 *Free* ⏲ *Sat.–Thurs. 8–5, except Muslim holy days* Ⓜ *Gongyuanqian.*

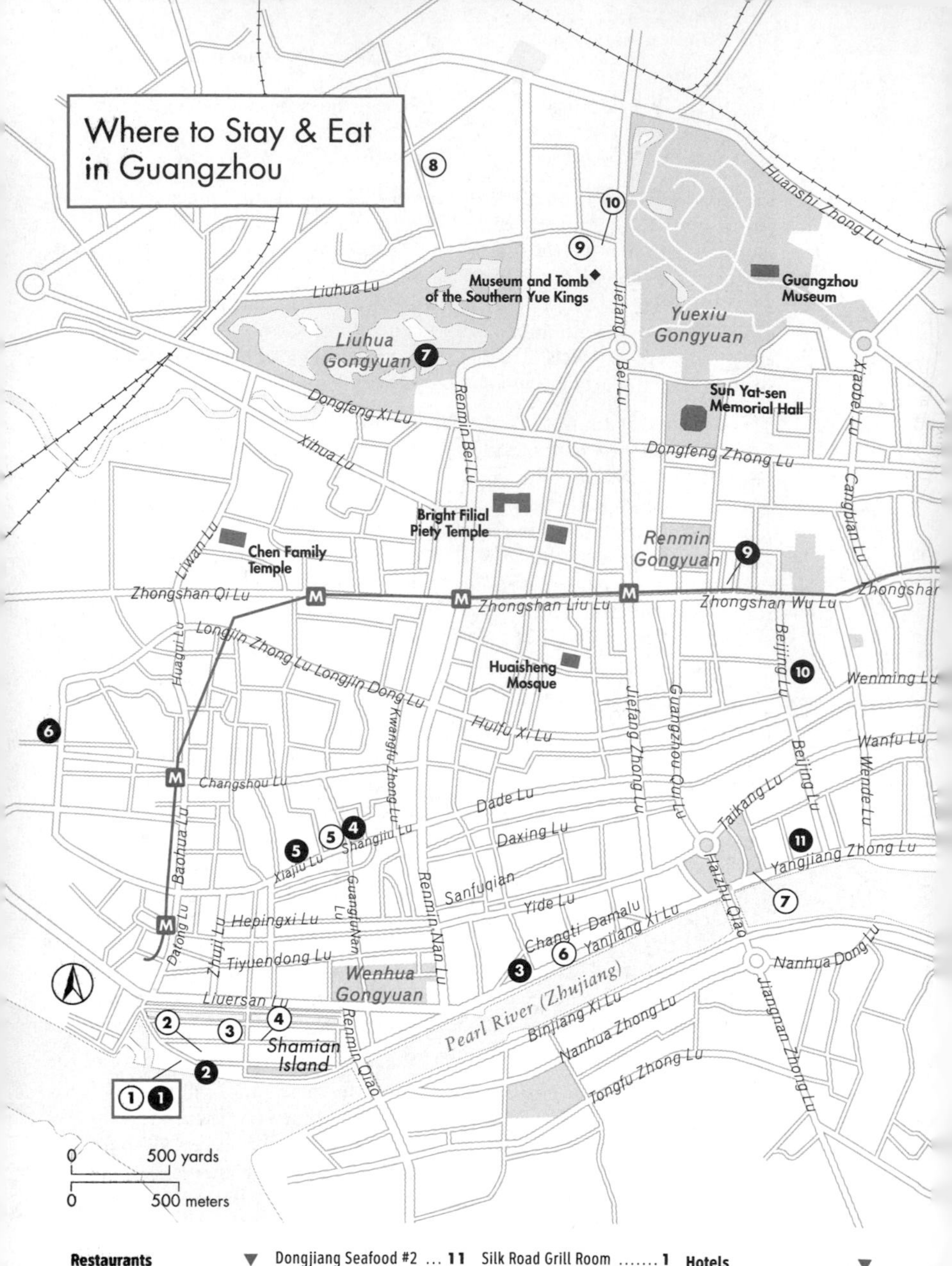

Restaurants ▼

- Back Street Jazz Bar & Restaurant 15
- Banxi Restaurant 6
- Connoisseur 12
- Da Chuan Japanese Food Restaurant 10
- Datong Restaurant 3
- Dongjiang Seafood #2 11
- Dongjiang Seafood Restaurant 9
- Guangzhou Restaurant 4
- The Italian Restaurant 14
- La Seine 16
- Lai Wan Market 13
- Lucy's 2
- Silk Road Grill Room 1
- Tang Yuan 7
- Tao Tao Ju 5

Hotels ▼

- Aiqun Hotel 6
- China Hotel 10
- Customs Hotel 4
- Dong Fang 9
- Elan Hotel 8
- Garden Hotel 12

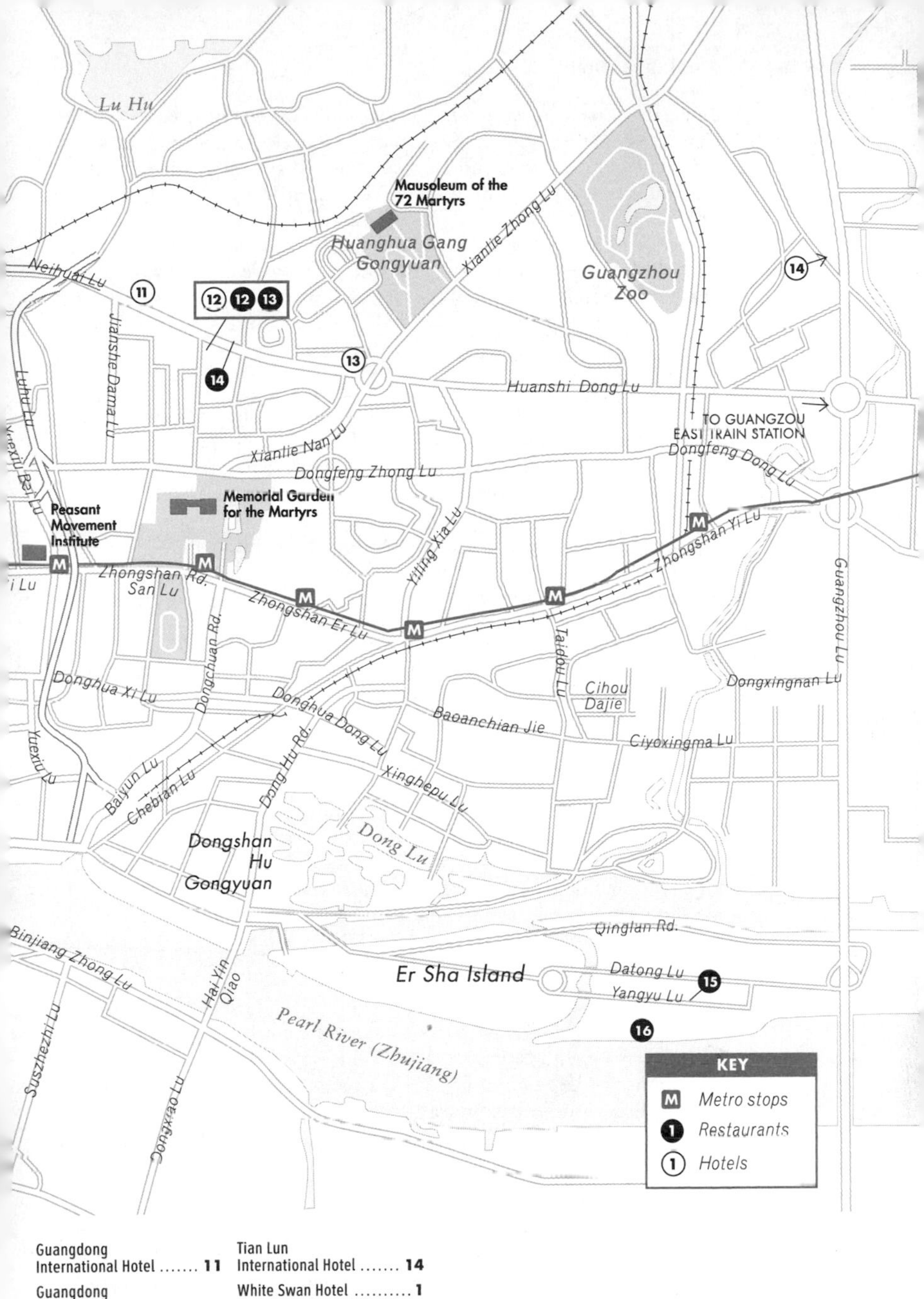

Guangdong International Hotel 11

Guangdong Victory Hotel 3

Holiday Inn City Centre ... 13

Holiday Inn Shifu 5

Landmark Canton 7

Shamian 2

Tian Lun International Hotel 14

White Swan Hotel 1

❺ **Guangxiao Temple** *(Guangxiao si)*. This impressively restored temple and city-gate complex, also known as the Five Celestials Shrine, was once the front gate for the wall that surrounded the city. The shrine and remaining sections of the wall in Yuexiu Park are the only standing remains of old Guangzhou's fortifications. There's also an impressive model of how the city looked when the air was clean, the roads were filled with horse-drawn carts, and foreigners were confined on pain of death to one small section of the city. ✉*Renmin Bei Lu, 3 blocks north of the Ximenkou metro, Liwan* Ⓜ*Ximenkou* 🎫*10* ⏲*Daily 8–5.*

PARKS AND MUSEUMS

MAIN ATTRACTIONS

❿ ★ **Orchid Garden** *(Lanpu)*. This garden offers a wonderfully convenient retreat from the noise and crowds of the city. It's spread over 20 acres, with paths that wind through groves of bamboo and tropical trees to a series of classic teahouses. Here you can sit and enjoy a wide variety of Chinese teas, brewed the traditional way. There are tables inside and on terraces that overlook the ponds. As for the orchids, there are 10,000 pots with more than 2,000 species of the flower, which present a magical sight when they bloom (peak time is May and June). ✉*Jiefang Bei Lu, Liwan* 🎫*Y5* ⏲*Daily 8:30 AM–11 PM.*

❾ ★ **Tomb of the Southern Yue Kings.** In 1983 bulldozers clearing ground to build the China Hotel uncovered the intact tomb of Emperor Wen Di, who ruled Nan Yue (southern China) from 137 BC to 122 BC. The tomb was faithfully restored and its treasures placed in the adjoining **Nan Yue Museum.**

The tomb contained the skeletons of the king and 15 courtiers—guards, cooks, concubines, and a musician—who were buried alive to attend him in death. Also buried were several thousand funerary objects, clearly designed to show off the extraordinary accomplishments of the southern empire. The tomb—built entirely of stone slabs—is behind the museum and is remarkably compact. ✉*867 Jiefang Bei Lu, around the corner from the China Hotel, Liwan* 🎫*Y15* ⏲*Daily 9:30–5:30.*

⓯ **Guangdong Museum of Art** is a major cultural establishment of the "new Canton," and regularly hosts the works of painters, sculptors, and other artists from around China and the world. An excellent sculpture garden surrounds the large complex. It's on Ersha Island; the Web site has a map to help you find your way—so print it out before you go. ✉*38 Yanyu Lu, Er Sha Island, Yuexiu* ☎*020/8735–1468* 🌐*www.GDMoA.org* ⏲*Tues.–Sun. 9–5.*

IF YOU HAVE TIME

⓫ ★ **Yuexiu Park** *(Yuexiu Gongyuan)*. To get away from the bustle, retreat into Yuexiu Park in the heart of town. The park covers 247 rolling acres and includes landscaped gardens, man-made lakes, recreational areas, and playgrounds. Children and adults get a kick out of the fish-feeding ponds.

Visit the famous **Five Rams Statue** *(Wuyang Suxiang)*, which celebrates the legend of the five celestials who came to Guangzhou riding on goats to bring grains to the people. Guangzhou families like to take each other's photo in front of the statue before setting off to enjoy the park. ✉*Jiefang Bei Lu, across from China Hotel, Liwan* ☎*020/8666–1950* 🌐*www.yuexiupark-gz.com* 🎫*Y5* ⏲*Daily* 6 AM–9 PM.

REVOLUTIONARY MEMORIALS

In the center of the city are memorials to people who changed Chinese history during the 20th century, using Guangzhou as a base of operations. The most famous were local boy Dr. Sun Yat-sen, who led the overthrow of the Qing Dynasty, and Communist Party founders Mao Zedong and Zhou Enlai.

⓭ **Mausoleum of the 72 Martyrs** *(Huanghua Gang Qishi'er Lieshi Mu)*. In a prelude to the successful revolution of 1911 a group of 88 revolutionaries staged the Guangzhou armed uprising, only to be defeated and executed by the authorities. Of those killed, 72 were buried here. Their memorial, built in 1918, incorporates a mixture of international symbols of freedom and democracy, including replicas of the Statue of Liberty. ✉*Xianlie Zhong Lu, Yuexiu* 🎫*Y10* ⏲*Daily* 6 AM–*8:30* PM.

⓬ **Memorial Garden for the Martyrs** *(Lieshi Lingyuan)*. Built in 1957, this garden has been planted around a tumulus that contains the remains of 5,000 revolutionaries killed in the 1927 destruction of the Guangzhou Commune by the Nationalists. This was the execution site of many victims. On the grounds is the **Revolutionary Museum,** which displays pictures and memorabilia of Guangdong's 20th-century rebellions. ✉*Zhongshan San Lu, Yuexiu* 🎫*Y5* ⏲*Daily* 6 AM–9 PM.

❽ **Sun Yat-sen Memorial Hall** *(Zhongshan Jinian Tang)*. Dr. Sun's Memorial Hall is a handsome pavilion that stands in a garden behind a bronze statue of the leader. Built in 1929–31 with funds mostly from overseas Chinese, the building is a classic octagon, with sweeping roofs of blue tiles over carved wooden eaves and verandas of red-lacquer columns. Inside is an auditorium with seating for 5,000 and a stage for plays, concerts, and ceremonial occasions. ✉*Dongfeng Zhong Lu, Liwan* 🎫*Y10* ⏲*Daily 8–5:30.*

TIANHE-DISTRICT SIGHTS

⓮ The Tianhe District is Guangzhou's newly designated business and upmarket residential area. Among the buildings is the 80-story **GITIC Plaza** which soars 396 meters (1,300 feet) and is China's second-tallest building. The **Guangzhou East Railway Station** (✉*Linhe Lu, Tianhe*), with its vast entrance hall is worth a peak, even if you don't have a train to catch. A hub for most of Guangzhou's sporting events, the **Tianhe Stadium Complex** (✉*Huanshi Dong Lu, East Guangzhou, Tianhe*) has two indoor and two outdoor arenas that are equipped for international soccer matches, track-and-field competitions, as well as pop concerts and large-scale ceremonies. The complex is surrounded by a pleasantly landscaped park, with outdoor cafés and tree-shaded benches. The park includes a bowling center with 38 lanes and lots of video games.

WHERE TO EAT

Guangzhou has more excellent Indian, Italian, Thai, and Vietnamese restaurants than you can shake a joss stick at, and owing to the recent influx of Middle Eastern traders, in some parts of town it's easier to find a falafel than a shrimp dumpling. Of course this isn't to say that Guangzhou's traditional delicacies have been usurped. Amazing seafood dishes and braised and barbecued meats are still available in delicious variety, and succulent dim sum still rules the roost as the city's hometown favorite.

$–$$$ ECLECTIC ✕**Back Street Jazz Bar and Restaurant.** Tall bamboo groves mask a space-age interior of glass walls, sliding-metal doors, and Plexiglas walkways in this cantina attached to the Guangdong Art Museum. Food is pure world fusion, with dishes like deep-fried salmon and lotus root, Thai chicken salad, and honey apple–foie gras. The softly lit red-neon bar serves mojitos, fruit martinis, and a wide selection of wines. Back Street has an in-house jazz band playing nightly from 10 until midnight, and often hosts international bands. ✉*38 Yanyu Lu, East Gate of the Guangdong Museum of Art, Er Sha Island* ☎*020/3839–9090* ▭*AE, DC, MC, V.*

$–$$$ CHINESE ✕**Banxi Restaurant.** On the edge of Liwan Lake, this restaurant has a series of teahouse rooms and landscaped gardens interconnected by zigzag paths and bridges that give the feel of a Taoist temple. One room is built on a floating houseboat. The food is as tasty as it looks with dishes such as scallop and crab soup and quail eggs cooked with shrimp roe on a bed of green vegetables. ✉*151 Longjin Xi Lu, Liwan Park* ☎*020/8181–5718* ▭*AE, MC, V.*

$$$$ CONTINENTAL ✕**Connoisseur.** This premier restaurant feels like regency France with its arched columns and gilded capitals, gold-framed mirrors, lustrous drapes, and immaculate table settings. The French chef specializes in lamb and steak dishes. ✉*Garden Hotel, 368 Huanshi Dong Lu, 3rd fl., Huanshi Road* ☎*020/3964–3962* ▭*AE, DC, MC, V* ⊙*No lunch.*

$ JAPANESE ✕**Da Chuan Japanese Food Restaurant.** This local eatery is in a busy shopping area on Beijing Road. The menu includes everything from à la carte dishes plucked straight off the rotating sushi bar, to ramen, tempura, and other Japanese specialties. ✉*294 Beijing Rd., 4th fl., Beijing Road Pedestrian Mall* ☎*020/8319–0283* ▭*No credit cards.*

$–$$ CHINESE ✕**Datong Restaurant.** Occupying all eight stories of an old riverfront building, with an open terrace on the top floor, this restaurant is popular with locals all hours of the day, so arrive early to be guaranteed a seat. The atmosphere is chaotic and noisy, but the morning and afternoon dim sum and huge menu are well worth it. Famous dishes include stewed-chicken claws (delicious, by the way), crispy-skin chicken, and roasted *Xishi* duck. ✉*Nanfang Dasha, 63 Yanjiang Xi Lu, Colonial Canton* ☎*020/8188–8988* ▭*AE, DC, MC, V.*

¢–$ CANTONESE ✕**Dongjiang Seafood Restaurant.** There are two Dongjiang Seafood restaurants in Guangzhou. Both are renowned for their culinary excellence and authentic Canton decor, but we recommend the Pearl River location (on Qiao Guang and Yan Jiang roads). It features a seafood market where you can wander around and choose your own meal. The staff will try to steer you toward the most expensive items first, so make sure you check prices beforehand. Some of our favorites include the braised duck stuffed with eight delicacies and glutinous rice, stuffed giant prawns, crab in black-bean sauce, and salt-roast chicken. ✉ *No.2 Qiao Guang Rd., Pearl River* ✣ *2 blocks SE of Haizhu Shichang metro* ☎ *020/8318–4901* ▭ *AE, DC, MC, V.*

$–$$$ CANTONESE ✕ **Guangzhou Restaurant.** Guangzhou Restaurant opened in 1936 and has had a string of culinary awards. The setting is classic Canton, with courtyards of flowery bushes surrounded by dining rooms of various sizes. The food is reputed to be among the best in the city, with house specialties like "Eight Treasures," a mix of fowl, pork, and mushrooms served in a bowl made of winter melon. Other Cantonese dishes include duck feet stuffed with shrimp, roasted goose, and of course, dim sum. Meals can be cheap or very expensive, depending on how exotic your tastes are. ✉ *2 Wenchang Nan Lu, Ancestral Guangzhou* ☎ *020/8138–0388* ▭ *AE, DC, MC, V.*

$ ITALIAN ✕ **The Italian Restaurant.** This aptly named restaurant has a cheerful home-away-from-home feel, complete with flags from various countries hanging from the ceiling and beers from around the world. The food is inexpensive and good, with pizzas, pastas, and excellent brochette prepared by an Italian chef. The owner is a number of other restaurants and bars in the neighborhood. ✉ *East Tower, Pearl Building, 3rd fl., 360 Huanshi Zhong Lu., 1 block west of Garden Hotel* ☎ *020/8386–6783* ▭ *AE, DC, MC, V* ⏲ *Daily.*

6

$$$–$$$$ CHINESE FUSION ✕ **Lai Wan Market.** A re-creation of the old Canton waterfront, this theme restaurant has booths shaped like flower boats and small wooden stools at low counters. The Market is known for its dim sum (which is served until 5.30 PM) and two kinds of rice, one made with pork, beef, fish, and seafood, the other with fish, beef, and pork liver. ✉ *Garden Hotel, 368 Huanshi Dong Lu, 2nd fl., Huanshi Road* ☎ *020/8333–8989 Ext. 3922* ▭ *AE, DC, MC, V.*

$$$$ FRENCH Fodor's Choice ★ ✕ **La Seine.** This upscale restaurant on Er Sha Island offers a daily lunch buffet. Dinner highlights include classic French fare, such as beef tenderloin, escargot, and foie gras. It's an ideal place to eat before or after a show. ✉ *Xinghai Concert Hall, 33 Qing Bo Lu, Er Sha Island-Guangzhou* ✣ *close to Xinghai Concert Hall and Guangzhou Museum* ☎ *020/8735–2531* ✍ *Reservations essential* ▭ *AE, DC, MC, V.*

$–$$ ECLECTIC ✕ **Lucy's.** With cuisines from so many cultures represented on its menu (Asian curries, mixed grills, Tex-Mex dishes, fish-and-chips, noodles, burgers, sandwiches, and much more), a UN–think tank could happily share a table. A favorite among foreigners, the outdoor dining area is lovely, and even the indoor dining area has a few trees growing through the roof. Take-out service is available. ✉ *3 Shamian Nan Jie, 1 block from White Swan Hotel* ☎ *020/8121–5106* ▭ *No credit cards.*

$$$$ ECLECTIC ✕ **Silk Road Grill Room.** This grill room in the White Swan Hotel has impeccable service. Choose between the set menu, which includes an appetizer, cold dish, soup, entrée, dessert, and drink (excluding wine), or à la carte. Highlight entrées include prime rib and sea-bass fillet. ✉ *White Swan Hotel, Yi Shamian Lu, Shamian Island* ☎ *020/8188–6968* ▭ *AE, DC, MC, V* ✍ *Reservations essential* ⏲ *No lunch.*

$$–$$$ CANTONESE ✕**Tang Yuan.** The location alone beats out most other restaurants in Guangzhou. It is in a faux colonial-style mansion on an island in Liuhuahu Park. Cuisine is pure old-school Cantonese, with expensive dishes like abalone and shark's fin soup being served alongside more rational staples like crispy fried pigeon, carbon-roasted mackerel, and stuffed garlic prawns. Naturally, there's plenty of dim sum, and the "Cantonese combo plate" features a variety of roasted meats. Although the food at Tang Yuan is excellent, most people come here for the opulence as well. Admission fee for the park is waived for guests of the restaurant, and a golf cart waits at the park's entrance on Liuhua Road to whisk diners to the restaurant's palatial front door. ✉*Lihuahu Park, Dongfeng Xi Lu and Renmin Bei Lu, 2 blocks west of Yuexiu Gongyuan metro station* ☎*020/3623–6993* ▭*AE, DC, MC, V.*

$$$$ CANTONESE ✕**Tao Tao Ju.** Prepare yourself for garish decor, shouted conversations of fellow diners, and a menu full of weird animal parts. Tao Tao Ju (which, roughly translated, means "house of happiness") is one of the most revered traditional Cantonese restaurants in the city. Soups are a favorite, and the menu (available in English) has many that you're unlikely to find elsewhere. The kudzu and snakehead soup is delicious, and they have more than 200 varieties of dim sum. They're also open from 6:30 AM to midnight. ✉*20 Dishipu Lu, Shangxiajiu* ☎*020/8139–6111* ▭*AE, DC, MC, V.*

WHERE TO STAY

¢ **Aiqun Hotel.** When it was built in the 1930s, this 16-story hotel was the tallest building in Pearl River Delta. Though it once hosted dignitaries of great importance during China's Republican era, these days this elegant art-deco hotel hosts visitors from around China and international travelers on a budget. Rooms are clean, comfortable, and tastefully furnished with rich mahogany, faux colonial-era furniture. The revolving restaurant on the 16th floor of the new wing offers great views of the surrounding area. **Pros:** interesting building and decor, cozy atmosphere. **Cons:** rooms are on the small side. ✉*No. 113 Yanjiang Rd., Pearl River District* ☎*020/8186–6668* 🌐*www.aiqunhotel.com* *330 rooms and suites* *In-room: Ethernet. In-hotel: 4 restaurants* ▭*AE, DC, MC, V.*

$$–$$$$ **China Hotel.** Managed by Marriott, this hotel is part of a multicomplex that includes office and apartment blocks, a shopping mall big enough to get lost in, and a range of restaurants to satisfy any appetite. The hotel is favored by business travelers because it's connected to the metro and close to the Trade Fair Exhibition Hall. The business center has 16 meeting rooms, and the piano bar in the lobby offers champagne brunches. **Pros:** close to metro, newly renovated rooms. **Cons:** very much a business person's hotel. ✉*Liuhua Lu Liwan* ☎*020/8666–6888* 🌐*www.marriott.com* *724 rooms, 126 suites* *In-room: Ethernet. In-hotel: 4 restaurants, 2 bars, tennis court, pool, gym* ▭*AE, DC, MC, V* Ⓜ *Yuexu Gongyuan metro.*

¢ **The Customs Hotel.** This newly opened four-story establishment has an attractive colonial facade that blends well with the surrounding area. The bright interior surrounds an inner courtyard. Standard rooms are tastefully decorated with Republican-era furniture made of dark wood, though the suites seem more cluttered. If possible, get a room facing Shamian Avenue, the quiet, tree-lined street, which runs the length of the island. There is a karaoke bar and a lovely backyard garden. **Pros:** quiet neighborhood, inexpensive. **Cons:** some prefer characterless hotels. ✉*No. 35 Shamian Ave., Shamian Island, Colonial Guangzhou* ☎*20/8110–2388* ✍*customshotel@126.com* *49 rooms, 7 suites* *In-room: Ethernet. In-hotel: 2 restaurants, bar, gym* *AE, DC, MC, V.*

TIGHTWAD TIP

All hotels in Guangzhou have in-room Internet access for those traveling with laptops. Although it's almost always free at the cheaper hotels, more expensive properties charge anywhere from Y100 to Y120 to "buy" a block of 24 hours of surfing time.

$–$$$$ **Dong Fang.** Across from Liuhua Park and the trade-fair headquarters, this complex is built around a 22½-acre garden with pavilions, carp-filled pools, and rock gardens. The lobby is done up in a Renaissance motif, complete with Romanesque pillars and gold-and-white floor tiling. The shopping concourse has Chinese antiques and carpets. The hotel has recently added an 86,000-square-foot convention center. Discounts of up to 30% for rooms in the off-season are not unheard of. **Pros:** spacious gardens, choice of restaurants. **Cons:** not for those who are averse to gigantic. ✉*120 Liuhua Lu* ☎*020/8666–9900, 852/2528–0555 in Hong Kong* *www.hoteldongfang.com* *699 rooms, 101 suites* *In-room: Ethernet. In-hotel: 6 restaurants, gym, spa* *AE, DC, MC, V.*

¢–$ **Élan Hotel.** If you like cheap, funky, and hip little hotels, this is the spot for you. Guangzhou's first attempt at a boutique hotel has compact, Ikea-inspired rooms with bold color palettes and clean lines. Celine Dion muzak wafting through the hallways can be annoying, but the warm, cozy beds guarantee a restful sleep. The small first-floor restaurant serves cheap northeast Chinese food that is as authentic as it is tasty. **Pros:** basic and clean, good value. **Cons:** small rooms. ✉*32 Zhan Qian Heng Rd.* *2 blocks south of Guangzhou main railway station* ☎*020/8622–1788* *www.hotel-elan.com* *76 rooms, 8 suites* *In-room: Ethernet. In-hotel: restaurant* *AE, DC, MC, V.*

¢–$ **Garden Hotel.** In the northern business suburbs, this huge, aging hotel is famous for its spectacular garden that includes an artificial hill, a waterfall, and pavilions. The cavernous lobby, decorated with enormous murals, has a bar–lounge set around an ornamental pool. Though long considered the standard of luxury in Guangzhou, other hotels are now giving the Garden a run for its money. **Pros:** spacious premises and gardens, pleasant staff. **Cons:** rooms in need of renovation; not the best neighborhood. ✉*368 Huanshi Dong Lu, Huanshi Road* ☎*020/8333–8989* *www.thegardenhotel.com.cn* *828 rooms, 42 suites* *In-room: Ethernet. In-hotel: 7 restaurants, bar, tennis courts, pool, gym* *AE, DC, MC, V.*

Grand Hyatt Guangzhou. "G" is the theme at the Grand Hyatt Guangzhou. For starters, there's "G" restaurant, a contemporary eatery decked out with tan wood floors that feature bay windows looking out onto the fabled Pearl River. Then there's "G" bar, with its burnished steel and lacquered wood decor, featuring a "walk through" wine cellar. Other highlights include a rooftop pool, six spa treatment facilities, and a 2,906-square-foot suite replete with a marble tub. Indeed, the size of the Hyatt's rooms also adds to its appeal — there are 375 rooms ranging from 484 square feet to a spacious 2,906 square feet. In a densely populated city, it's key to offer spots of respite with lots of personal space, and clearly, the Grand Hyatt Guangzhou is on top of this trend. **Pros:** Guanxi lounge offers one of the most unique meeting grounds in the city. **Cons:** hailing a taxi outside the hotel proves difficult; constructions sites surround the hotel. ✉ *12 Zhujiang West Rd., Pearl River, Guangzhou* ☎ *020/8396–1234 or 020/8550–8234* 🌐 *www.guangzhou.grand.hyatt.com* *375 rooms, 28 suites* *In-room: safe, minibar, Wi-Fi. In-hotel: 1 restaurant, bar, room service, pool, gym, spa, public Wi-Fi, laundry service, concierge* *AE, D, DC, MC, V.*

IN THE NEWS

Some good publications to check out for regularly updated info on ongoing cultural happenings are *City Weekends,City Guide,South China City Talk*, and *That's PRD*.

$–$$$ **Guangdong International Hotel.** This towering hotel in the finance district is somewhat of an institution in Guangzhou, but it has a tired feel, as if the leap from state to private ownership hasn't been made in full. The hotel does have extensive recreation facilities and an indoor gym. For the money though, the nearby City Centre Holiday Inn is a better buy. **Pros:** friendly staff, good views from the top floors. **Cons:** uninteresting location. ✉ *339 Huanshi Dong Lu, Huanshi Road* ☎ *020/8331–1888* 🌐 *www.gitic.com.cn* *333 rooms, 270 suites* *In-room: Ethernet. In-hotel: 3 restaurants, bar, tennis court, pool, gym* *AE, DC, MC, V.*

¢–$$$$ Fodor's Choice ★ **Guangdong Victory Hotel.** Over the past few years, this Shamian Island hotel has undergone upgrades that have bumped it up from budget class. The two wings, both originally colonial guesthouses, have been beautifully renovated. The main building has a pink-and-white facade, an imposing portico, and twin domes on the roof, where you'll find a pool and an excellent sauna facility. Standard rooms are more than adequate, and the hotel still retains a fairly inexpensive dining room on the first floor. **Pros:** historic, elegant building; peaceful area; great view of the city from the rooftop pool. **Cons:** shabby fitness center. ✉ *53 Yi Shamian Lu, Shamian Island* ☎ *020/8121–6802* 🌐 *www.vhotel.com* *328 rooms* *In-room: Ethernet. In-hotel: 3 restaurants, pool, gym* *AE, DC, MC, V.*

$$–$$$$ **Holiday Inn City Centre.** This centrally located hotel has large tasteful rooms are arranged according to Chinese feng-shui principles. The top three executive floors have suites and a lounge–restaurant area with stellar views of smog-shrouded Guangzhou. In addition to all of its lovely facilities, the hotel also has enough meeting rooms to host a small Tony Robbins seminar. **Pros:** good-sized rooms, central location. **Cons:** not what you'd call quaint. ✉ *28 Guangming Rd., Overseas Chinese Village, Huanshi Dong* ☎ *020/6128–6868* 🌐 *www.guangzhou.*

holiday-inn.com ⇆*430 rooms, 38 suites* *In-room: Ethernet. In-hotel: restaurant, bar, pool, gym* ▭*AE, DC, MC, V.*

$–$$$$ **Holiday Inn Shifu.** The newest hotel in Guangzhou, and the only four-star hotel in the popular tourist area Shangxiajiu, Holiday Inn Shifu is 14 stories, with a lovely rooftop pool and a bar with views of old Guangzhou. The Shifu is a stone's throw from the Qingping Market, which is a must-see for first-time visitors. **Pros:** good service, friendly staff. **Cons:** beds are too hard. ✉*No. 188 Di Shi Fu Rd., Xiangxi ajiu Liwan,* ✥*signs from Changshou metro exit point the way* ☎*020/8138–0088* ⇆*278 rooms, 28 suites* *In-room: Ethernet. In-hotel: 2 restaurants, bar, pool, gym* ▭*AE, DC, MC, V* Ⓜ*Changshuo.*

CABARET, CHINESE-STYLE

If you only go to one multimedia cabaret dinner–theater in Guangzhou, it has to be *The Magic Phantom* at Guangzhou's Mo Li Fang Theater. This original, quirky, and very well-executed production is the only example of multimedia cabaret dinner–theater we've yet to come across in Guangzhou (or anywhere else in China). The performance is in Chinese, but the combination of elements from traditional Beijing Opera, Hong Kong Cinema, puppetry, karaoke, acrobatics, dancing, and computer animation makes it a feast for the senses regardless of linguistic skill.

¢–$ **Landmark Canton.** Towering above Haizhu Square and the main bridge across the river, this hotel is in the heart of central Guangzhou. It's managed by China Travel Service of Hong Kong, so a lot of its guests tend to be Hong Kongers on holiday. There's a great chocolate shop in the lobby, and a small but very pretty Chinese garden and carp pond in the courtyard. The Landmark's location allows it to boast that most guest rooms have great views of the river and city. **Pros:** view of the Pearl River; decent restaurants nearby. **Cons:** small pool. ✉*8 Qiao Guang Lu, Haizhu Square* ☎*020/8335–5988* 🌐*www.hotel-landmark.com.cn* ⇆*566 rooms* *In-hotel: 2 restaurants, bar, pool, gym* ▭*AE, DC, MC, V* Ⓜ*Haizhu Guangchang.*

$$$ **Ritz-Carlton Guangzhou.** Bringing five-star luxury to Guangzhou's emerging Pearl River New City, the Ritz-Carlton Guangzhou features posh rooms with marble baths, a smattering of international restaurants and bars, and a swank spa. In addition to its hundreds of standard guest rooms, the Ritz offers 35 suites and 58 club-level rooms — all of which feature featherbeds draped with gentle Egyptian cotton linens. After a day of exploring the city, rest your tender soles at the spa, which pampers guests with treatments such as aqua therapy beds and a wet lounge with a sauna. **Pros:** in-house Terra restaurant offers unique cuisine; Churchill Bar offers fine cognacs and cigars. **Cons:** during the seasonal Canton Fairs during April and October, the city's hotel occupancy is heavily impacted; booking early is paramount. *3 Xing An Rd., Pearl River New City, Guangzhou, China 20/3813–6888 or 20/3813–6666* 🌐*www.ritzcarlton.com In-room: safe, refrigerator, DVD, Wi-Fi. In-hotel: 4 restaurants, room service, 2 bars, pool, gym, spa, concierge, executive floor, public Wi-Fi 351 rooms, 35 suites AE, V, MC, DC.*

¢ **Shamian.** This is a great hotel for visitors on a budget. Its rooms are a little spartan and the lobby cramped, but it is clean and friendly and the location—right in the middle of Shamian Island—is second to none. **Pros:** great location. **Cons:** no restaurant in hotel. *52 Shamian Nan Jie, Shamian Island 020/8121–8288 www.gdshamianhotel.com 58 rooms, 20 suites AE, DC, MC, V.*

$$–$$$ **Tian Lun International Hotel.** A new, upscale boutique hotel located next to Guangzhou East Railway Station offers large luxury rooms with a sleek edge. The colors are kept to soft blacks, grays, and beige. The buffet in the second-floor café is beautifully arranged around a centerpiece of coral, and the high ceilings lend an air of sophistication. **Pros:** near metro and train stations, clean and comfortable rooms. **Cons:** lack of English TV channels. *172 Linhe Lu Central, Tianhe District next to Guangzhou East Railway Station 020/8393–6388 www.tianlun-hotel.com 382 rooms, 23 suites In-room: Ethernet. In-hotel: 3 restaurants, pool, gym AE, DC, MC, V.*

¢–$$$ **White Swan Hotel.** Occupying a marvelous site on Shamian Island, beside the Pearl River, this huge luxury complex has landscaped gardens, two pools, a jogging track, and a separate gym and spa. Its presidential suite is just that: reserved for heads of state, it has been occupied by such "luminaries" as Richard Nixon and Kim Jong-Il. Its restaurants are second to none; the windows of the elegant lobby bar and coffee shop frame the panorama of river traffic. **Pros:** quiet neighborhood, good view of Pearl River. **Cons:** dated decor. *Yi Shamian Lu, Shamian Island, Colonial Canton 020/8188–6968, 852/2524–0192 in Hong Kong www.whiteswanhotel.com 843 rooms, 92 suites In-room: Ethernet. In-hotel: 9 restaurants, bar, pools, gym AE, DC, MC, V.*

NIGHTLIFE AND THE ARTS

PUBS AND BARS

Bingjiang xilu (*South of Shamian Island, across the Pearl River*) is *the* street for barhopping. Very popular with a younger crowd, it has great views, and if you get bored with looking north across the river you can always cross the bridge to **Yanjiang Xilu** and drink at some of the bars on that side.

Huanshi Dong Lu. Yuexiu and the area behind the Garden Hotel are popular with locals and expats (short- and long-term). Two favorites are **Gypsy** and **Cave,** both located on opposite ends of the Zhujiang Building. Cave has a distinct meat-market vibe and features nightly performances by a scantily clad woman whose specialty is dancing with snakes. Gypsy reeks of hashish and is much mellower.

The Paddy Field (*38 Huale Lu, behind Garden Hotel 020/8360–1379*) makes you long for Ireland. There are darts, pints of Guinness and Kilkenny, and football matches on a massive screen.

1920 Restaurant (*183 Yanjiang Zhong Lu 020/8333–6156 www.1920cn.com*) serves up Bavarian food and imported wheat beers on a lovely outdoor patio. Entrées start at Y60, beers at Y22.

The **Café Lounge** (✉ *China Hotel, lobby* ☎ *020/8666–6888*) has a mellow vibe, big comfortable bar stools, quiet tables for two, live music on weekends, and a fine selection of cigars.

The big attraction of the **Hare and Moon** (✉ *White Swan Hotel, Yi Shamian Lu, Shamian Island* ☎ *020/8188–6968*) is the panorama of the Pearl River as it flows past the picture windows.

DANCE CLUBS

Though normally thought of as inauspicious in Chinese culture, the number 4 is anything but at Guangzhou's newly renovated **Yes Club** (✉ *132 Dongfeng Xi Lu, across from Liuhua Lake Park* ☎ *020/8136–8688* 🎫 *Free*), which actually has four separate clubs under one roof for four distinctly different clubbing experiences. **Super Yes** has techno and electronica, whereas **Mini Yes** offers house and break beat. **Funky Yes** offers a more eclectic mixture of R&B and hip-hop, and **Club Yes** is a total chill-out zone, with softer music and lighting, and a fine selection of wine and cigars.

Deep Anger Music Power House (✉ *183 Yanjiang Lu* ☎ *020/8317–7158* 🎫 *Free* ⏲ *Daily 8* PM–2 AM) is a cool dance club located in a building that was a theater back in the days of Sun Yat-sen. Lounge lizards and history buffs will enjoy sipping a beer here.

6

ART AND CULTURE

If you think Guangzhou's high culture begins and ends with Cantonese opera, think again, pilgrim—the art and performance scene here is vibrant, and getting more so every day. The city is undergoing a cultural broadening, as evidenced by the opening of small art spaces, more eclectic forms of theater, and more national attention being focused on the city's major museums. Of course, purists need not panic; the Cantonese opera has hardly disappeared.

Xinghai Concert Hall (✉ *33 Qing Bo Lu, Er Sha Island* ☎ *020/8735–2222 Ext. 312 for English* 🌐 *www.concerthall.com.cn*) is the home of the Guangzhou Symphony Orchestra, and puts on an amazing array of concerts featuring national and international performers. Their Web site, unfortunately, is only in Chinese, but your hotel should be able to call to find out what's going on. The concert hall is surrounded by a fantastic sculpture garden, and is next door to the Guangzhou Museum of Art, making the two an excellent mid-afternoon to evening trip.

Guangdong Puppet Art Center (✉ *21 Fenyuan St.* ☎ *020/8431–0227*) hosts live puppet shows every Saturday and Sunday at 10:30 AM and 3 PM.

Guangdong Modern Dance Company (✉ *13 Shuiyinhenglu, Shaheding* ☎ *020/8704–9512* 🌐 *www.gdmdc.com*) is mainland China's first professional modern-dance company, and the troupe is regularly praised by publications such as the *New York Times* and the *Toronto Sun*. This theater is their home base. Their English-language Web site has a full performance schedule.

Continued on page 454

21ST
CENTURY
CHINA

Since the late 1970s, China and its billion-plus population have been moving from a centrally planned socialist economy to a market-oriented consumer society on a scale and at a speed unparalleled in history.

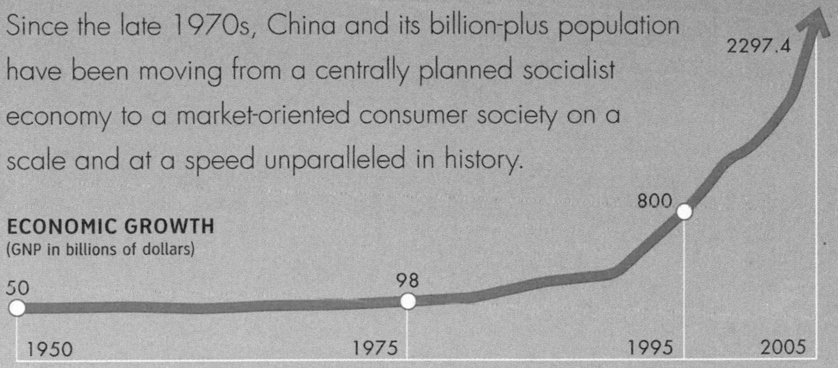

ECONOMIC GROWTH
(GNP in billions of dollars)

Year	GNP (billions of dollars)
1950	50
1975	98
1995	800
2005	2297.4

Source: http://news.bbc.co.uk/

SHANGHAI

A Chinese Century?

The SARS hiccup aside, China's economy has been red-hot since joining the World Trade Organization in 2001. One of the engines driving the global economy, it helped revive Japan's sagging economy and the slumping international shipping industry. Worldwide commodities markets have also been boosted by China's increasing hunger for everything from copper to coffee.

GDP-ANNUAL GROWTH RATE

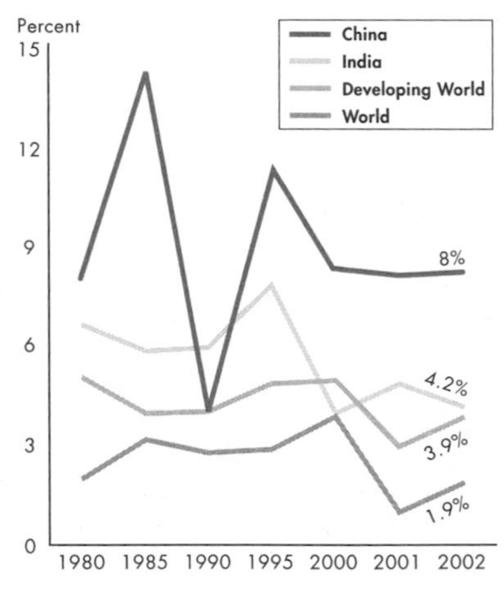

Source: World Bank/Earth Trends

The country that was long written off as just a cheap exporter is now a net importer. It's the fourth-largest economy in the world after the United States, Japan, and Germany, whose economies are growing at less than half the rate.

Such development is nothing short of remarkable, but national problems such as energy, the environment, and wealth inequality are threatening the country.

Internationally, it's how China and the United States cooperate on global issues, and how they manage their own complex relationship, that may have the greatest impact on the rest of the century. Since Nixon first opened the door in 1972, the two countries have managed to forge a working relationship. But Yuan revaluation, trade issues, energy supply (especially oil), and both countries' military role in the Asia-Pacific region are all issues that could sour this budding friendship.

(top) Architectural stars (or starchitects) like Rem Koolhaas, Li Hu, Paul Andreu, and Jacques Herzog and Pierre de Meuron (Olympic Stadium, above) are descending on Beijing for construction of state-of-the-art Olympic venues. (right) Hong Kong skyline.

Fueling the Chinese Dream

China is now the number–two energy consumer in the world, after the United States. Its consumption has exploded by an average of 5% yearly since 1998. This thirst for fuel is evident on roads all over the country. The land of the bicycle is now car-crazy. Three million vehicles were recently sold, and higher sales are predicted in the coming years.

Back in 2005, the country consumed 320 million tons of crude oil, roughly one third of which was imported. It's expecting to import 500 million tons by 2020, two thirds of its projected total imports.

Where will China get this oil? Much comes from countries with troubled relations with the West such as Iran and Sudan, but it is also working on importing more from traditional U.S. suppliers such as Saudi Arabia.

There's also a growing demand for electricity, 75% of which comes from coal. In the coming 25 years, the greenhouse gases produced by China's coal burning will probably exceed that of all industrial nations combined. And the country will continue to rely on coal for electricity in the years to come, despite large hydropower projects and a plan to increase the number of nuclear power plants.

Aside from developing clean, renewable energy sources, China needs to improve its poor energy efficiency—it uses nine times the energy Japan does to produce one GDP unit. But plans are being made to improve energy efficiency by 20% by 2010.

WORLD OIL CONSUMPTION

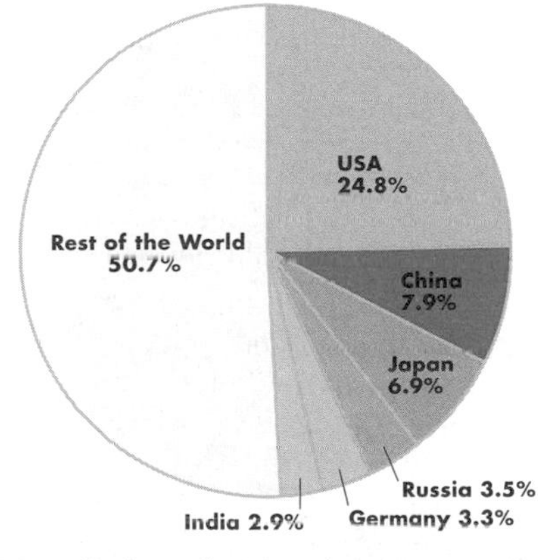

Source: http://www.nationmaster.com/

Can China Go Green?

A devastated environment is a major result of China's economic transformation. For example, because of deforestation around the capital, Beijing is threatened by the encroaching Gobi Desert, which dumped 300,000 tons of sand on the city in one week in 2006. Industrial carelessness and lack of regulation result in accidents such as the 50-mile benzene spill in a river near Harbin in late 2005.

Cities have been smoggy for decades because of pollution from factories, vehicles, and especially coal. But air quality is now becoming obscured by water issues. In mid-2006 the Water Resources Ministry reported that 320 million urban residents—more than the population of the United States—did not have access to clean drinking water.

Much of this is the result of a development-at-any-cost mentality, particularly in the wake of economic reform. Companies and factories, many of which are foreign-owned, have only recently had to deal with environmental laws— "scoff laws"—that are often circumvented by bribing local officials. And average citizens don't have freedom of speech or access to political tools to fight environmentally damaging projects.

Is the central government waking up? In 2006 the vice-chairman of China's increasingly outspoken State Environmental Protection Agency put it bluntly: "We will face tremendous problems if we do not change our development patterns."

Mind the Gap

China has come a long way from the days when everyone had an "iron rice bowl," or a state-appointed job that was basically guaranteed regardless of one's abilities or work performance.

Since 1980, the country has quadrupled per capita income and raised more than 220 million of its citizens out of poverty. A belt of prosperity is emerging along the coast, but hundreds of millions still live on less than $1 per day.

(left) Owning a car is the new Chinese dream. (top right) The Three Gorges Dam will be the largest in the world, supplying the hydroelectric power of 18 nuclear plants. (bottom right) China's cities are some of the most polluted in the world.

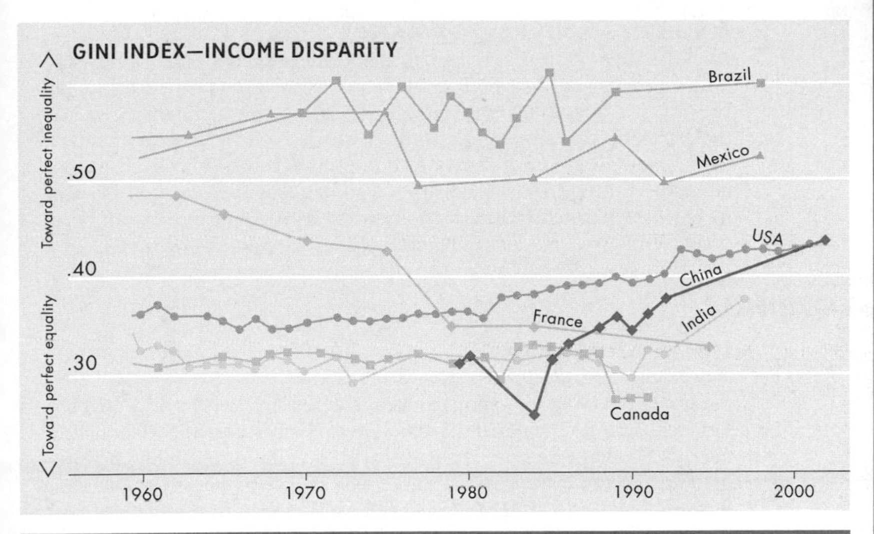

Economists use a statistical yardstick known as the Gini coefficient to measure wealth inequality in a society, with zero being perfect equality and one being perfect inequality. The World Bank estimates that China's national Gini coefficient rose from 0.30 to 0.45 from 1982, a 50% jump in two decades. In 2006, some academics estimated China's current Gini coefficient to be closer to, or even higher, than Latin America's 0.52.

As economic inequality has grown, so has discontent, particularly in rural areas. The country recorded 87,000 public protests in 2005, an increase of 11,000 over the year before.

Many of these protests are incited by the acts of local, particularly rural, officials whose corruption policies are sometimes beyond Beijing's sphere of influence.

Most protests are focused on specific incidents or officials rather than general dissent against the government, but the growing frequency of such events is not going unnoticed by the central government. In 2005, 8,400 officials were arrested on corruption-related charges.

CHINA IN NUMBERS

	CHINA	U.S.
Area in sq km:	9,560,960	9,631,420
Population	1.3 bil	300 mil
Men (15–64 yrs)	482 mil	100 mil
Women (15–64 yrs)	456 mil	101 mil
Population growth	0.59%	0.91%
Life expectancy: men	70.8	75
Life expectancy: women	74.6	80.8
GDP per head	$1,090	$37,240
Health spending, % GDP	5.8	14.6
Doctors per 1000 pop.	1.6	3.0
Hospital beds per 1000 pop.	23.12	6.43
Infant mortality rate per 1000 births	2.1	5.7
Education spending, % GDP	95.1%	99%
Adult literacy: men	86.5%	
Adult literacy: women		99%
Internet users	111 mil	204 mil

GALLERIES AND PERFORMANCE SPACES

If eclectic art is your thing, then **Vitamin Creative Space** (✉ *29 Hengyi Jie, inside of Xinggang Cheng, Haizhu District* ☎ *020/8429–6760* 🌐 *www.vitamincreativespace.com* ⏲ *Mon.–Sat. 10 AM–6 PM*) might be worth the trip. But be warned, it's located in the back of a semi-enclosed vegetable market and not easy to find even if you speak Chinese. Call first (the curator speaks English) and someone will escort you from in front of the market. Hours are somewhat erratic, but the art can be as wonderfully weird as anything you're likely to find in China.

SHOPPING

MALLS AND MARKETS

Shangxiajiu (✉ *Follow signs from Changshoulu metro*) is a massive warren of old buildings and shops and considered the user-friendly heart of old Guangzhou. The half-mile main street is a pedestrian mall boasting nearly 250 shops and department stores. The buildings in Shangxiajiu are old, but the stores are the same ones as in "modern Guangzhou." Even though the overall decibel level hovers around deafening, the area isn't without its charms. Our favorite shops are the small storefronts offering dried-fruit samples, which are very addictive. The area draws a big, younger crowd, but there are a few quiet back alleys that keep it from feeling too overwhelming. There's also a wide variety of street stalls selling a large selection of delicious edibles.

Beijing Road Pedestrian Mall (✉ *Follow signs from Gongyuanqian metro*) offers an interesting contrast to Shangxiajiu. Shangxiajiu offers new stores in old buildings, whereas Beijing Road makes no pretense at being anything other than a fully modern, neon-draped pedestrian mall, similar to Beijing's Wangfujing Street or Shanghai's Nanjing Street. Pedestrianized and open from around 10 AM until 10 PM, this is where city teenagers buy sensible, midrange Hong Kong–style clothes and increasingly garish local brands. Noisy and fun, the street is lined with cheap food stalls, cafés, and fast-food chains like.

Haizhu Plaza (✉ *Haizhu Sq., north of Haizhu Bridge, Haizhu* Ⓜ *Guangchang metro* ⏲ *Daily 10–6*) is a massive, two-story flea and souvenir market where casual shoppers and wholesale buyers alike bargain for kitsch—think toys, faux antiques, and cultural revolution–themed knickknacks. Merchants keep calculators at hand for entering figures in the heat of negotiation, and vendors sell a variety of snacks from carts located by the exits.

The **Friendship Store** (✉ *369 Huanshi Dong Lu, across from the Garden Hotel*) is an old stalwart, dating back from days of post-revolutionary China's earliest flirtation with capitalism. The Guangzhou Friendship Store occupies a five-story building with departments selling designer wear, children's wear, luggage, and household appliances.

La Perle (✉ *367 Huanshi Dong Lu, across from the Garden Hotel* ⏲ *Daily10–10*) is next to the Friendship Store, and a bit more upscale. They have genuine designer clothes at expensive rates, with shops such as Versace, Louis Vuitton, Polo, and Prada.

ANTIQUES AND TRADITIONAL CRAFTS

On Shamian Island, the area between the White Swan and Victory hotels has a number of small family-owned shops that sell paintings, carvings, pottery, knickknacks, and antiques.

Guangzhou Arts Centre (✉ *698 Renmin Bei Lu* ☎ *020/8667–9898*) has a fine selection of painted scrolls.

The **South Jade Carving Factory** (✉ *15 Xia Jiu Lu, Shangxiajiu* ☎ *020/8138–8040*) offers a wide variety of jade and jadeite products at reasonable prices. On the second floor visitors can watch jade being carved.

The **White Swan Arcade** (✉ *White Swan Hotel, Yi Shamian Lu, Shamian Island*) has some of the city's finest upmarket specialty shops. They sell genuine Chinese antiques, traditional craft items, works of modern and classical art, Japanese kimonos and swords, jewelry, cameras, and books published in and about China.

BOOKSTORES

Guangzhou Books Center (✉ *123 Tianhe Lu* ☎ *020/3886–4208 Chinese only*) is a chain with seven floors of books on every subject, including some bargain-priced art books in English.

Xinhua Bookstore (✉ *276 Beijing Rd.* ☎ *020/8333–2636*) sells an extensive catalog of books at very affordable prices.

6

SIDE TRIP TO WHITE CLOUD MOUNTAIN

17 km (10½ mi) north of Guangzhou.

White Cloud Mountain gets its name from the halo of clouds that, in the days before heavy pollution, appeared around the peak following a rainstorm. The mountain is part of a 28-square-km (17-square-mi) resort area and consists of 6 parks, 30 peaks, and myriad gullies. **Santailing Park** is home to the enormous Yuntai Garden, of interest to anybody with a thing for botany. **Fei'eling Park** has a nice sculpture garden, and **Luhu Park** is home to Jinye Pond, as pure and azure a body of water as you're likely to find within 100 mi. All in all, a trip to White Cloud Mountain is a good way to get out of the city—maybe for a day of hiking—without traveling too far. 🌐 *www.baiyunshan.com.cn* 🎫 *20Y* ⏲ *Daily 9–5.*

GETTING HERE AND AROUND

Bus 24 leaves from Dongfeng Zhonglu, just north of Renmin Gongyuan, and travels to the cable car at the bottom of the hill near Luhu Park. The 15-km (9-mi) trip takes between half an hour and one hour, depending on traffic. A taxi shouldn't set you back more than Y100.

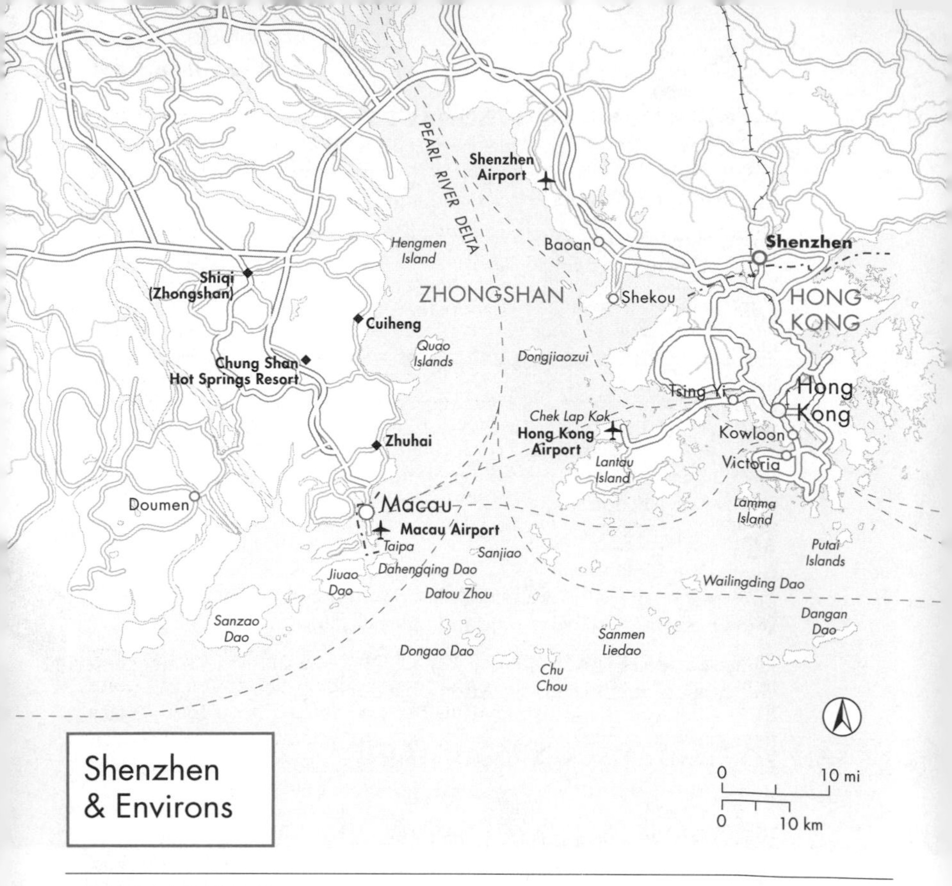

SHENZHEN

112 km (70 mi; 1 hr by express train, 2½ hrs by express bus) from Guangzhou. Walk across border from Hong Kong's Luohu KCR (Kowloon–Canton Railway) train station.

Shenzhen may be China's youngest city, but this is one metropolis that's definitely come of age. A small farming town until 1980, Shenzhen was chosen by Deng Xiaoping as an incubator in which the seeds of China's economic reform were to be nurtured. The results are the stuff of legend; a quarter century later, Shenzhen is now China's richest, and, according to some, its most vibrant city.

Until recently, most visitors thought of China's youngest city as a place to pass through on the way from Hong Kong to Guangzhou. But over the last several years, this has changed as more expats chose to call Shenzhen home, and more travelers discover that the city is a unique destination in itself.

GETTING HERE AND AROUND

Tens of thousands of people cross from Hong Kong into Shenzhen (and back) daily, usually over the Luohu border crossing. Over the weekends, numbers can triple. Most visitors take the KCR train from Kowloon to the crossing and walk into Shenzhen. A more expensive—but infinitely more pleasant—way to is by taking the ferry from Hong Kong or Kowloon into Shekou Harbor. Here, immigration lines are a fraction of what they can be in Luohu.

BY AIR Shenzhen Airport is very busy, with flights to 50 cities. There is commuter service by catamaran ferries and buses between the airport and Hong Kong. Bus service links the Shenzhen Railway Station, via Huaren Dasha, direct to Shenzhen Airport for Y25 (one-way).

BY BOAT AND FERRY Shenzhen Party maintains an updated schedule for trains and ferries on its Web site. The Turbojet Company runs regular ferries connecting Hong Kong, Shenzhen, Macau, and Zhuhai. Check their Web site for schedules and prices.

BY BUS Air-conditioned express buses crisscross most of the Pearl River Delta region several times a day. Buses for Hong Kong leave from a number of places, including the China Travel Service branches in Central and Wan Chai.

BY SUBWAY Shenzhen's metro, the newest in China, has two lines, and tickets range between Y2 and Y8.

BY TRAIN Shenzhen can easily be reached from Hong Kong by taking the KCR light railway from Hong Kong's Kowloon Tong KCR station to Luohu Railway Station and then crossing over to Shenzhen on foot. Trains depart from Luohu to Hong Kong every five minutes. Trains between Guangzhou East Railway Station and Shenzhen's Luohu Railway Station depart every hour and cost between Y80 and Y100.

6

ESSENTIALS

Air Contacts Civil Aviation Administration of China, CAAC represented by China Southern (✉ *181 Huanshi Lu, on left as you exit Guangzhou railway station [Guangzhou main station metro]* ☎ *020/8668–2000, 24-hr hotline*). **Shenzhen Airport** (☎ *0755/2777–7821* 🌐 *www.szairport.com*).

Banks HSBC (✉ *Shop No. 9, Shangri-la Hotel, 1002 Jianshe Rd.* ☎ *755/8266–3228* 🌐 *www.hsbc.com.cn*). **Bank of China** (✉ *International Finance Building, 2022 Jianshe Road, Luohu District* ☎ *755/2233–8888* 🌐 *www.boc.cn*).

Boat and Ferry Contacts Macau Ferry Terminal (✉ *Shun Tak Centre, Connaught Rd., Central* ☎ *853/2546–3528*). **Shenzhen Party** (🌐 *www.shenzhenparty.com/travel*). **The Turbojet Company** (☎ *852/2921–6688, press 3 for English)* 🌐 *www.ctshk.com*).

Bus Contacts Shenzhen Luohu Bus station (✉ *1st–2nd fls., East Plaza, Luohu District* ☎ *755/8232–1670*).

Medical Assistance Shenzhen People's Hospital (✉ *Dongmen Rd. N* ☎ *0755/2553–3018 Ext. 2553, 1387 (Outpatient Dept.)*.

Subway Contact Shenzhen Metro (☎ *020/8310–6622 for information in English, 020/8310–6666*).

Train Contacts The Mass Transit Rail (MTR) (☎ *852/2881–8888* 🌐 *www.mtr.com.hk*). **Shenzhen Railway Station** (✉ *Luohu District* ☎ *020/8232–8647*).

EXPLORING SHENZHEN

Sprawling Shenzhen is composed of six districts. Luohu and Futian are the "downtown" districts, with most of the major shopping areas, financial districts, and hundreds of hotels. If beautiful beaches and Soviet-era aircraft carriers-cum-theme parks are your thing, you won't want to miss the Yantian district. Shekou District is an area extremely popular for its waterfront dining and many bars and restaurants. Nanshan is Shenzhen's arts and theme-park district. Surrounding these smaller districts like a misshapen croissant are Shenzhen's two largest (and least urban) districts: Bao'an to the east and Longgang to the west.

LUOHU AND FUTIAN

Though Luohu and Futian are the smallest districts in the city, for many it is this urban jungle of skyscrapers, markets, restaurants, and hotels that defines Shenzhen. Luohu (*Lo Wu* in Cantonese) begins right at the border crossing with Hong Kong. Jienshi Road is the street that ends at the border, and like many border areas, has a rough feel about it. Single men walking on this road (which parallels the train tracks leading north to Guangzhou and south to Hong Kong) will be harassed by countless women shouting out "massage" and "missy" (ironically, this street also has a number of good, reputable massage parlors as well as a number of excellent restaurants).

Futian, Shenzhen's trading hub, is also where the Shenzhen's gourmands go for a night of gastronomic pleasure. The Zhenhua Road–restaurant district in Futian is where scores of excellent restaurants compete for the patronage of Shenzhen's very discriminating diners.

NANSHAN AND SHEKOU

Nanshan is where you'll find Shenzhen's most stylish district, Huaqiao Cheng, or Overseas Chinese Town (often called the OCT District). Here you will find the **OCT park,** an urban expanse of greenery and sculpture (whose highlights include pieces like Fu Zhongwang's "Earth Gate," a Gothic-looking locked iron door buried in the ground, and French sculptor Bernar Vernet's *230.5*, a postmodern monument of forged steel that fits well with Shenzhen's industrious nature). There are two excellent museums, the **Hexiangning Museum of Contemporary Chinese Art,** and the more underground-feeling **OCAT** (Overseas Chinese Art Terminal). The OCT also has three popular theme parks.

Shekou was the first Special Economic Zone, marking the earliest baby step of modern China's transformation from state planned to market economy. Nowadays the neighborhood is best known for **Sea World Plaza,** a pedestrian mall featuring restaurants, bars, and a completely landlocked oceangoing vessel (now transformed into a bar, hotel, and nightclub complex), and the Shekou bar street.

MAIN ATTRACTIONS

Splendid China features China's 74 best-known historical and geographical sights collected and miniaturized to 1:15 scale. Built in 1991 and popularized by Deng Xiaoping (who stopped in for a photo op on his famous 1992 journey south promoting free enterprise), it is still a big draw with the patriotic camera-wielding masses, and not a few Westerners "doing China" in a day. The 74-acre site includes a waist-high Great Wall, a fun-size Forbidden City, and little Potala Palace. ✉ *OCT District, Shenzhen* ☎ *0755/2660–0626* 🌐 *www.cn5000.com.cn* 🎫 *Y120* ⏲ *Daily 9–9:30* Ⓜ *Windows of the World metro station.*

Windows of the World gives a similar miniature makeover to 130 of the world's most famous landmarks and is China's biggest and busiest homegrown theme park. Divided into eight geographical areas interconnected by winding paths and a full-size monorail, it includes randomly scaled Taj Mahal, Mount Rushmore, Sydney Harbor Opera House, and a 100-meter-high (328-foot-high) Eiffel Tower that can be seen from miles away. There is also a fireworks show at 9 PM on weekends and holidays which, for adults, is best viewed from across the street at the Crowne Plaza's rooftop V-Bar. ✉ *OCT, Nanshan District, Shenzhen* ☎ *0755/2660–8000* 🌐 *www.szwwco.com (in Chinese only)* 🎫 *Y120* ⏲ *Daily 9 AM–10:30 PM* Ⓜ *Windows of the World metro station.*

IF YOU HAVE TIME

In addition to its statue-filled Overseas Chinese Town Park, the OCT neighborhood is packed with other museums.

The **He Xiangning Art Museum** is free on Friday and features contemporary and classical art from all over China. ✉ *Shenzhen shi Huaqiaocheng Shennan Dadao 9013 hao, OCT, Nanshan District* ☎ *0755/2660–4540* 🌐 *www.hxnart.com* ⏲ *Tues.–Sun. 10–6* Ⓜ *Huaqiaocheng metro station.*

The **OCT Contemporary Art Terminal.** Shenzhen shi Huaqiaocheng Enping Lu is where you'll find works from the hippest artists from Beijing and beyond. ✉ *OCT, Nanshan District* ☎ *0755/2691–6199* 🌐 *www.ocat.com.cn* 🎫 *Free* ⏲ *Tues.–Sun. 10–5:30* Ⓜ *Huaqiaocheng metro station.*

YANTIAN, LONGGANG AND BAO'AN

Though these three districts make up the bulk of Shenzhen's land area, most casual visitors to the city never hear of them, let alone visit them. We think this is a pity, as it's these outer regions where you'll find the prettiest scenery and the most culturally edifying places in the Pearl River Delta, not to mention China's most famous golf course, Mission Hills.

Just east of Luohu, Yantian is Shenzhen's beach district. **Dameisha** and **Xiaomeisha** are two beaches adjacent to one another, which offer sun, surf, and strange statues of colorful winged men doing what appears to be beachfront tai chi. Dameisha is a public beach, whereas Xiaomeisha has a Y20 admission price. Both are about 40 minutes from Luohu by taxi. Yantian is also the home of **Minsk World,** a decommissioned Soviet-era aircraft carrier turned into a tourist attraction.

Longgang, Shenzhen's ancient heart, is where you'll find the sights that belie the city's reputation as a place of new money and no history. **Dapeng Fortress** is a Ming Dynasty–era walled city where visitors can wander down narrow cobblestone streets and walk on parapets that were ancient even in the days of the last Qing empress. The **Hakka Folk Customs**

Museum and Enclosures is another walled town. This one was built (and formerly occupied) by the Hakka—Han Chinese who are said to have migrated from north to south ages ago, bringing with them their own cuisine and traditions; not to mention peculiar building design. Both of these slices of ancient China are about an hour away from the modern heart of Luohu by taxi.

MAIN ATTRACTIONS

Minsk World. When a group of Shenzhen businessmen bought a decommissioned Soviet-era aircraft carrier in the late 1990s, Western intelligence agencies wondered if it was a military move by the Chinese. But the truth was revealed when these savvy entrepreneurs turned this massive warship into Minsk World, Shenzhen's most popular—and perhaps strangest—tourist attraction. Parked in perpetuity on the top deck of the ship (which is as long as three football fields placed end to end, and gets wickedly hot in the summer) are several Soviet fighter planes and helicopters. Every hour on the hour comely young ladies in military costumes perform a dance routine combining sensuality with martial flair and twirling rifles. ✉*Shatoujiao, Dapeng Bay, Yantian District, Shenzhen* ☎*0755/2535–5333* 🌐*www.szminsk.com (Chinese only)* 🎫*Y110* ⏲*Daily 9:30–7:30.*

Dapeng Fortress was built more than 600 years ago, and is an excellent example of a Ming Dynasty–military encampment (1368–1644). The fortress was originally built to resist Japanese pirates who'd been harassing the southern coastal areas of Guangdong. However, the fortress is best known as the site of the British Naval attack of September 4, 1839, in which British forces attacked China in what is widely considered the beginning of the Opium Wars. As local legend goes, Chinese troops in fishing boats, led by General Lai Enjue, defeated the better-equipped enemy. Today, visitors flock to the fortress to admire the inside of the walled town, which is replete with ornately carved beams and columns, with poetic couplets painted over each door. ✉*Pengcheng Village, Dapeng Town, Longgang District, Shenzhen* ☎*No phone* 🎫*Y20* ⏲*Daily 10–9.*

Hakka Folk Customs Museum and Enclosures is a large series of concentric circular homes built inside of an exterior wall that basically turns the whole place into a large fort. Inside of the enclosure are a large number of old Hakka residences, some of which are still filled with tools and furniture left over from the Qing Dynasty. The site is somewhat feral; once you pass the ticket booth, you're pretty much on your own and free to stroll around the grounds and explore inside the residences themselves, many of which seem to have been left in a mostly natural state. Although some restoration projects pretty things up to the point of making the site look unreal, the opposite is true here. Parts of the enclosures are so real as to seem downright spooky; visitors might get the feeling that the original inhabitants may return at any moment, crossbows cocked. ✉*Luoruihe Village, Longgang Township, Longgang District, Shenzhen* 🎫*Y20* ⏲*Daily 10–6.*

IF YOU HAVE TIME

If you're interested in watching art in the making, spend an afternoon at the **Dafen Oil Painting Village,** a small town 20 minutes by taxi from Luohu, which employs thousands of artists painting everything from originals to copies of classics. Where do all those oil paintings you find in motels come from? Visit Dafen and you'll know. Be aware, opening hours are sporadic. ✉ *Shen Hui Rd., Bu Ji St., Longgang District* ☎ *0755/8473–2622* ⏱ *Daily 10–6:30.*

WHERE TO EAT

From the heavy mutton stews of Xinjiang to the spicy seafood dishes of Fujian, Shenzhen is home to thousands of restaurants existing not to please the fickle palates of visitors, but to alleviate the homesickness of people pining for native provinces left behind. Furthermore, over the past few years, Shenzhen has attracted a slew of restaurateurs from abroad.

$$–$$$$ ECLECTIC Fodor'sChoice ★ ✕ **360.** The newest (and possibly brightest) star on the Shenzhen haute-cuisine scene, 360 takes up the top two floors of the Shangri-la hotel, and offers sumptuous dishes like homemade pasta with eggplant, zucchini, and pesto sauce and ginger-crusted-salmon fillet with couscous and lemon celery sauce. Ambience is chic, and the view from any table in the house is breathtaking. For food, decor, and view we can't recommend this place highly enough. ✉ *31st fl., Shangri-la hotel, 1002 Jianshi Rd., Luohu* ☎ *0755/8396–1380* ▭ *AE, DC, MC, V* Ⓜ *Luohu*

$$$–$$$$ ITALIAN ★ ✕ **Blue Italian Seafood & Grill.** Arguably one of the finest Italian restaurants in China, the decor, as the name suggests, is blue—blue walls, ceilings, and mellow indigo lighting. The food is expensive but worth every penny. If you're really in the mood for decadence, try the dessert tray—chocolates, pastries, and eight different types of mousse surround a caramelized sugar statue of David. ✉ *Crowne Plaza Hotel, 3rd fl., 9026 Shen Nan Rd., OCT District* ☎ *0755/2693–6888 Ext. 8022, 8023, or 8106* ▭ *AE, DC, MC, V.*

¢–$ CHINESE FUSION ✕ **Foodfeast.** This is the only place in Shekou for genuine Hakka cuisine, including rich soups made with pork and bitter melon, serious Hakka-style dumplings, stewed clay-pot dishes and roasted chicken, duck, and fatty pork. Try the durian pancake, if you're a fan of the enormously smelly "king of fruits." (Durian's odor is so strong that it is sometimes banned from subways.) Foodfeast is unpretentious, the sort of place where Sun Yet-sen might have taken tea while plotting the revolution against the Manchu Dynasty ✉ *Sea World Hotel, 1st fl., Taizi Rd. #7, Shekou District* ☎ *0755/2540–4730* ▭ *No credit cards.*

$$$$ CONTEMPORARY ✕ **Greenland Lounge.** This favorite is known for its international-style buffet and truly unique selection of Chinese teas. The glass-domed roof and smart-casual ambience make this a popular spot for Shenzhen's movers and shakers. ✉ *Lobby, Pavilion hotel, 4002 Huaqiang Rd. N, Futian District* ☎ *0755/8207–8888* ▭ *AE, DC, MC, V.*

$$$ INDIAN ✕ **Little India.** This is definitely more than your average curry house. The Nepalese chef offers cuisine from both northern India and Nepal. The restaurant is especially known for its tandoori dishes, and for its

6

selection of baked *nan* breads. Little India is also the only restaurant in the Sea World Plaza that offers hookahs, though they'll gently ask you to smoke on the outdoor pavilion during peak hours. ✉*Shop 73–74, Sea World Plaza, Shekou District* ☎*0755/2685–2688* ▭*MC, V.*

$$–$$$$ CHINESE FUSION ✕ **Sunday Chiu Chow King.** The dim sum and other Cantonese dishes are good, but what really sets this place apart is the excellent Chaozhou (or Chiu Chow) cuisine. Well known on both sides of the border, this restaurant is usually packed on the weekends with noisy diners from Hong Kong. Try the crispy fried tofu and steamed seafood balls, or the yin-yang soup (it's the soup that looks like a yin-and-yang symbol, made up of rice congee on one side and creamed spinach on the other, just point to the picture on the menu). All of these are Chaozhou specialty dishes. ✉*Jen Shi Rd. 1076, 9th–10th fls., Luohu* ✣*2 blocks north of Shangri-La Hotel* ☎*0755/8231–0222* ▭*V* Ⓜ*Luohu metro station.*

¢ JAPANESE ★ ✕ **Yokohama.** Enjoy excellent sushi and amazing views of the fishing boats and ferries of Shekou Harbor to the east, and the hills of Shekou to the north. Sashimi is the freshest around, and other dishes are the real deal. The clientele is mostly Japanese, which is always a good sign. Try a side dish of *oshinko* (traditional Japanese pickles)—unlike many lesser Japanese restaurants in China, Yokohama takes no shortcuts with its oshinko and offers eight different types. ✉*Shekou Harbor, Nanhai Hotel, 10th fl., Shekou District* ☎*0755/2669–5557* ▭*AE, DC, MC, V.*

WHERE TO STAY

$$$$ Fodor'sChoice ★ **Crowne Plaza.** This hotel holds its own among the best hotels in Asia. The theme is pure Italian Renaissance, right down to the Venetian-gondolier uniforms worn by the staff, and the wide spiral staircases and long hallways gives the place an M.C. Escher aura. The Crowne's swimming pool is the largest in Shenzhen, and extends from an indoor pool under a domed roof to a connected outdoor pool with a swim-up bar. One regular patron told us that she comes back "because anywhere you look in this hotel there's something interesting." The Crowne also has a number of excellent restaurants. **Pros:** near metro, stylish decor. **Cons:** you may not have been thinking Italy when you came to China. ✉*OCT District* ✣*across from Windows of the World metro station* ☎*0755/2693–6888* 🌐*www.crowneplaza.com* *400 rooms, 47 suites* *In-hotel: 4 restaurants, bars, pool, gym* ▭*AE, DC, MC, V.*

Crowne Plaza Hotel and Suites Landmark Shenzhen. Since completing its ambitious renovation program in 2006, The Landmark has become Shenzhen's first *all-suites* hotel; every room is a suite, boasting a 42-inch plasma television and extra large bathrooms. In addition, the hotel has three excellent restaurants, as well as a wine and cigar bar with a walk-in humidor. However, what makes this hotel truly unique is its personalized butler service, managed by Robert Watson, director of the Guild of Professional English Butlers and the former principal tutor at the Lady Apsley School for Butlers in London. As for amenities, this hotel basically has it all. If you're looking to experience the life of China's new elite, this is the place to do it. **Pros:** good restaurants, good amenities, personal butler service, near metro. **Cons:** not for those who like quaint.

✉3018 Nanhu Lu, 3 blocks NE of Shenzhen main station, Shenzhen ☎0755/8217–2288 🌐www.szlandmark.com.cn ⇆319 suites ♁In-hotel: 3 restaurants, bar, pool, gym ▭AE, DC, MC, V.

$$–$$$$ **Cruise Inn.** Pearlescent tiled floors and stained-glass ceilings are the first thing you'll notice in the lobby of this newly opened hotel inside of the landlocked and permanently docked ship *Minghua,* the central feature of Shekou's Sea World Plaza. Rooms are clean, comfortable, and nautically themed. The Romantic Sea View room has a waterbed and a view of the ocean and driving range; the Captain's Suite looks out over the bar street, and has two plasma-screen televisions and a Jacuzzi. If a whimsical maritime *Alice in Wonderland*–style inn is what you're looking for, then look no farther. **Pros:** a fun, quirky place to stay. **Cons:** best if you like things nautical. *✉Minghua Ship, Sea World, Shekou ☎0755/2682–5555 🌐www.honlux.com ⇆110 rooms, 1 suite ♁In-hotel: 3 restaurants, bars, bicycles ▭AE, DC, MC, V.*

¢–$ **Nan Hai.** This hotel's retro space-age exterior, featuring rounded balconies that look as if they might detach from the mother ship at any moment, is the first sight greeting visitors on the Hong Kong–Shekou ferry. Although one of Shenzhen's older luxury hotels, the Nan Hai still holds its own in the moderate-luxury class, offering a lobby piano bar, attractive rooms with balconies and sea views, and a number of excellent restaurants. **Pros:** near pier for ferries to Hong Kong International Airport. **Cons:** dated decor. *✉1 Gongye Yilu, Shekou ☎0755/2669–2888 🌐www.nanhai-hotel.com ⇆396 rooms and suites ♁In-hotel: 1 restaurant, bar, gym, tennis courts, pool ▭AE, DC, MC, V.*

6

$–$$$$ **The Pavilion.** With a great location in the heart of the Futian business district, and a gorgeous interior (check out the domed-glass roof over a central piano bar–teahouse), the Pavilion is one of the top international-class hotels in Shenzhen. Service is good, especially for a locally managed hotel, and most staff members speak English. The meeting rooms have everything an international traveler could need. **Pros:** good location and service. **Cons:** rooms don't have much character. *✉4002 Huaqiang Bei Lu, Futian District ☎0755/8207–8888 🌐www.pavilionhotel.com ⇆294 rooms and suites ♁In-hotel: 4 restaurants, pool, gym ▭AE, DC, MC, V.*

¢–$ **Seaview O City Hotel Shenzhen.** Staying in the OCT District but can't afford the Crowne Plaza? The nearby Seaview hotel is a good bet, albeit far less luxurious. Though rack prices are steep, discounts of up to 40% are usually available. The Sea view is clean, comfortable, has a water view, and as it's across the street from the He Xiangning Art Museum, it's popular with visiting artists. The second-floor restaurant serves excellent Western food, and the third-floor Cantonese restaurant is good for dim-sum. **Pros:** affordable, water views. **Cons:** pretty standard. *✉No. 3–5 Guangqiao St., OCT, Nanshan District, Shenzhen ✥Directly in front of Huaqiao Cheng metro ☎0755/2660–2222 🌐www.octhotels.com ⇆436 rooms, 17 suites ♁In-hotel: 2 restaurants, gym ▭AE, DC, MC, V.*

$$$$ ★ **Shangri-La Shenzhen.** The location (practically straddling the border with Hong Kong) has made it a popular meeting place, and it's a city landmark. Rooms are first class, hospitality is excellent, and the hotel

features in-house wireless Internet and top-notch spa facilities. What really makes Shangri-La worth a visit is the 360 Lounge and Restaurant, which takes up the top two floors of the hotel and offers a view of Shenzhen. The Shangri-La also has a number of other excellent restaurants, making it a good choice for visitors who might not want to come into contact with the neighborhood's rougher edges. **Pros:** near Lowu shopping malls. **Cons:** noisy and crowded neighborhood. ☒*1002 Jianshe Lu, Luohu District, Shenzhen* ✣*Luohu, east side of train station* ☎*0755/8233–0888* ⊕*www.shangri-la.com* *523 rooms, 30 suites* *In-hotel: 5 restaurants, bar, pool, gym* *AE, DC, MC, V.*

¢–$$$ **Shanshui Trends Hotel.** This budget hotel in the Futian District appeals mostly to business travelers. With a round bed and view of the interior food court, the Romance Suite is a bit musty and distinctly unromantic. However, the Japanese Suite, with its wooden tub and traditional tatami-mats is much nicer. Shanshui Trends is good deal for travelers on a shoestring, located in one of Shenzhen's most happening food districts. Discounts of up to 30% are available. **Pros:** good price, good district for food. **Cons:** nothing special. ☒*No. 1 Hua Fa Bei Lu, Futian District* ✣*2 blocks north of Hua Qiang metro station* ☎*0755/6135–8802 or 0755/6135–5555* *197 rooms, 2 suites* *In-hotel: gym, spa* *AE, DC, MC, V.*

NIGHTLIFE AND THE ARTS

Shenzhen's nightlife is so happening that it's not unusual to run into people—expats and Chinese—who have come in from Hong Kong and Guangzhou just to party. The two major nightlife centers are the Luohu District and Shekou District (Luohu tends to be flashier and Shekou a bit more laid-back), but a couple of cool spots are in the OCT District as well.

Baby Face (☒*Beside Lushan Hotel, Luohu District* ☎*0755/9234–2565* ⊕*www.babyface.com.cn*) is the Shenzhen branch of one of China's most popular nightspots, offering imported DJs, a late-night-party scene, and extremely chic clientele (so don't show up in sandals).

True Colors (☒*3F Dongyuan Mansion, 1 Dongyuan Lu, Futian District* ☎*0755/8212–9333*) has one of the coolest party scenes in Shenzhen and attracts top-name international DJs. Musical tastes range from trance to house, and the party usually doesn't break up until dawn.

V-Bar (☒*Crowne Plaza Hotel, rooftop OCT District* ☎*0755/2693–6888*) is without a doubt the hottest nightspot in the OCT, featuring a live band, a holographic globe hovering over a circular bar, and a fireworks show on the weekends at 9 PM courtesy of the Windows of the World theme park across the street. The V-Bar is the only bar in town with an attached swimming pool.

Browns Wine Bar and Cigar House (☒*Portofino, OCT District, Shenzhen* ☎*0755/8608–2379*) is the perfect, low-key place for quiet conversation over a bottle of wine and a Cuban cigar. Browns has an admirable stock of vintage wines, cognacs, and Armagnacs, and a walk-in humidor to insure that all cigars are kept fresh.

Soho Nightclub (✉*TaiZi Bar St, Shekou District* ☎*0755/2669–0148 or 0755/2669–2148*) is the place in Shekou to dance, drink, and party. If you need a rest from dancing, slip out to the outdoor garden for a cocktail.

3 colors Bar (✉*Jing Yuan Building, 2nd fl., SongYuan Rd., Luohu District* ☎*0755/2588–7000*) is a lively dance club that's very in with Shenzhen's gay crowd. It's a fun place so there's a wide mix of people.

Er Ding Mu (✉*Jiang Nan Chun Hotel, 3rd fl., Ai Hua Rd. No.23, Futian District* ✣*at Nanyuan and Ai Hua Rds.* ☎*0755/8365–1879 or 131/4883–9798*) is another popular gay club, offering a more relaxed spot for a mostly younger male crowd to unwind and hook up.

SHOPPING

Dongmen Shopping Plaza (✉*Laojie Metro Station, Luohu District, Shenzhen* ☎*No phone*) is Shenzhen's oldest shopping area. It's a sprawling pedestrian plaza with both large shopping centers for name-brand watches, shoes, bags, cosmetics, and clothes, and plenty of smaller outdoor shops. Foot fetishists won't want to miss the huge **Dongmen Shoes City,** close to the east side of the plaza. If you're into people-watching, grab a glass of bubble-milk tea and soak up the sights—the plaza is like a low-rent version of the fashionista youth culture in Tokyo's Ginza.

CITIC City Plaza (✉*1095 Shennan Rd., Shenzhen* ☎*0755/2594–1502* ⏲*Daily 10:30* AM *to 10* PM Ⓜ*Kexueguan metro station*) offers upscale shopping for the time-conscious business traveler. Shops include Japanese department stores **Seibu and Jusco,** and **Louis Vuitton, Polo,** and **Tommy Hilfiger.** There's also a food court on the lower level that's not a bad place to take a break over some coffee or a bowl of noodle soup.

Luohu (*Lo Wu Commercial City* ✉*Adjacent to the Hong Kong Border Crossing/Luohu metro station, Shenzhen* ☎*No phone* ⏲*Daily 10* AM*–10* PM) is a venerable stalwart of Shenzhen mixed-bag shopping. On one hand, its location (straddling the Hong Kong–Shenzhen border) makes it a good place to do last-minute shopping for pirate DVDs, shoddy electronics, and phony versions of just about any name brand you can think of, and stalls selling semiprecious stones and feng-shui knickknacks on the second floor is pretty cool. On the other hand, Luohu Commercial City has some of the most aggressive touts you're likely to find in Shenzhen. If having "DVD? Rolex watch?" shouted every 20 seconds doesn't bother you, this place might be worth the trip.

San Dao Plaza (✉*Jen Shi Rd. 1076, Luohu, Shenzhen* ⏲*9* AM*–8* PM Ⓜ*Luohu metro station*). This four-story extravaganza is the area's best market for medicinal herbs, tea, and tea-related products. The top two floors contain a series of stalls where merchants sell a wide range of Chinese teas. Visitors are generally invited to *lai, he cha,* or come drink tea. Don't worry, it isn't considered rude to have a cup without buying anything, but you'll find it hard to leave empty-handed. Downstairs, there is also a large vegetable market and small shops selling traditional Chinese herbal medicines, incense, and religious items.

GOLF

The **Guangzhou Luhu Golf and Country Club** (✉*Lujing Rd.* ☎*020/8350–7777*) has 18 holes spread over 180 acres of Luhu Park, 20 minutes from the Guangzhou Railway Station and 30 minutes from Baiyun Airport. The 6,820-yard, par-72 course was designed by renowned course-architect Dave Thomas. The club has a 75-bay driving range and a clubhouse with restaurants, pro shop, and a gym. Members' guests and those from affiliated clubs pay Y637 in greens fees on weekdays, Y1,274 on weekends. Nonmembers pay Y849 and Y1,486, respectively. These prices include a caddie. Clubs can be rented for Y265. The club is a member of the International Associate Club network.

The **Lakewood Golf Club** (✉*Da'nan Mountain, Jinding District* ☎*0756/338–3666*) is about 20 minutes from the Zhuhai Ferry Terminal, and is the most popular of the city's five golf clubs. Both its Mountain Course and its Lake Course are 18 holes, and are said to be challenging. Visitor packages, including greens fees and a caddy are Y420 for weekdays and Y820 weekends. Golf carts cost Y200.

The **Sand River Golf Club** (✉*1 Baishi Lu, Nanshan District Shenzhen* ☎*0755/2690–0111* ⊙*Daily 7 AM–9 PM*) is another popular club, though not nearly as large as Mission Hills. Sand River offers two courses, one of which is designed by Gary Player and floodlighted for night playing. Other facilities include a large driving range, a lake, and various resort amenities. Greens fees: 9-holes Y330 weekdays and Y550 weekends. Greens fees: Y660 weekdays and Y1,100 weekends; caddies Y160 to Y180.

Mission Hills Golf Club (✉*Nan Shan, Da Wei, Sha He, Bao'an District, Shenzhen* ☎*0755/2690–9999, 852/2826–0238 in Hong Kong* 🌐*www.missionhillsgroup.com*) has 10 celebrity-designed 18-hole courses (two of which offer nighttime playing), as well as a spectacular clubhouse, a tennis court, two restaurants, and an outdoor pool. There's also a five-star hotel on the premises for golfers serious about trying every course. Mission Hills offers a shuttle bus service from Hong Kong and Shenzhen (call Shenzhen: 0755/2802–0888 or Hong Kong: 852/2973–0303 for schedule). Greens fees: Y600 weekdays and Y1,000 weekends; caddies Y150.

White Swan Hotel Golf Practice Center (✉*White Swan Hotel, Yi Shamian Lu Shamian Island* ☎*020/8188–6968*) is a good driving range on Shamian Island if you are pressed for time or don't want to leave the city. Admission is Y70, a rental of one club is Y30, and a box of 20 balls is Y10.

SIDE TRIPS TO ZHONGSHAN AND ZHUHAI

Two other cities worth visiting in the Pearl River Delta are Zhongshan and Zhuhai. Though some casual visitors might chose to spend more than one day in this region, both are small enough to be seen in an afternoon.

Zhongshan is 78 km (48 mi) from Guangzhou and 61 km (38 mi) northwest of Macau. Until recently it was a picturesque port, where a cantilever bridge over the Qi River was raised twice a day to allow small freighters to pass. Today, the old town has been all but obliterated by modern high-rises, and the surrounding farms are now factories. However, there are still a few spots of historical note worth seeing.

Zhongshan is the birthplace of Sun Yat-sen and home to the **Sun Yat-sen Memorial Hall** (✉*Sunwen Zhong Lu* *Y10* *Daily 8–4:50*). Considered the father of the Chinese revolution that overthrew the corrupt Qing Dynasty, he is one of the few political figures respected on both sides of the Taiwan Straits. The **Xishan Temple** (✉*Xishan Park* *Y5* *Daily 8–5*) is a beautifully restored temple that's also worth a visit. Probably the most popular spot in town is **Sunwen Xilu,** a pedestrian mall lined with dozens of restored buildings. At the end of the street is the lovely **Zhongshan Park,** where there is the seven-story Fufeng Pagoda and the world's largest statue of . . . you guessed it, Sun Yat-sen.

Bordering Macau, and a little over an hour away by ferry from Hong Kong and Shenzhen, most people don't see **Zhuhai** as a major destination in its own right. The city does, however, have a nice long coastline and many small offshore islands. Lover's Road, a 20-km (12½-mi) stretch of road hugging the shoreline, is Zhuhai's signature attraction, as beachside drives are a rarity in China. The road leads to the **Macau Crossing** and has enough bars and restaurants to draw a steady crowd of Macau partygoers. Near the Macau border, across from the bus station, is **Yingbin Street,** a popular shopping area. Cheap seafood restaurants stay open well after midnight and, thanks to a variety of hawkers, street musicians, and food stalls, it makes for a fascinating, if slightly earthy, evening stroll.

GETTING HERE AND AROUND

Regular bus service to Zhongshan and Zhuhai runs from Guangzhou's three long-distance bus stations: Liuhua bus station, Guangdong long-distance bus station, and Haizhu Passenger Station.

Bus Contacts Zhuhai Gongbei Bus Station (✉*No.1 Lianhua Rd., Gongbei District* ☎*756/888–8554*). **Zhongshan Bus Station** (✉*Fuhua Rd., Shiqiben West District* ☎*760/863–3825*).

6

ENGLISH	PINYIN	CHINESE CHARACTERS
GUANGZHOU	GUĀNGZHŌU	广州
1920 Restaurant and Bar	Yījiŭèrlín Cānbā	1920 餐吧
A Thousand And One Nights	Yī Qiān Lín Yī Yè	一千 零一夜
Aiqun Hotel	Āiqún Jiŭdiàn	爱群酒店
Anger Music Power House	Páoxiào	咆哮
Australian Consulate	Àodàlìyà Lĭngshìguăn	澳大利亚领事馆
Baby Face Club	Baby Face Jùlèbù	Baby Face 俱乐部
Back Street Jazz Bar & Restaurant	Hòujiē Cāntīng	后街餐厅
Baiyun Bowling Center	Báiyuánshān Băolíngqiú Zhōngxīn	白云保龄球中心
Banxi Restaurant	Bànxī Jiŭjiā	泮溪酒家
Beijing Road Pedestrian Mall	Běijīng Lù Bùxíngjiē	北京路步行街
Bingjiang West Road	Bīnjiāng Xī Lù	滨江西路
Bright Filial Piety Temple	Guāngxiào Sì	光孝寺
British Consulate	Yīngguó Lĭngshìguăn	英国领事馆
Café Elles	Mùzĭ Bā	木子吧
Canadian Consulate	Jiānádà Lĭngshìguăn	加拿大领事馆
Can-Am International Medical Centre	Jiāměi Guójì Yīliáo Zhōngxīn	加美国际医疗中心
Chen Family Temple	Chénjiā Cí	陈家祠
China Hotel	Zhōngguó Dàjiŭdiàn	中国大酒店
Citybus Hong Kong Office	Xiānggăng Chéngbā Bàngōngshì	香港城巴办公室
Civil Aviation Administration of China	Zhōngguó Mínháng Zŏngjú	中国民航总局
Club Tang	Tánghuì	唐会
Connoisseur	Míng Shì Gé	名仕阁
Da Chuan Japanese Food Restaurant	Dàchuān Rìběn Liàolĭ	大川日本料理
Datong Restaurant	Dàtóng Jiŭdiàn	大同酒店
Dong Fang Hotel	Dōngfāng Bīnguăn	东方宾馆
Dongjiang Seafood Restaurant	Dōngjiāng Hăixiān Cāntīng	东江海鲜餐厅
Elan Hotel	Mĭlánhuā Jiŭdiàn	米兰花酒店
English Language Directory Inquiries	Yīngwén Cídiăn	英文词典
Five Rams Statue	Wŭyáng Sùxiàng	五羊塑像
Friendship Store	Yŏuyí Shāngdiàn	友谊商店
Friendship Theatre	Yŏuyí Jùyuàn	友谊剧院

ENGLISH	PINYIN	CHINESE CHARACTERS
Garden Hotel	Huāyuán Jiǔdiàn	花园酒店
GITIC Plaza	Zhōngxìn Guǎngchǎng	中信广场
Guang Ming Theatre	Guāngmíng Yǐngyuàn	光明影院
Guang Zhi Lu Agency	Guǎngzhīlǔ Lǚxíngshè	广之旅旅行社
Guangdong CITS	Guǎngdōng Guólǚ Guójì Lǚxíngshè	广东国旅国际旅行社
Guangdong CTS	Guǎngdōngshěng Zhōngguó Lǚxíngshè	广东省中国旅行社
Guangdong International Hotel	Guǎngdōng Jiāyì Guójì Jiǔdiàn	广东嘉逸国际酒店
Guangdong International Travel	Guǎngdōng Guójì Lǚxíngshè	广东国际旅行社
Guangdong Modern Dance Company	Guǎngdōng Xiàndàiwǔ Tuán	广东现代舞团
Guangdong Museum of Art	Guǎngdōng Měishù Guǎn	广东美术馆
Guangdong Provincial Bus Station	Guǎngdōng Shěn Chángtú Qìchēzhàn	广东省长途汽车站
Guangdong Puppet Art Center	Guǎngdōng Mùǒu Yìshù Zhōngxīn	广东木偶艺术中心
Guangxiao Temple	Guāngxiào Sì	光孝寺
Guangzhou Arts Centre	Guǎngzhōu Yìshù Zhōngxīn	广州艺术中心
Guangzhou Book Center	Guǎngzhōu Gòushū Zhōngxīn	广州购书中心
Guangzhou Books Center	Guǎngzhōu Gòushū Zhōngxīn	广州购书中心
Guangzhou Bus Station	Guǎngzhōu Qìchēzhàn	广州汽车站
Guangzhou East Railway Station	Guǎngzhōu Dōngzhàn	广州东站
Guangzhou East Railway Station	Guǎngzhōu Dōngzhàn	广州东站
Guangzhou Emergency Treatment Centre	Guǎngzhōu Jíjiù Zhōngxīn	广州急救中心
Guangzhou Ji Ya Zhai	Guǎngzhōu Jíyǎ Zhāi	广州集雅斋
Guangzhou Luhu Golf & Country Club	Guǎngzhōu Lùhú Gāoěrfūqiú Xiāngcūn Jùlèbù	广 州 麓 湖 高 尔 夫 球 乡 村 俱 乐 部
Guangzhou Museum	Guǎngzhōu Bówùguǎn	广州博物馆
Guangzhou Railway Station	Guǎngzhōu Huǒchēzhàn	广州火车站
Guangzhou Restaurant	Guǎngzhōu Jiǔjiā	广州酒家
Haizhu Plaza	Hǎizhū Guǎngchǎng	海珠广场
Hare & Moon Bar	Yuètù Jiǔbā	月兔酒吧
Haveli Restaurant and Bar	Táng Yuè Gōng	唐乐宫
Holiday Inn City Centre	Wénhuà Jiàrì Jiǔdiàn	文化假日酒店
Holiday Inn Shifu	Shífǔ Jiàrì Jiǔdiàn	十甫假日酒店

ENGLISH	PINYIN	CHINESE CHARACTERS
Hong Kong Trade Development Council	Xiānggǎng Màoyì Fāzhǎn Jú	香港贸易发展局
Huaisheng Mosque	Huáishèng Sì	怀圣寺
Huanshi East Road	Huánshì Dōng Lù	环市东路
Kathleen's Café	Kǎisèlín Kāfēi	凯瑟林咖啡
Kowloon Station	Jiǔlóng Chēzhàn	九龙车站
La Perle	Lìbǎi Guǎngchǎng	丽柏广场
La Seine	Sàinàhé Fǎguó Xīcāntīng	塞纳河法国西餐厅
L'Africain Bar	Fēizōu Bā	非洲吧
Lai Wan Market	Lìwān Tíng	荔湾亭
Landmark Canton	Huáxià Dà Jiǔdiàn	华夏大酒店
Liuhua Park	Liúhuāhú Gōngyuán	流花湖公园
Lucy's	Lùsī Jiǔbā	露丝酒吧
Mausoleum of the 72 Martyrs	Huánghuā Gǎng Qīshí'èr Lièshì Língyuán	黄花岗七十二烈士陵园
Memorial Garden for the Martyrs	Lièshì Língyuán	烈士陵园
Metro	dìtiě	地铁
Mo Li Fang Theater	Mólìfāng Jùyuàn	魔立方剧院
Nan Yue Museum	Nányuè Bówùguǎn	南岳博物馆
Nile Restaurant	Níluóhé Cāntīng	尼罗河餐厅
Orchid Garden	Lánpǔ Gōngyuán	兰圃公园
Our Lady of Lourdes Catholic Church	Shāmiàn Táng	沙面堂
Park 19	Park Yāojiǔ Yìshù Kōngjiān	Park 19 艺术空间
Peasant Movement Institute	Nóngmín Yùndòng Jiǎngxī Suǒ	农民运动江西所
Public Security Bureau	Gōngānjú	公安局
Qingping Market	Qīngpíng Shìchǎng	清平市场
Revolutionary Museum	Qǐyì Bówùguǎn	起义博物馆
Shamian Hotel	Shāmiàn Bīnguǎn	沙面宾馆
Shamian Island	Shāmiàn Dǎo	沙 面 岛
Shangxiajiu Street	Shàng Xià Jiǔ	上下九
Silk Road Grill Room	Sīchóu ZhīLù	“丝绸之路” 扒房
Six Banyan Temple	Liùróng Si	六榕寺
South Jade Carving Factory	Nánfāng Yùdiāo Chǎng	南方玉雕厂
Sportsman's American Bar and Restaurant	Xiūxián Bā Xīcāntīng	休闲吧西餐厅
Sun Yat-sen Memorial Hall	Sūn Zhōngshān Jìniàn Táng	孙中山纪念堂

ENGLISH	PINYIN	CHINESE CHARACTERS
Tang Yuan	Táng Yuàn	唐苑
Tao Tao Ju	Táotáo Jū	陶陶居
Taxis	chūzū chē	出租车
Teem Plaza	Tiānhé Chéng	天河城
That's PRD	Chéngshì Mànbù Zhūjiāng Sānjiǎozhōu	《城市漫步》珠江三角洲
The Customs Hotel	Hǎiguān Bīnguǎn	海关宾馆
The Italian Restaurant	Xiǎojiē Fēngqíng	小街风情
The Paddy Field Bar	Àiěrlán Cānbā	爱尔兰餐吧
The Roof	Lín Xiāo Gē	凌宵阁
Tian Lun International Hotel	Tiānlún Wànyí Jiǔdiàn	天伦万怡酒店
Tianhe Bus Station	Tiānhé Bāshì Zhàn	天河巴士站
Tianhe District	Tiānhé Qū	天河区
Tianhe Stadium Complex	Tiānhé Tǐyù Zhōngxīn	天河体育中心
Tomb of the Southern Yue Kings	Nányuè Wáng Mù	南岳王墓
Tower Controlling the Sea	Zhènhǎi Lóu	镇海楼
Trade fair information	Guǎngjiāohuì Xìnxī	广交会信息
U.S. Consulate	Měiguó Lǐngshìguǎn	美国领事馆
Victory Hotel	Shènglì Bīnguǎn	胜利宾馆
Vitamin Creative Space	Wéitāmìng Yìshù Kōngjiān	维他命艺术空间
White Cloud Mountain	Báiyúnshān	白云山
White Swan Hotel	Báitiāné Jiǔdiàn	白天鹅酒店
White Swan Arcade	Báitiānér Shāngchǎng	白天鹅商场
White Swan Hotel Golf Practice Center	Báitiān É Gāoěrfū Liànxíchǎng	白天鹅酒店高尔夫练习场
Xinghai Concert Hall	Xīnghǎi Yīnyuètīng	星海音乐厅
Xinhua Bookstore	Xīnhuá Shūdiàn	新华书店
Yan Yang Tian Agency	Yàn Yáng Tiān Lǚxíngshè	广州艳阳天旅行社
Yes Club	Yīnyuè Gōngchǎng	音乐工厂
Yidu restaurant	Yìdū Jiǔjiā	艺都酒家
Yuexiu Park	Yuèxiù Gōngyuán	越秀公园
SHENZHEN	**SHENZHÈN**	**深圳**
Huaqiaocheng station	Huánqiáochéng Zhàn	华侨城站
OCT district	HuáQiáo Chéng	华侨城
3 colors Bar	Sānyuánsè Jiǔbā	三原色酒吧
360 Degree Bar	Sānbǎi Liùshí Dù Jiǔbā	360度酒吧

6

ENGLISH	PINYIN	CHINESE CHARACTERS
Bao'an	Bǎoān	保安
Blue Italian Seafood & Grill	Yìdàlì Cāntīng	意大利餐厅
Boao Scenic Zone	Bóáo fēngjǐng Qu	博鳌风景区
Browns Wine Bar& Cigar House	Bùlǎngshì Pútáojiǔ Xuějiābā	布朗士葡萄酒雪茄吧
Chiu Chow Cuisine	Cháozhōu Cài	潮洲菜
CITIC City Plaza	Shēnzhèn Zhōngxìn Dàshà	深圳中信大厦
Crowne Plaza	Wēinísī Huángguān Jiàrì Jiǔdiàn	威尼斯皇冠假日酒店
Dafen Oil Painting Village	Dàfēn Yóuhuà Shìjiè	大芬油画世界
Dapeng Fortress	Dàpéng Gǔchéng	大鹏古城
Dongmen Shopping Plaza	Dōngmén Lǎojiē	东门老街
Er Ding Mu	Èrdīngmù	二丁目
Foodfeast	Lǎolóng Fēngwèi Shífǔ	老隆风味食府
Foshan	Fóshān	佛山
Futian	Fútián	福田
Futian district Shenzhen	Shēnzhèn Fútián	深圳福田
Grand Bay View	Zhūhǎi Hǎiwān Dà Jiǔdiàn	珠海海湾大酒店
Greenland Lounge	Lǜjiànláng Dàtángbā	绿涧廊大堂吧
Haikou	Hǎikǒu	海口
Hainan Island	Hǎinán Dǎo	海南岛
Happy Kingdom	Huānlè Gǔ	欢乐谷
He Xiangning Art Museum	Héxiāngníng Měishùguǎn	何香凝美术馆
Holiday Inn Zhuhai	Zhūhǎi Yuècái Jiàrì Jiǔdiàn	珠海粤财假日酒店
Huaqiao Cheng Metro	Huáqiáochéng Dìtiězhàn	华侨城地铁站
Jinye Hotel	Jīnyè Jiǔdiàn	金叶酒店
Lakewood Golf Club	Zhūhǎi Cuìhú Gāoěrfú Qiúhuì	珠海翠湖高尔夫球会
Lakewood Golf Club	Zhūhǎi Cuìhú Gāoěrfú Qiúhuì	珠海翠湖高尔夫球会
Landmark Shenzhen	Fùyuàn Jiǔdiàn	富苑酒店
Lao Yuan Zi	Láo Yuànzī	老院子
Little India	Xiǎo Yìndù Cāntīng	小印度餐厅
Lo Wu Commercial City	Luóhú Shāngyè Chéng	罗湖商业城
Longgang	Lónggǎng	龙岗
Longgang Hakka Customs Museum	Lónggǎng Kèjiārén Bówùguǎn	龙岗客家人博物馆
Lover's Road	Qínlu Lù	情侣路
Luohu	Luóhú	罗湖
Macau Ferry Terminal	Àomén Mǎtóu	澳门码头

ENGLISH	PINYIN	CHINESE CHARACTERS
Minghua Cruise Inn	Mínghuálún Jiǔdiàn	明华轮酒店
Minsk World	Míngsīkè Hángmǔ	明思克航母世界
Mission Hills Golf Club	Guānlán Gāoěrfū	观澜高尔夫
Nan Hai	Nánhǎi	南海
Nanshan	Nánshān	南山
OCT Contemporary Art Terminal	OCT Dāngdài Yìshù Zhōngxīn	OCT当代艺术中心
Outer Shenzhen	Shēnzhèn zhōubiān,	深圳周边
Overseas Chinese Town	Huáqiáo Chéng	华侨城
Paradise Hill	Shíjǐngshān Lǚyóu Zhōngxīn Dà Jiǔdiàn	石景山旅游中心大酒店
Pengcheng Village	Péngchéng Cūn	鹏城村
San Dao Plaza	Sāndǎo Zhōngxīn	三島中心
Sand River Golf Club	Shāhé agāoěrfū Qiúhuì	沙河高尔夫球会
Sanya	Sānyà	三亚
Shangri-La Shenzhen	Shēnzhèn Xiānggélǐlā Jiǔdiàn	深圳香格里拉酒店
Shangri-La Zhongshan	Zhōngshān Xiāng Gé Lǐ Lā Jiǔ Diàn	中山香格里拉酒店
Shanshui Trends Hotel	Shānshuǐ Hánguó Jiǔdiàn	山水韩国酒店
Shekou	Shékǒu	蛇口
Shenzhen Airport	Shēnzhèn Jīchǎng	深圳机场
Shenzhen Longgang Tourist Bureau	Shēnzhènshì Lónggǎng Lǚyóujú	深圳市龙岗区旅游局
Shenzhen North Sea Restaurant	Shēnzhèn Běihǎi Yúcūn Jiǔjiā	深圳北海渔村酒家
Shenzhen Sea view	Shēnzhèn Huáqiáochéng Hǎijǐn JiǔDiàn	深圳华侨城海景酒店
Splendid China	Jǐnxiù Zhōnghuá	锦绣中华
Sun Yat-sen Memorial Hall	Zhōngshān Jìniàntáng	中山纪念堂
Sunday Chiu Chow King	Sāndǎo Cháohuáng Yuècài Jiǔlóu	三岛潮皇粤菜酒楼
Sunwen West Road	Sūnwén Xīlù	孙文西路
TaiZi Bar Street	Tàizǐlù Jiǔbājiē	太子路酒吧街
The Pavilion	Shèngtíngyuàn Jiǔdiàn	圣廷苑酒店
True Colors	Běnsè Yīnyuè	本色音乐
Turbojet Company	Jīchǎng pēnshè fēiháng	机场喷射飞航
V-Bar	Ūī Bā	V 吧
Windows of the World	Shìjiè Zhīchuāng	世界之窗
Xishan Temple	Xīshān Miào	西山庙

ENGLISH	PINYIN	CHINESE CHARACTERS
Yantian	Yántián	盐田
Yingbin Street	Yínbīn Dàdào	迎宾大道
YOKOHAMA	Héngbīn Rìběn Liàolǐ	横滨日本料理
Zhongshan City	Zhōngshān Shì	中山市
Zhongshan Fuhua Hotel	Zhōngshān Fùhuá Jiǔdiàn	中山富华酒店
Zhongshan Hot Springs Resort	Zhōngshān Wēnquán Bīnguǎn	中山温泉宾馆
Zhuhai	Zhūhǎi	珠海
Zhuhai Hotel	Zhūǎl Bīnguǎn	珠海宾馆
Zhuhai International Airport	Zhūhǎi Guójì JīChǎng	珠海国际机场

The Southwest

GUANGXI, GUIZHOU & YUNNAN

A lazy ride down the Li River at sunset, Guilin.

WORD OF MOUTH

"[V]isit Longshen rice fields from Guilin. It is a great day trip with unforgettable sights (not just the rice fields themselves but the trip there as well). The 'Dragon back' is one of the most impressive visual experiences I have encountered."

—Paulchili

WELCOME TO THE SOUTHWEST

Miao Minority during their New Year Celebration in Kaili, Guizhou province.

TOP REASONS TO GO

★ **Lose Yourself in Lijiang:** Treasured by the Chinese and home to a UNESCO World Heritage Site, the winding cobblestone lanes of Lijiang beckon to all.

★ **Lush Xishuangbanna Rain Forests:** Hugging the borders of Laos and Myanmar, this small city in Yunnan is home to the legendary Dai minority people, who make you feel far from the rest of China.

★ **Trek Tiger Leaping Gorge:** Explore the deepest gorge in the world, and one of the most scenic spots in all of Yunnan, and possibly China.

★ **Guizhou's Eye-Popping Huangguoshu Falls:** Travel to the Baishui River in Guizhou, where the largest waterfall in China plummets 230 feet.

★ **Ballooning Yangshuo:** Float over this strange lunarlike landscape of limestone karsts.

1 Guangxi. Having inspired countless paintings and poems in the past, the spectacular karst scenery of Guilin and Yangshuo today inspires travelers who are in search of an unforgettable Chinese experience. Capital city Nanning is being groomed as China's gateway to Vietnam. Guangxi is officially Guangxi Zhuang Autonomous Region, not a province.

2 Guizhou. Off the beaten path, this fascinating province is known for its undulating mountains, terraced fields, traditional villages, frequent festivals, and China's largest waterfall, Huangguoshu. More than a third of the population is made up of Dong, Hui, Yao, Zhuang, and Miao (known in the West as the Hmong) peoples.

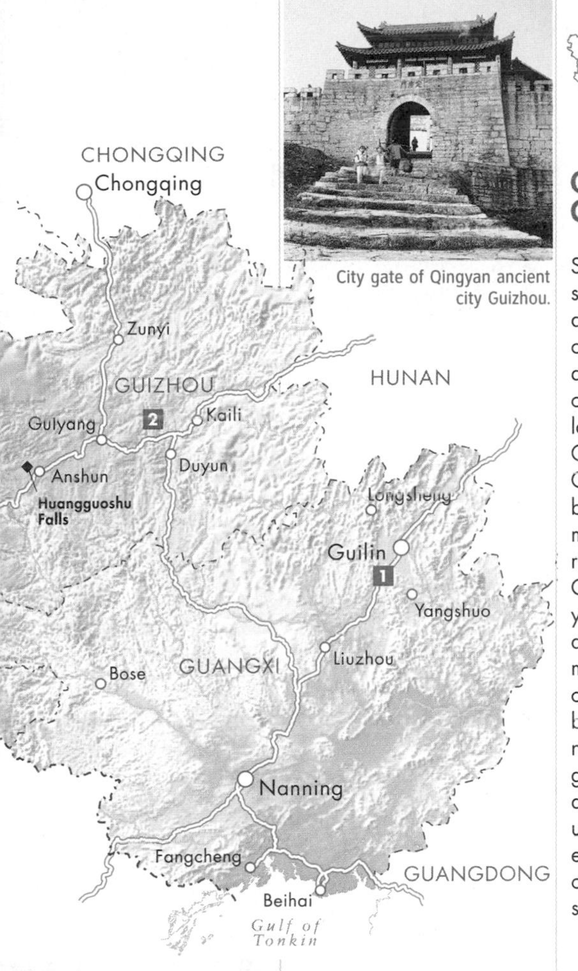

City gate of Qingyan ancient city Guizhou.

GETTING ORIENTED

Southwest China can be summed up by one word: diversity. The regions of Guangxi, Guizhou, and Yunnan offer some of China's most singular travel experiences. Guilin and Yangshuo in Guangxi are surrounded by otherworldly karst mountains and idyllic rivers. Qianling Park in Guizhou's capital, Guiyang, has a beautiful Buddhist temple, hundreds of monkeys, and amazing city views. Stretching between Tibet and Vietnam, Yunnan province's geographic, biological and ethnic diversity is unparalleled anywhere else in China. This part of the world must be seen to be believed.

3 Yunnan. The sleepy towns of Lijiang and Dali offer glimpses into the centuries-old traditions of the Naxi and Bai ethnic groups. For a more rugged experience, hike through the breathtaking Tiger Leaping Gorge. If a slow boat on the Mekong appeals, head south to Jinghong and chill out in the tropics.

An old bridge in Lijiang.

THE SOUTHWEST PLANNER

On the Menu

From sour and spicy Dai dishes with fresh pepper to chicken steamed in clay pots and bitter melon served with eggs, Southwest China's cuisine is unique.

Bordering Sichuan and Hunan provinces to the north and Myanmar, Laos, and Vietnam to the south, the region is sandwiched between some of the spiciest cuisines on earth. Yet meals retain a palatable earthiness, defined by river fish, terraced rice, mountain medicinal herbs, and wild mushrooms.

Particularly popular are soup-based dishes served with thin, spaghetti-like rice-noodles that come with fresh mint, oil, slices of pork, carrots, and corn. Other amazing delicacies involve steaming sticky rice inside bamboo. The province sees its fair share of Tibetan delights, too, including yak meat and yoghurt-wine.

Guangxi's Silver-Toothed Touts

Aggressive touts are a fact of life for Western travelers in hyper-capitalist China. Guangxi province is known for the tenacity of its touts—mostly older, tribal women with silver teeth (as is the local custom). To these wandering merchants, a Western traveler is a coin purse with legs.

It's not uncommon for half a dozen of these women to surround you at any given site, shouting "water" and "postcard." They'll follow you around until you buy something from each of them.

It's hard for travelers to maintain equilibrium when confronted with a gaggle of old women who seem doggedly intent on turning a hiking trip around, say, the Longsheng Rice Terraces into a no-win trinket-buying binge. Polite "no, thank you's" can soon become expletive-laden tirades, inevitably leading to remorse for cursing a poverty-stricken old woman.

What's worse, cursing accomplishes nothing. No sooner will the last bitter word leave your lips than Granny will thrust a pack of commemorative postcards at you and shout "10 yuan!"

Consider the purchasing of minor souvenirs or unwanted sodas as part of the experience, keep a few yuan handy for just that, and to deal with it smilingly. Failing that, you can always run. But remember, these old women know all the shortcuts, and you'll tire out and need to buy a beverage anyway. And maybe some postcards as well.

Money Matters

Money can be changed in the major hotels or at the Bank of China. The Guilin and Nanning airports have branches and ATMs, and all Bank of China ATMs take international cards.

Foreign bank cards on the Cirrus or Plus systems can be used at ATMs displaying their respective logos. Bank of China and ICBC are your best bets. When traveling to remote parts of the region, have cash on hand, as ATMs accepting foreign cards are rare.

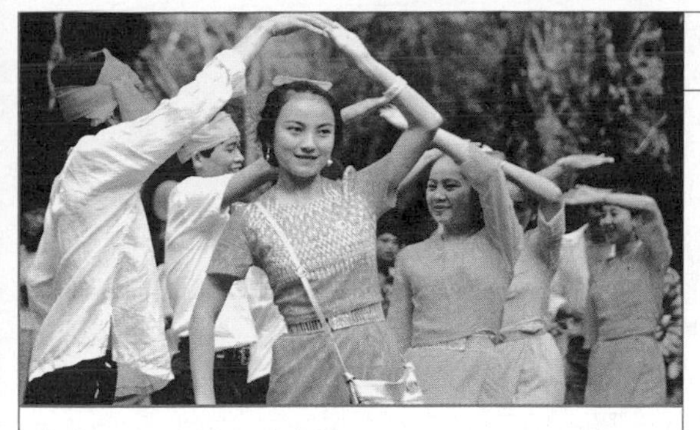

Minority Festivals

In Kunming, Dali, and villages around Yunnan, the Yi and Bai peoples hold their Torch Festivals on the 24th day of the sixth lunar month. They throw handfuls of pine resin into bonfires, alighting the night sky with clouds of sparks. The Dai Water Splashing Festival in the rain forests of Xishuangbanna on the 22nd day of the third lunar month is liquid pandemonium. Its purpose is to wash away the sorrow of the old year and refresh you for the new.

Dali has two festivals of note: the Third Moon Fair (middle of third lunar month) during which people from all around Yunnan come to Dali to sell their wares; and the Three Temples Festival (usually May). The Sister's Meal Festival, celebrated in the middle of the third lunar month by Miao people throughout Guizhou, is dedicated to unmarried women. During the great rice harvest, special brightly colored dishes are made and at nightfall, there's much ado about courtship, dancing, and old-fashioned flirting. The Zhuang Singing Festival turns Guangxi's countryside into an ocean of song. On the third day of the third lunar month, the Zhuang gather and sing to honor Liu Sanjie ("Third Sister Liu"), the goddess of song. Singing "battles" ensue between groups who sing—often improvising—at each other until a group concedes.

DINING AND LODGING PRICE CATEGORIES IN YUAN

¢	$	$$	$$$	$$$$
Restaurants				
under Y25	Y25–Y49	Y50–Y99	Y100–Y165	over Y165
Hotels				
under Y700	Y700–Y1,099	Y1,100–Y1,399	Y1,400–Y1,800	over Y1,800

Restaurant prices are for a main course, excluding tips (there is no sales/retail tax in China). Hotel prices are for a standard double room, including taxes.

Three Climates

When you are packing for travel in Southwest China, think of the region as three distinct zones separated by altitude. Steamy tropical lowlands spread across the southern halves of Yunnan and Guangxi. The mountainous highlands of central and northwest Yunnan are characterized by intense, high-UV sun, long rainy seasons, and cold winters. Somewhere in between are the cloudy mountain scenes found throughout Guizhou and northern Guangxi. Each zone requires a different packing strategy.

In summer, the monsoon rains can be heavy. Keep abreast of weather reports on the Internet at any of the numerous cafés, hostels, and hotels. Temperatures don't get as hot as the tropics or as cold as the highlands, but summers can be quite hot in Guilin and Yangshuo, and winters in Guiyang can be cold enough for snow. The best time of year is spring, in April or early May. Winter months can be surprisingly cold (except in southern Guangxi and Yunnan), and the summertime heat is stifling. Mid-September can also be a comfortable time to travel. The falls at Huangguoshu are at their best in the rainy season from May through October.

By Joshua Samuel Brown and Christopher Horton

THE SOUTHWESTERN PROVINCES ARE THE most alluring destinations in the country. This region lays claim to some of the most breathtaking scenery in all of China—the moonscape limestone karsts and river scenery of Yangshuo, China's mightiest waterfall in Guizhou, to Yunnan's tropical rain forests and spectacular Tiger Leaping Gorge.

Rich in ethnic diversity and culture, Yunnan is home to almost a third of China's ethnic minorities. In 1958, Guangxi became an autonomous region in an attempt to quell the friction between the Zhuang minority and the ethnic Han majority. Yunnan, Guanxi, and Guizhou represent the complex tapestry of China's ethnic diversity.

GUANGXI

Known throughout China for its fairy-tale scenery, Guangxi's rivers, valleys, and stone peaks have inspired painters and poets for centuries. From the distinctive terraced rice fields of Longsheng, which resemble a dragon's spine, to the karst rock formations that surround Guilin and Yangshuo and rise from the coastal plain in the south, Guangxi is quite possibly the most picturesque of China's regions.

A significant portion of Guangxi's population consists of ethnic minorities: the Dong, Gelao, Hui, Jing, Miao, Shui, Yao, Yi, and, in particular, the Zhuang people, who constitute about a third of the province's population. Guangxi has often been the object of struggle between these indigenous peoples and the Han, who established their rule only in the 19th century. Today it is one of five autonomous regions, which, in theory, have an element of self-government.

The climate is subtropical, affected by seasonal monsoons, with long, hot, humid, and frequently wet summers and mild winters. Guangxi is one of the most popular travel destinations in China.

LONGSHENG LONGJI RICE TERRACES

120 km (74 mi; 3 hrs by bus) northwest of Guilin.

A mesmerizing pattern of undulating fields has been cut into the hills up to a height of 2,625 feet at the **Longsheng Longji Rice Terraces.** These terraces, known as the "Dragon's Backbone," are amazing in both their scale and their beauty. They are worked, and have been for generations, by rice farmers from the local Yao, Dong, Zhuang, and Miao communities, who build their houses in villages on the terraced hills. *Y30.*

GETTING HERE AND AROUND

Buses are the best way to get to Longsheng. The only alternative to a bus is to pay a premium to retain a taxi's services for the day, which will set you back at least Y500.

Buses heading to Longsheng from Guilin's bus station leave every 15 minutes and take about 4 hours (Y15). The express bus back to Guilin takes 3 hours and departs Longsheng every two hours (Y20).

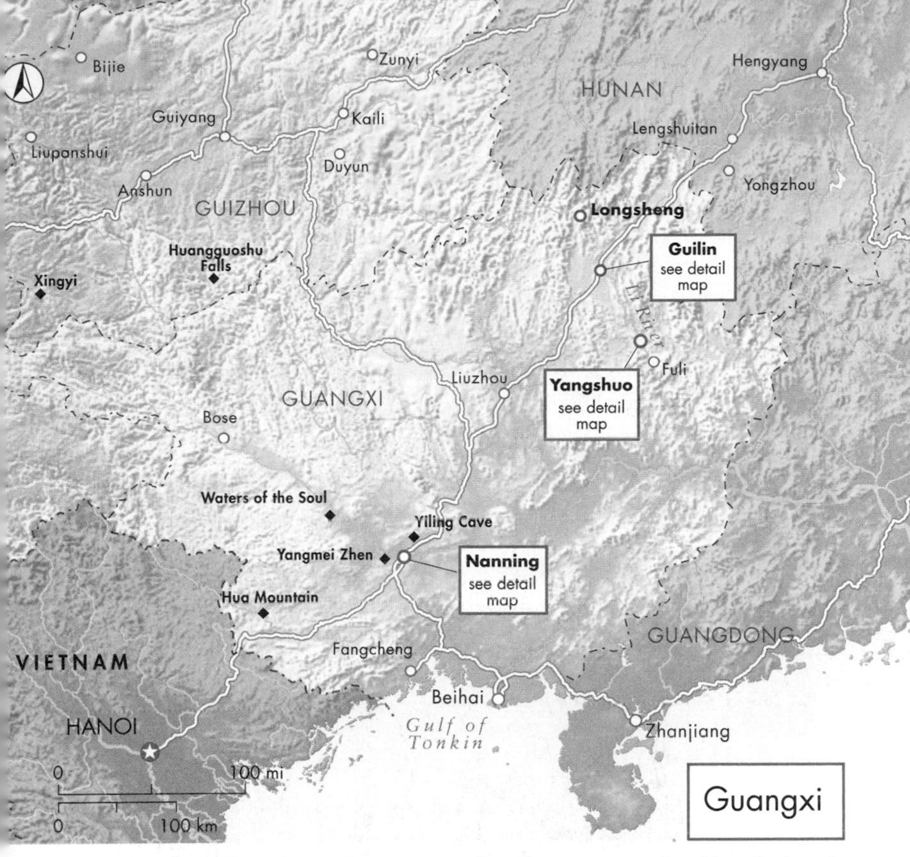

Longsheng is not home to any local tour companies. Travel plans in Longsheng are best arranged through Guilin travel agencies, and the stretch of Binjiang Lu south of the Sheraton has several English-speaking travel agencies.

WHERE TO STAY AND EAT

¢–$ **Li Qing Restaurant.** This extremely popular restaurant, in addition to more well-known Chinese dishes, serves a number of traditional dishes like bamboo stuffed with sticky rice, and stir-fried mountain vegetables. *Ji Lu, Ping'an* *0773/758–3048* *No credit cards.*

¢ **Li Qing Guesthouse.** In the nearby village of Ping'an, the Li Qing Guesthouse is run by sisters Liao Yan Li and Liao Yan Qing. The guesthouse is two houses; the older one has dorm-style rooms, and the newer one has single and double rooms with private baths. **Pros:** friendly staff caters well to Western guests. **Cons:** can be noisy on weekends. *Ji Lu, Ping'an* *0773/758–3048* *12 rooms* *In-hotel: restaurant, public Internet, no elevator* *No credit cards.*

GUILIN

> **WORD OF MOUTH**
>
> "The rice terraces are absolutely stunning. This was definitely the highlight of my month in China. I could easily see myself staying for an entire summer." —Lil1210

500 km (310 mi; 13 hrs by train) northwest of Hong Kong; 1,675 km (1,039 mi; 22 hrs by train) southwest of Beijing.

Guilin has the good fortune of being situated in the middle of some of the world's most beautiful landscapes. This landscape of limestone karst hills and mountains, rising almost vertically from the earth, has a dreamy, hypnotic quality. They were formed 200 million years ago, when the area was under the sea. As the land beneath began to push upward, the sea receded, and the effects of the ensuing erosion over thousands of years produced this sublime scenery.

Architecturally, the city lacks charm, having been heavily bombed during the Sino-Japanese War and rebuilt in the utilitarian style popular in the 1950s. Still, the river city is replete with beautiful parks and bridges, and has a number of historical sites that make it worthy of exploration. It's also a good base from which to explore Northern Guangxi.

GETTING HERE AND AROUND

BY AIR About 28 km (17 mi) southwest of the city center, Guilin Liangjiang International Airport has flights to cities throughout China as well as throughout Asia. An airport shuttle bus, which operates daily from 6:30 AM to 8 PM, runs between the airport and the Aviation Building located at 18 Shanghai Lu, across the street from the main bus station. The cost is Y20 per person.

BY BUS The main bus station in Guilin is just north of the train station on Zhongshan Nan Lu. Short- and long-distance buses connect Guilin to nearby cities, including Yangshuo, Longsheng, Liuzhou, and Nanning. Long-distance sleeper coaches travel to cities throughout the Pearl River Delta.

BY TRAIN Guilin is linked by daily rail service with most major cities in China. Most long-distance trains arrive at Guilin's South Railway Station.

ESSENTIALS

Air Contacts Guilin Liangjiang International Airport (☎ *0773/284–5359*).

Banks Bank of China (✉ *5 Shanhu Bei Lu* ☎ *0773/280–2867* ✉ *Guilin Liangjiang International Airport* ☎ *0773/284–4020*).

Bus Contacts Guilin Bus Station (✉ *Off Zhongshan Nan Lu* ☎ *0773/382–2153*).

Medical Assistance Guilin People's Hospital (✉ *12 Wenming Lu* ☎ *0773/282–8712*).

Public Security Bureau PSB Guilin (✉ *16 Shi Jia Yuan Rd.* ☎ *773/582–9930*).

Train Contacts Guilin Railway Station (✉ *Off Zhongshan Nan Lu* ☎ *0773/383–3124*).

Exploring ▼

- Elephant Trunk Hill 1
- Ming Tomb 3
- Peak of Solitary Beauty 2
- Seven Star Park 4

Hotels & Restaurants ▼

- Golden Elephant Hotel .. 1
- The Here 6
- Inaka 2
- Lijiang Waterfall Guilin 3
- Rosemary Cafe 5
- Sheraton Guilin 4
- Wang Cheng Fan Dian 7

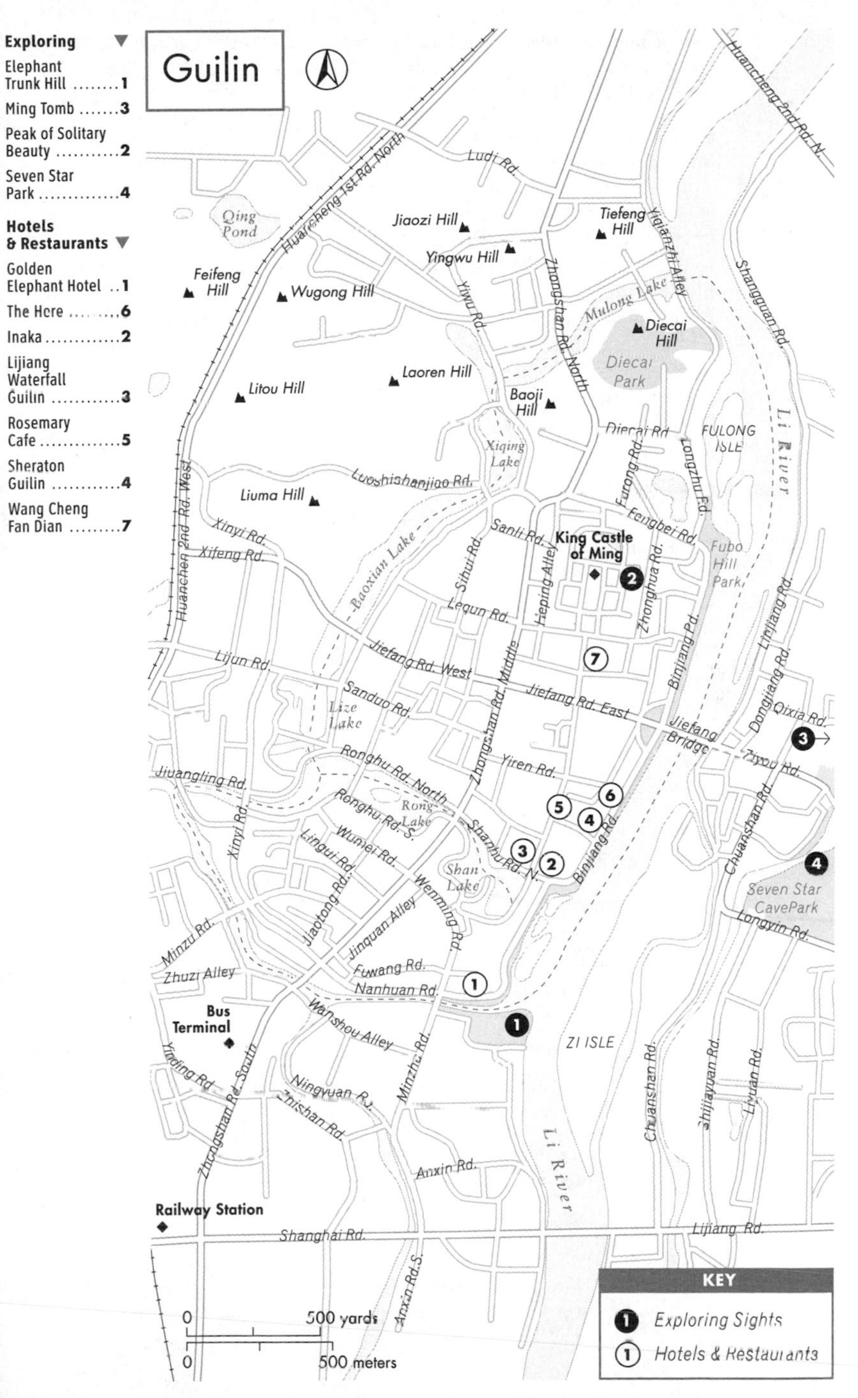

Visitor and Tour Info **China International Travel Service (CITS)** (✉ *11 Binjiang Lu* ☎ *0773/288–0319*). **China Travel Service (CTS)** (✉ *11 Binjiang Lu* ☎ *0773/283–3986* 🌐 *en.guilincits.com*).

EXPLORING GUILIN

MAIN ATTRACTIONS

❷ The 492-foot **Peak of Solitary Beauty** *(Duxiu Feng)*, with carved stone stairs leading to the top, offers an unparalleled view of Guilin. It's one of the attractions of the **Princess City Solitary Beauty Park.** Surrounded by an ancient wall outside of which vendors hawk their wares, sits the heart of old Guilin. Inside are the decaying remains of an ancient Ming Dynasty palace built in 1393 and Guilin's Confucius temple. Sun Yat-sen lived here for a few months in the winter of 1921 (a fact duly noted on the wall by the outside gate). Cixi, the last empress of China, inscribed the character for "longevity" on a rock within these walls. ✉ *Heart of Old Guilin, in center of city, 2 blocks north of Zhengyang Lu pedestrian mall* ☎ *No phone* *Y50* *Daily 8–6.*

❹ **Seven Star Park** *(Qixing Gongyuan)* gets its name from the arrangement of its hills, said to resemble the Big Dipper. At the center of this huge park on the east side of the Li river is **Putuo Mountain** (Putuoshan), atop of which sits a lovely pavilion housing a number of famous examples of Tang calligraphy. Indeed, calligraphy abounds on the side of this hill, mostly the work of Ming Dynasty Taoist philosopher Pan Changjing. Nearby is **Seven Star Cliff** (Qixing Dong) with several large caves open for exploration. The largest contains rock formations that are thought to resemble a lion with a ball, an elephant, and other figures. An inscription in the cave dates from AD 590. Seven Star Park also contains Guilin City Zoo, which is only worth a stop if you have kids in tow. It costs an additional Y30. ✉ *1 km (½ mi) east of downtown Guilin* ☎ *No phone* *Y30* *Daily 8–5.*

❶ **Elephant Trunk Hill** *(Xiangbi Shan)* once appeared on Chinese currency bills. On the banks of the river in the southern part of the city, it takes its name from a rock formation arching into the river like the trunk of an elephant. Nearby is a grotto covered in poetic inscriptions inspired by the beauty of the place, some by the greatest poets of the Song Dynasty. ✉ *Binjiang Lu, across from Golden Elephant Hotel* ☎ *0773/258–6602* *Y25* *Daily 7 AM–7 PM.*

IF YOU HAVE TIME

❸ East of the town is the **Ming Tomb** *(Zhu Shouqian Ling)*, the tomb of Zhu Shouqian, the nephew of the first Ming emperor, who founded a principality here. It makes a pleasant excursion by bicycle. To get here, take Jiefang Dong Lu east about 9 km (5 mi). ✉ *Jiefang Dong Lu* ☎ *No phone* *Y40* *Daily 8:30–5:30.*

WHERE TO EAT

Guilin's notable local dishes are limited to horsemeat and rice noodles. Freshwater fish is popular with locals, but eat it only if you dare. The Zhengyang Lu pedestrian street has the best variety of dining spots.

CLOSE UP

The Zhuang & the Miao

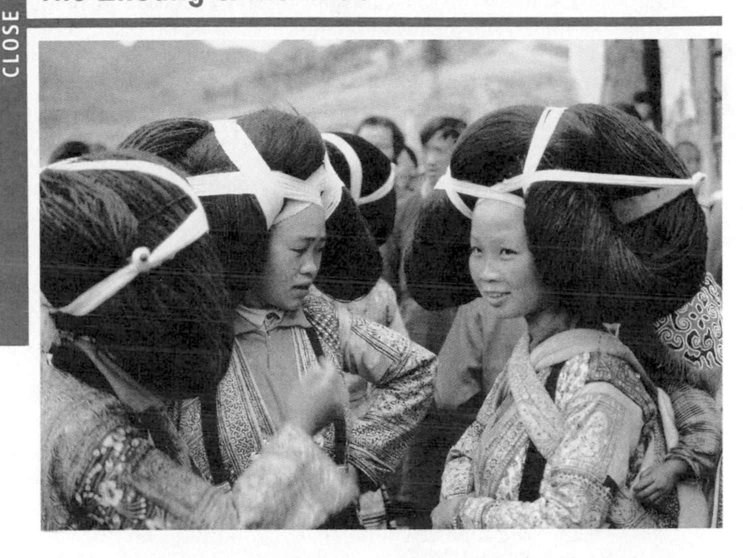

The Zhuang are China's largest minority population, totaling more than 16 million. Most Zhuang are in Guangxi Zhuang Autonomous Region (where they constitute more than 85% of the population), Guizhou, Yunnan, and Guangdong provinces. The Zhuang language is part of the Tai-Kadai family, related to Thai and fellow Chinese minority the Dai. Historically, the Zhuang have had almost constant friction with China's Han majority, but that's improved since the Guangxi Zhuang Autonomous region was established in 1958. In many ways the Zhuang are becoming assimilated into the dominant Han Chinese culture, but they have still preserved their strong culture and its music and dance traditions. Clothing varies from region to region but mostly consists of collarless, embroidered jackets buttoned to the left, loose wide trousers or pleated skirts, embroidered belts or black square headbands.

The Miao are also a large minority group and spread across much of southern China. Throughout their history, the Miao have had to deal with Han China's southward expansion, which drove them into marginal, chiefly mountainous areas in southern China and northern areas of Myanmar, Thailand, Laos, and Vietnam. Living in such isolated regions, the Miao group developed into several subsets, including Black, Red, Green, and Big Flowery Miao. Most of China's nearly 10 million Miao are in Guizhou province, where local markets feature the intricate and expert craftsmanship of the Miao, who specialize in jewelry, embroidery, and batik. The Miao are also renowned for their festivals, particularly the Lusheng festival, which occurs from the 11th to the 18th of the first lunar month. Named after a Miao reed instrument, Lusheng is a week of lively music, dancing, horse races, and bullfights. The Guizhou city of Kaili is the center of Miao festivals, hosting more than 120 each year.

$–$$ ITALIAN ★ **The Here.** Although the sign outside says LITTLE ITALIAN, this is one of three The Here restaurants in Guangxi. Branches are in Yangshuo and Nanning. The menu is straightforward: pizza, pasta, and sandwiches made fresh when you order. The cozy urban decor creates an ideal environment for reading a book, checking your e-mail, or planning the next step in your trip. Most of the young, friendly staff speaks English. *1–4, 18 Binjiang Lu 0773/311–1068 No credit cards.*

$$–$$$ JAPANESE **Inaka.** Resembling a Japanese home, this excellent restaurant sits at the southern end of Zhengyang Lu pedestrian mall. The interior, which recalls a temple-style building, has a low-key vibe. The sashimi and sushi—not easy to find in cities away from the coast—are fresh and excellent. The best deals are the four-course lunch specials, which begin with miso soup and end with a dessert made from sweetened bean curd. *1 Zhengyang Lu 0773/280–2888 MC, V.*

¢–$$ AMERICAN **Rosemary Café.** Every city has at least one restaurant that serves as a home away from home for expats. The kitchen serves up a wide selection of familiar dishes, including soups like vegetarian vegetable and chicken noodle. There are great hamburgers and sandwiches. *Yiren Lu, 1 block east of clock tower on Zhengyang Lu pedestrian street 0773/281–0063 No credit cards.*

¢–$ CHINESE **Wang Cheng Fan Dian.** This restaurant south of the Peak of Solitary Beauty is extremely popular with students from the nearby college. It serves a wide variety of dishes, including many made with horse, including noodles stir-fried with horse and a spicy hotpot with horse and vegetables. *56 Zhengyang Lu, 1 block north of pedestrian mall 0773/282–2284 No credit cards.*

WHERE TO STAY

¢ ★ **Golden Elephant Hotel.** If you're on a budget, this clean, comfortable hotel will fit the bill. The guest rooms are on the frumpy side, and the beds are hard; however, many have terrific views of Elephant Trunk Hill. The Korean restaurant on the first floor is good. **Pros:** decent value, good location. **Cons:** lackluster decor, not much English spoken. *8 Binjiang Lu 0773/289–2821 50 rooms In-room: Ethernet. In-hotel: 2 restaurants, no-smoking rooms AE, MC, V.*

$$$–$$$$ **Lijiang Waterfall Guilin** *(Lijiang Da Pubu Jiudian).* Overlooking the river, this luxury hotel also has breathtaking views of Elephant Trunk Hill and Seven Star Park. Rooms are clean, spacious, and as the hotel is one of the city's newest, extremely modern. Five excellent restaurants offer Asian and Western cuisine. Every night at 8:30 the hotel hosts a 15-minute watershow that turns the back of the building into a massive waterfall. **Pros:** reasonable rooms for reasonable rates. **Cons:** staff doesn't speak much English. *1 Shanhu Bei Lu South end of Zhengyang Lu pedestrian street 0773/282–2881 www.waterfallguilin.com 430 rooms, 23 suites In-room: safe, Ethernet, refrigerator. In-hotel: 5 restaurants, bar, pool, gym, concierge, laundry service, airport shuttle, no-smoking rooms AE, MC, V.*

$$–$$$$ ★ **Sheraton Guilin** *(Guilin Dayu Dafandian).* This recently renovated Sheraton is easily the nicest. The lobby is very chic, with its sunny atrium and glass elevators that whisk you up to your room. Rooms are clean and spacious, and the new club lounge on the top floor offers

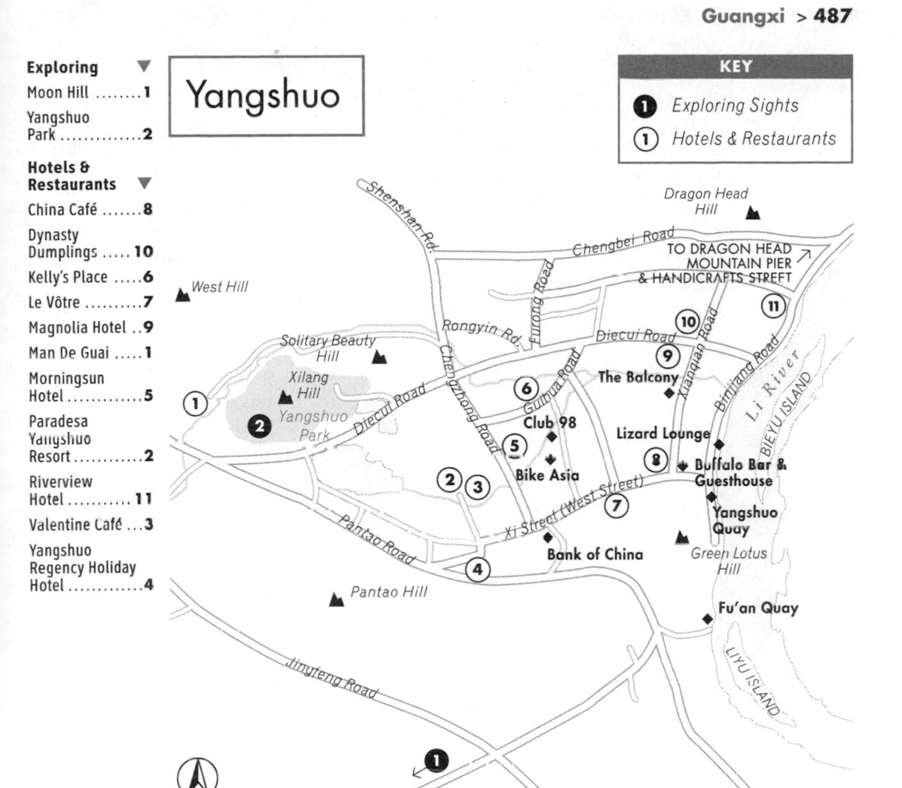

rooftop seating with some of the best views of the city and the surrounding mountains. The Chinese restaurant on the first floor offers a delicious culinary tour of China, while the Western restaurant on the second floor offers creative dishes such as Peking duck quesadillas and standards including Australian rack of lamb. **Pros:** professional management, English-speaking staff. **Cons:** slightly overpriced. ⊠ *15 Binjiang Lu, on west bank of Li River* ☎ *0773/282–5588* 🌐 *www.sheraton.com/guilin* *411 rooms, 19 suites* *In-room: safe, Ethernet, refrigerator. In-hotel: 3 restaurants, room service, bar* ▭ *AE, MC, V.*

NIGHTLIFE AND THE ARTS

For a quieter evening of drinks and conversation, try **Paulaner** (⊠ *2 Zhengyang Lu* ☎ *0773/286–8698*), which has a good selection of mostly German and Chinese beers plus pizza, pasta, and sandwiches. Just next door, **Paddie's** (⊠ *4 Zhengyang Lu* ☎ *0773/285–1239*) is a no-frills pub selling big mugs of draft beer for Y25. Both Paulaner and Paddie's have outdoor seating.

YANGSHUO

70 km (43 mi; 1 hr by bus) south of Guilin.

Yangshuo has taken center stage as the province's top tourist destination. At the heart of the city is West Street, a pedestrian mall extending to the Li River. Many visitors are content to spend a few days wandering up and down the main drag, eating, drinking, and gazing over the low-slung traditional structures facing toward the fang-shaped peaks that surround the town. Yangshuo is fast becoming a destination for adventure travel, and the countryside is filled with opportunities for biking, hiking, rock climbing, caving, and even hot-air ballooning.

GETTING HERE AND AROUND

Arriving via train or airplane means traveling through Guilin (⇨*above*). You can also get from Guilin to Yangshuo by bus or minibus or via a costly but pleasant boat trip.

BY AIR Guilin Liangjiang International Airport is the gateway to Yangshuo. Taxis from Guilin Airport to Yangshuo cost around Y200.

BY BOAT The boat that traverses the Li River from Guilin to Yangshuo takes approximately four hours. At Y380 for a round-trip ticket, it's costlier than other modes of travel, but the trip is a pleasant and scenic. Tickets are available from any of the countless travel agents in Guilin or Yangshuo.

BY BUS Departing from the Guilin Train Station, express luxury buses travel between Guilin and Yangshuo every half hour between 7 AM and 8 PM. The trip takes just over an hour in these air-conditioned and smoke-free buses that cost Y15.

TOURS

If getting wet and muddy underground is your idea of a good time, look no farther than Water Cave, the deepest and largest underground grotto in the area. Accessible only by a flat-bottom boat, Water Cave has hikes among stalactites, a mud bath, and a number of crystal-clear pools perfect for washing off all that mud. Tours can be arranged through any of the many travel agencies in the Xi Jie area. Charm Yangshuo Tour is recommended.

ESSENTIALS

Banks Bank of China (✉ *93 Pantao Lu* ☎ *0773/882–0260*).

Bus Contacts Yangshuo Bus Station (✉ *Pantao Lu, across from Yangshuo Park* ☎ *0773/882–2188*).

Public Security Bureau PSB Yangshuo (✉ *Pan Tao Lu* ☎ *0773/882–2178*).

Visitor and Tour Info China International Travel Service (CITS) (✉ *Xi Jie, near Pantao Lu* ☎ *0773/882–7102*). **Charm Yangshuo Tour** (✉ *Pantao Lu* ☎ *0773/881–4355*).

EXPLORING YANGSHUO

❶ Probably the most popular destination in Yangshuo, **Moon Hill** *(Yueliang Shan)* is named after the large hole through the center of this karst peak. More than a dozen rock-climbing routes are on the northwest side. ✉ *Yangshuo–Gaotian Lu* ☎ *No phone* 🎫 *Y15* ⏲ *Daily 7 AM–7 PM.*

❷ In the center of town, **Yangshuo Park** *(Yangshuo Gongyuan)* is where older people come to play chess while children scamper about in small playgrounds. The park has a number of statues and ponds worth seeing, and Yangshuo Park Peak has a small pagoda offering excellent views of the surrounding town. For a more intense climb with even better views, ascend the television tower, across the street from the park's entrance. ✉*Diecui Lu, at Pantao Lu, across from Yangshuo Bus Station* *Free* *Daily.*

BACKPACKER'S PARADISE

Yangshuo is bliss for hipster backpackers. Yangshuo's 20,000 surrounding karst lime mountains are part and parcel of the Southeast Asia backpacker circuit that was forged in the 1970s and remain well trodden to this day. Today, Yangshuo's main strip known as "Xijie" or "West Street" throbs with the commingling cacophony of Hong Kong canto-pop, reggae, hip-hop, and classic rock. You can order everything from lasagna to enchiladas to pad-thai noodles. It's also the ideal place to get the low down on the best deals from English-speaking waitstaff or expats.

WHERE TO EAT

¢–$$ ECLECTIC **China Café.** In addition to shepherd's pie and baguette sandwiches, China Café serves an addictive rotisserie chicken that is made from a highly guarded local recipe. The kitchen roasts between 12 and 18 chickens each night, so diners in the know call the chef's mobile number (☎*1380/783–0498*) at least an hour in advance. One chicken will set you back Y50. ✉*34 Xi Jie* ☎*1380/783–0498* *No credit cards.*

¢–$$ NORTHERN CHINESE ★ **Dynasty Dumplings.** This local favorite serves some of the best northern-style dumplings in the area. Don't leave without trying them, either steamed or fried. You'll also find excellent local specialties like *pi jiu yu* (beer fish) and *tian luo niang* (stuffed river snails). English menus are available. ✉*21 Xianqian Jie, across from Magnolia Hotel* ☎*0773/890–2058* *No credit cards.*

¢–$ ECLECTIC **Kelly's Place.** Beloved by expats, this closet-size café is an escape from the hustle and bustle of West Street. On any given night, English teachers can be found drinking beer on the cobblestone pavilion. There are tasty Chinese-style dumpling soups. This is the only place in town to find vegetarian burgers. ✉*43 Guihua Lu, 1 block north of Xi Jie* ☎*0773/881–3233* *No credit cards.*

¢–$ CHINESE **Man De Guai.** At this family-owned restaurant, popular with locals but almost unknown to travelers, you'll find an amazing array of local dishes. There are no English menus, but the owners will bring you into the kitchen and let you pick out what you want. This place is hard to find: look for it on the small street two blocks north of the bus station, next to the large statue of Guanyin, the Buddha of Compassion. ✉*41 Yangshuo Xie Bilian Dong* ☎*0773/691–0959* *No credit cards.*

$$–$$$ FRENCH **Valentine Café.** Featuring a French chef and one of the most upscale menus in Southwest China, Valentine Café is aiming for Yangshuo's growing fine dining market. Smoked salmon with broccoli terrine, empanadas, gazpacho, quiche, and lamb cutlets are but some of the unexpected surprises on the menu in this comfortable multistory restaurant

designed with intimacy in mind. ✉83D Xi Jie ☎0773/882–6147 ▭No credit cards.

$–$$ FRENCH ✕**Le Vôtre.** A restored building dating from the Qing Dynasty is the setting for this French restaurant. The dining room looks more like a museum than a restaurant. The restaurant serves excellent Western-style specialties like grilled lamb chops and pasta primavera, as well as fine pizza. ✉*79 Xi Jie* ☎*0773/882–8040* ▭*No credit cards.*

WORD OF MOUTH

"Go straight to Yangshuo and hire a small boat to take you along the best part of the Li River, the section between the nearby village of Xingping and Yangdi. It's widely acknowledged that this section of the Li River has the best scenery, and a small boat cruise is much more peaceful than a ride aboard the noisy cruise boats from Guilin." —Lil1210

WHERE TO STAY

¢ **Magnolia Hotel** *(Baiyulan Jiudian).* Built around a traditional courtyard, the Magnolia has a glass-roofed lobby overlooking a lovely carp pond. Rooms have big windows, with most having amazing views of the mountains, the river, or both. The family suite is particularly nice: two adjoining rooms that give parents and children a little privacy. **Pros:** comfortable rooms, off the beaten path. **Cons:** uninspiring decor. ✉*7 Diecui Lu* ☎*0773/881–9288* *magnoliahotel@hotmail.com* *26 rooms, 1 suite* *In-room: Ethernet. In-hotel: Wi-Fi, laundry service, no-smoking rooms, no elevator* ▭*AE, MC, V.*

¢ Fodor's Choice ★ **Morningsun Hotel** *(Chenguang Jiudian).* With a lovely enclosed courtyard, the Morningsun Hotel has the look of a Ming Dynasty guesthouse. The guest rooms also carry on the traditional style (except for the brass and glass bathrooms). The staff at this family-run establishment is extremely friendly. Reserve ahead, as the hotel tends to fill up on weekends and holidays. **Pros:** friendly staff, near Xi Jie. **Cons:** rooms feel a bit "cold." ✉*4 Chengzhong Lu* ☎*0773/881–3899* *www.morningsunhotel.com* *23 rooms* *In-hotel: restaurant, laundry service, public Internet, no-smoking rooms, no elevator* ▭*AE, MC, V.*

$–$$$ **Paradesa Yangshuo Resort** *(Yangshuo Bailelai).* Once the premier hotel of Yangshuo, the Paradesa now has a lot of competition. The guest rooms are comfortable and some have nice views of the surrounding peaks. This is the only hotel in town with a babysitting service. Ask about seasonal and group discounts. **Pros:** central location, spacious grounds. **Cons:** slightly overpriced rooms. ✉*116 Xi Jie* ☎*0773/882–2109* *www.paradesahotel.com* *145 rooms* *In-room: Ethernet, refrigerator. In-hotel: 2 restaurants, pool, gym, laundry service, public Internet, no-smoking rooms, no elevator* ▭*AE, MC, V.*

¢ **Riverview Hotel** *(Wangjianglou Kezhan).* With its curvaceous tile roof and balconies with stunning views of the Li River, the Riverview is one of the town's nicest budget hotels. The guest rooms are tastefully appointed with dark-wood furniture. The first-floor restaurant, with alfresco seating and a great river view, is a lovely place to get breakfast or a coffee even if you're staying somewhere else. **Pros:** comfortable restaurant seating, river view. **Cons:** slightly isolated from the rest of town. ✉ *11 Binjiang Lu,* ☎ *0773/882–2688* 🌐 *www.riverview.com.cn* *38 rooms* *In-hotel: restaurant, bar, laundry service, public Internet, no elevator* ▭ *AE, MC, V.*

¢ **Yangshuo Regency Holiday Hotel.** At the entrance to the tourist district, this hotel has clean rooms with soft beds and nice views of the surrounding mountains. Its location makes it a good base for exploring the area. It faces the main road through town, so some rooms are noisy. **Pros:** central location, nice scenery. **Cons:** noisy area, touts offering everything from taxis to sex wait outside at night. ✉ *117 Xi Jie,* ☎ *0773/881–7198* 🌐 *www.ys-holidayhotel.com* *52 rooms* *In-room: Ethernet. In-hotel: 2 restaurants, laundry service, public Internet, no-smoking rooms, minibar* ▭ *AE, MC, V.*

NIGHTLIFE

With a good selection of imported and local beers, **Buffalo Bar** (✉ *50 Xianqian Jie* ☎ *773/881–3644*) is popular with expats. You can meet a few around the pool table. **Club 98** (✉ *42 Guihua Jie* ☎ *773/881–4605*) serves mixed drinks and imported beers in a pleasant atmosphere.

THE OUTDOORS

BIKING

Cheaply made mountain bikes are available for rent all over Yangshuo at a cost of about Y10 per day. However, if you want a better quality mountain bike, **Bike Asia** (✉ *42 Guihua Lu* ☎ *0773/882–6521* 🌐 *www.bikeasia.com*) rents them for Y30 per day. The company leads short trips to the villages along the Li River.

BOATING

Starting as a humble spring at the top of Mao'er Mountain, the majestic Li River snakes through Guangxi, connecting Yangshuo to many other towns along the way. One of the country's most scenic—and thus far, unpolluted—rivers, its banks are filled with stone embankments where people practice tai chi. The best spots for swimming can be found north of the city, where the stone walls give way to sand. Several local companies offer rides on bamboo rafts along the Li River and on the Yulong River, a smaller tributary. You can bargain with them at the stone quay at the end of West Street.

HOT-AIR BALLOONING

Guilin Flying Hot Air Balloon (☎ *0773/881–4919* 🌐 *www.chinahotairballoon.cn*) glides above the winding rivers and stunning peaks of Yangshuo—an unforgettable experience that will be a highlight of your trip. Hourlong trips cost US$290 per person.

ROCK CLIMBING

Yangshuo is the undisputed rock-climbing capital of China. The oldest and most trusted climbing club in Yangshuo is **Chinaclimb** (✉ *45 Xianqian Jie* ☎ *0773/881–1033* 🌐 *www.chinaclimb.com*). Led by a mostly Australian staff, climbs are perfect for novices and experts alike. Half-day treks cost between Y200 and Y300, including equipment and transportation.

SHOPPING

West Street is filled with shops selling everything from batik tapestries to T-shirts with cheesy sayings like I SURVIVED SARS. Also explore Dragon Head Mountain Pier Handicrafts Street (Longtou Shan Matou Gongyi Jie), a cobblestone street running along the river. You can bargain merchants down to half of the original asking price or even less.

Yangshuo does have a great place to buy mostly second-hand books. **Johnny Lu's Café and Books** (✉ *7 Chengzhong Jie* ☎ *1323/783–1208*) has a full selection of travel books.

SIDE TRIPS FROM YANGSHUO

Yangshuo is an exceptional base from which to explore the villages along the Li River, many of which date back hundreds of years. About 8 km (5 mi) southeast of Yangshuo sits **Fuli,** a Ming Dynasty town built on the river's northern banks. Fuli has narrow, winding cobblestone streets and a number of ancient temples worth exploring. This village is where you'll find the **Peng Family Painted Scroll Factory** (✉ *55 Fuling Bei Jie* ☎ *0773/894–2416*), a family-run shop that's been producing handmade scrolls and painted fans for generations. You'll find these for sale in Yangshuo for two or three times the price you can get them for here. From Fuli you can travel up the river to other villages such as Xinzhai, Degongzha, and Puyi, which has a large weekend market. Many of the people living in these villages still dress in traditional clothing.

NANNING

350 km (217 mi; 5 hrs by train) southwest of Guilin; 440 km (273 mi; 24 hrs by train) southeast of Guiyang; 600 km (372 mi; 16 hrs by train) west of Hong Kong.

Built along the banks of the Yong River, Nanning is the capital of Guangxi Zhuang Autonomous Region. The city isn't a major tourist draw, but it is a pleasant place to stop for a day or two. Many travelers come here for a visa before continuing into Vietnam.

GETTING HERE AND AROUND

Nanning is most accessible by bus from elsewhere in Guangxi. For anything beyond, it's a flight or an overnight train.

BY AIR Nanning Wuxu International Airport is 31 km (19 mi) southwest of Nanning and has flights throughout China, including to Guilin, though not to Yangshuo.

BY BUS There are frequent buses between Nanning and Guilin (4+ hours). There is no direct service between Nanning and Yangshuo, meaning a change of buses in Guilin.

BY TRAIN Nanning's station is at the northwestern edge of town, and offers frequent service to Guilin. The fastest of these takes 4 hours.

ESSENTIALS

Air Contacts Nanning Wuxu International Airport (☎ *0771/209–5160*).

Banks Bank of China (✉ *39 Gu Cheng Lu* ☎ *0771/281–1267* ✉ *Nanning Wuxu International Airport* ☎ *0771/482–4538*).

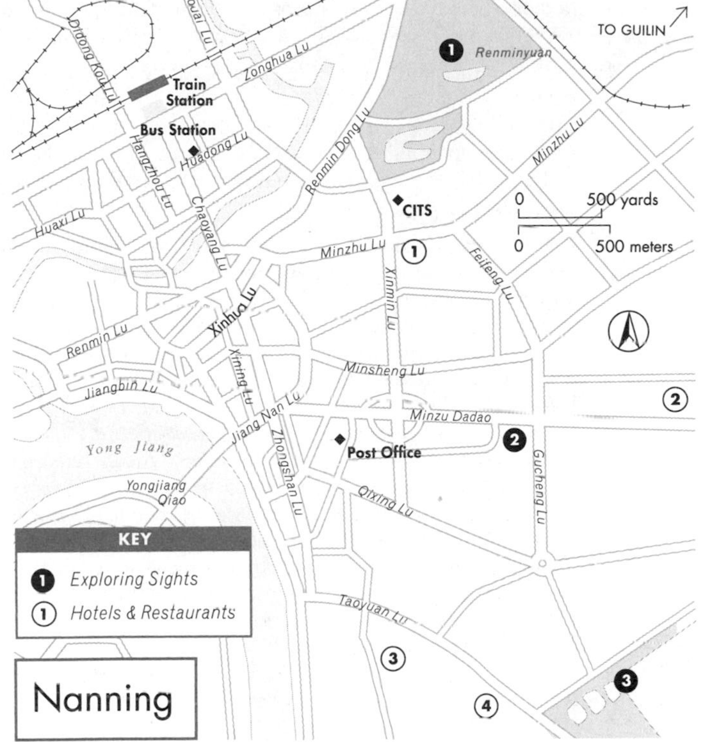

Bus Contacts **Nanning Bus Station** (✉ *65 Huadong Lu* ☎ *0771/242–4529*).

Medical Assistance **Nanning First Municipal People's Hospital** (✉ *89 Qixing Lu* ☎ *0771/267–7885*).

Public Security Bureau **PSB Nanning** (✉ *5 Ke Yuan East Rd, Xi Xiang Tang* ☎ *110* ☎ *0771/289–1302*).

Train Contacts **Nanning Station** (✉ *North end of Chaoyang Lu* ☎ *0771/243–2468*).

Visitor and Tour Info **China International Travel Service (CITS)** (✉ *40 Xinmin Lu* ☎ *0771/532–0165*).

EXPLORING NANNING

Surrounding White Dragon Lake, **White Dragon Park** *(Bailong Gongyuan)* has some 200 species of rare trees and flowers. Here you'll find the remains of fortifications built by a warlord in the early part of the 20th century. ✉ *Renmin Dong Lu* *Y5* *Daily 8:30–6.*

The **Guangxi Zhuang Autonomous Region Museum** *(Guangxi Zhuang Zizhiqu Bowuguan)* focuses on Guangxi's numerous ethnic minorities. In the back is a magnificent life-size reconstruction of houses, pagodas, and drum towers set among attractive pools and bridges. A collection

of more than 300 bronze drums made by local people is also on display. ✉ *34 Minzu Dadao* 💳 *Y5* ⏲ *Daily 8:30–11:30 and 2:30–5.*

3 In the southeastern part of the city, **South Lake** *(Nan Hu)* covers more than 200 acres. There's a bonsai exhibition and an orchid garden in the surrounding park. The park is encircled by a wide path that's ideal for strolling or jogging. A small number of bars have also begun to pop up along the lake's north side. ✉ *Gucheng Lu* 💳 *Free* ⏲ *Daily.*

WHERE TO EAT

$–$$ CHINESE ✕ **Beifang Renjia.** Tired of eating the local rice noodles? This is where many of Nanning's transplants from Northeastern China come to dine on traditional *dongbei cai.* A large dumpling menu is complemented by a full range of northeastern favorites such as *disanxian* (potato, eggplant, and green pepper in brown sauce), moo shu pork, plus a long list of unique breads and noodle dishes. Wash it all down with a cold Harbin beer. Staff is friendly but can't speak English. ✉ *86 Taoyuan Lu* ☎ *0771/530–4263* ▭ *No credit cards.*

$–$$ ITALIAN ★ ✕ **The Here.** One of the city's hidden gems, The Here Nanning features the same lineup of sandwiches, pizza, and pasta as its sister restaurants in Guilin and Yangshuo, the Nanning location is the most comfortable of the three. Sit in the shade on the patio or cool off in an air-conditioned private room while grabbing a meal or reading with a cup of fresh Yunnan coffee. Although the restaurant's official address is in the back of the labyrinthine Xinzhu residential area, save yourself the hassle and take the street entrance just west of the northwest corner of Minzu Dadao and Chahuayuan Lu. ✉ *Xinzhu Lu, Xinzhu Xiaoqu, Block 71, Room 102* ☎ *0771/588–7183* ▭ *No credit cards.*

WHERE TO STAY

$–$$ ★ **Majestic Hotel** *(Mingyuan Xindu Jiudian).* This older luxury hotel, close to the main square, has been refurbished reasonably well and is efficiently run. Its low price, excellent location, and fine gym make it a top choice in Nanning. **Pros:** one of Nanning's nicest swimming pools, professional staff/management. **Cons:** one of the tougher places in town to catch a cab. ✉ *38 Xinmin Lu* ☎ *0771/283–0808* *298 rooms* *In-room: safe, Ethernet, refrigerator. In-hotel: 2 restaurants, bar, pool, gym, laundry service* ▭ *AE, DC, MC, V.*

¢ **Taoyuan Hotel** *(Taoyuan Fan Dian).* The guest rooms at this budget hotel are clean and comfortable. There is a decent gym, a travel agency, and a pair of restaurants, one serving good Cantonese dim sum, the other spicy Sichuanese cuisine. **Pros:** good value. **Cons:** poor sound insulation. ✉ *74 Taoyuan Lu* ☎ *0771/209–6868* *400 rooms* *In-room: Ethernet. In-hotel: 2 restaurants, room service, bar, gym, concierge, laundry service, refrigerator, airport shuttle* ▭ *AE, DC, MC, V.*

Continued on page 502

FOR ALL THE TEA IN CHINA

Legend has it that the first cup dates from 2737 BC, when Camellia sinensis leaves fell into water being boiled for Emperor Shenong. He loved the result, tea was born, and so were many traditions.

Historically, when a girl accepted a marriage proposal she drank tea, a gesture symbolizing fidelity (tea plants die if uprooted). Betrothal gifts were known as "tea gifts," engagements as "accepting tea," and marriages as "eating tea." Today the bride and groom kneel before their parents, offering cups of tea in thanks.

Serving tea is a sign of respect. Young peo-ple proffer it to their parents or grandparents; subordinates do the same for their bosses. Pouring tea also signifies submission, so it's a way to say you're sorry. When you're served tea, show your thanks by tapping the table with your index and middle fingers.

And forget about adding milk or sugar. Not only is most Chinese tea best without it, but why dilute and sweeten a beverage long known by herbalists to be good for you? Even modern medicine acknowledges that tea's powerful antioxidants reduce the risk of cancer and heart disease. It's also thought to be such a good source of fluoride that Mao Zedong es-chewed toothpaste for a green-tea rinse. Smiles, everyone.

HISTORICAL BREW

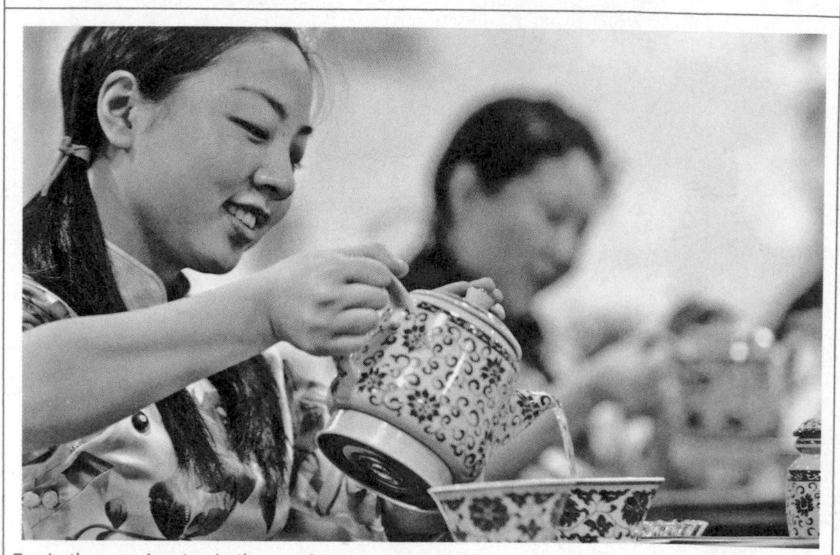

Tea in the morning; tea in the evening, tea at suppertime…

The Rise and Fall of Empires

Tea has a long and tumultuous history, making and breaking empires in both the East and the West. Bricks of tea were used as currency, and Chinese statesmen kept rebellious northern nomads in check by refusing to sell it to them.

Rumor has it that tea caused the downfall of the Song Empire. Apparently, tea-whisking was Emperor Huizong's favorite pastime: he was so obsessed with court tea culture that he forgot all about trivial little matters like defense. The country became vulnerable to invasion and fell to the Mongols in 1279.

Genghis preferred *airag* (fermented mare's milk), but after the Mongol's defeat, the drink of kings returned with a vengeance to the court of the Ming Dynasty (1368–1644). Tea as we know it today dates to this period: the first Ming emperor, Hongwu, set the trend of using loose-leaf tea by refusing to accept tea tribute gifts in any other form.

Tea Goes International

The first Europeans to encounter the beverage were navigators and missionaries who visited China in the mid-16th century. In 1610, Dutch traders began importing tea from China into Europe, with the Portuguese hot on their heels. It was initially marketed as a health drink and took a while to catch on. By the 1640s, tea had become popular amongst both the Dutch and Portuguese aristocracy, initially the only ones who could afford it.

Although we think of tea as a quintessentially British drink, it actually arrived in America two years before it appeared in Britain. When the British acquired New Amsterdam (later New York) in 1664, the colony consumed more tea than all the British isles put together.

Tea was available in Britain from about 1554 onward, but Brits were wary of the stuff at first. What tipped the scales in tea's favor was nothing less than celebrity product endorsement.

King Charles II married the Portuguese princess Catherine of Braganza in 1662. She arrived in England with tea and fine porcelain tea ware in her dowry and a healthy addiction to the stuff. Members of the royalty were the 16th-century's trendsetters: tea became the thing to drink at court; pretty soon the general public was hooked, too.

Storms in a Teacup

Tea quickly became a very important—and troublemaking—commodity. Religious leaders thought the drink sinful and doctors declared it a health risk. In Britain, ale-brewers were losing profits and pressure-groups successfully persuaded the government to tax tea at 119%. On top of all this, the immensely powerful British East India Company held the monopoly on tea importation.

Tea's value skyrocketed: by 1706, the retail price of green tea in London was equivalent to $300 for 100 g (3.5 oz), far beyond the reach of normal people. Tea-smuggling quickly became a massive—and often cut-throat—business. To make sought-after tea supplies stretch even further, they were routinely mixed with twigs, leaves, animal dung, and even poisonous chemicals.

Back in the New World, Americans were fed up with paying taxes that went straight back to Britain. Things came to a head when a group of patriots dressed as Native Americans peacefully boarded British ships in Boston harbor and emptied 342 chests of tea into the water. The act came to be known as the Boston Tea Party and was a vital catalyst in starting the American Revolution.

The War of Independence wasn't the only war sparked by tea. In Britain, taxes were axed and, as tea was suddenly affordable for everyone, demand grew exponentially. But China remained the world's only supplier so that by the mid-19th century, tea was causing a massive trade deficit. The British started exporting opium into China in exchange for tea, provoking two Opium Wars. In the 1880s, attempts to grow tea in India were finally successful and Indian tea began to overtake Chinese tea on the market.

These days, over 3.2 million tonnes of tea are produced annually worldwide. After water, tea is the world's favorite drink. Though Britain and Ireland now consume far more tea per capita than China, tea is still a regular presence at the Chinese table and is inextricably bound to Chinese culture.

ANCIENT TRADE ROUTES

The Ancient Tea and Horse Caravan Road, also known as the Southern Silk Road, is a trade corridor dating back to the Tang Dynasty (618–907). The 4,000-km route emerged more than 1,200 years ago and was actually still in use until recently.

Back in the heyday of the Caravan Road, Xishuangbanna, Dali, Lijiang, and many other parts of Yunnan were important outposts on the route. Tea, horses, salt, medicinal herbs, and Indian spices all featured prominently in this massive network.

During World War II, the route was used to smuggle supplies from India into the interior of Japanese-occupied China.

DRINKING IN THE CULTURE

The way tea was prepared historically bears little resemblance to the steep-a-teabag method many westerners employ today. Tea originally came in bricks of compressed leaves bound with sheep's blood or manure. Chunks were broken, ground into a powder, and whisked into hot water. In the first tea manual, *Cha Jing (The Way of Tea)*, Tang-dynasty writer Lu Yu describes preparing powdered tea using 28 pieces of teaware, including big brewing pans and shallow drinking bowls.

The potters of Yixing (near Shanghai) gradually transformed wine vessels into small pots for steeping tea. Yixing pottery is ideal for brewing: its fine unglazed clay is highly porous, and if you always use the same kind of tea, the pot will take on its flavor.

Today the most elaborate Chinese tea service—which requires only two pots and enough cups for all involved—is called *gong fu cha* (skilled tea method). Although you can experience it at many teahouses, most people consider it too involved for every day. They simply brew their leaf tea in three-piece lidded cups, called *gaiwan*, tilting the lid as they drink so that it acts as a strainer.

Gaiwan

THE CEREMONY

1. Rinse teapot with hot water.
2. Fill with black or oolong to one third of its height.
3. Half-fill teapot with hot water and empty immediately to rinse leaves.
4. Fill pot with hot water, let leaves steep for a minute; no bubbles should form.
5. Pour tea into small cups, moving the spout continuously over each, so all have the same strength of tea.
6. Pour the excess into a second teapot.
7. Using the same leaves, repeat the process up to five times, extending the steeping time slightly.

TEA TIMELINE

Yunnan Pu-erh Tea Bricks

350 AD	"Tea" appears in Chinese dictionary.
618–1644	Tea falls into and out of favor at Chinese court.
7th c.	Tea introduced to Japan.
1610–1650	Dutch and Portuguese traders bring tea to Europe.
1662	British King Charles II marries Portugal's Catherine of Braganza, a tea addict. Tea craze sweeps the court.
1689	Tea taxation starts in Britain; peaks at 119%.
1773	Boston Tea Party: Americans dump 342 chests of tea into Boston Harbor, protesting British taxes.

HOW TEA IS MADE

Chinese tea is grown on large plantations and nearly always picked by hand. Pluckers remove only the top two leaves. A skilled plucker can collect up to 35 kg (77 lbs) of leaves in a day; that's 9 kg (almost 20 lbs) of tea, or 3,500 cups. After a week, new top leaves will have grown, and bushes can be plucked again. Climate and soil play an important role on a tea plantation, much as they do in a vineyard. But what really differentiates black, green, and oolong teas is the way leaves are processed.

1784	British tea taxes slashed; consumption soars.
1835	Tea cultivation starts in Assam, India.
1880s	India and Ceylon produce more tea than China.
1904	Englishman Richard Blechynden creates iced tea at St. Louis World's Fair.
1908	New York importer Thomas Sullivan sends clients samples in silk bags—the first tea bags.
2004	Chinese tea exports overtake India's for the first time since the 1880s.

TYPES OF TEA

Some teas are simply named for the region that produces them (Yunnan or Assam); others are evocatively named to reflect a particular blend. Some are transliterated (like Keemun); others translated (Iron Goddess of Mercy). Confused? Keep two things in mind. First, the universal word for tea comes from *one* Chinese character—pronounced either "te" (Xiamen dialect) or "cha" (Cantonese and Mandarin). Second, all types of tea come from *one* plant.

	BLACK	PU-ERH	GREEN
Overview	It's popular in the West so it makes up the bulk of China's tea exports. It has a stronger flavor than green tea, though this varies according to type.	Pu-erh tea is green, black, or oolong fermented from a few months to 50 years and formed into balls. Pu-erh is popular in Hong Kong, where it's called Bo Le.	Most tea grown and consumed in China is green. It's delicate, so allow the boiling water to cool for a minute before brewing to prevent "cooking" the tea.
Flavor	From light and fresh to rich and chocolatey	Rich, earthy	Light, aromatic
Color	Golden dark brown	Reddish brown	Light straw-yellow to bright green
Caffeine per Serving	40 mg	20–40 mg	20 mg
Ideal Water Temperature	203°F	203°F	160°F
Steeping Time	3–5 mins.	3–5 mins.	1–2 mins.
Examples	Dian Hong (chocolatey aftertaste; unlike other Chinese teas, can take milk). Keemun (Qi Men; mild, smoky; once used in English breakfast blends). Lapsang Souchong (dried over smoking pine; strong flavor). Yunnan Golden (full bodied, malty).	Buying Pu-erh is like buying wine: there are different producers and different vintages, and prices vary greatly.	Bi Luo Chun (Green Snail Spring; rich, fragrant). Chun Mee (Eyebrow; pale yellow; floral). Hou Kui (Monkey Tea; nutty, sweet; floral aftertaste). Long Ding (Dragon Mountain; sweet, minty). Long Jing (Dragon's Well; bright green; nutty).

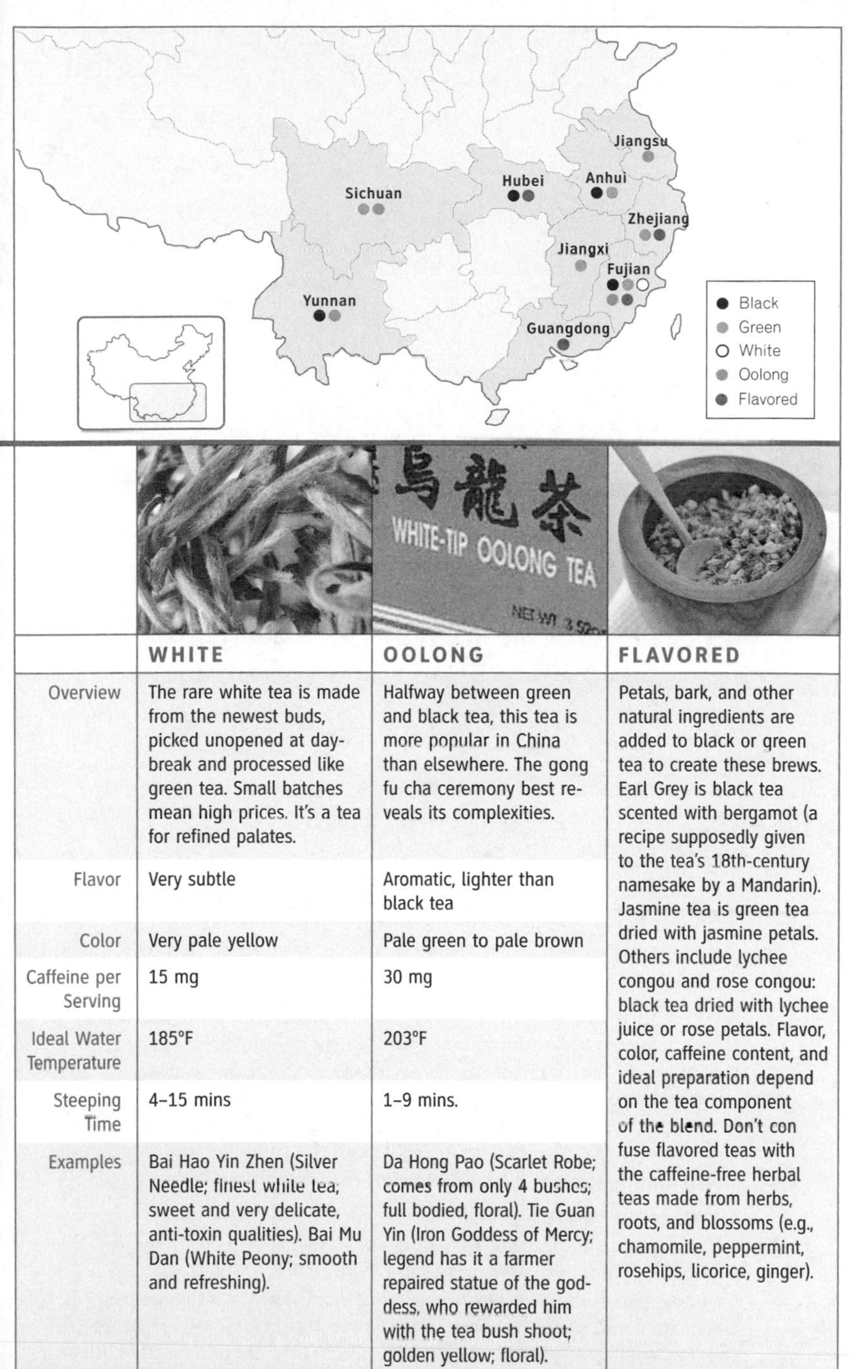

	WHITE	OOLONG	FLAVORED
Overview	The rare white tea is made from the newest buds, picked unopened at daybreak and processed like green tea. Small batches mean high prices. It's a tea for refined palates.	Halfway between green and black tea, this tea is more popular in China than elsewhere. The gong fu cha ceremony best reveals its complexities.	Petals, bark, and other natural ingredients are added to black or green tea to create these brews. Earl Grey is black tea scented with bergamot (a recipe supposedly given to the tea's 18th-century namesake by a Mandarin). Jasmine tea is green tea dried with jasmine petals. Others include lychee congou and rose congou: black tea dried with lychee juice or rose petals. Flavor, color, caffeine content, and ideal preparation depend on the tea component of the blend. Don't con fuse flavored teas with the caffeine-free herbal teas made from herbs, roots, and blossoms (e.g., chamomile, peppermint, rosehips, licorice, ginger).
Flavor	Very subtle	Aromatic, lighter than black tea	
Color	Very pale yellow	Pale green to pale brown	
Caffeine per Serving	15 mg	30 mg	
Ideal Water Temperature	185°F	203°F	
Steeping Time	4–15 mins	1–9 mins.	
Examples	Bai Hao Yin Zhen (Silver Needle; finest white tea; sweet and very delicate, anti-toxin qualities). Bai Mu Dan (White Peony; smooth and refreshing).	Da Hong Pao (Scarlet Robe; comes from only 4 bushes; full bodied, floral). Tie Guan Yin (Iron Goddess of Mercy; legend has it a farmer repaired statue of the goddess, who rewarded him with the tea bush shoot; golden yellow; floral).	

GUIZHOU

With its undulating mountains, terraced fields, and traditional villages, Guizhou is among China's most interesting provinces. Although beautiful, it has less tourism infrastructure than neighboring Guangxi or Yunnan. One of the least visited provinces in southern China, Guizhou attracts those intent on heading off the beaten path.

Guizhou is home to many different ethnic minorities, including the Dong, Hui, Yao, Zhuang, and Miao (known in the west as the Hmong) peoples. More than a third of Guizhou's population comes from these groups. The countryside is sprinkled with villages dominated by impressive towers. The province is known for its festivals, and frequent travelers claim that you can't travel through the province without running into at least one or more celebration.

REGIONAL TOURS

Quite possibly the only multilingual identical-twin tour guides operating in China, **Jennifer and Louisa Wu** (☎ *1370844–3445* ✉ *wujennife@gmail.com or wuminlouisa@gmail.com*) are members of the Miao minority and speak English, Mandarin, and a number of other Chinese languages fluently. They are both highly familiar with Guizhou and Yunnan, and divide their time leading short- and long-term tours around these provinces. Rates for a group are negotiable, but generally average around Y250 per day.

GUIYANG

350 km (217 mi; 17 hrs by fastest train) northwest of Guilin; 425 km (264 mi; 17½ hrs by train) northwest of Nanning; 850 km (527 mi; 26 hrs by train) northwest of Hong Kong; 1,650 km (1,023 mi; 29 hrs by train) southwest of Beijing.

The capital city of Guiyang is a pleasant place to begin an exploration of the province. Like most cities in China it is fast losing its older quarters, however enough remain to make a short stay here worthwhile. The main streets of the sprawling town are Zunyi Lu, Ruijin Lu, Zhonghua Lu and Yan'an Lu.

GETTING HERE AND AROUND

BY AIR Guiyang Airport lies 9 mi (15 km) to the southeast of the city. There are direct flights between Guiyang and most of the main cities in China.

BY BUS From Guiyang's station there is regular bus service to Anshun (2 hrs), Kaili (2 hrs), and Xingyi (approximately 12 hrs over very bad roads). There are also special tour buses to Huangguoshu Falls from the Guiyang Railway Station that take about two hours and cost Y45.

BY TRAIN Direct trains link Guiyang with Chongqing (9 hrs), Guilin (16½ hrs), Kunming (10 hrs), Liuzhou (13 hrs), Nanning (24½ hrs), and Shanghai (30 hrs). The train station is at the southwest edge of the city at the southern end of Zunyi Lu.

ESSENTIALS

Air Contacts Guiyang Airport (✉ *Southeast of the city* ☎ *0851/549–8908*).

Bank Bank of China (✉ *30 Dusi Lu* ☎ *0851/581–5261*).

Bus Contacts Guiyang Station (✉ *Yan'an Xi Lu* ☎ *0851/685–5336*).

Public Security Bureau PSB Guiyang (✉ *5 Zhuxin Lu* ☎ *0851/676–5230*).

Train Contacts Guiyang Railway Station (✉ *Zunyi Lu* ☎ *0851/818–1222*).

Visitor and Tour Info China International Travel Service (CITS) (✉ *20-40 Yan'an Zhong Lu* ☎ *0851/581–6348*). **Guizhou Overseas Travel Service** (✉ *20 Yan'an Zhong Lu* ☎ *0851/657–3212*).

EXPLORING GUIYANG

MAIN ATTRACTIONS

Just outside the city, **Qianling Park** *(Qianling Gongyuan)* covers 740 acres. It has a bit of everything, including thousands of plants and a collection of birds and monkeys (many of whom roam wild through the park). Dominating the park is a 4,265-foot-high mountain that has fine views of the town from its western peak. The **Unicorn Cave** *(Qilin Dong)*, discovered in 1531, was used as a prison for the two Nationalist generals Yang Hucheng and Chang Xueliang, who were accused by the Guomindang of collaborating with the Communists when Chiang

Kai-shek was captured at Xian in 1937. ✉1 *Zaoshan Lu 2½ km (1 mi) northwest of city* 🎫*Y5* ⏲*Daily 8* AM*–10* PM.

★ **Underground Gardens** *(Dixia Gongyuan)* is the poetic name for a cave about 25 km (15 mi) south of the city. In the cave, at a depth of 1,925 feet, a path weaves its way through the various rock formations, which are illuminated to emphasize their similarity with animals, fruit, and other living things. ✉*25 km (15 mi) south of Guiyang* ☎*0851/511–4014* 🎫*Y5* ⏲*Daily 8:30–11:30 and 2:30–5.*

IF YOU HAVE TIME

With bamboo groves, **Hebin Park** *(Hebin Gongyuan)*, sits on the banks of the Nanming River. For the children, there are a Ferris wheel and other rides. In the park you'll find the **Hua Jia Pavilion** *(Hua Jia Lou)*, an attractive Ming Dynasty pagoda painted with dragons and phoenixes. Also within the park is the colorful Ming Dynasty **Wen Chang Pavilion** *(Wen Chang Lou)*, surrounded by buildings that house a collection of ancient coins and tools. ✉*Ruijin Nan Lu* 🎫*Free* ⏲*Daily 9–5.*

Filled with ornamental gardens, **Huaxi Park** *(Huaxi Gongyuan)* sits on the banks of the Huaxi, known as the River of Flowers. The Huaxi Waterfall is nearby. ✉*18 km (11 mi) south of Guiyang* 🎫*Y5* ⏲*Daily 8–6.*

WHERE TO EAT

Every province has a number of dishes that locals are fiercely proud of. In Guizhou, this is unquestionably *suan tang yu*, or sour fish soup. It combines a mouth-numbing number of herbs, spices, and local vegetables to make a dish that is at once spicy and savory. Another wonderfully named dish is *lian ai doufu guo*, or "the bean curd in love." It's a strip of vegetable- or meat-stuffed tofu toasted to a golden brown and sprinkled with sesame oil. It's a popular dish with couples.

¢–$ SEAFOOD ★ ✕**Old Kaili Sour Sour Fish Restaurant** *(Lao Kaili Suan Tang Yu)*. This is where you can order the city's signature dish, sour fish soup. It's cooked at your table, so you are able to add just the right amount of seasonings. Should yours be too spicy, remember that a bit of white rice—*not* water—is the best method of dousing culinary flames. ✉*55 Shengfu Lu* ☎*0851/584–3665* ▭*No credit cards.*

$–$$ INTERNATIONAL ✕**Nell's Yard Café.** A small, comfortable restaurant featuring a basic Chinese menu and a smaller Western menu that includes some spaghetti dishes. Coffee is on the pricey side, starting at Y28, but it is the alcohol selection that makes Nell's standout. An extensive—and sometimes expensive—selection of wines from France, Italy, and Spain is complemented by a variety of imported German beers. Service is friendly. ✉*166 Zhonghua Bei Lu* ☎*0851/682–2502* ▭*No credit cards.*

WHERE TO STAY

¢ **Guizhou Park Hotel** *(Guizhou Fandian)*. The most luxurious hotel in town is this sleek glass tower close to Qianlingshan Park. The rooms are well appointed, but you'd be hard-pressed to find anything in them that lets you know you're in China. **Pros:** comfortable rooms, staff is familiar with Western travelers. **Cons:** somewhat isolated. ✉*66 Beijing Lu* ☎*0851/682–3888* *410 rooms* *In-room: safe, refrigerator. In-hotel: 2 restaurants, bar, pool* ▭*AE, DC, MC, V.*

CLOSE UP

Festivals of Guizhou

Since the province is comprised of various ethnic groups—including the Dong, Hui, Yao, Zhuang, and Miao peoples—Guizhuo is a gallery of traditional customs. Festivals are held throughout the year in Guiyang and elsewhere in the province. Many of these festivals are named after the dates on which they're held. These dates are according to a lunar calendar, so the festival called "Eighth Day of the Fourth Month" is not on April 8, but on the eighth day of the fourth lunar month (usually sometime in May).

Siyueba, which translates as "Eighth Day of the Fourth Month," is when the Miao, Buyi, Dong, Yao, Zhuang, Yi, and other peoples of the province celebrate spring. Similar to Mardi Gras (but without the drinking or bawdy behavior), the festival is a major holiday in the region. Guiyang is a great place to check out the festival. The area around the fountain in the city center erupts with music, dancing, and general merrymaking.

An important traditional festival of Guiyang's Buyi population is **Liuyueliu,** or "Sixth Day of the Sixth Month." Held in midsummer, as the name implies, this festival sees thousands of Buyi people from the region gathering on the banks of the Huaxi River. As the story goes, a beautiful Buyi maiden embroidered an image of mountains and rivers of immense beauty. It was so inspiring that a miscreant devised to steal it, and on the sixth day of the sixth lunar month he sent his minions to take it by force. The maiden cast her embroidery into the air, where it was transformed into the beautiful mountains and rivers seen here today.

Among the Miao people who live in and around Kaili, a bullfight is a contest between the bulls themselves. The **Miao Bullfight Festival** traditionally takes place between the planting of rice seedlings and their harvest a few months later, usually between the sixth and eighth lunar month. Owners of bulls meet beforehand to size up the competition prior to agreeing to the fight. The atmosphere on fight day is lively, with drinking, music, and exchanging of gifts. Fireworks entice the bulls into combat until one falls down or runs away.

An important fertility festival among the Miao people is the **Sister's Meal Festival** when unmarried women harvest rice from the terraced fields and prepare a special dish of sticky rice colored blue, pink, and yellow. Men arrive to serenade the women, and the women offer gifts of rice wine and small packets of rice wrapped in cloth. In the evenings, women dress up for a night of dancing.

7

¢–$ **Nenghui Jiudian.** This handsome modern hotel has accommodations and facilities above its official three-star designation. Guest rooms are large and bright with high ceilings, big firm beds, modern furniture, and sparkling bathrooms. Its central location makes it a good base for exploring the city. **Pros:** central location for not much money. **Cons:** noisy part of town. ✉*38 Ruijin Nan Lu* ☎*0851/589–8888* *117 rooms* *In room: safe, Ethernet, refrigerator. In-hotel: restaurant, bar, gym, concierge, laundry service* *AE, DC, MC, V.*

$$$–$$$$ ★ **Sheraton Guiyang Hotel.** Today's undisputed best five-star hotel in Guiyang the Sheraton Guiyang has everything a high end traveler needs: a bar with amazing city views, a full-service spa, the best international dining in town, and attentive English-speaking staff. Rooms are very comfortable, with excellent views of the city and the surrounding mountains from rooms located on the 20th floor or up. **Pros:** by a small park, excellent city views. **Cons:** not for B&B lovers. ✉ *49 Zhonghua Nan Lu* ☎ *0851/588–8888* 🌐 *Sheraton.starwoodhotels.com/Guiyang* *305 rooms, 41 suites* *In-room: safe, Ethernet, refrigerator. In-hotel: restaurants, bar, spa, gym, concierge, laundry service* 💳 *AE, DC, MC, V.*

SIDE TRIP TO HUANGGUOSHU FALLS

Fodor's Choice ★ The Baishui River streams over nine sets of rocks, creating nine waterfalls over a course of 2 km (1 mi). At the highest point, **Huangguoshu Falls** *(literally, Yellow Fruit Trees Falls)* drops an eye-popping 230 feet. The largest in China, these falls are set in lush countryside where you'll find numerous villages. You can enjoy them from afar or by wading across the **Rhinoceros Pool** *(Xiniu Jian)* to the **Water Curtain Cave** *(Shuilian Dong)* hidden behind the main falls. Seven kilometers (4½ mi) downstream is the **Star Bridge Falls** *(Xingqiao Pu)*. The falls are at their best from May through October. Buses from Guiyang's main bus terminal make the trip here in two to three hours. Any travel agent can help you with the arrangements. ✉ *160 km (99 mi) southwest of Guiyang* ☎ *No phone* *Y90* *Daily, dawn–dusk.*

KAILI

200 km (124 mi; 3 hrs by train) east of Guiyang.

Capital of the Qian Dongnan Miao and Dong Autonomous Region, Kaili serves as the starting point for a journey to the Miao and Dong villages that dominate eastern Guizhou. More than two-thirds of the population is Miao, and their villages are along the eastern and northeastern outskirts of Kaili. The Dong communities are to the southeast. To get a real flavor for these peoples, one of the more than 100 annual festivals.

GETTING HERE AND AROUND

The fastest way to get from Guiyang to Kaili is by bus. The bus trip takes two hours while the train takes more than three.

BY BUS The long-distance bus station outside Guiyang train station has buses leaving every 20 minutes or so for Kaili. Buses usually don't leave until they're full. Bus tickets run from Y40 to Y60.

BY TRAIN Kaili's small train station is three hours from Guiyang. Trains passing through Kaili connect to Guilin, Kunming, Beijing, Shanghai, and much of the rest of China.

ESSENTIALS

Bank Bank of China (✉ *Beijing Donglu near the city's main roundabout*).

Bus Contacts Kaili Bus Station (✉ *Beijing Xi Lu* ☎ *No phone*).

Train Contacts Kaili Train Station (✉ *Qingjiang Lu* ☎ *No phone*).

EXPLORING KAILI

In Jinquanhu Park, the **Drum Tower** *(Gu Lou)* is the Dong people's gathering place for celebrations.

The **Minorities Museum** (*Zhou Minzu Bowuguan* ✉ *5 Guangchang Lu* *Y10* *Mon.–Sat. 9–5*) displays arts, crafts, and relics of the local indigenous peoples.

Outside town the local villages are of great interest. To the north is the Wuyang River, which passes by many mountains, caves, and Miao villages. At **Shibing,** you can take boat rides through spectacular limestone gorges and arrange stops at these towns. South of Kaili are the Dong villages of **Leishan, Rongjiang,** and **Zhaoxing.** The latter village, set in a beautiful landscape, is known for its five drum towers.

WHERE TO STAY AND EAT

¢ **Guotai Dajiudian.** This hotel, in the center of town, is the best in Kaili. The guest rooms are extremely comfortable, and the bathrooms are squeaky clean. The staff—mostly made up of members of the Miao minority group—is very friendly. The restaurant serves a variety of traditional Miao dishes, as well as many from the rest of the country. **Pros:** good rooms, friendly staff. **Cons:** restaurant service can be less than responsive. ✉ *6 Beijing Dong Lu* ☎ *0855/826–9888* *73 rooms* *In-room: Ethernet. In-hotel: 2 restaurants, room service, laundry service* *No credit cards.*

YUNNAN

Hidden deep in southwestern China, Yunnan is one of the country's most fascinating provinces. Its rugged and varied terrain contains some of China's most beautiful natural scenery, as well as the headwaters of three of Asia's most important rivers: the Yangtze, Mekong, and Salween. Stunning mountains, picturesque highland meadows, and steamy tropical jungles are inhabited by Bai, Dai, Naxi, Hani, and dozens of other ethnic groups, many of which can only be found in Yunnan.

Yunnan sits atop the Yunnan-Guizhou Plateau, with the Himalayas to the northwest and Myanmar, Laos, and Vietnam to the south. Yunnan was central to the Ancient Tea and Horse Caravan Route, an important trade route that connected China with the rest of Southeast Asia for thousands of years. Today, Yunnan is one of the top travel destinations in China, with Lijiang, Dali, and Jinghong getting most of the attention. Countless lesser-known but equally amazing places are throughout the province.

Roughly the size of California, Yunnan is becoming increasingly accessible to the outside world. More convenient air travel makes it possible to have breakfast by the Mekong in Jinghong and dinner overlooking the old mountain town of Lijiang the same day. Yunnan still has plenty of places that are off the beaten path.

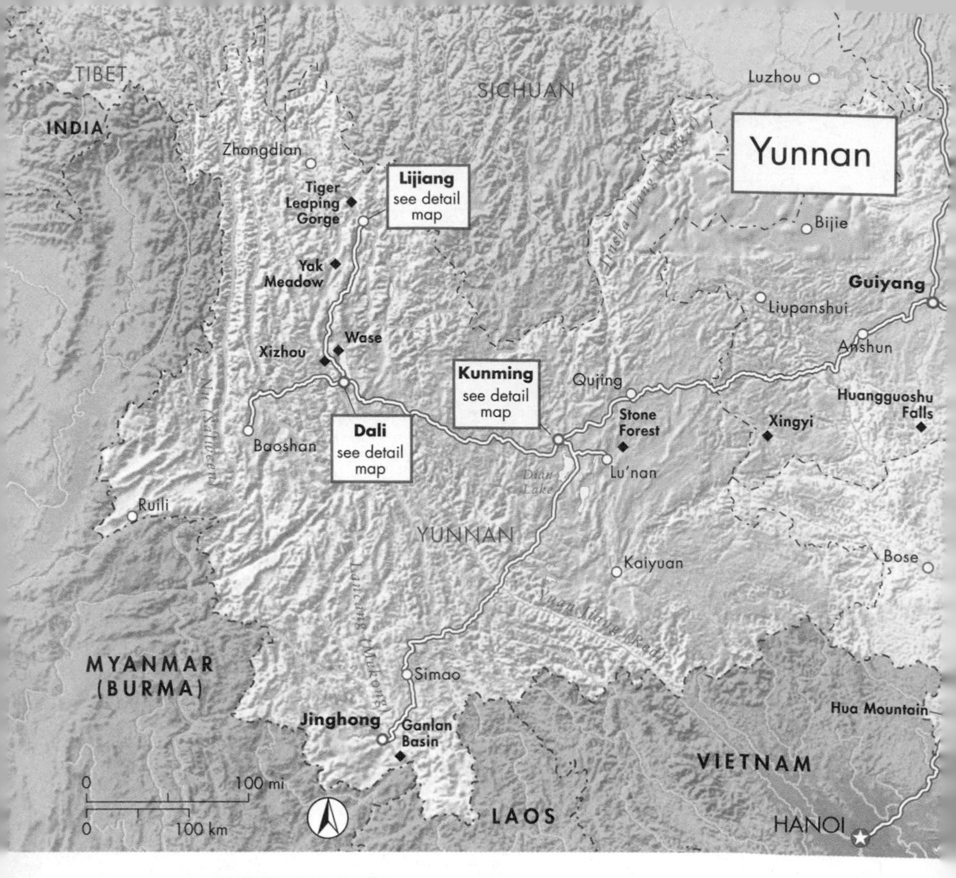

REGIONAL TOURS

China Minority Travel offers multiple-destination tours of Yunnan with visits to the province's lesser-known gems including Yuanyang, Lugu Lake, and Zhongdian (Shangri-la). The agency, which is based in Dali, has been organizing Yunnan tours for more than a decade. Multiple-day treks, family-oriented tours and custom itineraries are all available (✉ *63 Bo'ai LuDali* ☎ *0872/267–9549* 🌐 *www.china-travel.nl*).

KUNMING

400 km (248 mi; 13 hrs by train) southwest of Guiyang; 650 km (403 mi; 21 hrs by train) southwest of Chengdu; 1,200 km (744 mi; 18 hrs by train) west of Hong Kong

With its cool mountain air and laid-back locals, Kunming is one of China's most comfortable big cities and is an ideal base for Yunnan travels. It's one of the few cities in the country that regularly has blue skies and is nicknamed the "Spring City." Weather can be gray and soggy during the summer monsoon season and gray and cold around January and February.

Kunming is changing rapidly as the city is transforming into China's gateway to Southeast Asia. But despite the disappearance of the old city and increasingly congested traffic, Kunming retains its unique character as a relaxed and somewhat idiosyncratic city.

GETTING HERE AND AROUND

BY AIR Kunming is a busy air hub with flight links all over China. The airport is at the southern end of Chuncheng Lu, in the city's southeast, about 20 minutes by taxi from the center of town. Taxi fare costs Y20 to Y30.

Kunming also has flights to Shangri-la (previously known as Zhongdian), which has daily flights to Lhasa, Tibet. Travelers to Tibet will need to have Tibet travel permits in hand to board the Lhasa flight.

BY BUS Kunming has two major long-distance bus stations: Xizhan Bus Station on Kunrui Lu and Nanyao Bus Station just north of the train station on the south end of Beijing Lu. Xizhan Bus Station is the more orderly of the two and tends to have better buses that cost more but are still a good value.

BY CAR If you need a car and driver while you're in Kunming, you can make arrangements through your hotel. Expect to pay at least Y500 for a car to the Stone Forest. Alternatively, if you speak a little Chinese or you luck into one of the few English-speaking cabbies in Kunming, you can haggle for a taxi that should be much cheaper than the hotel option.

BY TRAIN The station is at the southern terminus of Beijing Lu.

TOURS

No group tours of Kumming are recommended, especially because most agencies in the city have little to no fluency in English and spend more time in shops than attractions.

ESSENTIALS

Air Contacts **Kunming Airport** (✉ *Changchun Lu* ☎ *0871/711–3232*).

Bank **Bank of China** (✉ *448 Beijing Lu*).

Bus Contacts **Xizhan Bus Station** (✉ *Kunrui Lu* ☎ *0871/532–6258*). **Nanyao Bus Station** (✉ *Beijing Lu* ☎ *0871/534–9414 or 0871/351–1534*).

Medical Assistance **Kunming First People's Hospital** (✉ *504 Qingnian Lu* ☎ *0871/318–8200*).

Public Security Bureau **PSB Kunming** (✉ *Beijing Lu* ☎ *110*).

Train Contact **Kunming Train Station** (✉ *Beijing Lu* ☎ *0871/534–9414 or 0871/351–1534*).

Visitor and Tour Info **China International Travel Service (CITS)** (✉ *220 Huancheng Nan Lu* ☎ *0871/313–2332*).

EXPLORING KUNMING

❷ Fodor'sChoice ★ In the north-central part of the city, **Green Lake Park** *(Cuihu Gongyuan)* is filled with willow- and bamboo-covered islands connected by stone bridges. Green Lake itself was once part of Dianchi Lake, but it was severed from that larger body of water in the late 1970s. The park is a favorite gathering place for Kunming's older residents, who begin to congregate in the park for singing and dancing around 2:30 PM and

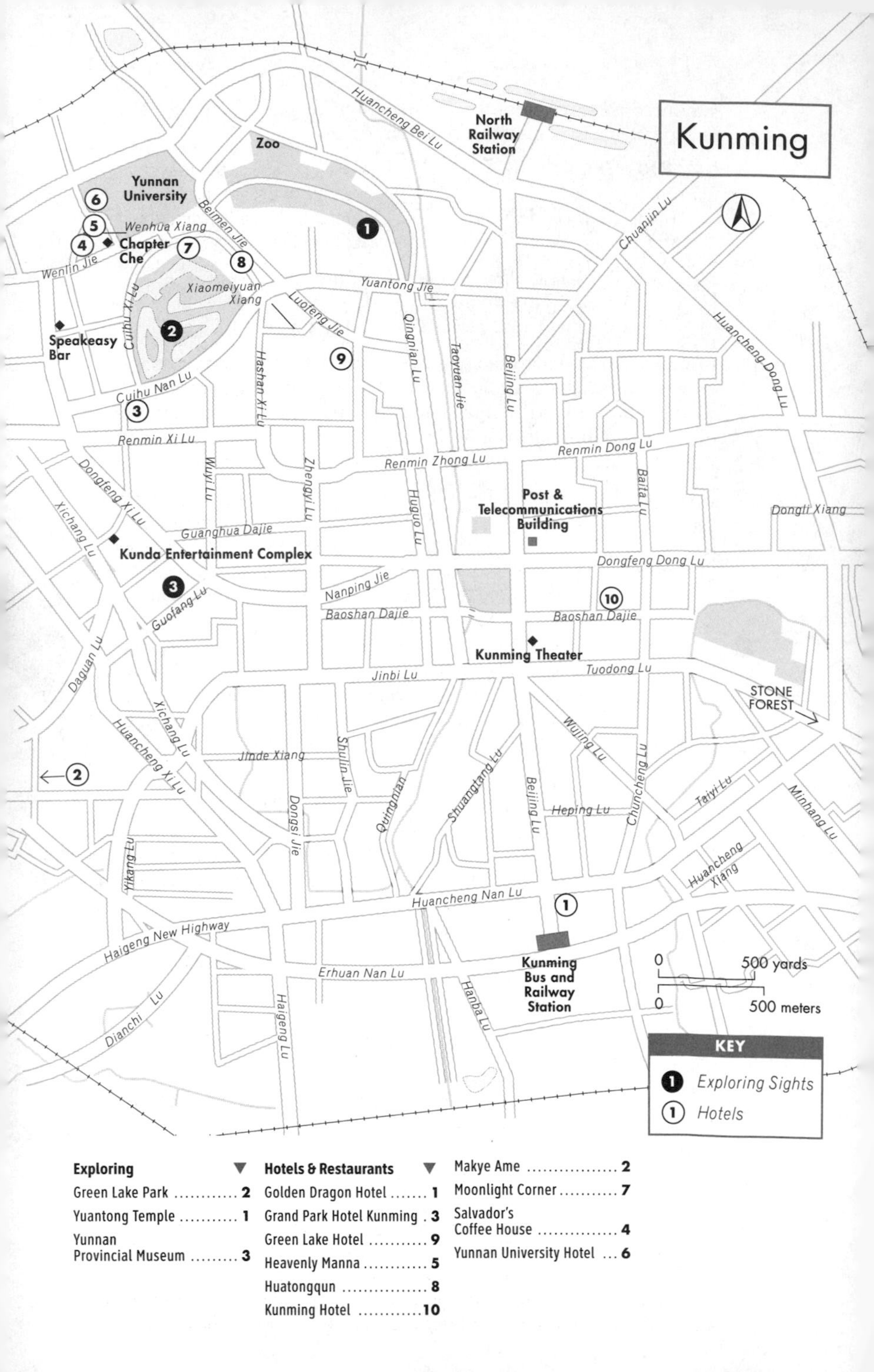
Kunming
North Railway Station
Huancheng Bei Lu
Zoo
Yunnan University
Wenhua Xiang
Beimen Jie
Chapter Che
Wenlin Jie
Xiaomeiyuan Xiang
Yuantong Jie
Luofeng Jie
Cuihu Xi Lu
Speakeasy Bar
Cuihu Nan Lu
Hashan Xi Lu
Qingnian Lu
Taoyuan Jie
Beijing Lu
Chuanjin Lu
Huancheng Dong Lu
Renmin Xi Lu
Renmin Zhong Lu
Renmin Dong Lu
Dongfeng Xi Lu
Xichang Lu
Wuyi Lu
Zhengyi Lu
Huguo Lu
Post & Telecommunications Building
Baita Lu
Dongli Xiang
Guanghua Dajie
Kunda Entertainment Complex
Dongfeng Dong Lu
Nanping Jie
Baoshan Dajie
Guofang Lu
Kunming Theater
Daguan Lu
Jinbi Lu
Tuodong Lu
STONE FOREST
Huancheng Xi Lu
Jinde Xiang
Shulin Jie
Wujing Lu
Shuangtang Lu
Chuncheng Lu
Taiyi Lu
Minhang Lu
Dongsi Jie
Quingnian
Heping Lu
Yikang Lu
Huancheng Xiang
Huancheng Nan Lu
Haigeng New Highway
Erhuan Nan Lu
Kunming Bus and Railway Station
Hanba Lu
Haigeng Lu
Dianchi Lu
0
500 yards
0
500 meters
KEY
Exploring Sights
Hotels
Exploring
Green Lake Park 2
Yuantong Temple 1
Yunnan Provincial Museum 3
Hotels & Restaurants
Golden Dragon Hotel 1
Grand Park Hotel Kunming . 3
Green Lake Hotel 9
Heavenly Manna 5
Huatongqun 8
Kunming Hotel 10
Makye Ame 2
Moonlight Corner........... 7
Salvador's Coffee House 4
Yunnan University Hotel ... 6

stay until the gates close at 11 PM. In summers, the lake is filled with pink and white lotus blossoms. In winter the park fills with migrating seagulls from Siberia. ✉ *Cuihu Nan Lu* 🎫 *Free* ⏲ *Daily 7–11.*

❶ ★ **Yuantong Temple** *(Yuantong Si)*, the largest temple in the city, dates back some 1,200 years to the Tang Dynasty. The compound consists of a series of gates leading to the inner temple, which is surrounded by a pond brimming with fish and turtles. The chanting of worshippers in the serene environment makes it hard to believe you're in a big city. In the back of the compound, a temple houses a statue of Sakyamuni, a gift from the king of Thailand. ✉ *30 Yuantong Jie* 🎫 *Y4* ⏲ *Daily 8–6.*

BIKING KUNMING

Kunming is one of the best cities in China for biking. Small brown signs point toward historical and cultural sights. The signs are in Chinese, but just follow the arrows. Start at Green Lake Park and explore the winding lanes shooting off in every direction from the park. Heading south you'll find the few remaining pockets of old Kunming. Continuing south there are several small parks, temples, and pagodas.

Group tours leave Saturday morning at 9 from **Xiong Brothers Bike Shop** (✉ *Unit 5, 51 Beimen Jie* ☎ *0871/519–1520*).

❸ The **Yunnan Provincial Museum** *(Yunnansheng Bowuguan)* is a window into Yunnan's history. The museum focuses primarily on the Dian Kingdom, which ruled much of Yunnan from 1000 BC to 1 BC. Most of what you'll see here is more than 2,000 years old. Exhibits have good English captions. ✉ *118 Wuyi Lu* ☎ *0871/362–7718* 🎫 *Y10* ⏲ *Daily 9–5:30.*

WHERE TO EAT

¢–$ CHINESE ✕ **Heavenly Manna.** Manna serves some of the best no-frills Chinese food in the city. There are delicious regional specialties such as steam-pot chicken, bitter melon with egg, and corn in duck egg yolks, as well as local interpretations of traditional Chinese dishes. Manna is a favorite lunch and dinner spot for locals and foreign students, so it can be difficult to find seating at peak hours. There's an English menu. ✉ *74 Wenhua Xiang* ☎ *0871/536–9399* ▭ *No credit cards.*

¢–$ CHINESE ✕ **Huatongqun.** This may be the best place in Kunming to enjoy Dai cuisine, which is known for intense flavors and chili peppers. If you want to go straight for the spice, try the *gui ji* or "ghost chicken," a cold chicken salad that is slightly sour and extremely spicy. Tamer options include pineapple rice, fennel omelets, dried beef, wild mushrooms, fried fish, and tapioca with cookies in coconut milk. Dai cuisine features many dishes and ingredients that are foreign even to coastal Chinese. The restaurant stops taking orders around 8 PM. ✉ *24 Qingyun Jie* ☎ *0871/510–6806* ▭ *No credit cards.*

$–$$$$ TIBETAN ✕ **Makye Ame.** As much a cultural experience as a gastronomical adventure, Makye Ame is known for its Tibetan and Indian song-and-dance performances. The shows are enjoyable, but loud. For a quieter meal, ask for one of the rooms in the back or the cozy teahouse upstairs. Foodwise, Makye Ame serves a large variety of Tibetan dishes, including

CLOSE UP

Ethnic Minorities of the Southwest

Yunnan is like no other place in China with 26 of the counties, 56 ethnic minorities living within its borders. Many of the groups in this region have long resisted Han influence.

NAXI

Primarily living in the area around Lijiang and neighboring Sichuan, the Naxi culture is unique, even when compared with other minority groups in China. The society is traditionally matriarchal, with women dominating relationships, keeping custody of children, and essentially running the show. Some Naxis practice Buddhism or Taoism, but it is the shamanistic culture of the Dongba and Samba that set their spiritualism apart from other groups. The Dongba (male shamans) and Samba (female shamans) serve their communities as mediators, entering trancelike states and communicating with the spiritual world in order to solve problems on earth. Naxi script, like Chinese script, is made up of ideograms. These pictographs are vivid representations of body parts, animals, and geography used to express concrete and abstract concepts. Despite numbering less than 300,000, the Naxi are one of the better-known ethnic groups in China.

BAI

The Bai, also known as the Minjia, are one of the more prominent minorities in Yunnan, although they are also found in Guizhou and Hunan provinces. Primarily centered around the Dali Bai Autonomous Region, the Bai are known for their agricultural skills and unique architecture style. The Bai also have some of the most colorful costumes, particularly the rainbow-colored hats worn by women. The Bai, along with the Yi people, were part of the Nanzhao Kingdom, which briefly rose to regional dominance in southwest China and Southeast Asia during the Tang Dynasty, before giving way to the Kingdom of Dali. The Dali region and the Bai have essentially been a part of the Chinese sphere of influence since the Yuan Dynasty, during which the Yuan's Mongolian armies conquered the area in the 13th century. The Bai's highly productive rice paddies were seen as an asset by the Yuan, who let them operate under relative autonomy. Today the Bai and their festivals, including the Third Moon Festival and Torch Festival, are major attractions for domestic and international tourists.

DAI

Related to Thais and speakers of languages belonging to the Tai-Kadai family, the Dai seem much more Southeast Asian than Chinese. In China, they are primarily located in the Xishuangbanna, Dehong, and Jingpo regions of southern Yunnan, but can also be found in Myanmar, Laos, and Thailand. They practice Theravada Buddhism, the dominant form of Buddhism in Southeast Asia. The linguistic, cultural, and religious connections with Southeast Asia give Dai-inhabited regions a decidedly un-Chinese feel. Within China, they are most famous for their spicy and flavorful food and their Water Splashing Festival (water is used to wash away demons and sins of the past and bless the future). Many grow rice and produce such crops as pineapples, so villages are concentrated near the Mekong (Lancang) and Red (Honghe) rivers. The Dai population here has ebbed and flowed with China's political tide and many are now returning after the turmoil of the 1960s and '70s.

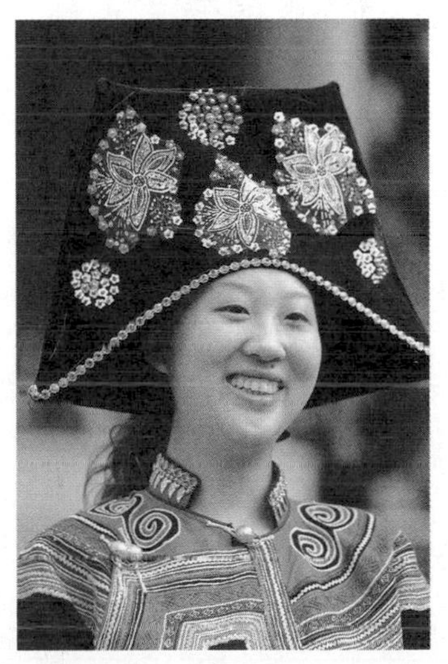

YI

Descendants of the Qiang people of northwestern China, the Yi (aka Sani) are scattered across southwestern China in Yunnan, Sichuan, and Guizhou provinces as well as Guangxi Zhuang Autonomous Region. The largest concentration of the more than 6.5 million Qiang descendants are in Sichuan's Liangshan region. They live in isolated, mountainous regions and are known for being fierce warriors. Notable traits include their syllabic writing system, ancient literature, and traditional medicine—all of which are still being used today. The Yi also sport extravagant costumes that vary according to geographical region. Massive black mortarboard-style hats, blue turbans, ornate red headdresses, and other headwear complement the brilliantly colored vests and pants. Their language is part of the Tibeto-Burman language family and similar to Burmese. Some Yi also live in Vietnam, where they are called the Lolo.

(left) Young unmarried Bai women. Yunnan province. (right) Yi Girl in traditional costume. Puge, Sichuan Province

CLOSE UP

Yunnan Cuisine

Dian cuisine is the term for Han Chinese cuisine found in Yunnan, especially around Kunming. Dian-style dishes are similar to Sichuan dishes and tend to favor spicy and sour flavors. Rice is a staple here, as is a type of rice noodle called *mixian.* A favorite dish is *guoqiao mixian,* a boiling oily broth served with raw pork and vegetables that you cook yourself. *Qiguo ji* (steampot chicken), another trademark Dian-style dish, uses a special earthenware pot to steam chicken and vegetables into a savory soup.

One thing that sets Dian cuisine apart from the rest of China is the dairy products. *Rubing* is made from goat's milk and is typically fried and served with dried chili peppers or sugar. It is a little drier and less pungent than regular goat cheese. *Rushan,* or "milk fan," is a long strip of a cheese that is spread with a salty or sweet sauce. Wrapped around a chopstick, it makes a handy snack.

Street barbecue is a major part of the Yunnan culinary experience. Every kind of meat and vegetable are on offer, as well as quail eggs, *chou doufu* (stinky tofu), and *erkuai* (rice pancakes with sweet or savory fillings). Most restaurants in Yunnan close early, but barbecue stands stay open until the wee hours, making them a good place for a late-night snack.

stone-cooked yak, *malai kafta* (large potato and cashew balls in a curried yogurt sauce), and an incomparable *xianggu* (shiitake-mushroom) platter. A cold Lhasa beer or some homemade yogurt wine rounds out one of the city's more memorable meals. ✉*Jinhuapu Lu, next to Yimen Hotel* ☎*0871/833–6300* ▭*No credit cards.*

$$$–$$$$ THAI

✕**Moonlight Corner.** With Thai owners, Thai chefs, and fresh imported Thai ingredients, Moonlight Corner is arguably the best Thai restaurant in China. Its original location in north Kunming was already quite popular, but this new location on the north side of Green Lake Park has been booming with locals and foreigners since it opened in late 2008. Try favorites such as Thai barbecued chicken, tom yam gong, pineapple fried rice, green papaya salad, or grilled fish, or go for lesser-known gems such as lemongrass salad or the Thai-style iced tea. If the sun is out, sit out front and enjoy one of the best park views in the area. ✉*16 Cuihu Dong Lu650031* ☎*0871/513–8088* ▭*No credit cards.*

¢–$$ AMERICAN Fodor'sChoice ★ ☺

✕**Salvador's Coffee House.** It has the city's best espresso drinks—made from local beans—but Salvador's is more than just a coffeehouse. Easily the best Western restaurant in Kunming, Salvador's makes its own ice cream, bagels, hummus, salsa—even the Indian chai is powdered on-site. Popular main dishes include burritos, quesadillas, and falafel. Salvador's has comfy sofas for lounging and outdoor seating ideal for people-watching on bustling Wenhua Xiang. Seats aren't easy to come by, as Salvador's fills up regularly. ✉*76 Wenhua Xiang650031* ☎*0871/536–3525* ▭*No credit cards.*

CLOSE UP

Kunming's Flying Tigers

Despite being in the hinterland of Southwest China, Kunming played a crucial role in World War II by preventing Japanese forces from taking control of all of China. At the center of this role was the American Volunteer Group, best known by its local nickname *feihu*, or the Flying Tigers, because of the shark faces painted on their fuselages.

The group of around 300 American servicemen was led by the mysterious Claire L. Chennault. A retired captain in the U.S. Air Force, Chennault first came to Kunming in 1938 when Madame Chiang Kai-shek, wife of the country's leader, asked him to organize a Chinese air force to counter the relentless attacks from the Japanese, who were busily bombing much of China with little opposition.

Supply routes to China's capital were being taken out one after another leaving just one road. Chennault argued that a group of American pilots could defend this crucial supply artery, as well as push the Japanese out of the region.

The Flying Tigers were tenacious fighters. They swept through much of China to combat the constant bombing by Japanese forces. Their record was second-to-none in World War II. They had over 50 enemy encounters and were never defeated.

7

WHERE TO STAY

$$–$$$ **Grand Park Hotel Kunming.** Formerly the Harbour Plaza Kunming, this hotel has improved levels of quality and service under its new Singaporean management. A stone's throw from Cuihu Park, the Grand Park's hotel buffet and its Japanese and Cantonese restaurants are solid dining options, but there are plenty of food and drink choices just a short stroll away. **Pros:** clean and comfortable rooms, central location. **Cons:** slightly overpriced. ✉ *20 Honghuaqiao* ☎ *0871/538–6688* 🌐 *www.parkhotelgroup.com/phkunming/phkunming00_index.html* *315 rooms, 14 suites* *In-room: safe, Ethernet. In-hotel: 2 restaurants, bar, pool, gym* ▭ *AE, DC, MC, V.*

$$–$$$$ **Green Lake Hotel** *(Cuihu Binguan)*. Adjacent to Cuihu Park, this hotel is probably Kunming's nicest. From the lobby to the guest rooms, it may be the only five-star hotel in Kunming that actually deserves the rating. The Western restaurant on the first floor is headed by a French chef, and the Cantonese restaurant across the lobby is a favorite of local businessmen and officials. The grand marble-and-wood lobby is filled with plush chairs and sofas, and the coffee shop has excellent coffee drinks and homemade ice cream. The guest rooms are Kunming's cleanest and most comfortable. The restaurant hosts regular performances of traditional music. **Pros:** great location, good service, comfortable rooms. **Cons:** many staff members speak little or no English. ✉ *6 Cuihu Nan Lu* ☎ *0871/515–8888* 🌐 *www.greenlakehotel.com.cn* *301 rooms, 6 suites* *In-room: satellite TV, safe, Ethernet. In-hotel: 2 restaurants, bar, pool, gym* ▭ *AE, DC, MC, V.*

¢–$ **Golden Dragon Hotel** *(Jinlong Fandian)*. Although a bit side, this locally owned hotel offers moderately priced rooms and a reasonable standard of service. It's conveniently close to the railway and bus stations. **Pros:**

close to train and bus stations. **Cons:** far from the city center. ✉*575 Beijing Lu* ☎*0871/313–3015* *150 rooms* *In-room: Ethernet. In-hotel: 2 restaurants, bar, pool* ▭*AE, DC, MC, V.*

¢ **Kunming Hotel.** The oldest of the luxury hotels in town is centrally located and has reasonably comfortable rooms, although they have not been renovated for some years. There is a pool and a practice range for golfers on the premises. **Pros:** central location. **Cons:** feels a little dated. ✉*52 Dongfeng Dong Lu* ☎*0871/316–2063* ⊕*www.kmhotel.com.cn/enhome.htm* *267 rooms, 53 suites* *In-hotel: 3 restaurants, bars, pool, gym* ▭*AE, DC, MC, V.*

¢ **Yunnan University Hotel.** In the heart of the university area, Yunnan University Hotel is one of the city's best bargains. Standard rooms all have clean bathrooms. On the west side of Yunnan University, the hotel has backdoor access to one of China's most beautiful college campuses. **Pros:** close to Wenlin Jie and Cuihu Park. **Cons:** minimal facilities and services, location is chaotic during rush hour. ✉*Yieryi Dajie,* ☎*0871/503–4195* *84 rooms* *In-room: no phone, no TV. In-hotel: restaurant, laundry facilities* ▭*V* *BP.*

NIGHTLIFE AND THE ARTS

NIGHTLIFE

When evening falls, Kunming's growing expat population tends to congregate at the bars, cafés, and restaurants of Wenlin Jie and Wenhua Xiang (literally Culture Forest Street and Culture Alley). **Chapter One** (✉*146 Wenlin Jie* ☎*0871/536–5635*) is a favorite bar for expats, as is **Speakeasy Bar** (✉*445 Dongfeng Xi Lu* ☎*0871/532–7047*), which often has live music.

THE ARTS

Kunming's nascent art scene can be taken in at **Chuangku** (✉*101 Xiba Lu* ☎*No phone*). A group of warehouses that have been converted into galleries, Chuangku is also home to a smattering of cafés and restaurants. **Yunart Gallery** (✉*16 Cuihu Dong Lu* ☎*No phone*) occupies the central area of the high-end Gingko Elité compound at the north end of Cuihu Park. The gallery highlights up-and-coming local artists.

Chinese dance legend Yang Liping may have retired after breaking her leg during her last tour in 2005, but the Yunnan native's award-winning dance and musical production **Dynamic Yunnan** (✉*Kunming Theater, 427 Beijing Lu* ☎*0871/319–2141*) still plays to full-capacity crowds. It's an impressive fusion of the storytelling, songs, and dances of indigenous groups.

SHOPPING

If you're looking for a good deal on tea, look no farther than the wholesale tea market at the southeast corner of Beijing Lu and Wujing Lu. Within the market you'll find an amazing variety of green teas, black teas, flower teas, and herbal teas. It's a wholesale market, but all vendors will sell you small quantities.

Qianju Jie is one of the more popular shopping streets in the city, near the intersection of Wenlin Jie and Wenhua Xiang. On Wenhua Xiang is **Mandarin Books** (✉*52 Wenhua Xiang 9–10* ☎*0871/551–6579*), one of the best foreign-language bookstores in all of China.

CLOSE UP

Dali & the Nanzhao Kingdom

The idyllic scenery belies Dali's importance as the center of power for the Nanzhao Kingdom. The easily defensible area around Erhai Lake was the Kingdom's birthplace, which began as the Bai- and Yi-dominated Damengguo in 649. Almost a century later, Damengguo was expanded to include the six surrounding kingdoms ruled by powerful Bai families. This expansion was supported by the ruling Chinese Tang Dynasty, and the kingdom was renamed Nanzhao.

The primarily Buddhist Nanzhao Kingdom was essentially a vassal state of the Tang Dynasty until AD 750, when it rebelled. Tang armies were sent in 751 and 754 to suppress the insurgents, but they suffered humiliating defeats. Emboldened by their victories, Nanzhao troops helped the kingdom acquire a significant amount of territory. Before reaching its high point with the capture of Chengdu and Sichuan in 829, the Nanzhao Kingdom had expanded to include all of present-day Yunnan, as well as parts of present-day Burma, Laos, and Thailand.

Although the capture of Chengdu was a major victory for Nanzhao, it appears to have led directly to its decline. The Tang Dynasty couldn't stand for such an incursion and sent large numbers of troops to the area. They eventually evicted Nanzhao forces from Sichuan by 873. About 30 years later, the Nanzhao leaders were finally overthrown, ending the story of their meteoric rise and fall.

SIDE TRIP TO THE STONE FOREST

Fodor'sChoice ★ One of the most interesting sites near Kunming is a geological phenomenon known as the **Stone Forest** *(Shilin)*. This cluster of dark gray-limestone karst formations has been twisted into unusual shapes since being formed beneath the sea 270 million years ago. Many have been given names to describe their resemblances to real or mythological animals (phoenixes, elephants, and turtles).

You can take walks through the park, which is dotted with small lakes and pools. Here you'll find plenty of Sani women eager to act as guides and sell you their handicrafts. The area where most tourists venture has, inevitably, become rather commercialized, but there are plenty of similar formations in other parts of the park if you wander off the main trail. The journey here takes you through the hilly countryside dotted with timber-frame architecture typical of the area. ⊠ *Lu'nan* 🎫 *Y80* ⏲ *24 hrs.*

GETTING HERE AND AROUND

The Stone Forest is 125 km (78 mi) southeast of Kunming. There are several ways to get here, the best being a car and driver. One can be arranged through your hotel and should cost between Y500 and Y600. Another option is the cheap bus tours (Y20 round-trip) that leave each morning from the area around the train station. Reservations aren't necessary. This trip takes at least four hours, as the driver makes numerous stops at souvenir stands and junk stores along the way.

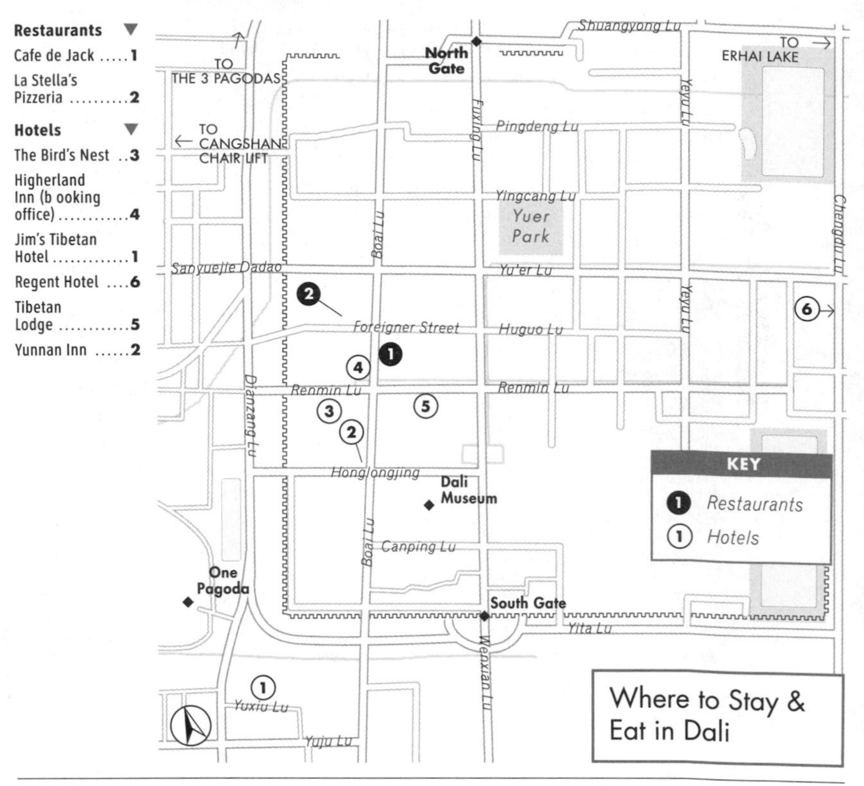

DALI

250 km (155 mi; 4 hrs by bus) northwest of Kunming; 140 km (87 mi; 3 hrs by bus) south of Lijiang.

Dali is one of those rare places that feels completely cut off from the rest of the world, yet has high-speed Internet access. The rustic town is perched at the foot of the towering Cangshan Mountains and overlooks lovely Erhai Lake. Its typically sunny weather, sleepy atmosphere, and gorgeous sunsets have made it one of Yunnan's most popular destinations.

Home to the Bai people, Dali has been inhabited for more than 4,000 years, serving as a major rice-production base for the region. Today, tourism is rejuvenating the town. The upside of this building boom is a greater variety of restaurants and hotels; the downside is that the old town is constantly being demolished and reconstructed, the most recent addition being a massive shopping complex called "Foreigner Street Plaza" that looks like it was copied from a strip mall.

GETTING HERE AND AROUND

BY AIR There are multiple daily flights from Kunming to Dali. Dali's airport is at the southern tip of Erhai Lake. Taxis between the airport and the old town cost Y90. The trip takes just under an hour.

BY BUS Buses from Kunming to Dali take four hours. Bus tickets are available at Kunming's Xizhan and Nanyao Bus stations. Most buses drop you off in "New Dali," the nondescript city of Xiaguan. A 25-minute cab ride gets you from the new town to the old town. It should cost Y35 to Y40, depending on your haggling skills.

BY TRAIN Train service between Kunming and Dali costs about the same as a bus, but the train trip takes seven hours, which is three hours longer than a bus trip.

THE TORCH FESTIVAL

One of the more exciting festivals in southwest China is the Torch Festival, which is celebrated by both the Yi and Bai minorities on the 24th day of the sixth lunar month (in June or July). Dali's old town is one of the best (and worst) places to catch the festival. The chaotic celebration is rivaled only by Chinese New Year. However, many local children like to frighten travelers with the flames, especially on Foreigner Street. Anyone who wants to see the festival without worrying about getting singed by pyromaniac children might want to go to Xizhou—the first town north of Dali.

TOURS

China Minority Travel lets you explore the villages surrounding Erhai Lake. The first stop on the day-trip is nearby Xizhou, a village that resembles Dali before the tourism boom. Afterward, enjoy lunch on the ferry across Erhai Lake before arriving at Wase to explore the village's market. The trip is $225 for up to five people, including a guide, transportation, and lunch. Prices may be higher during Chinese holidays.

ESSENTIALS

Air Contacts **Dali Airport** (☎ *0872/242-8909*).

Medical Assistance **Dali First Municipal People's Hospital** (✉ *217 Tai'an Lu, Dali* ☎ *0872/212-4462*).

Banks **Bank of China** (✉ *Fuxing Lui*). **ICBC** (✉ *Huguo Lu*).

Public Security Bureau **PSB Dali** (✉ *Huguo Lu* ☎ *110*).

Train Contact **Xiaguan Train Station** (✉ *Dianyuan Lu, Xiaguan*).

Visitor and Tour Info **China Minority Travel** (✉ *63 Bo'ai Lu* ☎ *0872/267-9549* 🌐 *www.china-travel.nl*).

EXPLORING DALI

Dali's old town, called Dali Gucheng, is surrounded by attractive reconstructions of the old city wall and gates. Go to the wall's southwest corner and take the stairs to the top for a great view of the city and the surrounding mountains. Outside of the bustling center of the old town are countless little alleys lined with old Bai-style homes.

Dali has two popular pedestrian streets, Huguo Lu and Renmin Lu, both of which run east–west, or uphill–downhill. Huguo Lu, better known as Foreigner Street, is lined with the cafés that made Dali famous in the 1990s, but the street has begun to lose its luster. High rents and cutthroat competition have taken a toll on quality and service.

The most famous landmark in Dali, the **Three Pagodas** *(Santa Si)*, appears on just about every calendar of Chinese scenery. The largest, 215 feet high, dates from AD 836 and is decorated on each of its 16 stories with Buddhas carved from local marble. The other two pagodas, also richly decorated, are more elegant in style. When the water is still, you can ponder their reflection in a nearby pool. A massive new Chan (Zen) Buddhist Temple has been built behind the pagodas. The pagodas are a 20-minute walk from the old town. ⊠*1 km (½ mi) north of Dali Gucheng* *Y121* *Daily 7 AM–8 PM.*

WHERE TO EAT

For a taste of authentic local Bai dishes like *paojiao zhurou* (pork with pickled peppers) or *chao rubing* (fried goat cheese), try any of the local restaurants on Renmin Lu just east of the intersection with Fuxing Lu. None of these restaurants have English menus or service, but they generally have their ingredients on display.

¢–$$ ECLECTIC **Café de Jack.** In business since 1989, Café de Jack still offers good breakfasts and friendly service. Get the strongest cup of Yunnan coffee in Dali and catch up with the rest of the world via the Wi-Fi or in-house net bar. All three floors are a bit different: the first floor feels like a bar, the second floor is more like a restaurant, and the rooftop is a perfect place to kick back with a beer. ⊠*82 Bo'ai Lu* *0872/267–1572* *No credit cards.*

¢–$$ PIZZA Fodor's Choice ★ **La Stella's Pizzeria.** Located at the top of Foreigner Street, Stella's has emerged as one of the best restaurants in town. The pizzas, cooked in a wood-fired oven, feature traditional toppings, as well as Chinese favorites such as corn. Other highlights include lasagna, nachos, and Greek salads. The Chinese food is also worth a try. ⊠*21 Huguo Lu 671003* *0872/267–9251* *No credit cards.*

WHERE TO STAY

¢ **The Bird's Nest.** Owned by a couple of young artists from northern China, the Bird's Nest is centered around a tranquil courtyard just behind the popular Bird Bar. The hotel offers comfortable rooms and friendly service at a reasonable price. An added bonus if you're traveling in a group or just want to live it up is the hotel's free-standing villa with courtyard across the street for Y800 a day. The Bird Bar's kitchen is open past midnight, should you get the munchies. **Pros:** comfortable rooms, chilled-out courtyard. **Cons:** Bird Bar can be noisy. ⊠*22 Renmin Lu* *0872/266–1843* *11 rooms, 1 villa* *In-hotel: restaurant, laundry service, Wi-Fi* *No credit cards.*

¢–$$ **Higherland Inn.** Up in the verdant mountains behind the old town sits the Higherland Inn. At 8,500 feet, it's the perfect place to start a hike or enjoy the view. The walls are a little thin, so it's not the best place for light sleepers. Meals are similar to those you'd find in town, and feature both Chinese and Western dishes. There is a booking office in Dali at 67 Bo'ai Lu, near Renmin Lu; reserve ahead to get a discount on the Y30 fee to ascend the mountains. **Pros:** beautiful scenery, clean air, quiet at night. **Cons:** not easy to get to. ⊠*Cangshan Daorendong* *0872/266–1599* *8 rooms* *In-hotel: restaurant, no elevator* *No credit cards.*

¢ **Jim's Tibetan Hotel.** Outside the south gate, this is one of the city's newest lodgings. It's in the quiet Yulu Xiaoqu neighborhood, making it ideal for those wanting to avoid the hubbub of the old town. Decorated in traditional Tibetan and Bai styles, the hotel is run by a Tibetan and Dutch couple who speak English. It's the only place in Dali with a playground. Ask about booking tours of Dali and beyond. **Pros:** kid friendly, clean. **Cons:** feels isolated from the old town. ✉ *13 Yuxiu Lu* ☎ *0872/267–7824* 🌐 *www.china-travel.nl* *13 rooms* *In-room: Wi-Fi. In-hotel: restaurant, bar* *No credit cards.*

¢–$$ **Regent Hotel.** Dali's only five-star hotel, the Regent seems unnecessary when compared to the highly affordable options in the old town. However, if you have to stay in a five-star, this is your place. **Pros:** good quality and service. **Cons:** feels isolated from the old town. ✉ *Yu'er Lu* ☎ *0872/266–6666* 🌐 *www.regenthotel.cn* *501 rooms* *In-room: Ethernet, laundry. In-hotel: restaurant, bar, pool, airport pickup* *AE, DC, MC, V.*

¢ **Tibetan Lodge.** Near the top of Renmin Lu, Tibetan Lodge puts you in the middle of a long stretch of bars and restaurants. The guest rooms are clean and well-equipped. Tibetan Lodge has bicycles for rent plus a variety of tour options. **Pros:** solid value, good location. **Cons:** can seem too "backpack-y" at times. ✉ *58 Renmin Lu* ☎ *0872/266–4177* *20 rooms* *In-hotel: restaurant, bar, bicycles, public Internet* *No credit cards.*

¢ ★ **Yunnan Inn.** Owned by acclaimed Chinese artist Fang Lijun, this guesthouse is in a class by itself. Eschewing traditional architecture for a more modern style, Fang has created one of the city's most pleasant places to stay. Great rooftop views and the chance to visit Fang's studio set this guesthouse apart. Even better, standard rooms start at just Y80. **Pros:** unique style, quiet at night. **Cons:** often booked, staff doesn't speak much English. ✉ *3 Honglongjing* ☎ *0872/266–3741* *10 rooms* *In-hotel: restaurant, bar, public Internet, no elevator* *No credit cards.*

THE WATER SPLASHING FESTIVAL

The Dai Water Splashing Festival is held in Dai-inhabited areas of southern Yunnan, including the cities of Jinghong and Ruili.

Originally, water was poured gently upon the backs of family members to wash away the sins of the past year and provide blessings for the coming year. Today, it has become a water war, replete with squirt guns, buckets of ice water, and other weapons. It is quite a bit of fun, and a great way to cool off. Just remember to leave any cameras, watches, or cell phones back in your room.

NIGHTLIFE

The **Bird Bar** (✉ *22 Renmin Lu* ☎ *0872/266–1843*) has a courtyard that's great for enjoying starry nights. **Café de Jack** (✉ *82 Bo'ai Lu* ☎ *0872/267–1572*) often has live music in the evenings.

SHOPPING

Foreigner Street is lined with Bai women who have been selling the same jewelry, fabrics, and Communist kitsch for nearly two decades. Don't be afraid to walk away when bargaining; vendors will often drop their prices at the last minute.

Bo'ai Lu and Renmin Lu are peppered with a variety of shops featuring outdoor clothing and equipment; handicrafts from India, Nepal, and Southeast Asia; as well as Chinese antiques. Fuxing Lu, aimed primarily at Chinese tourists, is where you'll find local teas, specialty foods, and most prominently, jade. Much of it is low quality, so buy only if you know something about jade.

SIDE TRIPS FROM DALI

★ With a peak that rises to more than 14,765 feet, **Cangshan** *(Green Mountain)* can be seen from just about any place in Dali. A 16-km (10-mi) path carved into the side of the mountain halfway between the summit and the old town offers spectacular views of Dali and the surrounding villages. There are also several temples, grottoes, and waterfalls just off the main trail. If you don't want to climb several thousand feet to get to the path, there is a cable car (more like a ski lift) that will take you up and back for Y60. To get to the cable car, follow Yu'er Lu to the foot of the mountain. The cost of taking the cable car up the mountain to Y90 and footing it to Y30.

Almost any street off Fuxing Lu will bring you to the shore of **Erhai Lake** *(Erhai Hu)*. You may catch a glimpse of fishermen with their teams of cormorants tied to their boats. In good weather, ferries are a wonderful way to see the lake and the surrounding mountains. The ferries cost between Y30 and Y70 (depending on your ability to bargain). More interesting perhaps—and cheaper—would be to hire one of the local fishermen to paddle wherever you want to go. Boats depart from the village of Zhoucheng.

DID YOU KNOW?

The cormorants have a collar around their necks that prevents them from swallowing the fish they have caught.

Among the prettiest towns in the area is **Xizhou**, about 20 km (12 mi) north of Dali. It has managed to preserve a fair amount of its Bai architecture. The daily morning market and occasional festivals of traditional music attract a fair number of tourists from neighboring Dali. Buses to Xizhou leave from Dali's west gate and cost Y4.

There are a handful of towns with markets known for local crafts, household goods, and antiques (beware of fakes!). **Shaping** has the most popular market, taking place every Monday morning. The town sits on the lake's northern shore and can be most easily reached by boat or by hiring a car and driver. **Wase** is another popular area market, featuring Bai clothing. The town is on the opposite side of the lake from Dali and can be reached by car or boat.

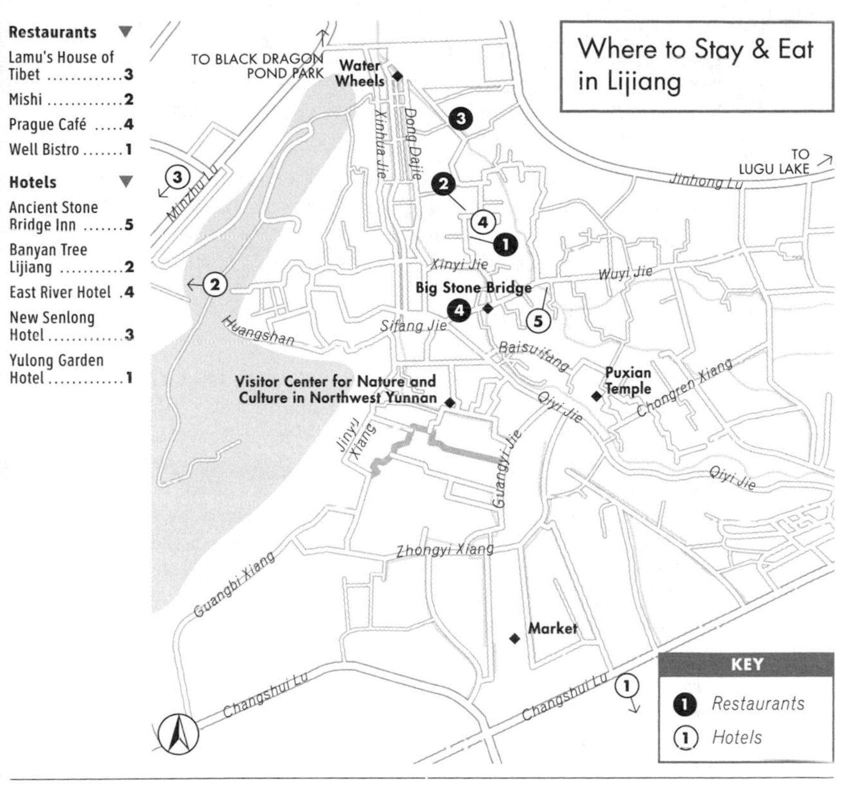

LIJIANG

150 km (93 mi; 3 hrs by bus) north of Dali; 320 km (198 mi; 7 hrs by bus) northwest of Kunming; 550 km (341 mi; 20 hrs by bus) southwest of Chengdu.

Lijiang is probably the most famous travel destination in Yunnan, as its old town was named a UNESCO World Heritage Site. At the base of majestic Jade Dragon Snow Mountain, Lijiang is home to the Naxi people, who are related to Tibetans but have their own language and culture.

Lijiang's old town is a labyrinth of winding alleys, fish-filled streams, and old Naxi houses with tile rooftops. Traditional Naxi singing and dancing are on display nightly at Sifang Jie, the square in old town's center.

GETTING HERE AND AROUND

BY AIR There are multiple daily flights between Lijiang and Kunming. The airport is 30 mi (a half-hour) south of Lijiang. A Y20 bus from the airport terminates on the edge of the old town. A taxi to the old town will run you Y80.

BY BUS Lijiang's main bus stations are on Xin Dajie and the south side of Xiangelila Dadao. Bus trips from Kunming to Lijiang take seven hours.

CLOSE UP

Naxi Music of Lijiang

The Naxi culture is rich in artistic elements—the Naxi pictographs, architecture, Dongba shamans, and, not least of all, the music. It is a complex and intricate musical blending of Han and Naxi musical traditions that has commonly served as entertainment, as well as a measuring stick for Confucian social relationships—Naxi musicians and members of social clubs related to the music were considered to be of a higher status than the average Naxi villager.

Today, Naxi music, with its 500 years of history, is a sonic time capsule, giving us the opportunity to hear songs dating as far back as the Tang, Song, and Yuan Dynasties. Most of the Naxi-inhabited counties around Lijiang feature their own orchestras specializing in the two extant versions of Naxi music: Baisha fine music and Dongjing music. A third type, Huangjing music, fell out of practice over the centuries and has since been lost.

THE ROOTS OF RHYTHM

Legend has it Baisha fine music developed as a result of Kublai Khan's gratitude for Naxi assistance during his conquest of Yunnan during the Yuan Dynasty. The Khan is believed to have left a group of his best musicians and their musical canon with the Naxi in Lijiang. Baisha fine music is one of the grander Chinese musical styles, with large orchestras including the Chinese flute, the lute, and the zither.

Dongjing music came to this region from central China during the Ming and Qing dynasties and is based on Taoist classics. It is the better preserved of the two musical styles, most likely because the Naxi incorporated more of their indigenous music into it.

BEAUTY IS IN THE EAR OF THE BEHOLDER

Naxi orchestras have their own standards for what makes for a quality Naxi musical experience, the key factor being age. In the eyes of the Naxi, the older the musicians, the better. Perhaps this is because fewer and fewer are learning the traditional styles. The musicians' instruments are also old, often much older than the septuagenarians playing the music—the craftsmanship 100 years ago was better than today. Naxi orchestras refuse to play any modern music. They only jam to centuries-old tunes.

For many travelers, Naxi music is an aural step back in time. Others find it screechy and grating. You can catch a show at a number of venues in Lijiang's old town and the new city. The most famous groups are the Baihua and Dayan orchestras. Tickets can typically be purchased starting at Y100 at most hotels and guesthouses.

ESSENTIALS

Air Contacts Lijiang Airport (☎ *0888/517–3088*).

Bank Bank of China (✉ *Dong Dajie*).

Bus Contacts Xianggelila Bus Station (✉ *Xiangelila Dadao*).

Medical Assistance Lijiang People's Hospital (✉ *Fuhui Lu* ☎ *0888/512–2393*).

Public Security Bureau PSB Lijiang (✉ *Fuhui Lu* ☎ *110*).

Visitor and Tour Info **China International Travel Service (CITS)** (✉*Xin Dajie* ☎*0888/512–3508*).

EXPLORING LIJIANG

With so many shops and markets, much of Lijiang's old town feels more like a Special Economic Zone than a UNESCO-protected site. However, it's still possible to get away for an interesting stroll. Helpful English maps around town help you navigate the maze.

The **Visitor Center for Nature and Culture in Northwest Yunnan** is a small but fascinating museum of the region's cultural and biological diversity. Exhibits include one in which area villagers were given cameras to document their daily lives. One exhibit compares photos taken in the 1920s with those taken more recently. The museum is funded by the Nature Conservancy. ✉*42 Xianwen Xiang, at Guangyi Jie* ☎*0888/511–5969* *Free* *Daily 9–6.*

If you can find it, the **Puxian Temple** *(Puxian Si)* is a tranquil place to get away from the crowds. You can refuel with some local snacks from the temple's vegetarian snack restaurant. Try fried Naxi potatoes (they're purple), *jidoufen,* a bean concoction that can be eaten hot as a porridge, or cold and cut up like noodles—the ubiquitous Naxi *baba* bread is also quite good. Wash it all down with a pot of Tibetan yak butter tea. ✉*Qi Yi Jie* *Free* *Daily 8–6.*

Outside the old town, the **Black Dragon Pool Park** *(Heilong Tan Gongyuan)* has a tranquil pavilion where locals come to play cards and drink tea. The park is home to the **Dongba Research Institute Museum** *(Dongba Yanjiu Suo),* a museum devoted to Naxi Dongba culture. ✉*Xinde Lu* *Y80* *Daily 6:30 AM–8 PM.*

7

WHERE TO EAT

¢–$ ECLECTIC **✕Lamu's House of Tibet.** One of the most consistent restaurants in the old town, Lamu's serves Tibetan, Chinese, and Naxi cuisine, as well as familiar dishes like lasagna and french fries. The pleasant atmosphere, traditional Tibetan decor, and helpful staff make Lamu's one of Lijiang's better dining options. ✉*56 Jishan Xiang, Xinyi Jie* ☎*0888/511–5776* *No credit cards.*

$$–$$$$ ECLECTIC Fodor'sChoice ★ **✕Mishi.** Easily the best restaurant in the old town, Swedish-owned Mishi serves the perfect balance of local and international cuisine. The relaxing environment combines Scandinavian design with traditional Naxi sensibilities. Standout dishes include sizzling yak meat on a roof tile, panfried salmon with lemon butter, and fried spareribs. In a town full of bars, Mishi has one of the best selections of liquor and beer, which go perfectly with the plush seating inside or the relaxing interior courtyard. ✉*52 Mishi Xiang, off Xinyi Jie* ☎*0888/518–7605* *No credit cards.*

¢–$ CAFE **✕Prague Café.** The town's top choice for good coffee, Prague Café also serves good food, especially the American breakfast. Favorite meals include Japanese-style *katsudon,* pork cutlets in a savory sauce. It also has a good book collection and free Internet access. ✉*80 Mishi Xiang, at Xinyi Jie* ☎*0888/512–3757* *No credit cards.*

¢–$ CAFE ✕ **Well Bistro.** Near the Old Well, this small eatery serves a nice variety of international food at reasonable prices in a pretty setting away from the town square. Its coffee is very good and it's a top choice for breakfast. This is one of the best places in town to hunker down with a hot drink and a good book on a cold or rainy day. ✉ *32 Mishi Xiang, at Xinyi Jie* ☎ *0888/518–6431* ▭ *No credit cards.*

WHERE TO STAY

¢ **Ancient Stone Bridge Inn.** Two of the rooms in this guesthouse look directly out over a brook, a small pedestrian street, and pair of bridges. It's a bit more expensive than the average guesthouse, but the perfect setting may justify the extra few yuan. The front door is locked at midnight. **Pros:** good location, inexpensive. **Cons:** in slight need of a renovation. ✉ *71 Wuyi Jie Xingrenxia* ☎ *0888/518–4001 or 139/8882–5829* *10 rooms* *In-hotel: laundry service, no elevator* ▭ *No credit cards.*

$$$$ **Banyan Tree Lijiang.** The only luxury resort near Lijiang, Banyan Tree is made up of villas designed to resemble Naxi courtyard homes. Each self-contained accommodation features its own hot tub or swimming pool. Located in the old Naxi capital of Baisha at the foot of mist-covered Jade Dragon Snow Mountain, the hotel has spectacular unobstructed views. It has all the amenities you would expect in a world-class resort, from Thai massage in the spa to fine dining in the Bai Yun restaurant. **Pros:** nearly perfect service and accommodations, breathtaking scenery. **Cons:** very expensive. ✉ *Yuerong Lu,* ☎ *0888/533–1111* ⊕ *www.banyantree.com* *55 villas* *In-room: safe, Ethernet. In-hotel: 2 restaurants, room service, bar, gym, spa, laundry service, airport shuttle, no elevator* ▭ *DC, MC, V.*

¢ ★ **East River Hotel** *(Dong He Ju)*. One of the newer guesthouses, East River Hotel offers some of the most comfortable rooms—and bathrooms—in the old town. Outside the modern comfort of the guest rooms, a traditional courtyard with a clear stream running through it beckons. Although a little more expensive than most of its competition, East River Hotel is worth it. Complimentary breakfast comes with the room. **Pros:** quiet, idyllic courtyard. **Cons:** hard to find. ✉ *68 Mishi Xiang, off Xinyi Jie* ☎ *0888/515–1668* *40 rooms* *In-hotel: restaurant, public Internet, no elevator* ▭ *No credit cards.*

¢ **New Senlong Hotel.** This five-star is located on the southwest edge of the old town and is the closest in style to traditional high-end accommodation you'll find in the area. A lovely garden area is in the courtyard, and the rooms are large and nicely furnished. The restaurant serves a variety of local dishes. **Pros:** comfortable rooms, old town location. **Cons:** noisy part of town. ✉ *Minzhu Lu* ☎ *0888/512–0666* *214 rooms* *In-hotel: restaurant* ▭ *No credit cards.*

¢ **Yulong Garden Hotel.** This hotel offers a pleasant combination of traditional architecture and modern convenience. It's a good option for visitors who want the amenities of a hotel, like an on-site restaurant and bar. It may not be special, but it is very clean and well maintained, and the hot water is reliable. **Pros:** more amenities than most guesthouses. **Cons:** staff can be hard to find when you need them. ✉ *Dinghong Lu* ☎ *0888/518–2888* *150 rooms* *In-hotel: restaurant, bar, laundry service, no elevator* ▭ *AE, MC, V.*

NIGHTLIFE AND THE ARTS

Traditional Naxi music and dancing can be found in the town square at Sifang Jie beginning in the afternoon and lasting into the evening. There is also a variety of cultural performances held daily around Lijiang.

The most impressive cultural event is **Lijiang Impression** (✉*Ganhai Scenic District* ☎*0888/888–8888*), produced by director Zhang Yimou (Beijing Olympics opening ceremony, *Red Sorghum, Raise the Red Lantern*). Zhang takes Lijiang's Dongba culture and beautiful surroundings as his muse. Set at the base of Jade Dragon Snow Mountain and using the mountain as an integral part of the scenery, this music and dance performance makes full use of its spectacular location. The show takes place daily at 1:20, and costs Y190.

At the Meeting Hall of Lijiang, the **Mountain Spirit Show** (✉*Minzu Lu* ☎*No phone*) offers fire eating and other extraordinary feats by the Yi shamen. The performance, daily at 8 PM, costs Y120.

SIDE TRIPS FROM LIJIANG

Towering majestically over Lijiang, the 18,360-foot **Jade Dragon Snow Mountain** *(Yulong Xue Shan)* is one of non-Tibetan China's most spectacular peaks. The mountain's jagged, snow-covered face is one of the defining sights of a trip to Lijiang. The well-maintained road to the scenic area is a nice drive, passing numerous villages and offering fine valley and mountain views. The park entrance is about a 30 minute drive from old town. Taxis should cost Y35 to Y40 one-way, and Y100 or more if you want the driver to wait for you. Most hotels and guesthouses can book trips to the mountain. *Y80 Daily 7–5.*

¢ **Wenhai Ecolodge.** Only accessible by foot or on horseback, Wenhai Ecolodge is one of the country's first "green" resorts. It's located in the mountain valley that is home to Lake Wenhai, a seasonal lake that appears between July and March. When the basin is filled, the lake is home to black-necked cranes, black storks, and several varieties of duck. There is excellent hiking in the valley, and the chance to come across some of the area's endangered plants and animals such as the giant laughing thrush and the winter wren. The 12-room lodge is designed to minimize environmental impact and has excellent views of nearby Jade Dragon Snow Mountain. It's highly recommended for nature lovers and conservation-minded travelers. Room price includes three meals per day. **Pros:** fascinating for nature lovers. **Cons:** remote, rougher than some travelers can handle. ✉*Lake Wenhai* ☎*1390/888–1817* *www.northwestyunnan.com/wenhai_ecolodge.htm* *12 rooms* *In hotel: restaurant, no elevator* *No credit cards* *FAP.*

★ A 2½-hour drive from Lijiang, **Tiger Leaping Gorge** *(Hutiao Xia)* is home to some of China's most breathtaking mountain scenery. Lucky for travelers who have not yet seen this spectacular scenery, plans to dam the gorge were scrapped by the government in late 2007. By water, the gorge winds about about 16 km (10 mi); following it by land on the uppertrail is a 40-km (25-mi) hike, which can be leisurely hiked in two days or done in one day if you're fit enough. The upper trail and a paved road below connect the towns of Qiaotou in the west and Daju in the east, and there is a ferry across the river near Daju that stops service at 5 PM. The easiest way to tackle the trek from Lijiang is to take the 8:30 AM or 9 AM bus on Xin Dajie to Qiaotou and hike toward Daju.

There are several guesthouses in the gorge, scattered at distances to accommodate hikers at any stage of their trek. All offer food, hot showers, and beds for Y10 to Y20. Many of the guesthouses have expanded and upgraded accommodations in the past couple of years, so there is more selection and even some higher-end rooms for Y150. The guesthouses have put up signs and arrows to let hikers know how much farther until the next lodging. If you don't mind not hiking the whole gorge, stop in Walnut Garden, where you can take one of the regular buses back to Lijiang. If you continue to Daju, there are only two buses a day to Lijiang, at 8:30 AM and 1 PM.

Nuisances along the trail include fake "toll collectors" who will attempt to take your money and aggressive local dogs. The former requires patience and politeness to deal with, the latter the ability to stand one's ground—and it's useful to have a large stick.

JINGHONG AND THE XISHUANGBANNA REGION

400 km (248 mi; 12 hrs by bus) southwest of Kunming; 425 km (264 mi; 12 hrs by bus) south of Dali.

Jinghong is the capital of southern Yunnan's Xishuangbanna Dai Autonomous Region, which borders Laos and Myanmar. Xishuangbanna is home to the Dai, a people related to Thais and Laotians who, like their cousins to the south, love very spicy food.

Jinghong sits on the banks of the muddy Mekong, although this stretch of the legendary river is known locally as the Lancang. This is where China meets Southeast Asia; it feels more and more like Laos or Thailand the farther you travel from Jinghong. Even inside the city, the architecture, the clothing, and even the barbecue seem much more like what you'd find in Vientiane or Chiang Mai.

Jinghong has experienced a small tourist boom; it now has its own airport with flights to Kunming and other cities. But despite the increase in economic activity, Jinghong still moves at about the same speed as the Mekong.

GETTING HERE AND AROUND

BY AIR Jinghong's international airport has service to Kunming and Chengdu, as well as destinations in Thailand, Cambodia, and Laos. It's about 15 minutes west of the city center. From the airport, take the Number 1 bus into town for Y2, or opt for a taxi for Y30.

BY BUS Jinghong's Number Two Bus Station, just north of the intersection of Mengle Dadao and Xuanwei Lu.

TOURS

Tours organized by Forest Café and Meimei Café are your best bet for a tailored English-language tour of Xishuangbanna.

ESSENTIALS

Air Contacts Jinghong Airport (☎0691/212–3003).

Bus Contacts Number Two Bus Station (✉Minhang Lu ☎0691/212–4427).

Medical Assistance Jinghong People's Hospital (✉41 Galan Zhong Lu ☎0691/212–3221).

Banks Bank of China (✉Mengle Dadao).

Public Security Bureau PSB Jinghong (✉Xuanwei Dadao ☎110).

Visitor and Tour Info China International Travel Service (CITS) (✉Galan Zhong Lu ☎0691/213–1165).

EXPLORING JINGHONG

Even a short walk around Jinghong reveals its colorful mix of Dai, Chinese, Thai, and Burmese influences. It's a small enough town that you can cover most of it on foot in a day. Bordered by the Lancang River to the east, the city quickly begins to thin out as you head west.

The **Lancang River** *(Lancang Jiang)* is the name of the Mekong River in China, where it originates before flowing into Southeast Asia. It is easiest to access the river from Jinghong at the Xishuangbanna Bridge—there is a path there that follows alongside the river and is ideal for strolling or biking. A growing number of local operations offer a variety of boat, raft, and dinghy trips along the famed river.

On the southeastern edge of Jinghong is **Manting Park** *(Manting Gongyuan)*, a pleasant park where you can have a closer look at some of the area's indigenous plants. Also worth exploring is the large peacock aviary. The park is especially lively around mid-April when people gather here to celebrate the Water Splashing Festival. ✉*Manting Lu* *Y40* *Daily 7:30 AM–7:30 PM.*

★ **Xishuangbanna Tropical Flower and Plant Garden** *(Xishuangbanna Redai Huahuiyuan)* is an interesting place to spend several hours walking among fragrant frangipani, massive lily pads, drooping jackfruit, and thousands of other colorful and peculiar plants. This is one of China's finest gardens, featuring a well-designed layout arranged into themed sections including tropical fruits, palms, and rubber trees. Don't walk through too fast or you'll miss out on some of the more unique plants such as *tiaowu cao*, or "dancing grass," which actually stands up if you sing at it. Each plant's placard features English and Latin names. ✉*99 Xuanwei Dadao* *Y40* *Daily 7:30–6.*

WHERE TO EAT

$–$$ CHINESE **✕Foguang Yuan.** Tucked away behind a school and a police station, Foguang Yuan is a hidden gem. The restaurant is actually several dining areas built around a patch of jungle. The Dai architecture and beautiful tropical setting alone merit a visit, but the restaurant also serves an excellent array of Dai and Chinese classics. There are no English menus, so venture into the kitchen and point to what looks good. Brave diners can sample the large selection of *paojiu*, or infused rice wines. ✉*2 Jiaotong Xiang, near Yiwu Lu* ☎*0691/213–8608* *No credit cards.*

¢–$ CHINESE **Forest Café.** Run by the brother-sister team of Sarah and Stone Chen, both of whom are fluent in English, this café serves the best Western-style breakfasts in town. The kitchen makes its own whole-wheat bread and uses only organic mountain rice in its dishes. The staff can also arrange trips to a variety of local villages. *Galan Nan Lu at Jingde Lu 0691/898–5122 No credit cards.*

¢–$$ CHINESE **Meimei Café.** Now at a new location at the north end of Manting Lu, Meimei is a good place to compare notes with other travelers, as many people come here to buy tickets or book tours. One of the few places in Jinghong with English-speaking staff, Meimei Café serves Western, Chinese, and Dai food, as well as good coffee and juice drinks. *Manting Lu 0691/212–7324 No credit cards.*

WHERE TO STAY

¢–$ **Crown Hotel.** In the heart of Jinghong, this hotel has several low-slung buildings in a parklike setting with a large swimming pool. Standard rooms start at Y480, but if you haggle a bit you can likely get a better rate. There is also a good night market outside the hotel. **Pros:** near night market, pool is perfect for cooling off. **Cons:** almost no English-speaking staff. *70 Mengle Dadao 0691/219–9888 88 rooms In-hotel: restaurant, laundry service No credit cards.*

¢ **Golden Banna Hotel.** Across the street from the Crown Hotel, Golden Banna is a decent, no-frills accommodation option in Jinghong. The standard rooms are clean and have private bathrooms. Don't expect much in the way of service or amenities, however. **Pros:** good value. **Cons:** drab decor. *55 Mengle Dadao 0691/212–4901 100 rooms In-hotel: restaurant AE, MC, V.*

SHOPPING

Zhuanghong Lu, in the northern part of town, is filled with Burmese jade and goods from Thailand. There is a massive night market by the Xishuangbanna Bridge in the city's northeast. There is a much smaller night market on Mengla Lu outside the Crown Hotel.

SIDE TRIPS FROM JINGHONG

One of China's first serious attempts at ecotourism, the 900-acre **Sanchahe Nature Reserve** is home to wild elephants. Two hours north of Jinghong, the park also features a butterfly farm and a cable car that offers breathtaking views. Lodging is in "tree houses" about 25 feet above ground—a unique place to spend a night. It is best to avoid visiting during the summer, when the weather can be rainy. Arrange transportation through your hotel.

One of the more scenic areas of Xishuangbanna is **Ganlan Basin** *(Ganlanba)*, 37 km (23 mi) from Jinghong. Minority peoples still live in bamboo huts here, amid the beautiful rain forest. The area is famous in Yunnan for its tropical flowers and the millions of butterflies that inhabit this valley. If you want to spend a few days hiking and investigating the basin, you can stay at one of the many village guesthouses, most of which accept foreigners.

ENGLISH	PINYIN	CHINESE
GUANGXI	GŬANXI	广西
GUILIN	Gùilín	桂林
Bank of China	Zhōnggúo yínháng	中国银行
China International Travel Service (CITS)	Zhōngguó guójì lǚxíngshè	中国国际旅行社
China Travel Service (CTS)	Zhōngguó lǚxíngshè	中国旅行社
Elephant Trunk Hill	Xiàngbíshān	象鼻山
Golden Elephant Hotel	Jīnxiàng dàfàndiàn	金象大酒店
Guilin Bus Station	Guìlín kèyùnzhàn	桂林客运站
Guilin People's Hospital	Guìlín rénmín yīyuàn	桂林人民医院
Guilin Railway Station	Guìlín huǒchēzhàn	桂林火车站
Inaka	Tángjiànlì	唐剑利
Lijiang Waterfall Guilin	Líjiāng dàpòbù fàndiàn	漓江大瀑布饭店
Ming Tomb	Jìngjiāngwáng líng	靖江王陵
Paddie's	Bànjiē bā	畔街街吧
Paulaner	Bǎilòng	柏龙
Peak of Solitary Beauty	Dúxiùfēng	独秀峰
Princess City Solitary Beauty Park	Jìngjiāngwáng chéng	靖江王城
Putuo Mountain	Pǔtuóshān	普陀山
Rosemary Cafe	Diédiéxiāng bǐshàbǐng diàn	迷迭香比萨店
Seven Star Cliff	Qīxīngyán	七星岩
Seven Star Park	Qīxíng gōngyuán	七星公园
Sheraton Guilin	Guìlín Dàyǔ dàfàndiàn	桂林大宇大饭店
The Here	zhè lǐ	這里
Wang Cheng Fan Dian	Wángchéng fàndiàn	王城饭店
YANGSHUO	Yángshuò	阳朔
Bank of China	Zhōngguó yínhàng	中国银行
Buffalo Bar	Niútóu bā cantīng	牛头吧餐厅
China Cafe	Yuánshǐrēn	原始人
China International Travel Service (CITS)	Zhōngguó guójì lǚxíngshè	中国国际旅行社
Club 98	jiǔbā jūlèbù	98俱乐部
Dynasty Dumplings	Yīpǐnjū	一品居
Kelly's Place	Dēnglóngfēngwèi guǎn	灯笼风味馆
Le Votre	Lèdéfǎshì cāntīng	乐得法试餐厅
Longsheng Longji Rice Terraces	Lóngshènglóngjǐ tītián	龙胜龙脊梯田

7

ENGLISH	PINYIN	CHINESE
Magnolia Hotel	Báiyùlán jiǔdiàn	白玉兰酒店
Man De Guai	Mǎndéguǎi	满得拐
Moon Hill	Yuèliàng shān	月亮山
Morningsun Hotel	Chénguāng jiǔdiàn	晨光酒店
Paradesa Yangshuo Resort	Yángshuò Bǎilèlái dùjià fàndiàn	阳朔百乐来度假饭店
Peng Family Painted Scroll Factory	Péngshì shànhuà gōngyìchàng	彭氏扇画工艺厂
Riverview Hotel	Wàngjiāng lóu	望江楼
Yangshuo Bus Station	Yángshuò kèyùnzhàn	阳朔客运站
Yangshuo Park	Yángshuò gōngyuán	阳朔公园
Yangshuo Regency Holiday Hotel	Lìjǐng jiàrì bīngguǎn	丽景假日宾馆
NANNING	Nánníng	南宁
Bank of China	Zhōngguó yínháng	中国银行
Beifang Renjia	Běifāngrénjiā	北方人家
China International Travel Service (CITS)	Zhōngguó guójì lǚxíngshè	中国国际旅行社
Guangxi Zhuang Autonomous Region Museum	Guǎngxī Zhuàngzhú zìzhìqū bówùguǎn	广西壮族自治区博物馆
Majestic Hotel	Mīngyuánxīndū dàjiǔdiàn	明园新都大酒店
Nanning Bus Station	Nánníng kèyùnzhàn	南宁客运站
Nanning First Municipal People's Hospital	Nánníng dìyī rénmín yīyuàn	南宁市第一人民医院
Nanning Station	Nánníng huǒchēzhàn	南宁火车站
Nanning Wuxu International Airport	Nánníng Wúyǔ guójì jīchǎng	南宁吴圩国际机场
South Lake	Nánhú	南湖
Taoyuan Hotel	Táoyuán dàjiǔdiǎn	桃源大酒店
The Here	zhè lǐ	這里
White Dragon Park	Báilóng gōngyuán	白龙公园
GUIZHOU	GUÌZHŌU	贵州
GUIYANG	Guìyáng	贵阳
Bank of China	Zhōngguó yínháng	中国银行
China International Travel Service (CITS)	Zhōngguó guójì lǚxíngshè	中国国际旅行社
Guiyang Bus Station	Guìyáng Kèyùnzhàn	贵阳客运站
Guiyang Longdongbao Airport	Guìyáng Lóngbǎodòng jīchàng	贵阳龙洞堡机场
Guiyang Railway Station	Guìyáng huǒchēzhàn	贵阳火车站
Guizhou Overseas Travel Service	Wénhǎi shēngtài lǚguǎn	文海生态旅馆

ENGLISH	PINYIN	CHINESE
Guizhou Park Hotel	guìzhōu fàndiàn	贵州饭店
Hebin Park	Héibīn gōngyuán	河滨公园
Huangguoshu Falls	Huángguǒshù pùbù	黄果树瀑布
Huaxi Park	Huāxī gōngyuán	花溪公园
Nell's Yard Café	Níěr xiǎoyuàn kāfēiwō	尼尔小院咖啡屋
Nenghui Jiudian	Xiónghuī Jiǔdiàn	能辉酒店
Old Kaili Sour Soup Fish Restaurant	Lǎokǎilǐ suānyútāng	老凯里酸汤鱼
Qianling Park	Qínlíng gōngyuán	黔灵公园
Sheraton Guiyang Hotel	Guìyáng Xǐláidēng jiǔdiàn	贵阳喜来登酒店
Underground Gardens	Guìyáng dìxià gōngyuán	贵阳地下公园
KAILI	Kǎilǐ	凯里
Bank of China	Zhōngguó yínháng	中国银行
Guotai Dajiudian	Guótài dàjiǔdiàn	国泰大酒店
Jinquanhu Park	Jīnquán hú	金泉湖
Kaili Bus Station	Kǎilǐ kèyùnzhàn	凯里客运站
Kaili Train Station	Kaǐlǐ huǒchēzhàn	凯里火车站
Minorities Museum	zhōu mínzhú bówùguǎn	州民族博物馆
YUNNAN	**YÚNNÁN**	**云南**
KUNMING	Kūnmín	昆明
Bank of China	Zhōngguó yínháng	中国银行
Chapter One		no chinese name
China International Travel Service (CITS)	Zhōngguó guójì lǚxíngshè	中国国际旅行社
Chuangku	Chuàngkù	创库
Golden Dragon Hotel	Jīnglóng fàndiàn	金龙饭店
Grand Park Hotel Kunming	Kūnmín Jūnlè jiǔdiàn (qián Hǎiyì jiǔdiandiàn)	昆明君乐酒店(前海逸酒店)
Green Lake Hotel	chuìhú bīngguǎn	翠湖宾馆
Green Lake Park	Chuìhū gōngyuán	翠湖公园
Heavenly Manna	Mānà	吗哪
Huatongqun	Huātǒngqún	花筒裙
Kunming Airport	Kūnmín jīchǎng	昆明机场
Kunming First People's Hospital	Kūnmín dìyī rénmín yīyuàn	昆明第一人民医院
Kunming Hotel	Kūnmín fàndiàn	昆明饭店
Kunming Train Station	Kūnmín huǒchēzhàn	昆明火车站
Makye Ame	Mǎjímāmī	玛吉阿米

ENGLISH	PINYIN	CHINESE
Mandarin Books	Kūnmín Mànlín shūyuàn	昆明漫林书苑
Nanyao Bus Station	Nányáo kèzhàn	南窑客站
Salvador's Coffee House	Sàěrwǎduō	萨尔瓦多
Speakeasy Bar	Shuō bā	说吧
Stone Forest	Shílín	石林
Xiong Brothers Bike Shop	Xióngshìxiōngdì zìxíngchē	熊氏兄弟自行车
Xizhan Bus Station	xīzhàn kèyùnzhàn	西站客运站
Yuantong Temple	Yuántōngsì	圆通寺
Yunart Gallery	Yunart huàláng	Yunart 画廊
Yunnan Provincial Museum	Yúnnán shéng bówùguǎn	云南省博物馆
Yunnan University Hotel	Yúndà bìn guǎn	云大宾馆
DALI	Dālǐ	大理
Bank of China	Zhōngguó yínháng	中国银行
Bird Bar	Liǎobā	鸟吧
Cafe de Jack	Yīnghuāyuǎn xīchāntīng	樱花园西餐厅
Cangshan	Chāngshān	苍山
China Minority Travel	Zhōngguó shǎoshùmínzhú lǚyóu gōngsī	中国少数民族旅游公司
Dali Airport	Dàlǐ jīchǎng	大理机场
Dali First Municipal People's Hospital	Dàlǐ shì dìyī rénmín yīyuàn	大理市第一人民医院
Erhai Lake	Erhǎi	洱海
Guiqu Laixi	Guīqùláixī	归去来兮
Higherland Inn	Gāodì	高地
ICBC	Gōngshāng yínháng	工商银行
Jim's Tibetan Hotel	Jīmǔ zhàngshì jiǔdiàn	吉姆藏式酒店
La Stella's Pizzeria	Xīnxīng bǐshà fáng	新星比萨房
Regent Hotel	Fēnghuāxuěyuè dàjiǔdiàn	风花雪月大酒店
The Bird's Nest	Laiǒwō	鸟窝
Three Pagodas	Sāntǎ sì	三塔寺
Tibetan Lodge	Qīngnián lǚguǎn	青年旅馆
Xiaguan Train Station	Xiàguān huǒchēzhàn	下关火车站
Yunnan Inn	Fēngyuèshānshuǐ kèzhàn	风月山水客栈
LIJIANG	Lìjiāng	丽江
Ancient Stone Bridge Inn	Dàshíqiáo kèzhàn	大石桥客栈
Bank of China	Zhōngguó yínháng	中国银行

ENGLISH	PINYIN	CHINESE
Banyan Tree Lijiang	Lìjiāng Yuèrōng zhuāng	丽江悦榕庄
Black Dragon Pool Park	Hēilóngtán gōngyuán	黑龙潭公园
China International Travel Service (CITS)	Zhōngguó guójì lǚxíngshè	中国国际旅行社
East River Hotel	Dōnghéjū	东河居
Jade Dragon Snow Mountain	Yùlóng xuěshán	玉龙雪山
Lamu's House of Tibet	Xīzàng xīcāntīng	西藏屋西餐馆
Lijiang Airport	Lìjiang jīchăng	丽江机场
Lijiang People's Hospital	Lìjiāng rénmín yīyuàn	丽江人民医院
Mishi	Mĭsīxiāng	米思香
New Senlong Hotel	Xīnshēnlóng dajiŭdiàn	新森龙大酒店
Prague Cafe	Bùlāgé kāfēitīng	布拉格咖啡馆
Puxian Temple	Pŭxiánshì	普贤寺
Tiger Leaping Gorge	Hŭtiàoxiá	虎跳峡
Visitor Center for Nature and Culture in Northwest Yunnan	Diănxīběi zìrán yŭ wēnhuà zhī chuāng jiē ŭyóu tuīguăng zhōngxīn	滇西北自然与文化之窗暨绿色旅游推广中心
Well Bistro	Jĭngzuó cāntìng	井卓餐馆
Wenhai Ecolodge	Wénhăi shēngtài guăn	文海生态旅馆
Xianggelila Bus Station	Xiānggélĭlā kèyùnzhàn	香格里拉客运站
Yulong Garden Hotel	Yùlóng huāyuán jiŭdiàn	玉龙花园酒店
JINGHONG	Jĭnghóng	景洪
Bank of China	Zhōngguó yínháng	中国银行
China International Travel Service (CITS)	Zhōngguó guójì lǚxíngshè	中国国际旅行社
Crown Hotel	Huángguān dàjiŭdiàn	皇冠大酒店
Foguang Yuan	Fóguāng yuán	佛光园
Forest Cafe	Shenlín kāfēiwō	森林咖啡屋
Ganlan Basin	Gănglăn bà	橄榄坝
Golden Banna Hotel	Jīnbănnà jiŭdiàn	金版纳酒店
Jinghong Airport	Jĭnghóng jīchăng	景洪机场
Jinghong People's Hospital	Jĭnghóng rénmín yīyuàn	景洪人民医院
Lancang River	Lánchāng jiāng	澜沧江
Manting Park	Màntīng gōngyuán	曼听公园
Meimei Cafe	Měiměi kāfēitīng	美美咖啡厅
Number Two Bus Station	èrhào kèyùnzhàn	二号客运站
Sanchahe Nature Reserve	Sānchàhé zìrán băohuìqū	三岔河自然保护区

ENGLISH	PINYIN	CHINESE
Xishuangbanna	Xīshuángbǎnnà	西双版纳
Xishuangbanna Tropical Flower & Plant Garden	Xīshuāngbǎnnà rèdài huāyuán	西双版纳热带花卉园

Sichuan & Chongqing

You're not in Kansas anymore! The Litang Horse Festival, Sichuan

WORD OF MOUTH

"Wenshu Monastery . . . was a great place to explore. The murals inside the buildings were very vivid and the relief carvings amazing. We relaxed in one if the tea houses inside the temple grounds before heading back to our street and our hotpot lunch."

—martha1953

WELCOME TO SICHUAN & CHONGQING

Medieval Buddhist cave art at Dazu

TOP REASONS TO GO

★ **Emeishan:** Hike 10,000 feet, to the top of one of China's holy mountains and UNESCO World Heritage Site.

★ **Giant Panda Breeding Research Base:** Stroll through the bamboo groves, bone up on the latest in genetic biology and ecological preservation, and check out cute baby pandas.

★ **Horseback riding in Songpan:** Marvel at the raw beauty of Northern Sichuan's pristine mountain forests and emerald-green lakes from the back of these gentle beasts.

★ **Liquid Fire:** Savor some of the spiciest food on the planet in Chongqing's many hotpot restaurants.

★ **An engineering miracle or madness:** Enjoy a lazy riverboat ride through the surreal Three Gorges, and stand in awe of one of China's latest engineering feats, the mighty Three Gorges Dam.

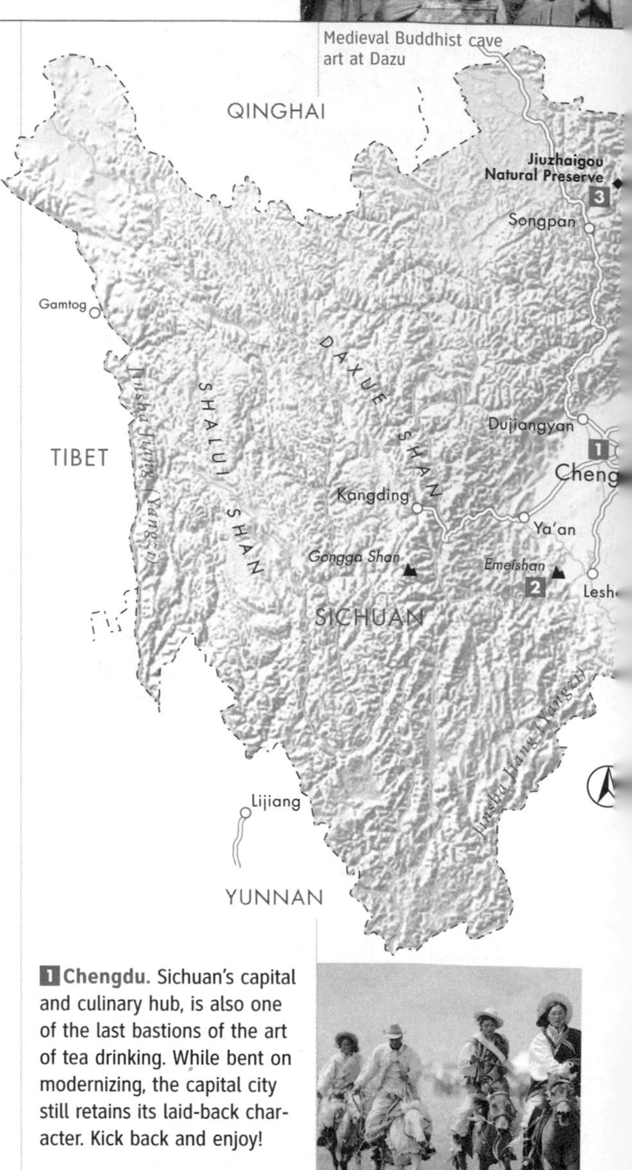

1 Chengdu. Sichuan's capital and culinary hub, is also one of the last bastions of the art of tea drinking. While bent on modernizing, the capital city still retains its laid-back character. Kick back and enjoy!

Horse race at the Litang Horse Festival, Sichuan Province.

2 Emeishan. One of China's holy mountains, it has almost 50 km (31 mi) of paths leading to the summit. Take time out to enjoy the lush mountains around Emeishan, which also produce some of the world's best tea.

Tourist boat at the Three Little Gorges, Yangzi River.

3 Juizhaigou Natural Preserve. Nestled between the snowcapped peaks of the Aba Autonomous Prefecture in northern Sichuan lies the Jiuzhaigou Reserve, a wonderland of turquoise.

4 Chongqing. Formerly part of Sichuan proper, Chongqing is its own exploding municipality with more than 15 million residents. Chongqing's meandering alleys will appeal to those who love getting lost in Venice-like twisting streets. This is also the jumping-off point for the Three Gorges river ride.

GETTING ORIENTED

If you're after a China experience where the cuisine is fiery and pandas can be found in the forests gnawing on bamboo, Sichuan province in Southwestern China is a good bet. Sichuan's capital of Chengdu is dab smack in the middle of the province and the logical point to begin your sojourn. Chengdu's flat, grid-like layout is ideal for strolls and biking. It's also acclaimed for its many outdoor gear shops that can equip one for any of Sichuan's local and neighboring natural wonders. For those interested in witnessing the mighty Three Gorges Dam, the city of Chongqing, 150 mi southeast of Chengdu, is where the best Yangtze tour boats begin their journey downriver, through the Gorges and to the dam.

SICHUAN & CHONGQING PLANNER

The Developing West

After the May 12, 2008, earthquake, even more development funds were designated for Sichuan. But the money has been slow to reach the province. Flooding and road washouts have become a major problem since the quake, and the Sichuan–Tibet highway suffered frequent closings in the months after the catastrophe. Rebuilding will take a long time.

The Weather

Chengdu and eastern Sichuan are hot and humid, with temperatures around 35° to 50°F in winter and 75° to 85°F in summer. Chongqing is known for its broiling summer temperatures—sometimes over 100°F. The western plateau is cold but intensely sunny (bring sunscreen and sunglasses). In winter temperatures drop to -15°F. Summers are around 65°F.

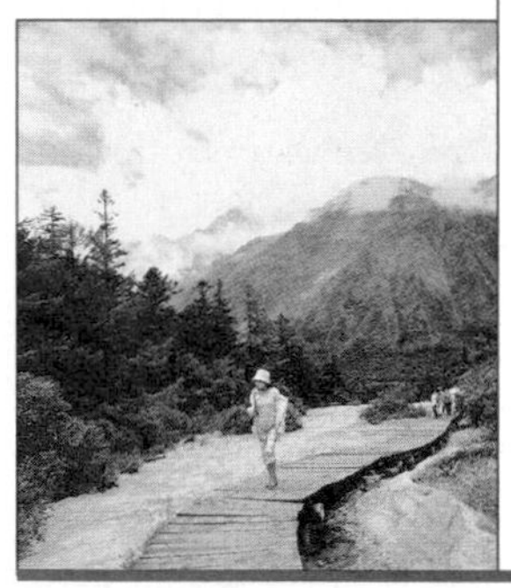

Walking Shoes

If you plan on spending time in Sichuan and Chongqing, bring good walking shoes or hiking boots. These two peppery provinces in Western China have everything from hardcore trekking to hilly urban strolls.

When visiting Chongqing, think of San Francisco and you'll have an idea of what to expect of the city's hilly streets. Thankfully, this charming conurbation on the Yangtze River is riddled with steps for ascending steep inclines.

Sichuan's capital of Chengdu couldn't be more different. The streets are broad, laid out in grid-fashion and ideal for biking and long urban treks.

If you're traveling between these two cities, be aware of the construction and reconstruction projects associated with the recovery from the Sichuan earthquake. It's not uncommon to wait for a few hours in a long traffic line.

2008 Sichuan Earthquake

The earthquake that struck Sichuan's Wenchuan County on May 12, 2008, killed about 90,000 people and left infrastructure near the epicenter severely damaged. Of the 4,000 plus scenic areas in Sichuan, almost 600 were badly damaged. The epicenter struck 50 mi northwest of Chengdu, though that city escaped major damage for the most part. Sichuan is a huge province and most of the major earthquake destruction was concentrated in a small area. The majority of tourist sites that were damaged have been repaired or soon will be. Most importantly, Sichuan's economy depends on tourists, so perhaps the best thing you can do to help the province recover is to go there. About 400,000 people work in tourism-related activities in Sichuan, and profits from tourism account for 11.6 percent of the province's gross domestic product.

Plight of the Panda

Mysterious, endangered, and cuddly are a few of the monikers typically associated with China's most well-known symbol. Dwindling in population would be another. Given China's recent economic reforms, pandas face a mixed future. On the one hand, economic growth and overpopulation are increasingly affecting their habitat. On the other hand, more state and international resources are pouring into special research institutes like Sichuan's Panda Breeding Research Base. What will be the ultimate fate of these stoic creatures? It's hard to say. One thing is certain though: those who visit ecological panda preserves are part of the solution.

DINING AND LODGING PRICE CATEGORIES IN YUAN

¢	$	$$	$$$	$$$$
Restaurants				
under Y25	Y25–Y49	Y50–Y99	Y100–Y165	over Y165
Hotels				
under Y700	Y700–Y1,099	Y1,100–Y1,399	Y1,400–Y1,800	over Y1,800

Restaurant prices are for a main course, excluding tax and tips. Hotel prices are for a standard double room, including taxes.

Chongqing and the Yangtze River

Some call the Yangtze China's dragon river, with its tail at Chongqing and mouth at Shanghai. The Yangtze is one of the richest rivers in terms of sites and the Three Gorges Damn is its signature draw.

If you're touring of this legendary river, you'll definitely spend some time in Chongqing. Some advice—take your time here. There are more than 30 million people in the Chongqing area and the city is ablaze with neon. For those interested in seeing a working river port, visit the Chaotianmen Docks. Historians will relish the U.S. Chiang Kai-shek Criminal Acts Exhibition Hall and SACO Prison.

Chongqing is brimming with a thriving food scene, teahouses, bookshops, and clubs. The adjacent villages are nestled in rolling hills, so before parachuting in to seize the Yangtze by the horns, allow a few days of proper Chongqing trekking.

Leaving from Chongqing allows for lots of daytime sightseeing through Yichang, Shashi and Qutang, Wu and Xiling gorges. However, this trip moves fast and can be frustrating for shutterbugs. Make sure that the tour goes to the Shennong section of the dam. Its steep, foliage-laden hills are some of the most majestic in China.

By Sascha Matuszak
Updated by Michael Standaert

SOUTHWEST CHINA HARKS BACK THOUSANDS of years to the trade routes that extended north from Burma and India through the sunny highlands of Yunnan and Guangxi into the wilds of Sichuan and Guizhou. The peoples that once ruled this wide swath of land can still be found in its valleys, hills, and mountains: the Yi, spanning the entire region with their cultural and political base in southern Sichuan; the Naxi, straddling the salt-, horse-, and tea-trade routes between Tibet, Sichuan, and Yunnan; the Miao, centered in Guizhou with close cousins as far away as the Hmong people of Vietnam; the Mosu, a matriarchal society gathered around Lugu Lake; and, of course, the Tibetans and the Han, arbiters of power in the region for millennia.

The snowcapped Himalayas march in from the west. Its lush foothills, green valleys, and spectacular gorges eventually smooth out into the central plains. Extremely diverse flora and fauna make the area a hotbed of scientific research—more than 100 panda reserves dot the mountains of Southwest China. But the people have made their mark, too. There are numerous UNESCO World Heritage Sites sprinkled throughout Southwest China, including dazzling Buddhist and Taoist monuments.

SICHUAN

Throughout history, Sichuan has been known as the "Storehouse of Heaven," due not only to its abundance of flora and fauna, but also to its varied cuisine, culture, and customs.

Geographically, it is dominated by the Sichuan Basin, which covers much of the eastern part of the province. The Sichuan Basin—also known as the Red Basin because of the reddish sandstone that predominates in the region—accounts for almost half its area. On all sides the province is surrounded by mountains: the Dabashan in the northeast, the Wushan in the east, the Qinghai Massif in the west, and the Yunnan and Guizhou plateaus in the south.

Sichuan's relative isolation made communication with the outside world difficult and fostered the development of valley, plains, and mountain cultures with distinct characteristics. The Tibetans living deep in the foothills of the Himalayas share space with Qiang, Hui, and Han settlers. In the mountains to the south toward Yunnan, there are dozens of peoples living side by side, such as the Yi, Naxi, Mosu, Miao, and Bai. These cultures all have their own religions and philosophies, with Buddhism and Taoism being the dominant religions in the area.

The mountain of Emeishan is a pilgrimage site for millions of Buddhists, as is the Great Buddha in nearby Leshan. Its distance from the epicenter spared the area from any major quake damage. In Songpan, north of the capital city of Chengdu, Muslims, Buddhists, Christians, and Taoists live alongside each other in harmony. One of China's most famous national parks is in Jiuzhaigou, far to the north in Aba Prefecture. The natural springs, dense forests, dramatic cliffs, and sprawling waterfalls make Jiuzhaigou Nature Reserve one of the country's most popular

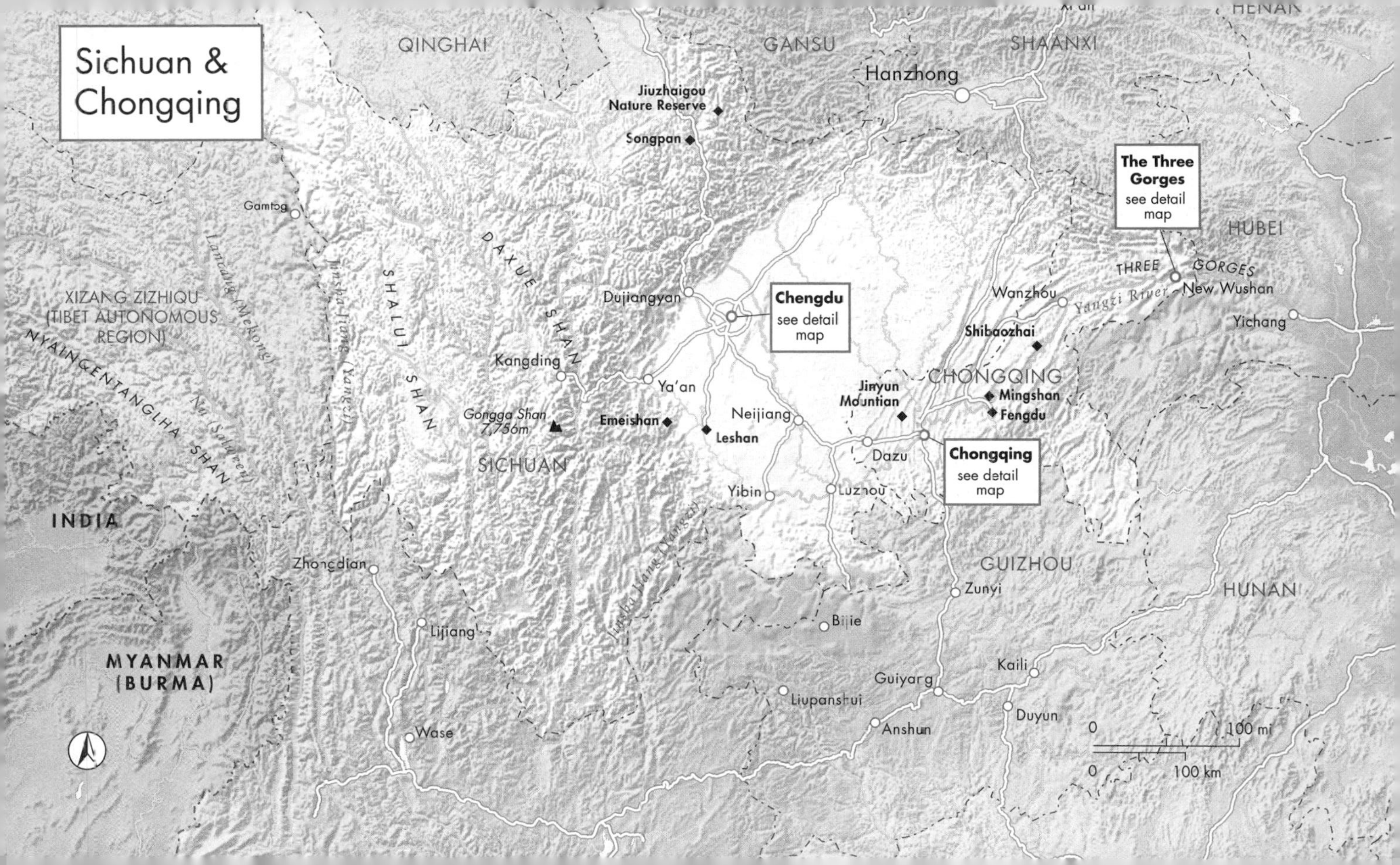
Sichuan & Chongqing
QINGHAI
GANSU
SHAANXI
Hanzhong
Jiuzhaigou Nature Reserve
Songpan
Gamtog
The Three Gorges see detail map
HUBEI
THREE GORGES
New Wushan
Yichang
Yangzi River
Wanzhou
XIZANG ZIZHIQU (TIBET AUTONOMOUS REGION)
NYAINGENTANGLHA SHAN
Lancang (Mekong)
Nu (Salween)
Jinsha Jiang (Yangzi)
SHALUI SHAN
DAXUE SHAN
Dujiangyan
Chengdu see detail map
Kangding
Ya'an
Gongga Shan 7,756m
Emeishan
Leshan
Neijiang
SICHUAN
Shibaozhai
CHONGQING
Jinyun Mountian
Mingshan
Fengdu
Dazu
Chongqing see detail map
Yibin
Luzhou
INDIA
Zhongdian
GUIZHOU
Zunyi
HUNAN
Bijie
Lijiang
MYANMAR (BURMA)
Kaili
Guiyang
Liupanshui
Duyun
Wase
Anshun
0
100 mi
0
100 km

tourist destinations. And if you need more urban comforts, Chengdu is an increasingly international city with food from all over the world, top-notch hotels, dizzying nightlife, and what must be more teahouses per square inch than any other city in the world.

REGIONAL TOURS

The China Culture Center in Beijing offers excellent custom tour options for Sichuan with English-speaking guides, including trips to the panda reserves. Visit *www.chinaculturecenter.org*.

CHENGDU

240 km (149 mi; 4 hrs by bus) northwest of Chongqing; 1,450 km (900 mi; 32 hrs by train) southwest of Beijing; 1,300 km (806 mi; 40 hrs by train) northwest of Hong Kong.

Don't go to Chengdu when you're young—is what the Chinese advise children who might be corrupted by this modern, energetic city. But despite the warnings, Chengdu is one of the most leisurely places in all of China. Most visitors end up joining the locals as they while away the day playing mah-jongg, sipping fragrant green tea, and cracking sunflower seeds.

The city is changing at a dizzying pace. Much of the old city has been razed to make room for modern high-rises. But there is still much to see in terms of history and culture. Temples and memorials demonstrate Chengdu's position as the cosmopolitan capital of western China. The city is also a great center for Sichuan cooking, which many believe is the best in China. The Sichuanese cuisine is famous for its spicy peppers and strong flavors. Chengdu has too many good restaurants to list and the hole in the wall around the corner may serve the most tasty Sichuan dishes you'll eat.

All roads into Southwest China lead through Chengdu. As the gateway to Tibet, this city is the place to secure the permits and supplies needed for your trip there. Journeys south to Yunnan or north to Xi'an pass through here as well. Lying in the middle of Sichuan Province, Chengdu is also a good base for excursions to the scenic spots dotting Sichuan.

As with many big cities in China, Chengdu is very polluted. Bring eyedrops, anti-bacterial wipes, and possibly even a face mask.

GETTING HERE AND AROUND

Chengdu is the transportation hub of Western China. Bus, train, and plane connections are as convenient as they get in China. ■**TIP→ The Chengdu Tourism Bureau has a shuttle bus between the city's three major sights: Du Fu's Cottage, the Memorial of the Marquis of Wu, and the Tomb of Emperor Wang Jian.** With your ticket stub, you can hop aboard the bus free of charge. The bus leaves every 20 minutes.

Chengdu is built along a main north–south artery and surrounded by two ring roads. Bikes are a great way to get around. If you are on foot, many of the city's sights are within walking distance of Tian Fu Plaza. Snag a cab or brave the buses if you are going farther afield.

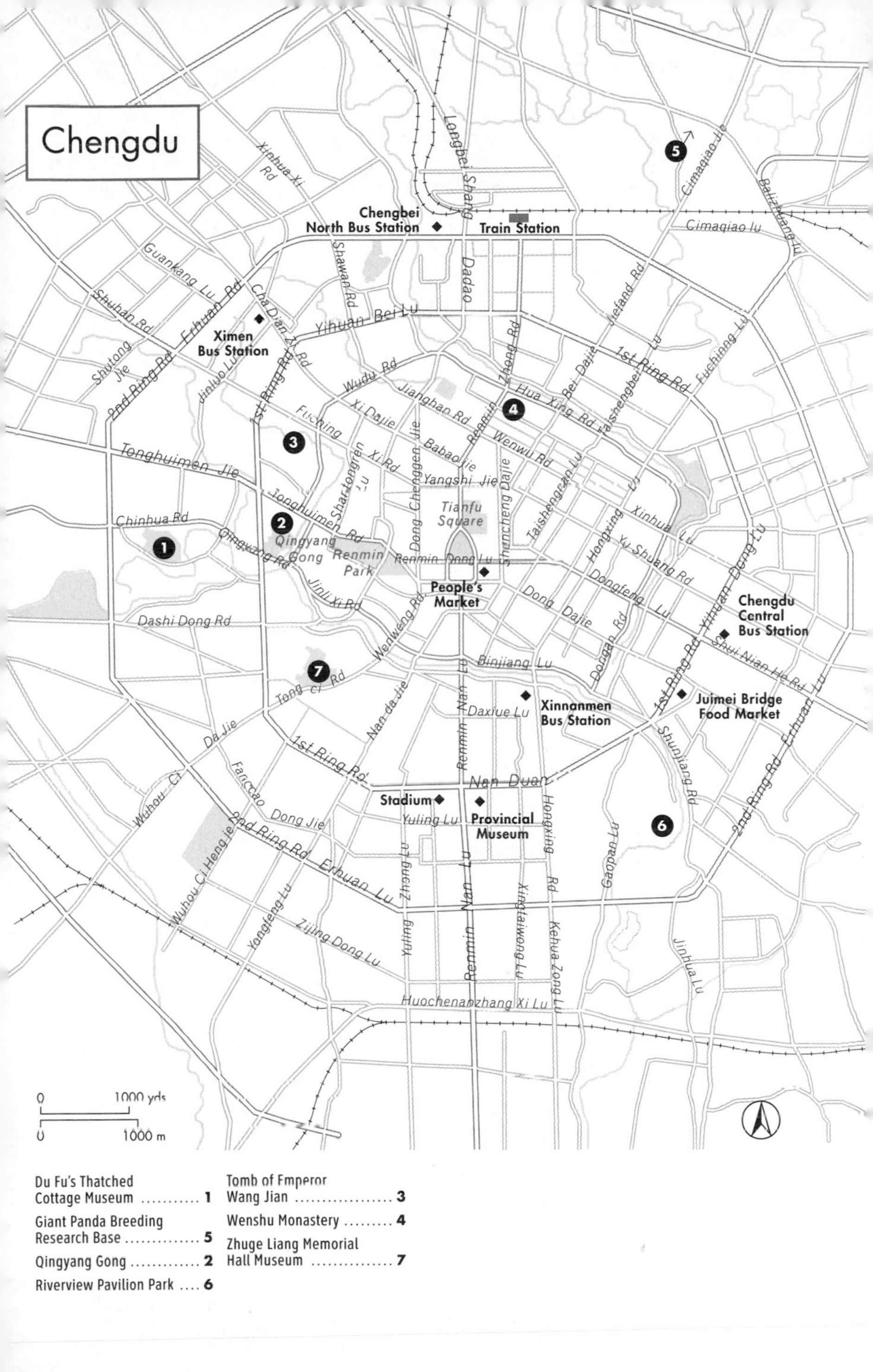

Chengdu
Chengbei North Bus Station
Train Station
Ximen Bus Station
Tianfu Square
People's Market
Qingyang Gong
Renmin Park
Chengdu Central Bus Station
Juimei Bridge Food Market
Xinnanmen Bus Station
Stadium
Provincial Museum
Xinhua Xi Rd
Longbei Shang
Dadao
Cimaqiao Jie
Cimaqiao Lu
Balizhuang Lu
Shawan Rd
Guankang Lu
Shuhan Rd
Erhuan Rd
Cha Dian Zi Rd
Yihuan Bei Lu
Shutong Jie
2nd Ring Rd
Jinluo Lu
1st Ring Rd
Wudu Rd
Jianghan Rd
Zhong Rd
Renmin
Hua Xing Rd
Bei Dajie
Jiefand Rd
Taishengbei Lu
Fuching Lu
Fuching
Xi Dajie
Babao Jie
Wenwu Rd
Tonghuimen Jie
Shantongren Lu
Xi Rd
Dong Chenggen Jie
Yangshi Jie
Shuncheng Dajie
Taishengnan Lu
Chinhua Rd
Tonghuimen Rd
Qingyang Rd
Renmin Dong Lu
Hongxing Lu
Xinhua Lu
Yu Shuang Rd
Yihuan Dong Lu
Jinli Xi Rd
Dongfeng Lu
Dong Dajie
Dashi Dong Rd
Wenweng Rd
Dongan Rd
Shui Nian He Rd
Binjiang Lu
Tong ci Rd
Nan da Jie
Daxiue Lu
Renmin Nan Lu
Da Jie
Shunjiang Rd
Wuhou Ci
Fanccao
Dong Jie
Nan Duan
Yuling Lu
Hongxing Rd
Gaopan Lu
Wuhou Ci Heng Jie
2nd Ring Rd Erhuan Lu
Zhong Lu
Yuling
Xingtaiwong Lu
Kehua Zong Lu
Yongfeng Lu
Zijing Dong Lu
Jinhua Lu
Huochenanzhang Xi Lu
2nd Ring Rd Erhuan Lu
0 1000 yds
0 1000 m
Du Fu's Thatched Cottage Museum 1
Giant Panda Breeding Research Base 5
Qingyang Gong 2
Riverview Pavilion Park 6
Tomb of Emperor Wang Jian 3
Wenshu Monastery 4
Zhuge Liang Memorial Hall Museum 7

BY AIR Chengdu Shuangliu International Airport is about 16 km (10 mi) southwest of the city. From here you can fly to Beijing (2½ hours), Canton (2 hours), Kunming (1 hour), Shanghai (2½ hours), or many other domestic destinations. There are a few international connections, but these may be canceled without notice.

Bus service links the airport terminal and downtown Chengdu, with Bus 303 traveling to the center of town. Taxis should cost about Y55.

BY BUS There are three main bus stations in Chengdu. The Xinnanmen Bus Station, in the city center, has buses to almost every town in Sichuan. The Wuguiqiao Bus Station, east of the city, is used mainly for travelers to Chongqing or Yibin. The Chadianzi Bus Station, in the northwestern part of the city, has buses to destinations in the mountains to the north and west (including Jiuzhaigou and Songpan).

BY TRAIN Chengdu sits on the Kunming–Beijing railway line, therefore connections are reliable. The Chengdu Railway Station is in the northern part of the city. It's a Y20 cab ride from Tian Fu Plaza.

TOURS

A good resource for package and individual tours in Chengdu and throughout Sichuan is the tour agency Intowestchina.

ESSENTIALS

Air Contacts **Chengdu Shuangliu International Airport** (☎ *028/8520–5555* 🌐 *www.cdairport.com*).

Bank **Bank of China** (✉ *Renmin Nan Lu*).

Bus Contacts **Chadianzi Bus Station** (✉ *Sanhuan Lu*). **Wuguiqiao Bus Station** (✉ *Dongguichun Sanzhu*). **Xinanmen Bus Station** (✉ *57 Linjiang Lu*).

Consulate **U.S. Consulate** (✉ *4 Lingshiguan Lu, Chengdu* ☎ *028/8558–3992*).

Medical Assistance For **emergency medical assistance** anywhere in China, dial 120; for all other emergencies call 110. (✉ *PSB; Foreigner's Police, Wenwu Lu, part of Xinhua Dong Lu; 40 Wenmiaohou Jie* ☎ *110 or 028/8674–4683*). **International Medical Center and Foreigners Clinic** (✉ *37 Guo Xue Lu, Chengdu* ☎ *028/8542–2408*).

Train Contacts **Chengdu Train Station** (✉ *Erhuan Lu* ☎ *028/8370–9580*).

Visitor and Tour Info **China International Travel Service** (*CITS* ✉ *65 Renmin Nan Lu, at Er Duan* ☎ *028/6648–8000 or 028/6648–8333*). **Intowestchina Holiday** (✉ *No. 501-12, 5th floor, Lianyi Mansion, No. 20 Jiangxi St.* ☎ *028/855–82963 or 028/855–82964* 🌐 *www.intowestchina.com*).

EXPLORING CHENGDU

MAIN ATTRACTIONS

❶ **Du Fu's Thatched Cottage Museum** *(Du Fu Caotang)* is named for the famous poet Du Fu (712–770) of the Tang Dynasty, whose poetry continues to be read today. A Manchurian, he came to Chengdu from Xi'an and built a small hut overlooking the bamboo and plum tree–lined Huanhua River. During the four years he spent here he wrote well over 240 poems. After his death the area became a garden; a temple was added during the Northern Song Dynasty (960–1126). A replica of his cottage now stands among several other structures, all built during the Qing Dynasty. Some of Du Fu's calligraphy and poems are on display here. English-speaking guides are available, as are English translations of his poems. ✉ *37 Qinghua Lu* ☎ *028/8731–9258* 🌐 *www.dfmuseum.org.cn* 🎫 *Y60* ⏲ *May–Oct., daily 7:30–7; Nov.–Apr., daily 8–6:30.*

WORD OF MOUTH

"We spent a very pleasant afternoon at the Chengdu panda center. They give you a tour on a tourist train through the area. We saw lots of adult and baby pandas—and also red pandas."

—JaneB

❺ ★ The **Giant Panda Breeding Research Base** *(Daxiongmao Bowuguan)* is worth the 45-minute drive to walk the peaceful bamboo groves, snap pictures of the lolling pandas, and catch a glimpse of the tiny baby pandas that are born with startling regularity. For those interested in efforts to save these creatures, the research center is excellent. Crews of scientists help pandas breed and care for the young in a safe, controlled environment. ■ **TIP→ Visit early in the morning, when the pandas are most active.** To get here, book a tour through your hotel for about Y70 per person. ✉ *26 Panda Road (Jiefang Lu)* ☎ *028/8351–0033* 🌐 *www.panda.org.cn* 🎫 *Y10* ⏲ *Daily 7–6:30.*

❷ Built during the Tang Dynasty, **Qingyang Gong** is the oldest Taoist temple in the city and one of the most famous in China. Six courtyards open out onto each other before arriving at the sculptures of two goats, which represent one of the earthly incarnations of Lao Tzu (the legendary founder of Taoism). If you arrive midmorning, you can watch the day's first worshippers before the stampede of afternoon pilgrims. The temple grounds are filled with nuns and monks training at the Two Immortals Monastery, the only such facility in Southwest China. A small teahouse is on the premises. ✉ *9 Yihuan Lu at Xi Erduan* ☎ *028/8776–6584* 🌐 *www.qingyanggong.com* 🎫 *Y10* ⏲ *Daily 8–6:30.*

❼ The **Zhuge Liang Memorial Hall Museum** *(Wuhou Ci)* is a shrine to the heroes that made the Shu Kingdom legendary during the Three Kingdoms Period. The temple here was constructed in 221 to entomb the earthly remains of Shu Emperor Liu Bei. During the Ming Dynasty, Liu Bei's subjects were also housed here, most notably Zhu Ge Liang. Liu Bei's most trusted advisor during the Three Kingdoms Period, Zhu Ge Liang is a legendary figure in Sichuan and, in some respects, more honored than his master. The temple burned during the wars that toppled the Ming Dynasty and was rebuilt in 1671–72 during the Qing Dynasty. The main shrine, Zhaolie Temple, is dedicated to Liu Bei; the rear shrine, Wu Hou Temple, to Zhu Ge Liang. There is also the Sworn Brotherhood Shrine, which commemorates Liu Bei, Zhang Fei, and Guan Yu's "Oath in the Peach Garden." English guides are available for Y80 for groups up to 10 people.

The Sichuan Opera performs here nightly from 7:30 to 9. The Y120 ticket is expensive, but the face-changing, fire-breathing, lyre-playing ensemble might make you forget that. If that doesn't work, get a free massage from one of the elegantly dressed masseuses touring the audience area. ✉*231 Wuhou Ci Da Jie* ☎*028/8555–2397* 🌐*www.wuhouci.net.cn* 🎫*Y60* ⏲*Daily 8–9.*

IF YOU HAVE TIME

❻ The four-story wooden pavilion in **Riverview Pavilion Park** *(Wangjiang Lou Gongyuan)*, dating from the Qing Dynasty, offers splendid views of the Fu River and the surrounding countryside. The poet Xue Tao, who lived in Chengdu during the Tang Dynasty, was said to have spent time near the river, from which she apparently drew water to make paper for her poems. The pavilion stands amid more than 120 species of bamboo, a plant revered by the poet. ✉*30 Wangjiang Lu* ☎*028/8522–3389* 🌐*www.wangjianglou.com* 🎫*Y20* ⏲*Daily 8–6.*

NEED A BREAK?

Not many people know that some of the best green tea comes from the mountains of western Sichuan. In Chengdu, *hua cha* (flower tea) is the most popular. Hua cha has such a potent aroma because it has been doctored up with jasmine or chrysanthemum. If you want to sample some good tea, head to People's Park, Wen Shu Temple, or Kuan Xiangzi, the last street of the old city that remains intact.

❸ In the northwest section of Chengdu stands the 49-foot-high, 262-ft-diameter **Tomb of Emperor Wang Jian** *(Wang Jian Mu)*, which honors the ruler of the Kingdom of Shu from AD 847 to 918. Made of red sandstone, it is distinguished by the male figures that support the platform for the coffin and the carvings of musicians, thought to be the best surviving record of a Tang Dynasty musical troupe. There are a lovely park and teahouse on the grounds, both quite popular among locals. ✉*Off Fuqin Dong Lu* 🎫*Y30* ⏲*Daily 8–4:50.*

❹ ★ In the northern part of town, the large **Wenshu Monastery** *(Wenshu Yuan)* is a major tourist attraction in Chengdu. It is currently undergoing extensive renovations, both inside and outside the temple walls. Originally constructed during the Sui Dynasty (617 BC–605 BC), the monastery fell in the flames of war during the Ming Dynasty. The temple was rebuilt during the Qing Dynasty. In this complex you can find a fine cup of green tea and the best vegetarian food in the city. ✉*15 Wenshu Yuan Jie off Renmin Zhong Lu* 🎫*Y5* ⏲*Daily 8–6.*

WHERE TO EAT

In Chengdu, hotpot is easy to find. A walk down just about any street will yield at least one restaurant serving this local specialty: a boiling vat of chili oil, red peppers, and mouth-numbing spices into which you dip duck intestines, beef tripe, chicken livers, or (for the less adventurous) bamboo shoots and mushrooms. Hotpot restaurants tend to be open-air affairs, often spilling out onto the sidewalk.

$$$–$$$$ SICHUAN ★ ✕**Chuan Jiang Hao Zi.** The most popular hotpot restaurant in Chengdu, Chuan Jiang Hao Zi is in the restaurant district of Yulin. Always crowded, you can spot this place by the line of people at the front door chewing sunflower seeds as they wait for a table. The hotpot here is

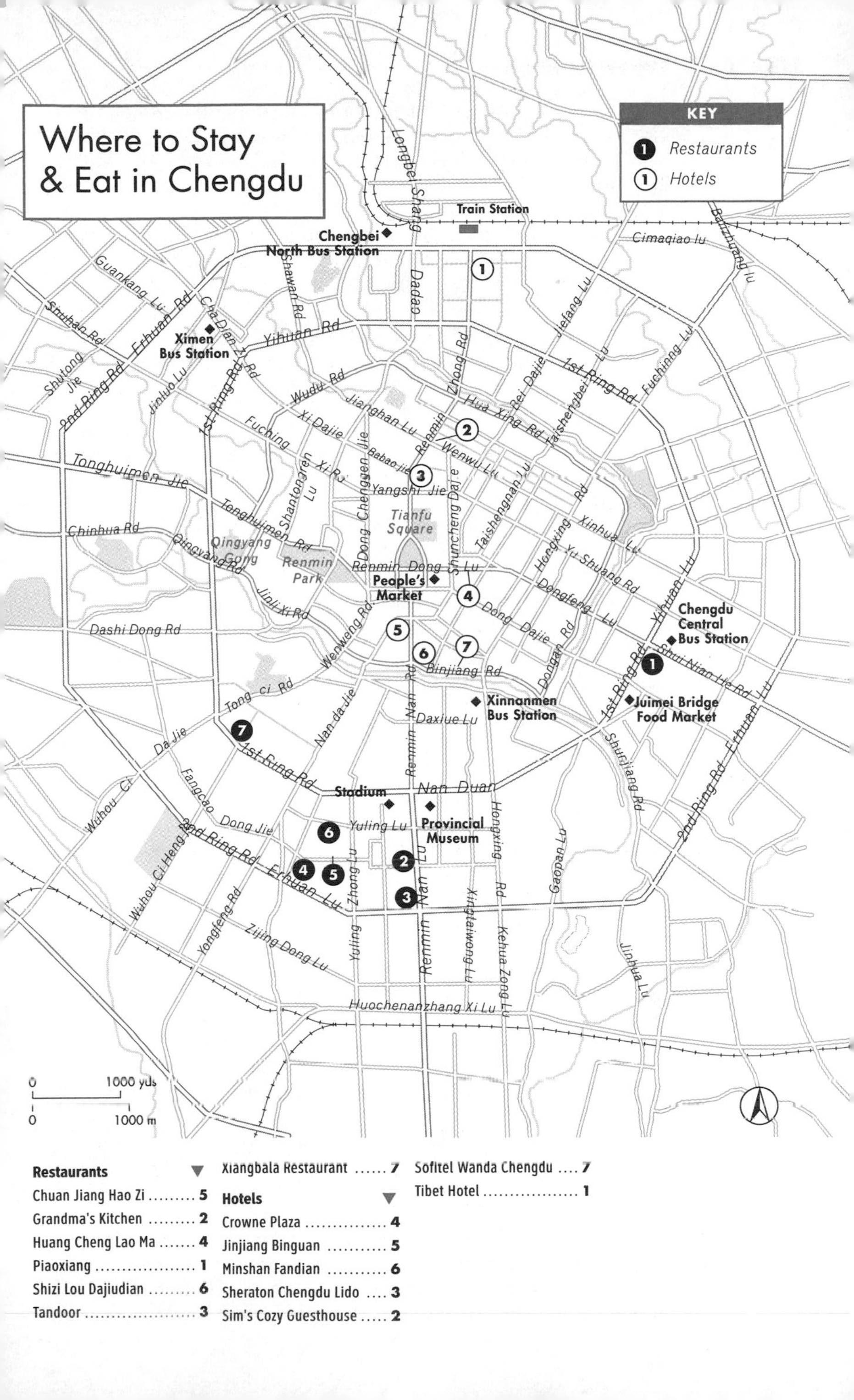
Where to Stay & Eat in Chengdu
KEY
Restaurants
Hotels
Train Station
Chengbei North Bus Station
Ximen Bus Station
Cimaqiao Lu
Longbei Shang
Dadao
Guankang Lu
Shuhan Rd
Shutong Jie
Erhuan Rd
2nd Ring Rd
Chadian Zi Rd
Shawan Rd
Yihuan Rd
Jinluo Lu
1st Ring Rd
Jiefang Lu
Fuching Lu
Taishengbei Lu
Bei Dajie
Zhong Rd
Wudu Rd
Jianghan Lu
Hua Xing Rd
Renmin
Wenwu Lu
Xi Dajie
Fuching
Xi Rd
Babao jie
Yangshi Jie
Tonghuimen Jie
Tonghuimen Rd
Shantongren Lu
Dong Chenggen Jie
Shuncheng Dajie
Taishengnan Lu
Hongxing Rd
Xinhua Lu
Xi Shuang Rd
Tianfu Square
Chinhua Rd
Qingyang Gong
Qingyang Rd
Renmin Park
Renmin Dong Lu
People's Market
Dongfeng Lu
Dong Dajie
Jinli Xi Rd
Wenweng Rd
Dashi Dong Rd
Dongan Rd
Yihuan Lu
Chengdu Central Bus Station
Shui Nian He Rd
Binjiang Rd
Tong ci Rd
Nan da Jie
Xinnanmen Bus Station
Daxiue Lu
Juimei Bridge Food Market
Da Jie
Renmin Nan Rd
Shufijiang Rd
Erhuan Lu
Fangcao Dong Jie
Stadium
Nan Duan
Provincial Museum
Wuhou Ci
Yuling Lu
Hongxing Rd
Gaopan Lu
Wuhou Ci Heng Jie
Zhong Lu
Renmin Nan Lu
Xingtaiwong Lu
Kehua Zong Lu
Yongfeng Rd
Zijing Dong Lu
Yuling
Jinhua Lu
Huochenanzhang Xi Lu
0 1000 yds
0 1000 m
Restaurants
Chuan Jiang Hao Zi 5
Grandma's Kitchen 2
Huang Cheng Lao Ma 4
Piaoxiang 1
Shizi Lou Dajiudian 6
Tandoor 3
Xiangbala Restaurant 7
Hotels
Crowne Plaza 4
Jinjiang Binguan 5
Minshan Fandian 6
Sheraton Chengdu Lido 3
Sim's Cozy Guesthouse 2
Sofitel Wanda Chengdu 7
Tibet Hotel 1

classic Sichuan style, with plenty of fresh meat and vegetables from which to choose. Even if you call ahead for a reservation, the policy seems to be first-come, first-served. ✉ *1 Hua Zi Lu, across from the Yulin Middle School* ☎ *028/8553–3111* 🌐 *www.chuanjianghaozi.com* ▭ *Credit cards accepted.*

¢–$$$ AMERICAN
✕ **Grandma's Kitchen.** If you're sick of hotpot, this is the place to go. Hamburgers and other American foods are served up at decent prices. It's an excellent choice for breakfast, but also a good standby any time of day. The Renmin Nan Lu branch is cozy (perhaps too cozy), but most people there are too busy enjoying their food to notice. ✉ *143 Kehua Bei Lu* ☎ *028/8524–2835* ✉ *22 Renmin Nan Lu at Si Duan* ☎ *028/8555–3856* ▭ *No credit cards.*

$$$–$$$$ SICHUAN ★
✕ **Huang Cheng Lao Ma.** Built and run by artists, this amazing restaurant on Second Ring Road South is a must for visitors to Chengdu. Huang Cheng Lao Ma is a massive brick-and-stone building with sculpted pillars rising up either side with a stone facade depicting scenes from old Chengdu. The hotpot here comes in traditional spicy varieties and also wild mushroom, seafood, and "soft/clear soup" styles (soft soup—*qing tang* means no spices!). Not only will you get an idea of the creativity in architecture and cuisine in modern China, but there are often photo exhibitions from local artists. The top floor is a high-end teahouse. ✉ *20 Erhuan Lu, Nan San Duan* ☎ *028/8513–9999* 🌐 *www.huangchenglaoma.com* ▭ *No credit cards.*

$$–$$$ SICHUAN ★
✕ **Piaoxiang.** This restaurant is renowned for its efforts to update Sichuanese dishes, transforming traditional into something wonderful. Simple fare like *dou hua* (soft tofu) and *hue guo rou* (twice-cooked pork) is fresh and tasty, and includes much less oil than your average spot. The menu is mostly ribs, tofu, and chili sauce, but more refined than the typical street stall. ✉ *60 Yihuan Lu, Dong San Duan* ☎ *028/8437–9999* ▭ *No credit cards.*

$$$–$$$$ SICHUAN
✕ **Shizi Lou Dajiudian.** The specialty here is Sichuan-style hotpot—very spicy and delicious. It's more expensive than your run-of-the-mill places, but worth it. Your visit might coincide with evening entertainment, often live local music. ✉ *2 Wannian Lu, off Er Xi Lu, Dong San Duan* ☎ *028/8438–9970* 🌐 *www.bwszl.com* ▭ *No credit cards.*

$$–$$$ INDIAN
✕ **Tandoor.** Just a couple of blocks from the American Consulate, this restaurant serves the city's best northern Indian fare. The decor, a sophisticated combination of wood and mirrors, makes a meal here seem like a special occasion. It's no surprise that the devoted Punjabi chef serves up delicious tandoori chicken, and there's also freshly baked breads. ✉ *Sunjoy Inn, 34 Renmin Nan Lu, Si Duan* ☎ *028/8555–1958* ▭ *AE, DC, MC, V.*

¢–$ TIBETAN
✕ **Xiangbala Restaurant.** For a taste of Tibet, come here. Groups of Tibetan cowboys crowd around tables shooting the breeze as solitary monks eat quietly in the corner. Everything is traditional—the kitchen makes its own yogurt and uses yak meat from the grasslands. The tea, which arrives in a big pot, is delicious. No English menus are available, but the staff does its best to assist you. Some bread, yak noodles, and a few dumplings will satisfy almost anyone. The restaurant sits on a street of Tibetan establishments near Southwest Nationalities

University. ✉ *Wuhou Ci Dong Jie Xin 3, Fu 3* ☎ *028/8553–8665 or 138/8181–1045* ▭ *No credit cards.*

WHERE TO STAY

$–$$ **Crowne Plaza.** In the heart of Chengdu, this luxury hotel puts you very close to attractions like Du Fu's Thatched Cottage. The guest rooms are among the most spacious that you'll find in the city, although the decor is a little staid. The restaurants are not as snazzy as at the other top-notch hotels, but they serve an interesting array of cuisines. **Pros:** friendly staff, near shopping. **Cons:** subpar pool facilities, rooms can be small for price. ✉ *31 Zong Fu Jie* ☎ *028/8678–6666 or toll-free 800/830–2628 (in U.S.)* ⊕ *www.crowneplaza.com* *434 rooms, 80 suites* *In-room: Ethernet. In-hotel: 4 restaurants, bars, gym, laundry service* ▭ *AE, DC, MC, V.*

$ **Jinjiang Binguan.** For years this was the city's best hotel—foreign dignitaries and bigwigs from Beijing could always be found milling around the lobby. Now with five-star hotels all over the city, the Jinjiang has lost a little of its luster. But the hotel has one of the finest Chinese restaurants in the city, as well as a dance club that is surprisingly popular. Although a bit dated, the guest rooms have cable TV, Internet, and spacious bathrooms. **Pros:** good base for exploring region, large rooms. **Cons:** basic, not very exciting. ✉ *80 Renmin Nan Lu, Er Duan* ☎ *028/8550–6666* ⊕ *www.jjhotel.com* *523 rooms* *In-room: Ethernet. In-hotel: 2 restaurants, bar, laundry service, public Internet* ▭ *AE, MC, V.*

¢–$ **Minshan Fandian.** In the heart of downtown, this gleaming white tower is one of the city's best hotels. The lobby is covered with gleaming marble, and the guest rooms enlivened by bold floral prints. The Taibai Lou restaurant, which opens out onto a lovely garden, is one of Chengdu's popular places for Sichuan cooking. **Pros:** good location, nice garden. **Cons:** service could be better. ✉ *55 Renmin Nan Lu, Er Duan* ☎ *028/8558–3333* ⊕ *www.minshan.com.cn* *422 rooms* *In-room: Ethernet. In-hotel: 2 restaurants, bar* ▭ *AE, DC, MC, V.*

$–$$ **Sheraton Chengdu Lido.** In a quiet section of the central business district, the Sheraton Chengdu Lido was one of the city's first luxury hotels. It's still among the best. The rooms are immaculate and very comfortable, and the service is very conscientious. Amenities, such as the glass-roofed swimming pool, are world-class. The location puts you closer to many popular attractions, including the Giant Panda Breeding Research Base. **Pros:** helpful staff, comfortable, large rooms. **Cons:** room decor is boring. ✉ *15 Renmin Zhong Lu, Yi Duan* ☎ *028/8676–8999 or toll-free 800/810–3088 (in U.S.)* ⊕ *www.sheraton.com/chengdu* *413 rooms* *In-hotel: 4 restaurants, bars, pool, gym, laundry service, Internet in lobby* ▭ *AE, DC, MC, V.*

¢ **Sim's Cozy Guesthouse** *(Laoshen Qingnian Lvshe).* Having served as the German Consulate at the beginning of the 20th century, this traditional building has survived longer than most in this modern-minded city. It's a beautiful, quiet place, with large comfortable rooms and clean common areas. The owners, from Singapore and Japan, having traveled extensively throughout the region are very helpful in planning your excursions. **Pros:** nice staff, great location. **Cons:** can be noisy. ✉ *42 Xizhushi Jie* ☎ *028/8691–4422* ⊕ *www.gogosc.com* *22 rooms*

8

In-room: no TV. In-hotel: restaurant, bar, laundry service, public Internet *No credit cards.*

$$–$$$ **Sofitel Wanda Chengdu.** One of Chengdu's finest luxury hotels, this concave glass tower sits beside the Fu Nan River. The restaurants are amazing—as might be expected from a European-based hotelier—so expect to be taken on a culinary journey that takes you from China to Japan to France. The reception area is magnificent, with skylight illuminating the marble corridors. The guest rooms are quiet and restful. **Pros:** clean, modern, good location. **Cons:** staff sometimes rude, food expensive, noise from street. *15 Binjiang Zhong Lu* *028/6666–9999 or toll-free 800/830–2688 (in U.S.)* *www.sofitel.com* *262 rooms, 91 suites* *In-room: safe, Ethernet. In-hotel: 3 restaurants, bars, pool, gym* *AE, MC, V.*

¢–$ **Tibet Hotel** *(Xizang Fandian).* Near the train station, this hotel built by the Tibet Autonomous Region Government is a good option for those planning trips to Tibet. There is a tourist office in the hotel lobby specializing in travel to Tibet. The Tibetan restaurant suffers from a surprising lack of Tibetan food. The guest rooms are clean and comfortable. **Pros:** nice rooms, convenient location. **Cons:** service could be better. *10 Renmin Bei Lu* *028/8318–3388 or 800/886–5333* *www.tibet-hotel.com* *260 rooms* *In-hotel: 3 restaurants, Wi-Fi in lobby. In-room: free cable Internet* *AE, DC, MC, V.*

NIGHTLIFE AND THE ARTS

One of the city's most popular discos is the **Babi Club** (*Er Huan Lu Nan San Duan* *28/6605–9955*). This and other clubs on the Second Ring Road South are packed with Chivas-chugging Chinese business executives. A crew of "beer girls" walk around serving Carlsberg, Heineken, and other imported beers for Y100 to Y120 for a six-pack. A huge entertainment complex known simply as **69** (*Ke Hua Lu*) sits just south of the Jiu Yuan Bridge. In addition to dancing, you can also enjoy tipsy locals crooning along to the karaoke machine.

TIP→ For goings-on check out the monthly English-language magazine *Go West,* **available at many bars.**

For the classic pub feel, the **Shamrock Irish Bar** (*15 Renmin Nan Lu, Si Duan* *028/8523–6158*) is an old standby around the corner from the U.S. Consulate. On weekends this pub is filled with expats, students, and a smattering of travelers to listen to live music or a DJ. Guinness on tap is Y40, and other beers range from Y10 to Y25. South of the U.S. Consulate is the **Bookworm** (*Yujie East Road 2-7, 28 Renmin Nan Lu* *028/8552–0117*), a relaxed spot with clinking classes, comfy chairs, and a thousand books.

SHOPPING

The main shopping street is **Chunxi Lu,** east of Tianfu Square. The best place to shop for souvenirs is **Song Xian Qiao Antique City** (*22 Huan Hua Bei Lu*), the country's second-largest antiques market, with more than 500 separate stalls selling everything from Mao-era currency to fake Buddha statues to wonderful watercolor paintings. It's near Du Fu's Cottage and Wu Hou Temple.

EMEISHAN

★ *100 km (62 mi; 3 hrs by train) southwest of Chengdu.*

The 10,000-foot-high Emeishan (literally, Lofty Eyebrow Mountain) sits in the southern part of Sichuan. One of the country's holiest places, the mountain is a pilgrimage site for Buddhists. The temples here survived the Cultural Revolution better than most others in China, due in part to courageous monks. Still, of the hundreds of temples that once were found here, only 20 remain.

MONKEY BUSINESS

The mountain is known for its wily golden monkeys who have been known to steal items (such as cameras) and hang them in trees. They will try to surround you, screaming, pointing, and jumping in an intimidating manner. A sound strategy is to walk quickly through the band before they can increase in numbers.

■TIP→ When coming to Emeishan, bring enough cash to last your whole visit. Although there are banks in Emei Town, the ATMs are unreliable when dealing with foreign banks. There Is no place to exchange money, except on the black market.

GETTING HERE AND AROUND

The get here, most people take a shuttle bus from Chengdu or Leshan to Emeishan, but you can also take the train. The trip from Chengdu takes about two to three hours by bus, or three hours by train. If you arrive by train, you'll have to catch a bus to visit the area's sites. Inexpensive public buses travel between destinations, but schedules vary.

BY BUS There are departures from Chengdu's Xinnanmen station every half hour and from Leshan every hour on the hour between 7 AM and 6 PM. One-way tickets on shuttle buses cost between Y35 and Y45, and the trip takes about two hours. Also departing from Leshan are buses that travel directly to Emeishan's Baoguo Si. They depart every half hour between 9 and 5. It'll cost you Y10 by shuttle bus, or just Y1 on the public bus.

BY TRAIN A train from the Chengdu North Railway Station bound for Kunming passes through Emei Town; it takes 3 hours and costs about Y22.

ESSENTIALS

Banks Agricultural Bank of China (✉ *Near Baoguo Monastary* ☎ *083/3559-3397*).

Medical Assistance Emeishan Renmin Hospital (✉ *94 Santaishan Jie* ☎ *083/3553-4524 or 083/3552-2725*).

Train Contacts Emeishan Station (☎ *083/3516-8609*).

Visitor and Tour Info Emeishan Travel Agency (✉ *94 Ningshan Lu at Zhongduan, Emeishan* ☎ *083/3552-4244*).

EXPLORING EMEISHAN

You can reach the Golden Summit of Emeishan in just over two days. It's a difficult climb—the stairs up the mountain somehow make it seem more arduous. On the first day, hike until a bit before nightfall and stay

8

in one of the temples along the way for Y15 to Y40 per person. Start out early on the second day, reaching the summit by nightfall. On the third day, rise early in the morning and walk to the Golden Summit, where you may catch a spectacular sunrise. It's a wonderful journey. You will find the natural surroundings as enchanting as the temples.

The most common route to the top is past Long Life Monastery. This route takes you past the Elephant Bathing Pool, the crossroads for tourists and pilgrims headed up or down the mountain. The pool was once used by Bodhisattva Puxian to wash the grime off his white elephant. This place is usually crowded, but once you ascend from here you will be mostly free of the madding crowd.

A recommended route down is the long shoulder of the mountain past Magic Peak Monastery, another highlight of the climb. The monks here personify the compassion and simplicity of Buddhism, and the scenery is beyond compare. After a hard climb down, sharing a simple meal in the courtyard then staying the night in the monastery is magical.

The best times to climb are in the spring or fall. The summer can be uncomfortably hot at the lower altitudes, but once you ascend to the mountain's upper reaches you might want to stay a few extra days to avoid the stifling summer heat below. The true beauty of Emeishan appears after the halfway point, when most of the tourists are below you. Bring a change of clothes for the sweaty part of the journey and a warm jacket for the summit. Water and food are available on the mountain, carried by pipe-puffing porters to the stalls along the way.

DID YOU KNOW?

The mountain is part of a range that stretches from Ya'an in the north to Xichang in the south. These mountains produce some of the world's best green tea. Emei's local tea is called Zhu Ye Qing (Jade Bamboo Leaf), and there are several types and grades. It's possible to buy organic Zhu Ye Qing around the mountain and in Emei Town. Look for the Long Dong Organic Brand.

For an easier pilgrimage, use the Y30 minibus service from Declare Nation Temple *(Baoguo Si)* up to **Jieyin Dian,** from where the climb to the top will take about two hours. To avoid climbing altogether, ride the cable car (Y40 up, Y30 down) to the summit from Jieyin Dian (although there are often long lines).

Direct bus (2 hours) service links Chengdu with Baoguo Si, at the foot of the mountain. Trains from Chengdu stop in the town of Emei, about 6 km (4 mi) from the mountain.

WHERE TO STAY AND EAT

$$–$$$ CAFE ★

✕ **Teddy Bear Café.** Arriving at the Emei Bus Station, you will likely be approached by touts offering to take you to the Teddy Bear Café. It's a good idea to go with them. Despite its odd name and spartan decor, the Teddy Bear is a great place to eat. The café has everything from hamburgers to Chinese dishes. The eggplant, crispy but not overcooked, is one of the best dishes. The sign outside says LOCAL PRICES, and it's the truth. The owners are friendly, know the area well, and will help you in any way they can, doing everything from loaning walking sticks to arranging guides. They even have an exceptionally clean and comfortable hotel in back. ✉ *43 Baoguosi Lu, Emei* ☎ *0833/559–0135* 🌐 *www.teddybear.com.cn* ▭ *No credit cards.*

¢ **Baoguo Monastery.** This monastery, at the foot of the mountain, is one of the many accommodations available to those journeying to the Golden Summit. Few people stay here because it sits near the start of the path up the mountain, but if you are arriving late then this quiet, if slightly damp, hotel is a good option. **Pros:** quiet, a monastic experience. **Cons:** pretty basic. ✉ *Baoguo Si,* ☎ *No phone* *20 rooms* *In-hotel: restaurant* ▭ *No credit cards.*

¢–$ **Emeishan Hotel** *(Emeishan Dajiudian).* This hotel sits at the foot of the mountain, offering good access for those going on early hikes. The rooms are comfortable, and have clean bathrooms. **Pros:** nice rooms, good location. **Cons:** staff could be more helpful. ✉ *Baoguo Si,* ☎ *0833/552–6888* 🌐 *www.emshotel.com.cn* *202 rooms* *In-hotel: restaurant, bar* ▭ *AE, MC, V.*

LESHAN

★ *165 km (102 mi; 3 hrs by bus) south of Chengdu.*

Leshan is famous for the Great Buddha, carved into the mountainside at the confluence of the Dadu, Qingyi, and Min rivers. The Great Buddha—a UNESCO World Heritage Site—was initiated by the monk Haitong, who never saw its completion. The statue, blissfully reclining, has overlooked the swirling, choppy waters for 1,300 years. The city's new museum, up the Dadu River from the Great Buddha, is worth a stop.

GETTING HERE AND AROUND

BY BUS Buses to Leshan leave from Chengdu's Xinnanmen station every 30 minutes between 7:30 AM and 7:30 PM. Buses from Chongqing to Leshan leave every hour from 6:30 AM to 6:30 PM. From Leshan's Xiao Ba Bus Station, take Bus 13 directly to the Grand Buddha's main gate.

BY TRAIN The train trip between Chengdu and Leshan takes between 1½ and 2½ hours and costs Y8 to Y109.

TOURS

Boats at a dock about 1,500 feet up the river from the main gate will take you for a bumpy ride to within camera distance of the Grand Buddha. The 40-minute trip is Y40 per person. From the boat you will be able to see two heavily eroded guardians that flank the main statue.

ESSENTIALS

Banks **Bank of China** (✉ *35 Huangjiashan* ☎ *0833/212–5246*).

Medical Assistance **Leshan Renmin Hospital** (✉ *76 Baita Jie* ☎ *0833/211–9304*).

Visitor and Tour Info **Leshan Information Office** (✉ *Huahuwan, Luzi Jie* ☎ *0833/230–2131*).

8

EXPLORING LESHAN

At 233 feet, the **Grand Buddha** *(Da Fo)* is the tallest stone Buddha and among the tallest sculptures in the world. The big toes are each 28 feet in length. The construction of the Grand Buddha was started in AD 713 by a monk who wished to placate the rivers that habitually took local fishermen's lives. Although the project took more than 90 years to complete, it had no noticeable effect on the waters. It's possible to clamber down, by means of a cliff-hewn stairway, from the head to the platform where the feet rest. You can also take a boat ride (about Y40) to see the statue in all its grandeur from the river. ☎*0833/230–2048* *Y70 (includes Wu You Temple)* *Daily 8 AM–6 PM.*

There are also several temples or pagodas in the vicinity, including **Wu You Temple** *(Wuyou Si)*, a Ming Dynasty temple with a commanding view of the city. You might find yourself staring at the lifelike figures and wonder about the person they were modeled after. *Y70 (includes Grand Buddha)* *Daily 8 AM–6 PM.*

WHERE TO STAY AND EAT

¢–$ CHINESE ✕**San Jiang.** This Chinese restaurant run by a husband and wife team serves up some great fish dishes. The buffets here are guaranteed to please; the food is primarily fish from the waters around the feet of the Grand Buddha and local specialties like *dou hua* (soft tofu) and bamboo shoots. The restaurant is one of several facing the water, so there's a nice view. ✉*North of the main gate to the Grand Buddha* ☎*130/0642–2361* *No credit cards.*

¢–$ **Jiazhou Hotel.** This "Hotel California" is on the opposite side of the river from the Grand Buddha and has comfortable accommodations and clean bathrooms. A café across the parking lot serves passable Western food. **Pros:** clean, good location. **Cons:** food could be better. ✉*19 Baitu Lu,* ☎*083/3213–9888* *083/3213–3233* *190 rooms* *In-hotel: restaurant* *No credit cards.*

JIUZHAIGOU NATURAL PRESERVE

★ *350 km (217 mi; 8–10 hrs by bus) north of Leshan; 225 km (140 mi; 4–6 hrs by bus) northwest of Chengdu.*

High among the snowcapped peaks of the Aba Autonomous Prefecture of northern Sichuan lies the **Jiuzhaigou Reserve** *(Jiuzhaigou Ziran Bao Hu Qu)*, a spectacular national park filled with lush valleys, jagged peaks, a dozen large waterfalls, and most famously, a collection of iridescent lakes and pools. Jiuzhaigou has become one of the country's most popular tourist destinations, with more than 1½ million people visiting every year.

The preserve's cerulean and aqua pools are among the most beautiful in the world, and the park's raw natural beauty has been compared to Yellowstone National Park. Also similar to Yellowstone are the crowds—throngs of Chinese tourists descend daily on this 800-km (497-mi) stretch of lush forests, piercing peaks, languid lakes, and clear pools. UNESCO has awarded the park heritage status for its "Man and Biosphere" program.

Jiuzhaigou Nature Reserve is a natural reserve and a collection of villages, mostly of Tibetan and Qinang origin. (The name Jiuzhaigou translates as "Nine Villages.") The dramatic increase in tourism has had a great impact upon the locals, many of whom have been removed from their homes in order to "protect" the park.

WORD OF MOUTH

"Jiuzhaigou was really something else—there aren't words to describe this place. It's superb scenery, absolutely gorgeous. What makes it even better is there are several beautiful Tibetan villages and temples in the valley where Tibetans go about their everyday lives." —Neil_Oz

Management of Jiuzhaigou Nature Reserve has been turned over to a private company, so admission is much more expensive than in previous years, but there are also more services available, such as the introduction of an environment-friendly transportation route through the park—plied by so-called green buses that have reduced emissions to protect the environment. For those who want to avoid tour buses and local guides, walkways and signs direct travelers along the way. There are now many hotels around the park, including a five-star resort tucked in the wilderness.

This region is spectacular, with limestone and karst formations, temperate rain forests, and dozens of bright turquoise, orange, and emerald-green pools. The park shelters 76 mammal species, including pandas, black bears, and deer. The climate is wet in the spring and fall, very snowy and cold in the winter, and bright and warm in the summer. *Y320 0837/773-9753 www.jiuzhai.com Apr. 1–No.v 15, daily 7 AM–7 PM; Nov. 16–Mar. 31, daily 7:30 AM–6:30 PM.*

8

GETTING HERE AND AROUND

BY AIR You can fly to Jiuhuang Airport, 2½ hours south of Jiuzhaigou in Huanglong. There are numerous shuttle buses that can take you from the airport to Songpan (2 hours) or to the Jiu Zhai Valley (2 hours). Your hotel should arrange a transfer; otherwise a shuttle bus will cost Y60 to Y80.

BY BUS Several buses a day shuttle passengers from Chengdu's Xinnanmen Bus Station or Chadianzi Bus Station.

TOURS

If you want to experience Jiuzhaigou as the Chinese do, sign up with any of the numerous package tours in Chengdu and Chongqing. A word to the wise: be prepared to be herded along by a guide armed with a flag and a bullhorn. General information on tours from Chengdu and Chongqing is available from China Travel Service.

ESSENTIALS

Air Contacts Jiuzhaigou Huanglong Airport (*0837/724-3700 www.jzairport.com*).

Banks Agricultural Bank of China (☎*0837/773–9717*).

Visitor and Tour Info China Travel Service (☎*028/6866–3866, 028/6866–3138, or 028/6655–1188*). **Jiuzhaiguo Park Office** (☎*0837/773–9753*).

EXPLORING JIUZHAIGOU

Exploring the park is made easier by frequent ranger stations and signs in English. As you explore the Y-shaped Jiuzhaigou Nature Reserve, your first stop will undoubtedly be the Zaru Valley, on your left. You'll find the Zaru Temple and the Hejiao Stockade farther up the Zaru Valley. Deeper in the valley you'll pass the stunning Shunzheng Terrace Waterfall before you reach Mirror Lake and Nuorilang Falls. On the right side of this path you'll find the fabled Nine Villages, where it is possible to have a meal with the locals. These sights alone are worth the trip, and many tourists head back after marveling at Mirror Lake.

From Mirror Lake, veer left to the Zechawa Village, an impossibly beautiful small Tibetan community. From the village, the path travels through a temperate rain forest interspersed with dozens of turquoise-colored pools. At the far end of the left branch of the Y is Long Lake, a beautiful and peaceful place that carries barely a trace of the modernization happening all around. Down the right branch of the Y is a series of amazing small lakes, including Five Flower Lake and Arrow Bamboo Lake, crisscrossed by wooden walkways.

WHERE TO STAY AND EAT

Did someone say yak? Near the main gate of Jiuzhaigou Reserve you'll find restaurants selling dried yak, cured yak, pickled yak, smoked yak, yak hotpot, fried yak, and—well, you get the point. Sample the *sampas* (barley-and-yak-butter tea cakes).

$$$–$$$$ **Intercontinental Resort Jiuzhai Paradise.** Tucked away in a valley 15 km (9 mi) from the Jiuzhaigou Nature Reserve, this is the region's most luxurious lodging. The sprawling complex was designed around a Qiang-style village that sits under a glass dome. The foyer is truly one of a kind, covered by a glass-and-metal dome that lets in sunlight during the day and allows glimpses of the moon at night. The rooms are extravagantly decorated, and there's a nightly performance by Tibetan dancers. A daily bus takes you to the national park's main gate. **Pros:** pretty location, nice rooms. **Cons:** less than stellar food and service, lack of hot water at times. ✉*Near Jiuzhaigou Nature Preserve,* ☎*0837/778–9999* 🌐*www.jiuzhaiparadise.com* *945 rooms, 45 suites* *In-hotel: 6 restaurants, room service, bar, pool, gym, spa, business center, public Internet* 💳*AE, MC, V.*

$$$–$$$$ **Sheraton Jiuzhaigou Resort.** This was the region's first luxury hotel, located about a thousand feet from the mouth of the Jiu Zhai Valley. With dozens of peaked roofs, the resort vaguely resembles an ancient castle. Surrounded by the mountains, the hotel has incredible views from its nicely decorated guest rooms. **Pros:** good service and location. **Cons:** dated rooms. ✉*Jiu Zhai Gou Scenic Spot, Jiuzhaigou,* ☎*0837/773–9988* 🌐*www.sheraton.com/jiuzhaigou* *482 rooms, 20 suites* *In-hotel: 3 restaurants, room service, bar, pool, gym, spa, laundry service, public Internet* 💳*AE, MC, V.*

¢ YouU Hostel. All things considered, this may be the best lodging in the area. The hostel is a 15-minute cab ride south of the Jiu Zhai Valley. The owners are artists and travelers—evident in their tasteful decor and their knowledge of the surrounding area. The rooms, which run the gamut from dorm-style to suites, are spotless, cozy, and comfortable. The café has the finest Western food in the area—not surprising, as the chef once ran the kitchen at Grandma's in Chengdu. The steaks are juicy and tender, the pasta is perfect, and the coffee is some of the best around. **Pros:** helpful staff, great food. **Cons:** a little far out. ✉*Building 4, Khampa Lingka Plaza,* ☎*0837/776–3111* 🖷*0837/776–3966* *60 rooms, 6 suites* *In-hotel: Wi-Fi in bar and café, 2 restaurants, laundry facilities, no elevator.* *No credit cards.*

WORD OF MOUTH

"Some of my relatives just came back from China, and suffered from some mild to moderate altitude sickness at Huanglong National Park in Sichuan province . . . If you're planning a trip to Jiuzhaigou and Huanglong, and flying directly from Chengdu, please give yourself a lot of time to acclimate before going to Huanglong."

– rkkwan

SONGPAN

350 km (217 mi; 6–8 hrs by bus) northwest of Chengdu.

Anyone who visited Songpan more than a few years ago won't recognize the place. The village with a couple of dirt roads and no accommodations has become a small town with several decent hotels and a fine restaurant. The locals have spruced up the streets and built nice new wooden signs, often with English translations. The old town is not that old any longer, but the mosque by the river is a beautiful sight in the morning when the sunlight reflects off of the minaret.

Most people visit Songpan for the horses, and they do not leave disappointed. These horseback-riding treks through the surrounding countryside go on and on, but four days seems to be the maximum.

GETTING HERE AND AROUND

BY AIR Don't be fooled by the name of Songpan's Jiuzhaigou Huanglong Airport—it's about 88 km (55 mi) from Jiuzhaigou. Shuttle buses make the 1½-hour trip.

BY BUS Buses from Chengdu's Chadianzi and Xinnanmen bus stations shuttle passengers every day from 6:30 AM to 7 PM.

HORSE TREKS

Shun Jiang Horse Treks (☎*139/0904–3513*) offers horseback tours into the mountains and past Tibetan villages that haven't changed for centuries. The trips cost Y160 per person, per day. Prices are somewhat negotiable.

8

WHERE TO STAY AND EAT

You can't leave Songpan without trying goat. Restaurants up and down the main drag prepare this local specialty. If you spy an Islamic crescent moon above the restaurant in question, it is a good bet the fare is excellent.

¢ **Songzhou Jiaotong Hotel.** When you want bang for your buck, this is the place. On the 2nd floor of the long-distance bus station, this hotel has clean private rooms and dorm-style accommodations. Another perk is the English-speaking manager. **Pros:** convenent location, helpful staff. **Cons:** no frills. ✉ *Long Distance Bus Station* ☎ *0837/723–1818* *20 rooms* *No elevator* *No credit cards.*

CHONGQING AND THE YANGTZE RIVER

After decades of lobbying for special economic status, in 1997 Beijing finally allowed Chongqing to formally separate from Sichuan. This maneuver facilitated Chongqing's rise from a stunted once-capital to the region's industrial powerhouse and allowed for the long-planned Three Gorges Dam Project to move forward.

Called the Mountain City (also the name of the local beer), Chongqing has features unlike any other Chinese city. Instead of the ubiquitous bicycle, Chongqing has the Stickman Army. Stickmen are peasants for hire who wander the streets of Chongqing carrying stuff up and down the hills. The city is also riddled with tunnels, many of which were dug during the sieges of WWII. Built on the side of a mountain, the city has an upper and a lower level, so it's not unusual for buildings to have two or more "ground floors."

The city is the major jumping-off point for the Three Gorges Cruise down the Yangtze River. The classic novel, *The Three Kingdoms,* takes place along this stretch of the river, and the cliffs are lined with caves and tombs dating back to the Yellow Emperor. The Three Gorges Dam is now complete and the water level is steadily rising—millions of people have been displaced, entire villages swamped, and countless historical artifacts lost forever—but China needs energy to keep its economic miracle running and the western regions need a reliable inland port with deep water capacity, therefore the dam stays.

DID YOU KNOW?

Chongqing is the heart of the BaYu Culture—vibrant, colorful, and proud—with its own version of Sichuan Opera, its own cuisine, and a history of rebelliousness. Chongqingese are known for their directness and fiery tempers.

REGIONAL TOURS

Tour Contacts Chongqing Dongfan Travel Service (✉ *5 Chaoqiang Lu, Chongqing* ☎ *0236/371–0326*).

Continued on page 567

A CULINARY TOUR OF CHINA

For centuries, the collective culinary fragrances of China have drifted far beyond its borders and tantalized the entire world. In the decades following the revolution, most Westerners couldn't get anything close to genuine Chinese cuisine. But with China's arms now open to the world, a vast variety of Chinese flavors are more widely accessible than ever.

Four corners of the Middle Kingdom

In dynasties gone by, a visitor to China might have to undertake a journey of a thousand li just to feel the burn of an authentic Sichuanese hotpot, and another to savor the crispy skin and juicy flesh of a genuine Beijing roast duck. Luckily for us, the vast majority of regional Chinese cuisines have made successful internal migrations. As a result, Sichuanese cuisine can be found in Guangzhou, Cantonese dim sum in Urumuqi, and the cumin-spiced lamb-on-a-stick, for which the Uigher people of Xinjiang are famous, is now grilled all over China.

Before you begin your journey, remember, a true scholar of Middle Kingdom cuisine should first eliminate the very term "Chinese food" from their vocabulary. It hardly encompasses the variety of provincial cuisines and regional dishes that China has to offer, from succulent Shanghainese dumplings to fiery Sichuanese hotpots.

To guide you on your gastronomic journey, we've divided the country's gourmet map along the points of the compass—North, South, East, and West. Bon voyage and *bon appétit!*

NORTH

THE BASICS

Cuisine from China's Northeast is called *dongbei cai,* and it's more wheat than rice based. Vegetables like kale, cabbage, and potatoes are combined with robust, thick soy sauces, garlic (often raw), and scallions.

Even though many Han Chinese from southern climates find mutton too gamey, up north it's a regular staple. In many northern cities, you can't walk more than a block without coming across a small sidewalk grill with *yang rou chua'r,* or lamb-on-a-stick.

NOT TO BE MISSED

The most famous of all the northern dishes is Peking duck, and if you've ever had it well prepared, you'll know why Beijingers are proud of the dish named for their city.

The fowl is cleaned, stuffed with burning millet stalks and other aromatic combustibles, and then slow-cooked in an oven heated by a fire made of fragrant wood. Properly cooked, Peking duck should have crispy skin, juicy meat, and none of the grease. Peking duck is served with pancakes, scallions, and a delicious soy-based sauce with just a hint of sweetness.

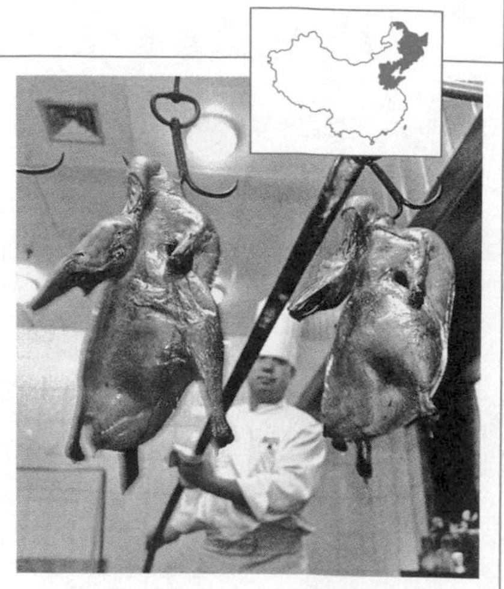

The ultimate window dressing.

LEGEND HAS IT

Looking for the best roast duck in Beijing? You won't find it in a luxury hotel. But if you happen to find yourself wandering through the Qianmendong hutong just south of Tiananmen Square, you may stumble upon a little courtyard home with a sign in English reading LI QUN ROAST DUCK. This small and unassuming restaurant is widely considered as having the best Peking roast duck in the capital. Rumor has it that the late leader Deng Xiaoping used to send his driver out to bring him back Li Qun's amazing ducks.

THE CAPITAL CITY'S NAMESAKE DISH

SOUTH

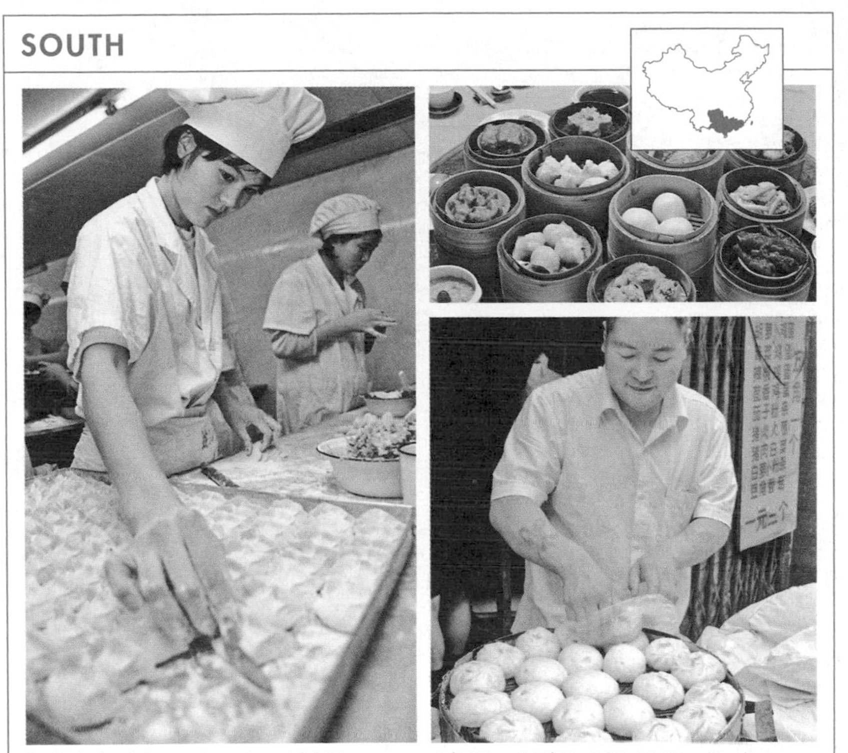

(left) Preparing for the feast. (top right) Dim sum as art. (bottom right) Meat-filled Beijing dumplings.

THE BASICS

The dish most associated with Southern Chinese cuisine is dim sum, which is found in great variety and abundance in Guangdong province, as well as Hong Kong and Macau. Bite-size dim sum is usually eaten early in the day. Any good dim sum place should have dozens of varieties. Some of the most popular dishes are *har gao*, a shrimp dumpling with a rice-flour skin, *siu maai*, a pork dumpling with a wrapping made of wheat flour, and *chaa-habao*, a steamed or baked bun filled with sweetened pork and onions. Adventerous eaters should order the chicken claws. Trust us, they taste better than they look.

The Cantonese saying *"fei qin zou shou"* roughly translates to "if it flies, swims or runs, it's food."

For our money, the best southern food comes from Chaozhou (Chiuchow), a coastal city only a few hours' drive north of its larger neighbors. Unlike dim sum, Chaozuo cuisine is extremely light and understated. Deep-fried bean curd is also a remarkably fresh Chaozuo dish.

NOT TO BE MISSED

One Chaozuo dish that appeals equally to the eye and the palate is the plain-sounding mashed vegetable with minced chicken soup. The dish is served in a large bowl, and resembles a green-and white yin-yang. As befitting a dish resembling a Buddhist symbol, a vegetarian version substituting rice gruel for chicken broth is usually offered.

SOUTHWEST AND FAR WEST

Southwest

THE BASICS

When a person from the Southwest asks you if you like spicy food, consider your answer well. Natives of Sichuan and Hunan take the use of chilies, wild pepper, and garlic to blistering new heights. These two areas have been competing for the "spiciest province in China" title for centuries. The penchant for fiery food is likely due to the weather—hot and humid in the summer and harshly cold in the winter. But no matter what the temperature, if you're eating Sichuan or Hunan dishes, be prepared to sweat.

Southwest China shares some culinary traits with both Southeast Asia and India. This is likely due to the influences of travelers from both regions in centuries past. Traditional Chinese medicine also makes itself felt in the regional cuisine. Theory has it that sweating expels toxins and equalizes body temperature.

As Chairman Mao's hometown province, Hunan has a number of dishes with revolutionary names. The most popular are red-cooked Hunan fish *(hongshao wuchangyu)* and red-cooked pork *(hongshao rou)*, which was said to have been a personal favorite of the Great Helmsman.

The hotter the better.

NOT TO BE MISSED

One dish you won't want to miss out on in Sichuan is *mala zigi*, or "peppery and hot chicken." It's one part chicken meat and three parts fried chilies and a Sichuanese wild pepper called *huajiao* that's so spicy it effectively numbs the tongue. At first it feels like eating Tiger Balm, but the hot-cool-numb sensation produced by crunching on the pepper is oddly addictive.

KUNG PAO CHICKEN

One of the most famous Chinese dishes, Kung Pao chicken (or gongbao jiding), enjoys a legend of its own.

Though shrouded in myth, its origin exemplifies the improvisational skills found in any good Chinese chef. The story of Kung Pao chicken has to do with a certain Qing Dynasty–era (1644-1911) provincial governor named Ding Baozhen, who arrived home unexpectedly one day with a group of friends in tow. His cook, caught in between shopping trips, had only the chicken breast and a few vegetables he was planning to cook for his own dinner. The crafty chef diced the chicken into tiny bits and fried it up with everything he could find in the cupboard—some peanuts, sugar, onion, garlic, bits of ginger, and a few handfuls of dried red peppers—and hoped for the best.

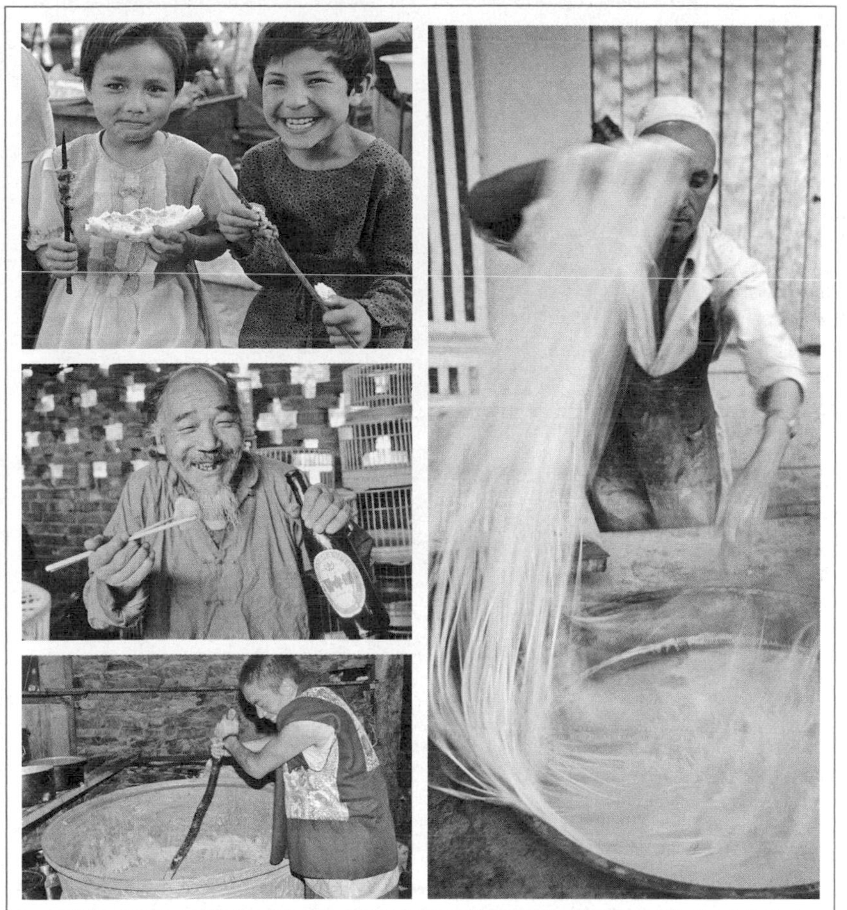

(top left) Chowing down at Kashgar's Sunday Market. (center left) Eat, drink, and be merry! (bottom left) Monk stirring tsampa barley. (right) Juggling hot noodles in the Xinjiang province.

Far West

THE BASICS

Religion is the primary shaper of culinary tradition in China's Far West. Being a primarily Muslim province, chefs in Xinjiang don't use pork products of any kind. Instead, meals are likely to be heavy on spiced lamb. Baked flat breads coated in sesame seeds are a specialty. Whole lamb roasted on a spit, fine spicy tomato salads, and lightly spiced mutton and vegetable soups are also favorites.

NOT TO BE MISSED

In Tibet, climate is the major factor dictating cuisine. High and dry, the Tibetan plateau is hardly suited for rice cultivation. Whereas a Han meal might include rice, Tibetan cuisine tends to include tsampa, a ground barley usually cooked into a porridge. Another staple that's definitely an acquired taste is yak butter tea. Dumplings, known as *momo*, are wholesome and filling. Of course, if you want to go all out, order the yak penis with caterpillar fungus.

EAST

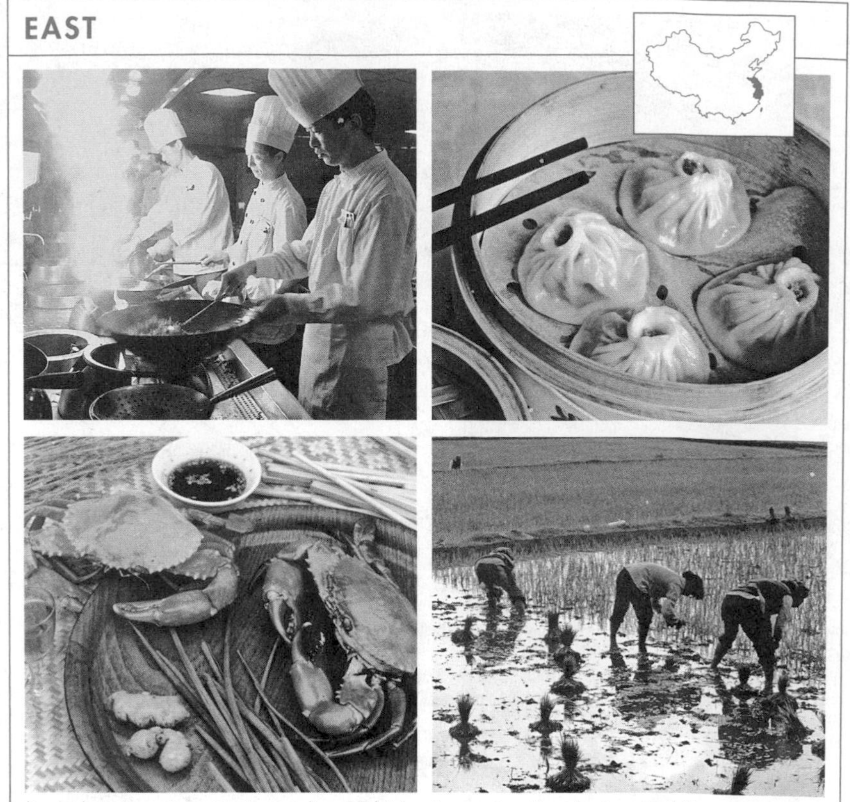

(top left) Flash cooking with the wok. (top right) Juicy steamer dumplings. (bottom right) Harvesting China's staple. (bottom left) Shanghai's sublime hairy crab.

THE BASICS

The rice, seafood, and fresh vegetable-based cooking of the southern coastal provinces of Zhejiang and Jiangsu are known collectively as *huiyang cai*. As the area's biggest city, Shanghai has become a major center of the culinary arts. Some popular dishes in Shanghai are stir-fried freshwater eels and finely ground white pepper, and red-stewed fish—a boiled carp in sweet and sour sauce. Another Shanghai favorite are *xiaolong bao*, or little steamer dumplings. Similar to Cantonese dim sum, xiaolong bao tend to be more moist. The perfect steamed dumpling is meant to explode in your mouth in a juicy burst of meat.

NOT TO BE MISSED

Drunken anything! Shanghai chefs are known for their love of cooking with wine. Dishes like drunken chicken, drunken pigeon, and drunken crab are all delectable meals cooked with prodigious amounts of Shaoxing wine. People with an aversion to alcohol should definitely avoid these. Another meal not to be missed is hairy freshwater crabs, which only come into season in October. One enthusiast of the dish was 15th-century poet and essayist Li Yu, who wrote of the dish in near-erotic terms. "Meat as white as jade, golden roe . . . to use seasoning to improve its taste is like holding up a torch to brighten the sunshine."

CHONGQING

240 km (149 mi; 4 hrs by bus) southeast of Chengdu; 1,800 km (1,116 mi; 3 hrs by plane) southwest of Beijing; 1,025 km (636 mi; 34 hrs by train) northwest of Hong Kong.

Contrary to popular opinion, Chongqing is not just a dump that's only visited as a jumping-off spot for the ride down the Yangtze. For starters, because of the summertime heat and humidity, Chongqing comes alive at night. Few places have as many night food markets with such delicious, diverse, and agreeably priced fare. There's a great club scene in all parts of the city, especially in the Jie Fang Bei area. And the hills that distinguish Chongqing don't stop at the city limits—the lush countryside is dotted with villages locked in time and the mountains are riddled with caves. Finally, Chongqing is rich in early-20th-century Chinese historical sites.

GETTING HERE AND AROUND

Chongqing is smack-dab in the middle of China, connected by rail, bus, and plane to every major city in the country. The Chongqing airport is well connected, with daily flights to all major cities in China. For travel between the east coast and Chongqing, flying is your most comfortable option. For trips to Chengdu, the express train is the best bet, although there are bus and plane connections as well.

Chongqing's light-rail line from the city center to the zoo in the south is worth the Y10 round-trip ticket price. The two stations in the city center (Jiao Chang Kou and Ling Jiang Men) are easily accessible from Liberation Monument. The line curves north to the Jialing River—above ground—and goes through six riverside stations before it heads south to the terminal station at the zoo.

BY AIR Traffic permitting, Chongqing's Jiangbei International Airport is a 1½-hour drive north by taxi from the city center. The airport flies to every major domestic, and some international hubs, mostly within Asia. Book tickets at any hotel or the travel agencies around Liberation Monument.

BY BOAT AND FERRY Boats go on the Yangtze from Chongqing all the way to Shanghai (seven days), but the most popular route is the cruise downstream from Chongqing to Yichang or Wuhan (three to four days) or upstream from Wuhan to Chongqing. Most major sights, including the Three Gorges and Three Little Gorges, lie between Chongqing and Yichang. Tourist boats offer air-conditioned cabins with a television and private bath; the ordinary passenger steamers used by most Chinese offer minimal comforts. Tickets can be arranged through CITS or your travel agent.

BY BUS The shared train and bus station may be the most inconvenient, crowded, and annoying station in the world. Once your taxi has maneuvered through the corrugated tin walls and piles of baggage, finding buses or trains is not hard, however.

From Chongqing to Chengdu is a well-trodden path. The bus departs every hour, takes five to six hours, and costs Y120. Buses are viable as

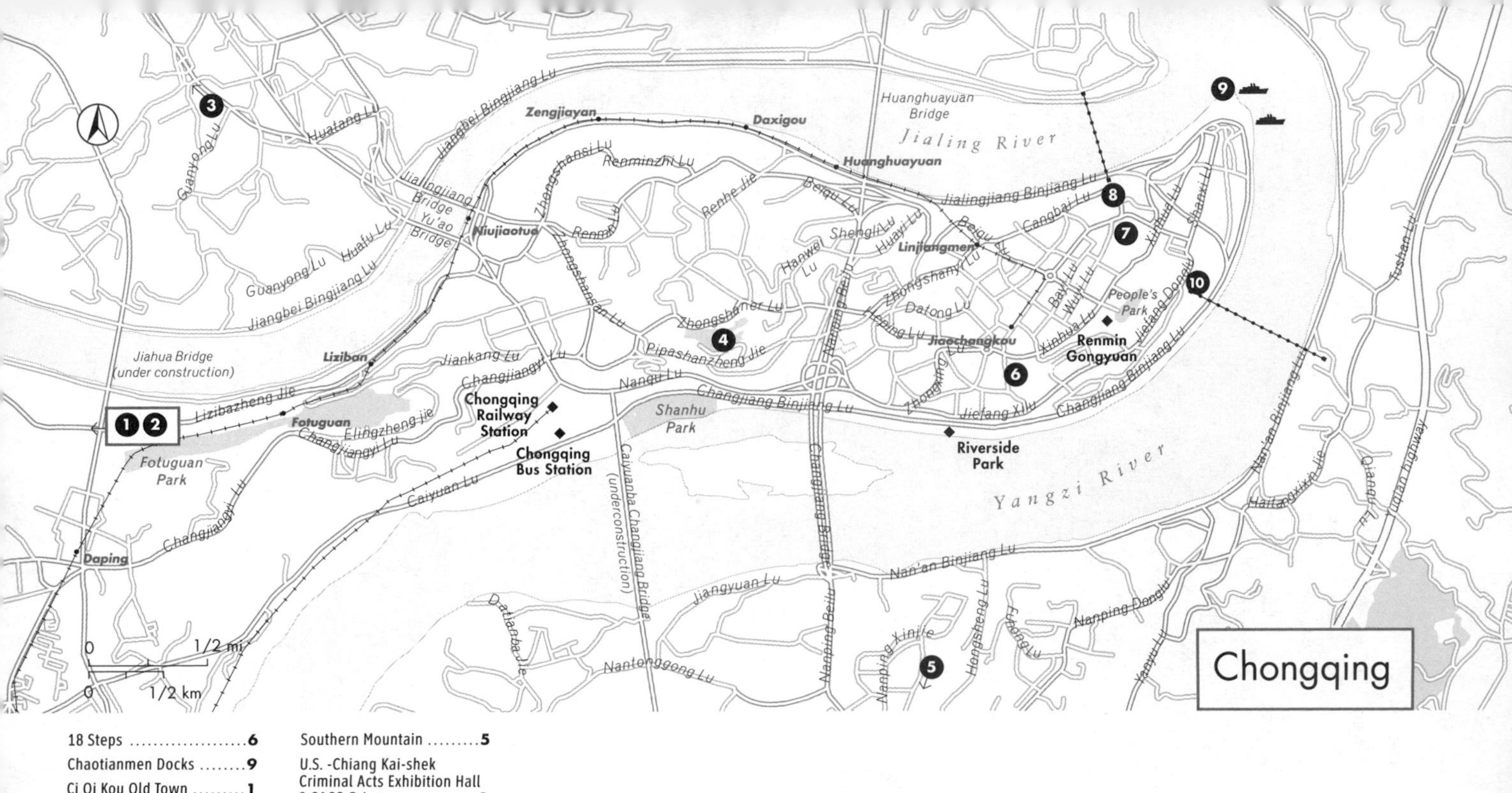

18 Steps 6
Chaotianmen Docks 9
Ci Qi Kou Old Town 1
Jiangling River Cable Car ..8
Jinyun Mountain 3
Loquat Hill 4
Luohan Temple 7
Southern Mountain 5
U.S. -Chiang Kai-shek Criminal Acts Exhibition Hall & SACO Prison 2
Yangtze River Cable Car .. 10

far as Yibin or within the municipality itself (Dazu and Beibei), but trains are recommended for all other destinations.

BY TRAIN The train and bus station (⇨*above*) share a location. Trains leave Chongqing every minute for every conceivable city in China. If you're going to Chengdu, we recommend the express train. It's a comfy, double-decker train with air-conditioning and good food. The trip only takes 4 hours. Trains leave every day from Chongqing North Station at 7:49 AM, 12:39 PM, 4:21 PM, and 6:35 PM. Tickets cost Y51 one-way for hard-seat class and Y81 for soft-seat class. Sleeper-seats cost Y98 to Y106.

18 STEPS

Chongqing has the dubious distinction of being the most-bombarded city ever. During WWII, people would hide in the tunnels throughout the city to escape devastation. One of these tunnels is located in the district known as 18 Steps, in present-day Jie Fang Bei District. The tunnel still exists today but serves a very different purpose. It emits a constant flow of cool air and area residents gather here to cool themselves on sweltering summer days.

TOURS

At night, the high-rises that ring the hills around the city, give off a glow that reflects off the rushing rivers below. A night boat cruise is a romantic way to appreciate the charms of the Mountain City. Tickets can be bought at any hotel, or at the **Chongqian Huanyu Travel Agency.** Cruises can be booked with or without dinner. ✉*18 Xingyi St., across from the port* ☎*023/6380–3350* *Y38–Y550* ⏲*24 hours.*

8

ESSENTIALS

Banks Bank of China (✉*Minzu Lu*).

Bus Contacts Chongqing Long Distance Bus Group (☎*023/6888–1939 or 023/8908–8458*).

Train Contacts Cai Yuan Ba Train Station (✉*Off of Nan Qu Lu* ☎*023/6168–1114*).

Internet Gao Shou Internet Bar (✉*Ci Qi Lu, Yu Zhong District, basement of De Yi World, around the corner from the Marriott and next to the Falling Club*).

■ TIP→ Most hotels in the city center are wired and there are Internet cafés in the smaller streets that radiate from the Liberation Monument.

Medical Assistance First Aid Emergency Medical Center (✉*1 Jiankang Lu* ☎*023/6369–2008*).

Visitor and Tour Info CITS (✉*151 Jiefangbei Zourong Lu, A8* ☎*400/887–7761 toll free or 023/6372–7120* 🌐*www.hikeyangtze.com*).

EXPLORING CHONGQING

MAIN ATTRACTIONS

18 Steps *(Shi Ba Ti)* is one of the coolest places in the city, literally and figuratively. The neighborhood is just south of Liberation Monument and hasn't changed since the early 20th century. The name refers to the steps leading from the upper level of Jie Fang Bei down to the slums below. The infamous 18 Steps tunnel, the scene of horrible carnage during WWII, serves as a congregation point for the whole neighborhood. Find the tunnel, pull up a mat, and sip tea while the locals stare at you incredulously. At the top of the steps is a teahouse with a treasure trove of WWII memorabilia. ✉ *18 Steps, Jie Fang Bei District, walk in a southerly direction from Liberation Monument and ask about "Shi Ba Ti" as you go.*

8 10 Be sure to ride on both of the **cable cars** that dangle above the city. One links the north and south shores of the Jialing River, from Canbai Lu to the Jinsha Jie station and gives excellent views of the docks, the city, and the confluence of the Jialing and Yangtze rivers. The other crosses the Yangtze itself and starts close to Xinhua Lu. Be sure to take a map and study the city while up in the air. It's a good opportunity to rise above it all and get a grip on the city. **Jiangling River Cable Car** (✉ *63 Cangbai Lu* ☎ *023/6383–4320* 🎫 *Y1.50* ⏲ *Daily 10 AM–6 PM*). **Yangtze River Cable Car** (✉ *24 Xinhua Lu* 🎫 *Y2* ⏲ *Daily 6:15 AM–10 PM*).

NEED A BREAK?

On top of a wall overlooking the Yangtze, the Unique Coffee House (✉ *100 Nan Bing Rd., Sunlight Pavilion* ▭ *No credit cards*) sits across from the evening cruise-boat launch. The view is splendid, the coffee is good, and the boss speaks English. There is also a small selection of cakes and muffins.

1 **Ci Qi Kou Old Town** *(Ci Qi Kou Gu Cheng)*. Perched in the west of the city overlooking the Jialing River, this refurbished old district dates back to the late Ming Dynasty. There is a main drag with dozens of souvenir and snack shops, including the peaceful Baolun Si temple, which dates back 1,500 years. If you stay until late into the evening, head down the alleys off the main drag and have a bowl of "Night Owl Noodles." It's spicy, meaty, and filling. ✉ *Take Bus 462 from Liberation Monument to Chongqing University and connect with one of dozens of minivans and small buses to Ci Qi Kou for Y1–Y2; the ride takes about 40 mins.*

3 ★ In Beibie Town, just north of the city, **Jinyun Mountain** *(Jinyun Shan)* has some pretty views and a smattering of pavilions from the Ming and Qing dynasties. Three contain imposing statues of the Giant Buddha, the Amitabha Buddha, and the famous general of the Three Kingdoms Period, Guan Yu. The park also has a set of **hot springs,** where it is possible to bathe in the 30°C (86°F) water, either in a swimming pool or in the privacy of cubicles with their own baths. ✉ *Jinyun Shan, 45 min (50 km [30 mi]) by bus north of city* 🎫 *Y15 for admission to the park, Y30–Y200 for use of the hot springs* ⏲ *Daily 8:30–6.*

7 Originally built about 1,000 years ago (Song Dynasty) and rebuilt in 1752, and again in 1945, the **Luohan Temple** *(Luohan Si)* is a popular place of worship and a small community of monks is still active here. One of the main attractions is the 500 lifelike painted clay arhats—Buddhist disciples who have succeeded in freeing themselves from the earthly chains of delusion and material greed. At the back of the temple, you can order tea, get a massage, and eat a vegetarian meal every day at 11 AM for Y2. ✉ *7 Louhan Si* 🎫 *Y10* ⏲ *Daily 8 AM–6 PM.*

5 **Southern Mountain** *(Nan Shan)* is the highest point in the city and at 935 feet, it's the most popular place from which to view Chongqing. For a thousand years Nan Shan has been the route over which travelers and traders of medicine, tea, spices, and silk entered the city and headed on to Sichuan. Besides spectacular views, the following sites are also on the mountaintop: **The Chongqing Anti-Japanese War Ruins Museum** (*Y20 Daily 8:30–5:30*) is a collection of new houses built where the Nationalist Army had its headquarters during WWII. There are a few pictures and maps here, but we found the price too steep for what was offered. For the highest view of Chongqing City, check out the **Viewing Pavilion** (*Y20 Daily 8* AM–*6* PM), a half-moon pavilion facing north across the Yangtze River. The **Luo Jun Cave Taoist Temple** (*Y6 Daily 7:30* AM–*4:30* PM) is a 1,700-year-old temple that has been completely renovated but still sees very little traffic. The main temple entrance is accessible from the far side of the mountain, but we recommend slipping through the back door, which is a nice walk up the mountain's main road. The main temple sits on top of five caves that were used by Taoist monks centuries ago for meditation and contemplation. ✉*Nanping District, south side of the city, near Nan An Bin Jiang Lu Daily 7* AM–*11* PM.

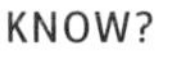
DID YOU KNOW?

There are dozens of hole-in-the-wall restaurants all along the stone steps that serve the cheapest, tastiest food in town.

IF YOU HAVE TIME

9 Perhaps not as busy and bustling as once upon a time, **Chaotianmen Docks** *(Chaotianmen Matou)* still offer an opportunity to get a glimpse of China at work and see the various boats departing for the Three Gorges river cruise. It's also a nice place to witness the unique merging of the muddy-brown Yangtze River and the blue-green Jialing River. ✉*Shaanxi Lu.*

4 The 804 foot **Loquat Hill** *(Pipa Shan)* has great views of the bustle on the river below. At night, enjoy the city lights. There's also a small park with no entrance fee. ✉*Zhongshan Er Lu Daily 8* AM–*7* PM.

2 **U.S.-Chiang Kai-shek Criminal Acts Exhibition Hall and SACO Prison** *(Zhongmei Hezuosuo)*. SACO stands for the Sino-American Cooperation Organization, a collaboration between Chiang Kai-shek and the U.S. government and dedicated to the training and supervision of agents for the Nationalist Party government that fought the Communists before retreating to Taiwan. It was jointly run by the Chinese and the Americans, who built prisons outside Chongqing where sympathizers of the Communist Party were imprisoned and tortured. The exhibition hall houses a few photographs and examples of the restraining devices used on the prisoners but has nothing in English. The prisons are a considerable walk from the exhibition hall. The SACO museum is a complex of four separate sites in the Sha Ping Ba suburb in northwest Chongqing at the foot of and atop Gele Mountain. There is also the option to hire a car and a guide with passable English for Y140. The prisons are not worth the price, but Gele Mountain is worth the climb; it is peaceful and often misty, and has several small pavilions, a playground,

8

and a monument to the Martyrs at the summit. ✉ *Foot of Gele Mountain, Sha Ping Ba District* 🎫 *Free* 🕑 *Daily 8:30–5.*

WHERE TO EAT

$$–$$$ FRENCH ✕ **Lao Sichuan.** The best-known restaurant in Chongqing because it's been in existence for as long as anyone can remember, the Old Sichuan has traditional and exotic food (for example, chili-braised frogs) at reasonable prices. The hot-pepper dishes are as spicy as you'd get in Sichuan. ✉ *186 Minzu Lu* ☎ *023/6382–6644* 💳 *No credit cards.*

$$–$$$ ITALIAN ✕ **Pizza Amalfi.** For weary travelers looking for some culinary familiarity, this pizzeria hits the spot. The food is pricey for what it is, but they speak English and offer take-out and delivery service. ✉ *Minzu Lu near Liberation Monument* ☎ *023/6381–7868 or 023/6091–4480* 💳 *No credit cards.*

$–$$$$ SICHUAN ✕ **Yizhishi Fandian.** This multilevel eatery is one of Sichuan's most famous. The food upstairs is more expensive but delicious—indulge in top-notch local dishes such as tea-smoked duck. The pastries and *jiaozi* (dumplings) downstairs are perfect breakfast nosh. ✉ *114 Zourong Lu* 💳 *No credit cards.*

WORD OF MOUTH

"We like spicy food and have experienced no problems with the spicy hotpots we've encountered before, but they are chicken broth compared to Chongqing hotpots! Your whole mouth goes numb. Your lips tingle." —Marija

WHERE TO STAY

¢ ★ 🏨 **Chongqing Fandian.** The well-equipped rooms make this hotel an excellent value and the restaurant, Chiao Tiang Gong—one of the city's older, more famous eateries—serves very good local and regional food in pleasant modern surroundings. It's in the center of town in an art-deco–style building. **Pros:** central location, good food. **Cons:** service could be better. ✉ *41–43 Xinhua Lu* ☎ *023/6191–6666 or 023/6399–2597* 📠 *023/6391–2599* *216 rooms* *In-hotel: 2 restaurants, café, bar. In-room: Free cable Internet* 💳 *AE, MC, V.*

$–$$ 🏨 **Hilton Hotel.** The Hilton is in a leafy, quiet neighborhood west of Liberation Monument. The hotel chain that gave Paris her fortune literally drips with class. Plush rooms have the firmest beds in town and fabulous bathrooms to boot. The rooftop pool is the perfect place to unwind. **Pros:** modern, clean, helpful staff. **Cons:** could be closer to shopping. ✉ *139 Zhongshan San Lu* ☎ *023/8903–9999* 🌐 *www.hilton.com.cn* *435 rooms and suites* *In-room: Internet. In-hotel: 4 restaurants, pool, spa* 💳 *AE, MC, V.*

¢–$ 🏨 **Holiday Inn Yangtze Chongqing** *(Yangzijiang Jiari Fandian).* This international standard hotel is just outside the city center. Try to reserve a room on the hotel's north side, where you can enjoy full views of

A SPOT OF TEA

Qi Xiang Ju (✉ *Liang Lu Kou Ti Yu Guan, next to the Liang Lu Kou Sports Facility*), which translates literally into "Strange Aroma Spot," is a small collection of tables and trees in the heart of the city. Some of the best tea in town is served here and it's a favorite hangout for artists, journalists, and the nouveau rich of Chongqing.

the Yangtze River. It's right across from the International Conference and Exhibition Center and there are lots of in-house amenities. **Pros:** courteous staff, very clean, comfortable. **Cons:** decor slightly dated. ✉*7 Nanping Xinjie* ☎*023/6280–3380* 🌐*www.holiday-inn.com.cn* *320 rooms* *In-hotel: 5 restaurants, Wi-Fi in lobby, bar, pool, gym* *AE, DC, MC, V.*

CHONGQING NOODLES

Southern China is not known for its noodles, as such fare is the domain of northerners. But during the mass migrations south and west over the past 100 years, noodle culture has been introduced to the Mountain City. Now, Chongqing has some of the tastiest bowls anywhere in the nation. Chongqing noodles come in all varieties and there are too many noodle stands to count.

$–$$$ **J.W. Marriott.** The Marriot is just off the main drag of the city within short walking distance to virtually any site near Liberation Monument. The service is impeccable, the rooms plush and comfy, and the amenities are first-class. The shopping arcade on the ground floor is a nice way to spend an hour or two, and if you're in the mood for steak and excellent views, visit the restaurant on the top floor. **Pros:** variety of food, good pool. **Cons:** bugs, air-conditioning problems. ✉*77 Qing Nian Lu, Yu Zhong District* ☎*023/6388–8888* 🌐*www.marriotthotels.com* *460 rooms and suites* *In-hotel: 5 restaurants, pool, spa, gym* *AE, DC, MC, V.*

¢ **Yu Du Da Jiu Dian.** A fine option if the foreign hotels are out of your price range but you still want to feel like royalty. The hotel's great location makes up for the mediocrity of the Chinese restaurant inside. The entire street down from the Liberation Monument is filled with food stands during the afternoon and evening hours, so you won't starve. Next door, on the third floor is the Newcastle Arms, an English-style pub with Y20 beers and Y300 bottles of booze. **Pros:** location. **Cons:** noise from outside. ✉*168 Bayi Lu* ☎*023/6382–8888* *023/6381–8168* *160 rooms* *In-hotel: 3 restaurants. In-room: free cable Internet* *AE, MC, V.*

NIGHTLIFE AND THE ARTS

Hong Ya Cave (*Hong Ya Dong* ✉*Bin Jiang Lu, south bank of the Yangtze, Nanping District*) is a recently built complex that fuses Ba Yu cultural performances with traditional Chinese architecture and elements of the American mall. It overlooks the Jialing River and has a brightly lit waterfall and paved streets built right into the mountainside. The main attraction is the Ba Yu dance performance, a dancing primer for Chongqing customs and folklore. At times it's racy, and the historical aspects of Ba Yu culture have been dumbed-down, but the costumes, choreography, and the bit on the Devil Town of Fengdu make it an evening well spent. For the **Ba Yu Theatre** (☎*023/6303–9968, 023/6303–9969 ticket reservations* *Y180–Y580* *Shows Sat. at 8* PM).

River Side Road (*Nan An Bing Jiang Lu* ✉*Nan An Bin Jiang Lu, south bank of the Yangtze, Nanping District*) stretches the length of the Yangtze River's south bank. The road is still under construction (with no definate date set for completion) and has not yet fulfilled its potential as the Champs Elysee of Chongqing, but there are a few good places to eat and a slew of enormous clubs along the road.

De Yi World (*De Yi Shi Jie* ✉ *Ci Qi Lu, Yu Zhong District, near Jie Fang Bei, around the corner from the Marriott Hotel*) is a large complex of bars, karaoke rooms, and dance clubs. If you want to party with the locals, we recommend **Falling** (✉ *Basement of De Yi World Complex* ☎ *No phone* 🎟 *Free* ⏲ *6 PM–sunrise*), a cramped club with a little dance floor that is packed on weekends. The music is good for Chinese club standards.

SHOPPING

Carrefour (*Jialefu* ✉ *Cangbai Lu* ⏲ *9 AM–11 PM*), near Chaotian Men port, is the largest foreign-owned department store in China. The France-based giant sells everything from congee to caviar plus a decent import section with all the goodies one misses from home. Carrefour is next to the largest fish market in the city.

SIDE TRIP TO DAZU

★ *3 hrs (160 km [99 mi]) by bus northwest of Chongqing.*

The Buddhist caves outside of this sprawling city were recently named a UNESCO site. They rival those at Datong, Dunhuang, and Luoyang. The sculptures, ranging from teeny-tiny to gigantic, contain unusual domestic detail, as well as purely religious works. There are two major sites at Dazu—Bei Shan and Baoding Shan. Work at the caves began in the 9th century (during the Song and Tang dynasties) and continued for more than 250 years.

Baoding Shan is the more impressive of the two sites and where the carvings were completed according to a plan. Here you will find visions of hell reminiscent of similar scenes from medieval Europe; the Wheel of Life; a magnificent 100-foot reclining Buddha; and a gold, thousand-armed statue of the goddess of mercy.

The best way to reach Dazu is to book a tour through your hotel or a travel agency. Every agency gives the Dazu tour for between Y220 and Y250, which includes transportation, lunch, and the entrance fee. If you would like to go it alone, there are minibuses by Liberation Monument that can take you there for about Y180 to Y230 round-trip. Leave early as seats sell out. 🎟 *Y85* ⏲ *Daily 8–5.*

WHERE TO STAY

¢ 🏨 **Dazu Binguan.** Most foreign guests end up staying in this clean but unimaginative hotel. The on-site travel agency can help you buy bus or train tickets. **Pros:** prime location. **Cons:** uncomfortable beds, dirty carpet. ✉ *350 Longgang Zhonglu,* ☎ *023/4372–1888* 📠 *023/4372–2907* 🛏 *132 rooms* 🖒 *In-hotel: 2 restaurants, bar. In-room: Free cable Internet* 💳 *AE, DC, MC, V.*

THE THREE GORGES

The third-longest river in the world after the Amazon and the Nile, the Yangtze cuts across 6,380 km (3,956 mi) and seven provinces before flowing out into the East China Sea. After descending from the mountain ranges of Qinghai and Tibet, the Yangtze crosses through Yunnan to Sichuan, winding its way through the lush countryside between Sichuan and Hubei before flowing northward toward Anhui and Jiangsu. Before the 20th century, many lost their lives trying to pass through the fearsome stretch of water running through what is known as the Three Gorges—the complicated system of narrow cliffs between Fengjie, in Sichuan, and Yichang, in Hubei.

> **WORD OF MOUTH**
>
> "The grottos in Baoding demonstrate Buddhist teachings and are absolutely incredible."
>
> —Marija

The spectacular scenery of the Three Gorges—Qutang, Wu, and Xiling—has survived the rising waters of the newly dammed Yangtze River. A trip through the Three Gorges offers a glimpse of a way of life that is rapidly disappearing: panoramas of hills covered with rice fields; fishermen scooping the waters with large nets from the shores; cliffs and clouds parting to reveal narrow passages of water barely wide enough for two boats—these images have persisted for centuries. If you can pull your mind away from the hype and hyperbole surrounding the Three Gorges project, you will find yourself dreaming of kung fu warriors, splendidly clad princes and princesses, and clashing armies from a bygone age. Even though the towns along the river—Fengdu, Shibaozhi, and others—have been conquered by the prevailing religion of today's mercantile China, the sites along the river are magical. How you experience your journey will depend on your mindset and on your preparation—this trip can be as amazing as you want it to be.

BOAT TOURS

Riverboat options depend on how much money you want to spend and how comfortably you want to travel. Riverboat rides essentially come in two forms: luxury and domestic. Domestic cruises are much cheaper and have fewer amenities. No matter which option you choose, book ahead as berths are limited.

LUXURY CRUISE BOATS

The foreign-owned ships, such as the Victoria Series boats, are big, quadruple-decker liners and by far the most comfortable option. In addition to spacious decks from which to soak up the breathtaking views, many boats are equipped with a gym, a ballroom, a business center with Internet connection, and bars and restaurants. There are also a few shops in case you run out of film or other necessities.

> **BEFORE YOU GO**
>
> The Three Gorges area is steeped in legends and history. To best appreciate the trip, read the classic book, *The Three Kingdoms.*

The ticket price includes the admission cost for most of the sites along

CLOSE UP

Dam the Yangtze

The Three Gorges dam project has been a dream for the Chinese leadership since Liberation in 1949. Harnessing the power of the mighty Yangtze River as it rushes through the gorges can help satiate China's appetite for energy as well as generate millions in income for provincial and central government coffers. At 607 feet high and more than 1 mi wide, the dam will produce enough electricity to supply the factories and cities of both the developed east and the underdeveloped heartland, hopefully putting an end to the rampant blackouts that threaten to choke China's economic revolution. The dam, when completed in 2009, will be the largest ever constructed, the cornerstone for the Communist Party's development program, and an international symbol of China's global power status. The reservoir created by the dam will increase Chongqing's ability to send freight down the Yangtze River and provide critical flood control for long-suffering downstream cities like Wuhan.

Since construction began, however, critics have railed against a project they consider a poorly planned attempt to impress the rest of the planet while destroying land, homes, and the history of a vast swath of China. Costs are difficult to assess in China, but estimates have been put as high as $75 billion. Rampant corruption has led to accusations of "tofu engineering," a serious allegation considering the millions of lives at stake if the dam were to collapse.

The project has been vilified by environmentalists worldwide. The reservoir, though instrumental in jump-starting hinterland exports to the outside world, will also back up the muddy Yangtze, potentially silting up the dam and thereby reducing electricity output. A more sinister possibility is the creation of a 300-mi long-cesspool, as the notoriously filthy and toxic towns of central China pour their wastes into a stagnant river.

The dam has also created a swarming diaspora of migrant workers and displaced persons who have swelled the nearby cities of Wuhan, Chongqing, Xi'an, and other cities as far away as Lanzhou and Urumqi. The submergence of entire towns and villages has coincided with the inundation of countless relics and artifacts from the cradle of Chinese civilization. The Three Gorges area is the site of some of the most famous battles of the Three Kingdoms period and has cliff-side tombs dating back to the dawn of civilization as we know it.

Regardless of the pitfalls and dangers, the Chinese are going through with their great project and banking that the benefits will outweigh the costs. Hopefully the dam will be a defiant success in the face of a wall of skepticism.

the way, except the Little Three Gorges. A one-way package tour ranges from Y4,583 to Y3,793 and the boats themselves are divided into three-, four-, and five-star service. Prices fluctuate so be sure to check ahead.

DOMESTIC BOATS

These less expensive, less luxurious boats are divided into four classes. Suites offer almost all of the amenities of Luxury Cruise Boats and are available for Y2,084 one-way. First-class sleeps two people and costs

Y1,042 one-way to Yichang. Spartan rooms come with two beds, a private bathroom, TV, and air-conditioning. Second-class sleeps four people and costs Y503 for a one-way ticket. Third-class sleeps six to eight people and costs Y347 one-way. Both second- and third-classes have bunk beds, shared bathrooms that aren't always kept clean, and views from lower decks are sometimes limited. Unlike the Luxury Cruise lines, these prices do not include the price of entry to sites along the way. The domestic boats serve good Chinese food, depending on the class you choose. Avoid any Western dishes that are on the menu. There are no shops on board, so stock up beforehand. If you go in winter, bring an extra blanket and dress warmly.

WORD OF MOUTH

"You definitely don't want to stay in Yichang more than you absolutely have to! It's claim to fame is that it's the end point of the Yangtze cruises. Nothing to see, nothing to do there, except wait for a flight out." —Marija

The tour operators have been consolidated into one company, and most tours get booked through them. Offices can be found throughout the Chaotianmen District.

Contact Chongqing Port International Travel Service (✉ *18 Xingyi St., Chaotianmen, Yu Zhong District, Chongqing* ☎ *023/6310–0595* 🌐 *www.cqpits.com*). Prices range from Y476 for the lease expensive tour to Y4,600 for the costliest.

HYDROFOIL

This option is used by those returning from Yichang to Chongqing, who don't want to do the whole trip over again, in reverse. Prices may vary, but currently it is Y280 from Yichang to Chongqing and takes about six hours. You have to get off at Wanxian and take a bus back into Chongqing. This costs Y120 and takes another 3½ hours. If you're pressed for time, an airport in Yinchang has daily flights to Chongqing at 7 PM for Y700.

8

SIGHTS EN ROUTE

On the banks of the Yangtze, **Fengdu,** also known as Guicheng or the "city of devils," is filled with temples, buildings, and statues depicting demons and devils. During the Tang Dynasty, the names of two local princely families, Yin (meaning "hell") and Wang (meaning "king"), were linked through marriage, making them known as Yinwang, or the "king of hell." Part of the old city has been submerged in the Three Gorges Dam project. You can take a series of staircases or a cable car to the top of the mountain. *Y60* ⊙ *Daily* 6 AM–6 PM.

The bamboo-covered **Ming Hill** *(Mingshan)* has a Buddhist temple, a pavilion, and pagodas with brightly painted dragons and swans emanating from the eaves. The hill has a nice view of the Yangtze River.

Stone Treasure Stronghold *(Shibaozhai)* is actually a rectangular rock with sheer cliffs, into which is built an impressive 12-story pagoda, constructed by Emperor Qianlong (1736–96) during the Qing Dynasty. Wall carvings and historical inscriptions describing the construction of the building can be seen along the circuitous stairway that leads

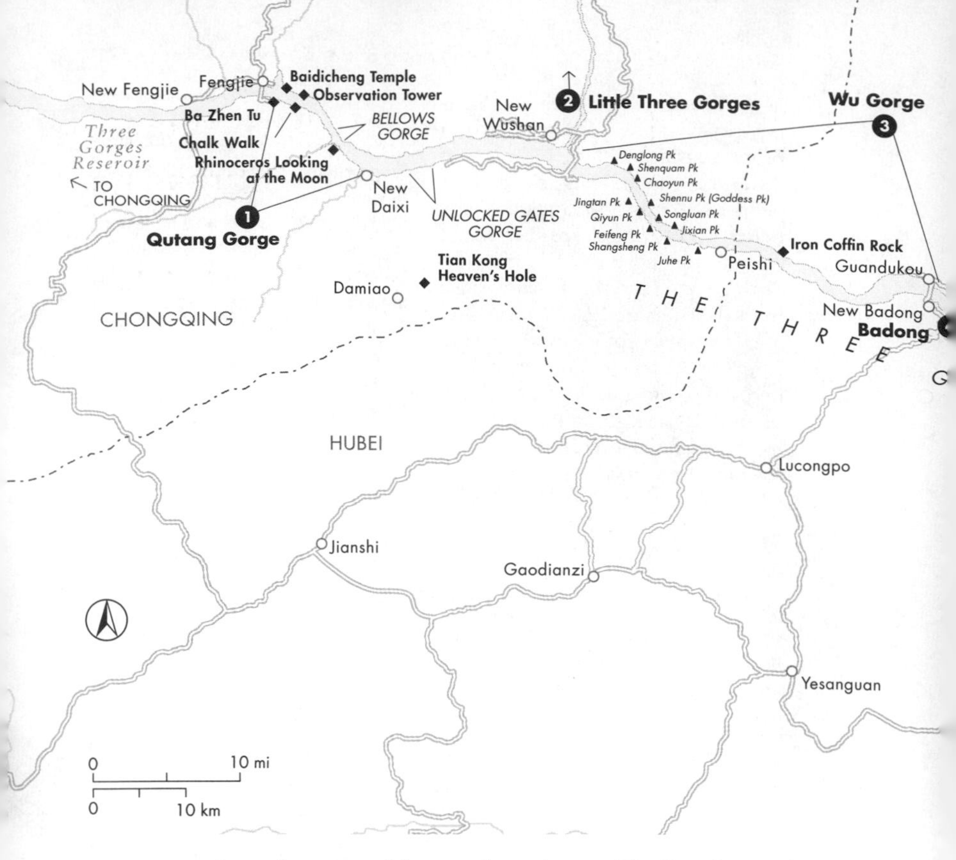

from the center of the pagoda to the top. The Pagado was damaged by the earth quake but is expected to be fixed up in early 2009. *Y50* *Daily 8 AM–7 PM.*

Three Gorges (San Xia). The Three Gorges lie in the heart of China, along the fault lines of what once were flourishing kingdoms. Those great kingdoms vanished into history and became, collectively, China.

1. The westernmost gorge, **Qutang Gorge** *(Qutang Xia)* is the shortest, at 8 km (5 mi). The currents here are quite strong due to the natural gate formed by the two mountains, Chijia and Baiyan. There are cliff inscriptions along the way, so be sure to have your guide point them out and explain their significance. Several are from the Warring States period over 1,000 years ago. Warriors' coffins from that period were discovered in the caves on these mountains, and some still remain.

2. Next, a short turn leads to Wushan, at the entrance to Wu Gorge. Here you can change to a smaller boat navigated by local boatmen to the **Little Three Gorges** (*Xiao San Xia* *Y150*). The Little Three Gorges (Dragon Gate Gorge, Misty Gorge, and Emerald Gorge) are spectacular and not to be missed. They are striking and silent, rising dramatically out of the river. If you have time, take a trip to the old town of Dachang near the end of the Little Three.

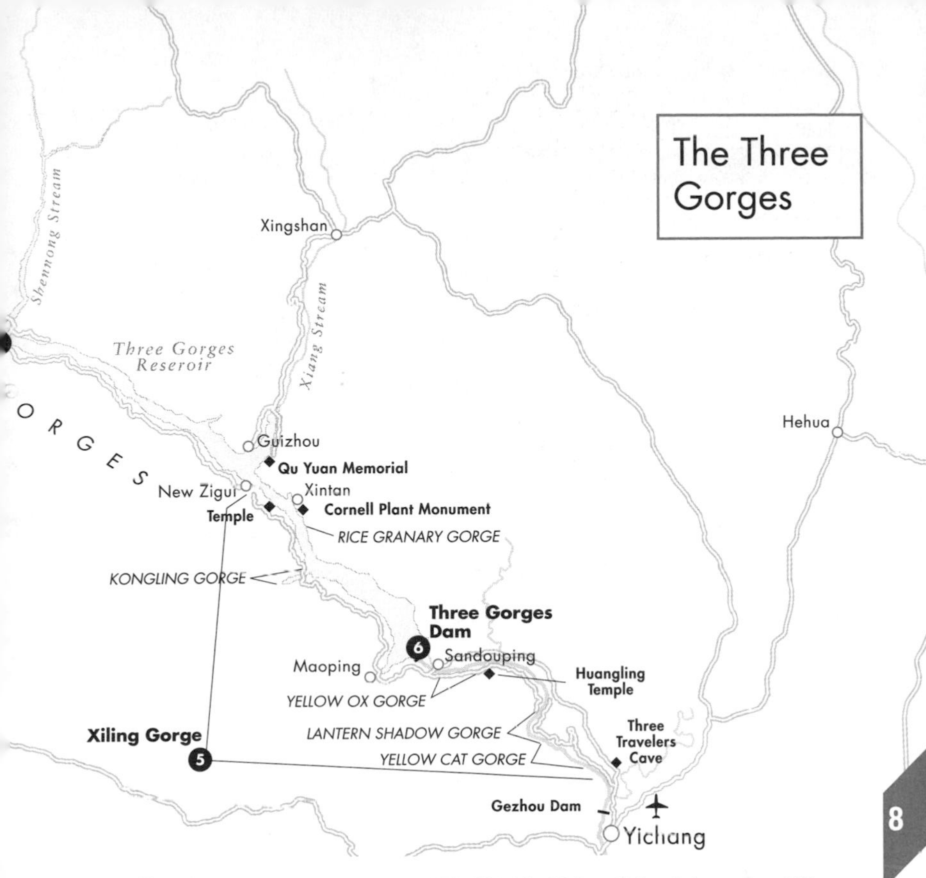

❸ The impressive **Wu Gorge** *(Wu Xia)* is 33 km (20 mi) long. Its cliffs are so sheer and narrow that they seem to be closing in upon you as you approach in the boat. Some of the cliff formations are noted for their resemblances to people and animals. Most notably is the Goddess Peak, a beautiful pillar of white stone.

❹ At the city of **Badong** in Hubei, just outside the eastern end of Wu Gorge, boats leave for Shennongjia on the Shennong River, one of the wildest and strangest parts of the country.

❺ **Xiling Gorge** *(Xiling Xia)*, 66 km (41 mi) long, is the longest and deepest of all the gorges, with cliffs that rise up to 4,000 feet. There are no stops along here and it is undoubtedly the most peaceful and contemplative leg of the journey.

❻ Xiling Gorge ends at the **Three Gorges Dam** *(San Xia Da Ba)*. Nothing that you've seen or read about this project can possibly prepare you for its massive scale. Sit back in awe as the boat approaches this great dam and then slowly slips into the lower reaches of the river. *Y190.*

ENGLISH	PINYIN	CHINESE CHARACTERS
SICHUAN	SÌCHUĀN	四川
CHENGDU	Chéngdū	成都
Anlan Cable Bridge	Ānlān suòqiáo	安澜索桥
Chen Mapo Doufu	Chénmápó dòufù	陈麻婆豆腐
Chengdu Chaoshou Canting	Chéngdūlóngchāoshǒu cāntīng	成都龙抄手餐厅
Chengdu Grand Hotel	Chéngdū dàfàndiàn	成都大饭店
Chengdu Zoo	Chéhngdū dòngwùyuán	成都动物园
Chunxi Lu	Chūnxī lù	春熙路
Chunxi Road	Chūnxī lù	春熙路
Du Fu's Cottage	Dùfǔ cǎotáng	杜甫草堂
Du River Canal Irrigation System	Dūjiāngyàn shuǐlì gōngchéng	都江堰水利工程
Dujiangyan	Dūjiāngyàn	都江堰
Giant Panda Breeding Research Base	dàxióngmāo bówùguàn	大熊猫博物馆
Grandma's Kitchen	Zhǔmú de chúfáng	祖母的厨房
Half Dozen Pub	Dàndāpíjiǔ	半打啤酒馆
Jiaotong Hotel	Jiaōotōngfàndiàn	交通饭店
Jinjiang Binguan	Jǐnjiāng bīngguǎn	锦江宾馆
Jinjiang Theater	Jǐnjiāng jùyuàn	锦江剧院
Memorial of the Marquis of Wu Zhuge Liang Memorial Hall	Wǔhóu sì	武侯祠
Minshan Fandian	Min Shan Fan Dian	岷山饭店
Old House	Lǎofángzǐ	老房子
Piaoxiang	Piāoxiāng	飘香
Qingyang Palace	Qīngyáng gōng	青羊宫
Renmin Park	rénmín gōngyuán	人民公园
Repeat Qingaong Palace	Qīngyánggōng	青羊宫
Riverview Pavilion Park	Wàngjiānglóu gōngyuán	望江楼公园
Shizi Lou Dajiudian	Shīzīlóu dàjiǔdiàn	狮子楼大酒店
Sim's Cozy Guest House	Guānhuá qīngnián lǔguǎn	观华青年旅馆 check
Tibet Hotel	Xīzàng fàndiàn	西藏饭店
Tomb of Emperor Wang Jian	Wángjiàn mù	王建墓
Two Princes Temple	Erwáng miào	二王庙
Wenshu Monastery	Wénshūyuàn	文殊院
Xiangbala Restaurant	Xiāngbālā cānguǎng	check
Zhaojue Temple	Zhāojué sì	昭觉寺

ENGLISH	PINYIN	CHINESE CHARACTERS
Ziyunxuan	Zhĭyúnxuān	紫云轩
EMEISHAN	Éméi shān	峨嵋山
Baoguo Monastery	Bàoguó sì	报国寺
Emeishan Hotel	Éméi dàfàndiàn	峨嵋山大酒店
Golden Summit Temple	Jīnding sì	金顶寺
Jieyin Dian	Jiēyĭndiàn	接引殿
Teddy Bear Cafe	Xiăoxióng kāfēi	小熊咖啡
LESHAN	Lèshān	乐山
Grand Buddha	Lèshān dàfó	乐山大佛
Jiuzhaigou	Jiŭzhàigōu	九寨沟
Lingyun Temple	Língyún sì	凌云寺
Wuyou Temple	Wūyóu sì	乌尤寺
SONGPAN	Sōngfān	松潘
Hailougou Glacier	Hăiluógōu bīngchuán	海螺沟冰川
Kangding	Kàngdìng	康定
CHONGQING	Chóngqìng	重庆
Badong	Bādōng	巴东
Baoding Shan	Băodìng shān	保定山
cable cars	diàn dăn chē	电缆车
Chaotianmen Docks	Cháotiānmén mătóu	朝天门码头
Chaotianmen Docks	Cháotiānmén mătóu	朝天门码头
Check Great Changjiang Bridge	Chóngqìng dàqiáo	重庆大桥
Chengdu Train Station	Chéngdū huŏchézhàn	成都火车站
Chongqing	Chóngqìng	重庆
Chongqing Fandian	Zhóngqìng fàndiàn	重庆饭店
Chongqing Fandian	Chóngqìng fàndiàn	重庆饭店
Chongqing Train Station	Chóngqìng huŏchē zhàn	重庆火车站
Dazu	Dàzú	大足
Dazu Binguan	Dàzú bīngguăn	大足宾馆
Fengdu	Fēngdū	丰都
Gezhou Dam	Gĕzhōubà	葛洲坝
Great Changjiang Bridge	Chángjiāng dàqiáo	长江大桥
Holiday Inn Yangtze Chongqing	Yángzhĭjiāng jiàrì fàndiàn	扬子江假日饭店
hot springs	wēnquán	温泉
Jinyun Mountain	Jìnyún shān	缙云山
Jinyun Mountain	Jìnyún shān	缙云山

8

ENGLISH	PINYIN	CHINESE CHARACTERS
Lao Sichuan	Lǎosìchuān	老四川
Lao Sichuan	Lǎosìchuān	老四川
Little Three Gorges	xiǎo Sānxiá	小三峡
Loquat Hill	Pípáshān	枇杷山
Loquat Hill	Pípá shān	枇杷山
Luohan Temple	Luóhàn sì	罗汉寺
Luohan Temple	Luóhàn sì	罗汉寺
Min Hill	Mǐn shān	岷山
Painters Village	Huànjiā zhīcūn	画家之村
Painters Village	Huàjiā zhīcūn	画家之村
Qutang Gorge	Qútángxiá	瞿塘峡
Red Crag Village	Hóngyán cūn	红岩村
Red Crag Village	Hóngyáncūn	红岩村
Renmin Binguan	Rénmín bīngguǎn	人民宾馆
Renmin Binguan	Rénmín bīnguǎn	人民宾馆
Shibaozhai	Shíbǎozhài	石宝寨
Three Gorges	Sānxiá	三峡
Tibet Tourism Office	Xīzàng lǚyóu bànshìchù	西藏旅游办事处
U.S. Consulate	Měiguó lǐngshìguǎn	美国领事馆
U.S.-Chiang Kai-shek Criminal Acts Exhibition Hall & SACO Prison	Zhōngměihézuòsuǒ	中美合作所
U.S.-Chiang Kai-shek Criminal Acts Exhibition Hall & SACO Prison	zhōngměi hézuòsuǒ	中美合作所
Wu Gorge	Wūxiá	巫峡
Wushan	Wūshān	巫山
Xiling Gorge	Xīlíngxiá	西岭峡
Yangzi River	Chángjiāng	长江
Yizhishi Fandian	Yìzhīshí fàndiàn	颐之时饭店

The Silk Road

SHAANXI, GANSU, QUINGHAI, XINJIANG

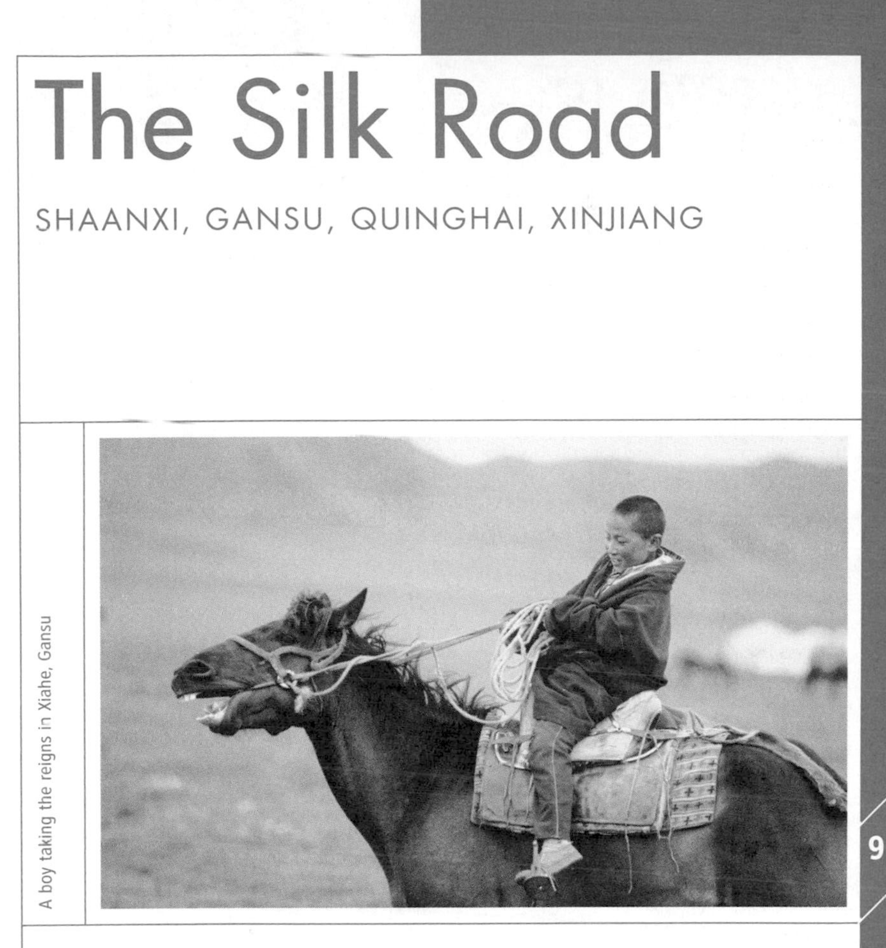

A boy taking the reigns in Xiahe, Gansu

WORD OF MOUTH

"We walked around the markets in the Muslim Quarter [in Shaanxi] which were fascinating, bought some wonderful dried fruit and little bean cakes, then got a bus back to the Big [Wild] Goose Pagoda just in time to see the end of the fountain and music show."

—Martha 1953

WELCOME TO THE SILK ROAD

Karakoram Highway.

TOP REASONS TO GO

★ **Terracotta Warriors:** Visit one of the nation's most haunting and memorable sites—the vast life-size army of soldiers, built to outlast death.

★ **Discover Dunhuang:** Satisfy your inner archaeologist at the magnificent Mogao caves and scale the shifting slopes of Singing Sand Mountain.

★ **Seek Solace at Kumbum Monastery:** Visit one of the six great monasteries of the Tibetan Buddhist sect known as Yellow Hat, reputedly the birthplace of the sect's founder, Tsong Khapa.

★ **Tour Turpan:** Discover the ruins of ancient city-states Jiaohe and Gaochang, destroyed by Genghis Khan and his unstoppable Mongol hordes.

★ **Kashgar and the Karakorum Highway:** Explore Central Asia's largest and liveliest bazaar before heading south to the snow-capped Pamir Mountains and crystal-clear Karakul Lake.

1 Shaanxi. Visit the tomb of China's first emperor and its army of thousands of terracotta warriors in Xian. Shaanxi is the starting point of the fabled Silk Road that brought silks and spices from China to Rome more than two millennia ago.

2 Gansu. Arid and mountainous, Gansu has served as a corridor to the West for thousands of years. Heralded sites include the Mogao Grottoes, Singing Sand Mountain, and the remote Labrang Monastery.

3 Qinghai. Away from the industrialized cities, on the vast open plains, seminomadic herders, clad in brown robes slashed with fluorescent pink sashes, still roam the grasslands.

Terracotta Soldiers.

GETTING ORIENTED

There was no single "Silk Road," but scores of trading posts that formed an overland trade network that linked China, Central Asia, and Europe. The current "Silk Road" received its moniker from German scholar Baron Ferdinand von Richtofen in the mid-19th century, when the Chinese section of the route stretched to Xian in Shaanxi Province. After passing through the famed Jade Gate, which divided China from the outside world, it webbed out in three directions to several key cities in Xinjiang: Ürümqi in the north, Korla in the center, Hotan in the south, and Kashgar in the west.

Kashgar bazaar.

4 Xinjiang. Chinese in name only, Xinjiang is a land of vast deserts and ancient Silk Road settlements, including legendary Kashgar. The region is populated by Uyghurs, China's largest minority group.

THE SILK ROAD PLANNER

Women's Wear

Many places along the Silk Road have large Muslim communities, and it's courteous to dress appropriately when there. Women in Xinjiang will feel less conspicuous if they dress as most locals do and wear long trousers and cover their shoulders. Scarves aren't necessary, but they can be good protection against dust.

Safety

In an emergency, Your first stop should be a good hotel. Even if you are not a guest, or if you don't speak Chinese or have a Chinese friend to call on, get a hotel involved to arrange treatment and provide translation. If you call them directly, you will find that the emergency services do not speak any English.

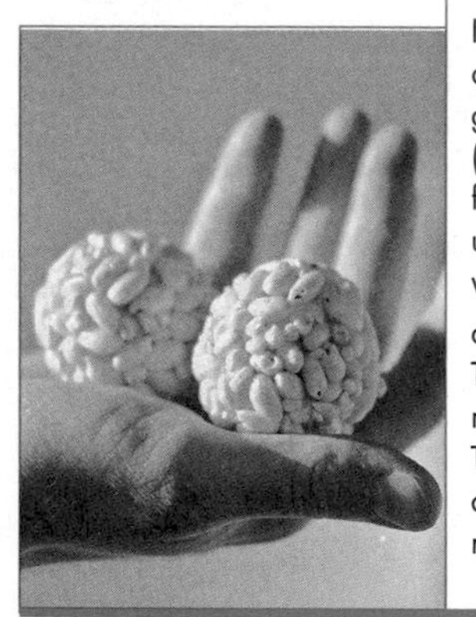

Northwestern Fare

The cuisine in Shaanxi revolves around noodles and *jiaozi* (dumplings) rather than rice, and lamb is the meat of choice. A Xian Muslim specialty is *yangroù paomo,* a spicy lamb soup poured over broken pieces of flat bread. Other popular Muslim street foods are *heletiao* (buckwheat noodles marinated in soy sauce and garlic) and *roùjiamo* (pita bread filled with beef or pork and topped with cumin and green peppers).

Gansu and Qinghai don't offer many culinary surprises, but in Xinjiang, where temperatures can reach scorching levels, you'll find a variety of local ices, ice cream, and *durap* (a refreshing mix of yogurt, honey, and crushed ice). Traditional Uyghur dishes like *bamian* (lamb and vegetables served over noodles) and *kevap* (spicy lamb kebabs) are ubiquitous. Grapes from Turpan and melons from the oasis town of Hami are famous throughout China.

Traveling in the Desert

Things change quickly from uncomfortable to painful to dangerous in the intense heat of northwest China's expansive deserts. Temperatures in the summer reach 100°F (40°C), with some areas—the depression around Turpan in particular—soaring to 120°F (50°C). Many of the sites you'll be visiting are remote and lack even the most basic facilities.

In conditions like these, it's unwise to travel without abundant water, as well as strong sunscreen, sunglasses, a good hat, toilet paper, and some heat-resistant snacks (dried fruit and nuts). If you're a fan of cold water, buy frozen plastic bottles in the morning and they'll stay cool until lunchtime.

Water and food are particularly important for the long trek across the Taklamakan Desert to the southern Silk Road. The cross-desert highway traverses hundreds of miles of the most inhospitable territory, with just a single gas station at Tazhong, the halfway point. Should your vehicle become disabled somewhere along that stretch of highway, you may have to wait a while before help arrives.

Getting Here and Around

The regional capital Ürümqi is the main travel hub: here it's possible to get flights across the province as well as train and bus services to every corner of the region. To avoid long and back-breaking journeys by bus, it's worth flying at least occasionally and with tickets often heavily discounted, there's not always a huge price differential. The train is also more comfortable than buses and extremely efficient—and with the great scenery, time passes quickly.

Money Matters

It is now possible to use foreign bank cards in all major cities in the region, including Xian, Ürümqi, and Lanzhou. But the farther away you get from industrialized places, the less likely it is that your card will work in a local ATM. Be sure to have a supply of cash to avoid getting stranded. Traveler's checks can be cashed and foreign currency converted at Bank of China branches and major hotels. This is completely unnecessary in restaurants and hotels: some more expensive hotels will add a service charge, but there is no need to add anything extra.

DINING AND LODGING PRICE CATEGORIES IN YUAN				
¢	$	$$	$$$	$$$$
Restaurants				
under Y25	Y25–Y49	Y50–Y99	Y100–Y165	over Y165
Hotels				
under Y700	Y700–Y1,099	Y1,100–Y1,399	Y1,400–Y1,800	over Y1,800

Restaurant prices are for a first course (*primo*), second course (*secondo*), and dessert (*dolce*). Hotel prices are for two people in a standard double room in high season, including tax and service.

How's the Weather?

The best time to visit is from early May to late October, when it's warm and the land is in bloom with grasses and flowers. It's also high tourist season, when many festivals take place.

In spring, wildflowers make a colorful, riotous appearance on the mountain meadows, rolling grasslands, and lush valleys. That said, much of northwest China is desert and spring is when warm winds whip across the land causing dust devils and sandstorms. By May most of the fury has died down.

Dry, sunny summers provide blue skies and long days, optimal for exploring and photographing the region. Lunchtime, however, can be insufferably hot and most tourists follow the locals' lead in taking a midday siesta. If you plan to explore mountain areas, summer gives the most access and fluctuates between chilly nights and warm, bright days.

Clear skies last usually through October. The changing leaves explode into a symphony of yellow, orange, and red, once again creating ideal opportunities for the shutterbug. Cold weather, however, comes quickly and unannounced

Winter brings sub-freezing temperatures and a dearth of travelers. Although solitude may have its charms, a few sights close for the off-season.

SHAANXI

By Michael Manning
Updated by Helena Iveson

SHAANXI HAS MORE OFTEN THAN not been the axis around which the Chinese universe revolved. It was here more than 6,000 years ago that Neolithic tribes established the earliest permanent settlements in China. In 221 BC, the territories of the Middle Kingdom were unified here under the Qin Dynasty (from which the word "China" is derived). Propitiously located at the eastern terminus of the famed Silk Road, Shaanxi later gave birth to one of the ancient world's greatest capitals, Changan, a city enriched financially and culturally by the influence of foreign trade.

But nothing lasts forever: as the Silk Road fell into disuse and China isolated itself from the outside world, Shaanxi's fortunes declined. Flood, drought, and political unrest among the province's large Muslim population made Shaanxi a very difficult place to live for most of the past 1,000 years. It's only since the founding of the People's Republic in 1949 that the area has regained some of its former prominence, both as a center of industry and as a travel destination.

REGIONAL TOURS

Sino NZ Tourism Group. This well-run travel agency, run out of the HQ Youth Hostel, offers Xian city and Terracotta Warrior tours. The tour around the Muslim Quarter, led by a local guide, is particularly recommended, as are trips farther afield to Hua Shan and the very untouristed and stunning Qinling Mountain range. Prices are set for backpackers and are up for negotiation in the off-season—for city tours expect to pay upwards of Y200. ✉*Hong Cheng Guoji Gong Yu Xi Hua Men* ☎*15829031947* 🌐*www.hqhostelxian.moonfruit.com.*

CITS. The Xian branch of China's state-run travel service gets much better reports than many other branches, thanks to the friendliness of its young, well-trained staff. CITS will cater tours to your requirements, and although they might be more expensive than options offered at youth hostels, they offer nicer cars and smaller groups. ✉*48 Changan Bei Lu* ☎*029/8539–9999* 🌐*www.citsxian.com.cn.*

XIAN

1½ hrs by plane or 12 hrs by train southwest of Beijing; 15 hrs by train west of Shanghai.

Many first-time visitors to Xian are seeking the massive terra-cotta army standing guard over the tomb of China's first emperor.

Xian was known in ancient times as Changan (meaning Long Peace) and was one of the largest and most cultured cities in the world. During the Tang Dynasty—considered by many Chinese to be the nation's cultural pinnacle—the city became an important center for the arts. Not surprisingly, this creative explosion coincided with the height of trade on the Silk Road, bringing Turkish fashions to court and foreigners from as far away as Persia and Rome. Although the caravan drivers of yesteryear have long since turned to dust, their memory lives on in the variety of faces seen in Xian.

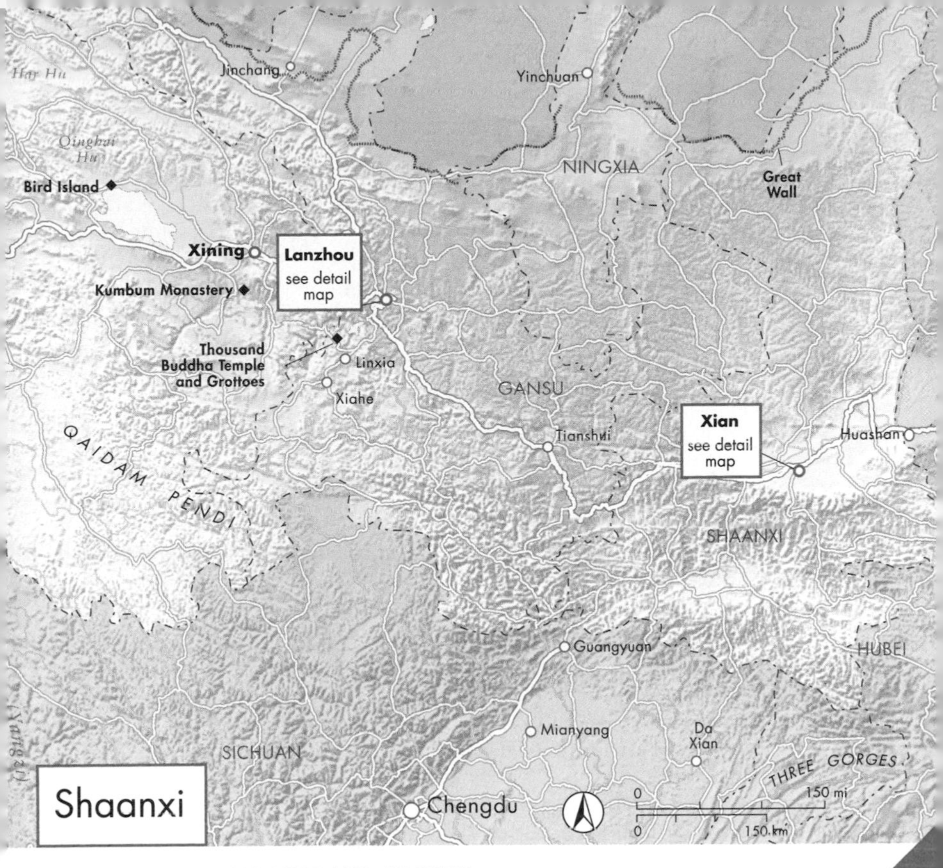

9

GETTING HERE AND AROUND

BY AIR Although Xian's Xianyang Airport is an inconvenient 50 km (30 mi) northwest of the city center in neighboring Xianyang, it has daily flights to and from Beijing, Shanghai, Hong Kong, Guangzhou, Chengdu, Kunming, Dunhuang, and Ürümqi. International destinations include Japan, Korea, Singapore, and Thailand.

If your hotel doesn't arrange transportation, taxis will try to squeeze every last yuan out of your wallet; a decent price is around Y120. Hourly buses are a far more economical option, costing Y25. There are six routes to choose from, so you should let the dispatcher know where you're staying—make sure you have the name in Chinese.

BY BUS Just about every bus in Xian passes through the traffic circle around the Bell Tower. If your Chinese is shaky, it's best to stick to taxis.

The long-distance bus station, on Jiefang Lu across the street and just west of the train station, has buses to Lanzhou, Xining, and other destinations throughout Shaanxi and Henan. Tourist destinations like the Terracotta Warriors Museum are served from the parking lot between the train station and the Jiefang Hotel.

BY CAR Because so many of the sights lie outside the city proper, hiring a taxi or a car and driver gives you the freedom to depart when you like instead of waiting for the rest of the tour. Prices start at about Y800 per day, but vary widely based on the type of vehicle and whether you need an English-speaking guide. Every major hotel can arrange car services.

BY TRAIN The train station lies on the same rail line as Lanzhou. Those arriving in Xian by train disembark north of the old city walls. The train station is close to most hotels; a taxi should cost less than Y10. The foreigners' ticket window, on the second floor above the main ticket office, is open daily 8:30 to 11:30 and 2:30 to 5:30. It sometimes closes without explanation. For a small booking fee, hotels can get tickets.

TOURS

Every hotel offers its own guided tours of the area, usually dividing them into eastern area, western area, and city tours. Most tour operators have special English-language tour guides.

Bargaining may get you a much better deal. And check more than one company to make sure you are being charged the going rate. One of the best places to comparison shop is on the second floor of the Bell Tower Hotel, where several tour companies vie for your business. Try Golden Bridge first, but there are other good options.

EASTERN TOUR By far the most popular option from Xian, tours that head east of the city usually visit the Tomb of the First Qin Emperor, the Terracotta Warriors Museum, and the Huaqing Hot Springs, all located in the town of Lintong. Many tours also stop at the Banpo Matriarchal Clan Village in eastern Xian. The China International Travel Service (CITS) offers this tour for Y300, which includes all admission tickets and an English-speaking guide. The journey takes most of the day; plan on leaving after breakfast and returning in time for dinner.

If you don't want a guide, you're better off taking one of the cheap buses that leave constantly from the parking lot between the Xian Train Station and the Jiefang Hotel. The 60-minute journey costs Y10. Make sure the driver knows where you want to be dropped off. To travel between any of the sites in Lintong, a taxi should cost between Y5 and Y10 (although drivers ask foreigners for Y15). To get back to Xian, simply wait along the road for a bus headed to the city.

WESTERN TOUR Less popular than the eastern tour, this excursion varies wildly from operator to operator. Find out what you're getting for the money. Amateur archaeologists and would-be tomb raiders will hardly be able to tear themselves away from the sites in what's been called China's own Valley of the Kings; others will appreciate some of the relics, but may tire of what appear to be mounds of dirt or holes in the ground.

Of the 18 imperial tombs on the plains west of Xian, a list of the best should include the Qian Tomb, resting place of Tang Dynasty Empress Wu Zetian, China's only female sovereign. A number of her relatives—many sentenced to death by her own decree—are entombed in the surrounding area. The tomb of Prince Yi De contains some beautifully restored frescoes. Other stops on the western tour might include the Xianyang City Museum in Xianyang and the Famen Temple in Famen. Sino NZ Tourism Group offers a customizable Western Tour for between Y500 to Y800 depending on the number of people. Plan on spending the whole day visiting these sites.

TREASURES OF SHAANXI

Shaanxi gave birth to 13 major Chinese dynasties, including the Zhou, Qin, Han, and Tang states. The Tang is considered China's Golden Age. Consider first hitting the Shaanxi History Museum. Once you've steeped yourself in its chronology, local "must-see" destinations like Xian's Drum Towers, Muslim Quarter, and Great Goose Pagodas will make much more sense. So, too, will the awe-inspiring army of terra cotta warriors at the tomb of China's first emperor. True fans of history can even make the trip to China's own "Valley of the Kings" near Xianyang.

Hua Shan. A few hours east of Xian lies one of China's five sacred mountains, a traditional watercolor come to life. The 7,218-foot mountain has lovely scenery, including pines reminiscent of a Dr. Seuss creation and sheer granite walls that rise shockingly out of the surrounding plains. The five peaks of Hua Shan reminded ancient visitors of flower petals, hence the name; translated it means "Flower Mountain". Climbing the mountain is not a trip for the fainthearted: unless you're an Olympic athlete, hiking the main trail to the top will take a good seven to nine hours, some of it along narrow passes on sheer cliffs. Thankfully, there's a cable car ride to North Peak that brings you most of the way up the trail (Y60 one-way, Y110 round-trip). Don't worry about looking like a wimp; there's plenty of climbing left to do from the cable car terminal. From Xian, you can take a train (3 hours, Y12) to Huashan Village, although you'll inconveniently disembark 15 km (9 mi) away in the neighboring town of Mengyuan; frequent minibuses (Y10) link the two places. A better choice is one of the tour buses that leave hourly every morning from the parking lot in front of the Jiefang Hotel, across from the train station. Round-trip bus tickets can be had for Y80, although they'd prefer you purchase the inclusive package with all necessary tickets for Y310. You will be required to provide your passport information when you buy a ticket. *Y100 entrance; Y60 one-way/Y110 round-trip cable car; Y20 round-trip minibus from Hua Shan Village to the cable car* *Cable car operates daily 7–7.*

9

ESSENTIALS

Air Contacts Xian Xianyang Airport (*029/8879–8450*).

Bank Bank of China (*396 Dong Da Jie* *157 Jiefang Lu* *21 Xianning Xi Lu* *38 Juhuayuan Beilin Qu*)

Bus Contacts Xian Bus Station (*Jiefang Lu* *029/742–7420*).

Internet Hai An Xian Internet Bar (*323 Jiefang Lu* *029/8741–0555* *Y1 per hour* *8 AM–midnight*). Bring your passport.

Medical Assistance In case of an emergency, contact your hotel manager for assistance. If you speak Chinese (or are traveling with someone who does), you can also call emergency numbers for an ambulance, call 120. **People's Hospital** (*214 Youyi Lu* *029/8525–1331*).

Police (*110*).

Train Contacts You can also purchase train tickets at the main CITS tourism office (48 Changan Bei Lu). **Xian Huochezhan** (*Huancheng Bei Lu and Jiefang Lu 029/8213–0402*).

Visitor and Tour Info CITS (*48 Changan Bei Lu 029/8539–9999 Bell Tower Hotel, 110 Nan Da Jie 029/8760–0227*). **Golden Bridge Travel** (*Bell Tower Hotel, 110 Nan Da Jie 029/8760–0219*). **Sino NZ Tourism Group** (*Hong Cheng Guoji Gong Yu, Xi Hua Men 15829031947 www.hqhostelxian.moonfruit.com*).

EXPLORING XIAN

MAIN ATTRACTIONS

Bell Tower. Xian's most recognizable structure, the Bell Tower was built in the late 14th century in what was then the center of the city. It's still good a reference point. The tower marks the point where Xi Da Jie (West Main Street) becomes Dong Da Jie (East Main Street) and Bei Dajie (North Main Street) becomes Nan Da Jie (South Main Street). To reach the tower, which stands isolated in the middle of a traffic circle, use any of eight entrances to the underground passageway. Once inside the building, you'll see Ming Dynasty bells on display. Concerts are given six times daily (9, 10:30, 11:30, 2:30, 4, and 5:30). For Y5 you can make your own music by ringing a copy of the large iron bell that gives the tower its name. Don't miss the panoramic views of the city from the third-floor balcony. *Junction of Dong Da Jie, Xi Da Jie, Bei Da Jie, and Nan Da Jie No phone Y40 includes admission to Drum Tower Apr.–Oct., daily 8:30* AM*–9:30* PM*; Nov.–Mar., daily 8:30* AM*–6* PM.

9 **Big Wild Goose Pagoda.** This impressively tall pagoda lies 4 km (2½ mi) southeast of South Gate, on the grounds of the still-active Temple of Thanksgiving (Da Ci'en Si). The pagoda was constructed adjacent to the Tang palace in the 7th century AD to house scriptures brought back from India by monk Xuan Zang. It's been rebuilt numerous times since then, most recently during the Qing Dynasty, in Ming style. A park and huge plaza were built around the temple in 2004, and locals gather here after work to fly kites, stroll hand in hand, and practice calligraphy. The main entrance gate to the temple is found on the plaza's southern edge. *Yanta Lu 029/8525–5141 Y25; additional Y25 to climb the pagoda Daily 8–6.*

2 **Drum Tower.** Originally built in 1380, this 111-foot-high Ming Dynasty building—which used to hold the alarm drums for the imperial city—marks the southern end of Xian's Muslim Quarter. Various ancient drums are on display inside the building, and concerts are given daily at 9, 10:30, 11:30, 2:30, 4, and 5:30. After passing through the tower's massive base, turn left down a small side street called Hua Jue Xiang to find everything from shadow puppets to Mao memorabilia—truly a souvenir heaven. After clearing that gauntlet, you'll find yourself deep inside the Muslim Quarter at the entrance to the Great Mosque. *Bei Yuan Men, 1 block west of the Bell Tower No phone Y40 includes admission to Bell Tower Apr.–Oct., daily 8:30* AM*–9:30* PM*; Nov.–Mar., daily 8:30* AM*–6* PM.

1 **Great Mosque.** This lushly landscaped mosque with four graceful courtyards may have been established as early as AD 742, during the Tang Dynasty, but the remaining buildings date mostly from the 18th century. Amazingly, it was left standing during the Cultural Revolution. Stone tablets mark the various pavilions, often bearing inscriptions in both Chinese and Arabic. Look above the doors and gates: there are some remarkable designs, including three-dimensional Arabic script that makes the stone look as malleable as cake frosting. Non-Muslims are not allowed in the prayer hall, as the mosque is still an active place of worship. The place is a bit hard to find. After passing through the Drum Tower, follow a small curving market street called Hua Jue Xiang on the left. (You'll see an English sign posted on a brick wall next to the street's entrance reading GREAT MOSQUE.) When you reach a small intersection, the mosque's entrance is on the left. The bustling **Muslim Quarter** surrounding the mosque is the center of the city's Hui (Chinese Muslim) community. It's a great place to wander, and you'll find endless food stalls offering everything from cold sesame noodles to pan-fried dumplings to spicy mutton kebabs. ✉ *30 Hua Jue Xiang* 🎫 *Y25* ⏲ *May–Sept., daily 8–7; Oct.–Apr., daily 8–5.*

8 **Shaanxi History Museum.** Although museums in China are often underwhelming, this is a notable exception. The works in this imposing two-story structure, built in 1991, range from crude Paleolithic stone tools to gorgeously sculpted ceramics from the Tang Dynasty. Several terra-cotta warriors taken from the tombs outside town are on display. The exhibits, which have English descriptions, leave no doubt that China has long been the world's most advanced culture. The museum no longer charges an admission fee; instead, a limited number of tickets are handed out in the morning and the afternoon. To secure tickets, visitors must arrive early to wait in line. ✉ *91 Xiaozai Dong Lu* ☎ *029/8525–4727* 🌐 *www.sxhm.com* 🎫 *Free* ⏲ *Tues.–Sun. 8:30–6.*

Fodor's Choice ★

9

South Gate. This is the most impressive of the 13 gates leading through Xian's 39-foot-high city walls. This was the original site of Tang Dynasty fortifications; the walls you see today were built at the beginning of the Ming Dynasty, and they include the country's only remaining example of a complete wall dating to this dynasty. Repairs mean you can travel the entire 14 km (9 mi) around the city on the top of the wall. The trip by bike takes about 2 hours. Rental bikes are Y15 for 90 minutes. An open-air shuttle bus costs Y50. ✉ *Nan Da Jie* ☎ *029/8727–1696* 🎫 *Y20* ⏲ *Daily 8 AM–9 PM.*

IF YOU HAVE TIME

Banpo Matriarchal Clan Village. About 5 km (3 mi) east of the city are the remains of a 6,000-year-old Yangshao village, including living quarters, a pottery-making center, and a graveyard. The residents of this matriarchal community of 200 to 300 people survived mainly by fishing, hunting, and gathering, although there is ample evidence of attempts at animal domestication and organized agriculture.

Stone farming and hunting implements, domestic objects, and pottery inscribed with ancient Chinese characters are all on display in small galleries near the entrance. There's also enough left in the ground—pottery, building foundations, and a few skeletons—to make things interesting. The archaeological site has been under renovation since 2003, with no end in sight, but there are, at last, English captions throughout. Unless you're interested in documenting one of China's great tourist oddities, avoid the awful model village that sits in a state of semi-disrepair toward the rear of the property. ✉ *139 Banpo Lu, off Changdong Lu* ☎ *029/8353–2482* 🎫 *Y35* ⏲ *Daily 8–5.*

❺ **Culture Street.** Located just inside the city wall, this lively, but very touristy pedestrian street is lined with houses that have been rebuilt in traditional Ming style. Shops sell a wide variety of wares, including charming calligraphy and watercolors. If you're coming from South Gate, halfway down the first block you'll find Guanzhong Academy, built in 1609. Take a peek through the gates, as entrance is forbidden. Continue east along the city wall to reach the Forest of Stone Tablets. ✉ *1 block north of South Gate.*

❹ ★ **Forest of Stone Tablets Museum.** As the name suggests, there is no shortage here of historical stone tablets engraved with content ranging from descriptions of administrative projects to artistic renditions of landscape, portraiture, and calligraphy. One of the world's first dictionaries and a number of Tang Dynasty classics are housed here. One tablet, known as the Popular Nestorian Stela, dates from AD 781 and records the interaction between the emperor and a traveling Nestorian priest. After presenting the empire with translated Nestorian Christian texts, the priest was allowed to open a church in Xian. English descriptions are rare. ✉ *15 Sanxue Jie, end of Culture St.* 🎫 *Y30* ⏲ *Mar.–Nov., daily 8:15–6:45; Dec.–Feb., daily 8:15–5:15.*

❼ ★ **Small Goose Pagoda.** Once part of the 7th-century AD Jianfu Temple, this 13-tier pagoda was built by Empress Wu Zetian in 707 to honor her predecessor, Emperor Gao Zong. Much less imposing than the Big Goose Pagoda, the smaller pagoda housed Buddhist texts brought back from India by the pilgrim Yiqing in the 8th century. A tremendous earthquake in 1555 lopped off the top two stories of what was originally a 15-story structure; climbing to the top lets you examine the damage. The new Xian Museum is part of the same complex and shows how the ancient capital changed over the centuries. ✉ *Youyi Xilu, west of Nanguan Zhengjie* ☎ *029/8525–3455* 🎫 *Y25; additional Y20 to climb the pagoda* ⏲ *Daily 8–8.*

AROUND XIAN

Famen Temple. Originally built in the 3rd century AD, the temple was the site of an amazing find during renovations in 1981. A sacred crypt housing four of Sakyamani Buddha's finger bones was discovered to hold more than 25,000 coins and 1,000 sacrificial objects of jade, gold, and silver. Many of these objects are now on display in the on-site museum. ✉ *125 km (80 mi) west of Xian in the town of Famen* 🎫 *Y60* ⏲ *Daily 8–6.*

Huaqing Hot Springs. A pleasure palace during the Tang Dynasty, the destination gets mixed reviews from visitors. The site contains General

Chiang Kai-shek's living quarters, where the infamous Xian Incident unfolded. Despite the name, the hot springs are often out of action leaving visitors to wander around the garden. You'll probably be happier spending your time on **Li Shan,** the small mountain directly behind Huaqing Hot Springs. It was on these slopes that Chiang was captured, and it has China's first beacon tower and a number of small temples. Many people take the cable car to the top and walk down. Tickets (Y25 one-way, Y45 round-trip) can be purchased at the hot springs; look for the blue metal gate just west of the ticket booth. ✉ *30 km (19 mi) east of Xian in the town of Lintong* 🎫 *Y70* ⏲ *Daily 8–6.*

WORD OF MOUTH

"In my opinion, there is no need for a guide in Xian. We took the bus from the train station to the warriors and back again. Only a few dollars each way. Met some nice people on the bus and ended up having dinner with them that night." —monicapileggi

Fodor'sChoice ★ **Terracotta Warriors Museum.** Discovered in 1974 by farmers digging a well, this archaeological site includes more than 7,000 terra-cotta soldiers standing guard over the tomb of Qin Shihuang, the first emperor of a unified China. The warriors, 1,000 of which have been painstakingly pieced together, come in various forms: archers, infantry, charioteers, and cavalry. Incredibly, each of the life-size statues is unique, including different mustaches, beards, and hairstyles. An exhibition hall displays artifacts unearthed from distant sections of the tomb, including two magnificently crafted miniature bronze chariots. Allow yourself at least three hours if you want to study the warriors in detail. ✉ *30 km (19 mi) east of Xian in the town of Lintong* ☎ *029/8139–9170* 🌐 *bj.bmy.com.cn* 🎫 *Mar.–Nov., Y90; Dec.–Feb., Y65* ⏲ *Daily 8:30–5:30.*

Tomb of the First Qin Emperor. The tomb—consisting mainly of a large burial mound—is a fairly disappointing visit these days, but must have been impressive in its heyday. According to ancient records, the underground palace took more than 40 years to build. You can climb to the top of the burial mound for a view of the surrounding countryside, although most visitors hurry off to see the Terracotta Warriors Museum after watching a mildly amusing ceremony honoring the emperor who united China. ✉ *30 km (19 mi) east of Xian in the town of Lintong* 🎫 *Y40* ⏲ *Apr.–Oct., daily 7–7; Nov.–Mar., daily 8–6.*

Xianyang City Museum. Formerly a Confucian temple, the museum now houses 3,000 miniature terra-cotta warriors unearthed in 1965. The museum isn't worth a special trip, especially if you will see the warriors in situ, but it is included on some tour itineraries. ✉ *28 km (16 mi) northwest of Xian in the city of Xianyang* 🎫 *Y20* ⏲ *Daily 8–6.*

9

WHERE TO EAT

¢–$ CHINESE ✕ **De Fa Chang Restaurant.** If you think dumplings are just occasional snack food, think again. De Fa Chang, one of Xian's most famous restaurants, is known for its dumpling banquet. Don't miss the pan-fried *guotie,* stuffed with pork and chives. For the dumpling banquet, head upstairs and choose between the preset menus. Considerably cheaper à

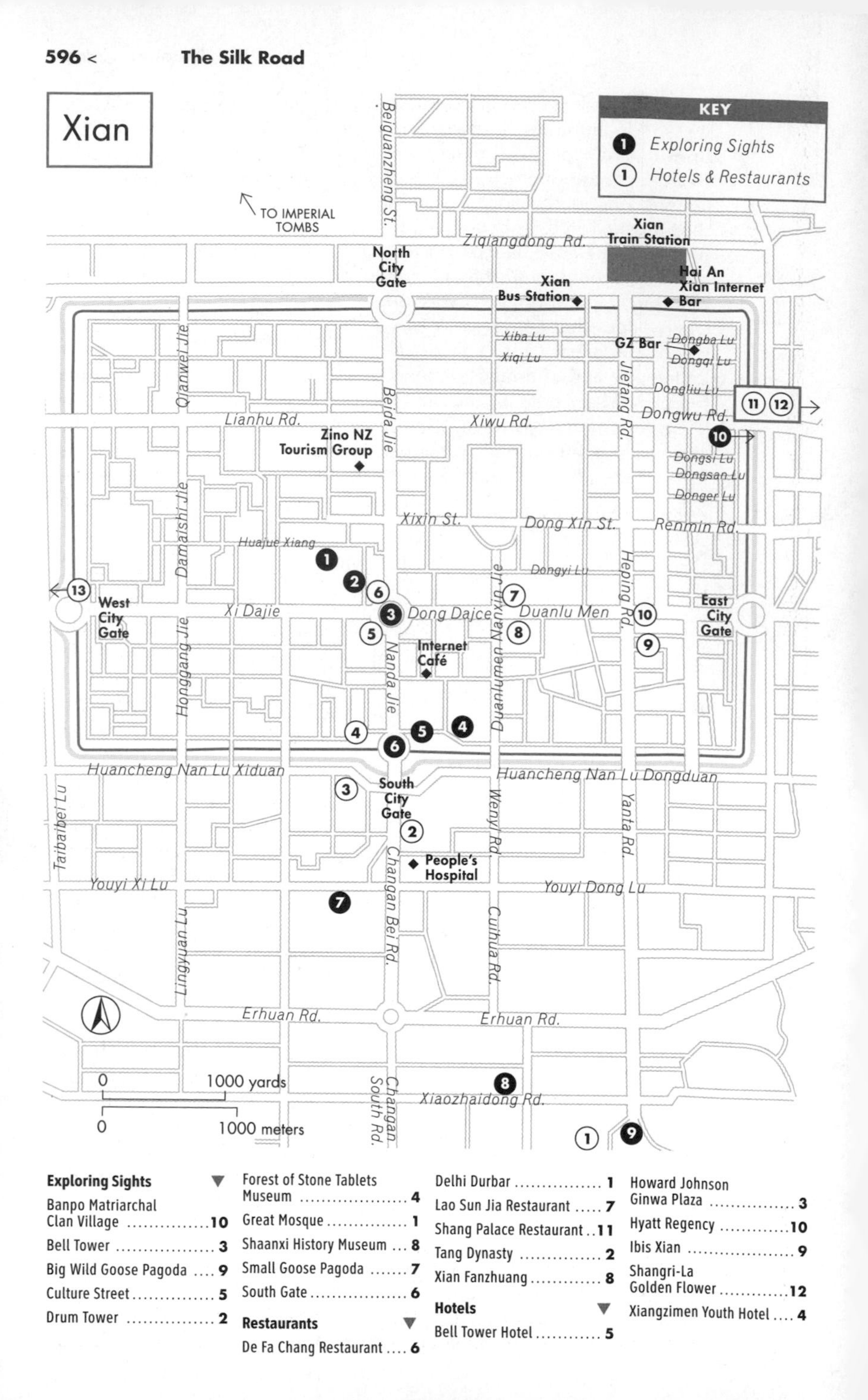
Xian
KEY
Exploring Sights
Hotels & Restaurants
TO IMPERIAL TOMBS
Beiguanzheng St.
Ziqiangdong Rd.
Xian Train Station
North City Gate
Xian Bus Station
Hai An Xian Internet Bar
Xiba Lu
Xiqi Lu
GZ Bar
Dongba Lu
Dongqi Lu
Dongliu Lu
Qianwei Jie
Beida Jie
Jiefang Rd.
Lianhu Rd.
Xiwu Rd.
Dongwu Rd.
Zino NZ Tourism Group
Dongsi Lu
Dongsan Lu
Donger Lu
Damaishi Jie
Xixin St.
Dong Xin St.
Renmin Rd.
Huajue Xiang
Heping Rd.
Dongyi Lu
West City Gate
Xi Dajie
Dong Dajce
Duanlu Men
East City Gate
Honggang Jie
Nanda Jie
Internet Café
Duanlumen Nanxin Jie
Huancheng Nan Lu Xiduan
Huancheng Nan Lu Dongduan
Taibaibei Lu
South City Gate
Wenyi Rd.
Yanta Rd.
People's Hospital
Youyi Xi Lu
Youyi Dong Lu
Lingyuan Lu
Changan Bei Rd.
Cuihua Rd.
Erhuan Rd.
Erhuan Rd.
0
1000 yards
0
1000 meters
Changan South Rd.
Xiaozhaidong Rd.
Exploring Sights
Banpo Matriarchal Clan Village ... 10
Bell Tower ... 3
Big Wild Goose Pagoda ... 9
Culture Street ... 5
Drum Tower ... 2
Forest of Stone Tablets Museum ... 4
Great Mosque ... 1
Shaanxi History Museum ... 8
Small Goose Pagoda ... 7
South Gate ... 6
Restaurants
De Fa Chang Restaurant ... 6
Delhi Durbar ... 1
Lao Sun Jia Restaurant ... 7
Shang Palace Restaurant ... 11
Tang Dynasty ... 2
Xian Fanzhuang ... 8
Hotels
Bell Tower Hotel ... 5
Howard Johnson Ginwa Plaza ... 3
Hyatt Regency ... 10
Ibis Xian ... 9
Shangri-La Golden Flower ... 12
Xiangzimen Youth Hotel ... 4

la carte dishes can be found downstairs; just grab a plate as a cart passes by your table and be ready to pay on the spot. With red lanterns hanging outside, this four-story behemoth attracts large groups of locals, who sometimes exit singing. ✉*Xi Dajie, north side of Bell Tower Sq.* ☎*029/8721–4060* ▭*No credit cards.*

$–$$ INDIAN ✕**Delhi Durbar.** When you need a change from Chinese food, try this place run by Indian ex-pats for spicy flavors and friendly service. Try the Palak Green Peas Masala with fluffy nan bread. Vegetarians will feel right at home—for once you can rely on waitresses to tell you if there is meat in a dish! ✉*3 Huan Ta Xi Lu* ☎*029/8525–5157* ▭*No credit cards.*

¢–$ NORTHERN CHINESE ✕**Lao Sun Jia Restaurant.** This traditional, family-run affair serves some of the best local Islamic lamb and beef specialties; it's become so popular that it's grown into a small Xian chain. The decor isn't special, but the food is popular with Xian's large Muslim community. A few famous offerings, such as the roasted leg of lamb or the spicy mutton spareribs, are pricey, but most dishes are inexpensive. Try *pao mo,* the mutton and bread soup. Ask for an English menu. ✉*364 Dong Da Jie, near the corner of Duanlu Men* ☎*029/8721–6929* ▭*No credit cards.*

$$–$$$$ CANTONESE ★ ✕**Shang Palace Restaurant.** All of Xian's top hotels have elegant eateries, but Shang Palace deserves special mention for its Cantonese and Sichuan dishes, which are authentic and approachable. On the menu, classics like honey-barbecued pork and stir-fried chicken with chili sit alongside less familiar dishes. As you dine, musicians pluck away in traditional costumes. Most of the staff speaks some English. ✉*Shangri-La Golden Flower Hotel, 8 Changle Xi Lu 710032* ☎*029/8323–2981 Ext. 4386* ▭*AE, MC, V.*

$$–$$$$ CHINESE Fodor's Choice ★ ✕**Tang Dynasty.** Don't confuse the cuisine served in the Tang Dynasty's popular dinner theater with the specialties available at the separate restaurant. While the former serves mediocre, tourist-friendly fare, the latter specializes in Tang Dynasty–imperial cuisine—a taste you're not likely to find back home at your local Chinese restaurant. Locals praise the abalone and other fresh fish dishes as the finest in Xian. You can reserve either for dinner, or for dinner and the show, which starts every night at 8:30 PM. Dinner costs Y220, and the full package will set you back Y500. ✉*75 Changan Bei Lu Xian, 710061* ☎*029/8782–2222* 🌐*www.xiantangdynasty.com* ▭*AE, MC, V.*

¢–$ CHINESE ✕**Xian Fanzhuang.** This restaurant specializes in Shaanxi snacks with a Muslim flavor as well as "small eats"—street food spruced up for the visitor. Business executives and T-shirt-clad college students alike head to the bustling first-floor dining room for the all-you-can-eat buffet (Y22). An adjacent entrance leads to a second-floor restaurant, where more exotic and expensive dishes—algae flavored with orchid, for example—are prepared. An English menu is available. ✉*Xian Hotel, 298 Dong Da Jie* ☎*029/8727–3185* ▭*No credit cards.*

WHERE TO STAY

$–$$ ★ **Bell Tower Hotel.** Relatively inexpensive compared to other hotels in its class, the very popular Bell Tower has spacious, airy rooms with views overlooking downtown Xian. Directly across from the Bell Tower, this hotel puts you within walking distance of many tourist sites. On the

Continued on page 604

THE TERRACOTTA SOLDIERS

DID YOU KNOW?

The thousands of life-size soldiers include charioteers, cavalrymen, archers, and infantrymen. They're all arranged according to rank and duty—exactly as they would have been for a real-life battle. Each one has individual facial features, including different mustaches, beards, and hairstyles.

In 1974, Shaanxi farmers digging a well accidentally unearthed one of the greatest archaeological finds of the 20th century—the Terracotta Soldiers of Qin Shihuang. Armed with real weapons and accompanied by horses and chariots, the more than 8,000 soldiers buried in Qin's tomb were to be his garrison in the afterlife.

Who was Qin Shihuang?

After destroying the last of his rivals in 221 BC, Qin Shihuang became the first emperor to rule over a unified China. He established a centralized government headquartered near modern-day Xianyang in Shaanxi Province. Unlike the feudal governments of the past under which regional officials developed local bases of power, the new centralized government concentrated all power in the hands of a godlike emperor.

Unfortunately for Qin Shihuang's potential heirs, the emperor's inexhaustible hunger for huge engineering projects created high levels of public unrest. These projects, including a precursor to the Great Wall, his own massive tomb, and numerous roads and canals, required the forced labor of millions of Chinese citizens. In 210 BC, Qin died from mercury poisoning during a failed attempt at making himself immortal. Only four years later, his son was overthrown and killed, bringing an ignominious end to China's first dynasty.

A Thankless Job

The construction of Qin Shihuang's gargantuan tomb complex—which includes the Terracotta Soldiers—was completed by more than 700,000 workers over a period of nearly 40 years. The warriors themselves are believed to have been created in an assembly line process in which sets of legs and torsos were fired separately and later combined with individually sculpted heads. Most workers were unskilled laborers; skilled craftsmen completed more delicate work such as the decoration of the tomb and the molding of heads. The soldiers were then painted with colored lacquer to make them both more durable and realistic. It's believed that all of the workers were buried alive inside the tomb (which hasn't yet been excavated) to keep its location and treasures a secret and protect it from grave robbers.

Discovering the Soldiers

Only five years after the death of Qin Shihuang, looting soldiers set fire to the thick wooden beams supporting the vaults. As wood burned and the structure became unsound, beams and earthen walls came crashing down onto the statues, crushing many soldiers and burying all. In many ways, though, the damage to the vaults was a blessing in disguise. The buried Terracotta Soldiers were forgotten to history, but the lack of oxygen and sunlight preserved the figures for centuries.

Since its rediscovery, only a part of the massive complex has been excavated, and the process of unearthing more warriors and relics continues. No one is sure just how many warriors there are or how far the figures extend beyond the already-excavated 700-foot-by-200-foot section. For the time being, most excavation work has stopped while scientists attempt to develop a method of preserving the figures' colored lacquer, which quickly deteriorates when exposed to oxygen.

VISITING THE SOLDIERS

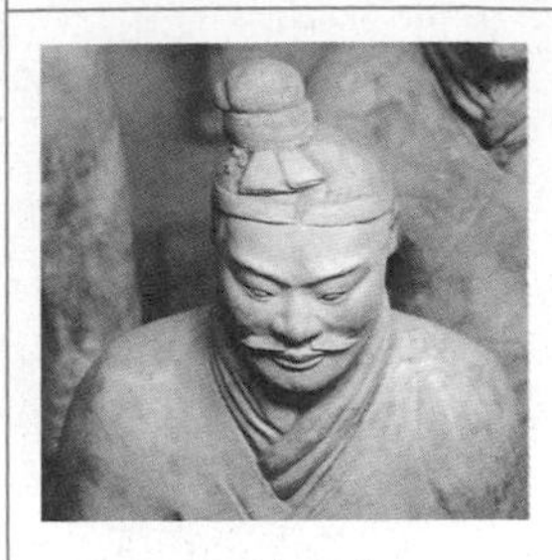

Be sure to walk around to the rear of Vault 1, which contains most of the figures that have already been unearthed. There you can see archaeologists reassembling the smashed soldiers. Vaults 2 and 3 contain unreconstructed warriors and their weapons and give you an idea of how much work went into presenting Vault 1 as we see it today.

Circle Vision Theater

Before heading to the vaults, stop by this 360-degree movie theater and learn how the army was constructed, destroyed, forgotten, and then rediscovered. Although the film is cheesy, it's nonetheless entertaining and informative. It gives a sense of what the area may have been like 2,200 years ago.

Vault 1

Here you'll find about 6,000 warriors, although only 1,000 have been painstakingly pieced together by archaeologists. The warriors stand in their original pits and can only be seen from the walkways erected around the digs. Those in the front ranks are well shaped and fully outfitted except for their weapons, whose wooden handles have decayed over the centuries (the chrome-plated bronze blades were still sharp upon excavation). Walk around to the rear of the vault where you can see terracotta soldiers in various states of reconstruction.

(right) Archaeologists have puzzled together almost 1,000 soldiers.

COLORATION

The colored lacquers that were used not only gave the terracotta soldiers a realistic appearance, but also sealed and protected the clay. Unfortunately, upon exposure to oxygen, these thin layers of color become extremely brittle and flake off or crumble to dust. Chinese scientists are devising excavation methods that will preserve the coloration of warriors unearthed in the future.

Ready on one knee with bow in hand, these archers are poised to rise and fire a deadly salvo at a moment's notice.

Every cavalry rider is accompanied by a life-size terracotta horse.

(top) Unreconstructed warriors in Vault 2. (right) The exhibition is a work of art in progress. (opposite page) Visit the museum to see the warrior detail up close.

Vault 2

This vault offers a glimpse of unreconstructed figures as they emerge from the ground. It has remained mostly undisturbed since 1999 when archaeologists found the first tricolor figures—look closely and you can still see pink on the soldiers' faces and patches of dark red on their armor. As with ancient Greek sculptures, the warriors were originally painted in lifelike colors and with red armor. Around the sides of the vault, you can take a close-up look at excellent examples of soldiers and their weaponry in glass cases.

Vault 3

Sixty-eight soldiers and officers in various states of reconstruction stand in what appears to be a military headquarters. Although the condition of the warriors are similar to those in Vault 2, there is one unique figure: a charioteer standing at the ready, though his wooden chariot has been lost to time.

Qinyong Museum

Near Vault 3, an imposing sand-colored pavilion houses two miniature bronze chariots unearthed in the western section of Qin Shihuang's tomb. Found in 1980, these chariots are intricately detailed with ornate gold and silver ornamentation. In the atrium leading to the bronze chariots, look for a massive bronze urn—it's one of the treasures unearthed by archaeologists in their 1999 excavation of an accessory pit near the still-sealed mausoleum. Other artifacts on display include Tang Dynasty tricolor pottery and Qin jade carvings.

GETTING THERE

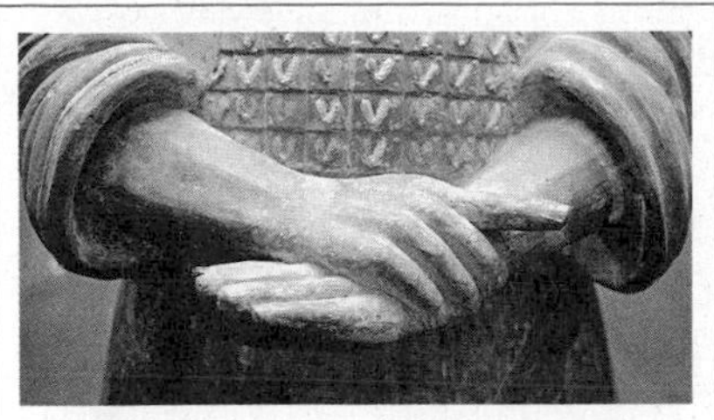

Practically every hotel and tour company in Xian arranges bus trips to the Terracotta Soldiers as part of an Eastern Tour package. If you aren't interested in having an English-speaking guide for the day, you can save a lot of money by taking one of the cheap buses (Y10 one-way) that leave for the town of Lintong from the parking lot between Xian's train station and the Jiefang Hotel. The ride to the Terracotta Warriors Museum should take between 90 and 120 minutes.

Opening Hours: Mar.—Nov., daily 8:30—5:30; Dec.—Feb., daily 8:30—5.

Admission: Mar.—Nov., Y90 ; Dec.—Feb., Y65. Price includes movie, access to three vaults, and entrance to the Qinyong Museum.

Phone: 029/8139-9001 (main office); 029/8139-9126 (ticket office).

VISITING TIPS

CAMERAS: You can shoot photographs and videos inside the vaults, a change from previous years when guards brusquely confiscated film upon seeing your camera. You still can't use a flash or tripod, however.

SOUVENIRS: You can buy postcards and other souvenirs in the shops outside the vaults and the Circle Vision Theater. Alternatively, you can face the fearsome gauntlet of souvenir hawkers outside the main gates; miniature replica terra-cotta soldiers can be found here for as little as Y1 each. If you're intimidated by the aggressive touts, however, there's nothing available here that you can't get back in Xian. So be strong, don't look them in the eyes, and most important, never stop walking.

TIME: You'll likely end up spending two to three hours touring the vaults and exhibits at the Terracotta Warriors Museum. The time spent here will probably be part of a long day-tour visiting a number of sites—the Hauqing Hot Springs and possibly the Banpo Matriachal Clan Village—clustered around the small city of Lintong, east of Xian.

RAIDERS OF THE LOST TOMB

Qin started construction on his enormous, richly endowed tomb, said to be booby-trapped with automatic crossbows, almost as soon as he took the throne. According to ancient records, this underground palace contained 100 rivers of flowing mercury as well as ceilings inlaid with precious stones and pearls representing the stars and planets. Interestingly enough, mercury levels in the area's soil are much higher than normal, indicating that there may be truth to those records. Though the site of the tomb was rediscovered to the east of Xian in 1974 (soon after the Terracotta Soldiers were unearthed), the government didn't touch it because it lacked the sophisticated machinery needed to excavate safely. Authorities also executed any locals foolish enough to attempt a treasure-seeking foray.

In 1999, archaeologists finally began excavations of the area around the tomb and unearthed some fabulous treasures. They've only scratched the surface, however. Most of the tomb still lies buried. In fact, no one is even certain where its main entrance—reportedly sealed with molten copper—is located. Authorities have delayed further excavations until the tomb can be properly preserved rather than risk damaging what may be China's greatest archaeological site.

second floor, you can compare rates offered by three experienced travel agencies, all competing aggressively for your business. Rooms at the front of the building are more expensive because they have views of the Bell Tower, but some visitors are disturbed by noise from the traffic. **Pros:** excellent location. **Cons:** absence of character. ⊠*110 Nan Da Jie* ☎*029/8760–0000* 🖷*029/8727–1217* *belltower@ihw.com.cn* *322 rooms, 11 suites* *In-room: safe, Ethernet. In-hotel: 2 restaurants, bar, laundry service, minibar* ▭*AE, MC, V.*

$ **Howard Johnson Ginwa Plaza.** Don't look for the familiar orange roof here. This is a five-star operation rivaling the best in the city, and it's conveniently located just outside the city walls near South Gate. Rooms are outfitted with top-quality European-style furnishings and feature separate workspaces that are much appreciated by travelers. **Pros:** attractive lobby, superb variety at mealtimes. **Cons:** language barriers with staff. ⊠*18 Huancheng Nanlu* ☎*029/8842–1111* *www.hojochina.com* *324 rooms* *In-room: safe, Ethernet. In-hotel: 2 restaurants, bar, spa, laundry service, minibar* ▭*AE, MC, V.*

$$$–$$$$ **Hyatt Regency.** Although there are newer luxury venues, people return here because of this hotel's friendly staff and location. Near the most popular sights, it's within walking distance of the Bell Tower and the East Gate. The beds are extremely comfortable and the large windows provide great views of the city. The guest rooms, however, are smaller than rooms at other comparably priced hotels; chirping birds in the atrium lobby can be annoying when you're trying to fall asleep. **Pros:** walking distance to the city's sights, fun bar, which is an ex-pat hangout. **Cons:** overpriced breakfast. ⊠*158 Dong Da Jie,* ☎*029/8723–1234* *www.hyatt.com* *382 rooms, 22 suites* *In-room: safe, Ethernet. In-hotel: 2 restaurants, bar, tennis court, gym, laundry service, airport shuttle, minibar* ▭*AE, MC, V.*

¢ **Ibis Xian.** The best bargain in Xian is part of a budget hotel chain. It offers excellent rooms and low prices and is run to Western standards, so the beds are comfortable and everything is clean. The hotel is inside the old city (within walking distance of the Confucius Temple), and a few Chinese bars are up the road. The hotel's travel agent can organize cars and so forth. **Pros:** great location, friendly service. **Cons:** unappealing breakfast. ⊠*59 Heping Lu* ☎*029/8727–5555* *www.accorhotels.com* *220 rooms* *In-room: safe, Ethernet. In-hotel: restaurant, bar, laundry service, minibar* ▭*AE, MC, V.*

$$$–$$$$ **Shangri-La Golden Flower.** One of the city's most luxurious hotels, the Shangri-La offers excellent service. Still, the hotel could do with a refit. The English-speaking staff is very helpful—you'll find yourself wondering how they manage to tidy up your room and turn down your bed during the half hour you spent swimming laps in the indoor pool. The hotel is 15 minutes northeast of the city center. **Pros:** spacious rooms, excellent room service. **Cons:** layout is confusing, rooms are beginning to show their age. ⊠*8 Changle Xi Lu* ☎*029/8323–2981, 800/8942–5050 in the U.S.* *www.shangri-la.com* *416 rooms, 16 suites* *In-room: safe, Ethernet. In-hotel: 2 restaurants, 2 bars, pool, gym, minibar* ▭*AE, MC, V.*

¢ **Xiangzimen Youth Hostel.** The historical building, a converted siheyuan house, and its location just steps away from the imposing south gate of the city, can't be beaten. Rooms are hostel-standard—pine furniture and dorm-style bathrooms—but the doubles are more appealing. The common room is lively every night and is always full of locals and travelers. **Pros:** great staff, great place to meet other travelers. **Cons:** showers in the shared bathrooms leak. ✉ *16 Xiang Zi Ta Jie,* ☎ *029/6286–7888* 🌐 *www.yhaxian.com* *40 rooms* *In-hotel: restaurant, bar, laundry service, business facilities* ▭ *AE, MC, V.*

NIGHTLIFE AND THE ARTS

Muslim Quarter. One of the busiest parts of town in the evening, this is where crowds converge to shop, stroll, and eat virtually every night of the week. Street-side chefs fire up the stoves and whip up tasty dishes, vendors ply the crowded lanes peddling their wares, and locals and tourists alike jostle in the frenetic pace.

The impressive song and dance performance at **Tang Dynasty** (✉ *75 Changan Bei Lu* ☎ *029/8782–2222* 🌐 *www.xiantangdynasty.com*) is the city's most popular evening of entertainment for foreign visitors. Shows begin at 8:30. **GZ Bar** (✉ *Dong Qi Dao Xiang* ☎ *133/5920–7823*), the only jazz bar of its kind in Xian, is worth seeking out for its nightly live music and cheap beers.

SHOPPING

Predictably, Xian is overloaded with terra-cotta souvenirs. There is more to buy in Xian, however. **Hua Jue Xiang Market** (✉ *Hua Jue Xiang*), the alley leading to the Great Mosque, is one of the best places to find interesting souvenirs. Expect the antique you're eyeing to be fake, no matter how vehemently the vendor insists your find is "genuine Ming Dynasty." The shops along **Culture Street** (✉ *Wenhua Jie*) are filled with carved jade, calligraphy, and Shaanxi folk paintings. Even if you don't buy anything, it's a nice place for a stroll.

GANSU

Gansu, the long, narrow province linking central China with the desert regions of the Northwest. For centuries, as goods were transported through the region, Gansu acted as a conduit between China and the Western world. As merchants made their fortunes from silk and other luxuries, the oasis towns strung along the Silk Road became important trade outposts of the Middle Kingdom. But beyond the massive fortress at Jiayuguan lay the end of the Great Wall, the oasis of Dunhuang, and then perdition. Gansu was the edge of China.

What has long been the poorest province in China is essentially dry, rugged, and barren. The decline of the Silk Road brought terrible suffering and poverty, from which the area has only very recently begun to recover as tourism boosts the local economy.

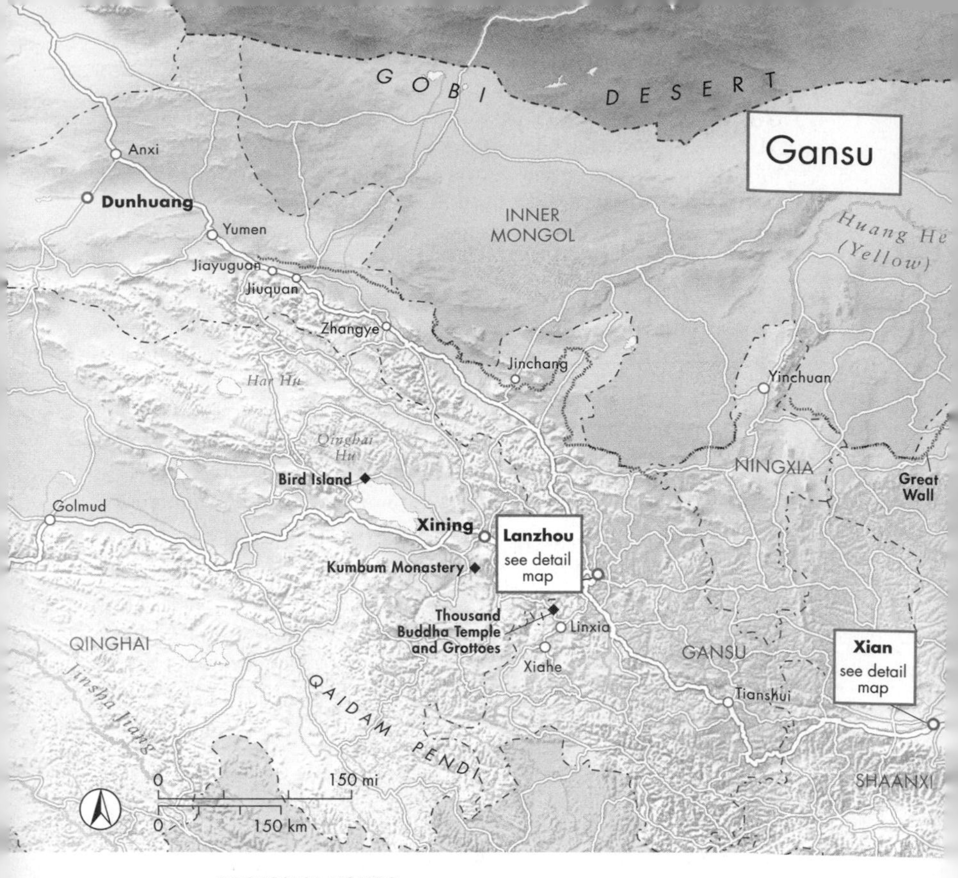

REGIONAL TOURS

John's Information Cafè. There isn't a lot of choice when it comes to tours in Gansu, but this branch of a small chain of cafés along the Silk Road offers tours to Dunhuang and the Mogao Caves led by English-speaking guides. Prices are negotiable and depend on the number of people traveling, but expect to pay about Y200 per day excluding admission (which adds up). They can also arrange tours of Lanzhou. ✉ *21 Mingshan Lu, north of the Feitian Hotel, Dunhuang* ☎ *1399/373–3106* 🌐 *www.johncafe.net.*

LANZHOU

8 hrs by train northwest of Xian; 22 hrs by train southeast of Ürümqi; 5 hrs by train east of Xining, 28 hours by train from Beijing.

Built on the banks of the Yellow River, the capital of Gansu extends along the base of a narrow gorge whose walls rise to 5,000 feet. A city with a long history, Lanzhou has been nearly ruined by rampant industrialization and is now one of the world's most polluted urban areas. The ethnic mix of the city's population makes the place interesting for a few hours, but plan to stay here only as long as it takes to arrange transportation to somewhere more pleasant, like Xiahe or Dunhuang.

GETTING HERE AND AROUND

The city's Zhongchuan Airport is 90 km (59 mi) north of town. Because of this, most people arrive by train.

BY AIR From Lanzhou, there are daily flights to Dunhuang, Beijing, Guangzhou, Shanghai, Chengdu, Ürümqi, and Xian. A public bus costing Y30 per person takes more than an hour to reach the airport from the China Northwest Airlines office at 512 Donggang Xilu.

BY BUS Long-distance buses arrive at the East Station (Qiche Dongzhan) on Pingliang Lu, north of the train station. Leaving the city can be a bit more complicated. Buses to major destinations like Xian, Xining, Jiayuguan, and Dunhuang usually leave from East Station, whereas lesser destinations are served by West Station (Qiche Xizhan). Buses to Xiahe depart from South Station (Qiche Nanzhan).

Buses originating in Lanzhou often require foreigners to show proof of travel insurance bought from the Chinese company PICC (The People's Insurance Company of China—a monsterously large insurance company) before purchasing tickets. It's unclear why this regulation exists, or why there's usually at least one daily bus to each destination that doesn't require the paperwork. You should be able to purchase insurance with your bus ticket, but this is often not the case. For peace of mind, head straight to the main PICC office on the north side of Qingyang Lu, just east of Jingning Lu. They'll know why you're there. A two-week policy costs Y40.

BY TRAIN The train station (Lanzhou Huochezhan) is at the southern end of Tianshui Lu, 1 km (½ mi) south of the city's hotels. Because few trains originate here, buying sleeper tickets in Lanzhou can be difficult; your best bet is to buy tickets early or hope for an upgrade onboard.

TOURS

Gansu Western Travel Service offers a day trip to Thousand Buddha Temple and Grottoes that includes all transportation and insurance for around Y400 per person. The company also has tours to Xiahe, including a five-day trip that visits the spectacularly beautiful Tibetan temples at Langmusi on the border with Sichuan. A basic two-day tour from Lanzhou costs between Y600 and Y750 per person, including hotel.

ESSENTIALS

Air Contacts China Northwest Airlines (✉ *512 Donggang Xilu* ☎ *0931/882–1964*). **Lanzhou Zhongchuan Airport** (✉ *Zhongchuan* ☎ *0931/896–8160*).

Bank Bank of China (✉ *589 Tianshui Lu* ☎ *0931/888–9942*).

Bus Contacts Lanzhou East Bus Station (✉ *Ping Yuang Lu* ☎ *0931/841–8411*). **Lanzhou West Bus Station** (✉ *458 Xijin Dong Lu* ☎ *0931/233–3285*). **Lanzhou South Bus Station** (✉ *Lanzhou Nan Gonggongqiche Zhan* ☎ *0931/234–1765*).

Train Contacts Lanzhou Train Station (✉ *Houche Zhan Dong Jian, at the southern end of Pingliang Lu and Tianshui Lu* ☎ *0931/882–2142*).

Visitor and Tour Info Gansu Western Travel Service (✉ *Lanzhou Hotel, 486 Donggang Xilu* ☎ *0931/885–2929 or 138/9331–8956*).

EXPLORING LANZHOU

WORD OF MOUTH

"Lanzhou, Gansu's capital, and Urumqi, Xinjiang's capital are both large, industrial, and heavily polluted cities worth avoiding."
—PeterN_H

Five Spring Mountain Park. In the park, you can sip tea among ancient temples and see impressive views of the city below. The five springs that gave the place its name, unfortunately, have dwindled to a trickle. *Y5 Daily 8–7.*

Fodor's Choice ★ **Gansu Provincial Museum.** The most famous item in the collection of this excellent museum is the elegant bronze "Flying Horse," considered a masterpiece of ancient Chinese art. Other notable objects include a silver plate indicating contact between China and Rome more than 2,200 years ago, and wooden tablets used to send messages along the Silk Road. Exhibits are uniformly subtitled in English. *3 Xijin Xilu, across from the Friendship Hotel Free Tues.–Sun. 9–5.*

Mountain of the White Pagoda Park. Laid out in 1958, the park covers the slopes on the Yellow River's north bank. It's more of a carnival than a place to relax, but it's a great place for people-watching. *Entrance at Zhongshan Qiao, the bridge extending over the Yellow River Y6 Daily 7:30–7:30.*

WHERE TO EAT

Many of the best restaurants in Lanzhou are in its upscale hotels; one to try is Zhong Hua Yuan in the Lanzhou Hotel, where an English menu is available. Another place to find a good meal is along Nongmin Xiang Lu, a street that runs behind the Lanzhou Hotel. This is a great place to try the *roujiamo,* a small sandwich filled with onion, chili, and flash-fried lamb or beef.

¢–$ SICHUAN **Chuanwei Wang.** You can often tell a good restaurant by the lack of empty tables; at mealtimes, this Sichuanese eatery is always packed. There's no English menu, but pictures of almost every dish make ordering simple. If you're stuck, order *gongbao jiding,* a slightly spicy dish of chicken stir-fried with peanuts. *26 Nongmin Xiang Lu, north of Tianshui Lu No phone No credit cards.*

$–$$$ CHINESE **Xinhai Restaurant.** One of Lanzhou's finest eateries, Xinhai is surprisingly affordable. Lanzhou specialties as well as Cantonese and Sichuanese dishes are pictured on the menu; you can also order from the text-only English menu. *499 Dongan Xi Lu, next to Legend Hotel 0931/886–6078 No credit cards.*

WHERE TO STAY

¢–$ **Jing Jiang Sun Hotel.** From the marble floors in the lobby to the plush furnishings, this is Lanzhou's top luxury hotel. On the west side of the building, the upper floors have sweeping views of the mountains; if you're trying to stay cool, however, be aware that the sun makes these rooms warmer than those on the east side. **Pros:** excellent value, reception staff speak English. **Cons:** expensive Internet and business center facilities are sparse. *481 Donggang Xilu 0931/880–5511 www.*

jjsunhotel.com *In-room: safe, Ethernet. In-hotel: restaurant, gym, laundry service, minibar* *MC, V.*

¢ **Lanzhou Hotel.** Built in 1956, this concrete behemoth's Sino-Stalinist exterior hides a modern, extensively refurbished interior. Pleasant service and clean, standard-size rooms make this hotel a good value; the older east and west wings house shabbier but still decent rooms for half the price. The hotel's renowned Chinese restaurant, Zhong Hua Yuan, offers great local cuisine. **Pros:** a local landmark that's easy to find. **Cons:** even the no-smoking rooms can be smokey. *486 Donggang Xilu, on the corner of Tianshui Lu* *0931/841–6321* *0931/841–8608* *476 rooms, 50 suites* *In-hotel: 5 restaurants, minibar* *AE, MC, V.*

SIDE TRIPS FROM LANZHOU

Fodor's Choice ★ One of the only day-trips worth taking from Lanzhou is the **Thousand Buddha Temple and Grottoes.** It's filled with Buddhist paintings and statuary, including an impressive 89-foot-tall Buddha carved into a cliff face. Although the art is disappointing compared to the Mogao Grottoes at Dunhuang, the location, in a 200-foot-high canyon dominated by spectacular cliff formations of porous rock, is stunning.

If you travel here on your own, you'll need to catch a bus, a ferry, and a jeep. Don't even try it. It's much easier to book a tour. Gansu Western Travel Service (⇨Tours, *above*) offers a popular day trip that includes all transportation and insurance for about Y400 per person. You can ask your hotel to make the arrangements. *Y50 entrance* *Daily 8–5.*

DID YOU KNOW?

The canyon is along one side of the Yellow River. The journey through a gorge lined by water-sculpted rocks is spectacular. When the canyon is dry you can travel 2½ km (1½ mi) by foot or four-wheel-drive vehicle to see the small community of Tibetan lamas at the Upper Temple of Bingling. The temple (Y10) is nothing special, but the twists and turns of the upper gorge are breathtaking, and the monks are friendly.

Fodor's Choice ★ **Labrang Monastery.** In the remote town of Xiahe, the monastery is a little piece of Tibet along the Gansu-Qinghai border. A world away from Lanzhou, Xiahe has experienced a dizzying rise in the number of travelers over the past decade. Even Tibetan monks clad in traditional fuchsia robes now surf the Internet, play basketball, and listen to pop music. Yet despite the encroaching modernity, Xiahe is still a wonderful place, attracting large numbers of pilgrims who come to study and to spin the 1,147 prayer wheels of the monastery daily, swathed in their distinctive costume of heavy woolen robes tied with brightly colored sashes. Foreign tourists were

DON'T MISS

A highlight is the daily gathering of monks on a lawn for religious debate in the liveliest fashion. The monks charge at each other in groups, hissing good-naturedly, as older monks supervise with a benevolent air. The debate takes place in the afternoon; ask at the ticket office for times. Another interesting daily event is the gathering of hundreds of chanting monks on the steps of the main prayer hall beginning at 11 AM.

9

banned from Xiahe after the police crackdown of antigovernment riots in Lhasa and Tibetan areas, including Xiahe. Travel restriction may be in place. The Labrang Monastery is the largest Tibetan lamasery outside Tibet. Founded in 1710, it once had as many as 4,000 monks, a number much depleted due in large part to the Cultural Revolution, when monks were forced to return home and temples were destroyed. Though the monastery reopened in 1980, the government's policy of restricted enrollment has kept the number of monks down to about 1,500.

There are two ways to reach Xiahe: by public bus or by private tour. Buses for Xiahe leave from Lanzhou's South Station (Qiche Nanzhan) every hour or two starting at 7:30 AM and take about 6 hours. Make sure to purchase tickets in advance, as some departures require travel insurance (*baoxian*). ✉ *2 km (1 mi) west of long-distance bus station* 🎫 *Free; Y25 for guided tour* ⏲ *Daily sunrise–sunset.*

DUNHUANG

17 hrs by bus northwest of Lanzhou; 6 hrs by bus west of Jiayuguan.

A small oasis town, Dunhuang was for many centuries the most important Buddhist destination on the Silk Road. Just outside of town, beyond the towering dunes of Singing Sand Mountain, you can see the extraordinary caves of the Mogao Grottoes, considered the richest repository of Buddhist art in the world.

Buddhism entered China via the Silk Road, and as Dunhuang was the point of entry to the Chinese world, it was not long before a temple was established here. By AD 366 the first caves were being carved and painted at the Mogao oasis. Work continued until the 10th century, after which they were left undisturbed for nearly a thousand years.

Adventurers from Europe, North America, and other parts of Asia began plundering the caves at the end of the 19th century, yet most of the statuary and paintings remain. By far the most astounding find was a "library cave" filled with more than 45,000 forgotten sutras and official documents. The contents were mostly sold to Sir Aurel Stein in 1907, and when translated they revealed the extent to which Dunhuang was an ancient melting pot of cultures and religions.

Today, you'll find a rapidly developing small city that is still, in some ways, a melting pot; tourists from every continent converge upon Dunhuang daily to visit one of the most impressive sites in all of China.

GETTING HERE AND AROUND

BY AIR The easiest and most expensive way to reach Dunhuang is by air, with regular flights from Beijing, Xian, Lanzhou, and Ürümqi. Dunhuang's airport is 13 km (8 mi) east of town, on the road to the Mogao Grottoes. A taxi ride from the airport costs Y20 to Y30.

BY BUS Buses from Lanzhou and Jiayuguan depart frequently for Dunhuang, dropping you off at the station in the center of town.

CLOSE UP

The Silk Road: Then & Now

The history of the Silk Road starts in 138 BC, when Emperor Wudi of the Han Dynasty sent a caravan of 100 men to the west, attempting to forge a political alliance with the Yuezhi people living beyond the Taklamakan Desert. The mission was a failure and only two men survived the 13-year return journey, but they brought back with them to Chang'an (present-day Xian) tales of previously unknown kingdoms: Samarkand, Ferghana, Parthia, and even Rome. More important, they told stories about the legendary Ferghana horse, a fast and powerful creature said to be bred in heaven. Believing that this horse would give his armies a military advantage over the Huns, Emperor Wudi sent a number of large convoys to Central Asia in order to establish contact with these newly discovered kingdoms—and to bring back as many horses as possible. These envoys of the Han emperor were the first traders on the Silk Road.

The extension of the Silk Road beyond Central Asia to the Middle East and Europe was due to another ill-advised foreign excursion, this time on the part of the Roman Empire. In 55 BC, Marcus Licinius Crassus led an army to the east against Parthia, in present-day Syria. The battle was one of Rome's greatest military defeats, but some of the survivors were able to obtain Chinese silk from the Parthians. Back in Rome, wearing silk became the fashion, and for the first time in history a trade route was established covering the arduous (5,000-mi) journey between East and West.

It might seem odd today, the two empires knew very little about the origins of their precious cargo. The reason for this common ignorance was the complicated supply chain that transported goods over the Silk Road. No one merchant made the entire journey, but wares were instead brought from kingdom to kingdom, switching hands in the teeming bazaars of wealthy oasis cities along the way.

Over time, the Silk Road became less important due to the opening of sea routes, and was dealt a deathblow by the isolationist tendencies of the Ming Dynasty in the 14th century. Yet today, the Silk Road is being resurrected to transport the modern world's most precious commodity: oil. China's rapid development has created an almost insatiable appetite for energy resources. In the last few years, pipelines have been completed from Kazakhstan and Xinjiang to Shanghai. There's even a long-term plan to create the world's longest pipeline, stretching from Saudi Arabia to China.

BY TRAIN Dunhuang's train station is 13 km (8 mi) northeast of he town and serves Lanzhou and Jiayuguan. A better connected station, with services to Beijing and Shanghai, is in the small town of Liuyuan, 120 km (74 mi) away. Taxis from Liuyuan to Dunhuang cost Y120, or you can ride one of the buses that leave hourly for Y15.

TOURS

If you only have time for one tour, head to the Mogao Grottoes (Y20). Don't bother with a tour to Singing Sand Mountain, as it's easy enough to reach on your own by taxi. If you're able to spend an extra day in town, take a tour of sites relating to ancient Dunhuang (Y130).

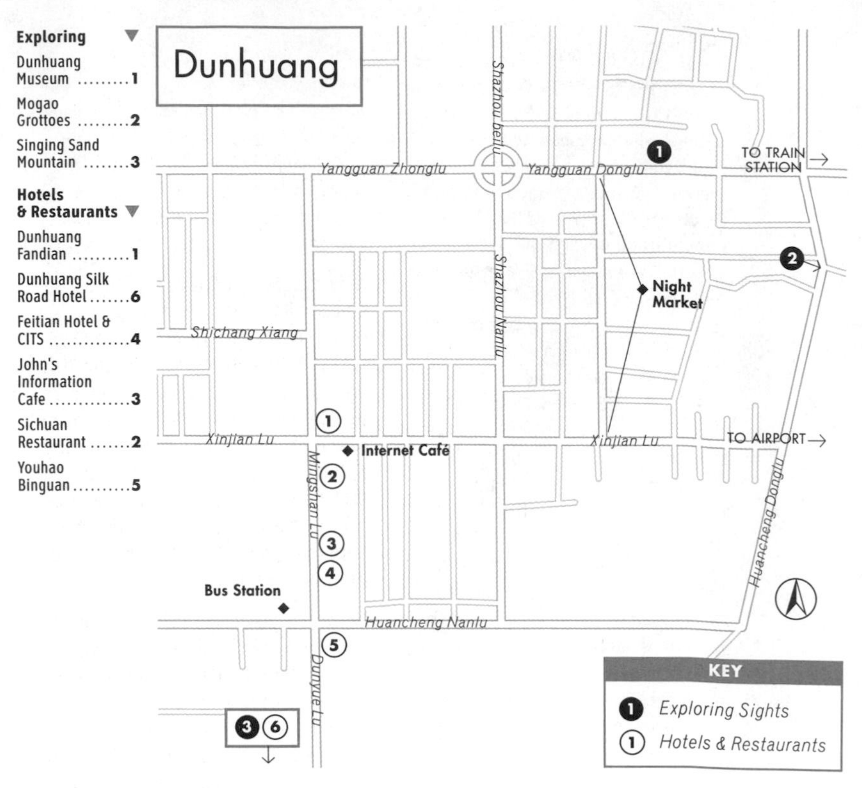

ESSENTIALS

Air Contacts **Dunhuang Airport** (✉ *13 km [8 mi] east of town, near the Mogao Grottoes* ☎ *0937/882–5292*).

Bank **Bank of China** (✉ *Yangguan Zhong Lu* ☎ *0937/263–0510*).

Bus Contact **Dunhuang Bus Station** (✉ *Dingzi Lu* ☎ *0937/882–2174*).

Train Contacts **Liuyuan Train Station** (✉ *Liuyuan Huoche Zhan* ☎ *0937/557–2995*).

Dunhuang Train Station (✉ *Dunhuang Huoche Zhan* ☎ *0937/ 882–2598*).

Visitor and Tour Info **Feitian CITS** (✉ *Feitian Hotel, 22 Mingshan Lu* ☎ *0937/883–2714*).

EXPLORING DUNHUANG

❶ **Dunhuang Museum.** The small museum displays objects recovered from nearby Silk Road fortifications. If you've visited the Jade Gate or Yangguan Pass, you may enjoy seeing what's been found. ✉ *8 Yangguan Dong Lu, east of the night market* *Free* ⏲ *Daily 8–1 and 2–6.*

❸ **Singing Sand Mountain.** South of Dunhuang, the oasis gives way to desert. Here you'll find a gorgeous sweep of sand dunes, named for the light rattling sound that the sand makes when wind blows across the surface. At 5,600 feet above sea level, the half-hour climb to the summit is a difficult climb but is worth it for the views, particularly at sunset. Nestled in the sand is **Crescent Moon Lake** *(Yueyaquan),* a lovely pool that by some freak of the prevailing winds never silts up. Camels, sleds, and various flying contraptions are available at steep prices; try your bargaining skills. ✉*Mingshan Lu, 5 km (3 mi) south of town* 🎫*Y120.*

RENT-A-BIKE

The best way to get around Dunhuang is by bicycle, and you can easily hire one from rental places around town.

❷ Fodor'sChoice ★ **Mogao Grottoes.** The magnificent Buddhist grottoes lie southeast of Dunhuang. At least 40 caves—dating from the Northern Wei in the 4th century AD to the Five Dynasties in the 10th century AD—are open to the public. Which caves are open on a given day depends on the whim of local authorities, but you shouldn't worry too much about missing something. Everything here is stunning. You'll almost certainly visit the giant seated Buddhas in caves 96 and 130, the Tang Dynasty sleeping Buddha in cave 148, and the famous "library" in caves 16 and 17 where 45,000 religious and political documents were uncovered at the turn of the 20th century. A flashlight is a useful item for your visit.

This is one site where you should hire an English-speaking guide. At a cost of only Y20 extra, your understanding of the different imagery used in each cave will increase immeasurably. Tours in English take place about three times a day in the high season, so you may have to wait to join one. Be sure to verify that the tour is of the same two-hour duration and covers the same number of caves (8–10) as the Chinese tours. After the tour, you'll have time to wander around and revisit any unlocked caves. A fine museum contains reproductions of eight caves not usually visited on the public tour. A smaller museum near the library cave details the removal of artifacts by foreign plunderers.

To get here, take a taxi (Y60 to Y80 round-trip) or take the half-hour bus ride that departs from Xinjian Lu, near the corner with Minshan Lu. The bus runs from 8 AM to 6 PM, and tickets cost Y8 each way. CITS at the Feitan Hotel also has a daily bus service, leaving Dunhuang at 8 AM and returning at noon. A round-trip costs Y20. ✉*25 km (17 mi) southeast of town* ☎*No phone* 🎫*Y160 for tour; additional Y20 for English-speaking guide* ⏲*Daily 8:30–6.*

WHERE TO EAT

Dunhuang's night market is a 10-minute walk from the most popular hotels. Located between Xinjian Lu and Yangguan Dong Lu, it's worth a visit for cold beer and flavorful lamb kebabs. Small restaurants are clustered together on Mingshan Lu in the center of town.

¢–$ AMERICAN ✕**John's Information Café.** Cool off after a full day of sightseeing on this trellised patio. Another option is to come before you start your day for a Western-style breakfast and a cup of joe. The restaurant also arranges overnight camel rides for Y200–Y300 per person, depending on group size, and trips to Yadan National Park and elsewhere. ✉*21 Mingshan*

Lu, north of the Feitian Hotel ☎*1399/373–3106* 🌐*www.johncafe.net* ▭*No credit cards.*

¢–$ SICHUAN ✕ **Sichuan Restaurant.** Delicious Sichuanese classics like chicken with peanuts, sweet and sour pork, and spicy fried potato strips are available here at very cheap prices. There's an English menu but prices are much higher than on the Chinese menu. ✉*75 Mingshan Lu, next to the Dunhuang Trade Union Hotel* ☎*No phone* ▭*No credit cards.*

WHERE TO STAY

$–$$ ★ **Dunhuang Silk Road Hotel.** This cross between a Chinese fortress and an alpine lodge is the most interesting place to stay in Dunhuang. The large, spacious rooms have historical touches like Ming reproduction furniture and traditional wooden shower buckets. The hotel arranges some great tours, including a sunrise camel ride to the sand dunes of Singing Sand Mountain. The fourth-floor café is the perfect spot to appreciate the dunes from a distance. The hotel's only drawback is its location 3 km (2 mi) south of the town center. **Pros:** rooftop terrace, good hotel food. **Cons:** touts approach guests all the time. ✉*Mingshan Lu,* ☎*0937/888–2088* 🌐*www.the-silk-road.com/hotel/dunhuanghotel* *292 rooms, 8 suites* *In-hotel: 2 restaurants, gym* ▭*AE, MC, V.*

¢ **Dunhuang Fandian.** If you're looking for something mildly luxurious, this lodging in the center of town will fit the bill. Rooms are nicer than at the Feitian Hotel, but without an elevator you'll have to climb the stairs to your room. Foreign currency and traveler's checks can no longer be exchanged in the lobby; go to the bank opposite the hotel. **Pros:** central location, excellent value. **Cons:** lackadasical staff. ✉*16 Mingshan Lu, corner of Xinjiang Lu* ☎*0937/882–2413* *In-hotel: restaurant, minibar* ▭*No credit cards.*

¢ **Feitian Hotel.** Dunhuang's most popular tourist hotel has a variety of clean, comfortable rooms. For a taste of the high life you could book yourself a deluxe suite. The hotel is home to the CITS travel office and the departure point for popular tour buses. Best of all, it's in the middle of town. **Pros:** inexpensive basic rooms. **Cons:** large deposits required. ✉*22 Mingshan Lu, ½ block north of the bus station* ☎*0937/882–2337* *0937/882–2337* *In-hotel: business center, restaurant, minibar* ▭*No credit cards.*

¢ **Youhao Binguan.** Across from the bus station, this is Dunhuang's best budget option. The three-bed dorm rooms on the fourth floor are acceptable at Y60 per person, but the better option are the doubles with air-conditioning, which start at Y80. Hot water flows from 7:30 PM until midnight. Whatever you do, don't use the sub-par laundry service. **Pros:** decent restaurant, good place to meet backpackers. **Cons:** slow service all around. ✉*25 Mingshan Lu* ☎*0937/882–3072* *In-hotel: laundry service* ▭*No credit cards.*

QINGHAI

A remote and sparsely populated province on the northeastern border of Tibet, Qinghai's sweeping grasslands locked in by icy mountain ranges are relatively unknown to most Chinese people. They tend to think of the province as their nation's Siberia, a center for prisons and work camps. Yet Qinghai shares much of the majestic scenery of Xinjiang combined with the rich culture of Tibet.

The opening of the railway that links Tibet with the rest of China in 2006 led to an influx of tourists to Qinghai, one of major stops before the train arrives in Lhasa. However, the number of foreigners who experienced the region's stunning scenery from the train came to a dramatic halt in March 2008 when China made Tibet off-limits after the riots in Lhasa. The area was reopened, visitors could not travel independently on the train or any other method of transport. The situation goes back and forth, so for the latest information, check out 🌐*www.chinatibettrain.com* for timetables and the news about permits and costs. A luxury service which promises to be akin to the *Orient Express* is scheduled to begin in April 2009; see 🌐*www.tangulaluxurytrains.com* for more details.

Visitors to the region should take in a few of Qinghai's must-see sites. The capital city of Xining is small and receives mixed reports, but it has some charming Tibetan flair. On the northwest edge of the city is the famed North Monastery, a solemn Daoist destination. The Kumbum Monastery is a testament of Tibetan tranquility. For a truly heavenly display, crane your neck skyward at Bird Island on Qinghai Lake several hundred miles to the west of Xining.

REGIONAL TOURS

Tibetan Connections. This locally owned tour company is run out of Xining and offers very interesting off-the-beaten-track hikes, camping trips, and tours through one of the region's most fascinating and beautiful Tibetan areas. ✉*International Village, Building 5, Lete Youth Hostel, Xining* ☎*0971/820–3271* 🌐*www.tibetanconnections.com.*

China International Travel Service. The main Xining branch of China's state-run travel service is located in the Xining Guesthouse and offers tours of the city as well as to Bird Island. Despite the services being aimed at international tourists, the office is staffed with people who speak limited English. ✉*215 Qiyi Lu, Xining* ☎*0971/823–8701.*

XINING

4 hrs (225 km [140 mi]) by train or 3 hrs by bus west of Lanzhou; 25 hours (1,900 km [1,200 mi]) by train northeast of Lhasa.

Its name means "Peace in the West," so it's no surprise that Xining started out as a military garrison in the 16th century, guarding the empire's western borders. It was also an important center for trade between China and Tibet. A small city by Chinese standards, with a population slightly more than 1.1 million, Xining is no longer cut off from the rest of China. But the city still feels remote; a far-flung metropolis wedged between dramatic sandstone cliffs, Xining is populated largely by Tibetan and Hui peoples.

For travelers, Xining is a convenient base for visits to the important Kumbum Monastery, which sits just outside the city, and the stunning

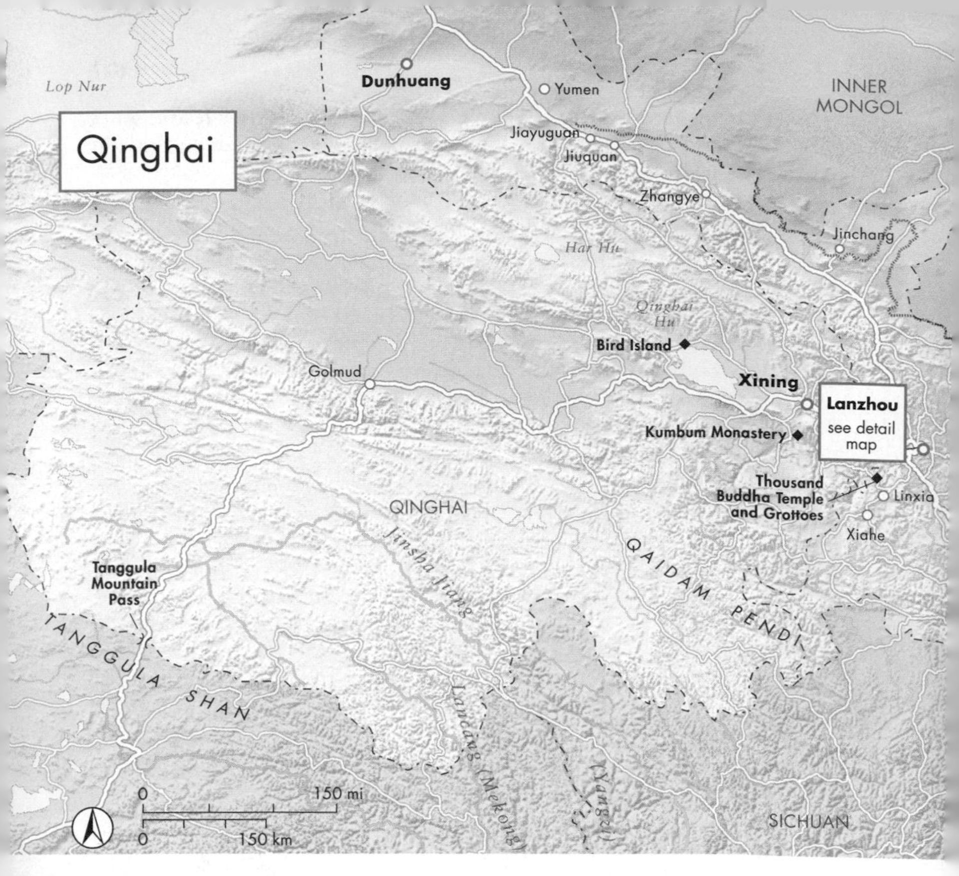

avian sanctuary of Bird Island, 350 km (217 mi) away on the shores of China's largest saltwater lake. Beginning in 2007, trains linking Tibet to Beijing and Shanghai stopped in Xining. Tibet was off-limits for much of the first half of 2008 after anti-Chinese riots in Lhasa, but now tourists are once again allowed on the train.

GETTING HERE AND AROUND

Xining Caojiabao Airport is 30 km (19 mi) east of the city. Shuttle buses costing Y16 per person can get you to or from the airport in about 40 minutes. If you're traveling with someone else, a taxi (Y50) is a better option. If you arrive by train or bus, you'll be within walking distance of the Post Hotel and the Station Hotel. You can reach the city's more upscale hotels by taking a taxi, a ride that should be less than Y10.

If you're planning on traveling to Tibet, use a well-established travel agent. Bureaucratic formalities mean that you'll still need help obtaining the proper permits.

BY AIR Daily flights link Xining with Beijing, Shanghai, Chengdu, Guangzhou, Xian, and Shenzhen. There is less frequent service to Lhasa, Ürümqi, Qingdao, and Golmud.

BY BUS Tickets for the long, bumpy bus ride to Lhasa can be purchased from any travel agent. Tickets for the journey to Lanzhou (3 hours) and Xian

(15 hours) are available at the long-distance bus station, a few minutes north of the train station. If your next stop is Dunhuang, but you don't want to backpedal to Lanzhou, take the bus to Jiuquan in Gansu and get a connection farther west; the mountain scenery and small Tibetan villages along the way are spectacular.

BY TRAIN The train to Lhasa began with much fanfare in 2007, but foreign travelers need to arrange permits before they can buy train tickets to Tibet.

TOURS

Xining's more upscale hotels have travel offices that can help you arrange expensive private tours to Kumbum Monastery or Bird Island with English-speaking guides. For less expensive group tours, head to the Station Hotel or the Post Hotel where the on-site travel agencies specialize in group tours. Be forewarned: you will probably be crammed into a minibus with Chinese tourists. A third option is to hire the services of an enterprising individual like Niu Xiaojun, who speaks good English and been leading foreigners to off-the-beaten-path destinations for years.

ESSENTIALS

Air Contact **Xining Caojiabao Airport** (✉ *30 km [20 mi] east of Xining* ☎ *0971/818–8222*).

Bus Contact **Xining Main Bus Station** (✉ *Jianguo Lu, south of the train station* ☎ *0971/711–2094*).

Medical Assistance **Qinghai People's Hospital** (✉ *143 Gonghe Lu* ☎ *0971/817–7911*).

Train Contact **Xining Railway Station** (✉ *Northern end of Jianguo Lu* ☎ *0971/814–9790*).

Visitor and Tour Info **Niu Xiaojun** (☎ *1319/579–1105*). **Spring & Autumn Travel Service** (✉ *Post Hotel, 138 Huzhu Lu, east of the train station* ☎ *0971/817–4957*). **Yicai Travel Service** (✉ *Station Hotel, Huochezhan Guanchang* ☎ *0971/814–2008*).

9

EXPLORING XINING

Although most travelers don't come to see Xining, there are a few sights in and around the city.

The most important site is the Taoist **North Monastery** *(Beishan Si)*, at the northwest end of town. Construction on this series of mountainside cloisters and pavilions began more than 1,700 years ago during the Northern Wei. Climbing the stairs to the white pagoda at the top gives a view of the entire city sprawled out beneath you. To get here, take a taxi. ✉ *North end of Chanjiang Lu* 🎫 *Y10* ⏲ *8:30* AM–6 PM.

AROUND XINING

★ The magnificent **Kumbum Monastery** *(Ta'Er Si)* lies 25 km (15 mi) southwest of Xining. One of the six great monasteries of the Tibetan Buddhist sect known as Yellow Hat—and reputedly the birthplace of the sect's founder, Tsong Khapa—construction began in 1560. A great reformer who lived in the early 1400s, Tsong Khapa formulated a new doctrine that stressed a return to monastic discipline, strict celibacy, and moral and philosophical thought over magic and mysticism. Tsong's followers have controlled Tibetan politics since the 17th century. Still a magnet for Tibetan pilgrims, Kumbum boasts a dozen prayer halls, an exhibition hall, and monks' quarters. Public buses (Y5) to Huangzhong leave frequently from Zifang Jie Bus Station. Get off at the last stop and walk 2 km (1 mi) uphill, or take a put-put (Y2) to the monastery's gates. Taxis from Xining are Y30. ✉ *Huangzhong* 🎫 *Y80* ⏲ *8 AM–5 PM.*

> **WORD OF MOUTH**
>
> "Luce Boulnois' history of the Silk Road has finally been translated from the French, Susan Whitfield's 'Life Along the Silk Road' is a very readable collection of first person accounts from individuals living at various points on the routes at different periods of its history."
>
> —PeterN_H

WHERE TO EAT

¢ INTERNATIONAL ✕ **Black Tent.** This place serves great Tibetan, Indian, and Nepali food. All of the workers are Tibetans from Amdo and are very friendly. The atmosphere is great. The menu is in Tibetan and English. ✉ *Wen Hua Jie Wen Miao Guang Chang Wenhua Jie* ☎ *0971/823–4029* 💳 *No credit cards.*

¢ ITALIAN ✕ **Casa Mia Italian Restaurant.** This restaurant is managed by a local Chinese woman but is financially backed by several European expats, who wanted a place to satisfy their cravings for western food. With free wireless Internet and excellent Italian food, including espresso coffee drinks, it is very popular among expats. Menus are in English and Chinese and the staff speaks English. ✉ *10-4 Wu Si Xi Lu* ☎ *0971/631–1272* 💳 *No credit cards.*

¢–$ ASIAN ✕ **Jianyin Revolving Restaurant.** Perched atop the 28-story Jianyin Hotel, this slowly revolving restaurant offers mediocre Asian-inspired cuisine. But the food is beside the point. People come here for the spectacular views of the city. There's no minimum, so sipping a cup of tea while enjoying the scenery or playing cards is perfectly acceptable. ✉ *Jianyin Hotel, 55 Xida Jie, southeast corner of the central square* ☎ *0971/826–1885* 💳 *No credit cards.*

WHERE TO STAY

¢ **Jianyin Hotel.** A pink-marble foyer greets you at this handsome hotel, the best mid-range option in Xining. The rooms are about the same as everywhere else in town, but with an extra layer of glitz. **Pros:** nice view from 28th floor revolving restaurant, good value rooms. **Cons:** staff's English is limited. ✉ *55 Xida Jie* ☎ *0971/826–1887* 📠 *0971/826–1551* *160 rooms, 20 suites* *In-hotel: 2 restaurants, laundry service, minibar* 💳 *MC, V.*

¢ **Lete Hostel.** This new hostel gets good feedback from guests because it's geared to what budget travelers want: inexpensive, clean rooms, helpful travel information, and a place to meet other backpackers. The tour agency Tibet Connections is based here. In addition to dorms, there are double rooms with private baths and small apartments. **Pros:** friendly staff, nice views over the city. **Cons:** dorms can be cold. ✉ *16th* *floor, International Village Building 5* ☎*0971/820–3271* *In-hotel: kitchen, Wi-Fi* *No credit cards.*

$ Fodor's Choice ★ **Yinlong Hotel.** This ultramodern hotel is hands-down the finest lodging between Xian and Ürümqi. There's an incredible attention to detail, from sound-activated lighting in the hallways to bathrooms with a tub and a separate shower. Rooms are exceptionally comfortable and quiet, with views overlooking Xining's central square. **Pros:** central location, good quality hotel restaurants, wireless Internet in rooms. **Cons:** expensive buffet breakfast, small gym. ✉*38 Huanghe Lu, north side of the central square, Xining* ☎*0971/616–6666* *www.ylhotel.net* *316 rooms* *In-room: safe. In-hotel: gym, hair salon, 5 restaurants, laundry service, minibar* *AE, MC, V.*

SHOPPING

Those interested in Tibetan handicrafts will want to stroll through Xining's excellent street markets. The **Jianguo Lu Wholesale Market** (✉*Jianguo Lu, opposite the main bus station*) sells everything from traditional Tibetan clothing and food to the latest CDs.

SIDE TRIP FROM XINING

★ **Bird Island** *(Niao Dao)* is the main draw at Qinghai Hu, China's largest inland saltwater lake. The name Bird Island is a misnomer: it was an island until the lake receded, connecting it to the shore. The electric-blue lake is surrounded by rolling hills covered with yellow rapeseed flowers. Tibetan shepherds graze their flocks here as wild yaks roam nearby. Beyond the hills are snowcapped mountains. An estimated 100,000 birds breed at Bird Island, including egrets, speckle-headed geese, and black-neck cranes; sadly, the numbers have been much depleted because of the country's efforts to suppress the spread of avian flu. There are two viewing sites: spend as little time as possible at Egg Island in favor of the much better Common Cormorant Island, where you can see birds flying at eye-level from the topof a cliff. The best months to see birds are May and June. If you're taking a tour to Qinghai Hu, make sure that you're headed here and not the much closer tourist trap known as Qinghai Hu 151. To get to Bird Island, either contact a tour agency, or if you prefer to go under your own steam, catch a tourist bus from Xining Railway Station for Y35 each way. ✉*350 km (215 mi) northwest of Xining* *Y78.*

XINJIANG

The vast Xinjiang Uyghur Autonomous Region, covering more than 1.6 million square km (640,000 square mi), is China's largest province. Even more expansive than Alaska, it borders Mongolia, Russia, Kazakhstan, Kyrgyzstan, Tajikistan, Afghanistan, and Pakistan. Only 40% of Xinjiang's 19.6 million inhabitants are Han Chinese. About 45% are Uyghur (a people of Turkic origin), and the remainder is mostly Kazakhs, Hui, Kyrgyz, Mongols, and Tajiks.

Xinjiang gets very little rainfall except in the northern areas near Russia. It gets very cold in winter and very hot in summer, especially in the

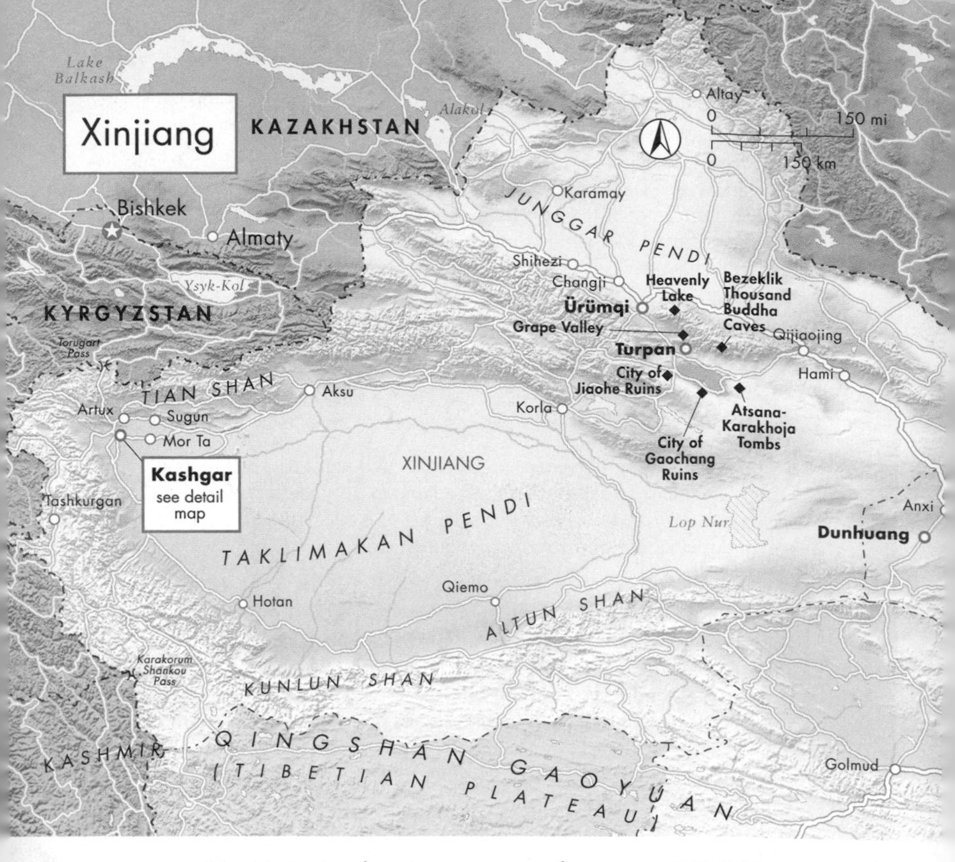

Turpan Basin where temperatures often sore to 120°F. Visitors usually forgive the extreme weather, however, as they're charmed by the locals and awed by the rugged scenery, ranging from the endless sand dunes of the desert to the pastoral grasslands of the north.

Long important as a crossroads for trade with Europe and the Middle East, Xinjiang has nevertheless seldom come completely under Chinese control. For more than 2,000 years, the region has been contested and divided by Turkic and Mongol tribes who—after setting up short-lived empires—soon disappeared beneath the shifting sands of time. In the 20th century, Uyghurs continued to resist Chinese rule, seizing power from a warlord governor in 1933 and claiming the land as a separate republic, which they named East Turkestan. China tightened its grip after the 1949 revolution, however, encouraging Han settlers to emigrate to the province to dilute the Uyghur majority. Today, Uyghurs concede that they have almost no chance of gaining independence, and you'll see little evidence of any remaining aspirations; speaking out against Beijing in public is just too risky.

DID YOU KNOW?

In the 1980s, archaeologists discovered dozens of tombs in various parts of Xinjiang, with bodies that had been buried for about 3,000 years yet remained remarkably preserved thanks to the arid desert climate. Many of

the mummies, believed to be forefathers of the Uyghurs, had northern European features, including fair hair and skin.

REGIONAL TOURS

Uyghur Tour & Travel Center. This excellent tour company based in Kashgar organizes tours of the Silk Road, as well as more unusual destinations like traditional Uyghur villages. Tour manager Abdul can also arrange cars to take you along the Karakorum Highway at prices significantly lower than the competition, and the company goes out of its way to tailor a tour to your requirements. ✉*Overseas Chinese Hotel 170 Seman Lu* ☎*0998/220–4012* 🌐*www.silkroadinn.com.*

CYTS. Based in Ürümqi, Ali, the English-speaking tour guide, offers interesting tailor-made tours to sights across the province, from two-day tours to Heavenly lake to multi-stop trips which can include Turpan and Kashgar. All prices are negotiable. ✉*Bogda Hotel, 10 Guangming Lu, Ürümqi* ☎*0991/232–1170.*

ÜRÜMQI

48 hours (2,250 km [1,400 mi]) by train, 4 hrs by plane northwest of Beijing.

Xinjiang's capital and largest city, Ürümqi is at the geographic center of Asia and has the distinction of being the most landlocked city in the world. It's a new city by Chinese standards, little more than barracks for Qing Dynasty troops when it was built in 1763. Once a sleepy trading post, Ürümqi has grown to a sprawling city with just over 2 million inhabitants. Yet despite this modernization, Ürümqi manages to conjure up the past, especially in the Uyghur-populated area near the International Grand Bazaar.

GETTING HERE AND AROUND

BY AIR Many people fly to Ürümqi from Beijing or Xian to begin a journey on the Silk Road. The airport is 20 km (12 mi) north of the downtown area and can be reached by taxi (about Y40) in 30 minutes or via frequent minibuses.

BY BUS Long-distance bus travel is often the only way to travel in Xinjiang if you don't want to wait a day or two for the next available train. Every city in the region is served at least daily by bus from Ürümqi. There's even bus service to Almaty, Kazakhstan.

It's usually a straightforward affair buying tickets from the only station in town, but Ürümqi is more complicated. Unless you're going to Hotan or Altai—which have their own separate bus stations—your best bet is to first look for tickets at Nianzigou Station. If you don't like what's available there, or if your destination is Turpan, head to the South Station (Nanjiao Qichezhan).

Buses (Y25 each way after bargaining) leave for Heavenly Lake (Tianchi Hu) at 9:30 AM from the north gate of Renmin Park. They usually leave the lake at 6 PM and arrive back in Ürumqi at 7:30 PM.

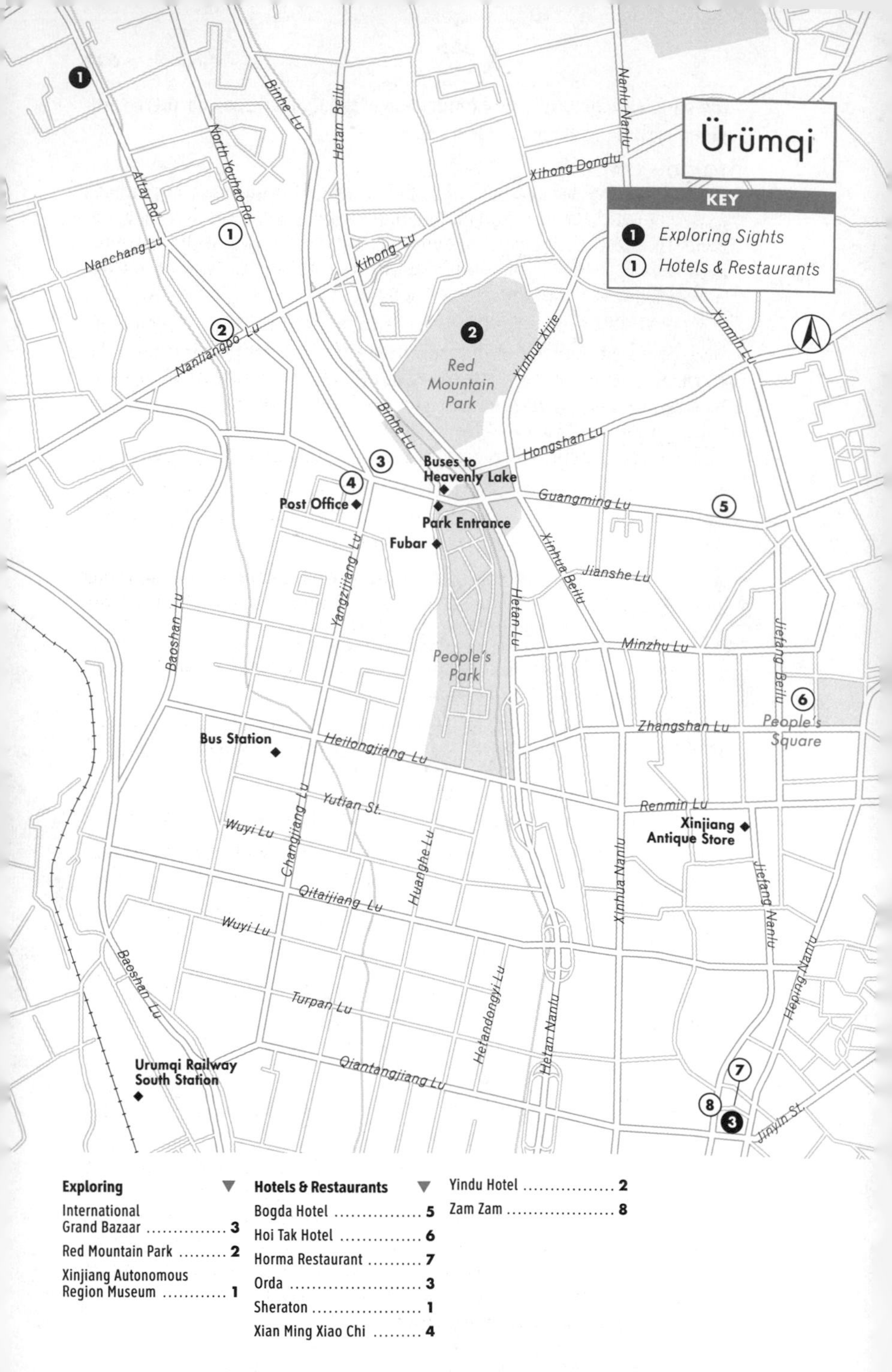

Exploring

International Grand Bazaar **3**

Red Mountain Park **2**

Xinjiang Autonomous Region Museum **1**

Hotels & Restaurants

Bogda Hotel **5**

Hoi Tak Hotel **6**

Horma Restaurant **7**

Orda **3**

Sheraton **1**

Xian Ming Xiao Chi **4**

Yindu Hotel **2**

Zam Zam **8**

BY TRAIN Those arriving by train will find themselves about 2 km (1 mi) southwest of the city center.

TOURS

Ürümqi is a popular place to begin a tour of Xinjiang's vast desert expanses. A private tour probably makes the most sense. Travel agencies are happy to let you pick and choose from a list of destinations. A four-wheel-drive vehicle will cost around Y1,300 per day; a smaller Volkswagen Santana is Y900 per day.

CYTS, in the parking lot of the Bogda Hotel, offers trips lasting from one day to more than three weeks. Seek out English-speaking guide Ali to talk you through the options. A tour of sites around Turpan or a trip to the Heavenly Lake can be accomplished in a single day.

ESSENTIALS

⚠ In China, there's no place more difficult to run out of money than in off-the-beaten-track Xinjiang. But there are ATMS in both Ürümqi and Kashgar, and all the machines accept international credit cards and debit cards. Most banks will also exchange currency and traveler's checks.

Air Contacts **China Southern Airlines** (✉ *26 Guangming Lu, Ürümqi* ☎ *0991/882–3300 or 0991/950–333*). **Ürümqi Airport** (✉ *16 km [10 mi] northwest of the city in Diwopu* ☎ *0991/380–1347*).

Bank **Bank of China** (✉ *343 Jiefang Nan Lu, at the corner of Minzhu Lu, behind the Hoi Tak Hotel* ☎ *0991/283–4222*).

Bus Contacts **Ürümqi Nianzigou Station** (✉ *Western end of Heilongjiang Lu* ☎ *0991/587–8898*). **Ürümqi South Station** (✉ *Yanerwo Lu* ☎ *0991/286–6635*).

Internet **Dragon Netbar** (✉ *190 Wuyi Lu* ☎ *No phone*) Y3/hr; open 24 hrs.

Medical Assistance **Chinese Medicine Hospital of Ürümqi** (✉ *60 Youhau Nan Lu* ☎ *0991/242–0963*).

Train Contact **Ürümqi Train Station** (✉ *Qiantangjiang Lu* ☎ *0991/581–4203*).

Visitor and Tour Info **CYTS** (✉ *10 Guangming Lu, in the parking lot of the Bogda Hotel* ☎ *0991/232–1170*). **Grassland Travel Service** (✉ *2 Renmin Gongyuan Beijie, southwest of the entrance gate to People's Park* ☎ *0991/584–1116*).

EXPLORING ÜRÜMQI

❸ **International Grand Bazaar.** The streets around the bazaar were once full of donkey carts and flocks of sheep. Men in embroidered skullcaps and women in heavy brown wool veils remain, and the whole area maintains the bustling atmosphere of a Central Asian street market. You can bargain for Uyghur crafts here, such as decorated knives, colorful silks, and carved jade. Small shops are tucked into every nook and cranny. The international bazaar itself has been heavily expanded and now includes a newly built minaret, which you can climb once you've paid the Y20 admission fee. The stalls, while interesting enough, are aimed firmly at tourists; the more authentic option are the streets nearby. ✉ *Jiefang Lu, 3 km (2 mi) south of the city center.*

9

CLOSE UP

China's Muslims

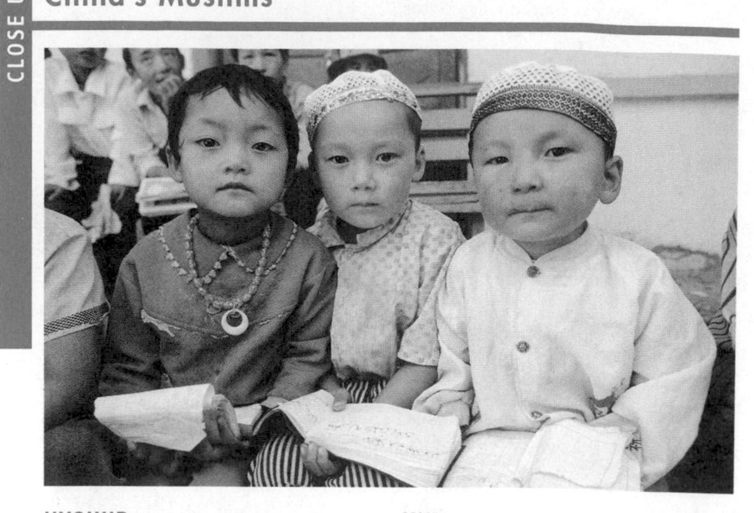

UYGHUR

The Muslim Turkic people known as Uyghurs (pronounced "WEE-grs") are one of China's largest—and in the eyes of Beijing, most troublesome—minority groups. Uyghurs mostly live in northwest China's Xinjiang, an "autonomous region" that is one of the most tightly controlled parts of the country after Tibet. Uyghurs are descendants of nomadic Turkic Central Asian tribes. Their language, food, music, dance, clothing, and other customs have little or no relation to those found elsewhere in China. Yet with a population of nearly 10 million people, most foreigners have never heard of them or their troubled independence movement. Protests and occasional violence in the region during the late 1990s caused Beijing to crack down severely, placing limits on religious education and executing hundreds of suspected Uyghur separatists. The attacks of September 11, 2001 gave the Chinese government further leverage to oppress Uyghurs in the name of fighting terrorism, and Xinjiang has been relatively quiet in recent years.

HUI

Primarily identifiable by their brimless white caps and headscarves, the Hui are ethnically Chinese Muslims. They are descendants of Middle Eastern traders who came to China via the Silk Road, settling down with a Chinese wife after her conversion to Islam. Over a thousand years' time, the Middle Eastern influence on the Hui appearance became diluted to the point where their facial features are now almost impossible to distinguish from those of Han Chinese. Yet because of cultural differences associated with their Islamic faith, Hui tend to associate with other Hui in largely Muslim neighborhoods. Hui reject the eating of several kinds of meat that are popular with Han Chinese, including pork, horse, dog, and several types of birds. In what could be seen as a form of respect by the business-savvy Han Chinese, Hui are also generally considered by the Han to be shrewd businesspeople, perhaps a vestige of their history as the descendants of foreign traders.

2 **Red Mountain Park.** Climbing to the top of the park gives you a picture-perfect view of the snowcapped Heavenly Mountains. An array of incongruously grouped objects—including an eight-story pagoda built by the emperor in 1788 to suppress an evil dragon—are reached via a long set of stairs. Come here in the early evening for the pleasure of seeing the cityscape bathed in the setting sun's golden light. Ignore the cheap carnival rides near the entrance. The park is hard to find, so take a taxi. ✉ *Off Hongshan Lu* *Free* *Daily 6* AM–*1* AM.

WHAT TIME IS IT?

A constant source of confusion for travelers in Xinjiang is figuring out the time. Uyghurs often speak in unofficial Xinjiang time, whereas Han Chinese use standard Beijing time. If in doubt, ask. No matter what time is spoken, you can count on everything in Xinjiang starting two hours later than in Beijing. That is, lunch in Kashgar is usually eaten at 2 PM Beijing Time.

1 **Xinjiang Autonomous Region Museum.** Don't miss the exhibition of perfectly preserved mummies at this superb museum, 4 km (2½ mi) northwest of the city center. The mummies—including the 4,000-year-old beauty of Loulan—were excavated from tombs in various parts of Xinjiang. In addition, the museum has a well-executed exhibition on the region's ethnic minorities. If you are lucky, one of the museum's English-speaking guides will accompany. There's no extra charge, and it's well worth doing. ✉ *132 Xibei Lu, 1 block west of the Sheraton Hotel* ☎ *0991/453–4453* *Free* *Weekdays 10* AM–*6* PM.

Fodor's Choice ★

WHERE TO EAT

Ürümqi is a good place to have your first taste of Uyghur cuisine. For cheap eats and a great scene, the Wuyi night market is best.

¢ NORTHERN CHINESE

✕ **Horma Restaurant.** This lunch spot serves classic Uyghur dishes at incredibly cheap prices. You can go with a standard like rice with lamb and raisins, or look at what other people are eating and point to indicate your selection. The *rounang* (flat bread baked with lamb inside) is especially good. Wash it all down with a can of Muslim-friendly Zam-Zam Cola, Xinjiang's answer to Coke. ✉ *185 Hanchi Lu, on the northern wall of the International Grand Bazaar* ☎ *No phone* ▭ *No credit cards.*

¢ NORTHERN CHINESE

✕ **Orda.** Next door to the Cornfield International Youth Hostel, this Kazakh-run restaurant offers exotic delicacies like horsemeat and intestines. Ignore those and enjoy a huge plate of tasty pilaf cooked in a stupendously large pot outdoors. There's no English menu. If pilaf runs out, try the laghman noodles or chicken stew, dapanji. ✉ *726 Youhao Nan Lu (south of Parksons shopping mall)* ▭ *No credit cards.*

¢ CHINESE

✕ **Xian Ming Xiao Chi.** If you need a change from Uyghur fare, this cheap and cheerful fast food joint offers tasty snacks from Xian. Do as the locals do when the temperature rises: try a cooling plateful of cold noodles with cucumber called *liang pi.* Say *bu la* if you don't want your noodles to be spicy. Other specialties include *rou jia mo,* or Chinese-style pork burgers—made from a meat rarely served in this part of the world. ✉ *33 Yangzi Jiang Lu* ▭ *No credit cards.*

9

CLOSE UP

The Jade Road

The residents of Xinjiang are apt to point out that the Silk Road isn't the first road they knew. That honor goes to the "Jade Road," which was established nearly 7,000 years ago. Running from Hotan into today's Qinghai and Gansu provinces, the Jade Road was the artery for Xinjiang's legendary white jade trade. Primarily mined from the Hotan River, Xinjiang jade comes in a number of hues, although small white stones with a reddish-brown exterior are the most highly valued.

Sensous and smooth to the touch, this "lamb's fat jade" is cloudy with translucent qualities. Chinese emperors have craved it for centuries. Good places to hunt around for all manner of jade in Ürümqi include the swirling International Grand Bazaar and the Xinjiang Antique Store.

Visitors who wish to know more about this region's heady history of jade, silk, and more should visit the Xinjiang Autonomous Region Museum. Here's a quick tip: buy fast. The availability of quality jade has dropped in recent years, and scientists fear the precious stone is being mined to exhaustion.

$ NORTHERN CHINESE **Zam Zam.** This smart Uyghur eatery looks as though it should be very pricey, but the excellent food is the best bargain in town. The ornate room is outfitted with carved wood and Arabic-style arches, and the smartly uniformed staff adds to the atmosphere. Few waiters speak Mandarin, let alone English, but there is a picture menu: try the pilaf or the lamb dumplings. No alcohol is served. *423 Heping Nan Luof, the International Bazaar 0991/843–0555 No credit cards.*

WHERE TO STAY

¢ **Bogda Hotel.** A good budget option if you don't want to stay in a dorm, this hotel has rooms that are cleaner and more comfortable than those offered in similarly priced lodgings. Rooms are discounted to Y200 if you ask nicely (in Chinese, because staff doesn't speak English). Most bathrooms even feature separate shower stalls. **Pros:** good selection of tours available, good value rooms. **Cons:** noisy lobby, little English spoken. *10 Guangming Lu 0991/886–3910 0991/886–5769 248 rooms In-hotel: 3 restaurants, gym, laundry service No credit cards.*

$–$$ ★ **Hoi Tak Hotel.** Popular with Chinese tour groups, this gleaming white tower offers first-rate views of the snowcapped Tian Shan Mountains. For the best views, request a room on the east side. Though not huge, standard rooms are tastefully appointed and have comfortable beds and ample closet space; Internet access is free. The lobby bar, while straight out of the '70s, make surprisingly good cocktails. **Pros:** staff speak English, rooms are good value. **Cons:** not near any attractions or good restaurants. *1 Dongfeng Lu, west side of People's Square 0991/232–2828 www.hoitakhotel.com 318 rooms, 38 suites In-room: safe, Ethernet. In-hotel: 7 restaurants, pool, gym, laundry service, refrigerator AE, MC, V.*

$–$$ **Sheraton.** The only foreign-run hotel in town, this reliable option opened in 2007 but the facilities are in not in as great shape as they should be. The lobby gleams and rooms are spacious, but the western-style food in the hotel's restaurants is not up to snuff. The pool is a lovely place to cool off after a day of sightseeing. **Pros:** keen staff, rooms have great bathrooms. **Cons:** inconvenient for Ürümqi's sights. ✉ *669 Youhao Bei Lu* ☎ *0991/699–9999* 🌐 *www.sheraton.com/Ürümqi* *420 rooms, 22 suites* *In-room: Internet. In-hotel: 4 restaurants, bar, gym, pool, laundry service, airport shuttle, minibar* *AE, MC, V.*

$–$$ **Yindu Hotel.** Xinjiang's finest hotel, the Yindu is testament to the influx of cash that has transformed Ürümqi over the past decade. The main drawback is that it's a couple of kilometers northwest of the city center. You may also be uneasy with the window between the shower and the bed, which the staff explains is "for your wedding night." **Pros:** comfortable rooms. **Cons:** bad location for exploring the sights. ✉ *39 Xibei Lu* ☎ *0991/458–0136* 🌐 *www.yinduhotel.com* *312 rooms* *In-room: safe. In-hotel: 6 restaurants, pool, gym, spa, laundry service, minibar* *AE, MC, V.*

NIGHTLIFE

As with most Chinese cities, every other block in Ürümqi is blighted by high-price karaoke parlors and blaring discos. But there are plenty of places to order a bottle of cold beer, and the best options are on Renmin Gongyuan Beijie where there is also a selection of gay bars.

★ The entertaining song and dance performance at the **International Grand Bazaar Banquet Performance Theater** (✉ *Jiefang Lu, 3 km [2 mi] south of the city center* ☎ *0991/855–5491* *Y168*) is preceded by a ho-hum buffet that unsuccessfully tries to capture the delights of Uyghur cuisine. Never mind the food, as this is your best chance to see Uyghur, Uzbek, Kazakh, Tajik, Tartar, and even Irish dancing all in one spectacular evening. Make reservations through your hotel.

Fubar (✉ *Renmin Gongyuan Beijie* ☎ *0991/584–4498* 🌐 *www.fubar.com.cn*) is the real thing: a tavern serving cold imported beer and authentic pub grub. The pizza is especially noteworthy as are the fish-and-chips. This is the best place in Ürümqi to relax after a day exploring the city. The foreign owners are happy to dispense free travel advice.

SHOPPING

The **International Grand Bazaar** (✉ *Jiefang Lu, 3 km [2 mi] south of the city center*) is the best place to go for Uyghur items like embroidered skullcaps, brightly colored carpets, and hand-carved knives. If it's inexpensive gifts you're after, you will find them here.

Xinjiang Antique Store (✉ *325 Jiefang Nan Lu, south of Renmin Lu* ☎ *0991/282–5161*) has a good selection of genuine antique Chinese bric-a-brac, including jade, jewelry, carpets, and porcelain. As all items come with a state-certified export certificate, you won't have to worry about getting your purchase through customs. A smaller branch is located inside the Xinjiang Autonomous Region Museum.

SIDE TRIPS FROM ÜRÜMQI

Fodor's Choice ★ **Heavenly Lake.** About a three-hour ride from Ürümqi is the not-to-be-missed lake, possibly the prettiest lake in China, surrounded by snow-sprinkled mountains. The water is crystal clear with a sapphire tint. In summer, white flowers dot the hillsides. Unfortunately, tourism has been leaving its ugly footprint. The lake's southern shore is crowded with tour groups posing for snapshots with Mount Bogda in the background. To better appreciate the lake's natural beauty, arrive before the hordes, or stay until after the last bus has departed.

Kazakh families still set up traditional felt tents along the shores of Heavenly Lake from early May to late October, bringing their horses, sheep, and cashmere goats. The Kazakh people have a long history as horse breeders and are known to be skilled riders.

■ TIP→ Most foreign visitors stay with the amiable Rashit (☎ *138/9964–1550* 🌐 *www.rashityurt.com*), who has been hosting tourists at his family yurt since 1980. For Y50, you get a spot in a cozy yurt and three freshly cooked if basic meals a day. They can also furnish horses and a guide for a day of riding around the lake. The sleeping quarters are communal, and there's no plumbing. However, you'll have a rewarding glimpse into the way your Kazakh hosts live.

From Ürümqi, day-tour buses (Y25 each way after bargaining plus Y100 entrance fee to the lake) to Heavenly Lake leave at 9:30 in the morning from a small street beside the north gate of People's Park *(Renmin Gongyuan)*. You'll have from about noon to 6 PM to explore the lake, arriving back in the city at 8 PM. Tickets—usually available up until the bus leaves—can be purchased near the buses.

TURPAN

2½–3 hrs (184 km [114 mi]) by bus southeast of Ürümqi

Turpan lies in a desert basin at the southern foot of the Heavenly Mountains. Part of the basin lies 505 feet below sea level, the hottest spot in China and the second-lowest point in the world after the Dead Sea. In summer, temperatures can soar to more than 50°C (120°F), so come prepared with lots of water and sunscreen.

Turpan's claim to fame is its location between the ruins of two spectacular ancient cities, Jiaohe and Gaochang. Most visitors don't linger in Turpan; the best five sites can easily be visited in a single day. But there are other attractions. Surrounded by some of the richest farmland in Xinjiang, Turpan's vineyards are famous for producing several varieties of candy-sweet raisins popular throughout China.

GETTING HERE AND AROUND

Too close to Ürümqi to have its own airport, Turpan is an inconvenient 60 km (38 mi) south of the nearest train station, in Daheyan. If you arrive by train, take a taxi (Y40) or a public bus (Y7.50) to reach the city. The easiest way to reach Ürümqi from Turpan is by bus (2½ hours). Buses leave every 20 minutes from 7:30 AM and 8:30 PM and cost Y40 one way. The terminal is in the center of town on the north side of Laocheng Lu. Leaving Turpan is more difficult than arriving: one bus daily departs at noon for Kashgar. For any other destination, you'll have to head back to Ürümqi.

TOURS

You could join an organized group tour around Turpan, but you'll likely spend too much time in annoying tourist traps. With a slightly more expensive taxi tour you can choose your own itinerary and spend hours roaming the ruins of Jiaohe and Gaochang. In the off-season you may be able to secure a taxi for the day for as little as Y150, although prices of Y250 are more common during the summer.

ESSENTIALS

Bus Contacts **Turpan Bus Station** (✉ *27 Laocheng Lu* ☎ *0995/852–2325*).

Train Contacts **Daheyan Train Station** (✉ *Huoche Zhan Lu, Daheyan* ☎ *0995/864–2233*).

Visitor and Tour Info **CITS** (✉ *Jiaotong Hotel, 125 Laocheng Lu* ☎ *0995/852–1352* 🌐 *www.xinjiangtour.com*).

EXPLORING TURPAN

Karez Irrigation System. The remarkable 2,000-year-old system allowed the desert cities of the Silk Road to flourish despite an unrelentingly arid environment. In the oasis cities of Turpan and Hami, 1,600 km (990 mi) of underground tunnels brought water—moved only by gravity—from melting snow at the base of the Heavenly Mountains. You can view the tunnels at several sites around the city. Most tour guides take visitors to the largely educational Karez Irrigation Museum. Despite being described as the "underground Great Wall," most visitors are completely underwhelmed by what are essentially narrow dirt tunnels. ✉ *888 Xincheng Lu, on the city's western outskirts* 🎫 *Y40* ⏲ *Daily 8–7.*

Sugong Mosque and the adjacent **Emin Tower** *(Emin Ta)* form Turpan's most recognizable image, often featured in tourist brochures. Built in 1777, it commemorates a military commander who suppressed a rebellion by a group of aristocrats. The 141-foot conical tower is elegantly spare, with bricks arranged in 15 patterns. The sunbaked roof of the mosque affords a view of the surrounding lush vineyards. Tours of the area often stop here, but if you've got a couple of hours you can visit on your own. Beware: the gate staff may force you to purchase a second ticket (Y20) to the adjoining "restored" residence of mosque founder Emin Hoja, but it's better skipped. This complex lies 4 km (2½ mi) from the city center at the southeast end of town. ✉ *Go east on Laocheng Lu, turn right on the last paved road before farmland, known as Qiu Nian Zhong Lu* 🎫 *Y50* ⏲ *Daily 8–8.*

AROUND TURPAN

★ **City of Gaochang.** The city ruins lie in a valley south of the Flaming Mountains. Legend has it that a group of soldiers stopped here in the 1st century BC on their way to Afghanistan, found that water was plentiful, and decided to stay. By the 7th century the city was the capital of the Kingdom of Gaochang, which ruled over 21 other towns, and by the 9th century the Uyghurs had moved into the area from Mongolia, establishing the Kingdom of Kharakojam. In the 14th century Mongols conquered and destroyed the kingdom, leaving only the ruins that can still be seen today. Only the city walls and a partially preserved monastery surrounded by muted, almost unrecognizable shapes remain, an eerie and haunting excursion into the pages of history. Despite repeated plundering of the site, in the early 1900s German archaeologists were able to unearth manuscripts, statues, and frescoes in superb condition. To make the best of your time here, take a donkey cart (time to use your bargaining skills!) to the monastery in the rear right corner; from there, you can walk back toward the entrance through the ruins. ✉ *30 km (19 mi) east of Turpan* 🎫 *Y40* ⏲ *Dawn–dusk.*

WORD OF MOUTH

"Turpan has the ancient ruins of two major cities, a well-sited if rather bare set of cave temples, and other sights. It is the lowest inland place after the Dead Sea."

—PeterN_H

Fodor's Choice ★ **City of Jiaohe.** On an island at the confluence of two rivers, these impressive ruins lie in the Yarnaz Valley west of Turpan. The city, established as a garrison during the Han Dynasty, was built on a high plateau, protected by the natural fortification of cliffs rising 100 feet above the rivers. Jiaohe was governed from the 2nd to the 7th century by the Kingdom of Gaochang and occupied later by Tibetans. Despite destruction in the 14th century by Mongol hordes, large fragments of actual streets and buildings remain, including a Buddhist monastery and Buddhist statues, a row of bleached pagodas, a 29-foot observation tower, and a prison. ✉ *8 km (5 mi) west of Turpan* 🎫 *Y40* ⏲ *Dawn–dusk.*

★ **Bezeklik Thousand Buddha Caves.** In a breathtaking valley inside the Flaming Mountains is this ancient temple complex, built between the 5th and 9th century by slaves whose entire lives went into the construction. Many of the fine examples of Buddhist sculpture and wall frescoes were destroyed after Islam came to the region in the 13th century. Other sculptures and frescoes, including several whole murals of Buddhist monks, were removed by 20th-century archaeologists like German Albert von Le Coq, who shipped his finds back to Berlin. Although they remain a feat of early engineering, the caves are in atrocious condition. Go just to see the site itself and the surrounding valley, which is magnificent. The views of the scorched, lunar landscape leading up to the site, which clings to one flank of a steep, scenic valley, make the trip worth the effort. Avoid the nearby Buddha Cave constructed in 1980 by a local artist; it isn't worth an additional Y20. ✉ *35 km (22 mi) east of Turpan* 🎫 *Y20* ⏲ *Dawn–dusk.*

WHERE TO EAT

Most visitors stick to the restaurants in and around the Turpan Hotel on Qingnian Lu, a pleasant side street shaded by grape vines. The bazaar across from the bus station is a good place to grab lunch for around Y5. A lively night market with rows of kebab and spicy hotpot stands is on Gaochang Lu, a 10-minute walk north from the Turpan Hotel, next to the huge public square and near the China Post building.

¢ AMERICAN **John's Information Café.** Part of a small family-run chain that operates in destinations along the Silk Road, his popular tourist hangout is far from authentic, but people flock here for the familiar Western choices and rock-solid travel advice. They can also rent bikes and wash laundry. *Qingnian Lu, rear of the Turpan Hotel 0998/258–1186 johncafe.net No credit cards.*

¢ NORTHERN CHINESE **Muslim Restaurant.** Like most hotel restaurants in the region, this one is poorly lighted and lacks ambience, but it does have a hearty variety of standard Uyghur dishes: lamb, noodles, and vegetables. *Turpan Hotel, 2 Qingnian Nan Lu No phone No credit cards.*

WHERE TO STAY

¢ **Jiaotong Hotel.** This budget option isn't a bad place to stay, despite noise from the bus station in the rear and the bazaar across the street. The on-site travel agency makes arranging tours a snap, although the staff can be a bit pushy. If you come to Turpan in the off-season, a deluxe suite with a small balcony overlooking the bazaar can be had for as little as Y200. **Pros:** bargain twin rooms (Y80), convenient location for early buses. **Cons:** unattractive and slightly dusty lobby. *230 Laocheng Lu, next to the bus station 0995/853–1320 67 rooms In-hotel: restaurant No credit cards.*

¢ **Turpan Hotel.** This study in basic geometry, covered in white tile, is the best lodging in town. That isn't saying much, however. Rooms are relatively clean and large. The Muslim Restaurant is quite good, and the gift shops are handy. Even if you're not staying here, the indoor swimming pool—open only in the summer—is a good place to cool off after a day in the desert sun, though the water looks a little grubby. Admission is Y20 per person. **Pros:** usually offers good discounts, friendly staff. **Cons:** if you can't get a discount, better values are available elsewhere. *2 Qingnian Nan Lu, south of Laocheng Lu 0995/856–8888 219 rooms, 5 suites In-hotel: 3 restaurants, pool, gym, laundry service V.*

KASHGAR

24 hrs (1,175 km [729 mi]) by train southwest of Ürümq or 1½ hours by plane.

Kashgar, the westernmost city in China, is closer to Baghdad than Beijing. More than 3,400 km (2,100 mi) west of the capital, the city has been a center of trade between China and the outside world for at least 2,000 years. Today, Kashgar is a hub for merchants coming in over the Khunjerab Pass from Pakistan and the Torugart Pass from Kyrgyzstan. When these two treacherous mountain passes are open between May 1 and October 30, Kashgar becomes a particularly colorful city, abuzz not only with curious Western tourists but also with visitors from every corner of Central Asia.

Despite an increasing Han presence in central Kasghar (symbolized by one of the largest Mao statues in the country), the city is still overwhelmingly Uyghur. A great deal of modernization has taken place here since the railway from Ürumqi arrived in 1999, yet parts of Kashgar remain in a time warp. Only a few blocks from newly built karaoke parlors and car dealerships, you can still find blacksmiths, bakers, and cobblers. Much of the city's Uyghur architecture has been demolished, but there are still some traditional houses with ornately painted balconies, as well as large remaining sections of the old city. Most visitors come to Kasghar for the amazing Sunday Market, the largest bazaar in Central Asia and one of the best photo-ops in all of China.

GETTING HERE AND AROUND

Daunted by the long train journey from Ürümqi, many tourists headed for Kasghar travel by air. The airport is 13 km (8 mi) north of the city center; a taxi to or from your hotel shouldn't cost more than Y30, and minibus will drop you off at your hotel for Y10. Trains between Ürümqi and Kashgar (24 or 28 hours) depart twice daily; the slow train is half the price of the fast train, but you'll have to do without air-conditioning. The station is 10 km (6 mi) east of town, not far from the livestock market. Taxis from here cost about Y15. Kasghar's long-distance bus station is just east of People's Park in the center of town, although many buses arriving in the city will stop somewhere less convenient to drop you off.

TOURS

Kasghar is a tourist-friendly city, so you shouldn't have any trouble arranging tours. Uyghur Tour and Travel Center (also known as Abdul's), in the lobby of the Overseas Chinese Hotel, opposite the Seman Hotel, offers a "money-back guarantee." It has received high marks from travelers for the past five years. A day-tour of sites within Kashgar will cost about Y400, not including admission tickets. If you're interested in spending a night in the area's only 1,000-star hotel—the Taklamakan Desert—the agency can arrange an all-inclusive overnight camel trek for Y850 per person.

ESSENTIALS

Air Contacts Kashgar Airport (✉ *13 km (8 mi) north of the city center* ☎ *0998/282–3204*).

Bus Contacts Kashgar Bus Station (✉ *Tiannan Lu, on the east side of People's Park* ☎ *0998/282–9673*).

Police Kashgar PSB (✉ *139 Yumulakexiehai Lu, south of the Qinibagh Hotel* ☎ *0998/282–2814*).

Medical Assistance Number One People's Hospital (✉ *Jichang Lu* ☎ *0998/296–2750*).

Train Contacts Kashgar Train Station (✉ *Kashi Huoche Zhan* ☎ *0998/256–1298*).

Visitor and Tour Info CITS (✉ *Qinibagh Hotel, 144 Seman Lu* ☎ *0998/298–3156* 🌐 *www.xinjiangtour.com*). **Uyghur Tour and Travel Center** (✉ *Overseas Chinese Hotel, 170 Seman Lu, at Renmin Lu* ☎ *0998/220–4012* 🌐 *www.silkroadinn.com*).

EXPLORING KASHGAR

❶ **Id Kah Mosque.** Start your tour of the city with a visit to the center of Muslim life in Kasghar. One of the largest mosques in China, the ornate structure of yellow bricks is the result of many extensions and

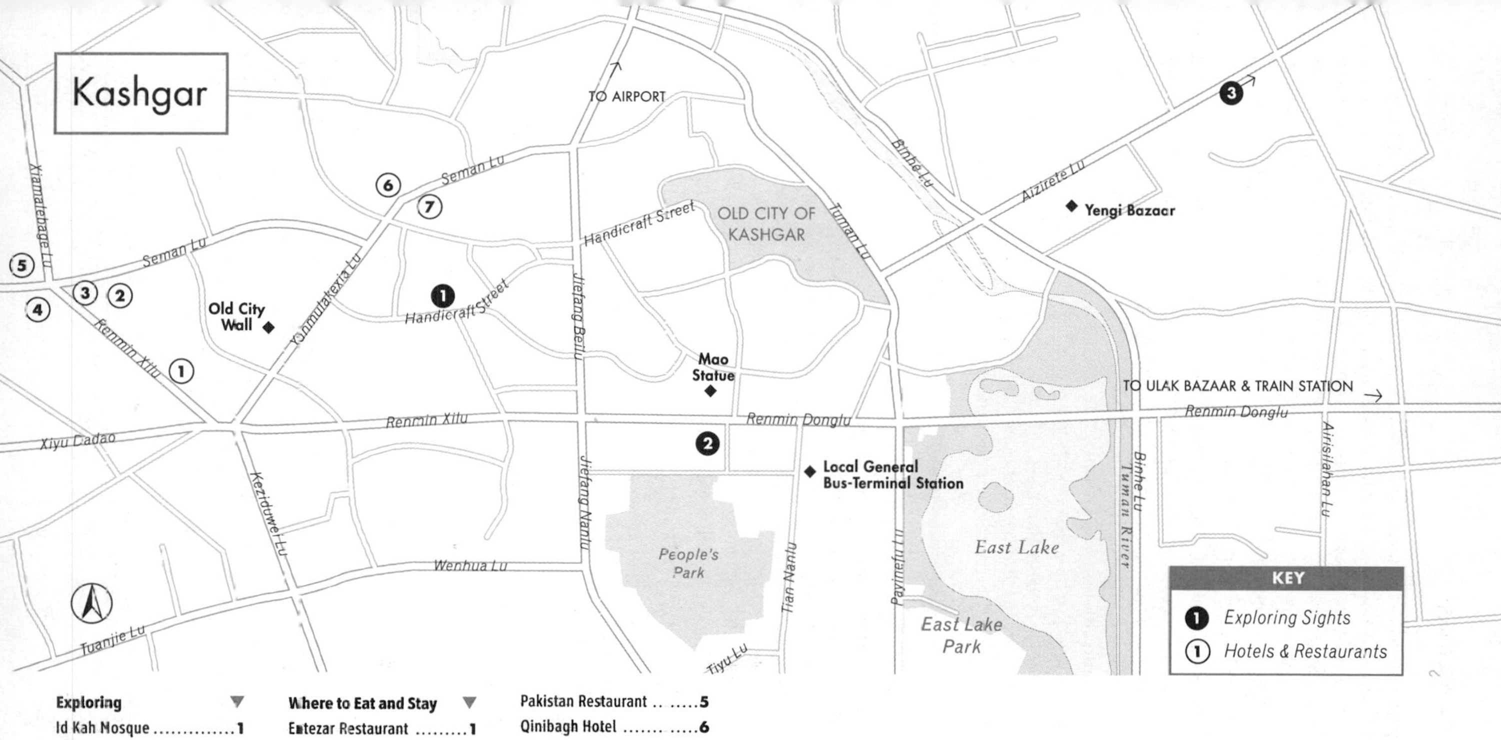

Exploring

Id Kah Mosque 1
People's Square 2
Tomb of Abakh Hoja 3

Where to Eat and Stay

Entezar Restaurant 1
Jalawan 3
Karakorum Cafe 7
Pakistan Restaurant 5
Qinibagh Hotel 6
Seman Hotel 4
Xiao Bei Dou 2

renovations to the original mosque, built in 1442 as a prayer hall for the ruler of Kashgar. The main hall has a ceiling with fine wooden carvings and precisely 100 carved wooden columns. When services aren't being held, you are free to wander the quiet shaded grounds and even to enter the prayer hall. As this is an active site of worship, visitors should dress modestly. ✉ *Ai Tiga'er Guangchang* ☎ *No Phone* 🎫 *Y20* ⏲ *Dawn–dusk.*

❸ **Tomb of Abakh Hoja.** About 5 km (3 mi) northeast of the city lies one of the most sacred sites in Xinjiang. The sea-green tiled hall that houses the tomb—actually about two dozen tombs—is part of a massive complex of sacred Islamic structures built around 1640. Uyghurs named the tomb and surrounding complex after Abakh Hoja, an Islamic missionary believed to be a descendant of Mohammed who ruled Kashgar and outlying regions in the 17th century. Excavations of the glazed-brick tombs indicate that the first occupant was Abakh Hoja's father, who is buried here along with Abakh Hoja and many of their descendants.

The Han, who prefer to emphasize the site's historical connection to their dynastic empire, call it the Tomb of the Fragrant Concubine. When the grandniece of Abakh Hoja was chosen as concubine by the Qing ruler Qianlong in Beijing, Uyghur legend holds that she committed suicide rather than submitting to the emperor. In the Han story, she dutifully went to Beijing and spent 30 years in the emperor's palace, then asked to be buried in her homeland. Either way, her alleged tomb was excavated in the 1980s, and found to be empty. The tomb is a bit difficult to locate, so take a taxi. ✉ *Off of Aizirete Lu, 2 km (1 mi) east of the Sunday Bazaar* ☎ *No phone* 🎫 *Y30* ⏲ *Daily 9–9.*

❷ **People's Square.** If you happen to forget which country Kashgar is located in, chances are you aren't standing in this square. A statue of Mao Zedong—one of the largest in China—stands with his right arm raised in perpetual salute. The statue is evidence of an unspoken rule in China that directly relates the size of a Mao tribute to its distance from Beijing; the only Mao statue larger than this one is located in Tibet. ✉ *Renmin Lu between Lu and Tian Lu* ☎ *No phone.*

WHERE TO EAT

¢–$ NORTHERN CHINESE ★

✕ **Entezar Restaurant.** Frequented by locals and outfitted with wooden paneling and chandeliers, Entezar is perhaps the most formal of Kashgar's Uighur restaurants. It offers a complete range of the great cuisine, and the menu is translated into English, including helpful descriptions of each dish. For those tired of typical Uyghur fare, Muslim-friendly stir-fry dishes are also available. Alcohol is not allowed on the premises. ✉ *320 Renmin Xilu, southeast of the Seman Hotel* ☎ *0998/258–3555* 💳 *No credit cards.*

¢–$ NORTHERN CHINESE

✕ **Jalawan.** It's very easy to join the crowds of locals relaxing at this restaurant especially underneath the (admittedly) fake trellises of grapes with tables grouped around a fountain. The staff will hand you an English language menu though prices are a few RMB higher than on the Chinese language menu! But when it's all so cheap you can't complain too much. Try the *lao hu cai,* or tiger salad, an evocatively named dish, or cucumber chilies and tomatoes, the pilaf with a cooling bowl of yoghurt. ✉*Seman Lu, on the roundabout opposite the Seman Hotel* ☎*0998/258–1001* ▭*No credit cards.*

WORD OF MOUTH

"You definitely don't need a headscarf for just walking around the city, even in Kashgar, and the mosques should provide you with one if they require it inside. On the other hand, a scarf is a good idea regardless because of the wind and sand in places like Dunhuang. I'd suggest you bring one." —rkkwan.

¢–$ AMERICAN **Karakorum Café.** If it's Western food you're craving, head straight to this brand new expat-run cafè—after weeks of eating noodles, you'll feel it's a veritable breath of fresh air on the Silk Road. The banana smoothies go down well, as does the roast eggplant focaccia. The friendly manager will give you travel advice if asked, or you could just relax in the bright and airy cafè. ✉*87 Seman Lu, opposite the Qinibagh Hotel's entrance gate* ☎*0998/258–2345* ▭*No credit cards.*

¢ MIDDLE EASTERN **Pakistan Restaurant.** Foreign restaurants are rare in Kasghar, so this dirt-cheap curry joint is a welcome addition. This is where the city's Pakistani residents wile away their evenings playing cards and sipping tea. There's an English menu, but its function seems to be primarily illustrative—we visited twice and got the wrong dishes both times, but in both cases they were delicious! Particularly good were the chickpea and beef and potato curries. There are no chopsticks here, as everything is scooped-up using delicious *roti* flat bread. Hot chai tea served with milk is the best way to wash down your meal. This restaurant's sign is covered by a large tree, so look for the tree instead. ✉*Seman Lu, opposite the Seman Hotel's rear gate* ☎*No phone* ▭*No credit cards.*

¢–$$ SICHUAN **Xiao Bei Dou.** When you've grown tired of mutton, head here for the best Sichuan-style dishes in Kashgar. Classic selections like sweet-and-sour pork (*tangcu liji*), chicken with peanuts (*gongbao jiding*), and scallion pancakes (*conghuabing*) are all well prepared. There's plenty of cold beer in the refrigerator, and the second-floor covered terrace is perfect on a warm summer evening. An English menu is available, but the selection is limited. ✉*285 Seman Lu, east of the Seman Hotel* ☎*No phone* ▭*No credit cards.*

WHERE TO STAY

¢ **Qinibagh Hotel.** Of Kasghar's two popular hotels, the Qinibagh is in much better shape. Located on the site of the former British consulate, this hotel has an interesting history. Constructed in 1908, the consulate building—now an attractive Uyghur restaurant—was home to diplomat extraordinaire Sir George McCartney and his wife for 26 years. Don't expect historic rooms though—the hotel buildings are '60s-style monstrosities. There are branches of CITS and John's Information Café, two travel resources, on the premises. Dorm rooms are a great bargain and are set around a reasonably attractive open-air courtyard. **Pros:** easy to find, good place to meet other foreigners. **Cons:** a little tatty around the edges. ✉*93 Seman Lu, northwest of Id Kah Mosque* ☎*0998/298–2103* 📠*0998/298–2299* *In-hotel: 4 restaurants, bar, laundry service, refrigerator, elevator* ▭*V.*

¢ **Seman Hotel.** Built in 1890 as the Russian consulate, this edifice served as a center of political intrigue for many years. The oldest wing of the hotel is the original consulate, where fans of the "Great Game" can stay in musty suites decorated with luxurious rugs and old furniture. The hotel's newer rooms range from comfortable to dilapidated, so be sure to look at a few before you decide. The worst rooms are adjacent to a large traffic circle; nicer ones surround a pleasant courtyard in the rear. The hotel is very popular with backpackers who come for the Y20 beds packed into dorm-style rooms. Travel agencies are clustered around the lobby. **Pros:** near some excellent restaurants, competitive prices from the lobby tour agencies. **Cons:** musty bathrooms in the cheaper rooms and dorms. ✉*170 Seman Lu, at Renmin Lu* ☎*0998/258–2129* 🖷*0998/258–2150* ♁*In-hotel: 3 restaurants, laundry service* ▭*No credit cards.*

SHOPPING

Kashgar's famous **Sunday Market** consists of two bazaars with a distance of almost 10 km (6 mi) between them. The **Yengi Bazaar** on Aizilaiti Lu, about 1½ km (1 mi) northeast of the city center, is open every day, but on Sunday the surrounding streets overflow with vendors hawking everything from boiled sheep's heads to trendy sunglasses. In the covered section you can bargain for decorative knives, embroidered fabrics, and all sorts of Uyghur-themed souvenirs. Behind the bazaar, rows of sleepy donkeys nod off in the bright sunlight, their carts lined up neatly beside them. For the best photos, however, you'll need to head over to the **Ulak Bazaar,** a 10-minute taxi ride to the east. Essentially a livestock market, farmers here tug recalcitrant sheep through the streets, scarf-shrouded women preside over heaps of red eggs, and old Uyghur men squat over baskets of chickens, haggling over the virtues and vices of each hapless hen. In the market for a camel? You can buy one here. On the outskirts of the market you can get an old-world-style straight-razor shave from a Uyghur barber or grab a bowl of *laghman* noodles, knowing that it's flavored with meat that is very, very fresh.

Running alongside the Id Kah Mosque is a narrow lane known as **Handicraft Street.** Walking in either direction you'll find merchants selling everything from bright copper kettles to wedding chests to brass sleigh bells. At the **Uyghur Musical Instruments Workshop** (✉*272 Kumdarwaza Rd.* ☎*0998/283–5378*) you can watch the owner or his apprentice working on Uyghur string instruments—stretching snakeskin or inlaying tiny bits of shell to make a Uyghur guitar called a *ravap.*

SIDE TRIPS FROM KASGHAR

The **Karakorum Highway,** a spectacular road winding across some of the most dramatic and inhospitable terrain in the world, traces one of the major ancient silk routes, starting in Kashgar and leading south for 2,100 km (1,300 mi) through three great mountain ranges over the Khunjerab Pass into Pakistan.

Fodor'sChoice ★ **Karakul Lake,**,Kālākùlēi Hú. Six hours south of Kasghar, having followed the Gez River valley deep into the heart of the Pamir Mountains, the highway passes alongside this picturesque lake. At an elevation of

3,800 meters (12,500 feet), this crystal-blue jewel of a lake is dominated on either side by stunning snowcapped mountains, including the 7,800-meter (25,600-foot) peak of **Muztagata**, the "Father of the Ice Mountains." Arriving at the lake, you'll practically be assaulted by would-be-hosts on camelback, horseback, and motorcycle. Avoid the expensive yurts near the entrance and head back along the road to the more secluded yurts, where it is possible to stay with a local family for Y50 including (basic) food. You can rent your own yurt for Y40. Standard food will be limited to bread and butter, tea, and fried rice dishes, but there is an expensive Chinese restaurant. Toilet facilities in this area count as some of the worst in China, and there are no showers, but the area's beauty makes it worthwhile. Tour the lake via camel, horse, or motorbike, or just walk around, which will take about three hours. Bring warm clothing even in the summer, as it can be downright chilly: during our visit in July, we were applying sunscreen in the morning and battling sleet in the afternoon.

Any travel agent can arrange tours to Karakul Lake, but most people make the breathtaking journey by public bus. Buses headed for Tashkurgan, two hours south of the lake, leave Kashgar's long-distance bus station every morning at 10 AM. You'll have to pay the full price of Y43 for your ticket even though you're not traveling the full distance. Bring your passport or you'll be turned back at a border checkpoint in Gezcun. To catch the bus, wait by the side of the highway and flag it down—the bus returning to Kasghar from Tashkurgan passes the lake between 11 AM and 1 PM. A seat should only cost Y40, but enterprising drivers will demand Y50. Either way, the bus is much cheaper than private tours, which will set you back about Y500 per day.

ENGLISH	PINYIN	CHINESE
SHAANXI	SHĂNXI	陕西
XIAN	Xī'ān	西安
Banpo Matriarchal Clan Village	Bànpō bówùguǎn	半坡博物馆
Bell Tower	Zhōnglóu	钟楼
Big Wild Goose Pagoda	Dàyàntǎ	大雁塔
Culture Street	Wénhuà jiē	文化街
Delhi Durbar	Yìndù fànguǎn	印度饭馆
Drum Tower	Gǔlóu	鼓楼
Famen Temple	Fǎménsì	法门寺
Forest of Stone Tablets Museum	Bēilín bówùguǎn	碑林博物馆
Great Mosque	Dàqīngzhēn sì	大清真寺
GZ Bar	GZ Jiǔba	GZ 酒吧
Hai An Xian Internet Bar	Hǎi'àn Xī'ān wǎngba	海岸西安网吧
Huaqing Hot Springs	Huáqīnghí	华清池
Ibis Xian	Xī'ān Yíbìsī jiǔdiàn	西安宜必思酒店
Shaanxi History Museum	Shǎnxī Lìshǐ bówùguǎn	陕西历史博物馆
Small Goose Pagoda	Xiǎoyàntǎ	小雁塔
South Gate	Nánmén	南门
Terracotta Warriors Museum	Bīngmǎyǒng bówùguǎn	兵马俑博物馆
Tomb of the Qin Emperor	Qínshǐhuánglíng	秦始皇陵
Xiangzimen Youth Hostel	Xiāngzimén Qīngnián lǚxíngshè	湘子门 青年旅行舍
Xianyang City Museum	Xiányáng shì bówùguǎn	咸阳市博物馆
GANSU	GĀNSÙ	甘肃
LANZHOU	Lánzhōu	兰州
Gansu Provincial Museum	Gānsù shěng bówùguǎn	甘肃省博物馆
Labrang Monastery	Lābǔléngsì	拉卜楞寺
Lanzhou East Bus Station	Lánzhōu Dōng qìchēzhàn	兰州东汽车站
Lanzhou South Bus Station	Lánzhōu Nán qìchēzhàn	兰州南汽车站
Lanzhou Train Station	Lánzhōu huǒchēzhàn	兰州火车站
Lanzhou West Bus Station	Lánzhōu Xī qìchēzhàn	兰州西汽车站
Lanzhou Zhongchuan Airport	Lánzhōu Zhōngchuān fēijīchǎng	兰州中川飞机场
Mountain of the White Pagoda Park	Báitǎshān gōngyuán	白塔山公园
Thousand Buddha Temple and Grottoes	Bǐnglíngsì shíkū	炳灵寺石窟
DUNHUANG	Dūnhuáng	敦煌

ENGLISH	PINYIN	CHINESE
Dunhuang Airport	Dūnhuáng fēijīchǎng	敦煌飞机场
Dunhuang Bus Station	Dūnhuáng qìchēzhàn	敦煌汽车站
Dunhuang Museum	Dūnhuáng bówùguǎn	敦煌博物馆
Mogao Grottoes	Mògāokū	莫高窟
Singing Sand Mountain	Míngshāshān	鸣沙山
QINGHAI	QĪNGHǍI	青海
XINING	Xīníng	西宁
Bird Island	Niǎo dǎo	鸟岛
Black Tent	Hēise Zhàngpeng	黑色帐篷
Casa Mia Italian restaurant	Yìdàlì Fànguǎn	意大利饭馆
Jianguo Road Wholesale Market	Jiànguó lù pīfā shìchǎng	建国路批发市场
Kumbum Monastery	Tǎ'ěrsì	塔尔寺
Lete Hostel	Xīníng Lìtǐ Qīngnián lǚshè	西宁理体青年旅舍
North Monastery	Běichán Sì	北禅寺
Qinghai Lake	Qīnghǎihú	青海湖
Shuijin Xiang Market	Shuǐjǐn xiàng shāngchǎng	水井巷商场
Xining Bus Station	Xīníng qìchēzhàn	西宁汽车站
Xining Caojiabao Airport	Xīníng Cáojiābǎo	西宁曹家堡飞机场
Xining Train Station	Xīníng huǒchēzhàn	西宁火车站
XINJIANG	XĪNJIĀNG	新疆
ÜRÜMQI	Wūlǔmùqí	乌鲁木齐
Karakorum Café	Kālākùli Kāfēitīng	卡拉库里咖啡厅
Bell Tower Square	Zhōnglóu guǎngchǎng	钟楼广场
Bezeklik Thousand Buddha Caves	Bòzīkèlǐkè qiānfódòng	柏孜克里克千佛洞
Cornfield Youth Hostel	Màitián Qīngnián lǚxíngshè	麦田青年旅行舍
Heavenly Lake	Tiānchí hú	天池湖
Id Kah Mosque	Àitígǎ'ér Qīngzhēn sì	艾提尕尔清真寺
International Grand Bazaar	Dàbāzā	大巴扎
Jalawan	ābùdūkādíěr	阿布都卡迪尔
Karakul Lake	Kālākùlēi hú	喀拉库勒湖
Karez Irrigation Museum	Kǎnérjǐng bówùguǎn	坎儿井博物馆
Kasghar	Kāshí	喀什
Kasghar Train Station	Kāshí huǒchēzhàn	喀什火车站
Kashgar Airport	Kāshí fēijīchǎng	喀什飞机场
Nianzigou Bus Station	Niǎnzǐgōu qìchēzhàn	碾子沟汽车站

ENGLISH	PINYIN	CHINESE
Old City of Gaochang	Gāochāng gùchéng	高昌故城
Old City of Jiaohe	Jiāohé gùchéng	交河故城
Orda Restaurant	Ěrdá	尔达
People's Park	Rénmín gōngyuán	人民公园
People's Square	Rénmín guǎngchǎng	人民广场
Red Mountain Park	Hóngshān gōngyuán	红山公园
Shaanxi	Shǎnxī	陕西
Sheraton	Xǐláidēng Wūlǔmùqí jiǔdiàn	喜来登乌鲁木齐酒店
Sugong Mosque & Emin Tower	Émǐn tǎ	额敏塔
Tomb of Abakh Hoja	Xiāngfēi mù	香妃墓
Turpan	Tǔlǔfān	吐鲁番
Ürümqi Airport	Wūlǔmùqí fēijīchǎng	乌鲁木齐飞机场
Ürümqi South Bus Station	Wūlǔmùqí nán qìchēzhàn	乌鲁木齐南汽车站
Ürümqi Train Station	Wūlǔmùqí huǒchēzhàn	乌鲁木齐火车站
Xinjiang Autonomous Region Museum	Xīnjiāng zìzhìqū bówùguǎn	新疆自治区博物馆

Tibet

THE ROOFTOP OF THE WORLD

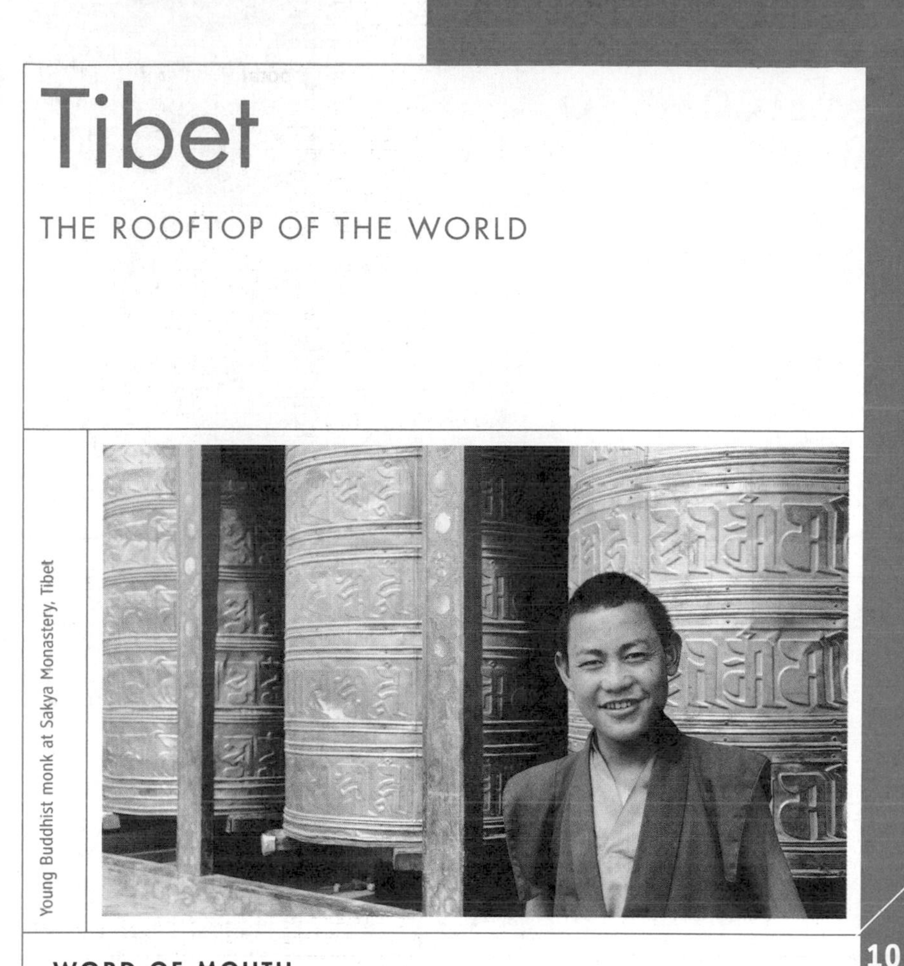

Young Buddhist monk at Sakya Monastery, Tibet

WORD OF MOUTH

"My advice is to stay on top of the permit situation on a day-to-day basis before you go. If you go in a group, you shouldn't run into any problems as long as you make sure that they are a reputable operator."

—travelguy120

www.fodors.com/forums

WELCOME TO TIBET

Gyantse Monastery.

TOP REASONS TO GO

★ **Barkhor:** Tibetan Buddhism's holiest pilgrimage circuit, the Barkhor is both the heart of old Lhasa and one of the liveliest people-watching spots in all of China.

★ **Potala Palace:** Towering over Lhasa, this still-impressive palace of the Dalai Lamas was once the world's tallest structure.

★ **Ganden Monastery:** The most remote of the capital's three great monasteries, Ganden offers stunning views of the Lhasa River Valley and surrounding Tibetan farmland from a height of 14,764 feet.

★ **Gyantse Dzong:** The site of fierce fighting between Tibetan and British troops in 1904, this fortress is one of the few remaining symbols of Tibetan military power.

★ **Everest Base Camp:** Stand in awe beneath the world's tallest mountain.

XINJIANG UYGUR ZIZHIQU
QINGSHAN GAOYUA (TIBETAN PLATEAU)
Wujang
Zhaxigang
XIZANG ZIZHIQU (TIBET AUTONOMO REGION)
GANGDISE SHAN
Dongco
Barga
INDIA
HIMALAYA
Nyima
Coqen
NEPAL
Everest Base Camp
Lhaze
Shigat
Tingri
4
Mt. Everest (Mt. Qomolangma)
0 100 mi
0 100 km

1 Lhasa. Despite the city's rapid modernization, Lhasa is still one of China's must-visit destinations. From the crowded back alleys of the Barkhor to the imposing heights of the Potala Palace, a mix of Westerners, local Tibetans, Nepalis, and Han Chinese give this city an atmosphere unlike any other place in the world.

2 Gyantse. Past the sapphire waters of Yamdrok Tso and endless fields of golden highland barley, this small city is the gateway to southern Tibet and the Himalayas. An abandoned fortress high above town is testament to the area's former military importance, while the unique architecture at Pelkor Chode Monastery speaks to the city's history as a melting pot of religious denominations.

Camp in the shadow of Mt. Everest.

GETTING ORIENTED

The Tibetan plateau is more than twice the size of France, sandwiched between two Himalayan ridges whose peaks reach an altitude of nearly 9 km (5½ mi). With the opening of the rail line and significantly improved roads, Tibet is more accessible than ever. Lhasa is the best base from which to take day-trips to the fertile Kyi-chu Valley or longer jaunts into the southwestern highlands of Tsang to visit Gyantse, Shigatse, and the Everest region. Every hotel and tour operator can arrange four-wheel-drive jeeps with a driver and/or a guide. Tibet is currently undergoing massive infrastructure improvements, and many roads that were once as bumpy as the steep mountain passes have been flattened into perfect stretches of blacktop. You'll still have to use a significant number of dirt roads, however.

3 Shigatse. Tibet's second-largest city, Shigatse, is the traditional capital of the Tsang region and home to the Panchen Lama's seat of power at Tashilhunpo Monastery. The ruined fortress on a hill above town has been rebuilt based on old photographs, but its concrete construction stands as one of the most glaring symbols of the modern world's encroachment on an ancient and sacred land.

4 Everest. You may have trouble breathing when you first see the majestic peaks of the Himalayas, and not only because of the high altitude. The roof of the world is a spectacular place, with roaring snow-melt rivers feeding Tibetan farms and fields of wildflowers below.

TIBET PLANNER

When to go

Choosing when to visit Tibet is a matter of balancing your tolerance for extreme weather with your tolerance for tourist hordes. The busiest months are July and August, but pleasant weather is common from May through October. If you come at the beginning or end of the high season you'll have plenty of breathing space to take in the golden roofs of Tibet's monasteries and the icy peaks of the Himalayas. You may want to schedule your trip to coincide with one of Tibet's colorful celebrations including the Birth of Buddha Festival (end of May), the Holy Mountain Festival (end of July), the Yogurt Festival (August), and the Bathing Festival (September). If you travel to Tibet in the off-season, many hotels and restaurants may be closed. Whenever you visit, warm clothing, sunglasses, and sunscreen are essentials for the high-altitude climate.

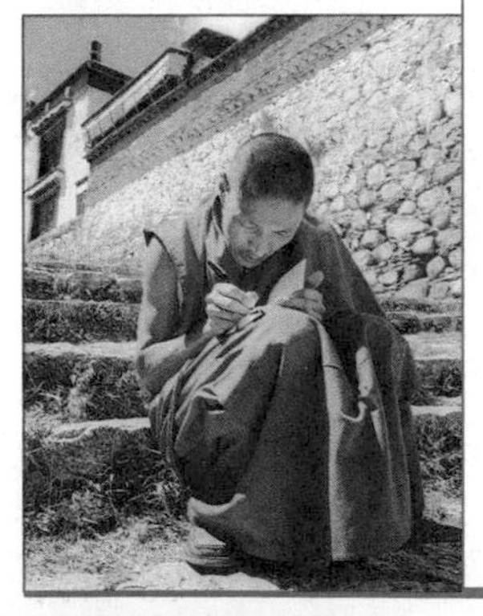

Lhasa Express

One of history's most audacious engineering projects, the rail line to Lhasa began construction in 2001 after more than 30 years of delays. Chairman Mao first proposed the railroad in the 1960s along with other infrastructure projects now being realized, like the massive Three Gorges Dam on the Yangtze River. The list of technical challenges confronting the rail line was daunting, as more than 966 km (600 mi) of track needed to be constructed at an altitude of more than 13,000 feet, topping out at Tangula Pass near 17,000 feet. Much of the track rests on semifrozen and constantly shifting permafrost. The line also crosses through six protected environmental reserves, home to endangered species like the Tibetan antelope and snow leopard.

Swiss engineers, experts on frozen terrain, said the project was impossible, but the Chinese government was having none of it. The first passenger train, carrying President Hu Jintao and a host of other dignitaries, rolled into Lhasa's shiny new station on July 1, 2006. The cultural implications of the railroad to ethnic Tibetans—already a minority in their own land—are obvious. The migration of Han Chinese will continue to expand as the traditional Tibetan way of life in many areas rapidly declines in the face of modernization. Politically, the railroad is another firm sign from Beijing that they have no intention of ever letting Tibet break off into a separate political entity; in fact, plans to extend the railway to Tibet's second-largest city, Shigatse, and over the Himalayas to Kathmandu in Nepal are already being developed.

However, the railway isn't completely negative for the locals. A large number of Tibetans make their livelihood from tourism in the region, which has increased dramatically since the opening of the line. The relatively cheap, quick, and comfortable ride by train has also made it possible for Tibetans working and studying in far away parts of China to return home and visit their families during holidays, something that was nearly impossible when the only practical way to reach Lhasa was an expensive flight.

Passports and Visas

A visa valid for the People's Republic of China is required. You will also need to get a Tibet Tourism Bureau travel permit, which is usually arranged by the travel agent who books your tour or transportation to Lhasa. Travel by train without a permit is possible, but you do so at your own risk. At the time of this writing, no independent travel to Tibet was permitted; only individuals booked on tours to Tibet could travel there. These restrictions change depending on the political situation in Tibet, so it is best to contact travel agents, tour groups or hotels in the region for information on current policies.

The Chinese government would always prefer that you join a guided tour. Groups find it easier to secure a TTB permit as well as permits to visit sites outside of Lhasa. A typical package includes flights to Lhasa and a guide to take you to a hotel. You will then be on your own until your departure, when the guide will take you back to the airport. There is no limit, aside from the validity of your Chinese visa, to the length of time you can stay in Tibet, except when the government decides not to allow foreigners in.

DINING AND LODGING PRICE CATEGORIES IN YUAN

¢	$	$$	$$$	$$$$
Restaurants				
under Y25	Y25–Y49	Y50–Y99	Y100–Y150	over Y150
Hotels				
under Y200	Y200–Y349	Y350–Y499	Y500–Y999	over Y1,000

Restaurant prices are for a main course. There is no sales tax in China and tipping is not expected. Hotel prices unless noted are for a standard double room, including taxes.

Cultural Conflict

No matter how remote and underdeveloped Tibet may seem, it's still a tempting destination for the more than one billion people in China's eastern half. As the region's infrastructure is built up and its small towns turn into cities, people looking for job opportunities gravitate here.

Tibetan exile groups accuse the Chinese government of actively encouraging Han migration into the region, but the continued influx of ethnic Chinese (Han) into Tibet is also the result of people escaping the east to look for opportunities in the west. Now, Han Chinese almost certainly outnumber locals living in the Tibet Autonomous Region (TAR).

Still, while The Barkhor in Lhasa and the area around Tashilhunpo Monastery in Shigatse are Tibetan islands in otherwise increasingly Han cities, the rest of Tibet remains relatively free of Chinese influence.

The increased presence of Han has created frictions and led to allegations that the new immigrants practice discrimination in their businesses because of cultural and linguistic differences. Some of this friction led to violent anti-Han riots in March 2008 during protests against the central government's influence over religious practice in the region.

By Michael D. Manning

TIBET IS ALL YOU'VE HEARD and everything you've imagined: a land of intense sunshine and towering snowcapped peaks, where crystal-clear rivers and sapphire lakes irrigate terraced fields of golden highland barley. The Tibetan people are extremely religious, viewing their daily toil and the harsh environment surrounding them as challenges along the path to life's single goal, the attainment of spiritual enlightenment. The region's richly decorated monasteries, temples, and palaces—including the Potala Palace—were not constructed by forced labor, but by laborers and artisans who donated their entire lives to the accumulation of good karma.

The death, destruction, and cultural denigration of Tibet that accompanied the Chinese invasion in the early 1950s changed this land forever, as did the Cultural Revolution in the late 1960s. Yet the people remain resilient. Colorfully dressed pilgrims still bring their offerings of yak butter to the temples, and monks work with zeal to repair the damage done to their monasteries. Many young Tibetans, attracted by the wealth and convenience brought by development, have abandoned their ancestors' traditional ways. Coca-Cola, fast food, and pulsing techno music are popular in Lhasa. Yet it would be a mistake to think that the changes have lessened Tibet's allure as a travel destination.

REGIONAL TOURS

Foreign travelers are required by law to book a tour when securing a Tibet Travel Bureau permit. Enforcement of this rule has increased in the wake of riots in Lhasa in March 2008. Now flexibility has disappeared. The five-day trip to Everest Base Camp (Y2,500–Y5,000, depending on group size) is the most popular tour, but others include the two-day trip to Nam Tso Lake (Y750–Y2,000), the two-day trip to Samye Monastery (Y800–Y2,500), and the 12-day trip to sacred Mount Kailash (Y5,250–Y14,000). One reliable local company is Tibet FIT Travel.

Agents should advise you on the latest changes to travel restrictions and permit requirements. Typically the cost of an organized tour for a week runs $1,000 to $2,000 per person. When booking a tour, be sure to get confirmation in writing with details about your hotel and meal arrangements.

Contacts Tibet FIT Travel aka Xizang Gaoyuan Sanke Guanli Jiedaizhongxin (✉ *Inside the Snowlands Hotel, 4 Zangyiyuan Lu, Lhasa* ☎ *0891/634-9239* 🌐 *www.tibetfit.com*).

LHASA

14 hrs by train south of Golmud, 48 hrs by train southwest of Beijing. 2 hrs by plane west of Chengdu, 5 hrs by plane southwest of Beijing.

The capital of Tibet, Lhasa is a treasure trove of monasteries, palaces, and temples. Geographically the city is divided into a Chinese Quarter to the west and a Tibetan Quarter to the east. The Chinese neighborhood is where you'll find older hotels and Norbulingka Summer Palace.

The more colorful Tibetan Quarter is full of small guesthouses, laid-back restaurants, bustling street markets, and Jokhang Temple. There is also a small Muslim Quarter to the southeast of the Barkhor. The old winding lanes in and around the Barkhor are immensely walkable and a great way to rub shoulders with the locals. Don't worry about getting lost: most of the thoroughfares are circular; if you follow the pilgrims, you'll make it back to the circuit.

GETTING HERE AND AROUND

With the opening of the railroad line in 2006, travelers can now travel easily and cheaply to Tibet from almost anywhere in China. You'll need a Tibet Travel Bureau permit—which should cost about Y200—to buy a train ticket, and this should arranged by your tour group. The new Lhasa Train Station is located 15 to 20 minutes southwest of the city center by taxi (Y50).

Booking an airline ticket to Lhasa is a complicated process involving a Tibet Tourism Bureau permit. You're better off letting a travel agent handle this for you.

BY AIR Air China, Sichuan Airlines, China Southern Airlines, and China Eastern Airlines all have frequent service to Lhasa. The easiest direct route is from Chengdu, which has as many as 10 daily flights during the summer months for about $200 each way. Flights to Lhasa depart from Beijing (5 hrs), Guangzhou (5 hrs), Xi'an (3½ hrs), Chongqing (3 hrs), and Chengdu (2 hrs). The airport is located 53 km (32 mi) southwest of Lhasa, which takes about 45 minutes by taxi (Y140) or more than an hour by shuttle bus (Y 25).

If you are coming from Kathmandu, the nonstop flights made three times a week will give you fantastic views of the Himalayas. You must show your permit from the Tibet Tourism Bureau when you check-in.

BY BUS Intercity travel by bus is not only long and uncomfortable, it's also illegal for foreigners in almost all of Tibet. You can, however, take the pilgrim buses that leave every day at 6:30 AM from Barkhor Square headed to Ganden Monastery

10

BY CAR Travel by car is the only permitted transportation throughout Tibet for foreigners. Travel agencies can arrange a driver and all of the necessary permits for any destination you can imagine, if you're willing to pay the price. If you're headed to Nepal, make sure you arrange a visa in Lhasa before your departure.

BY TRAIN The train line to Lhasa has rewritten many of the world's records for extreme engineering. It's the world highest railway, with more than 966 km (600 mi) of track above 13,000 feet, reaching above 16,500 feet in several locations. The line is also home to the world's highest railway station, which at Tangu-la Pass sits at almost 17,000 feet.

The train is comfortable and inexpensive, with free oxygen supplies beneath every seat to combat altitude sickness. Traveling by rail is also the perfect way to see the vast uninhabited expanse of the northern Qinghai-Tibet Plateau, with yaks and antelopes roaming the hills.

Tibet
KUNLUN SHAN
XINJIANG UYGUR ZIZHIQU
QAIDAM PENDI
Golmud
QINGHAI
QINGSHAN GAOYUAN (TIBETIAN PLATEAU)
Wujang
Zhaxigang
XIZANG ZIZHIQU (TIBET AUTONOMOUS REGION)
GANGDISE SHAN
Dongco
Barga
Nyima
Coqen
Amdo
Doba
Siling Co
Nam Co
TANGGULA SHAN
Nagqu
SICHUAN
Gamtog
Lancang (Mekong)
Jinsha (Yangzi)
Qamdo
NYAINQENTANGLHA SHAN
Nu (Salween)
Bangda
Bayizhen
Yarlung Zangbo
Lhasa see detail map
Yangbajain
Ganden Monastery
Gonggar
Shigatse
Lhaze
Sakya
Everest Base Camp
Shegar
Gyantse
Kangmar
Guru
Diggye
Yamdrok Tso
HIMALAYA
NEPAL
INDIA
Kathmandu
Mt. Everest (Mt. Qomolangma)
Thimbu
BHUTAN
INDIA
YUNNAN
Ganges
0 150 mi
0 150 km

SAFETY

Don't openly talk politics with Tibetans. If they speak out against the government they may be charged with treason and receive a 20-year jail term. Public Security Bureau personnel are everywhere, sometimes in uniform, sometimes in civilian clothes or even in monks' robes. The PSB monitors civil unrest, visa extensions, crime, and traffic. Beware of the charming Tibetan who may be a secret policeman trying to entrap you into giving him a photograph of the Dalai Lama. You could be detained, deported, and even risk being beaten. PSB offices are in all towns and many of the smaller townships.

ABOUT THE WEATHER

From November to January, temperatures become frightfully cold (–10°F), but the climate is dry and the skies are blue. Many tourist sights in Lhasa shorten their opening hours in winter months. From June to August highs reach 80°F, although it can feel hotter. Summer sees a bit of rain, and occasionally roads will be closed to popular tourist destinations, including the Everest Base Camp. The best touring conditions occur from mid-April through May as wildflowers bloom and snow begins to melt. September through early November, with its mild weather, is another good option.

TOURS

Lhasa is overflowing with travel agencies, any one of which can arrange transportation and an English-speaking guide for sites in and around Lhasa. Most foreign travelers have already purchased tours along with their airline or train tickets, as it is required by Chinese law. Once you're here, you can book other tours if you find there's something else you want to see. A good local agency is Tibet FIT Travel.

ESSENTIALS

Air Contacts Gongga Airport (*Gongga Feijichang ✉ Airport Rd., Gongga County ☎ 0891/624–6114 or 0891/624–6009*).

Bank Bank of China (*✉ 28 Lingkor Xi Lu ✉ 20 Beijing Dong Lu ☎ 0891/682–8547 or 0891/683–5311*).

Medical Assistance Tibet Military General Hospital (*Xizang Junqu Zongyiyuan ✉ 3 Zhaji Lu ☎ 0891/685–8122*).

Train Contacts Tibet Autonomous Region Tourism Office (*Zizhiqu Luyouzhu ✉ 3 Luobulingka Lu ☎ 0891/683–5472 ⏲ Daily 8:30—6:30*).

Visitor and Tour Info Mountain and River International Travel Services *(aka Shanshui Luxingshe)* (*✉ 27 Beijing Donglu ☎ 0891/633–3819*). **Tibet FIT Travel** *(Xizang Gaoyuan Sanke Guanli Jiedaizhongxin)* (*✉ Inside the Snowlands Hotel, 4 Zangyiyuan Lu, Lhasa ☎ 0891/634–9239 🌐 www.tibetfit.com*).**Tibet Tourism Bureau** (*✉ 3 Luobulingka Lu, Lhasa ☎ 0891/655–3176 information*).

EXPLORING

Your main axis of orientation in Lhasa is Beijing Lu, a street that stretches from the Barkhor in the east to as far as Drepung Monastery in the west, passing right in front of the Potala Palace. The easiest way to get from site to site is by taxi, which costs a flat Y10 between most locations in the city. Pedicabs are also available, but agreeing on a price before you hop on is essential; most trips should cost about Y10. Many of the most popular attractions are concentrated in and around the Barkhor area, so walking is always an option.

WORD OF MOUTH

"For anyone with an interest in Tibet, I highly recommend the documentary *Tibet: Cry of the Snow Lion*. You'll learn what really happened in Tibet when the Chinese invaded and what's happening even now. I didn't see it until after we returned but wish I had seen it before going." —PIPERPAT

❷ **Ani Tsangkung Nunnery.** This colorful convent has a livelier atmosphere than what you'll find at Lhasa's monasteries. Beaming nuns encourage you to wander through the courtyards, listen to their chanting, and watch them make ornamental butter flowers. There's a simple outdoor restaurant—popular at lunchtime—where nuns serve up inexpensive bowls of noodles and *momos* (dumplings). The chief pilgrimage site is the meditation hollow where Songtsen Gampo concentrated his spiritual focus on preventing the flood of the Kyi River in the 7th century. ✉ *Waling Lam* ✣ *southeast of Jokhang Temple* 🎫 *Y30* ⊙ *Daily 9–6.*

❹ **Barkhor.** Circling the walls of the Jokhang Temple, the Barkhor is not only Tibetan Buddhism's holiest pilgrimage circuit but is also the best spot in Lhasa for people-watching. Look for monks sitting before their alms bowls while the faithful constantly spin their prayer wheels. Unless you want to shock the devout with your blatant disregard for tradition, flow with the crowd in a clockwise direction. This wide pedestrian street is also souvenir central, crammed with stalls where vendors sell prayer shawls, silver jewelry, wall hangings, and just about anything that screams, "I've been to Tibet!" Don't even think about paying what the vendors ask; many of the items can easily be bargained down to less than a quarter of the original price.

❽ **Palha Lupuk Temple.** Religious rock paintings dating from as early as the 7th century can be seen at this grotto-style temple. On the third floor you'll find an entrance to a cave with sculptures carved into the granite walls, mostly by Nepalese artists more than a millennium ago. It's a decent temple, but probably only worth the visit if you find yourself in the area with an hour or so to kill. ✉ *South face of Iron Mountain* ✣ *on a small street opposite the western end of the Potala Palace* 🎫 *Y20* ⊙ *Daily 9–8.*

❸ **Jokhang Temple** *(Da Zhao Si)*. This temple is the most sacred building in Tibet. From the gentle flicker of a butter-lamp light dancing off antique murals, statues, tapestries, and *thangkhas* (scroll paintings), to the air thick with incense and anticipation as thousands of Tibetans pay homage day and night, the temple contains a plethora of sensory delights. Most likely built in 647 during Songtsen Gampo's reign, the Jokhang stands in the heart of the old town. The site was selected by Queen Wengcheng, a princess from China who became Songtsen Gampo's second wife. His first wife, Princess Bhrikuti from Nepal, financed the

Fodor's Choice ★

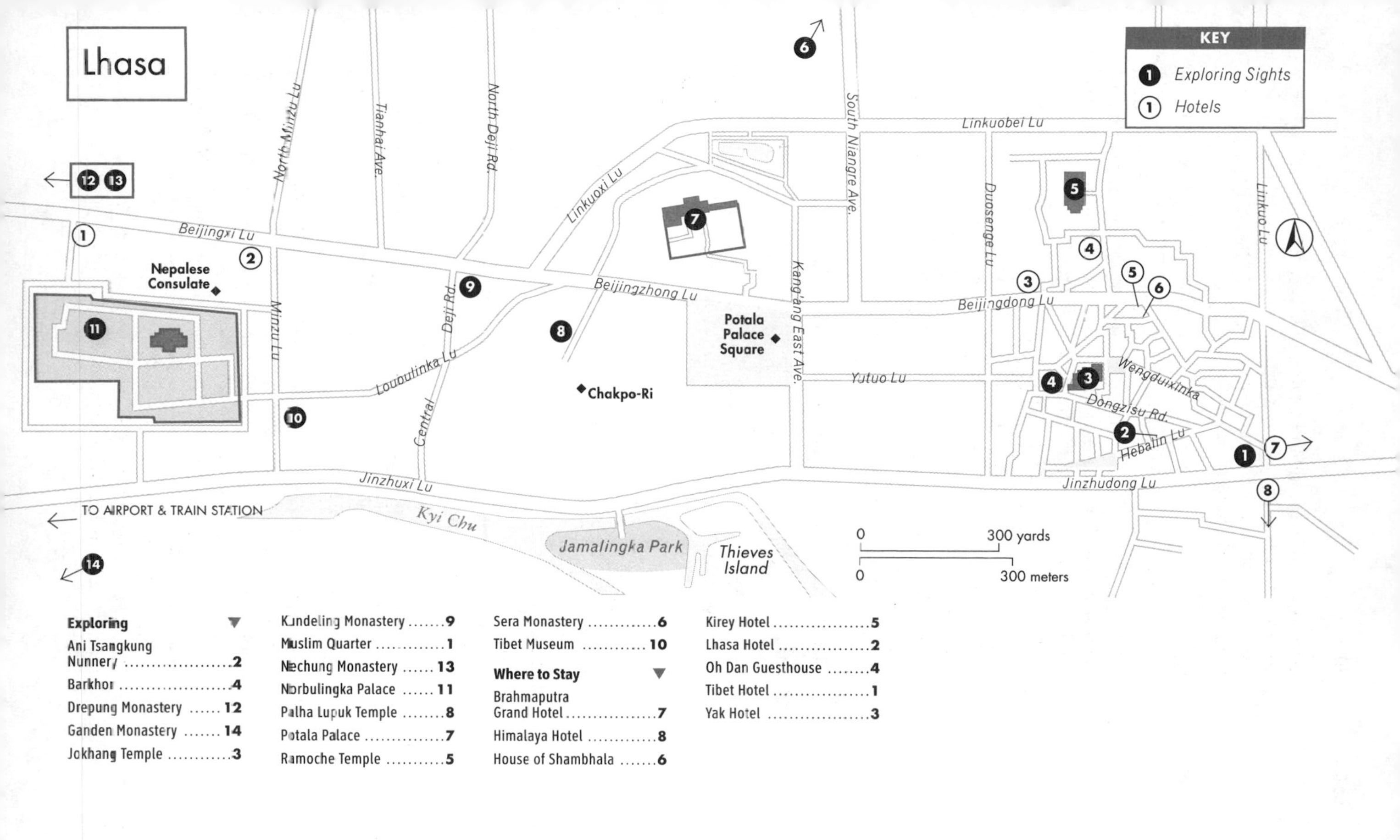

Lhasa
KEY
Exploring Sights
Hotels
Linkuobei Lu
Linkuo Lu
South Niangre Ave.
Duosenge Lu
North Minzu Lu
Tianhai Ave.
North Deji Rd.
Linkuoxi Lu
Beijingxi Lu
Beijingzhong Lu
Beijingdong Lu
Nepalese Consulate
Minzu Lu
Deji Rd.
Central
Luobulinka Lu
Potala Palace Square
Kang'ang East Ave.
Yutuo Lu
Chakpo-Ri
Wengduixinka
Dongzisu Rd.
Hebalin Lu
Jinzhuxi Lu
Jinzhudong Lu
TO AIRPORT & TRAIN STATION
Kyi Chu
Jamalingka Park
Thieves Island
0
300 yards
0
300 meters
Exploring
Ani Tsangkung Nunnery 2
Barkhor 4
Drepung Monastery 12
Ganden Monastery 14
Jokhang Temple 3
Kundeling Monastery 9
Muslim Quarter 1
Nechung Monastery 13
Norbulingka Palace 11
Palha Lupuk Temple 8
Potala Palace 7
Ramoche Temple 5
Sera Monastery 6
Tibet Museum 10
Where to Stay
Brahmaputra Grand Hotel 7
Himalaya Hotel 8
House of Shambhala 6
Kirey Hotel 5
Lhasa Hotel 2
Oh Dan Guesthouse 4
Tibet Hotel 1
Yak Hotel 3

building of Jokhang. In her honor, and in recognition of Tibet's strong reliance on Nepal, the Jokhang's main gate faces west, toward Nepal. Among the bits remaining from the 7th century are the four door frames of the inner temple, dedicated to different deities.

Over the centuries, renovations have enlarged the Jokhang to keep it the premier temple of Tibet. Its status was threatened in the 1950s when the Chinese Army shelled it and the Red Guards of the Cultural Revolution ransacked it. During this period, the temple was used for various purposes, including a pigsty. Much of the damage has since been repaired, but a portion of it has been lost forever.

Before entering the Inner Jokhang, you should walk the Nangkhor Inner Circuit in a clockwise direction. It's lined with prayer wheels and murals depicting a series of Buddhist scenes. Continue on to the large Entrance Hall, whose inner chapels have murals depicting the wrathful deities responsible for protecting the temple and the city. Straight ahead is the inner sanctum, the three-story **Kyilkhor Thil,** some of whose many columns probably date from the 7th century, particularly those with short bases and round shafts.

The chapels on the ground floor of the Kyilkhor Thil are the most rewarding. The most revered chapel of the inner hall is **Jowo Sakyamuni Lhakhang,** opposite the entrance. Inside rests a bejeweled -foot statue of Jowo Rinpoche—representing the Buddha at age 12—surrounded by adoring disciples. It was brought to Tibet by Queen Wengcheng and somehow has survived, despite a history of being plastered over and buried in sand. On busy days you may wait in line to enter this shrine, but it's worth it. On the second floor there are a number of small chapels, although many are closed to visitors. Before you leave, climb the stairs next to the main entrance up to the Jokhang's ornately decorated golden roof. You'll be rewarded with sweeping views of the Barkhor, the Potala Palace, and the snowcapped mountains beyond Lhasa. ✉ *Barkhor* ☎ *0891/632–3129* 🎫 *Y70* ⏲ *Daily 9–6.*

NEED A BREAK?

Located on the eastern leg of the Barkhor Circuit, Sun Tribe Restaurant (✉ *39 Barkhor Dong Jie* ☎ *0891/634–1990* ▭ *No credit cards*) is a good place to take a break after a visit to the Jokhang Temple. Monks sit around the low tables, chatting and sipping tea. The Tibetan dishes served here—everything from fried yak hooves to mutton with spring onion—are praised by locals as "the real thing."

9 **Kundeling Monastery** *(Gongdelin Si)*. This monastery is often overlooked by tourists, so it's less crowded than others around Lhasa. If you arrive in the morning, climb to a second-floor chapel to see monks chanting, beating drums, and playing long bronze prayer trumpets. This temple also contains examples of sand painting, in which millions of colorful grains of sand are arranged in a complex pattern over the course of hours or even days. ✉ *Beijing Zhong Lu and Deji Lu* ✢ *west of the Potala Palace* ☎ *0891/685–1973* 🎫 *Y10* ⏲ *Daily 9–8.*

GETTING AROUND

Taxis are plentiful in Lhasa. A set fare of Y10 will get you almost anywhere within the city limits. Getting to Drepung Monastery will cost about Y40. Minibuses ply a fixed route with fares of about Y2. Bicycle rickshaws are also available for short trips and normally cost Y3, although they're famous for trying to charge foreigners higher prices.

1 **Muslim Quarter.** In perhaps the most Buddhist of cities, the Muslim Quarter—centered around Lhasa's Great Mosque—is a bit of an anomaly. The district was originally intended for immigrants arriving from Kashmir and Ladakh. The Great Mosque (Da Qingzhen Si) was completed in 1716, but very little of the original structure remains. The area is now primarily of interest for its distinct atmosphere and the large concentration of pork-free halal restaurants. ⊠ *Lingkor Nan Lu ✣ west of Lingkor Dong Lu.*

11 **Norbulingka Palace.** The 7th Dalai Lama (1708–57), a frail man, chose to build a summer palace on this site because of its medicinal spring, and later had his whole government moved here from the Potala Palace. Successive Dalai Lamas expanded the complex, adding additional palaces, a debating courtyard, a pavilion, a library, and a number of landscaped gardens. The most recent addition, built by the current Dalai Lama between 1954 and 1956, is an ornate two-story building containing his private quarters. It turned out to be the place from which, disguised as a soldier, he fled to India on March 17, 1959, three days before the Chinese massacred thousands of Tibetans and fired artillery shells into every building in the complex. Only after searching through the corpses did they realize that the Dalai Lama had escaped.

The repair work in the aftermath of the March 1959 uprising is not of high caliber and much of Norbulingka feels run-down. That said, a collection of the Dalai Lama's carriages and automobiles housed in the **Changsam Palace** is worth a look. More fascinating are the personal effects of the current Dalai Lama housed in the **New Summer Palace,** including his radio and phonograph. You can even peek into the Dalai Lama's bathroom. Look closely at the murals surrounding the current Dalai Lama's throne; on the left behind the throne is perhaps the only portrait of him you'll see anywhere in Tibet. ⊠ *Western end of Luobulingka Lu* 🎫 *Y60* ⏲ *Daily 9–6:30.*

7 **Potala Palace** *(Pudala Gong).* Virtually nothing remains of the original 11-story Potala Palace, built in 637 by Songtsen Gampo. What you see today is a 17th-century replacement. The Fifth Dalai Lama, anxious to reestablish the importance of Lhasa as the Tibetan capital, employed 7,000 workers and 1,500 artisans to resurrect the Potala Palace on the 7th-century foundation. The portion called the White Palace was completed in 1653. The Red Palace was not completed until 1694, 12 years after the Dalai Lama's death (which was kept secret by the regent in order to prevent interruption of the construction). The Potala Palace has been enlarged since then, and has been continually renovated. Once the headquarters of Tibet's theocracy, the vast complex is now a museum.

Fodor's Choice ★

10

The Potala Palace was the world's tallest building before the advent of modern skyscrapers. Towering above the city from the slopes of Mount Marpori, the structure is 384 feet high; its 1,000 rooms house some 200,000 images. The outer section, the White Palace, was the seat of government and the winter residence of the Dalai Lama until 1951. Inside you can pass through the Dalai Lama's spartan quarters. On either side of the palace are the former offices of the government. The Red Palace, looming above the White Palace, is filled with murals that chronicle Buddhist folklore and ancient Tibetan life. Interspersed among the chapels are eight spectacular tombs covered in nearly five tons of gold. These bejeweled rooms contain the remains of the 5th through 13th Dalai Lamas.

ALTITUDE ALERT

At 12,000 feet, shortness of breath and mild headaches are common during the first few days in Lhasa. These symptoms can be managed by use of a small oxygen canister, herbal remedies, or an aspirin or two. Drink plenty of water. Severe altitude sickness should be immediately brought to the attention of a physician.

The increasing number of visitors makes it difficult to secure tickets for the Potala Palace. Only 500 visitors are allowed in each day. If you're not part of a tour group, here's the drill: arrive at the palace's western gate at 7:30 AM and line up to receive a number; return at 11:30 AM with your passport in order to receive a voucher for the *following day*; return to the palace's front gate the next day at the time indicated on your voucher, when you'll be able to buy a ticket and finally tour the Potala Palace. Don't get discouraged; the Potala Palace is worth the trouble. Expect to spend about two hours here. ✉*Beijing Zhong Lu, Gongtian Xian* ☎*0891/683–4362* 🎫*Y100* ⏲*By appointment, which must be made one day in advance; Low season (Nov.–Apr.), 9:30–3; high season (May–Oct.), 9–4.*

❺ **Ramoche Temple** *(Xiao Zhao Si)*. This temple was founded by Queen Wengcheng at the same time as the Jokhang Temple. Its three-story structure dates from the 15th century. Despite restorations in the 1980s, it lost much of its former glory after the Chinese used it to house the Communist Labor Training Committee during the Cultural Revolution.

The Ramoche Temple was intended to house the most revered statue of Jowo Rinpoche. A threat of a Chinese invasion in the 7th century induced Queen Wengcheng to hide the statue in the Jokhang Temple. Some 50 years later it was rediscovered and placed within the Jokhang Temple's main chapel. As a substitute, Jokhang reciprocated with a Nepalese statue of Jowo Mikyo Dorje—representing Buddha as an eight-year-old—richly layered in gold and precious stones. It was decapitated during the Cultural Revolution and its torso lost in Beijing. Both head and body were found in 1984, put back together again, and placed in a small chapel at the back of the Ramoche Temple's Inner Sanctum. Be sure to climb to the temple's roof for a spectacular view of the Potala Palace perched high above the rooftops of Lhasa. ✉*Xiao*

Zhao Si Lu, off the north side of Beijing Dong Lu ☎*0891/633–6163* *Y20* ⏲*Daily 8–4:30.*

10 **Tibet Museum.** For the Chinese interpretation of Tibetan history, politics, and culture, visit this modern museum. The free personal audio guide provides commentary on important pieces from prehistoric times, Chinese dynasties, and traditional Tibetan life. If you are a scholar of history, you may find some of the explanations intriguing. ✉*Corner of Luobulingka Lu and Minzu Nan Lu* ✣*across from the entrance to Norbulingka Palace* ☎*0891/681–2210* *Y30* ⏲*May–Oct., daily 9–6:30, Nov.–Apr., daily 10:30–5.*

DID YOU KNOW?

Underneath the 13-story, 1,000-room fortress are the dungeons, inaccessible to tourists. Justice could be harsh—torture and jail time were the punishments for refusing to pay taxes, displaying anger, or insulting a monk. The worst place to be sent was the Cave of Scorpions, where prisoners were the targets of stinging tails.

WHERE TO EAT

Take advantage of the competitive market of hybrid restaurants that serve Chinese, Indian, Nepali, Tibetan, and Western fare. Most have sprung up from backpacker haunts serving perennially favorite dishes, from banana pancakes to yak burgers to chicken masala. The most dependable eateries are on hotel or guesthouse premises.

$$–$$$ ECLECTIC ✗**Dunya.** Meaning "The World" in 10 languages, Dunya serves a melting pot of international dishes. The Western food here is disappointing, but the Indian and Nepalese dishes are first rate; both can be complemented by a bottle of Australian wine or a cup of real coffee—both rarities in Tibet. With its exposed-brick interior and a polite English-speaking staff, Dunya feels like a real restaurant, not another hole-in-the-wall eatery. Upstairs is a well-stocked bar with a balcony where you'll often find the Dutch proprietor chatting with customers. ✉*100 Beijing Dong Lu* ✣*next to the Yak Hotel* ☎*0891/633–3374* ▭*No credit cards* ⏲*Closed Nov.–Apr.*

¢–$ ECLECTIC ✗**Makye Ame** *(Ma Ji A Mi).* Ask to be seated by the second-floor windows or on the rooftop terrace for some of the best views of the pilgrims on the Barkhor, which passes right by this legendary corner restaurant. Meat eaters will enjoy the fried yak slices, and vegetarians rave about the spinach-tofu ravioli topped with homemade tomato-basil sauce as well as the Indian-style bread stuffed with potato and served with curry and yogurt sauces. Ask the staff to explain the legend of Makye Ame, a mysterious woman immortalized in a poem penned by the Sixth Dalai Lama, who spied her in a bar where the café now stands. To find this place, look for a hand-painted sign reading RESTAURANT. ✉*Southeast corner of Barkhor* ☎*0891/632–8608* ▭*No credit cards.*

$$–$$$ TIBETAN ★ ✗**Shangrila.** Make time in your busy tour schedule for dinner at the Shangrila. As dancers perform traditional routines, your taste buds will be treated to an 18-course Tibetan buffet—a superb opportunity to try indigenous food such as sautéed yak lung, cold yak tongue, and

wild sweet potatoes. The colorful scroll paintings that line the walls, the dark-wood furniture, and the congenial staffers that happily explain the dishes sets this place apart from other dinner-and-a-show restaurants. Reservations are necessary—sometimes a day in advance—and you should arrive by 7 PM for the best seats. The performance and buffet are a set price of Y50. ✉ *122 Beijing Dong Lu* ✣ *inside the Kirey Hotel* ☎ *0891/636–3880* ▭ *No credit cards.*

¢–$ ECLECTIC Fodor's Choice ★ ✕ **Snowlands** *(Xueyu Canting)*. The well-traveled menu at the Snowlands—covering Chinese, Nepalese, Tibetan, Indian, Italian, and even Mexican cuisine—is your guide to the finest meals in Tibet. Join foreign aid workers, local business executives, and the small tour groups who flock in droves to this cozy café near Barkhor. Try the chicken masala with a freshly baked *naan* bread, or feast on grilled yak steak with garlic-butter sauce. This place is hugely popular, and the service can be slow, but the food is worth the wait. Fresh cinnamon rolls, apple pie, and croissants are also available. ✉ *4 Danjielin Lu* ✣ *north of Barkhor* ☎ *0891/633–7323* ▭ *No credit cards.*

$$–$$$ ECLECTIC ✕ **Tashi** *(Daxi Xiaochi)*. A popular hangout for foreigners, Tashi is the kind of restaurant where conversations with other diners are inevitable. The most popular dish here is the *bobi*, a kind of tortilla into which sautéed chicken, vegetables, and cream cheese are stuffed. If you're looking to add heft to your meal, try the delicious cauliflower croquettes, which are deep-fried patties of cauliflower, potato, peas, and carrots. The yak burger is also tasty. ✉ *131 Beijing Dong Lu, at Danjielin Lu* ☎ *0891/633–7305* ▭ *No credit cards.*

WHERE TO STAY

Hotel options in Lhasa have improved significantly in recent years. Ask and you may be shown rooms ranging from a depressing 20-person dormitory to a deluxe suite with private bath, balcony, and minibar. Many of the more expensive hotels even equip their rooms with oxygen machines to ease the effects of altitude sickness. Tibetan guesthouses are staffed by locals, and are more personable but some of the shared bathing facilities at the lower-end options can be archaic.

$$$$ **Brahmaputra Grand Hotel** *(Yaluzangbu Dajiudian)*. The Brahmaputra Grand is by far the finest hotel in Lhasa. Opened in 2006, it's billed as the world's only "museum hotel," with every nook and cranny displaying gorgeous Tibetan antiques and artifacts. The only difference here is that everything's for sale. Be careful what you set your heart on—some of the items go for as much as $15,000. The hotel's exterior is a strange mix of Russian and Tibetan architecture, but inside it's all class. From the smartly clad Nepali bellmen to the gently scented hallways with perfect lighting and dark-wood paneling, you'll be impressed every minute of your stay. The hotel is 2½ km (1½ mi) east of the Barkhor. **Pros:** authentic, spacious rooms, helpful staff. **Cons:** a little far from center, beds are hard. ✉ *Gongbutang Lu, Yangcheng Plaza D* ☎ *0891/630–9999* 🖷 *0891/630–9888* 🌐 *www.tibethotel.cn* *185 rooms* *In-room: Ethernet, minibar. In-hotel: 2 restaurants, laundry service* ▭ *AE, DC, MC, V.*

$$–$$$ **Himalaya Hotel** *(Ximalaya Jiudian).* Sliding-glass doors open onto a lavishly appointed foyer defined by four soaring columns, a marble floor, and a central chandelier. The rooms here range from budget rooms to luxurious suites, all featuring Tibetan woodwork and bedding in soothing earth tones. Ask for a room with a view of the Potala Palace. If you want to stay near the Barkhor area, this is your best bet. As a bonus, there are also occasional performances of Tibetan opera. **Pros:** good location. **Cons:** business service could be better. ✉*6 Lingkor Dong Lu* ☎*0891/632–1111* 📠*0891/633–2675* *133 rooms* *In-hotel: 3 restaurants, laundry service, no elevator* *AE, MC, V.*

$$$–$$$$ ★ **House of Shambhala** *(Xiangbala Gong).* If you want to stay in a traditional Tibetan dwelling, this quiet boutique hotel is a good choice. The building, which dates back to the 7th century, was once the home of a high-ranking Tibetan general under the 13th Dalai Lama. Suites are decorated with tangerine-colored walls, hardwood floors, sheepskin rugs, and exposed roof beams. The king-size beds are covered with hand-beaded duvets, and the bathrooms are tiled in local slate. The staff is attentive, but few speak much English. On the rooftop terrace you can lounge on a daybed and order from the downstairs restaurant. This hotel is very small, so reserve far in advance. It's on a small alley next to the Kirey Hotel. **Pros:** friendly staff, less touristy location, nice decor. **Cons:** appliances sometimes don't work. ✉*7 Jiri Erxiang* ☎*0891/632–6533* 📠*0891/632–6695* 🌐*www.houseofshambhala.com* *10 suites* *In-hotel: spa, gym, restaurant, laundry service, no elevator. In-room: free Internet* *AE, MC, V.*

¢ **Kirey Hotel** *(Jiri Binguan).* A popular budget hotel, the Kirey is filled with everyone from backpackers to bicyclists to tour groups. Rooms here are spotless, but otherwise unremarkable. Something that is special, however, is that the staff here will wash and dry your laundry free of charge. The location, north of Jokhang Temple, can't be beat. Two excellent restaurants are located in the courtyard. **Pros:** free laundry service. **Cons:** more of a hostel than a hotel. ✉*105 Beijing Dong Lu* ☎*0891/632–3462* *35 rooms* *In-hotel: 2 restaurants, bar, bicycles, public Internet, no elevator* *No credit cards.*

$$$$ **Lhasa Hotel** *(Lasa Fandian).* If you stay here in July and August, you'll be pleased with the swimming pool—a rare find in Lhasa. The rest of the year you will pay premium rates for an average hotel where the building and the gardens look largely ignored. The hotel is north of the entrance to Norbulingka Palace. **Pros:** good shops, friendly staff. **Cons:** old wing is run down, shabby. ✉*3 Minzu Lu Zhong Lu* ☎*0891/683–2221* 📠*0891/683–5796* 🌐*www.lhasahotel.com* *453 rooms, 12 suites* *In-hotel: 5 restaurants, room service, bar, pool, laundry service, minibar* *AE, DC, MC, V.*

¢–$ **Oh Dan Guesthouse** *(Oudan Binguan).* An excellent budget choice, this small hotel sits on a busy pedestrian street between the Jokhang and Ramoche temples, only a few minutes north of the Barkhor. Rooms are simple, but comfortable and clean. On the rooftop terrace, you can sip tea and enjoy an awesome view of Lhasa. Avoid the third or fourth floor, as there is no elevator. **Pros:** great views, well-kept. **Cons:** rooms are a bit small. ✉*15 Xiao Zhao Si Lu or 15 Ramoche Rd.* ☎*0891/634–4999*

🖷0891/633–0823 ⇆32 rooms ♘In-hotel: restaurant, laundry service, no elevator. In-room: Internet charge ▭No credit cards.

$$$–$$$$ **Tibet Hotel** *(Xizang Binguan)*. The rooms in this well-maintained hotel feature a touch of Tibetan style, from the vibrant blue carpeting to the golden silk pillows on the crimson sofas. Couples who want to maximize their time will appreciate the separate tubs and showers in the bathrooms. There are 10 restaurants serving Western and Asian food, but their opening hours are erratic (a problem, as you're a ways from downtown). Many on the staff speak a little English, but their enthusiasm makes it easy to bridge the communication gap. Rooms in the hotel's rear building are bigger, but slightly older. **Pros:** caring staff, great views. **Cons:** lower level rooms are not as good. ✉*64 Beijing Xi Lu* ☎*0891/683–4966* 🖷*0891/683–1039* ⇆*333 rooms* ♘*In-room: safe, Ethernet. In-hotel: 5 restaurants, sauna, laundry service* ▭*AE, DC, MC, V.*

SLIDING PRICE SCALES

Don't be too shy about bargaining. Room rates are negotiable from October to March and then tend to soar and become inflexible in the high season.

$–$$$ **Yak Hotel** *(Ya Binguan)*. Once the first choice for travelers on a tight budget, the Yak now appeals to travelers of all levels. Regardless of what kind of room you choose, it will be immaculate. Even in the most economical of rooms you will find nice touches like Tibetan chests as bedside tables. If you're sensitive to noise, try to get a room toward the back. Dunya restaurant is to the right of the courtyard. **Pros:** central location, outdoor breakfast terrace. **Cons:** noise, staff could be more helpful. ✉*100 Beijing Dong Lu* ☎*0891/632–3496* 🖷*0891/630–0191* ⇆*120 rooms* ♘*In-hotel: 2 restaurants, bar, laundry service, public Internet* ▭*No credit cards.*

NIGHTLIFE AND THE ARTS

If you're looking for a bit of excitement, look no farther than **Neeway Nangma** (✉*13 Lingkor Bei Lu*), the city's most popular disco. An hour spent here watching the dance performances set to both pop and traditional folk songs will clear away any ideas you may have about Tibetan culture being stuck in the past. If you're looking for a quiet spot near the Barkhor to enjoy a drink or a cup of tea after a long day, try **Ganglamedo** (✉*127 Beijing Dong Lu*), across from the Yak Hotel. The bar stocks a wide range of liquors.

Tibetan operas are performed by the **Tibet Shol Opera Troupe** (✉*6 Lingkor Dong Lu* ☎*0891/632–1111*) in a theater at the Himalaya Hotel. Tickets cost Y100, and reservations are required.

SHOPPING

ARTS AND CRAFTS

For souvenirs varying from prayer flags to jewel-encrusted horse bridles, stop by one of the hundreds of open-air stalls and small shops that line the roads leading to the Jokhang Temple. Bargain in a tough but friendly manner and the proprietors may throw in extra items for luck. Many of the goods come from around Tibet and Nepal. For quality Tibetan handicrafts, visit **Dropenling** (✉ *11 Chak Tsal Gang Lu* ☎ *0891/636–0558* 🌐 *www.tibetcraft.com*), down an alley opposite the Muslim Quarter's main mosque. Unlike other souvenir shops, all the products here are made by Tibetans and all the profits are returned to the local artisan community.

OUTDOOR EQUIPMENT

West of the Potala Palace, **The Third Pole** (✉ *6 Luobulingka Lu* ☎ *0891/682–0549*) can outfit you with everything you'll need to enjoy the great outdoors, from good hiking shoes to walking sticks to sunglasses. **Wilderness Outside Sports Club** (✉ *182 Beijing Zhong Lu* ☎ *0891/682–9365*) features a wide selection of outdoor equipment, as well as warm clothing if you're planning a trip to the mountains.

AROUND LHASA

Many of Lhasa's best sites are clustered around the city center, but three of the most important are a bit more remote. This trio of monasteries are known as the "three pillars of Tibetan Buddhism," having all been founded by religious patriarch Tsongkhapa at the beginning of the 15th century. All three are worth the effort it takes to reach them, especially Ganden Monastery, located 90 minutes east of Lhasa.

⓮ Fodor'sChoice ★ **Ganden Monastery.** If you only have time for one side trip from Lhasa, this rambling monastery with ocher-color walls is your best bet. Established in 1409 by Tsongkhapa, the founder of the Gelugpa sect, its abbot is chosen on merit rather than heredity. Of the six great Gelugpa monasteries, Ganden was the most seriously damaged by Chinese during the Cultural Revolution. Since the early 1980s, Tibetans have put tremendous effort into rebuilding the complex. Some 400 monks are now in residence. Pilgrims come daily from Lhasa to pay homage to the sacred sites and religious relics.

The monastery comprises eight major buildings. The most impressive structure is the **Gold Tomb of Tsongkhapa** (Serdhung Lhakhang) in the heart of the complex, easily recognized by the recently built white *chorten*, or small shrine, standing before the red building. On the second floor is the chapel of **Yangchen Khang,** with the new golden chorten of Tsongkhapa. The original (1629), made of silver, later gilded, was the most sacred object in the land. In 1959 the Chinese destroyed it, although brave monks saved some of the holy relics of Tsongkhapa, which are now inside the new gold-covered chorten. Be careful walking around this shrine: the buttery wax on the floor is thick and slippery.

A path that circumambulates the monastery starts from the parking lot. From the path, which leads to the spot where Tsongkhapa was cremated in 1419, you'll be treated to breathtaking views of the Lhasa River Valley. You'll need about an hour to complete the circuit. Buses (Y20 round-trip) to Ganden leave from Barkhor Square in front of Jokhang Temple every morning at 6:30 AM, returning to Lhasa at 3 PM.

CLOSE UP

The Tibetans

They live primarily on the Tibet-Qinghai Plateau, but they also make their homes in southern Gansu, western and northern Sichuan, and northwestern Yunnan. Their culture is influenced both by Tibet's extreme geography and their unique interpretation of Buddhism, the line between the two often blurred by a "sacred geography," which deifies many of the region's mountains and lakes. Compared with other forms of Buddhism, Tibetan Buddhism (also known as "Lamaism") places far more emphasis on the physical path to enlightenment. This is why the sight of pilgrims prostrating around the base of a sacred mountain or temple for days or weeks on end is a common one in the region.

When Tibet was annexed by China (or "liberated") in 1959, their supreme spiritual leader the Dalai Lama fled in disguise to India where he set up a Tibetan government-in-exile in Dharamsala, which became known as "little Lhasa." Since then the Dalai Lama has become an international celebrity and has succeeded in making the struggle for Tibetan independence a focus of global attention, drawing strong condemnation—and brutal crackdowns—from Beijing. Few people know that the Dalai Lama has actually for many years no longer insisted on independence, but a more moderate form of autonomy like that enjoyed by Hong Kong and Macau. Yet despite international pressure—and perhaps even because of the attention—there seems little hope that Tibet's status will change in the near future.

Meanwhile, Tibet continues to modernize at full-speed, with seemingly every road between Lhasa and Mount Everest being upgraded simultaneously. The rail link between Beijing and Lhasa completed in 2006 is expected to promote "Hanification," or a major increase in the Han Chinese population. With only 2.5 million Tibetans living in the Tibet Autonomous Region—and 800 million impoverished Han Chinese nationwide looking for a better way of life—it's only a matter of time before ethnic Tibetans become a small minority in their own homeland.

The beautiful 90-minute ride from Lhasa will give you a glimpse of life in rural Tibet. ✉*36 km (22 mi) southeast of Lhasa on main Tibet–Sichuan Hwy.* 🎫*Y35* ⏲*Daily 8:30–6.*

> **WORD OF MOUTH**
>
> "Remember just about everything you do in Lhasa requires lots of walking and uphill. Potala Palace is incredibly taxing, even if you are in great shape. So too with the other monasteries. We saw lots of people really struggling with breathing. It is very hard work in the high altitude." —Don

❻ ★ **Sera Monastery** *(Sela Si)*. This important Gelugpa monastery, founded in 1419, contains numerous temples filled with splendid murals and icons. Originally it was a hermitage for Tsongkhapa and a few of his top students. Within a couple hundred of years it housed more than 5,000 monks.

On the clockwise pilgrimage route, start at the two buildings that will take up most of your visit. **Sera Me Tratsang,** founded in 1419, has a *dukhang* (assembly hall) rebuilt in 1761 with murals depicting Buddha's life. Among the five chapels along the north wall, the one with its exterior adorned with skeletons and skulls is unforgettable. The complex's oldest surviving structure, **Ngagpa Tratsang,** is a three-story college for tantric studies. Here you'll find statues of famous lamas and murals depicting paradise.

Continue to the four-story-high **Sera Je Tratsang,** where Manjashuri, the God of Wisdom, listens to monks engaged in philosophical debate in a courtyard just beyond the temple walls. The extremely animated debates—during which emphatic hand movements signify agreement or disagreement—take place daily starting at 3 PM. Whatever your feelings are about the excitement of debates, this is one you don't want to miss. ✉*At the base of Mt. Phurbuchok, 5 km (3 mi) north of Lhasa* ☎*0891/638–7453* 🎫*Y50* ⏲*Daily 9–5.*

⓬ **Drepung Monastery** (☎*0891/686–3149*). The largest of the Gelugpa monasteries was the residence for lesser lamas. Founded in 1416, it was enlarged in the 16th century by the Second Dalai Lama. By the era of the Fifth Dalai Lama it had become the largest monastic institution in the world, with 10,000 residents. During the Cultural Revolution it suffered only minimally because the army used the building as its headquarters and therefore didn't ransack it as much as other temples. The monastery was reopened in 1980, although the number of resident monks has been severely depleted.

The monastery's most important building is the Tshomchen, whose vast assembly hall, the **Dukhang,** is noteworthy for its 183 columns, atrium ceiling, and ceremonial banners. Chapels can be found on all three floors, as well as on the roof. In the two-story **Buddhas of Three Ages Chapel** (Düsum Sangye Lhakhang), at the rear of the Dukhang on the ground floor, the Buddhas of past, present, and future are each guarded by two bodhisattvas. To get here, you can hire a taxi from town for between Y40 and Y50. ✉*Off Beijing Xi Lu, 8 km (5 mi) west of Lhasa* 🎫*Y50* ⏲*Daily 9–6.*

CLOSE UP

Festivals & Celebrations

Try to time your visit with one of the brilliantly colorful traditional Tibetan festivals. Dancing monks whip up a frenzy to dispel the evil spirits of the previous year at the Year End Festival on the 29th day of the 12th lunar month. The first week of the first lunar month includes Losar (New Year Festival), when Lhasa is filled with Tibetan drama performances, incense offerings, and locals promenading in their finest wardrobe. Grand butter lanterns light up the Barkhor circuit during the Lantern Festival on the 15th of the 1st month. On the seventh day of the fourth month you can join the pilgrims in Lhasa or Ganden to mark the Birth of Sakyamuni (Buddha), or you may want to wait until the 15th for the celebrations of Saga Dawa (Sakyamuni's enlightenment) and join the pilgrims who climb the Drepung Monastery to burn juniper incense. Picnics at the summer palace of Norbulingka are common during the Worship of the Buddha in the second week of the fifth month. During Shötun (Yogurt Festival) in the first week of the seventh month, immerse yourself in the operas, masked dances, and picnics from Drepung (6½ km [4 mi] out of Lhasa) to Norbulingka. During the festival, giant thangkas of the Buddha are unveiled in Drepung Monastery and Tibetan opera troupes perform operas at Norbulingka.

The Tibetan calendar is the same as the lunar calendar, so exact dates as they relate to the Western calendar are only published a year in advance. The approximate dates are as follows: Tibetan New Year (February); the Butter Lantern Festival (late February/early March); the Birth of Buddha Festival (late May/early June); the Holy Mountain Festival (late July/early August); the one-week Yogurt Festival (August); and the Bathing Festival (September).

⓭ **Nechung Monastery.** Many people skip this 12th-century monastery, but that's a big mistake. With a strong focus on beasts, demons, and the afterlife, Nechung is unlike anything else you'll see in Tibet. Murals on the monastery's walls depict everything from humans being dismembered by dogs and vultures to demons wearing long belts of human skulls engaged in passionate sexual intercourse. Until 1959 this monastery was home to the highly influential Nechung Oracle. Every important decision by a Dalai Lama is made after consulting this oracle, which currently resides in Dharamsala as a member of the government-in-exile. The monastery is 1 km (½ mi) southeast of Drepung Monastery. ✉ *Off Beijing Xi Lu, 8 km (5 mi) west of Lhasa* 🎫 *Y20* 🕒 *Daily 9–5.*

TSANG PROVINCE

The Tibetan province of Tsang includes some of the region's most important historical sites outside of Lhasa, but it's also rich in stunning scenery and dotted with small villages and terraced barley fields filled with brightly decorated yaks. This is your chance to get out of the city and experience rural Tibet, where life seems to have changed little over the past hundred years.

TOURS

If you're trying to find the majestic valleys and towering peaks that Tibet conjures up in the imagination, a journey through Tsang should be part of your itinerary. Typically lasting five days, these tours hit all of the hot spots: the brilliant blue waters of Yamdrok Tso Lake, the Dzong Fortress and Pelkor Chode Monastery in Gyantse, the Tashilhunpo Monastery in Shigatse, and the Base Camp below the world's highest peak at Mount Everest.

RUSTIC CUISINE

Outside the capital, the variety of food leaves something to be desired, but in areas commonly visited by tourists you should be able to find a simple meal. You can even order a picnic from your hotel for a countryside trip.

Every travel agency in Lhasa can arrange this tour for you, but for the best deals check out the message boards in the courtyards of the Snowlands and Kirey hotels in the Barkhor area. A good price is in the range of Y1,000 per day, which includes all necessary travel permits. Food, lodging, and admission charges to attractions are not included.

GYANTSE

6 hrs (180 km [110 mi]) by jeep southwest of Lhasa over the Yong-la Pass. 1½ hrs (90 km [55 mi]) southeast of Shigatse.

With small villages of stone houses beside fields of highland barley, Gyantse feels far removed from Lhasa, although the drive is only about six hours. Home to two of Tsang's most impressive sights—the massive tiered Gyantse Kumbum at Pelkor Chode Monastery and the Gyantse Dzong where British soldiers defeated Tibetans in 1904—Gyantse is an essential stop on the journey toward Everest. Tourist dollars have transformed what was once a small village into a small one bustling with hotels, restaurants, and Internet cafés. However, the sites remain impressive and the journey to get here over the Yong-la Pass is unforgettable.

GETTING HERE AND AROUND

Coming from Lhasa, don't let your driver take the longer but faster route through Shigatse to reach Gyantse. Insist on being taken via the dirt road over the Yong-la Pass, where the views are absolutely stunning. Few tourists take this route, and the locals will be genuinely surprised to see you. Once in Gyantse, don't feel the need to rush on to Shigatse the same day; you can spend the night and see the sites in the morning without significantly throwing off your touring schedule.

EXPLORING

Gyantse is easily navigable on foot. Most hotels and restaurants are located along Yingxiong Nan Lu, a few minutes south of the unmistakable Dzong Fortress. The Pelkor Chode Monastery is located 10 minutes' walking northwest of the fortress; both can easily be visited and toured over the course of about three hours.

Gyantse Dzong. In the 14th and 15th centuries, Gyantse rose to political power along with the rise of the Sakyapa monastic order. To get an idea of the amount of construction during this period, make the steep climb to the top of this old fortress on the northern edge of town. The building isn't in great shape, but you'll be treated to staggering views of the town and the surrounding Nyang Chu Valley. Signs reading JUMP OFF CLIFF aren't making a suggestion, but pointing to the location where Tibetan warriors jumped to their deaths rather than surrendering to British troops in 1904. The best way to see everything here is to wind around the fortress clockwise toward the top, using the long concrete staircase to descend. Be careful, as there's a slippery bit of concrete at the bottom of the stairs. The **Anti-British Imperialist Museum,** just inside the front gate, is worth a visit for a distorted yet amusing account of the British invasion, sprinkled with obvious propaganda. ✉ *North end of Yingxiong Lu* ☎ *0892/817–2263* 🎫 *Y30* ⏲ *Daily 9–6:30.*

★ **Pelkor Chode Monastery.** One of the few multidenominational monastic complexes in Tibet—housing Gelugpa, Sakyapa, and Bupa monks—Pelkor Chode is home to the **Gyantse Kumbum.** Built in AD 1427, this building with its glittering golden dome and four sets of spellbinding eyes rising over uniquely tiered circular architecture is one of the most beautiful in Tibet. Inside there are six floors, each a labyrinth of small chapels adorned with Nepalese-influenced murals and statues. A steep ladder at the rear of the fifth floor provides access to the roof. Impressive in itself, you'll appreciate this complex even more after you've seen it from the heights of Gyantse Dzong. ✉ *Northwest end of Pelkor Lu* ☎ *0892/817–2680* 🎫 *Y40* ⏲ *Daily 8–7.*

WHERE TO STAY AND EAT

¢–$$ CHINESE — ✕ **Fuqi Sichuan.** If you're getting tired of the same old Western–Tibetan hybrid cuisine, there are lots of well-prepared traditional Chinese dishes here from which you can choose. Best of all, there's an English menu, although the prices on it are nearly double what you'd pay ordering in Chinese. ✉ *10 Yingxiong Nan Lu* ✣ *near the Gyantse Hotel* ▭ *No credit cards.*

¢–$ ECLECTIC — ✕ **Tashi.** Although it shares the same name and a similar menu with an old favorite in Lhasa, this restaurant is unrelated. Still, the Indian, Tibetan, and Western dishes served in the second-floor dining room are well liked by visitors, with the yak being highly recommended. ✉ *North end of Yingxiong Lu, near Pelkor Lu* ▭ *No credit cards.*

$$–$$$$ — **Gyantse Hotel** *(Jiangzi Fandian).* In business since 1986, this government-run hotel is still the top choice in Gyantse. Rooms here are clean and comfortable, if a bit dark and dreary. Amazingly, televisions here have CNN and the BBC available. Make sure to reserve a room in advance, especially during the busy summer months. If no doubles are available, consider sharing a suite with your traveling companions; each contains two bedrooms with king-size beds and separate bathrooms. **Pros:** tV options, nice interior design, helpful staff. **Cons:** food isn't great. ✉ *2 Shanghai Dong Lu* ✣ *near Yingxiong Lu* ☎ *0892/817–2222* 📠 *0892/817–2366* ♿ *In-hotel: 3 restaurants, bar, laundry service, no elevator* ▭ *No credit cards.*

CLOSE UP

A Once Mighty Empire

The Tibet Autonomous Region (TAR) bears only a passing resemblance to what was once a massive empire that encompassed all of Tibet, Qinghai (except for the area around Xining), western Sichuan, and parts of northern Yunnan. Historically, despite their modern-day reputation for being a peaceful people, Tibetans were known as fierce warriors and feared by their neighbors. They even sacked the Chinese capital of Changan, now Xi'an, in the 8th century.

When the Mongols conquered China in the 13th century and founded the Yuan Dynasty, they also took control of Tibet, adopting Tibetan Buddhism as their official religion. This relationship came back to haunt Tibetans—it was used by China's successive dynasties and governments to legitimize the nation's claim to Tibet. In 1950, with almost 10 years of experience fighting first the Japanese and then the Nationalist government, the People's Liberation Army entered Tibet and quickly crushed all resistance.

$ **Jian Zang Hotel** *(Jianzang Fandian)*. Less expensive than the Gyantse Hotel, the Jian Zang is where most backpackers spend the night. The rooms here are clean but otherwise unremarkable, and hot water is always available. **Pros:** cheap. **Cons:** spartan. ✉*14 Yingxiong Nan Lu* ☎*0892/817–3720* 📠*0892/817–3910* *In-hotel: Restaurant, laundry service, no elevator* *No credit cards.*

SHIGATSE

4½ hrs (280 km [170 mi]) west of Lhasa by jeep. 1½ hrs (90 km [55 mi]) northwest of Gyantse. 6 hrs (240 km [150 mi]) northeast of Shegar.

Tibet's second-largest city, Shigatse, is the traditional capital of Tsang and home to the Tashilhunpo Monastery, Tibet's largest functioning monastic institution. The Tsang kings once ruled over the region from the fortress north of town. On its foundations you'll find a newly constructed luxury hotel built to resemble the Potala Palace. Most people only spend a day in Shigatse, visiting the monastery and wandering up and down the city's Walking Street, a tourist-friendly section of Qingdao Lu. Shigatse is quite pleasant, but you haven't traveled all the way to Tibet to see another unremarkable Chinese city.

GETTING HERE AND AROUND

The perfectly smooth road from Lhasa to Shigatse travels alongside the picturesque Tsangpo River beneath the towering walls of Nimo Gorge. Rather than stopping in Shigatse the first time you pass through, consider visiting the city on the way back from Everest Base Camp. Driving from Gyantse all the way to Shegar in a single day will maximize the time you have to spend at the mountain by getting a significant chunk of driving out of the way. Shigatse is the only city outside of Lhasa that foreigners can reliably reach by public transportation. Buses leave starting at 7 AM across from the Kirey Hotel in Lhasa.

EXPLORING

Everything of interest to foreign visitors, including most hotels and restaurants, is located on the stretch of road between the monastery and the fortress, namely Walking Street, which you can recognize by the Chinese-style gates on either end.

> **LODGING OPTIONS**
>
> In the major towns outside Lhasa you usually have a choice between bland Chinese hotels and rundown guesthouses, about half of which have hot running water.

Tashilhunpo Monastery. One of the six great Gelugpa institutions, this monastery is the seat of the Panchen Lama and one of the few religious sites in Tibet not destroyed during the Cultural Revolution. The Chapel of Maitreya houses an 85-foot-high statue of the Future Buddha—the largest in the world—covered in more than 600 pounds of gold. More than a thousand more images are painted on the surrounding walls. You will also be able to visit the Panchen Lama tombs, many of which are lined with photos and sculptures of their later reincarnations. The beautiful stupa of the 10th Panchen Lama, built in 1990 after his death in 1989, is topped with a remarkable likeness of his unmistakable fat, jocular face done in pure gold. As this is the largest functioning monastery in Tibet, the police presence can be a bit heavy at times. Refrain from discussing politics or the Dalai Lama. Don't try to take unauthorized photos, as monks here have been known to manhandle those unwilling to pay for a snapshot. ✉ *Qingdai Xi Lu* ☎ *0892/882–2114* *Y55* *Daily 9:30–7.*

WHERE TO STAY AND EAT

$ ECLECTIC — ✕ **Tashi** *(Daxi Canting).* Another in a series of unrelated restaurants with the same name, this Nepali-managed eatery specializes in excellent Indian dishes such as chicken butter masala. There's also Western fare. ✉ *Eastern end of Walking St.* ✣ *near Qingdao Lu* ☎ *0892/883–5969* *No credit cards.*

¢–$$ TIBETAN — ✕ **Yakhead Tibet** *(Niutou Zangcan).* Located in the middle of Walking Street, this restaurant has the most extensive Tibetan menu in town. Only a few words on the menu have been translated into English, but luckily there's also a photograph of every dish. The yak burgers and fried potato momos are especially popular. Look for the sign with a huge carved yak's head above the entrance. ✉ *14 Walking St.* ☎ *0892/883–7186* *No credit cards.*

$–$$ — **Manasarovar Hotel** *(Shenhu Jiudian).* Until the luxury hotel upon the remains of Shigatse's old fortress opens in a year or two, this will remain the best hotel in town. Unfortunately, it's more than a mile east of the restaurants and shops of Walking Street. Nevertheless, the pleasant rooms have hardwood floors with colorful Tibetan rugs. **Pros:** clean, good Western restaurant. **Cons:** a bit far off, poor service. ✉ *14 Qingdao Lu* ☎ *0892/883–9999* *0892/883–1111* *78 rooms* *In-hotel: restaurant, laundry service, no elevator* *No credit cards.*

SHEGAR

6 hrs (240 km [150 mi]) southwest of Shigatse. 3½ hrs (110 km [70 mi]) northeast of Rongbuk Monastery and Everest Base Camp.

There isn't much of anything to see in Shegar—which also goes by the name New Tingri—a town so small that its two intersecting streets don't even have names. Nevertheless, it's the best place to spend the night before heading down to Rongbuk Monastery for the hike to Everest Base Camp. Supplies in Shegar are more expensive than what you'd pay in Shigatse, but the gouging here is nothing compared to what you'll find closer to Everest. If the accommodations near Everest sound too rough for you, consider making Base Camp a day-trip and spending both nights in the relatively luxurious lodgings in Shegar.

GETTING HERE AND AROUND

The long drive from Shigatse to Shegar is necessary if you want to maximize your time at Everest Base Camp. On the way to Mount Everest, you'll encounter a border area checkpoint about 15 minutes outside of town, so don't forget to bring your passport. About 45 minutes later you'll reach Bang-la Pass, with perhaps the world's best view of the Himalayas. On a clear day you can see 4 of the world's 10 highest peaks including Everest, Lhotse, Makalu, and Cho Oyu.

WHERE TO STAY AND EAT

¢–$$ CHINESE ✕**Chengyu Friendship Restaurant** *(Chengyu Youyi Canting).* This Sichuanese restaurant is overpriced, but so is almost everything in Shegar. Stick to simple classics like stir-fried egg with tomato or sweet-and-sour pork, which can be ordered from an English menu. ✉*Opposite the gas station* ☎*0892/894–7121* ▭*No credit cards.*

$–$$ **Qomolongma Hotel** *(Zhufeng Binguan).* A mediocre government-run hotel, this is nevertheless the best place to stay anywhere near Mount Everest. You'll be well rested for your assault on Base Camp the next day, and the walk to your room down what is perhaps the longest hallway on earth will help you get used to the altitude. The restaurant serves both Chinese and Western fare, although we'd recommend sticking with the former. A mountaineering shop can provide you with any last-minute supplies, although water here is three times as expensive as you'll pay at the small shops near the town's gas station. **Pros:** Only show in town. **Cons:** Only show in town. ✉*From the intersection, go west over a small bridge and turn left into the entrance* ☎*0892/826–2775* *0892/826–2818* *80 rooms* *In-hotel: restaurant, bar, laundry service, public Internet, no elevator* ▭*No credit cards.*

10

EVEREST BASE CAMP

14 hrs (670 km [420 mi]) southwest of Lhasa by jeep. 3½ hrs (110 km[70 mi]) southwest of Shegar (New Tingri).

"Because it's there," mountaineer George Mallory quipped in 1922 when asked why he wanted to climb the tallest mountain on the planet. The fabled peak is located in the world's highest national park, Qomolangma Nature Reserve, which is a visual delight that alone is worth the trek from Lhasa. After the monsoon rains in June the hillsides are covered with a variety of blooming flowers and butterflies. Even from April to June the light snow blanketing the rugged ground and along babbling brooks is striking.

GETTING HERE AND AROUND

If you only have eyes for Everest, you can make it here from Lhasa and back in three days. But you spend about 10 hours driving every day, skip all the sites along the way, and hang out for only an hour or so at Everest Base Camp. Most people make this a five-day trip. Not included in the price of your tour will be the Y65 per person entrance fee, plus Y405 per vehicle, usually split among the passengers.

You can also visit the world's highest monastery, **Ronguk Monastery,** on your way to Base Camp. There were once 500 monks living here, but now there are only 20 monks and 10 nuns who delight in the company of visitors. It is 8 km (5 mi) along a dirt road from the monastery to Base Camp. The 15-minute drive from the monastery is no longer officially allowed, but plenty of jeeps get through with a little cajoling and perhaps a bit of cash. It's more thrilling, however, to make the three-hour walk, even if it is just to say that you trekked the Everest region. Horse-drawn carts are also available for Y30 per person one-way, making the trip in about an hour. Everest Base Camp is a simple plateau where a number of Tibetan entrepreneurs set up tent hotels where you can have a meal, drink a hot cup of tea, and even spend the night.

WHERE TO STAY AND EAT

Sleeping near Mount Everest is a treat, despite that the lodgings are underwhelming. The Chinese hotel near Rongbuk Monastery is extremely overpriced, and the monastery's own guesthouse is a run-down flophouse popular with backpackers. If you're tough and up for a once-in-a-lifetime experience, stay in one of the tents at Everest Base Camp. Every tent hotel has a kitchen serving up decent food.

¢ **Rongbuk Monastery Guesthouse.** This dingy little guesthouse is the most popular lodging near Mount Everest, mainly because it's the only affordable option with four solid walls. Notable is the guesthouse's prison-style lighting system—lights out at 11 PM—and lack of electrical outlets. Still, the restaurant off of the courtyard is an excellent place to warm up and chat with fellow adventurers after a long day of trekking. **Pros:** Social atmosphere. **Cons:** Basic. *Across from Rongbuk Monastery* *No phone* *25 rooms* *In-hotel: restaurant* *No credit cards, no elevator.*

$ **View Station Hotel.** This pink box not far from Rongbuk Monastery is the only hotel-like lodging near Everest Base Camp. Still, for the price you'd expect private bathrooms and consistently hot water, neither of which is available. If you're insistent on staying in a hotel near Mount Everest this place will have to do, but you'd probably be happier heading back to Shegar. **Pros:** It's actually a hotel. **Cons:** Nothing to brag about. *North of Rongbuk Monastery* *No phone* *40 rooms* *In-hotel: restaurant* *No credit cards.*

ENGLISH	PINYIN	CHINESE
TIBET	Xīzàng	西藏
LHASA	Lāsà	拉萨
Ani Tsangkung Nunnery	Āní cāngkōng nīgū ān	美洲黑杜鹃女修道院
Barkhor	bākuò	八廓
Brahmaputra Grand Hotel	Yǎlǔzàngbù dàjiǔdiàn	雅鲁藏布大酒店
Drepung Monastery	Zhébàng sì	哲蚌寺
Ganden Monastery	Gāndān sì	甘丹寺
Himalaya Hotel	Xǐmǎlāyǎ jiǔdiàn	喜玛拉雅酒店
House of Shambhala	Xiānbālā dàjiǔdiàn	眾議院的香巴拉
Jokhang Temple	Dàzhāo sì	大昭寺
Kirey Hotel	Jírì Lǔguǎn	基列伊酒店
Kundeling Monastery	Kūndélīn sì	修道院
Lhasa Gonggar Airport	Gònggá fēijīchǎng	贡嘎飞机场
Lhasa Hotel	Lāsà fàndiàn	拉萨饭店
Lhasa Train Station	Lāsà huǒchēzhàn	拉萨火车站
Muslim Quarter	Mùsīlín xiǎoqū	穆斯林小区
Nechung Monastery	Nǎiqióng sì	修道院
Norbulingka Palace	Luóbùlínkǎ gōng	罗布林卡宫
Oh Dan Guesthouse	Ōudān bīnguǎn	欧丹宾馆
Palha Lupuk Temple	Pàlālǔfǔ Shíkū Miao	寺廟
Potala Palace	Bùdálā Gōng	布达拉宫
Ramoche Temple	Xiǎozhāo sì	小昭寺
Sera Monastery	Sèlā sì	色拉寺
Shangrila	Xiāng Gé Lǐ Lā	香格里拉
Tashi	Zāxī	扎西
Tibet Hotel	Xīzàng bīnguǎn	西藏宾馆
Tibet Museum	Xīzàng bówùguǎn	西藏博物馆
tibet museum	Xīzàng Bówùguǎn	西藏博物館
Yak Hotel	Yà Lǔ Guǎn	牦牛旅館
TSANG PROVINCE	Hōu Zàng Dì Qū	曾蔭權省
GYANTSE	Jiāngzī	江孜
Gyantse Dzong	Jiāngzī Xiàn	江孜镇
Gyantse Hotel	Jiāngzī fàndiàn	江孜饭店
Pelkor Chode Monastery	Bái Jū Sí	修道院
Tashi	Zāxī	扎西
Tashilhunpo Monastery.	Zhāshílúnbù Sì	扎什倫布寺

10

ENGLISH	PINYIN	CHINESE
SHIGATSE	Rìkāzé	日喀则
Tashi	Zāxī	扎西
SHEGAR (NEW TINGRI)	Xīn Dìngrì	新定日
MT EVEREST (QOMOLANGMA)	Zhūmùlǎngmǎfēng	珠穆朗玛峰
Ronguk Monastery	Róngbù Sì	修道院

UNDERSTANDING CHINA

CHINA AT A GLANCE

FAST FACTS

Capital: Beijing
National anthem: March of the Volunteers
Type of government: Communist
Administrative divisions: 23 provinces (including Taiwan), 5 autonomous regions, 4 municipalities, 2 special administrative regions (Hong Kong and Macau)
Independence: October 1, 1949
Constitution: December 4, 1982
Legal system: A mix of custom and statute, largely criminal law, with rudimentary civil code
Suffrage: 18 years of age
Legislature: Unicameral National People's Congress; 2,985 members elected by municipal, regional, and provincial people's congresses to serve five-year terms; next elections scheduled for late 2007 or early February 2008
Population: 1.3 billion; the largest in the world
Population density: 138 people per square km (361 people per square mi)
Median age: Female 31.7, male 31.2
Life expectancy: Female 74.3, male 70.3
Infant mortality rate: 25.3 deaths per 1,000 live births
Literacy: 86%
Language: Standard Chinese or Mandarin (official), Yue (Cantonese), Wu (Shanghainese), Minbei (Fuzhou), Minnan (Hokkien-Taiwanese), Xiang, Gan, Hakka dialects
Ethnic groups: Han Chinese 92%; Zhuang, Uygur, Hui, Yi, Tibetan, Miao, Manchu, Mongol, Buyi, Korean, and other nationalities 8%
Religion: Officially atheist but Taoism, Buddhism, Christianity, and Islam are practiced.
Discoveries & Inventions: Decimal system (1400 BC), paper (100 BC), seismograph (AD 100), compass (200), matches (577), gunpowder (700), paper money (800), movable type (1045)

GEOGRAPHY & ENVIRONMENT

Land area: 9.3 million square km (3.6 million square mi), the fourth-largest country in the world, and slightly smaller than the United States
Coastline: 14,500 km (9,010 mi) on the Yellow Sea, the East China Sea, and the South China Sea
Terrain: Mostly mountains, high plateaus, deserts in west; plains, deltas, and hills in east
Islands: Hainan, Taiwan, many smaller islands along the coast
Natural resources: Aluminum, antimony, coal, hydropower, iron ore, lead, magnetite, manganese, mercury, molybdenum, natural gas, petroleum, tin, tungsten, uranium, vanadium, zinc
Natural hazards: Droughts, earthquakes, floods, land subsidence, tsunamis, typhoons
Environmental issues: Air pollution (greenhouse gases, sulfur dioxide particulates), especially from China's reliance on coal, which is used to generate 70% of the country's electric power. Acid rain is also a consequence of the burning of China's high-sulfur coal, particularly in the north; deforestation; soil erosion and economic development have destroyed one-fifth of agricultural land since 1949; desertification; trade in endangered species; water pollution from untreated wastes; water shortages

China is an attractive piece of meat coveted by all . . . but very tough, and for years no one has been able to bite into it.

— Zhou Enlai, Chinese Premier, 1973

ECONOMY

Currency: Yuan
Exchange rate: Y8.28 = $1
GDP: $6 trillion
Inflation: -0.4%
Per capita income: Y4,329 ($523)
Unemployment: 9%
Workforce: 744 million; agriculture 50%; industry 22%; services 28%
Debt: $149.4 billion
Major industries: Armaments, automobiles, cement, chemical fertilizers, coal, consumer electronics, food processing, footwear, iron and steel, machine building, petroleum, telecommunications, textiles and apparel, toys
Agricultural products: Barley, cotton, fish, millet, oilseed, peanuts, pork, potatoes, rice, sorghum, tea, wheat
Exports: $325.6 billion
Major export products: Footwear, machinery and equipment, mineral fuels, sporting goods, textiles and clothing, toys
Export partners: U.S. 21.5%; Hong Kong 18%; Japan 14.9%; South Korea 4.8%
Imports: $295.3 billion
Major import products: Chemicals, iron and steel, machinery and equipment, mineral fuels, plastics
Import partners: Japan 18%; Taiwan 11%; South Korea 10%; U.S. 9%; Germany 6%

POLITICAL CLIMATE

Since the Chinese Communist Party (CCP) took control of the government in 1949, it has shown little tolerance for outside views. Other major political parties are banned and the government is quick to crack down on movements that it doesn't approve of, most recently the Falun Gong. China's size and diversity complicate national politics, with party control weaker in rural areas, where most of the population lives. Successful politicians have sought support from local and regional leaders and must work to keep influential nonparty members from creating a stir. The decade-long struggle for democracy, which ended in the bloody Tiananmen Square protests of 1989, has fragmented and lost much of its power. The party blamed its rise on foreign agitators and reminds the population that political stability is essential for China's economic growth. The poor handling of the SARS outbreak in early 2003 prompted new calls for government reform.

DID YOU KNOW?

China has nearly 13 million more boys than girls, leading demographers to fear that 40 million Chinese men will remain single in the 21st century.
The country dropped its Soviet-style centralized economy for a more market-oriented system in 1978. As a result, its GDP had quadrupled by 1998.
China is the world's largest producer of red meat and rice.
One out of every three cigarettes in the world is smoked in China.
The nation consumes more than three times the cigarettes puffed away by U.S. smokers.
Since the revolution, China has had four constitutions in less than 60 years. The first three couldn't keep up with the rapid pace of change, particularly during the Cultural Revolution.
China executed more than 17,500 people between 1990 and 1999, more than the rest of the world put together.

CHINESE VOCABULARY

	CHINESE	ENGLISH EQUIVALENT	CHINESE	ENGLISH EQUIVALENT
CONSONANTS				
	b	**b**oat	p	**p**ass
	m	**m**ouse	f	**f**lag
	d	**d**ock	t	**t**ongue
	n	**n**est	l	**l**ife
	g	**g**oat	k	**k**eep
	h	**h**ouse	j	an**d y**et
	q	**ch**icken	x	**sh**ort
	zh	ju**dge**	ch	chur**ch**
	sh	**sh**eep	r*	**r**ead
	z	see**ds**	c	do**ts**
	s	**s**eed		
VOWELS				
	ü	**you**	ia	**ya**rd
	üe	**you + e**	ian	**yen**
	a	f**a**ther	iang	**young**
	ai	k**i**te	ie	**yet**
	ao	n**ow**	o	**a**ll
	e	**ea**rn	ou	g**o**
	ei	d**ay**	u	w**oo**d
	er	c**ur**ve	ua	**wa**ft
	i	y**ie**ld	uo	**wa**ll
	i (after z, c, s, zh, ch, sh)	thunde**r**		

WORD ORDER

The basic Chinese sentence structure is the same as in English, following the pattern of subject-verb-object:

He took my pen.	Tā ná le wŏ de bĕ.
s v o	s v o

NOUNS

There are no articles in Chinese, although there are many "counters," which are used when a certain number of a given noun is specified. Various attributes of a noun—such as size, shape, or use—determine which counter is used with that noun. Chinese does not distinguish between singular and plural.

a pen	yìzhī bǐ
a book	yìběn shū

VERBS

Chinese verbs are not conjugated, and they do not have tenses. Instead, a system of word order, word repetition, and the addition of a number of adverbs serves to indicate the tense of a verb, whether the verb is a suggestion or an order, or even whether the verb is part of a question. Tāzaì ná wǒ de bǐ. (He is taking my pen.) Tā ná le wǒ de bǐ. (He took my pen.) Tā you méi you ná wǒ de bǐ? (Did he take my pen?) Tā yào ná wǒ de bǐ. (He will take my pen.)

TONES

In English, intonation patterns can indicate whether a sentence is a statement (He's hungry.), a question (He's hungry?), or an exclamation (He's hungry!). In Chinese, words have a particular tone value, and these tones are important in determining the meaning of a word. Observe the meanings of the following examples, each said with one of the four tones found in standard Chinese: mā (high, steady tone): mother; má (rising tone, like a question): fiber; mā (dipping tone): horse; and mà (dropping tone): swear.

PHRASES

You don't need to master the entire Chinese language to spend a week in China, but taking charge of a few key phrases in the language can aid you in just getting by.

COMMON GREETINGS		
	Hello/Good morning	Nǐ hǎo/Zǎoshàng hǎo
	Good evening	Wǎnshàng hǎo
	Good-bye	Zàijiàn
	Title for a married woman or an older unmarried woman	Tàitai/Fūrén
	Title for a young and unmarried woman	Xiǎojiě
	Title for a man	Xiěnshēng
	How are you?	Nǐ hǎo ma?
	Fine, thanks. And you?	Hěn hǎo. Xièxie. Nǐ ne?
	What is your name?	Nǐ jiào shénme míngzi?
	My name is . . .	Wí jiào . . .
	Nice to meet you	Hěn gěoxìng rènshì nǐ
	I'll see you later.	Huítóu jiàn.
POLITE EXPRESSIONS		
	Please	Qǐng.
	Thank you	Xièxiè.

Thank you very much.	Fēicháng gănxìe.
You're welcome.	Bú yòng xiè.
Yes, thank you.	Shì de, xièxiè.
No, thank you.	Bù, xièxiè.
I beg your pardon.	Qĭng yuánliàng.
I'm sorry.	Hěn baòqiàn.
Pardon me.	Dùibùqĭ.
That's okay.	Méi shénme.
It doesn't matter.	Méi guěnxi.
Do you speak English?	Nĭ shuō Yĭngyŭ ma?
Yes.	Shì de.
No.	Bù.
Maybe.	Huòxŭ.
I can speak a little.	Wĭ néng shūo yī diănr.
I understand a little.	Wĭ dĭng yì diănr.
I don't understand.	Wĭ bù dĭng.
I don't speak Chinese very well.	Wĭ Zhōngwén shūo de bù haĭ.
Would you repeat that, please?	Qĭng zài shūo yíbiàn?
I don't know.	Wĭ bù zhīdaò.
No problem.	Méi wèntí.
It's my pleasure.	Lèyì er wéi.

NEEDS AND QUESTION WORDS

I'd like . . .	Wĭ xiăng . . .
I need . . .	Wĭ xūyào . . .
What would you like?	Nĭ yaò shénme?
Please bring me . . .	Qĭng gěi wĭ . . .
I'm looking for . . .	Wĭ zài zhăo . . .
I'm hungry.	Wĭ è le.
I'm thirsty.	Wĭ kĭukě.
It's important.	Hěn zhòngyào.
It's urgent.	Hěn jĭnjí.
How?	Zěnmeyàng?
How much?	Duōshăo?
How many?	Duōshăo gè?
Which?	Nă yí gè?
What?	Shénme?

	What kind of?	Shénme yàng de?
	Who?	Shuí?
	Where?	Năli?
	When?	Shénme shíhòu?
	What does this mean?	Zhè shì shénme yìsi?
	What does that mean?	Nà shì shénme yìsi?
	How do you say . . . in Chinese?	. . . yòng Zhōngwén zĕnme shūo?
AT THE AIRPORT		
	Where is . . .	. . . zài năr?
	customs?	Hăigūan
	passport control?	Hùzhào jiănyàn
	the information booth?	Wènxùntái
	the ticketing counter?	Shòupiàochù
	the baggage claim?	Xínglĭchù
	the ground transportation?	Dìmìan jiĕotōng
	Is there a bus service	Yĭu qù chéng lĭ de gōnggòng
	to the city?	qìchē ma?
	Where are . . .	. . . zài năr?
	the international departures?	Guójì hángbĕn chūfĕ diăn
	the international arrivals?	Guójì hángbĕn dàodá diăn
	What is your nationality?	Nĭ shì nĕi guó rén?
	I am an American.	Wĭ shì Mĕiguó rén.
	I am Canadian.	Wĭ shì Jiĕnádà rén.
AT THE HOTEL, RESERVING A ROOM		
	I would like a room . . .	Wĭ yào yí ge fángjiĕn.
	for one person	dĕnrén fáng
	for two people	shuĕngrén fĕng
	for tonight	jīntīan wănshàng
	for two nights	liăng gè wănshàng
	for a week	yí ge xīngqī
	Do you have a different room?	Nĭ hái yĭu bié de fángjiĕn ma?
	with a bath	dài yùshì de fángjiĕn
	with a shower	dài línyù de fángjiĕn
	with a toilet	dài cèsuĭ de fángjiĕn
	with air-conditioning	yĭu kōngtiáo de fángjiĕn

How much is it?	Duōshăo qián?
My bill, please.	Qĭng jiézhàng.

AT THE RESTAURANT

Where can we find a good restaurant?	Zài năr kĕyĭ zhăodào yìjiĕ hăo cĕnguăn?
We'd like a(n) . . . restaurant.	Wĭmen xiăng qù yì gè . . . cĕnguăn.
elegant	gĕo jí
fast-food	kuàicĕn
inexpensive	piányì de
seafood	hăixiĕn
vegetarian	sùshí
Café	Kĕfeī diàn
A table for two	Liăng wèi
Waiter, a menu please.	Fúwùyuán, qĭng gĕi wĭmen càidĕn.
The wine list, please.	Qĭng gĕi wĭmen jĭudĕn.
Appetizers	Kĕiwèi shíwù
Main course	Zhŭ cài
Dessert	Tiándiăn
What would you like?	Nĭ yào shénme cài?
What would you like to drink?	Nĭ yào hē shénme yĭnliào?
Can you recommend a good wine?	Nĭ néng tūijiàn yí ge hăo jĭu ma?
Wine, please.	Qĭng lăi diăn jĭu.
Beer, please.	Qĭng lăi diăn píjiŭ.
I didn't order this.	Wĭ méiyĭu diăn zhè gè.
That's all, thanks.	Jiù zhèxie, xièxiè.
The check, please.	Qĭng jiézhàng.
Cheers!/Bottoms Up!	Gĕnbēi! Zhù nĭ shēntì
To your health!	jiànkĕng.

OUT ON THE TOWN

Where can I find . . .	Năr yĭu . . .
an art museum?	yìshù bówùguăn?
a museum of natural history?	zìránlìshĭ bówùguăn?
a history museum?	lìshĭ bówugŭan?
a gallery?	huàláng?
interesting architecture?	yĭuqù de jiànzhùwù?

	a church?	jiàotáng?
	the zoo?	dòngwùyuán?
	I'd like . . .	Wǐ xiǎng . . .
	to see a play.	kàn xì.
	to see a movie.	kàn diànyǐng.
	to see a concert.	qù yīnyuèhuì.
	to see the opera.	kàn gējù.
	to go sightseeing.	qù guěnguěng.
	to go on a bike ride.	qí děnchē.
SHOPPING		
	Where is the best place to go shopping for . . .	Mǎi . . . zuì hǎo qù nǎr?
	clothes?	yīfu
	food?	shíwù
	souvenirs?	jìniànpǐn
	furniture?	jīajù
	fabric?	bùliào
	antiques?	gǔdǐng
	books?	shūjí
	sporting goods?	yùndòng wùpǐn
	electronics?	diànqì
	computers?	diànnǎo
DIRECTIONS		
	Excuse me. Where is . . .	Duìbùqǐ . . . zài nǎr?
	the bus stop?	Qìchēzhàn
	the subway station?	Dìtiězhàn
	the rest room?	Xǐshǐujiěn
	the taxi stand?	Chūzū chēzhàn
	the nearest bank?	Zùijìn de yínháng
	the hotel?	Lüˇguǎn
	To the right	Zài yòubiěn.
	To the left.	Zài zuǐbiěn.
	Straight ahead.	Wǎng qián zhízǐu.
	It's near here.	Jìuzài zhè fùjìn.
	Go back.	Wǎng húi zǐu.
	Next to . . .	Jǐnkào . . .

TIME		
	What time is it?	Xiànzài shénme shíjiěn?
	It is noon.	Zhōngwŭ.
	It is midnight.	Bànyè.
	It is 9:00 a.m.	Shàngwŭ jĭu diăn.
	It is 1:00 p.m.	Xiàwŭ yì diăn.
	It is 3 o'clock.	Sĕn diăn (zhōng).
	5:15	Wŭ diăn shíwŭ fēn.
	7:30	Qī diăn sĕnshí (bàn).
	9:45	Jĭu diăn sìshíwŭ.
	Now	Xiànzài
	Later	Wăn yì diănr
	Immediately	Măshàng
	Soon	Hĕn kuài

DAYS OF THE WEEK		
	Monday	Xīngqī yī
	Tuesday	Xīngqī èr
	Wednesday	Xīngqī sĕn
	Thursday	Xīngqī sì
	Friday	Xīngqī wŭ
	Saturday	Xīngqī lìu
	Sunday	Xīngqī rì (tiĕn)

MODERN CONNECTIONS		
	Where can I find . . .	Zài năr kĕyĭ shĭ yòng . . .
	a telephone?	dìanhuà?
	a fax machine?	chuánzhēnjī?
	an Internet connection?	guójì wănglù?
	How do I call the United States?	Gĕi Mĕiguó dă diànhuà zĕnme dă?
	I need . . .	Wĭ xūyào . . .
	a fax sent.	fĕ chuánzhēn.
	a hookup to the Internet.	yŭ guójì wănglù liánjiē.
	a computer.	diànnăo.
	a package sent overnight.	liányè bă bĕoguĭ jìchū.
	some copies made.	fùyìn yìxiē wénjiàn.
	a VCR and monitor.	lùyĭngjī he xiănshiqì.

	an overhead projector and markers.	huàndēngjī he biěoshìqì.

EMERGENCIES AND SAFETY

	Help!	Jìumìng a!
	Fire!	Jìuhuǐ a!
	I need a doctor.	Wǐ yào kàn yīshēng.
	Call an ambulance!	Mǎshàng jiào jìuhùchē!
	What happened?	Fěshēng le shénme shì?
	I am/My wife is/My husband is/	Wǐ/Wǐ qīzi/Wǐ Zhàngfu/
	My friend is/Someone is . . . very sick.	Wǐ péngyǐu/Yǐu rén . . .
	having a heart attack.	bìng de hěn lìhài.
	choking.	yēzhù le.
	losing consciousness.	yūndǎo le.
	about to vomit.	yào ǐutù le.
	having a seizure.	yòu fěbìng le.
	stuck.	bèi kǎ zhù le.
	I can't breathe.	Wǐ bù néng hūxī.
	I tripped and fell.	Wǐ bàn dǎo le.
	I cut myself.	Wǐ gē shěng le.
	I drank too much.	Wǐ jǐu hē de tàı duo le.
	I don't know.	Wǐ bù zhīdào.
	I've injured my . . .	Wǐ de . . . shòushěng le.
	head	toú
	neck	bózi
	back	Bèi
	arm	shǐubèi
	leg	tuǐ
	foot	jiǎo
	eye(s)	yǎnjīng
	I've been robbed.	Wǐ bèi qiǎng le

NUMBERS

	0	Líng
	1	Yī
	2	Er
	3	Sěn
	4	Sì

	5	Wŭ
	6	Lìu
	7	Qī
	8	Bĕ
	9	Jĭu
	10	Shí
	11	Shíyī
	12	Shí'èr
	13	Shísĕn
	14	Shísì
	15	Shíwŭ
	16	Shílìu
	17	Shíqī
	18	Shíbĕ
	19	Shíjĭu
	20	Ershí
	21	Ershíyī
	22	Ershí'èr
	23	Eshísĕn
	30	Sĕnshí
	40	Sìshí
	50	Wŭshí
	60	Lìushí
	70	Qīshí
	80	Bĕshí
	90	Jĭushí
	100	Yìbăi
	1,000	Yìqiĕn
	1,100	Yìqiĕn yìbăi
	2,000	Liăngqiĕn
	10,000	Yíwàn
	100,000	Shíwàn
	1,000,000	Băiwàn

Travel Smart China

WORD OF MOUTH

". . . I don't remember exact ATM locations at Shanghai, but they should be clearly visible in the arrivals hall. Making the gesture of inserting your card into a machine will anyway get you pointed in the right direction."

—PeterN_H

GETTING HERE & AROUND

Make no mistake: this is one HUGE country. China's efficient train system is a good way of getting around if you're not in a hurry. The growing network of domestic flights is a quicker travel option.

China's capital, Beijing, is in the northeast. Financial capital Shanghai is halfway down the east coast. The historic city of Nanjing is upriver from Shanghai; head much farther inland and you'll hit the erstwhile capital Xi'an, home to the Terracotta Warriors.

Limestone mountains surround the Guilin area, in southern China. The region's hubs are Guangzhou, capital of Guandong province, and Shenzhen, an industrial boomtown on the border with Hong Kong. Though part of China, Hong Kong is a Special Autonomous Region, and functions as if it were another country.

Smack bang in the middle of China is Sichuan province. Its capital, Chengdu, is an important financial center, and is a transport hub connecting eastern and western China. Kunming is the capital of the southwestern province of Yunnan. Once the gateway to the Silk Road, it's now a gateway to the bordering countries of Myanmar, Laos, and Vietnam.

Despite ongoing international controversy, Tibet, in the far west of the country, remains a special Chinese autonomous region. Its capital, Lhasa, the historical center of Tibetan Buddhism, is a mind-blowing 3,650 meters (11,975 feet) above sea level on the northern Himalayas.

Vast deserts and grassy plains make up much of northwest China. Here, autonomous Xinjiang province is home to a largely Muslim population. Its capital city, Ürümqi, is the farthest city inland on earth. Nei Mongolia, or Inner Mongolia, is a great swath of (mostly barren) land that runs across much of the north of China.

Maps with street names in Pinyin are available in most Chinese cities, though they're not always up to date. A few crucial words of Chinese can help decode street names. *Lu* means road, *jie* means street, *dalu* is a main road, and *dajie* is a main street. Those endings are often preceded by a compass point: *bei* (north), *dong* (east), *nan* (south), *xi* (west), and *zhong* (middle). These distinguish different sections of long streets. So, if you're looking for Beijing Xi Lu, it's the western end of Beijing Road.

TRAVEL TIMES FROM BEIJING

To	By Air	By Train
Shanghai	2¼ hours	10–22 hours
Xi'an	2 hours	11–15 hours
Guangzhou	3 hours	20–27 hours
Hong Kong	3¾ hours	21–28 hours
Guilin	3¼ hours	22–27 hours
Kunming	3¼ hours	38–47 hours
Nanjing	1¾ hours	8–16 hours
Lhasa	6 hours	46 hours
Ürümqi	4 hours	40 hours
Chengdu	3¾ hours	25–31 hours

BY AIR

If you are flying into Asia on a SkyTeam airline (Delta or Continental, for example), you're eligible to purchase their Asia Pass. It covers over 15 Chinese cities (including Beijing, Shanghai, Xi'an, and Hong Kong) as well as destinations in 20 other Asian and Australasian countries. The pass works on a coupon basis; the minimum of three coupons costs $600, and six coupons come to $1,128.

Beijing, Xiamen, and Hong Kong are three of the cities included in the One World Alliance Visit Asia Pass. Cities are grouped into zones, and a flat rate is levied for each flight based on the zone in which the city is located. It doesn't include flights from the United States, however. Inquire through American Airlines, Cathay Pacific, or any other One World member. It won't be the cheapest way to get around, but you'll be flying on some of the world's best airlines.

If you're planning to travel to several different Asian destinations, Cathay Pacific's All Asia Pass is an excellent deal. For $1,500 you get a round-trip ticket from New York (JFK), Los Angeles, or San Francisco to Hong Kong, plus 21 days of unlimited travel to up to four other Asian cities. You can pay supplements to add cities that aren't included and to extend the pass: $400 buys you up to 90 days and/or additonal cities cost $300. If you just want to combine Hong Kong and one other Cathay destination, though, go for a regular ticket: the airline generally allows a free Hong Kong stopover.

China Southern Airlines's China Air Pass is excellent value if you're planning to fly to several destinations within the country: the minimum 3-coupon pass comes to $394, and the 10-coupon pass costs $1,116. The catch? You have to be flying in from abroad on one of their flights. Hong Kong isn't included in the pass, but Shenzhen, just over the border, gets you close enough. Bear in mind that Chinese domestic flight schedules can be very flexible—flights may be changed or canceled at a moment's notice.

Air Pass Info All Asia Pass (*Cathay Pacific ☎ 800/233–2742 🌐 www.cathay-usa.com*). **Asia Pass** (*SkyTeam ☎ 800/523–3273 Continental, 800/221–1212 Delta 🌐 www.skyteam.com*). **China Air Pass** (*China Southern Airlines ☎ 323/653–8088 🌐 www.flychinasouthern.com*). **Visit Asia Pass** (*OneWorld Alliance ☎ 800/233–2742 Cathay Pacific 🌐 www.oneworld.com*).

Beijing, Shanghai, and Hong Kong are China's three major international hubs. You can catch nonstop or one-stop flights to Beijing from New York (13¾), Chicago (13–14 hours), San Francisco (11½–12½ hours), Los Angeles (11½–13 hours), Sydney (14–16 hours), and London (10½–11½ hours). Though most airlines say that reconfirming your return flight is unnecessary, some local airlines cancel your seat if you don't reconfirm.

Airlines & Airports Airline and Airport Links.com (*🌐 www.airlineandairportlinks.com*) has links to many of the world's airlines and airports.

Airline-Security Issues Transportation Security Administration (*🌐 www.tsa.gov*) has answers for almost every question that might come up.

AIRPORTS

Northern China's main hub is the efficient Beijing Capital International Airport (PEK), 27 km (17 mi) northeast of the Beijing city center. Shanghai has two airports: Pudong International Airport (PVG) is newer and flashier than scruffy Hongqiao International Airport (SHA), but Hongqiao is more efficient and closer to downtown. The main hub in southern China is the fabulous Hong Kong International Airport (HKG), also known as Chek Lap Kok.

There are also international airports at Guangzhou (CAN), Kunming (KMG), Xiamen (XMN), Shenzhen (SZX), Xi'an (XIY), Chengdu (CTU), and Guilin (KWL), among others.

Clearing customs and immigration in China can take a while, especially in the mornings, so arrive at least two hours before your scheduled flight time.

While wandering Chinese airports, someone may approach you offering to carry your luggage, or even just give you directions. Be aware that this "helpful" stranger will almost certainly expect payment. Many of the X-ray machines used for large luggage items aren't film-safe, so keep films in your carry-on.

Airport Information Beijing Capital International Airport (*☎ 010/6454 1100* www.en.bcia.com.cn). **Chengdu Shuangliu International Airport** (028/8525-6360 www.cdairport.com). **Guangzhou Baiyun International Airport** (020/3606-6999 www.gbiac.net/en/). **Guilin Liangjiang International Airport** (077/3284-5114 www.airport-gl.com.cn). **Hong Kong International Airport** (852/2181-8888 www.hongkongairport.com). **Kunming Wujiaba Airport** (0871/711-4300). **Shanghai Hongqiao International Airport** (021/6268-8899 www.shanghaiairport.com). **Shanghai Pudong International Airport** (021/6834-1000 www.shanghaiairport.com). **Shenzhen Bao'an International Airport** (0755/9500-0666 www.eng.szairport.com). **Xi'an Xianyang International Airport** (029/0500-2327 www.xian-airport.com). **Xiamen Gaoqi International Airport** (0592/570-6017 www.xiagc.com.cn).

FLIGHTS

TO & FROM CHINA

Air China is China's flagship carrier. It operates nonstop flights from Beijing and Shanghai to various North American and European cities. Although it once had a sketchy safety record, the situation has improved dramatically, and it is now part of Star Alliance (an "alliance" of airlines worldwide that helps facilitate travel between them). Don't confuse it with the similarly named China Airlines, which is operated out of Taiwan.

Air Canada has daily flights to Beijing and Shanghai from Vancouver and Montréal. Cathay Pacific flies to Beijing via Hong Kong. China Eastern and China Southern airlines fly from China to the West Coast of the United States. Japan Airlines and All Nippon fly to Beijing via Tokyo. Northwest and United both have service to Beijing from the United States, and United has a nonstop flight to Shanghai and Beijing from Chicago.

WITHIN CHINA

China Southern is the major carrier for domestic routes, flying to over 80 cities in China. Its main rival is China Eastern. Smaller Shanghai Airlines has a growing number of national routes, mostly out of Shanghai.

The service on most Chinese airlines is on par with low-cost American airlines—be prepared for limited legroom, iffy food, and possibly no personal TV. More importantly, always arrive at least two hours before departure, as chronic overbooking means latecomers just don't get on.

You can make reservations and buy tickets for flights within China through airline Web sites or with travel agencies. It's worth contacting a Chinese travel agency like China International Travel Service (CITS) (⇨ *Visitor Information, above*) to compare prices.

Airline Contacts **Air China** (800/982-8802 in New York, 800/986-1985 in San Francisco, 800/882-8122 in Los Angeles www.airchina.com). **China Eastern** (800/200-5118, 626/583-1500, 310/646-1849 in Los Angeles, 415/982-5115, 650/875-2367 in San Francisco www.ce-air.com). **China Southern** (888/338-8988 www.cs-air.com/en). **China Southwest Airlines** (028/8666-8080 in China www.cswa.com/en). **Shanghai Airlines** (800/620-8888 www.shanghai-air.com).

BY BIKE

For millions of Chinese people, bicycles are still the primary form of transport, although the proliferation of cars is making biking less pleasant. Large cities like Beijing, Chengdu, Xi'an, Shanghai, and Guilin have well-defined bike lanes, often separated from other traffic. Travel by bike is extremely popular in the countryside around Guilin, too. Locals don't rate gears much—take your cue from them and just roll along at a leisurely pace. Note that bikes have to give way to motorized vehicles at intersections. If a flat tire or sudden brake failure strikes, seek out the nearest street-side mechanic (they're everywhere), easily identified by their bike parts and pumps.

In major cities, some lower-end hotels and hostels rent bikes. Otherwise inquire at bike shops, CTS or even corner shops. The going rental rate is Y15 to Y30 a day, plus a refundable deposit. Check the seat and wheels carefully.

Most rental bikes come with a lock, but they're usually pretty low quality. Instead, leave your wheels at an attended bike park—peace of mind costs a mere Y0.50. Helmets are just about unheard of in China, though upmarket rental companies catering to foreign tourists usually rent them. They charge much more for their bikes, but they're usually in better condition.

If you're planning a lot of cycling, note that for about Y150 to Y200 you can buy your own basic bike, though expect to pay three or four times that for a mountain bike with all the bells and whistles or for a "Flying Pigeon," the classic heavy-duty model Beijing was once famous for.

The U.S. company Backroads has a China bike tour suitable for families. Bike China Adventures organizes trips of varying length and difficulty all over China. The Adventure Center runs cycling trips along the Great Wall, in Guilin, and out of Hong Kong.

BIKES IN FLIGHT

Most airlines accommodate bikes as luggage, provided they are dismantled and boxed; check with individual airlines about packing requirements. Some airlines sell bike boxes, which are often free at bike shops, for about $20 (bike bags can be considerably more expensive).

Tour Operator Backroads (☎ *800/462-2848* 🌐 *www.backroads.com*). **Bike China Adventures** (☎ *800/818-1778* 🌐 *www.bikechina.com*). **The Adventure Center** (☎ *800/228-8747* 🌐 *www.adventurecenter.com*).

LUCKY NUMBER

Sichuan Airlines bought the number 28-8888-8888 for 2.33 million yuan ($280,723) during an auction of more than 100 telephone numbers in 2003, making it the most expensive telephone number in the world. The number 8 (*ba* in Chinese), is considered lucky in China, as it is similar to the Cantonese word for "getting rich."

BY BOAT

Trains and planes are fast replacing China's boat and ferry services. Four- to seven-day cruises along the Yangtze River are the most popular, and thus the most touristy of the domestic boat rides. Both local and international companies run these tours, but shop around as prices vary drastically.

See chapter 8 for specific details on the Yangtze River Cruise information. The Shanghai Ferry Company and the China-Japan International Ferry Company both operate weekly services to Osaka, Japan, from Shanghai. You can purchase tickets for both international and domestic services (in Chinese) at local terminals, or through CITS for a small surcharge.

Information China-Japan International Ferry Company (✉ *908 Dongdaming Lu, Shanghai* ☎ *021/6325-7642* 🌐 *www.shinganjin.com*). **Shanghai Ferry Company** (☎ *021/6537-5111* 🌐 *www.shanghai-ferry.co.jp*).

BY BUS

China now has some fabulous luxury long-distance buses with air-conditioning and movies. Most of these services run out of Beijing and Shanghai. However, buying tickets can be complicated if you don't speak Chinese—you may end up on one of the cramped old-style affairs, much like an old-fashioned school bus (or worse). The conditions on sleeper buses are particularly dire. Taking a train or an internal flight is easier and safer, especially in rural areas where bad road conditions make for dangerous rides.

Big cities often have more than one bus terminal, and luxury services sometimes leave from the private depot of the company operating the service. Services are frequent and usually depart and arrive punctually. You can buy tickets for a small surcharge through CITS.

Bus Information **CITS** offices are located in every city; see specific city listings for contact information. **Hong Kong Tourist Association** (*HKTA information hotline* ☎ *852/2807-6177* 🌐 *www.hkta.org*).

BY CAR

Driving oneself is not a possibility when vacationing in mainland China, as the only valid driver's licenses are Chinese ones. However, this restriction should be cause for relief, as city traffic is terrible, drivers manic and maniacal, and getting lost inevitable for first-timers. Conditions in Hong Kong aren't much better, but you can drive there using a U.S. license.

A far better idea is to put yourself in the experienced hands of a local driver and sit back and watch them negotiate the tailbacks. All the same, consider your itinerary carefully before doing so—in big cities, taking the subway or walking are often far quicker for central areas. Keep the car for excursions farther afield.

The quickest way to hire a car and driver is to flag down a taxi and hire it for the day—if you're happy with a driver you've used for a trip around town, ask him. After some negotiating, expect to pay between Y350 and Y600, depending on the type of car. Most hotels can make arrangements for you, though they often charge you double that rate.

Another alternative is American car-rental agency Avis, which includes mandatory chauffeurs as part of all rental packages. A car and driver usually cost Y740 to Y850 ($93 to $110) per day. They have offices in Beijing, Hong Kong, Shanghai, Guangzhou, and Shenzhen.

BY TRAIN

China's enormous rail network is one of the world's busiest. Trains are usually safe and run strictly to schedule. There are certain intricacies to buying tickets, which usually have to be purchased in the city of origin. You can buy most tickets 10 days in advance; 2 to 3 days ahead is usually enough time, except during the three national holidays—Chinese New Year (two days in mid-January–February), Labor Day (May 1), and National Day (October 1).

The cheapest place for tickets is the train station, where they only accept cash and English is rarely spoken. Most travel agents, including CITS, can book your tickets for a small surcharge (Y20 to Y50). You can also buy tickets through online retailers like China Train Ticket. They deliver the tickets to your hotel but you often end up paying much more than the station rate.

The train system offers a glimpse of old-fashioned socialist euphemisms. There are four classes, but instead of first class and second class, in China you talk about hard and soft. Hard seats (*yingzuo*) are often rigid benchlike seats guaranteed to numb the buttocks within seconds; soft seats (*ruanzuo*) are more like the seats in long-distance American trains. For overnight journeys, the cheapest option is the hard sleeper (*yingwo*), open bays of six bunks, in two tiers of three. They're cramped, but not uncomfortable; though you take your own bedding and share the toilet with everyone in the wagon. Soft sleepers (*ruanwo*) are more comfortable: their closed compartments have four beds with bedding. Trains between Beijing, Shanghai, Hong Kong, and Xi'an have a deluxe class, with only two berths per compartment and private bathrooms. The nonstop Z-series trains are even more luxurious.

Train types are identifiable by the letter preceding the route number: Z is for non-stop, T is for a normal express.

Overpriced dining cars serve meals that are often inedible, so you'd do better to make use of the massive thermoses of boiled water in each compartment and take along your own noodles or instant soup, like locals do. Trains are always crowded, but you are guaranteed your designated seat, though not always the overhead luggage rack. Note that theft on trains is increasing; on overnight trains, sleep with your valuables or else keep them on the inside of the bunk.

You can find out just about everything about Chinese train travel at Seat 61's fabulous Web site. China Highlights has a searchable online timetable for major train routes. The tour operator Travel China Guide has an English-language Web site that can help you figure out train schedules and fares.

Information China Highlights (*www.chinahighlights.com*). **Seat 61** (*www.seat61.com/China.htm*). **Travel China Guide** (*www.travelchinaguide.com/china-trains/*).

SERIOUS TRAINING

The most dramatic Chinese train experience is the six-day trip between Beijing and Moscow, often referred to as the Trans-Siberian railway, though that's actually the service that runs between Moscow and Vladivostok. Two weekly services cover the 8,047 km (5,000 mi) between Moscow and Beijing. The Trans-Manchurian is a Russian train that goes through northeast China, whereas the Trans-Mongolian is a Chinese train that goes through the Great Wall and crosses the Gobi Desert. Both have first-class compartments with four berths (Y2,500), or luxury two-berth compartments (Y3,000). Trains leave from Beijing Station—the cheapest place to buy tickets, though it's easier to get them through CITS.

ESSENTIALS

GREETINGS

Chinese people aren't very touchy-feely with one another, even less so with strangers. Stick to handshakes and low-key greetings when you are first meeting local people. Always use people's title and surname until they invite you to do otherwise.

SIGHTSEEING

By and large, the Chinese are a rule-abiding bunch. Follow their lead and avoid doing anything signs advise against. Although you won't be banned from entering any sightseeing spots on grounds of dress, you'd do well to avoid overly skimpy or casual clothes.

China is a crowded country; pushing, nudging, and line-jumping are commonplace. It may be hard to accept, but it's not considered rude, so avoid reacting (even verbally) if you're accidentally shoved.

OUT ON THE TOWN

It's a great honor to be invited to someone's house, so explain at length if you can't go. Arrive punctually with a small gift for the hosts; remove your shoes outside if you see other guests doing so. Eating lots is the biggest compliment you can pay the food (and the cook).

Smoking is one of China's greatest vices. No-smoking sections in restaurants used to be nonexistent, but they are becoming more prevalent in cities like Beijing and Shanghai.

Holding hands in public is OK, but keep passionate embraces for the hotel room.

DOING BUSINESS

Time is of the essence when doing business in China. Make appointments well in advance and be extremely punctual, as this shows respect. Chinese people have a keen sense of hierarchy in the office: if you're visiting in a group, the senior member should lead proceedings.

Suits are still the norm in China, regardless of the outside temperature. Women should avoid plunging necklines, heavy makeup, overly short skirts or high heels. Pants are completely acceptable. Women can expect to be treated as equals by local businessmen.

Face is ever-important. Never say anything that will make people look bad, especially in front of superiors. Avoid being pushy or overly buddylike when negotiating: address people as Mr. or Ms. until they invite you to do otherwise, respect silences in conversation and don't hurry things or interrupt. When entertaining, local businesspeople may insist on paying: after a slight protest, accept, as this lets them gain face.

Business cards are a big deal: not having one is like not having a personality. If possible, have yours printed in English on one side and Chinese on the other (your hotel can usually arrange this in a matter of hours). Proffer your card with both hands and receive the other person's in the same way, then read it carefully and make an admiring comment.

Many gifts, like clocks and cutting implements, are considered unlucky in China. Food—especially presented in a showy basket—is always a good gift choice, as are imported spirits. Avoid giving four of anything, as the number is associated with death. Offer gifts with both hands, and don't expect people to open them in your presence.

LANGUAGE

For language fundamentals, see Language Notes in the back of the book for an explanation of pronunciation and a vocabulary list. Translations of specific place names are located at the end of every chapter. Nearly everyone in mainland China speaks Putonghua (*pǔtōnghuà*, the "common language") another name for Mandarin Chinese. It's written using ideograms, or characters; in 1949 the government also introduced a phonetic writing system that uses the Roman alphabet. Known as Pinyin, it's widely used to label public buildings and station names. Even if you don't speak or read Chinese, you can easily compare Pinyin names with a map.

In Hong Kong the main language spoken is Cantonese, although many people speak English. There are many other local Chinese dialects. Some use the same characters as Putonghua for writing, but the pronunciation is so different as to be unintelligible to a Putonghua speaker. The Chinese government actively discourages mainlanders from using dialects in front of foreigners. There are several non-Chinese languages (such as Mongolian, Uyghur, and Tibetan) spoken by China's ethnic minorities.

Chinese grammar is simple, but a complex tonal system of pronunciation means it usually takes a long time for foreigners to learn Chinese. Making yourself understood can be tricky; however, the Chinese will appreciate your making the effort to speak a few phrases understood almost everywhere. Try "Hello"—*"Ní hǎo"* (nee how); "Thank you"—*"Xiè xiè"* (shee-yeh, shee-yeh); and "Good-bye"—*"Zai jian"* (dzai djan). When pronouncing words written in Pinyin, remember that "q" and "x" are pronounced like "ch" and "sh," respectively; "zh" is pronounced like the "j" in "just"; "c" is pronounced like "ts."

English isn't widely spoken, though the staff in most hotels, travel agencies, and upscale restaurants in major cities is the exception. If you're lost and need help, look first to someone under 30, who may have studied some English in school. In shops, calculators and hand gestures do most of the talking.

A great place to start learning online before your trip is ChinesePod.com, which has free podcasts you can download and listen to any time.

WORD OF MOUTH

"We were on our own for a week in Beijing and 5 days in Shanghai, and any difficulties we encountered were minor. Once we realized how easy it was to get around Beijing and do what we wanted to do we were very pleased that we hadn't signed up for a tour." –Neil Oz

Language Resources *Business Companion: Chinese*, by Tim Dobbins and Paul Westbrook, **Living Language/Random House Inc** (☎ *800/726–0600* 🌐 *www.livinglanguage.com*). *I Can Read That! A Traveler's Introduction to Chinese Characters*, by Julie Mazel Sussman, **China Books and Periodicals, Inc** (☎ *415/282–2994* 📠 *415/282–0994* 🌐 *www.chinabooks.com*). *In the Know in China*, by Jennifer Phillips, **Living Language/Random House Inc** (☎ *800/726–0600* 🌐 *www.livinglanguage.com*).

ACCOMMODATIONS

The forums on Fodors.com are a great place to start your hotel investigations.

Location is the first thing you should consider. Chinese cities are usually big, and there's no point schlepping halfway across town for one particular hotel when a similar option is available more conveniently.

In major urban centers, many four- or five-star hotels belong to familiar international chains, and are usually a safe—if pricey—bet. You can expect swimming pools, a concierge, and business services here. Locally owned hotels with four stars or less have erratic standards both in and out of big cities, as bribery plays a big part in star acquisition. However, air-conditioning, color TV, and private Western-style bathrooms are the norm for three to four stars, and even lone-star hotels have private bathrooms, albeit with a squatter toilet. Extra-firm beds are a trademark of Chinese hotelerie even in luxury chains.

(⇨Restaurant & Hotel price charts appear at the beginning of each chapter.)

■TIP→ Assume that hotels operate on the European Plan (EP, no meals) unless we specify that they use the Breakfast Plan (BP, with full breakfast), Continental Plan (CP, Continental breakfast), Full American Plan (FAP, all meals), Modified American Plan (MAP, breakfast and dinner), or are all-inclusive (AI, all meals and most activities).

APARTMENT & HOUSE RENTALS

There's an abundance of furnished rental properties for short- and long-term lets in Beijing, Guangzhou, Hong Kong, Shanghai, and some other cities, too. Prices vary wildly. At the top end are luxury apartments and villas, usually far from the city center and accessible by (chauffeur-driven) car. Usually described as "serviced apartments" or "villas," these often include gyms and pools, and rents are usually well over $2,000 a month.

There are a lot of well-located mid-range properties in new apartment blocks. They're usually clean, with new furnishings, with rents starting at $500. Finally, for longer, cheaper stays, there are normal local apartments. These are firmly off the tourist circuit and often cost only a third of the price of the midrange properties. Expect mismatched furniture, erratic amenities, and varying insect populations, although what you get for your money fluctuates, so shop around.

Property sites like Move and Stay, Sublet, and Primacy Relocation have hundreds of apartments in major cities. The online classified pages in local English-language magazines or on expat Web sites are good places to look for cheaper properties.

Contacts Asia Expat (🌐 *www.asiaxpat.com*). **Primacy Relocation** (🌐 *www.worthenpacific.com*). **Move and Stay** (🌐 *www.moveandstay.com*). **Sublet.com** (🌐 *www.sublet.com*).

HOMESTAYS

Single travelers can arrange homestays (often in combination with language courses) through China Homestay Club. Generally these are in upper-middle-class homes that work out to be at least as expensive as a cheap hotel—prices start from $175 to $235 a week. Nine times out of 10, the family has a small child in need of daily English-conversation classes. ChinaHomestay.org is a different organization that charges a single placement fee of $875 for a stay of three months or less.

Organizations China Homestay Club (🌐 *www.homestay.com.cn*). **ChinaHomestay.org** (🌐 *www.chinahomestay.org*).

HOSTELS

Budget accommodation options are improving in China. However, the term "hostel" is still used vaguely—the only thing guaranteed is shared dorm rooms aimed at backpackers; other facilities vary. Backpacking hot spots like Yangshuo have lots of options. Beijing, Shanghai, Hong Kong, and Xi'an all have a few decent hostels, but flea-ridden dumps are also common, so always ask to see your room before paying. New places open all the time, so try to get recommendations from fellow travelers as you go. Note that a private room in a low-end hotel is often just as cheap as so-called hostels; some guesthouses and hotels also have cheaper dorm beds in addition to regular rooms.

China's small but growing Youth Hostelling Association is based in Guangzhou and has a growing list of affiliates. Backpackers.com is a useful resource for booking budget accommodations online, as is HostelWorld.com. Their prices are sometimes higher than the walk-up rate, but it's good to know you have a bed reserved when you arrive.

Information Backpackers.com (🌐 *www.backpackers.com*). **Hostelling International—USA** (☎ *301/495–1240* 🌐 *www.hiusa.org*). **HostelWorld.com** (🌐 *www.hostelworld.*

com). **Youth Hostel Association of China** (☎ *020/8734–5080* 🌐 *www.yhachina.com*).

HOTELS

All hotels listed have private bath unless otherwise noted. Remember that water is a precious resource in China and use accordingly.

When checking in to a hotel, you need to show your passport—the desk clerk records the number before you're given a room. Unmarried couples may occasionally have problems staying together in the same room, but simply wearing a band on your left finger is one way to avoid this complication. Friends or couples of the same sex, especially women, shouldn't have a problem getting a room together. There may, however, be regulations about who is allowed in your room, and it's also normal for hotels to post "visitor hours" inside the room.

BUSINESS SERVICES & FACILITIES

Your hotel (or another nearby mid- to top-end one) is the best place to start looking for business services, including translation. Most are very up-to-speed on businesspeople's needs and can put you in touch with other companies if necessary. Regus and the Executive Centre are international business-services companies with several office locations in Beijing, Shanghai, and Hong Kong. They provide secretarial services, meeting and conference facilities, and office rentals.

Contacts The Executive Centre (🌐 *www.executivecentre.com*). **Regus** (☎ *800/819–0091* 🌐 *www.regus.cn*).

COMMUNICATIONS

INTERNET

China's major cities are very Internet-friendly for those bearing laptops. Most mid- to high-end hotels have in-room Internet access; if the hotel doesn't have a server but you have a room phone, you can usually access a government-provided ISP, which only charges you for the phone call. Wi-Fi is growing exponentially—many hotels and even cafés provide it free.

Many hotels also have a computer with Internet access that you can use. Internet cafés are ubiquitous in big cities, and are rapidly spreading to smaller destinations. Known as *wang ba* in Chinese, they're not usually signposted in English, so ask your hotel to recommend one nearby. Prices (and cleanliness) vary considerably, but start at about Y3 to Y10 per hour.

Remember that there is strict government control of the Internet in China. There's usually no problem with Web-based mail, but you may be unable to access news and even blog sites. To get around the restrictions, you can subscribe to a Virtual Private Network or use proxy servers to access certain sites. AnchorFree offers a free VPN called Hotspot Shield, though the service includes annoying pop-up ads. A more reliable service, like those from WiTopia, will cost about $40 a year for safe, fast surfing. If you're going to be in China a while, investing in a VPN is worth the cost.

PHONES

The country code for China is 86; the city code for Beijing is 10, and the city code for Shanghai is 21. Hong Kong has its own country code: 852. To call China from the United States or Canada, dial the international access code (011), followed by the country code (86), the area or city code without the initial zero, and the eight-digit phone number.

Numbers beginning with 800 within China are toll-free. Note that a call from China to a toll-free number in the United States or Hong Kong is a full-tariff international call. If you need to call home, use your computer and a service like Skype or a Web messenger service with phone access. Beware though and be sure to download the U.S. version of Skype—the

Chinese TOM-Skype is constantly monitored by government cyberpolice.

CALLING WITHIN CHINA

The Chinese phone system is cheap and efficient. You can make local and long-distance calls from your hotel or any public phone on the street. Some pay phones accept coins, but it's easier to buy an integrated circuit (IC) calling card, available at convenience stores and newsstands (⇨ *see Calling Cards, below*). Local calls are generally free from landlines, though your hotel might charge a nominal rate. Long-distance rates in China are very low. Calling from your hotel room is a viable option, as hotels can only add a 15% service charge.

Chinese phone numbers have eight digits—you only need to dial these when calling somewhere within the city or area you're in. In general, city codes appear written with a 0 in front of them; if not, you need to add this when calling another city within China.

For directory assistance, dial 114. If you want information for other cities, dial the city code followed by 114 (note that this is considered a long-distance call). For example, if you're in Beijing and need directory assistance for a Shanghai number, dial 021–114. The operators do not speak English, so if you don't speak Chinese you're best off asking your hotel for help.

To make long-distance calls from a public phone you need an IC card (⇨ *Phone Cards*). To place a long-distance call, dial 0, the city code, and the eight-digit phone number.

CALLING OUTSIDE CHINA

To make an international call from within China, dial 00 (the international access code within China) and then the country code, area code, and phone number.

The United States country code is 1.

IDD (international direct dialing) service is available at all hotels, post offices, major shopping centers, and airports. By international standards prices aren't unreasonable, but it's vastly cheaper to use a long-distance calling card, known as an IP card (*see Calling Cards, below*). These cards' rates also beat AT&T, MCI, and Sprint hands-down. If you do need to use these services, dial 108 (the local operator) and the local access codes from China: 11 for AT&T, 12 for MCI, and 13 for Sprint. Dialing instructions in English will follow.

Access Codes AT&T Direct (☎ *800/874–4000 from China: Call 108–11 from southern China or 108–888 from northern China*). **MCI WorldPhone** (☎ *800/444–4444 from China: 108–12*). **Sprint International Access** (☎ *800/793–1153 from China: 108–13 from south China or 108–713 from north China*).

CALLING CARDS

Calling cards are a key part of the Chinese phone system. There are two kinds: the IC card (integrated circuit; *àicei ka*), for local and domestic long-distance calls on pay phones; and the IP card (Internet protocol; *aipi ka*) for international calls from any phone. You can buy both at post offices, convenience stores, and street vendors.

IC cards come in denominations of Y20, Y50, and Y100, and can be used in any pay phone with a card slot—most urban pay phones have them. Local calls using them cost around Y0.30 a minute, and less on weekends and after 6 PM.

To use IP cards, you first dial a local access number. You then enter a card number and PIN, and finally the phone number, complete with international dial codes. When calling from a payphone, both cards' minutes are deducted at the same time—one for local access (IC card) and one for the long-distance call you placed (IP card). There are countless different card brands; China Unicom is one that's usually reliable. IP cards come with face values of Y20, Y30, Y50, and Y100.

However, the going rate for them is up to half that, so bargain vendors down.

CELL PHONES

If you have a tri-band GSM or a CDMA phone, pick up a local SIM card (*sim ka*) from any branch of China Mobile or China Unicom: there are often branches at international Chinese airports. You'll be presented with a list of possible phone numbers, with varying prices—an "unlucky" phone number (one with lots of 4s) could be as cheap as Y50, whereas an auspicious one (full of 8s) could fetch Y300 or more. You then buy prepaid cards to charge minutes onto your SIM—do this straight away as you need credit to receive calls. Local calls to landlines cost Y0.25 a minute, and to cell phones Y0.60. International calls from cell phones are very expensive. Remember to bring an adapter for your phone charger. You can also buy cheap handsets from China Mobile—if you're planning to stay even a couple of days this is probably cheaper than renting a phone.

Contacts Cellular Abroad (☎ *800/287-5072* 🌐 *www.cellularabroad.com*) rents and sells GMS phones and sells SIM cards that work in many countries. **Mobal** (☎ *888/888-9162* 🌐 *www.mobalrental.com*) rents cell phones and sells GSM phones (starting at $49) that will operate in 140 countries. Per-call rates vary throughout the world.

CUSTOMS & DUTIES

Except for the usual prohibitions against narcotics, explosives, plant and animal material, firearms, and ammunition you can take anything into China that you plan to take away with you. Cameras, video recorders, GPS equipment, laptops, and the like should pose no problems. However, China is very sensitive about printed matter deemed seditious, such as religious, pornographic, and political items, especially articles, books, and pictures of Tibet. All the same, small amounts of English language reading matter aren't generally a problem. Customs officials are for the most part easygoing, and visitors are rarely searched. It's not necessary to fill in customs declaration forms, but if you carry in a large amount of cash, say several thousand dollars, you should declare it upon arrival.

WORD OF MOUTH

"I really enjoyed being in China on my own; I did a lot of reading before I went and I'm glad I did, as nothing can truly prepare you for the reality . . . but it sure does help to have that background!" –Amy

You're not allowed to remove any antiquities dating to before 1795. Antiques from between 1795 and 1949 must have an official red seal attached—quality antiques shops know this and arrange it.

U.S. Information U.S. Customs and Border Protection (🌐 *www.cbp.gov*).

EATING OUT

In China, meals are really a communal event, so food in a Chinese home or restaurant is always shared—you usually have a small bowl or plate to transfer food from the center platters into. Although cutlery is available in many restaurants, it won't hurt to brush up on your use of chopsticks, the utensil of choice.

The standard eating procedure is to hold the bowl close to your mouth and shovel in the contents without any qualms. Noisily slurping up soup and noodles is also the norm. Covering the tablecloth in crumbs, drips, and even spat-out bones is a sign you've enjoyed your meal. It's considered bad manners to point or play with your chopsticks, or to place them on top of your rice bowl when you're finished eating (place the chopsticks horizontally on the table or plate). Avoid, too, leaving your chopsticks standing up in a bowl of rice—they look like the two incense sticks burned at funerals.

If you're invited to a formal Chinese meal, be prepared for great ceremony, endless toasts and speeches, and a grand variety of elaborate dishes. Your host will be seated at the "head" of the round table, which is the seat that faces the door. Wait to be instructed where to sit. Don't start eating until the host takes the first bite, and then simply help yourself as the food comes around, but don't take the last piece on a platter. Always let the food touch your plate before bringing it up to your mouth; eating directly from the serving dish is bad form.

For information on food-related health issues, see Health, below.

MEALS & MEALTIMES

Food is a central part of Chinese culture, and so eating should be a major activity on any trip to China. Breakfast is not usually a big deal—congee, or rice porridge (*zhou*) is the standard dish. Most mid- and upper-end hotels do big buffet spreads, whereas blooming café chains provide lattes and croissants in China's major cities.

Snacks are a food group in themselves. There's no shortage of steaming street stalls selling kebabs, grilled meat or chicken, bowls of noodle soup, and the ubiquituous *baozi* (stuffed dumplings). Many visitors seem to loath eating from stalls—you'd be missing out on some of the best nibbles around, though. Pick a place where lots of locals are eating to be on the safe side.

The food in hotel restaurants is usually acceptable, but vastly overpriced. Restaurants frequented by locals always serve tastier fare at better prices. Don't shy from trying establishments without an English menu—a good phrase book and lots of pointing can usually get you what you want.

If you're craving Western food (or sushi or a curry), rest assured that big cities have plenty of American fast-food chains, and sometimes world-class international restaurants, too. Most higher-end Chinese restaurants have a Western menu, but you're usually safer sticking to the Chinese food.

Meals in China are served early: breakfast until 9 AM, lunch between 11 and 2, and dinner from 5 to 9.

Unless otherwise noted, the restaurants listed in this guide are open daily for lunch and dinner.

PAYING

At most restaurants you ask for the bill at the end of the meal, like you do back home. At cheap noodle bars and street stands you often pay up front. Only very upmarket restaurants accept payment by credit card.

RESERVATIONS & DRESS

Regardless of where you are, it's a good idea to make a reservation if you can. In some places (Hong Kong, for example), it's expected. We only mention them specifically when reservations are essential (there's no other way you'll ever get a table) or when they are not accepted. For popular restaurants, book as far ahead as you can (often 30 days), and reconfirm as soon as you arrive. (Large parties should always call ahead to check the reservations policy.) We mention dress only when men are required to wear a jacket or a jacket and tie.

WINES, BEER & SPIRITS

Forget tea, today the people's drink of choice is beer. Massively popular among Chinese men, it's still a bit of a no-no for Chinese women, however. Tsingtao, China's most popular brew is a 4% lager that comes in liter bottles and is usually cheaper than water. Many regions have their own local breweries, too, and international bands are also available.

When you see "wine" on the menu, it's usually referring to sweet fruit wines or distilled rice wine. The most famous brand of Chinese liquor is Maotai, a distilled liquor ranging in strength from 35%

to 53% proof. Like most firewaters, it's an acquired taste.

There are basically no licensing laws in China, so you can drink anywhere, and at any time, provided you can find somewhere open to serve you.

ELECTRICITY

The electrical current in China is 220 volts, 50 cycles alternating current (AC) so most American appliances can't be used without a transformer. A universal adapter is especially useful in China as wall outlets come in a bewildering variety of configurations: two- and three-pronged round plugs, as well as two-pronged flat sockets. Although blackouts are not common in Chinese cities, villages occasionally lose power for short periods of time.

Consider making a small investment in a universal adapter, which has several types of plugs in one lightweight, compact unit. Most laptops and cell-phone chargers are dual voltage (i.e., they operate equally well on 110 and 220 volts), so require only an adapter. These days the same is true of small appliances such as hair dryers. Always check labels and manufacturer instructions to be sure. Don't use 110-volt outlets marked FOR SHAVERS ONLY for high-wattage appliances such as hair dryers.

Contacts **Steve Kropla's Help for World Travelers** (*www.kropla.com*) has information on electrical and telephone plugs around the world. **Walkabout Travel Gear** (*www.walkabouttravelgear.com*) has a good coverage of electricity under "adapters."

EMERGENCIES

If you lose your passport, contact your embassy immediately. Embassy officials can also advise you on how to proceed in case of other emergencies. The staff at your hotel may be able to provide an interpreter if you need to report an emergency or crime to doctors or the police. Most police officers and hospital staff members don't speak English, though you may find one or two people who do.

Ambulances generally offer just a means of transport, not medical aid; taking a taxi is quicker and means you can choose the hospital you want to go to. Where possible, go to a private clinic catering to expats—prices are sky-high but so are their hygiene and medical standards. Most have reliable 24-hour pharmacies.

U.S. Embassy & Consulate **United States Consulate** (*1469 Huaihai Zhong Lu, Xuhui District, Shanghai 021/6433-6880, 021/6433-3936 for after-hours emergencies Citizen Services Section, Westgate Mall, 8th fl., 1038 Nanjing Xi Lu, Jingan District 021/3217-4650 shanghai.usembassy-china.org.cn*). **United States Embassy** (*55 Anjialou Lu, Chaoyang District, Beijing 010/8531-4000 beijing.usembassy-china.org.cn*). **United States Citizens Services** (*4 Ling Shi Guan Rd., Chengdu 028/8558-3992 chengdu.usembassy-china.org.cn 1 South Shamian St., Guangzhou 020/8518-7605, 020/8121-6077 for after-hours emergencies guangzhou.usembassy-china.org.cn*).

General Emergency Contacts **Ambulance** (*120*). **Fire** (*119*). **Police** (*110*).

HEALTH

The most common types of illnesses are caused by contaminated food and water. Especially in developing countries, drink only bottled, boiled, or purified water and drinks; don't drink from public fountains

WORD OF MOUTH

Was the service stellar or not up to snuff? Did the food give you shivers of delight or leave you cold? Did the prices and portions make you happy or sad? Rate restaurants and write your own reviews in "Travel Ratings" or start a discussion about your favorite places in "Travel Talk" on www.fodors.com. Your comments might even appear in our books. Yes, you, too, can be a correspondent!

or use ice. You should even consider using bottled water to brush your teeth. Make sure food has been thoroughly cooked and is served to you fresh and hot; avoid vegetables and fruits that you haven't washed (in bottled or purified water) or peeled yourself. If you have problems, mild cases of traveler's diarrhea may respond to Imodium (known generically as loperamide) or Pepto-Bismol. Be sure to drink plenty of fluids; if you can't keep fluids down, seek medical help immediately. Tap water in major cities like Beijing and Shanghai is safe for brushing teeth, but buy bottled water to drink and check the bottle is sealed.

Infectious diseases can be airborne or passed via mosquitoes and ticks and through direct or indirect physical contact with animals or people. Some, including Norwalk-like viruses that affect your digestive tract, can be passed along through contaminated food. If you are traveling in an area where malaria is prevalent, use a repellant containing DEET and take malaria-prevention medication before, during, and after your trip as directed by your physician. Condoms can help prevent most sexually transmitted diseases, but they aren't absolutely reliable and their quality varies from country to country. Speak with your physician and/or check the CDC or World Health Organization Web sites for health alerts, particularly if you're pregnant, traveling with children, or have a chronic illness.

SHOTS & MEDICATIONS

No immunizations are required for entry into China, but it's a good idea to be immunized against typhoid and Hepatitis A and B before traveling, as well as routine tetanus-diphtheria and measles boosters. In winter, a flu vaccination is also smart, especially you're infection-prone or are a senior citizen. ■ **TIP→ In summer months malaria is a risk in tropical and rural areas, especially Hainan and Yunnan provinces—consult your doctor four to six weeks before your trip as preventative treatments vary.** The risk of contracting malaria in cities is small.

Health Warnings National Centers for Disease Control & Prevention (*CDC ☎ 877/394–8747 international travelers' health line* *www.cdc.gov/travel*). **World Health Organization** (*WHO* *www.who.int*).

SPECIFIC ISSUES IN CHINA

Even at China's public hospitals foreigners need to pay fees to register, to see a doctor, and then for all tests and medication. Prices are cheap compared to the fancy foreigner clinics that exist in major cities, where you pay $100 to $150 just for a consultation. However, most doctors at public hospitals don't speak English and hygiene standards are low—all the more reason to take out medical insurance.

Hong Kong has excellent public and private healthcare. Foreigners have to pay for both, so insurance is a good idea. Even for lesser complaints private doctors charge a fortune: head to a public hospital if money is tight. In an emergency you'll always receive treatment first and get the bill afterward—Y570 is the standard ER charge.

The best place to start looking for a suitable doctor is through your hotel concierge, then the local Public Security Bureau. If you become seriously ill or are injured, it is best to fly home, or at least to Hong Kong, as quickly as possible. In Hong Kong, English-speaking doctors are widely available.

Pneumonia and influenza are common among travelers returning from China—talk to your doctor about inoculations before you leave. If you need to buy prescription drugs, try to go to the pharmacies of reputable private hospitals. Do *not* buy them in street-side pharmacies as the quality control is unreliable.

Avian Influenza, commonly known as Bird Flu, is a form of influenza that affects birds (including poultry) but can be passed to humans. It causes initial flu symptoms, followed by respiratory and organ failure. Although rare, it's often lethal. There've been several outbreaks in Hong Kong and China since 2003. The Hong Kong Government now exercises strict control over poultry farms and markets, and there are signs all over town warning against contact with birds. Things aren't so well-controlled in the mainland, however, so ensure any poultry or eggs you consume are well cooked.

Severe Acute Respiratory Syndrome (SARS), also known as atypical pneumonia, is a respiratory illness caused by a strain of coronavirus that was first reported in parts of Asia—notably Hong Kong—in early 2003. Symptoms include a fever greater than 100.4°F (38°C), shortness of breath, and other flulike symptoms. The disease is thought to spread by close person-to-person contact, particularly respiratory droplets and secretions transmitted through the eyes, nose, or mouth. SARS hasn't returned to Hong Kong or China, but many experts believe that it or other contagious, upper-respiratory viruses will continue to be a seasonal health concern.

OVER-THE-COUNTER REMEDIES

Most pharmacies in big Chinese cities carry over-the-counter Western medicines and traditional Chinese medicines. By and large, you need to ask for the generic name of the drug you're looking for, not a brand name. Acetominophen—or Tylenol—is often known as paracetomol in Hong Kong. In big cities, reputable pharmacies like Watsons are usually a better bet than no-name ones.

HOURS OF OPERATION

Most banks and government offices are open weekdays 9 AM to 5 PM or 6, although close for lunch (sometime between noon and 2). Some bank branches and most CTS tour desks in hotels keep longer hours and are open Saturday (and occasionally Sunday) mornings. Many hotel currency-exchange desks stay open 24 hours. Museums open from roughly 9 AM to 6 PM, six or seven days a week. Everything in China grinds to a halt for the first two or three days of Chinese New Year (sometime in mid-January to February), and opening hours are often reduced for the rest of that season.

Pharmacies are open daily from 8:30 or 9 AM to 6 or 7 PM. Some large pharmacies stay open until 9 PM or even later. Shops and department stores are generally open daily 8 AM to 8 PM; some stores stay open even later in summer, in popular tourist areas, or during peak tourist season.

HOLIDAYS

National holidays in mainland China include New Year's Day (January 1); Spring Festival aka Chinese New Year (late January/early February); Qingming Jie (April 4); International Labor Day (May 1); Dragon Boat Festival (late May/early June); anniversary of the founding of the Communist Party of China (July 1); anniversary of the founding of the Chinese People's Liberation Army (August 1); and National Day—founding of the People's Republic of China in 1949 (October 1); Chongyang Jie or Double Ninth Festival (9th day of 9th lunar month). Hong Kong celebrates most of these festivals, and also has public holidays at Easter and for Christmas and Boxing Day (December 25 and 26). (⇨*Festivals & Seasonal Events in Chapter 1.*)

MAIL

Sending international mail from China is extremely reliable. Airmail letters to any place in the world should take 5 to 14 days. Express Mail Service (EMS) is available to many international destinations. Letters within any city arrive the next day, and mail to the rest of China takes a day or two longer. Domestic mail can be subject to search so don't send sensitive materials, such as religious or political literature, as you might cause the recipient trouble.

Service is more reliable if you mail letters from post offices rather than mailboxes. Buy envelopes here, too, as there are standardized sizes in China. You need to glue stamps onto envelopes as they're not self-adhesive. Most post offices are open daily between 8 AM and 7 PM; many keep longer hours. Your hotel can usually send letters for you, too.

You can use the Roman alphabet to write an address. Do not use red ink, which has a negative connotation. You must also include a six-digit zip code for mail within China. Sending airmail postcards costs Y4.50 and letters Y5 to Y7.

Long-term guests can receive mail at their hotels. Otherwise, the best place to receive mail is at the American Express office. Most major Chinese cities have American Express offices with client-mail service. Be sure to bring your American Express card, as the staff will not give you the mail without seeing it

SHIPPING PACKAGES

It's easy to ship packages home from China. Take what you want to send *unpacked* to the post office—everything will be sewn up officially into satisfying linen-bound packages, a service that costs a few yuan. You have to fill in lengthy forms—enclosing a photocopy of receipts for the goods inside isn't a bad idea, as they may be opened by customs along the line. Large antiques stores often offer reliable shipping services that take care of customs in China. Large international couriers operating in China include DHL, Federal Express, and UPS—next-day delivery for a 1-kilogram (2.2-pound) package starts at about Y300. Your hotel can also arrange shipping parcels, but there's usually a hefty markup.

Express Services **DHL** (☎ *800/810–8000* 🌐 *www.cn.dhl.com*). **FedEx** (☎ *800/988–1888* 🌐 *www.fedex.com*). **UPS** (☎ *800/820–8388* 🌐 *www.ups.com*).

MONEY

China is a cheap destination by most North Americans' standards but expect your dollar to do more for you in smaller cities than pricey Shanghai or Beijing. The exception to the rule is Hong Kong, where eating and sleeping prices are on a par with the United States.

In mainland China the best places to convert your dollars into yuan are at your hotel's front desk or a branch of a major bank, such as Bank of China, CITIC, or HSBC. All these operate with standardized government rates—anything cheaper is illegal, and thus risky. You need to present your passport to change money.

ITEM	AVERAGE COST
Cup of coffee at Starbucks	Y20–Y25
Glass of local beer	Y10–Y30
Cheapest subway ticket	Y2
2-km (1-mi) taxi ride in Beijing or Shanghai	Y10–Y11
Set lunch in a cheap restaurant	Y20
Hourlong foot massage	Y50
Fake Chloé purse	Y200

Prices throughout this guide are given for adults. Substantially reduced fees are almost always available for children, students, and senior citizens.

Although credit cards are gaining ground in China, for day-to-day transactions cash is definitely king.

Currency Conversion **Google** (🌐 *www.google.com*). **Oanda.com** (🌐 *www.oanda.com*). **XE.com** (🌐 *www.xe.com*).

ATMS & BANKS

Your own bank will probably charge a fee for using ATMs abroad; the foreign bank you use may also charge a fee.

Nevertheless, you'll usually get a better rate of exchange at an ATM than you will at a currency-exchange office or even when changing money in a bank.

■ TIP→ PIN numbers with more than four digits are not recognized at ATMs in many countries. If yours has five or more, remember to change it before you leave.

ATMs are widespread in major Chinese cities. The most reliable ATMs are HSBC's. They also have the highest withdrawal limit, which offsets transaction charges. Of the Chinese banks, your best bet for ATMs is the Bank of China, which accepts most foreign cards. That said, machines frequently refuse to give cash for mysterious reasons—move on and try another. On-screen instructions appear automatically in English.

ATMs are widely available throughout Hong Kong—most carry the sign ETC instead of ATM. Subway stations are a good place to look.

CREDIT CARDS

American Express, MasterCard, and Visa are accepted at most hotels and a growing number of upmarket stores and restaurants. Diners Club is less widely accepted.

Throughout this guide, the following abbreviations are used: **AE,** American Express; **DC,** Diners Club; **MC,** MasterCard; and **V,** Visa.

It's a good idea to inform your credit-card company before you travel. Otherwise, the credit-card company might put a hold on your card owing to unusual activity—not a good thing halfway through your trip. Record all your credit-card numbers—as well as the phone numbers to call if your cards are lost or stolen—in a safe place, so you're prepared should something go wrong. Both MasterCard and Visa have general numbers you can call (collect if you're abroad) if your card is lost, but you're better off calling the number of your issuing bank, since MasterCard and Visa usually just transfer you to your bank; your bank's number is usually printed on your card.

If you plan to use your credit card for cash advances, you'll need to apply for a PIN at least two weeks before your trip. Although it's usually cheaper (and safer) to use a credit card abroad for large purchases (so you can cancel payments or be reimbursed if there's a problem), note that some credit-card companies *and* the banks that issue them add substantial percentages to all foreign transactions, whether they're in a foreign currency or not. Check on these fees before leaving home, so there won't be any surprises when you get the bill.

■ TIP→ Before you charge something, ask the merchant whether or not he or she plans to do a dynamic currency conversion (DCC). In such a transaction the credit-card *processor* (shop, restaurant, or hotel, not Visa or MasterCard) converts the currency and charges you in dollars. In most cases you'll pay the merchant a 3% fee for this service in addition to any credit-card company and issuing-bank foreign-transaction surcharges.

Dynamic currency conversion programs are becoming increasingly widespread. Merchants who participate in them are supposed to ask whether you want to be charged in dollars or the local currency, but they don't always do so. And even if they do offer you a choice, they may well avoid mentioning the additional surcharges. The good news is that you *do* have a choice. And if this practice really gets your goat, you can avoid it entirely thanks to American Express; with its cards, DCC simply isn't an option.

Reporting Lost Cards **American Express** (☎ *800/992–3404 in the U.S., 336/393–1111 collect from abroad* 🌐 *www.americanexpress.com*). **Diners Club** (☎ *800/234–6377 in the U.S., 303/799–1504 collect from abroad* 🌐 *www.dinersclub.com*). **MasterCard** (☎ *800/622–7747 in the U.S., 636/722–7111 collect from abroad, 800/110–7309 in*

China 🌐 *www.mastercard.com).* **Visa** *(☎ 800/847-2911 in the U.S., 410/581-9994 collect from abroad, 800/711-2911 in China* 🌐 *www.visa.com).*

CURRENCY & EXCHANGE

The Chinese currency is officially called the yuan (Y), and is also known as *renminbi* (RMB), or "People's Money." You may also hear it called *kuai*, an informal expression like "buck."

Old and new styles of bills circulate in China, and many denominations have both coins and bills. The Bank of China issues bills in denominations of 1 (burgundy), 2 (green), 5 (brown or purple), 10 (turquoise), 20 (brown), 50 (blue or occasionally yellow), and 100 (red). There are 1 yuan coins, too. The yuan subdivides into 10-cent units called *jiao* or *mao*; these come in bills and coins of 1, 2, and 5. The smallest denomination is the *fen*, which comes in coins (and occasionally tiny notes) of 1, 2, and 5. Counterfeiting is rife in China, and even small stores inspect notes with ultraviolet lamps. Change can be a problem—don't expect much success paying for a Y13 purchase with a Y100 note.

Exchange rates in China are fixed by the government daily, so it's equally good at branches of the Bank of China, at big department stores, or at your hotel's exchange desk. Any lower rates are illegal, so you're exposing yourself to scams. A passport is required. Hold on to your exchange receipt, which you need to convert your extra yuan back into dollars.

In Hong Kong, the only currency used is the Hong Kong dollar, divided into 100 cents. Three local banks (HSBC, Standard Chartered, and the Bank of China) all issue bills and each has their own designs. At this writing, the Hong Kong dollar was pegged to the U.S. dollar at approximately 7.75 Hong Kong dollars to 1 U.S. dollar. There are no currency restrictions in Hong Kong. You can exchange currency at the airport, in hotels, in banks, and through private money changers scattered through the tourist areas. Banks usually have the best rates, but as they charge a flat HK$50 fee for non-account holders, it's better to change large sums infrequently. Currency-exchange offices have no fees, but they offset that with poor rates. Stick to ATMs whenever you can.

■ TIP→ Even if a currency-exchange booth has a sign promising no commission, rest assured that there's some kind of huge, hidden fee. (Oh . . . that's right. The sign didn't say no *fee*.) And as for rates, you're almost always better off getting foreign currency at an ATM or exchanging money at a bank.

PASSPORTS & VISAS

All U.S. citizens, even infants, need a valid passport with a tourist visa stamped in it to enter China (except for Hong Kong, where you only need a valid passport). It's always best to have at least six months' validity on your passport before traveling to Asia.

Getting a tourist visa to China (known as an "L" visa) in the United States is straightforward. Standard visas are for single-entry stays of up to 30 days, and are valid for 90 days from the day of issue (NOT the day of entry), so don't get your visa too far in advance. The cost for a tourist visa issued to a U.S. citizen is $130; citizens of other countries can expect to pay between $30 and $90.

Travel agents in Hong Kong can also issue visas to visit mainland China—though this was disrupted during the Olympics and regulations can change during times of unrest. Note: The visa application will ask your occupation. The Chinese government doesn't look favorably upon those who work in publishing or the media. People in these professions routinely state "teacher" under "occupation." Before you go, contact the embassy or consulate of the People's Republic of China to gauge the current mood.

Hong Kong Travel Agents China Travel Service (*CTS* ☎ *852/2851–1700* 🌐 *www.ctshk.com*) has 22 branches all over Hong Kong.

Children traveling with only one parent do not need a notarized letter of permission to enter China. However, as these kinds of policies can change, being overprepared isn't a bad idea.

Under no circumstances should you overstay your visa. To extend your visa, stop by the Entry and Exit Administration Office of the local branch of the Public Security Bureau a week before your visa expires. The office is known as the PSB or the Foreigner's Police; most are open weekdays 9 to 11:30 and 1:30 to 4:30. The process is extremely bureaucratic, but it's usually no problem to get a month's extension on a tourist visa. You need to bring your registration of temporary residency from your hotel and your passport, which you generally need to leave for five to seven days (so do any transactions requiring it beforehand). If you are trying to extend a business visa, you'll need the above items as well as a letter from the business that originally invited you to China saying it would like to extend your stay for work reasons. Rules are always changing, so you will probably need to go to the office at least twice to get all your papers in order.

The Web site 🌐 *www.visatoasia.com/china.html* provides up-to-date information on visa applications to China.

Chinese Visa Information Chinese Consulate, New York (☎ *212/244–9456* 🌐 *newyork.chineseconsulate.org*). **Visa Office of Chinese Embassy, Washington** (☎ *202/328–2500* 🌐 *www.china-embassy.org*). **Visa to Asia** (🌐 *www.visatoasia.com/china.html*).

WORD OF MOUTH

". . . unless you'll be attending a formal business or social meeting you will NOT need dressy clothing in China. The Chinese themselves tend to dress quite casually. I would just take one 'smart casual' outfit for eating out, theater performances and the like." –Neil Oz

GENERAL REQUIREMENTS FOR MAINLAND CHINA

Passport	Must be valid for six months after date of arrival
Visa	Required for U.S. citizens ($130)
Required Vaccinations	None
Recommended Vaccinations	Hepatitis A and B, typhoid, influenza, booster for tetanus-diphtheria
Driving	Chinese driver's license required

China officially denies visas (and thus entry) to anyone suffering from infectious diseases, including leprosy, AIDS, venereal diseases, and contagious tuberculosis. You must complete information regarding these on applications and on entering the country. However, this information is never checked for tourist visas, though medical tests are required for longer visas.

PACKING

Most Chinese people dress for comfort, so you can plan to do the same. There's little risk of offending people with your dress: Westerners tend to attract attention regardless of their attire. Fashion capitals Hong Kong and Shanghai are the exceptions to the comfort rule: slop around in flip-flops and worn denims and you WILL feel there's a neon "tourist" sign over your head. Opt for your smarter jeans or capri pants for sightseeing there.

Sturdy, comfortable walking shoes are a must: go for closed shoes over Tevas as dust and toe-stomping crowds make them impractical. Northern Chinese summers are dusty and baking hot, so slacks, capris, and sturdy shorts are best. A raincoat, especially a light Goretex one or a fold-up poncho, is useful for an onset of rainy weather, especially in Southern China. During the harsh winters, thermal long johns are a lifesaver—especially in low-star hotel rooms.

That said, in urban centers you can prepare to be unprepared: big Chinese cities are a clothes shopper's paradise. If a bulky jacket's going to put you over the airline limit, buy one in China and leave it behind when you go. All the other woollies—and silkies, the local insulator of choice—you'll need go for a song, as do brand-name jackets. Scarves, gloves, and hats, all musts, are also easy to find.

Most good hotels have reliable overnight laundry services, though costs can rack up on a long trip. Look outside your hotel for cheaper laundries, and bring some concentrated travel detergent for small or delicate items. Note that it's often cheaper to buy things than have your own laundered, so if you're even a little interested in shopping, consider bringing an extra, foldable bag to cart purchases home in.

Keep packets of Kleenex and antibacterial hand wipes in your day pack—paper isn't a feature of Chinese restrooms, and you often can't buy it in smaller towns. A small flashlight with extra batteries is also useful. The brands in Chinese pharmacies are limited, so take adequate stocks of your potions-n-lotions, feminine-hygiene products (tampons are especially hard to find), and birth control. All of these things are easy to get in Hong Kong.

In your carry-on luggage, pack an extra pair of eyeglasses or contact lenses and enough of any medication you take to last a few days longer than the entire trip.

If you're planning a longer trip or will be using local tour guides, bring a few inexpensive items from your home country as gifts. Popular gifts are candy, T-shirts, and small cosmetic items such as lipstick and nail polish—double-check that none were made in China. Be wary about giving American magazines and books as gifts, as these can be considered propaganda and get your Chinese friends into trouble.

RESTROOMS

Public restrooms abound in mainland China—the street, parks, restaurants, department stores, and major tourist attractions are all likely locations. Most charge a small fee (usually less than Y1), but seldom provide Western-style facilities or private booths. Instead, expect squat toilets, open troughs, and rusty spigots; WC signs at intersections point the way to these facilities. Toilet paper is a rarity, so carry tissues and antibacterial hand wipes in your day pack. The restrooms in the newest shopping plazas, fast-food outlets, and deluxe restaurants catering to foreigners are generally on a par with American restrooms. In post-SARS Hong Kong, public restrooms are well maintained. Alternatively, dip into malls or the lobby of big international hotels to use their loos.

Find a Loo The Bathroom Diaries (🌐 *www.thebathroomdiaries.com*) is flush with unsanitized info on restrooms the world over—each one located, reviewed, and rated.

SAFETY

There is little violent crime against tourists in China, partly because the penalties are severe for those who are caught—China's yearly death-sentence tolls run into the thousands. Single women can move about without too much hassle. Handbag-snatching and pickpocketing do happen in markets and on crowded buses or trains—keep an eye open and your money safe and you should have no problems. Use the lockbox in your hotel room to store any valuables, but always carry your passport with you for identification purposes.

China is full of people looking to make a quick buck. The most common scam involves people persuading you to go with them for a tea ceremony, which is often so pleasant that you don't smell a rat until several hundred dollars appear on your credit card bill. "Art students" who pressure you into buying work is another common scam. The same rules that apply to hostess bars worldwide are also true in China. Avoiding such scams is as easy as refusing *all* unsolicited services—be it from taxi or pedicab drivers, tour guides, or potential "friends."

TIP→ Distribute your cash, credit cards, IDs, and other valuables between a deep front pocket, an inside jacket or vest pocket, and a hidden money pouch. Don't reach for the money pouch once you're in public.

Chinese traffic is as manic as it looks, and survival of the fittest (or the biggest) is the main rule. Crossing streets can be an extreme sport. Drivers rarely give pedestrians the right-of-way and don't even look for pedestrians when making a right turn on a red light. Cyclists have less power but are just as aggressive.

The severely polluted air of China's big cities can bring on, or aggravate, respiratory problems. If you're a sufferer, take the cue from locals, who wear surgical masks, or a scarf or bandana as protection.

Contact Transportation Security Administration (*TSA*; *www.tsa.gov*).

TAXES

There is no sales tax in China or Hong Kong. Mainland hotels charge a 5% tax; bigger, joint-venture hotels also add a 10% to 15% service fee. Some restaurants charge a 10% service fee.

TIME

The whole of China is 8 hours ahead of London, 13 hours ahead of New York, 14 hours ahead of Chicago, and 16 hours ahead of Los Angeles. There's no daylight saving time, so subtract an hour in summer.

Time Zones Timeanddate.com (*www.timeanddate.com/worldclock*) can help you figure out the correct time anywhere in the world.

TIPPING

Tipping is a tricky issue in China. It's officially forbidden by the government, and locals simply don't do it. In general, follow their lead without qualms. Nevertheless, the practice is beginning to catch on, especially among tour guides, who often expect Y10 a day. Official CTS representatives aren't allowed to accept tips, but you can give them candy, T-shirts, and other small gifts. You don't need to tip in restaurants or in taxis.

In Hong Kong, hotels and major restaurants usually add a 10% service charge; in almost all cases, this money does not go to the waiters and waitresses. Add on up to 10% more for good service. Tipping restroom attendants is common, but it is generally not the custom to leave an additional tip in taxis and hair salons.

TOURS

Most guided tours to China take in three or four major cities, often combined with a Yangtze River cruise or a visit to far-flung Tibet. You get a day or two in each place, with the same sights featured in most tours. If you want to explore a given city in any kind of depth, you're better doing it by yourself or getting a private guide.

Shopping stops plague China tours, so inquire before booking as to when, where, and how many to expect. Although you're never obliged to buy anything, they can take up big chunks of your valuable travel time, and the products offered are always ridiculously overpriced. Even on the best tours, you can count on having to sit through at least one or two.

Small groups and excellent guides are what Overseas Adventure Travel takes pride in. The Adventure Center has a huge variety of China packages, including trekking, cycling, and family tours. China Focus Travel has 10 different China tours—they squeeze in a lot for your money. Ritz Tours is a mid-range agency specializing in East Asian tours. R. Crusoe & Son is an offbeat company that organizes small group or tailor-made private tours. For something more mainstream, try Pacific Delight; for serious luxury, head to Artisans of Leisure or Imperial Tours. If you're concerned about responsible tourism, try Wild China, a high-caliber local company with some of the most unusual trips around. For example, one of their cultural trips explores China's little-known Jewish history.

Not all of the companies we list include air travel in their packages. Check this when you're researching your trip.

Recommended Companies **Artisans of Leisure** (☎ *800/214–8144* 🌐 *www.artisansofleisure.com*). **China Focus Travel** (☎ *800/868–7244* 🌐 *www.chinafocustravel.com*). **Imperial Tours** (☎ *888/888–1970* 🌐 *www.imperialtours.net*). **Overseas Adventure Travel** (☎ *800/493–6824* 🌐 *www.oattravel.com*). **Pacific Delight** (☎ *800/221–7179* 🌐 *www.pacificdelighttours.com*). **R. Crusoe & Son** (☎ *800/585–8555* 🌐 *www.rcrusoe.com*). **Ritz Tours** (☎ *626/289–7777* 🌐 *www.ritztours.com*). **The Adventure Center** (☎ *800/228–8747* 🌐 *www.adventurecenter.com*). **Wild China** (☎ *010/6465–6602* 🌐 *www.wildchina.com*).

SPECIAL-INTEREST TOURS

ART

Ethnic folk art and the Silk Road are two of the focuses of Wild China's art and architecture tours.

Contacts **Wild China** (☎ *010/6465–6602* 🌐 *www.wildchina.com*).

BIKING

Wild China runs an eight-day bird-watching tour in Yunnan, southwest China.

Contacts **Wild China** (☎ *010/6465–6602* 🌐 *www.wildchina.com*).

CULTURE

Local guides are often creative when it comes to history and culture, so having an expert with you can make a big difference. Learning is the focus of Smithsonian Journeys' small-group tours, which are led by university professors. China experts also lead National Geographic's trips, though all that knowledge doesn't come cheap. Wild China is a local company with some of the most unusual trips around, including visits to ethnic minority groups, Tibet, and little-known Xinjiang province as well as more conventional historical trips and journeys focusing on traditional festivals.

Contacts **National Geographic Expeditions** (☎ *888/966–8687* 🌐 *www.nationalgeographicexpeditions.com*). **Smithsonian Journeys** (☎ *877/338–8687* 🌐 *www.smithsonianjourneys.org*). **Wild China** (☎ *010/6465–6602* 🌐 *www.wildchina.com*).

CULINARY

Artisans of Leisure's culinary tour takes in Shanghai and Beijing from the cities' choicest establishments, with prices to match. Intrepid Travel is an Australian company specializing in budget, independent travel. Their China Gourmet Traveler tour includes market visits, cooking demonstrations, and lots of eating at down-to-earth restaurants. Imperial Tours Culinary Tour combines sightseeing with cooking lectures and demonstrations, and lots of five-star dining.

Contacts **Artisans of Leisure** (☎ *800/214–8144* 🌐 *www.artisansofleisure.com*). **Imperial Tours** (☎ *888/888–1970* 🌐 *www.imperialtours.net*). **Intrepid Travel** (☎ *203/469–0214 in the U.S.* 🌐 *www.intrepidtravel.com*).

ECOTOURS

Wild China's nature-trekking tours include a weeklong hike through a Sichuan nature reserve, home to the Giant Panda.

Contacts Wild China (☎ *010/6465-6602* 🌐 *www.wildchina.com*).

GOLF

China Highlights organize short golf packages that combine sightseeing with golfing in Beijing, Shanghai, Kunming, Guangzhou, and Guilin.

Contacts China Highlights (☎ *800/268-2918* 🌐 *www.chinahighlights.com*).

HIKING

The Adventure Center's China hikes include an eight-day walk along the Great Wall, a three-week walk along the route of the Communists' 1934 Long March, and a trip that combines mild hikes with Yangtze cruises and sightseeing. Wild China runs ecologically responsible treks in different parts of China, including Tibet.

Contacts The Adventure Center (☎ *800/228-8747* 🌐 *www.adventurecenter.com*). **Wild China** (☎ *010/6465-6602* 🌐 *www.wildchina.com*).

VISITOR INFOMATION

For general information before you go, including advice on tours, insurance, and safety, call or visit the Web site of the China National Tourist Office.

The two best-known Chinese travel agencies are the state-run China International Travel Service (CITS) and China Travel Service (CTS), both under the same government ministry. Although they have some tourist information, they are businesses, so don't expect endless resources if you're not buying a tour or flight through them. In theory, CTS offices cater to sightseeing around their area, and CITS arranges packages and tours from overseas; in reality, their services overlap.

The Hong Kong Tourism Board has stacks of online information about events, sightseeing, shopping, and dining in Hong Kong. They also organize tour packages from the United States, and local sightseeing tours.

Contacts China International Travel Service (*CITS* ☎ *626/568-8993* 🌐 *www.citsusa.com*). **China National Tourist Office** (☎ *888/760-8218 New York* ☎ *800/670-2228 Los Angeles* 🌐 *www.cnto.org*). **China Travel Service** (*CTS* ☎ *800/899-8618* 🌐 *www.chinatravelservice.com*). **Hong Kong Tourist Board** (*HKTB* 🌐 *www.discoverhongkong.com*).

ONLINE TRAVEL TOOLS

The Web sites listed in this book are in English. If you come across a Chinese-language site you think might be useful, copy the URL into Google, then click the "Translate this page" link. Translations are literal, but generally work for finding out information like opening hours or prices.

ALL ABOUT CHINA

China Digital Times (🌐 *chinadigitaltimes.net*): an excellent Berkeley-run site tracking China-related news and culture in serious depth. **China National Tourism Office** (🌐 *www.cnto.org*): a general overview of traveling in China. **China International Travel Service (CITS)** (🌐 *www.cits.net*): the largest travel agency in China. **China Travel Services (U.S. site)** (*CTS* 🌐 *www.chinatravelservice.com*): the state-run travel agency is a helpful starting place when planning trips.

Chinese Government Portal (🌐 *english.gov.cn*). **China Site** (🌐 *www.chinasite.com*): a comprehensive portal with links to thousands of China-related Web sites. **Hong Kong Government** (🌐 *www.info.gov.hk*). **The Oriental List** (🌐 *www.datasinica.com*): a free Internet mailing list giving extremely reliable information about travel in China.

BUSINESS

Business in Hong Kong (🌐 *www.business.gov.hk*): a government-run site packed with advice. **China Business Weekly** (🌐 *www.chinadaily.com.cn/english/bw/bwtop.html*): a weekly magazine from *China Daily* newspaper. **Chinese Government Business**

Site (*english.gov.cn/business.htm*) provides news, links, and information on business-related legal issues from the Chinese government.

CULTURE & ENTERTAINMENT

Chinese Culture (*www.chinaculture.org*): detailed, searchable database with information on Chinese art, literature, film, history and more. The **Leisure and Cultural Services Department** (*www.lcsd.gov.hk*) has access to Web sites for all of Hong Kong's museums and parks through this government portal.

LOCAL INSIGHT

Asia Expat (*www.asiaxpat.com*) gives advice and listings from foreigners living in Beijing, Hong Kong, Guangzhou, and Shanghai. **Asia City Magazines** (*www.asia-city.com*): an online version of quirky weekly rags with the lowdown on everything happening in Shanghai and Hong Kong.

NEWSPAPERS

China Daily (*www.chinadaily.com.cn*): the leading English-language daily. *People's Daily* (*english.peopledaily.com.cn*): English edition of China's most popular—and most propagandistic—local daily. *South China Morning Post* (*www.scmp.com*): Hong Kong's leading English-language daily.

GREAT CHINESE READS

Big Name Fiction: Gao Xinjiang's *Soul Mountain,* Ha Jin's *Waiting,* and Dai Sijie's *Mr. Muo's Traveling Couch.* **China 101:** *The China Reader: The Reform Era,* edited by Orville Schell and David Shambaugh; *The Search for Modern China,* by Jonathan Spence; and *A History of Hong Kong,* by Frank Welsh. **How about Mao:** Dr. Li Zhisui's *The Private Life of Chairman Mao.*

INDEX

N

O

P

Q

R

S

T

U

V

W

X

Photo Credits: 5, Dennis Cox/age fotostock. 9 (left), JLImages/Alamy. 9 (right), John W. Warden/age fotostock. 10 (top), Martyn Vickery/Alamy. 10 (bottom), Keren Su/China Span/Alamy. 11, Sylvain Grandadam/age fotostock. 12, Dennis Cox/Alamy.13 (left), Lon Linwei/Alamy. 13 (right), China National Tourist Office. 14, Luis Castañeda/age fotostock. 15 (left), Dbimages/Alamy. 15 (right), San Rostro/age fotostock. 23, SuperStock/age fotostock. 24 (top right), José Fuste Raga/age fotostock. 24 (bottom right), Mary Evans Picture Library/Alamy. 25 (top left), China National Tourist Office. 25 (bottom left), Visual Arts Library (London)/Alamy. 25 (right), Panorama Media (Beijing) Ltd./Alamy. 26 (left), Popperfoto/Alamy. 26 (top right), Eddie Gerald/Alamy. 26 (bottom right), North Wind Picture Archives/Alamy. 27 (left), Beaconstox/Alamy. 27 (top right), Bruno Perousse/age fotostock. 28 (left), Kevin O'Hara/age fotostock. 28 (bottom right), A.H.C./age fotostock. 29 (top left), Tramonto/age fotostock. 29 (bottom left), ImagineChina. 29 (right), Iain Masterton/Alamy. **Chapter 1: Beijing:** 31, Superstock/age fotostock. 32, Tina Manley/Alamy. 34, Tim Graham/Alamy. 42-43, ImagineChina. 43 (bottom), Juan Carlos Muñoz/age fotostock. 44, Luis Castañeda/age fotostock. 45 (top), Dennis Cox/age fotostock. 45 (top center), Richard T. Nowitz/age fotostock. 45 (bottom center), ImagineChina. 45 (bottom left), Wendy Connett/Alamy. 45 (bottom right), Jon Arnold Images/Alamy. 46 (top), Robert Harding Picture Library/Alamy. 47 (top), Scott Kemper/Alamy. 94-95, Dennis Cox. 96, ImagineChina. 97 (left), Superstock/age fotostock. 97 (right), Sun Liansheng/age fotostock. 98 (all), ImagineChina. 99, Superstock/age fotostock. 113, Lucid Images/age fotostock. 114, Mary Evans Picture Library/Alamy. 115, Liu Jianmin/age fotostock. 118, Peter Bowater/Alamy. 119, ImagineChina. 120, Nic Cleave Photography/Alamy. 121, ImagineChina. **Chapter 2: Beijing to Shanghai:** 133, ImagineChina. 134, Dennis Cox/Alamy. 135 (top), Juan Carlos Muñoz/age fotostock. 135 (bottom), JTB Photo Communications, Inc./Alamy. 136, Sylvain Grandadam/age fotostock. 137, View Stock/Alamy. 184, Juan Carlos Muñoz/age fotostock. **Chapter 3: Shanghai:** 203-04, ImagineChina. 205, ImagineChina. 271, ImagineChina. 272 (top and center), Elyse Singleton. 272 (bottom), Pat Behnke/Alamy. 273 (top left and bottom right), Elyse Singleton. 273 (top right), ImagineChina. 273 (bottom left), ImagineChina. 274 (top), Kevin O'Hara/age fotostock. 274 (bottom), Pixonnet.com/Alamy. 275 (left), ImagineChina. 275 (right), Ulana Switucha/Alamy. 276, Elyse Singleton. **Chapter 4: Eastern China:** 285, Sylvain Grandadam/age fotostock. 286, Pat Behnke/Alamy. 287 (top), SuperStock/age fotostock. 287 (bottom), Hemis/Alamy. 288, Zhao Yong/age fotostock. 289, Tina Manley/Alamy. 306, La Belle Aurore/Alamy. 307, Wojtek Buss/age fotostock. 308 (top), Wojtek Buss/age fotostock. 308 (bottom), iStockphoto. 309 (top), Imagine-

China. 309 (center), ImagineChina. 309 (bottom), Serge Kozak/age fotostock. 310-311, iStockphoto. **Chapter 5: Hong Kong:** 323, David Crausby/Alamy. 324, Sean David Baylis/Alamy. 399, Andrew McConnell/Alamy. 400, Rough Guides/Alamy. 401, ImagineChina. 402-03, John Jay Cabuay. **Chapter 6: Pearl River Delta:** 423, ImagineChina. 424, Wojtek Buss/age fotostock. 425, Bruno Perousse/age fotostock. 426, Doug Scott/age fotostock. 427, JTB Photo/Alamy. 448-49, SuperStock/age fotostock. 450-51, ImagineChina. 452 (left and top right), ImagineChina. 452 (bottom right), Bruno Perousse/age fotostock. **Chapter 7: The Southwest:** 475, J.D. Heaton/age fotostock. 476, ImagineChina. 477 (top), Panorama Media (Beijing) Ltd./Alamy. 477 (bottom), ImagineChina. 478, Bjorn Svensson/age fotostock. 479, ImagineChina. 485, Li Xin/age fotostock. 495 (top and bottom) and 496, ImagineChina. 497, Richard T. Nowitz/age fotostock. 498 (top), Panorama/age fotostock. 498 (center), Wikimol/Wikipedia. 498 (bottom), ImagineChina. 499, North Wind Picture Archives/Alamy. 500 (top), Christine Gonsalves/iStockphoto. 500 (bottom left), Profimedia.CZ/Alamy. 500 (bottom center), TH Foto/Alamy. 500 (bottom right), wikipedia.org. 501 (left), Fuding Bai Hao Yin Zhen/Wikipedia. 501 (right), Sue Wilson/Alamy. 512, Dennis Cox/age fotostock. 513, Tom Allwood/Alamy. **Chapter 8: Sichuan & Chongqing:** 537, Bjorn Svensson/age fotostock. 538 (top), Jon Bower/Alamy. 538 (bottom), Craig Lovell/Eagle Visions Photography/Alamy. 539, Andrew McConnell/Alamy. 540, JTB Photo Communications, Inc./Alamy. 541, Steve Bloom Images/Alamy. 561, Peter Adams/age fotostock. 562 (top and bottom), ImagineChina. 563 (left), ImagineChina. 563 (top right), JTB Photo/Alamy. 563 (bottom right), Iain Masterton/Alamy. 564 (top), ImagineChina. 564 (bottom), Profimedia.CZ/Alamy. 565 (top left), Iain Masterton/Alamy. 565 (center left), Tim Graham/Alamy. 565 (bottom left), Craig Lovell/Eagle Visions Photography/Alamy. 565 (right), Cephas Picture Library/Alamy. 566 (top and bottom left), ImagineChina. 566 (top right), Doug Scott/age fotostock. 566 (bottom right), ImagineChina. **Chapter 9: The Silk Road:** 583, Bjorn Svensson/age fotostock. 584, Gonzalo Azumendi/age fotostock. 585 (top), Terry Fincher/Alamy. 585 (bottom), Gonzalo Azumendi/age fotostock. 586, Antonio D'Albore/age fotostock. 587, Eye Ubiquitous/Alamy. 598, Val Duncan/Kenebec Images/Alamy. 599 (left), Lee Foster/Alamy. 600-01, Alain Machet/Alamy. 601 (top and bottom inset), ImagineChina. 602 (top), Lou Linwei/Alamy. 602 (bottom), ImagineChina. 603, Tina Manley/Alamy. 624, Gonzalo Azumendi/age fotostock. **Chapter 10: Tibet:** 641, Angelo Cavalli/age fotostock. 642, Michele Falzone/Alamy. 643, Colin Monteath/age fotostock. 644, Nick Cobbing/Alamy. 645, Bjorn Svensson/age fotostock. 660, ImagineChina. **Color section:** The Juyongguan section of the Great Wall of China: John Henshall/Alamy. The Bailin Buddhist Temple in Shijiazhuang, Hebei: Dennis Cox/Alamy. Camel trip on the Silk Road in Dunhuang, Gansu: JTB Photo Communications, Inc./Alamy. Pudong, Shanghai: ImagineChina. Labrang Monastery, Xiahe, Tibet: Bruno Morandi/age fotostock. Chinese New Year, Beijing: Keren Su/China Span/Alamy. Longsheng Longji Rice Terraces in Guangxi: Dennis Cox/Alamy. Native son Chow Yun-Fat in Crouching Tiger, Hidden Dragon: Pictorial Press Ltd/Alamy. Cormorant fishermen on the Li River near Guilin: Dennis Cox/Alamy. Flagstaff House Museum of Tea Ware, Hong Kong: Pat Behnke/Alamy. Manpower sculpture by Rosanna Li, Grotto Fine Art gallery, Hong Kong: Grotto Fine Art. The new China is crackling with energy and crossing the street can sometimes be dangerous sport: Hong Kong Tourism Board. The Bund, Shanghai: José Fuste Raga/age fotostock. Cantonese Opera: Sylvain Grandadam/age fotostock. The Great Buddha in Leshan, Sichuan: SuperStock/age fotostock. Architects and designers strive for auspicious feng shui in Hong Kong: Bernd Mellman/Alamy. In the countryside, the traditional blue Mao uniforms are still fairly common: Wang Rui/age fotostock. Nine-Dragon Wall at Beihai Park in Beijing: Luis Castañeda/age fotostock.

ABOUT OUR WRITERS

Chris Horton first came to China in 1998 to study Chinese in Beijing. Since then he has worked in Dali as a cafe manager, Shanghai as a magazine and book editor and Kunming as a business consultant. Work aside, he travels around Yunnan whenever he has free time, preferably by bike. Chris updated the Yunnan section of the Southwest chapter, wrote China in the 21st Century, and the ethnic minorities articles that are scattered throughout the book.

Helena Iveson has called China home for 5 years. She packed her bags moved there after finishing a Masters in International Journalism in London. She is a freelancer for the *South China Morning Post,* the *Independent on Sunday* and *The Australian* and has started a company called Bespoke Beijing (www.bespoke-beijing.com) which offers personalised advice on visiting Beijing. Helena updated the Silk Road chapter and the Nightlife section of the Beijing chapter.

Hannah Lee is a Hong Kong native but grew up in the UK. She left her life as an accountant in London to return to Hong Kong where she pursued a career in journalism. She now reports for the *South China Morning Post* and TVB, the city's top TV station. In her spare time, Hannah has traveled throughout China, Mongolia, Europe, and South East Asia. She currently tutors undergraduate Journalism students at the University of Hong Kong. Hannah updated the Pearl River Delta chapter of this guide.

Michael D. Manning made the move to Xinjiang in 2005, where he taught English for a year before helping to set up China's largest sundried tomato operation. He has worked for media outlets as diverse as NBC News, High Times, and China Central Television (CCTV), maintaining a popular blog focused on the country's remote western regions (http://china.notspecial.org). Michael updated the Beijing to Shanghai chapter and the Experience and Neighborhoods sections in the Beijing chapter.

Michael Standaert is a writer, journalist and editor based in Beijing where he lives with his wife and his dog. In Beijing he's been an editor at a state-run magazine, and most recently a staff writer and editor at *Asia Weekly.* He is the author of two books and has contributed to a wide range of media during the past decade including the *Los Angeles Times, San Francisco Chronicle,* and *Christian Science Monitor,* He is also a regular blogger at Huffington Post. Michael helped update the Beijing and China Essentials sections, as well as the Tibet and Sichuan chapters.

Having lived and traveled throughout China for the past six years, **David Taylor** has spent the last four working as a writer and editor, mostly in the fields of travel, hospitality, and food and beverage. While Shanghai has many fine hotels and restaurants, he is still more often to be found hunched over *gou bao rou* and *jiaozi* at his favorite Dongbei restaurant than sipping champagne over the Bund. David updated the Eastern China chapter and the dining and lodging chapters in Shanghai.

Beijing Contributors

Zoe Li left her native Hong Kong for mainland China and bravely faced the annihilation of all her foodie preconceptions as she boldly tackled the wholloping animal that is Chinese food cultureShe updated the Beijing Restaurants section. **Eileen Wen Mooney** has lived in Taiwan, Hong Kong, and China for more than 20 years—the last 12 have been in Beijing. She lent her incredible know-how and insider secrets to the Where to Eat and Where to Stay sections. **Paul Mooney**, a New York native, is a freelance writer who has studied and worked in Asia for more than 25 years. He is the author of several travel books and updated the Experience and Neighborhoods section for this book.

Hong Kong Contributors

Liana Cafolla is a Hong Kong–based freelance journalist and editor who writes for the *South China Morning Post, AsiaSpa, Business Traveller,* and other publications. She updated the Where to Eat section.**Cherise Fong,** a freelance writer originally from San Francisco, currently lives in Hong Kong, where she contributes regularly to CNN.com International's Digital Biz. Cherise updated the Experience, Neighborhoods, Cultural Sights, and Side Trip to Macau chapters of this book. **Helen Luk** is a veteran journalist, globetrotter, and fervent food lover. She previously worked for the *South China Morning Post* and the Associated Press in Hong Kong and now runs a business and accounting magazine. Helen contributed to the Where to Eat section. **Zoe Mak** now writes a weekly beauty column for the *South China Morning Post.* She considers herself a full-time bargain hunter and she updated the shopping section of this for the Hong Kong chapter. **Dominique Rowe** After working as chief editor of *JUICE,* a trendy Hong Kong fashion and nightlife magazine, Dominique is now a freelance writer, contributing to *AsiaSpa* and *TIME* in addition to the nightlife and shopping sections of Hong Kong.

Shanghai Contributors

Lisa Movius has written extensively about China's contemporary art, culture, society and economy. She updated the Arts & Nightlife. Back in the U.S. after serving as a foriegn newspaper correspondent in Shanghai, **Elyse Singleton** has been living in Shanghai since 2001. She has traveled extensively through China as a writer and photographer and wrote the Experience and Neighborhoods section, as well as the Markets piece.